HANDBOOK OF
EXPERIMENTAL ECONOMICS RESULTS

HANDBOOKS IN ECONOMICS

1

Series Editors

KENNETH J. ARROW
MICHAEL D. INTRILIGATOR

NORTH-HOLLAND

AMSTERDAM NEW YORK OXFORD TOKYO

HANDBOOK OF EXPERIMENTAL ECONOMICS RESULTS

Edited by

CHARLES R. PLOTT
California Institute of Technology

and

VERNON L. SMITH
Chapman University

NORTH-HOLLAND
AMSTERDAM NEW YORK OXFORD TOKYO

North-Holland is an imprint of Elsevier
Radarweg 29, PO Box 211, 1000 AE Amsterdam, The Netherlands
Linacre House, Jordan Hill, Oxford OX2 8DP, UK

First edition 2008

Copyright © 2008 Elsevier B.V. All rights reserved

No part of this publication may be reproduced, stored in a retrieval system or transmitted in any form or by any means electronic, mechanical, photocopying, recording or otherwise without the prior written permission of the publisher

Permissions may be sought directly from Elsevier's Science & Technology Rights Department in Oxford, UK: phone (+44) (0) 1865 843830; fax (+44) (0) 1865 853333; email: permissions@elsevier.com. Alternatively you can submit your request online by visiting the Elsevier web site at http://elsevier.com/locate/permissions, and selecting *Obtaining permission to use Elsevier material*

Notice
No responsibility is assumed by the publisher for any injury and/or damage to persons or property as a matter of products liability, negligence or otherwise, or from any use or operation of any methods, products, instructions or ideas contained in the material herein. Because of rapid advances in the medical sciences, in particular, independent verification of diagnoses and drug dosages should be made

Library of Congress Cataloging-in-Publication Data
A catalog record for this book is available from the Library of Congress

British Library Cataloguing in Publication Data
A catalogue record for this book is available from the British Library

ISBN: 978-0-444-82642-8
ISSN: 1574-0722

For information on all North-Holland publications
visit our website at books.elsevier.com

Printed and bound in China

08 09 10 11 12   10 9 8 7 6 5 4 3 2 1

Working together to grow
libraries in developing countries

www.elsevier.com | www.bookaid.org | www.sabre.org

ELSEVIER   BOOK AID International   Sabre Foundation

Introduction

INTRODUCTION TO THE SERIES

The aim of the *Handbooks in Economics* series is to produce Handbooks for various branches of economics, each of which is a definitive source, reference, and teaching supplement for use by professional researchers and advanced graduate students. Each Handbook provides self-contained surveys of the current state of a branch of economics in the form of chapters prepared by leading specialists on various aspects of this branch of economics. These surveys summarize not only received results but also newer developments, from recent journal articles and discussion papers. Some original material is also included, but the main goal is to provide comprehensive and accessible surveys. The Handbooks are intended to provide not only useful reference volumes for professional collections but also possible supplementary readings for advanced courses for graduate students in economics.

Kenneth J. Arrow and Michael D. Intriligator

PREFACE

Introduction

The organization of this book and even the title reflect our views about the state of experimental economics in relation to the field of economics in general. Experimental methods in economics seem to respond to circumstances that are not completely dictated by accepted theory or even outstanding problems found in the discipline. Where the field of economics seems to make sharp distinctions, the work of experimental economics sometimes seems to produce a blur. Where traditional economics produces a sharp and precise theory, experiments may produce results that vary from strong support to little or only "partial" support of the relevant theory. The cup is often half empty (and therefore half full) with authors varying as to whether they emphasize the former (or the latter). Where traditional economics draws clear methodological lines, experiments might say little or nothing about method, or follow a different methodology. For example, when results are very robust but do not support the theory experimentalists may ask, contrary to the Friedman (1953) methodology, what assumptions of the theory failed. After all, the assumptions can embody principles useful for the construction of new models. On the other hand, an experimentalist's reply to a critic who claims that some experiment is "invalid" or "incoherent" because the assumptions of theory were not satisfied might be that theory predictions and not assumptions represent the relevant considerations. Experimenters seem to be opportunistic, attempting to find replicable results even though the experiments might involve mixes of methodology, theory and institutions.

In a recent conference, a question was asked about where experimental methods might be more useful than field methods. The answer is that many questions of interest to economists cannot be answered by experimental methods. For example, if the question is related to the behavior of some unique economic entity or event, such as General Motors Corporation in relation to an economic downturn, then it might well be impossible to create an experiment in which the entities of interest can be put under laboratory conditions. However, there are also important questions that can only be answered by experiments. In the field it is difficult to study situations that have not occurred or institutions that do not exist because there is no natural experiment. For example, in the laboratory it is just as easy to study the effects of auction market rules that have never been observed in the economy as to study those that have. When left on her own, nature may never create a situation that clearly separates the predictions of competing models or may never create a situation that allows a clear view of the underlying principles at work. Indeed, much of the progress of experimental methods involves the posing of new questions or the posing of old questions in a way that experimental methods can be applied. It is this sense of discovery, the discovery of how to pose a question, which the book hopes to capture through the presentation of examples as opposed to a roadmap or a guide on how to do experiments.

In many respects the title of the book reflects the spirit of adventure that experimentalists share. Rather than an attempt to focus on experiments in general and force an organization into traditional categories that do not fit, the book is called Experimental *Results* and the emphasis reflects the fact that the results do not necessarily demonstrate a consistent theme but instead reflect bits and pieces of progress as opportunities to pose questions become recognized. In this context Mayo (1996) argues that in every field of science there exists a body of knowledge known and developed by experimentalists that is unknown to the theory and to theorists. Of course knowledge of experimental results can become a foundation for new theory, but an independent body of experimental knowledge of technique and practice always tends to flourish out of practicing experience.

Where should we begin, with the individual or with the group? Economic theory seems to be governed by two separate bodies of principles. The most prominent body of theory, especially the most recent developments based on game theory, begins with the individual as the locus of principles. A second body of principles is focused on groups of individuals such as markets, voting bodies and organizations. In some respects it might seem more natural to begin the book with studies of individuals, but instead the book begins with studies that take place within a specific set of institutions. Why not follow what might seem to be a natural progression from general principles of individual choice and then focus on how those principles operate in the context of institutions? While there are elements of theory that attempt to connect the individual and the group (auction and contract theory are examples), the fact is that theory does not perform this function consistently or well.

If institutions are to play a prominent role, why not begin with categories of institutions. Parts of the book are organized along such lines but the reader will notice that the institutions are not in one-to-one correspondence with those found naturally occurring in the world around us. Instead, experimentalists have focused on "parts" of institutions and special institutions that they feel give insights to the behavior that emerges from systems of institutions. In many respects this mirrors the evolution of the study of institutions that has been taking place in economics. Hayek (1973) noticed a difference between institutions that are discovered (emergent order) and institution that are constructed (designed order). The former involved the recording of the customs and procedures that were not written but were nevertheless followed. Scholars observed such processes and committed the practice to oral, and later, written statements. Similarly, experimentalists implemented institutions in the laboratory even though they were not found in documents, but constituted the "essence" of what seems to exist in social practice. Such institutions are sometimes embodied in the laboratory procedures and only later reveal themselves as institutions worthy of independent study. On the other hand, both the constructed and the discovered institutions of Hayek are combined in the process of institutional and process design that characterizes much of the more complex experimental work found today. That work uses elements of theory and learning from previous experiments to help create the initial new design, but neither is considered so reliable that experimentalists would use a design that had not been thoroughly tested in the new framework.

One might think that a proper organization of experiments would be classified by the applicable theories. According to such a view, one should list the theories and then proceed to list the evidence for and against them. Part of the book is indeed organized this way but it does not work as a general organizing principle. Many of the problems of interest to experimentalists and practitioners are beyond the reach of a fully articulated theory. Examples include electric power markets, spectrum auctions and the dynamics of market convergence based on individual behavior. In addition to problems of refining theories in sufficiently operational terms to produce empirical implications, there are also ambiguities in what might constitute tests. Indeed, such a "theory first" organization would be substantially at odds with many successful experimental methods. Some experiments involve what might be called a "measurement methodology" in which all variables but one are held constant and the influence of a change in one condition (the "treatment") is measured. Measurements that coincide with the direction of predicted influence are considered to be support for the theory and otherwise the theory is challenged. By contrast, other experiments pose multiple models that can be applied to a single experiment with the methodology being focused on posterior odds and contests among a series of models (all of which might be rejected). According to some research strategies, the question is not which model is right, since there is a strong presumption that each is incorrect in some substantive sense. Instead, the question posed is which is most accurate. Econometricians who deal with field methods will certainly recognize the difference, but when scholars consider experimental methods this approach is sometimes forgotten.

Theory and institutions meet at an interesting junction when the issue is one of institutional design. In one sense the focus in experiments is on institutions unlike any that have existed in history. In another sense the focus is on theory that is sometimes very reliable but at other times might have only vestiges of accuracy in the sense that the "glass of evidence" is less than half full. These two starting points are joined by the fact in some cases, that the institutions will be applied as policy under circumstances and at a scale and environments that might be substantially different from those studied in the laboratory.

How can laboratory methods be of use? The challenge of answering that question is the domain of the test-bed methodology. In essence, three different questions are posed. The first is whether or not the institutions produce acceptable outcomes in the normative sense of what the desirable properties of a social decision process might be. This first is a "proof of principle" or "proof of concept." The second question is more probing for it asks if the performance takes place for understandable reasons. This step is called "design consistency" because it asks if the reasons for the performance are sufficiently consistent to support the conjecture that the system would work as it is observed to work. Tests of design consistency ask if the dynamics of the system and the behavior of individuals within the system are consistent with the theory or principles of behavior that lead to the design. The third question is one of robustness. Are the principles at operation in the simple environment reliable at larger and more complex scale in which numbers, institutions, events and general environment are different? The questions are about the robustness of the model.

The Book Organization

The papers are organized in eight major headings. In some cases the positioning of a paper under one heading as opposed to another is only a matter of judgment. The categories emerged from the papers that were submitted.

The first three of the major headings are related to markets. Each of the three areas involves substantial differences in experimental procedures due to the differences in institutions. Not only do the institutions differ but the environments also differ so different principles might be at work. The fourth section is devoted to principles of game theory. Here the focus is primarily on the underlying principles at work as opposed to applications within any particular institutional context. Section Five has as a focus the creation of new forms of social organization and their implementation. As economics and game theory mature it becomes possible to create new forms of organization and study them under laboratory conditions. This section provides summaries of how that has taken place. Section Six reflects a shift to a different set of institutions and the special circumstances presented by public goods and externalities. Section Seven examines individual behavior and Section Eight focuses on methods.

This book is a result of an invitation sent from the editors to a broad range of experimenters asking them to write brief notes describing specific experimental results that they feel are important. The challenge to each author was to produce pictures and tables that were self-contained; i.e., the reader could understand quickly the essential nature of the experiments and the results by viewing the pictures and tables and reading a short text directly attached thereto. If interested, the reader could learn more by reading the text of the report. Any reader wishing to study the subject further could then consult the references. Authors were invited according to their expertise so that a wide range of research would be represented. The idea was to create a work readily accessible to a wide range of economists, social scientists, and others.

References

Friedman, M. (1953). "Essays in Positive Economics". University of Chicago Press, Chicago.
Mayo, D. (1996). "Error and the Growth of Experimental Knowledge". University of Chicago Press, Chicago.
Hayek, F. (1973). "Law, Legislation, and Liberty". Rules and Order, vol. 1. University of Chicago Press, Chicago.

CONTENTS OF VOLUME 1

Introduction to the Series	vii
Preface	ix
Introduction	ix
The Book Organization	xii
References	xii

PART 1: MARKETS

Markets	3
	3
1.1. Institutional Environments	3
1.2. Imperfect Competition	8
1.3. Dynamics of Market Adjustments	11
References	13

PART 1.1: INSTITUTIONAL ENVIRONMENTS

PART 1.1.1: PROPERTIES OF THE DOUBLE AUCTION

Chapter 1
Properties of Disequilibrium Adjustment in Double Auction Markets
CHARLES R. PLOTT … 16
References … 20

Chapter 2
From Market Jaws to the Newton Method: The Geometry of How a Market Can Solve Systems of Equations
PETER BOSSAERTS AND CHARLES R. PLOTT … 22
References … 24

Chapter 3
Exogenous Uncertainty Increases the Bid–Ask Spread in the Continuous Double Auction
VERNON L. SMITH AND MARK VAN BOENING … 25
1. Experimental Design … 25

2. Exogenous Uncertainty and the Bid/Ask Spread — 27
  3. Conclusion — 30
  References — 30

Chapter 4
Zero-Intelligence Robots and the Double Auction Market: A Graphical Tour
PAUL J. BREWER — 31
  1. Environment — 32
    1.1. Values and Costs — 32
    1.2. Profits — 32
    1.3. Limitations on Trading — 32
    1.4. Market Rules — 32
    1.5. Budget Constraints — 33
    1.6. Trades Involve Arbitrage; No Speculative Trades — 33
  2. Robot Agents — 34
    2.1. Zero Intelligence Robots – Trading Algorithm — 34
    2.2. UNIT Robots – Trading Algorithm — 34
    2.3. Kaplan's Parasitic Robots[1] – Trading Algorithm — 35
  3. Literature – Robots and the Double Auction — 35
    3.1. Types of Questions — 35
    3.2. Major Results from the Literature – A Chronology — 37
  References — 44

Chapter 5
Effect of Non-binding Price Controls in Double Auction Trading
VERNON L. SMITH AND ARLINGTON W. WILLIAMS — 46
  1. Introduction — 46
  2. Experimental Design — 46
  3. Experimental Results — 48
  4. Why Do Non-binding Price Controls Interfere with the DA Market Process? — 53
  5. Conclusions — 53
  References — 53

PART 1.1.2: PROPERTIES OF POSTED OFFER PROCESSES

Chapter 6
Fairness and Short Run Price Adjustment in Posted Offer Markets
PRAVEEN KUJAL AND VERNON L. SMITH — 55
  1. Introduction — 55
  2. Market Experiments — 55
    2.1. Extension: Posted Bid vs Posted Offer — 56
    2.2. Our Experiments — 57
  3. Hypothesis and Experimental Results — 57

Contents of Volume 1

4. Discussion	58
4.1. What is Fairness?	60
References	61

Chapter 7
Mixed Strategy Nash Equilibrium Predictions as a Means of Organizing Behavior in Posted-Offer Market Experiments
DOUGLAS D. DAVIS AND BART J. WILSON

	62
1. Introduction	62
2. Equilibrium Mixed Strategy Pricing Distributions	63
3. Pricing Performance with Market Power	64
4. Pricing Densities Relative to Static Nash Equilibrium Predictions	67
5. Performance of Alternative Theories	68
6. Summary	69
References	69

Chapter 8
Simulated and Real Buyers in Posted Offer Markets
JAMIE BROWN KRUSE

	71
1. Introduction	71
2. Summary of the Experimental Design	71
3. Results	72
Acknowledgements	76
References	76

Chapter 9
The Performance of Double-Auction and Posted-Offer Markets with Advance Production
STUART MESTELMAN

	77
References	82

PART 1.1.3: CALL MARKETS AND SEALED BIDS

Chapter 10
Strategy-Proof Equilibrium Behavior in Two-Sided Auctions
VERNON L. SMITH

	84
1. Strategy-Proof Equilibria in the Sealed Bid-Offer Auction	85
2. Strategy-Proof Equilibria in the Uniform Price Double Auction (UPDA)	88
3. Summary	89
References	91

Chapter 11
First Price Independent Private Values Auctions
JAMES C. COX   92

1. Tests of the RNM with Market Prices	92
2. Tests of the RNM with Subject Payoff Data	94
3. Tests of the CRRAM and the RNM with Individual Bid Data	95
4. Tests of the LCM with Individual Bid Data	96
5. Summary of the Test Results	98
Acknowledgement	98
References	98

PART 1.1.4: ALTERNATIVE MARKET INSTITUTIONS

Chapter 12
The Walrasian Auction
CORINNE BRONFMAN, KEVIN MCCABE, DAVID PORTER, STEPHEN RASSENTI AND VERNON SMITH — 100

1. Introduction	100
2. Experimental Environments	100
2.1. Baseline	100
2.2. Multi-unit Non-stationary Supply and Demand Environment	101
3. Walrasian Auction Design and Computerized Implementation	102
4. Experimental Results	104
4.1. The E1 Environment Replication	104
4.2. Baseline and Treatment Effects	104
4.3. Individual Behavior	105
References	108

Chapter 13
The Matching Market Institution
DANIEL FRIEDMAN AND CHANGHUA RICH — 109

1. Experimental Procedures	109
2. Results	111
3. Discussion	114
References	114

Chapter 14
Tatonnement
CHARLES R. PLOTT — 115
Reference — 117

PART 1.2: IMPERFECT COMPETITION

PART 1.2.1: MARKET POWER

Chapter 15
Wage Differentials in Experimental Efficiency Wage Markets

ERNST FEHR AND SIMON GÄCHTER	120
1. Wage Differentials: Experiments Help to Test Explanations	120
2. The Fair Wage-Effort Version of Efficiency Wage Theory	121
2.1. Experimental Design	121
2.2. Results	121
3. The Shirking Version of Efficiency Wage Theory	123
3.1. Design	123
3.2. Results	124
4. Summary	125
References	126

Chapter 16
The Paradox of Power

YVONNE DURHAM, JACK HIRSHLEIFER AND VERNON L. SMITH	127
1. The Model	128
2. Implementing the Model	132
3. Experimental Procedures and Design	132
4. Results	133
4.1. Nash vs Cooperative Comparisons	133
4.2. Predictions of the Model	135
4.3. Charting the Observations	136
References	136

Chapter 17
The Exercise of Market Power in Laboratory Experiments

DOUGLAS D. DAVIS AND CHARLES A. HOLT	138
1. Introduction	138
2. Market Power	139
3. Applications of Market Power	143
References	145

Chapter 18
The Classical Experiments on Cournot Oligopoly

ANTONI BOSCH-DOMÈNECH AND NICOLAAS J. VRIEND	146
1. Sauermann and Selten's Results	146
2. Hoggatt's Results	148
3. Fouraker and Siegel's Results	149
References	152

Chapter 19
Experiments in Decentralized Monopoly Restraint

JAMES C. COX AND R. MARK ISAAC	153
1. Market Institutions for Monopoly Restraint	153

2. Contestable Markets	155
3. The Loeb–Magat Mechanism	156
4. The Finsinger–Vogelsang Mechanism	157
5. The Cox–Isaac Mechanism	159
Acknowledgement	161
References	161

PART 1.2.2: COLLUSION

Chapter 20
Price Signaling and "Cheap Talk" in Laboratory Posted Offer Markets
TIMOTHY N. CASON — 164
1. Multi-Market versus Single-Market Competition — 165
2. The Importance of the Signaling Language — 167
3. Summary — 168
References — 168

Chapter 21
The Effects of Collusion in Laboratory Experiments
DOUGLAS D. DAVIS AND CHARLES A. HOLT — 170
1. Introduction — 170
2. Collusion with and without Secret Discounts — 171
3. Recent Work — 175
References — 176

Chapter 22
Predatory Pricing: Rare Like a Unicorn?
ROSARIO GOMEZ, JACOB K. GOEREE AND CHARLES A. HOLT — 178
1. Introduction — 178
2. Single Market Designs — 178
3. Multiple Market Designs — 180
4. Summary — 183
References — 184

Chapter 23
Some Results on Anti-Competitive Behavior in Multi-Unit Ascending Price Auctions
KATERINA SHERSTYUK — 185
1. Experiments on Demand Reduction — 186
2. Experiments on Bidder Collusion — 192
Acknowledgement — 197
References — 197

Contents of Volume 1

PART 1.2.3: NON-CONVEXITIES

Chapter 24
Non-Convexities, Economies of Scale, Natural Monopoly and Monopolistic
Competition
CHARLES R. PLOTT   200
References   205

Chapter 25
Avoidable Cost Structures and Competitive Market Institutions
MARK V. BOENING AND NATHANIEL T. WILCOX   206
1. A Simple Avoidable Cost Structure   206
2. Three Market Institutions   208
3. The Results   209
4. A Next Step: Cooperative Arrangements?   211
References   211

PART 1.3: DYNAMICS OF MARKET ADJUSTMENTS

Chapter 26
Principles of Market Adjustment and Stability
CHARLES R. PLOTT   214
1. Theory   214
   1.1. Cobweb Dynamics   215
   1.2. The Walrasian (Hicks, Samuelson) Dynamics   216
   1.3. Marshallian Dynamics   216
2. Experiments   217
   2.1. Instability does not Occur under Conditions Predicted by the Cobweb Model   217
   2.2. Walrasian Dynamics and not Marshallian Dynamics Capture the Backward-Bending Case   219
   2.3. The Marshallian Model and not the Walrasian Model Best Describes Market Behavior
      in the Case of a Marshallian Externality or a "Fad"   223
3. Summary   226
References   227

Chapter 27
Off-floor Trading, Market Disintegration and Price Volatility in Bid/Ask Markets
VERNON L. SMITH AND MARK VAN BOENING   228
1. The Problem   228
2. The Environment   228
3. Results   229
4. Discussion: Implications for, and Barriers to, Institutional Redesign   232
References   232

Chapter 28
Quantitative Restrictions in Experimental Posted-offer Markets
PRAVEEN KUJAL   234
1. Introduction   234
    1.1. Quotas   234
2. Quota Experiments   235
3. Experimental Design   236
    3.1. Market equilibrium   237
4. Experimental Results   238
5. Conclusion   240
References   241

Chapter 29
Price Bubbles in Large Financial Asset Markets
ARLINGTON W. WILLIAMS   242
References   246

Chapter 30
Price Bubbles
DAVID PORTER AND VERNON L. SMITH   247
1. Introduction   247
2. Empirical Results from Laboratory Asset Markets   247
References   255

Chapter 31
Experiments with Arbitrage Across Assets
ERIC O'N. FISHER   256
References   259

Chapter 32
Bubbles and Crashes in Experimental Asset Markets: Common Knowledge Failure?
CHARLES NOUSSAIR AND CHARLES PLOTT   260
References   263

Chapter 33
A Comparison of Market Institutions
TIMOTHY N. CASON AND DANIEL FRIEDMAN   264
1. Market Institutions   264
2. Market Environment   266
3. Related Work   266
4. Results   267
    4.1. Market Efficiency   267

Contents of Volume 1   xxi

    4.2. Transaction Prices   269
    4.3. Transaction Volume   271
5. Discussion   271
References   271

Chapter 34
Coordination Success in Non-cooperative Large Group Market Entry Games
AMNON RAPOPORT AND DARRYL A. SEALE   273
1. The Market Entry Game   273
2. Results   274
    2.1. Sundali, Rapoport, and Seale (1995)   274
    2.2. Rapoport et al. (1998)   281
    2.3. Rapoport, Seale, and Winter (1997)   282
3. Adaptive Learning   293
Acknowledgement   294
References   294

PART 2: MARKET ECONOMICS OF UNCERTAINTY AND INFORMATION

Market Economics of Uncertainty and Information   299

Chapter 35
Learning to Forecast Rationally
HUGH KELLEY AND DANIEL FRIEDMAN   303
1. Introduction   303
2. The Tasks   303
    2.1. Orange Juice Forecasting (OJ)   303
    2.2. The Medical Diagnosis Task (MD)   305
3. Results   305
    3.1. Rolling Regressions   305
    3.2. OJ Learning Curves   306
    3.3. MD Learning Curves   308
4. Discussion   308
References   310

Chapter 36
Laboratory Tests of Job Search Models
JAMES C. COX AND RONALD L. OAXACA   311
1. Basic Search Experiments   311
2. Precommitment/No Precommitment Experiments   313
3. Recall Experiments   316
4. Extensions of the Standard Search Model   318
Acknowledgements   318

References   318

Chapter 37
Reciprocity and Contract Enforcement
SIMON GÄCHTER AND ERNST FEHR   319
1. The Contract Enforcement Problem   319
2. Experimental Design and Results of Fehr and Gächter (1998a)   320
   2.1. Design   320
   2.2. Results   320
3. Contract Enforcement with an Imperfect Verification Technology   323
4. Summary   324
References   324

Chapter 38
Reciprocity in Experimental Markets
ERNST FEHR AND ARMIN FALK   325
1. Introduction   325
2. Experimental Design   326
   2.1. Common Features of All Treatments   326
   2.2. The One-sided Auction-treatment   327
   2.3. The Double Auction-treatment   327
   2.4. The Bilateral Bargaining-treatment   328
   2.5. Standard Predictions   328
3. Results   328
4. Reciprocity Under Conditions of High Stakes   329
5. Related Experiments   330
Acknowledgement   333
References   334

Chapter 39
Information Cascade Experiments
LISA R. ANDERSON AND CHARLES A. HOLT   335
1. Cascades   335
2. Market Applications and Alternative Institutions   340
References   342
Further reading   343

Chapter 40
Markets and Information Aggregation Mechanisms
KAY-YUT CHEN AND CHARLES R. PLOTT   344
1. Are The Lessons From The Simple Cases Useful?   348
References   352

PART 3: GENERAL EQUILIBRIUM AND THE ECONOMICS OF MULTIPLE MARKET SYSTEMS

General Equilibrium and Multiple Market Systems   355

Chapter 41
Comparative Advantage and International Trade
CHARLES R. PLOTT   358
Reference   363

Chapter 42
Asset Pricing
PETER BOSSAERTS   364
1. What the Theory Predicts   364
2. The Empirical Question   365
3. What the Field Data Teach Us   365
4. What the Experiments Teach Us   366
References   369

Chapter 43
Price Discovery and Allocation in Chains and Networks of Markets
CHARLES R. PLOTT AND JACKIE YEUNG   370
Reference   375

Chapter 44
Multiple Market Systems and the Classical Principles of Price Dynamics in General Equilibrium
CHARLES R. PLOTT   376
References   382
Further reading   383

PART 4: GAMES

Games   387
    4.1. Accuracy of the Nash Model   387
    4.2. Learning in Games   389

PART 4.1: ACCURACY OF THE NASH MODEL

Chapter 45
Experimental Beauty Contest Games: Levels of Reasoning and Convergence to Equilibrium
ROSEMARIE NAGEL   391
1. Introduction   391

2. Variations on the Beauty Contest Game — 392
3. Bounded Rational Behavior — 401
   3.1. Iterated Best Reply Model — 401
   3.2. Learning — 404
Appendix A: Instructions (from Duffy and Nagel, 1997) — 407
   A.1. General — 407
   A.2. The Rules — 407
   A.3. What is the Median — 408
   A.4. Payoffs — 408
   A.5. Explanation Sheet — 408
Appendix B: — 408
References — 409

Chapter 46
Reciprocity in Ultimatum and Dictator Games: An Introduction
ELIZABETH HOFFMAN, KEVIN MCCABE AND VERNON SMITH — 411
1. Motivation — 411
2. Ultimatum and Dictator Games Described — 412
3. Experimental Designs and Summary Results — 412
4. Interpretations and Discussion — 414
References — 415

Chapter 47
Preferences and Property Rights in Ultimatum and Dictator Games
ELIZABETH HOFFMAN, KEVIN MCCABE AND VERNON SMITH — 417
1. Property Rights Defined — 417
2. Experimental Design — 417
3. Ultimatum Results — 419
4. Dictator Games and Results — 420
5. Discussion — 421
References — 422

Chapter 48
Prompting Strategic Reasoning Increases Other-regarding Behavior
ELIZABETH HOFFMAN, KEVIN MCCABE AND VERNON SMITH — 423
1. Introduction — 423
   1.1. Previous Results — 423
   1.2. The Current Experiment — 425
2. Experimental Design and Subject Recruitment — 425
3. Experimental Results — 426
4. Discussion — 426
References — 428

Chapter 49
Social Distance and Reciprocity in Dictator Games
ELIZABETH HOFFMAN, KEVIN MCCABE AND VERNON SMITH 429
1. Defining Variations on Perceived Social Distance in Dictator Games 429
2. Experimental Design 429
   2.1. Replicating Forsythe et al. (1994) 430
   2.2. FHSS-V 431
   2.3. Double Blind 2 (DB2) 433
   2.4. Single Blind 1 (SB1) 433
   2.5. Single Blind 2 (SB2) 433
3. Experimental Design and Research Hypothesis 434
4. Results 435
References 435

Chapter 50
Fairness in Ultimatum Bargaining
J. KEITH MURNIGHAN 436
1. Defining and Investigating the Impact of Fairness Concerns 437
2. "My Offer is Fair" 440
3. Fairness, Anger, and Spite 445
4. Ultimatum Bargaining by Children 449
5. Ultimatums Dividing Money and M&Ms 449
6. Conclusions 451
Acknowledgements 452
References 452
Further reading 453

Chapter 51
Coordination Failure in Market Statistic Games
JOHN VAN HUYCK AND RAYMOND BATTALIO 454
1. Introduction 454
2. Strategic Uncertainty and Coordination Failure 455
3. The Influence of Out-of-Equilibrium Payoffs 457
4. The Influence of Group Size, Grid Size, and Order Statistic 458
5. The Separatrix 459
Acknowledgements 461
References 461

Chapter 52
The Problem of Common Choice in Symmetric N-person Coordination Games
CARL M. RHODES AND RICK K. WILSON 463
1. The Problem 463
2. Experimental Design 464

3. Single Stage Results	466
4. Repeated Play Results	467
5. Conclusion	470
Acknowledgements	471
References	471

Chapter 53
Equilibrium Convergence in Normal Form Games
NICOLE BOUCHEZ AND DANIEL FRIEDMAN

	472
1. Laboratory Procedures and Treatments	472
2. Results	475
3. Discussion	479
References	479

Chapter 54
Analyzing Choice with Revealed Preference: Is Altruism Rational?
JAMES ANDREONI AND JOHN H. MILLER

	481
1. Introduction	481
2. The Choice Task	483
3. Checking GARP	483
4. Conclusion	486
References	487

Chapter 55
Testing Theories of Other-regarding Behavior: A Sequence of Four Laboratory Studies
GARY E. BOLTON, JORDI BRANDTS, ELENA KATOK, AXEL OCKENFELS AND RAMI ZWICK

	488
1. Introduction	488
2. Bolton and Zwick (1995): Reputation Building versus Self-centered Fairness in an Ultimatum Game	489
3. Bolton, Katok and Zwick (1998): The Nature of Giving Behavior in Dictator Games	492
4. Selten and Ockenfels (1998) and Ockenfels and Weimann (1999): The Fixed Total Sacrifice Effect in the Solidarity Game	494
5. Bolton, Brandts, and Ockenfels (1998): Distribution versus Intentions in a 2-person Dilemma Game	495
6. Summary: Regularities for Theory Building	498
References	498
Further reading	499

Chapter 56
Focal Points and Bargaining

KEN BINMORE AND JOSEPH SWIERZBINSKI 500
References 507

PART 4.2: ALTERNATIVES TO NASH

Chapter 57
Differences in the Economic Decisions of Men and Women: Experimental Evidence
CATHERINE C. ECKEL AND PHILIP J. GROSSMAN 509
Abstract 509
1. Public Goods Experiments 510
2. Ultimatum Experiments 513
3. Dictator Experiments 515
4. Conclusions 518
References 518

Chapter 58
Emergent Conventions in Evolutionary Games
JOHN VAN HUYCK 520
1. Introduction 520
2. Inefficient Conventions 521
3. Coordination Conventions: Labels and Populations 522
4. Unequal Division Bargaining Conventions 527
Acknowledgements 529
References 529
Further reading 530

Chapter 59
Self-centered Fairness in Games with More Than Two Players
GARY E. BOLTON AND AXEL OCKENFELS 531
1. Introduction 531
2. Sketch of ERC Preferences 532
3. Evidence in Games with More Than Two Players 534
   3.1. The Güth–van Damme Bargaining Game 534
   3.2. Market Game 537
   3.3. The Fixed Total Sacrifice Effect 538
4. Summary 539
References 540

Chapter 60
Quantal Response Equilibria: A Brief Synopsis
RICHARD D. MCKELVEY AND THOMAS R. PALFREY 541
1. Introduction 541
2. The Model 541

3. Properties of the QRE	542
4. Fit to Experimental Data	543
4.1. Learning to Play Nash Over Time	543
4.2. Systematic Bias Away from the Nash Equilibrium	543
4.3. Nash Equilibrium Selection	544
Acknowledgement	547
References	548

Chapter 61
Logit Equilibrium Models of Anomalous Behavior: What to do when the Nash Equilibrium Says One Thing and the Data Say Something Else
SIMON P. ANDERSON, JACOB K. GOEREE AND CHARLES A. HOLT   549

1. Background: The Logit Approach	551
2. How to Find a Logit Equilibrium	552
3. Comparative Static Properties	554
Acknowledgement	557
References	557

PART 4.3: LEARNING IN GAMES

Chapter 62
Asymmetric Two-person Bargaining Under Incomplete Information: Strategic Play and Adaptive Learning
AMNON RAPOPORT, TERRY E. DANIEL AND DARRYL A. SEALE   560

1. Most Participants Behave Strategically in General Accordance with the Linear Equilibrium Strategy	561
2. There is an Information Advantage Exceeding the Predictions of the LES	563
3. Repeated Play with a Fixed Partner Enhances Strategic Advantages	565
4. Explanation of the Findings in Terms of Adaptive Learning	565
References	571

Chapter 63
The Effect of Message Space Size on Learning and Outcomes in Sender–Receiver Games
ANDREAS BLUME, DOUGLAS V. DEJONG AND GEOFFREY B. SPRINKLE   572

1. Introduction	572
2. The Games	572
3. Results	574
3.1. Game 1	574
3.2. Game 2	575
4. Summary	584
References	584

Contents of Volume 1

Chapter 64
Learning in Entry Limit Pricing Games
DAVID J. COOPER   585
1. Introduction   585
2. The Limit-pricing Game   585
3. Experimental Procedures   588
4. Adaptive Learning   588
5. Experimental Results   592
6. Conclusions   592
References   597

Chapter 65
Payoff Uncertainty and Cooperation in Finitely-repeated Prisoner's Dilemma Games
LAWRENCE M. KAHN AND J. KEITH MURNIGHAN   598
1. Methods   599
2. The Experimental Design   599
3. Results   602
4. Discussion and Conclusions   604
Acknowledgements   605
References   605

Chapter 66
Learning and Equilibrium in Games
COLIN F. CAMERER, TECK H. HO AND JUIN-KUAN CHONG   607
1. Introduction   607
2. Adaptive EWA and Other Learning Models   607
3. Sophisticated EWA and Equilibrium Models   611
References   615

PART 5: MECHANISM DESIGN AND POLICY APPLICATIONS

Mechanism Design and Policy Applications   619
   5.1. Abstract, Theory Driven   619
   5.2. Applied, Problem Driven   620
   5.3. From the Lab to the Field   622
References   623

PART 5.1: ABSTRACT, THEORY DRIVEN

Chapter 67
Incentive-compatible Mechanisms for Pure Public Goods: A Survey of Experimental Research

YAN CHEN 625
1. Introduction 625
   1.1. Theoretical Results and Unresolved Issues 625
   1.2. Economic Environments in Experiments 627
2. Dominant Strategy Mechanisms 628
3. Nash-efficient Mechanisms 630
4. Mechanisms Using Refinements of Nash as Implementation Concepts 635
   4.1. Perfect Nash Mechanisms 635
   4.2. Subgame Perfect Mechanisms 637
5. Other Mechanisms 638
6. Concluding Remarks 639
Acknowledgements 640
References 640

Chapter 68
The Combinatorial Auction
STEPHEN J. RASSENTI AND VERNON L. SMITH 644
1. The Environment 645
   1.1. Two Market Mechanisms: The Independent Auction and the Combinatorial Auction 646
2. The After Market 649
3. Results 649
References 653

PART 5.2: APPLIED, PROBLEM DRIVEN

Chapter 69
Share Trading and Coupon Banking Interact to Improve Performance in Emission Trading Markets
STUART MESTELMAN AND R. ANDREW MULLER 655
References 659

Chapter 70
Trading Institutions and Emission Allowances
TIMOTHY N. CASON 661
1. The Federal Sulfur Dioxide Allowance Program and the EPA Emissions Trading Auction 661
2. Other Emission Allowance Trading Assessments: China, Ontario and Los Angeles 665
3. Summary 667
References 667

Chapter 71
Procurement Contracting

JAMES C. COX AND R. MARK ISAAC   669
1. A Model of Cost Information Asymmetry   669
2. Linear Contracts   670
3. Testable Hypotheses   670
4. Experimental Results   671
Acknowledgements   674
References   675

Chapter 72
Electric Power Market Design Issues and Laboratory Experiments
STEPHEN RASSENTI AND VERNON SMITH   676
1. Nodal Price Theory for Lossy Lines   677
Acknowledgements   679
References   679

Chapter 73
Energy, Reserve and Adjustment Market Behavior With Industry Network, Demand and Generator Parameters
MARK A. OLSON, STEPHEN RASSENTI AND VERNON L. SMITH   681
1. Modeling Generators   681
2. Modeling Demand   685
3. Market Design   687
4. Sealed Bid Day-Ahead Energy Market   687
5. Reserve Market   688
6. Load Adjustment Market   689
7. Continuous Double Auction Energy Market   690
8. The Network   690
9. Optimization   691
10. Subjects   691
11. Data Analysis: Questions and Answers   692
    11.1. What is the Competitive Efficiency of the Two Markets Based on Marginal Energy Costs?   692
    11.2. Do SBO Prices and CDA Weighted Average Prices Converge to Comparable Levels?   694
    11.3. What are the Profitability Levels for the Various Agents in the System?   694
    11.4. Do Nodal Prices Reflect Distance Sensitivity and Line Constraints?   694
Reference   699

Chapter 74
Transmission Constraints, Incentive Auction Rules and Trader Experience in an Electric Power Market
STEVEN BACKERMAN, STEPHEN RASSENTI AND VERNON L. SMITH   700
1. Experimental Network Environment   700
2. Experimental Design   703
3. The Mechanism: A Continuously Updated Nodal Uniform Price Auction   703

4. Hypotheses and Tests	705
5. Regression Results	707
6. Further Results	707
7. Conclusions	708
References	709

Chapter 75
A Smart Market for the Spot Pricing and Pricing of Transmission Through a Power Grid
HUNG-PO CHAO AND CHARLES R. PLOTT

	710
1. Kirchoff's Law and Resource Constraints	710
2. The Mechanism	711
2.1. Notation	712
2.2. Notation	713
2.3. Dual Linear Program for Continuous-time Double Auction	713
3. Parameter and the Testbed	714
4. Performance	715
Reference	718
Further reading	718

PART 5.3: FROM THE LAB TO THE FIELD

Chapter 76
Asset Market Manipulation: A Field Experiment with Racetrack Betting
COLIN F. CAMERER

	720
1. Experimental Design	720
2. Experimental Results	722
3. Conclusion	723
References	724

Chapter 77
Pre-testing International Climate Change Policies: Methods and Results
PETER BOHM

	725
1. Testing Gains from Emissions Quota Trade among a Few Countries (Bohm, 1997)	726
1.1. Test Design	726
1.2. Test Results	727
2. Testing International Acceptability of a 'Global' Tradable-quota Treaty with Diplomats as Subjects (Bohm, 1997b)	730
References	732

Chapter 78
Quasi-experimental Evaluation of Regional Employment Subsidies

PETER BOHM	733
1. Experimental Design	733
2. Results	734
Further reading	735

Chapter 79
Field-test Elicitations of Demand for Public Goods
PETER BOHM	736
References	740

Chapter 80
Results from a Dozen Years of Election Futures Markets Research
JOYCE BERG, ROBERT FORSYTHE, FORREST NELSON AND THOMAS RIETZ	742
1. Introduction and Description of Election Futures Markets	742
2. Market Mechanism	743
3. Results from Share Markets	744
3.1. Absolute Market Accuracy	744
3.2. Accuracy Relative to Polls	746
4. How and why do Election Futures Markets "Work?"	748
5. Other Issues Studied and Future Research Potential	749
Acknowledgements	750
References	751

Chapter 81
Experimental Evidence on the Existence of Hypothetical Bias in Value Elicitation Methods
GLENN W. HARRISON AND E. ELISABET RUTSTRÖM	752
1. The CVM Literature and Tests with Private Goods	753
2. The CVM Literature and Tests with Public Goods	755
3. Open-ended Elicitation in the Lab	758
4. Dichotomous Choice Elicitation in the Lab	760
5. Social Elicitation in the Lab	761
6. Constructive Solutions	762
6.1. Instrument Calibration	762
6.2. Statistical Calibration	763
7. Conclusions	765
References	766

PART 6: NON-MARKET AND ORGANIZATIONAL RESEARCH

Non-market and Organizational Research	771
Introduction	771

6.1. Public Goods and Externalities	771
6.2. Committees and Voting Groups	773
Reference	774

PART 6.1: PUBLIC GOODS, EXTERNALITIES AND COMMON POOLS

Chapter 82
Partners versus Strangers: Random Rematching in Public Goods Experiments
JAMES ANDREONI AND RACHEL CROSON

	776
1. Introduction	776
2. Partners versus Strangers	777
3. A Closer Look	777
4. Partners, Strangers, Warm-glow and Confusion	781
5. What is Next?	781
References	782

Chapter 83
Differentiating Altruism and Reciprocity
RACHEL T.A. CROSON

	784
1. Introduction	784
2. Hypotheses	785
3. The Experiments and Results	785
4. Types of Reciprocity	788
5. Discussion and Conclusion	789
References	791

Chapter 84
Voluntary Provision of Public Goods: Experimental Results with Interior Nash Equilibria
SUSAN K. LAURY AND CHARLES A. HOLT

	792
1. Introduction	792
2. Dominant Strategy Designs	793
3. Non-dominant Strategy Designs	795
4. Treatment Effects	799
5. Final Observations	800
Acknowledgements	800
References	800

Chapter 85
Spiteful Behavior in Voluntary Contribution Mechanism Experiments
TATSUYOSHI SAIJO

	802
1. Saijo–Nakamura Experiments	803
2. Non-excludable Public Good Experiments	810

Acknowledgement 816
References 816

Chapter 86
Explaining the Comparative Statics in Step-Level Public Good Games
ARTHUR SCHRAM, THEO OFFERMAN AND JOEP SONNEMANS 817
1. Introduction 817
2. Basic Experimental Tools 818
3. Treatments 818
4. Interpreting the Results 821
References 824

Chapter 87
Cooperation in VCM Experiments: Results Using the Contribution Function Approach
JORDI BRANDTS AND ARTHUR SCHRAM 825
1. Introduction 825
2. Description of the Design 825
3. Results 826
4. Some Insights 829
References 829

Chapter 88
Voluntary Provision of Public Goods
KENNETH S. CHAN, STUART MESTELMAN AND R. ANDREW MULLER 831
References 835

Chapter 89
Intrinsic Motivation in a Public Good Environment
FRANS VAN WINDEN, FRANS VAN DIJK AND JOEP SONNEMANS 836
1. Introduction 836
2. Experimental Design 837
3. Main Observations 841
   3.1. Different Intrinsic Motivation for Contributing 841
   3.2. Intrinsic Motivation Changes with Social Interaction 841
   3.3. Effect of Success of Social Interaction (Social Ties) 841
   3.4. Group Formation 844
4. Conclusions 844
References 844

Chapter 90
Theoretical Explanations of Treatment Effects in Voluntary Contributions Experiments

CHARLES A. HOLT AND SUSAN K. LAURY — 846
1. Introduction — 846
2. Generalized Preferences — 848
3. Noisy Decision Making — 850
4. Evolution and Adaptation — 851
    4.1. Cooperation and Signaling — 852
5. Final Observations — 854
Acknowledgement — 854
References — 854

PART 6.2: COMMITTEES AND VOTING GROUPS

Chapter 91
Institutional Modifications of Majority Rule
WILLIAM P. BOTTOM, RONALD A. KING, LARRY HANDLIN AND GARY J. MILLER — 857
1. General Introduction — 857
2. Agenda Control — 858
    2.1. One-dimensional Agenda Control — 858
    2.2. Decentralized Agenda Control — 861
3. Extraordinary Majorities and the Veto — 864
4. Bicameralism — 867
Acknowledgements — 870
References — 870

Chapter 92
Endogenous Properties of Equilibrium and Disequilibrium in Spatial Committee Games
RICK K. WILSON — 872
1. Theoretical Background — 872
2. Experimental Design — 873
3. Endogenous Preferences — 874
    3.1. The Core — 874
    3.2. Star Preferences — 875
    3.3. Skew Star Preferences — 877
4. Discussion — 878
Acknowledgements — 878
References — 879

Chapter 93
Structure Induced Equilibrium in Spatial Committee Games
RICK K. WILSON — 880
1. Theoretical Basics — 880

2. Experimental Design	881
3. Monopoly Agenda Setting	882
4. Backward Voting Agenda	884
5. Conclusion	887
Acknowledgements	888
References	888

Chapter 94
Three-way Experimental Election Results: Strategic Voting, Coordinated Outcomes and Duverger's Law
THOMAS RIETZ 889

1. Introduction	889
2. The Experiments	891
2.1. Common Procedures	891
2.2. Equilibria	891
2.3. Specific Treatments	892
3. Results	893
3.1. Candidate Winning Frequencies	893
3.2. Other Results	895
4. Conclusions and Other Issues Studied with Similar Experiments	895
Acknowledgements	896
References	896

Chapter 95
Participation Game Experiments: Explaining Voter Turnout
JOEP SONNEMANS AND ARTHUR SCHRAM 898

References	901

PART 6.3: BEHAVIOR AND ORGANIZATIONS

Chapter 96
Growing Organizational Culture in the Laboratory
COLIN F. CAMERER AND ROBERTO WEBER 903

References	907

PART 7: INDIVIDUAL CHOICE, BELIEFS AND BEHAVIOR

Individual Choice, Beliefs and Behavior	911
Risk: Effect of Stakes and Sex	911
Endowment effects	912
References	913

Chapter 97
Motivation Theory and Experimental Behavior under the Decision Cost Hypothesis
VERNON L. SMITH AND JAMES M. WALKER   914
1. Payoffs and Behavior   914
   1.1. Decision Making and Decision Cost Under Uncertainty   915
   1.2. Two-person Interactive Model of Decision Cost   917
References   920

Chapter 98
Intertemporal Choice under Habit Formation
ERNST FEHR AND PETER K. ZYCH   923
1. Introduction   923
2. Experimental Design   923
3. Results   924
4. Conclusions   927
References   928

Chapter 99
Preference Reversal: Now You See it, Now You Do Not!
PETER BOHM   929
Concluding remarks   937
References   938

Chapter 100
The Endowment Effect: Evidence of Losses Valued More than Gains
DANIEL KAHNEMAN, JACK L. KNETSCH AND RICHARD H. THALER   939
1. Experimental Verification   940
2. Exchanges   941
3. Repeated Trials   943
4. Buy, Sell, and Choose   943
5. Market Transactions   946
6. Summary   946
References   947

Chapter 101
The Endowment Effect
PRAVEEN KUJAL AND VERNON L. SMITH   949
1. The Background   949
2. The Experiments   950
   2.1. Kahneman–Knetsch–Thaler Choice Experiments   950
   2.2. Franciosi et al. Choice Experiments   950
   2.3. Kahneman, Knetsch and Thaler (1991) Exchange Experiments   952

2.4. Mug Exchange Experiments using Uniform Price Double Auction	953
References	955

Chapter 102
The Becker–DeGroot–Marschak Mechanism is not Generally Incentive-Compatible in Practice
PETER BOHM 956
1. Experimental design 956
2. Conclusions 957
References 957

Chapter 103
Utility Maximization
JAMES C. COX 958
1. The Utility Hypothesis 958
2. A Complete, Disaggregated Data Set 960
3. Test Results and Power 961
4. Are the Inconsistencies with Utility Maximization Significant? 963
Acknowledgement 965
References 965

Chapter 104
Preference Reversals
JAMES C. COX 967
1. Seminal Experiments 968
2. Independence Axiom Treatments 969
3. Incentive Treatment 971
4. Transitivity Treatments 972
5. Risk Neutrality Treatment 973
6. Market Treatment 974
Acknowledgement 975
References 975

Chapter 105
Rationality the Fast and Frugal Way: Introduction
GERD GIGERENZER AND PETER M. TODD 976
1. Heuristics 977
2. A Fast and Frugal Heuristic 977
3. The Adaptive Toolbox 979
   3.1. Heuristic Principles for Guiding Search 979
   3.2. Heuristic Principles for Stopping Search 980
   3.3. Heuristic Principles for Decision Making 980
4. Emergency Room Decisions 981

5. Ecological Rationality	983
6. What is to Come	984
References	985

Chapter 106
The Recognition Heuristic and the Less-Is-More Effect
DANIEL G. GOLDSTEIN AND GERD GIGERENZER   987

1. Accuracy of the Recognition Heuristic	988
2. The Less-is-More Effect	988
3. Do People Use the Recognition Heuristic?	990
4. Does the Less-is-More Effect Occur in Human Reasoning?	991
5. The Underpinnings of the Recognition Heuristic	992
References	992

Chapter 107
The Recognition Heuristic: A Fast and Frugal Way to Investment Choice?
ANDREAS ORTMANN, GERD GIGERENZER, BERNHARD BORGES
AND DANIEL G. GOLDSTEIN   993

1. Investment Theory and Practice	993
2. Recognition-based Investment Decisions	994
2.1. When Choosing a Subset from a Larger Set, Choose Those Objects in the Larger Set That are Highly Recognized	994
3. Study 1	994
3.1. Study Design	994
3.2. How Did High Recognition Portfolios Perform Relative to Low Recognition Portfolios?	997
3.3. How Did High Recognition Portfolios Perform Relative to Market Indices?	997
3.4. How Did High Recognition Perform Relative to Managed Funds?	998
3.5. How Did High Recognition Portfolios Perform Relative to Random Stock Picks?	999
3.6. How Did High Recognition Portfolios Perform Relative to Individuals' Investment Choices?	1000
4. From Recognition to Riches?	1000
5. Study 2	1000
5.1. Study Design	1001
5.2. How Did High Recognition Portfolios Perform Relative to Low Recognition Portfolios?	1001
5.3. How Did High Recognition Portfolios Perform Relative to Various Benchmarks?	1002
5.4. What About Gender Effects?	1002
5.5. From Recognition to Riches?	1002
6. Conclusion	1003
References	1003

Chapter 108
One-Reason Decision Making
GERD GIGERENZER, LAURA MARTIGNON, ULRICH HOFFRAGE,
JÖRG RIESKAMP, JEAN CZERLINSKI AND DANIEL G. GOLDSTEIN   1004

1. "Take The Best" and Minimalist — 1004
2. Simple Rules for Search — 1006
3. Predicting Homelessness — 1008
4. Fast and Frugal Heuristics Versus Linear Models: A Competition — 1008
5. Fast and Frugal Heuristics Versus Bayesian Methods — 1009
6. Why is Take The Best so Robust? — 1010
7. Ecological Rationality: Which Environmental Structures Can Take The Best Exploit — 1011
8. Non-compensatory Information — 1011
9. Scarce Information — 1012
10. Abundant Information — 1013
11. Do People Intuitively Adapt Heuristics to Environmental Structures? — 1013
12. Does the Use of Lexicographic Strategies Depend on Time Pressure? — 1014
13. An Intelligent System Must Ignore Information — 1015
References — 1016

Chapter 109
Cognitive Illusions Reconsidered
GERD GIGERENZER, RALPH HERTWIG, ULRICH HOFFRAGE AND PETER SEDLMEIER — 1018
1. Base Rate Fallacy Reconsidered — 1018
2. The Ecological Argument — 1019
3. Helping John Q. Public — 1020
4. Helping Physicians — 1021
5. Helping AIDS Counselors — 1023
6. Helping Lawyers and Judges — 1023
7. How to Teach Bayesian Reasoning — 1024
8. Overconfidence Bias Reconsidered — 1025
9. Conjunction Fallacy Reconsidered — 1027
10. Availability Reconsidered — 1030
11. Conclusion — 1033
References — 1033

Chapter 110
Social Heuristics
PETER M. TODD, JÖRG RIESKAMP AND GERD GIGERENZER — 1035
1. Social Heuristics for Cooperation — 1035
2. Detecting Cheaters — 1037
3. Cheater Detection Versus Social Contracts — 1040
4. Cheater Detection Versus Logical Reasoning — 1041
5. Searching for Mates — 1042
6. Conclusion — 1045
References — 1045

Chapter 111
Payoff Scale Effects and Risk Preference Under Real and Hypothetical Conditions
SUSAN K. LAURY AND CHARLES A. HOLT — 1047
1. Introduction — 1047
2. Incentive Effects for Choices Involving Gains — 1048
3. Choices in the Loss Domain, and the Reflection Effect — 1050
4. Conclusion — 1052
References — 1053

Chapter 112
Rewards and Behavior in First Price Auctions
VERNON L. SMITH AND JAMES M. WALKER — 1054
1. The First Price Auction — 1054
2. The Experimental Environment — 1055
3. Behavior — 1056
References — 1060

Chapter 113
Men, Women and Risk Aversion: Experimental Evidence
CATHERINE C. ECKEL AND PHILIP J. GROSSMAN — 1061
1. Abstract Gamble Experiments — 1062
2. Contextual Environment Experiments — 1066
3. Evidence From Field Studies — 1069
4. Discussion — 1071
References — 1072

PART 8: METHODS

8. Methods — 1077

Chapter 114
Experimetrics: The Use of Market Experiments to Evaluate the Performance of Econometric Estimators
JAMES C. COX AND RONALD L. OAXACA — 1078
1. Designing Experiments to Study the Properties of Estimators — 1079
2. Performance of the Estimators — 1080
3. Explanation of the Posted Offer Results — 1083
Acknowledgement — 1085
References — 1086

Chapter 115
On the Performance of the Lottery Procedure for Controlling Risk Preferences
JOYCE E. BERG, THOMAS A. RIETZ AND JOHN W. DICKHAUT — 1087

1. Introduction	1087
2. Inducing Risk Preferences in Theory	1087
3. Evidence	1090
3.1. Inducing Risk Neutrality: Evidence from Sealed Bid Auctions	1090
3.2. Inducing Risk Aversion and Risk Seeking: Evidence from Paired Choice Tasks	1092
3.3. Inducing Risk Aversion and Risk Seeking: Evidence from the Becker–DeGroot–Marshak Procedure	1093
4. Summary	1094
Acknowledgements	1096
References	1096
Author Index of Volume 1	I-1
Subject Index of Volume 1	I-19

PART 1

MARKETS

1. MARKETS

More than anything else in the history of the development of economic thought, experimental economics is about "the extended order of markets" whose outcomes are not part of the intentions of the participants.

It is accurate to say that markets emerged out of the dim past of social and economic exchange as an inscrutable human social "propensity to truck, barter and exchange," rather than to describe them as having been invented. Even today, as in the experimental subfield of economic system design and testing, although "invention" appears to be prominent initially, all designs are subject to continuous change and adaptation in the light of experience and feedback; first in lab testing, then ongoing in the field. For example, the Chicago Mercantile Exchange has a book of rules, consisting of a three ring loose-leaf notebook, symbolizing the persistence of change based on experience that characterizes institutions. This is the central feature of markets in this Handbook.

1.1. Institutional Environments

1.1.1. Properties of the Double Auction

The double auction is a dynamic, real-time bid/ask continuous trading mechanism. It appears to have evolved originally as a two-sided generalization of the open outcry progressive auction, but was co-opted in the form of various electronic versions beginning in 1976 in both the lab (A. Williams at Arizona) and the field (the Toronto stock exchange). The term itself comes from the "old finance" descriptive literature, and was introduced to economics only through laboratory experiments that, from their inception, had to come to terms with the microstructure of trading. As an institution it continues to be subject to ongoing modification and selection for a great variety of new applications.

The laboratory discovery of the double auction's remarkable convergence properties to static equilibrium and its ability to track random (and other) shifts in the supply and demand environment has invited many experimental investigations supplemented by much data analysis. Plott here summarizes six properties, suggestively and graphically labeled (Sawtooth, Beacon, Pushing, etc.) that characterize some of the endogenous features of this mechanism's facilitation of price discovery. These features spotlight the extent to which empirical discoveries from experiments have greatly outrun the development of adequate dynamic theories of price discovery in economics that are institution-specific.

In asset trading environments, it was found that a positive or negative excess of bids over asks – revealed as a natural part of the trader message interaction process and using a Walrasian interpretation of adjustment – foreshadows movements in contract price formation. Bosserts and Plott exploit this discovery and subsequent elaboration and extension to the within-period and across-period motion of prices on the road to finding the equilibrium in controlled supply and demand experiments. The predictive information content of the bid/ask arrival structure enables one to apply numerical methods (here, it is Newton's) and via successive updated approximations in real time to describe the convergence to equilibrium.

In this development it is crucial to note that convergence processes, like the traders, are completely ignorant of the state to which the market converges. This fact continues to mystify the economics profession, although experimentalists were forced to incorporate it into their thinking long ago. The mystery that remains is to fully characterize this convergence process. How and why the bid/ask arrival process is able to provide the discovery procedure that anticipates price movements and the unknown equilibrium is unknown and not yet formally modeled. It is clear, however, that if the price is below the equilibrium of unknown conditions of supply and demand, the number of buyers who would want to buy at that price exceeds the number who want to sell. Hence is it natural to expect a greater intensity of bid activity than ask activity. At the margin, this differential activity is a correct predictor of change toward the unknown equilibrium.

These articulations are an important step in replacing the standard economic story – market participants need complete information – with the more realistic fact that such information cannot – and demonstrably does not – need to be given to any one mind in order to achieve efficient realizations for resource allocation. The complete information requirement stems from Jevons (1888/1871). If it were otherwise, how could the economy even function in the manner traditionally believed in professional and applied discourse?

A partial equilibrium approach to modeling the bid/ask spread from the perspective of optimal individual trader choice introduces a probability distribution that a contract resulting from any given submitted bid (ask) will be accepted. Consistent with this model, Smith and Van Boening show that a behavioral empirical property of double auction trading is that if you increase uncertainty in the supply and demand environment this increases the observed bid/ask spread standing whenever a contract occurs; i.e., increased uncertainty in the environment increases the bid/ask spread.

Brewer studies further the important finding by Gode and Sundar that institutions carry some of the intelligence that enables individuals to discover equilibrium in a market, relieving them from dependence on full rationality. The finding has been confined to isolated single-commodity markets, and its robustness to multiple commodity markets is unknown. However, Brewer looks at robustness where the buyer/seller limit price bounds are continuously refreshed, and expands somewhat the limited intelligence of the traders who are nevertheless of limited rationality. He also provides a nice guide to the development of this literature including the theoretical work pioneered by Hurwicz and his coworkers.

The hypothesis that institutions provide algorithms that assist traders is very powerful. The challenge ultimately is to understand how the algorithmic behavior of traders interacts with institutions as algorithms to yield socially optimal outcomes approximated by what we observe; this interaction occurs outside of anyone's conscious intention.

Smith and Williams demonstrate and articulate the anatomy of the response of double auction markets to external price controls, either ceilings or floors, binding or non-binding. The key discovery from experimental probes by Isaac and Plott was that both binding and non-binding controls slowed convergence to the competitive equilibrium. Why is this? It seemed transparent from traditional static supply and demand theory that the market (1) should quickly lock on to the control price – ceiling or floor – if it is binding and (2) have no effect whatsoever if it is not binding. Both propositions are robustly false and in the report of their work, Smith and Williams show why: it is implicit in the dynamics of the double auction process. In double auction processes, buyers and sellers, not knowing anything about an "equilibrium price" or what might constitute a realizable trade, start from an initial advantageous position of strength – they bid low, and ask high relative to their respect induced values and costs. Then they concede competitively, narrowing the bid/ask spread. But a price ceiling asymmetrically limits the buyer and seller strategy spaces: it has no effect on the capacity of buyers to begin bargaining from advantageously low bids, while sellers can start no higher than the ceiling. The normal tendency to concede then yields contracts lower than would prevail if there were no ceiling. The process is reversed if there is a floor price control. This discovery sheds important new light on the importance of understanding how institutions mediate the market price discovery process. It was only one of the dozens of discoveries that changed the way experimentalists think about economics and markets.

1.1.2. Properties of Posted Offer Processes

Even where alternative institutions yield equilibrium convergence, the dynamics differ greatly, and there is wide variation in the ability of different pricing processes to track changes in the environment.

Posted offer pricing was one of the early trading institutions examined in the laboratory, and it played a central role in alerting experimentalists to the significance and role of institutions in understanding economic behavior in markets. It is the pricing mechanism most often put forward by economists when they seek to model oligopoly behavior or think about market power. Posted offer pricing is particularly visible because of its ubiquity in retail markets.

The simplicity of posted offer relative to double auction trading has invited more theoretical modeling, but in the tradition of standard price theory the models abstract from strategic behavior by buyers; i.e., demand is given and fully revealed by buyers who are (in effect) modeled as robots in the standard theory. This qualification and limitation is not always evident in proposed policy and other applications of market power theory. Relevance is sometimes justified on the basis that in some applications there are a great many buyers, who by assumption are usually thought to reveal demand. But this assumption has never been tested so far as we are able to determine.

How might buyers, whatever their number relative to sellers, influence seller posted offer prices? There are two ways: (1) sellers may expect that buyers may overreact (retaliate) to an increase in price; (2) buyers may react by withholding demand, particularly at the margin, which has been observed in experimental markets, and prominently in monopoly markets with multiple buyers. As documented in experiments, demand withholding even at the margin has strong disciplinary power in cases of decreasing marginal and average cost (since the marginal units are the most profitable), leading firms to compete brutally for volume.

The first entry in this section deals with an issue concerning possible retaliatory buyer behavior in markets due to perceived "unfairness." It has been found in questionnaire response studies that buyers resist changes in posted offer prices that are not cost justified, that arise from external changes in the environment, because these increases are perceived as "unfair" based on available information. Kujal and Smith manipulate information to investigate this "fairness" argument in a market context, and ask whether fairness affects the path or the equilibrium if the latter is modified for a taste for "fairness" in the sense of preference for more equal outcomes: the path is affected, but "fairness" washes out in determining the new equilibrium which is based on traditional, competitive, profit-maximizing behavior.

In posted offer pricing, where a competitive equilibrium outcome is not supported by a Nash pure strategy equilibrium there is a potential for unilateral self-interested action to lead to behavior that is natural to define as market power. "Edgeworth cycles" are a prominent example, and this suggests the possibility of a mixed strategy Nash equilibrium defined on the premise that buyers have no role in influencing posted prices. Davis and Wilson explicitly consider this approach for characterizing seller behavior in posted offer markets. They find that this approach poorly organizes seller behavior. Since they control for any effects due to buyer behavior by simulating fully revealing buyers, the failure cannot be due to buyer responses.

Kruze directly addresses the issue of buyer influence on seller posted price behavior. She compares posted offers by two sellers in markets using robot demand-revealing buyers with markets using human buyers. Mean posted prices are significantly higher when the robot buyers fully reveal demand.

As a means of having close experimental control on the expression of demand, experimentalists remove the effect of seller inventories on pricing behavior by treating all trades as applying to contracts for sales to order. Since most of the gross national product and a growing share of it are for services, this is not an oversimplification. Nevertheless, it is important to ask how price formation in posted offer and double auction institutions is affected by the need for sellers to manage inventory simultaneously in order to facilitate sales. Mestelman reports many experiments comparing the two institutions in this environment. One important finding is that the advantage that the posted price procedure has over double auction (for sellers) *disappears* when they have to manage inventory to make sales.

Just as price controls, both binding and non-binding, impact the dynamics of market convergence processes, quantity controls or quotas affect market convergence behavior. Kujal summarizes experiments examining this phenomenon in posted offer markets, demonstrating how quotas interfere with the price–quantity equilibrium discovery process.

1.1.3. Call Markets and Sealed Bids

Smith reports a robustly replicable example of a remarkable property of two-sided bid-offer trading institutions. In this example, all trades clear at a uniform price and traders closely approximate the predicted competitive equilibrium: many accepted bids and asks are tied or nearly tied at the equilibrium clearing price. Consequently, the equilibrium is strategy-proof. This emergent property enables each side of the market to "regulate" the ability of the other side to extract more favorable terms. No trader can influence the price by withholding some of his or her units from the market. The market frequently achieves 100 percent efficient allocations, but only 5–10 percent of the induced supply and demand surplus is revealed in the bids (asks).

In this section Cox provides a summary of the theory – various risk preference models – of the first- or high-price sealed bid auction developed in response to experimental tests. All these auctions build upon the pioneering work of Vickery. Cox also summarizes the principal results from experimental tests of these models. Auctions have been a particularly fruitful success story for non-cooperative equilibrium theory after the original models of Vickery were modified for risk aversion.

1.1.4. Alternative Market Institutions

Walras observed in the 1870s that the French bourse used a trading procedure that avoided the occurrence of trades at different prices. Economic theorists thereafter were attracted to studying the dynamic properties of the "tatonnement" mechanism Walras used to describe general multi-market equilibrium determination. The idea was to use an iterative procedure to discover equilibrium clearing prices that would avoid non-equilibrium trades that changed endowments and generated complex path dependent trajectories. The London gold market used the same procedure (adding unanimity as a stopping rule), but it was not an institution adopted in other market applications. This long history was reason enough to invite experimental testing and comparison with the other institutions discussed in this section.

Bronfman et al. and Plott report experiments making it plain that the tatonnement is inefficient and yields volatile outcomes. There is no suggestion that the French were somehow missing something obvious, as Walras's version may well have ignored additional institutional structure supplied by the auctioneer, who was not modeled. The episode is a mystery, leaving unexplained why a procedure with such flawed incentive properties has survived so long.

Friedman and Rich examine an unusual institution which was created by government and other agents without benefit of either an equilibrium theory or a testing methodology. In this case, the "Matching Market" (some versions have been called a "buyers' bid auction") in which the highest remaining bid is matched with the lowest offer in order and filled at the bid price so long as that price is greater than the matching ask. They find this mechanism to be inefficient relative to the uniform price sealed bid-offer clearing market. This contribution illustrates the hazards of market design proposals that are offered without test-bedding their properties to determine if they have undesirable outcomes or are dominated by well-known alternatives.

Plott discusses two methods of implementing the Walrasian adjustment mechanism that have been tested in the experimental literature. Although both have performed satisfactorily in isolated single commodity markets with linear excess demand, neither does well in nonlinear or multiple market settings. Part of the poor performance is a consequence of strategic misrepresentation of the excess demand, and part comes from coordination failure across markets. The problems are especially evident – even in the single market case – where there is no price that yields zero excess demand, although there is a price above which excess demand is negative, and below which it is positive. Such markets converge in the continuous double auction, but fail to do so with the tatonnement.

1.2. Imperfect Competition

The theory of perfect competition stemming from W.S. Jevons specified conditions so restrictive and impractical that both theory and public policy were destined to deal extensively with market imperfections in the achievement of static market equilibrium. Although Jevons imagined that complete information on supply and demand was essential for market participants to reach a competitive equilibrium, neither he nor his followers have produced a theorem showing that competition prevails with such information and fails in its absence. Instead we have a proliferation of cases in which competition is compromised depending upon the dearth of firms, market power, whose conditions depend more critically on the intra-firm cost-capacity structure than the number of firms, collusion, various information asymmetries, entry barriers, and so on.

Contestable markets theory and laboratory experiments independently brought new insights to the notion that the world was inherently non-competitive. The former focused on the cost of entry relative to its value to the entrant thereby linking competition in a completely natural way with decision in the context of opportunity cost. The world defined the opportunity set of the firm whose location-entry decision was in response to everything in the environment that could potentially yield benefits in excess of the cost of entry. Industrial organization went dynamic, but also returned to fundamental economic decision-making as it applied to entry and exit.

Experimental economists discovered: (1) complete information on the conditions of supply and demand, as proposed by Jevons and thereafter accepted, are not necessary nor even sufficient for agents to discover a competitive equilibrium; (2) the institution of trading significantly impacted competitive outcomes through its implicit information revelation properties; (3) competitive outcomes were mediated by agent choice governed by opportunity cost comparisons in single markets that varied the cost of entry, and multiple market participation choice by buyers and sellers; (4) the predicted potential for profit to be left on the table because of information asymmetries were overcome by reputation formation, warranties, and participant monitoring of those who had the inside asymmetric information, as agent behavior signaled the need for more comprehensive models of the role of information in equilibrium; (5) contestable market theory performed as predicted; (6) it was difficult to show that concepts of rational predatory pricing described observed behavior in market experiments.

These developments together had straight-forward implications for public policy: reduce all artificial entry barriers such as restrictions on trade foreign or domestic, impediments to new business formation, nontransferable management and worker benefits, and so on.

1.2.1. Market Power

Fehr and Gachter use laboratory experiments to examine two models that have been offered to explain the persistent residue of inter-industry wage differentials after controlling for job, worker and demographic characteristics. Is the residue a consequence of not having identified all the factors determining the differentials or a failure of the law of one price in a market? Experiments control for "other characteristics," and therefore provide an independent approach to hypothesis testing. Fehr and Gachter test two versions of the theory of efficiency wage differentials: reference fair-wage effort, and shirking, where the wage differential is paid to reduce shirking. Both versions survive the laboratory tests. For example, firms with better profit alternatives (higher value for the work) pay wages above the competitive wage to induce more effort (or to prevent shirking).

The paradox of power is that in many instances, such as in the distribution of income, the strong do not grow ever more powerful relative to the weak. Thus the poor who have more votes than the rich have not appropriated any substantial share of the latter's resources. Durham, Hirshleifer and Smith test a Nash–Cournot model resolving the paradox in terms of diminishing returns to appropriative effort. The results show good conformance with the several predictions of the model.

The paper by Davis and Holt provides the basic primer on market power, its definition and manifestation in experiments, and the emergence of collusive behavior by market participants. Since entry cost is infinite by experimental design, these partial equilibrium exercises demonstrate the mischief that can persist in the complete absence of any discipline of entry.

Bosch-Domenèch and Vriend examine the path-breaking early literature on oligopoly behavior (1959–1961) summarizing the effect of information and institutional form (quantity vs price adjusting) on the occurrence of cooperative or competitive outcomes.

This literature not only launched experimental economics, but it also defined the laboratory protocols that continue to influence how experiments are designed and executed.

Cox and Isaac's entry shows how and why institutions, contestability, and incentive designs can matter in the decentralized restraint or control of monopoly behavior. It was this theme – institutional design for monopoly control – that originally inspired Vickrey's investigation of incentive compatibility, and his contributions to auction theory.

1.2.2. Collusion

Cason provides a brief but comprehensive discussion of results in the literature on price signaling, conspiracies and their often observed transient impact on competitive outcomes He also reports that the airline industry, which has been plagued by profit troubles, uses its multiple market participation to squeeze some profits from collusion. Airlines are an interesting example in which specific airlines dominate certain airports, but most have persistently failed to convert such apparent market power into profitable operations.

Gomez, Goeree and Holt report the results of laboratory experiments designed to elicit predatory pricing behavior. The question is whether an incumbent can gain by temporarily pricing below marginal cost, drive out the entrant, and then enjoy an unmolested and profitable monopoly. It turns out that such behavior was difficult to find. They report three replications of a single contrary experiment that yielded predation, found none, and then report a simpler design in which predatory behavior emerged. The theoretical and experimental literature on predation is deficient in failing to fully model entry/exit cost: for example the effect of predatory behavior on the target firm's asset value. Thus, where the sunk cost of an entrant is high because of specialized, long-lived capital, predatory behavior destroys asset value by forcing its resale price to be discounted by the predation, and any new buyer (public policy should not allow purchase by the incumbent predator) enters at a lower cost so that it can effectively compete against predation. Otherwise – hat is, when there is a low entry cost and high contestability – predation carries little advantage: every price increase after effective predation attempts to pick its monopoly fruits and invites new highly contestable entrants whose entry cost is low.

Sherstyuk provides an extensive discussion of the literature dealing with the special anti-competitive issues arising in multiple unit progressive auctions because of incentive incompatibility ("demand reduction") arising in a naturally occurring institution. She also indicates how these effects can be mitigated by redesigning the institution and eliminating the signaling culprit – open bidding by the agents – for example by using English clock procedures including the combinatorial clock. This work illustrates the principle that less information and a truncated message space may improve performance. For example, "jump bidding," in which bidders raise the standing bid by more than the bid increment, is eliminated by the English clock. A high degree of uncertainty regarding identity and number of bidders is particularly important for efficiency and the control of collusion.

1.2.3. Non-classical Cost Environments

Traditionally, non-convexities have been thought to undermine the efficiency properties of the competitive model as derived in the neo-classical synthesis. Where an industry was characterized by scale economies that were large enough to exhaust all demand, natural monopoly was thought to be the state that would emerge. J.B. Clark (1904) stated the idea of potential competition but failed to develop its full analytical implications: the plant that is not built but could be built provides a limit on price. Contestable market theory formally introduced the concept of "hit and run" entry, with prices limited by entry opportunity cost.

Plott reports the results of competing firms that choose between two markets. One market is characterized by scale economies, and he finds that among the various possible imperfect competition models, a single firm emerges in the industry, and prices are Ramsey competitive as predicted by contestable markets theory.

But certain non-convexities can create severe price discovery problems in certain institutions, such as double auction, that in classical environments are exceptionally effective. The problem is at the foundation: any institution that converges to yield the law of one price in a market will fail to be efficient because no price line or hyper plane cleanly separates the two sides of the market. Efficiency requires nonlinear, disjoint or multi-part pricing such as might be included in directly negotiated contracts.

Van Boeing and Wilson summarize experiments providing a particularly compelling example of non-convex supply in which firms incur only avoidable fixed costs – costs that do not vary with the level of output, but must be incurred if any output is produced. The structure is such that demand passes through a gap in the supply function. With double auction trading, convergence to a single price allows a higher cost firm to enter, but demand cannot support the entry, and market allocation is inefficient. The authors preclude entry, which can (but need not) provide a solution in some parameterizations. Indeed, entry cost itself can be an avoidable fixed cost. How behavior in their environment would evolve if the troublesome "entrant" in their market had an outside option is an open question.

1.3. Dynamics of Market Adjustments

In this section, the papers report work on market price stability, market disintegration, asset market price bubbles and entry decision coordination.

Hypotheses governing adjustment in price–quantity space and the stability of competitive equilibrium points in that space captured alternative modes of thinking about agent responses in disequilibrium states. Supply quantity lags behind the current price, the current price change depends on excess demand at that price, or the current quantity change depends on the gap between the demand and supply prices (marginal surplus) for that quantity. Since traditional economic theory was not institution-specific, this void was filled in by the experimenters. Plott uses the double auction to test the quantity and price adjustment hypotheses in an environment with multiple equilibria, each stable or unstable by one or the other hypotheses tested.

Organized exchanges in Chicago, New York and elsewhere have rules prohibiting or controlling the occurrence of "off floor" trades, that is, outside the designated hours and locus on the exchange floor. Are these rules functional in terms of market performance and maintenance, or are they only an obvious manifestation of the exchange firm's desire to collect its service fees? The problem posed for study by Smith and Van Boening is described by a parable:

> In the beginning, traders were dispersed in space and time, and it was transaction-costly for the traders to find each other and to negotiate private trades; a fee-for-trades exchange firm was formed where traders congregate to negotiate, and the multilateral double auction was born with public display of prices in real time; traders are now in close proximity to each other and find it natural to defect from the exchange and trade bilaterally at low negotiation cost since they can free-ride on the prices discovered by the market (such information being a public good). This compromises the viability of the exchange firm in facilitating central markets.

Smith and Van Boening report experimental results in which subjects in electronic double auction exchange are given the opportunity to easily make bilateral "off floor" trades that bypass the organized market. A growing number of such trades occur over time. These trades tend predominantly to split the available gains from exchange at prices inside the standing bid/ask spread. Moreover, the standing bid/ask spread tends to widen, and prices become more volatile, as the price discovery process fragments.

Price bubbles are as old as asset trading, and have characterized organized stock markets since their inception in the nineteenth century. This phenomenon motivated the idea of creating a "transparent" asset trading market where shares had a well-defined, intrinsic value based on common trader information concerning share expected, or average, dividend value. Using these experimental results as a baseline, the research program originally was expected to inquire if price bubbles – trading away from intrinsic value – could be created by controlling information or other elements.

But a funny thing happened at the very beginning: the baseline environment generated huge price bubbles and the research program turned to questions of replication and to the study of a great variety of treatments that were conjectured might mitigate the phenomena These treatments include experience within or across diverse groups; homogeneity of endowments; the imposition of price change limits based on the previous period's close; subject sophistication (business executive and even over-the-counter market makers); allowing subjects to buy on margin and to sell short; futures trading; dividend certainty; recruiting subjects who were required to bring their own money to mitigate an alleged "house money" effect; varying the supply of money relative to shares; preventing resale of previously purchased shares; and so on.

Replication by others proved that it was not a peculiar "Arizona" phenomenon and none of the mitigating treatments eliminated bubbles except one: experience in the same group – bring the same group to the lab three times, and prices in the third session deviate little from dividend value and volume slows to a trickle. Some of the treatments reduced somewhat various measures of the severity of the bubble; others made the bubble worse on one or more measures. For example the bubble is smaller or greater depending on whether subjects are endowed with less or more cash, confirming the observation that the stock market is sensitive to changes in monetary policy; futures trading is accompanied by a reduction in spot share price bubbles, consistent with the hypothesis that there is a problem with common dividend information being sufficient to induce common expectations. Bubbles are exacerbated by margin and short trading, but are nevertheless eliminated by experience across three sessions of experience.

The results reported by Williams, Porter and Smith, by Fisher and by Noussair and Plott document many of these findings. Not all of the reported treatment effects range across all three levels of experience.

Rapoport and Seale study a class of (0, 1) entry games in which the average number of entries tracks with remarkable if not perfect accuracy the Nash equilibrium. These results look "like magic" to Kahneman who introduced the game to cognitive psychologists, and "like magic" to economists. They look this way to anyone who accepts the implicit hypothesis that desirable individual and social outcomes are unattainable except by cognitive self-awareness, focused attention and prolonged deliberation. Welcome to the world of experimental economics: this Handbook is filled with examples of this kind of "magic" replicated over and over in a great variety of contexts during the last half century. Rapoport and Seale find these particular entry game results replicable and robust with respect to a number of treatment and parameter changes. It is like the bubble results, intransigent, but here the results support "rational" economic performance.

It is not magic. Rather, it is simply not understood by any of the constructivist models in the standard toolkits of either economists or psychologists because those models deal with outcomes not processes. Asking the subjects does not help, for they do not understand it either, any more than they can tell you how they are able to drive a car while thinking about their term paper.

References

Clark, J.B. (1904). "The Problem of Monopoly". Macmillan, London.
Jevons, W.S. (1888/1871). "The Theory of Political Economy", third ed. Macmillan, London, online, Library of Economics and Liberty.

PART 1.1

INSTITUTIONAL ENVIRONMENTS

PART 1.1.1

PROPERTIES OF THE DOUBLE AUCTION

Charles R. Plott, "Properties of Disequilibrium Adjustment in Double Auction Markets"

Peter Bossaerts and Charles R. Plott, "From Market Jaws to the Newton Method: The Geometry of How a Market Can Solve Systems of Equations"

Vernon L. Smith and Mark Van Boening, "Exogenous Uncertainty Increases the Bid–Ask Spread in the Continuous Double Auction"

Paul J. Brewer, "Zero Intelligence Robots and the Double Auction Market: A Graphical Tour"

Vernon Smith and Arlington Williams, "Effect of Non-binding Price Controls in Double Auction Trading"

Chapter 1

PROPERTIES OF DISEQUILIBRIUM ADJUSTMENT IN DOUBLE AUCTION MARKETS

CHARLES R. PLOTT

California Institute of Technology

The tendency of double auction markets to converge to the equilibrium of the associated competitive equilibrium model is well known, but the equilibration process is not understood. The reason for adjustment and the processes that are actively involved with the adjustment process are still a mystery. However, the study of many markets reported over the years by many different research groups have provided some properties of disequilibria and the dynamics of the adjustment process.

Double auction markets have properties that are closely associated with certain institutional and environmental features and have been studied extensively. First, there is a period structure to the markets: an open and a close. Second, major changes, such as parameter changes, occur between the close of one period and the open of the next and this fact is public information. That is, parameter changes do not occur during a period. Third, the commodity traded is like a service that does not have a life of over one period. Redemption values and costs are active for only one period at a time. If the commodity does have a time life – like a security – it will systematically change its value between periods, such as a dividend that is paid at the end of a period. While the discussion that follows does not specifically explore the dynamics of adjustment that occur in other market structures, the properties listed below are characteristic of the asset markets that have been studied: speculative markets, and economies characterized by overlapping generations.

1. *The "sawtooth" property of transactions price equilibration*: period open to period open, period close to period close, period open to period close and period close to period open relationships.

Markets that are not "near" the equilibrium price and quantity exhibit characteristic "sawtooth" properties of equilibration. Equilibration can be detected within periods and between periods; however, the process is not monotonic. It has a sawtooth property such as the illustrated line drawn in Figure 1.

Periods two, three and four of Figure 2 represent a typical pattern. The opening prices of a period are further from the equilibrium than are the closing prices. That is, during a period the movement of prices tends to be in the direction of the equilibrium price. However, while the movement within a period is generally toward the equilibrium, the transaction-to-transaction movement is up and down. This is like moving along a single tooth on the blade of a saw that has many smaller teeth built into it. This movement

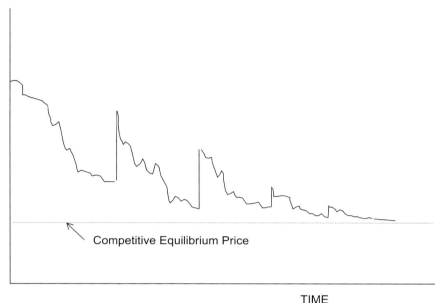

Figure 1. The sawtooth nature of the price adjustment path. Prices begin high and converge toward the competitive equilibrium price during a period. The following period prices start at prices above the price that existed at the end of the previous period.

within a period is often modeled as an exponential adjustment path and while such models capture much of the data, negative serial correlation is evident. Third period opening prices are closer to the equilibrium than were the opening prices of the second period. But the opening prices of the second period are further from the equilibrium than the closing price of the first period. After the open, the prices again move toward the equilibrium price, while following an up and down pattern. Typically opening price in period $t + 1$ is closer to the equilibrium price than was the opening price in period t. So, in each period the opening prices are closer to the equilibrium. The teeth of the saw get smaller and smaller until all data are near the equilibrium price. Ordinarily, the prices do not overshoot the equilibrium, but it can happen as in Figure 1 for periods two and six. Prices start slightly above equilibrium in period one; they then settle below equilibrium in period two and begin to work their way upward, overshooting equilibrium slightly in period six.

2. *The "beacon" property of end of period trades.* The last price movements in a period tend to point in the direction of the competitive equilibrium price (Aliprantis and Plott, 1992). If the prices are above the competitive equilibrium then the final prices

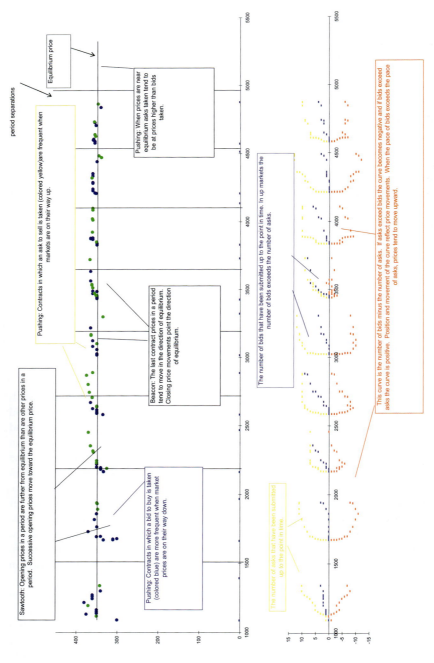

Figure 2. The time series of contract prices show the properties of adjustment in double auction markets: Markets that are in disequilibrium exhibit dynamic properties of adjustment.

tend to be lower than the other prices of the period. If prices are below equilibrium, then the final prices tend to increase relative to earlier prices. This property can be seen in Figure 2. Notice that the last price movements in almost every period are in the direction of the competitive equilibrium. The movement is down at the end of periods four, five (notice that overshooting points in the proper direction), six and seven. In these periods prices are above equilibrium as the end of the period approaches. The final movement is up in periods one, two, eight and nine. In these periods the prices have wandered below equilibrium near the end of the period so the movement is in an upward direction at the end.

3. *The "pushing" property of sale-making actions.* The market price is pushed away from the interests of the side that takes the final action in a transaction. To understand this property it is necessary to distinguish between offers that come in the form of bids to buy, offers that come in the form of asks to sell, and the market orders or actions that actually make a sale/transaction. These sale/transaction actions can be viewed as asks taken and bids taken. In the language of the Street, the sale is made when an ask is hit or a bid is hit. For example, a buyer who takes an ask pushes the price in a direction (up) that the buyer would prefer that the prices not go. Similarly a seller that takes a bid pushes the price in a direction (down) the seller would prefer that the market not go. Sometimes this property is interpreted as an "adverse selection" property of continuous, open outcry markets, in the sense that the person that made the original offer, the offer that was hit, would prefer to have waited.

3.1. *In stationary or equilibrated markets the prices of asks taken dominate prices of bids taken.* This is property is related to the work of Roll (1984) who noticed that such a dominance relationship exists in the U.S. securities markets.[1] In these previous studies the need for the market to be near equilibrium in order for the property to be clearly present was not fully appreciated.

3.2. *Markets with rising prices are characterized by asks taken and markets with falling prices are characterized by bids taken (Plott and Turocy, 1994).* It is this property that leads to the adverse selection interpretation of the pushing property of closing actions can be understood. An individual placing an order is frequently going to be disappointed. A seller placing an order will make a sale if the market is on the way up and will thus "regret" having placed the order. Similarly a buyer who places an order and is hit will regret placing the order because the market is on the way down and thus the buyer could imagine himself/herself having been made better off by waiting.

---

[1] This relationship has also been studied by Cason and Friedman (1993).

4. *Relative volumes of bids and asks have predictive power*. That is, the difference between bid and ask volume predicts price movement. If the quantity of bids in period t is greater than the quantity of asks in period t, then there is a tendency for the average price in period $t + 1$ to be greater than the average price in period t. This was one of the first properties of the market equilibration process to be identified (Smith, Suchanek and Williams, 1988).

The lower panel of Figure 2 represents this property in a little different manner than has typically been used in the literature. The time structure of the graph is the same as in upper panel so the periods in the upper graph correspond to the sequences in the lower graph. The blue curve is the number of bids that have been tendered in the period; this curve grows as the period continues. The green curve is the total number of asks. The red curve is the number of bids that have occurred minus the number of asks. As the figure shows, the number of asks tends to exceed the number of bids as the market is involved in a downward trend in period one and the beginning of period two, but when the direction tends to reverse in period three the difference falls and the curve begins to move upward. In this experiment there is a general tendency for asks to exceed the bids. The general activity levels can differ from experiment to experiment. However, when the market is clearly pulling upward as it is at the end of periods three and four the relative number of bids is dramatically increasing. The market is holding slightly above the equilibrium in period six when the bids and asks are paced about equally and then, when the market starts its decent, the asks again exceed the bids in period seven and eight.

5. *The principle of full revelation*. The last bid and ask in a period tend to be demand revealing (Jamison and Plott, 1997). This property of markets was first postulated as an axiom by Easley and Ledyard (1993). The idea is that buyers and sellers facing the possibility of no trade at all will reveal their willingness to trade at the end of a period.

6. *Negative serial correlation exits*. Price changes are negatively correlated (Cason and Friedman, 1993). The small teeth in the sawtooth pattern show the sequential up and down pattern of individual transaction prices. This property could be interpreted as a consequence of the pushing property of contract completing actions as the action comes from a buyer who takes an ask and then from a seller who takes a bid. If a market is near equilibrium then the number of asks taken and the number of bids taken tend to be about equal and there seems to be no order in which these actions are exercised. Since bids taken are at prices below asks taken, negative serial correlation can be generated.

References

Aliprantis, C.D., Plott, Charles R. (1992). "Competitive equilibria in overlapping generations experiments". Economic Theory 2, 389–426.

Cason, T.N., Friedman, Daniel (1993). "An empirical analysis of price formation in double auction markets". In: Friedman, D., Rust, J. (Eds.), The Double Auction Market: Institutions, Theory and Evidence. Addison–Wesley.

Easley, D., Ledyard, John (1993). "Theories of price formation and exchange in double oral auctions". In: Friedman, D., Rust, J. (Eds.), The Double Auction Market: Institutions, Theory and Evidence. Addison–Wesley.

Jamison, Julian C., Plott, Charles R. (1997). "Costly offers and the equilibration properties of the multiple unit double auction under conditions of unpredictable shifts of demand and supply". Journal of Economic Behavior and Organization 32, 591–612.

Plott, Charles R., Turocy III, Theodore L. (1994). "Intertemporal speculation under conditions of uncertain future demand and an endogenous, nonpublic number of speculators and speculative activity: Experimental results". Social Science Working Paper 911, California Institute of Technology, 1994.

Roll, R. (1984). "A simple implicit measure of the effective bid–ask spread in an efficient market". Journal of Finance 39 (4), 1127–1139.

Smith, Vernon L., Suchanek, Gerry L., Williams, Arlington W. (1988). "Bubbles, crashes and endogenous, expectations in experimental spot asset markets". Econometrica 56 (5), 1119–1151.

Chapter 2

FROM MARKET JAWS TO THE NEWTON METHOD: THE GEOMETRY OF HOW A MARKET CAN SOLVE SYSTEMS OF EQUATIONS

PETER BOSSAERTS and CHARLES R. PLOTT

Since market equilibrium can be interpreted as a solution to a system of equations, "price discovery," as it called in the language of market makers, can be viewed as having "found" the solution. Of course the information needed to even formulate the equations does not exist in one place so the idea that markets are "searching" for the solution to a system of equations as a numerical process would search, cannot be taken literally. Nevertheless, it is interesting that the language that has evolved from the world of practical markets has such an interpretation and curiosity alone makes one wonder how markets settle on the particular pattern of prices that solve a particular system of equations.

The substance of this note is to take seriously the analogy between market processes and the numerical methods of mathematics. The analogy is made in Figures 1 and 2. Figure 1 is a picture familiar to experimental economists. At any time, in many forms of continuous markets there exists an order book in which all standing orders to buy and sell are listed. If new orders are such that trades are possible, the trades are executed. In some cases the book is an "open book" in which all traders see the book and place orders with a full knowledge of existing orders. In other markets, the book is held by a specialist who operates under rules about what aspects of the book must be exposed to the market and how orders are executed.

It is known that in markets such as the multiple unit double auction, the shape of the book is a good indicator of the directions price changes are likely to take. In particular, when the sell order builds up, the sell order book extends beyond the buy order book and price movements down are likely. The opposite happens when the market goes up. The movement of the book when displayed (as in Figure 1) appear as "jaws" that move in a direction that anticipate which way the market is going to move.

The empirical foundation for jaws can be found in many forms.[1] When markets are on the way up the number of bids typically exceeds the number of asks. When markets are on the way down, the number of asks typically exceeds the number of bids. This is exactly the concept of "pushing" referred to Plott. When the speed of arrival of bids is greater than the speed of arrival of asks the buy order book builds and the lower jaw "juts out." When the sell orders arrive more rapidly, the sell order book builds and the upper jaw juts out. Thus the shape of the book reflects the underlying arrival rates of orders and the arrival rates in turn reflect an underlying excess demand or supply that will force price movement.

---

[1] The reader should refer to Plott (2008, this volume).

Handbook of Experimental Economics Results, Volume 1
Copyright © 2008 Elsevier B.V. All rights reserved
DOI: 10.1016/S1574-0722(07)00002-9

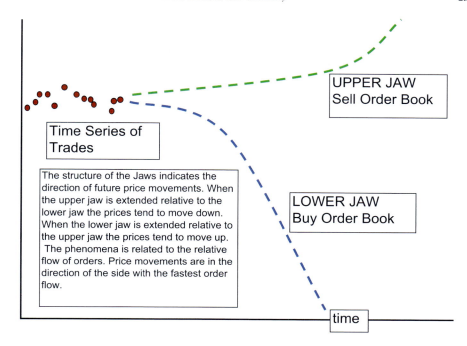

Figure 1. The market jaws can be used to predict future price changes.

The suggestion of Figure 2 is that the information in market jaws has important aspects of the information needed to apply the Newton method of solving equations. It is known that, under a wide range of conditions, the Newton method will converge to the solution to a system of equations. In general to find the value of z that solves the equation $G(z) = 0$ one needs to start at some value of z and then make small changes in z that satisfy the equation

$$dz/dt = -G'(z)^{-1} G(z).$$

The information needed is $G(z)$ and the derivative of G at the point z.

Notice that if we let $z = P$, and if $G(z) = D(P) - S(P)$, then the problem of equilibration is to find the solution of the equation

$$D(P) - S(P) = 0.$$

To apply Newton's method one needs to know for some P^*, $D(P^*) - S(P^*)$ and the value of the derivatives. Notice further that approximations of these magnitudes are given by the market jaws.

It is interesting to compare this formulation with the classical notion of Walrasian adjustment in which

$$dP/dt = A\big[D(P) - S(P)\big],$$

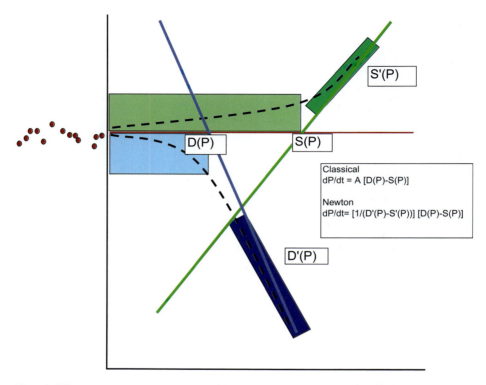

Figure 2. The relationship between the Newton method and the market jaws is that the latter is the source of information that is needed by the former.

where A is a positive constant. Thus to connect the models one only needs to recognize that the variable A needs to be the inverse of the derivative of the function. In the classical theory of price adjustment, this derivative is absent and in the classical metaphor about tatonnement, the information is not needed.

Does such a model of price adjustment work? That it does is exactly the result reported in Asparouhova, Bossaerts and Plott (2003).

References

Asparouhova, Elena, Bossaerts, Peter, Plott, Charles (2003). "Excess demand and equilibration in multi-security financial markets: The empirical evidence". Journal of Financial Markets 6 (1), 1–21.

Plott, Charles (2008). "Properties of disequilibrium adjustment in double auction markets". In: Plott, C., Smith, V. (Eds.), Handbook of Experimental Economic Results. Elsevier Science, Amsterdam.

Chapter 3

EXOGENOUS UNCERTAINTY INCREASES THE BID–ASK SPREAD IN THE CONTINUOUS DOUBLE AUCTION

VERNON L. SMITH and MARK VAN BOENING

Traditional theories of the bid–ask spread are of two kinds: (1) the bid–ask spread is a transactions cost of the dealer or a specialist for providing the services of immediacy (see Demsetz, 1968), and (2) the bid–ask spread is due to the existence of traders with superior information to that of the specialist (see Copeland and Galai, 1983; Glosten and Milgrom, 1985). One should be aware that these models provide sufficient – not necessary – conditions for the existence of a positive bid–ask spread. That these conditions are not necessary is shown by the hundreds of experimental double auction markets and our experiments reported here, in which a positive bid–ask spread persists; yet these are principals markets, without intermediate dealers or specialists, and transactions costs are minuscule. In many of these experiments, all individuals have identical (although uncertain) information on the value of the securities traded (see Smith, Suchanek, and Williams, 1988), so asymmetric information is not necessary for observing a bid–ask spread. A third theory is based on establishing that "...the probability of a limit order executing does not rise to unity as the price at which the order is placed gets infinitesimally close to a counterpart (bid or ask) market quote" (see Cohen et al., 1981, p. 300). In terms of this theory, the success reported below in inducing a wider bid–ask spread by increasing uncertainty in the environment may be attributed to the fact that we shifted the probability distribution of executing a limit order.

1. Experimental Design

Our experimental design uses the supply and demand schedules shown in Figure 1. These schedules are known to the experimenter but are not known by any subject. Price is measured in deviations from the center of the set of competitive equilibrium prices. There are five buyers and five sellers. Three of the buyers (B_1, B_3, B_5) each have a capacity to buy up to 6 units, while two of the buyers (B_2, B_4) have a capacity to buy up to 3 units in any single trading period. Symmetrically, three sellers (S_1, S_3, S_5) can sell up to 6 units and two (S_2, S_4) can sell up to 3 units. Any particular buyer or seller subject was assigned randomly to one of the step positions (1, 2, 3, 4, 5) at the beginning of each of the three weeks (5 day trading periods) in an experiment.

In experiments 4 and 5 (Table 1) subjects were not only assigned randomly by 5-day weeks to the steps shown in Figure 1, but in addition a random constant (positive or negative) was added each period to all buyer values and all seller costs. Consequently,

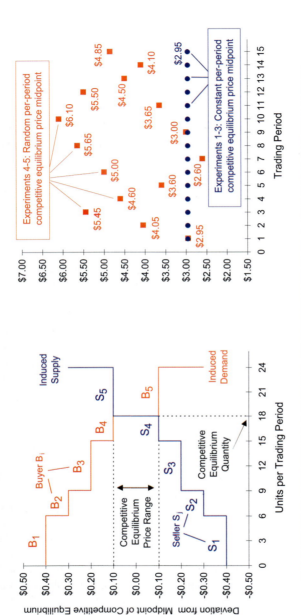

Figure 1. Experimental per period induced supply and demand schedules.

The competitive equilibrium (CE) price range is ± $0.10 from the CE midpoint, and the CE quantity is 18 units (left panel). In experiments 1-3, the midpoint of the CE price range is constant at $2.95 each period, while in experiments 4 and 5 the CE midpoint is randomly shifted each period (right panel).

Source: Campbell et al. (1991); see Tables 1 and 2, Baseline 2 experiments 2-4 (constant) and 7-8 (random).

Table 1
Experimental design

Experiment number	Market size	Competitive equilibrium price per period	Value/cost assignment per period	Number of periods
1, 2, 3	5 buyers 5 sellers	Constant	Random	15
4, 5	5 buyers 5 sellers	Random	Random	15

in these experiments, the competitive equilibrium price was shifted randomly each period. This provided greatly increased price and transaction uncertainty relative to those experiments (1–3) in which only the step assignments were randomized.

2. Exogenous Uncertainty and the Bid/Ask Spread

In experiments 1–3 the competitive equilibrium price and quantity were constant over all periods, while in experiments 4 and 5 the competitive equilibrium price level shifted at random each period. Our a priori prediction was that the second condition would yield a greater bid–ask spread than the first. We define the spread as the difference between the "standing (lowest) bid" and the "standing (highest) ask" at the time of a contract. Here, we evaluate our prediction by comparing the per-period mean and median spreads of experiments 1–3 with those of experiments 4 and 5, and by comparing the distribution of spreads in 1–3 with those in 4 and 5.

A measurement problem associated with our prediction is that contracts may and often do occur without a defined bid–ask spread or before that spread has a chance to narrow. Thus, a bid may be entered and accepted before an ask price is established. We measure the spread two ways. First, we exclude any observations where there is either no bid or no ask at the time of contract, and compute the mean spread using the remaining observations (this is the measure of central tendency reported in Campbell et al., 1991). Second, we define the spread as follows. Where a bid is accepted to form a contract but no ask is entered, we define the standing offer as $9.99; if there is an offer price being accepted, but no bid, we define the standing bid as $0.01. In this way we are able to utilize all the information content in our data; it requires only the weak assumption that any seller would be willing to sell for $9.99 (the maximum allowable) and any buyer would be willing to buy for $0.01 (the minimum allowable). Defining the spread in this way leads to some large erratic observations under all treatment conditions. In order not to weight such observations unduly, we use the median as the measure of central tendency.

Figure 2 shows the mean and median spreads per period across the constant (experiments 1–3) and randomly shifting (experiments 4 and 5) per period supply and demand

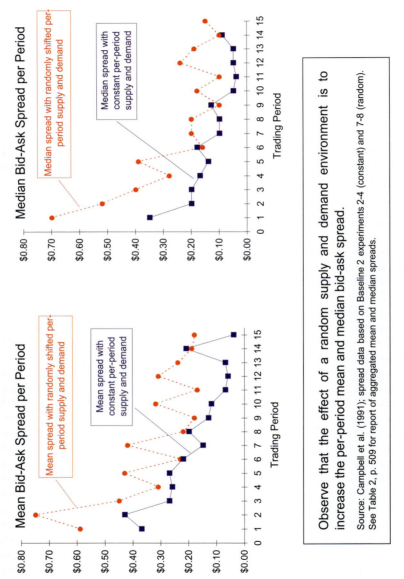

Figure 2. Mean and median bid–ask spreads for constant and randomly shifted per-period supply and demand.

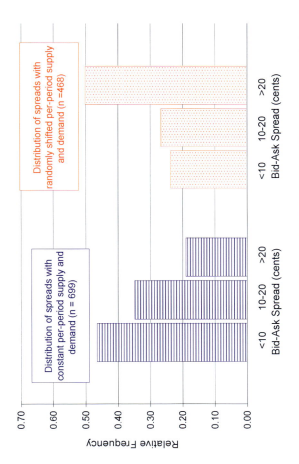

Figure 3. Distribution of bid-ask spreads for constant and randomly shifted per period supply and demand.

conditions. The upper panel shows that in 14 of the 15 trading periods, the mean spread with randomly shifting supply and demand is greater than the mean spread with constant supply and demand. The lower panel shows that in 13 of the 15 trading periods, the median spread with randomly shifting supply and demand is greater than when the supply and demand are constant. These data suggest that the effect of increased uncertainty in the supply and demand environment is to increase the per-period mean and median bid–ask spread.

Figure 3 shows our observed distributions of bid–ask spreads for the two treatment conditions. The data are shown for spreads less than 10 cents, spreads in the 10–20 cent range, and spreads greater than 20 cents. There is clearly a difference in the two empirical distributions: smaller spreads are much more likely in the constant supply and demand treatment. Closer comparison reveals that under constant per period supply and demand, about 45% of the spreads are less than 10 cents, whereas under the randomly shifting supply and demand, the amount is less than 25%. Furthermore, with constant supply and demand, less than 20% of the spreads are greater than 20 cents, while half (50%) of all spreads in the random environment fall in this interval. The data indicate that relative to a constant supply and demand, the effect of a random supply and demand environment is to decrease the frequency of small spreads and increase the frequency of large spreads.

3. Conclusion

These experiments demonstrate that exogenous uncertainty can increase the bid–ask spread in the continuous double auction. We observed greater mean and median spreads, and a greater probability of a large spread in double auctions with randomly shifting per-period supply and demand than in double auctions with constant supply and demand. These results, and many others, demonstrate that even in the absence of transaction cost or information asymmetry, positive bid–ask spreads are observed and wider spreads are observed when there is greater uncertainty in the environment.

References

Campbell, Joseph, LaMaster, Shawn, Smith, Vernon L., Van Boening, Mark (1991). "Off-floor trading, disintegration and the bid–ask spread in experimental markets". Journal of Business 64, 495–522.
Cohen, Kalman J., Maier, Steven F., Schwartz, Robert A., Whitcomb, David K. (1981). "Transaction costs, order placement strategy, and existence of the bid–ask spread". Journal of Political Economy 89, 287–305.
Copeland, Thomas E., Galai, Dan (1983). "Information effect on the bid–ask spread". Journal of Finance 38, 1457–1469.
Demsetz, Harold (1968). "The cost of transacting". Quarterly Journal of Economics 82, 33–53.
Glosten, Lawrence R., Milgrom, Paul R. (1985). "Bid, ask and transaction prices in a specialist market with heterogeneously informed traders". Journal of Financial Economics 6, 71–99.
Smith, Vernon L., Suchanek, Gerry L., Williams, Arlington W. (1988). "Bubbles, crashes and endogenous expectations in experimental spot asset markets". Econometrica 56, 1–34.

Chapter 4

ZERO-INTELLIGENCE ROBOTS AND THE DOUBLE AUCTION MARKET: A GRAPHICAL TOUR

PAUL J. BREWER

Hong Kong University of Science and Technology

Experimental evidence has established that prices and volumes in markets populated by humans generally converge towards the outcome predicted by the competitive model. Earlier chapters in this text demonstrate this phenomenon at work over and over again. Yet, casual observations together with a variety of experiments suggest that humans are not perfect maximizers. This raises some interesting questions, such as:

- Is profit maximization really necessary for the functioning of such economic principles as the law of supply and demand?
- Could some lower form of "rationality," such as agents who follow simple rules and/or stay within their budget constraint, lead to markets that converge to the competitive outcomes?

The pictures in this chapter illustrate the behavior of *Zero-Intelligence* (ZI) *Robots* in double auction markets and offer some comparison with humans. Later, we will add a little more intelligence to the ZI's. As with the human markets described in earlier chapters, we will designate each robot as a buyer robot or a seller robot. The behavior of these robots is very simple: they simply choose a random bid or ask over a range of prices constrained by their budget and the market improvement rules.[1] This is made formal later in the descriptions below.

The goal of this chapter is to compare the behavior of markets populated with simple robots to markets populated by humans. As there is clearly a lot more that could be done, sufficient detail about the market, environment, and robots are provided so that an advanced undergraduate or graduate student could easily develop their own ZI robot and market software. After providing this detail, the literature surrounding robots in double auctions is reviewed.

A series of graphs summarizes some important features of various humans and robots in a variety of double auction environments. In particular, these graphs are an attempt to both show some of the more important phenomena reported in the several papers by Gode and Sunder (1993a, 1993b) as well as show new results where the ZI robots are pushed into environments that are quite different from Gode and Sunder (1993a, 1993b), and similar experimentalists. These environments involve flows (or "recycling") of costs

---

[1] There is precedent for such random behavior in earlier work. The ZI robots can be seen as similar to the Hurwicz, Radner, and Reiter (1975a, 1975b) *B*-process, where agents negotiate by randomly choosing points that are jointly preferred.

and redemption values and can be seen as a primitive step away from environments with fixed gains from trade towards environments involving the continuous order flows of financial markets. After "breaking" the ZI robots in the new environment, the UNIT robots are introduced to show how making robot behavior dependent on the previous market transaction price can yield stability in situations with continuously order flow.

1. Environment

1.1. Values and Costs

Robots are assigned a role as either a buyer or a seller and retain this role throughout the market simulation. As with experiments involving human markets, buyers receive a value indicating how much a unit of good X is worth to them and sellers receive a cost for a unit of the good X. The robots might then be programmed to maximize their profits, as defined below, or perhaps behave in some other way (e.g., the ZI's do not actively maximize anything). Typically the experimenter will set a variety of buyer's values and seller's costs in the market in order to create sloping demand and supply curves.

1.2. Profits

BUYERS   profit = unit value (set by experimenter) − price paid in market,
SELLERS profit = price received in market − production cost
         (set by experimenter).

1.3. Limitations on Trading

Normally in a double auction market, seller's costs and buyer's redemption values may only be used once. This makes the gains from trade in a market finite and insures that supply and demand can be constructed in the usual way from sellers' costs and buyers' values. However, the case where costs and values appear again and again as in a flow can yield some new insights into how markets work. We call this latter case *continuously refreshed supply and demand* and will refer to this later in the text and graphs.

Normal – robots may produce or consume at most one unit of X.

Continuously refreshed – robots may produce or consume over and over again as new redemption values and costs appear.

1.4. Market Rules

The rules of the double auction market place some limits on what agents (robot or human) may do. The market operates under four basic rules:

1.4.1. Improvement rule

At any time, buyers may send a new bid to the market indicating the price they are willing to pay. Sellers may send a new ask to the market indicating the price they are willing to accept. To become the market bid or market ask the new bid or ask must be an improvement over any existing market bid/ask. That means bids must go up and asks must go down until a trade takes place. Trades reset the market, allowing any new bid or ask to become the market bid or market ask without regard to previous prices.

(Note: Bids and asks that are "beaten" are not saved for later use. Only the best bid and ask are retained by the market. Buyers and sellers may bid/ask again when they are beaten.)

1.4.2. Trading at ask price (new bid > market ask)

If a buyer sends a bid that is greater than the market ask price, the unit is traded at a price equal to the ask. The market bid and ask are reset to allow more trades.

1.4.3. Trading at bid price (new ask < current bid)

If a seller sends an ask that is less than the market bid price, the unit is traded at a price equal to the bid. The market bid and ask are reset to allow more trades.

1.4.4. Access to market

With humans, access to the market is generally first-come, first-served. Small groups (<100) of humans are usually, though not always, slower than the technology on which the markets are implemented, but computerized robots could overwhelm their marketplace if left to act asynchronously. Typically with robots one uses a random number generator to decide which robot will act next in the market, with each robot having an equal chance.

1.5. Budget Constraints

Robots are not allowed to trade at a loss. In the market, this means that buyers may not bid above their value and sellers may not ask below their cost. In many trading experiments, humans can and do trade at a loss. Usually these are mistakes (e.g. hitting wrong keys on unfamiliar trading software a subject uses for the first time, confusion over bid vs ask).

1.6. Trades Involve Arbitrage; No Speculative Trades

The environment is basically one of arbitrage between one's cost or value, which is private information, and the available market price, which is public information. Only buyers may buy and only sellers may sell, no one may do both – this rules out many forms of speculation. Many, though not all, of the early trading experiments with humans are similarly structured.

2. Robot Agents

2.1. Zero Intelligence Robots – Trading Algorithm

The ZI robots basically act randomly within what their budget constraints and the market rules allow. In particular, the ZI's have no memory and do not mimic, anticipate or respond to other robots, strategize, or maximize anything. Their behavior is totally determined by their value or cost, the current market bid/ask, and the outcome of a random number generator.

ZI buyers: If redemption value > market bid, send a new bid chosen from a uniform random distribution between the current market bid[2] and the buyer's redemption value. Otherwise, if redemption value $\leqslant$ market bid, the robot is not allowed to send a bid because no profit is possible.

ZI sellers: If marginal cost < market ask, send a new ask chosen from a uniform random distribution between the seller's marginal cost and the current market ask.[3] Otherwise, if market ask $\leqslant$ marginal cost, the robot is not allowed to send an ask because no profit is possible.

2.2. UNIT Robots – Trading Algorithm

The UNIT robots bid or ask at a price equal to, one unit above, or one unit below the previous transaction price, so long as this is within what their budget constraints allow. Like the ZI's, the UNIT's do not anticipate or respond to other robots, strategize, or maximize anything. Unlike the ZI's, they do have a memory and retain the previous transaction price. It is this link to previous transaction prices that results in market behavior that can be quite different from what is observed in markets with ZI robots.

UNIT buyers: Choose at random a bid B equal to one of 3 values $\{P-1, P, P+1\}$, where P is the previous[4] transaction price in the market. Each choice has an equal $(1/3)$ probability. If B is less than or equal to the robot's redemption value and greater than the current bid (if any), send the bid. Otherwise, do not send the bid – because it violates either the buyer's budget constraint or the market improvement rule.

---

[2] If there is no market bid then we use 0 as the lower limit.

[3] If there is no market ask then we use a number well above the highest buyers' value for the maximum possible ask. We cannot use ¥ because the resulting uniform random distribution would be ill defined.

[4] A pre-existing price $P0$ must be chosen by the experimenter to seed the simulation. From the graphs we will see that in environments with continuously refreshed supply and demand, the effect of this choice of $P0$ dies away as market prices converge towards instantaneous competitive equilibrium.

UNIT sellers: Choose at random an ask A equal to one of 3 values $\{P-1, P, P+1\}$, where P is the previous transaction price in the market. Each choice has an equal (1/3) probability. If A is greater than or equal to the robot's cost and less than the current ask (if any), send the bid. Otherwise, do not send the bid – because it violates the seller's budget constraint or the market improvement rule.

2.3. Kaplan's Parasitic Robots[5] – Trading Algorithm

Kaplan's robots follow a 'steal the deal' strategy, waiting for a low bid–ask spread before accepting beneficial trades. Thus, they require a market populated by other participants (other kinds of robots or humans) who are actively submitting bids and asks.

Parasitic buyers: Wait until (current ask < redemption value) and (current ask − current bid) < target, then send a bid equal to the current ask. This causes a transaction.

Parasitic sellers: Wait until (current bid > cost) and (current ask − current bid) < target, then send an ask equal to the current bid. This causes a transaction.

3. Literature – Robots and the Double Auction

3.1. Types of Questions

Robot populated markets are interesting artifacts of study for many reasons. The range of questions that can be asked is broad. The list below is a humble attempt at some categorization of these questions. Necessarily incomplete, it does provide a starting point from which to understand the research.

- *Phenomenology* involves questions about 'How are market phenomena similar or different when the types of agents or other parameters of a market environment are changed?' In what ways are markets populated by ZI robots, for example, similar to markets populated by humans and in what ways are they different? The questions are about phenomena rather than about models. Of course such a question requires many details about the market institution and economic environments to be meaningful. Once the question is well defined, *similarities* can mean any of several things: humans and certain types of robots are exhibiting some similarity in behavior within some domain; institutional rules such as the double auction improvement rule or budget constraints filter different individual behaviors to reach common types of market behavior; other factors in the economic environment (existence of a Marshallian path) are causing the similar market behavior even though the agents' individual behaviors are different. Sorting out these different causes and effects requires a great deal of future work and could yield new insights to market

---

[5] In the graphics section we do not show any examples of markets with Kaplan's robots, but they are discussed in the literature section below.

phenomena in general. As will be shown in the graphical section, similarities and differences in market behavior can exist at the same time – for instance closing prices might be similar but the path by which these prices are reached might be very different.

- *Simulation* involves questions such as 'Can we use robot markets to simulate the behavior of human markets?' 'To what extent?' and 'How?' Markets populated by robots are governed by some of the same natural principles that govern markets populated by humans. In some cases, it may be easier to calculate the competitive equilibria of complex systems of markets by robot simulation than by formally solving complex sets of equations. It might not be practical to even identify all the appropriate equations for fully rational agents in some theoretically complex game theoretic market setting, but – given some leeway with agent's rationality – we might be able to easily set up a robot simulation. As a means of obtaining information about markets populated by agents who follow rules that can be formalized as a robot algorithm, computer simulation (as opposed to, say, explicit analysis of the math behind the behavior) is sensible and merely a means of bringing these robots to life so that economists can observe them. The extent to which robot simulations can answer questions about human markets is a matter of controversy to be resolved through future research.
- *Model building, testing and refinement* involves many kinds of questions, often controversial, that are related to models (e.g., specification, comparison, rejection, usefulness). Particular robot algorithms can be thought of as mathematical models of individual behavior. Through analysis or simulation one can determine the aggregate behavior of particular kinds of robots within a market setting. The results can be compared to the predictions of other mathematical models – whether they be from other types of robots or from more traditional sources such as classical economics or game theory, e.g., Cason and Friedman (1993, 1996). Robots allow us the flexibility to alter agents' behavior in very exact and particular ways to examine various aspects of economic phenomena that might otherwise be difficult to probe.
- *Applied philosophy* involves questions such as 'How much rationality is required for markets to converge to competitive equilibrium predictions?' If the answer is "not much," then this may have broad policy reaching implications about such issues as deregulation and consumer protection. Of course, this calls to issue such basic matters as 'What is rationality?' as well as what rationality means in a market context.
- *Tournaments* involve questions about comparative performance of different robot strategies in a particular market setting. Robots allow a formalization of strategies and computer simulation becomes an easy means of comparison. Of course, there are a number of important factors that could be varied in a tournament and that might affect the results – period length, distribution of costs and values, types of private and public knowledge, methods of reward in the tournament (e.g., genetic algorithms that reproduce profitable robots and kill those with low profits, cash to

the author of the robot), etc. Tournaments can become interesting to economists when we try to explain the relative performance of strategies or what elements of strategies are important, because these issues can require pushing economic principles and ideas into new areas – sometimes beyond their normal realms of applicability.

3.2. Major Results from the Literature – A Chronology

The issues and questions which have motivated market research via robot simulation lie quite early in the literature and underpin some of the early laboratory experimental work as well. The reader should consult earlier chapters of this volume to get a fuller appreciation of the breadth of market phenomena.

- Becker (1962). *Downward sloping demand can result from purely random behavior limited by budget constraints.* Theoretical work showing that rationality at the level of utility maximizing agents is not required for the demand side of markets to function as generally expected.
- Hurwicz, Radner and Reiter (1975a, 1975b). *A particular resource allocation process, called the B-process which is stochastic in nature will almost surely result in Pareto-optimal outcomes.* This theoretical paper can be seen as a precursor to the Gode and Sunder (1993a, 1993b) work below. The *B*-process operates by iterative improvements: in each iteration, agents reveal subsets of allocations preferred to the current status quo and a market-maker chooses randomly over any possible Pareto-improvements.
- Gode and Sunder (1993a). *'Zero-intelligence' robots that behave randomly within their budget constraint when placed in a double auction environment reach high trading efficiencies and exhibit prices converging towards competitive equilibrium outcomes.* This was the first journal publication of computer simulations with ZI robots. It is a combination of the private costs/values environments of experiments, the double auction trading institution, and ideas about randomness inspired by Becker, and shows that rationality on the order of human rationality is not necessary for markets to converge to an equilibrium: Randomness constrained by budgets and market rules will suffice. Some of the results of this study are replicated in Figure 1 of this chapter.
- Gode and Sunder (1993a). *The marketplace can be seen as a partial substitute for individual rationality.* This is a matter of philosophy advocated by Gode and Sunder (1993b) that is still important today. If purely random behavior under a budget constraint yields the same market behavior in terms of competitive prices and allocations that would occur under ideal rationality and foresight, then this has important implications for public policy regarding matters such as deregulation and consumer protection. It also suggests that economists need not worry so much about individual behavior and how it differs from ideal rationality – in a market setting the differences may not really matter in the aggregate.

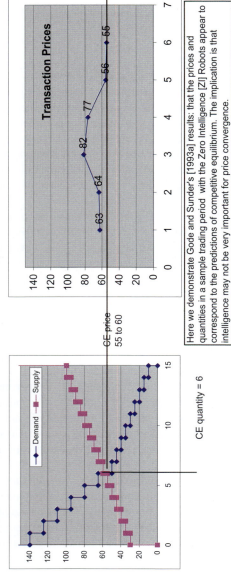

Figure 1.

- Cason and Friedman (1993, 1996). *Laboratory investigations with human-populated markets show negative autocorrelation of returns similar to those observed in ZI-populated markets.* This is the first paper comparing ZI robots as a *model* of human behavior against other more traditional models from the literature. Cason and Friedman (1993) examine the trade-by-trade returns $R_t = P_t - P_{t-1}$ from human traders, ZI traders, and two alternative models of market behavior obtained from game theory. They acknowledge that the price distribution for the ZI traders will change from one trade to the next, but claim that it can be approximated by independent draws. In the case of independent draws, it is easy to show that the autocorrelation of returns would be -0.5.[6] While prices are clearly not IID (e.g., see the first set of graphs here and note the differences in probability distribution of prices for initial and final trades), autocorrelations of returns are typically negative in ZI simulations. Laboratory data from humans also shows a negative autocorrelation of returns, which agrees with the ZI simulations and disagrees with the other alternatives examined by Cason and Friedman.
- Gode and Sunder (1993b, 1997a). *Double auction trading reaches high efficiencies of allocation because it creates a tradeoff between the size vs probability of inefficiencies.* Using ZI traders in a simple private values environment of 1 buyer, 1 inframarginal seller and N extramarginal sellers, it is shown via analytical methods that the probability of an inefficient trade involving an extramarginal seller goes down as the amount of lost surplus increases. The relationship between the shape of the extramarginal portions of the supply and demand curves to inefficient trading is also explored.
- Rust, Miller and Palmer (1993). *Markets populated by heterogeneous collections of robots exhibit price convergence to competitive equilibrium and high efficiency of allocations. Kaplan's simple parasitic robots are highly effective even against very sophisticated learning algorithms.* Reports the results of a double auction based robot-trading tournament held in 1990 at the Santa Fe Institute. The first result can be seen as support for the idea that the environment, budget constraints and market rules inherent in the double auction institution are more important for determining outcomes than individual agent behavior. The second result caused some concern: Kaplan's very simple design, illustrated in the robots section above, outperformed submissions from a number of prominent researchers in artificial

---

[6] Following an argument given by Cason and Friedman (1993), suppose transaction prices are IID with finite positive variance V and mean M. Thus $E(P_{t+k}^2) = V$ and $E(P_{t+j} P_{t+k}) = 0$ for $j \neq k$. Since prices are IID, all autocorrelation coefficients for the prices themselves are zero. For returns, or price differences, this is not true. The first-order autocorrelation coefficient for returns is $\rho_1 = E(R_{t+1} R_t)/E(R_t^2)$ where $R_t = P_t - P_{t-1}$. We can reduce the numerator: $E(R_{t+1} R_t) = E((P_{t+1} - P_t)(P_t - P_{t-1})) = E(P_{t+1} P_t - P_{t+1} P_{t-1} - P_t^2 + P_t P_{t-1}) = E(P_{t+1} P_t) - E(P_{t+1} P_{t-1}) - E(P_t^2) + E(P_t P_{t-1}) = 0 - V - 0 + 0 = -V$. Similarly the denominator is $E(R_t^2) = E((P_{t+1} - P_t)(P_{t+1} - P_t)) = 2V$. Thus, for any finite V and M, the autocorrelation $\rho_1 = -V/2V = -0.5$. For $k > 1$, $\rho_k = 0$ since there will be no overlapping P terms in the numerator.

Continuously Refreshing the Demand and Supply Parameters Confuses the Ro

Initial Supply and Demand parameters

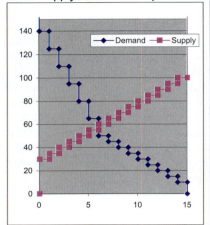

What is continuously refreshed S/D?

Standard S/D - When a buyer and a seller trade, their redemption values and costs are used up. A seller must pay a higher cost for the next unit. A buyer's next unit is worth less to him. These diminimishing returns to scale result in an upward sloping market supply and downward sloping market demand that *initially* looks like the figure at left but shrinks back over time as agents trade. Gains from trade are finite.

Continuously Refreshed S/D - When a buyer and a seller trade, their redemption values and costs are recycled to other agents, who may trade again. This results in a *stationary instantaneous supply and demand* that looks like the figure at left and never shrinks back. Its unusual properties include infinite gains from trade and a constant instantaneous clearing price.

The ZI robots behave as if the first trade is being repeated over and over again.
(to save space, only the best bid and ask are shown for each trade)

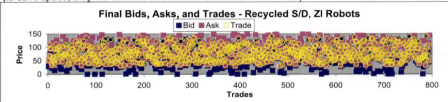

Zooming in, we see that the end is as random as the beginning as well as some interesting details.

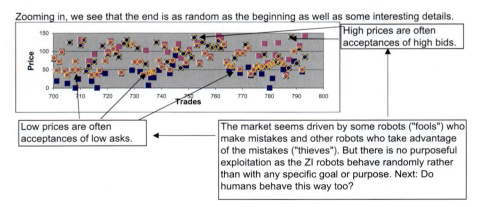

Low prices are often acceptances of low asks.

High prices are often acceptances of high bids.

The market seems driven by some robots ("fools") who make mistakes and other robots who take advantage of the mistakes ("thieves"). But there is no purposeful exploitation as the ZI robots behave randomly rather than with any specific goal or purpose. Next: Do humans behave this way too?

Figure 2.

Ch. 4: *Zero-Intelligence Robots and the Double Auction Market: A Graphical Tour* 41

Human Markets Equilibrate, even with continuously refreshed supply and demand.
Human intelligence adds a robustness to the dynamics that the Zis do not possess.

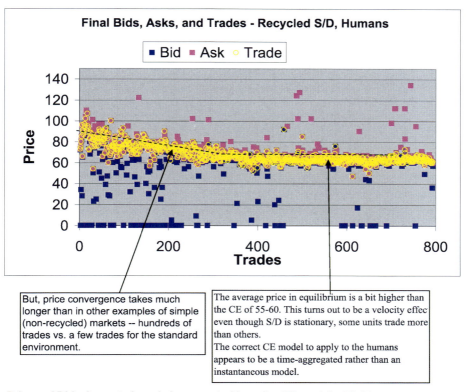

But, price convergence takes much longer than in other examples of simple (non-recycled) markets -- hundreds of trades vs. a few trades for the standard environment.

The average price in equilibrium is a bit higher than the CE of 55-60. This turns out to be a velocity effec even though S/D is stationary, some units trade more than others.
The correct CE model to apply to the humans appears to be a time-aggregated rather than an instantaneous model.

Prices of Bids Accepted vs. Asks accepted is quite different for ZIs/Humans.

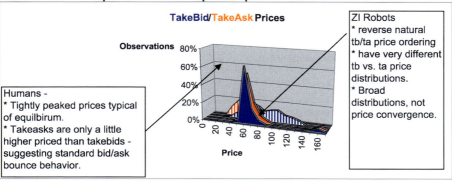

Humans -
* Tightly peaked prices typical of equilbirum.
* Takeasks are only a little higher priced than takebids - suggesting standard bid/ask bounce behavior.

ZI Robots
* reverse natural tb/ta price ordering
* have very different tb vs. ta price distributions.
* Broad distributions, not price convergence.

Figure 3.

Can we make the ZI robots "smarter" like the Humans?
Yes -- by having them randomize their bids/asks about previous prices!
We will call these new agents "UNIT robots" for reasons that are made clear in the key.

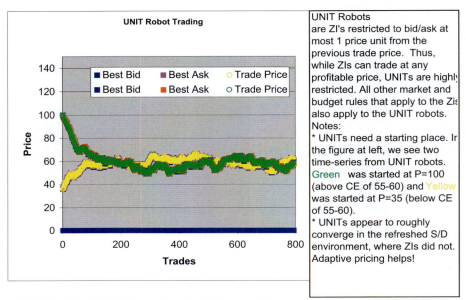

UNIT Robots are ZI's restricted to bid/ask at most 1 price unit from the previous trade price. Thus, while ZIs can trade at any profitable price, UNITs are highly restricted. All other market and budget rules that apply to the ZIs also apply to the UNIT robots.
Notes:
* UNITs need a starting place. In the figure at left, we see two time-series from UNIT robots. Green was started at P=100 (above CE of 55-60) and Yellow was started at P=35 (below CE of 55-60).
* UNITs appear to roughly converge in the refreshed S/D environment, where ZIs did not. Adaptive pricing helps!

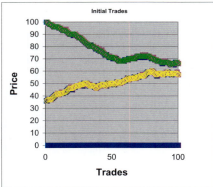
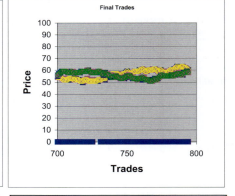

It takes the UNITs about 100 trades to converge. The yellow rising prices are mostly takebids, while the green falling prices are mostly takeasks. This is a bit different from the fool/thief dynamic with ZI.

After several hundred trades, the behavior of green and yellow markets are essentially indistinguishable. Both have found an equilibrium around 50-65, with substantial periods of drift. This is slightly off the Inst-CE.

Figure 4.

But there are still differences...
Consider the following two choices of continuously refreshed supply and demand environments

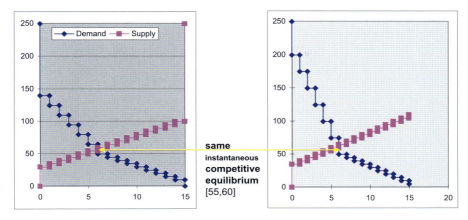

same instantaneous competitive equilibrium [55,60]

But different types of market behavior depending on what kind of agents populate the market...
(averages over 500 or more trades in each case; source: Brewer, Huang, Nelson, Plott 1999 and recent simulatio

Average Trading Prices in Environment A		Average Trading Prices in Environment B
63.4	Humans	75.9
78.3	ZI Robots	95.0
56.9	UNIT robots	57.4

Even though the parameters in the left and right panes result in the same instantaneous competitive equilibrium they elicit different market behaviors that are sensitive to agent type. (We summarize and provide average price here rather than provide a set of six additional graphs). First, notice that the markets populated by UNIT robots are not affected and appear to trade near the instantaneous CE. The markets populated by humans or zi robots both show a higher average price for environment B. In the human markets, we think there is a velocity effect i the price convergence that can be reconciled with velocity adjusted supply and demand as described by Brewer, et.al. 1999. With the ZIs, there is no price convergence in this continuously refreshed environment but there is shift in the stationary IID probability distribution of prices favoring higher prices.

Another place to look for differences is in autocorrelations of trading prices - 1 parameter set is enough
Environment "A" parameters (left pane)

	1st order autocorrelation of Prices $Corr(P_n, P_{n+1})$	1st order autocorrelation of Returns $Corr(P_{n+1}-P_n, P_n-P_{n-1})$
ZI robots	-0.015	-0.494
UNIT robots	0.988	-0.06
Humans	0.722	-0.468

Here we see the ZI robots and the UNIT robots are on different "corners" of Price vs. Return autocorrelation. The ZI robots show return autocorrelation but no price autocorrelation as prices are IID. The UNIT robots show no return autocorrelation, by their Martingale-like design, but significant price autocorrelation. Humans show both kinds of autocorrelations: a ZI-like autocorrelation of returns together with a level of price autocorrelation that is a bit less than the UNIT robots.

Figure 5.

intelligence, economics, psychology, and the physical sciences. By trading only at low bid–ask spreads, Kaplan's robots avoided making mistakes that were possible in other robot designs.

- Gode and Sunder (1997b). *The effects of non-binding price ceilings and floors that occur in human markets can also be observed in markets populated by ZI robots.* The effect of non-binding price ceilings and floors was first discovered experimentally by Isaac and Plott (1981). A price ceiling is an upper limit price for allowable bids, asks, and trades. Similarly, a price floor is a lower limit. These limits are called 'non-binding' when they do not preclude trades at the competitive equilibrium price. While non-binding, these floors and ceilings do affect the process of market negotiation because they affect the prices at which bids and asks may be made – an effect that can apparently be studied and observed with either human agents or the ZI robots.
- Brewer et al. (1999). *In environments where supply and demand is continuously refreshed, as in a flow, ZI robot traders will not exhibit price convergence but instead transaction prices will be independent, identically distributed draws from a random distribution. In contrast, markets populated by human traders will converge.* This is the first paper to introduce a continuously refreshed double auction environment where instantaneous supply and demand curves are held stationary by giving buyers and sellers new costs and redemption values as they trade. Velocity of units affects the price towards which the transaction prices seem to converge – suggesting that the equilibrium model for these environments may be a time-aggregated concept of equilibrium rather than an instantaneous concept of equilibrium. Figures 2–5 show some of the data from this research along with recent extensions of the research obtained through additional robot simulations.

References

Becker, Gary S. (1962). "Irrational behavior and economic theory". Journal of Political Economy 70, 1–13.
Brewer, Paul J., Huang, Maria, Nelson, Brad, Plott, Charles R. (1999). "Price formation in markets with continuously refreshed supply and demand: Human convergence and robot randomness". Mimeo.
Cason, Timothy N., Friedman, D. (1993). "An empirical analysis of price formation in double auction markets". In: Friedman, D., Rust, J. (Eds.), The Double Auction Market: Institutions, Theories, and Evidence, pp. 253–283.
Cason, Timothy N., Friedman, D. (1996). "Price formation in double auction markets". Journal of Economic Dynamics and Control 20, 1307–1337.
Gode, Dhananjay K., Sunder, S. (1993a). "Allocative efficiency of markets with zero-intelligence traders: Market as a partial substitute for individual rationality". Journal of Political Economy 101, 119–137.
Gode, Dhananjay K., Sunder, S. (1993b). "Lower bounds for efficiency of surplus extraction in double auctions". In: Friedman, D., Rust, J. (Eds.), The Double Auction Market: Institutions, Theories, and Evidence, pp. 199–219.
Gode, Dhananjay K., Sunder, S. (1997a). "What makes markets allocationally efficient?" Quarterly Journal of Economics 112, 603–630.
Gode, Dhananjay K., Sunder, S. (1997b). "Double auction dynamics: Structural consequences of non-binding price controls". In: Santa Fe Institut Studies in the Sciences of Complexity, Proceedings.

Hurwicz, L., Radner, R., Reiter, S. (1975a). "A stochastic decentralized resource allocation process: Part 1". Econometrica 43, 187–221.
Hurwicz, L., Radner, R., Reiter, S. (1975b). "A stochastic decentralized resource allocation process: Part 2". Econometrica 43, 363–393.
Isaac, R.M., Plott, C.R. (1981). "Price controls and the behavior of auction markets: An experimental examination". American Economic Review 71, 448–459. Reprinted in Smith, Vernon L. (Ed.), Experimental Economics. Edward Elgar Publishing Ltd., UK, 1990, pp. 187–198, Chapter 8.
Rust, John., Miller, John H., Palmer, Richard (1993). "Behavior of trading automata in a computerized double auction market". In: Friedman, D., Rust, J. (Eds.), The Double Auction Market: Institutions, Theories, and Evidence, pp. 155–198.

Chapter 5

EFFECT OF NON-BINDING PRICE CONTROLS IN DOUBLE AUCTION TRADING

VERNON L. SMITH and ARLINGTON W. WILLIAMS

1. Introduction

There are two primary reasons for examining the effect of non-binding price controls (floors or ceilings) on experimental double auctions (DA) trading.

 1. The DA institution yields convergence to a competitive equilibrium at least as rapidly, and in most cases distinctly more rapidly, with fewer participating agents, than any other institution to which it has been compared. (See Smith, 1982; for an exception; see McCabe, Rassenti and Smith, 1993 for a version of the real time uniform price DA with open display). As a vehicle to better understand this important characteristic, it is desirable to explore conditions that might interfere with, or otherwise modify, this convergence process. The pathbreaking work of Isaac and Plott (1981) set the stage for expecting that non-binding price controls, contrary to static competitive equilibrium theory, would extensively modify the convergence properties of DA trading. (See Smith and Williams, 1981 for a more detailed treatment of the results reported here.)

 2. Commodity trading often occurs at prices just below ceilings and just above floors set by the exchanges who "... often set limits on price fluctuations during any single day ... (and when such limits are achieved) ... no further trading for the day is permitted" (Labys, 1976, p. 162). Consequently, ceilings and floors routinely have application to DA exchange.

2. Experimental Design

The research task is to isolate the treatment effect of non-binding price controls on competitive market outcomes including market dynamics. The design used for this exercise has the following key features.

 1. All experiments use an electronic (computerized) DA mechanism characterized by a bid/ask continuous market in which bids (asks) were required to improve; i.e., once a standing bid (ask) was entered any new bid (ask) must be higher (lower) to become standing. When the standing bid (ask) is accepted, the resulting contract ends the auction, and the computer awaits a new bid (ask), and so on. There is also an electronic "specialist's" book. Any new bid (ask) that is lower (higher) than the standing bid (ask) cannot replace it, but is entered into an electronic queue, lexicographically ordered with higher bids (lower asks) having priority, and tied bids (asks) ordered chronologically – the first in having priority over a second at the same price.

Handbook of Experimental Economics Results, Volume 1
Copyright © 2008 Elsevier B.V. All rights reserved
DOI: 10.1016/S1574-0722(07)00005-4

Table 1

Incentives for subjects units. Listed are the typical unit values (costs) in dollars for each subject buyer (seller), with the competitive equilibrium (CE) surplus for each subject shown in the last column. In addition to the surplus realized in a trading period, a commission of $0.10 is paid for each trade as a means of providing a minimal incentive for a unit to trade at its value (cost). The market CE price in this example is $ 4.65 with 15 units trading since all buyer (seller) units are predicted to trade whose value (cost) is equal to or above (below) the CE price

Subject	1	2	3	4	5	6	Individual competitive equilibrium surplus
Buyer 1	5.35	5.10	4.70	4.60	4.50	–	1.20
Buyer 2	5.60	4.90	4.80	4.65	4.55	–	1.35
Buyer 3	5.60	4.90	4.80	4.65	4.60	4.50	1.35
Buyer 4	5.35	5.10	4.70	4.65	4.55	–	1.20
Seller 1	3.95	4.20	4.60	4.65	4.75	–	1.20
Seller 2	3.70	4.40	4.50	4.65	4.75	–	1.35
Seller 3	3.95	4.20	4.60	4.70	4.80	–	1.20
Seller 4	3.70	4.40	4.50	4.65	4.70	4.80	1.35
Total market surplus							10.20

2. All subjects in these experiments had participated in at least one previous DA market experiment without price controls in which the induced supply and demand were characterized by parameters distinct from those reported below.

3. The induced values and costs for a typical experiment are shown in Table 1 for each of four buyers and four sellers. Also listed is the competitive equilibrium (CE) surplus that would be earned by each subject, where the CE price is $4.65 and exchange volume is 15 units. To provide incentives for units to trade at their value (cost) a 10 cent commission is paid to the buyer (seller) on each trade. This provides a minimum, or normal, profit to be made on the marginal values and costs at the CE price.

4. Each experiment consisted of three five-day "weeks" of trading. Week 1 provided the baseline set of observations without a price control. If any particular subject sample is characterized by strong bargaining buyers (sellers) this is measured in the baseline by the difference between the surplus earned by buyers and that earned by the sellers. Since the design is symmetrical in the sense that at the CE differential surplus is zero, this measure reflects only the relative bargaining strength of buyers (sellers if negative) in a particular experiment.

5. Following the first five periods (week 1) of trading, a prespecified constant is added algebraically to all values and costs to yield a uniform shift up or down. (A trading period, or "day," is 6.5 minutes). Also, the assignment of unit values (costs) to individual buyers (sellers) in Table 1 is rerandomized. Trading is resumed in week 2, periods 6 to 10 (or 9 in some cases). In eight experiments a price ceiling is imposed, in four experiments a price floor is imposed, and in four others no price control is used. This allows any effect of the shift in supply and demand to be separated from the effect of the ceiling or floor.

Table 2
Experiments and conditions price control variable. Listed are the number of markets conducted under each experimental condition. The unit values (costs) are shifted up (down) or down (up) in week 2 (3). In the baseline control experiments there are no price controls in any week. In week 2 either a price ceiling or floor is imposed at 5 cents above or below the CE price; in week 3 the price controls are reversed, yielding a symmetric treatment design

Supply and demand shift in week 2 (3)	No price control in week 2 or week 3	Week 2 price ceiling 5 cents above CE week 3 price floor 5 cents below CE	Week 2 price floor 5 cents below CE week 3 price ceiling 5 cents above CE
Up (up)	1	2	1
Up (down)	1	2	1
Down (up)	1	2	1
Down (down)	1	2	1

6. After five periods of trading in week 2, the values (costs) are again shifted and rerandomized among the subjects. Trading resumes in week 3, period 11–15, with a price floor in eight experiments, a ceiling in four, and with no price control in four experiments. The number of experiments concluded under each week 2 (or week 3) shift condition with or without a ceiling or floor is shown in Table 2.

The price hypotheses were that, after correcting for shifts in supply and demand and group specific differential bargaining ability, a price ceiling 5 cents above the CE benefits buyers at the expense of sellers,

3. Experimental Results

Define: $B(\tau) - S(\tau) \equiv D(\tau) \equiv$ differential DA bargaining strength of buyers over sellers, period τ of week 2 ($\tau = t = 6, 7, \ldots, 10$) or week 3 ($\tau = t' = 11, 12, \ldots, 15$), $B(\tau)$, buyer realized surplus in period τ, $S(\tau)$, seller realized surplus in period τ, $X_i^c = 1$, if ceiling price is imposed in week i; 0 otherwise, $X_i^f = 1$, if floor price is imposed in week i; 0 otherwise, $Y_i = 1$, if supply and demand shift down in week i; 0 otherwise.

We estimate the following OLS regression equations:

$$D(t) = 0.236 D(t-5) + 0.464 X_2^c - 2.02 X_2^f + 1.09 Y_2,$$
$$(3.41) \quad (2.08) \quad (-6.03) \quad (4.81)$$
$$R^2 = 0.55, \ N = 70, \ t = 6, 7, \ldots, 10, \quad (1)$$

$$D(t') = 0.111 D(t'-10) + 2.32 X_3^c - 1.19 X_3^f + 0.260 Y_3,$$
$$(1.94) \quad (8.47) \quad (-6.54) \quad (1.38)$$
$$R^2 = 0.74, \ N = 67, \ t' = 11, 12, \ldots, 15. \quad (2)$$

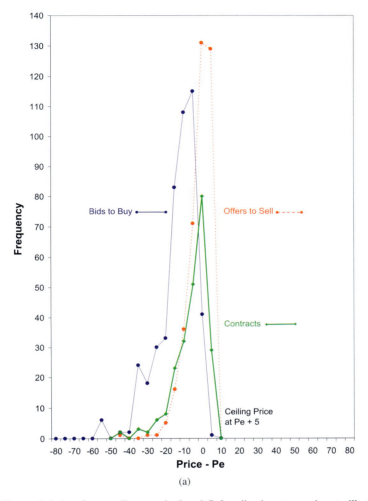

(a)

Figure 1. The pooled data from trading rounds 6 and 7 for all relevant experiments illustrate that a non-binding price ceiling (Pe) 5 cents above the competitive equilibrium truncates the distribution of buyer's bids (blue), seller's offers (red), and thus contract prices (green). The effect on the offer distribution is quite pronounced, since sellers are required to begin their bargaining with offers that are at or below the ceiling price, and much below the levels at which they would begin their contract negotiations in the absence of the ceiling. (This is seen by comparing with panel (b)). The effect on the bid distribution is less pronounced since a ceiling does not interfere with buyer inclinations to start their contract negotiations at low levels. Comparing the bid distribution in panel (a) with that in panel (b) it is seen, however, that the effect of the price ceiling is to shift the bid distribution somewhat lower than in an unconstrained market. This is because buyers, seeing lower offers from sellers (under the price ceiling), find it in their self interest to begin negotiations at a lower level when there is a ceiling. Hence, the main result is evident in panels (a) and (b): non-binding ceilings in DA trading distort prices, and retard convergence to the CE, because the ceiling truncates seller offers and lowers the distribution of both offers and bids, but most particularly the offers.

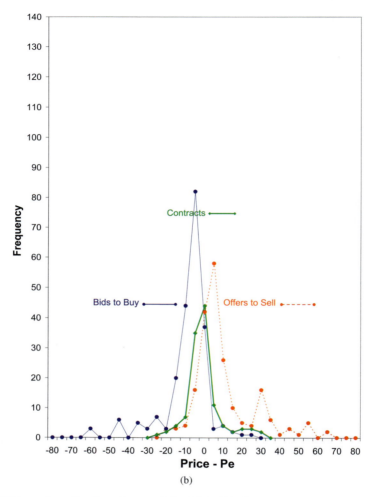

(b)

Figure 1. With no price ceiling, in trading rounds 6 and 7 the bid (blue), offer (red), and contract (green) distributions are not truncated by the non-binding ceiling price, as in panel (a). The chart illustrates an important property of unconstrained DA trading: the distribution of the contract prices is largely contained within the intersection of the distribution of bids and offers. This means that most of the bids accepted by sellers to form contracts are below the level at which 'sellers' make offers. That is, sellers can contract by accepting any bid entered by a buyer, but generally sellers wait to accept bids that are near or above their offers. The opposite is true for buyers. When there is a price ceiling (panel (a)) this property is somewhat compromised by the effect of the ceiling in truncating the bid and offer distributions.

Equations (1) and (2) support the following conclusions:

1. Price ceilings marginally transfer 46 cents per period in surplus from sellers to buyers in week 2 and $2.32 during week 3, while floors transfer $3.03 per period from

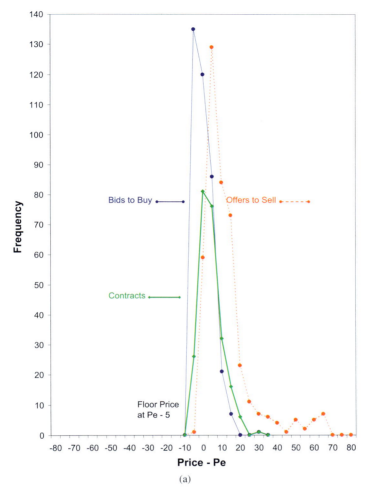

Figure 2. Data from trading rounds 11 and 12 illustrate that a price floor 5 cents below the competitive equilibrium truncates the distribution of buyer's bids (blue), seller's offers (red), and thus contract prices (green). Just as the ceiling in Figure 1a, truncates the distribution of bids, and especially the offers from above, here the effect of the floor is to truncate the offers, but especially the bids, from below. Thus, a floor interferes more with the bargaining strategies of buyers than those of sellers. But sellers definitely shift their offer price upward relative to the offers tendered when there is no floor, as in panel (b).

buyers to sellers in week 2 and $1.19 during week 3. These results are significant ($P < 0.025$, one-tailed test).

2. The positive differential bargaining strength of buyers over sellers tends to persist in successive trading periods, and weeks, but with declining strength. The persistent ten-

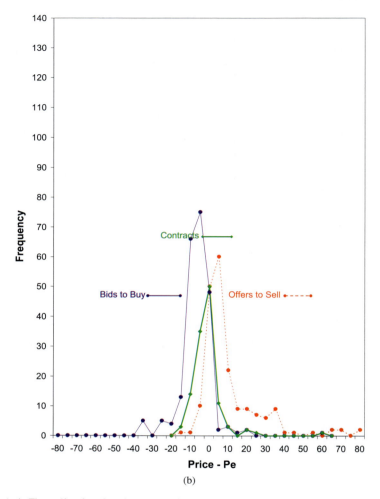

Figure 2. As in Figure 1b, when there is no constraint on free multilateral negotiation in DA markets – in this case no floor – the distributions are not truncated and are more symmetrical. The contract distribution tends to be contained within the intersection of the bid and offer distributions.

dency of buyers to be slightly stronger bargainers in DA trading has been documented in other independent experimental designs. (See Smith and Williams, 1982.)

3. A uniform shift, up or down, in demand and supply (and rerandomization among individuals) produces an overreaction (overshooting of the CE price), but with diminished effect in week 3 relative to week 2.

4. Why Do Non-binding Price Controls Interfere with the DA Market Process?

There is a simple reason why a non-binding price ceiling (floor) retards convergence to the static CE price, biasing prices below (above) the equilibrium.

A price ceiling strongly truncates the asking price distribution of sellers in the bid/ask negotiation process. Thus, in an unconstrained market, sellers start their negotiation at high prices, buyers start low. The ceiling limits seller initial asking prices much more than buyer bid prices. The bid distribution, however, is shifted down somewhat, as buyers bid lower in response to lower seller asking prices. A price floor has the opposite effect, limiting the buyer's negotiation stance more than that of the sellers. This is made plain by the pooled distribution of bids and offers in Figures 1a and 1b comparing all the price ceiling experiments, periods 6 and 7, with the experiments with no price ceilings. The same comparison for price floors is shown in Figures 2a and 2b.

5. Conclusions

Static price theory predicts that non-binding price ceilings and floors will have no effect on price determination in double auction markets. In fact they have substantial effects on price dynamics. Ceilings limit the negotiation strategies of sellers, while floors limit the strategies of buyers. The buyer side of the market responds with lower bids (in the ceiling case), and the sellers with higher offers (in the floor case) than would otherwise prevail, slowing convergence. Sellers have to learn to begin negotiation at the ceiling and concede only slightly, and similarly, buyers must learn to start at the floor and resist price concessions.

References

Isaac, Mark R., Plott, Charles (1981). "Price controls and the behavior of auction markets: An experimental examination". American Economic Review 71 (3), 448–459.

Labys, W.C. (1976). "Bidding and auctioning on international commodity markets". In: Amihud, Y. (Ed.), Bidding and Auctioning for Procurement and Allocation. New York University, New York, pp. 43–64.

McCabe, Kevin A., Rassenti, Stephen J., Smith, Vernon L. (1993). "Designing a uniform price double auction: An experimental evaluation". In: Friedman, D., Rust, J. (Eds.), The Double Auction Market: Institutions, Theories and Evidence. Addison–Wesley/SFI, Reading, pp. 307–332.

Smith, Vernon L. (1982). "Microeconomic systems as an experimental science". American Economic Review 72 (5), 923–955.

Smith, Vernon L., Williams, Arlington W. (1981). "On nonbinding price controls in a competitive market". American Economic Review 71 (3), 467–474.

Smith, Vernon L., Williams, Arlington W. (1982). "Effect of rent asymmetries in experimental auction markets". Journal of Economic Behavior and Organization 3 (1), 99–116.

PART 1.1.2

PROPERTIES OF POSTED OFFER PROCESSES

Praveen Kujal and Vernon L. Smith, "Fairness and Short Run Price Adjustment in Posted Offer Markets"

Douglas D. Davis and Bart J. Wilson, "Mixed Strategy Nash Equilibrium Predictions as a Means of Organizing Behavior in Posted-Offer Market Experiments"

Jamie Brown Kruse, "Simulated and Real Buyers in Posted Offer Markets"

Stuart Mestelman, "The Performance of Double-Auction and Posted-Offer Markets with Advanced Production"

Chapter 6

FAIRNESS AND SHORT RUN PRICE ADJUSTMENT IN POSTED OFFER MARKETS

PRAVEEN KUJAL
Universidad Carlos III de Madrid

VERNON L. SMITH
University of Arizona

1. Introduction

In the context of pricing in retail markets, using questionnaire survey studies, Kahneman, Knetsch, and Thaler (1986a, 1986b) indicate that fairness norms imply that any change in price in the short run that is not justified by a cost increase is unfair. Moreover, they argue that many people would follow fair policies in the absence of enforcement through punishment. They further argue that this kind of (fair) behavior may imply that markets may not clear if excess demand is not justified by an increase in supply costs (Kahneman, Knetsch, and Thaler, 1986a, p. 213). This is due to the "principle of dual entitlements" where customers have a right to the terms of a reference transaction, while the firm has a right to a reference profit (Zajac, 1985, pp. 139–141), implying that recent posted prices may serve to define the reference transaction.

Fairness in Kahneman, Knetsch, and Thaler (1986a) can be interpreted as an adaptation; i.e., any persistent state of affairs over some period of time may be accepted as fair. Thus a given state may come to be accepted as a reference transaction that may form the benchmark in evaluating any future changes. An implication of these considerations could be the following: the short-run price response to situations of excess demand may be sluggish if a price increase is not justified by an increase in unit supply cost. However, if excess demand persists, only higher new prices would be sustainable, and people will adapt by redefining the reference transaction. As we interpret it, the equilibrium may still be what is predicted from economic theory in the absence of a utility payoff from fairness.

In this paper we hypothesize that any short-run failure of markets to clear depends upon buyers knowing that increased profits result from higher prices. In the absence of this knowledge buyers may give in quickly to the equilibrating tendencies of the market.

2. Market Experiments

Kachelmeier, Limberg, and Schadewald (1991) report laboratory experiments designed to measure the effect of fairness considerations on actual price responses and convergence behavior in experimental markets using buyer-posted bid pricing. In their experiments five buyers and five sellers trade for 10 periods under stationary value/cost conditions. Buyers independently post bid prices and sellers respond with individual sales by accepting bids. Then a change is introduced for a new ten period sequence. In the first sequence the sellers are subject to a 50% profit tax such that, at the competitive equilibrium price and volume, the seller's share of total surplus is exactly 50%. In the second stage (10 periods), the profit tax is replaced by a 20% sales tax on each seller's revenue. The effect of this is to raise the previous marginal cost, $MC(q)$, to $1.25 * MC(q)$. This raises the competitive equilibrium price, lowers the volume, and increases the seller's share of the total profit with respect to the earlier design. They replicate each of the different information treatment three times with different subjects (90 subjects total):

(1) *Seller marginal cost information is disclosed to all the subjects*: with the sales tax buyers are informed that prices must increase to cover the new seller costs.
(2) *Seller's share of aggregate profit is disclosed to all the subjects*: with profit disclosure buyers are fully informed, compared with the previous ten reference transaction periods, that the change to a sales tax regime has shifted net surplus from buyers to sellers.
(3) *No marginal cost or profit information is disclosed.*

Information revelation in those treatments corresponds to the Kahneman, Knetsch, and Thaler (1986a) conjectures that:

(a) under profit revelation, because sellers are only entitled to their previous reference profit, it would be 'unfair' for the sellers to profit from the tax and,
(b) under marginal cost disclosure, any price increase would be justified by a unit cost increase. Treatment (1) with no marginal cost or profit disclosure provides experimental control. These experiments generate the following prediction hypotheses (based on Kahneman, Knetsch, and Thaler, 1986a and Kachelmeier, Limberg, and Schadewald, 1991, p. 697).

H1: price response to changing from an income to a sales tax will be greater under marginal cost disclosure than under profit disclosure.
H2: faster under marginal cost disclosure.
H3: slower under profit disclosure.

Kachelmeier, Limberg, and Schadewald (1991) report statistical support for all three hypotheses.

2.1. Extension: Posted Bid vs Posted Offer

The institution used by Kachelmeier, Limberg, and Schadewald (1991) is posted bid pricing. They defend this on the ground that as the preliminary interest is to look at fairness perceptions and responses of buyers an institution where buyer responses are directly measurable is suitable (Kachelmeier, Limberg, and Schadewald, 1991, p. 700).

We examined the robustness of the Kachelmeier, Limberg, and Schadewald (1991) results using the posted offer retail institution (Ketcham, Smith, and Williams, 1984).

Primarily this is the institution that Kahneman, Knetsch, and Thaler (1986a) have in mind in their consumer market examples (although they do discuss implications for labor markets where wage bids are made by the firm). Kahneman, Knetsch, and Thaler (1986a) talk of retail incentives to behave fairly (Kahneman, Knetsch, and Thaler, 1986a, p. 212) if consumer response to 'unfair' pricing would be to switch firms. If the firms anticipate this, they will have an incentive to price fairly. As a result, in the Posted-Offer market institution we can study the tendency of firms to price fairly and of buyers to punish firms that depart from fair pricing.

In our experiments sellers could not see each other's prices. This was done so as to reduce seller undercutting and thus separate lower prices due to competition from lower prices due to fairness. This was intended to give the Kahneman, Knetsch, and Thaler (1986a) hypothesis its best shot.

2.2. Our Experiments

We used essentially the same parameter configurations and information disclosure treatments as did Kachelmeier, Limberg, and Schadewald (1991). Our design differed in the following respects.

1. We used six buyers and sellers rather than five each.
2. Each treatment was replicated four times instead of three times.
3. The length of our experiments varied. In stage 1 the control experiment was run for twelve periods while the marginal cost and profit disclosure experiments were run for ten periods each. In stage 2 the profit disclosure experiments were run for twenty periods while the others were run for ten periods each. The longer profit disclosure experiment enables us to determine whether equilibrating tendencies continued after the first ten periods.
4. Between stage 1 and stage 2, Kachelmeier, Limberg, and Schadewald (1991) scheduled a break allowing buyers and sellers to be separated (ostensibly to pay them privately) and given the required separate instructions for stage 2 regime, sales tax/(no disclosure). We simply chose to pass out different instruction forms to buyers than to sellers in the control experiment; since everyone received handouts this disguised the different treatment of sellers. The instructions to buyers informed them that their redemption value in stage 2 were the same as in stage 1, while it explained to the sellers that starting in the next period they would pay a sales rather than a profits tax.

The subjects earned non-trivial amounts of money. Payoffs for the experiments ranged from $8.75 to $62.50.

3. Hypothesis and Experimental Results

We examine the following hypotheses (see Franciosi et al., 1995 for formal hypothesis tests):

H1: In stage 2, the first period of trading under the sales tax regime, the Kahneman, Knetsch, and Thaler (1986a) fairness argument will yield prices ordered as follows:
  prices (marginal cost disclosure) > prices (no disclosure)
              > prices (profit disclosure).
H2: By period 10, stage 2, the prices under the various treatment conditions will be indistinguishable.
H3: Under the profit disclosure treatment, the two experiments that continue for twenty periods in stage 2 will show convergence to the competitive equilibrium.

Looking at Figure 2, it is clear that in stage 2 there is initially a clear separation of mean observed prices in accordance with H1. Under the marginal cost disclosure treatment, plotted in green, the mean price jumps immediately to the competitive equilibrium, while under profit disclosure, plotted in red, the price does not change from its earlier 'reference' transaction level. With no disclosure, plotted in blue, the mean price is above that for profit disclosure, and below the mean for marginal cost disclosure. By period ten, mean prices under all three information conditions have converged to near the competitive equilibrium ($2.90). Finally, the two profit disclosure treatments that were run for twenty periods yield mean prices that stabilize near the competitive equilibrium.

It is clear that the profit disclosure treatment has slower price convergence than the other treatments. Further, in the early parts of stage 2, profit disclosure softens the profit seeking behavior of the sellers relative to the other experiments. However, prices under the control and the marginal cost disclosure treatments are indistinguishable after the first three periods in stage 2.

Another consequence of the Kahneman, Knetsch, and Thaler (1986a) hypothesis was that buyers, upon seeing unfair prices, may choose punishing strategies. In our experiments this would be manifest by buyer withholding. Withholding occurs if a buyer fails to purchase a unit of a good that is offered for sale at a price less than the buyer redemption value. The incidence of withholding in the profit disclosure treatment (23 units) was much greater than in the sales tax treatment (4 units). However, 22 of the cases were from one experiment in the profit disclosure treatment. Note that this observed withholding was an uncontrolled treatment variable and that mean prices in the experiment with the high withholding were not higher than in the other experiments with the sales tax. In our experiments withholding did not manifest itself in the form of lower efficiencies because mostly marginal units were withheld.

4. Discussion

Experimental work such as ours and that of Kachelmeier, Limberg, and Schadewald (1991) has studied the effect of alternative information disclosures on the prices posted by a seller subsequent to an exogenous shift in seller marginal costs (a sales tax). If buyers will resist any price increase that is not cost justified then, recognizing this, sellers

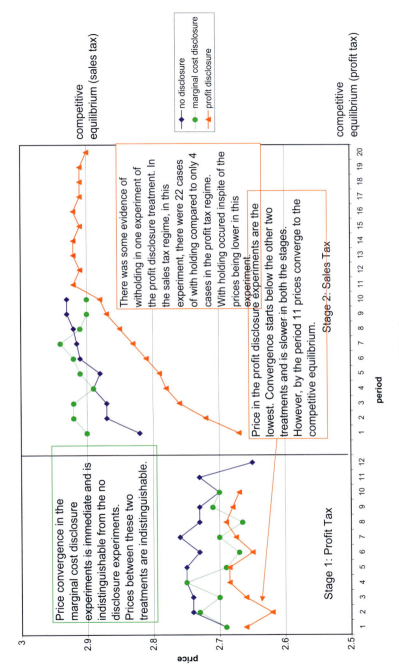

Figure 1.

Figure 2. The experiments use 6 buyers and 6 sellers in the posted-offer trading institution. Each of the two treatments, stage 1 and stage 2, were replicated 4 times. In stage 1 two control experiments with no cost or profit disclosure, were run for 12 price/purchase periods; the others, marginal cost and profit disclosure, were run for 10 periods. In stage 2 two profit disclosure experiments were run for 20; the others, marginal cost and control, for 10 periods. In the profit disclosure experiments all subjects were informed about the aggregate profits of the sellers. Further, after the imposition of the sales tax they were informed that sellers' share of total surplus has now increased. In the marginal cost disclosure treatment seller marginal cost was disclosed to all the subjects. In stage 2 buyers were also informed that prices will have to increase to cover the new (increased) seller costs. In stage 1 sellers pay a 50% profit tax such that, at the competitive equilibrium they have exactly 50% of the net surplus. In stage 2 sellers pay a 20% sales tax that raises their marginal cost schedule. The sales tax increases the competitive equilibrium price, lowers the volume and increases the sellers' share of the total profits. In the no disclosure treatment, sellers were informed privately that in stage 2 they will pay a sales tax rather than a profit tax. The buyers were simply informed that their redemption values will stay the same. Mean prices for no disclosure are plotted in blue, for marginal cost disclosure in green, and for profit disclosure in red. In stage 2, as hypothesized, the mean price is highest under marginal cost disclosure, next highest under no disclosure and lowest under profit disclosure. But over time, we observe convergence to the competitive equilibrium in all treatments, by period 10. Moreover, under profit disclosure the price hovers near the competitive equilibrium in periods 11–20. Conclusion: fairness considerations effect initial prices as expected, but over time prices reflect the underlying supply and demand conditions.

will post lower prices under profit disclosure than under marginal cost disclosure. However, these lower prices need not persist over time if fair prices result in situations of excess demand. That is, equilibrium behavior may allow the establishment of new reference transactions that will prevail in the long run. Our results support this interpretation of fairness. Consequently, the prediction that equilibrium outcomes will reflect the rational behavior of standard economic models is supported. However, the transition path to a new equilibrium will be affected by 'fairness' considerations.

4.1. What is Fairness?

In the context in which we study fairness it is clear that self-interested maximizing behavior dominates disequilibrium fair prices in the long run. This implies that fairness considerations do not belong in the utility function as an externality that alters equilibrium behavior in a sustainable way as predicted by the own utility maximizing model.

We suggest that 'fairness' in our context is best characterized as affecting agent expectations and not their utility functions. (Also see Binmore et al., 1993.) That is, buyers feel that price increases resulting from cost increases 'should not' produce higher profits for sellers. Sellers, accepting this norm of fair treatment, do not initially attempt to raise prices and extract higher profit. In the absence of obtaining utility from being 'fair,' over time, sellers gradually raise prices and reap higher profits. This adaptation to a higher price is due to the competitive behavior of both buyers and sellers. Some buyers realize that there are gains (higher consumer surplus) from trade from buying at slightly higher prices. Sellers on the other hand are able to subsequently charge higher prices as buyers battle for gains in surplus from the marginal units. Thus, what alters over time, and adapts as a social norm, are the expectations of the buyers and sellers as to what is fair.

This also explains why fairness dominates the Kahneman, Knetsch, and Thaler (1986a) questionnaire response of subjects. Their answers are based upon their expectations, not on the unanticipated adjustments that can occur along a convergence path. This happens because the market participants do not know, and cannot anticipate the new equilibrium and its possible effect on what is fair.

Finally, questionnaire data summarizes average – and not marginal – opinion, while competitive outcomes are driven by marginal analysis. In markets like ours, as was reflected in buyer behavior, the gains from trade on the marginal units determined the eventual transition to the market equilibrium. Eventually, self-maximizing behavior dominates, overcoming the initial resistance based on what is thought to be fair prices.

References

Binmore, K., Swierzbinski, J., Hsu, S., Proulx, C. (1993). "Focal points and bargaining". International Journal of Game Theory 4 (22), 381–409.

Franciosi, R., Kujal, P., Michelitsch, R., Smith, V., Deng, G. (1995). "Fairness: Effect on temporary and equilibrium prices in posted-offer markets". The Economic Journal 105 (431), 938–950.

Kachelmeier, S., Limberg, S., Schadewald, M. (1991). "A laboratory market examination of the consumer price response to information about producers' cost and profits". The Accounting Review 66 (4), 694–717.

Kahneman, D., Knetsch, J., Thaler, R. (1986a). "Fairness as a constraint on profit seeking: Entitlements in the market". American Economic Review 76, 728–741. Reprinted in Thaler, R., Quasi Rational Economics. Russell Sage Foundation, New York, 1991, pp. 199–219.

Kahneman, D., Knetsch, J., Thaler, R. (1986b). "Fairness and the assumptions of economics". Journal of Business 59, S285–S300. Part 2, reprinted in Thaler, R., Quasi Rational Economics. Russell Sage Foundation, New York, 1991, pp. 199–219.

Ketcham, J., Smith, V., Williams, A. (1984). "A comparison of posted offer and double auction pricing institutions". Review of Economic Studies 51, 595–614.

Zajac, E. (1985). "Perceived economic justice: The example of public utility regulation". In: Young, H.P. (Ed.), Cost Allocation: Methods, Principles and Applications. North-Holland, Amsterdam.

Chapter 7

MIXED STRATEGY NASH EQUILIBRIUM PREDICTIONS AS A MEANS OF ORGANIZING BEHAVIOR IN POSTED-OFFER MARKET EXPERIMENTS

DOUGLAS D. DAVIS and BART J. WILSON[†]

Virginia Commonwealth University and George Mason University

1. Introduction

In posted-offer markets the competitive outcome for a market, defined by the intersection of market supply and market demand curves, is frequently not a Nash equilibrium for the market viewed as a stage game. Rather, one or more sellers often have incentives to deviate unilaterally from the competitive outcome. A simple example illustrates. Consider a market with two sellers, $S1$ and $S2$, and a single, fully revealing buyer. Sellers $S1$ and $S2$ can each offer two units for sale at a constant cost of c. The buyer will purchase up to three units at a maximum price of v_h per unit, and will pay up to v_l for a fourth unit, with $v_h > v_l > c$. In the competitive prediction for this market, four units trade at a price of v_l, and earnings for each seller are $2(v_l - c)$. But this competitive outcome is not a Nash equilibrium if $v_h - c > 2(v_l - c)$, since in this case either seller could increase earnings unilaterally by posting a price of v_h and selling a single unit.

Holt (1989) defines sellers as having market power in this instance when the competitive price is not a pure strategy Nash equilibrium. When market power arises, a Nash equilibrium in pure strategies typically does not exist. Notice above, for example, that the price v_h cannot be supported as a pure strategy Nash equilibrium, since a posting of v_h, by, say, seller $S1$ will induce seller $S2$ to post $v_h - \varepsilon$, thereby guaranteeing $S2$ a sale of two units. Incentives to undercut remain for any price down to the point where earnings from selling two units as the low price seller are equal to earnings from selling a single unit at a price v_h. Defining this lowest price as $p_{\min}$, sellers will undercut each other until $p_{\min} = (v_h + c)/2$.[1] A common price of $p_{\min}$ also cannot be supported as a pure strategy Nash equilibrium because only three units will trade at this price, and one of the sellers will fail to earn the security earnings available at the price v_h. Any static equilibrium for this market must involve mixing over the range $p_{\min}$ to v_h.

Market power can arise inadvertently in posted-offer markets. One can easily imagine, for instance, that the competitive outcome in a market consisting of many units and

---

[†] This work was funded in part by the National Science Foundation (SBR 93-19842).
[1] Price $p_{\min}$ is found by solving the equation $2(p_{\min} - c) = v_h - c$.

Handbook of Experimental Economics Results, Volume 1
Copyright © 2008 Elsevier B.V. All rights reserved
DOI: 10.1016/S1574-0722(07)00007-8

many sellers might include the incentives illustrated above.[2] A wide variety of treatment changes within laboratory markets can also introduce or remove market power. Instances where treatments have intentionally affected market power include mergers (Davis and Holt, 1994), demand shifts (Wilson, 1998), changes in the buying queue (Kruse, 1993), and cost synergies (Davis and Wilson, 2000).

Market power has long been shown to affect prominently market performance (e.g., Dolbear et al., 1968; Ketcham, Smith and Williams, 1984; Holt, Langan and Villamil, 1986; Alger, 1987; Isaac and Reynolds, 2002; Davis and Williams, 1991; Kruse et al., 1994; Wellford, 1990). The purpose of this chapter is to describe generally how sellers behave in such contexts, and to evaluate the organizing power of mixed strategy Nash equilibrium predictions relative to alternative theories for organizing the data.

Prior to proceeding, we stress that the behavior of sellers in such markets should not be viewed as a direct test of Nash mixed strategy equilibrium predictions. The oligopoly issues that are typically of interest to researchers conducting posted-offer market experiments focus on the interactions of a fixed collection of sellers who engage in repeated interactions, often under conditions of less than complete information about the market. The consequent interdependencies in actions and informational imperfections violate the assumptions underlying the Nash equilibrium. Thus, the project is not to assess generally the behavioral relevance of static Nash mixing predictions, but rather to consider the organizing power of such predictions in a particular context somewhat outside the domain of the theory.

2. Equilibrium Mixed Strategy Pricing Distributions

Holt and Solis-Soberon (1992) develop a method for calculating mixing distributions for posted-offer markets when market power exists.[3] The procedure involves three steps. First, a range over which sellers will price is found. Second, a "security" point in that range, where seller earnings are assured is identified. Finally, the price distributions that each seller must use in order to make other sellers indifferent to every price over the range of randomization is calculated.

To illustrate, consider the example developed in the introduction. The first two steps have been completed already. Sellers $S1$ and $S2$ will each mix over the range $p_{\min}$ to v_h, and the limit price v_h ensures each seller of security earnings of $v_h - c$. For the third step, define $F(p)$ as the cumulative pricing distribution that, say, seller $S1$ must follow in order to make seller $S2$ indifferent between the security price and any other price in the mixing range. For any price p, $p_{\min} \leqslant p \leqslant v_h$, expected earnings must just exactly equal those available at v_h, or $v_h - c = [1 - F(p)](2p - 2c) + [F(p)](p - c)$. Solving,

---

[2] Indeed the authors know from their own research experience that market power is almost insidious, and can arise when completely unintended.

[3] Kruse et al. (1994) also develop an alternative method for calculating mixed strategy equilibria in posted-offer markets with many small buyers, and nearly smooth demand curves.

$F(p) = (2p - v_h - c)/(p - c)$. In a symmetric equilibrium, seller $S2$ must also price according to $F(p)$, in order to make seller $S1$ indifferent to mixing over the support $p_{\min} \leqslant p \leqslant v_h$.

In this case, calculating the equilibrium mixing distributions is straightforward. However, even relatively minor cost asymmetries, and/or additional demand steps complicate quickly these calculations. For designs using the pronounced cost and value asymmetries typical of posted-offer market experiments with "normal" looking supply and demand arrays, a closed form solution for a well-defined cumulative distribution function often does not exist, making infeasible the calculation of the equilibrium mixing distributions. Thus, although the Nash equilibrium differs from the competitive outcome in many markets, only a carefully designed subset of those instances permits direct evaluation of static Nash predictions.

3. Pricing Performance with Market Power

When significant power exists, and when sellers realize their power, pricing patterns typically involve a series of price cycles that deteriorate as the session progresses. The upper left panel of Figure 1 illustrates the sequence of price postings for a representative market. The market, taken from Davis and Holt (1994), involves a design where two sellers have power, and one or more sellers have no power. Market power exists for two sellers because each can sell profitably a single unit at a limit price $p_{\lim}$, independent of the actions of the other sellers. Power sellers can sell up to four units, and theoretically these sellers will mix over the range $p_{\lim}$ to a lower bound $p_{\min}$, where earnings from selling four units as the low price seller equal earnings from selling a single unit at the limit price. Capacities for the sellers without power range between one and three units, but these sellers sell nothing with a unilateral deviation above the prices of the other sellers. In this experiment, demand was simulated, sellers had complete information about both demand and costs, and the market lasted for 60 periods. Solid dots (seller $S1$) and hollow blue dots (seller $S2$) illustrate the price choices for sellers with power. Price choices for sellers without power are illustrated by red, green and black dots. As is evident from the chart only a single no-power seller was present in the first 30 periods, while three sellers without power participated in the second 30 periods. While it is not obvious from the figure, the change in the number of sellers without power is theoretically irrelevant because it does not affect the mixing predictions for either the sellers with power or those without power.[4] Calculation of the theoretical mixing distribution is rather involved (see Davis and Holt, 1994 for details), and sellers with and without power have different distributions. Power sellers $S1$ and $S2$ mix over the range $p_{\min}$ to $p_{\lim}$. In equilibrium, no-power sellers $S3$–$S5$ mix over a range from $p_{\min}$ to slightly above $p_{\min}$.

---

[4] But behaviorally, reducing the number of sellers without power did result in a small but significant mean price increase. See Davis and Holt (1994).

Ch. 7: *Mixed Strategy Nash Equilibrium Predictions as a Means of Organizing Behavior* 65

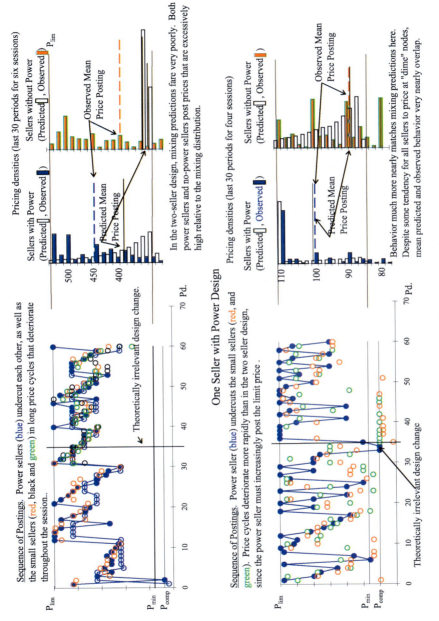

Figure 1. Two sellers with power design.

In the first twelve periods, power seller $S1$ and no-power seller $S3$ gradually undercut each other while power seller $S2$, prices generally below them. (Incidentally, seller $S3$'s aggressive behavior was rather costly for this seller. Fairly aggressive behavior by large no-power sellers was not uncommon.) In period 13 seller $S1$ raises his price to p_{lim} and maintains that posting for three periods, again drawing up seller $S3$. Seller $S1$ then undercuts $S3$, starting another cycle that persists until period 20. Seller $S1$ again posts the limit price in period 21, starting another cycle that lasts until the treatment change in period 30. A fourth cycle occurs between periods 30 and 40. After period 40, however, the cycles deteriorate somewhat, and are more difficult to characterize.

"Edgeworth" price cycles of this type are typical of such markets, and have been commonly observed by researchers who have investigated market power in the laboratory (see, e.g., Kruse, 1993; Kruse et al., 1994; Davis and Holt, 1994; Wilson, 1998; Davis and Wilson, 2000). But both the amplitude and the regularity of such cycles vary considerably from experiment to experiment. Although the sources of cycle variability have not been studied formally, cycles are undoubtedly affected by design and procedural factors such as subject experience, session length, the amount of information given to sellers, and the obviousness of the endowed power in the supply and demand schedules.[5]

The sequence of postings shown in the lower left portion of Figure 1 illustrates some of the variability in pricing patterns possible across experiments. This sequence, taken from Davis and Wilson (2000), involves a single seller with power, $S1$, represented by the solid blue dots, and two sellers without power, $S2$, and $S3$, shown as hollow green and hollow red dots, respectively. Seller $S1$ can with certainty sell a single unit at p_{lim}, independent of the other sellers' choices. Seller $S1$ has a capacity of three units, and will find undercutting $S2$ and $S3$ profitable down to the price p_{min}. The market consists of 60 trading periods, although a theoretically irrelevant design change was imposed after period 30 (in this case the cost fell on $S1$'s inframarginal unit). Sellers were given full information about demand, but only private cost information.[6]

Notice that the cycles are much less regular in this sequence than in the first sequence presented. After two more or less regular cycles in the first twenty periods, pricing becomes quite erratic, as seller $S1$ alternates between the limit price and a series of lower

---

[5] Full information probably facilitates exercise of market power. For example, although power was clearly exercised when present in each of 12 full-information sessions reported by Davis and Holt (1994), and in each of six full-information sessions conducted in a variant of the Davis and Holt design reported by Wilson (1998), Wilson reports that competitive performance was observed in four of 12 power sequences conducted under conditions of private information. This result complements the findings of researchers dating to Fouraker and Siegel (1963) who have observed that incomplete information tends to facilitate competitive outcomes. Notably, competitive outcomes have also been generated in some other incomplete information markets where some power existed (e.g., Ketcham, Smith and Williams, 1984, design 1 and Davis and Holt, 1998, baseline sessions).

[6] It is doubtful that sellers had less useful information here than in Davis and Holt (1994). The cost structure was simple, and sales quantities were revealed publicly *ex post* each period. After several periods, sellers undoubtedly knew the consequences of price changes on their and their rivals' sales quantities.

prices, in an effort to lure sellers $S2$ and $S3$ into higher postings. At the same time sellers $S2$ and $S3$ become very leery being of caught pricing above $S1$, suffering exclusion from the market. Observe in particular that repeated postings at the competitive price by $S1$ in periods 33 and 34 prominently affect the pricing decisions of $S2$ and $S3$ for the next 10 periods. Following $S1$'s competitive choices, neither seller $S2$ nor $S3$ regularly post prices above the competitive threshold again until period 48, this despite $S1$'s persistent postings at $p_{\lim}$.

4. Pricing Densities Relative to Static Nash Equilibrium Predictions

The price autocorrelations evident in both of the illustrated price sequences obviously invalidate any strict interpretation of Nash mixing predictions. However, the mixing distributions may still possibly organize the distribution of observed prices fairly well. A reasonable behavioral conjecture in this context is that sellers try to anticipate the actions of the others in making pricing decisions each period. This process becomes more difficult over time, as revealed by the decay of the price cycles. Eventually such a process could drive sellers to the predicted equilibrium mixing distributions.

In several instances, some rough conformity between predicted and observed distributions has been found. Pricing densities for the final 30 periods of the four sessions conducted in the one-seller-with-power design are displayed in the bottom right quadrant of Figure 1. Postings by the power sellers, illustrated by the blue bars, reveal an apparent tendency for pricing at the dime nodes of 80, 90 and 100 cents. These deviations are enough to drive a rejection of a distributional test.[7] However, a strong mode at the limit price is observed, as predicted, and only a relatively small portion of the pricing density occurs below the lower limit $p_{\min}$. Moreover, the observed mean of the pricing distribution for power sellers shown as a dashed blue line (101.54 cents), is only slightly below the predicted mean, shown as a thin line (103.14 cents). Similarly, the observed mean for sellers without power, shown as a dashed red line (93.22 cents) deviates only slightly from the predicted mean, shown as a thin line (92.47 cents), despite some tendency for the sellers without power to post prices below $p_{\min}$ and to post at even-dime nodes. Similar results have been observed in very different designs (e.g., Kruse et al., 1994; Kruse, 1993) and have given rise to the conjecture that perhaps at least the central moments of predicted mixing distributions may characterize behavior reasonably well.

The glaring discrepancies between predicted and observed densities for the last 30 periods of six sessions conducted in two-sellers-with-power design, which are shown in the upper right quadrant of Figure 1, suggest that such conjectures are preliminary. Consider first the power sellers, illustrated by the blue bars. Not only do they exhibit a tendency to price at prominent 50 cent nodes (e.g., in this case 400, 450 and 500 cents),

---

[7] For example, the Kolmogorov–Smirnov Test statistic for the large sellers 0.158, which exceeds the $p = 0.05$ critical value (240 d.f.).

but hardly any prices were observed at the predicted price mode, and far too much density was observed at the upper end of the distribution. The observed mean, shown as a dashed blue line (455 cents) far exceeds the predicted mean, shown as a thin line (388 cents). Similarly, the no-power sellers priced well above the predicted distribution, with the observed mean, which is displayed as a red dashed line (407 cents), far exceeding the thin-line predicted mean (335 cents). Wilson (1998) observes comparable results in a variation of the Davis and Holt (1994) design.

The wide discrepancies between predicted and observed performance in the Davis and Holt (1994) design merit some reflection. To the best of our knowledge, such wide discrepancies between observed and predicted performance in posted-offer markets are unique to this design.[8] It is possible that this particular type of design interacts with the sellers' decision-making process in a way that generates persistent deviations from static Nash-predicted outcomes. Sellers, for example, may generally make decisions with errors, but the error-process may generate persistent deviations from Nash-predicted outcomes only when the asymmetric sellers are sufficiently balanced. The central moments of static Nash mixing distributions may summarize pricing choices quite well either when sellers are symmetric (as in by Kruse, 1993; and Kruse et al., 1994) or when the asymmetries are so pronounced that the decision process is again simple (as in Davis and Wilson, 2000). Gaining some understanding of this apparent anomaly remains an important unanswered question.[9]

5. Performance of Alternative Theories

The somewhat erratic performance of Nash mixing predictions should be considered in light of the available alternative theories. Perhaps most obviously, competitive predictions do not characterize outcomes well in this context. Market power raises prices above the competitive prediction, and in the direction of the Nash equilibrium.[10] It is also difficult to ascribe the observed performance to some type of collusion. As illustrated in the sequences illustrated on the left side of Figure 1, prices rise above the competitive prediction, but prices tend neither to the joint profit maximizing price (p_{lim}

---

[8] Davis and Reilly (1998), however, do observe rather wide discrepancies between bids and static mixing predictions in asymmetric variants of an all-pay auction. Anderson, Goeree and Holt (1998) argue that the deviations observed in the Davis and Reilly auction can be explained in a logit-equilibrium with decision errors.

[9] The capacity of each no-power seller relative to total market capacity may also affect performance, as was observed above in the discussion of the sequence of postings for the two-sellers with power design, shown in Figure 1.

[10] There are, of course exceptions. In markets, of relatively short duration, where market power is slight, and where participants have only limited information about market costs and market demand, market power does not always generate deviations from competitive prediction. See, for example, the references listed at the end of note 5.

in each case), nor to any other stable outcome. Notice further that the kind of price-cutting behavior observed does little to suggest that sellers mete out punishments for defections with their cuts, as would be a part of any repeated game collusive strategy. [In a clever duopoly experiment, Kruse (1993) demonstrates that static predictions outperform dynamic predictions in repeated games.] A final possible means of organizing such data suggested by Figure 1, would be some variant of a standard theory of price cycles (Edgeworth, 1925). This final alternative is more promising, as was observed by Kruse et al. (1994). Although changes in the frequency and amplitude of the cycles invalidate any mechanical application of a static theory of price cycles, a modified version of the Edgeworth cycle theory may provide a good model for disequilibrium price formation. Notably, a modified Edgeworth cycle theory is not necessarily inconsistent with a distribution of prices that eventually approximates the static Nash mixing distributions.

6. Summary

Market power arises in many posted-offer markets and drives a distinction between the competitive prediction and the Nash equilibrium for the market viewed as a stage game. Pricing patterns in such markets tend to be characterized by "Edgeworth cycles" that deteriorate as the sessions progress. The amplitude and frequency of the cycles are sensitive to design and procedural details, and vary considerably from experiment to experiment. Although persistent serial correlation in pricing proscribe any direct test of static Nash mixing predictions, rough correspondence between the central moments of predicted and observed densities has been observed in a variety of different instances. However, the persistent and very prominent deviations observed in an asymmetric design by Davis and Holt (1994) suggest that Nash mixing predictions do not uniformly organize behavior well. The circumstances under which mixing predictions may organize outcomes well merits further investigation.

References

Alger, Dan (1987). "Laboratory tests of equilibrium predictions with disequilibrium data". Review of Economic Studies 54, 105–145.
Anderson, Simon P., Goeree, Jacob K., Holt, Charles A. (1998). "Rent seeking with bounded rationality: An analysis of the all-pay auction". Journal of Political Economy 106, 828–853.
Davis, Douglas D., Holt, Charles A. (1998). "Conspiracies and secret discounts in laboratory markets". Economic Journal 108, 76–756.
Davis, Douglas D., Holt, Charles A. (1994). "Market power and mergers in laboratory experiments with posted prices". RAND Journal of Economics 25, 467–487.
Davis, Douglas D., Reilly, Robert J. (1998). "Do too many cooks always spoil the stew? An experimental analysis of rent-seeking and the role of a strategic buyer". Public Choice 95, 89–115.
Davis, Douglas D., Williams, Arlington A. (1991). "The Hayek hypothesis in experimental auctions: Institutional effects and market power". Economic Inquiry 24, 261–274.

Davis, Douglas D., Wilson, Bart J. (2000). "Firm-specific cost savings and market power". Economic Theory 16 (3), 545–565.

Dolbear, F.T., Lave, L., Bowman, L.B., Lieberman, A., Prescott, E., Rueter, F., Sherman, R. (1968). "Collusion in oligopoly: An experiment on the effect of numbers and information". Quarterly Journal of Economics 82, 240–259.

Edgeworth, Francis Y. (1925). "Papers Relating to Political Economy I". Macmillian, London.

Fouraker, L., Siegel, S. (1963). "Bargaining Behavior". McGraw–Hill, New York.

Holt, Charles A. (1989). "The exercise of market power in laboratory experiments". Journal of Law and Economics 32 (2). s107–30.

Holt, Charles A., Langan, Loren, Villamil, Anne P. (1986). "Market power in oral double auctions". Economic Inquiry 24, 107–123.

Holt, Charles A., Solis-Soberon, Fernando (1992). "The calculation of equilibrium mixed strategies in posted-offer auctions". In: Isaac, M. (Ed.), Research in Experimental Economics, vol. 5. JAI Press, Greenwich, CT, pp. 189–229.

Isaac, Mark, Reynolds, Stanley (2002). "Two or four firms: Does it matter?" In: Holt, Charles A., Isaac, R. Mark (Eds.), Experiments Investigating Market Power: Research in Experimental Economics, vol. 9. JAI Press, Boston.

Ketcham, J., Smith, Vernon L., Williams, Arlington (1984). "A comparison of posted-offer and double-auction pricing institutions". Review of Economic Studies 51, 595–614.

Kruse, Jamie Brown (1993). "Nash Equilibrium and buyer rationing rules: Experimental evidence". Economic Inquiry 31, 631–646.

Kruse, Jamie Brown, Rassenti, Stephen, Reynolds, Stanley S., Smith, Vernon L. (1994). "Bertrand–Edgeworth competition in experimental markets". Econometrica 62 (2), 343–371.

Wellford, Charissa P. (1990). "Horizontal mergers: Concentration and performance". Takeovers and Horizontal Mergers: Policy and Performance. Doctoral dissertation, University of Arizona.

Wilson, Bart J. (1998). "What collusion? Unilateral market power as a catalyst for countercyclical markups". Experimental Economics 1 (2), 133–145.

Chapter 8

SIMULATED AND REAL BUYERS IN POSTED OFFER MARKETS

JAMIE BROWN KRUSE
Texas Tech University

1. Introduction

This chaper uses the data from three previously published studies to examine the effect of real versus simulated buyers on laboratory outcomes. Real buyers can and occasionally do strategically deviate from full demand revelation. Further, the threat of strategic behavior appears to temper the pricing decisions by sellers. The next section presents the experimental design and a discussion of demand withholding as a buyer strategy. This is followed by results and discussion.

2. Summary of the Experimental Design

The data reported here come from Coursey, Isaac, and Smith (1984), Coursey et al. (1984), and Brown-Kruse (1991). Although each study had a distinct research thrust, all had many design and procedural features in common. This commonality in experimental design and procedures allow for a powerful test of the effect of real buyers on experimental market outcomes. The three studies are early tests of contestability theory as described in Baumol, Panzar, and Willig (1982). One implication of contestability theory is that in the case of a natural monopoly, competitive prices will prevail even when a single seller serves the market. This result that runs counter to the monopoly price prediction, is supported by the threat of entry by potential competitors.

Coursey, Isaac, and Smith (1984), Coursey et al. (1984), and Brown-Kruse (1991) chose a design that used two potential sellers with natural monopoly cost structures. The cost structure of a natural monopoly is such that scale economies provide declining average cost over the relevant range of the demand curve. With declining average costs and no price discrimination, the firm's marginal profit increases with each additional unit sold. In a posted offer market, sellers post a take-it-or-leave-it price. Buyers cannot negotiate over price, they can only choose to buy or not. The standard assumption is buyers will purchase all units that yield positive net benefit (full demand revelation). Under-revelation or demand withholding is defined as the case in which a buyer chooses not to purchase a unit when his/her marginal value exceeds the price. Buyers can use demand withholding as a punishment strategy. For example, if there is an increase in price, buyers can withhold demand and reduce the seller's profit. The natural monopoly setting provides the best opportunity for buyers to use withholding as a punishment because the last units sold yield the highest marginal profit. The ability of buyers to withhold demand countervails the market power concentrated in two potential sellers.

Coursey, Isaac, and Smith (1984), Coursey et al. (1984), and Brown-Kruse (1991) have many identical design features which permits analysis of the pooled data for the purpose of comparing simulated and real buyers. All three studies were conducted at the University of Arizona using the PLATO posted offer trading mechanism programmed by Jonathon Ketcham. A detailed description of the PLATO Posted Offer protocol is contained in Ketcham, Smith, and Williams (1984). For a discussion of the behavioral properties and history of laboratory posted offer markets, see Davis and Holt (1993, Chapter 4, pp. 173–239). Coursey, Isaac, and Smith (1984), Coursey et al. (1984) and Brown-Kruse (1991) used the same marginal unit costs and buyer marginal valuations expressed in deviation from average variable cost of unit 10 as shown in Figure 1. [See also Figures 1 in Coursey, Isaac, and Smith (1984), Coursey et al. (1984), and Brown-Kruse (1991).] Subjects were drawn from the pool of undergraduates at the University of Arizona. The conversion rate from accumulated laboratory dollar balances to U.S. currency was 1:1 that was paid in cash at the conclusion of a session. Marginal cost schedules were private information. Sellers were informed whether they faced human subject buyers or computer simulated demand. Sellers did not know *a priori* the demand schedule or the end period of an experiment.

The three contestability papers did impose different entry costs. Entry cost ranged from zero to $0.50 per period. Sellers in the six Coursey, Isaac, and Smith (1984) duopoly experiments incurred zero entry cost. Coursey et al. (1984) imposed a sunk entry cost in the form of a $2.00 permit that applied to five periods. At the end of five periods, the seller could renew for five more periods with another $2.00 investment. Brown-Kruse (1991) induced a sunk opportunity cost of entry by offering a risk-free alternate market with $0.50 per period payment in six of the nine experiments reported. The remaining three sessions reported in Brown-Kruse (1991) had zero opportunity cost of entry.

Table 1 summarizes the 27 experimental sessions used for this analysis. The three studies provide 14 sessions which used human buyers and 13 sessions which simulated demand-revealing buyers. In order to compare the prices from experiments with different entry costs, trading prices for all experiments are reported in terms of deviation from the competitive (zero profit) outcome. Therefore, the zero entry cost experiments are reported in deviation from average variable cost of unit 10, AVC(10). Prices from sessions with $2.00 entry permits are reported in deviation from $AVC(10) + \$2/(5 \times 10)$. Sessions with $0.50 per period opportunity cost of entry are reported in deviation from $AVC(10) + \$0.50/10$.

3. Results

Figure 2 shows the mean prices for the eighteen potentially contestable trading periods common to all experiments. Clearly, the presence of possibly strategic human buyers

Ch. 8: Simulated and Real Buyers in Posted Offer Markets

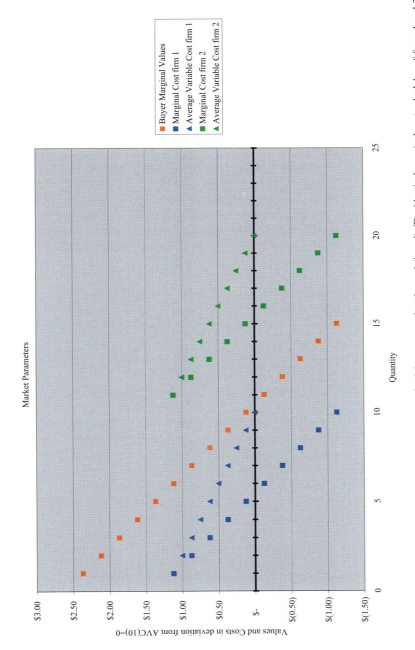

Figure 1. Figure illustrates the marginal valuations that comprise laboratory market demand (in red). The identical marginal cost schedules of firms 1 and 2 generate average variable cost curves as shown (blue for firm 1 and green for firm 2). This is a natural monopoly cost structure. A single firm can serve the entire market demand more efficiently than two competing sellers. At the efficient price, a single seller will earn zero profit selling 10 units whereas two firms each selling a fraction of the 10 units will incur losses.

Table 1
Data sources and experimental design characteristics

Author(s)	# of sessions/ID #	Demand	Entry cost
Coursey, Isaac, and Smith (1984)	6 sessions 37, 45, 47, 48, 51, 52	Human	Zero
Coursey et al. (1984)	6 sessions 70, 79, 82, 87, 96, 97	Human	$2.00 for 5 periods
	6 sessions 113, 114, 115, 116, 118, 119	Computer simulated	$2.00 for 5 periods
Brown-Kruse (1991)	3 sessions 210, 211, 237	Computer simulated	Zero
	2 sessions 194, 236	Human	$0.50 opportunity cost per period
	4 sessions 179, 181, 206, 207	Computer simulated	$0.50 opportunity cost per period

affects the laboratory market outcome. A Wilcoxon non-parametric test for paired samples indicates that the mean prices from human buyer sessions are significantly different from simulated demand sessions at the 1% significance level. A two-sample z-test for differences in means uses each trading period as a cross section. We can reject the null hypothesis of equal mean prices in seventeen of the eighteen trading periods at the 5% significance level. Table 2 contains the resulting p-values by trading period.

Is strategic demand withholding observed? Coursey et al. (1984) report that withholding of demand occurred at the low rate of 1.24% of full revelation. This is consistent with 1.16% observed in the Coursey, Isaac, and Smith (1984) duopoly experiments. Brown-Kruse (1991) identified a single buyer that withheld demand after a substantial price increase. Brown-Kruse (1991) partitions the Coursey, Isaac, and Smith (1984) sample of human buyer experiments into sessions with demand-revealing real buyers and sessions in which real buyers withheld demand. Using a Wilcoxon non-parametric test for matched samples, the hypothesis that the prices from experiments with strategic withholding and from demand revealing human buyers arose from the same distribution can be rejected at the 1% significance level. Further, using sessions in Brown-Kruse (1991) to compare demand revealing human buyers with demand revealing computer simulated buyers, the hypothesis that prices arose from the same distribution can be rejected at the 5% level. Evidently, the possibility that buyers may retaliate is sufficient to discipline the market.

Is the effect of human buyers experimentally robust in other designs? Davis and Williams (1991) report successful buyer withholding in a five seller market-power design. In two of four human buyer posted offer sessions, considerably lower price paths prevailed. The strategic behavior by buyers provides a countervailing force to the tac-

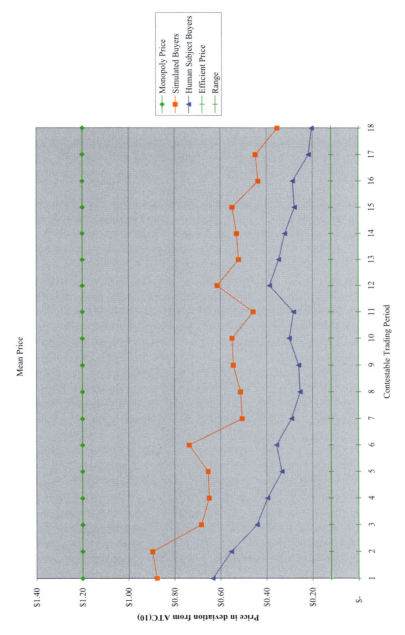

Figure 2. The figure plots the period-by-period mean prices of 14 sessions with real buyers and the mean prices of 13 sessions with computer-simulated demand. When the prices arising from a trading period are taken as a cross section, mean prices are significantly different at the 5% level in 17 of 18 trading periods. When the threat of strategic buyer behavior is absent, sellers initiate and sustain higher prices.

Table 2
P-values for a two sample z-test for differences in means by trading period

Trading period	$P(Z \leqslant z)$ two tail	Trading period	$P(Z \leqslant z)$ two tail
Period 1	0.012	Period 10	0.009
Period 2	0.005	Period 11	0.021
Period 3	0.004	Period 12	0.038
Period 4	0.003	Period 13	0.050
Period 5	0.000	Period 14	0.021
Period 6	0.011	Period 15	0.012
Period 7	0.021	Period 16	0.061
Period 8	0.009	Period 17	0.013
Period 9	0.003	Period 18	0.030

itly collusive efforts of sellers. At this point, oligopoly theory largely ignores buyers' ability to punish by choosing not to buy. As experimental evidence mounts, theory will eventually catch up.

Acknowledgements

I wish to thank Don Coursey, R. Mark Isaac, Margaret Luke, and Vernon L. Smith for providing data from their laboratory research.

References

Baumol, William J., Panzar, John C., Willig, Robert D. (1982). "Contestable Markets and the Theory of Industrial Organization". Harcourt, Brace, Jovanovich, Inc., New York.
Brown-Kruse, Jamie L. (1991). "Contestability in the presence of an alternate market: An experimental examination". RAND Journal of Economics 22, 136–147.
Coursey, Don, Isaac, R. Mark, Smith, Vernon L. (1984). "Natural monopoly and the contested markets: Some experimental results". Journal of Law and Economics 27, 91–113.
Coursey, Don, Isaac, R. Mark, Luke, Margaret, Smith, Vernon L. (1984). "Market contestability in the presence of sunk (entry) costs". RAND Journal of Economics 15, 69–84.
Davis, Douglas D., Holt, Charles A. (1993). "Experimental Economics". Princeton University Press, Princeton, NJ.
Davis, Douglas D., Williams, Arlington (1991). "The Hayek hypothesis in experimental auctions: Institutional effects and market power". Economic Inquiry 29, 261–274.
Ketcham, Jon, Smith, Vernon L., Williams, Arlington (1984). "A comparison of posted-offer and double-auction pricing institutions". Review of Economic Studies 51, 595–614.

Chapter 9

THE PERFORMANCE OF DOUBLE-AUCTION AND POSTED-OFFER MARKETS WITH ADVANCE PRODUCTION

STUART MESTELMAN
McMaster University

Mestelman and Welland (1988) argue that laboratory environments which use double-auction and posted-offer trading institutions typically do not require producers to incur production costs prior to entering into contracts to deliver units of their product to consumers. They add to the available information about the performance of these institutions by introducing an advance production condition, under which producers must incur production costs before entering into contracts to deliver their product to consumers. The markets they examine are markets for perishable goods. Inventories of unsold goods may not be carried from period to period. The decisions made by producers and consumers in this environment are influenced by the inability of producers or consumers to carry goods from one period to another.

The sunk cost incurred in the advance production environment, coupled with the inability of sellers to lower prices within a trading period in the posted-offer institution leads to lower prices in markets with advance production than in posted-offer markets with production to demand. The added complexity of the advance production environment leads to a reduction in the share of the gains from trade realized by participants in these markets from that realized in the less complex, production-to-demand environments. The double-auction institution, however, continues to perform better than the posted-offer institution with respect to the gains realized from trade.

Mestelman and Welland (1991a) extend their earlier work to consider an environment in which producers must make production decisions in advance of sale, but in which they are able to carry inventories of their products costlessly from period to period. The ability to carry inventories should offset the uncertainty associated with advance production, and should aid producers in realizing the potential gains from trade.

Increased market efficiency is not generally realized with the introduction of inventory carryover. The performance of the double-auction institution does improve when inventories may be carried. Inventory carryover, however, introduces a level of complexity which does not permit efficiency gains to be realized by traders in the posted-offer institution.

The laboratory sessions run by Mestelman and Welland (1988, 1991a) use subjects who are inexperienced with the trading institutions within which they must make production and consumption decisions. This inexperience is a possible source of the inefficiencies realized by traders in the posted-offer environments. Another source of inefficiency in the posted-offer institution, relative to the double-auction institution, is provided by the small amount of price information available to producers and consumers in posted-offer environments. Mestelman and Welland (1994) present a new set of laboratory sessions which reproduce the results of the earlier work and extend it by adding experienced traders and by introducing a second price-posting (clearance sales) in the posted-offer environment.

The introduction of experienced traders does not have a substantial effect on the performance of either market institution. This suggests that repeated trading provides enough experience to traders that the participation in more than one session of trading may not be necessary for subjects to benefit from learning effects in laboratory environments. The second price posting does, however, improve the performance of the posted-offer institution. This added price flexibility provides sufficient information to producers and consumers to permit producers to effectively manage any inventories that may accumulate. In addition, sufficient price information is revealed – and sufficient opportunity to vary prices exists – with a second posting that the posted-offer institution will generate trade gains matching those in double-auction markets (which permit multiple, and nearly continuous, price postings).

Figure 1 summarizes the price performance of double-auction and posted-offer markets generated in 120 laboratory sessions and more than 1800 trading periods. It shows that the mean contract price differences between double auction and posted offer institutions, which are common in production-to-demand markets, narrow with production in advance of sale. Furthermore, the consideration of inventory carryover in advance-production markets results in a further reduction of contract prices. Finally, the introduction of a second price posting in the posted-offer markets tends to reduce the contract prices in these markets and together with trading experience generates prices in the posted-offer environment comparable to those in the double-auction market with advance production and inventory carryover. At this point, price performance differences between the two trading institutions disappear.

Figure 2 shows that the efficiency of the posted-offer institution with a single price posting is systematically lower than the efficiency of the double-auction institution regardless of production characteristics, whether inventories may or may not be carried or trader experience. The efficiency of the posted-offer institution is improved significantly, however, if sellers are permitted a second price posting in each trading period. Although this is very different from the continuous price posting and contract formation by both buyers and sellers characteristic of the double-auction institution, it ultimately leads to comparable efficiency levels in both double-auction and posted-offer markets when production is in advance of sale, inventories may be carried from period to period, and traders are experienced.

The success of the posted-offer markets with a second price posting is best understood by comparing the pattern of inventories summarized in Figure 3. When traders are inexperienced, significantly more inventories are carried by sellers in posted-offer markets than by sellers in double-auction markets. In these environments, the perfect foresight, competitive equilibrium production for the market is eleven units. Nothing should be carried as inventories from period to period. With inexperienced traders, inventories in posted-offer markets (with single price postings) tend to be at least twice as large as in

Ch. 9: *The Performance of Double-Auction and Posted-Offer Markets with Advance Production* 79

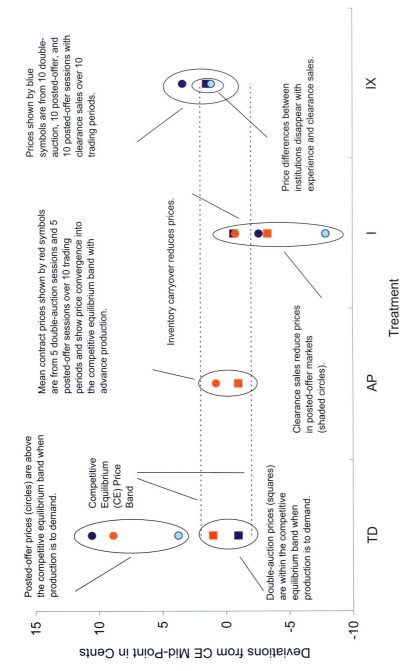

Figure 1. Mean contract price differences between double-auction and posted-offer institutions in production-to-demand markets narrow with advance production and disappear when clearance sales are introduced into posted-offer markets with experienced traders.

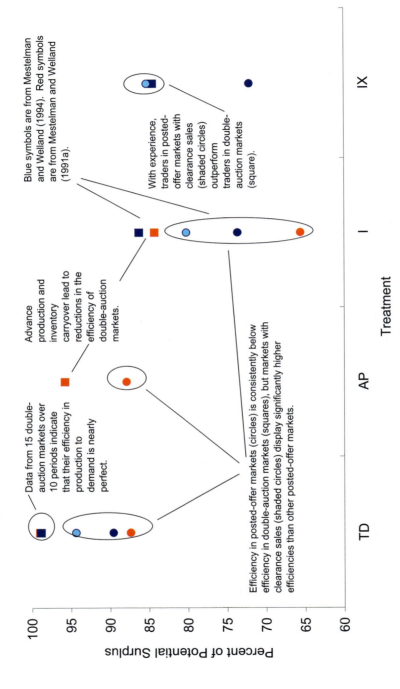

Figure 2. Market efficiency differences between double-auction and posted-offer institutions persist in environments with advance production and inventory carryover. Clearance sales temper the difference and with the introduction of experienced traders lead to the elimination of the differences between the two institutions.

Ch. 9: *The Performance of Double-Auction and Posted-Offer Markets with Advance Production* 81

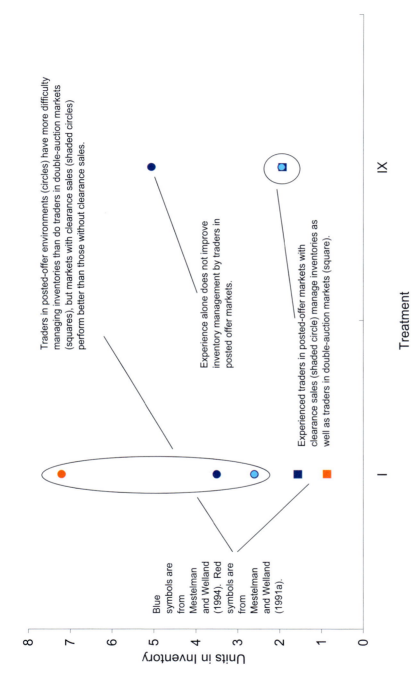

Figure 3. Clearance sales result in improved inventory management in posted-offer markets and with experience lead to performance comparable to that in double-auction markets.

double-auction markets. The introduction of a second price posting in posted-offer markets with inexperienced traders results in fewer units carried in inventory. When traders are experienced, the second price posting leads to reductions in inventories carried to the level realized by experienced traders in double-auction markets. It is interesting to note that average inventory carryover did not fall when experienced traders were used in the posted-offer markets with a single price posting.

The series of laboratory sessions reported in these papers suggest that trader experience may not be an important factor in explaining differences between the performance of double-auction and posted-offer trading institutions. The additional characteristics of the environment into which these institutions are placed are substantially more important.

Advance production leads to an elimination of the advantage sellers enjoy in posted-offer markets relative to double-auction markets. This is reflected by the convergence of the time series of prices (for additional analysis of rent asymmetries see Mestelman and Welland, 1991b). The introduction of inventory carryover does not improve market efficiencies in double-auction markets, but substantially reduces the efficiency of posted-offer markets. Laboratory sessions suggest that the management of inventories is a particularly difficult task in the posted-offer environment. Experience does not improve the management of inventories, but the ability to post a second price during a production period does substantially improve efficiency. The second price posting (or clearance sale) in the posted-offer institution is sufficient to lead to efficiency gains which rival those realized by experienced traders in double-auction markets who must make advance production decisions and who may carry inventories. In this environment, the double-auction trading institution no longer dominates the posted-offer institution.

References

Mestelman, Stuart, Welland, Douglas (1988). "Advance production in experimental markets". Review of Economic Studies 55, 641–654.

Mestelman, Stuart, Welland, J. Douglas (1991a). "Inventory carryover and the performance of alternative market institutions". Southern Economic Journal 57, 1024–1042.

Mestelman, Stuart, Welland, Douglas (1991b). "The effects of rent asymmetries in markets characterized by advance production". Journal of Economic Behavior and Organization 15, 387–405.

Mestelman, Stuart, Welland, Douglas (1994). "Price flexibility and market performance in experimental markets". Economic Theory 4, 105–129.

PART 1.1.3

CALL MARKETS AND SEALED BIDS

Vernon L. Smith, "Strategy-Proof Equilibrium Behavior in Two-Sided Auctions"

James C. Cox, "First Price Independent Private Values Auctions"

Chapter 10

STRATEGY-PROOF EQUILIBRIUM BEHAVIOR IN TWO-SIDED AUCTIONS

VERNON L. SMITH

Although we can think of an allocation mechanism as an institutional procedure that allows the preferences of individuals to be mapped into final allocations, this abstract formulation does not account for the fact that preferences are private and unobservable, and institutions have to rely upon the messages reported by agents, not their true preferences. Consequently, the standard theoretical proposition is that it is possible for an agent to affect prices and outcomes in a market by strategically misreporting his or her preferences. A buyer with a maximum willingness-to-pay of $10, $8 and $7, respectively, for three units of a good, who believes sellers are willing to sell for less, might strategically bid for all three units at $6 in an attempt to lower his or her purchase cost of the three units. Thus, allocation mechanisms are actually mappings from preferences, and each agent's information or beliefs about other agents, into allocations. This state of affairs has motivated the study of strategy-proof mechanisms designed to overcome the problem of strategic misrepresentation, but the results are not encouraging. Thus, stated informally, "an allocation mechanism is strategy-proof if every agent's utility-maximizing choice of what preferences to report depends only on his own preferences and not on his expectations concerning the preferences that other agents will report" (Satterthwaite, 1987, p. 519). This comes down to the strong requirement that each agent has a dominant strategy to report true preferences, and has led to impossibility theorems establishing the nonexistence of such a mechanism under certain minimal requirements (Gibbard, 1973; Satterthwaite, 1975).

Given these negative results, it is of particular interest to ask what people actually do in experimental environments in which the experimenter induces preferences on individual subjects so that the experimenter knows each agent's preferences but the subjects know only their own preferences. Although it is possible that an agent can obtain an advantage by strategically underrevealing his/her demand or supply, whether or not such action is successful depends upon the actions – possibly countervailing – of others. In particular, has society devised institutions in which forms of behavior arise that practically solve the problem of strategy-proofness in classical environments?

The best known example in which the answer to this question is "yes" is the continuous double oral (now widely computerized) auction used extensively in stock, bond, commodity, currency, futures and options markets. Since this institution is examined elsewhere in this volume, I will merely record here that in all but certain extreme classical environments (Smith, 1965; Holt, Langan, and Villamil, 1986; Davis and Williams, 1991) with a constant excess supply of only one or two units, convergence to competitive equilibria is rapid and leads to efficiencies of 100% or close thereto. Note that:

Handbook of Experimental Economics Results, Volume 1
Copyright © 2008 Elsevier B.V. All rights reserved
DOI: 10.1016/S1574-0722(07)00010-8

(1) this is not a counter example to the impossibility results – the exceptions, although rare, confirm the generality claimed by the theorems; (2) the problem is never-the-less solved by the continuous double auction institution in an extremely wide class of environments in the practical workday world of organized exchange markets. Our theoretical understanding of why and how this is so is weak, and represents one of the outstanding unsolved problems in economic/game theory.

Are there other examples, offering a practical (if not perfect) solution to the problem of achieving strategy-proof equilibria? If so, what are the behavioral mechanisms that solve this problem? The answer is in the form of two versions of uniform price auctions: the uniform-price sealed bid-offer auction, and the uniform-price double auction (UPDA).

1. Strategy-Proof Equilibria in the Sealed Bid-Offer Auction

Figure 1 plots the normalized uniform price, period by period, for an 11 period sealed bid-offer auction with five buyers and five sellers. The exchange quantity, Q, and efficiency E, is indicated for each period at the bottom of the chart. Note the poor efficiency in the early periods and slow convergence of the blind bidding process even in a stationary supply and demand environment. See Smith et al. (1982); Friedman and Ostroy (1991); Van Boening (1991) for studies of the sealed bid-offer mechanism, sometimes called the Clearing House mechanism.

The bid-offer array cross for period 11, shown in Figure 2, reveals the strategies that each side evolves to insulate themselves from manipulation by the other side: on the buy side, bid units 9 through 15 in the ordered set of bids are only one cent or less above the clearing price ($7.14); offer units 9 through 14 are one cent below the clearing price. Each side gives the other only a cent or two of room for price manipulation. Since no buyer or seller has more than three intramarginal units, the seven units bid, and the six units offered that are within a cent of the clearing price prohibit any one (or two) buyers or sellers from manipulating the price. Thus, subjects grope around and latch on to a behavioral strategy-proof equilibrium.

The true induced supply (S) and demand (D) overlaying the bid-offer cross illustrates the extent of under-revelation. All buyer units are under-revealed; all but the first three seller units are under-revealed. Three seller units are over-revealed – essentially offered safely "at market," as all other units on the sell side protect against manipulation by buyers. By offering these units "at market" these sellers free ride on the under-revealing messages of other sellers who erect a barrier to strategic manipulation by the buyers. Of particular interest is the empirical observation that this free riding is rare. As long as someone on your side of the market incurs the risk of offering their intramarginal units near the clearing price, your incentive is to guarantee to trade the maximum number of profitable units by revealing your demand or supply.

These experimental results make it plain that the theoretical condition for a strategy-proof equilibrium – that each agent have a dominate strategy to reveal true willingness-

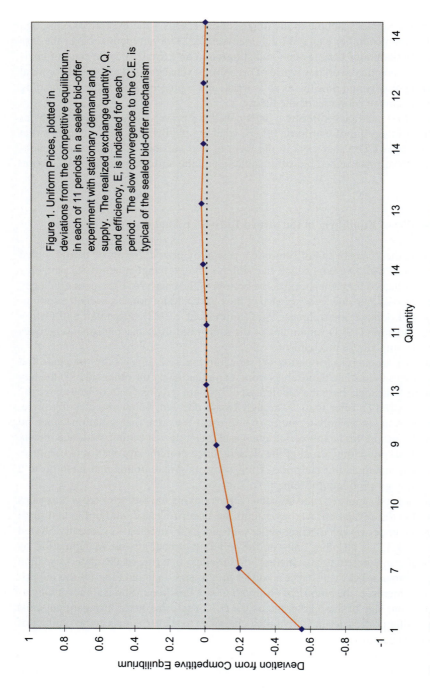

Figure 1. Uniform prices, plotted in deviations from competitive equilibrium, in each of 11 periods in a sealed bid-offer experiment with stationary demand and supply. The realized exchange quantity, Q, and efficiency, E, is indicated for each period. The slow convergence to the C.E. is typical of the sealed bid-offer mechanism.

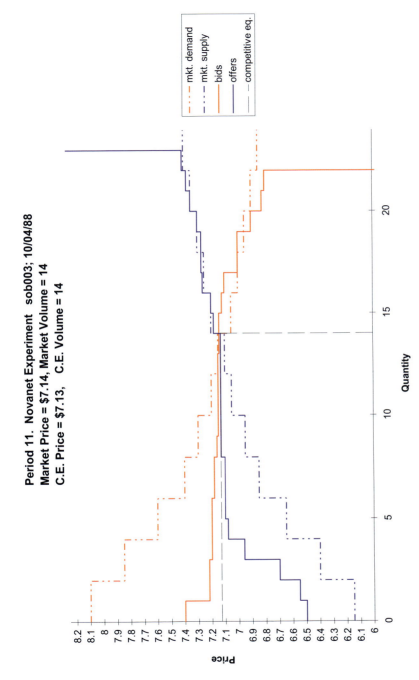

Figure 2. Chart shows the true supply (*S*) and demand (*D*) overlaid by the reported array of bids and offers for period 11 of the experiment shown in Figure 1. Bid units 9 to 15 are within one cent of the clearing price ($7.14) and offer units 9 to 14 are one cent below this price. Since no buyer or seller has more than 3 intramarginal units, each side of the market prevents the other side from moving the price by more than one cent.

to-pay or willingness-to-accept for all units, and not just units near the margin – is much too strong. The above results from blind two-sided auctions, however, also show that there is a cost to the achievement of a strategy-proof equilibrium: blind two-sided auctions converge more slowly to the competitive equilibrium than continuous double auctions, and upon converging, are somewhat less efficient.

2. Strategy-Proof Equilibria in the Uniform Price Double Auction (UPDA)

UPDA is a real-time, continuous feedback mechanism clearing all trades at a single price in each trading period. It comes in several forms depending upon whether there is a fixed time, or endogenous, close rule (the market closes if there is no new trade after a prespecified period), an open or closed book (the list of all bids and offers is displayed or not), and whether accepted bids enjoy a conditional time priority (a better bid or offer cannot displace an accepted one unless it meets the offer or bid on the other side). See McCabe, Rassenti and Smith (1991, pp. 311–316) for a report of 49 UPDA experiments comparing these different versions with double auction; also Friedman (1991), Cason and Friedman (1996). All of these versions yield even more under-revelation of demand and supply than the blind two-sided auction discussed above, but efficiency tends to be higher and, in one form (endogenous close, open book, the "other side" rule with conditional time priority), exceeds that of the continuous double auction.

Table 1 lists a period-by-period summary of the results from a typical experiment (up 43 with 5 buyers and 5 sellers). The market used a fixed close time, open book and the conditional time priority ("other side") rule. The environment is particularly demanding in that a random constant is added to all buyer values and seller costs, and the individual value/cost assignments are re-randomized, in each of 15 trading periods. Column 2 in Table 1 lists the fluctuating competitive equilibrium prices, P_e, induced by these random shifts (the competitive equilibrium quantity remains constant at $Q_e = 18$). Note that this equilibrium shifts randomly in a range of realizations from 260 to 610 across the 15 trading periods and thereby exposes the subjects to extreme exogenous uncertainty. Column 3 shows the realized clearing price, P_r, and quantity, Q_r, based on the reported bids and offers from all subjects. Finally, column 4 contains the market efficiency, Eff_e, achieved in each period, and the percentage of the true surplus that is revealed in the reported bids and offers, Eff_r. Efficiencies of 100% are achieved three times with less than 10% of the surplus revealed – periods 2, 5, and 14; in period 14 only 5% is revealed. Efficiency averages 95% across all 15 periods, while the average percentage of the surplus revealed is only 27%.

Figure 3 plots the true demand and supply (shown dashed) and the realized bid (B) and offer (O) arrays (shown solid) for period 14. Note that the true demand and supply has the following property: if all agents reveal their true demand or supply with the exception of one intramarginal buyer or seller, then that agent can manipulate the price to his or her advantage.

Table 1
Summary of results: up 43; 5,5

	P_e	Q_e	P_r	Q_r	Eff$_e$	Eff$_r$
1	295	18	300	16	91%	22%
2	405	18	400	18	100%	7%
3	545	18	540	18	100%	14%
4	460	18	448	18	92%	14%
5	360	18	350	18	100%	9%
6	500	18	500	18	98%	12%
7	260	18	250	17	96%	26%
8	565	18	553	15	92%	28%
9	300	18	300	18	100%	28%
10	610	18	610	18	100%	33%
11	365	18	350	15	85%	88%
12	550	18	558	15	88%	55%
13	450	18	450	18	100%	31%
14	410	18	410	18	100%	5%
15	485	18	484	19	89%	39%
			$\mu = 17.3$		95%	27%
			$\sigma = 1.3$		5	21

Notes. The trading period 1–15 is shown in column 1. The randomly shifting midpoint of the set of competitive equilibrium prices is listed under P_e, Q_e. The reported UPDA outcomes are listed under P_r, Q_r. Market efficiency is shown under Eff$_e$, while Eff$_r$ is the percentage of the available surplus that is revealed by the reported bid and offer arrays. μ and σ are the means and standard deviations of the column data.

Thus, if the agent is a buyer, he or she has only to reveal all units except the last and bid that unit at $4. But this truth is irrelevant. The relevant question is what behavior is manifest when all agents have the potential for manipulating the price. In Figure 3 we observe that bid and offer units 6 through 18 are all tied at the competitive equilibrium clearing price at $4.10, and no agent has nearly enough capacity to alter this price. In effect each side erects a solid barrier against manipulation by the other side. In this example only 5% of the true surplus is revealed, yet the participants capture 100% of the possible gains from exchange.

3. Summary

The experimental evidence from three prominent auction trading institutions: (1) the continuous double auction, (2) the uniform-price sealed bid-offer auction, and (3) the uniform-price double auction (with continuous feedback of real time information on the acceptance status of bids and offers), shows that subjects are able to work out a behavioral equilibrium which is strategy-proof. In institutions (2) and (3) this is achieved by a groping process which (a) approximates the competitive equilibrium, and (b) produces

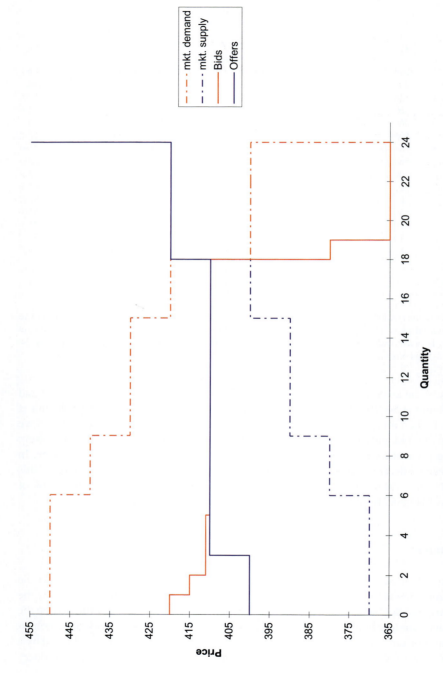

Figure 3. Chart shows the true supply (*S*) and demand (*D*) and the reported array of bids (*B*) and offers (*O*) for period 14 of UPDA experiment 43 with 5 buyers and 5 sellers (Table 1). *S* and *D* shift randomly each period, each buyer (seller) has all the units on a step, with the steps reassigned to buyers (sellers) each period.

a large number of bids and offers that are tied, or nearly tied. In (3) there are typically a great many tied bids and offers at the clearing price. The number of such ties often greatly exceeds the capacity of any one – typically several – agents. Consequently, no individual can take action that can strategically move the price to his or her advantage. This grid-lock, non-cooperative equilibrium is a form of unconscious order, in the sense that subjects are not cognizant of having achieved a strategy-proof equilibrium, and would not in fact know the meaning of such a statement.

Impossibility theorems provide important insight as to why the above two-sided mechanisms have difficulty achieving perfection, but they do not address the question as to why such field mechanisms, when studied in the laboratory, perform so well – in fact surprisingly well given the theorems and the fact that we observe massive under-revelation in the experiments. Fresh new theory, addressing the regularities in behavior that produce such good empirical outcomes, is much needed.

References

Cason, T., Friedman, D. (1996). "Price formation and exchange in thin markets: A laboratory comparison of institutions". Trento Conference in honor of Robert W. Clower, May 9–10.
Davis, D., Williams, A. (1991). "The Hayek hypothesis in experimental auctions: Institutional effects and market power". Economic Inquiry 29, 261–274.
Friedman, D. (1991). "How trading institutions affect financial market performance: Some laboratory evidence". Working Paper 22, Department of Economics, University of California at Santa Cruz.
Friedman, D., Ostroy, J. (1991). "Competitivity in auction markets: An experimental and theoretical investigation". Working Paper #633, Department of Economics, University of California at Los Angeles.
Gibbard, A. (1973). "Manipulation of voting schemes: A general result". Econometrica 41, 587–602.
Holt, C.A., Langan, L., Villamil, A.P. (1986). "Market power in oral double auctions". Economic Inquiry 24, 107–123.
McCabe, K.A., Rassenti, S.J., Smith, V.L. (1991). "Designing a uniform-price double auction: An experimental evaluation". In: Friedman, D., Rust, J. (Eds.), The Double Auction Market Institutions, Theories, and Evidence. Addison–Wesley, Reading, MA, pp. 307–332.
Satterthwaite, M. (1975). "Strategy-proofness and Arrow's conditions: Existence and correspondence theorems for voting procedures and social welfare functions". Journal of Economic Theory 10, 187–217.
Satterthwaite, M. (1987). "Strategy-proof allocation mechanisms". In: Eatwell, J., Milgate, M., Newman, P. (Eds.), The New Palgrave: A Dictionary of Economics. MacMillan Press, London.
Smith, V.L. (1965). "Experimental auction markets and the Walrasian hypothesis". Journal of Political Economy 73, 387–393.
Smith, V.L., Williams, A., Bratton, K., Vannoni, M. (1982). "Competitive market institutions: Double auctions versus sealed bid offer auctions". American Economic Review 72, 58–77.
Van Boening, Mark (1991). "Call versus continuous auctions: An experimental study of market organization". PhD dissertation, University of Arizona.

Chapter 11

FIRST PRICE INDEPENDENT PRIVATE VALUES AUCTIONS

JAMES C. COX
University of Arizona

The first price sealed bid auction is the market institution in which the high bidder acquires ownership of the auctioned item and pays a price equal to the amount of the highest bid. This market institution is distinguished from the second price sealed bid auction in which the high bidder obtains the auctioned item and pays an amount equal to the second highest bid. Bids in sealed bid auctions are often literally sealed in envelopes but need not be; the essential distinction is from a real time (or "oral") auction in which the time at which bids are submitted during the auction is an essential feature of the market institution. For example, in the English "oral" (or progressive or increasing-price) auction, a bid is admissible only if it is higher than the standing bid, and the last bid is the winning bid. In the Dutch "oral" (or decreasing-price) auction, the first and only bid is the winning bid.

The independent, private-values information environment is the one in which each bidder knows with certainty his own value for the auctioned item but knows only the probability distribution from which each of the other bidders' values are independently drawn. Vickrey (1961) first derived Nash equilibrium bid functions for the first price, second price, English, and Dutch auctions for bidders with independent private values of the auctioned item.

We are here concerned with experimental tests, using independent private values, of the consistency of bidding behavior in the first price auction with three nested Nash equilibrium bidding models. The risk neutral model (RNM) was developed by Vickrey (1961). The constant relative risk averse model (CRRAM) was developed by Cox, Roberson, and Smith (1982) and Cox, Smith, and Walker (1982). The log concave model (LCM) was developed by Cox, Smith, and Walker (1988) and Cox and Oaxaca (1996). These models are "nested," in that LCM contains CRRAM as a special case and CRRAM contains RNM as a special case. Of course a more specialized model places more restrictions on data than does a more general model; thus tests for consistency of the nested models with bidding in first price auctions are concerned with identifying those theoretical restrictions that are consistent with the patterns of empirical regularity in the auction data. Such tests have been conducted with data for market prices, subject payoffs, and individual bids and values.

1. Tests of the RNM with Market Prices

The model of the first price auction developed by Vickrey is based on the following set of assumptions: (a) the bidders are risk neutral, expected utility maximizers (and

Table 1
Market price tests (5% significance). Three tests with auction market prices imply rejection of the risk neutral model in favor of the risk averse alternative for all numbers of bidders and experiment series except one series of three-bidder experiments

Number of bidders	Experiment series	Number of auctions	t-Test	Binomial test	Kolmogorov–Smirnov test
3	1	70	Accept	Accept	Accept
3	1'	100	Reject	–	–
4	2	60	Reject	Reject	Reject
4	3	30	Reject	–	–
4	4	250	Reject	–	–
5	5	60	Reject	Reject	Reject
5	6	30	Reject	–	–
6	7	60	Reject	Reject	Reject
9	8	30	Reject	Reject	Reject

they all know this); and (b) the bidders' values for the auctioned item are independently drawn from the uniform distribution on the $[v_\ell, v_h]$ interval (and they all know this). These assumptions imply that the Nash equilibrium bid function is

$$b_i = v_\ell + \frac{n-1}{n}(v_i - v_\ell), \qquad (1)$$

where b_i is the amount bid by bidder i when her value for the auctioned item is v_i.

Bid function (1) immediately implies that the auction market price, p, is

$$p = v_\ell + \frac{n-1}{n} \max_i (v_i - v_\ell). \qquad (2)$$

Vickrey also first demonstrated that if all bidders are identically risk averse then the probability distribution of market prices (first-order) stochastically dominates the market price distribution of the risk neutral model.

Table 1 presents market price tests reported in Cox, Roberson, and Smith (1982) and Cox, Smith, and Walker (1988). Three types of tests are reported: t-tests comparing mean market prices with the RNM's predicted mean prices; Kolmogorov–Smirnov tests comparing the cumulative distributions of market prices with the cumulative distributions implied by the RNM; and binomial tests of the differences between market prices and prices predicted by the RNM conditional on auctioned item values. All three one-sided tests imply the same conclusion: except for one series of three bidder auctions, the hypothesis that market prices are the same as the RNM's predicted prices is rejected in favor of the hypothesis that they are higher. This result is consistent with bidding theory for risk-averse bidders.

2. Tests of the RNM with Subject Payoff Data

Harrison (1989) argued that researchers should test bidding models with subject payoff data, not market price or individual subject bid and value data. He applied "metrics" to (only) the median payoffs in experiments. Friedman (1992) developed a loss function that uses all of the subject payoff data to answer the question of whether the actual payoffs in an experiment differ significantly from the payoffs that would result from bidding according to a theoretical model.

Cox and Oaxaca interpreted Friedman's loss function in the context of first price auctions as follows. If all $n - 1$ of a representative bidder's rivals bid according to the risk neutral bid function in Equation (1), then the probability that a bid in amount b by the representative bidder will be a winning bid is given by the composition of the inverse bid function and the cumulative distribution function for the $(n - 1)$st order statistic for a sample of size $n - 1$ from the uniform distribution on $[v_\ell, v_h]$, which is $[n(b - v_\ell)/(n - 1)(v_h - v_\ell)]^{n-1}$. Multiplying the preceding expression by the difference between the value of the auctioned item and the amount of the bid gives one the expected payoff from bidding the amount b. The loss function then evaluates the expected payoff implications of unilateral deviation from the RNM bids to the observed bids. Thus the loss function is

$$L_{it} = \left[\frac{n}{(n-1)(v_h - v_\ell)} \right]^{n-1} \times \left[(b_{it}^{RN} - v_\ell)^{n-1}(v_{it} - b_{it}^{RN}) - (b_{it} - v_\ell)^{n-1}(v_{it} - b_{it}) \right], \qquad (3)$$

where b_{it} and v_{it} are the observed bid and value for subject i in auction t and b_{it}^{RN} is the bid given by the risk neutral bid function, Equation (1), for the observed value. The test statistic is

$$x_{it} = Z_{it} L_{it}, \qquad (4)$$

where

$$Z_{it} = \begin{cases} +1 & \text{for } b_{it} > b_{it}^{RN}, \\ 0 & \text{for } b_{it} = b_{it}^{RN}, \\ -1 & \text{for } b_{it} < b_{it}^{RN}. \end{cases} \qquad (5)$$

Cox and Oaxaca's results from tests with (their interpretation of) Friedman's loss function are exhibited in Figure 1. The furthest-right bar in Figure 1 shows that 90% of the subjects had significantly positive foregone expected earnings from submitting bids higher than RNM bids. Thus this test based on foregone expected earnings leads to the same conclusion as the three tests based on market prices: the risk neutral model is rejected.

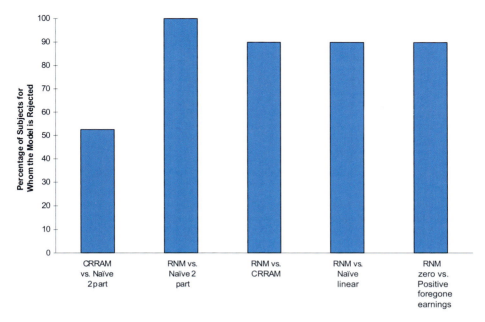

Figure 1. This figure reports tests using bid data of Nash equilibrium bid function parameter restrictions for the constant relative risk averse model (CRRAM) and the risk neutral model (RNM). It also reports a test of RNN using subjects' expected foregone earnings. The bar graph shows the rejection rates at 10% significance. CRRAM is rejected for 52.5% of the subjects in favor of a naïve two-part bid function that places no restrictions on the bid function slope and does not impose consistency of the slope with the location of the knot joining the two parts of the bid function. RNM is rejected in favor of the naïve two-part bid function for 100% of the subjects. RNM is rejected in favor of CRRAM for 90% of the subjects. RNM is rejected for 90% of the subjects in favor of a naïve linear bid function that places no restrictions on the bid function slope and intercept. Zero foregone expected earnings from bidding higher than RNM bids is rejected in favor of positive foregone earnings for 90% of the subjects. Thus, CRAMM is rejected for slightly more than one-half of the subjects by tests using bid data. RNN is rejected for 90–100% of the subjects by tests using either bid data or earnings data.

3. Tests of the CRRAM and the RNM with Individual Bid Data

The theory can be generalized to the environment where bidders can have preferences that exhibit any degree of constant relative risk aversion (and/or constant relative risk preference) and the bidders are not required to have the same preferences (Cox, Roberson, and Smith, 1982; Cox, Smith, and Walker, 1982). Let bidder i have power function utility for monetary payoff, y_i, such that $u(y_i) = y_i^{r_i}$, for $i = 1, 2, \ldots, n$. The r_i are independently drawn from a probability distribution with integrable cdf $\Psi(\cdot)$ on $(0, r_h]$. Note that if $r_h \geq 1$ then the risk neutral model is the special case where $\Psi(\cdot)$ places all of its probability mass at $r = 1$.

If auctioned item values are drawn from the uniform distribution on $[v_\ell, v_h]$ then the Nash equilibrium bid function for this model has two parts that are joined together at a "knot," v_i^*. The linear part of the bid function is

$$b_i = v_\ell + \frac{n-1}{n-1+r_i}(v_i - v_\ell) \quad \text{for } v_i \in [v_\ell, v_i^*], \tag{6}$$

and the knot is

$$v_i^* = v_\ell + \frac{n-1+r_i}{n-1+r_h}(v_h - v_\ell). \tag{7}$$

The upper part of the bid function, with domain $(v_i^*, v_h]$, is strictly concave but does not have a closed form.

Note that both Equations (6) and (7) contain r_i and n. If we assume that the least risk averse bidder in the population is risk neutral, then $r_h = 1$, and Equations (6) and (7) imply

$$b_i = v_\ell + \frac{(n-1)(v_h - v_\ell)}{n(v_i^* - v_\ell)}(v_i - v_\ell) \quad \text{for } v_i \in [v_\ell, v_i^*]. \tag{8}$$

As explained in Cox and Oaxaca (1996), the stochastic version of the two part bid function can be estimated by searching for the value of the knot and the parameters of a polynomial approximation of the upper part that minimize the sum of squared residuals. Data limitations made it impossible to use a polynomial of higher order than the quadratic.

Figure 1 exhibits test results reported by Cox and Oaxaca (1996) using data from experiments reported in Cox, Smith, and Walker (1988). The left-most bar in Figure 1 shows the results from testing the parameter restrictions implied by CRRAM against an unrestricted (or naive) two-part bid function. CRRAM is rejected for 52.5% of the subjects by this test. The second-to-the-left bar in Figure 1 reports results from applying this same test to RNM. We observe that RNM is rejected for 100% of the subjects by this test. The middle bar in Figure 1 shows results from testing RNM against CRRAM. Note that RNM is rejected in favor of CRRAM for 90% of the subjects. The second-from-the right bar in Figure 1 shows results from testing RNM against an unrestricted (or naïve) linear bid function. By this test, RNM is rejected for 90% of the subjects.

4. Tests of the LCM with Individual Bid Data

The theory can be generalized further (Cox, Smith, and Walker, 1988) by letting a bidder's utility for monetary income, y_i, depend on an $(M-1)$-dimensional characteristic vector, θ_i, that is drawn from a probability distribution with integrable cdf, Φ, on a convex set, Θ. Bidders' preferences are required to be strictly log-concave but not necessarily concave; that is, $\ln u(y_i, \theta_i)$ must be strictly concave in monetary income, y_i, for all $\theta_i \in \Theta$. This means that different bidders can be risk averse, risk neutral, or risk

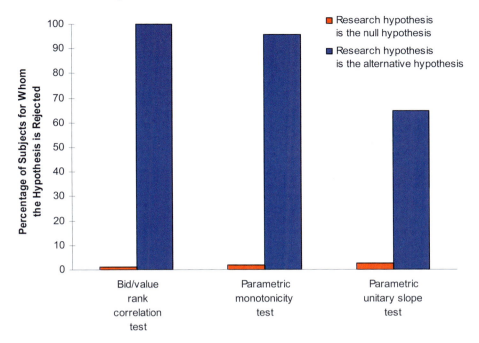

Figure 2. This figure reports tests using observed bids of Nash equilibrium bid function parameter restrictions for the log-concave model. The bar graph shows the rejection rates at 10% significance. Three tests imply very low rejection rates of 0%, 0.1%, and 2.6% when the log-concave model's properties ("the research hypotheses") are the null hypotheses of the tests. Three tests imply very high rejection rates of 100%, 95.7%, and 64.9% of the null hypotheses when the research hypotheses are the alternative hypotheses of the tests. The tests are for positive or negative rank correlation of bids and values, positive or negative slope of the estimated cubic bid function, and estimated bid function slope less than or greater than 1.

preferring. Furthermore, an individual bidder can be risk neutral in some parts of the payoff space, risk averse in some other parts, and/or risk-preferring in other parts. The only restriction on risk preferences is that $u(y_i, \theta_i)$ be everywhere less convex than the exponential function of y_i.

The Nash equilibrium bid function for LCM, $b(v_i, \theta_i)$, does not have a closed form. However, it does have testable implications. Cox, Smith, and Walker (1988) demonstrate that more risk averse bidders will bid more than less risk averse bidders with the same item value. Cox and Oaxaca (1996) demonstrate that the slope of the bid function with respect to v_i is everywhere contained in the interval (0, 1); that is, bids must be monotonically increasing in the value of the auctioned item but can never increase faster than that value.

Figure 2 shows results from tests of LCM reported by Cox and Oaxaca. The red bars show results from tests that use the research hypothesis as the null hypothesis while the blue bars are for tests where the research hypothesis is the alternative hypothesis.

The left-most pair of bars show the results from rank correlation tests of the positive monotonicity property of the LCM. Positive rank correlation of bids and values is not rejected for any of the subjects whereas negative rank correlation is rejected for 100% of the subjects. The middle pair of bars shows results from parametric monotonicity tests. Positive monotonicity of the estimated bid function slopes can be rejected for only 0.1% of the subjects. Non-positive monotonicity of bid function slopes can be rejected for 95.7% of the subjects. The right-most bars in Figure 2 show results from tests of the unitary slope property of LCM. Note that the restriction that the bid function slope be everywhere less than 1 can be rejected for only 2.6% of the subjects. The hypothesis that the bid function slope is everywhere greater than 1 can be rejected for 64.9% of the subjects.

5. Summary of the Test Results

The reported tests have the following implications for the three nested models. Depending on which test is used, data for only 0–10% of the subjects are consistent with the risk neutral model. This conclusion is the same regardless of whether one conducts the tests with market prices, individual subjects' bids and values, or subjects' expected foregone earnings. Tests with individual subjects' bids and values indicate that data for about 48% of the subjects are consistent with the constant relative risk averse model and data for almost all subjects are consistent with the log-concave model.

Acknowledgement

Todd Swarthout provided valuable assistance by preparing the table and figures.

References

Cox, James C., Oaxaca, Ronald L. (1996). "Is bidding behavior consistent with bidding theory for private value auctions?" In: Isaac, R. Mark (Ed.), Research in Experimental Economics, vol. 6. JAI Press, Greenwich.

Cox, James C., Roberson, Bruce, Smith, Vernon L. (1982). "Theory and behavior of single object auctions". In: Smith, Vernon L. (Ed.), Research in Experimental Economics, vol. 2. JAI Press, Greenwich.

Cox, James C., Smith, Vernon L., Walker, James M. (1982). "Auction market theory of heterogeneous bidders". Economics Letters 9, 319–325.

Cox, James C., Smith, Vernon L., Walker, James M. (1988). "Theory and individual behavior of first-price auctions". Journal of Risk and Uncertainty 1, 61–99.

Friedman, Daniel (1992). "Theory and misbehavior of first-price auctions: Comment". American Economic Review 82, 1392–1412.

Harrison, Glenn W. (1989). "Theory and misbehavior of first-price auctions". American Economic Review 79. September.

Vickrey, William (1961). "Counterspeculation, auctions, and competitive sealed tenders". Journal of Finance 16, 8–37.

PART 1.1.4

ALTERNATIVE MARKET INSTITUTIONS

Corinne Bronfman, Kevin McCabe, David Porter, Stephen Rassenti and Vernon L. Smith, "The Walrasian Auction"

Daniel Friedman and Changhua Rich, "The Matching Market Institution"

Charles R. Plott, "Tatonnement"

Chapter 12

THE WALRASIAN AUCTION

CORINNE BRONFMAN, KEVIN MCCABE, DAVID PORTER, STEPHEN RASSENTI, VERNON SMITH

1. Introduction

Joyce (1984) reports the results of experiments with a Walrasian tatonnement auction showing that the mechanism is stable, exhibits strong convergence properties and generates efficiencies that average better than 97%.[1] He also found that when subjects could see part of the order flow (excess demand), prices tended to be lower. His experiments consisted of a stationary environment where subjects were provided single-unit supply and demand functions. We examine the robustness of his results in a more general multi-unit per subject setting and systematically investigate the effect of various order flow information and message restriction rules on the performance of the Walrasian auction.

2. Experimental Environments

2.1. Baseline

Consider the environment charted in Figure 1. Each buyer has a value for a discrete single unit. Each seller has the capacity to supply only one discrete unit to the market for a specified cost.

In this environment goods are to be allocated using the following Walrasian auction:
1. An initial price $P_0 > 0$ is selected by an auctioneer.
2. Each buyer and seller indicates to the auctioneer whether they wanted to buy or sell a single unit at the announced price.
3. If the number of buyers demanding a unit equals the number of sellers supplying a unit at that price, the process stops.
4. If there is an imbalance of supply and demand at that price, i.e. excess demand $E(P)$ is non-zero, the auctioneer updates the price using the following formula:

$$\Delta P = \begin{cases} \$0.05 E(P) & \text{if } |E(P)| > 1, \\ \$Z E(P) & \text{if } |E(P)| = 1, \\ & \text{where } Z < \$0.05 \text{ is decided by auctioneer.} \end{cases}$$

---

[1] *Efficiency* is defined as the percent of the theoretical producer plus consumer surplus realized by a trading mechanism.

Handbook of Experimental Economics Results, Volume 1
Copyright © 2008 Elsevier B.V. All rights reserved
DOI: 10.1016/S1574-0722(07)00012-1

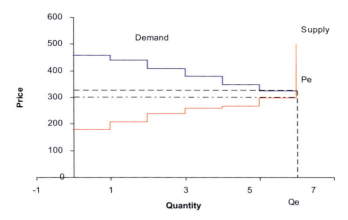

Figure 1. Simple single unit environment (E1). The figure shows an experimental environment with six buyers and six sellers. Each buyer has a resale value for one unit only and is represented by one of the steps on the demand function graphed in blue. Each seller has a cost for one unit only and is represented by one of the steps on the supply function graphed in red. The market equilibrium is given by the price tunnel P_e and quantity Q_e of six units.

When individuals have demands or supplies for one unit, non-revelation is a risky strategy since, should the market clear, the individual will fail to make a profitable transaction. In a single play of the game defined by this process, any pure strategy Nash equilibrium must be at (Q_e, P_e).

2.2. Multi-unit Non-stationary Supply and Demand Environment

When there are multiple units demanded/supplied by individual traders, the typical Nash equilibrium of the Walrasian auction results in underrevealation (see Hurwicz, 1972 and Otani and Sicilian, 1990). Consider the demand and supply configuration charted in Figure 2. The aggregate supply and demand arrays are step functions where each step identifies a particular buyer's or seller's value or cost. Only one trader is assigned to a step on these functions. In addition, each participant has multiple units to bid or to offer all on the same step. As shown in Figure 2, there are three buyers ($B1$, $B3$, $B5$) and three sellers ($S1$, $S2$, $S3$) with six units and two buyers ($B2$, $B4$) and two sellers ($S2$, $S3$) with three units. Thus, there are twenty-four buy and sell units in the market; of these, eighteen are potentially tradable in the equilibrium price tunnel (450, 470).

During an experiment, buyers remained buyers and sellers remained sellers, period to period, although two important changes occurred each period:

1. The equilibrium prices were changed by parallel and equal shifts in the aggregate demand and supply arrays. In particular, from period to period, a random constant from the interval [100, 490] is added to (or subtracted from) each step on the aggregate demand and supply functions.

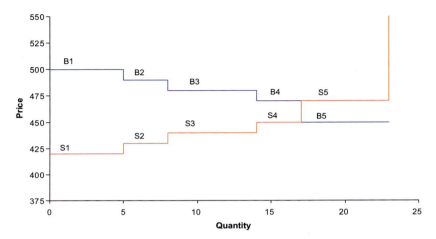

Figure 2. Multi-unit demand and supply environment (E2). This figure represents a multi-unit environment with five buyers and five sellers. The aggregate supply and demand arrays are step functions where each step identifies a particular buyer's or seller's value or cost. Only one subject is assigned to a step on these functions. In addition, each participant has multiple units to bid or to offer all on the same step. As shown in the figure, there are three buyers ($B1$, $B3$, $B5$) and three sellers ($S1$, $S2$, $S3$) with six units and two buyers ($B2$, $B4$) and two sellers ($S2$, $S3$) with three units. Thus, there are twenty-four buy and sell units in the market; of these, eighteen are potentially tradable in the equilibrium price tunnel (450, 470).

2. Within each period, buyers are assigned (by a random rotation procedure) to one of the demand steps ($B1$)–($B5$), and sellers are assigned to one of the supply steps ($S1$)–($S5$). Each period they are assigned to a new step. For example, buyer 1 with the right to resell up to 6 units at a price of 500, could be reassigned a step with 6 units, but with no tradable units within the equilibrium price tunnel, as is buyer 5. Alternatively, he or she could be on a step with only three units, as is buyer 4.

This experimental environment, which we will identify as E2, allows us to assess the performance of the Walrasian auction where participants have multiple units and where relative competitiveness is variable period to period. This environment has been used in previous experimental studies (see Campbell et al., 1991; McCabe, Rassenti, and Smith, 1992), and clearly stresses the price discovery process. The environment, from the participants' perspective, seems to be changing each period and thus relying on past market experience can hinder price discovery.

3. Walrasian Auction Design and Computerized Implementation

A Walrasian tatonnement must specify the following rules in order to implement the auction:

(i) The process must determine a starting or *initial price* P_0.

(ii) The *price adjustment function* we used in our experiments was the following piecewise rule:

$$P_t = P_{t-1} + \text{rnd}\left(4\left[\frac{1}{2(1+\{t/4\})}\right][D(P_{t-1}) - S(P_{t-1})]\right),$$

where $\{y\}$ denotes the greatest integer less than or equal to y, t is the current iteration in the period, and rnd(y) is the nearest integer to y. For example, in iteration 11 with an announced price of 200 and reported excess demand of 10, the price next period will be 207. Unlike the experiments conducted by Joyce, our experiments are computerized and thus there is no human auctioneer judging the "appropriate" price changes.

(iii) We consider two alternative information structures:
   (a) *minimum information*: subjects are informed of the current trial price, the adjustment factor for the current trial, the number of seconds remaining for the current trial, and a full history of past trial prices and past order flow imbalances;
   (b) *complete order flow information*: In addition to the information in (a), subjects are provided on each trial with the real-time updated buy and sell orders as they arrived during the current price iteration, and what the next iteration price would be, based on the current imbalance information.

(iv) A *message restriction* specification limits the messages that can be sent. We used an improvement rule where a buyer who was willing to purchase m units at a price Y must be willing to purchase at least m units at prices lower than Y. Similarly, a seller who was willing to sell n units at price Z must be willing to sell at least n units at prices above Z.[2] The motivation for this rule was to restrict manipulation and obvious misrevelation (see McAfee, 1992). This rule restricts the potential buy and sell orders that can be placed during iteration t as a function of past responses.

(v) The stopping rule used in our experiments has two dimensions. First, during an iteration, the time remaining to submit an order is endogenous. A clock is set at 15 seconds when the iteration price is posted. Any new order quantity submitted at the price reinitializes the clock to 15 seconds. This rule provided an implementation of a "soft close" procedure. A soft close enforces a unanimity requirement in that no one can guarantee himself or herself the last say. The second dimension dealt with the exact close of the market period. We close the market period, at trial t^*, when $P_{t^*} = P_{t^*-1}$ or $E(P_{t^*}) = 0$. Notice that given

---

[2] In addition, in all replications we placed the following restrictions on the messages participants could send at each iteration:
1. Individuals could not sell short or buy on margin. Thus, individuals were not permitted to offer more units than their maximum declared capacity to buy or sell.
2. Once an order was sent to the market it could not be canceled.

Table 1
Experimental treatments* (number of experiments is listed in each cell)

Message restriction	Information	
	Minimal	Order flow
No	4	5
Yes	3	3

Notes. The experiments consist of two information treatments in which either *minimal information* is provided to subjects during an iteration,[3] i.e., subjects are informed of the current trial price, the adjustment factor for the current trial, the number of seconds remaining for the current iteration, and a full history of past trial prices and past order flow imbalances; or *complete order flow information* where subjects are provided, at each iteration, with real-time updated buy and sell orders as they arrived during the price iteration, and what the next iteration price would be, based on the current imbalance information. The other treatment uses a *message restriction* improvement rule placed on subject orders where a buyer who was willing to purchase m units at a price Y must be willing to purchase AT LEAST m units at prices lower than Y. Similarly, a seller who is willing to sell n units at price Z must be willing to sell AT LEAST n units at prices above Z. This rule restricts the potential buy and sell orders that can be placed during iteration t as a function of past responses.

our price adjustment rule, this stopping rule does not guarantee $E(P) = 0$. Thus, if at t^*, $E(P_{t^*}) = 0$, we ration by time priority.

Table 1 provides an overview of the experimental treatments and the number of experiments conducted per cell in our design. The design consists of two factors (improvement rule and order flow information) which are either present or not in each experiment.

4. Experimental Results

4.1. The E1 Environment Replication

Using E1 we replicated the Joyce experiments with a computer implementation of the Walrasian Tatonnement mechanism. Table 2 shows the mean efficiency and competitive price deviation in the later periods of the experiments. There is no significant difference in efficiency and price between the oral and computerized treatments.

4.2. Baseline and Treatment Effects

For the remainder of this paper, we will use the following abbreviations for the treatments in our design: FINI = full information with no bid-offer improvement; NINI =

---

[3] An iteration is the time between two successive price changes based on the buyer and seller responses on the amounts they are willing to purchase and sell at the stated price.

Table 2
Oral versus computerized treatment for E1

	Oral implementation	Computerized implementation
Mean efficiency	96.3	97.7
Mean price deviation	5.7	5.3

Notes. The statistics presented in the table are: Average efficiency, which is the percentage of the maximum of the producer and consumer surplus attained by the oral and computerized implementation of the Walrasian auction, and the average deviation of prices from the competitive equilibrium price, for the simple E1 environment in Figure 1, attained by each mechanism.

no information with no bid-offer improvement; FII = full information with bid-offer improvement; NII = no information with bid-offer improvement.

Figure 3 shows the efficiency distribution (boxplots) for each of the four treatments in our implementation of the Walrasian auction in the E2 environment. The boxplots show the median (the dot), interquartiles (the box), the 10th and 90th percentiles (bars below and above each box). In addition to the Walrasian treatments, we report the results of 6 baseline double auction (DA) experiments using the E2 environment.

The DA outperforms each of the Walrasian auction designs we tested. FINI performs best among the Walrasian auction treatments. The following efficiency rankings, for periods 7+, show that only the full information no improvement (FINI) treatment approaches the efficiency of the double auction: DA $\geqslant$ FINI $\geqslant$ NII = FII = NINI.

We summarize the following comparative static results.
(i) Conditional on having no bid-offer restriction rule, full information helps in obtaining more efficient allocations.
(ii) Conditional on only minimal information being provided, the improvement rule helps in obtaining more efficient allocations. However, the level of efficiency does not approach that of FINI or DA.

With respect to price formation, Figure 4 shows the price dispersion relative to the competitive equilibrium price tunnel. From the boxplots it is easy to see that each treatment results in prices that lie within the tunnel ($-10, +10$). However, the low efficiencies reported in Table 2 show that the supply and demand match is not correct, and suggests the presence of significant underrevelation on both sides of the market: if either side underreveals to gain an advantage, the other side underreveals to neutralize that advantage.

4.3. Individual Behavior

Three types of individual behavior can be identified in our experiments:

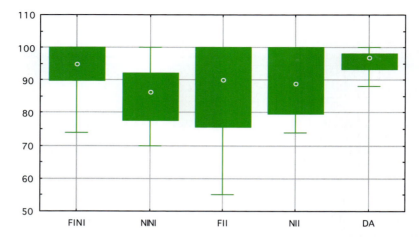

Figure 3. Distribution of efficiency across treatments. The figure shows the efficiency (the percentage of the maximum of the producer and consumer surplus attained) distribution for each of the four treatments in our implementation of the Walrasian auction in the E2 environment. The boxplots show the median (the dot), interquartiles (the box), the 5th and 95th percentiles (bars below and above each box). In addition to the Walrasian treatments, we report the results of 6 baseline double auction (DA) experiments using the E2 environment. The treatments are: FINI = full information with no bid-offer improvement; NINI = no information with no bid-offer improvement; FII = full information with bid-offer improvement; NII = no information with bid-offer improvement. *No information* means subjects are informed of the current trial price, the adjustment factor for the current trial, the number of seconds remaining for the current trial, and a full history of past trial prices and past order flow imbalances, while *full information* subjects were provided at each iteration with the real-time updated buy and sell orders as they arrived during the current price iteration, and what the next iteration price would be, based on the current imbalance information. The bid-offer improvement rule requires a buyer who was willing to purchase m units at a price Y must be willing to purchase AT LEAST m units at prices lower than Y. Similarly, a seller who was willing to sell n units at price Z must be willing to sell AT LEAST n units at prices above Z. This rule restricts the potential buy and sell orders that can be placed during iteration t as a function of past responses.

(1) *Overrevelation*: A buy or sell response that can result in a marginal loss in profit if the process stops, i.e., for each iteration t and participant i at the price P_t [4]

$$D_t^i(P_t) > d_t^i(P_t), \qquad S_t^j(P_t) > s_t^j(P_t).$$

(2) *Underrevelation*: A buy or sell response that is less than the number of units that are profitable at the current price

$$D_t^i(P_t) < d_t^i(P_t), \qquad S_t^i(P_t) < s_t^j(P_t).$$

---

[4] We define $D_t = (D_O(P_O), D_1(P_1), \ldots, D_t(P_t))$, $S_t = (S_O(P_O), S_1(P_1), \ldots, S_t(P_t))$ as the aggregate supply and demand responses for each price iteration up to P_t and D_t^i, S_t^j the individual supply and demand responses for each price iteration up to P_t. We will represent the true demands and supplies with the lower case letters, d_t, s_t, d_t^i, s_t^j.

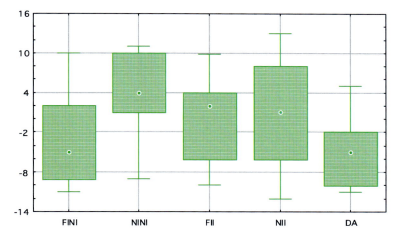

Figure 4. Distribution of prices relative to competitive equilibrium. The figure shows the distribution of the deviation of prices, in cents, from the competitive equilibrium price for each of the four treatments in our implementation of the Walrasian auction in the E2 environment. The boxplots show the median (the dot), interquartiles (the box), the 10th and 90th percentiles (bars below and above each box). In addition to the Walrasian treatments, we report the results of 6 baseline double auction (DA) experiments using the E2 environment. The treatments are: FINI = full information with no bid-offer improvement; NINI = no information with no bid-offer improvement; FII = full information with bid-offer improvement; NII = no information with bid-offer improvement. *No information* means subjects are informed of the current trial price, the adjustment factor for the current trial, the number of seconds remaining for the current trial, and a full history of past trial prices and past order flow imbalances, while *full information* subjects were provided at each iteration with the real-time updated buy and sell orders as they arrived during the current price iteration, and what the next iteration price would be, based on the current imbalance information. The bid-offer improvement rule requires a buyer who was willing to purchase m units at a price Y must be willing to purchase AT LEAST m units at prices lower than Y. Similarly, a seller who was willing to sell n units at price Z must be willing to sell AT LEAST n units at prices above Z. This rule restricts the potential buy and sell orders that can be placed during iteration t as a function of past responses.

(3) *Revelation*: A buy or sell response that contains all profitable units and no unprofitable units at the current price

$$D_t^i(P_t) = d_t^i(P_t), \qquad S_t^i(P_t) = s_t^j(P_t).$$

Overrevelation rarely occurs (3% of responses), however, both buyers and sellers underreveal nearly one-third of the time. In FII, over 65% of the buyer responses are consistent with underrevelation.

Notice that under our improvement rule, in later periods, once a buyer (seller) has revealed a willingness to purchase (sell) x units at a particular price, he or she is required to purchase (sell) that many units at a lower (higher) price; therefore, underrevealing at the beginning of a period is the only way to obtain strategic bargaining room later in a period. Consequently, the improvement rule fosters underrevelation by motivating people to begin their bargaining from a more "advantageous" position.

References

Campbell, J., LaMaster, S., Smith, V., Van Boening, M. (1991). "Off-floor trading, disintegration and the bid–ask spread in experimental markets". The Journal of Business 64, 495–522.
Hurwicz, L. (1972). "On informationaly decentralized systems". In: McGuire, C.B., Radner, R. (Eds.), Decisions and Organization. North-Holland, Amsterdam.
Joyce, P. (1984). "The Walrasian tatonnement mechanism and information". RAND Journal of Economics 15, 416–425.
McAfee, P. (1992). "A dominant strategy double auction". Journal of Economic Theory 56 (2), 434–450.
McCabe, K.A., Rassenti, S.J., Smith, V.L. (1992). "Designing call auction institutions: Is double dutch best?" Economic Journal 102, 9–23.
Otani, Y., Sicilian, J. (1990). "Limit properties of equilibrium allocations of Walrasian strategic games". Journal of Economic Theory 51, 295–312.

Chapter 13

THE MATCHING MARKET INSTITUTION

DANIEL FRIEDMAN and CHANGHUA RICH
University of California, Santa Cruz

The matching market (MM) institution is a two-sided auction procedure that collects bids from buyers and asks from sellers, and iteratively matches the highest remaining bid with the highest remaining ask less than or equal to it. Each buyer pays his bid price and the seller receives the bid price. Rich and Friedman (1998) and Rich (1996) document recent use of the MM by the Chinese Environmental Protection Agency and occasional use in various financial markets.[1]

The MM institution maximizes the number of agreeable matches (i.e., transactions) in a given set of bids and asks, and gives the seller the best agreeable price in each transaction. However, buyers and sellers in the MM have strong incentives to bid and ask strategically so as to underreveal willingness to transact (Rich and Friedman, 1998). Actual performance, in terms of efficiency as well as transaction volume and seller's surplus, therefore is a question of theoretical and practical interest.

In this chapter we summarize a first laboratory experiment comparing the MM institution to the natural alternative, the uniform price (UP) or single call market. The procedures and results are reported more fully in Rich and Friedman (1998). We find that, compared with UP, MM has lower efficiency, has about the same average volume but greater variability, and gives sellers a *smaller* fraction of the surplus.

1. Experimental Procedures

The experiment consisted of ten sessions; five conducted by hand at Wuhan University (WU) in China and five conducted over a computer network at University of California, Santa Cruz (UCSC). Each session involved 16 or more trading periods, roughly half under MM and half under UP. Three sessions at each site used inexperienced subjects, four buyers and four sellers, and the other two sessions used experienced subjects, six buyers and four sellers. Figure 1 shows the induced value and cost parameters; note that experienced buyers received the higher value schedule B' in some periods. On average subjects earned about $10 per hour at UCSC and 25 Yuan at WU, well in excess of average opportunity cost.

---

[1] A general definition is that a matching market is a mechanism for pairing individuals for mutual benefit. In one well-known special case, often referred to as the marriage market, utility is non-transferable and the value of a potential match depends nonlinearly on the characteristics of the two parties (Gale, 1968; Becker, 1973; Roth and Sotomayor, 1990; Shimer and Lones, 2000). Our MM is a polar case of transferable utility in which the value of a match is simply the difference between buyer's value and seller's cost.

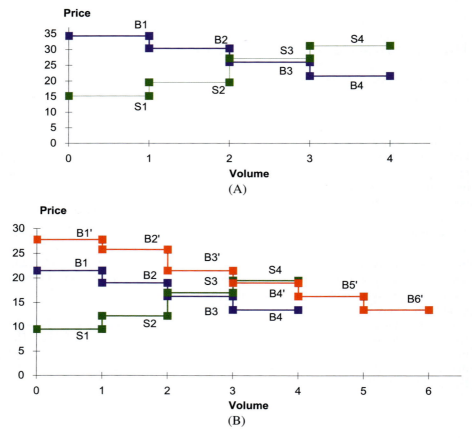

Figure 1. (A) Induced values and costs in inexperienced sessions. In sessions with inexperienced subjects, supply is induced each period using cost schedule $S1–S4$. Demand is induced each period using value schedule $B1–B4$, producing the competitive equilibrium (CE) price = 27.2, the CE volume = 2, and the total CE profit = 30 each period. (B) Induced values and costs in experienced sessions. In sessions with experienced subjects, supply is induced each period using cost schedule $S1–S4$. Demand is induced in some periods using value schedule $B1–B4$, producing CE price = 17.0, CE volume = 2, and CE total profit = 18.75. In other periods demand is induced using $B1'–B6'$, producing CE price = 19.5, CE volume = 3, and CE total profit = 36.25.

To illustrate the two market institutions, suppose that the bids of the four buyers are 4.60, 3.75, 2.25, and 1.50, and that sellers' asks are 6.00, 4.00, 2.81, and 1.40. In the MM, the highest ask would be rejected since it is above the highest bid, and the other three asks would be matched respectively with the three highest bids. The outcome is three transactions at prices 4.60, 3.75, and 2.25 with revealed surplus $4.60 - 4.00 = 0.60$, $3.75 - 2.81 = 0.94$, and $2.25 - 1.40 = 0.85$. The actual surplus, of course, depends on the three buyers' true values and the three sellers' true costs; presumably the actual surplus exceeds the total revealed surplus of $0.60 + 0.94 + 0.85 = 2.39$.

The same bids and asks lead to a different outcome in the UP institution. Here the two highest bids are matched with the two lowest asks at the highest market clearing price, 3.75. In this case the two transactions yield a revealed surplus of $4.60 - 1.40 = 3.20$ plus $4.00 - 3.75 = 0.25$ for a total of 3.45. See the Cason and Friedman chapter in this Handbook and the citations therein for a complete description of the UP institution, referred to there as the "$k = 1$ SCM."

In each period of the experiment, the trading institution, MM or UP, was announced (and typically held constant for 4–8 periods) and each trader privately submitted a bid or ask. The collected bids and asks and resulting transactions then were publicly displayed; true values and costs remained private information.

2. Results

We focus here on how the market institution (MM or UP) affects three performance variables: efficiency, trading volume, and surplus split. The variables are measured in 264 market periods in ten sessions, 133 MM periods and 131 UP periods. Efficiency is defined each period as the observed total profits as a fraction of the competitive equilibrium (CE) profit shown in Figure 1. The overall mean efficiency is 80 percent under the matching market compared to 92 percent under the uniform price market. Figure 2 shows the trends for the first eight periods averaged over all six inexperienced sessions in Panel A. In each of these periods the average efficiency is higher in UP than in MM. Panel B shows the corresponding averages over all four experienced sessions. Here the data are more erratic and in three periods the MM has higher efficiency, but overall UP is still clearly the more efficient market institution.

Volume deviation is defined in percentage terms each period as observed trading volume minus competitive equilibrium volume and then divided by CE volume. These values are quite small on average in both institutions: -0.6% in MM and -5% in UP. But volume is considerably more variable in MM, where the absolute value of volume deviation (VDVAB) averages 21% in MM and 5% in UP. That is, positive and negative deviations are both large in the MM but tend to offset each other, while positive deviations are extremely rare in UP and negative deviations are rather moderate. Figure 3 shows the trends in VDVAB. In each of the first eight periods the average absolute volume deviation in the six inexperienced sessions is larger in MM than in UP. Again the experienced data are more erratic – MM has smaller average absolute deviation in one period and equal in another. The overall conclusion is the same: the MM institution is less reliable than the UP in delivering the CE trading volume.

Why are the experienced session averages more erratic than the inexperienced?

Partly it is simply the difference in sample size, with four experienced versus six inexperienced sessions. The other part of the explanation is that both institutions perform erratically. In a stationary repetitive environment, traders in the UP institution tend to

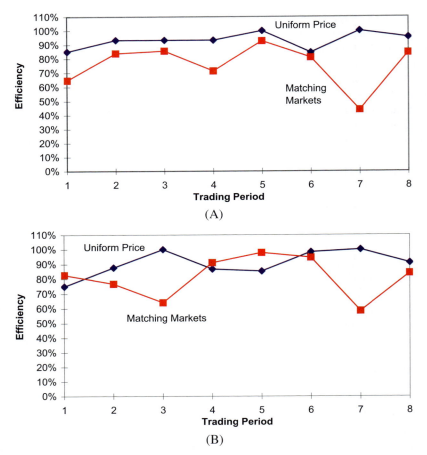

Figure 2. (A) Average efficiency in inexperienced sessions. The first eight periods are averaged over all six inexperienced sessions; see Figure 1 Panel A for induced values and costs. Note that average efficiency in every period is higher in the uniform price institution than in the matching institution. (B) Average efficiency in experienced sessions. The first eight periods are averaged over all four experienced sessions; see Figure 1 Panel B for induced values and costs. Note that overall UP is more efficient although the MM has slightly higher efficiency in three periods.

shade their bids and offers closer and closer to the anticipated clearing price, and occasionally they overshoot the price and fail to transact, with a drastic impact on efficiency and volume (Friedman and Ostroy, 1995; Smith et al., 1982). The UP data in Figures 2 and 3 reflect this strategic behavior, and also reflect the fact that the MM also encourages strategic behavior and produces even more erratic outcomes.

The final performance measure we consider is the surplus split. Define ratio of sellers' profit (RSP) as actual profits earned by all sellers in a given market period as a percent-

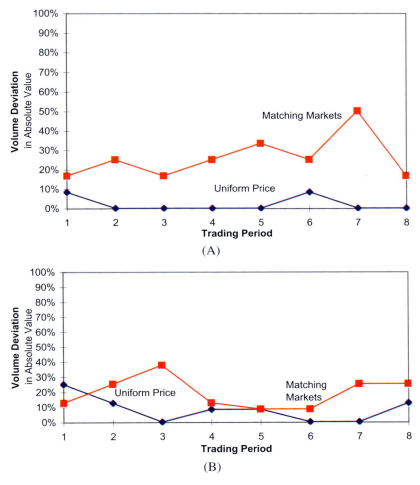

Figure 3. (A) Average volume deviation in inexperienced sessions. The first eight periods are averaged over all six inexperienced sessions; see Figure 1 Panel A for induced values and costs. Note that volume is considerably more variable in MM compared to UP. (B) Average volume deviation in experienced sessions. The first eight periods are averaged over all four experienced sessions; see Figure 1 Panel B for induced values and costs. Note that the MM is again less reliable than the UP in delivering the CE volume.

age of profits that sellers would earn in competitive equilibrium. Likewise, define RBP as the ratio of buyers' actual profit to CE profit. Overall, average RBP is 91.2% in MM versus 99.9% in UP, while average RSP is 72.9% in MM versus 86.6% in UP. Thus the profits of both buyers and sellers are notably lower in MM than in UP. To assess the relative loss (or surplus split *per se*) we consider the ratio of average RSP to average RBP.

The ratio is 79.9% in MM and 86.7% in UP. Thus the MM impairs sellers' relative, as well as absolute, profitability.

3. Discussion

Our findings offer little encouragement to advocates of the MM in field markets. Compared either to the competitive equilibrium (CE) theoretical benchmark or to the actual performance of the uniform price (UP) market institution, the MM institution fails to deliver on its main selling point: that it will generate higher trading volume. It does generate considerably more variable volume but average trading volume is quite close to the CE benchmark and to the UP average. A secondary selling point is that the MM will offer sellers a larger share of the surplus. However, our data show that sellers in the MM get a smaller slice of a smaller pie than in UP.

Rich and Friedman (1998) show that prices were also more variable in MM, even after averaging across transactions within a period. The main problem with the MM in practice is that it is much less efficient; loss of potential gains from trade averaged about 8% in UP and about 20% in MM. Rich and Friedman (1998) argue that the reason for the poor showing is that buyers substantially understate their willingness to pay and sellers understate their willingness to accept in both institutions but especially in the MM institution. These results serve as a caution to those who contemplate field use of the MM, and serve as a challenge to theorists who wish to construct general models of price formation.

References

Becker, Gary (1973). "A theory of marriage, Part I". Journal of Political Economy 81 (4), 813–846.
Friedman, Daniel, Ostroy, Joseph (1995). "Competitivity in auction markets: An experimental and theoretical investigation". The Economic Journal 105 (428), 22–53.
Gale, David (1968). "Optimal assignments in an ordered set: An application of matroid theory". Journal of Combinatorial Theory 4, 176–180.
Rich, Changhua Sun (1996). "An experimental investigation of two systems of emission permits trading". Dissertation chapter, University of California, Santa Cruz.
Rich, Changhua Sun, Friedman, Daniel (1998). "The matching market institution: A laboratory investigation". American Economic Review 88 (5), 1311–1322.
Roth, Alvin, Sotomayor, Marilda (1990). "Two-sided Matching: A Study in Game-Theoretic Modeling and Analysis". Cambridge University Press, New York.
Shimer, Robert, Lones, Smith (2000). "Assortative matching and search". Econometrica 68 (2), 343–369.
Smith, Vernon L., Williams, Arlington W., Bratton, Kenneth, Vannoni, Michael (1982). "Competitive market institutions: Double auctions versus sealed bid-offer auctions". American Economic Review 72 (1), 58–77.

Chapter 14

TATONNEMENT

CHARLES R. PLOTT

The concept of tatonnement evolved to embody a methodology for determining price – a "price discovery process" – without disequilibrium trades taking place. It has been viewed as an auctioneer calling out prices, observing behavior and calling out new prices in response to the behavior. The process is imagined as continuing until an equilibrium is reached. For "well behaved" economic environments, such systems can function effectively. However, the behavioral principles that operate within such mechanisms are not those imagined by those who introduced the concept as a theoretical tool, and as a result, the tatonnement mechanisms are not generally reliable. That is, the tatonnement mechanism is not reliable as a market discovery tool in single or multiple markets.

Two different forms of tatonnement adjustment processes have been tested in the literature. The classical model holds that prices adjust proportionally to excess demand. That is, it is a process drawn from the model

$$dP/dt = \alpha[D(P) - S(P)].$$

In the practical world of an experiment the time variable is discrete so the model becomes $P_{t+1} - P_t = \alpha[D(P_t) - S(P_t)]$, where t is a "round" in which agents submit demands and supplies contingent on the price announced. Of course the demand and supply functions are not observed by the mechanism. Only the quantities X_t^D and X_t^S are observed, where these quantities are the buy orders and sell orders that are tendered in response to the price announced. These quantities replace the functions in the formula. The stopping rule, unless an alternative convention is adopted, is where the buy and sell orders are equal.

The second tatonnement method of price discovery was first introduced and tested by Plott and George (1992) and is based on the "secant" algorithm for finding the zeros of an equation. It is based on the Newton model

$$dP/dt = [1/(D'(P) - S'(P))](D(P) - S(P)).$$

Again, the practical world of an experiment requires an operational interpretation of the system, which was:

$$P_{t+1} = P_t + \left|[(P_t - -P_{t-1})/(X_t - X_{t-1})]\right|X_t \quad \text{if } X_t \neq X_{t-1} \quad \text{and}$$
$$P_{t+1} = P_t + (P_t - P_{t-1}) \quad \text{if } X_t = X_{t-1},$$

where X_t is the difference between buy and sell orders in response to the announced price. Notice that the absolute value imposed in the formula follows Walras's fundamental principle that the direction of price change is dictated by the sign of the excess

Handbook of Experimental Economics Results, Volume 1
Copyright © 2008 Elsevier B.V. All rights reserved
DOI: 10.1016/S1574-0722(07)00014-5

demand. Of course, in the unstable case that is exactly what does not happen so because of this feature of the mechanism the mechanism itself would seem to be inconsistent with the underlying forces at work.

Both mechanisms have performed successfully as price discovery mechanisms in cases in which only a single market existed and that market the demand and supplies were essentially linear, leading smoothly to a unique equilibrium. By contrast, when a single market environment has a slightly more complex structure or when multiple markets are involved the tatonnement mechanism either operates inefficiently or does not work at all in the sense that it does not converge.

When multiple markets are involved two problems exist. The first is "cheap talk" in the sense that agents are not bound to the quantities they express at a price unless the system happens to terminate at that moment. They also know that the price announced in the next period is influenced by the price this period. The resulting pattern of responses does not necessarily lead the process to an efficient equilibration. The second problem is related to coordination. Agents might coordinate themselves and tender responses that might get the adjustment process in one market to be close to a termination configuration but then the second market is typically nowhere near termination. When attention is diverted to the second market the first market will move in a manner that signals non-termination. Experiments ended with subjects frustrated and never achieving a trade.

The basic problem with tatonnement is illustrated in Figure 1. The demand and supply configuration is the classical "swastika" design first studied by Smith, in which the demand curve is perfectly inelastic and cuts the supply where the latter is perfectly elastic. It a technical sense there is no classical competitive equilibrium in this environment because at no price does the quantity demanded exactly equal the quantity supplied in the absence of some sort of selection mechanism that picks the supply units to be allocated to the demanders when the price announced is the competitive equilibrium. At the competitive equilibrium price of 195, there are 16 units demanded and 35 units offered as supply. Since the suppliers make zero profit at that price they are indifferent, according to theory, and submit a supply correspondence as shown in Figure 1. It is well-established that when the exchange mechanism is the oral double auction or the multiple unit double auction, the market will converge to the competitive equilibrium and the allocation will be one hundred percent efficient.

Data from the application of the tatonnement (the secant method that was shown to work in Plott and George, 1992), are contained in the figure. Notice first that the allocations were not necessarily efficient. The volumes are often above the 16 units of the competitive equilibrium. Demanders are seen buying units that had no value for them. That is, units with zero redemption value were purchased. Second, the prices need not be at the competitive equilibrium level. In two cases, the prices are above 300. Third, cases exist in which the mechanism terminated without demand equaling supply. The iterations stopped due to the algorithm reaching its maximum precision for an iteration.

Why does this happen? When the system stops because the quantity expressed as demand equaled the quantity expressed as supply it is because demanders were willing to buy more than they wanted and suppliers were compromising on the quantities they

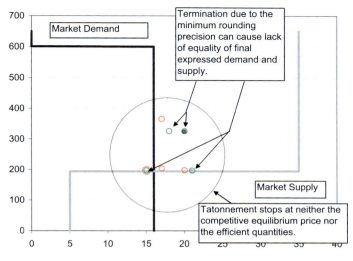

Figure 1.

wanted to sell. The agents were modifying their requests in the light of what they really wanted in order to get the mechanism to stop iterating. Agents realized that the system was using much resource time in iterations and in the interest of acquiring some gains from the exchange, as opposed to continuous iteration terminating with no trade, they compromised in a negotiating fashion. Thus, when the system did terminate, it was due to a process of negotiation that ended in an inefficient allocation. This feature is exacerbated when many markets are involved. The "negotiations" and "compromises" are attempted but in a multiple market system they are not successfully coordinated. The iterations continue without termination until the system is arbitrarily stopped and no exchanges take place.

Reference

Plott, R. Charles, George, Glen (1992). "Marshallian vs Walrasian stability in an experimental market". The Economic Journal 102, 437–460.

PART 1.2

IMPERFECT COMPETITION

PART 1.2.1

MARKET POWER

Ernst Fehr and Simon Gächter, "Wage Differentials in Experimental Efficiency Wage Markets"

Yvonne Durham, Jack Hirshleifer and Vernon L. Smith, "The Paradox of Power"

Douglas D. Davis and Charles A. Holt, "The Exercise of Market Power in Laboratory Experiments"

Antoni Bosch-Domènech and Nicolaas J. Vriend, "The Classical Experiments on Cournot Oligopoly"

James C. Cox and R. Mark Isaac, "Experiments in Decentralized Monopoly Restraint"

Chapter 15

WAGE DIFFERENTIALS IN EXPERIMENTAL EFFICIENCY WAGE MARKETS[1]

ERNST FEHR and SIMON GÄCHTER
University of Zurich

1. Wage Differentials: Experiments Help to Test Explanations

In recent years, many econometric studies have confirmed the existence of inter-industry wage differentials. Even after controlling for a large number of job- and worker-related characteristics, and demographic variables, large and statistically significant industry wage differences remain. Moreover, these differences exist for union as well as for non-union workers and seem to be remarkably similar (i) across countries with different labor market institutions, (ii) across occupations, and (iii) across time. Two particularly interesting facts are that (a) high profit industries tend to pay high wages and (b) if one occupation in an industry is highly paid, all other occupations in that industry also tend to be paid high wages (Dickens and Katz, 1987; Katz and Summers, 1989).

Even though the empirical fact of wage differentials is largely undisputed, the *explanation* of it is not. Some writers (e.g., Thaler, 1989; Thaler's article also provides a summary of the most important findings) have assigned these differentials even the status of an "anomaly." Put differently, some economists see the fact of inter-industry wage differentials to be at odds with neoclassical labor market theory. Basically, there are two rival explanations. One tries to reconcile the facts with neoclassical labor market theory by claiming that the observed wages compensate for *unobserved* abilities and/or working conditions (Murphy and Topel, 1990). An alternative approach rejects the neoclassical view and invokes an efficiency wage explanation (e.g., Krueger and Summers, 1987, 1988).

With field data, it has so far been impossible to sharply discriminate between rival explanations. Unambiguous measurement of job rents requires reliable information about reservation wages, working conditions and skill levels. While these variables can in general only be crudely approximated with field data they can be controlled in the laboratory. Here we report on experimental tests of two leading efficiency wage theories, which have been invoked as an explanation of observed wage differentials, namely the Fair Wage-Effort version and the Shirking version of efficiency wages. In these experiments, the test methodology has been to implement an environment (i) that allows for the emergence of efficiency wages and (ii) that gives competitive forces the best shot.

---

[1] This paper is part of a research project on social norms in labor markets. It has been financed by the Swiss National Science Foundation under the project No. 12-43590.95.

2. The Fair Wage-Effort Version of Efficiency Wage Theory

This version of Efficiency Wage Theory goes back to Akerlof (1982, 1984) and in particular to Akerlof and Yellen (1990). The basic hypothesis in this model is that if wages fall short of a fair reference wage, a rise in wages will raise workers' effort. As a consequence, firms have an incentive to pay wages that are close to workers' fair reference wage. Two kinds of social comparison processes may affect the level of the fair reference wage and, hence, the wage-effort relation: (i) If workers' perception of what constitutes a fair wage level is positively correlated with firms' profit opportunities, high profit firms are forced to pay a higher wage to elicit a *given* level of effort. Moreover, if higher profit opportunities are associated with a higher marginal product of effort, firms with high profit opportunities have an incentive to elicit higher effort levels. Both reasons may be responsible for the observed positive correlation between profits and wages in the field data. (ii) Fair reference wages may also be influenced by what other workers in closely related occupations earn. In the following we describe an experiment by Fehr, Gächter, and Kirchsteiger (1996) in which point (i) and its implication for persistent wage differentials was investigated.

2.1. Experimental Design

In the experiment, subjects acted in the roles of firms and workers, respectively. The design consisted of three elements: (a) *a competitive bid market* with an excess supply of workers to create a lot of competitive pressure; this market institution has well-known features of convergence to the competitive equilibrium (see Plott, 1989), (b) *firms which differ according to the profitability of an employed worker* to be able to test point (i) above, (c) *incomplete contracts*, that is, workers have some discretion in exerting work effort; this is regarded to be an essential characteristics of naturally occurring labor relations and a precondition for reciprocity to become effective. The experiment consisted of 16 trading days in each of which a three-stage game was played. Table 1 summarizes the design. An important design feature concerns the information about payoffs and the anonymity of trading partners. Payoff functions of firms and workers were common knowledge. Individual firms and individual workers could develop no reputation across periods because all interactions were fully anonymous.

2.2. Results

At the *third stage* firms actually rewarded or punished despite this being costly for the firm, which is evidence for firm's reciprocity (for a definition of reciprocity see, e.g., Rabin, 1993). At the *second stage* workers show a highly significantly positive wage-effort relation even if one controls for firms' redemption values. Put differently, the higher wages are, the higher are the effort levels put forward, despite their increasing costliness. At the *first stage* firms pay wages that are positively correlated with their profit opportunities (i.e., their redemption value).

Table 1
The Fair Wage-Effort Efficiency Wage Theory: The design of Fehr, Gächter, and Kirchsteiger (1996)

A. Sequence of events during a trading day	
Stage 1	1. Each firm (which differ in their assigned redemption values q (= profitability of an employed worker)) simultaneously posts a binding wage offer $w \in [f, q]$. f is a fixed cost for the worker of accepting an offer.
	2. Workers observe all wages and choose among the available offers in a randomly determined order. There are more workers than jobs (= firms) to create competition.
Stage 2	3. Workers who accept an offer are informed about the redemption value q of their firm and choose an effort level e. They incur effort costs $c(e)$ with $c(e^{\min}) = 0$, $c'(e) > 0$ and $c''(e) > 0$.
Stage 3	4. Firms are informed about the effort choice of their worker and can punish ($p < 1$) or reward ($p > 1$) their worker at some cost $k(p)$; $k(p = 1) = 0$; $k'(p < 1) < 0$; $k'(p > 1) > 0$.

B. Payoffs	
Firms	$\pi = (q - w)^* e - k(p)$
Workers	$u = [w - c(e) - f]^* p$

C. Main predictions

In the absence of fairness motives (*null hypothesis*)	In the presence of fairness motives
No systematic wage and job rent differentials because workers' effort choices are *not* affected by wages and firms' profit opportunities	Firms with higher profit opportunities pay higher wages and higher job rents because workers' effort choices are affected by wages and firms' profit opportunities

Figure 1 demonstrates that the null hypothesis of no wage differentials has to be rejected in favor of the fair wage-effort hypothesis that wages are positively related to profit opportunities. The black bars show the average wages over all 16 periods per redemption value (profit opportunity). The white bars are evidence for the temporal stability of observed wage differentials. They depict the average wages in the last three periods. Notice that they are almost identical to the averages over all periods.

In the empirical literature there is no doubt that wage differentials exist. However, an important open question is whether the observed differentials are *compensating* wage differentials. Notice that in this experiment unobserved abilities and other worker heterogeneities – which are invoked as explanations for observed field data (see Murphy and Topel, 1990) – are excluded by design. Therefore, a relevant question is whether the observed wages contain a pure rent element as argued by, e.g., Krueger and Summers (1988). It turns out that firms pay positive job rents at *all* redemption values. Yet,

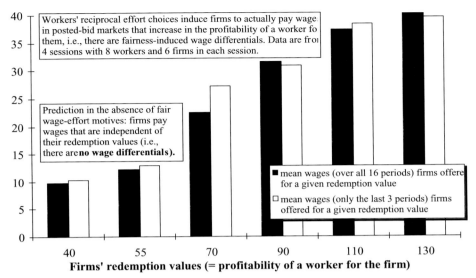

Source: Fehr, Gächter, and Kirchsteiger (1996).

Figure 1. Intertemporally stable wage differentials in the Fair Wage-Effort Model: Firms' wage payments increase in the redemption value because workers' effort levels depend positively on the rent share.

there are also large job rent differentials. Firms with higher profit opportunities pay significantly higher job rents. The picture with job rents mimics Figure 1.

3. The Shirking Version of Efficiency Wage Theory

This version of Efficiency Wage Theory has been developed by Shapiro and Stiglitz (1984), Bowles (1985), Fehr (1986), MacLeod and Malcomson (1989), and others. The shirking version is essentially a theory of involuntary unemployment that arises because of a *moral hazard* problem. In these models, firms pay incentive compatible efficiency wages to prevent workers from shirking. Fehr, Kirchsteiger, and Riedl (1996) have developed a simplified version of the shirking model and subjected it to an experimental test.

3.1. Design

Their design is summarized in Table 2.

Despite its simplicity the efficiency wage model of Fehr, Kirchsteiger and Riedl contains many testable predictions. Among them are the following: (i) wages are incentive compatible, i.e., they satisfy the so-called "no-shirking condition" (ii) employed workers receive a job rent and the firms with the lowest redemption values make no job offer

Table 2
The shirking version of Efficiency Wage Theory: The design of Fehr, Kirchsteiger, and Riedl (1996)

	A. Sequence of events during a trading day
Stage 1	1. Firms (which differ in their assigned *redemption values* q (= profitability of an employed worker)) simultaneously post employment contracts $[w, \hat{e}, p]$, where w is the wage, $\hat{e}$ is the *desired* effort and p is a penalty in case the worker is caught shirking ($e < \hat{e}$). p is bounded from above.
	2. Workers observe all contracts and choose among the available offers in a randomly determined order. There are more workers than jobs to create competition among workers.
Stage 2	3. Workers who accept an offer choose an effort level e and incur effort costs $c(e)$ with $c(e^{\min}) = 0$, $c'(e) > 0$ and $c''(e) > 0$.
	4. A random mechanism determines whether the actual effort e is verifiable. In case the worker has shirked, she has to pay the penalty p to the firm.
	B. Payoffs
Firms	$\pi = q^*\hat{e} - w$ if the worker does not shirk ($e = \hat{e}$)
	$\pi = q^*e - w[+p]$ if the worker shirks [and gets caught]
Workers	$u = w - c(\hat{e})$ if the worker does not shirk ($e = \hat{e}$)
	$u = w - c(e)[-p]$ if the worker shirks [and gets caught]
	C. Main predictions

The equilibrium wage w^* and equilibrium job rents are increasing in the redemption value q. The reason is that firms with higher redemption values demand higher effort levels and therefore have to pay higher wages to prevent shirking.

which leads to endogenous involuntary unemployment, (iii) firms choose the maximal punishment possible, (iv) the desired effort level is positively correlated with a firm's redemption value, (v) there are non-compensating wage differentials, that is, the higher a firm's redemption value, the higher is the optimal wage that is paid by the firm.

3.2. Results

All five predictions are qualitatively borne out by the data. For the purpose of this paper, the most important result is related to (v), which predicts redemption value-dependent wage differentials.

This figure contains the actual average wage (white bars) and the theoretical prediction for each redemption value. As Figure 2 shows, the actual data match the predictions qualitatively quite well. Quantitatively, wages are a little bit too low compared to the theoretical prediction. With regard to job rents the picture is very similar. Job rents are increasing in the redemption value and somewhat lower than predicted. A regression

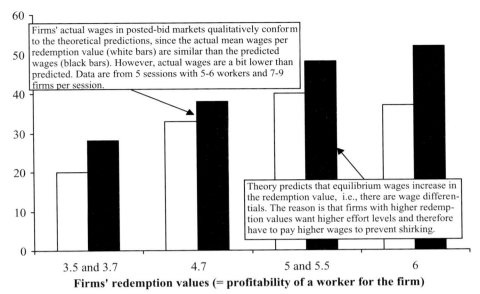

Source: Fehr, Kirchsteiger, and Riedl (1996).

Figure 2. Wage differentials in the Shirking-Model: Theoretically predicted (black bars) and actual wages (white bars).

analysis confirms that the observed positive relationship between wages (job rents) and redemption values is indeed highly significant.

4. Summary

This chapter reports on two experiments that were designed to test whether efficiency wage theories receive support in the laboratory. The idea is that theories which have no explanatory power even under the controlled circumstances of the laboratory, will not apply to the much more complicated field. The investigated efficiency wage theories – the fair wage-effort hypothesis and the shirking version – are often invoked to explain certain labor market phenomena, as involuntary unemployment and (non-compensating) wage differentials. Both variants of efficiency wage theories considered here "survived" the laboratory tests and may, therefore, be considered as possible explanations for field observations. In this sense, the reported experimental results can be viewed as complementary to field work in this area.

References

Akerlof, George (1982). "Labor contracts as partial gift exchange". Quarterly Journal of Economics 97, 543–569.

Akerlof, George (1984). "Gift exchange and efficiency-wage theory: Four views". American Economic Review 74, 79–83.

Akerlof, George, Yellen, Janet (1990). "The fair wage-effort hypothesis and unemployment". Quarterly Journal of Economics 105, 255–283.

Bowles, Samuel (1985). "The production process in a competitive economy: Walrasian, neo-Hobbesian and Marxian models". American Economic Review 75, 16–36.

Dickens, William, Katz, Lawrence (1987). "Inter-industry wage differences and industry characteristics". In: Lang, K., Leonhard, J. (Eds.), Unemployment and the Structure of Labour Markets. Basil Blackwell, New York.

Fehr, Ernst (1986). "A theory of involuntary equilibrium unemployment". Journal of Institutional and Theoretical Economics 142, 405–430.

Fehr, Ernst, Gächter, Simon, Kirchsteiger, Georg (1996). "Reciprocal fairness and noncompensating wage differentials". Journal of Institutional and Theoretical Economics 152, 608–640.

Fehr, Ernst, Kirchsteiger, Georg, Riedl, Arno (1996). "Involuntary unemployment and non-compensating wage differentials in an experimental labour market". Economic Journal 106, 106–121.

Katz, Lawrence, Summers, Lawrence (1989). "Industry rents: Evidence and implications". Brookings Papers on Economic Activity (Microeconomics), 209–290.

Krueger, Alan, Summers, Lawrence (1987). "Reflections on the inter-industry wage structure". In: Lang, K., Leonhard, J. (Eds.), Unemployment and the Structure of Labour Markets. Basil Blackwell, New York.

Krueger, Alan, Summers, Lawrence (1988). "Efficiency wages and the inter-industry wage structure". Econometrica 56, 259–294.

MacLeod, Bentley, Malcomson, James (1989). "Implicit contracts, incentive compatibility, and involuntary unemployment". Econometrica 57, 447–480.

Murphy, Kevin, Topel, Robert (1990). "Efficiency wages reconsidered: Theory and evidence". In: Weiss, Y., Fishelson, G. (Eds.), Advances in the Theory and Measurement of Unemployment. Macmillan, London.

Plott, Charles (1989). "An updated review of industrial organisation: Applications of experimental methods". In: Schmalensee, R., Willig, R. (Eds.), Handbook of Industrial Organization, vol. 2. North-Holland, pp. 1109–1176.

Rabin, Matthew (1993). "Incorporating fairness into game theory and economics". American Economic Review 83, 1281–1302.

Shapiro, Carl, Stiglitz, Joseph (1984). "Equilibrium unemployment as a worker discipline device". American Economic Review 74, 433–444.

Thaler, Richard (1989). "Interindustry wage differentials". Journal of Economic Perspectives 2, 181–193.

Chapter 16

THE PARADOX OF POWER

YVONNE DURHAM
University of Arkansas

JACK HIRSHLEIFER
University of California at Los Angeles

VERNON L. SMITH
Economic Science Laboratory
University of Arizona

Individuals and organizations – if rational and self-interested – will equalize the marginal returns of two ways of generating income: (1) production and exchange, versus (2) 'appropriative' efforts for capturing resources previously controlled by other parties (or to defend against appropriation by others). For example, management and labor jointly generate the output of the firm, but also are in contention over the distribution of the firm's net revenues. This balancing problem has been examined in a number of theoretical studies, among them Haavelmo (1954), Skogh and Stuart (1982), Hirshleifer (1989, 1991), Skaperdas (1996), and Grossman and Kim (1995).

Following the model proposed by Hirshleifer (1991) in our experimental investigation, decision-makers simultaneously interact through *joint production* (requiring cooperation) and a *distributive struggle* (conflict).

It might be expected that in appropriative struggles between stronger and weaker contenders, the strong would grow ever stronger and the weak always weaker. The "paradox of power" (POP) is the observation that in actual contests, poorer or smaller combatants often end up improving their position relative to richer opponents. A notable instance is the political struggle over income redistribution. Although citizens in the upper half of the income spectrum surely have more political strength than those in the lower half, modern governments have mainly been attempting to transfer income from the former to the latter group (Browning, and Browning, 1994, pp. 259–261).

The theoretical explanation is that the marginal payoff of appropriative effort relative to productive effort is typically greater at low levels of income. Thus, while the rich always have the capability of exploiting the poor, it often does not pay them to do so.

Nevertheless, in some contexts, initially richer contestants do exploit weaker rivals. So the question is, when does POP occur? The crucial factor is a parameter (m) reflecting the *decisiveness* of conflictual effort. When decisiveness is low, the rich are content to concentrate upon producing a larger social pie of income even though the poor will be gaining an improved share thereof. But when conflictual preponderance makes a sufficiently weighty difference for achieved income, the rich cannot afford to let the poor win the contest over distributive shares.

1. The Model

Each of two contenders ($i = 1, 2$) must divide his/her exogenously given resource endowment R_i between productive effort E_i and appropriative ('fighting') effort F_i:

$$E_1 + F_1 = R_1, \qquad E_2 + F_2 = R_2. \tag{1}$$

The efforts (E_i) are inputs to a joint production function. For simplicity here we have assumed the simple additive form:

$$I = E_1 + E_2. \tag{2}$$

Thus, the parties can cooperate by combining their productive efforts so as to generate a common pool of income, I, available to the two of them jointly. But the respective shares p_1 and p_2 (where $p_1 + p_2 = 1$) are determined in a conflictual process: the contest success function (CSF) takes the fighting efforts F_i as inputs, yielding the distributive shares:

$$p_1 = F_1^m / (F_1^m + F_2^m), \qquad p_2 = F_2^m / (F_1^m + F_2^m). \tag{3}$$

Here, m is a 'decisiveness parameter' controlling the mapping of the input ratio F_1/F_2 into the success ratio p_1/p_2. For $m \leq 1$ the CSF is characterized by diminishing marginal returns as F_1 increases with given F_2, or vice versa. However, for $m > 1$ there will be an initial range of increasing returns before diminishing marginal returns set in.

The resulting incomes are:

$$I_1 = p_1 I, \qquad I_2 = p_2 I. \tag{4}$$

For each level of fighting effort by contender 2, there is a corresponding optimal effort for contender 1 (and vice versa). Thus, 1's optimization problem is to choose $F_1 \geq 0$ so as to solve:

$$\text{Max } I_1 = p_1(F_1|F_2) \times I(E_1|E_2) \quad \text{subject to} \quad E_1 + F_1 = R_1.$$

The solution is similar for side 2.

For an interior equilibrium, the Nash–Cournot reaction functions are defined by

$$\frac{F_1}{F_2^m} = \frac{m(R_1 + R_2 - F_1 - F_2)}{F_1^m + F_2^m}, \qquad \frac{F_2}{F_1^m} = \frac{m(R_1 + R_2 - F_1 - F_2)}{F_1^m + F_2^m}. \tag{5}$$

The right-hand sides being identical, $F_1 = F_2$ is always a solution of these equations. That is, the reaction curves intersect along the 45° line between the F_1 and F_2 axes. In fact, this is the sole intersection in the positive quadrant.

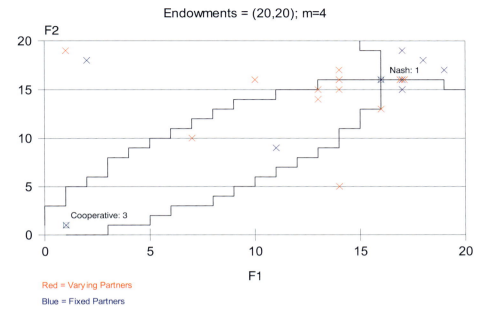

Figure 1. The step function in Figures 1–3 are the optimal reaction functions for each of the two protagonists for various resource endowments and value for the decisiveness parameter, m. Thus in this figure, the lower step function defines the optimal fighting effect, F_1, for player 1 for each fighting effort F_2 chosen by player 2 and vice versa for the upper step function. The Nash equilibrium is at the intersection (16, 16), while the joint maximizing cooperative outcome is at (1, 1). The ×s in this figure plot the observations on the 16th round of play in experiments 13 and 14 for varying partners, shown in red, and experiments 15 and 16 for fixed partners, shown in blue. Note the tendency for the observations to cluster nearer to the Nash equilibrium than to the cooperative; this tendency is stronger for varying, than for fixed partners; also, the error relative to Nash tends to the cooperative side.

If however the boundary constraint is binding for the poorer side (which we always take to be contender 2), the second equation would be replaced by

$$F_2 = R_2. \tag{5a}$$

In that case, at equilibrium, F_1 and F_2 are in general unequal, but the intersection of the reaction functions still determines the Nash–Cournot equilibrium values of the fighting efforts. Figures 1–3 plot the integer valued reaction functions in (5) and (5a) for the different values of (R_1, R_2) and m used in the experiments we report here. In each figure the lower reaction function is for subject 1, the upper one for subject 2. Thus, for each level of fighting effort by 2, we read off the conditionally optimal fighting effort for 1 using the lower step function. Each figure corresponds to a different parameterization of the model.

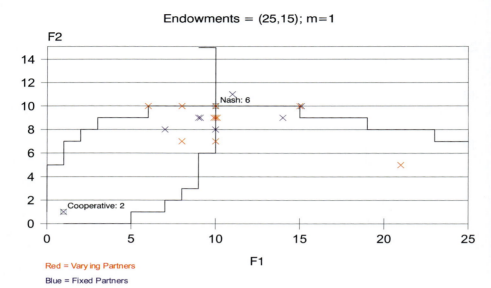

Figure 2. The ×s plot the final observations in experiments 5 and 6 for varying partners, shown in red, and experiments 7 and 8 for fixed partners, shown in blue. The tendency toward Nash is strong, stronger for varying than fixed partners, with many error deviations from Nash tending to occur on the cooperative side.

The experiments were intended in part to challenge a number of specific predictions derived from the model.

(i) *Fighting intensities*: If the decisiveness parameter m is increased, it pays both sides to 'fight harder.' As the F_i increase the ultimate achieved incomes (I_i) must fall. (Compare Figure 1 with Figures 2 and 3.)

(ii) *Conflict as an equalizing process (paradox of power), strong vs weak form*. For sufficiently low values of the decisiveness parameter m, disparities in achieved income will be smaller than the initial disparities in resource endowments. Letting contender 1 be the initially better endowed side:

$$R_1/R_2 > I_1/I_2 \geqslant 1. \qquad (6)$$

When the *equality* on the right holds we have the 'strong form' of the POP. It can be shown that there will be interior solutions up to some critical value ρ of the resource ratio:

$$\rho = (2+m)/m. \qquad (7)$$

When $m = 1$ for the decisiveness parameter, the prediction is that the strong form of the POP will hold for low resource ratios, specifically for $R_1/R_2 \leqslant 3$. For resource ratios larger than $\rho = 3$, only the weak form, i.e., the strict *inequality* on the right of Equation (6), is predicted.

Ch. 16: The Paradox of Power

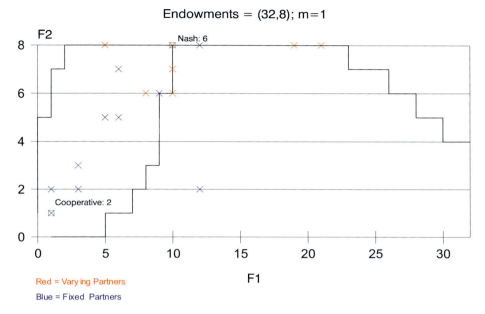

Figure 3. The data are from the last round of experiments 9–12. In comparison with Figures 1 and 2, the observations are not as strongly supportive of Nash, with many errors tending to the cooperative side of Nash. This is explained by the boundary Nash equilibrium for subjects 2. If they err relative to Nash it must be toward cooperation. Also, subjects 2 are limited by this boundary in responding with punishing choices. These elements encourage cooperation attempts although it is rarely achieved.

(iii) *Conflict as an inequality-aggravating process.* The model also indicates that for sufficiently high values of the decisiveness coefficient m and the resource ratio R_1/R_2, the POP will *not* apply. The rich would get richer and the poor poorer. Specifically, for our experiments using the high decisiveness coefficient $m = 4$, the critical value τ of the resource ratio for this condition is approximately 2.18. (The value of τ was obtained by finding the resource ratio where the condition $I_1/I_2 = R_1/R_2$ was met for $m = 4$.) Also, from (7), when $m = 4$ the critical ρ separating the weak from the strong forms of the POP equals 1.5. Thus in our experiments using the low resource ratio $25/15 = 1.67$ we expect the weak form of the POP to hold, since 1.67 lies between ρ and τ. However, for the experiments with $R_1/R_2 = 32/8 = 4 > \tau = 2.18$, the prediction is that the initially better endowed party will improve its relative position compared to the less well endowed side:

$$I_1/I_2 = (F_1/F_2)^m > R_1/R_2. \tag{8}$$

2. Implementing the Model

Certain game-theoretic and implementational concerns are also addressed in our experimental test of the above model. In the strict game-theoretic sense, the non-cooperative equilibrium is about strangers who meet once, interact strategically in their self-interest, and will never meet again. Such conditions control for repeated game effects, since the protagonists have no history or future. Yet in many contexts individuals interact in repeated games, where they can signal, punish, and build reputations. In the particularly simple version where the one-shot game is iterated with the same payoffs each round, we have a supergame. The study of such games has been motivated by the intuition or "folk theorem" that repetition makes cooperation possible (Mertens, 1984).

Consequently, in addition to testing the substantive predictions associated with the paradox of power, we address some of these issues that have arisen in the experimental and game-theoretic traditions. Specifically, we will be comparing the results of experiments in which the partners are randomly varied in each round with experiments in which the partners are fixed throughout the supergame. As suggested by previous experimental studies and the "folk theorem," we anticipate that the condition of fixed partners will favor somewhat more cooperative behavior.

3. Experimental Procedures and Design

We conducted 24 experiments using a total of 278 subjects. No subject participated in more than one experiment. There were 6 bargaining pairs in each experiment, except for a few cases with only 4 or 5 pairs. Each experiment involved repeated play, the payoffs being constant in each round. Within each round, each subject pair chose simultaneously a (row, column) in a payoff matrix. Subjects were not informed how many rounds would take place; in fact, in each experiment there were 16 or 17 rounds before termination. Subjects were recruited for two-hour sessions but the experiments took much less time, making credible the condition of an unknown horizon.

In every round each subject allocated his/her initial endowment of tokens between an "Investment Account" (IA) and a "Rationing Account" (RA). (We deliberately avoided using any terminology suggestive of "fighting".) Tokens contributed to the IA corresponded to productive effort, E_i, in the theoretical model: the paired IA contributions generated an aggregate pool of income (in the form of 'experimental pesos') in accordance with Equation (2) above. Funds put into the RA corresponded to fighting effort, F_i, and determined the respective distributive shares p_1 and p_2 in accordance with Equations (3). For simplicity, only integer choices were permitted. (More precisely, each subject could allocate, within his/her resource constraint, amounts in integral hundreds of tokens to invest in the IA, the remainder, of course, going into the RA.) The totals of pesos ultimately achieved were converted into actual dollars at the end of the experiment, so subjects had a substantial motivation to make self-interested choices. (The payoffs ranged from $.25 to $75.25, not including the $5 show-up fee. The average payoff was $17.66.)

Table 1

There are two classes of experimental treatment variables: (1) model parameters which include resource endowments (R_1, R_2), and decisiveness, m; (2) pairing protocol, either with "variable partners" (subjects randomly rematched on each round) or "fixed partners" (subjects randomly matched once who then play repeatedly). Two experiments were run under each parameterization with variable, and two with fixed, partners. Most sessions were run in groups of 6 pairs (12 subjects), but in a few experiments not all subjects appeared on time, and were run with 4 or 5 pairs. Each experiment was run for either 16 or 17 repeat rounds

Model parameters		Number of experiments (subjects)		
Endowments (R_1, R_2)	Decisiveness m	Variable pairing	Fixed pairing	Totals
20, 20	1	2(24)	2(24)	4(48)
25, 15	1	2(24)	2(24)	4(48)
32, 8	1	2(22)	2(24)	4(46)
20, 20	4	2(22)	2(22)	4(44)
25, 15	4	2(20)	2(24)	4(44)
32, 8	4	2(24)	2(24)	4(48)
	Totals	12(136)	12(142)	24(278)

To challenge the implications of the model, we manipulated the resource endowments R_1 and R_2 and also the decisiveness coefficient m. Four experiments were run with each of the three endowment vectors $(R_1, R_2) = (20, 20)$, $(25, 15)$, and $(32, 8)$ – the first series using a low value $m = 1$ of the decisiveness parameter, and the next using a high value $m = 4$. Thus there were 24 experiments in all.

Also, in view of the well-established results (e.g., McCabe, Rassenti, and Smith, 1996) that cooperation is promoted by repeated play with the same partners, each group of four experiments was further subdivided into alternative matching protocols. In the first ('varying partners') protocol, partners were randomly changed each round. Under the second ('fixed partners') protocol, subjects were randomly paired at the beginning of the experiment but played repeatedly with the same partner throughout.

Overall there were eight experiments under each of the three endowment conditions. Four of the eight involved varying partners, and four fixed partners. There was an analogous subdivision between experiments conducted using $m = 1$ and using $m = 4$. The design is summarized in Table 1. The pairing treatment and model parameters for each of the 24 experiments are listed in columns 1–7 of Table 2.

4. Results

4.1. Nash vs Cooperative Comparisons

Column 8 in Table 2 lists the results of each experiment as measured by the average fighting efforts (F_1, F_2) of the 4 to 6 pairs participating in each experiment. Columns 9–

Table 2

Each experiment listed in column 1, consists of 4 to 6 pairs of subjects (Table 1). Columns 2–5 list the corresponding model parameters, and columns 6 and 7 the Nash solution. In columns 8–10, are listed the average of the 4 to 6 observations on (F_1, F_2) occurring in round 16, and the ratios F_1/F_2, and I_1/I_2. The last two columns list the values of S_1 and S_2, the index of average slippage toward cooperation for the type 1 and 2 players respectively, where $S_i = (N_i - F_i)/(N_i - C)$. The S_i are mostly positive indicating that errors in hitting Nash tend to be biased in the direction of the cooperative solution at $(1, 1)$. When the parameter m increases from 1 to 4 (column 2), the POP model predicts an increase in (F_1, F_2); in the 48 comparisons between the bottom and top halves of the table, 45 observations satisfy this prediction. When $m = 1$, POP predicts $I_1/I_2 < R_1/R_2$ for the 8 experiments with $R_1 > R_2$. As is seen in rows 5–12, all 8 observations conform to this prediction. See text for additional predictions only partially conforming to the data

Exp. #	Treatment parameters				Nash solution		Avg. results (16th obs.)			Avg. slippage	
	m	Pairing	R_1, R_2	R_1/R_2	N_1, N_2	N_1/N_2	F_1, F_2	F_1/F_2	I_1/I_2	S_1	S_2
1	1	V	20, 20	1	10, 10	1	7.83, 6.83	1.15	1.15	0.24	0.35
2	1	V	20, 20	1	10, 10	1	8, 9	0.89	0.89	0.22	0.11
3	1	F	20, 20	1	10, 10	1	8.67, 6.67	1.30	1.30	0.15	0.37
4	1	F	20, 20	1	10, 10	1	4, 5	0.8	0.8	0.67	0.56
5	1	V	25, 15	1.67	10, 10	1	10.83, 8.5	1.27	1.27	−0.09	0.17
6	1	V	25, 15	1.67	10, 10	1	9, 9.17	0.98	0.98	0.11	0.09
7	1	F	25, 15	1.67	10, 10	1	10.17, 9	1.13	1.13	−0.02	0.11
8	1	F	25, 15	1.67	10, 10	1	7.67, 6.83	1.12	1.12	0.26	0.41
9	1	V	32, 8	4	10, 8	1.25	11.83, 7.67	1.54	1.54	−0.20	0.05
10	1	V	32, 8	4	10, 8	1.25	10.33, 7.5	1.38	1.38	−0.04	0.07
11	1	F	32, 8	4	10, 8	1.25	5.17, 3.17	1.63	1.63	0.54	0.69
12	1	F	32, 8	4	10, 8	1.25	5.4, 4.6	1.17	1.17	0.51	0.46
13	4	V	20, 20	1	16, 16	1	10.33, 12.83	0.81	0.42	0.38	0.21
14	4	V	20, 20	1	16, 16	1	14.67, 15.33	0.96	0.84	0.09	0.04
15	4	F	20, 20	1	16, 16	1	11.67, 13.83	0.84	0.51	0.29	0.15
16	4	F	20, 20	1	16, 16	1	10, 9.2	1.09	1.40	0.40	0.45
17	4	V	25, 15	1.67	16, 15	1.07	15.5, 11.83	1.31	2.95	0.33	0.23
18	4	V	25, 15	1.67	16, 15	1.07	16.5, 12.5	1.32	3.04	−0.03	0.18
19	4	F	25, 15	1.67	16, 15	1.07	16.17, 13.83	1.17	1.87	−0.01	0.08
20	4	F	25, 15	1.67	16, 15	1.07	13.5, 12.33	1.10	1.44	0.17	0.19
21	4	V	32, 8	4	12, 8	1.5	11.67, 7.33	1.59	6.42	0.03	0.10
22	4	V	32, 8	4	12, 8	1.5	11.67, 7	1.67	7.72	0.03	0.40
23	4	F	32, 8	4	12, 8	1.5	10.5, 7.5	1.4	3.84	0.14	0.07
24	4	F	32, 8	4	12, 8	1.5	11, 4.67	2.36	30.76	0.09	0.48

12 are calculations derived from (F_1, F_2). Thus, F_1/F_2 and I_1/I_2 are ratios of the average fighting efforts and the attained incomes of the protagonists in each experiment. Since the cooperative solution is $(C_1, C_2) = (1, 1)$, column 8 allows a comparison between the observed average outcome (F_1, F_2) and the Nash and cooperative solutions. It is immediately evident that most of the observations are closer to the Nash than the cooperative solution. However, the error relative to Nash tends toward the cooperative

side. This "slippage" (S_i), indicated in the last two columns, is defined as:

$$S_i = (N_i - F_i)/(N_i - C).$$

A positive S_i indicates that error with respect to Nash is tending toward the cooperative solution while a negative S_i indicates that the error is tending away from the cooperative solution.

4.2. Predictions of the Model

Various predictions of the model can be evaluated from Table 2.

PREDICTION 1. Higher values of the decisiveness parameter m will lead to larger fighting efforts on both sides.

The upper half of Table 2 shows the results for $m = 1$, and the lower half for $m = 4$. There are 48 comparisons, of which a remarkable 45 are in the direction predicted.

PREDICTION 2A. At the low value $m = 1$ of the decisiveness parameter, the initially poorer side will always end up improving its position.

At $m = 1$ the attained income ratio I_1/I_2 should exceed the resource ratio R_1/R_2. This is the "paradox of power." The requirement of unequal initial endowments limits the relevant data to rows 5 through 12 of Table 2. Here all 8 of the 8 comparisons show the predicted relative improvement – that is, $I_1/I_2 < R_1/R_2$.

PREDICTION 2B. For $m = 1$ the poorer side should attain approximate equality of income (strong form of the POP) for initial resource ratios $R_1/R_2 < 3$, but only some relative improvement, $1 < I_1/I_2 < R_1/R_2$, for larger resource ratios (weak form of the POP).

Looking only at the unequal endowments cases, rows 5 through 12 of Table 2, the average of the tabulated results is $I_1/I_2 = 1.125$, on the high side of the predicted $I_1/I_2 = 1$. By way of comparison, for rows 9 through 12 $I_1/I_2 > 1$ is predicted, the average outcome is $I_1/I_2 = 1.43$. In a relative sense, the predicted comparison of the strong form versus weak form predictions is supported.

PREDICTION 2C. At the specific high value $m = 4$ of the decisiveness coefficient, the paradox of power should continue to hold (in its weak form) for $\rho < R_1/R_2 < \tau$, where $\rho = 1.5$ and $\tau = 2.18$. But for higher resource ratios the richer side should end up actually improving on its relative position. That is, in this range $I_1/I_2 = (F_1/F_2)^4$ should exceed R_1/R_2.

For the unequal-endowments rows 17 though 20 of Table 2, the resource ratio is $R_1/R_2 = 25/15 = 1.67$, lying between ρ and τ. So the paradox of power is predicted in these cases. However, for rows 21 through 24 the resource ratio is $R_1/R_2 = 32/8 = 4 > 2.18 = \tau$, so we expect the rich to become richer still.

Taking up the latter group first, 3 of the 4 cases support the prediction $I_1/I_2 = (F_1/F_2)^4 > 4$. In fact, the average of the observed results was a much higher $I_1/I_2 = 12.19$. That is, the model predicted that here the rich would get richer – and they did. Turning to the first group, however, all 4 cases violate the prediction! Quantitatively, the predicted Nash outcome $(N_1, N_2) = (16, 15)$ implies $I_1/I_2 = (16/15)^4 = 1.29 < 1.67$ while the average of the observed results was $I_1/I_2 = 2.32 > 1.67$. Here the poor should have improved their position, but did not. On the whole the rich behaved about as expected, whereas the poor fell short of the fighting effort $F_2 = 15$ predicted for them. But notice that the Nash prediction for the poorer side required them to devote 100% of their resources to fighting. Thus, any error whatsoever could only take the form of a deficiency of fighting effort. Such outcomes commonly occur in experiments with boundary equilibria (Smith and Walker, 1993).

4.3. Charting the Observations

The final period (16) observations are plotted for four experiments in each of three parameter classes: Figure 1, experiments 13–16; Figure 2, experiments 5–8; Figure 3, experiments 9–12. Each "×" symbol plots the values (F_1, F_2) chosen by the 12 bargaining pairs in round 16, along with the reaction step functions defined for integer outcomes. The computed Nash equilibrium at the intersection, and cooperative solution at $(1, 1)$ are as shown. The red symbols are the final outcomes for varying partners, while the blue symbols are for fixed partners.

To summarize: (1) as predicted, the outcomes tend to support (are closer to) Nash. (The statistical tests, both classical and Bayesian, strongly support Nash against cooperation for both fixed and varying partners; see Durham, Hirshleifer, and Smith, 1998); (2) but the error deviation or "slippage" from Nash tend to be biased toward cooperation; (3) as predicted by the "folk theorem" the slippage toward cooperation is stronger in the case of fixed than varying partners, as some pairs attempt to coordinate on the cooperative outcome; (4) the predictions of the POP model are broadly supported.

References

Browning, Edgar F., Browning, Jacquelene M. (1994). "Public Finance and the Price System", fourth ed. Prentice Hall, Englewood Cliffs, NJ.

Durham, Yvonne, Hirshleifer, Jack, Smith, Vernon L. (1998). "Do the rich get richer and the poor poorer? Experimental tests of a model of power". American Economic Review 88, 970–983.

Grossman, Herschel, Kim, Minseong (1995). "Swords or plowshares: A theory of the security of claims to property". Journal of Political Economy 103, 1275–1288.

Haavelmo, Trygve (1954). "A Study in the Theory of Economic Evolution". North-Holland Publishing Co., Amsterdam.

Hirshleifer, Jack (1989). "Conflict and rent-seeking success functions: Ratio vs. difference models of relative success". Public Choice 63, 101–112.

Hirshleifer, Jack (1991). "The paradox of power". Economics and Politics 3, 177–200.

McCabe, Kevin, Rassenti, Stephen, Smith, Vernon (1996). "Game theory and reciprocity in some extensive form experimental games". Proceedings National Academy of Science 93, 13421–13428.

Mertens, J. (1984). "Repeated games". In: Eatwell, J., Milgate, M., Newman, P. (Eds.), The New Palgrave. MacMillan Press, London, pp. 151–152.

Skaperdas, Stergios (1996). "Contest success functions". Economic Theory 7, 283–290.

Skogh, Goran, Stuart, Charles (1982). "A contractarian theory of property rights and crime". Scandinavian Journal of Economics 84, 27–40.

Smith, Vernon L., Walker, James M. (1993). "Monetary rewards and decision cost in experimental economics". Economic Inquiry 31, 245–261.

Chapter 17

THE EXERCISE OF MARKET POWER IN LABORATORY EXPERIMENTS

DOUGLAS D. DAVIS and CHARLES A. HOLT[†]

1. Introduction

Many aspects of antitrust policy are influenced by the possibility that sellers in concentrated markets may have the power to raise prices above competitive levels. Of course, anyone can raise prices, so the issue is whether a change in structure, e.g., a merger, will allow one or more sellers to raise price profitably. A price increase by one seller diverts sales to others, so a firm is more likely to have market power when its competitors have limited capacity to expand their sales. Thus a merger that reduces competitors' capacity may create market power.

In laboratory experiments, any treatment that reassigns "units" of capacity from one seller to another may create or destroy market power, even if the aggregate supply curve is unchanged. For example, giving one seller a relatively large endowment of inframarginal, low-cost units may make it less risky for this seller to raise price and forego the sale of high cost units. Thus it is not surprising that experiments with apparently similar supply and demand structures may yield different price outcomes. As discussed below, there are a number of other ways in which structural changes can affect the degree of power that sellers enjoy.

Market power can also be sensitive to the trading institution, and this is the context that power issues first arose in experimental economics. For example, the public posting of uniform prices in a posted offer auction eliminates the incentive to offer discounts on marginal units that arises in a double auction. In fact, Smith (1981) found that even monopolists are sometimes unable to maintain prices above competitive levels in double auctions, whereas supra-competitive prices are the norm in posted-offer monopolies. Similarly, Holt, Langan, and Villamil (1986) found that sellers in concentrated double auctions were sometimes able to raise prices, but that prices fell to competitive levels in about half of the sessions, despite the high concentration of seller capacity. Davis and Williams (1991) replicated the Holt, Langan, and Villamil results for double auctions, and then used the same market structure in a parallel series of posted-offer markets, where price increases above the competitive levels were strong and persistent.

Relatively high prices in posted-offer auctions are not surprising, since experimental economists have long noticed that prices in such markets tend to be above competitive levels, and will converge from above if they converge at all. One issue is whether

[†] This work was funded in part by the National Science Foundation (SBR 93-19842 and SBR 96-617784).

this upward bias can be explained by standard game theory. Holt (1989) offered a game-theoretic definition of market power, i.e., that at least one seller has a unilateral incentive to raise price above a common competitive price. Thus the presence of market power means that the competitive equilibrium is not a Nash equilibrium. Ketcham, Smith, and Williams (1984) report data for a posted-offer experiment in which the Nash equilibrium price was identifiably above the competitive price, and prices were also above competitive levels. For most posted-offer experiments, however, the Nash predictions are difficult to calculate because of the complex supply and demand structures that are typically used. Nevertheless, some market power frequently exists, and in these cases, the Nash equilibrium typically involves randomization over some range of supra-competitive prices (Holt and Solis-Soberon, 1992). The first experiment that explicitly considered the behavior in markets with a mixed-strategy equilibrium were reported by Kruse et al. (1994). They found Edgeworth cycles at prices above competitive levels, up in the range of randomization, but subjects did not appear to be choosing prices randomly.

The posted offer experiments discussed to this point did not directly address the issue of whether supra-competitive prices are really due to market power, or whether other factors such as the number of sellers or the shapes of supply and demand drive the observed data patterns. This question led to investigations in which numbers effects and other factors are held constant, and market power is created or destroyed by reallocating capacity in a way that leaves the shapes of supply and demand unchanged (Davis and Holt, 1994). This work is discussed in detail in the next section. The final section surveys a number of contexts in which power issues have arisen in experimental investigations of other issues, e.g., the trading of pollution permits or the design of computerized auction markets

2. Market Power

We begin with a simple example that shows how market power can be created by capacity constraints, and how the mixed-strategy Nash equilibrium can be calculated in this case. Consider a market composed of two sellers and a single buyer. Each of the sellers has a capacity to produce two units at zero cost. The buyer will purchase three units at any price at or below a reservation price r. Thus the seller with the low price will sell both units of capacity, and the one with the high price will only sell one unit. Under these conditions, each seller would want to undercut the other's price, if it were known, until the other's price was so low that gains from selling two units as the low pricing seller no longer exceeded the profits from selling a single unit at price r. As is easily shown, there is no Nash equilibrium in pure strategies for this type of structure. Rather the equilibrium must involve mixing.

For any equilibrium in mixed strategies, sellers must be willing to choose price randomly, which can only be the case if the expected payoff is constant for all prices in the range of randomization. Thus, the first step in the analysis is to find the expected payoff function, and the second step is to equate expected payoffs to an appropriate constant.

In order to evaluate expected payoffs, let the common equilibrium distribution of prices be denoted by $F(p)$. Thus if one seller chooses a price of p, the probability that the other is below p is $F(p)$. Just as $F(p)$ is the probability that p is high, $1 - F(p)$ is the probability that a price p is low. Only 1 unit is sold with a high price and 2 units are sold with a low price, so the expected payoff is $pF(p) + 2p[1 - F(p)]$. (We ignore the possibility of ties, which occur with probability zero since the distributions are continuous.)

The second step in finding the mixed-strategy equilibrium is to equate this expected payoff to a constant. Since the high-priced seller will sell a single unit, the person considering making a very high price should raise it to the buyer reservation value r, which yields a payoff of r. The seller would be indifferent between this high price and any other if expected payoffs are equal to r, or if: $pF(p) + 2p[1 - F(p)] = r$. This equation is solved for the equilibrium price distribution: $F(p) = (2p - r)/p$, which equals zero when $p = r/2$. Thus the lowest price in the range of randomization, denoted $p_{\min}$, is half of the buyer reservation value in this example, and the range of randomization is from $r/2$ to r.

This simple example illustrates the steps that are typically involved in finding a mixed-strategy equilibrium: calculating the expected payoffs, equating them to a constant, and solving for the equilibrium price distribution. These calculations become more tedious very quickly as more sellers, more cost and demand steps, and asymmetries are introduced. Holt and Solis-Soberon (1992) contains a step-by-step guide to finding mixed-strategy Nash equilibria with more complicated step-function designs that result from the discrete units of capacity that are used in laboratory experiments.

Davis and Holt (1994) exploited these solution techniques to design an experiment that allowed the isolation of market power as motivation for price increases. Consider the asymmetric cost structure in Figure 1. The green supply function and the red demand function overlap on a range of competitive prices, the highest of which is indicated by a horizontal dotted line. In a no-power treatment, the price indicated by the dotted line is also a Nash equilibrium. To see this, consider the structure of supply for the no power design: Each of the five sellers, S1–S5, has a single low-cost unit, as shown on the lower-left step of the green supply function. In addition, sellers S1, S2, and S3 also have two high-cost units each, on the upper-right step. (Please ignore the italicized S1 and S2 indicators below upper step for now.) In total, no seller has more than three units out of the industry capacity of 11 units in the no-power design. Since the demand is only for 8 units at prices above the competitive level, any seller who raises price above a common competitive level will sell nothing. Hence such a unilateral price increase is unprofitable, and the highest competitive price is a Nash equilibrium.

Market power is created by reallocating seller S3's high-cost units to S1 and S2, as indicated by the parenthetical (S1) and (S2) notations below the high-cost step of supply in Figure 1. For the two large sellers, the aggregate capacity of their competitors has gone down by 1 unit, so a unilateral price increase to r will result in sales of 1 unit

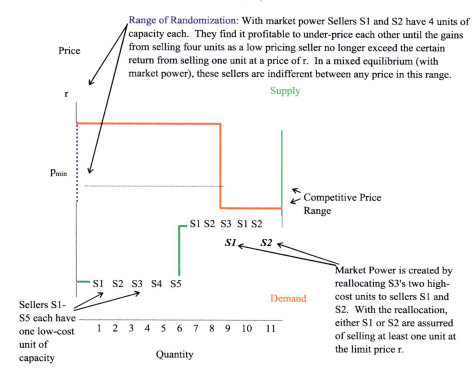

Figure 1.

instead of 0 units. The calculations are much more complicated for this design than for the example discussed above, but the same general approach can be used to show that the two large sellers will choose prices randomly on a range from p_{min} to r, as shown by the thick blue band on the vertical axis of Figure 1.

To summarize, the reallocation of seller S3's high-cost units to S1 and S2 gives them the unilateral incentive to raise price above the competitive level, which raises the Nash equilibrium prices up into the range of randomization. This allows an evaluation of the effects of creating market power, without changing the shapes of supply and demand. We conducted six posted-offer sessions with this setup. Three of these began with 30 periods of trading in the power design, followed by 30 periods in the no-power design. The treatment order was reversed in the other three sessions. The five subjects playing the seller roles were provided with complete information about demand and cost. The demand side was simulated by the experimenters (see Davis and Holt, 1994, for details).

Figure 2 shows the price sequences for a session that began with the power treatment. The prices of the two large sellers, S1 and S2, are colored as red and blue, respectively. The prices of the other three sellers are stars. Notice that the "red seller" is choosing the highest price of r for most of the first ten periods, which gradually brings the other

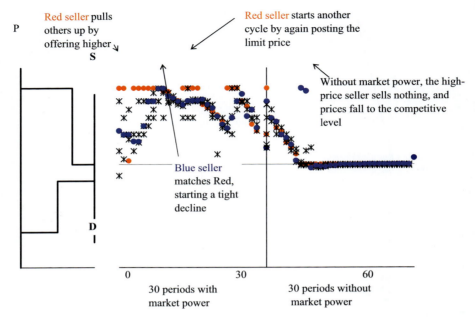

Figure 2.

sellers up. In period 10, the red seller undercuts the blue one, which starts a tight price decline for the next several periods, until red returns to choosing the highest price. This stops the price decline, but without an increase in others' prices, red becomes frustrated and drops price, which leads to a second tight decline. The price cycles continue, becoming a little more erratic, until period 30 where units are transferred from the two large sellers to seller S3, thereby destroying market power. Notice that prices start a steep decline after period 30, and there is no rebound after the blue seller briefly tries to signal with the highest price. With no power, this high-price gesture results in no sales for that seller, and an intense competition reigns throughout the rest of the session.

A similar pattern was observed in the other sessions that begin with the power treatment, shown by the blue dashed lines in Figure 3. The price average for these sessions, the bold blue line, rises and stays well above the theoretical prediction of the mixed equilibrium, as shown by the upper horizontal black line in the figure. (This line is the median of the price distributions for the large sellers, who make most of the sales.) Prices for these power/no-power sessions fall toward competitive levels when power is removed after period 30, as shown on the right side of the figure. A reversal of the order of treatments, with no power first, is shown by the red dashed lines for individual sessions and by the red bold line for the average across sessions. Note that there is some inertia, as prices do not always fall all the way to the competitive prediction in a no-power treatment that follows high prices in a power treatment.

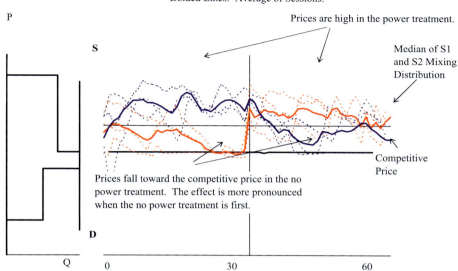

Figure 3.

Davis and Holt (1994) also ran six additional sessions in which a "merger" of the three small sellers was effected in the power design. Thus the treatments were: the pre-merger power design from before (five sellers with power) and the post-merger structure (three sellers with power). The interesting thing about the design is that the theoretical price distributions in the mixed equilibrium did not change, so the merger reduces the number of sellers without changing the extent of market power in a theoretical sense.[1] This pure-numbers effect did increase prices by a small, but statistically significant, amount; however the magnitude of this "pure numbers" effect was much smaller than the "market power" effect.

3. Applications of Market Power

Market power can have important implications in a wide variety of contexts where experimental analysis has played a role. For example, McCabe, Rassenti, and Smith (1993) consider the optimal design of computerized "call markets." The price is determined in these markets by letting buyers' submit bids and sellers' submit asks, which

---

[1] The merger, however, raises the Herfindahl index by about 450 points, just as the initial change from no-power to power raised the index by 450 points.

are then arrayed in supply and demand functions that are crossed to find the clearing price when the market is called. Overall these call markets tend to be quite efficient, almost on a par with standard double auctions. Nevertheless, some cost and/or valuation combinations may create market power that a trader could exercise by altering the bid or ask on a unit that is near the crossing, in order to make more money on an infra-marginal unit. For example, a buyer may lower a bid in the neighborhood of the anticipated crossing price in an attempt to lower the market price, and raise earnings on an infra-marginal unit for which a high bid has been submitted to ensure a purchase. McCabe, Rassenti, and Smith (1993) recognized the efficiency-reducing attempts of such possibilities, and suggested some trading rule variations to minimize the damage (such as keeping a closed bid/ask book).

A second instance where market power has arisen in the area of market design involves the construction of markets for pollution emission permits. In most instances where such markets have been introduced in the United States, market power has not been a concern, since the number of producers interested in buying and selling permits has been quite large. However, in some smaller countries, permit markets, if introduced, would be much thinner. Building on theoretical work by Misiolek and Elder (1989) and Hahn (1984), Godby (1997) shows that market power effects can cause sizable distortions in simple markets with structures that parallel those that would exist in some Canadian emissions permit markets, if established. The extent of the problem is a function not only of the relative size of the producers, but also the competitive conditions in producers' downstream markets, and on the initial distribution of permits. Based on his experiments, Godby (1997) suggests that careful attention to the market structure and to the way permits are distributed is warranted.

Market power also provides a fairly plausible explanation for "price-stickiness" observed in the U.S. economy (e.g., Rotemberg, 1982): Reynolds and Wilson (1997) provide a persuasive explanation for these counter-cyclical markups based on unilateral market power. Reynolds and Wilson show that unilateral market power can arise as a result of a demand shift, which may occur during a business cycle. In the design shown in Figure 1, for example, the power treatment produces high prices because the earnings from selling a single unit at the buyer's reservation value r are high enough to compensate for the lost sales of high cost units at the competitive price. However, a vertical upward shift in the demand curve raises the opportunity cost of foregoing the sale of marginal units, and, therefore, may eliminate market power. Thus, prices may not fall in recessionary times, because the demand reductions create some market power. An experiment reported by Wilson (1998) confirms that demand shifts of this type can introduce and remove market power.

We close by mentioning briefly one final application that again pertains directly to antitrust considerations. Recently, antitrust authorities have paid increased attention to synergies as a potential justification for mergers, if the efficiency gains are likely to be at least partially passed on to consumers in the form of lower prices. One possible standard would be to view more favorably proposed consolidations, if respondents can show that efficiency improvements in the recent past resulted in lower prices. An experiment by

Davis and Wilson (1998) shows that such a standard would be overly simplistic, because synergies and market power can be interrelated: For a given market structure, a synergy of a particular size can introduce market power where it did not previously exist, can take away market power that existed previously, or leave power conditions unchanged. The relationship between synergies and market power turns on whether the synergy affects the infra-marginal, low cost units, or higher cost marginal units. Results of the Davis and Wilson study suggest strongly that a policy that considers synergies as a justification for mergers must also consider carefully how the synergy will affect the combined firm's cost schedule.

References

Davis, Douglas D., Holt, Charles A. (1994). "Market power and mergers in laboratory experiments with posted prices". RAND Journal of Economics 25, 467–487.
Davis, Douglas D., Williams, Arlington W. (1991). "The Hayek hypothesis in experimental auctions: Institutional effects and market power". Economic Inquiry 29, 261–274.
Davis, Douglas D., Wilson, Bart (1998). "The effects of synergies on the exercise of market power". Working paper, Middlebury College.
Godby, Robert (1997). "Market power in emission permit double auctions". In: Holt, C.A., Isaac, R.M. (Eds.), Research in Experimental Economics, vol. 7, JAI Press. Greenwich, CT, in press.
Hahn, Robert W. (1984). "Market power and transferable property rights". Quarterly Journal of Economics 99, 753–765.
Holt, Charles A. (1989). "The exercise of market power in laboratory experiments". Journal of Law and Economics 32, s107–s130.
Holt, Charles A., Solis-Soberon, Fernando (1992). "The calculation of mixed-strategy equilibria in posted-offer markets". In: Isaac, R.M. (Ed.), Research in Experimental Economics, vol. 5. JAI Press, Greenwich.
Holt, Charles A., Langan, Loren, Villamil, Anne P. (1986). "Market power in oral double auctions". Economic Inquiry 24, 107–123.
Ketcham, Jon, Smith, Vernon L., Williams, Arlington W. (1984). "A comparison of posted-offer and double-auction pricing institutions". Review of Economic Studies 51, 595–614.
Kruse, Jamie Brown, Rassenti, Stephen, Reynolds, Stanley S., Smith, Vernon L. (1994). "Bertrand–Edgeworth competition in experimental markets". Econometrica 62 (2), 343–371.
Misiolek, W.S., Elder, H.W. (1989). "Exclusionary manipulation of the market for pollution rights". Journal of Environmental Economics and Management 16, 156–166.
McCabe, Kevin A., Rassenti, Stephen J., Smith, Vernon L. (1993). "Designing a uniform-price double auction, an experimental evaluation". In: Friedman, D., Rust, J. (Eds.), The Double Auction Market: Institutions, Theory, and Evidence, SFI Studies in the Sciences of Complexity, Proceedings, vol. 15. Addison–Wesley, Reading, MA.
Reynolds, Stanley S., Wilson, Bart J. (1997). "Market power, price markups and capacity investment under uncertain demand". Manuscript, University of Arizona.
Rotemberg, J. (1982). "Sticky prices in the United States". Journal of Political Economy 90, 1187–1211.
Smith, Vernon L. (1981). "An empirical study of decentralized institutions of monopoly restraint". In: Quirk, J., Horwich, G. (Eds.), Essays in Contemporary Fields of Economics in Honor of E.T. Weiler, 1914–1979. Purdue University Press, West Lafayette, pp. 83–106.
Wilson, Bart J. (1998). "What collusion? Unilateral market power as a catalyst for countercyclical markups". Experimental Economics 1, 133–145.

Chapter 18

THE CLASSICAL EXPERIMENTS ON COURNOT OLIGOPOLY

ANTONI BOSCH-DOMÈNECH

Universitat Pompeu Fabra, Barcelona

NICOLAAS J. VRIEND

Queen Mary, University of London

Moving beyond the development of game theory and the exercise games for managers that inspired them, two papers – Hoggatt (1959) and Sauermann and Selten (1959, 1960) – explicitly set up controlled experiments on quantity adjusters (or Cournot) oligopolists. "*The experiment can be constructed in such a way that decision-making can be observed throughout, and the assumptions about human behavior implicit in economic theories can be tested.*" claim Sauermann and Selten (1960, p. 85). "*We focus on using game situations as a research tool for studying the behavior of human beings in conflict situations*" asserts Hoggatt (1959, p. 192). With these papers, experimental research on oligopolies was born, reaching maturity soon, with Fouraker, Shubik, and Siegel (1961), and Fouraker and Siegel (1963).

Fouraker and Siegel's work is indistinguishable in method and purpose from recent oligopoly experiments. The oligopolistic market used in Fouraker and Siegel's experiments is as simple as it can be, the purpose – comparing the results of two treatments – is clearly stated, while the problems confronted and the solutions applied are not different from today's. It is instructive to note how in a matter of a few years, simplification is preferred to realism. In Sauermann and Selten (1960), firms are complex, decision-making units with several managers, each specializing in a different task. In Hoggatt (1959), firms are simple, one-person, one-decision units, but different among themselves, and the inverse demand function depends not only on current quantities but also on amounts traded in the past. In Fouraker and Siegel (1963), firms are identical one-person one-decision units, and the inverse demand function is linear in current quantities. Clearly, the purpose of Fouraker and Siegel's experiments was to study human behavior, not to decipher the complexities of oligopolistic markets or the behavior of complex organizations.

1. Sauermann and Selten's Results

Although their main task is to explore the motives behind the observed decisions, one of the questions Sauermann and Selten (1959, 1960) focus on is whether tacit cooperation prevails in their experiments.

Handbook of Experimental Economics Results, Volume 1
Copyright © 2008 Elsevier B.V. All rights reserved
DOI: 10.1016/S1574-0722(07)00018-2

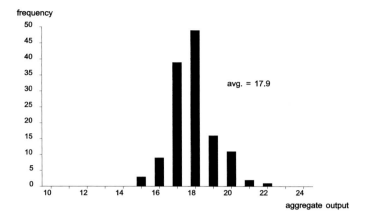

Figure 1. (Based on Sauermann and Selten (1959), Table 8.) *Aggregate output frequencies*. The results correspond to the last 10 periods of 13 experimental sessions of 30 periods each. In the experiments, three firms are involved which cannot communicate among each other. The aggregate output levels that are Pareto optimal are in the 10 to 14 range, but aggregate output seems to stabilize at higher volumes – and, therefore, at lower joint profits – mainly around the Cournot–Nash equilibria, corresponding to aggregate output levels from 16 to 18.

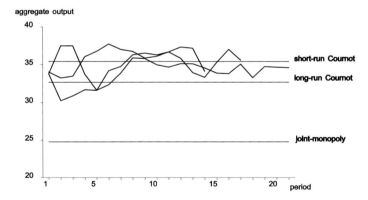

Figure 2. (Based on Hoggatt (1959), Figures 4, 5 and 6.) *Observed time path of aggregate output*. The three curves correspond to the three experimental sessions. In each, three firms confront an industry inverse demand function dependent on quantities traded in the period and in the previous two periods. Firms are informed about the industry demand function and their own costs, but are not told how many firms are competing in the same market. After each period, subjects are told the market price, the total amount supplied and their profits in the period. The three horizontal lines indicate the output levels of the short-run Cournot equilibrium (myopically not taking into account the dynamic nature of the demand function), the long-run Cournot equilibrium (choosing a best-reply to the current output levels, to maximize profits two periods from the current one), and the joint-monopoly profit maximizing output level.

Table 1
Hypotheses (Fouraker and Siegel, 1963, p. 101)

Numbers of bargainers	Possible combinations of bargaining types or signals	Predicted aggregate output Q	
		Incomplete information	Complete information
$N = 2$	CC	$Q =$ Cournot	$Q <$ Cournot
	CM	$Q =$ Cournot	$Q <$ Cournot
	CR	$Q =$ Cournot	$Q <$ Cournot
	MM	$Q =$ Cournot	$Q =$ Cournot
	MR	$Q =$ Cournot	$Q >$ Cournot
	RR	$Q =$ Cournot	$Q >$ Cournot
$N = 3$	CCC	$Q =$ Cournot	$Q <$ Cournot
	CCM	$Q =$ Cournot	$Q <$ Cournot
	CCR	$Q =$ Cournot	$Q <$ Cournot
	CMM	$Q =$ Cournot	$Q <$ Cournot
	CMR	$Q =$ Cournot	$Q =$ Cournot
	CRR	$Q =$ Cournot	$Q >$ Cournot
	MMM	$Q =$ Cournot	$Q =$ Cournot
	MMR	$Q =$ Cournot	$Q >$ Cournot
	MRR	$Q =$ Cournot	$Q >$ Cournot
	RRR	$Q =$ Cournot	$Q >$ Cournot

Note. $C =$ cooperative, $M =$ simple maximizer, $R =$ rivalistic.

From a questionnaire that subjects had to answer, Sauermann and Selten conclude that a successful theory of oligopoly has to contain explicitly *qualitative* motives (and not only quantitative maximizing arguments). In addition, they claim, *learning* should be incorporated in the theory as the simplest mode of behavior. In their own words, "*learning from experience must be mathematically formulated as a stochastic learning model*" (p. 102). See Figure 1.

2. Hoggatt's Results

Hoggatt (1959) runs three simultaneous experimental sessions in order to observe how the subjects' actual behavior compares with various types of maximizing behavior postulated by economic theory. In particular, he wants to test the Cournot model as a predictor of the outcome of group behavior; the hypothesis being that aggregate output would converge to the short-run Cournot equilibrium. See Figure 2.

Hoggatt (1959) mentions that different treatments may yield different results and suggests further research with treatments involving information and communication, as well as an analysis of learning behavior.

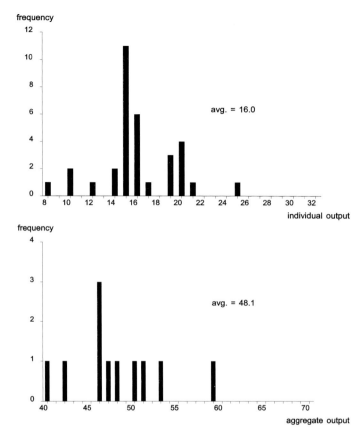

Figure 3. (Based on Fouraker and Siegel (1963, p. 134).) *Quantity choices, triopoly with incomplete information, 11 sessions*. In the triopolies, Pareto's individual output is at 10 (aggregate output at 30), Cournot's at 15 (aggregate at 45) and Walras' at 20 (aggregate at 60). In 9 of the 11 triopolies the aggregate output is closer to Cournot than to either of the alternative solutions.

3. Fouraker and Siegel's Results

Fouraker and Siegel view oligopolies as an example of human conflict between cooperation and defection. Their goal is to infer useful generalizations from the experiments of the effects of information conditions on the resolution of this conflict. While Fouraker and Siegel also consider Bertrand competition, we focus here on their symmetric Cournot games, with subjects – randomly and anonymously matched at the start of the experiment – deciding the amount of output they bring to the market. The market is characterized by a linear demand function, while marginal costs are zero at all output levels, and there are no fixed costs. These specifications are not given

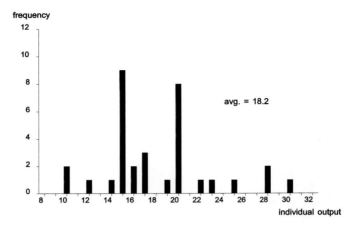
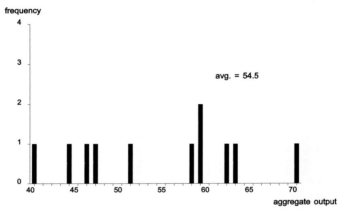

Figure 4. (Based on Fouraker and Siegel (1963, p. 140).) *Quantity choices, triopoly with complete information, 11 sessions*. No clear tendency is revealed by the data. The observations are mainly split between Cournot and Walras, about half favoring the Cournot solution.

to the subjects. Instead the players get a *profit matrix*, which is based on these functions.

In all treatments, 25 periods were played. The first 3 periods were trial periods without payoff, the other 22 were with monetary reward. The number of periods to be played was not announced in advance. But after round 21, it was announced that the next round would be the last one, possibly inducing end effects in round 22. Most results analyzed in Fouraker and Siegel concern period 21. Fouraker and Siegel distinguish three possible attractors. The joint-monopoly output level (Pareto from here on), the Nash (Cournot) output level, and the competitive (Walras) output level. From Table 1, we

Table 2
(Fouraker and Siegel, 1963, p. 150) *Number of times the three alternative solutions were supported*. First, under conditions of *incomplete* information, more choices supported the Cournot prediction than all alternative predictions combined. Under *complete* information conditions, more choices favored alternative predictions than favored the Cournot values. Second, oligopolistic transactions negotiated under complete information are more variable than oligopolistic transactions negotiated under incomplete information

Solution	Experimental session							
	Triopoly, incomplete information		Triopoly, complete information		Duopoly, incomplete information		Duopoly, complete information	
	q_i	Q	q_i	Q	q_i	Q	q_i	Q
Pareto (C)	4	0	3	0	2	0	10	5
Cournot (M)	20	9	15	5	26	14	12.5	7.5
Walras (R)	9	2	15	6	4	2	9.5	3.5

can see that quantity setting oligopolistic behavior depends on the *information available* and the *number* of opponents. Fouraker and Siegel conjecture that there are three types of players: Cooperators C, simple Maximizers M, and Rivalists R. In the case of oligopolies under incomplete information, for the two sizes of N and regardless of the bargaining types, the hypothesis is that the Cournot equilibrium will prevail, because if an individual player does not know the relation between her output and the profit of the other players, she will act as if those profits are some constant and concentrate on naively maximizing her own profit.[1] Under complete information instead, the hypothesis is that the solution is a function of the number of participants, the composition of bargaining types, and the dynamics of the interaction between the players, with the possible outcomes ranging from Pareto to Walras.

Fouraker and Siegel's work – and that of Sauermann and Selten (1959) and Hoggatt (1959) – clearly differentiates between hypotheses, tests and conclusions. Their hypotheses are stated in terms of two characteristics. First, the degree of information available to the subjects, which appears as two treatments called incomplete information (subjects are told of their own profits and *aggregate* output of others) and complete information (they are told about everybody's decisions and profits), and second, the number of players, N, per market, with two different treatments for $N = 2$ and $N = 3$.

---

[1] Notice that from a game-theoretic point of view, going for the Walrasian output level is the dominant strategy for a Rivalistic player. Hence, while Fouraker and Siegel' hypotheses are formulated with respect to the players' preferences, what they must have had in mind as well is the beginning of a bounded rationality kind of explanation. Fouraker and Siegel do not explicitly consider learning, but they do observe, for example, that a player might be motivated solely by his own profits, and employ the rivalistic *signal* as a means of increasing those profits. Hence, what Fouraker and Siegel call "*the dynamics of the interaction between the players*" seems related to an adaptive learning process concerning the behavior of one's opponents.

We choose to report, for symmetry with the previous results, the triopoly experiments, $N = 3$:

From Figures 3 and 4 it may be concluded, as hypothesized, that oligopolists bargaining under complete information as quantity adjusters show a greater variability of decisions than under incomplete information.

For a summary of Fouraker and Siegel results on Cournot oligopoly we refer to Table 2.

References

Fouraker, L.E., Shubik, M., Siegel, S. (1961). "Oligopoly bargaining: The quantity adjuster models". Research Bulletin 20. Pennsylvania State University, Department of Psychology.
Fouraker, L.E., Siegel, S. (1963). "Bargaining Behavior". McGraw–Hill, New York.
Hoggatt, A.C. (1959). "An experimental business game". Behavioral Science 4, 192–203.
Sauermann, H., Selten, R. (1959). "Ein oligopolexperiment". Zeitschrift für die gesamte Staatswissenschaft 115, 427–471.
Sauermann, H., Selten, R. (1960). "An experiment in oligopoly" (translation of Sauermann and Selten (1959)). General Systems 5, 85–114.

Chapter 19

EXPERIMENTS IN DECENTRALIZED MONOPOLY RESTRAINT

JAMES C. COX and R. MARK ISAAC
University of Arizona

In this chapter, we report on laboratory experimental examinations of a particular class of institutions, policies or mechanisms of monopoly control. These are mechanisms which take the existence of a monopoly as a given and ask how might the "abuses" of monopoly be controlled in a decentralized manner. As such, we will be excluding from our analysis experiments in the discouragement or dismemberment of monopoly ("antitrust" experiments).

The most prevalent form of monopoly control in the United States for many decades was cost-based "rate of return" regulation. The academic and practitioner critics of rate of return regulation were numerous. In general, the arguments were that the incentives in the rate of return regulatory process itself led to distortions relative to standard measures of efficiency (for a more detailed discussion see Isaac, 1982). It is not surprising that there were many explorations for alternatives to rate of return regulation. We will focus exclusively on experiments that do more than simply reform centralized price regulation, that is, we examine *decentralized* forms of monopoly control.

1. Market Institutions for Monopoly Restraint

Smith (1981) conducted a series of laboratory market experiments designed to investigate whether the structure of some market trading institutions might discipline a monopolist. If some market institutions were to limit the exercise of monopoly power, then the charge to a regulatory body could be implementation of an appropriate design of the market itself rather than regulation of price or quantity. Smith looked at four market trading institutions: double auction, offer auction, posted bid, and posted offer. Two different measures of monopoly effectiveness for the eight Smith experiments are presented in Figure 1 (three double auction experiments, one posted offer experiment, one offer auction experiment, and three posted bid experiments, respectively). The yellow bars show the deviations of average prices in experiments from the quantity conditional monopoly prices (the demand prices for the actual average quantities traded). This measure, called "δ" in the paper, is a measure of the seller's effectiveness in obtaining high prices for the actual number of units sold. The second measure is overall market efficiency, which is inversely related to reductions in trading quantity below the competitive level. (These efficiency data are averaged across periods 5–10.)

Smith reported that some forms of market organization facilitated the disciplining of monopoly sellers by buyers. In one case, the offer auction, this conclusion is unam-

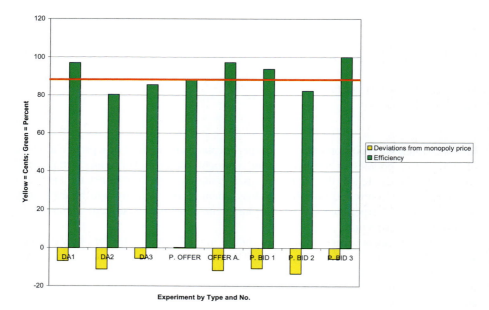

Figure 1. Smith (1981) asked whether some market institutions are decentralized mechanisms that enable buyers to effectively constrain the market power of monopolists. This figure presents results from Smith's experiments with the double auction (DA), posted offer (P. OFFER), offer auction (OFFER A.), and posted bid (P. BID) market institutions. The yellow bars show the deviations of average prices in experiments from the quantity conditional monopoly prices (the demand prices for the actual average quantities traded). This is a measure of the seller's effectiveness in obtaining high prices for the actual number of units sold. Note that sellers were highly monopoly price effective in the posted offer experiment, less effective in the posted bid experiments, even less effective in the double auction experiments, and least monopoly price effective in the in the offer auction experiment. Thus the posted offer market is the least effective institution for constraining the ability of a monopolist to charge high prices and the offer auction is the most effective. The green bars show the efficiency of the experimental market allocations, measured as the realized sum of consumer and producer surplus, divided by the surplus that would result from the competitive equilibrium allocation, multiplied by 100. The horizontal red line indicates the efficiency of the theoretical monopoly allocation, 88.5 percent. Note that the offer auction allocation is highly efficient, the average posted bid allocation less efficient, the posted offer allocation even less efficient, and the average double auction allocation the least efficient. Thus the offer auction allowed the buyers to effectively constrain the ability of a monopolist to charge high prices without sacrificing much market surplus from witheld demand.

biguous – this market had high efficiency and prices were well below the monopoly prediction. In other cases, the conclusions are more ambiguous. The double auction, for example, allowed buyers to keep prices well below theoretical monopoly prices but at the cost of greatly reduced trade and hence low market efficiency. The market institution that was most conducive to the seller obtaining the theoretical monopoly price and quantity was the posted offer market, arguably the one closest to what may be the "natural" organization of most retail markets of concern to regulators.

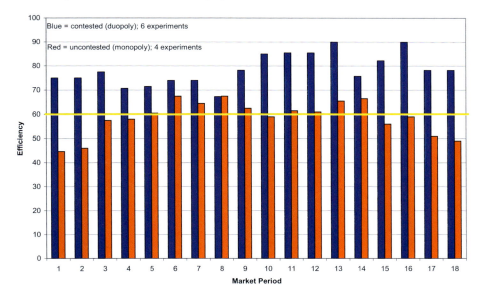

Figure 2. Coursey, Isaac, and Smith (1984) reported results from experiments with contested and uncontested markets for sellers with decreasing marginal costs and zero sunk costs. The red bars show the average allocative efficiencies in each of the 18 periods of four experiments with uncontested markets. The blue bars show the average allocative efficiencies in six experiments with the same decreasing costs but with markets contested by a second firm. The theoretical monopoly allocation has an efficiency of 60 percent, denoted by the yellow line. Market efficiency is increased notably by the contesting actions of the second firm.

2. Contestable Markets

Another regulatory approach which would also not require centralized price regulation is the promotion of contestable markets. The idea of what became known as the "contestable markets" hypothesis (see, for example, Baumol, Panzar, and Willig, 1982) is that even a market with a cost structure which satisfies the conditions of a "natural monopoly" may be lacking in traditional definitions of "market power" if there is a second firm with access to identical technology ready to contest the market. Thus the power to charge monopoly prices can be constrained in a market that is contested even if only one firm is observed to be serving the entire market.

There have been several experimental market tests of the contestable markets hypothesis (e.g., Coursey, Isaac, and Smith, 1984; Harrison and McKee, 1985; Brown-Kruse, 1991). The results generally support the conclusion that laboratory markets with conditions required for contestability perform reasonably like the predictions of the contestable markets hypothesis. Figure 2 summarizes the results from Coursey, Isaac, and Smith (1984).

Much of the debate in the regulatory arena was not over the contestable markets hypothesis, *per se*, but rather over the applicability of the conditions of the theory to field

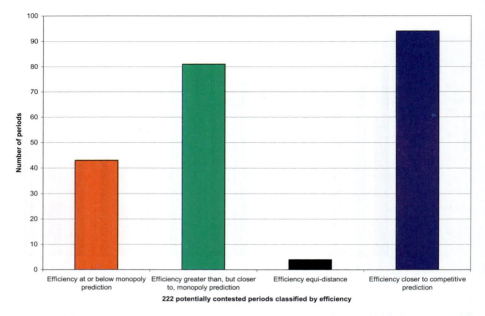

Figure 3. Coursey et al. (1984) added small sunk costs to the design in Coursey, Isaac, and Smith (1984) to ascertain whether the greater efficiency of the contested markets with decreasing cost firms was robust. The bars in this figure report the number of experimental market periods out of 222 with efficiencies closer to monopoly or competitive predictions. Contestable market efficiency is greater than the theoretical monopoly efficiency in 179 out of the 222 periods and in 94 of those periods it is closer to the competitive market prediction than to the monopoly prediction.

environments. One limiting condition of the pure form of the contestable markets hypothesis is the assumption of zero sunk costs. Coursey et al. (1984) provided additional empirical information by adding small sunk costs to their previous design. They found that the results of contestability were not "brittle"; that is, adding a small amount of sunk costs caused only a modest amount of deviation from the predictions of the contestability theory. Market performance did not suddenly "jump" to the monopoly outcomes. Figure 3 illustrates this conclusion.

3. The Loeb–Magat Mechanism

In some markets, perhaps those in which the cost conditions are significantly different from those specified by the contestable markets hypothesis, it may be that some form of explicit regulatory process is inevitable. [We ignore alterations in centralized price regulations, such as the "price cap" scheme discussed in Isaac (1991).] A theoretically optimal regulatory mechanism was offered by Loeb and Magat (1979). It is a reformulation of the Groves (1973) and the Groves and Loeb (1975) demand revealing process.

In the Loeb–Magat process [as described in Cox and Isaac (1987)], total profits of the firm are represented as:

$$pQ(p) - C(Q(p)) + S^{LM}(p) + A, \tag{1}$$

where $C(\bullet)$ is the firm's cost function, $Q(\bullet)$ is the demand function, $S^{LM}(\bullet)$ is a subsidy function that depends on p, and A is a lump-sum transfer that does *not* depend on p. The subsidy function is defined as:

$$S^{LM}(p) = \int_0^{Q(p)} \rho(x)\,dx - pQ(p), \tag{2}$$

where $\rho(\bullet)$ is the inverse demand function. That is, net of some lump-sum transfer A, the regulated firm receives as a subsidy all of the consumers' surplus at its chosen price. The dominant strategy of a profit-maximizing firm that is regulated by the Loeb–Magat mechanism is to set price equal to marginal cost.

There are two possible objections to the Loeb–Magat process. First, the subsidy function may pose a political barrier to acceptance of the process. Several remedies have been proposed to address this problem (see Cox and Isaac, 1986). The second problem is that the regulators would have to know the demand function for the monopolist's product in order to implement the Loeb–Magat mechanism's subsidy formula. But the regulators would only have observations of market demand within the sample of historical prices, not over the domain of the demand function.

Harrison and McKee (1985) report on five experimental sessions combining the Loeb–Magat mechanism with a franchise auction to dissipate expected monopoly rents back to the regulator. One of the sessions allows collusion, and in only one of the remaining four experiments do the firms know their own demands (although the regulatory operation of the Loeb–Magat mechanism necessarily incorporates demand information). Harrison and McKee report that by a standard measure of "monopoly effectiveness," their implementation of the Loeb–Magat mechanism approaches full dissipation of economic rents. Cox and Isaac (1986) conducted four L–M experiments, half with and half without the firm knowing its own demand. Like Harrison and McKee, Cox and Isaac found that the Loeb–Magat mechanism worked largely as advertised. Figure 4 presents the price and quantity path from two of these experiments.

4. The Finsinger–Vogelsang Mechanism

Regardless of the implementation of the information condition regarding the firm's knowledge of demand, the problem of the *regulators'* need to know the demand function is present in any case. This implementation problem is not alleviated by the presence or absence of a franchise auction to reduce the net transfers. Finsinger and Vogelsang (1981) reported an iterative alternative to the Loeb–Magat subsidy formula with much weaker information requirements. Let p_r be the price of the monopolist's product upon introduction of the F–V mechanism. The firm is free to choose price in each subsequent

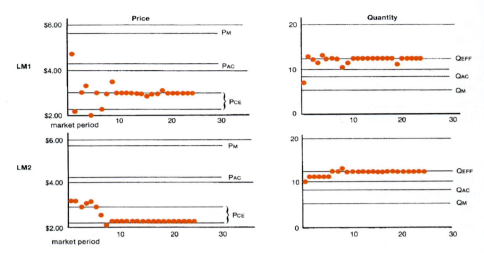

Figure 4. Cox and Isaac (1986) reported experiments with the Loeb–Magat subsidy mechanism applied to monopoly sellers with decreasing marginal costs. The size of the subsidy under this mechanism is equal to the area under the seller's demand curve plus a (positive or negative) lump sum. Implementation of the subsidy requires the regulator to know the demand function for the seller's product. This subsidy formula makes the fully-efficient ("competitive") outcome profit-maximizing for the same reason that the perfectly-discriminating monopoly outcome is fully efficient. Price and quantity outcomes from two representative experiments (LM1 and LM2) are shown. Prices converge quickly to be within the range of competitive market-clearing prices. Quantities converge to the efficient quantity.

period $0, 1, \ldots, t \ldots$. The general formula of the Finsinger–Vogelsang subsidy is

$$S_t^{FV} = \sum_{\tau=0}^{t} Q_{\tau-1}[p_{\tau-1} - p_\tau]. \qquad (3)$$

Since Equation (3) contains only observed prices and quantities, it is clear that the regulator need not have any *a priori* knowledge of the demand function in order to implement the Finsinger–Vogelsang subsidy. This is the great practical advantage of the Finsinger–Vogelsang (hereafter, F–V) subsidy mechanism over the Loeb–Magat (hereafter, L–M) mechanism.

The critical empirical question is whether the F–V mechanism can actually induce efficient allocation by a monopolist. The F-V theory states that the optimal price path for the regulated firm will converge to the social optimum. However, note from Equation (3) above that, if a firm ever raises its price, it is penalized in the current period and *in all future periods*. This suggests the importance of the question of what happens if the firm errs and raises price. Even if the firm realizes it has made a mistake and lowers price, the firm has permanently lowered its potential subsidy. The possible deleterious effect of price cycles on the performance of the F–V mechanism was first noticed by Seagraves (1984). Cox and Isaac (1986) presented the results of four laboratory experiments with

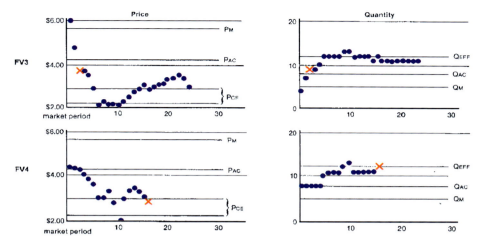

Figure 5. Cox and Isaac (1986) reported experiments with the Finsinger–Vogelsang subsidy mechanism applied to monopoly sellers with decreasing marginal costs. The size of the subsidy under this mechanism is calculated from observed quantities and price changes; thus the regulator does not need prior knowledge of the seller's demand function. The theory for this mechanism predicts that, starting from any price greater than marginal cost, the profit-maximizing prices and quantities will monotonically converge to the fully-efficient, competitive price and quantity. But the subsidy formula permanently penalizes any price increase in all subsequent periods. Thus the actual performance of this mechanism can be vulnerable to deviations from optimal monotonic price decreases. The figure shows results from two representative experiments. In experiment FV3, the seller decreased price too quickly and would have been bankrupt in the third period (with prices and quantities marked with a red ×). In this experiment, the seller's losses were forgiven and the experiment was restarted. The further results were that the seller's prices and quantities did not converge to efficient outcomes before the experiment ended in period 25. Prices and quantities in experiment FV4 did not converge to efficient levels before the subject went bankrupt in period 17 from the penalty for the non-monotonic price path.

the F–V mechanism and found that, indeed, these profit-destroying cycles were a robust occurrence. Results from two of these experiments are presented in Figure 5.

5. The Cox–Isaac Mechanism

Cox and Isaac (1987) reported an alternative subsidy formula that is similar to F–V in its information requirements but offers superior incentives to converge to the social optimum. The subsidy function is based on a revealed measure of surplus, and the penalty for raising price in the Cox and Isaac (hereafter, C–I) subsidy formula is "forgiving," unlike the F–V formula. The C–I subsidy formula is defined as:

$$S_t^{CI}(p_r, p_0, p_1, \ldots, p_t) = [p_r - p_t]Q_r, \quad \text{for } p_t \geq p_r$$
$$= \int_0^{Q(p_t)} M_t(q \mid p_r, p_0, p_1, \ldots, p_t) \, dq - p_t Q(p_t), \quad \text{for } p_t < p_r, \qquad (4)$$

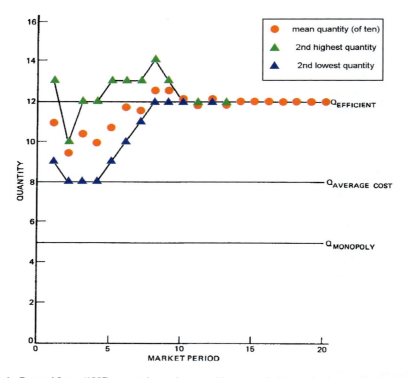

Figure 6. Cox and Isaac (1987) reported experiments with a new subsidy mechanism applied to monopoly sellers with the same decreasing marginal costs as in their other experiments. The size of the subsidy under this mechanism is also calculated from observed quantities and prices and theory predicts monotonic convergence to the fully-efficient, competitive price and quantity. But this subsidy formula is forgiving of non-monotonic price cycles. The figure shows quantity results from ten experiments. Mean quantities are denoted by red circles. Second-highest quantities are represented by green triangles and second-lowest quantities are denoted by blue triangles. As shown, quantities converge to the efficient quantity.

where p_r is the extant price and Q_r the extant quantity before the subsidy is first implemented and the function $M(\bullet)$ is defined as

$$M_t(q \mid p_r, p_0, p_1, \ldots, p_t) = \min\left\{p_r, \max_{p_\tau, \tau \leqslant t}[p_\tau \mid Q(p_\tau) \geqslant q]\right\}. \tag{5}$$

Cox and Isaac (1987) prove that the optimal path for a firm with subsidy formula (4) is convergence to the social optimum.

Cox and Isaac (1987) conducted laboratory tests with the new subsidy formula and reported that it did induce efficient allocations by monopoly sellers. They reported ten laboratory sessions, and all ten of the laboratory monopolists regulated with the C–I mechanism converged to the social optimum. Figure 6 reports the mean and dispersion of prices in the ten experiments; Figure 7 reports the same for quantities. In a later

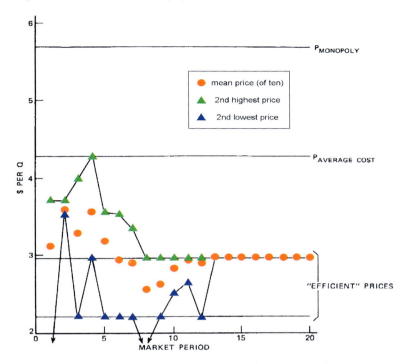

Figure 7. Mean, second-highest, and second-lowest prices in the Cox and Isaac (1987) experiments with the new subsidy formula are reported in this figure. Prices converge to the efficient price.

paper, Cox and Isaac (1992) found similarly robust results when there was an (uncertain) opportunity for cost reduction.

Acknowledgement

Toby Isaac provided valuable assistance by preparing the figures. Figures 4 and 5 are a modified representation of the same data as they appeared in Cox and Isaac (1986). Figures 6 and 7 are a modified representation of the same data as they appeared in Cox and Isaac (1987).

References

Baumol, William J., Panzar, John C., Willig, Robert D. (1982). "Contestable Markets and the Theory of Industry Structure". Harcourt–Brace–Jovanovich, New York.
Brown-Kruse, Jamie L. (1991). "Contestability in the presence of an alternate market: An experimental examination". RAND Journal of Economics 22, 136–147.

Coursey, Don, Isaac, R. Mark, Smith, Vernon L. (1984). "Natural monopoly and the contested markets: Some experimental results". Journal of Law and Economics 27, 91–113.

Coursey, Don, Isaac, R. Mark, Luke, Margaret, Smith, Vernon L. (1984). "Market contestability in the presence of (sunk) entry costs". RAND Journal of Economics 15, 69–84.

Cox, James C., Isaac, R. Mark (1986). "Incentive regulation: A case study in the use of laboratory experimental analysis in economics". In: Moriarity, S. (Ed.), Laboratory Market Research. Center for Economic and Management Research, Norman, OK.

Cox, James C., Isaac, R. Mark (1987). "Mechanisms for incentive regulation: Theory and experiment". RAND Journal of Economics 18, 348–359.

Cox, James C., Isaac, R. Mark (1992). "Incentive regulation and innovation". In: Isaac, R. Mark (Ed.), Research in Experimental Economics, vol. 5. JAI Press, Greenwich, CN.

Finsinger, Jörg, Vogelsang, Ingo (1981). "Alternative institutional frameworks for price incentive mechanisms". Kyklos 34, 388–404.

Groves, Theodore (1973). "Incentives in teams". Econometrica 41, 617–633.

Groves, Theodore, Loeb, Martin (1975). "Incentives and public inputs". Journal of Public Economics 4, 211–226.

Harrison, Glenn W., McKee, Michael (1985). "Monopoly behavior, decentralized regulation, and contestable markets: An experimental evaluation". RAND Journal of Economics 16, 51–69.

Isaac, R. Mark (1991). "Price cap regulation: A case study of some pitfalls of implementation". Journal of Regulatory Economics 3, 193–210.

Isaac, R. Mark (1982). "Fuel cost adjustment mechanisms and the regulated utility facing uncertain fuel prices". Bell Journal of Economics 13, 158–170.

Loeb, Martin, Magat, Wesley (1979). "A decentralized method for utility regulation". Journal of Law and Economics 22, 399–404.

Seagraves, J. (1984). "Regulating utilities with efficiency incentives". Public Utilities Fortnightly, 18–23.

Smith, Vernon L. (1981). "An empirical study of decentralized institutions of monopoly restraint". In: Quirk, J., Horwich, G. (Eds.), Essays in Contemporary Fields of Economics in Honor of E.T. Weiler (1914–1979). Purdue University Press, West Lafayette, IN.

PART 1.2.2

COLLUSION

Timothy N. Cason, "Price Signaling and "Cheap Talk" in Laboratory Posted Offer Markets"

Douglas D. Davis and Charles A. Holt, "The Effects of Collusion in Laboratory Experiments"

Rosario Gomez, Jacob K. Goeree and Charles A. Holt, "Predatory Pricing: Rare Like a Unicorn?"

Katerina Sherstyuk, "Some Results on Anti-competitive Behavior in Multi-unit Ascending Price Auctions"

Chapter 20

PRICE SIGNALING AND "CHEAP TALK" IN LABORATORY POSTED OFFER MARKETS

TIMOTHY N. CASON

Purdue University

Adam Smith's observation that "sellers of the same trade seldom meet together ... but the conversation ends in a conspiracy against the public ..." has enjoyed widespread support among economists and has strongly influenced antitrust policy in the U.S. and many other nations.[1] More controversial, however, is the appropriate definition of a "meeting," in terms of the type of communication that could have an adverse impact on market performance. Due to "folk theorem" considerations, theoretical predictions are imprecise when oligopolists interact repeatedly. Moreover, non-binding "cheap talk" between firms may facilitate price coordination, but this communication does not eliminate any theoretical equilibria present in the game without communication. Consequently, the impact of communication is an empirical question.

Several recent laboratory studies have assessed the impact of various forms on non-binding price signaling on market performance in posted offer markets with a small number of sellers. Unlike some earlier research featuring explicit conspiracies implemented through face-to-face verbal communication (e.g., Isaac and Plott, 1981; Isaac, Ramey, and Williams, 1984), these studies of price signaling implement communication that is legal or possibly legal under U.S. antitrust law. In some cases, the type of communication implemented in the laboratory was under investigation in specific antitrust cases.[2]

Certain types of non-binding price communications increase transaction prices modestly in some environments. This price increase is more likely to be sustained across transaction periods when sellers compete in multiple markets simultaneously (Cason and Davis, 1995), or when the price signaling language is structured to permit repeated price change proposals and "consensus-building" agreement or disagreement signals by rival sellers (Harstad, Martin, and Normann, 1997). In many other settings, however, the positive price impact due to price signaling is transitory and declines across periods

---

[1] Smith (1937, p. 128).

[2] This review focuses on market games with preplay communication, rather than bimatrix games such as those studied in Cooper et al. (1989, 1992). In a battle of the sexes game, Cooper et al. (1989) find that one-way communication significantly increases the frequency of equilibrium play. Cooper et al. (1992) demonstrate that this one-way communication increases play of the Pareto-dominant equilibrium in a cooperative coordination game, but that two-way communication is more effective in a simple coordination game when greater risk is associated with the Pareto-dominant equilibrium.

Handbook of Experimental Economics Results, Volume 1
Copyright © 2008 Elsevier B.V. All rights reserved
DOI: 10.1016/S1574-0722(07)00020-0

– especially with free-form price signaling or with a very restricted signaling language (Cason, 1995; Holt and Davis, 1990).

The first laboratory study to examine a specific form of price signaling was motivated by a U.S. Federal Trade Commission (FTC) complaint against the producers of certain gasoline additives (Grether and Plott, 1984). The FTC was concerned that the advance price notification practiced by sellers in this industry, along with some other practices, had an anticompetitive impact on prices. In the field, these announcements were usually made several days prior to their required 30-day advance notice, which permitted sellers to rescind proposed price increases that were not followed by others. In this sense, the advance price notices could be interpreted as non-binding price signals.

Unlike the experiments summarized below, Grether and Plott's experiment employed human buyers, and trading did not occur using the standard posted offer institution.[3] In the price announcement treatment each seller posts prices publicly, and then actual trades are executed following verbal negotiation over the telephone. All sessions employed four sellers. The results suggest that in this trading institution, the price signaling operationalized through this advance price notification increased prices. However, Grether and Plott did not attempt to isolate the impact of advance price notification, because their interest concerned how this practice interacted with other practices cited in the FTC complaint (e.g., most favored nation clauses). More recent studies have focused on identifying the marginal impact of price signaling, holding all other environmental and institutional factors constant.

1. Multi-Market versus Single-Market Competition

Researchers have recognized for several years that multi-market contact can facilitate collusion, because it allows sellers to exploit slack incentive constraints arising in the single-market setting (Edwards, 1955; Bernheim, and Whinston, 1990). Airlines compete in dozens (and in some cases hundreds) of city-pair markets simultaneously, and a recent antitrust case against the major U.S. airlines focused on non-binding price communications that the airlines routinely posted on their shared electronic tariff publishing system (United States v. Airline Tariff Publishing Company et al., 1993). This case inspired two laboratory experiments that determine the impact of similar free-form price communications on market prices in single-market and multi-market environments.

In Cason (1995) four sellers compete in a single market, and in Cason and Davis (1995) three sellers compete simultaneously in three markets. In both studies, the baseline treatment was the standard posted offer trading institution. In the price signaling treatment, sellers were free to post public, non-binding price proposals for one or two

---

[3] All the studies cited below employ simulated, non-strategic buyers in order to allow the seller subjects to focus on their strategic interaction with the other sellers.

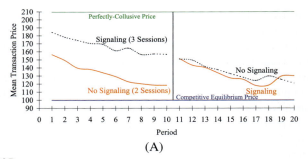

Source: Cason (1995).

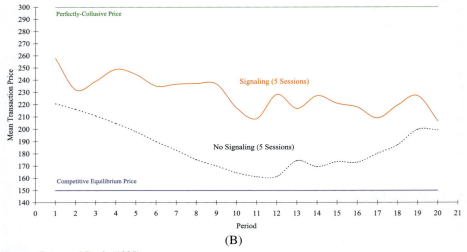

Source: Cason and Davis (1995).

Figure 1. (A) Single-market competition in the price signaling treatment sellers could continuously change multiple non-binding prices prior to their final posted prices; the impact of signaling is temporary when sellers compete in a single market. (B) Multi-market competition with the same continuous, non-binding price signaling rules, signaling has a more persistent impact when 3 sellers compete in 3 markets simultaneously. Prices are similar in both treatments in the final period.

minutes before submitting binding price offers.[4] Figure 1 illustrates that in the single-market setting (Panel A), mean prices are higher with signaling only in the first ten periods. Prices decline in both treatments, and *do not* decline more slowly when signaling is permitted. Therefore, the higher prices with price signaling in the early periods

---

[4] Cason (1995) employs a within-session treatment switchover design, while Cason and Davis (1995) fixes the treatment for each session and evaluates the treatment effect across sessions.

is due to the higher initial prices in this treatment. By contrast, in the multi-market setting (Panel B), mean prices are always higher in the signaling treatment. Nevertheless, the impact of price signaling appears temporary even the multi-market setting, as the prices in the two treatments are very similar toward the end of the sessions. Unlike the field application of the airline market, in both of these laboratory studies the sellers did not develop an obvious "language of conspiracy." Rather, conspiracies were more successful when a subset of sellers support the others with supercompetitive prices.

2. The Importance of the Signaling Language

In contrast to the free form price signaling implemented in Cason (1995) and Cason and Davis (1995), other studies have imposed more structure on the permissible price signals. Holt and Davis (1990) reports posted offer triopolies with very restrictive price signaling. Each period before sellers submitted binding price offers, one seller (chosen in sequence) made a "price announcement." This announcement was displayed to the other two sellers, who then publicly indicated one of three possible responses: (1) *agreement* with the announcement; (2) prices should be *lower* than the announcement; and (3) prices should be *higher* than the announcement. Neither the announcements nor responses were binding. The signaling treatment was always introduced following 15 periods of trading without price signaling.

Holt and Davis find that prices increase substantially after signaling opportunities are introduced, but that this impact is temporary. Prices in the two treatments are nearly identical after about 10 periods. Similar to the single-market, free-form price communication in Cason (1995), after several periods the price signaling becomes irrelevant cheap talk. Subjects propose high, collusive prices, but submit much lower binding offer prices. Within a few periods the proposals lose credibility and are ignored.

Harstad, Martin, and Normann (1997) manipulate the price signaling language as a treatment variable. Their experiment employs four sellers in each session. In one treatment sellers publicly post free form price proposals for 30 to 120 seconds before they submit binding price offers, similar to Cason (1995) and Cason and Davis (1995). In another treatment sellers propose specific price changes, which are followed by agreement or disagreement responses by the remaining sellers. This signaling structure is similar to the Holt and Davis (1990) language, except that in Harstad, Martin, and Normann (1997) any seller can propose price changes at any time, and multiple proposals are permitted per period. This structured price signaling is intended to give the conscious parallelism theory of MacLeod (1985) the best chance of describing behavior. Sellers in these latter structured signaling sessions are then brought back for another session with free form price signaling.

Relative to their no signaling benchmark treatment, Harstad, Martin, and Normann (1997) find that free form price signaling has a small but usually temporary impact on prices. This is consistent with the earlier results summarized above. But in contrast to the one-shot structured signaling of Holt and Davis (1990), prices are higher in their structured signaling treatment for 17 periods or longer. Prices decline slowly for 2 out of the 3 sessions in this treatment (and rise substantially beginning in period 13 in the other session), but prices typically remain above the static Nash equilibrium until the ending periods. When these subjects who have gained experience in the structured signaling treatment return for a session with free form price signaling, they tend to set prices significantly higher than the free form signaling sessions with inexperienced subjects. This suggests that they have learned some "collusive language" in their structured signaling session that translates in some way to the free form signaling environment.

3. Summary

Three main conclusions can be drawn from this experimental literature on non-binding price signaling.
1. Although price signaling often increases transaction prices, this increase is very often temporary. *Equilibrium* behavior may be unaffected by non-binding price signaling in many environments.
2. Price increases due to price signaling are more likely when sellers compete in multiple markets. Conspiracies are more successful when a subset of sellers forego short term gains by repeatedly offering supercompetitive prices.
3. The market impact of price signaling depends on the signaling language available to sellers. Very restrictive language (e.g., one price proposal by one seller per period) does not have a lasting impact on prices. By contrast, multiple-round structured signaling – in which many sellers per period can propose price changes with specific responses required of other sellers – can generate persistently higher prices compared to free form price signaling.

References

Bernheim, B. Douglas, Whinston, Michael (1990). "Multimarket contact and collusive behavior". RAND Journal of Economics 21, 1–26.
Cason, Timothy (1995). "Cheap talk price signaling in laboratory markets". Information Economics and Policy 7, 183–204.
Cason, Timothy, Davis, Douglas (1995). "Price communications in a multi-market context: An experimental investigation". Review of Industrial Organization 10, 769–787.
Cooper, Russell, DeJong, Douglas, Forsythe, Robert, Ross, Thomas (1989). "Communication in the battle of the sexes game: Some experimental results". RAND Journal of Economics 20, 568–587.
Cooper, Russell, DeJong, Douglas, Forsythe, Robert, Ross, Thomas (1992). "Communication in coordination games". Quarterly Journal of Economics 107, 739–771.
Edwards, Corwin (1955). "Conglomerate Bigness as a Source of Power". NBER, Business Concentration and Price Policy. Princeton University Press, Princeton.
Grether, David, Plott, Charles (1984). "The effects of market practices in oligopolistic markets: An experimental examination of the ethyl case". Economic Inquiry 22, 479–507.
Harstad, Ronald, Martin, Stephen, Normann, Hans-Theo (1997). "Experimental tests of consciously parallel behaviour in oligopoly". In: Phlips, L., (Ed.), Applied Industrial Economics, Cambridge University Press, Cambridge, in press.

Holt, Charles, Davis, Douglas (1990). "The effects of non-binding price announcements on posted offer markets". Economics Letters 34, 307–310.
Isaac, R. Mark, Plott, Charles (1981). "The opportunity for conspiracy in restraint of trade". Journal of Economic Behavior and Organization 2, 1–30.
Isaac, R. Mark, Ramey, Valerie, Williams, Arlington (1984). "The effects of market organization on conspiracies in restraint of trade". Journal of Economic Behavior and Organization 5, 191–222.
MacLeod, W. Bentley (1985). "A theory of conscious parallelism". European Economic Review 27, 25–44.
Smith, Adam (1937). "The Wealth of Nations". Random House, Modern Library, New York (original 1776).

Chapter 21

THE EFFECTS OF COLLUSION IN LABORATORY EXPERIMENTS

DOUGLAS D. DAVIS and CHARLES A. HOLT[†]

1. Introduction

At least since the time of Smith (1976), economists have believed that sellers are likely to discuss common price strategies, but that incentives to defect may be strong enough to break down collusive agreements. Collusion is difficult to study in naturally occurring markets, since sellers will try to hide illegal activities from buyers and from antitrust authorities. Even when a conspiracy can be established, the effective dates, the exact identities of all participants, and the real effects on prices are typically difficult to prove. In particular, price-fixing may result in stable common prices, but it is usually impossible to say what prices would have been without collusion, at least in the absence of precise cost and demand conditions. Even when markets seem to alternate between collusive and non-collusive phases, the price differences are difficult to interpret since a breakdown in collusion may be caused by a demand decrease that would have reduced prices in any case. This makes the laboratory an ideal setting to study factors that facilitate or hinder illegal price fixing.

The main result from the experimental economics literature is that the market trading institutions are crucial in determining whether or not collusion will be successful in raising prices above competitive levels. The initial paper on this topic was Isaac and Plott (1981), who examined the effects of seller discussions between rounds of a continuous double auction. In particular, the sellers were allowed to come together to a corner of one of the rooms and confer after the close of one trading period and before the start of another. Attempts to collude were as ineffective as they were inevitable. The problem is that each seller has a strong private incentive to defect and lower the asking price during the course of the double auction trading (Clauser and Plott, 1993).

In some sense, the Isaac and Plott (1981) result is consistent with Smith's (1981) finding that even a single-seller monopolist could not always find and enforce near-monopoly prices when trading with a number of buyers in a continuous double auction. Smith, however, did observe consistent supra-competitive prices, sometimes approaching monopoly levels, in posted-offer monopolies with the same supply-and-demand design. The posted-offer trading rules preclude price cuts during the course of the trading, which facilitates monopoly pricing. This raises the issue of what would happen in a posted-offer conspiracy with more than one seller. Isaac, Ramey, and Williams (1984)

[†] This work was funded in part by the National Science Foundation (SBR 93-19842 and SBR 96-617784).

Handbook of Experimental Economics Results, Volume 1
Copyright © 2008 Elsevier B.V. All rights reserved
DOI: 10.1016/S1574-0722(07)00021-2

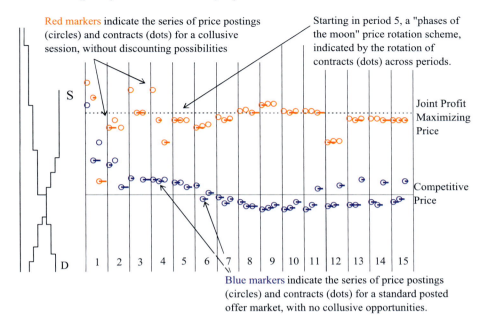

Figure 1.

addressed this issue and found that sellers were much more effective when conspiring about prices that were posted on a take-it-or-leave-it basis.

Many markets of interest to industrial organization economists do not fit exactly into the double-auction or posted-offer category. Sometimes sellers post list prices, for example, and then consider offering discounts if sales are falling behind expectations or if there is other evidence that others are offering secret discounts. The next section summarizes some experiments that illustrate the dramatic effects of opportunities to collude without discounts, and the opportunities to offer secret discounts even if there is collusion. Then the effects of collusion in some other auction and securities market trading institutions are considered in the final section.

2. Collusion with and without Secret Discounts

The dramatic effects of conspiracy in a posted-offer auction are shown in Figure 1, which summarizes two sessions reported in Davis and Holt (1998). There were six subjects in each session, randomly assigned to the three buyer and seller roles. Subjects were visually isolated and interacted over a network of personal computers. The supply and demand arrays are reproduced on the left side of the figure, and the theoretical competitive and joint-profit maximizing prices are indicated by horizontal dashed lines.

First look at the blue series for the standard posted offer market without collusion. The posted prices for the three sellers are indicated by small circles, and contracts (units actually sold) are shown as dots to the right of the corresponding circle. The price data for each period are separated by vertical lines, with the period number (from 1 to 15) shown at the bottom. Within the slot for each period, the price for seller S1 is plotted to the left, the price for S2 in the middle, and the price for seller S3 is on the right. Thus the blue circle for seller 1 in the first period is above the monopoly price (sellers were not given information about the demand curve or others' costs). Seller S2 has the low price in period 1, as shown by the blue circle with the three dots that indicate sale of three units. By the third period, all sellers' prices are nearing competitive levels, and the average price actually falls somewhat below the highest competitive price in periods 6 to 13. As intended, this is a very competitive supply and demand design.

The upper red price sequence in Figure 1 shows a parallel session in which price collusion among sellers was permitted prior to the start of each period. Buyers were taken from the room under the guise of using a random device to assign them to buyer roles, B1, B2, or B3. As buyers entered the hall to return, an experimenter alerted the sellers, who ceased discussions and slid their chairs back into their visually isolated booths before entering their prices for the next period. After some initial bouncing around in early periods, sellers agreed on a common price in period 5, but all three buyers purchased from seller S1, which may be due to the focalness of the "1" key, despite the fact that this seller had been offering higher prices in earlier periods.[1] Seller S1 then suggested a price rotation scheme, with him going first! Incredibly enough, the other sellers agreed, and S1 sold all three units at a price slightly below the others, as indicated by the red dots attached to the left-hand circle in the period 6 slot. This "phases-of-the-Moon" rotation continued, as the sellers experimented with different prices over the next several periods.[2] Prices were raised above the joint monopoly level in period 9, which resulted in only two units sold, and sellers returned to an exact monopoly outcome in period 10. The price reduction experiment in period 12 did not increase sales, so prices returned to near-monopoly levels for the final rounds. The industry cost structure was such that this rotation is very inefficient, since each seller had a low-cost unit, but only one of these would get produced and sold under price rotation. Interestingly, sellers moved to the more profitable equal-division arrangement in period 15, even though they had no way of knowing that was the final period.

The pattern effects of collusion in Figure 1 were replicated and were significant using a non-parametric test applied to the session price averages. A particularly interesting collusion session is plotted by the red sequence at the top of Figure 2. As before, there is some price variation in the initial periods before a common price is established in period 4. Seller S2, however, does not sell anything, and they then agree to limit sales to

---

[1] Here we see one of the advantages of using human buyers, since simulations may introduce too much uniformity or too much randomness relative to human behavior.

[2] The defendants in the celebrated electrical equipment price-fixing case of the early sixties had used phases of the moon to determine which one would submit the low bid.

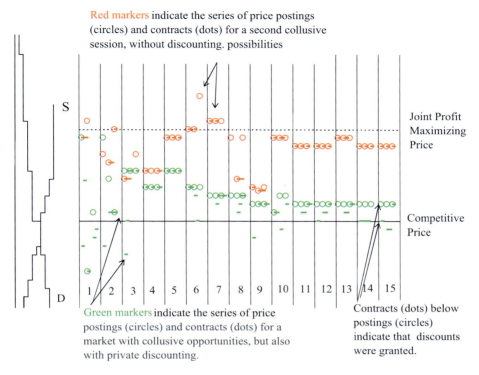

Figure 2.

one unit each in an effort to solve the "random selection problem." This split is honored in the next period, but the agreement breaks down as seller S2 prices aggressively in periods 8 and 9, thereby making all of the sales. In period 10 sellers finally coordinate a uniform, high price. Despite the fact that there was an understanding that each would limit sales to one unit, S2 cheated and sold two units, as indicated by the two dots attached to the middle circle for that period. Seller S3 was "not happy," but S2 covered up the defection by claiming that they should have expected sales to be lower when price is higher. Whether believed or not, this deceptive claim let them to agree on a uniform price reduction, with equal splits being honored in periods 11 and 12. They decided to try another increase in period 13, and seller 2 defected again, and again claimed deceptively that the failure of S3 to sell a unit was due to the demand reduction at a higher price. This only resulted in a slight price decline, with high prices and efficient market splitting the rule in the final two periods.

The next issue is the effect of opportunities to offer secret discounts from list prices that come out of a conspiracy. The setup for these "list-discount" sessions was the same as before, with the buyers being taken from the room while (without their knowledge) sellers discussed prices. The sellers then returned to their personal computers and entered their prices as buyers returned to the room. The main difference between this treatment and the previous conspiracy setup is that buyers could select a seller and direct a discount request to that seller by pressing a specific key. The seller selected would respond by typing in the original price or a lower one. Other sellers could not tell by the number of keystrokes whether the response was a discount or not. A buyer who was not satisfied with the seller's response could switch to another seller, which resulted in a "switching cost" of 5 cents that was deducted from the buyer's earnings for each switch (see Davis and Holt, 1998, for details).[3]

The price data for a typical session with discounting is shown in green in the lower part of Figure 2. When a discount price is accepted, the dot indicating that sale may lies below the green circle directly above, which marks the seller's list price. The opportunity to discount clearly causes a breakdown in the effectiveness of the conspiracy, but the breakdown process is particularly interesting. As in the previously discussed collusion sessions, there is considerable price variation in the initial period before a common price is selected in period 3. Seller S2 sells nothing, however, so they agree to a price reduction at which all sell at least one unit in period 4. This success emboldens them to raise prices. The prospects for high earnings start to fade when seller two discounts from the common list price in periods 6–8. Notice that these are not small discounts, indicating that seller S2 is suspicious that the others may do the same. Seller S1, who sells nothing in periods 7 and 8, offers a deep discount in period 9 and defects from the list price agreement in period 10. This results in persistent discounts for the remaining periods, despite the fact that sellers are able to agree on a common list price. Finally, note that the price fixed in these final periods was only slightly above competitive levels.

The next issue considered was whether providing more information to sellers about market shares may facilitate collusion, even in the presence of discounting. In particular, we ran a parallel series of sessions in which we provided *ex post* sales quantity information to each seller. This information, which is of the type sometimes disseminated by a trade association, makes it possible for sellers to monitor sales quantity agreements. In fact, this type of sales information did result in prices increases: prices in the conspiracy/discounting/sales-information sessions were about halfway between the low prices for the conspiracy/discount treatment and the high prices for the conspiracy/no-discount treatment.

The conclusion emerging from these and other sessions is that seller conspiracies can raise prices to near-monopoly levels, even in environments that yield competitive prices in a standard posted offer market. Second, this success of this price-fixing tends to evaporate when colluding sellers are given the chance offer secret discounts to individual buyers. This research suggests that antitrust hostility to contracts and codes that impede or discourage price discounts is justified. Moreover, it is now known that contracts which reduce sellers' flexibility to offer buyer-specific discounts may have

---

[3] To ensure comparability across treatments, this switching cost was assessed in each of the other treatments as well.

the effect of raising prices, even in the absence of explicit collusion (Grether and Plott, 1984).

3. Recent Work

One critical issue in the study of collusion is how to infer whether or not it exists. As seen above, successful conspirators may rotate bids (the red markers in Figure 1), or may split the market at fairly constant prices (the red markers in Figure 2). Neither of these pricing patterns, however, is uniquely a result of conspiratorial behavior. Consider, for example, sealed-bid auctions, such as those that are typically used to let construction subcontracts, and in government procurement auctions.[4] In these contexts, sellers may be relatively small, and may face sharp capacity constraints. Under these conditions, competitive bidders may find themselves rotating winning bids, since the bidder who has waited the longest since winning the last contract may have the most idle capacity, and may therefore have the lowest costs. In other contexts, where capacity constraints are less of an issue, competitive sellers may post identical prices, given sufficient excess supply. Davis and Wilson (2002) explore the extent to which collusion can be discerned from competitive behavior through observed bidding patterns in sealed bid procurement auctions. This research also allowed insight into other empirical means of detecting collusion through bidding patterns, such as the conjecture by Porter and Zona (1993) that collusion in sealed bid auctions can be detected by the correlation between losing bids and costs. With collusion, the correlation between bids and costs should break down.

A second direction of the relevant experimental work continues with the theme explored above, of assessing the interrelationship between explicit communications opportunities, and the institutional features of a market. Cason (2000), for example, examines the effects of collusive opportunities among subjects who are put into the position of dealers in asset markets. Cason's market structure was designed to parallel critical features of NASDAQ markets, where the dealer's long-standing convention of setting spreads on "even eighths" led recently to allegations of collusion. (See, for example, Christie and Schultz, 1994a, 1994b.) Cason finds that the combination of explicit discussions by dealers, combined with the capacity to monitor all dealer quotes on a computer screen can substantially increase dealer spreads. Cason also reports that the SEC's response to the alleged collusion by NASDAQ dealers – allowing traders to publicly post limit orders – narrows spreads even when dealers are allowed to communicate. This policy tool, however, is a rather blunt instrument, in that it has the undesirable characteristic of making dealer profits negative. Cason's experimental results suggest

---

[4] Isaac and Walker (1985) examine the effects of explicit conspiratorial opportunities in sealed bid auctions, and find results very similar to those for the standard posted offer markets illustrated by the red markers in Figures 1 and 2.

that the practice of publishing limit orders may have the undesirable consequence of eliminating liquidity-enhancing market making services.

To this point, our focus has been exclusively on verbal forms of collusion. The rise in the use of computerized auction and sales systems opens up the opportunity for a number of near-collusive types of signals. For example, bidders in the recent Federal Communications Commission bandwidth auctions allegedly used the decimal places in bids to identify zip codes, sparking concerns that such communications generated artificially low bids. In a related incident, several major airlines attached letter combinations (e.g., FU) to fare quotes listed electronically in the Airline Tariff Publishing (ATP) system network that seemed to effectively communicate particular messages to other competitors. This feature, combined with sellers capacity to costlessly and quickly submit non-binding, non-public advance price quotes led to allegations of conspiratorial behavioral in the airline industry. Cason (1995) and Cason and Davis (1995) examine the price-increasing effects of some of the pricing practices used by airlines in the ATP system.[5] In a single-market environment, Cason (1995) finds that extensive non-binding price-signaling opportunities raise prices, but only temporarily. This parallels results observed by Holt and Davis (1990) in an posted-offer environment with less robust communications opportunities: Although price-signaling can temporarily raise prices, it is difficult for sellers to implement stable agreements, absent opportunities for explicit discussion. Cason and Davis (1995) report that high prices were more consistently observed in a multi-market setting with extensive price-signaling opportunities. However, even here it was not the case that sellers were able to communicate successfully with non-binding signals, despite some persistent efforts. Rather, high prices were the result of one seller supporting high prices despite continued defections by the others.[6]

References

Cason, Timothy N. (1995). "Cheap talk and price signaling in laboratory markets". Information Economics and Policy 7, 183–204.
Cason, Timothy N. (2000). "The opportunity for conspiracy in asset markets organized with dealer intermediaries". Review of Financial Studies 13, 385–416.
Cason, Timothy N., Davis, Douglas D. (1995). "Price communications in laboratory markets: An experimental investigation". Review of Industrial Organization 10, 769–787.
Christie, William, Schultz, Paul (1994a). "Why do NASDAQ market makers avoid odd-eighth quotes?" Journal of Finance 49, 1813–1840.
Christie, William, Schultz, Paul (1994b). "Why did NASDAQ market makers stop avoiding odd-eighth quotes?" Journal of Finance 49, 1814–1850.

---

[5] Many of the questionable practices were prohibited via a 1994 consent decree between the ATP, the major airlines, and the Department of Justice.

[6] Results of these experiments, as well as the capacity of other types of non-binding communications to affect prices are reviewed elsewhere in this Handbook by Timothy Cason.

Clauser, Laura, Plott, Charles R. (1993). "On the anatomy of the 'nonfacilitating' features of the double auction institution in conspiratorial markets". In: Friedman, D., Genakopolos, S., Lave, D., Rust, J. (Eds.), Double Auction Market: Institutions, Theories, and Laboratory Evidence. Addison–Wesley, Reading.

Davis, Douglas D., Holt, Charles A. (1998). "Conspiracies and secret price discounts". Economic Journal 108, 736–756.

Davis, Douglas D., Wilson, Bart J. (2002). "Collusion in procurement auctions: An experimental examination". Economic Inquiry 40, 213–230.

Grether, David M., Plott, Charles R. (1984). "The effects of market practices in oligopolistic markets: An experimental examination of the ethyl case". Economic Inquiry 24, 479–507.

Holt, Charles A., Davis, Douglas D. (1990). "The effects of non-binding price announcements on posted offer markets". Economics Letters 34, 307–310.

Isaac, R. Mark, Plott, Charles R. (1981). "The opportunity for conspiracy in restraint of trade". Journal of Economic Behavior and Organization 2, 1–30.

Isaac, R. Mark, Walker, James M. (1985). "Information and conspiracy in sealed bid auctions". Journal of Economic Behavior and Organization 6, 139–159.

Isaac, R. Mark, Ramey, Valerie, Williams, Arlington (1984). "The effects of market organization on conspiracies in restraint of trade". Journal of Economic Behavior and Organization 5, 191–222.

Porter, Robert H., Zona, J. Douglas (1993). "Detection of bid rigging in procurement auctions". Journal of Political Economy 101, 79–99.

Smith, Adam (1976). "The Wealth of Nations, E. Cannan, ed.". University of Chicago Press, Chicago (original 1776).

Smith, Vernon L. (1981). "An empirical study of decentralized institutions of monopoly restraint". In: Quirk, J., Horwich, G. (Eds.), Essays in Contemporary Fields of Economics in Honor of E.T. Weiler, 1914–1979. Purdue University Press, West Lafayette, pp. 83–106.

Chapter 22

PREDATORY PRICING: RARE LIKE A UNICORN?[1]

ROSARIO GOMEZ[†], JACOB K. GOEREE[‡] and CHARLES A. HOLT[‡]

1. Introduction

Despite the discovery of predatory intent in several widely cited antitrust cases, many industrial organization economists have argued that predatory pricing is irrational and rarely observed. For example, one of our colleagues, Kenneth Elzinga, in an address to the American Bar Association posed the question of whether predatory pricing is rare like an old stamp or "rare like a unicorn." The argument is that pricing below cost in order to drive competitors out of the market will be irrational for two reasons: (1) there are more profitable ways (e.g., acquisitions) to eliminate competitors, and (2) future price increases will result in new entry.

Decisions in antitrust cases have often resulted from documented predatory intent, which is sometimes attributed to an "irrational" motive for management to eliminate rivals. In the absence of a "smoking gun," arguments turn on Areeda–Turner cost-based tests, which are difficult to apply given the multi-product nature of most business operations. For these reasons, the issue of predatory pricing is a natural topic for laboratory studies where costs are induced directly.

2. Single Market Designs

The first experiment designed to investigate the possibility of predation is reported by Isaac and Smith (1985). They conducted a series of posted offer markets with a large seller that has a cost advantage over a small seller. Besides having a larger cash endowment to cover initial losses, the incumbent was given a higher capacity and lower costs, as shown in Figure 1. In order to construct the market supply function, consider the average costs for the two sellers, shown on the left side of the figure, in red for the large seller and in green for the small seller. Since the large seller's minimum average cost is at $2.50, no units would be supplied at lower prices, and the (thick) market supply function (in yellow on the right) follows the vertical axis up to $2.50. At this price, the large seller would supply the seven units with decreasing costs shown on the left side of the figure. The small seller would not supply any units until the price rises to $2.66,

---

[1] This research was supported in part by a grant from the National Science Foundation (SBR 0094800).
[†] Gomez: University of Malaga.
[‡] Goeree and Holt: University of Virginia.

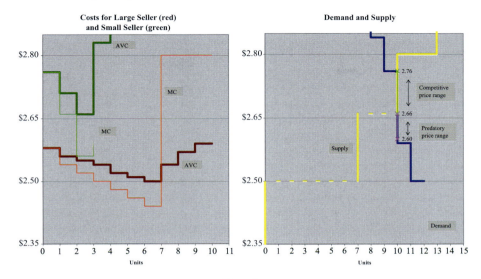

Figure 1.

the minimum of the small seller's average cost. So the market supply curve is vertical at seven units between $2.50 and $2.66, a price at which the small seller provides the three units with decreasing costs shown on the left side of the figure. Supply overlaps market demand in the vertical range from $2.66 to $2.76, which is labeled the competitive price range.

The most obvious case of predation would be where the large seller chose a price below the small seller's minimum average cost of $2.66 and supplied a quantity such that market demand is exhausted. Such a price together with a quantity of ten units would not result in a loss if the price is above the large seller's average cost, as would be the case in the "predatory price range" shown on the demand curve in Figure 1. This action, which leaves no room for positive earnings for the small seller, is predatory in the sense that price is below the $2.80 marginal cost of the 10th unit. It is inefficient for the large seller to sell ten units, since the large seller's three extra-marginal units are more costly than the three infra-marginal units of the small seller. Therefore, this design permits an inefficient predatory outcome that does not require the predator to sustain losses, although profits during the predation phase are lower than would be the case in a competitive equilibrium. A predatory action that drives the other seller out of the market *may* result in much higher, monopoly profits if entry does not occur. The small seller in Isaac and Smith's design can ensure earnings of zero by exiting the market, although there is only one active market in this setup.

Predatory pricing was not observed in any of the Isaac and Smith markets, even after they introduced several design variations (e.g., sunk costs) intended to be progressively more favorable to such pricing, and hence the provocative title "In Search of Predatory Pricing." Since subjects may not want to be left out of the market trading activity, this raises the issue of whether predation might occur in the presence of a reasonable alternative activity for the "prey," which is the topic of the next section.

Jung, Kagel, and Levin (1994) report an experiment that implements repetitions of a simple signaling game in which one of the equilibrium outcomes can be given a predatory pricing interpretation. Each play of the game involved a subject monopolist who encountered a different potential entrant in a series of eight periods. In each period, the potential entrant would choose to enter or stay out, and the monopolist would choose to fight or accommodate. The monopolist's decision was observed by the prospective entrants. The entrants earned more by staying out, unless the monopolist chose to accommodate. Following Kreps and Wilson (1982), the monopolist was given one of two possible cost structures: a strong monopolist would prefer to fight and a weak monopolist would prefer to accommodate in a single period. The monopolist was informed of her cost type that was determined randomly at the start of the eight-period sequence, but a prospective entrant would have to infer the monopolist's type on the basis of observed responses to previous entrants. There is a sequential equilibrium in which a weak monopolist will fight entry in early periods in order to deter subsequent entry. This "predatory" response by weak monopolists was commonly observed.

The market interpretation of this pooling equilibrium is that there may be a monopolist with costs so low that the profit-maximizing choice in the presence of entry would be below the entrant's average cost (that depends on the opportunity cost of foregoing earnings in the alternative market). Thus the theoretical possibility that behavior with a predatory flavor can exist in equilibrium is confirmed in the experiments. The setting used was rather abstract, e.g., the monopolist was called a "type-B player," and there was no mention of prices, quantities, entry, etc. Thus the Jung, Kagel, and Levin (1994) results are suggestive, although somewhat difficult to evaluate in the context of the industrial organization literature on predatory pricing.

3. Multiple Market Designs

Harrison (1988) modified Isaac and Smith's (1985) market structure in a clever manner. He implemented five simultaneous posted-offer markets with eleven sellers, each of whom could enter only one market at a time. Seven of the sellers were given the Isaac and Smith small-seller cost function, shown in green on the left side of Figure 1. Each of the other four sellers had a preferred market in the sense that they were a low-cost seller in that market, but they would become high-cost sellers if they entered any other market. There was only one potential low-cost seller in each of four markets. The efficient entry pattern required each of the four potential low-cost sellers to go to their own market and share it with a high-cost seller, and for the remaining high-cost sellers to congregate in the only market for which no seller had low costs. Demand in each market was simulated and corresponded to the demand in Isaac and Smith's (1985) setup.

Although Harrison only ran one session with this multi-market version of Isaac and Smith's design, he found evidence of predatory pricing. For example, the large seller in one market offered ten units at a price of $2.64, which is below the minimum average cost of the small seller and below own marginal cost. This predatory behavior drove the small seller out of the market, and the incumbent took advantage of the resulting monopoly position by posting high, profitable prices in the following periods. Since price and market entry decisions were made simultaneously, the large sellers had no way of knowing when entry would occur. For instance, one large seller posted a predatory price/quantity combination in period 10, presumably in an attempt to counter or deter entry, which occurred anyway in the next period.

In a survey of experimental work on predation and contestable markets, Holt (1995) concludes that Harrison's "behavioral existence proof" for predatory pricing would be more convincing with replication. Goeree and Gomez (1998) report such a replication, using Harrison's five-market design (see Capra et al., 1998, for a similar setup).[2] Subjects were provided with an experience profile similar to that used by Harrison (1988). In particular, each subject in the Goeree and Gomez replication began as a monopolist for several periods. These monopoly periods were followed by several periods of competition in which two or three identical sellers were exogenously assigned to one of four markets. Finally, all eleven subjects participated in the asymmetric cost, multi-market setup. In each market, the demand schedule was that used by Isaac and Smith.[3]

Overall, there was little evidence of predatory pricing from the three sessions conducted. One low-cost seller did select a price of $2.65 with a quantity of ten, but this was in the final period of the experiment. Since the number of periods had been announced in advance, this price could not have had a predatory intent unless the subject was confused about the endpoint. In another session, there were three cases in which a low-cost seller offered prices below the minimum average cost of $2.66, but the quantity was set at seven units in all cases, which would allow the entrant to earn positive profits.[4]

In a second series of experiments, Goeree and Gomez (1998) modified Harrison's five-market design in two important dimensions. Recall that prices and entry decisions are made at the same time in the Harrison setup, so the incumbent would not know whether a monopoly price is appropriate or whether an aggressive low price is needed to induce exit. Since price choices are more quickly changed than entry decisions in most markets, a reasonable alternative design is to have sellers choose their markets, with the entry choices announced prior to the posting of prices. Large sellers were required

---

[2] Although Harrison's instructions for the five-market design were unavailable, Harrison's monopoly instructions from an earlier paper were modified to allow entry, exit, and cost asymmetries.

[3] The demand schedule in each of the five markets was $3.92, 3.72, 3.52, 3.35, 3.21, 3.07, 2.97, 2.90, 2.84, 2.76, 2.59, 2.50, 2.32, 2.10, 1.88, 1.66, 1.44, 1.22, 1.11 and 1.00 for units 1–20, respectively. These values were assigned in descending order to buyers 1, 2, 3, 4, 5, 5, 4, 3, 2, 1, 1, 2, 3, 4, 5, 5, 4, 3, 2 and 1.

[4] Harrison classifies such prices as "type 2" predatory prices, because they are above the large seller's average cost, and moreover, are below $2.60.

to stay in their home markets, which should speed the adjustment process. A second change made by Goeree and Gomez involved a simplification of the demand structure. In Harrison's original setup, there were many steps in the market demand function, and this situation was further complicated by the fact that sellers were told nothing about market demand. Goeree and Gomez provide large sellers with complete information about demand, and simplified demand to a three step function: one at the monopoly price of $3.55, one at the highest competitive price of $2.85, and one at $2.60. Since the lowest cost for the small sellers was $2.80 and the lowest cost for the large sellers was $2.60, any price in the $2.60–$2.80 range would be predatory, as long as the quantity offered by the large seller was large enough (ten) to preclude sales by the small seller. The incumbents had seven units with costs of $2.60, and the three remaining units had higher marginal costs, which pulled average costs up to $2.72 for ten units, so entry could be deterred without pricing below average cost. This new design makes it clear what the monopoly price is and when it can be charged safely, thereby increasing the rewards from driving out entrants. Moreover, the incumbents knew the entrants' costs, which made it clear what price would preclude profitable entry.[5]

Sessions with these design changes resulted in a consistent pattern of predatory pricing in most markets, as shown in Figure 2. There are three parts to the graph; the top two panels plot prices in the two markets with a natural incumbent, and the bottom panel shows the prices for the remaining market with no natural low-cost seller. The Y-axis shows prices in pennies, with the upper predatory price ($2.80) indicated with a horizontal dashed line. Prices are plotted for the 12 periods in the 12 vertical columns. The prices selected by the natural incumbents are connected by solid lines (blue for seller 1 in the top panel and red for seller 2 in the middle panel). The prices chosen by the high-cost floating seller 3, for instance, are given by the yellow squares, regardless of which market seller 3 entered.

The prices for the low-cost sellers in the top two panels were often at predatory levels (below the dashed line) in periods when an entrant was present. Pricing at the monopoly level of $3.55 was generally observed in periods with no entry. Smaller sellers sometimes set high prices in initial periods, but undercutting drove prices down toward competitive levels in later periods, as can be seen in the bottom panel of Figure 2. Overall, these sessions show a clear picture of predatory behavior in a market setting.

---

[5] The small sellers did not know the large sellers' costs. This informational asymmetry was to a large extent present in Harrison's setup because the large sellers were told what their costs would be if they stayed in their home market and what the costs would be if they became a "type A" seller in another market. This information about the high cost structure provided a very strong hint, if not complete information, about entrants' costs in one's own market.

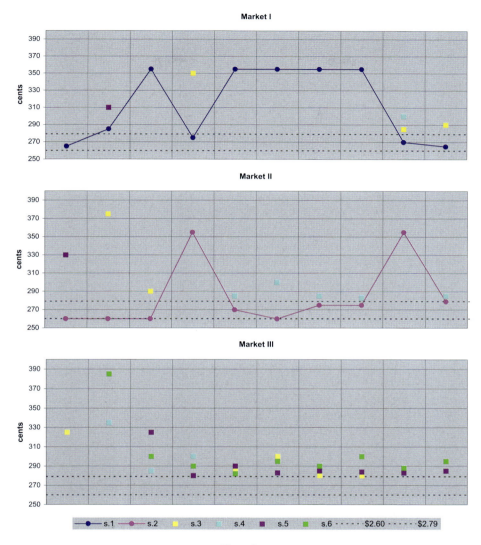

Figure 2.

4. Summary

Isaac and Smith's (1985) single market design did not produce predatory pricing. Such pricing was observed in the single multi-market session reported in Harrison (1988), but this pattern did not emerge in three replications run by Goeree and Gomez (1998). In a simpler design with prices being chosen after entry decisions are made and announced, the incumbents knew when to enjoy monopoly profits and when to punish entrants. This setup resulted in reliable predation in most markets. The lesson that predatory pricing experiments provide to date depends on an assessment of the realism of the design characteristics. What is clear is that predatory prices can be generated reliably, both in stylized signaling games and in rich market settings.

References

Capra, C.M., Goeree, J.K., Gomez, R., Holt, C.A. (1998). "Predation, asymmetric information and strategic behavior in the classroom: An experimental approach to the teaching in industrial organization". International Journal of Industrial Organization 18, 205–225.
Goeree, J.K., Gomez, R. (1998). "Predatory pricing in the laboratory". Working paper, University of Virginia.
Harrison, G.W. (1988). "Predatory pricing in a multiple market experiment. A note". Journal of Economic Behavior and Organization 9, 405–417.
Holt, C.A. (1995). "Industrial organization: A survey of laboratory research". In: Kagel, J., Roth, A. (Eds.), Handbook of Experimental Economics. Princeton University Press, Princeton, pp. 349–443.
Isaac, R.M., Smith, V.L. (1985). "In search of predatory pricing". Journal of Political Economy 93, 320–345.
Jung, Y.J., Kagel, J.H., Levin, D. (1994). "On the existence of predatory pricing: An experimental study of reputation and entry deterrence in the chain-store game". RAND Journal of Economics 25, 72–93.
Kreps, D.M., Wilson, R. (1982). "Reputation and imperfect information". Journal of Economic Theory 27, 253–279.

Chapter 23

SOME RESULTS ON ANTI-COMPETITIVE BEHAVIOR IN MULTI-UNIT ASCENDING PRICE AUCTIONS

KATERINA SHERSTYUK

Anti-competitive behavior is a concern for economists since if it occurs, it is detrimental to the performance of market institutions in terms of both social efficiency and auctioneer's revenue. Traditionally, experimentalists investigated possibilities of anti-competitive behavior in (1) two-sided auction markets trading multiple units and (2) single-unit one-sided auctions (see Holt, 1995 and Kagel, 1995 for reviews). A number of recent experimental studies turned to one-sided multi-unit auctions. The interest is generated by both theoretical developments in auction theory, and by the growing use of multi-unit auction mechanisms in practice, such as government procurement and privatization programs and Internet auctions.

Two frequently discussed kinds of anti-competitive behavior in multi-object auction markets are demand reduction and bidder collusion. Although the two are closely interrelated, distinction is often made along the following lines. Demand reduction occurs due to monopsony power of a buyer demanding multiple units of a homogeneous good in a uniform price auction. The buyer is essentially able to affect auction prices by reducing his or her demand. Coordination among buyers may not be necessary.[1] (Related earlier studies are market power experiments in two-sided auctions; e.g., Holt, Lagan, and Villamil, 1986; Davis and Williams, 1991.) Bidder collusion involves explicit or implicit coordination among more than one bidders demanding single or multiple units of a homogeneous or heterogeneous goods, usually in an attempt to suppress price competition. (Earlier studies focus on successful or unsuccessful attempts of bidder collusion in single-unit auctions and double auction markets; e.g., Isaac and Walker, 1985; Isaac and Plott, 1981; Clauser and Plott, 1993.)

Depending on the environment and institutional details, demand reduction and bidder collusion may occur under both ascending-price and sealed bid type markets. Here we focus on ascending auction institutions. Many researchers argue that, due to a richer action space and a superior information feedback that bidders get in the process of bidding in ascending auctions, these institutions have an advantage over the sealed bid procedures in solving complex allocation problems efficiently (such as allocation of airwave licenses; McAfee and McMillan, 1996). However, it is also well recognized that these very features of ascending auctions make them more susceptible to anti-competitive behavior (Milgrom, 1987; Cramton and Schwartz, 2000). The reason is two-fold. First,

---

[1] In other cases, several bidders need to coordinate on a demand reduction equilibrium, and distinction between demand reduction and collusion becomes less pronounced; see, e.g., Grimm and Engelmann (2001) discussed below.

some anti-competitive outcomes may be supported as equilibria in the ascending auctions, but not in their sealed-bid analogs (Milgrom, 1987; Brusco and Lopomo, 2002). Second, in cases where the same outcome may result from equilibrium play in both institutions, dynamic features of ascending auctions may allow bidders to learn their equilibrium strategies better.[2]

In this review we discuss whether experimental research on multi-unit auctions supports the claims made above. We focus on ascending price auctions; results on the sealed bids are mentioned only for comparison. Unless stated otherwise, we consider independent, private value auctions.

1. Experiments on Demand Reduction

In the research extending from single-unit to multi-unit auctions, the first question was whether and when desirable efficiency properties of single-unit auctions generalize to multiple units. Vickrey (1961) provided an original theoretical insight that this is the case for English and sealed bid uniform-price auctions as long as each bidder has use for at most one unit. McCabe, Rassenti, and Smith (1990) confirm, theoretically and experimentally, that with single-unit demands, the properties of English and Dutch clock auctions generalize to uniform-price multiple-unit institutions.[3]

Vickrey also made it clear that if bidders demand multiple units of the good, the strong incentive properties of single-unit English (and second price) auctions do not carry over to uniform-price multi-unit auctions: "It is not possible to consider a buyer wanting up to two units as merely an aggregation of two single-unit buyers: combining the two buyers into one introduces a built-in collusion and community of interest, and the bid offered for the second unit will be influenced by the possible effect of this bid on the price to be paid for the first, even under the first-rejected-bid method" (p. 27). This insight was later developed by theorists (Noussair, 1995; Ausubel and Cramton, 1996; Engelbert-Wiggans and Kahn, 1998) and tested by experimentalists who confirmed that multi-unit uniform-price institutions create incentives for demand reduction. Uniform-price K-unit English clock (EC) and sealed bid (SB) auctions work as follows. In the EC auction, the price starts at zero and then increases by small increments; bidders report their quantities demanded at each price. The bidders are informed about the total

---

[2] Thus in single-unit auctions, ascending (English) and sealed bid second price auctions are strategically equivalent: bidding according to the bidder's true value is a dominant strategy in both institutions. Yet, while observed behavior in English auctions closely conforms to the theory, overbidding is a persistent phenomenon in second price auctions. It is likely that dynamic nature of the English auction makes the dominant strategy more transparent than in the second price auction (Davis and Holt, 1993; Kagel, 1995).

[3] See also Cox, Smith, and Walker (1984). McCabe, Rassenti, and Smith (1988) report that open outcry auctions for multiple units are not as well behaved as their English clock analogs due to "jump bidding." Isaac and James (2000) confirm that strong incentive properties of the sealed bid Vickrey auctions hold in combinatorial auctions with multiple heterogeneous units.

demand at current price. The auction stops when there is no excess demand, and the uniform market-clearing price is then charged for every unit sold. In single-unit demand environments, each bidder has a dominant strategy to drop out of bidding once the price reaches his value; the outcome is therefore efficient with the price approximately equal to $(K + 1)$st highest valuation. With multi-unit demands, however, there may be incentives for bidders to reduce their demands, i.e., to drop out of bidding on lower-valued units early in order to buy higher-valued units at lower prices. In the SB auction, each subject submits sealed bids for every unit they wish to buy; K highest bids win the auction at the price equal to the highest rejected bid (or the lowest accepted bid). Similarly to the EC institution, the equilibria in the SB auctions under single-unit demands result in efficient allocations, whereas under multi-unit demands, there may exist strategic incentives to understate bidder willingness to pay for lower valued units, resulting in inefficiency and decreased seller revenue.[4]

Alsemgeest, Noussair, and Olson (1998) were the first to observe the demand reduction phenomenon in the experimental laboratory.[5] They conducted multi-unit English clock (EC) auctions and sealed bid (SB) auctions with lowest-accepted-bid pricing, in both single-unit and two-unit demand environments, in markets with either six or three bidders. Alsemgeest, Noussair, and Olson observed that whereas the outcomes of the EC under single-unit demands confirmed to the competitive prediction, there was a considerable amount of under-revelation under the two-unit demands: subjects attempted to influence prices by exiting the bidding process at prices below their valuations. Consequently, the EC generated less revenue under the two-unit demand than under the single-unit demand environment. Consistent with the theory, under-revelation most frequently occurred for the lower-valued unit in the two-unit demand environment. Interestingly, the authors observed no under-revelation in the two-unit demand environments in the SB auctions; the revenues and efficiencies in the SB were not significantly different between the single- and two-unit demand environments.[6]

Kagel and Levin (2001) further study demand reduction in uniform price EC and SB auctions. They employed a design which freed the environment of strategic uncertainty regarding other bidders' behavior: In their two-unit auctions, a human subject with a flat demand for two units competed with a number of computer rivals with single-unit demands; the computer rivals were programmed to follow their dominant strategy of

---

[4] We illustrate incentives for demand reduction with the following complete information example. Suppose that a bidder in the EC uniform-price auction demands two units, which he values at 70 each, and his only competitor demands one unit, which she values at 50. Two units are offered for sale. Assume the bidder demanding a single unit bids according to her valuation, which is her dominant strategy. If the bidder demanding two units bids for both units, the auction stops with his competitor dropping out at the price of 50, and the bidder gains 40 in profits. However, he can do better by dropping out of bidding for the second unit at the very start of the auction; the auction then stops at the price of zero, yielding this bidder the profit of 70.

[5] Miller and Plott (1985) studied multi-unit demand uniform and discriminative price sealed bid auctions. Under their design, there was no incentives for demand reduction for bidders.

[6] Theoretical properties of the sealed bid uniform price auctions under multi-unit demands were unknown at the time the study was conducted.

bidding according to their true value. The environment was chosen so that both EC and SB uniform price auctions yielded the same equilibrium prediction, with the human bidder bidding according to the true value on the first unit, and reducing demand to zero on the second unit. Kagel and Levin observe substantial demand reduction in both EC and SB auctions. However, similarly to earlier studies of single-unit auctions (Kagel, Hastard, and Levin, 1987; Kagel and Levin, 1993), they find that the behavior in the EC is closer to the equilibrium prediction than in the SB; see Figure 1, sessions 3 and 5. Additional variations on the EC and SB were then considered to study how the features of the English auction help bidders better learn the equilibrium strategies. The outcomes of these treatments[7] allowed the authors to conclude that "the closer conformity to equilibrium outcomes in the clock auctions results from both the information inherent in observing others' drop out prices and the ability of the clock to provide this information in a highly salient way" (p. 414).

Kagel and Levin also compare the bidding behavior in the uniform price auction with the Ausubel, or dynamic Vickrey, auction (Ausubel, 1997) designed to eliminate the demand reduction incentives. The latter auction works similarly to the EC ascending price auction, except winning bidders in the Vickrey auction do not pay a common price, but the price at which they have "clinched" an item (see Ausubel for details). Thus a bidder in the dynamic Vickrey auction cannot affect the price he pays for one unit by misrepresenting demand for another unit. In equilibrium, the auction results in full demand revelation and full efficiency.

Kagel and Levin report that the dynamic Vickrey auction does eliminate demand reduction and thus improves efficiency as compared to uniform-price auctions (Figure 1, session 9). However, they find that it raises less average revenue than the uniform price SB auctions, due to the bidders in the SB auction bidding less strategically than the theory predicts. They conclude that "there is a potential tradeoff between revenue and efficiency, unanticipated theoretically between the dynamic Vickrey auction and the uniform price sealed bid auction" (pp. 452–453).

In a related paper, Kagel and Levin (2005) investigate demand reduction incentives in multi-unit demand uniform price EC and SB auctions in environments with synergies. They observe less demand reduction in the EC uniform price auctions in the environment with synergies than in the no-synergy environment, and also find that demand reduction decreases with an increased number of rivals. As in the previous study (Kagel and Levin, 2001), the behavior is closer to the equilibrium play in the EC than in the SB auctions, but there is a large amount of out-of-equilibrium behavior under both institutions. The EC in these experiments not only generate less revenue than SB auctions, but they are also no more efficient.

---

[7] "Outcomes in the clock auction with no feedback are essentially the same as in the sealed bid auctions .... Sealed bid auctions with the second highest computer value announced begin to approach behavior in the clock auctions with feedback once the environment is structured so that the information inherent in announcing the computer's value is more salient" (p. 451).

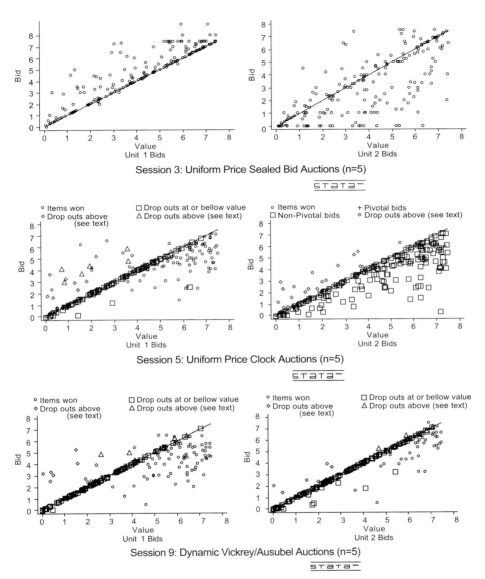

Source: Kagel and Levin (2001), © The Econometric Society.

Figure 1. Human bidder behavior in auctions with 5 computerized rivals. Session 3: Uniform price sealed bid auctions. Session 5: Uniform price clock auctions. Session 9: Ausubel (dynamic Vickrey) auctions.

Porter and Vragov (2000) compare Vickrey and uniform-price sealed bid (SB) with the English clock (EC) multi-unit auctions.[8] Unlike Kagel and Levin (2001), they use a setting with two human bidders, each demanding two units, competing in a market with a total supply of two units. They also find that EC results in more demand reduction than other institutions. As an explanation, Porter and Vragov hypothesize that "the low information content in sealed bid auctions tempers the amount of demand reduction that actually occurs."

Grimm and Engelmann (2004) investigate a similar setting, where two human bidders with a flat demand for two units each compete in a market with a total supply of two units. They compare five different multi-unit auction formats, including uniform EC and SB auctions, Ausubel auction, and sealed-bid Vickrey and discriminative auctions. An interesting feature of Grimm and Engelmann is that in their setting, the uniform price EC and SB auctions are characterized by multiple equilibria, including the truthful revelation, or the "incentive compatible" (IC) equilibrium which prescribes bidding according to the true value on both units, as well as the full demand reduction (DR) equilibrium, which prescribes reducing bidders' demands on the second unit down to zero.[9] Grimm and Engelmann report that three out of ten pairs in uniform EC auctions played almost the DR equilibrium strategy; in almost half of the cases bidders in the EC auctions acted in line with demand reduction incentives and dropped out of bidding on one unit immediately after the other bidder's drop-out. Given that bidders in these experiments played ten auctions only and did not have much time to learn to coordinate on DR equilibrium, the amount of demand reduction appears to be quite substantial. Slightly less demand reduction was observed in the uniform SB auction, with the bids often being noisier and further away from equilibrium than in the EC auctions. Grimm and Engelmann also report that Ausubel auctions exhibited more truthful bidding and higher efficiency than any other institutions considered, although some demand reduction was observed in the Ausubel auctions as well.

Manelli, Sefton, and Wilner (2000) consider two mechanisms which are not theoretically subject to demand reduction incentives. They compare Vickrey and Ausubel mechanisms in a 3-unit supply environment with 3 bidders, each demanding 2 units, in both private value and common value component environment. With private values, sincere bidding is an equilibrium in both mechanisms, and they should both yield, in

---

[8] Porter and Vragov also test the robustness of the findings of List and Lucking-Reiley (2000), who compared demand reduction in uniform price sealed bid and Vickrey auctions in a field Internet experiment. Their results are largely consistent with List and Lucking-Reiley.

[9] Note that playing the DR equilibrium requires certain coordination between the two bidders; hence, this setting comes very close to studies of bidder collusion. The differences between such DR equilibria and collusive equilibria (to be discussed below) are small. One distinction is that in the EC multi-unit settings usually employed to study demand reduction, only one bidder demanding multiple units may be left active at some point of the game. He then has a monopsony power and faces the exact DR incentives as discussed at the beginning of this section. In the open outcry-type auctions that are typically used to study collusion, activity rule restrictions are absent, and hence market power may be sustained only through continuous coordination among bidders in the auction (see below).

theory, the same revenue and efficient allocations. Manelli, Sefton, and Wilner (2000) report that neither mechanism conforms to the theoretical predictions. There was significant overbidding on the first unit in both Vickrey and Ausubel auctions (with more overbidding in Vickrey), and some underbidding (demand reduction) on the second unit in Vickrey auctions. Further, Ausubel auction exhibited another, unexpected, type of aggressive bidding. In the experiments, all bidders were allowed to demand up to three units, even though the third unit always had a value of zero. In Ausubel auctions bidders often bid for all three units until they secured the two units they desired; this sometimes led to a bidder acquiring all three units, leading to "too concentrated" allocations and therefore disturbing the efficiency. Manelli, Sefton, and Wilner (2000) note that while the amount of overbidding in Vickrey auctions was sensitive to small variations in the environment, aggressive over-demanding in Ausubel auctions persisted; in sum Vickrey auctions were always as efficient as Ausubel auctions, and yielded more or less revenue depending on the environment.

Kagel, Kinross, and Levin (2001) also compare multi-unit sealed-bid Vickrey with Ausubel (dynamic Vickrey) auctions, but in an environment with no strategic uncertainty. Unlike Manelli, Sefton, and Wilner (2000), they report that the Ausubel auction with drop out information comes significantly closer to sincere bidding than other institutions. It is then useful to compare the results of Manelli, Sefton, and Wilner (2000) with others' findings on Ausubel auctions. Kagel and Levin (2001) and Kagel, Kinross, and Levin (2001) find that in environments where a single human subject competes with computer rivals, Ausubel auctions work well in terms of efficiency, outperforming other auction formats. Grimm and Engelmann also find that Ausubel auctions perform well in a setting where several human bidders interact but by design are precluded from overly aggressive bidding. On the other hand, Manelli, Sefton, and Wilner (2000) report that Ausubel auctions may suffer from efficiency losses caused by aggressive bidding, which appears to be strategic in nature and therefore may be quite persistent. These results suggest that, at least in some environments, the presence of human rivals and strategic uncertainty associated with it may have significant effect on bidder behavior and therefore on performance characteristics of the Ausubel auction.

What have we learned? First, demand reduction is a well-documented phenomenon in the lab. Second, multi-unit uniform price ascending clock auctions exhibit demand-reduction behavior closest to equilibrium predictions as compared to corresponding sealed-bid institutions. Thus in uniform price clock auctions, the dynamic nature of the institution helps bidders to learn their equilibrium strategies better. Third, it may not be a universal phenomenon that dynamic multi-unit auctions unambiguously result in outcomes closer to the theoretical predictions than their sealed-bid analogs. While the Ausubel (dynamic Vickrey) auction, designed to eliminate demand reduction incentives, performs well in some environments (as in Kagel and Levin, 2001 and Grimm and Engelmann, 2004), it may become subject to new kinds of disequilibrium behavior in other settings (as in Manelli, Sefton, and Wilner, 2000), and lead to considerable efficiency losses.[10] These findings suggest that there is room for further research on multi-unit auction institutions that could eliminate demand-reduction incentives and improve efficiency.

2. Experiments on Bidder Collusion

Until recently, the evidence of outright bidder collusion in auctions under standard experimental procedures without communication was scarce (Kagel, 1995). Multi-unit ascending auctions present new opportunities for bidders to collude that are non-existent in single-unit auctions or even multi-unit sealed bid auctions.[11] Burns (1985) observed some collusion attempts in multi-unit sequential English auction with three bidders; yet collusion in her experiment was unstable and in the end all prices converged to competitive equilibrium. A number of recent studies report sustainable collusion in ascending auctions. The issues being addressed are: possibility of collusion under "standard" procedures; role of various institutional details or auction formats in preventing or facilitating collusion; and the role of communication. All studies discussed here consider collusion in open outcry ascending bid auctions, or their computerized analogs; collusion in experimental English clock auctions (often used to study demand reduction, as discussed above) has been rarely reported.[12]

Sherstyuk (1999, 2001) studies the role of bid improvement rules for safe-guarding against collusion in multi-unit ascending bid auctions. If bid improvement rules are absent in an ascending auction, bidders may sustain supra-competitive pricing as equilibria by matching each other's low bids. Deviations are deterred by the threat to switch to competitive bidding, and in equilibrium objects are allocated to bidders randomly at a low price. Experimental design employed to test this prediction had three bidders in the market, each demanding a single unit, and a supply of two units. During the bidding process, the subjects were allowed to submit bids no lower than the outstanding bid in the market; when the bidding was over, the two objects were allocated to two highest bidders, with ties in the bids of acceptance broken randomly. Explicit communication among bidders was not allowed. Sherstyuk reports persistent and mostly stable tacit collusion in such auctions, with occasional competitive outbreaks, first in a setting where all bidders had equal and commonly known valuation for the good (1999), and later in private value settings (2001).[13] In contrast, the sealed bid sessions conducted under

---

[10] Manelli, Sefton, and Wilner (2000) go as far as writing: "Just as theoretical properties of single-unit auctions do not always carry over to multi-unit environments in a simple way, so too behavioral regularities observed in single-unit environments do not always carry over to the multi-unit environment. For example, the transparency of sincere bidding in private value English auctions, that results in efficient allocations in laboratory environments, does not appear to be a characteristic shared by its multi-unit analogue."

[11] Kwasnica (2000) studies bidder collusion in multi-unit sealed bid auctions with communication.

[12] Grimm and Engelmann (2001) is a notable exception; see footnote 9 above.

[13] McCabe, Rassenti, and Smith (1988) also noted that allowing for bid matches may lead to low price equilibria in some versions of multi-unit English auction. However, in their settings, the low price prediction was not supported by the experimental data (p. 57).

identical supply and demand conditions converged to the competitive equilibrium. In the ascending auctions, bidders actively used the bid matching possibilities to communicate their intention to collude and to achieve and sustain collusive outcomes; Figure 2 presents an example of such "bid matching" auction. However, some collusion was also observed in the standard ascending price auctions with no bid matches allowed, relying on the repeated nature of the auction (2001). This indicates that institutional features of ascending auctions allow highly motivated bidders to find ways to achieve and sustain tacit collusion that are inaccessible in the sealed bid auctions; collusion may take various forms, with bidders splitting markets either within periods (using bid matching), or across periods (using bid rotation schemes).

Kwasnica and Sherstyuk (2001) provide the first systematic evidence of bidder collusion in simultaneous ascending price auctions under "standard" procedures without communication.[14] There were two objects offered for sale in each auction period, and two or five of bidders, each demanding both objects. Each good was auctioned in a separate computerized ascending bid auction, with the auctions run simultaneously for both goods. Brusco and Lopomo (2002) show that there exist collusive equilibria in such auctions where bidders split the markets and secure objects to themselves, each in their "designated" market, at lower than competitive prices; such equilibria may be sustained even in the presence of large but common complementarities between objects. Kwasnica and Sherstyuk do observe a large amount of collusive behavior in two-bidder markets without complementarities and in the presence of moderate complementarities, especially among experienced bidders. Yet, markets with large complementarities were all competitive. As predicted by the theory, collusion never emerged in any of the five-person markets. Figure 3 illustrates the actual price dynamics in a 2-bidder market with no complementarities, 2-bidder market with large complementarity, and 5-bidder market with no complementarity.

Kwasnica and Sherstyuk present an analysis of bidder behavior in these markets that sheds some light on how collusion was achieved and sustained. Two interesting features were characteristic of bidding in markets that resulted in low (collusive) prices. First, bidders in two-person markets often signaled to each other with their bids to decide on how to split markets.[15] Signaling involved either placing an opening bid in their preferred market first, or placing a strictly higher initial bid in the preferred market. Second, retaliation in the sense of bidding high, and often above own values, was used to punish non-collusive behavior of others.[16] Further (similarly to Sherstyuk, 2001), they provide evidence that bidders were able to adopt various collusive schemes to maximize their gains from collusion. In particular, in treatments with complementarities, the

---

[14] The auction studied in this paper closely resembles the one used in practice by FCC to auction off airwave licenses.
[15] This is in line with theoretical predictions by Brusco and Lopomo.
[16] Kwasnica and Sherstyuk report that the about 20% of inexperienced bidders and over 30% of experienced bidders bid above their value at least twice during the experiment. In our knowledge, this is the first study where consistent overbidding is reported in private value ascending price pay-your-bid auctions.

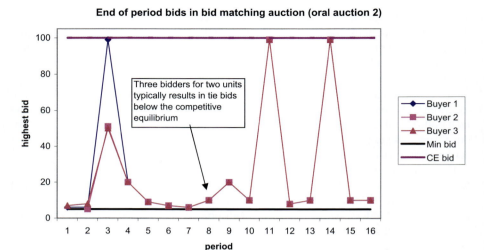

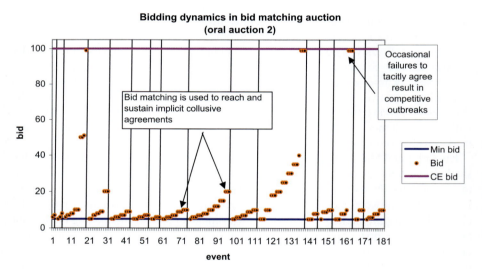

Source: Constructed with data from Sherstyuk (1999).

Figure 2. End-of-period bids (top) and bidding dynamics (bottom) in bid matching oral auction, session 2. In the absence of strict bid improvement rule, bidders used bid matches to suppress price competition. The prices averaged at 25.2 cents, compared with the competitive equilibrium prediction of 100 cents.

predominant collusive scheme was bid rotation across periods, rather than splitting markets within a period; the former scheme allowed bidders to capture the complementarity term.

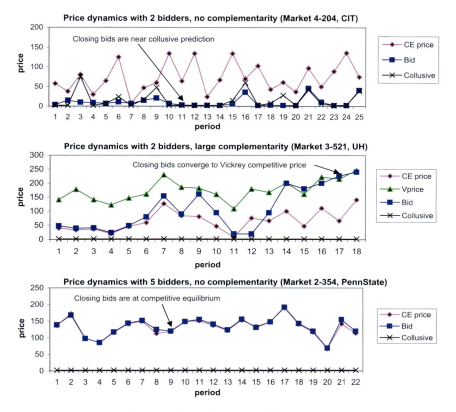

Source: Constructed with data from Kwasnica and Sherstyuk (2001).

Figure 3. Price dynamics for two objects in a 2-bidder market with no complementarity (top), 2-bidder market with large complementarity (middle), and 5-bidder market with no complementarity (bottom). "Bid" – actual price; "CE price" – competitive equilibrium price without complementarity; "Vprice" – competitive (Vickrey) price with complementarity; "Collusive" – collusive equilibrium prediction.

Sherstyuk and Dulatre (2001) consider whether simultaneous ascending price auctions are more susceptible to collusion than sequential ones, as some theories predict. They study a setting with four bidders and four heterogeneous goods; explicit face-to-face communication was allowed between auction series to facilitate collusion. Curiously, Sherstyuk and Dulatre report that even with communication, in some markets collusion never emerged.[17] Further, collusive agreements took place more often

---

[17] Archibald, Boening, and Wilcox (2002) report that collusion in some settings may be very hard to achieve except under a stringent set of procedures. They investigate posted-offer auctions in avoidable cost environments where collusion among firms is necessary to obtain efficiency.

in sequential than in simultaneous auctions. They conjecture that the reason was that sequential auctions were not as complex as the simultaneous ones, and advantages of collusion were easier to realize and learn under the former auction format. Sherstyuk and Dulatre further observe that the auction ending rules had a significant effect on bidder behavior. The "hard" closing rule led bidders in simultaneous auctions to focus on end-of-period bidding and possibly distracted the bidders' attention away from collusion. Collusion was somewhat more frequent under the soft closing rule.

Phillips, Menkhaus, and Coatney (2001) report on successful collusive practices in repeated sequential English auctions for homogeneous goods, in markets with two and six bidders.[18] Unlike in Sherstyuk and Dulatre, bidders in their design had identical downward sloping demands for the good, and the number of units offered for sale by the auctioneer was large enough to allow every bidder to buy most of their higher-valued units; thus the success of collusion may be due, to a large degree, to low competitive pressures from the market. An interesting finding they report is the absence of "high numbers effect" on collusion in auctions with communication (administered through email). Bidders in their six-person auctions were able to depress prices as effectively as in two-person auctions. A possible reason, Phillips, Menkhaus, and Coatney (2001) suggest, is that in the six-buyer markets, a sharing arrangement where each took a turn winning was focal; whereas in two-buyer markets there were many discussions on how much the subjects were earning, which complicated coordination between bidders. Phillips, Menkhaus, and Coatney (2001) also find that in two-buyer markets, knowing the quantity of goods for sale alone was as an effective collusion-facilitating device as communication.

In summary, the emerging experimental research on collusion in multi-unit ascending auctions clearly demonstrates that stable collusive outcomes can and do emerge under certain settings.

Yet, collusion proves to be difficult in other settings. Ascending open auctions appear to be more susceptible to collusion than sealed bids. Many interesting issues are under-explored or not yet explored. First, while all studies discussed here consider collusion in open outcry type auctions, in many cases the vulnerability of these institutions to collusion may be remedied by adopting an ascending English clock procedure instead. English clock auctions may make collusion among bidders much harder to achieve due to coordination problems.[19] Second, many other institutional aspects of ascending auctions that may affect collusion need further investigation, such as: "activity rules" in simultaneous auctions, information feedback to bidders, knowledge of quantity supplied, and communication. Other interesting issues include effects of eliminating

---

[18] See also Menkhaus, Phillips, and Coatney (2001).

[19] McCabe, Rassenti, and Smith (1988) and Banks et al. (2003) note that multi-unit English open-outcry-type auctions also suffer from other behavioral problems, such as "jump bids," or bid increases higher than the minimum required increment. Such "jump bidding" was observed even in single-unit-demand environments, and often resulted in efficiency losses. The problem is solved by disallowing bids from the floor – using the English clock.

repeated interaction with the same group of bidders; comparison between homogeneous and heterogeneous goods markets; effects of numbers; equilibrium selection in settings with multiple (collusive and competitive) equilibria; and behavioral foundations of collusion. Finally, one might expect to see a closer connection between demand reduction and bidder collusion literature.

Acknowledgement

I thank Jeremy Dulatre for research assistantship.

References

Alsemgeest, P., Noussair, C., Olson, M. (1998). "Experimental comparisons of auctions under single- and multi-unit demand". Economic Inquiry 36, 87–97.

Archibald, G., Boening, M., Wilcox, N. (2002). "Avoidable cost: Can collusion succeed where competition fails". In: Holt, C., Isaac, R.M. (Eds.), Research in Experimental Economics, vol. 9. JAI Press, New York.

Ausubel, L.M. (1997). "An efficient ascending-bid auction for multiple objects". Mimeo, University of Maryland.

Ausubel, L.M., Cramton, P.C. (1996). "Demand revelation and inefficiency in multi-unit auctions". Mimeo, University of Maryland.

Banks, J., Olson, M., Porter, D., Rassenti, S., Smith, V. (2003). "Theory, experiment and the Federal Communications Commission spectrum auctions". Journal of Economic Behavior and Organization 51, 303–350.

Brusco, S., Lopomo, G. (2002). "Collusion via signaling in simultaneous ascending bid auctions with heterogeneous objects, with and without complementarities". Review of Economic Studies 69, 407–436.

Burns, Penny (1985). "Market structure and market behavior: Price adjustment in a multi-object progressive oral auction". Journal of Economic Behavior and Organization 6, 275–300.

Clauser, L., Plott, C.R. (1993). "On the anatomy of the 'nonfacilitating' features of the double auctions institutions in conspiratorial markets". In: Friedman, D., Rust, J. (Eds.), The Double Auction Market. In: SFI Studies in the Science of Complexity, Proc., vol. 14. Addison–Wesley, chap. 12.

Cox, J., Smith, V., Walker, J. (1984). "Theory and behavior of multiple unit discriminative auctions". Journal of Finance 39 (4), 983–1010.

Cramton, P., Schwartz, J.A. (2000). "Collusive bidding: Lessons from the FCC spectrum auctions". Journal of Regulatory Economics 17, 229–252.

Davis, D., Holt, C. (1993). "Experimental Economics". Princeton University Press, Princeton, NJ.

Davis, D., Williams, A. (1991). "The Hayek hypothesis in experimental auctions: Institutional effects and market power". Economic Inquiry 29, 261–274.

Engelbert-Wiggans, R., Kahn, C.M. (1998). "Multi-unit auctions with uniform prices". Economic Theory 12, 227–258.

Grimm, Veronica, Engelmann, Dirk (2004). "Bidding behavior in multi-unit auctions – An experimental investigation". Working paper No. 2004-12, Instituto Valenciano de Investigaciones Económicas, S.A. (Ivie).

Holt, Charles A. (1995). "Industrial organization: A survey of laboratory research". In: Kagel, J., Roth, R. (Eds.), Handbook of Experimental Economics. Princeton University Press, pp. 349–443.

Holt, C.A., Lagan, L., Villamil, A. (1986). "Market power in oral double auctions". Economic Inquiry 24, 107–123.

Isaac, R. Mark, James, Duncan (2000). "Robustness of the incentive compatible combinatorial auction". Experimental Economics 3, 31–54.

Isaac, M.R., Plott, C.R. (1981). "The opportunity for conspiracy in restraint of trade". Journal of Economic Behavior and Organization 2, 1–30.

Isaac, M.R., Walker, J. (1985). "Information and conspiracy in sealed bid auctions". Journal of Economic Behavior and Organization 6, 139–159.

Kagel, John (1995). "Auctions: A survey of experimental research". In: Kagel, J., Roth, R. (Eds.), Handbook of Experimental Economics. Princeton University Press, Princeton, NJ, pp. 501–585.

Kagel, J., Hastard, R., Levin, D. (1987). "Information impact and allocation rules in auctions with affiliated private values: A laboratory study". Econometrica 55, 1275–1304.

Kagel, John H., Levin, D. (2001). "Behavior in multi-unit demand auctions: Experiments with uniform price and dynamic Vickrey auctions". Econometrica 69, 413–454.

Kagel, J., Levin, D. (2005). "Multi-unit demand auctions with synergies: Behavior in sealed bid versus ascending bid uniform price auctions". Games and Economic Behavior 53, 170–207.

Kagel, J., Kinross, S., Levin, D. (2001). "Comparing efficient multi-object auction institutions". Mimeo, Ohio State University.

Kwasnica, A. (2000). "The choice of cooperative strategies in sealed bid auctions". Journal of Economic Behavior and Organization 42, 323–346.

Kwasnica, A., Sherstyuk, K. (2001). "Collusion via signaling in multiple object auctions with complementarities: An experimental test". Mimeo, Penn State University.

List, J., Lucking-Reiley, D. (2000). "Demand reduction in multi-unit auctions: Evidence from a sportscard field experiment". American Economic Review 90 (4), 961–972.

Manelli, A., Sefton, M., Wilner, B. (2000). "Multi-unit auctions: A comparison of static and dynamic mechanisms". Center for Decision Research and Experimental Economics Working Paper, University of Nottingham.

McAfee, R.P., McMillan, J. (1996). "Analyzing the airwaves auctions". Journal of Economic Perspectives 10, 159–175.

McCabe, Kevin A., Rassenti, Stephen J., Smith, Vernon L. (1988). "Testing Vickrey's and other simultaneous multiple unit versions of the English auction". In: Isaac, R.M. (Ed.), Research in Experimental Economics 4, 1991. JAI Press, Greenwich, CT, pp. 45–79.

McCabe, Kevin A., Rassenti, Stephen J., Smith, Vernon L. (1990). "Auction institutional design: Theory and behavior of simultaneous multiple-unit generalizations of the Dutch and English auctions". American Economic Review 80 (5), 1276–1283.

Menkhaus, D., Phillips, O., Coatney, K. (2001). "Shared agents and competition in laboratory English auctions". Mimeo, University of Wyoming.

Milgrom, P. (1987). "Auction theory". In: Bewley, T. (Ed.), Advances of Economic Theory, Fifth World Congress. Cambridge University Press, Princeton, NJ, pp. 1–32.

Miller, G., Plott, C. (1985). "Revenue generating properties of sealed bid auctions: An experimental analysis of one-price and discriminative processes". In: Smith, V.L. (Ed.), Research in Experimental Economics, vol. 3. JAI Press, Greenwich, CT.

Noussair, Charles (1995). "Equilibria in a multi-object uniform-price auction with multi-unit demand". Economic Theory 5, 337–351.

Phillips, O., Menkhaus, D., Coatney, K., 2001. "Collusive practices in repeated English auctions: Experimental evidence on bidding rings." Mimeo, University of Wyoming.

Porter, D., Vragov, R. (2000). "An experimental examination of demand reduction in multi-unit versions of the uniform-price, Vickrey, and English auctions." Mimeo, University of Arizona.

Sherstyuk, K. (1999). "Collusion without conspiracy: An experimental study of one-sided auctions". Experimental Economics 2, 59–75.

Sherstyuk, K. (2001). "Collusion in private value ascending price auctions." Journal of Economic Behavior and Organization, in press.

Sherstyuk, K., Dulatre, J. (2001). "Auction format and bidder collusion in multi-object ascending price auctions." Mimeo, University of Hawaii.

Vickrey, W. (1961). "Counterspeculation, auctions, and competitive sealed tenders". Journal of Finance 16 (1), 8–37.

PART 1.2.3

NON-CONVEXITIES

Charles R. Plott, "Non-Convexities, Economies of Scale, Natural Monopoly and Monopolistic Competition"

Mark V. Van Boening and Nathaniel T. Wilcox, "Avoidable Cost Structures and Competitive Market Institutions"

Chapter 24

NON-CONVEXITIES, ECONOMIES OF SCALE, NATURAL MONOPOLY AND MONOPOLISTIC COMPETITION

CHARLES R. PLOTT

The behavior of markets characterized by non-convexities has been the subject of debate for almost a century. Marshall, for example, thought that the existence of large economies of scale in an industry would be a sufficient condition to guarantee that with any initial competition, the industry would ultimately result in monopoly. The great discussions between Joan Robinson and Edward Chamberlain were focused the principles that lie beneath the process of adaptation when non-convexities are present. A major question was whether monopoly or some constellation of oligopolies would evolve when competing firms had falling average costs throughout the range of demand. Much of industrial organization theory is built upon the principles of Cournot behavior. The theory predicts that Cournot prices will emerge from oligopolized markets and that such behavior will approach competitive behavior as the size of the economy grows large.

The classical discussion of the consequences of non-convexities took a new form as principles of game theory became joined with the structural features of large economies of scale. New models suggest that the threat of competition, as opposed to the existence of an actual competitor, serve to control monopolistic practices. The issues found in the literature explore and debate both the basic behavioral principles that might be at work as well as the application of those principles in particular situations.

The implications of these new models were first explored experimentally by Coursey et al. (1984) and by Coursey, Isaac, and Smith (1984). They studied markets with two potential competitors who were making decisions in a market with posted prices. (It is known that the textbook monopoly pricing model can predict the behavior of a single seller if the seller operates in a posted price institution.) The experiments produced the following results:

1. The existence of a single potential competitor has a clear influence on the pricing policies of a monopolist.
2. The prices that emerge are best modeled by contestable market theory. That is, monopoly emerges and the prices charged are close to the "limit price" that would make entry by the potential competitor unprofitable. The presence of sunk cost somewhat weakens this tendency.
3. While sales are monopolized, the industry is not. There is a tendency for the potential competitor to be a real competitor in that the competitor pays a price to expose its units to the market, even though it makes no sales.

A paper by Plott, Sugiyama, and Elbaz (1994) provides a replication and generalization of the earlier experiments. Agents had a choice between participation in a multiple unit double auction market in which they could acquire rents with almost certainty, and a market in which each agent had economies of scale and a potential for being the only seller. The generalization of previous work involves (i) the number of markets (expanded to prevent the possibility that entry might occur due to boredom), and (ii) a choice of scale, which allows the theoretical possibility of several different forms of industrial organization.

Figure 1 shows the cost structure of a representative agent seller in the Plott, Sugiyama and Elbaz experiments, should the agent sell in the market in which economies of scale existed. The cost functions conform to the classical notion of economies of scale and the related non-convexity of the production function. As Figure 1 shows, the costs are characterized by a series of short run cost functions. The agent had a choice of twenty-four short run cost functions (given in tabular form), which can be interpreted as different possible scales of plant. The figure shows that "long run" average costs were falling throughout the range of the demand function. An approximate market demand function was public information for the sellers. (It was redemption values of buyers minus a small transactions cost.) Sellers could only participate in one of the two markets that existed in the experiment. Thus, if a seller chose to enter this market, an opportunity cost of profits foregone in the other market should be added to the cost function shown in Figure 1. The added cost is not shown but is included in the equilibrium calculations for the models that are applied.

Sellers made private decisions about which of the two markets to enter. If the market with scale economies was chosen, then the seller chose three variables: the scale of plant that would be operated, the price to be posted and the maximum quantity to be offered. All decisions were made public simultaneously. After decisions were made public, sellers had the option of reducing their maximum quantity sold to zero. This, in effect, took the seller out of the market and prevented the possibility of selling only a small quantity, which would be very costly because of the falling nature of average costs. Cancellation announcements were made simultaneously and the sellers who chose cancellation incurred no cost, other than the profits foregone by not participating in the competitive market.

Figure 2 illustrates the predictions of three of several competing models.
(1) The monopoly model is shown with the lowest quantity and the highest prices.
(2) Several oligopolistic and monopolistic competitive organizations are compatible with the parameters in the market. Shown in the figure is the market price predicted by the Cournot model if a symmetric duopoly evolved. The market could also support a monopolistically competitive configuration of either three or four symmetric competitors following Cournot price and quantity strategies. These are not shown in the figure but the prices are about the same as would be the case of duopoly. Each agent would simply choose a smaller scale of plant and offer less quantity on the market. The market cannot support five symmetric sellers that are following Cournot behavior.
(3) The limit price of contested market theory is the case in which monopoly exists and charges a price equal to average cost of the optimal scale (given the market

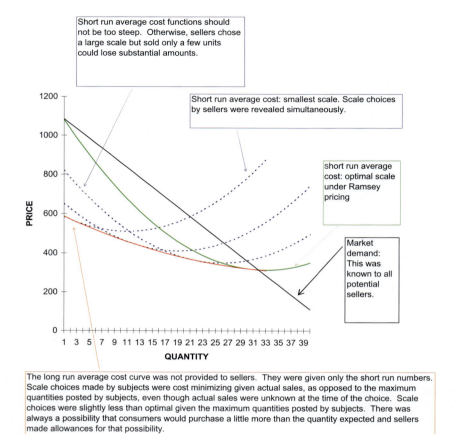

Figure 1. Identical average costs: subjects were given tables with the average cost and marginal cost associated with each of twenty four scales of plant. Each potential seller chose whether or not to leave a competitive market and enter this market, and if entry was chosen then a scale of plant and a maximum quantity offered and a (posed) price were also chosen.

demand and including the opportunity cost of foregone profits from the competitive market).

(4) A model of market collapse would predict that the threat of uncoordinated competition and resulting losses might prevent anyone from entering.
(5) A model of collusion would predict that some subset of firms would enter and through a coordination of strategies over time manage to hold prices at a monopoly level. Each, knowing that the benefits of collusion would disappear if

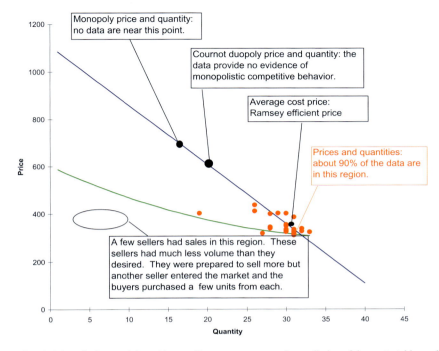

Figure 2. Model predictions and data: Almost all outcomes are near the prediction of the contestable markets model. Monopoly almost always emerges. Prices of the monopolist are always near average cost. There is no evidence of market collapse. There is no evidence of collusion. There is no evidence of monopolistic competition. The policing of the monopoly is done by entrants that stand ready to undercut the single seller should it attempt to charge monopoly level prices. This "contingent entry" is costly and can be viewed as a loss of efficiency due to the policing of the single seller.

any deviation from cooperation was detected by others, would hold to the implicit collusion and thereby render the organization stable.

The results of three experiments with seven agents are contained in Figure 2:

1. Under the conditions of non-convexities – and in particular the conditions of economies of scale and no institutional barriers to entry – the organizational form that emerged was monopoly; all sales were made by a single seller.
2. No evidence exists for any form of organization other than monopoly. No oligopolies or monopolistically competitive agents emerged. No conspiracies developed although some of the pricing might have represented attempts to collude or signal a willingness to collude.
3. There was an instance of market collapse in which no seller entered the market or all sellers canceled their decision after observing the choices of other sellers. This occurred only one time out of all periods.
4. Prices were near the limit price predicted by contestable market theory.

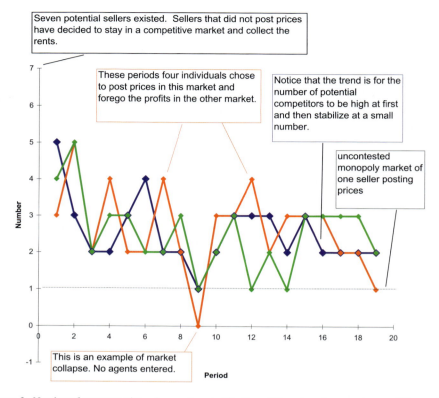

Figure 3. Number of agents posting prices each period for three different market experiments. This number provides a measure of both potential competition and the resources used to police monopoly pricing. If more than one seller posts price then the monopolist might be the single seller but there are other agents that have invested to become a seller should the monopolist post price that is sufficiently high to give them sales.

That is, prices were near the Ramsey optimal average cost.
5. Scale choices and quantity choices reflected the expectation of sellers that they would be the only seller and that they planned to sell at prices near average cost. Scale choices were near the optimal given market demand.

Figure 3 provides an insight about the process through which the contestable markets work. The figure shows the number of sellers that posted prices in the contested market for each period of each experiment. As shown, in almost all periods of all experiments there existed more than one agent that paid the opportunity cost to compete in the contested market and was prepared to sell. That is, the contested market was actually contested. The prices prepared by the potential entrants ranged from near average cost to substantially above average cost, perhaps reflecting the hope that the monopolist would get "greedy" and charge prices substantially above cost. This phenomenon leads the conclusion that follows.

6. The cost of policing the monopoly decreases with time. The fact that entrants always existed in the market indicates an efficiency cost of policing the monopolized market in terms of product foregone in the competitive market. As the number of posting firms decreases, the efficiency loss decreases.

The results of the Plott, Sugiyama and Elbaz experiments illustrated in the figures are consistent with the earlier experiments. Of course how these results might change if the scale decisions were made and announced before the pricing decision was made is unknown. Other variables of interest might involve longer term investment decisions and/or no ability to cancel quantity decisions, etc. but to date, these have not been studied.

References

Coursey, Don, Isaac, R. Mark, Luke, Margaret, Smith, Vernon L. (1984). "Market contestability in the presence of sunk (entry) cost". RAND Journal of Economics 15 (2), 69–84.

Coursey, Don, Isaac, R. Mark, Smith, Vernon L. (1984). "Natural monopoly and contested markets: Some experimental results". Journal of Law and Economics 27 (1), 91–113.

Plott, Charles R., Sugiyama, Alexandre Borges, Elbaz, Gilad. (1994). "Economies of scale, natural monopoly, and imperfect competition in an experimental market". Southern Economic Journal 61 (2), 261–287.

Chapter 25

AVOIDABLE COST STRUCTURES AND COMPETITIVE MARKET INSTITUTIONS

MARK V. BOENING and NATHANIEL T. WILCOX

Relatively simple, avoidable cost structures can undermine the trading efficiency of otherwise efficient competitive market institutions. The continuous double auction, often considered an empirical benchmark (e.g., Friedman and Rust, 1992), exhibits "efficiency roller coasters" in avoidable cost structures. Those same structures are problematic even for market institutions that are designed to eliminate, or at least alleviate, market inefficiency (Van Boening and Wilcox, 1997; Durham et al., 1996). Other research involving "lumpy" or non-convex cost structures indicates that market institutions are generally more efficient that non-market mechanisms (Ledyard, Porter, and Wessen, 1998), and that the relative performance of market institutions may depend on both supply and demand conditions (Ledyard, Porter, and Rangel, 1997). Non-convex cost structures appear to pose a significant challenge for institutional design, and experimental data can be useful in meeting this challenge (e.g., Plott, 1997). This paper summarizes results from some competitive experimental markets with a simple avoidable cost structure.

1. A Simple Avoidable Cost Structure

Avoidable costs (Telser, 1978) are not fixed costs. While fixed costs cannot be avoided by shutting down a plant, an existing plant sometimes has a minimum positive output level and substantial variable cost associated with producing at that level. As this cost can be avoided by foregoing production, it is called a plant's avoidable cost. One example is the recurring maintenance cost of shutting down and then bringing back on line electricity generators; they are sometimes "mothballed" to avoid this cost. Another example is airline flight costs, as the bulk of variable costs are those required to fly the aircraft, and the marginal cost of passengers and freight typically account for a small portion of total variable cost.

Figure 1 shows avoidable cost structures in two experimental market environments. There are four sellers, and each has an avoidable cost and a capacity constraint. A seller does not incur her avoidable cost if she does not sell any units, but if she sells as many as one unit, she incurs the avoidable cost. As there are no marginal costs, a seller's total production cost equals her avoidable cost, regardless of whether she sells one unit or her entire capacity. A seller's average cost at capacity is her avoidable cost divided by her capacity. For example, Figure 1 shows Seller 1 with an eight-unit capacity and an avoidable cost of 960, so her average cost at capacity is $960 \div 8 = 120$. At any price

Handbook of Experimental Economics Results, Volume 1
Copyright © 2008 Elsevier B.V. All rights reserved
DOI: 10.1016/S1574-0722(07)00025-X

Ch. 25: Avoidable Cost Structures and Competitive Market Institutions 207

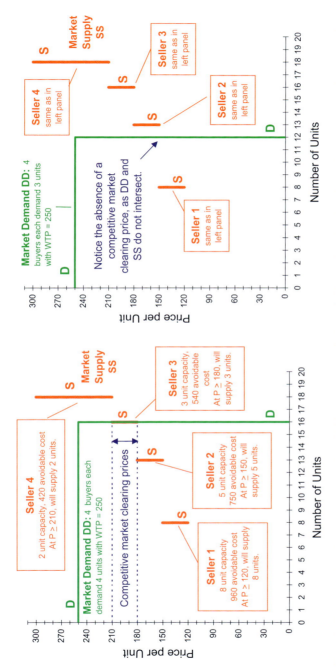

Figure 1. Experimental market environments with avoidable cost structures. Left panel: Observe that when the 4 buyers demand 4 units each, any price in the open interval (180, 210) is a competitive market clearing price, and the maximum demand of 16 units exactly exhausts the capacity of the three most efficient sellers (Sellers 1, 2 and 3). Right panel: Observe that when the 4 buyers demand only 3 units each, there is no competitive market clearing price, and the maximum demand of 12 units does not exhaust the capacity of the two most efficient sellers (Sellers 1 and 2).

greater than or equal to 120, she will provide all eight of her units to the market, and at any price below 120, she will provide zero units to the market. Similarly, at any price at or above 150, Seller 2 will provide five units to the market. Seller 3's average cost at capacity is 180 (three unit capacity, 540 avoidable cost), and Seller 4's is 210 (two unit capacity, 420 avoidable cost).

In Figure 1, the market supply curve SS is a series of spikes at each seller's average cost at capacity. At any price below 120, none of the four sellers will supply units to the market. At any price between 120 and 150, Seller 1 will enter the market and supply her eight units, but none of the other three sellers will supply units. Thus the market supply curve is horizontal from 120 to 150, above eight units. At a price between 150 and 180, market supply is thirteen units: Sellers 1 and 2 will supply eight and five units, respectively, while Sellers 3 and 4 each supply zero units. Seller 3 will add her three units to market supply at any price above 180, and Seller 4 will enter the market with her two units at any price above 210.

In the market environments shown in Figure 1, there are four buyers with a demand capacity of either four units each (left panel) or three units each (right panel). All four buyers have a maximum willingness to pay, or WTP of 250 for any one unit. Thus the market demand curve DD is horizontal at 250 until maximum demand is reached, and then it drops vertically to the axis. In the left panel, the maximum demand is 16 units, as each of the four buyers has a demand capacity of four units. In the right panel, each of the four buyers demands at most three units, so maximum demand is 12 units.

In the left panel of Figure 1, market demand and supply intersect on the open interval (180, 210), so any price in that range is a competitive market clearing price, and the maximum demand exactly exhausts the capacity of the three most efficient sellers (Sellers 1, 2 and 3). In the right panel, each of four buyers has a three-unit demand capacity, so the maximum demand is only 12 units. Note the absence of a competitive market clearing price or prices, as the market demand and supply curves do not intersect. Also note that the maximum demand (12 units) does not exhaust the capacity output of the two efficient sellers (Sellers 1 and 2, total capacity of 13 units).

2. Three Market Institutions

The multiple unit double auction, or MUDA (Plott, 1991), is an electronic double auction. Buyers and sellers bargain multilaterally and publicly over contract prices, with buyers making bids and sellers making asks sequentially as they wish. The highest (or standing) bid and lowest (or standing) ask are instantaneously updated and displayed to the entire market via private computer screens. Binding contracts occur when any buyer accepts the standing ask or when any seller accepts the standing bid. One important feature of MUDA is that a buyer (seller) who accepts an ask (bid) can purchase (sell) any or all of the units offered at that ask (bid). That is, bids and asks can be for multiple or "blocks" of units at a given per-unit bid/ask price, but agents are not obliged to accept all the units in a multiple unit bid/ask. For instance, a buyer may accept just one unit of a three-unit block offered by some seller.

The bundled unit double auction, or BUDA (Van Boening and Wilcox, 1997), is a variation of MUDA that allows all-or-none bids, asks and contracts for 1-, 2- or 3-unit bundles. For example, if a buyer accepts a 2-unit ask, he is obliged to purchase both units at the given per-unit ask price. Additionally, in the "restricted BUDA" or RBUDA, 1-unit trading is not allowed, so that all bid, ask and contract activity is for 2-unit and 3-unit blocks. In the avoidable cost structure shown in the right panel of Figure 1, theoretically efficient outcomes require non-linear prices and that no 1-unit trades occur (Van Boening and Wilcox, 1997). BUDA and RBUDA were designed to promote nonl-inear prices, and so they should be more efficient institutions than MUDA, as the double auction has a stylized tendency towards "the law of one price." And RBUDA should be more efficient than BUDA, as RBUDA explicitly prohibits the 1-unit trades that are ruled out by theory.

The Smart Market (Durham et al., 1996) is a version of the posted-offer market in which each seller submits a two-part price: a fixed vendor's fee, which must be paid before any units can be sold, and a per-unit price and a corresponding quantity. Automated buyers are programmed to reveal demand. A smart-market computing center then maximizes total surplus subject to the price, quantity and vendor fee constraints. Sellers can protect themselves from losses by simply by charging their avoidable cost as their vendor fee. Additionally, if each seller offers her capacity and the per-unit prices do not exceed the buyers' value, the Smart Market will choose the most efficient sellers and demand will be exhausted. Thus this institution is expected to consistently achieve (near) 100% efficiency.

3. The Results

Figure 2 compares the per-period trading efficiency of a standard marginal cost structure to the two avoidable cost structures under double auction (MUDA) trading (see Van Boening and Wilcox, 1996). Trading efficiency is defined in the usual manner, as total trading profit across all buyers and sellers divided by the maximum possible gains from trade. In Figure 2, just over 80% of the trading periods in the marginal cost structure are 90–100% efficient. This contrasts sharply with both of the avoidable cost structures, where less than half of the trading periods are 90–100% efficient (relative frequency 0.44 with a competitive market clearing equilibrium, 0.35 without a competitive equilibrium). In fact, when there is no competitive equilibrium, efficiency is as likely to be less than 70% as it is to be 90–100%: 37% ($= 0.27 + 0.10$) of the trading periods are less than 70% efficient, and 35% of the trading periods are 90–100% efficient.

Figure 3 shows per-period trading efficiency data for MUDA, BUDA, RBUDA and the Smart Market in the avoidable cost structure with no competitive equilibrium (summarized from Van Boening and Wilcox, 1997; Durham et al., 1996). Recall that BUDA,

Figure 2. Per-period trading efficiency in marginal cost and avoidable cost structures. Observe that: (a) In the marginal cost baseline, just over 80% of the trading periods are 100–90% efficient, but in the avoidable cost double auctions, less than 50% of the trading periods are 100–90% efficient (relative frequencies of 0.44 and 0.35). (b) In the absence of a competitive equilibrium, the trading efficiency in avoidable cost double auctions is equally likely to be less than 70% (relative frequency of $0.27 + 0.10 = 0.37$) as it is to be 90% or more (relative frequency of 0.35).

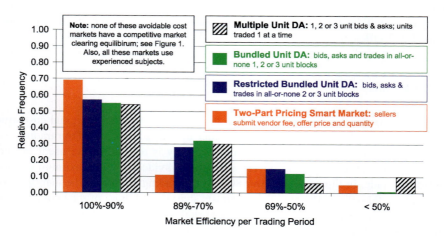

Figure 3. Per-period trading efficiency in four different institutions with avoidable cost structures. Observe that the new institutions (BUDA, RBUDA and Smart Market) each have a greater frequency of trading periods in the 100–90% interval than does the standard double auction (MUDA), but (a) all four institutions have a frequency less than 0.70 in this interval, which is unusual for experienced subjects, and (b) the greatest difference is only 15% (0.54 for MUDA, 0.69 for Smart Market). Also observe that in all four institutions, well over 10% of the trading periods have efficiency less than 70%. This is also unusual for experienced subjects.

RBUDA and the Smart Market were specifically designed to facilitate efficient outcomes efficiency in avoidable cost structures. The trading efficiencies for all four institutions are relatively low, at least compared to what one would expect in a comparable marginal cost structure with experienced subjects. Relative to the double auction, the two-part pricing Smart Market does increase the frequency of trading periods that are 90–100% efficient (relative frequencies of 0.54 for MUDA, 0.69 for Smart Market), but even in the Smart Market almost a third of the trading periods are less than 90% efficient. BUDA and RBUDA only marginally improve trading efficiency relative to MUDA. On a positive note, BUDA, RBUDA and the Smart Market all have a lower frequency of trading periods in the "<50% efficient" range than does MUDA. However, in all four institutions over 10% of the trading periods are less than 70% efficient, even though all of the markets summarized in Figure 3 used twice or three times experienced subjects. The failure to consistently achieve high trading efficiency is perplexing.

4. A Next Step: Cooperative Arrangements?

The search continues for a competitive institution that will consistently yield high trading efficiency in these avoidable cost structures. But frequently, such institutions have a uniform pricing tendency that cannot implement surplus shares that are in the core of the underlying cooperative game (Van Boening and Wilcox, 1996). This suggests that cooperative arrangements that allow for greater transfer flexibility might also implement stable, efficient outcomes, particularly when no competitive equilibrium exits (Telser, 1988). Archibald, Van Boening, and Wilcox (2002) allow experienced subjects to make explicit arrangements as to per-unit prices, output quantity and division of aggregate seller profit (i.e., side payments) in avoidable cost markets. In one of three different experimental protocols, efficient outcomes were consistently observed. However, under the other two protocols, collusion often resulted in inefficient production. Given the sensitivity of those results to changes in protocol, cooperative market institutions also remain an area of fruitful research.

References

Archibald, Glen, Van Boening, Mark V., Wilcox, Nathaniel T. (2002). "Avoidable cost: Can collusion succeed where competition fails?" In: Research in Experimental Economics: Experiments Investigating Market Power, vol. 9. JAI Press, Stamford, CT.
Durham, Yvonne, Rassenti, Stephen, Smith, Vernon, Van Boening, Mark, Wilcox, Nathaniel T. (1996). "Can core allocations be achieved in avoidable fixed cost environments using two-part pricing competition?" Annals of Operation Research 68, 61–88.
Friedman, Daniel, Rust, John (Eds.) (1992). "The Double Auction Market: Institutions, Theories, and Evidence". Proc. of the Santa Fe Institute, vol. XIV. Addison–Wesley, Reading, MA.
Ledyard, John O., Porter, David, Rangel, Antonio (1997). "Experiments testing multiobject allocation mechanisms". Journal of Economics and Management Strategy 6 (3), 639–675.

Ledyard, John O., Porter, David, Wessen, Randii (1998). "A market-based mechanism for allocating space shuttle secondary payload priority". Experimental Economics 2 (3), 173–195.

Plott, Charles R. (1991). "A computerized laboratory market system and research support systems for the multiple unit double auction". Social Science Working Paper 783, California Institute of Technology.

Plott, Charles R. (1997). "Laboratory experimental testbeds: Application to the PCS auction". Journal of Economics and Management Strategy 6 (3), 605–638.

Telser, Lester G. (1978). "Economic Theory and the Core". University of Chicago, Chicago, IL.

Telser, Lester G. (1988). "A Theory of Efficient Cooperation and Competition". Cambridge University Press, Cambridge, UK.

Van Boening, Mark V., Wilcox, Nathaniel T. (1996). "Avoidable cost: Ride a double auction roller coaster". American Economic Review 86 (3), 461–477.

Van Boening, Mark V., Wilcox, Nathaniel T. (1997). "Generalizing the double auction for nonconvexitites: An experimental exploration". Tms, University of Houston.

PART 1.3

DYNAMICS OF MARKET ADJUSTMENTS

Charles R. Plott, "Principles of Adjustment and Stability"

Vernon L. Smith and Mark Van Boening, "Off-Floor Trading, Market Disintegration and Price Volatility in Bid/Ask Markets"

Praveen Kujal, "Quantitative Restrictions in Experimental Posted-Offer Markets"

Arlington W. Williams, "Price Bubbles in Large Financial Asset Markets"

David Porter and Vernon L. Smith, "Price Bubbles"

Eric O'N. Fisher, "Experiments with Arbitrage Across Assets"

Charles Noussair and Charles Plott, "Bubbles and Crashes in Experimental Asset Markets: Common Knowledge Failure?"

Timothy N. Cason and Daniel Friedman, "A Comparison of Market Institutions"

Amnon Rapoport and Darryl A. Seale, "Coordination Success in Non-cooperative Large Group Market Entry Games"

Chapter 26

PRINCIPLES OF MARKET ADJUSTMENT AND STABILITY

CHARLES R. PLOTT

California Institute of Technology

Data produced in market experiments exhibit a process of convergence to near the levels predicted by the static competitive equilibrium model. The major result reported in this section is that classical models of market dynamics explain important features of that convergence process. That is, the (current) answer to the question of how markets manage to find the competitive equilibrium is that price movements are governed by a set of principles outlined by classical models of dynamics as opposed to technical aspects of the equilibrium itself.[1] Those principles tend to guide a process of equilibration to the competitive equilibrium.

Market stability can be used as a window to understand dynamics because the circumstances of stability and instability provide an opportunity to clearly separate the principles that govern convergence. Theoretical instances in which instability can be observed typically require some sort of "perverse" market conditions, such as a downward-sloping supply or an upward-sloping demand. Thus part of the experimental problem is the creation of circumstances in which such conditions exist.

1. Theory

Three distinct classical models of dynamics are found in the literature and these models make very sharp predictions about stability. By studying competing predictions about stability, one can perform a clear test between the models. Each of the three is illustrated in Figure 1. The models are all founded on a limited number of parameters relative to modern game theory. Basically, the only variables are demand price, demand quantity, supply price, supply quantity and time. The relationships assumed are of the form

$$D(P_d, Q_d) = 0 \quad \text{and} \quad S(P_s, Q_s) = 0, \tag{1}$$

which characterizes the behavior of the demand and supply sides of the market, respectively. The demand side of the market is characterized as a demand price, P_d, and a demand quantity, Q_d. The supply side has a similar characterization (P_s, Q_s). Time is

---

[1] For example, the equilibrium itself could be defined as the quantity demanded at a price equals quantity supplied (Walras) or demand price equals supply price (Marshall) or as the intersection of demand and supply correspondences (Debreu). The choice of which definition is used in a model might not be as important as the implications the definition holds for price movements.

Handbook of Experimental Economics Results, Volume 1
Copyright © 2008 Elsevier B.V. All rights reserved
DOI: 10.1016/S1574-0722(07)00026-1

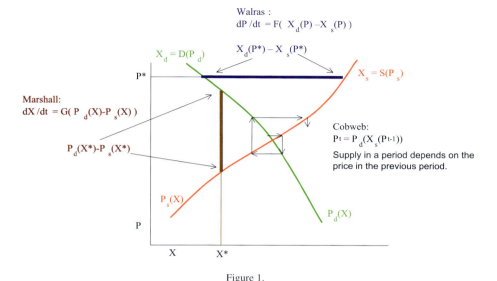

Figure 1.

not clearly defined and could be any of: clock time, time measured in trading periods, or time measured in number of trades. The functions themselves suffer from some ambiguity as to whether or not they characterize a stock or a flow. Similarly, prices are not defined operationally by the theory. In the experiments reported below, the assumptions about these variables are made both explicitly and implicitly in terms of the experimental procedures, parameters and measurements.

1.1. Cobweb Dynamics

The model assumes that only one price exists in a market, so demand price equals supply price equals P. However, the supply is not determined by the price in the current period. It is determined by the prices of the past, such as the previous period. Thus the equation defining the system balancing of demand and supply is

$$D(P_t) - S(P_{t-1}) = 0. \tag{2}$$

That is, the quantity demanded responds to the price at the current instant while the quantity supplied lags, dictated by the price of the previous period. According to the model the market is unstable if the slope of the demand curve is sufficiently greater than the slope of the supply curve. The possibility of instability is illustrated in Figure 1, in which initial prices move away from the equilibrium in a manner that can be interpreted as a spiral (prices cycle from high to low as periods progress).

1.2. The Walrasian (Hicks, Samuelson) Dynamics

The Walrasian model assumes that only one price exists in a market, so demand price equals supply price equals P. Equilibrium balancing occurs when the quantity demanded at a price equals the quantity supplied at that price. The dynamic of adjustment is characterized by the principle

$$dP/dt = F(D(P) - S(P)). \tag{3}$$

As illustrated in Figure 1, the principle asserts that prices will adjust to reflect the difference between the quantity demanded at that price and the quantity supplied. The principle seems to assume the law of one price in a market; if the quantity demanded at a price equals the quantity supplied, then prices do not change.

In the cases in which the supply curve is downward sloping (and demand also downward sloping) the condition under which an equilibrium is stable is that the demand curve crosses the supply curve coming from below the supply curve. Similarly, if demand is upward sloping and supply is also upward sloping, the condition under which an equilibrium is stable is again that the demand curve cross the supply curve coming from below the supply curve. If an equilibrium is not stable, then it is unstable (neglecting boundary cases).

1.3. Marshallian Dynamics

The Marshallian model assumes that demand quantity equals supply quantity equals Q. Equilibrium is defined by the equating of demand price and supply price. The system dynamics is characterized by the principle

$$dQ/dt = F(P_d(Q) - P_s(Q)). \tag{4}$$

The principle asserts that markets adjust by changes in the quantity. Quantity in the market will adjust to reflect the profitability of the marginal unit. As illustrated in Figure 1, if the demand price of the marginal unit is greater (less) than the supply price, then quantity will increase (decrease). As stated, the principle asserts nothing specific about prices but it does appear to assume that units are exchanged in the order of maximum surplus for otherwise the marginal units would not be well defined.

According to the model, if the demand curve crosses the supply curve coming from above the supply curve, then the equilibrium is stable. If the demand curve crosses the supply curve from below the supply curve, then the equilibrium is unstable. Notice that the conditions for stability can be exactly the opposite of those for the Walrasian model.

2. Experiments

2.1. Instability does not Occur under Conditions Predicted by the Cobweb Model

The experiments create a favorable condition for observing the type of instability predicted by the model by structuring an experimental market in which a lag could arise. The experiments reported in Figure 2 demonstrate that the cobweb model fails to make reliable predictions. The fact that market adjustments do not follow the lag assumed by the model was first demonstrated by Carlson (1967), so in essence, the experiments from Johnson and Plott (1989), referenced here, are replications and (substantial) extensions of Carlson's results. In the experiment suppliers made a decision on the quantity to supply before a period began and paid for the quantity chosen regardless of the number of units sold or the price they brought in the market. Thus, the supplier could lose money.

The first period the demand curve was at the lower of the two levels shown in Figure 2. After the first period, the demand curve shifted to the larger demand. This was implemented so that the suppliers were completely unaware of the shift. The shift was employed so the quantity supplied would be low (in the period just after the shift) and thereby producing prices above the equilibrium and starting a process of divergence according to the model. The solid green line is the competitive equilibrium predicted by the static model.

Two separate market institutions are studied. The first is the double auction and the second is the one-price sealed bid/sealed offer institution in which buyers and sellers submit orders. The orders are arrayed as in demand and supply the appropriate trades are made at the equilibrium price.

Typical results from the double auction are reproduced in the top panel. The red lines plot the competitive equilibrium given the production that took place in the period. The cobweb model predicts that the cycles will explode to a limit cycle. As can be seen the second period (the first period of high demand after the low demand experience) has only small supply. The supply is represented by the length of the red line. This small supply is exactly what was hoped for in the design. Prices move up rapidly, but not close to the competitive equilibrium given the supply. In the next period a large supply is forthcoming. Prices move up and then crash near the end of the period. In the third period, supplies are slightly above the static competitive equilibrium supply and prices hover near the static competitive equilibrium with sell-offs near the end of the period. As can be seen, supplies change over the succeeding periods but the general levels of activity are near the competitive equilibrium. The data are nearer to the static competitive equilibrium than the limit cycle predicted by the cobweb model.

The lower display in Figure 2 contains data from a sealed bid/offer process. The evidence of a cycle is greater under this institution than the double auction. However, the data do not explode to near the limit cycle predicted by the cobweb model. Indeed, the market activity is much closer to the static competitive equilibrium.

218   C.R. Plott

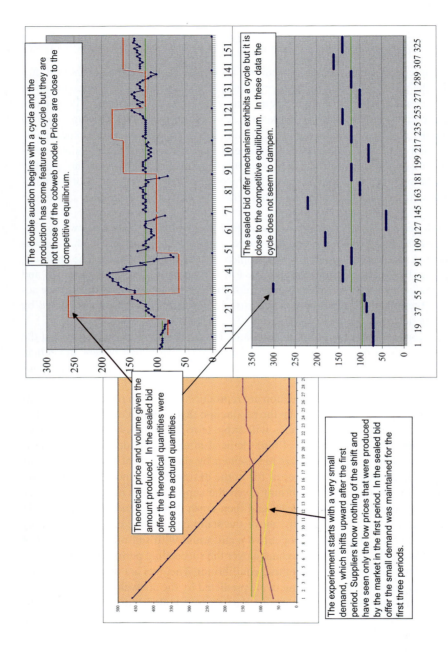

Figure 2. Both the double auction and the sealed bid offer mechanism converge to the competitive equilibrium price. Some small cycles are evident but the tendency is convergence.

2.2. Walrasian Dynamics and not Marshallian Dynamics Capture the Backward-Bending Case

The classic case of the backward-bending supply has been studied in Plott (2000) and the major result is represented here. Preferences of a subject with a capacity to supply x are induced using incentives roughly like those in the left panel of Figure 3. Those who could supply sold units of x and were paid in francs. Prices in the market were prices per unit of x. Where f is the total franc income of a supplier and x is the number of units supplied, the incentives given suppliers were of the form $U(f, x) = \$$. That is, the dollars earned by a subject were a function of the amount of x he/she supplied and the total francs received from the sale. The level surfaces (indifference curves) were similar to those in the left panel. Application of the competitive model produced a backward-bending supply curve like the one shown in the right panel.

The demand curve was structured to yield several equilibria which differed in stability properties. A stylized demand curve is shown in Figure 3 and the actual parameters used in experiments are shown in Figure 4. The experiment called for initial periods to operate under the parameters in the left panel of Figure 4. After equilibration, or sufficient movement for purposes of the experiment, the demand curve was shifted so the stability properties of all equilibria were reversed. Thus, if the data moved to an equilibrium before the shift then it became unstable after the shift according to the same theory that predicted it would go there in the first place. Such an experiment demonstrates that the model predicts movements both to and from an equilibrium.

The data from a typical experiment are in Figure 5. From the discussion and the preferences in Figure 3, the reader can imagine how differently shaped indifference curves can be induced and, in particular, can imagine how shapes can be chosen such that they produce the theoretical supply curve found in Figure 4. The experiment begins with the parameters represented by the supply curve S and the demand curve D_1. Then, after several periods the demand curve is changed to D_2 with the supply curve remaining at S. After a few more periods, the demand curve shifts back to D_1 and the supply curve still remains at S. As these shifts are made, all equilibria shift between stability and instability.

Notice first that there are several equilibria. On the left, points a, b and d are all equilibria but the stability properties differ. Under conditions D_1, points a and d are Walrasian stable and Marshall unstable. Point b is Walrasian unstable and Marshallian stable. By contrast, under conditions D_2 the equilibria are points a, b and c. Points b and c are Walrasian stable and Marshallian unstable. Point a is Walrasian unstable and Marshallian stable. Thus, for each of these equilibria the two models always give exactly the opposite predictions about stability. Other equilibria exist on the boundaries but these will not be discussed.

The nature of the exercise is to start with the parameters D_1 and S. If the market converges to one of the equilibria it will be a stable equilibrium according to one of the models. Prices should only converge to a stable equilibrium and thus convergence to one of the points will lend support for one of the models and serve as evidence against

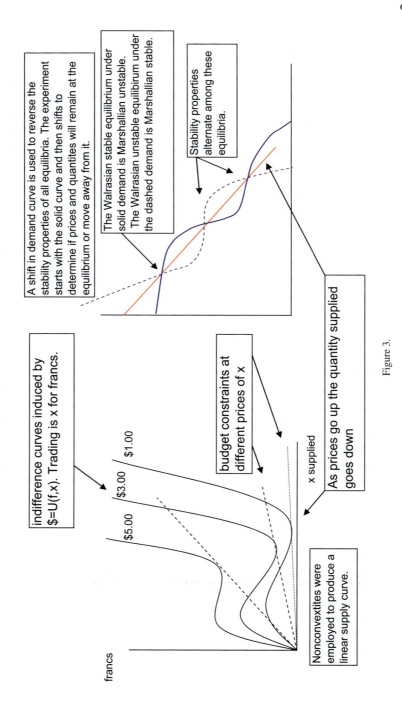

Figure 3.

Ch. 26: Principles of Market Adjustment and Stability

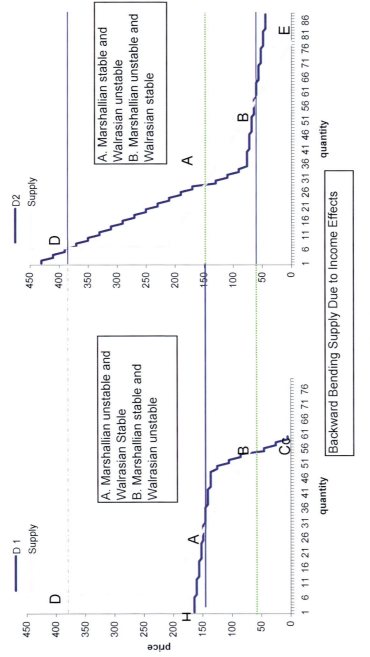

Figure 4.

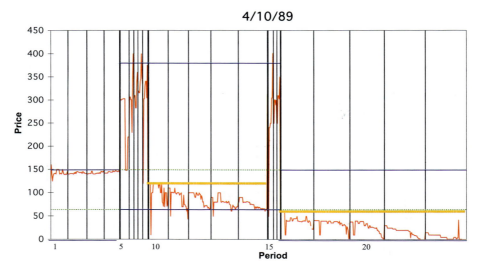

Figure 5.

the others. After the shift, the stability properties of all equilibria are reversed so the equilibrium where the prices exist will become unstable according to the model that had previously been supported. Thus, if the principles of the model were active then one would expect the prices to move away from the equilibrium toward one of the other stable equilibria of the model.

The basic result is that the data from experiments support the Walrasian model and not the Marshallian model. As can be seen in Figure 5, when the markets begin under demand condition D_1, prices converge to point a, an equilibrium that is stable according to the Walrasian model and unstable according to the Marshallian model. When the demand shifts to D_2 and point a becomes an unstable equilibrium according to Walras (stable according to Marshall) and the data move rapidly upward toward the stable Walrasian equilibrium that exists at point c. Such exercises produce strong evidence for the Walrasian model.

Additional exercises represented in the figure give additional support for Walras. About period 12 under demand conditions D_2 a price ceiling was imposed on the system just below the Walrasian unstable equilibrium at a and as can be seen prices bumped against the ceiling and then immediately fell to the nearest Walrasian stable equilibrium at b. The price ceiling was removed during period 16 and prices jumped over the unstable equilibrium at a and moved toward the stable equilibrium at c. To complete the demonstration, the demand parameters were returned to D_1 and a price ceiling was imposed just below the resulting unstable Walrasian equilibrium at b. The result was that prices fell to the Walrasian stable equilibrium at d. Removal of the price ceiling in the final period resulted in prices jumping away from the Walrasian stable d equilibrium to the stable a equilibrium. Thus the behavior is rather unintuitive, since high prices forced down by a price ceiling and without and demand or supply change resulted in prices falling still further. When the (non-binding) ceiling was removed, prices jumped up,[2] moving toward and then through an unstable equilibrium and then on to a different stable equilibrium.

Such an exercise demonstrates three points. First, market equilibria can exhibit instability. Second, the nature of the instability and stability in this type of environment is captured by Walrasian adjustment as opposed to Marshallian. Third, there is something wrong with the theory because jumps across unstable equilibria should not occur. But, such jumps are observed. Evidently the principles of dynamics are not restricted to "local" dynamics. Thus, the theory is partially misspecified.

2.3. *The Marshallian Model and not the Walrasian Model Best Describes Market Behavior in the Case of a Marshallian Externality or a "Fad"*

In order to study the second environment that leads to "perversely shaped" curves, an externality must be introduced. In the case of a fad this is accomplished in Plott and Smith (1999) by letting the redemption values of the individual buyers be a function of own purchases as well as the total volume of purchases of others. Of course, the supply case could be studied just as well as it was in Plott and George (1992). Let X_i be the consumption of individual i and let X_{-i} be the total consumption of agents other than individual i. Redemption values are of the form $R(X_i, X_{-i})$ and let X^e_{-i} be the expectations of individual i about the consumption of others.

According to theory market demand is derived from the incentives $R(X_i, X_{-i})$ through the decision problem defined by (5) and (6).

$$\max R(X_i, X^e_{-i}) - PX, \qquad (5)$$

$$X^e_{-i} = X_{-i}. \qquad (6)$$

The problem defined by (5) says that the individual attempts to maximize money income based on the redemption values and the expectations of the consumption of others. Equation (6) is a form of rational expectations, which says that the expectations of individuals are correct. From these equations an upward sloping demand can be computed as shown in Figure 6, although this demand curve is a much more complex theoretical construction than the ordinary demand curve since it has an element of rational expectations. Indeed it is more of an equilibrium curve than a demand curve in the usual sense.

All experiments with the upward-sloping supply curve are with the double auction. The downward-sloping supply curve with a Marshallian externality was studied in Plott

---

[2] Isaac and Plott (1981) were the first to report the fact that a non-binding price control can have surprising effects on a market. The fact that removal of the non-binding controls could cause a switch in the equilibrium selected was new with the demonstration shown in the figure.

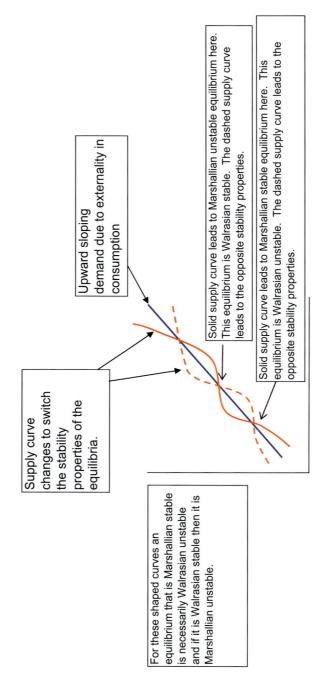

Figure 6. Market demand and supply for the case of a fad or other externality that causes an upward slope demand.

Ch. 26: Principles of Market Adjustment and Stability

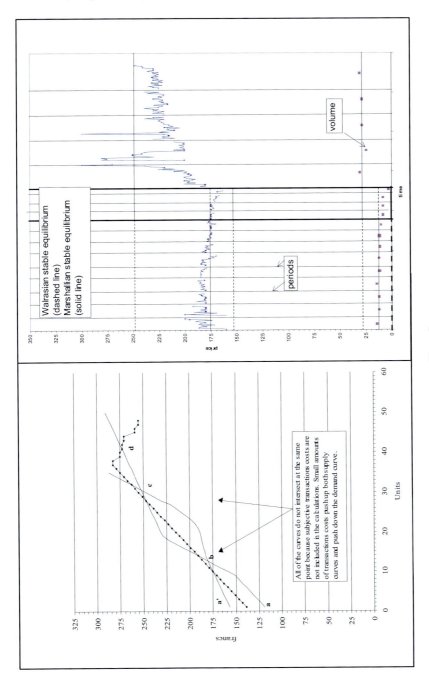

Figure 7.

and George under the double auction, the sealed bid/offer and a form of tatonnement with results similar to those reported here.

The structure of the experimental environment is shown in Figure 7. The demand curve is held constant over periods while the supply curve is shifted to create different stability conditions of the equilibria.

The results of three different conditions are reproduced in the right hand panel of Figure 7. First, the markets were opened under supply conditions such that the equilibrium at point b is stable according to Marshall but is unstable according to Walras. The supply conditions are then changed so that the stability conditions are reversed. Finally, a "volume guarantee" is added so the individuals get redemption values as if the volume was slightly above the volume at point b even though the volume might have been less. This started the system to the "right" of the equilibrium volume at b, which is an unstable equilibrium according to Marshall.

As can be seen in Figure 7, the data move toward the stable Marshallian (unstable Walrasian) equilibrium at point b. When point b becomes an unstable Marshallian (stable Walrasian) equilibrium, the market immediately moves to one of the nearby stable Marshallian equilibria (at the boundary). The volume completely dries up to zero. Then, when the process is started above the unstable equilibrium at b, the market immediately moves toward the nearest stable Marshallian (unstable Walrasian) equilibrium above b.

3. Summary

First, market prices can exhibit the type of instability predicted by classical dynamic models.[3] Second, the conditions under which instability is observed are not captured by the cobweb model but such conditions are captured by models of the form developed by Marshall and Walras in which the market has "perversely shaped" curves, such as an upward-sloped demand or downward-sloped supply. Third, the appropriate model, Marshall or Walras, depends on properties of the underlying demand and supply. If the special shape is due to the existence of an externality such as a fad or a Marshallian external economy, then experiments have demonstrated that the Marshallian model is the appropriate model. If the special shape is due to income effects, then the appropriate model is the Walrasian model and not the Marshallian model. That is, if the special shape is due to income effects such as Giffen goods or a backward-bending supply of labor, then the Walrasian model reflects the appropriate principles. In summary, the mystery of the price discovery process is solved, in part, by classical models of adjustment.

---

[3] In a very early paper Smith (1965) conducted experiments on the nature of dynamic adjustment but his design was inadequate for separating the competing theories and his econometric analysis misled him about the phenomena. He mistakenly rejected the Walrasian model.

References

Carlson, John A. (1967). "The stability of an experimental market with a supply-response lag". Southern Economic Journal 33 (3), 305–321.
Isaac, R. Mark, Plott, Charles R. (1981). "Price controls and the behavior of auction markets: An experimental examination". American Economic Review 71, 448–459.
Johnson, Michael D., Plott, Charles R. (1989). "The effect of two trading institutions on price expectations and the stability of supply-response lag markets". Journal of Economic Psychology 10, 189–216.
Plott, Charles R. (2000). "Market stability: Backward bending supply in a laboratory market". Economic Inquiry 38 (1), 1–18.
Plott, Charles R., George, Glen (1992). "Marshallian vs. Walrasian stability in an experimental market". Economic Journal, 437–460.
Plott, Charles R., Smith, Jared (1999). "Instability of equilibria in experimental markets: Upward-sloping demands, externalities, and fad-like incentives". Southern Economic Journal 65 (3), 405–426.
Smith, Vernon L. (1965). "Experimental auction markets and the Walrasian hypothesis". Journal of Political Economy 73, 387.

Chapter 27

OFF-FLOOR TRADING, MARKET DISINTEGRATION AND PRICE VOLATILITY IN BID/ASK MARKETS

VERNON L. SMITH and MARK VAN BOENING

1. The Problem

This study was commissioned by a futures market Exchange firm plagued by members' trading off-floor in strict violation of the Exchange's rules requiring transactions to be made on the Exchange floor during trading hours in the assigned trading areas. Any violation of these rules is a major offense, and penalties have been and are levied on violators. (See Campbell et al., 1991 for a complete report.) Although violators are often discovered and penalized, the prohibition itself assures that there exists no systematic field data from the Exchange that can help inform the circumstances that produce off-floor trading. Hence, experimental evidence is the only feasible source of relevant observations.

Why do Exchange members engage in bilateral trades that bypass the public trading pits? Such trades are not guaranteed by the Exchange, and therefore run the risk of failure due to contract non-compliance by one party or the other. Exchange officials conjectured that the bid/ask spread in pit trading was sufficiently wide to provide an incentive for both parties to trade inside the spread at savings to each that justified this risk. This would be especially applicable to traders who knew each other well, and each was comfortable with the trustworthiness of their trading partner.

2. The Environment

To examine this hypothesis it was necessary to first find treatments that would affect the size of the bid/ask spread. In experimental double auction trading with static induced supply and demand schedules, the bid/ask spread converges to near one cent – the minimum quotation increment. Accordingly, we conducted three baseline experiments in an environment in which individuals were randomly reassigned values (or costs) from period to period but the aggregate supply and demand schedules were constant, and two experiments in which a random shift occurred each period in addition to reassignment (Campbell et al., 1991, pp. 500–502, 507–508; see also Smith and Van Boening, "Exogenous Uncertainty Increases the Bid/Ask Spread in Double Auction Markets," this volume, for a summary of this data). These experiments established that an increase in exogenous uncertainty in a double auction market causes an increase in the average bid/ask spread. This provided an appropriate environment to see if subjects would trade "off-floor" in bilateral direct exchanges as an alternative to the electronic double auction market (which used a double auction software program written in the tutor language for the PLATO operating system by Arlington Williams; this program, written originally in 1976 and modified many times thereafter, was the first electronic double auction).

Bilateral off-floor trading was implemented by providing each subject with copies of a standard contract form, referred to as a buyer bid (seller offer) ticket. Subjects were seated at terminals so that buyers and sellers alternated. If a buyer (seller) wished to initiate an off-floor trade the bid (offer) price and quantity were written into the blanks on the ticket form and handed to his or her left or right (or over the partition for subjects seated at an end terminal). One of the experimenters placed it on the table of the adjacent subject who was required to accept or reject it immediately, and the ticket was then returned to the initiator of the bid (offer). Off-floor trades and profits were recorded manually in tables supplied to each subject. In one previously twice-experienced group, each subject recorded the standing clock time at the moment a bid (offer) was initiated and when it was accepted or rejected. This allowed a determination of whether the bid (offer) was inside or outside the bid/ask spread when it was initiated, and, shortly thereafter, when it was accepted or rejected.

3. Results

Figure 1 provides an overall summary of the results across five experiments using experienced ($\times$) or twice-experienced ($\times\times$) subjects. In two experiments, off-floor trading was restricted to single units (experiment 1$\times$ with constant per period supply and demand, experiment 2$\times$ with random per period supply and demand); and in three experiments off-floor trading was in blocks of three units (3$\times$, 4$\times$, and 5$\times\times$ all with randomly shifting supply and demand). (In Campbell et al., 1991, the corresponding experiments are labeled, 5$\times$, 6$\times$ and 9$\times$, 10$\times$, and 11$\times\times$.) The left panel plots the overall variance in transaction prices (on and off-floor combined) by experiment against the volume of off-floor trades as a percentage of total trading volume. Note that in both single and block off-floor trading price volatility increases with the percentage of off-floor trading, which in turn increases with experience. The right panel plots trading profit as a percent of the maximum possible (i.e., efficiency) against off-floor trades as a percentage of total volume. We observe a tendency for efficiency to decline with block trading and experience level.

Figure 2 plots data from our session with twice-experienced subjects (experiment 5$\times\times$), where the standing clock time was recorded for each off-floor trade. The left panel plots off-floor activity in five-period intervals relative to the mean bid/ask spread at the time the off-floor proposals were initiated. It is apparent that as off-floor activity inside the spread increases, the spread widens, both in absolute number and as a percent. (Also note that wider mean spreads are observed later in the experiment, whereas the spread normally narrows with experienced subjects in a double auction.) The right panel plots period-by-period off-floor trading volume as a percent of total trading volume. Thus the phenomenon of off-floor trading does not diminish with experience and in fact

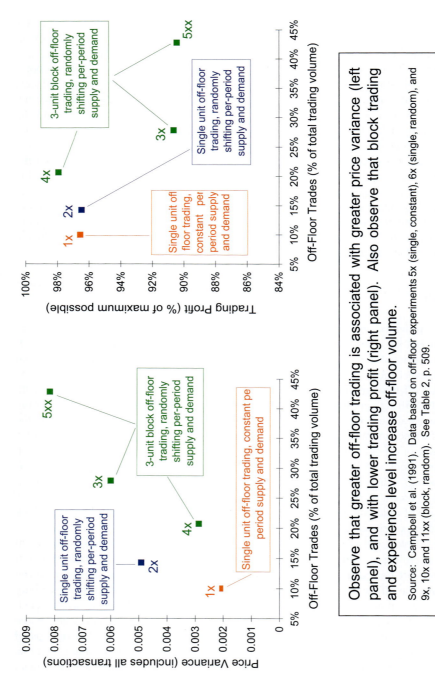

Figure 1. Price variance, trading profit and off-floor trading volume per experimental session.

Observe that greater off-floor trading is associated with greater price variance (left panel), and with lower trading profit (right panel). Also observe that block trading and experience level increase off-floor volume.

Source: Campbell et al. (1991). Data based on off-floor experiments 5x (single, constant), 6x (single, random), and 9x, 10x and 11xx (block, random). See Table 2, p. 509.

Ch. 27: Off-floor Trading, Market Disintegration and Price Volatility in Bid/Ask Markets

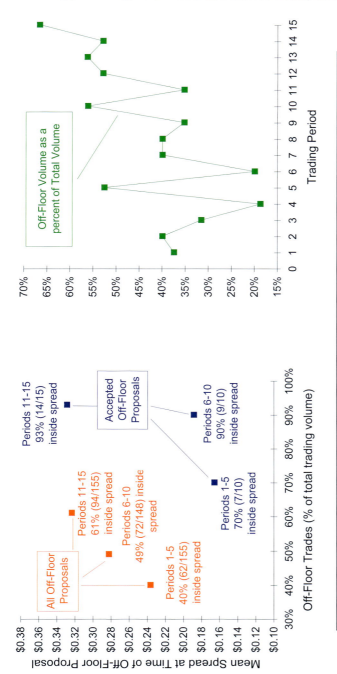

Figure 2. Mean bid-ask spreads, off-floor activity and off-floor trading volume in experimental session 5××.

Observe that as off-floor activity inside the bid/ask spread increases the spread widens (left panel), and that off-floor volume accounts for an increasing portion of total volume in later periods (right panel).

Source: Campbell et al. (1991). Data based on off-floor experiment 11xx. See Figure 7, p. 514 and Table 3, p. 515.

increases as subjects become more skilled at executing such contracts. These results are consistent with the Exchange officials conjecture that a sufficiently wide bid/ask spread facilitates off-floor activity, especially where traders are familiar with the practice.

4. Discussion: Implications for, and Barriers to, Institutional Redesign

The reported experiments demonstrate that bid/ask institutions on an Exchange can be invaded by the ancient tradition of bilateral bargaining. Yet historically we know that Exchange trading can invade and displace more informal over-the-counter trading in dealer markets. For example, prior to the 1970s, stock options (puts and calls) were traded over-the-counter (by such well known firms as Filor and Schmidt). After the Chicago Board of Trade started listing and trading options in 1973 (Schwartz, 1988, p. 77), followed soon thereafter by listing on other Exchanges, over-the-counter options trading declined rapidly. But trading on centralized Exchanges cannot resist invasion by block traders who can utilize public price information to efficiently negotiate private deals inside the bid/ask spread and share the savings. Hence, the long history of Exchange firm prohibitions on off-floor trading backed up by severe penalties for violations by Exchange members.

The Exchange solution is that of the typical centralized hierarchy – one that consumes monitoring and enforcement resources. Is there a decentralized institutional design solution to this problem, a change in the rules that gives traders an incentive to do the right thing (trade on floor) without anyone having to force them to do so? Experimental research suggests that the answer is yes: use a uniform price double auction (UPDA) call market (McCabe, Rassenti, and Smith, 1991). The incentive to trade inside the bid/ask spread is eliminated by doing away with the bid/ask spread. This is an academic proposal that engineers an incentive solution that would (i) reduce price volatility, and (ii) eliminate the monitoring and enforcement cost of rules prohibiting off-floor trading, and appears to yield a Pareto improvement. Why is it not acceptable to any existing exchange? Because it is the bid/ask spread in member–dealer markets that is the source of their livelihood. For such traders, reduced volatility is not necessarily welcome if it causes a reduction in trading (and retrading) volume. A revolutionary change from a continuous bid–ask auction to a uniform price call auction creates new uncertainties for Exchange members, and they cannot be expected to support it.

If such an institutional change is to occur, it would have to involve entry by a new Exchange whose advantages allow it to invade and displace existing Exchanges, much as occurred in the 1970s in the options market. We know precious little about the conditions under which one trading institution can invade and displace another.

References

Campbell, Joseph, LaMaster, Shawn, Smith, Vernon L., Van Boening, Mark (1991). "Off-floor trading, disintegration, and the bid–ask spread in experimental markets". Journal of Business 64, 495–522.

McCabe, Kevin, Rassenti, Stephen J., Smith, Vernon L. (1991). "Designing a uniform-price double auction: An experimental evaluation". In: Friedman, D., Rust, J. (Eds.), The Double Auction Market Institutions, Theories and Evidence. Addison–Wesley, Reading, MA.

Schwartz, Robert A. (1988). "Equity Markets". Harper and Row, New York.

Chapter 28

QUANTITATIVE RESTRICTIONS IN EXPERIMENTAL POSTED-OFFER MARKETS

PRAVEEN KUJAL

Universidad Carlos III

1. Introduction

Despite the prevalent use of quota restrictions, little experimental work exists on the effect on market performance of quotas. In this chapter I first elaborate on the different types of quota that can exist and how they are applied in the real world. This is then followed by the some experimental results.

1.1. Quotas

The effect of a particular quantity restriction depends on how it is applied. There are two ways to impose quantity restrictions. First, a quantity restriction can be imposed at the level of a firm such that the firm as a unit can only sell up to a maximum of the quantity allowed under the quota. This has been known to occur both in planned and market economies; wine imports, production of hops, or peanuts in the U.S. economy are some examples of this kind. Quantity restrictions of this kind can be called "firm-specific" quotas. The second kind of quota occurs when a quantity restriction is imposed on a group of firms in a market or upon an importing/exporting country. For example, voluntary export restraints (VERs) that put an upper bound on the total amount of the good that can be sold by a group of firms from a country fall in this category. Given that under such quotas the incentive to defect is very high (as is evidenced by the marketing agreements in the U.S. in the 1930s) innovative ways have been devised so that they end up functioning like firm-specific quotas. For example, in the marketing agreements that are prevalent in the U.S., the quotas are assigned to co-operatives at the state level. The co-operatives then assign quotas to the individual members on the basis of past history.[1] In the end, the effect is *as if* firm-specific quotas were being used. Thus, many of the quota applications end up being as the firm-specific kind. Further, firm-specific quotas are of greater interest as they increase market power of incumbent firms.

---

[1] This is made possible because the federal government can regulate inter-state and not intra-state commerce. As a result the federal government regulates the inter-state flow while the co-operatives assign in state quotas.

2. Quota Experiments

Plott (1983) was among the first ones to study quota restrictions. He studied the effect of (pollution) standards in the presence of externalities in a Double-Oral auction market. The maximum pollution that all the sellers could 'produce' in the market was fixed.[2] In his experiments, Plott observed that prices showed little or no tendency to converge when standards were used. Therefore, the standards approach was not as efficient as using a tax policy for pollution but was more efficient than using no policy at all.

Kujal (1994) conducted experiments where he studied whether non-binding/binding firm-specific quantity controls affect market performance in the same way as price ceilings. These experiments were important for the many reasons. Earlier experiments on price controls had shown consistent qualitative properties (see Isaac and Plott, 1981; Smith and Williams, 1981; and Coursey and Smith, 1983). The removal of price ceilings resulted in prices jumping upwards after the removal of controls. Further, price controls have an impact on market performance even after their removal (see Isaac, 1988 for a good discussion on remnants of regulation). Thus, because prices and quantities are sometimes used as alternative modes of regulation, it is important to study whether the qualitative results carry across the two different modes of regulatory control.

In his experiments, Kujal (1994) found that after the removal of firm-specific quantity controls there was no evidence of a discontinuous jump in prices (neither in the experiments with binding quotas or "BQ," nor in the experiments with non-binding quotas or "NBQ"). However, tests on aggregate data show that quotas do affect prices. Tests on individual experimental data were mixed. Further, a surprising property of prices was observed in these experiments. Prices converged from below the competitive[3] equilibrium. This result contradicted the well-established empirical regularity that price convergence is from above the competitive equilibrium in posted-offer markets. Thus, the asymmetric distribution of surplus, or the imposition of quotas themselves, affected price convergence in the quota experiments. Further, given that the experimental design had market power price convergence for both the BQ and NBQ experiments was from below the non co-operative equilibrium. However, as the experiments progressed prices converged to the Nash Equilibrium.

Quota experiments also showed interesting behavioral characteristics. Efficiencies in the short run were lower than that observed in the price control experiments. This is important because if the effect on market efficiency is not the same in the short run then one needs to be careful in employing these two alternative modes of regulatory control.[4] From the experimental evidence it seems that, given the quotas, the sellers take some time to find the market price. However, under price controls it seems much

---

[2] This kind of quota restriction would come under market quotas where the total quantity for a group of sellers is fixed.
[3] The competitive equilibrium is defined as the price that gives 100% total surplus.
[4] This is related to the question raised by Weitzman (1974) where he asks why quantities, and not prices, are the preferred modes of control for internal transfer of firms.

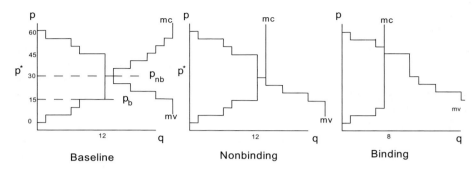

Figure 1. Marginal cost and marginal valuations.

easier to locate the profit maximizing quantity. The answer to this lies in the manner in which the two market controls affect seller search space. This is discussed later in the chapter.

3. Experimental Design

The experiments used the posted-offer exchange mechanism.[5] There were three different experimental designs: (I) the baseline (with no quantity restrictions); (II) nonbinding quota experiments (the sum of seller capacities equals the total quantity sold at the competitive outcome); and (III) binding quota experiments (the sum of the seller capacities is less than the competitive volume under the baseline design). In designs (II) and (III) the quotas were removed midway in period 10.

Five experiments were run for each treatment. Each experiment had four sellers and four buyers. Seller prices were arranged in ascending order with the seller with the lowest price selling first. The buyers were queued randomly to purchase the goods after the sellers post the prices. The next period would start after all the buyers had stopped purchasing the good. A buyer could purchase a unit of the good as long as the purchase price did not exceed the seller valuation of the good. As the focus of the paper was to study seller behavior due to the imposition of the quota buyers were simulated. The buyers revealed perfectly and accepted zero profit.

(I) Baseline (BSL) experiments (Figure 1): This design was characterized by four sellers and four buyers each capable of buying and selling five units each. Assuming everyone prices at the competitive equilibrium, the surplus was divided between the buyers and sellers symmetrically.

---

[5] For details on the functioning of the posted offer institution see Ketcham, Smith, and Williams (1984).

(II) Non-binding quotas (NBQ) (Figure 1): In this design, the sum of sellers' total capacity equals thirteen. This leaves the competitive price and the quantity unchanged from the baseline experiments.[6]

(III) Binding quota experiments (BQ) (Figure 1): The sum of sellers' capacity equals eight. The competitive outcome is in a 5-cent range, 15–20 cents above the competitive equilibrium in the NBQ/BSL design. Binding quotas distribute the total surplus in the favor of sellers.

The subjects receive a special announcement that quantity controls will be in effect when appropriate. If any seller attempts to violate the quota restriction this will result in the rejection of the sellers' offer until the output constraint (quota) is satisfied. Subjects are also told that their capacity is determined by a central authority. This announcement is made to all the subjects. They are also given individual (private) announcements that state their capacities. The announcement at the start of the experiment reads: "*Your capacity is determined by a central authority. Your capacity is . . . . Please make sure that the number on the screen coincides with the capacity stated.*"

One period prior to the removal of quotas, the subjects are told about the forthcoming change in capacity. Subjects are told individually what their "new" capacities are. Everyone knew that individual capacities have been changed, however, individual capacity changes are private information. The announcement read as follows: "*The central authority has now decided to change your capacities. You now have a capacity of FIVE units. Please make sure that the monitor screen shows the correct amount.*" The purpose behind the announcement was to emulate an environment where a regulatory authority decides on individual capacities.

3.1. Market equilibrium

Before the discussion of the experimental results it will be in order to discuss the "predicted" market equilibrium (as the non-cooperative price is not the competitive price) in the experiments. The competitive equilibrium has been defined as the price that gives efficiency of 100% for the following reasons. The experimental design gives market power to the sellers. Looking at Figure 1, and Table 1, it is easy to see that if all the sellers charge a price of 30, sellers 2 and 3 can each gain by selling at a price 9 cents higher (1 cents less than the two high cost units of sellers 1 and 2). At this price configuration, the two other sellers sell 3 units at 30 each. Now, sellers 1 and 2 can each charge 4 cents above the competitive equilibrium and sell all their units thereby getting higher profits. Thus, no seller charges a price of 30, as it is always profitable to deviate from this price for all sellers. This implies that a unique Nash equilibrium in prices does not exist due to the asymmetric allocation of the out-of-equilibrium units for the sellers. It is for this reason the competitive equilibrium is defined to be at 30, i.e., the price that maximizes total market surplus. Further, note that a similar analysis applies for the non-binding quota experiments.

---

[6] The effect of such restrictions on price outcomes is discussed in detail later.

Table 1
Marginal cost and marginal valuations

	Unit 1	Unit 2	Unit 3	Unit 4	Unit 5
Buyer 1	60	55	45	20	20
Buyer 2	55	50	45	25	15
Buyer 3	55	50	45	25	15
Buyer 4	60	55	45	30	20
Seller 1	00	05	15	30	40
Seller 2	05	10	15	35	45
Seller 3	00	05	15	35	55
Seller 4	05	10	15	40	50

Educated guesses on price can be made to show the approximate price equilibrium in the experiments. This is useful because it gives us a price prediction for the experiments. If a seller prices at 45 the minimum amount he or she sells is 2 units. The gain (30) dominates the loss on the unsold unit (15). Now assume that everyone prices at 45. At this price some sellers gain by lowering the price and selling 4 units. In fact all sellers gain by lowering their price and selling additional units. It is important to determine at what price is each seller willing to lower his or her price such that the net gain from undercutting and selling more is positive. This can be done individually for all the sellers. Seller 4 only finds it profitable to undercut until the price reaches 40 but not below. The maximum the seller gains from undercutting is 56, from pricing at 44 and selling 4. Now, sellers 2 and 3 can price at 39, sell 4 units and gain 36 cents (which is greater than the 30 gained from selling 2 units). The only seller who will undercut them at this price is seller 1 because he or she has the only available extra unit at 30. Seller 4 will never undercut below 40 cents and sellers 2 and 3 never undercut below 37.5 cents. (With a gain of 7.5 cents on each unit, selling 4, it makes them indifferent between pricing at 45 and pricing at 37.5.) Now, all we need to do is to see if seller 1 wants to price below 37.5. At any price below 37.5, selling 4 units, seller 1 earns less ($7 \times 4 = 28$) than the 30 cents he or she would earn at a price of 45. Hence, we know that no seller prices below 38 cents (as prices in decimals are not admitted). This simple exercise gives us an idea that the approximate range of equilibrium prices lies in [38, 45].

4. Experimental Results

Results are reported from five experiments: for the baseline, binding quotas and non-binding quotas.

In the non-binding quota and binding quota experiments, two results are of interest. The number of contracts remains well below the competitive level of 12 and as a result efficiency levels are lower in the earlier periods (Figure 2). After the non-binding quotas are removed, output in the subsequent periods remains lower and slowly starts to con-

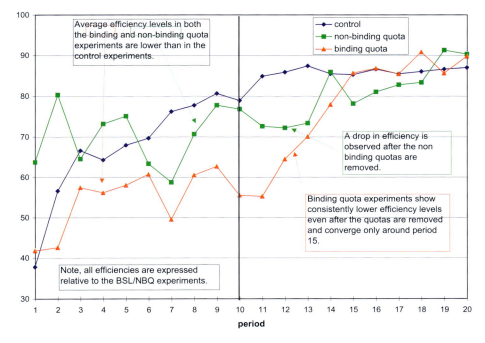

Figure 2.

verge to the competitive equilibrium. Similar results are also obtained for the binding quota experiments. Low output realization is reflected in low efficiency levels observed in the binding quota experiments (Figure 2). This is reminiscent of what Isaac (1988) calls remnants of regulation and is also observed in the price control experiments (see, Coursey and Smith, 1983; Isaac and Plott, 1981; and Smith and Williams, 1981).

In the binding quota experiments, when the quotas are in effect the average contracted price converges from below the competitive equilibrium (Figure 3). This result contradicts the well-established empirical regularity of posted-offer markets where the contract price converges from below the competitive equilibrium. However, if instead we use posted prices to study price convergence (Kujal, 1992) price convergence is observed from above the competitive equilibrium (Figure 4). Moreover, as economic theory predicts, posted prices it seems reasonable to use posted prices to study institutional characteristics.

Looking at efficiencies we see that experiments with binding quotas show a tendency toward lower surplus realization even after the quantity controls are removed. However, by the end of period, fifteen efficiencies for the baseline, non-binding quota experiments and binding quota experiments converge. It is clear that both binding and non-binding quotas clearly affect market performance after their removal. (This result is also reflected in all the price control experiments where a discontinuous jump in prices was

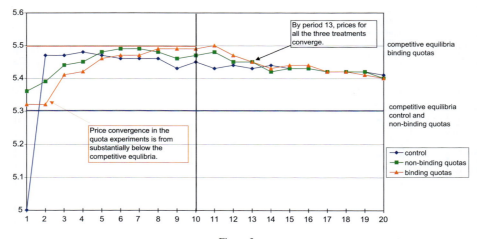

Figure 3.

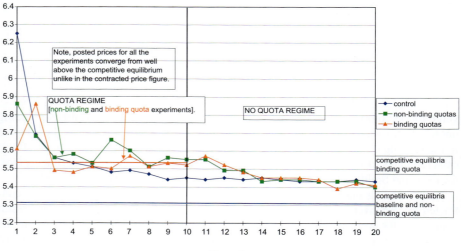

Figure 4.

witnessed after the removal of the price controls.) It is clear that market controls affect market performance even after their removal in our static framework.

5. Conclusion

Quota experiments have shown two interesting results. First, as was also seen in the price control experiments, both non-binding and binding quantity controls tend to affect institutional performance even after their. This lends support to the "remnants of regulation hypothesis" (Isaac, 1988). Second, in the case of binding quotas, average contract price convergence is observed from below the competitive equilibrium. This result goes against the observed empirical regularity of price convergence from above the competitive equilibrium in posted offer markets.

Unlike price control experiments, no discontinuous jump in prices is observed after the quotas are removed in either posted offer or oral double auctions. Another surprising characteristic of the binding quota experiments is that sellers have low efficiency levels on the average. This is observed despite the fact that the surplus distribution favors the sellers. It is evident that quotas, binding or non-binding, affect market performance while they are in place and after they have been removed.

References

Coursey, Don, Smith, Vernon L. (1983). "Price controls in a posted offer market". American Economic Review 73 (1), 218–221.
Isaac, R. Mark (1988). "Remnants of regulation". In: Libecap, Gary (Ed.), Advances in The Study of Entrepreneurship, Innovation and Economic Growth, vol. 2. JAI Press, Greenwich, CT, pp. 173–191.
Isaac, R. Mark, Plott, Charles R. (1981). "Price controls and behavior of auction markets: An experimental examination". American Economic Review 71 (3), 448–459.
Ketcham, Jon, Smith, Vernon L., Williams, Arlington (1984). "A comparison of posted-offer and double auction pricing institutions". Review of Economic Studies 51 (4), 595–614.
Kujal, Praveen (1992). "Asymmetric surplus distribution and the price convergence path in posted-offer markets: A note". Economics Letters 39 (1), 33–36.
Kujal, Praveen (1994). "Firm specific output limit in a posted-offer market: Distributive and efficiency effects". Journal of Economic Behavior and Organization 25 (2), 257–269.
Plott, Charles (1983). "Externalities and corrective policies in experimental markets". The Economic Journal 93 (369), 106–127.
Smith, Vernon L., Williams, Arlington (1981). "On non-binding price controls in a competitive market". American Economic Review 71 (3), 467–474.
Weitzman, Martin L. (1974). "Prices vs. quantities". Review of Economic Studies 41 (4), 477–491.

Chapter 29

PRICE BUBBLES IN LARGE FINANCIAL ASSET MARKETS

ARLINGTON W. WILLIAMS

Indiana University

The propensity for long-lived financial asset markets to exhibit price bubbles relative to the per-share expected dividend stream was first documented in experimental double auctions reported by Smith, Suchanek, and Williams (1988). Subsequent research by King et al. (1993) explored the robustness of this phenomenon to short selling opportunities, margin buying opportunities, limit price-change rules, informed insider trading, and increasing levels of subject experience with the double auction asset trading environment. It was found that the only reliable way to generate prices that approximately reflect the intrinsic dividend value of an asset share is to bring the same group of traders back for a series of three 15-round markets. In the first two markets, prices tended to bubble above intrinsic value and then crash back to intrinsic value prior to the final trading round. Prices in the third market tended to track the intrinsic dividend value much more accurately, reflecting the fact that traders learn through market experience to have common price expectations that are rooted in the expected dividend earnings associated with an asset share. This leads to an approximation of a risk-neutral rational expectations market equilibrium. Van Boening, Williams, and LaMaster (1993) document that the price bubble-crash phenomenon observed in double auctions is also found with regularity in 15-round closed-book call markets. All of the experiments referred to above utilized a cash reward structure and were relatively small markets with fifteen or fewer traders who were seated in the same computing lab together during the entire duration of the market.

This paper documents some open-book call asset markets that have a very large number of traders relative to traditional laboratory markets. The markets were conducted as out-of-class fully computerized extra-credit exercises in microeconomic theory classes at Indiana University. (This is one of three such exercises described by Williams and Walker, 1993.) Trading occurred over fifteen rounds lasting a total of approximately eight weeks. Round 1, which includes completing the computer-based instructions, was typically 7–10 days long, but rounds 2 through 15 were all 3.5 days long. Students could access the market software at a time of their own choosing and as often as they wanted during each trading round in order to view the market bid and ask arrays, the tentative market price and volume, and edit their personal bid or ask. All traders in a particular market received the same initial endowment of asset shares and cash. A common dividend was declared at the end of each round and all traders in the market had the same rectangular dividend distribution.

Performance-based extra-credit points were awarded using a rank-order tournament focusing on the traders' final cash holdings. Participation-based extra-credit points were

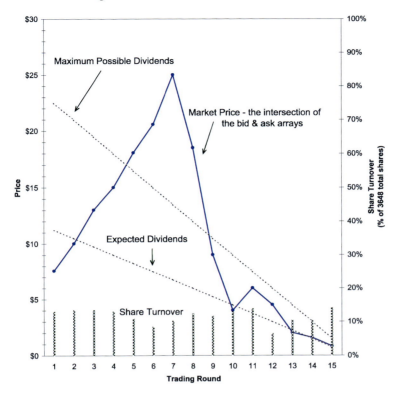

Figure 1. Asset market with 304 traders: a rising-price bubble and crash. Each trader is endowed with $150 and 12 asset shares at the beginning of round 1. At the end of each round, a per-share dividend is drawn from a uniform distribution bounded at $1.50 and $0. The expected dividend is thus $.75. In round 1, the expected dividend stream is 15 × $.75 = $11.25 per-share and falls by $.75 in each subsequent round.

also awarded in keeping with the educational goals of the exercise. Students participating in the market were encouraged to discuss the market with one another and to ask the instructor any questions they might have about the trading procedures, dividend earnings, or the extra-credit reward structure. However, the instructor refused to reveal the range of traders' share or cash holdings since this information is unlikely to be available in a naturally occurring market.

From a research perspective, these markets are important to the basic methodology of experimental economics since very few experiments have addressed the potentially critical issues of whether stylized results of typical small-group laboratory interactions are robust to: (1) substantial increases in group size, (2) the endogenous inter-trader information flows that may exist outside of the strict privacy that is possible in laboratory environments, (3) the enhanced cognition processes that may exist in decision rounds lasting several days rather than a few minutes, and (4) non-monetary reward structures.

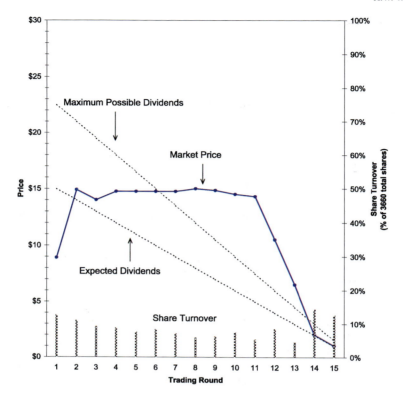

Figure 2. Asset market with 244 traders: a flat-price bubble and crash. Each trader is endowed with $225 and 25 asset shares at the beginning of round 1. At the end of each round, a per-share dividend is drawn from a uniform distribution bounded at $1.50 and $.50. The expected dividend is thus $1. In round 1, the expected dividend stream is 15 × $1 = $15 per-share and falls by $1 in each subsequent round.

(See Isaac, Walker, and Williams, 1994 for further discussion of these methodological issues in the context of public goods experiments.)

Figures 1, 2, and 3 illustrate the market-clearing price (determined by the intersection of the submitted bids to buy and asks to sell), trading volume (as a percentage of total shares outstanding), expected dividend stream, and maximum dividend stream for markets with 304, 244, and 310 traders, respectively. The outcomes depicted in these figures are characteristic of many such large call markets conducted over the past five years. The basic price bubble-crash phenomenon is by far the most typical outcome. This result is consistent with the cash-reward, small-group, strict-privacy lab experiments reported in the literature for inexperienced or once-experienced traders. One of the more astonishing aspects of the large-group results is that the price bubble dynamic appears to be unaffected by classroom discussions of the graph showing the market price relative to the expected dividend stream (very similar to those shown in the figures) for

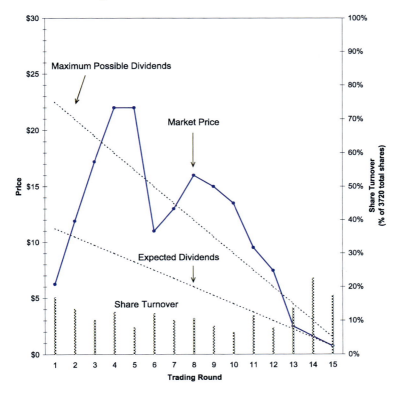

Figure 3. Asset market with 310 traders: a rare double bubble and crash. As in Figure 1, each trader is endowed with $150 and 12 asset shares at the beginning of round 1. At the end of each round, a per-share dividend is drawn from a uniform distribution bounded at $1.50 and $0. The expected dividend is thus $.75. In round 1, the expected dividend stream is $15 \times \$.75 = \$11.25$ per-share and falls by $.75 in each subsequent round.

a market that is still in progress. After viewing an on-line computer projection of the market data and listening to a quick summary of the graph's content, students frequently ask questions like "Why are people buying at such high prices?" This instructor's response is basically, "I really don't know, but they must believe that they will be able to profit from this action through dividend earnings and perhaps eventually selling the share to someone else." The traders who are doing the buying rarely choose to comment publicly on their market strategy.

The lack of total control over inter-trader information flows and the ongoing interaction between subject (student) and experimenter (teacher) embodied in these educationally oriented large-group markets is atypical of pure-research endeavors. The results are meaningful to the research methodology of experimental markets, however, since they provide an explicit example of a very complex, and somewhat counter-intuitive, laboratory phenomenon. This phenomenon generalizes to a less controlled environment that captures some critical elements of market interactions in the naturally-occurring world.

References

Isaac, R. Mark, Walker, James M., Williams, Arlington W. (1994). "Group size and the voluntary provision of public goods: Experimental evidence utilizing very large groups". Journal of Public Economics 54, 1–36.
King, Ronald R., Smith, Vernon L., Williams, Arlington W., Van Boening, Mark (1993). "The robustness of bubbles and crashes in experimental stock markets". In: Day, Richard H., Chen, Ping (Eds.), Nonlinear Dynamics and Evolutionary Economics. Oxford University Press, Oxford, pp. 183–200.
Smith, Vernon L., Suchanek, Gerry L., Williams, Arlington W. (1988). "Bubbles, crashes and endogenous expectations in experimental spot asset markets". Econometrica 56, 1119–1151.
Van Boening, Mark, Williams, Arlington W., LaMaster, Shawn (1993). "Price bubbles and crashes in experimental call markets". Economics Letters 41, 179–185.
Williams, Arlington W., Walker, James M. (1993). "Computerized laboratory exercises for microeconomics education: Three applications motivated by experimental economics". Journal of Economic Education 24, 291–315.

Chapter 30

PRICE BUBBLES

DAVID PORTER and VERNON L. SMITH

1. Introduction

Smith, Suchanek, and Williams (1988) report the results of laboratory asset markets in which each trader receives an initial portfolio of cash and shares of a security with an earnings life of 15 trading periods. Before the tth trading period, the expected dividend value of a share, e.g., $0.24(15-t+1)$, is computed and reported to all subjects to guard against any possibility of misunderstanding. Each trader is free to trade shares of the security using double auction trading rules. At the end of the experiment, a sum equal to all dividends received on shares, plus initial cash plus capital gains minus capital losses is paid in U.S. currency to the trader.

The data in Figure 1 shows a typical result from a laboratory asset market. With inexperienced traders, bubbles and crashes are standard fare. However, these phenomena disappear as traders become experienced. That is, traders who have experienced trading twice in a laboratory asset market will trade at prices that reflect fundamental value.

2. Empirical Results from Laboratory Asset Markets

Figure 1 supplies the structure of the baseline experiment of Smith, Suchanek, and Williams (1988) where the theory would predict prices that track the fundamental value line (see Tirole, 1982). In this environment, inexperienced traders produced high amplitude[1] bubbles that are 2 to 3 times intrinsic value. In addition, the span of a boom tends to be of long duration (10 to 11 periods) with a large turnover of shares (5 to 6 times the outstanding stock of shares over the 15-period experiment). In nearly all cases, prices crash to fundamental value by period 15.

The baseline market developed by Smith, Suchanek, and Williams (1988) omits many institutional features that are present in the field. Since some of these factors may very well dampen bubbles, they have provided the impetus for several new experiments reported in two recent studies: (1) King et al. (1993) report experiments that introduce short selling, margin buying, brokerage fees, informed "specialists," equal portfolio endowments, and limit price change rules; (2) Porter and Smith (1995) report new experiments examining the effect of a futures market and the effect of dividend certainty.

---

[1] We calculate amplitude as the difference between the highest deviation of mean contract price from its fundamental value and the lowest deviation of mean contract from its fundamental value. This value is then normalized by 360, the expected dividend value over 15 periods.

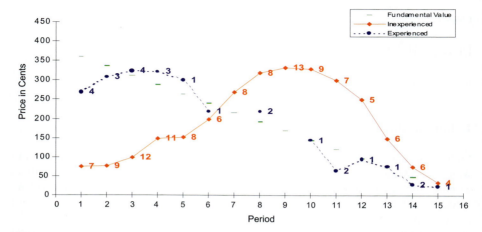

Figure 1. Mean contract price and total volume. The experiments graphed have nine subjects who can both buy and sell a security using the double auction trading rules. Each subject is endowed with cash and shares of the security (a third of the subjects had $9.45 in cash and one share; another third had $5.85 and two shares; one third had $2.25 and three shares) that pays a dividend at the end of each of 15 trading periods (the dividend is either $.00, $.08, $.28, $.60 with equal probability which is drawn at the end of each trading period). Thus the security has an expected dividend of $.24 for each period. If held for all fifteen periods it would pay $3.60 in dividends on average. The security's dividend or fundamental value decreases $.24 each trading period. This declining fundamental value is shown by the green dashed values in the graph. The red data points and red numbers next to them are the mean contract prices and volume, respectively, for an experiment in which subjects participated for the first time. The blue data points and associated number are the mean contract prices and volume, respectively, for an experiment in which these same subjects participated in the market for a second time.

Table 1 lists these structural changes, the associated data, and the predictions of the effect of these treatments on the market. Such structural changes have been suggested by others as an explanation of the bubbles reported in Smith, Suchanek, and Williams (1988). Table 1 lists the treatments discussed herein along with their hypothesized effect on the bubble's characteristics. Table 2 lists the mean values of amplitude, duration and turnover for each treatment.

The baseline experiments have individual traders endowed with different initial portfolios. A common characteristic of first-period trading is that buyers tend to be those with low share endowments, while sellers are those with relatively high share endowments. This suggests that risk-averse traders might be using the market to acquire more balanced portfolios. If liquidity preference accounts for the low initial prices, which in turn lead to expectations of price increases, then making the initial trader endowments equal across subjects would tend to dampen bubbles.

RESULT 1. Observations from four experiments with inexperienced traders show no significant effect of equal endowments on bubble characteristics.

Ch. 30: Price Bubbles							249

Table 1
Treatments and hypothesis

Treatment	Description	Hypothesis
Baseline	Declining dividend value (see Figure 2)	Rational expectations equilibrium has trading at fundamental values
Short-selling	Traders are given the capacity to sell units to be covered by last period	Traders can leverage sales and counter ebullient expectations
Margin buying	Traders are given interest free loan to be paid back at last period	Purchases can be leveraged to raise prices that are below dividend value
Equal portfolios	Each traders is given the identical initial amounts of cash and shares	Traders do not need to use the market to balance portfolios
Brokerage fees	Buy and seller in a transactions pay 10 cents each for the trade	Should reduce trading based on boredom or playing
Informed insiders	Specially trained traders who are given bid ask adjustment model	Expert traders aware of bubble characteristics engage in arbitrage
Dividend certainty	Security pays a fixed and known amount each period	Trading based on expectations/risk preference is virtually eliminated
Futures contracting	Traders are given a mid-horizon (period 8) security	Futures contracts should give read on traders price expectations
Limit price change rule	Asset price can only change a fixed percentage amount based on previous period prices	This rule has been recommended by expert advisory groups to reduce price volatility and crashes

If risk aversion about price expectations due to dividend uncertainty causes a divergence of common expectations, then the elimination of such uncertainty should reduce the severity of bubbles. The Porter and Smith (1995) experiments demonstrate otherwise (see Figure 2 for an example).

RESULT 2. *When the dividend draw each period is set equal to the one period expected dividend value, so that the asset dividend stream is certain, bubbles still occur and are not significantly different from the case with dividend uncertainty.*

Results 1 and 2 are directed at changing the underlying induced value parameters of the baseline experiments but not the basic structure of the market. Stock markets in the field provide margin rules that allow traders to take a position on either side of the market and leverage their sales by taking a short position or leverage their purchases by buying with borrowed funds. Consequently, a small number of traders who have counter cyclical expectations would be able to offset the ebullient expectations of others.

RESULT 3. *Short-selling does not significantly diminish the amplitude and duration of bubbles, but the volume of trade is increased significantly; Figure 3 provides an example.*

Table 2
Mean values by treatment

Treatment	Inexperienced			Once-experienced			Twice-experienced		
	Amplitude	Duration	Turnover	Amplitude	Duration	Turnover	Amplitude	Duration	Turnover
Baseline	1.21 $n=19$	9.23	5.79	.75 $n=4$	5.51	3.00	.10 $n=3$	3.00	1.60
Short-sell	1.61 $n=4$	9.50	6.67	.76 $n=5$	5.80	4.19	.40 $n=3$	3.67	1.74
Margin buy	3.64 $n=2$	8.00	5.48	1.15 $n=1$	2.00	2.33			
Equal portfolios	1.87 $n=4$	10.00	6.29						
Broker fees	.73 $n=2$	10.00	5.56	.63 $n=3$	4.00	4.92			
Informed insiders	.63 $n=2$	13.00	2.68	.25 $n=3$	6.00	4.05			
Dividend certain	1.10 $n=3$	11.00	8.84	.52 $n=3$	9.67	2.71			
Futures contract	.92 $n=3$	10.00	6.85	.60 $n=2$	5.50	2.63			
Limit price change	2.51 $n=2$	10.50	4.84	1.77 $n=2$	5.50	2.22	.70 $n=2$	1.50	1.89

RESULT 4. Margin buying opportunities cause a significant increase in the amplitude of bubbles for inexperienced ($p < 0.01$), but not for experienced subjects.

RESULT 5. A brokerage fee of 20 cents on each trade (10 cents each on the buyer and seller) had no significant effect on the amplitude, duration, or share turnover.

These results suggest that bubbles are robust against significant structural and environmental changes. The endogenous process by which expectations are being formed has no difficulty surviving these first-order changes. The observation that individuals do not form common expectations, given common information on asset value, raises the question of whether these bubbles are sensitive to the subject pool. Most of the experiments have been conducted at the University of Arizona and Indiana University, using volunteers from the student population.[2] Could the use of professional traders

---

[2] Bubbles have been observed with inexperienced student traders in two experiments at the California Institute of Technology and three experiments at the Wharton School.

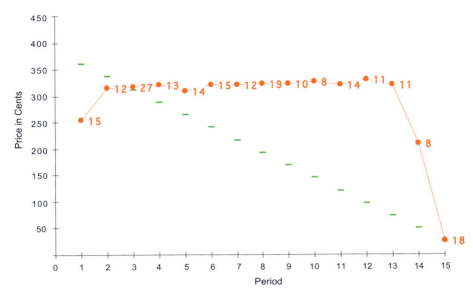

Figure 2. Mean contract price and total volume: Certain dividend. This experiment had nine subjects endowed with cash and shares of the security (a third of the subjects had $9.45 in cash and one share; another third had $5.85 and two shares; one third had $2.25 and three shares) that pays a certain $.24 dividend at the end of each of 15 trading periods. If held for all fifteen periods it would pay exactly $3.60 in dividends. The security's dividend or fundamental value decreases $.24 each trading period since the security has only a fifteen period life. This declining fundamental value is shown by the green dashed values in the graph. The red data points and red numbers next to them are the mean contract prices and volume, respectively for each trading period.

and business executives eliminate this uncertainty concerning the rationality of other's behavior?

RESULT 6. *The use of subject pools of small business persons, mid-level corporate executives, and over-the-counter market dealers has no significant effect on the characteristics of bubbles with first time subjects.*

Rational expectations theory predicts that if irrational trading patterns create profitable arbitrage, then knowledgeable traders will take advantage of these opportunities and this will eliminate such trading patterns. This hypothesis was tested by having three graduate students read the Smith, Suchanek, and Williams (1988) paper. In addition to seeing past data on laboratory bubbles, these "experts" were given information on the bid and offer count each period. As discovered in Smith, Suchanek, and Williams (1988), the excess of bids over offers was found to be a leading indicator of average price changes. These informed subjects then participated in a market with 6 or 9 uninformed traders recruited in the usual way.

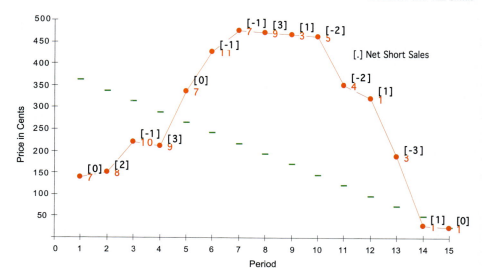

Figure 3. Mean contract price, volume and short sales. This experiment had nine subjects with endowments and dividend distribution the same as in Figure 1, but in addition, each subject was also given the capacity to short sell up to two shares. These shares had to be covered or a penalty of $4.00 would be paid for uncovered shares at the end of the experiment. The red data points and red numbers next to them are the mean contract prices and volume, respectively for each trading period. The black numbers in brackets are the net short sales of the all the subjects. Thus, a positive number implies that units in the short sale inventory have been used in that trading period; a negative number indicates net units have been bought to cover short positions.

RESULT 7. The results support the rational expectations prediction provided that the informed traders are endowed with a capacity to sell short and the uninformed traders are once experienced. When the uninformed traders are inexperienced, the bubble forces are so strong that the expert traders are swamped by the buying wave; by period 11 they reach their maximum selling capacity, including short sales.

The failure of the informed traders to eliminate the bubble when the uninformed traders are inexperienced is illustrated by the experiment in Figure 4.

It should be noted in Figure 4 that since short sales had to be covered by purchases to avoid penalties, when facing inexperienced traders short covering by expert traders prevented the market from crashing to dividend value in period 15. Thus, short selling against the bubble prevented convergence to the rational expectations value at the end.

A futures contract provides a mechanism by which each trader can get a reading on all traders' expectations concerning a future event. In effect, one runs a future spot market in advance. If a price bubble arises because of the failure of common information to induce common expectations, but the latter are achieved through repeat experience, then a futures contract should have the effect of speeding up this expectations homogenizing process. To test this hypothesis, Porter and Smith (1995) ran two sequences of two

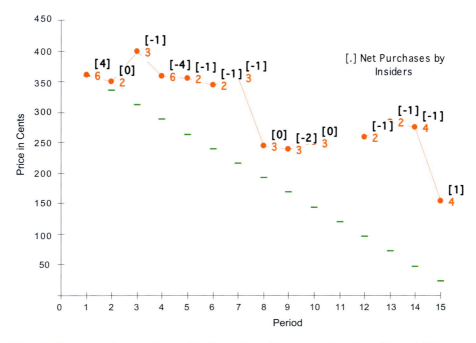

Figure 4. Mean contract price, volume and insider purchases (inexperienced uninformed traders). This experiment had 12 subjects (9 subjects had not participated in this type of market previously and 3 subjects were informed of this market and its characteristics). The nine inexperienced subjects were endowed with cash and shares of the security (a third of the subjects had $9.45 in cash and one share; another third had $5.85 and two shares; one third had $2.25 and three shares) that pays a dividend at the end of each of 15 trading periods. The three informed subjects, who were given information on the number of bids and asks tendered each market period, were endowed with $5.85 and two shares along with the ability to short sale up to 4 shares. These shares had to be covered or a penalty of $4.00 would be paid for uncovered shares at the end of the experiment. The red data points and red numbers next to them are the mean contract prices and volume, respectively for each trading period. The black numbers in brackets are the net short sales of the insiders. Thus, a positive number implies that units in the short sale inventory have been used in that trading period; a negative number indicates net units have been bought to cover short positions.

experiments with the same subjects trained in the mechanics of a futures market. In the new experiments, a futures contract due in period 8 was utilized, where agents could trade both the spot and futures contracts in periods 1–8; after period 8, only the spot market was active. Figure 5 shows the results of one these futures market experiments.

RESULT 8. *Futures markets dampen, but do not eliminate, bubbles by speeding up the process by which traders form common expectations.*

In the wake of the worldwide stock market crash of October 19, 1987, it was widely recommended by various investigatory groups that limit price change rules be imple-

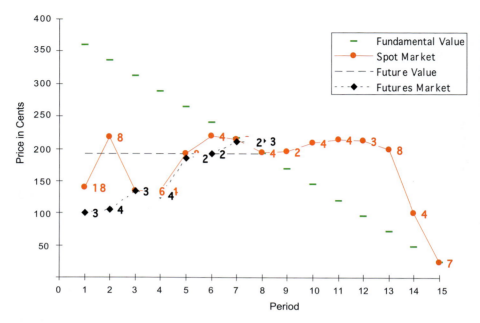

Figure 5. Mean spot and futures contract prices and total volume. This experiment had 9 subjects with endowments and dividends as in Figure 1. The fundamental value is shown by the green dashed values in the graph. In addition, each subject could sell up to 3 futures contracts. The futures contracts came due in period 8. That is, any futures contracts purchased beyond the 3 shares in inventory would becomes spot shares and begin earning dividends from period 9 and beyond. Thus, the fundamental value of the a futures contract is $1.92 ($.24 times 8 periods) and is the dashed black line in the figure. Any short futures at period 8 would pay a penalty of $4.00. Subjects were also given an interest-fee loan (margin account) to buy shares beyond their initial cash endowment. Any margin funds used had to be repaid at the end of the experiment. The red data points and red numbers next to them are the mean spot contract prices and volume, respectively for each trading period. The black data points and numbers are the mean futures prices and volume.

mented on U.S. stock market exchanges. King et al. (1993) report six experiments in which ceiling and floor limits were placed at plus (or minus) twice the expected one period dividend value.

RESULT 9. *Price limit change rules do not prevent bubbles.*

King et al. (1993) conjecture that bubbles are more severe with limit price change rules because traders perceive a reduced down-side risk inducing them to ride the bubble higher and longer. But, of course, when the market breaks, it moves down by the limit and finds no buyers. Trading volume is zero in each period of the crash as the market declines by the limit each period (see Figure 6 for example).

Ch. 30: Price Bubbles

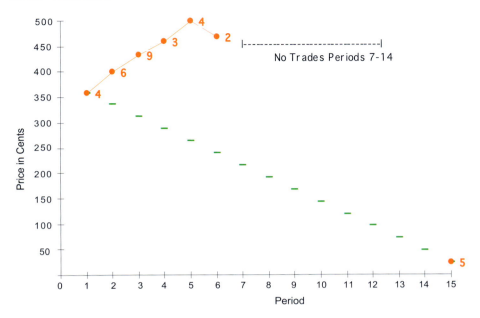

Figure 6. Mean contract price and total volume: Limit price change rule. This experiment had nine subjects endowed with cash and shares of the security (a third of the subjects had $9.45 in cash and one share; another third had $5.85 and two shares; one third had $2.25 and three shares) that pays a dividend at the end of each of 15 trading periods. If held for all fifteen periods it would pay exactly $3.60 in dividends. The security's dividend or fundamental value decreases $.24 each trading period since the security has only a fifteen period life. This declining fundamental value is shown by the green dashed values in the graph. In this experiment, prices could move up or down from the previous period mean contract price by only twice the expected one-period dividend value, i.e., $.48. The red data points and red numbers next to them are the mean contract prices and volume, respectively for each trading period.

References

King, Ronald R., Smith, Vernon L., Williams, Arlington W., Van Boening, M. (1993). "The robustness of bubbles and crashes in experimental stock markets". In: Prigogine, I., Day, R.H., Chen, P. (Eds.), Nonlinear Dynamics and Evolutionary Economics. Oxford University Press, New York.

Porter, David, Smith, Vernon L. (1995). "Futures contracting and dividend uncertainty in experimental asset markets". The Journal of Business 68 (4), 509–541.

Smith, Vernon L., Suchanek, Gerry L., Williams, Arlington A. (1988). "Bubbles, crashes, and endogenous expectations in experimental spot asset markets". Econometrica 56, 1119–1151.

Tirole, Jean (1982). "On the possibility of speculation under rational expectations". Econometrica 50, 1163–1181.

Chapter 31

EXPERIMENTS WITH ARBITRAGE ACROSS ASSETS

ERIC O'N. FISHER

European University Institute

The Johns Hopkins University

The Ohio State University

Theoretical finance is essentially the study of inter-temporal arbitrage, but it is often interesting also to analyze relationships between asset prices. Cross-sectional analysis makes it possible to purge both field and laboratory data of unobservable changes in time-varying fundamentals. Also, although backward induction is at the heart of asset-pricing theory, subjects may find its logic dauntingly complex. They may be able to perceive cross-asset arbitrage opportunities much more readily.

Caginalp and Constantine (1995) study two closed-end funds traded on the New York Stock Exchange, consisting of essentially identical portfolios under the same manager. They show that the relevant relative price is statistically significantly different from unity. Using a simple model of market momentum calibrated from their field data, they explain bubbles in experimental asset markets reported in Porter and Smith (1989). O'Brien and Srivastava (1991) use treatments with complex informational where several assets were traded. They found that markets did not aggregate information efficiently, but it is not always possible to detect these inefficiencies using standard statistical tests. In some treatments, two assets' dividends were perfectly negatively correlated, and a simple pricing relationship that was confirmed in the data. Another more subtle connection between two asset prices received some but not overwhelming support in these experiments.

Foreign exchange markets are also environments where arbitrage across assets is salient. Indeed, purchasing power parity, uncovered interest parity, and covered interest parity are all descriptions of arbitrage across currencies, goods, and interest-bearing assets. Since field data on international transactions are among the oldest economic statistics and since scholars as illustrious as Ibn Khaldoun (1375) and David Hume (1752) have written on exchange rates, it is somewhat surprising that the first foreign exchange market experiments were conducted only in this decade.

Fisher and Kelly (2000) explored foreign exchange markets in the laboratory by running sessions based upon the classic treatment of Smith, Suchanek, and Williams (1988). Fisher and Kelly's treatments capture two important aspects of field foreign exchange markets. First, subjects trade blue and red assets for dollars, just as foreign exchange traders use a key currency for most international transactions. Second, there are no goods markets; indeed, only a negligible fraction of foreign exchange transactions in the field is used for imports. The main finding of these experiments is that both the blue and red assets experience significant bubbles, but they are highly correlated.

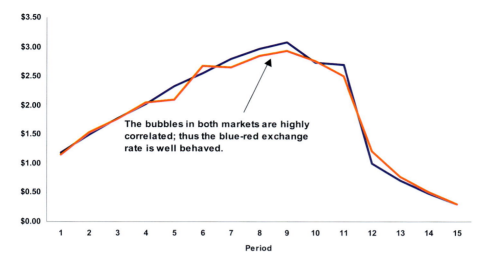

Figure 1. 11 November 1993: actual prices.

Thus a simple theory of cross-asset arbitrage predicts the blue–red exchange rate well, while the dollar price of each asset is quite different from its fundamental. Triangular arbitrage, a fundamental aspect of exchange rate theory, holds in these data, while a simple notion of inter-temporal arbitrage is soundly refuted.

Figure 1 shows the data from a typical session. Each experiment had twelve subjects with heterogeneous endowments of blue assets, red assets, and initial cash on hand. In this session, the blue dividend was an independent and identically distributed multinomial random variable with support {$0.00, $0.08, $0.28, $0.60}; each element occurred with probability 1/4. The red dividend was an identical random variable, independent of its blue analog. Since each asset has an expected dividend of $0.24 per period, both assets have the same fundamental, a line with intercept $3.60 and slope −$0.24. (This line is not shown to keep the figure uncluttered.) Since the two assets are identical, the natural prediction is that the blue-red exchange rate is unity. Figure 1 shows this is true, even in the initial periods.

Investigating the origins of these bubbles is still an active area of research. Lei, Noussair, and Plott (2001) show that bubbles occur even when there is no possibility of making profits from anticipated capital gains. In a fascinating exploration of the "active participation hypothesis," they construct a treatment where a static market and a dynamic asset market are open simultaneously. The data in the static market conform to theoretical predictions, but the asset market still experiences bubbles, albeit with attenuated volume.

Building on Morris (1996), Fisher (1998) posits that the subjects are Bayesians who have heterogeneous prior beliefs about the assets' dividends. Even though each experiment's instructions spend a good deal of time describing the true processes, Fisher

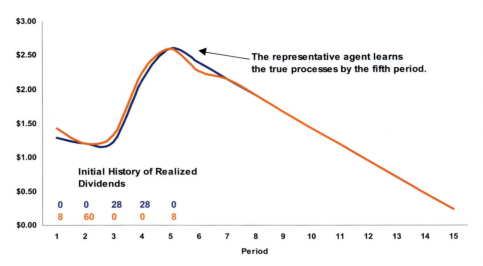

Figure 2. 11 November 1993: predicted prices.

(1998) argues that the subjects may not initially believe the directions, though agents typically do learn the truth. Figure 2 shows the predictions for the data from the session shown before; it is derived from a calibration akin to a minimum distance estimator. In this case, there is one representative agent participating in both the blue and red asset markets. It is apparent that the agent learns the true processes by about the fifth period. Also, this person's prior beliefs are sufficiently pessimistic so that the calibrations fit the data well in the initial periods.

Even though bubbles are ubiquitous in the laboratory, subjects often get cross-asset prices right. Why is this? Two reasons seem salient. First, cross-asset arbitrage may be a simpler cognitive task than inter-temporal arbitrage. This conjecture is supported by the fact that the exchange rates are uniformly accurate in Fisher and Kelly's treatments with two identical assets; in other cases, where the predicted exchange rate is one-half, the data are more variable. Second, after the bubbles burst, usually about two-thirds of the way through a session, the assets are priced according to their fundamental values and then the data predict the exchange rate almost perfectly.

Why does a model with Bayesian updating predict the asset price ratios well? Again two reasons stand out. First, the calibrated priors are often highly correlated across the two markets; thus the initial predictions for the blue and red assets are close, and the exchange rate is predicted well in the early periods. Second, most posterior beliefs converge to the truth. Thereafter the model fits the exchange rate perfectly, although it usually predicts convergence to fundamental values earlier than in the data.

References

Caginalp, Gunduz, Constantine, Greg (1995). "Statistical inference and modeling of momentum in stock prices". Applied Mathematical Finance 2, 225–242.
Fisher, Eric O'N. (1998). "Explaining bubbles in experimental foreign exchange markets". Unpublished manuscript, The Ohio State University.
Fisher, Eric O'N., Kelly, Frank S. (2000). "Experimental foreign exchange markets". Pacific Economic Review 5, 365–387.
Hume, David (1752). "Political Discourses". Reprinted in Rotwein, E., David Hume: Writings on Economics, Nelson, London, 1955.
Ibn Khaldoun (1375). "The Muqadimmah, vol. II". Especially the excerpts in: *Les textes économiques de la Mouqaddima* (1375–1379), translated into the French by G.H. Bousquet, Librarie Marcel Rivière et Compagnie, Paris.
Lei, Vivian, Noussair, Charles, Plott, Charles R. (2001). "Non-speculative bubbles in experimental asset markets: Lack of common knowledge of rationality vs. actual irrationality". Econometrica 69, 831–859.
Morris, Stephen (1996). "Speculative investor behavior and learning". Quarterly Journal of Economics 111, 1111–1134.
O'Brien, John, Srivastava, Sanjay (1991). "Dynamic stock markets with multiple assets: An experimental analysis". Journal of Finance 46, 1811–1838.
Porter, David P., Smith, Vernon L. (1989). "The scope of bubbles and crashes in experimental asset markets". Unpublished manuscript, University of Arizona.
Smith, Vernon L., Suchanek, Gerry L., Williams, Arlington W. (1988). "Bubbles, crashes, and endogenous expectations in experimental asset markets". Econometrica 56, 1119–1152.

Chapter 32

BUBBLES AND CRASHES IN EXPERIMENTAL ASSET MARKETS: COMMON KNOWLEDGE FAILURE?

CHARLES NOUSSAIR

Department of Economics, Emory University, Atlanta, GA 30322, USA

CHARLES PLOTT

Division of the Humanities and Social Sciences, California Institute of Technology, Pasadena, CA 91125, USA

As described earlier in this volume, experimental markets for long-lived assets have a tendency to generate price bubbles, which are prices much higher than fundamental values, and crashes, which are rapid drops in price. This result, originally due to Smith, Suchanek, and Williams (1988), is one of the most striking of modern experimental economics. Smith, Suchanek, and Williams (1988) offer the following insightful conjecture about the origin of the bubble phenomenon. "What we learn from the particular experiments reported here is that a common dividend, and common knowledge thereof, is insufficient to induce initial common expectations. As we interpret it, this is due to agent uncertainty about the behavior of others." The authors thus posit a lack of common knowledge of the rationality of market participants as the origin of the bubble phenomenon. Although the experimenter can control much of the underlying structure and some parameters of the market, he cannot control the beliefs participants have about each other. If some subjects believe that there are irrational traders in the market who might make purchases at high prices, speculative demand can push prices above fundamentals. Thus, even if all traders are rational, departures of prices from fundamental values could be observed, if the rationality is not common knowledge.

On the other hand, the bubble and crash phenomenon may also be due in part to actual decision errors on the part of subjects. That is, some of the purchases at high prices may not be due to speculative demand, but rather to other reasons that are inconsistent with rational behavior of purchasers. If this is the case, the rationality of traders is not common knowledge because some traders will in fact fail to act rationally when inexperienced with asset markets. Lei, Noussair, and Plott (2001) construct an asset market in which errors in decision-making on the part of the subjects in the experiment are the only way that bubbles can arise. The experiment differs from the other asset market experiments described in this section of the volume in that each participant is assigned one of two possible roles, a "buyer" or a "seller," in a continuous double auction market for the asset. A buyer is endowed with cash but no units of the asset. He has the capacity to purchase, but not to make sales. A seller is endowed with units of the asset and the capacity to make sales, but has no initial cash and no ability to make purchases. Purchase for resale is not possible, so there can be no speculative demand for the asset. Any

Handbook of Experimental Economics Results, Volume 1
Copyright © 2008 Elsevier B.V. All rights reserved
DOI: 10.1016/S1574-0722(07)00032-7

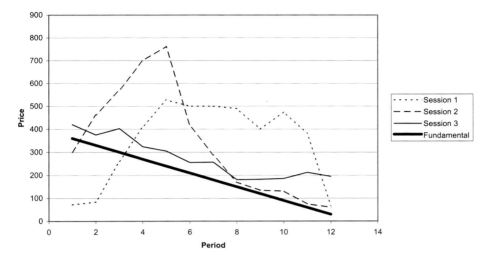

Figure 1. Median transaction price by period: Markets with speculation prohibited.

purchase at a price higher than the maximum possible realization of the future dividend stream results in certain losses and is therefore a dominated transaction. Even if a trader believed that there might be irrational traders in the market, it would be irrational on his own part to make such a purchase.

In the experiment, subjects have tables at their disposal that indicate the expected future dividend stream, which corresponds to the fundamental value, at any time. Subjects take a quiz on how to read the table before the market opens. Thus the fundamental value of the asset is common knowledge at all times during the experiment. Nonetheless, a considerable fraction of total transactions (45.3%, 41.6%, and 27.5% in the three sessions) take place at prices higher than the maximum possible realization of the future dividend stream. These are dominated purchases that can only be classified as errors on the part of the buyer. Furthermore, the time series of transaction prices exhibits the bubble and crash pattern, suggesting that the errors are of a type that has a role in generating bubbles in markets when resale is allowed.

Figure 1 displays the median transaction price in the three sessions of the "NoSpec" treatment of Lei, Noussair, and Plott (2001). The bold black line indicates the fundamental value and the bold gray line the maximum possible realization of the future dividend stream. The figure illustrates the bubble and crash pattern in sessions 1 and 2. In session three prices remain too high throughout the time horizon as a crash fails to occur. The presence of bubbles in the NoSpec treatment indicates that the possibility of speculation is not necessary to cause the bubble and crash price dynamics. It also shows that in fact there is no reason for the rationality of traders to be common knowledge, since subjects are indeed prone to making errors in their trading decisions.

Why do these purchases at high prices occur? The excess volume of trade in the experiment suggests the origin of some of the errors. The sellers sell 85.5% of the total stock of units in the NoSpec treatment to the buyers. In contrast, if risk attitudes were on average the same among buyers and sellers, approximately 50% of the units would change hands on average given that there are an equal number of buyers and sellers.

One possible explanation for the excess volume is that the procedures of the experiment encourage participants to make too many trades. Consider a subject who is recruited to participate in an experiment, and is trained in the mechanics of buying and selling. The subject may be predisposed to participate actively in the experiment in some manner and to use his training. That is, the subject may believe that he is "supposed" to buy and sell because he is placed in a market environment in the role of a trader, and there is no activity available other than buying or selling. If that is the case, when faced with a choice between an unprofitable transaction and not trading, a subject may choose the unprofitable transaction. In short, some of the activity in the asset market may be due to the fact the protocol of the experiment encourages subjects to be active, and the only way to be active is to make trades in the asset market. Lei, Noussair, and Plott (2001) explore this possibility in their "TwoMarket/NoSpec" treatment.

In the TwoMarket/NoSpec treatment, there are two markets, both organized as continuous double auctions, and each market trades a different commodity. In one of the markets a commodity called Y with a life of one period, as in Smith (1962), is traded. The market for Y is repeated under stationary conditions for 15 periods. In the other market an asset called X, with the same structure as the asset in the NoSpec treatment, is traded. The asset market opens in period 4, has a life of 12 periods, pays an expected dividend of 30 each period, and has zero terminal value after period 15. The instructions to subjects emphasize that participation is optional and that it may be in their best interest to participate in none, one, or both of the markets. The second market and the language in the instructions are intended to reduce any feeling of compulsion toward active participation that subjects may have.

Overall, 54.7% of the units were sold to the buyers, indicating that the change in the procedures served to greatly reduce the excess volume. Figure 2 shows the time series of median transaction prices by period in the three sessions of the TwoMarket/NoSpec treatment. A bubble occurs in only in session one. In the other two sessions, only 2.8% and 4.9% of all transactions were at prices higher than the maximum possible realization of the future dividend stream. Thus it appears that the excess volume and the incidence of the type of decision error that accompany bubble formation are related. However, it is also clear that the particular techniques Lei, Noussair, and Plott (2001) employ to reduce the bias toward active participation do not totally eliminate the possibility of a bubble.

In these asset markets, departures of prices from fundamental values are not only due to the lack of common knowledge of rationality, but also to the existence of traders who actually do behave irrationally. It certainly does appear that other traders speculate when they realize that some participants are prone to errors. The findings presented here suggest that the appropriate modeling approach to explaining the bubble and crash

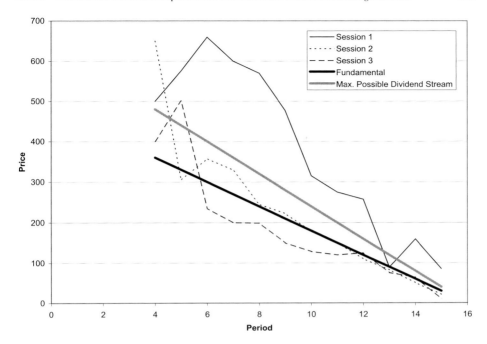

Figure 2. Median transaction price by period, TwoMarket/NoSpec treatment.

phenomenon requires the presence of errors in decision making on the part of agents, in addition to the absence of common knowledge of rationality.

References

Lei, V., Noussair, C., Plott, C. (2001). "Non-speculative bubbles in experimental asset markets: Lack of common knowledge of rationality vs. actual irrationality". Econometrica 69 (4), 831–859.
Smith, V. (1962). "An experimental study of competitive market behavior". Journal of Political Economy 70 (1), 111–137.
Smith, V., Suchanek, G., Williams, A. (1988). "Bubbles, crashes, and endogenous expectations in laboratory asset markets". Econometrica 56 (6), 1119–1152.

Chapter 33

A COMPARISON OF MARKET INSTITUTIONS

TIMOTHY N. CASON
Purdue University

DANIEL FRIEDMAN
University of California, Santa Cruz

This chapter summarizes a laboratory experiment comparing four different trading institutions, illustrated in Figure 1, in a random values environment with four single unit buyers and four single unit sellers. Figure 2 summarizes the main findings on efficiency: the continuous double auction (CDA) and high-frequency multiple-call market (MCM) are the most efficient institutions, followed by the low-frequency MCM and the single call market (SCM), with our implementation of uniform price double auction (UPDA) trailing the pack. Figures 3 and 4 summarize the main findings on transaction prices and volume. Price deviations from competitive equilibrium tend to be smallest in the SCM. Volume is highest in CDA, decreases with call frequency in MCM and SCM, and is lowest in UPDA. The body of this chapter describes the institutions, environment, performance measures, and results.

1. Market Institutions

The CDA is the richest trading institution in terms of within-period information feedback, trading opportunities and strategic complexity. The CDA sessions were conducted using multiple-unit double auction (MUDA) trading software (Plott, 1991), constrained to a single market and a single unit per trader. Every trader's screen displays the current market bid and ask. Buyers (sellers) are free to accept the market ask (bid) at any time, and the transaction is executed immediately. A transaction immediately removes both the market bid and ask. At any time during a trading period, buyers (sellers) who have not yet transacted are free to seize the market bid (ask) by posting a bid exceeding (ask below) the current market bid (ask). Traders perform their record-keeping by hand. Each period consists of 110 seconds of trading, which was sufficient for the typical 2- to 3-unit trading volume in our environment.

The SCM is the simplest trading institution in that it offers only one trading opportunity and minimal information within each trading period. The SCM sessions were conducted using a variant of the software employed in Friedman (1993) and several other studies. The SCM institution solicits a bid (or highest acceptable purchase price for a single unit) b_i from each buyer i and an ask (or lowest acceptable sale price) a_j

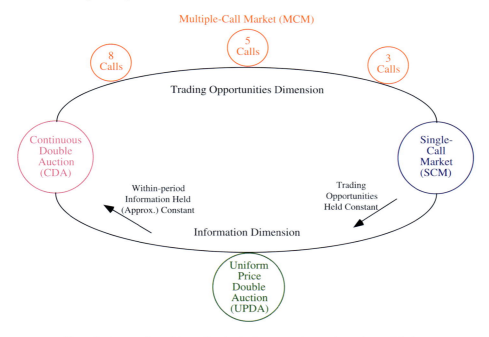

Figure 1. An overview of the trading institution comparison and experimental design.

from each seller j. The solicitations are simultaneous and private during the trading period. The demand revealed in $\{b_i\}$ and the supply revealed in $\{a_j\}$ then are cleared at a uniform equilibrium price p^*. With indivisible units, there often is an interval $[p_l, p_u]$ of market clearing prices, in which case the chosen price is $(1-k)p_l + kp_u$, where $k = 0$, $k = 0.5$ or $k = 1$. At the conclusion of the trading period traders observed p^* and the bids, asks, values, costs and profits of all other traders. Detailed analysis presented in Cason and Friedman (1997) indicates that trader behavior is generally insensitive to the pricing rule k, so for this institutional comparison we pool the data across the three k treatments.

As illustrated in Figure 1, the remaining two trading institutions link these polar institutions in two different ways. The MCM is just like the $k = 0.5$ SCM except that it has several calls (clearings) per period so traders have more trading opportunities. The number of calls is preannounced to be 3, 5, or 8 each period, with the length of the trading period is fixed at 120 seconds. Unaccepted bids and asks are automatically renewed for the next call, although traders can revise them at any time as in the CDA. After each call, all traders see whether their own offer was successful, and observe the transaction price (if any) as well as the best-rejected bid and best-rejected ask. At the end of the period subjects receive the same "full information" as in the SCM.

The UPDA market provides continuous information feedback as in the CDA, while limiting the number of trading opportunities to one per period as in the SCM. In the

UPDA, one call is held at the end of the trading period, but during the period traders submit and revise market bids and offers while observing changes in the possible terms of trade. A variety of information conditions are possible in the UPDA, many of which were explored in different environments from ours by McCabe, Rassenti, and Smith (1993) and by Friedman (1993). The choices made for this experiment reflect a desire to approximate the information conditions and environment of the CDA. Therefore, we provided subjects with the current "indicated market price" and the current best rejected bid and best rejected offer, which corresponds most closely to the CDA information concerning the current market bid and offer and available terms of trade. Moreover, the sessions allow traders to cancel bids and offers (which is allowed by many computerized CDA implementations including ours) and calls the market after 90 seconds. The UPDA sessions were conducted using the same market software (again appropriately modified) that was used in the SCM and MCM sessions. Once again, traders received complete information regarding the other traders values, costs, bids asks and profits at the conclusion of each period, and all sessions used the pricing rule $k = 0.5$.

2. Market Environment

To maintain comparability across institutions, we held constant several features of the environment. All sessions take place in a random values environment: in each trading period the buyers' redemption values and the sellers' costs are independently drawn from the uniform distribution with range [$0.00, $4.99]. This fact is publicly announced at the beginning of the session, and subjects have no other information regarding other subjects' drawn values during the trading period. The same sequences of drawn values were used in each session and across institutions to limit between-session variability. When the same subjects are brought back as experienced we employed a different set of random values, and these values were held constant across all experienced sessions.

All sessions used four buyers and four sellers, each with a trading capacity of only one unit. All inexperienced sessions ran 30 trading periods, and all experienced sessions ran 40 trading periods. In the 30-period inexperienced sessions, traders switched buyer and seller roles before period 9 and before period 25; in the 40-period experienced sessions, traders switched roles before period 11 and before period 31. This switch was preannounced, as was the number of buyers and sellers in each session. For each institution except SCM we conducted 3 sessions with inexperienced subjects and 2 sessions with experienced subjects. For the SCM we used three sessions (two employing inexperienced subjects) in each of the three k treatments.

3. Related Work

Several laboratory experiments have also compared these trading institutions in alternative environments. Smith et al. (1982) compares performance of the CDA to several variants of the SCM in a repetitive stationary environment. Price formation was more rapid and reliable in the CDA but a multiple-unit recontracting version of the SCM had equivalent allocational efficiency. Friedman and Ostroy (1995) find that both the CDA and the SCM eventually produce highly efficient allocations even when the induced values and costs are chosen to encourage strategic misrepresentation. McCabe, Rassenti, and Smith (1993) study UPDA in an environment with additive random shifts superimposed each period on otherwise repetitively stationary demand and supply schedules. Friedman (1993) examines another variant of the UPDA institution as well as the MCM institution in an asset market environment. These studies find that the best variants of UPDA and MCM are almost as reliable as the CDA in producing prices and allocations near competitive equilibrium. The interested reader should consult our previous work (Cason and Friedman, 1996, 1997) for more details of additional experimental treatments in the CDA and SCM environments, respectively.

Two caveats are in order. First, we chose a thin, random-values environment because it provided the clearest view of the price formation process. It is not necessarily the most representative of important field environments, and the environmental robustness of our conclusions is not yet established. Second, several of the institutions have variants that may have different performance characteristics. In particular, McCabe, Rassenti, and Smith (1993) find that UPDA efficiency depends fairly sensitively on implementation details, and is not enhanced by two details we chose to maintain comparability to the CDA, viz., a fixed closing time and a two-side update rule.

4. Results

4.1. Market Efficiency

Define market *inefficiency* as the percentage of the maximum possible gains from exchange which traders fail to realize. Figure 2 summarizes the outcomes. Our most surprising finding is that UPDA is the most inefficient trading institution in this thin volume, random-values environment. In statistical tests based on a random effects model reported in Cason and Friedman (1999), we show that the UPDA inefficiency is significantly greater than the CDA inefficiency and is marginally significantly greater than the SCM inefficiency. UPDA inefficiency is also significantly greater than the inefficiency in all three MCM treatments.

Like UPDA, the SCM has only one transaction opportunity per period and has lower efficiency than the other institutions in both experience conditions. This provides some evidence that multiple trading opportunities are important to generate increases in efficiency. However, the differences between SCM efficiency and CDA and MCM efficiency are not statistically significant. Finally, note that the MCM institution generates efficient outcomes that compare favorably with (and are not statistically distinguishable from) the CDA outcomes, so it would appear that 3 to 5 calls per period are sufficient to generate market efficiency comparable to the CDA benchmark.

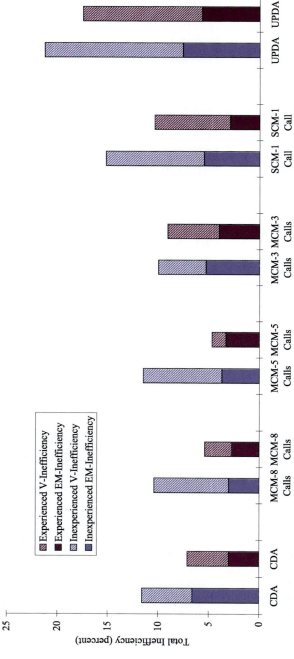

Figure 2. Trading inefficiency is greatest for the two institutions that permit only one transaction opportunity per period (UPDA and SCM), and inefficiency is lowest for the two institutions that permit multiple transaction opportunities per period (CDA and MCM).

Note: CDA denotes continuous double auction; MCM denotes multiple call market; SCM denotes single call market; UPDA denotes uniform price double auction. Inefficiency falls with experience in all trading institutions. V-inefficiency arises when volume falls below the competitive equilibrium volume, and EM-inefficiency arises when extra-marginal units displace.

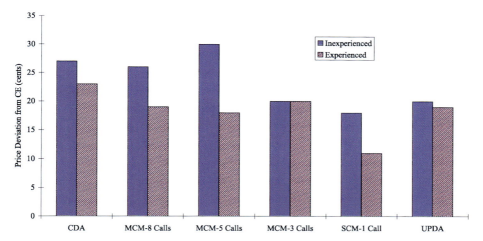

Note: CDA denotes continuous double auction; MCM denotes multiple call market; SCM denotes single call market; UPDA denotes uniform price double auction.

Figure 3. Mean absolute deviations from the competitive equilibrium are lowest in the SCM, in which all trades occur at one price; deviations tend to be greatest in the institutions that permit multiple transaction opportunities per period (CDA and MCM).

Efficiency can fall short of 100 percent if (a) traders with extra-marginal units transact (EM-inefficiency), or (b) profitable trades are not executed (low volume or V-inefficiency). The bars of Figure 2 distinguish the mix of V and EM inefficiency across institutions (see Cason and Friedman (1999) and Rust, Palmer, and Miller (1993) for details of this inefficiency decomposition). Both types of inefficiency are common, and in the inexperienced sessions the low volume efficiency losses exceed the extra-marginal efficiency losses in four of the six institutions. In all institutions the increase in efficiency due to experience generally occurs because of reductions in both types of inefficiency. In the 5-call and 8-call MCM, the reduction in V-inefficiency is quite pronounced. V-inefficiency is lowest for the CDA and MCM sessions, probably due to the multiple transaction opportunities permitted by these institutions.

4.2. Transaction Prices

The standard benchmark for price is the competitive equilibrium (CE), which equates true demand and true supply for the value and cost realization that period. In our thin, random values environment in nearly every period there exists a *range* of CE prices. Mean transaction prices in a period are within the CE range in less than one-half of the periods for all institutions. (The CDA and MCM final transaction prices, not shown here, are within the CE range no more often.)

Figure 3 presents the mean absolute deviation of average transaction prices (each period) from the nearest endpoint of the CE range. Of course, the price deviation is 0 if

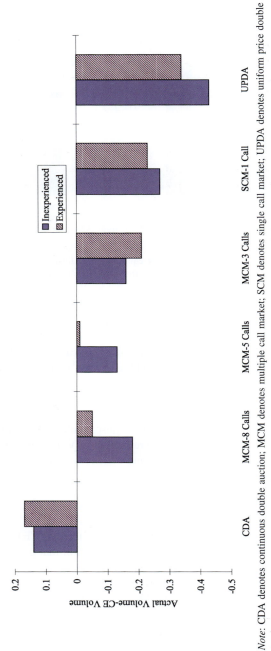

Figure 4. Trading volume increases with experience, and exceeds the CE volume in the CDA; volume roughly declines with the number of transaction opportunities in the MCM, and is lowest in the UPDA.

Note: CDA denotes continuous double auction; MCM denotes multiple call market; SCM denotes single call market; UPDA denotes uniform price double auction.

average prices are within the CE range. Price deviations are smallest in the SCM, and are largest (at least for experienced traders) in the CDA. Statistically speaking (again, see Cason and Friedman (1999) for details), the CDA mean price deviation exceeds: (1) the UPDA mean price deviation; (2) the 3-call MCM mean price deviation; and (3) the SCM mean price deviation. The SCM mean price deviation is also lower than the 5-call MCM mean price deviation and the 8-call MCM mean price deviation. The other mean price deviations are not significantly different.

4.3. Transaction Volume

The competitive equilibrium (CE) also provides a benchmark for trading volume. CE volume ranges from 0 to 4 units but usually is 2 or 3. Figure 4 shows that actual transaction volume increases with experience in every institution, with the minor exception of the 3-call MCM. Volume is highest in the CDA, where it exceeds the CE benchmark. Volume falls below the CE benchmark in the other institutions and declines almost monotonically with the number of calls in MCM and SCM. It is lowest in UPDA. Cason and Friedman (1999) report that most of these differences are statistically significant.

5. Discussion

The comparison of four trading institutions in a thin market, random values environment supports the following general conclusions. First, trading efficiency in the uniform price double auction is lowest, and the single call market efficiency is second lowest. This suggests that multiple trading opportunities, as in the continuous double auction and the multiple call market, help generate high efficiency. Second, the primary source of efficiency losses in these (single opportunity) institutions is insufficient trading volume. Third, transaction prices are less accurate on average (in that they deviate more from competitive equilibrium levels) in the continuous double auction and multiple call market. Taken together, these results highlight a key tradeoff when the trading institution permits multiple transaction opportunities. Multiple transaction opportunities substantially reduce (low volume) inefficiency due to underrevelation of traders' true values and costs, but also reduce pricing accuracy because traders allow more noise when negotiating transactions.

References

Cason, T., Friedman, D. (1996). "Price formation in double auction markets". Journal of Economic Dynamics and Control 20, 1307–1337.
Cason, T., Friedman, D. (1997). "Price formation in single call markets". Econometrica 65, 311–345.
Cason, T., Friedman, D. (1999). "Price formation and exchange in thin markets: A laboratory comparison of institutions". In: de Antoni, E., Howitt, P., Leijonhufvud, A. (Eds.), Money, Markets and Method: Essays in Honour of Robert W. Clower. Edward Elgar, Cheltenham, UK, pp. 155–179.

Friedman, D. (1993). "How trading institutions affect financial market performance: Some laboratory evidence". Economic Inquiry 31, 410–435.

Friedman, D., Ostroy, J. (1995). "Competitivity in auction markets: An experimental and theoretical investigation". Economic Journal 105, 22–53.

McCabe, K., Rassenti, S., Smith, V. (1993). "Designing a uniform price double auction: An experimental evaluation". In: Friedman, D., Rust, J. (Eds.), The Double Auction Market. Addison–Wesley, Reading, MA, pp. 307–332.

Plott, C. (1991). "A computerized laboratory market system and research support systems for the multiple unit double auction". Social Science Working Paper 783, California Institute of Technology.

Rust, J., Palmer, R., Miller, J. (1993). "Behavior of trading automata in a computerized double auction market". In: Friedman, D., Rust, J. (Eds.), The Double Auction Market. Addison–Wesley, Reading, MA, pp. 155–198.

Smith, V., Williams, A., Bratton, W.K., Vannoni, M. (1982). "Competitive market institutions: Double auctions vs. sealed bid–offer auctions". American Economic Review 72, 58–77.

Chapter 34

COORDINATION SUCCESS IN NON-COOPERATIVE LARGE GROUP MARKET ENTRY GAMES

AMNON RAPOPORT

University of Arizona

DARRYL A. SEALE

University of Nevada Las Vegas
e-mail: dseale@unlv.edu

When several firms independently consider entry into a new market, tacit coordination becomes critical for solving the problem of multiple equilibria. Several recent studies (Kahneman, 1988; Erev and Rapoport, 1998; Rapoport, 1995; Rapoport et al., 1998; Rapoport, Seale, and Winter, 1997; Sundali, Rapoport, and Seale, 1995) have shown that tacit coordination in a class of non-cooperative market entry games with a large number of agents is accounted for remarkably well by the Nash equilibrium solution. To Kahneman, who first introduced this game, the behavioral regularities found in the game looked "like magic" (1988, p. 12). Subsequent experimental studies of the market entry game by Rapoport and his associates, which systematically manipulated the information structure of the game, compared behavior in the domains of gains and losses, or introduced private information and asymmetry between players, have shown that this "magic" is robust. Under a wide variety of experimental conditions, interacting players in large groups playing the market entry game with no communication among them rapidly achieve coordination success that is accounted for on the aggregate level by a Pareto deficient equilibrium solution.

1. The Market Game

To study tacit coordination, we devised a class of iterated market entry games (Selten and Güth, 1982) played by a group N for T periods (trials), where the values of $n = |N|$ and T are common knowledge. At the beginning of each period (stage game) t, $t = 1, \ldots, T$, a possibly different positive integer c ($1 \leq c \leq n$), interpreted as the "known capacity of the market," is publicly announced. Each player i ($I \in N$) is then privately informed of her entry fee h_i ($h_i \geq 0$) for that period. After the value of c becomes common knowledge, each player i must decide privately and anonymously whether to enter the market ($d_i = 1$) or stay out of it ($d_i = 0$). Communication before or during the game is prohibited. Individual payoffs for each period are determined by

$$H_i(\mathbf{d}) = \begin{cases} v, & \text{if } d_i = 0, \\ k + r(c - m) - h_i, & \text{if } d_i = 1, \end{cases}$$

where v, k, and r are real-valued, commonly known constants that remain fixed across iterations, m ($0 \leqslant m \leqslant n$) is the actual number of entrants for that period, and $d = (d_1, d_2, \ldots, d_n)$ is the vector of n (binary) decisions. At the end of each period, players may or may not be informed of the value of m and, consequently, their individual payoff for that period. Information about the decisions and payoffs of other members of the group is not disclosed.

When $h_i = 0$ for all $I \in N$ (Erev and Rapoport, 1998; Rapoport, 1995; Rapoport et al., 1998; Sundali, Rapoport, and Seale, 1995), the resulting game is characterized by symmetric players, complete information, and zero entry fees in which the incentive to enter the market decreases linearly with the number of entrants. When the entry fee is private information, and only the distribution of entry fees in the population is known (Rapoport, Seale, and Winter, 1997), the effects of asymmetry between players can be studied. Whether players are symmetric or not, each player is faced on each period with a binary choice between earning a fixed payoff, regardless of the actions taken by the other players, or an uncertain payoff which is a linear function of the difference cm.

2. Results

2.1. Sundali, Rapoport, and Seale (1995)

Sundali, Rapoport, and Seale (1995), conducted two different computer-controlled experiments. In both experiments the value of c in each period was chosen randomly and without replacement from the set of market capacities $C = \{1, 3, \ldots, 19\}$. This determined a block of ten trials. The same procedure was then repeated, with a different random selection of market capacities, for six blocks in Experiment 1 ($T = 60$) and ten blocks in Experiment 2 ($T = 100$). The parameter values for Experiment 1 were $v = k = 1, r = 2, n = 20$, and $h_i = 0$ for all $i \in N$. What characterizes Experiment 1 is that no information about the number of entrants, m, and the individual payoff, $H_i(d)$, was given at the end of each trial to prevent learning. Table 1 presents the number of entries by block of ten trials and market capacity values across the twenty subjects. The values of c are presented in an ascending order, not in the random order of their presentation, which differed from block to block. The correlations between c and m for each block separately, and across the six blocks, are shown in the bottom row of the table. The means and standard deviations of number of entries across blocks, computed for each value of c separately, are presented in the two right-hand columns of the table.

For the market entry game played in Experiment 1, there are $r!/c!(n-c)!$ pure strategy equilibria in which $m^*(c) = c$ players enter and $n!/(c-1)!(n-c+1)!$ pure strategy equilibria in which $m^*(c) = c - 1$ players enter. There is also a symmetric mixed-strategy equilibrium in which, given c and assuming players to be risk-neutral, each player enters with probability $(c-1)/(n-1)$. Although no trial-to-trial feedback was provided, the aggregate results in Table 1 are accounted for surprisingly well by the equilibrium solutions. First, there is a positive and highly significant correlation

Table 1

Reports the number of entries by market capacity across the six blocks of trials for Experiment 1 of Sundali, Rapoport, and Seale (1995), where subjects made entry decisions without feedback. The correlation between the number of entries and market capacity is shown in the last row of the table. The shaded cells indicate those trials where the number of entries was within ±1 of the pure strategy equilibrium prediction

Capacity	Prediction	Block of ten trials						Total	Mean	SD
		1	2	3	4	5	6			
1	[0, 1]	1	0	0	1	0	0	2	0.33	0.47
3	[2, 3]	4	4	4	5	4	3	24	4.00	0.58
5	[4, 5]	7	7	6	6	7	7	40	6.67	0.47
7	[6, 7]	11	11	10	12	11	8	63	10.50	1.26
9	[8, 9]	13	10	11	12	9	13	68	11.33	1.49
11	[10, 11]	9	8	8	11	11	7	54	9.00	1.53
13	[12, 13]	15	12	11	11	9	12	70	11.67	1.80
15	[14, 15]	15	16	14	14	12	11	82	13.67	1.70
17	[16, 17]	15	16	14	14	16	17	92	14.83	0.90
19	[18, 19]	17	18	18	18	19	17	107	17.83	0.69
Total		107	102	96	104	98	95	602		
Correlation		0.93	0.94	0.94	0.92	0.93	0.91	0.92		

Key findings: (1) Positive and highly significant correlations between the number of entries m and market capacity c, (2) mean number of entries is accounted for by the pure strategy equilibrium prediction, (3) 62% (37 out of 60) of the trials are within ± of the equilibrium prediction.

between c and m. In equilibrium this correlation is 1, whereas in actuality it ranged between 0.91 and 0.94, accounting for approximately 85% of the variance. Second, the mean number of entries is well approximated by the equilibrium solution. We used the measure $d(c) = |m^*(c) - m(c)|$ to assess the goodness of fit, and found $d(c) = 0$ for 22 out of the 60 trials, $d(c) = 1$ for 15 trials, and $d(c) = 2$ for 12 more trials. $d(c) > 2$ in only 18% of all trials.

On the individual level, we find considerable differences between players. Table 2 shows the number of entries, summed across the six blocks of ten periods each, by subject and value of c. The total number of entries (out of a maximum of 60), shown in the bottom row of Table 2, varies considerably from 5 (Subject 10) to 52 (Subject 16), and the individual profiles support in general neither a mixed-strategy equilibrium nor cutoff decision rules of the type "enter if and only if $c \geq c^*$," where c^* is some cutoff value constant across blocks.

Table 2

The table reports the total number of entries by market capacity for each of the twenty subjects in Experiment 1 of Sundali, Rapoport, and Seale (1995). Subjects are arranged by the index s. This index is a measure of decision consistency, where $0 \leq s \leq 30$, and takes its largest value when subjects approach a cutoff-type decision rule

Capacity	Subject																			
	S08	S04	S16	S06	S05	S10	S12	S17	S14	S20	S11	S03	S18	S07	S15	S13	S19	S01	S09	S02
1	0	0	0	0	0	0	1	0	0	0	0	0	0	0	0	0	1	0	0	0
3	0	0	4	0	0	0	6	1	1	1	0	0	6	0	0	0	1	0	1	3
5	0	0	6	0	0	0	0	6	0	4	1	0	6	1	4	1	4	1	1	5
7	6	0	6	0	0	0	6	6	0	4	2	0	6	4	5	2	5	4	3	4
9	6	0	6	2	1	0	6	4	0	5	5	3	5	4	6	3	4	3	1	4
11	6	0	6	6	1	1	1	0	2	5	3	2	1	3	4	2	4	2	2	3
13	6	1	6	6	6	0	0	3	3	6	6	3	2	1	4	2	5	4	2	4
15	6	6	6	6	6	0	6	6	6	6	6	6	2	1	1	2	2	3	3	2
17	6	6	6	6	6	2	2	6	6	6	6	6	4	6	3	3	4	4	3	3
19	6	6	6	6	4	5	5	6	6	6	6	6	4	6	3	6	4	5	5	5
Total	42	19	52	32	26	5	33	38	24	43	35	26	36	26	30	21	34	26	21	33
s Index	30	29	28	28	28	27	25	24	24	23	23	22	20	20	16	15	14	14	13	11

Key findings: (1) Substantial individual differences in the total number of entry decisions and propensity to enter, given various market capacities, (2) individual decision profiles support neither a mixed strategy equilibrium nor rules of the type "enter only if $c \geq c^*$, where c^* is some cutoff value constant throughout the experiment.

Table 3

Reports the aggregate number of entries by market capacity across the ten blocks of trials for the three twenty-subject groups of Experiment 2 of Sundali, Rapoport, and Seale (1995), where subjects made entry decisions with trial-to-trial feedback. The correlation between the number of entries and capacity is shown in the last row of the table

Capacity	Prediction	Block of ten trials										Total	Mean	SD
		1	2	3	4	5	6	7	8	9	10			
1	[0, 1]	4	2	4	4	1	2	6	3	4	1	31	1.03	1.60
3	[2, 3]	17	12	9	9	7	12	11	11	10	12	110	3.67	2.67
5	[4, 5]	29	15	12	17	13	18	13	14	11	12	154	5.13	5.27
7	[6, 7]	20	21	26	21	18	23	23	25	21	25	223	7.43	2.54
9	[8, 9]	11	34	30	31	27	23	25	27	28	24	260	8.67	6.24
11	[10, 11]	42	34	28	33	32	36	30	29	40	31	335	11.17	4.62
13	[12, 13]	34	35	41	41	34	32	39	38	32	37	363	12.10	3.40
15	[14, 15]	34	45	42	38	49	45	45	40	43	43	424	14.13	4.22
17	[16, 17]	48	50	48	48	50	53	46	50	51	50	494	16.47	1.96
19	[18, 19]	54	55	56	55	56	53	54	54	54	55	546	18.20	0.97
Total		293	303	296	297	287	297	292	291	294	290	294		
Correlation		0.86	0.99	0.99	0.99	0.99	0.98	0.99	0.99	0.98	0.99	0		

Key findings: (1) The differences between the mean number of entries and the equilibrium prediction are very small, and (2) with the exception of the first block, the correlations between the number of entries and capacity are equal to or higher than 0.98.

Experiment 2 of Sundali, Rapoport, and Seale (1995) introduced three major changes. First and most importantly, trial-to-trial feedback about the number of entrants (m) and individual payoff ($H_i(d)$) was given, thereby allowing for learning. Second, the value of T was increased from 60 to 100. Third, the subjects were allowed to keep track of the history of the game. Three different groups, each including $n = 20$ subjects, were recruited. Table 3, which uses the same format as Table 1, shows the number of entries by block and market capacity across the sixty subjects. Basically, Table 3 shows the same aggregate results as Table 1: the differences between the mean number of entries and the value of c are very small, and the correlations between c and m are equal to or greater than 0.98 (except of Block 1).

Figures 1a, 1b, and 1c display the individual number of entries for each subject in Groups 1, 2, and 3, respectively. The decisions of each subject in Blocks 2 to 10 (Block 1 is omitted) are displayed by a rectangular bar, called a profile. The horizontal axis of each bar is divided into nine equal intervals (not shown in the figure), and the vertical axis shows the ten values of c ordered from 1 to 19. The total number of entries can take any integer from 0 to 90. (For example, Subject 1 in Group 1 only entered once on $c = 17$ and six times on $c = 19$ for a total of seven entries.) Within each group, the twenty subjects are ordered in terms of an index $s = \sum |4.5 - v|, v = 0, 1, \ldots, 9$, which assumes its maximum value when each of the ten rows of the profile includes either 0's or 1's. The profiles in Figures 1a, 1b, and 1c display the individual differences

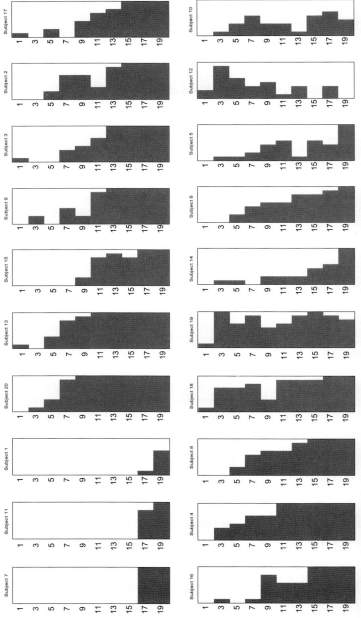

Key findings: (1) Substantial individual differences in entry rules, and (2) no evidence that the majority of subjects use a cutoff-type rule, or mix their decisions as prescribed by the mixed strategy equilibrium solution.

Figure 1a. Displays the number of entries by market capacity for each subject in Group 1 of Sundali, Rapoport, and Seale (1995). These individual profiles are arranged by the index s (not shown), a measure of decision consistency.

Ch. 34: Coordination Success in Non-cooperative Large Group Market Entry Games

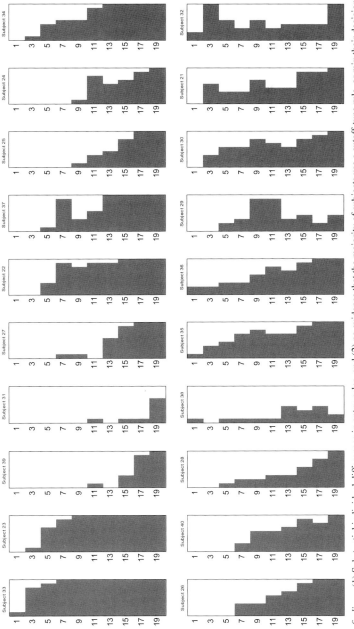

Key findings: (1) Substantial individual differences in entry rules, and (2) no evidence that the majority of subjects use a cutoff-type rule, or mix their decisions as prescribed by the mixed strategy equilibrium solution.

Figure 1b. Displays the number of entries by market capacity for each subject in Group 2 of Sundali, Rapoport, and Seale (1995). These individual profiles are arranged by the index s (not shown), a measure of decision consistency.

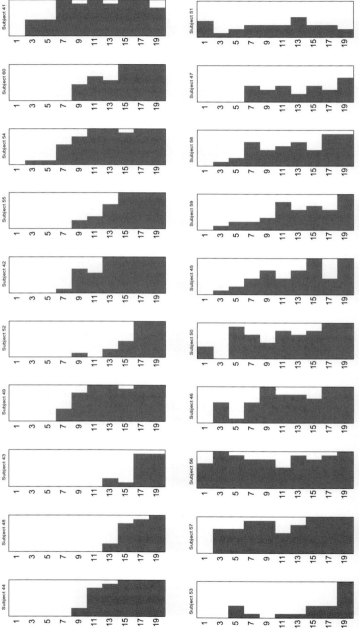

Key findings: (1) Substantial individual differences in entry rules, and (2) no evidence that the majority of subjects use a cutoff-type rule, or mix their decisions as prescribed by the mixed strategy equilibrium solution.

Figure 1c. Displays the number of entries by market capacity for each subject in Group 3 of Sundali, Rapoport, and Seale (1995). These individual profiles are arranged by the index s (not shown), a measure of decision consistency.

in the total number of entries and in the degree of consistency of decisions with a fixed cutoff decision rule across blocks. Clearly, different subjects in each group use different decision rules (with much switching in decision between adjacent blocks for the same value of c), but on the aggregate level the results are orderly and very close to the Nash equilibrium solution.

2.2. Rapoport et al. (1998)

Using the same experimental design as Sundali, Rapoport, and Seale (1995), Rapoport et al. (1998), extended the investigation to the case $v \neq k$. In particular, they focused on two cases: in the first case $v < 0 < k$, and in the second $v > k > 0$. In the former case, each player faces a choice between staying out and losing a certain amount v with certainty or entering the market and earning an uncertain payoff that is likely to be negative because of excessive entry. In the latter case, the tension is between receiving a positive payoff v with certainty and receiving an uncertain payoff that is likely to be positive because of too few entrants. Phenomenologically, the difference between these two domains of losses and gains is considerable (see Kahneman and Tversky, 1979).

Rapoport et al. (1998) included three conditions in a between-subjects design. In all three conditions $k = 1$, $r = 2$, and $n = 20$. The "staying out" parameter v assumed the values 6, −6, and −10, for Conditions 1, 2, and 3, respectively. Initial endowments were −$69.9, $110.1, and $170.0, for Conditions 1, 2, and 3, respectively. They were set in such a way that if a subject stayed out on all 100 trials, her payoff would have been $20.1. As before, ten different values of c were presented randomly in each of ten blocks of trials ($T = 100$).

The pure strategy asymmetric equilibria specify $c - 3$, $c + 3$, and $c + 5$ entrants for Conditions 1, 2, and 3, respectively. Clearly, they do not specify which subjects should enter. There exists a symmetric mixed-strategy equilibrium, in which each player enters with probability $[r(c - 1) + k - v]/[r(n - 1)]$. These equilibria are Pareto deficient; players can increase their payoff substantially by entering with a smaller probability.

Figure 2 presents the actual and predicted number of entries summed over the ten values of c by condition and block. The actual number of entries increases from 95.2 in Condition 1 through 118.7 in Condition 2 to 125.5 in Condition 3. In comparison, the predicted number of entries per block are 89, 115, and 125, respectively. The correlations $r_{(c,m)}$, (not shown) are very high (median = 0.91) and in agreement with the equilibrium solution. With respect to the fit provided by the equilibrium solution to the aggregate data, we find no difference between the three conditions, or between the results of Rapoport et al. (1998) and those reported earlier in Experiment 2 of Sundali, Rapoport, and Seale (1995).

The three panels of Figure 3 display the mean observed and predicted number of entries for each value of c in Conditions +6, −6, and −10, respectively. Note that the ten values of c vary from condition to condition, depending on the value of v. Each panel of Figure 3 shows that, as a first approximation, the Nash equilibrium solution – in either pure or mixed strategies – organizes the total number of entries very well:

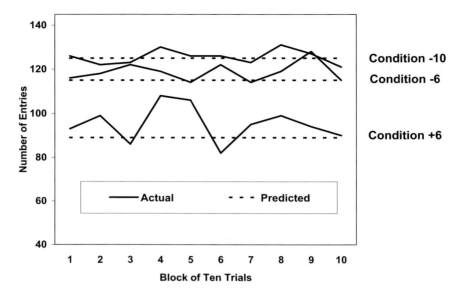

Key findings: The predicted number of entries tracks the actual mean number of entries in each condition. Mean entries increase from 95.2 in Condition +6 through 118.7 in Condition −6 to 125.5 in Condition −10. Predicted number of entries are 89, 115 and 125, respectively.

Figure 2. Actual and predicted number of entries for Conditions +6, −6 and −10 in Rapoport et al. (1998).

the observed mean increases linearly in c, and the absolute difference between observed and predicted values is rather small. There is a slight tendency to enter more often than predicted on low values of c and less often than predicted on high values of c.

Figures 4a, 4b, and 4c display the individual profiles for each condition separately. The only difference from the profiles in Figures 1a, 1b, and 1c is that the horizontal axis of each profile is divided now into ten rather than nine equal intervals. Similarly to Figures 1a to 1c, Figures 4a to 4c show that very few subjects used cutoff decision rules consistently across all ten blocks. Indeed, there are many profiles (e.g., Subjects 11 and 16 in Figure 4a) that defy a simple characterization. Similar to the previous study by Sundali, Rapoport, and Seale (1995), the individual results portrayed in Figures 4a to 4c support neither a cutoff decision rule, which remains unaltered across the 100 trials, nor a symmetric mixed-strategy equilibrium in which the probability of entry increases in c. Additional analyses of the data, not reported here, suggest that the remarkable coordination success on the aggregate level is achieved through some sort of adaptive learning.

2.3. Rapoport, Seale, and Winter (1997)

In yet another major extension of the basic market entry game, Rapoport, Seale, and Winter (1997), introduced asymmetry between players by charging differential entry

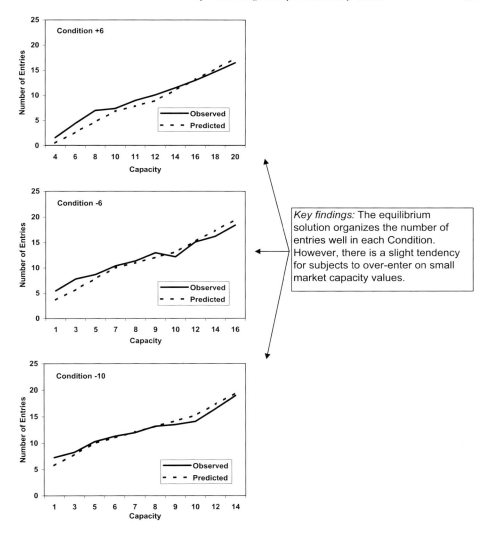

Figure 3. Observed and predicted number of entries by market capacity for Conditions +6, −6, and −10 in Rapoport et al. (1998).

fees. The parameter values were the same as in Experiment 2 of Sundali, Rapoport, and Seale (1995), namely, $v = 1$, $k = 1$, $r = 2$, $T = 100$, and $c \in \{1, 3, \ldots, 19\}$. In addition, the twenty subjects in each group were divided into $J = 5$ types, with four members each, and privately charged entry fees which assumed the values $h_j = 1, 2, 3, 4$, and 5, respectively ($j = 1, 2, \ldots, J$). The distribution of entry fees was common knowledge. Two different groups of $n = 20$ participated in this study. At the

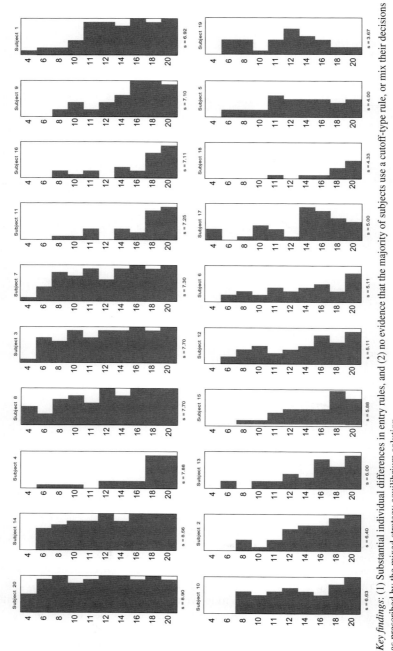

Key findings: (1) Substantial individual differences in entry rules, and (2) no evidence that the majority of subjects use a cutoff-type rule, or mix their decisions as prescribed by the mixed strategy equilibrium solution.

Figure 4a. Displays the number of entries by market capacity for Condition +6 of Rapoport et al. (1998). These individual profiles are arranged by the index s, a measure of decision consistency.

Ch. 34: Coordination Success in Non-cooperative Large Group Market Entry Games

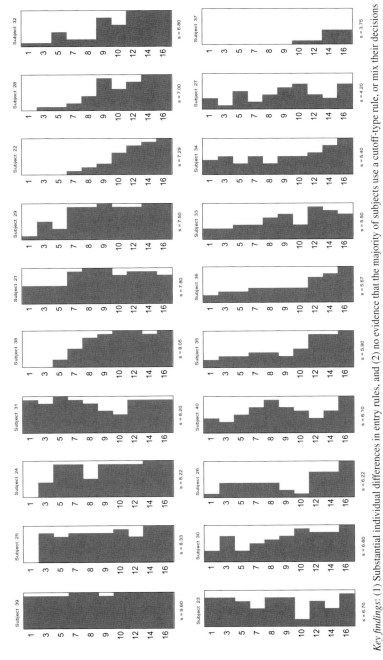

Key findings: (1) Substantial individual differences in entry rules, and (2) no evidence that the majority of subjects use a cutoff-type rule, or mix their decisions as prescribed by the mixed strategy equilibrium solution.

Figure 4b. Displays the number of entries by market capacity for Condition −6 of Rapoport et al. (1998). These individual profiles are arranged by the index s, a measure of decision consistency.

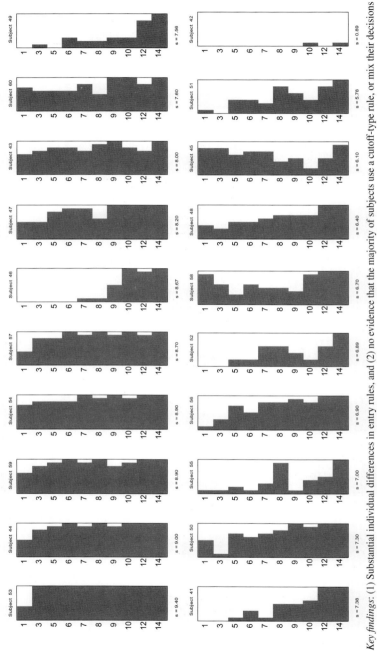

Key findings: (1) Substantial individual differences in entry rules, and (2) no evidence that the majority of subjects use a cutoff-type rule, or mix their decisions as prescribed by the mixed strategy equilibrium solution.

Figure 4c. Displays the number of entries by market capacity for Condition −10 of Rapoport et al. (1998). These individual profiles are arranged by the index s, a measure of decision consistency.

Ch. 34: Coordination Success in Non-cooperative Large Group Market Entry Games   287

Table 4
Reports the total number of entries by market capacity across the ten blocks of trials for the two groups of Rapoport, Seale, and Winter (1997). The correlation between the number of entries and capacity is shown in the last row of the table. The shaded cells indicate those trials where the number of entries was within ±1 of the equilibrium prediction

Capacity	Prediction	Block of ten trials										Total	Mean	SD
		1	2	3	4	5	6	7	8	9	10			
Group 1														
1	[0]	2	0	0	0	0	1	0	0	0	0	3	0.3	0.67
3	[2]	0	1	2	2	3	4	2	1	2	2	19	1.9	1.10
5	[4]	7	6	2	3	5	3	3	4	5	4	42	4.2	1.55
7	[5, 6]	1	9	3	7	6	7	7	5	4	5	54	5.4	2.32
9	[7, 8]	9	3	11	9	8	7	8	8	7	7	77	7.7	2.06
11	[9]	9	7	16	9	11	8	10	9	10	9	98	9.8	2.44
13	[11]	11	10	10	8	13	11	11	10	12	12	108	10.8	1.40
15	[12, 13]	7	16	15	10	13	12	13	13	15	12	126	12.6	2.63
17	[14, 15]	12	15	12	11	15	15	15	15	14	16	140	14.0	1.70
19	[16]	13	18	14	14	16	16	17	17	17	16	158	15.8	1.62
Total	[80, 84]	71	85	85	73	90	84	86	82	86	83	825		
Correlation		0.86	0.90	0.86	0.95	0.99	0.98	0.99	0.99	0.99	0.99	1.00		

(*continued on next page*)

end of each period, each subject was informed of the total number of entries and her payoff for the period.

When players are not symmetric, there exist no mixed-strategy equilibria which are symmetric within type. There exist multiple pure strategy equilibria, some of which are monotonic (i.e., $m_j^* \geq m_{j+1}^*$, $j = 1, 2, 3, 4$, where m^* is the equilibrium number of entrants of type j, $0 \leq m^* \leq 4$) and some are not. Efficient equilibria are the ones maximizing the group payoff associated with equilibrium play.

Table 4 shows the number of entrants by block and c value for each group separately. Similarly to previous tables, the ten values of c appear in ascending order, not in the actual order of their presentation. The total number of entries across the ten blocks is presented in column 13, the means and standard deviations are shown in columns 14 and 15, and the efficient equilibrium number of entrants (predictions) are presented as the first number in the second column from the left. The difference between the predicted and observed mean number of entries is not significant in 19 of 20 comparisons

Table 4
(Continued)

Capacity	Prediction	Block of ten trials										Total	Mean	SD
		1	2	3	4	5	6	7	8	9	10			
Group 2														
1	[0]	5	1	1	0	1	0	1	0	0	0	9	0.9	1.52
3	[2]	2	4	1	4	2	1	2	3	2	1	22	2.2	1.14
5	[4]	3	4	4	5	4	6	2	3	3	4	38	3.8	1.14
7	[5, 6]	6	7	5	6	8	7	7	9	6	5	66	6.6	1.26
9	[7, 8]	14	8	11	7	6	9	5	6	8	8	82	8.2	2.66
11	[9]	9	12	8	10	8	11	9	8	10	8	93	9.3	1.42
13	[11]	12	11	13	11	12	9	13	10	12	10	113	11.3	1.34
15	[12, 13]	14	15	11	14	13	14	12	15	11	15	134	13.4	1.58
17	[14, 15]	16	14	15	17	13	15	15	13	14	15	147	14.7	1.25
19	[16]	15	17	18	16	16	17	17	15	16	17	164	16.4	0.97
Total	[80, 84]	96	93	87	90	83	89	83	82	82	83	868		
Correlation		0.88	0.98	0.96	0.98	0.97	0.97	0.97	0.94	0.98	0.98	0.99		

Key findings: (1) Positive and highly significant correlations between the number of entries and market capacity that increase over block, (2) mean number of entries is accounted for by the equilibrium prediction, (3) 76% (152 out or 200) of the trials are within ±1 of the equilibrium prediction.

(10 values of c times 2 groups), and the correlations $r_{(c,m)}$ increase across blocks from 0.86 and 0.88 in Block 1 to 0.99 and 0.98 in Block 10. Similarly to all previous studies, we observe remarkable coordination success on the aggregate level – which increases with experience – even in the presence of private information about entry fees and considerable asymmetry between types of players.

However, we do not observe the expected differences between types. Table 5 presents the total number of entries across the ten blocks of trials partitioned into the $J = 5$ types of players. The frequencies are displayed by value of c for each type separately. The results shown in this table reject the equilibrium as an explanatory concept. For example, whether the equilibria are monotonic or not, all four players of type 1 are predicted to always enter if $c \geq 9$, all four players of type 5 are not expected to enter if $c \leq 15$, and the total number of entries should decrease in j. All of these predictions are violated. Similarly, examination of the individual profiles and the frequency of switches in decision for the same value of c across adjacent blocks clearly rejects the Nash equilibrium solution.

Ch. 34: *Coordination Success in Non-cooperative Large Group Market Entry Games* 289

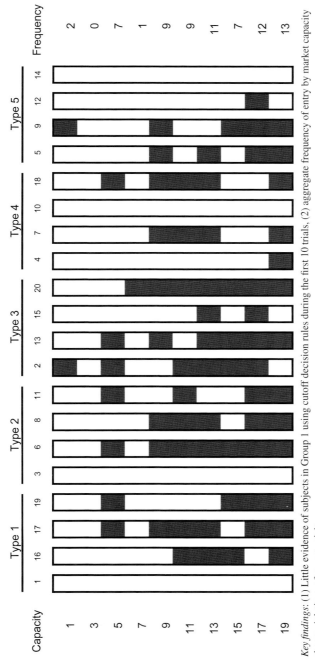

Key findings: (1) Little evidence of subjects in Group 1 using cutoff decision rules during the first 10 trials, (2) aggregate frequency of entry by market capacity shows violations of monotonicity.

Figure 5a. Displays the individual decisions for the first 10 trials for each subject in Group 1 of Rapoport, Seale, and Winter (1997). The shaded areas indicate entry decisions for a given market capacity. Type indicates the per-trial entry cost, whereas frequency refers to the aggregate number of entry decisions.

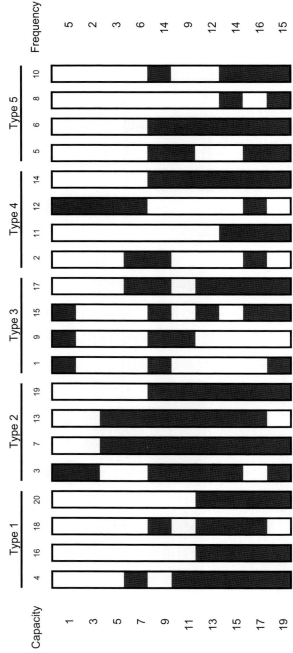

Key findings: (1) Little evidence of subjects in Group 2 using cutoff decision rules during the first 10 trials, (2) aggregate frequency of entry by market capacity shows violations of monotonicity.

Figure 5b. Displays the individual decisions for the first 10 trials for each subject in Group 2 of Rapoport, Seale, and Winter (1997). The shaded areas indicate entry decisions for a given market capacity. Type indicates the per-trial entry cost, whereas frequency refers to the aggregate number of entry decisions.

Ch. 34: Coordination Success in Non-cooperative Large Group Market Entry Games

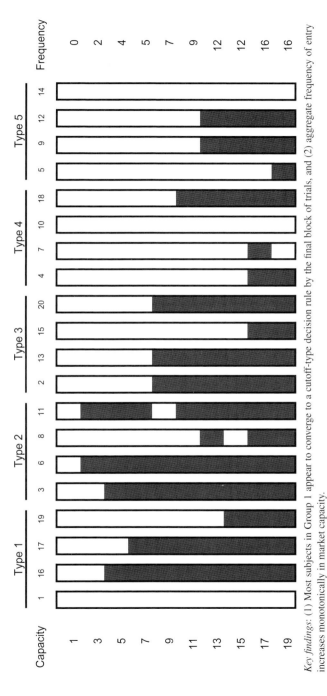

Figure 6a. Displays the individual decisions for the last 10 trials for each subject in Group 1 of Rapoport, Seale, and Winter (1997). The shaded areas indicate entry decisions for a given market capacity. Type indicates the per-trial entry cost, whereas frequency refers to the aggregate number of entry decisions.

Key findings: (1) Most subjects in Group 1 appear to converge to a cutoff-type decision rule by the final block of trials, and (2) aggregate frequency of entry increases monotonically in market capacity.

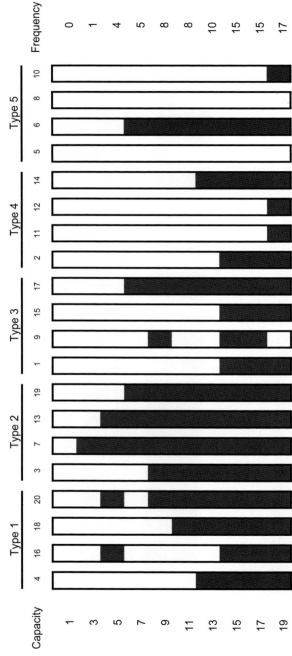

Key findings: (1) Most subjects in Group 2 appear to converge to a cutoff-type decision rule by the final block of trials, and (2) aggregate frequency of entry increases monotonically in market capacity.

Figure 6b. Displays the individual decisions for the last 10 trials for each subject in Group 2 of Rapoport, Seale, and Winter (1997). The shaded areas indicate entry decisions for a given market capacity. Type indicates the per-trial entry cost, whereas frequency refers to the aggregate number of entry decisions.

Table 5
Reports the number of entries by market capacity and player type for the two groups of Rapoport, Seale, and Winter (1997). Within each group, four players were assigned to each type, where type refers to the per-trial cost of entry. The number of entries within each cell may vary from 0 to 40

c	Type 1	Type 2	Type 3	Type 4	Type 5	Across types
Group 1						
1	0	0	1	0	2	3
3	0	14	2	0	3	19
5	11	22	6	1	2	42
7	13	19	13	3	6	54
9	14	26	17	9	11	77
11	18	30	27	13	10	98
13	18	30	30	14	16	108
15	29	27	32	20	18	126
17	29	35	36	22	18	140
19	30	39	37	29	23	158
Total	162	242	201	111	109	825

c	Type 1	Type 2	Type 3	Type 4	Type 5	Across types
Group 2						
1	0	2	6	1	0	9
3	5	13	2	1	1	22
5	5	20	6	7	0	38
7	12	29	10	8	7	66
9	16	32	15	7	12	82
11	22	38	13	8	12	93
13	34	35	19	11	14	113
15	37	37	22	22	16	134
17	39	39	33	21	15	147
19	38	39	34	35	18	164
Total	208	284	160	121	95	868

Key findings: The equilibrium solution is rejected as (1) entries are expected to decrease in type, (2) players of type 1 are predicted to always enter if the capacity is $\geqslant 9$, and (3) players of type 5 are predicted to never enter if the capacity is $\leqslant 15$.

3. Adaptive Learning

Taken together, the results of the market entry game experiments discussed above show remarkable coordination success in terms of the total number of entries for each value of c separately as well as the correlations between observed and predicted number of entries across values of c. These results stand in sharp contrast to the coordination failure reported by Van Huyck, Battalio, and Beil (1990, 1991, 1993) in a different class of coordination games. The Nash equilibrium is clearly rejected as a descriptive concept when the data are broken down by type or by player. There is considerable within-subject variability in the decision whether or not to enter a market with the same capacity, which is not due to randomization. In all the studies except Experiment 1 of Sundali, Rapoport, and Seale (1995) (where learning was not possible), there is evidence for a steady decline in the number of switches across blocks and convergence of individual behavior to cutoff decision rules with a cutoff point c^* that may change from block to block. This convergence is illustrated by comparing the individual profiles in Figures 5a and 5b to the ones in Figures 6a and 6b. Figures 5a and 5b display the individual profiles of all the forty subjects of Rapoport, Seale, and Winter (1997) in the first block of ten trials (Block 1), whereas Figures 6a and 6b portray the decision profiles of the same subjects in Block 10. Whereas there is only scant evidence for cutoff decision rules in Figures 5a and 5b, with experience most of the subjects (34 out of 40) converge to cutoff decision rules in Block 10 with marked individual differences in the value of c^* between and within types. The distribution of the cutoffs is a sufficient condition for coordination success. Reinforcement-based adaptive learning models of the kind proposed by Roth and Erev (1995) or by Daniel, Seale, and Rapoport (1998) account for the dynamics of play on both the individual and aggregate levels, thereby providing an explanation for the coordination success achieved in our experiments.

Acknowledgement

This research was supported by NSF Grant No. SBR-9512724 to Amnon Rapoport and Ken Koput.

References

Daniel, T.E., Seale, D.A., Rapoport, A. (1998). "Strategic play and adaptive learning in the sealed bid bargaining mechanism". Journal of Mathematical Psychology 42, 133–166.
Erev, I., Rapoport, A. (1998). "Coordination, "magic", and reinforcement learning in a market entry game". Games and Economic Behavior 23, 145–176.
Kahneman, D. (1988). "Experimental economics: A psychological perspective". In: Tietz, R., Albers, W., Selten, R. (Eds.), Bounded Rational Behavior in Experimental Games and Markets. Springer-Verlag, Berlin, pp. 11–18.
Kahneman, D., Tversky, A. (1979). "Prospect theory: An analysis of decision under risk". Econometrica 47, 263–291.
Rapoport, A. (1995). "Individual strategies in a market-entry game". Group Decision and Negotiation 4, 117–133.
Rapoport, A., Seale, D.A., Winter, E. (1997). "Coordination and learning behavior in large groups with asymmetric players". Games and Economic Behavior 39, 111–136.
Rapoport, A., Seale, D.A., Erev, I., Sundali, J.A. (1998). "Coordination success in market entry games: Tests of equilibrium and adaptive learning models". Management Science 44, 129–141.
Roth, A.E., Erev, I. (1995). "Learning in extensive-form games: Experimental data and simple dynamic models in the intermediate term". Games and Economic Behavior 8, 164–212.

Selten, R., Güth, W. (1982). "Equilibrium point selection in a class of market entry games". In: Deistler, M., Fürst, E., Schwödiauer, G. (Eds.), Games, Economic Dynamics, Time Series Analysis: A Symposium in Memoriam of Oskar Morgenstern. Physica-Verlag, Berlin, pp. 101–116.

Sundali, J.A., Rapoport, A., Seale, D.A. (1995). "Coordination in market entry games with symmetric players". Organizational Behavior and Human Decision Processes 64, 203–218.

Van Huyck, J., Battalio, R., Beil, R. (1990). "Tacit coordination games, strategic uncertainty, and coordination failure". American Economic Review 80, 234–248.

Van Huyck, J., Battalio, R., Beil, R. (1991). "Strategic uncertainty, equilibrium selection, and coordination failure in average opinion games". Quarterly Journal of Economics 106, 885–910.

Van Huyck, J., Battalio, R., Beil, R. (1993). "Asset markets as an equilibrium selection mechanism: Coordination failure, game form auctions, and tacit coordination". Games and Economic Behavior 5, 485–504.

PART 2

MARKET ECONOMICS OF UNCERTAINTY AND INFORMATION

2. MARKET ECONOMICS OF UNCERTAINTY AND INFORMATION

In the decades of the 1970's and 1980's economic theory experienced an evolution of the economic problem from simply "allocating scarce resources" to a problem of the "proper use of knowledge" as Hayek put it. Allocation efficiency began to be supplemented with informational efficiency. The principles based on purposeful behavior, which have always been at the foundations of economics, began to expand to explain the acquisition of information and its use, including both the information that might be carried in the actions of others and in the behavior of markets. This evolution was accompanied by the development of more precise principles of behavior as well as modifications of those of classical origin.

This section on uncertainty and information contains six contributions in which the evolving principles cover increasingly complex phenomena. The section begins with two papers focused on the ability of individuals to acquire information and on how they behave when doing so. The last three papers deal with the interaction of human behavioral tendencies with the special instruments and institutions that are designed to facilitate commerce and use information in the light of individual decisions.

Kelly and Friedman report on the expectations development of individuals and in particular the capacity of individuals to condition their expectations of some events on the observation of multiple other events. That is, they measure the implicit conditional subjective probabilities of events that have a stochastic dependence on other observable events. Unlike other modeling of expectations the environments they study have no prominent lag structure. Specifically they test the ability of beliefs to accurately reflect an equation of the form

$$y_t = a_0 + a_1 x_{1t} + a_2 x_{2t} + v e_t,$$

where x_{1t} and x_{2t} are observed and subjects are asked to estimate y_t. That is, the subject observes the pair (x_{1t}, x_{2t}) and then asked to predict the value of y_t, which is then used to statistically estimate the coefficients of the equation. The estimated coefficients are then interpreted as subjective conditional probabilities and are compared to the true coefficients, the true conditional probabilities. Kelly and Friedman report that for the most part the estimates are accurate but the analysis goes deeper to provide insights about the dynamics of the adjustment process. The tendency is for the estimates to be exaggerated at first, in the sense that the conditional means are as if they were multiplied by a positive scalar. They call this property "over-response." From this position of exaggeration the beliefs tend to slowly converge toward the truth. The potential for exaggeration is exacerbated by increased noise and when subjects are faced by a change in parameters of the data generating equation, the response is slow but in the proper direction. Thus, the new set of parameters is approached from the direction of the old set of parameters.

Cox and Oaxaca focus on information acquisition that shares a deep relationship with concepts of search and sequential decisions. Motivations are found in models of job search, search for lowest prices, and decisions to invest. Their focus is on classical models, which is appropriate because of the connection of those models to many areas of economics. The experiments thus provide a vehicle through which the consequences of any inaccuracies of the basic theory can be traced through to other contexts. They report that when put to the task of predicting when a person will stop searching and choose in a stationary environment, the classical, risk neutral model captures the behavior of a large proportion of subjects but subjects typically stop short and choose sooner than the model suggests. The abbreviated search is a property of the risk-averse model.

During the course of the research they successfully tested a method of measuring expectations during the search process, a variable which if measured would be an important tool for assessing model inaccuracies. They force subjects to precommit to a termination strategy and discover that this process has no effect on decisions after subjects become experienced. The effect exists at first but then wears off. Thus the methodology provides an opportunity to compare observed stopping rules with those predicted by theory. The risk averse model survived direct tests. They end the summary with a paradox. When subjects are allowed to return to previously passed over opportunities, like returning to a job offer that was previously refused, they behave as if they were facing a more risky task rather than less.

The third (Gachter and Fehr) and fourth (Fehr and Falk) papers illustrate the effects of other regarding attitudes and the importance of such attitudes in the design of institutions and in the behavior of markets. Their study is focused on attitudes of reciprocity in the context of contracts and in markets.

The concept of a contract is at the heart of information and uncertainty. Under conditions of certainty, the contract plays a mechanical role, acting something like an escrow account in which a third party inspects the deliveries to both sides of a contract before either can take the contracted amount away. The person who buys knows the delivery has taken place and inspects the goods before the money is released and the person who delivers the goods knows that payment has taken place before the goods are released. The structure of the relationship is so tight that it can be imagined as physical.

Under conditions of uncertainty the contract acquires additional dimensions. Payments can precede delivery and in such cases there may be no physical guarantee that appropriate delivery will take place. The success of the contract depends on incentives. The fundamental issue raised by the two papers is whether other regarding preferences act to enforce contracts that are otherwise unenforceable. The answer they give is "yes, to some degree" and that an understanding of this fact can be used to suggest ways to improve contract performance.

The interpretation of the research tends to be a relationship between an employer and a worker who can deliver effort that is costly to the worker and not monitored by the employer. The data demonstrate that subject employers who offer high wages can depend on subject workers to deliver more than the minimum (best Nash response) work. While the worker response is less than it would be if the contract were fully enforced, the workers do engage in reciprocity.

Can this tendency toward reciprocity be enhanced by additional features of a contract or by a change in the market organization? The second paper demonstrates that the power of reciprocity survives several market organizations. When focused on the terms of the contract the relationships prove to be delicate and intuitions drawn from economic theory alone can be misleading. A contract can include the possibility for retribution by a dissatisfied employer or reward by a satisfied employer. In a subgame perfect equilibrium, a reward would not be forthcoming and a costly retribution would not be exercised. Game theory suggests that the contract would make no difference – but it does. Not only do the employees deliver more, the employers also anticipate that they will deliver more. On the other hand, if enforcement is exercised through fines for shirking that results from randomized inspections, the benefits of reciprocity are reduced.

The patterns of these results emphasize several important points. First, from the individual level to the system level the basic principles of economics and game theory organize important features of how individual and systems cope with uncertainty. Secondly, they demonstrate that individual can be other-regarding. Importantly, for the next parts of this section, people have a tendency to understand the behavior of other people and factor that into their own decisions. We have seen how that property finds its way into contracts. The next papers demonstrate how that factors into the way in which information becomes transferred from one individual to another in the context of the operation of an economic system. Not only do individuals act purposefully, but they also see others as acting purposefully. By using a principle of invertability they incorporate the information held by others into their own information. This property of invertability is the amazing feature of rational expectations.

The Anderson and Holt paper reviews data on "cascades." The early discussions of cascades viewed them as a "herd," an odd, undesirable and even irrational behavior that was compared to mechanical, mimic-like or even thoughtless behavior that leads to disastrous lemming-like consequences. In part, it was thought to be related to a preference for conformity. Now the phenomenon can be seen in a completely different light as a remarkable demonstration of the invertability principle and how it facilitates information through social relationships. A pure preference for conformity can be ruled out.

The cascade experiment is deceptively simple. Each individual receives a private signal about the state of nature. In sequence, individuals make a guess about the state, and at the time of the guess know the private signal and the guess of all previous individuals. Since the reward is for being correct an individual can infer the information of others but "inverting" a postulated decision rule. A guess of "X" suggests that the individual believed that X would occur thereby revealing the belief to an observer who can add that information to whatever other information might be available and thus make better-informed decisions. Interestingly enough, people do not trust the decisions of others completely. It is as though they do not trust the rationality of others and thus, to the extent that errors exist, they reflect the fact that people rely on their private information too much.

Aside from an analysis of individuals, the questions posed are related to the magnitude and accuracy of this information transfer and how it is influenced by incentives and organization. When decisions are sequential, a cascade develops in which information held by individuals other than the first few never finds its way into the system. While individual decisions are better than if based on private information alone, the system is not "informationally efficient." All available information does not become public and incorporated into individual decisions. A change in the institution, for example to a majority rule voting system, dramatically improves the informational efficiency. Changes in the incentives to, say, one that rewards conformity, dramatically reduce the informational efficiency.

The basic principles of economics as applied to information and uncertainty merge naturally into a theory of rational expectations. The models suggest that markets can collect and aggregate information that is dispersed in small bits across many individuals. According to some models, the prices contain a summary of all economically relevant information that exists anywhere in the system. Of course the full force of that powerful claim is not supported by experiments but the claim has many elements of truth. The paper by Chen and Plott illustrates the implementation of experiments to study the phenomena of information in markets and demonstrate the operation of aspects of the principles through a series of experiments that are more complex than any reported in the literature. Two important points are made. First the development of rational expectations is a dynamic process, as reflected in a process of equilibration. The process can be contrasted with the instantaneous equilibrium selection presupposed in some game theoretic models. Secondly, the capacity of markets to perform the task is sensitive to the instruments that exist in the market. While the paper does not demonstrate it, the suggestion is that the nature of successful instruments could be closely related to the nature of the uncertainty that exists and how information is distributed.

The final section of the paper demonstrates that the concept of mechanism design can be extended to what Chen and Plott call Information Aggregation Mechanisms. These are market processes that have no other purpose than to collect information. The concept is developed and a field application is reviewed, demonstrating not only the scientific feasibility, but also the practical relevance of the idea.

Chapter 35

LEARNING TO FORECAST RATIONALLY

HUGH KELLEY and DANIEL FRIEDMAN

Economics Department, University of Santa Cruz, Santa Cruz, CA 95064, USA

1. Introduction

Economists routinely assume that all participants in the economy are rational forecasters who can correctly incorporate all available information when they form expectations of price and other variables that matter to them. Economists such as Marcet and Sargent (1989) point out that, when assessing the relevance of rational expectations models, researchers must ask whether or not repeat experience allows people to closely approximate rational forecasts. If people exhibit systematic departures from rational forecasts, then much of economic theory needs reconstruction.

The empirical literature on forecast rationality is surprisingly thin. Surveys of consumers, professional economists, and other market participants generally find that forecast errors have a non-zero mean, are correlated with other observable information, and follow an adaptive process (Camerer, 1995, pp. 609–611). Laboratory experiments with discrete forecasting tasks often indicate persistent biases (e.g., Grether, 1990). The most relevant previous experiment, Williams (1987, pp. 1–18) finds autocorrelated and adaptive errors when laboratory market participants forecast next period's market price. Other ties to existing literature can be found in Kelley (1998) and Kitzis et al. (1997).

The experiment described in this chapter isolates the forecasting process in two different stochastic individual choice tasks. The first task is based on Roll (1984), who finds that even in a very simple field financial market (Florida Orange Juice futures) where only two news variables are relevant (Florida weather hazard and competing supply, mainly from Brazil), the news can only account for a small fraction of the price variability. The second task is a variant of psychologists' standard discrete Medical Diagnosis task, e.g., Gluck and Bower (1988).

2. The Tasks

2.1. Orange Juice Forecasting (OJ)

In each trial, a subject views two continuous variables on her monitor: x_1 (called weather hazard) and x_2 (called Brazil supply), as in the upper-left corner of Figure 1. The values of x_1 and x_2 are independent random draws from the uniform distribution on (0, 100). The task is to forecast the dependent variable y (called orange juice futures price). The

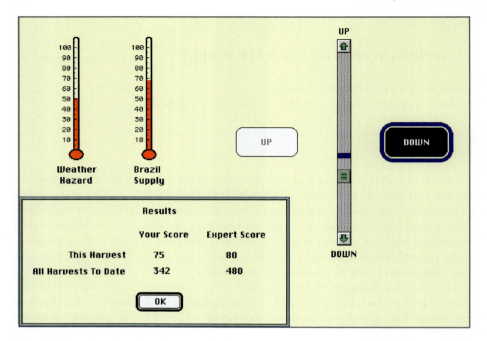

Figure 1. The values of x_1 (Weather Hazard) and x_2 (Brazil Supply) are random draws from the uniform distribution on (0, 100). The subject uses the slide bar on the right side of the display to enter her forecast. She uses the mouse to slide the small box up or down to enter her forecast. Then the realized value of the price appears on the same slide bar as a blue (dark) bar. Finally, in some treatments a score box is provided in the lower left of the screen. Score calculations are described in the text.

subject uses the slide bar on the right side of the monitor display to enter the forecast. The realized value of y appears on the same vertical display as the slide bar, as indicated in Figure 1. The realized value on trial t is

$$y_t = a_o + a_1 x_{1t} + a_2 x_{2t} + v e_t, \tag{1}$$

where the coefficients a_1 and a_2 are unknown to the subject (implicitly – they are the objects of learning) with baseline values 0.4 and −0.4, v is the noise amplitude (typically $v = 10$), e_t is an independent random variable drawn each trial from the uniform distribution on (−1, 1), and a_o is the intercept used to center the data so that y_t falls at the middle of the vertical scale when $e_t = 0$ and $x_{1t} = x_{2t} = 50$.

In one treatment (called History), before entering her forecast the subject can view a summary of price outcomes from previous trials where values of x_1 and x_2 are close to current values. In another treatment (called Score), at the end of each trial the monitor displays a score S as shown at the bottom of Figure 1, computed from the continuous forecast c and the actual price p according to the quadratic scoring rule $S(c, p) =$

$80 - 280(c - p)^2$. [The "expert score" in Figure 1 uses the forecast c obtained from Equation (1) with e_t set to 0.]

Sessions last 480 trials, and so far 57 subjects have been tested. Most subjects' cumulative scores fall between 36,000 and 37,000, with a theoretical maximum score of $480 * 80 = 38,400$. Additional treatments include high noise ($v = 20$ instead of 10), asymmetric weights (e.g., $(a_1, a_2) = (0.24, -0.56)$ instead of $(0.40, -0.40)$) and structural breaks (e.g., weights shift from symmetric to asymmetric in trial 241). See Kelley (1998) for a more complete description of the task and treatments.

2.2. The Medical Diagnosis Task (MD)

The medical diagnosis task also is a stochastic individual choice task with 480 trials for each subject, two independent variables (the symptoms) and one dependent variable (the disease). The user interface is quite similar to that in the OJ task. However, the independent variables (temperature and blood pressure) are discrete with four possible values (high, medium high, medium low and low), and the dependent variable is binary (the disease is either Autochus or Burlosis). Conditional on the realized disease, the symptoms are independently drawn according to likelihoods unknown to the subject.

Subjects' continuous response c_t in trial t consists of naming the disease deemed more likely and indicating (with the slide bar) the degree of confidence. The response is coded as a continuous variable between 0 (completely confident that the disease is B) and 1 (completely confident that the disease is A). Kitzis et al. (1997) show that the true Bayesian relationship between symptoms and diseases can be very closely approximated by the linear equation

$$y_t = a_o + a_1 x_{1t} + a_2 x_{2t}, \qquad (2)$$

where now y_t is the posterior log odds of disease A over disease B, and x_{it} is the discrete variable with values 1, 0.3, −0.3 and −1 respectively for high, medium high, medium low and low values of symptom $i = 1, 2$. The unknown coefficients a_1 and a_2 again are the implicit objects of learning; the true values are 1.39 and −2.30.

We tested 123 subjects in a 2 × 3 factorial design with the treatments History (vs No History) and Score (vs No Score and vs Score + Pay) with 20+ subjects in each cell.

3. Results

3.1. Rolling Regressions

Although a subject may think of the task in various idiosyncratic ways, the analyst can summarize the subject's beliefs by seeing how he responds to the current stimuli x_{it}. Moreover, the analyst can summarize the learning process by seeing how the subject's response to stimuli changes with experience.

Given Equations (1) and (2), learning thus can be seen in the changes over time in a subject's implicit subjective values of the coefficients a_1 and a_2. The data analysis reconstructs the implicit values of these coefficients and tracks their changes over time.

The reconstruction proceeds as follows. For the OJ task, take the subject's actual forecast c_t in trial t as the dependent variable, and take the actual values of x_{it} as independent variables. Then, run a rolling regression of c_t on the two independent variables over a moving window of 160 consecutive trials, incrementing the last trial T from 160 to 480. The procedure in the MD task is the same except that the dependent variable is the log odds of the continuous choice, $L(c_t) = \ln[(c_t + .01)/1.01 - c_t)]$; c_t is shifted by .01 away from 0 and 1 to avoid taking the log of zero. The intercept coefficient is constrained to its objective value in the results shown below in order to reduce clutter and to improve statistical efficiency.

Effective learning is indicated by rapid convergence of the coefficient estimates a_{iT} (as T increases) to the objective values a_i. Obstacles to learning are suggested by slow convergence, convergence to some other value, or divergence of the coefficient estimates. This empirical approach embodies some of the theoretical ideas on learning in Marcet and Sargent (1989) as explained in Kelley and Friedman (2002).

3.2. OJ Learning Curves

Figure 2 presents two examples. Top panel shows the simulated performance of a Marcet–Sargent econometrician who uses realized prices for all trials observed so far to estimate the coefficients a_1 and a_2 and then uses these coefficients in Equation (1) with $e_t = 0$ to forecast the current price. Learning seems immediate (within 160 trials). The R^2 for the first 160 trial window of data was 0.93 and ended at the same level, 0.93, for the last window.

Bottom panel shows that the actual subject who earned the top score came fairly close to the Marcet–Sargent ideal. The coefficient estimates indicate that he slightly overresponded to current symptoms throughout the session, but the overresponse was negligible by the last 160 trials. His R^2 for the first 160 trial window of data was 0.94 and increased to 0.96 by the last window. This high scoring subject is fairly representative; coefficient estimates for other subjects in most treatments sometimes indicate overresponse and sometimes underresponse, but on average are quite close to or slightly beyond objective values.

Table 1 summarizes the main departures from effective learning detected so far. Coefficient estimates indicating "Significant" under and overresponse by the end of the session ($T = 480$) are about equal in the baseline and asymmetric treatments, but underresponse is much more prevalent than overresponse in the structural break treatments. In the high noise treatment (amplitude $v = 20$ instead of $v = 10$), overresponse is much more common than underresponse. Figure 3 presents the corresponding histograms, which clearly show that coefficient estimates for subjects in the high noise environment tend strongly toward overresponse.

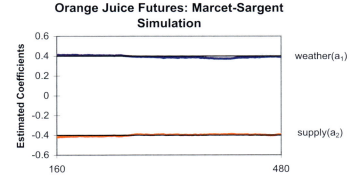
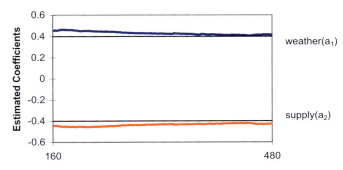

Figure 2. (Top) Coefficient estimates from rolling regression $y_t = a_1 x_{1t} + a_2 x_{2t} + ve_t$ on trials $\{T - 159, T - 158, \ldots, T\}$ for $T = 160$ to 480. The equation is estimated using the Marcet–Sargent Model to generate the forecasts y_t. (Bottom) Coefficient estimates from rolling regression $c_t = a_1 x_{1t} + a_2 x_{2t} + ve_t$ on trials $\{T - 159, T - 158, \ldots, T\}$ for $T = 160$ to 480. The equation is estimated using forecasts c_t from Subject 44.

Table 1
Over and under-response in Orange Juice forecasting

	Under response	Objective	Over response
Symmetric weights	20	11	21
Asymmetric weights	10	1	9
High noise	5	3	12
Structural break	13	2	7

Note: Coefficients a_1 and a_2 are estimated at $T = 480$ for all Ss for the equation $c_t = a_1 x_{1t} + a_2 x_{2t}$. Responses for each subject are classified as over or underresponse if the estimate differs from the objective value by more than $1.96 *$ std error.

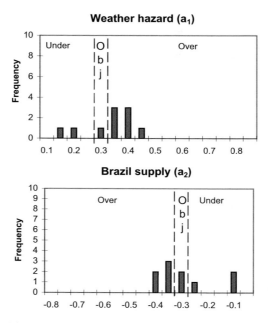

Figure 3. Distribution of final ($T = 480$) coefficient estimates in high noise treatment for the Orange Juice Futures experiment. "Obj" indicates estimates near objective values of (0.33, −0.33) respectively. "Under" (and "Over") refer to cases where the absolute value of the estimate is less (and more) than the objective value.

3.3. MD Learning Curves

Figure 4 provides two examples from the second experiment, Medical Diagnosis. Top panel simulates a Bayesian econometrician (the MD counterpart of Marcet–Sargent) who uses realized disease outcomes for all trials observed so far to estimate the coefficients a_1 and a_2 and then uses these coefficients in Equation (2) with $e_t = 0$ to predict the current disease. Ideal learning is a bit slower and more erratic than in the OJ task, but it still converges to the true values $a_1 = 1.39$ and $a_2 = -2.3$ quite rapidly.

Bottom panel shows that the actual subject who earned the top score differs noticeably from the Bayesian ideal. The coefficient estimates for this subject indicate persistent overresponse and are quite representative of the subject pool. The histograms in Figure 5 confirm that overresponse is indeed the prevailing bias in our MD data.

4. Discussion

Kelley (1998) reports several robustness checks. OJ specifications designed to capture prior beliefs and non-linear responses to news detected some transient effects in many subjects, but for the most part the final regression is indistinguishable from the basic

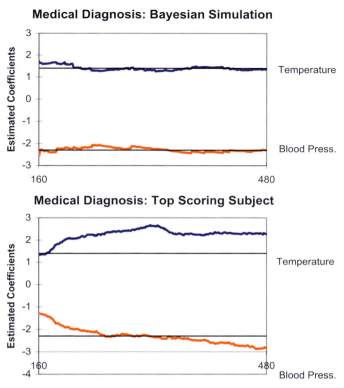

Figure 4. (Top) Coefficient estimates from rolling regression $y_t = a_1 x_{1t} + a_2 x_{2t}$ on trials $\{T-159, T-158, \ldots, T\}$ for $T = 160$ to 480. The equation is estimated using the Bayesian model to generate the forecasts y_t. (Bottom) Coefficient estimates from rolling regression $c_t = a_1 x_{1t} + a_2 x_{2t}$ on trials $\{T-159, T-158, \ldots, T\}$ for $T = 160$ to 480. The equation is estimated using the forecasts ct from Subject 28.

specification presented above. Eight parameter MD specifications that allow separate learning for each level of each symptom also converged roughly to the basic specification presented above, but we detect a general bias towards overresponding to the more informative symptom levels and underresponding to the less informative symptom levels.

We draw three conclusions from the data analysis. First, the rationality assumption is a good first approximation to subjects' forecasts at the end of 480 learning trials. Second, systematic biases towards under or overresponse can be detected in specific circumstances, e.g., overresponse in the noisier OJ environment. Third, more experiments are needed in a wider variety of tasks and environments in order to understand more fully when people can learn to forecast rationally. We anticipate that the rolling regressions and learning curves featured in this chapter will continue to be a useful tool in that research.

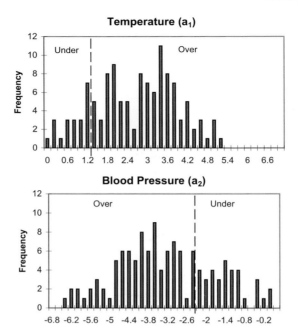

Figure 5. Distribution of final ($T = 480$) coefficient estimates for the Medical Diagnosis experiment. Objective values indicated by vertical dashed line. Objective values are (1.39) for Temperature and (-2.3) for Blood Pressure.

References

Camerer, C. (1995). "Individual decision making". In: Kagel, J.H., Roth, A.E. (Eds.), The Handbook of Experimental Economics. Princeton University Press, Princeton, NJ, pp. 587–703.

Gluck, M.A., Bower, G.H. (1988). "From conditioning to category learning: An adaptive network model". Journal of Experimental Psychology: General 117, 225–244.

Grether, D.M. (1990). "Testing Bayes rule and the representativeness heuristic: Some experimental evidence". Journal of Economic Behavior and Organization 17, 31–57.

Kelley, H. (1998). "Bounded rationality in the individual choice experiment". Unpublished thesis, Economics Department, University of California, Santa Cruz.

Kelley, H., Friedman, D. (2002). "Learning to forecast price". Economic Inquiry 40, 556–573.

Kitzis, S., Kelley, H., Berg, E., Massaro, D., Friedman, D. (1997). "Broadening the tests of learning models". Journal of Mathematical Psychology 42, 327–355.

Marcet, A., Sargent, T. (1989). "Convergence of least squares learning mechanisms in self referential linear stochastic models". Journal of Economic Theory 48, 337–368.

Roll, R. (1984). "Orange juice and weather". American Economic Review 74, 861–880.

Williams, A.W. (1987). "The formation of price forecasts in experimental markets". Journal of Money, Credit, and Banking 19, 1–18.

Chapter 36

LABORATORY TESTS OF JOB SEARCH MODELS

JAMES C. COX and RONALD L. OAXACA
University of Arizona

This chapter is concerned with laboratory tests of job search models. Formal models of job search specify certain common elements, i.e., the length of the search horizon, the searcher's discounting rate of interest, the net costs (subsidies) to search in each period of the search horizon, and the searcher's knowledge about the wage offer distribution he or she faces. Because these factors are difficult, if not impossible, to observe in the naturally-occurring economy, controlled laboratory tests of the search model offer the only practical means for formally testing search models.

A basic job search model of interest to economists specifies a finite search horizon. Searchers know the (discrete) wage offer distribution and must accept or decline an offer when it is received. The search model has sharp predictions for a utility maximizing, risk neutral agent. In this case the agent seeks to maximize the expected present value of the income from search. This can be accomplished by choosing an appropriate (minimally acceptable) reservation wage each period. The optimal reservation wage in any given period will equate (or, for discrete wage rates, appropriately order) the incremental benefits of searching an additional period with the incremental costs. Conditional on the draws, the model can predict precisely when an optimizing risk neutral searcher should terminate his or her search. By contrast the model does not have as sharp predictions for an individual with weakly risk averse (i.e., "concave") utility. Such an agent seeks to maximize the expected present value of his or her utility. In doing so the agent will select optimal reservation wages that are either less than or never greater than those that would be selected by an optimizing risk neutral agent. The implication of risk aversion is that the duration of search would on average be no longer than that of an optimizing, risk neutral agent.

1. Basic Search Experiments

Cox and Oaxaca (1989) report on a set of experiments with the basic search model. In these experiments there is a baseline design and several alternative treatments: Interest, Subsidy, Risk, Cost, Probability, and Horizon. The baseline consists of a 20 period search horizon in which the probability of an offer being generated is 0.5 each period. Conditional upon receiving an offer, the searcher faces a discrete uniform distribution defined over integer values 1 through 10. In the baseline design the induced discounting rate of interest is 0 and subsidies and costs are 0. In the Interest treatment the induced rate of interest is 10%. The Subsidy treatment offers a subsidy of 10 points for

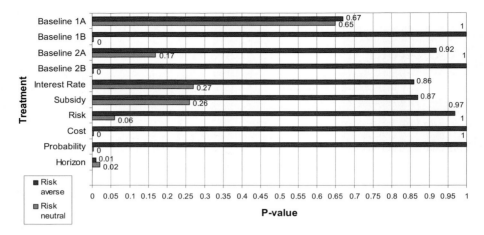

Figure 1. This figure reports the results of tests of the risk neutral (linear) model and the risk averse (concave) model based on mean search durations for treatments under the basic search model. The risk neutral model offers precise predictions for search terminations, conditional on the draws. Hence, the statistical tests are two-tailed. On the other hand, the risk averse model predicts only that search will terminate at or before the period predicted by the risk neutral model. The red bars indicate the p values associated with tests of the risk averse model and the blue bars indicate the p values associated with tests of the risk neutral model. Of the ten treatments, the risk averse model would be rejected at conventional levels in only one case (the horizon treatment). The risk neutral model would be rejected at conventional levels in six of the ten treatments.

each period searched. The Risk treatment consists of replacing the baseline conditional wage offer distribution with a discrete uniform distribution defined over integer values 4 through 7. This treatment reduces the riskiness (dispersion) of wage offers while holding constant the expected wage offer. In the Cost treatment subjects were charged 10 points for each period they searched. In the Probability treatment the probability of an offer being generated was reduced to 0.25 each period. The Horizon treatment consisted of halving the search horizon from 20 periods to 10 periods.

Figure 1 reports the test results for the risk neutral (linear) model and for the risk averse (concave) model. The experimental results were quite consistent with the predictions of the risk neutral model and were highly consistent with the risk averse model. 77% of the experimental searches terminated when predicted by the risk neutral model, conditional on the draws received, while 94% of the experimental searches terminated in periods consistent with the predictions of the risk averse model. Another indication of the strength of the test outcomes for search duration is the p value scores for paired differences between subject search durations and predicted durations for each subject conditional on their offers received. Out of 10 experimental treatments or baseline experiments, the p values exceeded 0.1 a total of 4 times for the risk neutral model and a total of 9 times for the risk averse model.

To examine treatment effects, a difference-in-difference comparison was made between each treatment and each baseline. The results of these difference-in-difference

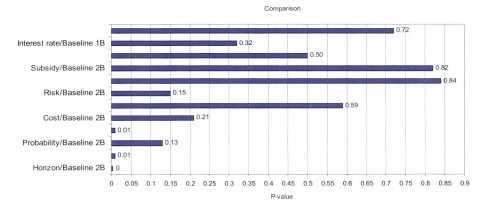

Figure 2. This figure reports the results of difference-in-difference tests in which observed differences in search terminations between each pair of treatments are compared against theoretically predicted differences, conditional on the draws. These tests are designed to capture treatment effects relative to the baseline treatments. The blue bars represent p values from matched pairs tests. There were two sets of baseline treatments (A and B) corresponding to different sets of subjects. The A baseline comparisons are not labeled but are reported above each corresponding B baseline comparison. The results show that treatment effects predicted by theory would be rejected in only three of the twelve comparisons.

tests are presented in Figure 2. Actual differences in each subject's search duration between a treatment and a baseline trial were compared to the expected difference predicted by theory, conditional on the draws. There were 12 comparisons (6 treatments and 2 baselines). Out of the 12 comparisons, 9 exhibited p values in excess of 0.1. In addition to tests based on mean durations of search, there were full distribution Kolmogorov–Smirnov tests. Out of 10 experimental treatments or baseline experiments, the risk neutral model could be rejected at the 5% level of significance only once and the risk averse model could never be rejected.

2. Precommitment/No Precommitment Experiments

The search duration tests presented in Cox and Oaxaca (1989) pertaining to the basic search model are indirect in as much as they are based on comparisons between actual stopping points and theoretically-predicted stopping points. A characteristic of the basic search model, however, is the existence of a reservation wage path. In other words the integer dynamic programming solution to the search problem specifies a minimally acceptable wage offer each period. In any given period all offers below the reservation wage will be rejected and all others accepted. A direct test of the search model would compare actual reservation wages with the theoretically predicted, optimal reservation wages. In the naturally-occurring economy, actual reservation wages used by searching workers are extremely difficult, if not outright impossible, to observe. In the laboratory it is possible to induce observable minimum acceptable wages that correspond to the theoretical notion of reservation wages.

Search experiments in which observable reservation wages were induced in the laboratory are reported in Cox and Oaxaca (1992a, 1992b). In some of these experiments subjects were required to precommit to a minimally acceptable offer in each period in advance of a draw. Any offer generated that was less than the precommitment wage was not available. All other offers resulted in search being terminated in that trial and the associated earnings being added to the subject's cumulative earnings during the experiment. Although such induced precommitment wages correspond to the theoretical notion of a binding reservation wage, there is always the possibility that subjects may precommitment to wages different than those they would implicitly use in the absence of the requirement to precommit in each period. This phenomenon stems from the possible existence of framing effects. Even though the decision problem is formally the same with or without precommitment, it is possible that the problem could be perceived as different depending on the presence or absence of the precommitment requirement. To the extent that this occurs one cannot accept the induced reservation wages at face value.

The scientific question raised by framing effects in this context is whether or not precommitment is itself a treatment. To answer this question the authors ran parallel precommitment and no precommitment treatments for the same group of subjects so that each subject would serve as his or her own control. The basic treatments consisted of the Baseline, Subsidy, and Probability treatments reported in Cox and Oaxaca (1989). The results reported in Cox and Oaxaca (1992b) suggest that initially subjects behaved as if the precommitment treatment was a riskier proposition. That is to say, the precommitment reservation wages were causing search to be terminated earlier than in parallel treatments without precommitment, after controlling for the offers received. After a few trials subjects returned to the baseline behavior observed in the parallel no precommitment experiments. Thus, the precommitment effects wore off as the subjects acclimated themselves to the precommitment design.

The direct tests themselves are reported in Cox and Oaxaca (1992a). In order to better gauge how well the risk neutral model is actually doing, a naive decision rule is used as a comparison case. The naive decision rule used specifies a reservation wage equal to the lowest integer value above the mean of the wage offer distribution except in the last period of the search horizon. In the last period the reservation wage would logically be 0.

Figure 3 reports the test results based on search terminations. When one combines the data from the precommitment and parallel no-precommitment treatments, it turns out that 2/3 of the subjects stopped at the theoretically-predicted risk neutral stopping periods 75% or more of the time. The naive model performed almost as well as the risk neutral model. In comparison, slightly in excess of 2/3 of the subjects stopped in periods consistent with the risk averse model 94% or more of the time. Nearly half of the subjects stopped at periods consistent with the risk averse model 100% of the time.

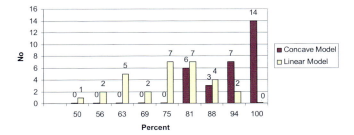

Figure 3. This figure reports the distribution of theoretically-correct search terminations across thirty subjects in the precommitment/no-precommitment experiments. With precommitment, subjects are required to commit to a minimally acceptable offer in advance of each draw. The red bars correspond to the number of subjects whose search terminations were consistent with the concave model at a given percentage, while the yellow bars correspond to the number of subjects whose search terminations were consistent with the linear model. The percentages were calculated over the combined precommitment and no-precommitment treatments. Thus 2/3 (20 out of 30) of the subjects had search durations that were consistent with risk neutrality at least 75% of the time. The figure also shows that slightly more than 2/3 (21 out of 30) of the subjects had search durations that were consistent with risk aversion at least 94% of the time.

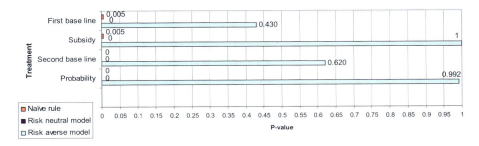

Figure 4. This figure reports the results of direct tests of the observed mean reservation wage paths for the precommitment treatments. In addition to the risk neutral (linear) model and the risk averse (concave) model, a naive model is also tested. The naive model predicts a search termination at any offer above the mean of the distribution except in the last period of the horizon in which case any offer would be accepted. The red bar corresponds to the p values associated with the naive model and the blue bar corresponds to the p values associated with the risk averse model. The risk neutral model exhibited a p value of 0 for every treatment and therefore can be rejected in every case. The naive model is also rejected for every treatment but the risk averse model is never rejected.

Figure 4 reports the test results based on mean reservation wage paths. Using only the data from the precommitment experimental trials, one can test whether the mean reservation wage path observed for each treatment is significantly different from the theoretically-predicted path for a risk neutral agent. On the basis of this direct test, Cox and Oaxaca (1992a) were able to reject both the risk neutral model and the naive model. At the same time the risk averse model survived the direct tests quite handily. The p values ranged from 0.43 to nearly 1.00.

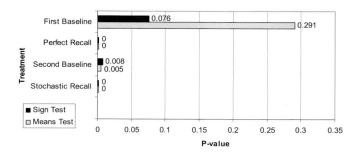

Figure 5. This figure presents the results of nonparametric (Fisher sign) and parametric (means matched pairs) tests of the risk neutral model in a recall search environment. In the perfect recall treatment every previously generated wage offer is available for recall in subsequent search periods. With stochastic recall, previously generated wage offers are available with probabilities that decline geometrically with the number of periods elapsed since the offers were originally generated. The purple bars report the p values for the sign test and the blue bars report the p values for the means tests. The risk neutral model can be rejected in all but one instance (the means test for the first baseline treatment.

3. Recall Experiments

In the basic search model, searchers do not have the option of recalling previously declined wage offers. The availability of a recall option makes search an inherently less risky enterprise. At the same time the presence of a recall option complicates the search environment. In each period of the search horizon, the optimizing searcher must consider the values of all previous offers and the probabilities of their continued availability. Laboratory experiments with recall are reported in Cox and Oaxaca (1996). These experiments examine both perfect recall (all previous offers are available) and stochastic recall (the availability of a past offer declines geometrically with the number of periods lapsed since the offer was generated). The experimental treatment sequence was as follows: Baseline (no recall), Perfect Recall, Baseline (no recall), Stochastic Recall.

Both parametric (matched pairs) and non-parametric (Fisher sign) tests of the linear and concave search models are reported in Cox and Oaxaca (1996). Figure 5 presents the results of tests of the risk neutral model. With the exception of the first baseline treatment, the risk neutral (linear) model is rejected by both sets of tests. The linear model for the first baseline is not rejected by the matched pairs test, although it is rejected at the 7.6% percent level by the Fisher sign test.

Figure 6 presents the results of tests of the risk averse model. As in the previous experiments, the risk averse (concave) model cannot be rejected for any treatment at conventional levels of significance. The lowest p value generated for the concave model is 0.854.

Figure 7 reports tests of treatment effects compared to the theoretical predictions and their implications for the risk neutral and risk averse models. As a first approximation one might conclude that risk aversion offers a satisfactory explanation of search behavior. Search duration is always less than the predictions of the risk neutral model,

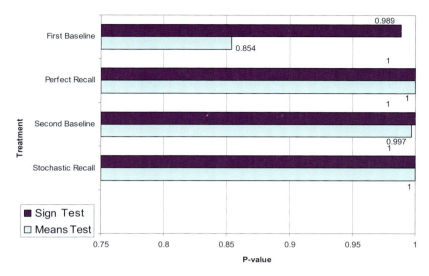

Figure 6. This figure presents the results of nonparametric (Fisher sign) and parametric (means matched pairs) tests of the risk averse model in a recall search environment. In the perfect recall treatment every previously generated wage offer is available for recall in subsequent search periods. With stochastic recall, previously generated wage offers are available with probabilities that decline geometrically with the number of periods elapsed since the offers were originally generated. The purple bars report the p values for the sign test and the blue bars report the p values for the means tests. The risk averse model is never rejected as the lowest p value is 0.854.

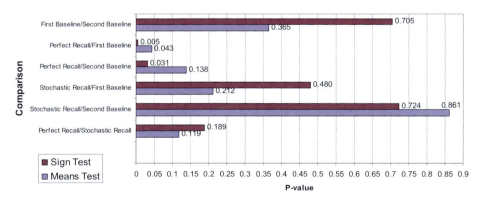

Figure 7. This figure reports the results of difference-in-difference tests in which observed differences in search terminations between each pair of treatments are compared against theoretically predicted differences, conditional on the draws. These tests are designed to capture treatment effects relative to the baseline treatments. The blue bars represent p values from matched pairs (means) tests and the red bars represent p values from the Fisher sign test. Theoretical predictions can be rejected for the perfect recall/baseline comparisons. The theory does not adequately predict subject behavior with the introduction of perfect recall.

conditional on the wage offers that were generated in the experiment. Conditional on the actual draws, theory predicts that search duration will rise under perfect recall relative to either baseline treatment. Although this is in fact observed, the increase in search duration under perfect recall is markedly less than the theoretical predictions.

Subjects are reacting to an inherently less risky search opportunity by behaving as if search were more risky. Thus the theory is not tracking how subjects respond to the introduction of perfect recall. Treatment effects are tested with the difference-in-difference methodology by comparing observed differences in search duration between all pairs of treatments with theoretically predicted differences in search duration. The only rejections of theoretical predictions occur when comparing perfect recall with the baseline treatments.

4. Extensions of the Standard Search Model

Experimental research with job search theory has been extended, beyond the questions discussed in this essay, to include search intensity (Harrison and Morgan, 1990) and search from unknown distributions (Cox and Oaxaca, 2000).

Acknowledgements

Charles Kiser provided valuable assistance by preparing the figures.

References

Cox, James C., Oaxaca, Ronald L. (1989). "Laboratory experiments with a finite-horizon job-search model". Journal of Risk and Uncertainty 2 (3), 301–330.

Cox, James C., Oaxaca, Ronald L. (1992a). "Direct tests of the reservation wage property". Economic Journal 102 (415), 1423–1432.

Cox, James C., Oaxaca, Ronald L. (1992b). "Tests for a reservation wage effect". In: Geweke, John (Ed.), Decision Making Under Risk and Uncertainty: New Models and Empirical Findings. Kluwer Academic Publishers, Dordrecht.

Cox, James C., Oaxaca, Ronald L. (1996). "Testing job search models: The laboratory approach". In: Polachek, Solomon W. (Ed.), Research in Labor Economics, vol. 15. JAI Press, Greenwich, CT.

Cox, James C., Oaxaca, Ronald L. (2000). "Good news and bad news: Search from unknown wage offer distributions". Experimental Economics 2 (3), 197–225.

Harrison, Glenn W., Morgan, Peter (1990). "Search intensity in experiments". Economic Journal 100, 478–486.

Chapter 37

RECIPROCITY AND CONTRACT ENFORCEMENT[1]

SIMON GÄCHTER and ERNST FEHR

University of Zurich

1. The Contract Enforcement Problem

The problem of contract enforcement is a central issue for the functioning of market economies. During the last two decades economic theory has made much progress in the understanding of the *endogenous* enforcement of contracts (see, e.g., Milgrom and Roberts, 1992). Almost all of these models assume that the parties involved in a contract enforcement problem are rational and *selfish*. The assumption that economic actors are *solely* driven by rationality and selfishness is a good starting point for a theoretical examination. It is, however, clearly refuted by many experiments. There is, in particular, a lot of experimental evidence that indicates that a considerable fraction of the population is driven by reciprocity motives (for an overview of results see Fehr and Falk, 1998 and Fehr and Gächter, 1998b). Being motivated by reciprocity means that one is willing to forgo some money in order to punish behavior that is considered as unfair and to reward behavior that is considered as fair.

In this chapter we report on experiments that were designed to test whether *reciprocity* is able to mitigate the contract enforcement problem. The experiments were set up in a labor market framework where the enforcement of workers' effort was problematic. However, we would like to stress that our argument is more general and applies also to contractual relations beyond the employment relationship. In our context a contract enforcement problem exists if, due to limitations in the enforcement technology, a firm which faces rational and purely selfish workers cannot enforce the efficient effort level. Instead, the firm can only enforce a minimal effort level, $e^{\min}$, that is below the efficient level.

To illustrate how reciprocity can, in principle, mitigate the effort enforcement problem consider the following example. Suppose that a firm stipulates a contract which specifies a wage w and a *desired* effort level $\hat{e}$. Once the worker accepts the contract she has to choose the actual effort e. If the worker is purely selfish the firm can only enforce $e^{\min}$. However, if the worker is motivated by reciprocity the firm can, by making a generous offer, induce the worker to respond with $e > e^{\min}$. If, after observing the worker's effort choice, the firm has the additional option to punish the worker even a selfish worker may be induced to provide $e > e^{\min}$. Of course, if the punishment of

---

[1] This chapter is part of a research project on social norms in labor markets. It has been financed by the Swiss National Science Foundation under the project No. 12-43590.95.

Handbook of Experimental Economics Results, Volume 1
Copyright © 2008 Elsevier B.V. All rights reserved
DOI: 10.1016/S1574-0722(07)00037-6

the worker is costly for the firm a selfish firm will never punish. Yet, if the firm is motivated by reciprocity it may well be willing to punish the violation of the contract by the worker even if that punishment is costly for the firm. As a consequence, if the worker anticipates that the firm is willing to punish she may not violate the contract in the first instance.

2. Experimental Design and Results of Fehr and Gächter (1998a)

2.1. Design

In the experiment, subjects acted in the roles of firms and workers, respectively. The design consisted of two major elements: First, *firms posted contracts in a posted bid market* with an excess supply of workers (in all experiments there were 8 workers and 6 firms) to create a lot of competitive pressure. Second, workers had some discretion in exerting work effort. This is regarded to be an essential characteristic of naturally occurring labor relations (see, e.g., Williamson, 1985; Milgrom and Roberts, 1992; Malcomson, 1999) and a precondition for reciprocity to become effective. The experiment consisted of 12 trading days. To determine the effectiveness of reciprocity as a contract enforcement device, two treatment conditions were designed. In the *two-stage treatment*, only workers could respond reciprocally. In the *three-stage treatment*, firms could punish or reward 'their' worker at the third stage after they have learned about workers' actual effort choice at the second stage. Hence, in the three-stage treatment both workers and firms could respond reciprocally. Table 1 summarizes the design and the predictions.

An important design feature concerns the information about payoffs and the anonymity of trading partners. Payoff functions of firms and workers were common knowledge. Individual firms and individual workers could develop no reputation across periods because all interactions were fully anonymous.

2.2. Results

In the *two-stage treatment* workers actually behaved reciprocally as it has been observed in many other similar experiments (see Fehr and Falk, 1998). The higher the wage payment, the higher the actual effort choice. Workers' reciprocity led firms to actually pay above minimum wages to induce higher than minimum effort levels. Figure 1a gives the most important result concerning contract enforcement. It depicts both firms' average desired effort levels ($\hat{e}$) and workers' actual average effort levels (e). The figure shows that the prediction of a minimum actual effort level (of $e = e^{\min} = 0.1$) derived under the assumption of selfishness, clearly receives no support. Workers are willing to provide above-minimum effort levels. However, firms cannot completely enforce their desired effort level. Firms demand, on average, an effort level of 0.65 and receive an

Table 1
Reciprocity and contract enforcement: the design of Fehr and Gächter (1998a)

	A. Sequence of events during a trading day
Stage 1	1. Firms choose wage $w \in [0, 100]$ and *desired* effort $\hat{e} \in [0.1, 0.2, \ldots, 1.0]$. 2. Workers observe all contracts $(w, \hat{e})$ and choose among the available contracts in a randomly determined order. There are more workers than jobs (= firms) to create competition among the workers.
Stage 2	3. Workers who accept a contract choose an *actual* effort level $e \in [0.1, \ldots, 1.0]$. They incur effort costs $c(e)$ with $c(e^{\min}) = 0$, $c'(e) > 0$ and $c''(e) > 0$. 4. Firms are privately informed about the worker's actual effort choice (e). In the two-stage treatment a trading day ends here.
Stage 3	5. (*In the three-stage treatment only!*) Firms decide whether they punish $p \in [-0.1, \ldots, -1]$ or reward $p \in [0.1, \ldots, 1]$ (no punishment/reward means $p = 0$) their worker at some cost $k(p) = 10 * |p|$, i.e., only $p = 0$ is costless.

	B. Payoffs	
Firms:	2-stage-treatment: $\pi = 100 * e - w$	3-stage-treatment: $\pi = 100 * e - w - k(p)$
Workers:	2-stage-treatment: $u = w - c(e)$	3-stage-treatment: $u = w - c(e) + 25p$

C. Main predictions

In the absence of reciprocity	In the presence of reciprocity
2-stage treatment: *2nd stage.* Workers choose $e = e^{\min} = 0.1$ because $e > e^{\min}$ is costly; *1st stage.* Firms pay the minimum wage $w = 0$.	*2-stage treatment*: *2nd stage.* Workers react reciprocally to firms' wage offers, i.e. $e'(w) > 0$. *1st stage.* Firms pay above-minimum wages $w > 0$ to induce $e > e^{\min}$.
3-stage treatment: *3rd stage.* Firms do not punish/reward (i.e., $p = 0$) because punishment is costly for them; *2nd stage.* Workers choose $e = e^{\min} = 0.1$ because $e > e^{\min}$ is costly for them; *1st stage.* Firms pay the minimum wage $w = 0$.	*3-stage treatment*: *3rd stage.* Firms punish shirking (i.e., $e < \hat{e}$ and reward contract fulfillment (i.e., $e = \hat{e}$); *2nd stage.* Workers choose $e > e^{\min}$ for reciprocal reasons and because of the expected reciprocity of firms at the third stage. *1st stage.* Firms pay above-minimum wages $w > 0$.
$\Rightarrow$ With selfishness, firms can only enforce the minimum effort level!	$\Rightarrow$ Reciprocity allows the enforcement of $e > e^{\min}$. Since in the 3-stage treatment both workers and firms can react reciprocally, actual effort levels in the 3-stage treatment are expected to be at least as high as in the two-stage treatment.

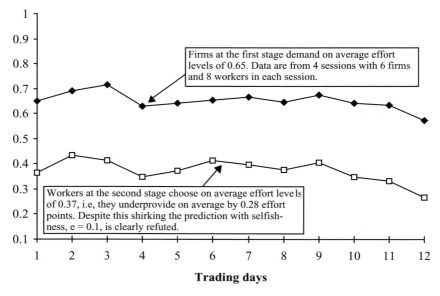

Source: Fehr and Gächter (1998a).

Figure 1a. Contract enforcement (i.e., workers' deviation from firms' desired effort level) in the TWO-stage treatment (workers can react to firms' contract offers).

actual average effort of 0.37. Therefore, one can conclude that workers' reciprocity partly mitigates the contract enforcement problem.

In the *three-stage treatment*, firms at the third stage actually rewarded or punished although this was costly for them. This is evidence for firm's reciprocity. At the second stage workers again showed a highly significantly positive wage-effort relation. Firms tried to induce reciprocity by offering generous contracts.[2] The most important result is that two-sided reciprocity further reduced the contract enforcement problem. As can be seen from Figure 1b, workers' average actual effort in the three-stage treatment was considerably higher than in the two-stage treatment. Moreover, the difference between firms' desired effort level and workers' actual effort level shrank from 0.28 in the two-stage treatment to 0.09 in the three-stage treatment.

Table 2 provides further evidence for the effectiveness of reciprocity as a contract enforcement device. Whereas in the two-stage treatment firms in only 17 percent of the trades were able to fully enforce the contract (i.e., to induce workers to actually choose $e = \hat{e}$), this number increased to 73.8 percent in the three-stage treatment.

---

[2] Gächter and Falk (1998), in a reanalysis of the data of Fehr and Gächter (1998b), find that workers' effort choice at the second stage is influenced by both workers' reciprocal reaction to the generosity of firms' contract offers at the first stage and of workers' anticipation of firms' reciprocal reaction at the third stage.

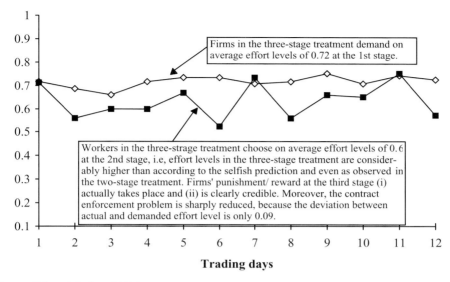

Source: Fehr and Gächter (1998a).

Figure 1b. Contract enforcement (i.e., workers' deviation from firms' desired effort level) in the THREE-stage treatment (firms can react to workers' actual effort choice).

Table 2
Contract enforcement (i.e., the deviation from $\hat{e}$) in the two- and three-stage treatment

Treatment	No. trades	Shirking $e < \hat{e}$		No shirking $e = \hat{e}$	Excess effort $e > \hat{e}$	
		% of trades with $e < \hat{e}$	Average amount of $(\hat{e} - e)$	% of trades with $e = \hat{e}$	% of trades with $e > \hat{e}$	Average amount of $(e - \hat{e})$
2-stage	141	82.98	0.31	14.18	2.84	0.18
3-stage	141	26.24	0.54	36.17	36.88	0.16

Note: $e(\hat{e})$ denotes actual (desired) effort; $e, \hat{e} \in [0.1, 0.2, \ldots, 1]$.

3. Contract Enforcement with an Imperfect Verification Technology

In the experiments of Fehr and Gächter (1998a) it was assumed that third parties (like, e.g., the courts) have no means to verify the underprovision (i.e., $e < \hat{e}$) of effort. Fehr, Gächter, and Kirchsteiger (1997) and Zanella (1998) conducted experiments where it was possible to verify the underprovision of effort with probability 0.5. Due to this verification possibility, firms could impose fines on shirking workers. They could offer contracts that consisted of (i) a wage payment, (ii) a desired effort level, and (iii) a fine the worker had to pay to the firm in case of verifiable shirking.

In this setup, Fehr, Gächter, and Kirchsteiger (1997) conducted two- and three-stage experiments similar to the procedures outlined in Table 1. *Again, it turns out that reciprocity is a very powerful contract enforcement device in the three-stage treatment. The authors report results that are qualitatively similar to those documented in Figure* 1b. It turns out that (i) shirking is drastically reduced relative to the two-stage treatment and (ii) firms are able to enforce effort levels that are far above the levels of both the two-stage treatment and the incentive compatible level under selfish preferences. In the two-stage treatments with fines, however, less reciprocal behavior and *lower* effort levels are observed compared to the two-stage treatments *without* fines. *This indicates that the explicit threat of fining shirking workers undermines reciprocal responses and reduces the average effort in the two-stage treatment.*[3]

4. Summary

This chapter reports the results of experiments that were designed to test the effectiveness of reciprocity as a contract enforcement device. It turns out that reciprocity generates a significant increase in effort levels relative to the prediction based on selfish preferences. Moreover, it gives rise to a considerable mitigation of the contract enforcement problem. The impact of reciprocity is particularly strong if both parties have possibilities to reciprocate. Hence, reciprocity can lead to considerable efficiency gains for the contracting parties. These results indicate that models that neglect reciprocity are likely to make wrong predictions and are, thus, seriously incomplete as a basis for normative advice.

References

Fehr, Ernst, Falk, Armin (1998). "Reciprocity in experimental markets". Mimeo, University of Zurich.
Fehr, Ernst, Gächter, Simon (1998a). "How effective are trust- and reciprocity-based incentives?" In: Ben-Ner, A., Putterman, L. (Eds.), Economics, Values and Organizations. Cambridge University Press, Cambridge.
Fehr, Ernst, Gächter, Simon (1998b). "Reciprocity and economics. The economic implications of Homo Reciprocans". European Economic Review 42 (3–5), 845–859.
Fehr, Ernst, Gächter, Simon, Kirchsteiger, Georg (1997). "Reciprocity as a contract enforcement device". Econometrica 65, 833–860.
Gächter, Simon, Falk, Armin (1998). "Work motivation, institutions and performance". In: Zwick, R., Rapoport, A. (Eds.), Experimental Business Research. Kluwer Academic, Dordrecht.
Malcomson, James (1999). "Individual employment contracts". In: Ashenfelter, O., Card, D. (Eds.), Handbook of Labor Economics, vol. 3B. Elsevier Science, Amsterdam, pp. 2291–2372.
Milgrom, Paul, Roberts, John (1992). "Economics, Organization and Management". Prentice Hall International, London.
Williamson, Oliver (1985). "The Economic Institutions of Capitalism". Free Press, New York.
Zanella, Beatrice (1998). "Die Verdrängung von Reziprozität durch Anreizverträge". Diploma thesis, University of Zurich.

---

[3] Zanella (1998) replicates and further analyses this result.

Chapter 38

RECIPROCITY IN EXPERIMENTAL MARKETS

ERNST FEHR and ARMIN FALK

Institute for Empirical Economic Research, University of Zürich,
Blümlisalpstrasse 10, CH-8006 Zürich, Switzerland
e-mail: efehr@iew.unizh.ch; falk@iew.unizh.ch

1. Introduction

This chapter summarizes main findings of five experimental studies. These studies (Fehr, Kirchsteiger and Riedl, 1993; Fehr and Falk, 1998; Fehr et al., 1998; Fehr and Tougareva, 1995) were primarily designed to test the fair wage–effort hypothesis in the context of competitive experimental markets. The fair wage–effort hypothesis (Akerlof, 1982; Akerlof and Yellen, 1990) stipulates that wage increases raise workers' effort levels. Facing the incompleteness of labor contracts it may, therefore, be profitable for firms to pay wages above the competitive level, which in turn may lead to involuntary unemployment. Besides this labor market interpretation, our experiments can however also be interpreted as stylized versions of incomplete goods or service markets. Suppose an incomplete market in which the price of the good or service is fixed before the good is produced or the service is rendered. If the quality of this good or service cannot be specified in the contract or if the quality is not verifiable by third parties the well-known *lemons* phenomenon may arise (Akerlof, 1970). Goods with quality levels above the minimum are driven out of the market and only goods with minimum quality are traded.

The common feature of all experiments reported in this paper is the so-called "Gift Exchange Game." This game consists of two stages. The first stage is a wage determination stage. Workers and firms trade for jobs with each other. This stage is followed by a second stage where those workers that have concluded a contract with a firm have to choose an effort level. The higher the chosen effort level the higher is the profit of the corresponding firm. Since effort levels above the minimum effort level are (increasingly) costly, workers have a pecuniary incentive to provide only the exogenously given minimum level irrespective of the wage they receive. Rational firms will anticipate that minimum effort choice. Firms' best response is, therefore, to pay the competitive wage that corresponds to the minimum effort level.[1]

Contrary to this prediction we found the following:
(1) Average wages are substantially above the competitive wage that corresponds to the minimum effort level. Moreover, firms' wage payments contain substantial

---

[1] Notice that for any given effort level there exists a competitive wage that just compensates workers for their effort costs.

rent elements, i.e., wages are much higher than the competitive wage that corresponds to workers' *actual* effort choices. There is no tendency for wages to converge towards the competitive level in late periods.
(2) There is a significantly positive relationship between wages and effort levels.
(3) This positive wage–effort relation turns out to be very robust not only within but also across different institutions. It drives results in markets that are organized as bilateral gift-exchange institutions as well as in one-sided and double auction markets.
(4) Even with rather high stake levels, no decline in the effects of fairness on market outcomes can be observed.

We find thus convincing evidence for the fair wage–effort hypothesis. Firms do not enforce competitive wages. Instead they voluntarily pay "fair" wages that is, wages that contain substantial rents. Since workers exhibit reciprocal effort choices a "fair" wage strategy earns higher profits than a "low" wage strategy. Due to sellers' (workers') reciprocal choices, average quality (effort) levels above the minimum are a persistent phenomenon. It is not the case that non-minimal quality levels are driven out of the market.

2. Experimental Design

2.1. Common Features of All Treatments

In all treatments, the game under study was a version of the so-called "Gift-Exchange Game." The Gift-Exchange Game is a sequential move game, which consists of two stages. In the first stage, firms and workers bargain over wages according to specified rules. In the second stage, all workers who conclude a contract with a firm have to choose an effort level e. A firm's payoff function in terms of experimental money, π, is given by

$$\pi = (v - w)e, \tag{1}$$

where v represents an exogenously given redemption value.[2]

A worker's payoff function, U, is simply the difference between the accepted wage, w, and the incurred effort costs $c(e)$ plus fixed costs c_0:

$$U = w - c(e) - c_0. \tag{2}$$

In case a firm or a worker does not conclude a contract, period income is zero. The available effort levels and their corresponding effort costs are depicted in Table 1.

---

[2] We implemented this payoff function instead of the more familiar function $\pi = ve - w$ to avoid the possibility of losses. It is a well-known fact that loss aversion can affect behavior (Tversky and Kahneman, 1992). In later experiments (Fehr and Gächter, 1998; Fehr, Gächter, and Kirchsteiger, 1997) the function $p = ve - w$ was implemented.

Table 1
Effort levels and costs of effort

Effort	0.1	0.2	0.3	0.4	0.5	0.6	0.7	0.8	0.9	1.0
$c(e)$	0	1	2	4	6	8	10	12	15	18

The roles of firms and workers were always randomly assigned to the experimental subjects. After subjects' roles were determined, workers and firms were located in two different, yet adjacent, rooms in which they sat remote from each other. Procedures and payoff *functions* were common knowledge. *Payoffs*, however, were always private information in the sense that a worker's effort choice was only revealed to the firm with which the worker had concluded a contract. Identities of trading partners were never revealed and subjects were informed that they would never learn a trading partner's identity. In all treatment conditions it was, therefore, impossible for individual subjects to develop a reputation.

The major differences between the various treatments (one-sided auction, double auction, bilateral bargaining) concern the wage determination and the matching process. Table 2 presents a summary.

2.2. The One-sided Auction-treatment

In the Fehr, Kirchsteiger and Riedl (1993, 1998) papers prices were determined by a *one-sided oral bid auction*.[3] Buyers publicly announced their price offers which had to obey the improvement rule. These offers could be accepted by any seller. Sellers could not make counteroffers. Buyers were allowed to revise their offers. In case an offer was accepted, a contract was concluded. Both, sellers and buyers could at most conclude one contract per period. The number of sellers always exceeded the number of buyers, i.e., there was always an excess supply.

2.3. The Double Auction-treatment

In the Fehr and Falk (1998) paper, the chosen institution is a *double auction*. Both firms and workers were free to submit and accept wage bids and offers at any time during the trading period. Bids and offers had to obey the improvement rule. Whenever a bid or an offer was accepted, a contract was concluded. As in the one-sided auction workers and firms could at most conclude one contract per period. Again, there was an excess supply of workers. The double auction treatment allows the explicit investigation of the impact of workers' underbidding on wage formation.

---

[3] In these experiments we did not use a labor frame. Instead a goods market language was used.

2.4. The Bilateral Bargaining-treatment

In this treatment condition (Fehr et al., 1998) there were always ten firms and ten workers who traded for ten periods. There was no competition among workers or firms, respectively. Instead, firms and workers were exogenously matched. Each worker was matched with the same firm exactly *once* and subjects knew that they were rematched in each period with a *different* person. In each period firms could propose a wage to "their" worker. In case of acceptance the worker had to choose his effort. If the worker rejected, no trade occurred.

2.5. Standard Predictions

The standard prediction rests on the assumption that rationality and selfishness of all agents are common knowledge. Notice that in all treatments effort levels above the minimum are not enforceable if workers are completely selfish. Since effort choices above the minimum of $e = 0.1$ are (increasingly) costly, rational and selfish workers will always choose the minimum effort independent of the wage they receive. Rational firms will anticipate the choice of that minimum effort level. This means that at the first stage the good that is traded is a well-defined homogeneous good, i.e., labor that provides an effort of $e = 0.1$. The firms' best response is to enforce the lowest wage a worker is just willing to accept. This equilibrium outcome yields low profits for both, firms and workers. Put differently, there is – in principle – a considerable scope for reciprocity-based cooperation to achieve a joint improvement compared to the equilibrium predicted by the standard approach.

3. Results

Across all treatments, average wages substantially exceed the equilibrium wage. Figure 1 shows that this deviation is systematic and stable across all periods, i.e., there is no tendency for wages to converge towards the equilibrium outcome in late periods. The natural question that arises is why do firms refuse to enforce lower wages?

The answer lies in the workers' effort behavior. As Figure 2 shows workers exhibit a positive wage–effort relation. The higher the wage paid the higher is the effort level a firm receives on average. Given workers' reciprocal effort behavior it is optimal for firms *not* to enforce low wages. Firms can substantially improve their profits if they pay "fair" wages. Therefore, our results provide convincing evidence for the validity of the fair wage–effort hypothesis.

Both results, wages that persistently exceed the equilibrium prediction and the positive wage–effort relation are remarkably robust. As Figures 1 and 2 show these regularities hold in a bilateral institution as well as in competitive market institutions. In view of the fact that double auctions are among the most competitive institutions we know it is remarkable that wages in the double auction are roughly similar to wages in the bilateral

Table 2
Parameters of the one-sided auction treatment, the double auction treatment and the bilateral bargaining treatment

Parameters	Treatments		
	One-sided auction (Fehr, Kirchsteiger, and Riedl, 1993)	Double auction (Fehr and Falk, 1998)	Bilateral bargaining (Fehr et al., 1998)
Redemption values v and fixed costs c_0	$v = 126$, $c_0 = 26$	$v = 120$, $c_0 = 20$	$v = 120$, $c_0 = 20$
Feasible effort levels e (quality levels q)	$q \in [0.1, 1]$	$e \in [0.1, 1]$	$e \in [0.1, 1]$
Feasible wages w (prices p)	$30 \leq p \leq 125$ (multiples of five)	$c_0 \leq w \leq v$	$c_0 \leq w \leq v$
Wage (price) determination	One-sided oral auction buyers are price setters	Double auction firms and workers are wage setters	Firms commit themselves to a wage level
Matching process	Via acceptance of price offers	Via acceptance of wage offers	Exogenous
# firms (buyers) # workers (sellers)	50–8 buyers 8–12 sellers (exogenous excess supply of at least 50%)	7 firms 11 workers	10 firms 10 workers
# sessions	4	4	4
# periods	12	10	10
Information conditions	v, $c(q)$, c_0, number of buyers and sellers were common knowledge; identity of trading partners unknown	v, $c(e)$, c_0, number of firms and workers were common knowledge; identity of trading partners unknown	v, $c(e)$, c_0, number of firms and workers were common knowledge; identity of trading partners unknown
Predictions with rational money maximizers	Convergence towards $p = 30$ and $q = 0.1$	Convergence towards $w = 20$ and $e = 0.1$	Convergence towards $w = 20$ and $e = 0.1$
Framing	Goods market	Labor market	Labor market

institution. This fact suggests that competition among workers in the double auction has a negligible impact on wage formation. It seems that wages are solely determined by firms' attempt to appeal to workers' reciprocity by paying "fair" wages.

4. Reciprocity Under Conditions of High Stakes

To what extent do *higher stake* levels change the results mentioned above? Fehr and Tougareva (1995) conducted gift-exchange experiments in Russia to examine whether

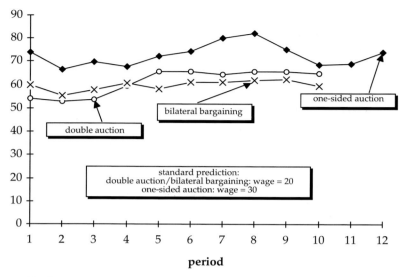

Figure 1. Evolution of average wages across market institutions as described in Table 2.

a large rise in stakes removes the impact of reciprocal fairness on the market outcome. The parameters of their high stake sessions were exactly as in the double-auction treatment described in Table 2. However, the wage determination process was organized as a one-sided auction. On average, subjects earned the income of *ten weeks* in a high stake session. In the control treatment subjects earned on average the income of *one week*. It turns out that despite this ten-fold increase in the stake level, no decline in the impact of reciprocal fairness can be observed. Instead, the high stake results are very similar to the results observed in the control treatment. This holds for the evolution of average wages (compare Figure 3) as well as for the wage–effort relationship (compare Figure 4). Moreover, the results in the high stake and the control sessions are both very similar to the results obtained with regular stake size as reported above (compare Figures 1 and 2).

5. Related Experiments

At first sight our results seem to suggest that competitive market institutions *in general* fail to promote convergence towards the competitive prediction if they are combined with incomplete contracts. However, a comparison with the results of other double

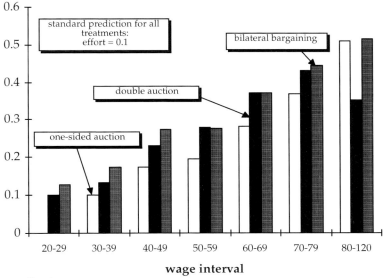

Figure 2. Wage–effort relationship across market institutions as described in Table 2.

Data base:
One-sided auction: Fehr, Kirchsteiger and Riedl (1993).
Double auction: Fehr and Falk (1998).
Bilateral bargaining: Fehr, Kirchler, Weichbold and Gächter (1998).

auctions with incomplete contracts reveals that the incomplete contracts feature is not sufficient for our results. In the Lynch et al. (1986, 1991) experiments[4] buyers also did not know the quality of the good they bought from sellers in a double auction market. The good purchased could either have a regular (i.e., low) quality or a superior (i.e., high) quality. High quality was more valued by the buyers but also more costly for the sellers. As in our experiments, quality was not contractible. In the Lynch et al. (1986, 1991) experiments high quality goods (called supers) were only traded in the early periods. In total 96 percent of the goods traded were low quality goods (called regulars). Moreover, these regulars were traded at prices that were very close to the competitive equilibrium price. In the context of our experiments the analogous (lemons-) result would be that workers almost always choose $e = 0.1$ and that firms pay wages that are very close to the corresponding competitive equilibrium wage.

---

[4] We refer here only to those treatment conditions in the Lynch et al. (1986, 1991) experiments that are similar to our double auction treatment.

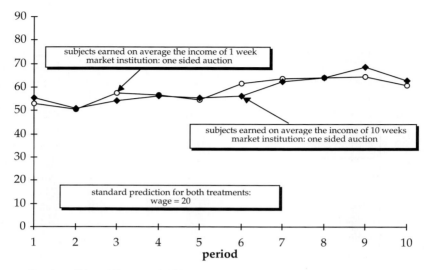

Data base: Fehr and Tougareva (1995).

Figure 3. Evolution of average wages under conditions of high stakes.

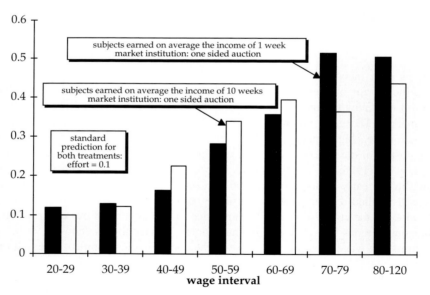

Data base: Fehr and Tougareva (1995).

Figure 4. Wage–effort relationship under conditions of high stakes.

Where does this remarkable difference between our results and the Lynch et al. (1986, 1991) results come from? In our view this difference is generated by the following three-parameter and design differences: *First* of all, and perhaps most importantly, in the competitive equilibrium[5] for both regulars and supers almost the whole surplus from trading is reaped by the sellers because there is an experimentally induced *excess demand*. In contrast, in our experiments the competitive equilibrium wage for any effort level[6] allocates the whole surplus from trading to the firm (buyer) because there is an *excess supply* of labor (sellers). This means that in the Lynch et al. (1986, 1991) experiments excess demand pressures forced buyers to pay high prices. As a consequence, they could not signal their generosity by voluntarily paying more than they had to pay according to demand and supply conditions. Buyers had thus in fact no opportunity to appeal to sellers' reciprocity, i.e., to elicit high quality choices. The *second* reason arises from the fact that buyers in the Lynch et al. (1986, 1991) experiments could easily experience *losses* if they offered prices above the competitive equilibrium price for regulars. Lynch et al. (1986, 1991) report that losses occurred in the first period. We conjecture that these losses deterred buyers from further attempts to elicit high quality choices from the sellers. Notice that in our experiments losses were ruled out and, thus, loss aversion could not inhibit firms' propensity to elicit reciprocity by paying high wages. A third reason stems from the fact that in the Lynch et al. (1986, 1991) experiments only two qualities could be chosen by the sellers and that the cost difference was rather big.[7] Binary effort (quality) choices with large cost differences are likely to inhibit reciprocity. Only those workers (sellers) with a large propensity to respond reciprocally will, under such conditions, *behave* reciprocally while those with a lower propensity will prefer the minimum effort (quality). If our arguments are valid the contrast between our results and the Lynch et al. (1986, 1991) results is very informative. Our experiments indicate the conditions under which one can expect noncompetitive outcomes in competitive markets whereas the Lynch et al. (1986, 1991) experiments indicate the conditions under which standard economic analysis provides good and reliable predictions.

Acknowledgement

Financial support by the Swiss National Science Foundation (project 12-43590.95) is gratefully acknowledged.

---

[5] By the competitive equilibrium price for high quality goods (supers) we mean the price that would be obtained for supers in the competitive equilibrium with full information and fully contractible and exogenously (by a third party) enforceable quality levels.

[6] The competitive equilibrium wage for effort levels above 0.1 is defined as the wage that would be obtained in the competitive equilibrium under full information and fully contractible and exogenously (by a third party) enforceable effort levels.

[7] For example, the choice of a high quality at the competitive equilibrium price for low quality goods would have reduced sellers' profits per trade from (approximately) 145 to 45.

References

Akerlof, G. (1970). "The market for lemons: Qualitative uncertainty and the market mechanism". Quarterly Journal of Economics 84, 488–500.

Akerlof, G. (1982). "Labor contracts as partial gift exchange". Quarterly Journal of Economics 97, 543–569.

Akerlof, G., Yellen, J.L. (1990). "The fair wage–effort hypothesis and unemployment". Quarterly Journal of Economics 105, 255–283.

Fehr, E., Falk, A. (1998). "Wage rigidities in a competitive incomplete contracts market". Journal of Political Economy 107, 106–134.

Fehr, E., Gächter, S. (1998). "How effective are trust- and reciprocity-based incentives?" In: Ben-Ner, A., Putterman, L. (Eds.), Economics, Values and Organizations. Cambridge University Press, Cambridge, UK, pp. 337–363.

Fehr, E., Tougareva, E. (1995). "Do high stakes remove reciprocal fairness – Evidence from Russia". Discussion paper, University of Zürich.

Fehr, E., Gächter, S., Kirchsteiger, G. (1997). "Reciprocity as a contract enforcement device, experimental evidence". Econometrica 65 (4), 833–860.

Fehr, E., Kirchsteiger, G., Riedl, A. (1993). "Does fairness prevent market clearing? An experimental investigation". Quarterly Journal of Economics 108 (2), 437–460.

Fehr, E., Kirchsteiger, G., Riedl, A. (1998). "Gift exchange and reciprocity in competitive experimental markets". European Economic Review 42, 1–34.

Fehr, E., Kirchler, E., Weichbold, A., Gächter, S. (1998). "When social norms overpower competition. Gift exchange in experimental labor markets". Journal of Labor Economics 16, 324–352.

Lynch, M., Miller, R.M., Plott, C.R., Porter, R. (1986). "Product quality, consumer information and 'lemons' in experimental markets". In: Ippolito, P.M., Scheffman, D.T. (Eds.), Empirical Approaches to Consumer Protection Economics. Federal Trade Commission, Bureau of Economics, Washington, DC, pp. 251–306.

Lynch, M., Miller, R.M., Plott, C.R., Porter, R. (1991). "Product quality, informational efficiency, and regulations in experimental markets". Research in Experimental Economics 4, 269–318.

Tversky, A., Kahneman, D. (1992). "Loss aversion in riskless choice: A reference dependent model". Quarterly Journal of Economics 106, 1039–1062.

Chapter 39

INFORMATION CASCADE EXPERIMENTS[1]

LISA R. ANDERSON
The College of William and Mary, Williamsburg, VA, USA

CHARLES A. HOLT
University of Virginia, Charlottesville, VA, USA

1. Cascades

The theoretical literature on "herding" pertains to situations where people with private, incomplete information make public decisions in sequence. Hence, the first few decision makers reveal their information, and subsequent decision makers may follow an established pattern even when their private information suggests that they should deviate. This type of "information cascade" can occur with perfectly rational individuals, when the information implied by early decisions outweighs any one person's private information. These theories have been used to explain fads, investment patterns, etc. (Bannerjee, 1992; Bikhchandani, Hirshleifer, and Welch, 1992). For example, a waiting line for a movie or restaurant may be enough to lure additional customers, even if they have heard mixed reviews from other sources. Economists are particularly interested in market and voting implications of herding behavior, e.g., the possibility that investment booms and busts are analogous to information cascades. This paper surveys the results of experiments designed to evaluate cascade behavior with human subjects, both in simple "ball-and-urn" settings and in more complex, asset-market environments.

The concept of an information cascade can be explained in the context of a specific numerical example that was used in initial laboratory experiments (Anderson and Holt, 1997). In this example, there are two states of nature, A and B, which are equally likely, *ex ante*. Each decision maker obtains an independent, private signal, a or b, which has a two-thirds chance of indicating the correct state, i.e. $\Pr(a|A) = \Pr(b|B) = 2/3$. The decision makers are selected in sequence and asked to predict the state, with a monetary reward paid for a correct prediction. The predictions are publicly announced as they are made, but individuals are not able to observe others' private signals. The first person in the sequence must predict only on the basis of private information. This person should predict the state indicated by the signal because, with a prior probability of $1/2$ for each state, the posterior probability is $2/3$ for the state that is signaled:

$$\Pr(A|a) = \frac{(1/2)\Pr(a|A)}{(1/2)\Pr(a|A) + (1/2)\Pr(a|B)} = \frac{(1/2)(2/3)}{(1/2)(2/3) + (1/2)(1/3)} = 2/3.$$

---

[1] This research was supported in part by grants from the National Science Foundation (SES93-20617).

Therefore, the first decision reveals that person's signal, even though subsequent individuals see only the prediction, not the private information on which the prediction was based.

Without loss of generality, suppose that the first person sees an "*a*" signal and predicts *A*. If the second decision maker in the sequence also sees an "*a*" signal, then it is obvious that the optimal prediction is *A*. If the second person sees a "*b*" signal, then the inferred and observed signals cancel each other, and the posterior probability is exactly 1/2, as can be verified by Bayes' rule. If we assume that people make a prediction based on their own private information when the posterior is 1/2, then the second decision also reveals the associated private signal, regardless of whether or not it conforms to the first prediction. Therefore, two initial predictions of *A* reveal two "*a*" signals, which loosely speaking, are more informative than the private signal seen by the third person in the sequence, even if this is a "*b*." Whenever the first two predictions match, the third person should follow.[2] This is how a cascade develops; the third person's decision does not reveal his or her private draw in this case, and the fourth person makes a decision based on the same prior information as the third. Thus a string of matching decisions can create a false degree of certainty, since all are driven by the first two predictions when they match.

Anderson and Holt (1997) implemented this setup in an experiment by putting balls labeled "*a*" or "*b*" in urns labeled *A* and *B*, with three labeled balls in each[3]:

Urn *A*: a, a, b,   Urn *B*: b, b, a.

The urns were equally likely to be chosen by the throw of a six-sided die. A throw of 1, 2, or 3 determined that urn *A* would be used for the draws, and a throw of 4, 5, or 6 determined that urn *B* would be used. Hence, each of the 6 balls was *ex ante* equally likely to be drawn. Since 2 of the 3 balls labeled "*a*" were in urn *A*, the posterior probability of event *A* given signal "*a*" is 2/3. Similarly, the posterior probability of event *A* given signal "*b*" is 1/3.[4]

---

[2] The argument given in the text is based on the assumption that, when the posterior is 1/2, the person bases the prediction on private information. This assumption is strongly supported by the laboratory evidence in Anderson and Holt (1997), who also note that relying on private information in this case is rational when the initial decision makers may have made a mistake. The cascade formation described in the text is unchanged if we make the alternative assumption that the prediction is equally likely to be an *A* or a *B* when the posterior is 1/2. Then the second prediction is also informative: a *B* prediction reveals a "*b*" signal, and an *A* prediction reveals that an "*a*" signal was more likely, since the "*a*" signal always results in an *A* prediction and the "*b*" signal only yields an *A* prediction half of the time. If the first two predictions match, then the third decision maker should reason: the first *A* prediction reveals an "*a*" signal, the second *A* prediction reveals that an "*a*" signal was more likely, and the total information content of these two observations is more favorable for state *A* than my own signal, even if it is a "*b*" signal. In this manner, the optimal decision of the third person in a sequence is to follow the first two predictions when they match, regardless of the signal observed.

[3] In the experiment, the balls were actually identified by a "light" or "dark" color, instead of being labeled by letters.

[4] In fact, this counting method of determining the posterior probability can be generalized to provide a natural and intuitive way of teaching Bayes' rule to students in a classroom setting. For example, suppose that

Subjects were chosen in a random order to see a private signal and make a public prediction about which urn was used. Once each subject made a prediction, a monitor announced which urn was actually used. Everyone who predicted correctly earned $2; others earned nothing. This process was repeated fifteen times for each group of six subjects with a new die throw to select the urn at the beginning of each repetition. New subjects were recruited for six different sessions of the experiment using the parameters described above.[5]

Sample results from one of these sessions are presented in Table 1. In period 1, the first two subjects in the sequence made conflicting predictions, based on their own private signals. Reading across the first row of the table, the next three subjects saw "a" signals and predicted A, and the final subject saw a "b" signal and followed the others with an A prediction. This was an incorrect cascade since urn B was actually being used for draws, as shown in the far right column of the table. Decisions made in an incorrect cascade are colored blue in the table. The second period begins with an error, as indicated by the red shading of the incorrect A prediction that followed a "b" signal. Cascades, indicated by green shading, formed in many of the subsequent periods. The longest cascade was the incorrect cascade in period 9, shown in blue. This session is atypical in the sense that cascades were possible in most of the periods. Over all sessions, the sequence of draws made cascades possible in about sixty percent of the periods, and cascades actually formed in seventy percent of the periods in which they were possible.[6]

Despite the overall consistency of the data with predicted behavior, mistakes are not uncommon. The first subject to make a decision in period 2 saw a "b" signal and predicted A. This type of error, which is inconsistent with Bayes' rule and private information, is probably the result of confusion or carelessness. Another type of error was committed by the third decision maker in period 8. This person saw a "b" signal and made a B prediction, consistent with the private information but inconsistent with the Bayesian posterior determined by the two previous A decisions. Perhaps it is not surprising that this particular subject relied on private information, since this person, who

---

the prior probability of Urn A is 2/3 instead of 1/2. To reflect the fact that Urn A is twice as likely in this case, just double the number of balls listed for Urn A, keeping the proportions unchanged: Urn A: a, a, b, a, a, b; Urn B: b, b, a. Now four of the five "a" balls are listed in Urn A, so the draw of an "a" ball results in a posterior of 4/5 for Urn A, as can be verified by Bayes' rule. Holt and Anderson (1996) show how this ball counting heuristic is related to the algebra of Bayes's rule, and how the relationship can be used in the teaching of Bayes' rule.

[5] Anderson and Holt (1997) report six additional sessions using an asymmetric design in which urns A and B contained different proportions of "a" and "b" balls.

[6] Information cascades have generally been observed in a number of different contexts, e.g., Willinger and Ziegelmeyer (1997) and Hung and Plott (2001), discussed below. With hypothetical payoffs the incidence of cascades is much lower, see Anderson (2001) and Huck and Oechssler (2000). The basic experimental design discussed here has been modified in several ways, e.g., continuous action spaces (Huck and Oechssler, 2000), option to purchase private signals (Kraemer and Nöth, 1999), random determination of the strength of the private signal (Nöth and Weber, 1999).

Table 1
Sample results from session 2 of Anderson and Holt (1997) experiments

Order in decision sequence	1st	2nd	3rd	4th	5th	6th	Urn used for draws
Period 1 decisions	A	B	A	A	A	*A*	Urn B
Private signal (probability of Urn A)	a (2/3)	b (1/2)	a (2/3)	a (4/5)	a (8/9)	b (4/5)	
Period 2 decisions	*A*	B	B	A	A	B	Urn B
Private signal (probability of Urn A)	b (1/3)	b (1/2)	b (1/3)	a (1/2)	a (2/3)	b (1/2)	
Period 3 decisions	A	A	*A*	A	A	A	Urn A
Private signal (probability of Urn A)	a (2/3)	a (4/5)	b (2/3)	a (4/5)	a (4/5)	a (4/5)	
Period 4 decisions	B	A	A	A	A	A	Urn A
Private signal (probability of Urn A)	b (1/3)	a (1/2)	a (2/3)	a (4/5)	a (8/9)	a (8/9)	
Periods 5 decisions	A	B	B	B	*B*	*B*	Urn B
Private signal (probability of Urn A)	a (2/3)	b (1/2)	b (1/3)	b (1/5)	a (1/3)	a (1/3)	
Period 6 decisions	A	A	*A*	*A*	A	A	Urn A
Private signal (probability of Urn A)	a (2/3)	a (4/5)	b (2/3)	b (2/3)	a (8/9)	a (8/9)	
Period 7 decisions	B	A	B	B	B	*B*	Urn B
Private signal (probability of Urn A)	b (1/3)	a (1/2)	b (1/3)	b (1/5)	b (1/9)	a (1/3)	
Period 8 decisions	A	A	*B*	A	*A*	A	Urn A
Private signal (probability of Urn A)	a (2/3)	a (4/5)	b (2/3)	a (4/5)	b (2/3)	a (4/5)	
Period 9 decisions	A	A	*A*	A	A	A	Urn B
Private signal (probability of Urn A)	a (2/3)	a (4/5)	b (2/3)	b (2/3)	b (2/3)	b (2/3)	
Period 10 decisions	A	B	B	B	B	B	Urn B
Private signal (probability of Urn A)	a (2/3)	b (1/2)	b (1/3)	b (1/5)	b (1/9)	b (1/9)	

Key: "Correct" cascade – correct prediction, inconsistent with private information, consistent with Bayes' rule. "Incorrect" cascade – incorrect prediction, inconsistent with private information, consistent with Bayes' rule. Error – inconsistent with Bayes' rule.

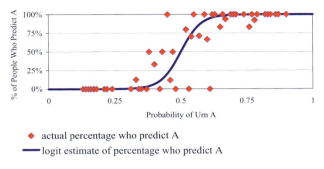

- ◆ actual percentage who predict A
- — logit estimate of percentage who predict A

Figure 1. Logistic error model of cascade data.

was the final decision maker in period 1, went against private information to follow the others in a series of predictions that turned out to be incorrect. Overall, this type of error occurred in about one-fourth of the cases where the optimal Bayesian decision differed from the decision implied by private information.

Anderson (2001) estimates error rates in these experiments using a logistic error model. If the error rate is very small, i.e. near perfect rationality, then the optimal decision is to predict urn A whenever the probability of urn A is greater than .5, and to predict urn B otherwise. The red data points in Figure 1 show the percentage of subjects who actually predicted urn A as a function of the Bayesian probability of urn A (as calculated in Anderson, 2001). Perfect rationality implies a step pattern, with data points on the horizontal axis to the left of 0.5, and with data points at the top of the figure when the probability of urn A is greater than 0.5. Notice that the actual pattern of data points only conforms approximately to this step pattern, which indicates some noise in the predictions. This pattern of errors was the motivation for estimating the logistic choice function, which is shown in blue in the figure. For example, when the probability of urn A is exactly 0.5, the blue line has a height of 0.5. This is because, when each urn is equally likely, either prediction has the same expected payoff, and the estimated probability of predicting urn A is 0.5. Notice that most of the errors in the data points occur at probabilities near the center of the graph, i.e. when the probability of urn A is close enough to 0.5 that the difference in the expected payoffs is relatively small.

The logistic model explains a number of other interesting patterns in the data. For example, when there is some chance that the first person in the sequence will make an error (a prediction that is inconsistent with the first observed signal), the second person should rely on private information when this information is inconsistent with the first decision. In this case, the logistic error model predicts that the second person will follow private information with a probability of .96. In fact, this reliance on private information occurred in ninety-five percent of the cases where the second person's signal differed from the first person's prediction.

Another prediction of the logistic error model is that increases in the payoff associated with a correct prediction will reduce the incidence of errors. Anderson (2001) replicates the basic cascade design with three different payoffs for a correct decision: $0 (no payoff), $2 (payoff), and $4 (double payoff).[7] Increasing payoffs from $0 to $2 resulted in a decrease in the number of errors, but the increase from $2 to $4 had no significant effect on errors.

Allsopp and Hey (2000) report the results of a cascade experiment based on the Banerjee (1992) model in which only one of a finite number of assets will have a positive payoff. Each subject receives a signal with probability α. A signal will reveal the correct asset with probability β. If two or more people have selected a particular asset that is different from the one indicated by a person's private signal, then it is optimal for that person to choose the most commonly selected asset, independent of the values of α and β. Cascades can form when it is optimal for people to ignore their private information and follow others.[8] Allsopp and Hey (2000) report that the incidence of observed cascades is lower in their experiments than would be predicted by the Banerjee model. Moreover, subjects' behavior is affected by the α and β parameters, despite the fact that theoretical predictions are independent of these parameters. The most common deviation from predicted behavior is the tendency for individuals to select the asset indicated by their own signal, even when it is irrational to do so. All of the analysis is based on the assumption that others do not make mistakes, and we conjecture that the anomalous behavior patterns may be explained by incorporating the possibility of decision error. When others may make errors, the option of following one's own information becomes more attractive. Moreover, the α and β parameters affect the relative costs of not following the herd, and therefore, these parameters affect behavior in a theoretical model with decision error.

2. Market Applications and Alternative Institutions

Hung and Plott (2001) alter the payoff structure of the basic cascade design in two ways: In their "majority rule institution," subjects receive a positive payment if the group decision (determined by the majority of public predictions) is correct. This reduces conformity among early decisions since each person has an incentive to reveal private information to subsequent decision makers. The second modification is a "conformity rewarding institution" in which a positive payment is received if one's own prediction matches that of the majority, whether or not the majority decision is correct. This is like a network externality or a coordination game in the sense that conformity matters, and the only role of the private signal is to facilitate uniformity. This treatment increases

---

[7] In all three designs, subjects were paid $5 for participation in the experiment. In addition, subjects in the no payoff treatment were paid a fixed amount, $20, independent of their decisions.

[8] Banerjee's result is based on a number of tie-breaking assumptions that are not listed here.

the tendency to cascade, since conformity *per se* is rewarded. The overall pattern of decisions in these treatments allows Hung and Plott to rule out a pure preference for conformity as an explanation of cascades in the basic design discussed in the previous section.

A natural application of cascade theory is in the context of voting, where the decisions are often binary (e.g., convict or acquit). Guarnaschelli, McKelvey and Palfrey (2001) report an experiment in which individuals have private signals about the state of nature (e.g., whether a defendant is guilty). Voting is simultaneous, which rules out cascade-like sequences. Following Hung and Plott (2001), Golladay (2001) allows subjects with private signals to vote in sequence, thereby generating cascade behavior. Her setup also differs from Buarnaschelli, McKelvey and Palfrey in that her payoffs make a distinction between the two types of errors, i.e., there is a higher payoff for acquitting a guilty person than for convicting an innocent person. With sequential voting, Golladay finds the frequency of incorrect group decisions to be approximately the same for unanimity and majority rule procedures, but there is some evidence that unanimity tends to avoid the worst error (convicting the innocent).

In a similar vein, some behavioral patterns in financial markets have been attributed to herd-like behavior. The connection between investment decisions and inferences drawn from other's investment decisions was noted by Keynes (1965), who compared investment decisions with a guessing game in which participants have to predict which contestant will receive the most votes in a beauty contest. This process is complicated if each person tries to think about what the others will find attractive, and what the others will think about what others find attractive, etc. Similarly, investors in financial markets will try to guess which stocks will become popular, even in the short term, perhaps by looking at others' purchases as revealed sequentially on a ticker tape. Note that the sequence of investment decisions usually is not exogenously specified, as was the case for the cascade experiments considered in the previous section. Here we review several papers in which the order of decisions is determined by the subjects in experiments, based on their own information.

Bounmy et al. (1997) conducted an experiment in which paired subjects each received a signal that pertained to the value of an asset. Moreover, the quality of the signal was apparent when the signal was received. The signal was either positive, indicating that it is better to buy, or negative, indicating that it better to sell. (Uninformative, zero, signals were also possible.) The magnitude of the signal indicated its quality, e.g., a large positive signal indicated that it is more likely that the correct decision is to buy. At each decision point, subjects could buy, sell, or incur a small cost by waiting. The prediction of the theoretical model is that subjects with less informative signals should wait and then imitate the decision made by the other person if that person decides earlier. These predictions tended to describe observed behavior.

Camerer and Weigelt (1991) report that imitation of earlier decisions may occur even if initial trades are not based on superior information. For example, randomness in initial decisions by uninformed traders may create a price movement that seems to indicate conformity of inside information. Then other traders may imitate these decisions, often resulting in an incorrect cascade.

Plott, Wit, and Yang (2003) present results from experiments that implement a type of parimutuel betting. The setup is analogous to a horse race where a cash prize is divided among those who bet on the winning horse in proportion to the amounts that they bet. In the experiment, there are six assets, and only the asset that corresponds to the true state has value to investors. Participants received private and imperfect information about the true state, and then decided how to allocate their endowment between purchases of each asset. Purchases were revealed as they occurred, so individuals could see others' purchases and make inferences about others' information. Information aggregation occurred to a large extent. In most cases, the asset corresponding to the true state was most heavily purchased. In some cases, however, heavy purchases of an asset that did not correspond to the true state induced others to imitate, which created a herding pattern, indicating an incorrect cascade.

This literature, which builds on simplified models of inference in sequential decision making, seems to be progressing toward more interesting applications, like the parimutuel betting example. Even though these applications are motivated by naturally occurring institutions, the usefulness of field data is limited by the fact that the private information of traders and/or betters typically cannot be observed. Laboratory experiments are particularly useful in examining herding behavior because private information is observed by the experimenter and the flow is information can be precisely controlled.

References

Allsopp, Louise, Hey, John D. (2000). "Two experiments to test a model of herd behavior". Experimental Economics 3 (2), 121–136.
Anderson, Lisa R. (2001). "Payoff effects in information cascade experiments". Economic Inquiry 39 (4), 609–615.
Anderson, Lisa R., Holt, Charles A. (1997). "Information cascades in the laboratory". American Economic Review 87 (5), 847–862.
Banerjee, A.V. (1992). "A simple model of Herd behavior". Quarterly Journal of Economics 107 (3), 797–817.
Bikhchandani, Sushil, Hirshleifer, David, Welch, Ivo (1992). "A theory of fads, fashion, custom, and cultural change as informational cascades". Journal of Political Economy 100 (5), 992–1026.
Bounmy, Kene, Vergnaud, Jean-Christophe, Willinger, Marc, Ziegelmeyer, Anthony (1997). "Information externalities and mimetic behavior with endogenous timing of decisions: Theoretical predictions and experimental evidence". Working paper, University Louis Pasteur, Strasbourg.
Camerer, Colin F., Weigelt, Keith (1991). "Information mirages in experimental asset markets". Journal of Business 64 (4), 463–493.
Golladay, K. Brett (2001). "An economic analysis of the jury system with focus on the experimental study of information cascades and juror preference diversity". Senior honors thesis, College of William and Mary.
Guarnaschelli, Serena, McKelvey, Richard D., Palfrey, Thomas R. (2001). "An experimental study of jury decision rules". American Political Science Review 94 (2), 407–427.
Holt, Charles A., Anderson, Lisa R. (1996). "Classroom games: Understanding Bayes' rule". Journal of Economic Perspectives 10 (2), 179–187.
Huck, Steffen, Oechssler, Jörg (2000). "Informational cascades in the laboratory: Do they occur for the right reasons?" Journal of Economic Psychology 21 (6), 661–671.

Hung, Angela A., Plott, Charles R. (2001). "Information cascades: Replication and an extension to majority rule and conformity rewarding institutions". American Economic Review 91 (5), 1508–1520.

Keynes, John Maynard (1965). "The General Theory of Employment, Interest, and Money". Harcourt, Brace & World, New York.

Kraemer, Carlo, Nöth, Markus (1999). "Information aggregation with costly signals and random ordering: Experimental evidence". Working paper, University of Mannheim.

Nöth, Markus, Weber, Martin (1999). "Information aggregation with random ordering: Cascades and over-confidence". Working paper, University of Mannheim.

Plott, Charles R., Wit, J., Yang, W.C. (2003). "Parimutuel betting markets as information aggregation devices: Experimental results". Economic Theory 22 (2), 311–351.

Willinger, Marc, Ziegelmeyer, Anthony (1997). "An attempt to shatter information cascades in the laboratory". Working paper, University Louis Pasteur, Strasbourg.

Further reading

Anderson, Lisa R. (1994). "Information cascades". Doctoral dissertation, University of Virginia.

Anderson, Lisa R., Holt, Charles A. (1996). "Classroom games: Information cascades". Journal of Economic Perspectives 10 (4), 187–193.

Huck, Steffen, Oechssler, Jörg (1998). "Informational cascades with continuous action spaces". Economics Letters 60 (2), 162–166.

Plott, Charles R., Sunder, Shyam (1982). "Efficiency of experimental security markets with insider information: An application of rational-expectations models". Journal of Political Economy 90, 663–698.

Plott, Charles R., Sunder, Shyam (1988). "Rational expectations and the aggregation of diverse information in laboratory security markets". Econometrica 56, 1085–1118.

Welch, Ivo (1992). "Sequential sales, learning, and cascades". Journal of Finance 47 (2), 695–732.

Chapter 40

MARKETS AND INFORMATION AGGREGATION MECHANISMS

KAY-YUT CHEN
Hewlett Packard Laboratories

CHARLES R. PLOTT
California Institute of Technology

The awareness that markets can be created specifically to aggregate information has roots in a long history of experimental economics research. Plott and Sunder (1982, 1988) made three central discoveries. The first is that markets can aggregate information when individuals have diverse preferences. The second is that the ability of markets to do so is related to the underlying architectures and instruments that exist in the market. If markets do not consist of a complete set of Arrow–Debreu, state contingent commodities, the aggregation might not occur. The third discovery is that if the preferences are homogeneous then markets can perform the task even if the instruments do not consist of a full set of state contingent commodities. An impressive literature has developed since (Copeland and Friedman, 1987, 1991, 1992; Forsythe and Lundholm, 1990; Friedman, 1993; Sunder, 1992, 1995; Nöth and Weber, 1996; Plott, 2000).

While this literature establishes the ability of markets to carry information from insiders to outsiders, it is also known that markets can make mistakes (Camerer and Weigelt, 1991). Furthermore the large literature on the winner's curse demonstrates that the logical possibility of conditioning on the information of others does not evolve naturally from strategic behaviors alone. Indeed, Kagel and Levine (1986) and Guarnaschelli et al. (2003) demonstrate that the existence and magnitude of a winner's curse are closely related to market architectures. Sealed bid processes, for example, and perhaps call markets in general, will not be an effective architecture for information aggregation, while the double auction is an effective architecture. The same message is found in the cascade literature, initiated by Anderson and Holt (1997). The information that becomes integrated into the pattern of social decisions is heavily influenced by incentives and procedures. Indeed the incentives and procedures such as majority rule can increase the information aggregation capacities of sequential observations and incentives to conform can destroy the capacity (Hung and Plott, 2001). The cause of mistakes systematically made by agents, the detectability of mistakes and the relationship between market architectures, market instruments and the information transmission process contains huge categories of unexplored issues.

The data reported here fill a gap in the literature. Roughly speaking, the literature suggests that markets with instruments consisting of a full set of Arrow–Debreu securities and organized as continuous, multiple unit double auctions have the capacity to collect and aggregate information. The ability to perform the function is related to replication of experiences similar to the convergence exhibited by all experimental markets. However, these suggestions are drawn from experiments with only a small number of states, a small number of traders and private information that contained "strong" signals. Such features of earlier experiments were dictated by the limitations of experimental technology but with the development of the Marketscape programs in the 1990s, much larger experiments became possible.

The experiments reported here were used as a test of the robustness of the earlier results referenced above. The purpose was to make sure that the lessons of the early experiments generalized to a more complex world that had features of the field exercise that was to be undertaken.

Figure 1 illustrates the information structure and the instruments created in the market. The experiment proceeds in a series of periods or "days." The economy consists of 10 states. A state is randomly drawn at the beginning of each period with all states are equally likely. The state drawn is unknown to subjects but each individual is given an independently drawn signal dependent on the state. The signal given to an individual consists of three draws with replacement from a distribution with the correct state having a probability of one fourth of being drawn and each of the other states having a probability of one of twelve. So, an individual with three draws of the same state has a posterior probability of 0.75 of knowing the state. If the individual has two draws the same then the probabilities are 0.45, 0.15 and 0.05 for the three types of states represented. If the individual gets three separate states drawn then the probabilities are 0.188 and 0.063 for those represented and those not represented, respectively.

Thus, each individual has very little information about the state. Even an individual with all three draws the same has a .25 chance of being wrong. However, if there are many individuals and if the draws of all individuals are pooled together then an application of Bayes Law to the pooled samples will give the true state with near certainty. Thus, the experimental environment is one in which each individual knows "very little" but "collectively" they know a lot. If the markets collect and reveal all information that is known to all individuals then the true state should be revealed in the prices with almost certainty. That is, the true state should be revealed with almost certainty if the principles of rational expectations information aggregation are in operation.

The instruments are Arrow–Debreu securities. Each state is represented by a security that pays $2.00 if the state occurs and $0 otherwise. Each agent is given an initial endowment consisting of a portfolio of 10 of each type of securities. By holding the full portfolio and making no trades at all, the portfolio would pay $20, which would allow the individual to repay the $10–$15 loan for the period. The rational expectations, fully revealing competitive equilibrium is for the price of the security representing the true state to be near $2.00 and the price of securities representing all other states to be near $0.

Figure 2 contains typical time paths from a single period of the ten markets when the agents in the markets have had some experience. Opening prices exhibit considerable variance with some prices being much too high, often due to computer entry errors but sometimes due to agents who had strong signals. All prices tend to drop and as the clus-

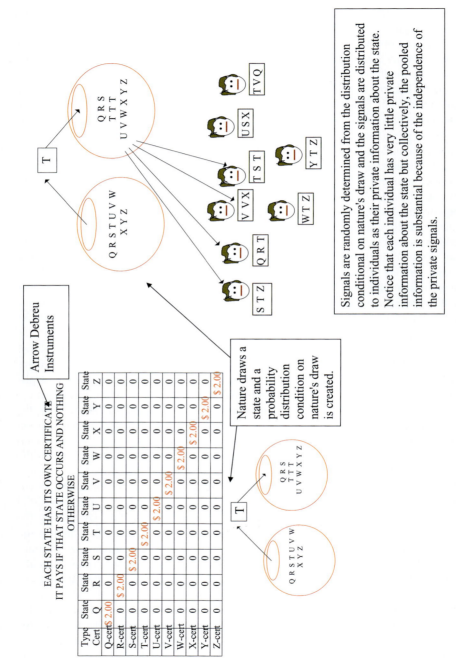

Figure 1. Market instruments correspond to states. States are randomly drawn and randomly generated private information is distributed to subjects.

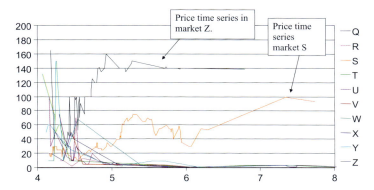

Figure 2. Given the aggregate of all private signals the probability of state z is .99. Market Z is shown in black. Arrow–Debreu markets are able to collect and publish information distributed over many agents: the market of the actual state emerges quickly with highest prices.

ter of prices drop and occasionally a price will move upward only to be competed back down. Eventually one price begins to emerge and move upward steadily and when this takes place it is almost always the market of the true state. In Figure 2 this is the Z market. State Z has a .99 chance of being the true state according to the pooled information that was sent privately to all agents. In the figure a second market, S, begins to emerge with a higher price. While the price of Z and the price of S sum to near the 200, the sum is not perfect and certainly the price of S is too high given the information in the system. In the sense of these time series, one can say that the markets managed to aggregate the information and make it available for all. The aggregation is not perfect but it is useful.

Figure 3 contains the results of an experiment with over 60 subjects for a number of periods. Subjects were located remotely, participating through the continuous Marketscape exchange over the Internet. Before a period opened, each subject received private information about the state as described above. They were given the initial endowment portfolio for the period, a loan of working capital, the results of any previous period states, and their own earnings. The figure contains the results of eight periods. The time sequence for each market is shown in the figure.

As can be seen, during the prices when the first period opens reveal very little. Almost all prices are roughly at the same level. However, even in the early periods a trained eye can detect the proper state by the behavior of the prices. Not shown in the figure are the bids and asks, which are known to be important carriers of information in addition to prices. By about the fourth period the price of the correct state emerges very quickly in the period and moves to near the rational expectations level. The prices of all other states fall toward zero. By the final periods the information becomes aggregated quickly in the prices and even those with no information at all can infer what others know from the behavior of the markets.

While experiments demonstrate that properly designed markets have the capacity to collect, aggregate and publish information the experiments also demonstrate that there

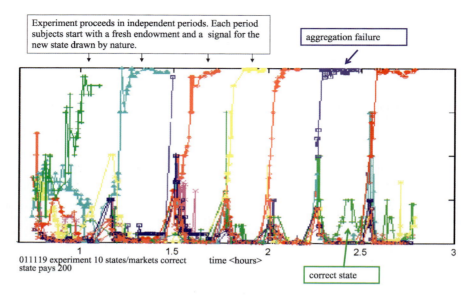

Figure 3. The time series for each trade in each market is contained in the figure. Each market is represented by a different color.

are limitations. Bubbles can be observed in experiments in which the wrong market emerges with a high price and strongly signals the wrong state. This can be seen in period six in which the wrong state emerges. However, it must be added that such events are rare, given strong underlying information and they are reduced with experience. It is also important to note that the market itself suggests that a bubble might be present and does so through the high prices that emerge for the X state shown in green.

1. Are The Lessons From The Simple Cases Useful?

The experimental work demonstrates that markets have the capacity to collect information through a process of equilibration and that fact suggests the feasibility of creating a system of markets that have only a purpose of gathering information. The laboratory work suggests that theory and experiments can be turned to the design and implementation of *Information Aggregation Mechanisms*.

The issue of whether or not laboratory methods are useful can now be brought into view. The idea of an information aggregation mechanism as a product of institutional design is a direct product of experimental work. Background laboratory work established the two important legs for an application.[1] First, the laboratory work established

---

[1] Considerable thought has been devoted to the methodology of using experiments in policy contexts. The concepts of "proof of principle" and "design consistency" are introduced by Plott (1994).

a "proof of principle" in the sense that when tested under laboratory conditions it performed as predicted. Second, the experiments established "design consistency" in the sense that the mechanism performed as it did for understandable reasons. The success of the mechanism has a theoretical underpinning and thus the success does not appear to be some sort of accident or accidental choice of parameters.

Experimentalists in Hewlett Packard Corporation were aware of the potential value of developing and deploying an Information Aggregation Mechanism. They decided that a field test would be appropriate and management was approached accordingly (Chen and Plott, 2000). Criteria for finding the appropriate problem were closely linked to the properties that existed in successful laboratory experiments. (i) The state of nature should be objective and not too far in the future, reflecting the fact that participant experience might be necessary for mechanism success. (ii) The state forecasted should be replicable in the sense that the same type of forecast should be undertaken repeatedly with the same participants. (iii) Those participating in the forecast should possess information that can be aggregated. The Information Aggregation Mechanism involves information collection and aggregation but not information creation. If no information existed to be collected, then there would be no reason to think that the forecast would be successful. (iv) The participants should have no interest that depended on the outcome of the exercise. The incentives should be to make money and not to manipulate the prediction.

The applied problem chosen for field tests was related to sales forecasting. In the context of the application, the company would like to obtain information about the sales of a particular piece of equipment a few months in the future. For purposes of the example used for this discussion the equipment will be called "Low" and the month for which sales were to be forecast was September. The month in which the markets operated was June. The possible sales were divided into ten intervals such as 0000–1500; 1501–1600; 1601–1700; etc. up to 2301-more. From the point of view of the theory and the market instruments, these intervals can be identified as the "states of nature" but of course that language was not used in the field. Thus, the mechanism was based on ten securities. Each state of nature was associated with a specific security and the associated security was given the name of the state. So, there was a security called, SEP-LOW-0000–1500 and one called SEP-LOW-1501–1600, etc. After the actual sales for the month of September were to become known the security associated with the state would pay a dollar per share to the holder. Those securities associated with all other states would pay zero. Thus, the situation is exactly a full set of Arrow–Debreu securities as described in the experiment above. Figure 4 contains the list.

Each of the individuals identified for the exercise was given a portfolio of approximately 20 shares of each security and some trading cash. The initial portfolio was designed with variations across subjects so as to promote trading. The timing of the markets, special screens, special training and online help were developed. Links to the company database were provided for those who wanted to study such data that the company had for processing and applications for forecasting. The time line of the exercise

Markets (Open 1st week of July)	000 1500	1501 1600	1601 1700	1701 1800	1801 1900	1901 2000	2001 2100	2101 2200	2201 2300	2301 MORE
SEP-LOW-0000-1500	$1.00	0	0	0	0	0	0	0	0	0
SEP-LOW-1501-1600	0	$1.00	0	0	0	0	0	0	0	0
SEP-LOW-1601-1700	0	0	$1.00	0	0	0	0	0	0	0
SEP-LOW-1701-1800	0	0	0	$1.00	0	0	0	0	0	0
SEP-LOW-1801-1900	0	0	0	0	$1.00	0	0	0	0	0
SEP-LOW-1901-2000	0	0	0	0	0	$1.00	0	0	0	0
SEP-LOW-2001-2100	0	0	0	0	0	0	$1.00	0	0	0
SEP-LOW-2101-2200	0	0	0	0	0	0	0	$1.00	0	0
SEP-LOW-2201-2300	0	0	0	0	0	0	0	0	$1.00	0
SEP-LOW-2301-MORE	0	0	0	0	0	0	0	0	0	$1.00

SEPTEMBER SALES OF "LOW"

Figure 4. Information aggregation markets for probable September sales of equipment called "low."

had to be consistent with the potential use of the data. In fact the exercise involved several different forecasts over a period of time.

Figure 5 contains the closing display on the software that participants used for trading. The prices listed there were part of the ingredients for the September-Low predictions. For each market the bid (best buy offer), ask (best sell offer) and the price of the last transaction in that market are displayed. For example, in the SEP-LOW-1601–1700 market the bid was 14 cents each for up to 5 units, the ask was 25 cents each for up to 10 units and the last trade was at 14 cents.

Since the security representing the correct state pays 100 cents. All prices should be between 0 and 100 and so prices can be interpreted as probabilities. In particular one can interpret the 14 cent price that existed in the SEP-LOW-1601–1700 markets as a "market belief" that with probability .14 the sales in September will be in the interval 1601–1700. With such an interpretation the mode of the predicted sales occurs at SEP-LOW-1901–2000 at a probability of .22. The distribution itself is skewed to the states higher than the mode. Thus, one could predict the most likely state, which would be the security with the highest closing price. Of course there are many other statistics that can be used, and the Information Aggregation Mechanism produces additional data such as the time series of trades, bids and asks, as well as the trading patterns of individual participants, all of which can be used as the basis for forecasts.

The mechanism has performed well inside Hewlett Packard Corporation with a total of twelve predictions. The predictions from the mechanism have been better than the official forecasts in all but two occasions. The complexity of field applications should not be minimized. There are many differences between the laboratory environment and

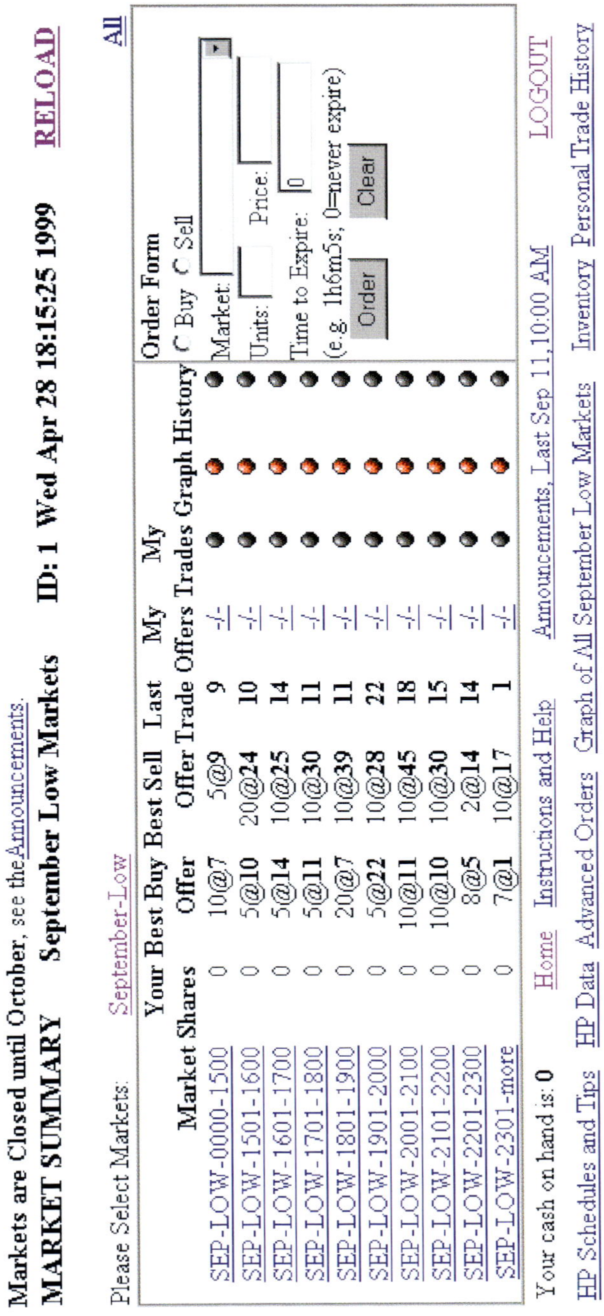

Ch. 40: *Markets and Information Aggregation Mechanisms* 351

Markets are Closed until October, see the Announcements.

MARKET SUMMARY   September Low Markets   **ID: 1 Wed Apr 28 18:15:25 1999**   **RELOAD**

Please Select Markets: September-Low   All

Market Shares	Your Shares	Best Buy Offer	Best Sell Offer	Last Trade	My Trade	My Offers	Trades	Graph	History
SEP-LOW-0000-1500	0	10@7	5@9	9	-/-	●	●	●	●
SEP-LOW-1501-1600	0	5@10	20@24	10	-/-	●	●	●	●
SEP-LOW-1601-1700	0	5@14	10@25	14	-/-	●	●	●	●
SEP-LOW-1701-1800	0	5@11	10@30	11	-/-	●	●	●	●
SEP-LOW-1801-1900	0	20@7	10@39	11	-/-	●	●	●	●
SEP-LOW-1901-2000	0	5@22	10@28	22	-/-	●	●	●	●
SEP-LOW-2001-2100	0	10@11	10@45	18	-/-	●	●	●	●
SEP-LOW-2101-2200	0	10@10	10@30	15	-/-	●	●	●	●
SEP-LOW-2201-2300	0	8@5	2@14	14	-/-	●	●	●	●
SEP-LOW-2301-more	0	7@1	10@17	1	-/-	●	●	●	●

Order Form
○ Buy ○ Sell
Market: [   ]
Units: [   ] Price: [0]
Time to Expire: [   ]
(e.g. 1h6m5s; 0=never expire)
[Order] [Clear]

Your cash on hand is: **0**   Home   Instructions and Help   Announcements, Last Sep 11,10:00 AM   **LOGOUT**

HP Schedules and Tips   HP Data   Advanced Orders   Graph of All September Low Markets   Inventory   Personal Trade History

Figure 5. Markets are closed until October, see the announcements.

the field environment. In the laboratory it was known that information exists to be collected. That is not the case in the field. In the laboratory, information is known to be independently distributed and there is a value to collection and aggregation. That is not known about the field. In the laboratory, the time, attention, and training of the subjects is controlled. Certainly that is not the case in the field. In the laboratory the subjects have no incentive to manipulate the outcome, but in the field they might. Thus, by no means does success in the laboratory guarantee success in the field.

References

Anderson, Lisa, Holt, Charles (1997). "Information cascades in a laboratory". American Economic Review 87 (5), 847–862.
Camerer, Colin F., Weigelt, Keith (1991). "Information mirages in experimental asset markets". Journal of Business 64 (4), 463–493.
Chen, Kay-Yut, Plott, Charles R. (2000). "Prediction markets and information aggregation mechanisms: A business application". California Institute of Technology.
Copeland, Thomas, Friedman, Daniel (1987). "The effect of sequential information arrival on asset prices: An experimental study". Journal of Finance 42 (3), 763–797.
Copeland, Thomas, Friedman, Daniel (1991). "Partial revelation of information in experimental asset markets". Journal of Finance 46 (1), 265–295.
Copeland, Thomas, Friedman, Daniel (1992). "The market value of information: Some experimental asset markets". Journal of Business 65 (2), 241–266.
Forsythe, Robert, Lundholm, Russell (1990). "Information aggregation in an experimental market". Econometrica 58, 309–347.
Friedman, Daniel (1993). "How trading institutions affect financial market performance: Some laboratory evidence". Economic Inquiry 31 (3), 410–435.
Guarnaschelli, Serena, Kvasnica, Anthony M., Plott, Charles R. (2003). "Information aggregation in double auctions: Rational expectations and the Winner's curse". Information Systems Frontier 5 (1), 63–77.
Hung, Angela, Plott, Charles R. (2001). "Information cascades: Replication and an extension to majority rule and conformity-rewarding institutions". American Economic Review 91 (5), 1508–1520.
Kagel, John H., Levin, D. (1986). "The winner's curse and public information in common value auctions". American Economic Review 76, 894–920.
Nöth, Markus, Weber, Martin (1996). "Insider detection in experimental asset markets". Zeitschrift für betriebswirtschaftliche Forschung 48, 959–982.
Plott, Charles R. (1994). "Market architectures, institutional landscapes and testbed experiments". Economic Theory 4, 3–10.
Plott, Charles R. (2000). "Markets as information gathering tools". Southern Economic Journal 67 (1), 2–15.
Plott, Charles R., Sunder, S. (1982). "Efficiency of experimental security markets with insider information: An application of rational expectations models". Journal of Political Economy 90, 663–698.
Plott, Charles R., Sunder, S. (1988). "Rational expectations and the aggregation of diverse information in laboratory security markets". Econometrica 56, 1085–1118.
Sunder, Shyam (1992). "Market for information: Experimental evidence". Econometrica 160, 667–695.
Sunder, Shyam (1995). "Experimental asset markets: A survey". In: Kagel, J., Roth, A.E. (Eds.), Handbook of Experimental Economics. Princeton University Press, Princeton.

PART 3

GENERAL EQUILIBRIUM AND THE ECONOMICS OF MULTIPLE MARKET SYSTEMS

3. GENERAL EQUILIBRIUM AND MULTIPLE MARKET SYSTEMS

Market interdependence is pervasive through all economies and it has attracted interest since the beginning of economics. Throughout history theories about the nature and consequences of interdependence have been the foundation of powerful and conflicting philosophies. The modern theory of general equilibrium that emerged from a century-long controversy holds that economies can be understood as a large system of simultaneous equilibrium equations. And, while the theory itself is highly technical, it holds profound implications about the role played by specialization and the law of comparative advantage in the creation of wealth. Almost all textbooks claim that self interest in response to profits promotes wealth-creating specialization and that prices serve as a key coordinating vehicle as described by the system of equilibrium equations. Yet, in spite of the importance and precision of the body of theory, skeptics remain and the reason they remain is obvious: the complexity of any economic system found in the field can always be used to produce a plethora of alternative theories that are impossible to discredit. Those who want to find an alternative theory to explain a pattern of facts can easily do so.

One does not need to look to the hotly debated political philosophies to find a need for a demonstration of the theory under controlled experimental conditions. Alternative theories are appearing as game theory advances. The alternative might be that the allocations are better described as the solution to a game as opposed to a general competitive equilibrium. In modern discussions that are heavily micro economic in nature, the possible influence of the background system of general equilibrium equations becomes lost. When interdependence is brought into the theory, data from multiple markets can be used to suggest a general pattern of randomness that seems to have no relationship to an underlying system of equations that might characterize equilibrium. The need for experiments stems from the fact that nature does not cooperate to create field circumstances that allow one to determine which theory from among many competing theories is the most accurate. Thus, the papers in this section are particularly important as demonstrations of the power of the theory and the underlying principles that are at work.

The need for experiments is so obvious that one wonders why they were not conducted many decades ago. The reason is easily discovered. Experiments with multiple markets and multiple agents with complex tasks like production were simply not possible. Two developments opened the possibilities, both of which are related to the development of the Internet and powerful local computers. The first was the development of electronic market systems that were capable of supporting multiple markets and large numbers of agents. Experiments with general equilibrium require a number of participants that far exceeds the capacity of early experimental methods and technology. The second was the development of experimental procedures and management tools that permitted subject recruitment, instruction and control together with the monitoring and instantaneous communication with remotely located subjects. The development of those laboratory experimental economics tools opened the door for a study of phenomena that had previously been impossible.

The papers in this section demonstrate the amazing fact that multiple markets have many of the properties found in classical writings in the field of general equilibrium. The first paper reviews applications in which the complexity of competing production technologies exists along with the interdependence caused by the operations of derived demand for inputs. The fundamental conclusion is that the law of comparative advantage can be observed operating in spite of such complexities. Specialization according to comparative advantage finds its way into most aspects of economics. Of course that is not surprising to an economic theorist because such specialization is fundamental to the wealth creating capacities of economic activity. The phenomenon is easy to see and understand in the context of a partial equilibrium model where it appears in models of industry entry with the most efficient firms (from a social point of view) being the first to enter. It appears again in exchanges where the resulting specialization in consumption can be viewed as an instance of the law of comparative advantage. However, in general equilibrium and especially in international trade context, the phenomena depend on sequences of interdependent patterns of specialization and thus become subtle. The first paper demonstrates how to study such complex issues and that the intuitions derived from the fundamental theories survive the tests.

The second paper explores the application of theory to the case in which risk must be allocated among those willing to bear it. The close relationship between modern finance and the theory of general equilibrium is often overlooked. Indeed, the study of asset markets has lead many to deny this relationship. However, experiments have indicated that the modern theory of finance and general equilibrium are closely related and this relationship can be directly observed in experimental markets.

The third paper extends the analysis to interdependencies that exist in networks of markets typical of location or vertical integration. Basic resource suppliers are located at the beginning of the chain and final product demanders are at the end of the chain and these are connected by a long sequence of intermediate (or transportation) links, each of which has its own separate market. The issue is whether and how the decentralized markets can coordinate the system. The result is a convergence toward the competitive equilibrium along a special path that starts with low prices at the "source" and high prices at the "sink" with the movement near equilibrium being a "lump" rather than an even flow.

Most general equilibrium theory is just that – a theory of equilibrium as opposed to a theory of what might happen in disequilibrium. Indeed, the modern dynamic models frequently have no disequilibrium at all but instead, the movement itself is assumed to be an equilibrium path. By contrast, the first three papers all demonstrate the capacity of markets to move toward the general equilibrium, but it is the movement itself, the disequilibrium as opposed to the equilibrium, that is prominent in the data. The final paper of the section outlines experiments designed to study disequilibrium in a general equilibrium setting. The findings are stunning in the sense that the classical theories of general equilibrium dynamics are found to produce models that capture many of the properties of the data even under conditions in which one might think that the theory would not apply. The message is that economic equilibrium must be understood in terms of events that take place when markets are in disequilibrium and major insights about how those event influence price discovery are contained in the classical models of multiple market dynamics.

Chapter 41

COMPARATIVE ADVANTAGE AND INTERNATIONAL TRADE

CHARLES R. PLOTT

The fundamental question addressed by this research is the degree to which the classical law of comparative advantage can be observed operating in experimental markets. The law holds that the local economic environments systematically influence, if not completely dictate, patterns of specialization and trade in this sense: local economies will experience economic pressures to specialize in the production and export of those commodities for which the local economy has a comparative advantage. This specialization is the engine that facilitates the gains from trade and the associated wealth that it produces. The issue is investigated in Noussair, Plott, and Riezman (1995).

Field evidence in support of the law is indirect at best. The law of comparative advantage predicts that countries will have a tendency to export the good that would have the lowest relative price in a situation of no international trade (autarky). Since autarkies do not exist, the theory cannot be tested directly in the field. Testing is further complicated by the fact that there are so many variables operating in the field that there are always many alternative explanations for any pattern of trade and specialization that might be observed. It is hard to reject the assertion that data in support of the law could simply be manifestations of some accident of history as opposed to being the footprint of a general and pervasive pattern of economic pressures.

The law of comparative advantage can be derived as a consequence of the competitive equilibrium model. In addition, the competitive equilibrium model can yield the property of factor price equalization. That is, if the economy is behaving as predicted by the competitive model then under certain parametric conditions, countries will specialize in predictable ways and the prices of factors of production among countries will be equalized by their flows of commodities even if the factors themselves cannot leave their home country. According to the model, the wages will be the same across all freely trading countries even though the countries produce different things and labor is not mobile.

The major results reported from experimental data are the following:
(1) The law of comparative advantage can be observed operating and the law accurately predicts trade patterns.
(2) Production and consumption output prices are observed moving toward the levels predicted by the competitive equilibrium. However, the levels of prices are not those predicted by the competitive equilibrium model.
(3) Within appropriate parametric conditions the property of factor price equalization predicted by the competitive model can be observed in operation.
(4) The imposition of tariffs restrict the volume of trade as predicted by the competitive model.

Ch. 41: *Comparative Advantage and International Trade* 359

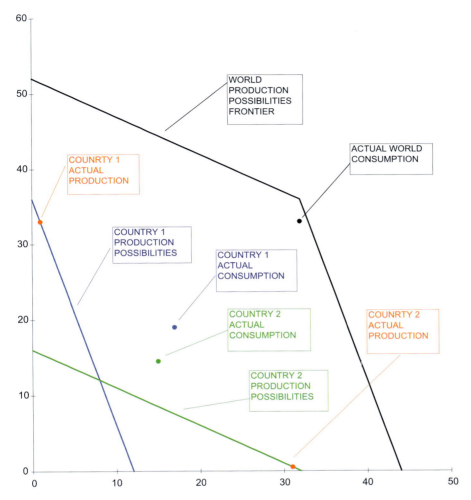

Figure 1. Comparative advantage at work: Specialization according to comparative advantage creates gains from trade and consumption by each country beyond its own production possibilities frontier. Total world consumption is near the efficient world production possibilities frontier.

The nature of the production and consumption data can be seen in Figure 1. In this experiment there are two countries, two different types of outputs (Z, Y) and one type of input (labor). Z is shown on the horizontal axis and Y is shown on the vertical axis. The labor is fixed in supply in each country and migration of labor is impossible. The labor can be used to produce either commodity according to a linear production function. The production possibilities curve for country 1 and the production possibilities curve for country 2 are shown in Figure 1. These country production possibility curves are dictated by the quantity of labor resources that exists in the country and the production function technology that exists in the country. The world production possibilities curve that would result from efficient production and specialization is shown in black.

The money in all of the economies was a commodity-based currency. The same currency was used in all countries and this currency had consumption value. Thus, there were no issues of exchange rates operating. Local producers in a country had the ability to buy labor in the local market and use it to produce the two outputs Y and Z consistent with the production functions implicit in the production possibility curves in Figure 1. Local markets were populated by local producers, local consumers and foreigners who might want to purchase and send units to the markets in their home countries. The countries operated in a world in which agents from country i could purchase commodities in country j and costlessly import them in country i and sell in the market in competition with goods that might have been produced in country i. Markets were organized by the multiple unit double auction.

Production took place in a country by purchasing labor in a home labor market and transforming it to one of the commodities (Y or Z) that is then sold in the home market. The computer regulated and controlled this production activity to make sure that the production was fast and violated no constraints. Thus in each country there were three active markets: labor, Y, and Z for a total of six active markets in the world. The buyers in these markets were agents from the home country, who could either consume the commodities or speculate for resale, and agents from the foreign country, who could either speculate by reselling or could ship commodities to their own home country for resale.

The law of comparative advantage holds that the countries would specialize. Given the production functions and preferences, country 1 should specialize in the production of Y shown as the vertical axis and country 2 should specialize in the production of Z, shown along the horizontal axis. The averages of actual production across several experiments and periods are shown in Figure 1. The average production in country one is near the upper left corner of the production possibilities frontier of country 1 and the average production of country 2 is in the lower right of the production possibilities frontier for country 2. That is, country 1 specializes in the production of Y and country 2 specializes in the production of Z, as is predicted by the law.

Country 1 is importing Z and exporting Y, and its average consumption after export and import in several periods of several experiments is shown as the blue dot. The consumption of country 2 is shown as the green dot. The gains from specialization and exchange are evident, since both countries are consuming far beyond their own productive capacity. The gains from specialization that emerged from the trade that took place in these economies is near the maximum possible. The black lines in Figure 1 constitute the world production possibilities frontier. The black dot represents the average of world consumption that emerged after trade. The level of consumption is near the production possibility frontier, which indicates that the production efficiency of the system is near 100%. The natural pressure of the competition was to coordinate production efforts in the most efficient manner.

Ch. 41: Comparative Advantage and International Trade

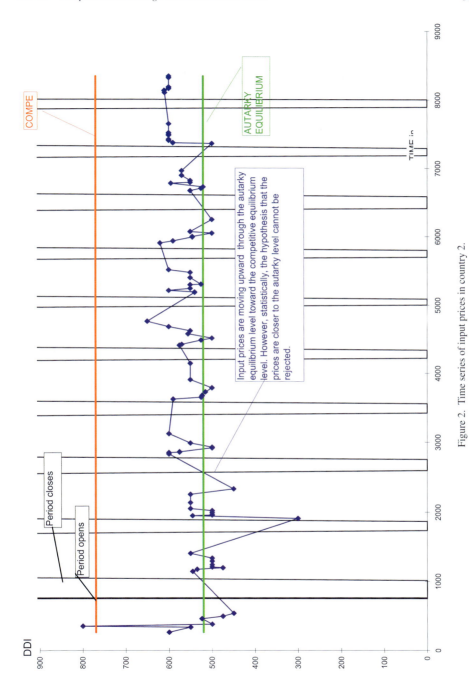

Figure 2. Time series of input prices in country 2.

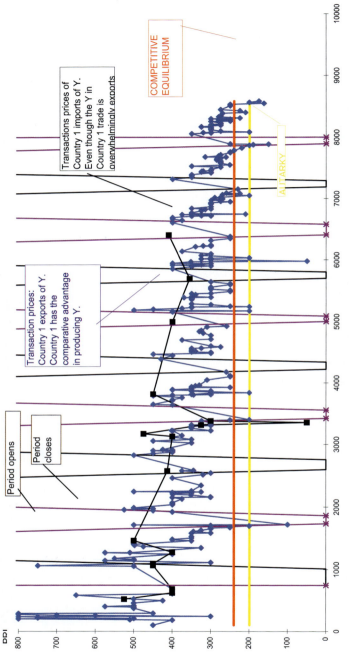

Figure 3. Prices in an output market. The time series for output Y is shown converging toward the competitive equilibrium prices. Prices start high but with time the variance of prices decrease and the prices get near the competitive equilibrium prices. Almost all trading takes place in country 1, which has a comparative advantage in producing Y but some product and trades take place in country 2, the volume is low and ultimately stops. This time series, like the input time series, was chosen to illustrate the difficulty that is occasionally encountered when attempting to test the predictions of the competitive model against autarky. While prices in the output market are closer to competitive equilibrium than the autarky, these data could also be used to support the autarky model. Consumption and production patterns clearly reject autarky.

While specialization occurred as predicted, the price predictions of the competitive model were not as accurate. The price time series from some representative markets are shown in Figures 2 and 3. Figure 2 shows the time series of labor in country 2 and Figure 3 contains the price time series for Z in both country 1 and country 2. The vertical lines are experimental "periods" that are similar to days. The parameters stayed constant for all periods, so the economies were like stationary systems of supply and demand. The lines on the figures correspond to the competitive equilibrium and to the autarky equilibrium, the equilibrium that theoretically exists if there is no international trade. As can be seen in both countries, the prices are moving in the direction of the competitive equilibrium; but, in the case of labor in country 2, the movement away from the autarky equilibrium toward the competitive equilibrium is very slow. In both cases the autarky prices receive very little support but the slow movement in country 2's labor market indicates that while the resource flows might well have been efficient, the prices that support those flows as equilibria may not have been "discovered" by the markets.

Overall, the competitive model predicted better than the autarky model. Several impacts of tariffs were observed to be consistent with the predictions of the competitive model. However, the competitive model was not completely accurate. The inaccuracies were conjectured to be due to risk aversion on the part of the producers. The producers of commodities bore some risk if they purchased labor and transformed it into Y or Z for sale. If the markets were not "deep," in the sense that the seller had difficulty moving product at expected prices, then the producer could lose money. This risk reduced demand for labor relative to the demand as reported in the risk neutral competitive model and thus depressed wages below those predicted by the risk neutral competitive model. This risk due to the natural randomness that exists in markets is not part of the competitive model, and so the errors remain somewhat a mystery until appropriate features are incorporated.

Reference

Noussair, Charles N., Plott, Charles R., Riezman, Raymond G. (1995). "An experimental investigation of the patterns of international trade". American Economic Review 85 (3), 462–491.

Chapter 42

ASSET PRICING

PETER BOSSAERTS

California Institute of Technology

1. What the Theory Predicts

A major evolution in the theory of asset pricing took place over the last century.
   (a) In 1900, Bachelier suggested the random walk hypothesis: price changes ought not to be predictable from past information (see Bachelier, 1900). In the 1960s and 1970s, this theory became known as the efficient markets hypothesis (Fama, 1970),[1] though some still refer to it as the random walk hypothesis (Malkiel, 1999).

   The random walk hypothesis is based on the idea that if price changes were predictable, profit opportunities emerge, and the ensuing speculation would eliminate them. The theory is very pragmatic. It does not specify a trading mechanism. It does not even explain why prices move; it only predicts that, if prices move, the movements ought not to be predictable. The random walk model is dynamic: it characterizes price changes.

   (b) Since about the 1950s, equilibrium asset pricing theory has been developing, based on the hypothesis that prices are determined by equilibrating supply and demand. Prices change when supply or demand changes. One distinguishes two (related) canonical models.

   (1) The Arrow–Debreu general equilibrium model, where the number of independent securities is assumed to equal the number of states. Implicit in the prices of the traded securities will be state prices: the prices of securities that pay one dollar in one state, and zero everywhere else. The Arrow–Debreu prediction is that the ranking of state security prices for equally likely states will be the inverse of the ranking of the aggregate wealth across those states. This translates into predictions about the pattern of expected returns (expected payoffs divided by prices) across securities.

   (2) The capital asset pricing model (CAPM). If quadratic expected utility is the appropriate representation of investors' preferences, then prices should be such that the market portfolio (supply of all risky securities) provides

---

[1] Fama and others would allow for a positive drift in the random walk, to capture risk aversion. But they did not quantify it and were even willing to allow the drift to vary over time. They did realize that if you were not able to explain why the drift should be there, you could potentially explain away any evidence of predictability.

maximal reward (expected return) per unit of risk (volatility). This also translates into predictions about the pattern of expected returns across securities. (Expected returns in excess of the risk-free rate should be proportional to covariances with the return on the market portfolio.)

Both are static equilibrium models. They are silent about how markets reach the equilibrium price (and hence, expected return) configuration. This also means that they do not make any prediction about price dynamics. There are multi-period extensions, but these only predict how one period-equilibrium changes to the next one. They are silent about what happens in between.

2. The Empirical Question

Which of these two theories provides the more appropriate view of the workings of financial markets: the relatively agnostic random walk theory or the more stylized equilibrium asset pricing models?

To compare the two theories, one could search for violations of the random walk hypothesis (if any can be found) and prove that these violations can be understood in light of equilibrium asset pricing models.

In field studies, it is customary to reject the random walk theory by identifying drift in prices. The drift is to be explained in terms of compensation for risk using some equilibrium asset pricing model. [A well-known example is Debondt and Thaler (1985), who find violations of the random walk hypothesis yet cannot identify them as reward for risk.]

An alternative would be to view drift as evidence that equilibration forces are at work, verify whether the drift points in the direction of a given asset pricing equilibrium, and whether it eventually leads markets to this equilibrium. In the experiments discussed below, the data can best be understood in this fashion.

3. What the Field Data Teach Us

There is plenty of evidence that it is hard to predict asset price changes, in support of the random walk theory. Still, there are well-documented violations (a number of them are reported in Lo and MacKinlay, 1999). Granted, the amount of predictability that is present in the field data is small, but they do not seem to be compensation for risk in any way equilibrium asset pricing models predict. Best known is the finding in Fama and French (1992) that the historical drift in prices across U.S. common stock cannot be explained in terms of differences in covariances with the market portfolio (as predicted by the CAPM).

While it is easy to verify the random walk hypothesis on field data, it is far more difficult to explain violations in terms of equilibrium models of asset pricing, because

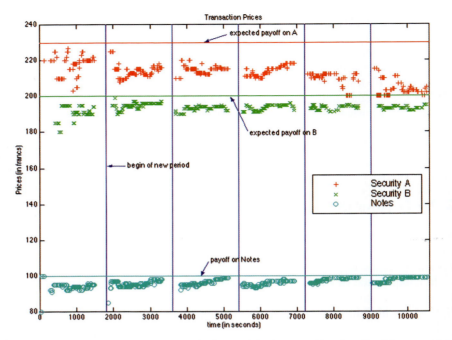

Note: Each observation corresponds to a transaction in one of the three securities; the price of the non-trading securities is taken to be the previous transaction price.

Figure 1.

these models require information that is hard to come by in the field (e.g., what is the aggregate wealth? What is the market portfolio? What are the expected returns? What did the market believe to be the covariances? What states did it perceive to be equally likely? Do investors have quadratic utility?).

4. What the Experiments Teach Us

Experiments make it easier to identify the forces of equilibrium asset pricing theory, because almost all parameters can be controlled (e.g., aggregate wealth, market portfolio, expectations).[2]

Figure 1 displays the evolution of transaction prices in a typical asset pricing experiment. Subjects were allocated three securities, two of which were risky. The payoff on these securities was determined by randomly drawing one out of three possible states.

---

[2] Quadratic utility can be assumed, as an approximation, provided risk is not too large and subjects have well-behaved preferences.

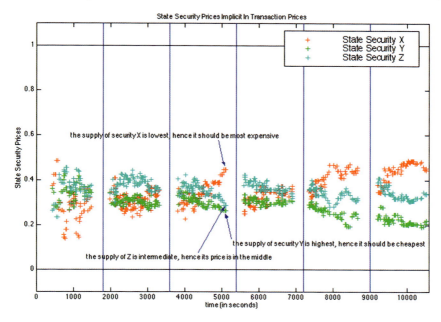

Figure 2.

Subjects could trade the securities over the Internet (using an anonymous open book trading mechanism) for about 25 minutes, after which payoffs were determined and distributed. Subjects were then given a fresh allocation of securities and a new period started. See Bossaerts and Plott (2004).

The prices of the risky securities in Figure 1 are below their expected payoff during the entire experiment, indicating the presence of risk aversion. The price of the risk-free security often starts below its payoff in a period; in equilibrium, its price should be 100 because of the presence of cash. This phenomenon emerges because of a cash-in-advance constraint: subjects need cash if they want to bid on the risky securities.

Inspection of Figure 1 reveals little predictability in changes in the prices of the risky securities. The price of one of the securities (A) seems to have a negative drift, but this is statistically insignificant. So, it appears as if the random walk hypothesis holds.

But there is more than meets the eye. Figure 2 displays the evolution of the state security prices (normalized to add up to one) implicit in the transaction prices of the traded securities. The aggregate payoff (wealth) was lowest in state X, followed by state Z and Y. Which means that the price of state security X should be highest; that of state security Y cheapest; and that of state security Z in the middle. Figure 2 reveals a clear tendency for state security prices to move in this direction. Confirming the visual impression, statistical tests confidently reject the random walk model in favor of a model where state security prices tend to re-arrange in accordance with the theory.

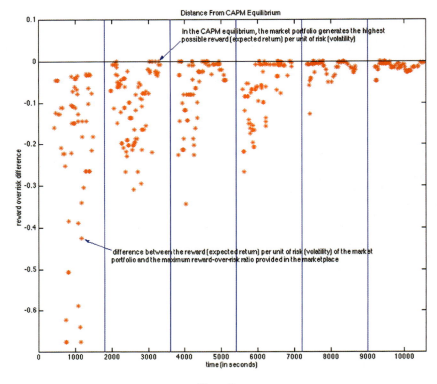

Figure 3.

Figure 3 summarizes the information in the prices in another way. It displays the difference between the reward (expected return) per unit of risk on the market portfolio and the maximum possible reward/risk ratio for any portfolio that investors could hold. In the CAPM equilibrium, this difference is zero. The question is: do prices change so that the difference disappears? Figure 3 demonstrates that there is this tendency, both within periods and over the duration of the experiment. Statistical tests confirm this: one can predict that transaction prices move in the direction of the CAPM (and hence, one can reject the random walk model).

Why can not we implement these prediction models in field data? Why can not we imply state security prices and predict where they are going as we can in the laboratory? Why can not we use the difference in reward/risk ratio between the market portfolio and the best portfolio and predict where prices will move next? Because unlike in the laboratory, we (the empiricists) know even less than investors.

Like investors, we do not know what the market portfolio or aggregate wealth is. Worse, we do not even know what investors' beliefs are. In the laboratory, we determine the nature of uncertainty, and hence, control subjects' beliefs. We know more than the subjects: we set the supplies, so we know aggregate wealth and the market portfolio. If we come down to the level of information of the subjects, or even below this level, as in field research, we cannot predict prices (Figure 1); if we use information that we do not have in field research, we can, as we can see in Figure 2 (using aggregate wealth in each state) and Figure 3 (knowing the market portfolio).

References

Bachelier, M.L. (1900). "Théorie de la spéculation". Annales de Ecole Normale 17 (3), 1–86.
Bossaerts, Peter, Plott, Charles (2004). "Basic principles of asset pricing theory: Evidence from large-scale experimental financial markets". Review of Finance 8, 135–169.
Debondt, W., Thaler, R. (1985). "Does the stock market overreact?" Journal of Finance 39, 793–805.
Fama, Eugene (1970). "Efficient capital markets: A review of theory and empirical work". Journal of Finance 25, 383–417.
Fama, E., French, K. (1992). "The cross-section of expected stock returns". Journal of Finance 47, 427–465.
Lo, A., MacKinlay, C. (1999). "A Non-Random Walk Down Wall Street". Princeton University Press, Princeton.
Malkiel, B. (1999). "A Random Walk Down Wall Street", fifth ed. Norton, New York.

Chapter 43

PRICE DISCOVERY AND ALLOCATION IN CHAINS AND NETWORKS OF MARKETS

CHARLES R. PLOTT and JACKIE YEUNG

The experiments reported in this chapter explore the interaction of networks of markets. The issue is whether, and how long, "chains" of markets separated in time, space and participants might behave. The setting can be interpreted in two different ways. One is a system of vertical markets in which tiers of intermediate goods are produced as inputs for the next, higher level on the way to a final consumption good. Another, and perhaps more graphic, interpretation is geographic, in which suppliers are located at one location and consumers are at a different location. They are connected by a series of "short" transportation hauls that must be undertaken by different transporters. No transporter can undertake a "long haul" from seller to consumer. Markets exist at the beginning and end of each short haul. That is, the first transporters/middlemen buy from sellers and transport to the first drop-off for sale there. At the first drop-off a different set of transporters/middlemen purchase the units in an open market and transport it to the second drop-off where a new set of transporters/middlemen have the capacity to negotiate, purchase and haul to the third drop-off, and so on.[1]

The structure of interdependence clearly creates a type of fragility in the system. Each link of the chain is crucial to the success of the whole. The system cannot work if it fails at any point. Two basic results appear in the data.

First, the markets do equilibrate to the general competitive equilibrium. The overall system efficiency is high.

Second, long chains of markets with vertical interdependencies exhibit a "backwards" process of convergence toward the competitive equilibrium. The time flow of economic activities through such systems when the system is near equilibrium is a "lump" that moves through the chain as opposed to a continuous, equal flow.

The nature of the observations is contained in Figure 1. A total of three experiments were conducted, and all of them exhibited the same qualitative properties.

The model is summarized in Figure 2. The classical equilibrium model of a network of markets making up a supply route holds that the prices between two markets should

---

[1] Interactive markets populated by randomly behaving robots in the first and only other study of the framework developed here, see Bosch-Domenech and Sunder (2000). Their remarkable conclusion was that the competitive equilibrium could be attained in the market even without the levels of rationality assumed by the competitive model. There are some differences when humans are the agents, which seem related to the speed with which the robots can interact. Aspects of the convergence structure reported here are also seen by Bosch-Domenech and Sunder (2000), but for the most part the human convergence process has properties not seen in the robots.

Handbook of Experimental Economics Results, Volume 1
Copyright © 2008 Elsevier B.V. All rights reserved
DOI: 10.1016/S1574-0722(07)00043-1

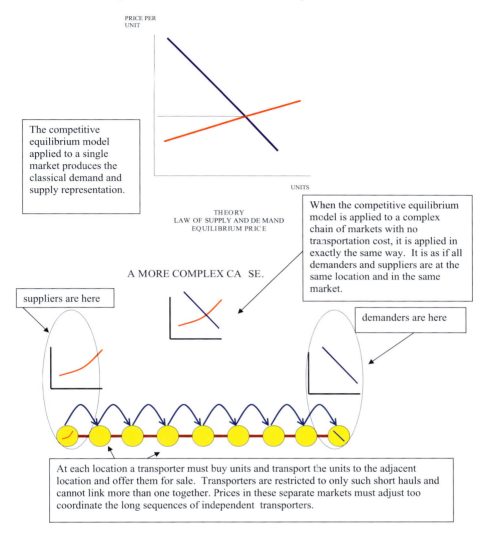

Figure 1. Prices and resource flows in chain-like networks of markets.

differ only by the transportation cost. So, if transportation costs are zero, then the prices at the source should equal prices at the sink. If there is a transport cost, then the price gradients will be as shown. Aggregate flow is constant across locations according to the equilibrium model.

The dynamics of price formation in networks is illustrated in Figure 3. As can be seen, two separate dynamics are at work. Markets near the source open first, followed

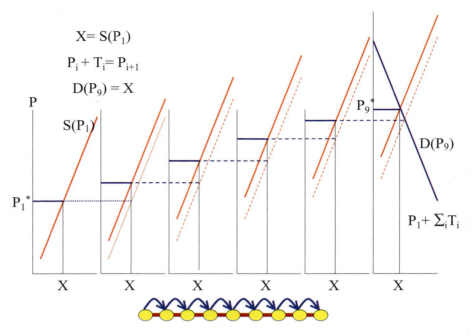

Figure 2. The competitive model applied to the chain of markets.

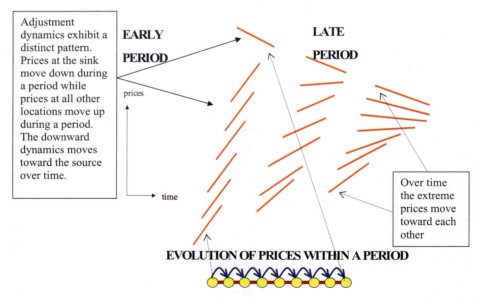

Figure 3.

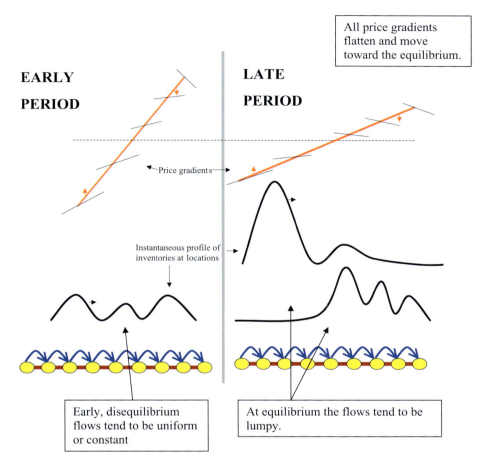

Figure 4. The structure of flow equilibration in relation to price equilibration in a networked chain of markets.

by the markets in the order of the chain. Within a market and within a period the price formation is as shown. The other dynamics operate across periods. The tendency is for prices across periods to equalize towards the competitive equilibrium.

While the prices tend to equalize as the system moves to an equilibrium, the flows have the opposite property (as is illustrated in Figure 4). Flows start rather constant over time but become lumpy as the system equilibrates. That is, all activity is concentrated in one location until all activity moves to the next location. This dynamic reflects the problems and cost minimization features of coordinated activities.

The relationship between prices and inventory location from an experiment that is illustrated in Figure 5. In the top panel, the average prices are shown for each location during period 3 and period 7. The price gradient across location becomes flatter over

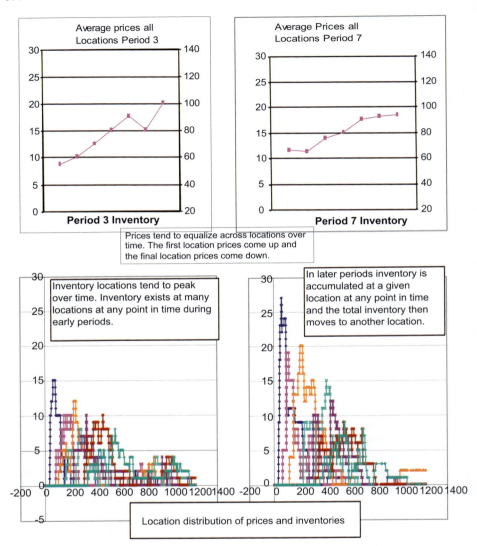

Figure 5. Location distribution of prices and inventories.

time. The bottom panel shows the location of inventory as a function of time (the horizontal axis). The quantity of inventory that exists at the particular location at the instant of time is shown. As can be seen inventory location in the disequilibrium period tends to be scattered in all locations, in a sense it is a constant flow through the system. In later periods the inventory accumulates at a location and then moves all at once. Thus, as the system approaches equilibrium, the flow is lumpy, reflecting the conservation of resources and coordination of agents required to move the units.

Reference

Bosch-Domenech, Antoni, Sunder, Shyam (2000). "Tracking the invisible hand: Convergence of double auctions to competitive equilibrium". Computational Economics 16, 257–284.

Chapter 44

MULTIPLE MARKET SYSTEMS AND THE CLASSICAL PRINCIPLES OF PRICE DYNAMICS IN GENERAL EQUILIBRIUM

CHARLES R. PLOTT

The study of the multiple equation structure of general equilibrium models seems to naturally motivate four questions:
   Can markets ever find a zero (an equilibrium) of a complex system?
   Will it always happen?
   Can markets find all of the zeros?
   If so, how does it happen?
   The answer to the first question is clearly yes. A mountain of data dealing with multiple market processes (Forsythe, Palfrey, and Plott, 1982, 1984; Plott, 1988, 2001; Plott and Sunder, 1988; Williams et al., 2000), derived demand (Goodfellow and Plott, 1990), finance (Asparouhova, Bossaerts, and Plott, 2003; Bossaerts, Kleinman, and Plott, 2001; Bossaerts and Plott, 2002, 2004; Bossaerts, Plott, and Zame, 2001), international trade (Noussair, Plott, and Riezman, 1995), international finance (Noussair, Plott, and Riezman, 1997), and macro economics (Lian and Plott, 1998) demonstrate that markets can sometimes find zeros. The answer to the third question is "no" as given by experiments on stability of markets. Markets will not find the unstable equilibria, only the stable ones.
   Fundamental issues posed by the second and fourth questions remain and between these two questions there is a clear scientific priority. The conditions under which markets will equilibrate, and therefore the frequency with which equilibration might be expected, depend on the nature of the process of equilibration and the underlying principles of dynamics. So, in order to answer the second question we need an answer to the fourth question, which will provide the tools needed to find the cases in which convergence is not expected to take place. Thus, in a sense, the last question is the most basic of them all and the subject of this note is the steps taken toward an answer.
   Scarf (1960), especially as extended by Hirota (1981), created an important platform from which to launch the study by producing an example demonstrating that if the price adjustment process is the classical tatonnement mechanism then the theoretical answer to the second question is "no." Theoretically, it is not the case that markets will necessarily equilibrate even when the equilibrium is a unique, interior equilibrium. In his example prices always orbit around the equilibrium and thus never converge. That platform thus provides the starting point of the research. For the parameters of his example, either the markets will not equilibrate, as predicted by theory, or the basic principle of dynamics he employed is substantially wrong. The Scarf example is ideal for a study of classical dynamics because in that situation the theory makes striking and unexpected predictions.

Handbook of Experimental Economics Results, Volume 1
Copyright © 2008 Elsevier B.V. All rights reserved
DOI: 10.1016/S1574-0722(07)00044-3

Table 1
Parameters for scarf environment experiments

Case	Type	Preferences	Initial endowments		
			X	Y	X
Convergence to equilibrium	I	40 min{y/20, z/400}	10	0	0
	II	40 min{x/10, z/400}	0	20	0
	III	40 min{x/10, y/20}	0	0	400
Counter clockwise orbit	I	40 min{y/20, z/400}	0	20	0
	II	40 min{x/10, z/400}	0	0	400
	III	40 min{x/10, y/20}	10	0	0
Clockwise orbit	I	40 min{y/20, z/400}	0	0	400
	II	40 min{x/10, z/400}	10	0	0
	III	40 min{x/10, y/20}	0	20	0

Anderson et al. (2003) focus directly on the issue by finding extensions of the environment in which the classical theory of dynamics predicts a clockwise orbit under one set of initial endowments, a counterclockwise orbit under another set of initial endowments and convergence to the unique interior equilibrium under a third set of endowments. Thus, according to theory the experimenter can change the direction of a price orbit or cause the markets to converge by simply changing the initial endowments alone, without preference, institution or procedural changes. That experiment is exactly the one performed.

The example is a three commodity general equilibrium, $\{x, y, z\}$, in which one of the commodity, $\{z\}$, serves as money. All trades are made in terms of the money. Agents have preferences that are perfect complement between two of the commodities and have no preferences for the third. Three types of preferences exist in the economy and are illustrated in Figure 1 and in Table 1. Type I person has preference for y and z while getting no utility at all for x. Specifically Type I has the utility function (and it is the one used in the experiments) $U(y, z) = 40 \min\{y/20, z/400\}$. Type II gets utility from x and z and receives no utility from y with the utility function $U(x, z) = 40 \min\{x/10, z/400\}$. Type III gets utility from only x and y, having utility function $U(x, y) = 40 \min\{1/10, y/20\}$. These are the actual incentives used each period with the units denoted in cents.

Table 1 organizes the parameters in terms of predictions. As shown, convergence to the equilibrium is predicted if each agent is endowed with units of the commodity that the individual does not want. If each individual is endowed with one of the commodities that the individual wants the prediction is an orbit in a particular direction (say clockwise). The predicted direction of the orbit is reversed (counter clockwise) if all individuals are endowed with the other commodity that they do not want.

Anderson et al. (2003) discovered that the market prices have all of the major features predicted by the classical model. Furthermore, they discovered that the features exist

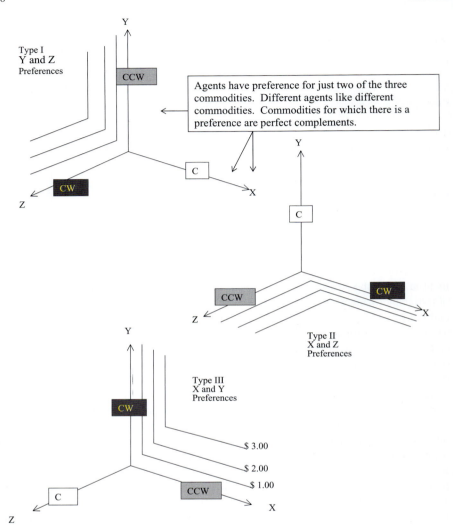

Figure 1. The three types of preferences in the scarf environment.

in markets organized as multiple unit double auctions. That is, while the theoretical markets studied by Scarf (1960) were constructed under tatonnement properties, with one price in the market and no trades at disequilibria the real, experimental markets studied by Anderson et al. (2003) did not. The experimental markets were organized as multiple unit double auctions so markets were populated by many prices and essentially no trades took place at equilibrium. Thus, the theoretical properties exhibit an amazing

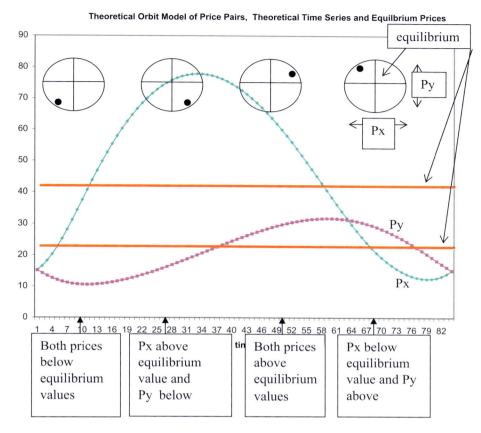

Figure 2. The circles at the top of the figure illustrate the position of the pair of prices relative to the equilibrium. The circle represents the theoretical orbit around the equilibrium. Horizontal and vertical lines partition space so angle to point representing price location indicates price movement directions. In first circle both prices are below equilibrium levels.

robustness in the face of market environments that could have impacts on the price discovery process.

The experiments reported here tests the robustness of the Anderson et al. (2003) result by employing a multiple unit double auction with an open book. Since the environment is one of strong complements the contracts reflect a preference for contingent contracts. A person does not want to transact in market A without assurance that of a transaction in market B. Since the open book allows market depths to be observed such coordination is easier. The issue is whether the open book form of market organization would remove the cycles and facilitate convergence. The markets studied in Anderson et al. (2003) had no order book and thus had limited possibility of planning.

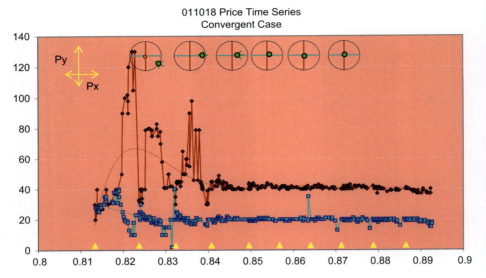

Figure 3.

The basic result reported here is that the open book makes no difference. The Anderson et al. (2003) results replicate. The predictions of the classical dynamic theory are illustrated in Figure 2. The bottom panel illustrates the price cycles as they would appear in a time representation, a time domain. The top of the figure illustrates the relationship between the predictions in the price pairs domain positioned over the relevant area in the time domain. Basically, these are two, related ways of representing a cycle.

Representative data are contained in Figures 3, 4 and 5. The data produced by an experiment in which convergence is predicted are contained in Figure 3. The equilibrium prices for X and Y are 40 and 20 respectively and as can be observed the data tightly converge to the predicted price pair. While this is only two markets the behavior here is not far from what is observed in the much more complex economies reported in the referenced materials. Figure 4 contains data from an economy where the classical dynamics predicts a counter clockwise cycle. As can be seen the data move in the predicted direction. The results of an experiment in which a clockwise cycle is predicted are represented in Figure 5. The data are moving in the clockwise direction as predicted.

Overall, the contrast among Figures 3, 4 and 5 are dramatic. When the classical dynamic model predicts convergence, that is what happens. When the classical model predicts counter clockwise cycles the data move in a counter clockwise direction. When the model predicts a clockwise orbit the data move in the clockwise direction predicted.

The results of these experiments move the science toward an answer to question four. From this step the presumption should be that markets are governed by the classical Walrasian dynamic. The rate of adjustment of the price in a market is directly related to the magnitude of its own excess demand. Of course, there are many other variables

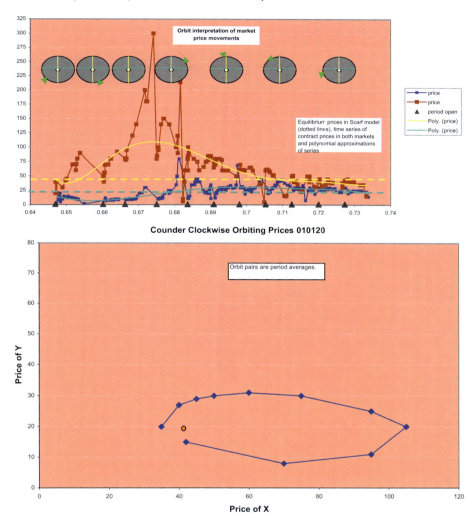

Figure 4.

that can enter into this equation but for now it is the place to start. The experiments demonstrate that it is not the case that markets will always find the equilibrium and the reason is because the market dynamics can fail to lead it there. To this basic conclusion there is a corollary and that is that the classical model of tatonnement, in which disequilibrium trades do not take place, can be used as an approximation of what to expect in the complex world of continuous, double auction markets in which disequilibrium trades do take place.

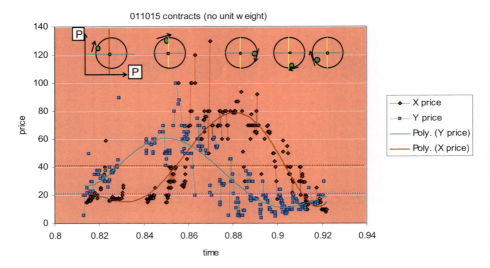

Figure 5.

References

Anderson, C., Granat, S., Plott, C., Shimomura, K. (2003). "Global instability in experimental general equilibrium: The scarf example". Journal of Economic Theory 115 (2), 209–249.

Asparouhova, Elena, Bossaerts, Peter, Plott, Charles R. (2003). "Excess demand and equilibration in multi-security financial markets: The empirical evidence". Journal of Financial Markets 6, 1–21.

Bossaerts, Peter, Kleinman, Daniel, Plott, Charles R. (2001). "Price discovery in financial markets: The case of the CAPM". In: Plott, Charles R. (Ed.), Information, Finance and General Equilibrium. Collected Papers on the Experimental Foundations of Economics and Political Science, vol. 3. Edward Elgar Publishing, Cheltenham, UK, pp. 445–492.

Bossaerts, Peter, Plott, Charles R. (2002). "The CAPM in thin experimental financial markets". Journal of Economic Dynamics and Control 26, 1093–1112.

Bossaerts, Peter, Plott, Charles R. (2004). "Basic principles of asset pricing theory: Evidence from large-scale experimental financial markets". Review of Finance 8, 135–169.

Bossaerts, Peter L., Plott, C.R., Zame, W. (2001). "The Role of Excess Demand in Determining Marginal Price Changes in the Equilibration of Competitor Markets". California Institute of Technology, Pasadena, CA.

Forsythe, R., Palfrey, T., Plott, C. (1982). "Asset valuation in an experimental market". Econometrica 50, 537–567.

Forsythe, R., Palfrey, T., Plott, C. (1984). "Futures markets and informational efficiency: A laboratory examination". Journal of Finance 39, 955–981.

Goodfellow, J., Plott, C. (1990). "An experimental examination of the simultaneous determination of input prices and output prices". Southern Economic Journal 56, 969–983.

Hirota, Masayoshi (1981). "On the stability of competitive equilibrium and the patterns of initial holdings: An example". International Economic Review 22, 461–467.

Lian, P., Plott, C. (1998). "General equilibrium, markets, macroeconomics and money in a laboratory experimental environment". Economic Theory 12 (1), 21–75.

Noussair, C., Plott, C., Riezman, R. (1995). "An experimental investigation of the patterns of international trade". American Economic Review 85, 462–491.

Noussair, C., Plott, C., Riezman, R. (1997). "The principles of exchange rate determination in an international finance experiment". Journal of Political Economy 105, 822–862.

Plott, Charles R. (1988). "Research on pricing in a gas transportation network". Office of Economic Policy Technical Report No. 88-2, Federal Energy Regulatory Commission, Washington, DC.

Plott, Charles R. (2001). "Equilibrium, equilibration, information and multiple markets: From basic science to institutional design". Nobel Symposium on Behavioral and Experimental Economics, Stockholm, Sweden, December 4.

Plott, Charles R., Sunder, Shyam (1988). "Rational expectations and the aggregation of diverse information in laboratory security markets". Econometrica 56 (5), 1085–1118.

Scarf, Herbert (1960). "Some examples of global instability of the competitive equilibrium". International Economic Review 1, 157–171.

Williams, A., Smith, V., Ledyard, J., Gjerstad, S. (2000). "Concurrent trading in two experimental markets with demand interdependence". Economic Theory 16 (3), 511–528.

Further reading

Hey, J., DiCagno, D. (1998). "Sequential markets: An investigation of Clower's dual decision hypothesis". Experimental Economics 1, 63–85.

Plott, Charles R. (2000). "Markets as information gathering tools". Southern Economic Journal 67, 2–15.

Plott, Charles R., Porter, David P. (1996). "Market architectures and institutional testbedding: An experiment with space station pricing policies". Journal of Economic Behavior and Organization 31 (2), 237–272.

PART 4

GAMES

4. GAMES

The three subparts of this part on games are focused on the accuracy of the Nash equilibrium (twelve entries), alternatives to the Nash theory (five) and the dynamics observed as games take place over time (five). Clearly, the Nash equilibrium concept has proved to be a powerful predictor of conflict situations, especially in non-zero sum environments but it is not perfect as a model. Other-regarding behavior surfaces naturally in conflicts and theoretically can be found in the form of assessments of the rationality of others, altruism, concepts of fairness, spite, etc. The chapters in this part reflect attempts to improve upon it and advance our understanding of why it works. The question becomes whether or not the principles of Nash equilibrium can be viewed in the behavior as modification of the attitudes or whether the attitudes themselves induce fundamentally different principles of behavior that can replace the strategic behavior of game theory. The substance of the papers is that strategic behavior is a deep and reliable property of human behavior in conflict environments.

4.1. Accuracy of the Nash Model

The first chapter, by Rosemarie Nagel, sets a proper stage for the section. The Nash theory ranges over many interpretations including reasoning, reasoning about the reasoning of others and a process of convergence. The "beauty contest" is an ingenious way to study the beliefs that agents have about the rationality of others and how those beliefs change over time, experience and insights about behavior. As an experimental environment it has special advantages because reasoning can be examined directly without intervention of altruism or other forms of unobservable incentives that are addressed in other parts of the section. Variations of the beauty contest game have proliferated as researchers discovered ways to use the game to explore new and increasingly complex phenomena.

Nagel puts it as follows. "In summary, experiments on the beauty-contest are easy to perform and are ideal for studying iterated dominance and numbers of levels of reasoning applied by real subjects. In the beginning, behavior is far away from equilibrium and converges to equilibrium over time. A simple bounded rational reasoning model describes the behavior in a consistent way across several treatments, especially in the first period. Convergence over time can be explained by various adaptive learning models and a continuous low level of rationality."

In a series of four entries, Hoffman, McCabe, and Smith test the many dimensions of ultimatum and dictator games. The ultimatum game has served as a challenge for at least two decades as game theorists ponder about why a person with the power to make a take it or leave it offer would not offer the minimum and why a person receiving such an offer might not take it. Concepts of fairness, the choice of language in describing the task, the context of the task (market or bargaining), the magnitude of the incentives and the possibility of reputation formation especially in terms of the presence of the experimenter are all examined. The influences of these variables are explored and the entries weave a theory attempting to explain the influences that are observed.

The general pattern of reports is set by Murnighan who reviews experiments from economics and from psychology that test the idea that people in ultimatum games are motivated by attitudes of fairness. A major tool employed is restricted information about the amount to be divided. In addition they study experiments in which third parties add fairness labels and they study children. The thrust of the findings is that anger, perhaps due to frustrated expectations accounts for rejections and that proposers tend to be aware of that source of motivation and use that awareness in crafting a strategy. Basically, it appears that people use concepts of fairness strategically trying to appear fair while pursuing self interest. The review includes studies of children as young as kindergarten.

Andreoni and Miller continue the analysis of compatibility between other-regardingness and game theory by demonstrating how rational choice, interpreted as classical consistency, can be used to recover preferences for non-observables, such as attitudes of altruism. Similarly, Bolton, Brandts, Katok, Ockenfels, and Zwick demonstrate how the attitudes of other-regardingness can be viewed as influencing the outcomes in a direction suggested by the equilibrium of the conflict once changed to include the preferences. The behaviors of altruism, fairness and reciprocity need not have the structure that the ethical and philosophical roots of these concepts suppose. People differ and therefore, their behavior differs.

Part of the mystery of other-regardingness lie in the dynamics of adjustments and specifically coordination. Van Huyck and Battalio study the development of coordination from two perspectives. One is the existence of a very special equilibrium that guarantees a level of security to be compared with the most efficient Nash. The other is the number of alternatives, where a dramatic increase in the number of alternatives is associated with a "smoothing" of the dynamic path. The thought is that "smoother" paths might facilitate convergence to the efficient outcomes. For Rhodes and Wilson, coordination problems are easily solved in the presence of institutional coordinating devices such as signals. On the other hand, when the institutions are ambiguous, there are obstacles to coordination that can become exacerbated by behaviors that seem to be attempts to compensate for the unpredictability of others and even punishments for unpredictable behavior. Bouchez and Friedman also focus on the convergence process and on theories of convergence processes in matrix games. The treatments include the amount of feedback about decisions and the payoff, whether it is the actual payoff that resulted from a match of the average of payoffs from a number of matches without the payoff from any particular match being known. Convergence, the speed of convergence and the patterns of individual strategies are studied in relation to evolutionary equilibria.

The final entry in this part is that of Binmore and Swierzbinski. Here the Nash bargaining environment is used to characterize outcomes with solution concepts based on different social or philosophical norms of fairness and placed in competition with the Nash equilibria. Manipulations of information were used to condition subjects to start near the prediction of one of the competing theories as a focal point. In this manner the research is able to identify the stability of the focal points and the extent to which the underlying norm of behavior gradually become transformed toward equilibrium play.

4.2. Learning in Games

Dynamics of adjustment are clearly related to learning. Rapoport and Seale, in a rare study of the effect of differing information about the others payoffs in games, demonstrate that the greater precision in understanding the preferences of the other side of the market results in higher prices. Furthermore, any "advantages" afforded one player or another through the information is exacerbated by repeated play with the same opponent. An adaptive learning model is applied to the dynamics. The theme of uncertainty about the payoff of the other is continued in Kahn and Murnighan who study the repeated prisoner's dilemma with differing information about the payoffs. The focus is on emerging cooperation and the conditions under which it takes place with an emphasis on the possible role of underlying psychological variables.

The theory becomes complex with the surfacing of different ideas about asymmetric information and different ways in which it might become resolved. Blume, DeJong, and Sprinkle study two person games with "partially conflicting" interests who can communicate. Using "a priori" meaningless messages in such games, they ask how agents attach meaning to the messages and extend the analysis to study outcomes, the learning process and the relationship between learning and the size of the message space.

Classical ideas of refinements are addressed by Cooper. The game studied is an entry game in which the incumbent can be a low cost or a high cost firm, a fact that will become known to an entrant only after a decision to enter. The entrant will profit if the incumbent is high cost but will lose if the incumbent is a low cost. Theoretical equilibrium refinements are studied and are poor models relative to adaptive learning.

Camerer and Ho outline one of the most successful of all learning models. A sophisticated experienced weighted learning model is compared to reinforcement learning and weighted fictitious play across a variety of games. The structure of these models is discussed together with interpretations of the measured parameters and areas of potential improvement.

PART 4.1

ACCURACY OF THE NASH MODEL

Rosemarie Nagel, "Experimental Beauty Contest-games: Levels of Reasoning and Convergence to Equilibrium"

Elizabeth Hoffman, Kevin McCabe and Vernon Smith, "Reciprocity in Ultimatum and Dictator Games: An Introduction"

Elizabeth Hoffman, Kevin McCabe and Vernon Smith, "Preferences and Property Rights in Ultimatum and Dictator Games"

Elizabeth Hoffman, Kevin McCabe and Vernon Smith, "Prompting Strategic Reasoning Increases Other-regarding Behavior"

Elizabeth Hoffman, Kevin McCabe and Vernon Smith, "Social Distance and Reciprocity in Dictator Games"

J. Keith Murnighan, "Fairness in Ultimatum Bargaining"

John Van Huyck and Raymond Battalio, "Coordination Failure in Market Statistic Games"

Carl M. Rhodes and Rick K. Wilson, "The Problem of Common Choice in Symmetric N-person Coordination Games"

Nicole Bouchez and Daniel Friedman, "Equilibrium Convergence in Normal Form Games"

James Andreoni and John H. Miller, "Analyzing Choice with Revealed Preference: Is Altruism Rational?"

Gary E. Bolton, Jordi Brandts, Elena Katok, Axel Ockenfels and Rami Zwick, "Testing Theories of Other-regarding Behavior: A Sequence of Four Laboratory Studies"

Ken Binmore and Joseph Swierzbinski, "Focal Points and Bargaining"

Chapter 45

EXPERIMENTAL BEAUTY CONTEST GAMES: LEVELS OF REASONING AND CONVERGENCE TO EQUILIBRIUM

ROSEMARIE NAGEL

Universitat Pompeu Fabra, Barcelona

1. Introduction

John Maynard Keynes (1936, p. 155) suggested that the behavior of investors in financial markets could be likened to newspaper beauty contests in which readers were asked to choose the six prettiest faces from 100 photographs. The winner was the person whose preferences were closest to the average preferences of all participants. Keynes reasoned that contest participants, like financial investors, do not choose faces (investments) that they personally find the most attractive but are instead guided by their expectations of others' expectations. We present data from a series of experiments with human subjects to test how individuals form expectations of others' expectations. The experiment has much in common with Keynes' insight regarding the behavior of investors in financial markets, and therefore the game is called 'beauty contest' game in honor of Keynes.

In the basic beauty contest game, a group of subjects is asked to guess a number from 0 to 100. The winner is the person(s) whose guess is closest to p times the mean of the choices of all players, with, e.g., $p = 2/3$; p is known to all players and is positive. The winners split a prize of $20. The same game is repeated several periods, and subjects are informed of the results in each period. In any period, for $p < 1$, in equilibrium all players should announce zero and thus everybody is a winner.[1] It is clear that deviating from zero would produce 0 payoffs for that player if all others choose zero. For $p > 1$, the upper bound of the interval is also an equilibrium.

The game is dominance solvable. Thus, as shown in Figure 1a, the process of iterated elimination of weakly dominated strategies, an important concept in game theory, with $p = 2/3$ and number chosen in the interval [0, 100] leads to the equilibrium choice of zero. A player might reason that the mean could be no higher than 100. Therefore, the winning number could be no greater than 2/3 of 100 or 66.667. Numbers above 66.667 are weakly dominated by 66.667 ($E(0)$ of Figure 1a, or 0-level of elimination of dominance). If our player believed that all others would choose 66.667, it would be rational for him to choose 44.444, approximately 2/3 of the new mean. Numbers between 66.667 and 44.444 are chosen by those players who eliminate dominated strategies, but

---

[1] If only integers are allowed, there is more than one equilibrium (see Lopez, 2002).

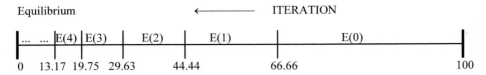

Figure 1a. Infinite process of iterated elimination of dominated strategies for $p = 2/3$-mean game (Infinite Threshold game). A choice in $E(0)$ means that a player is not rational (chooses a weakly dominated number), $E(1)$ is the interval of choices which indicates that the player is rational (does not choose dominated choices) but thinks that the other players are not rational and that they choose numbers which are in $E(0)$. $E(2)$ means that he believes that all others also think that everybody is rational, etc.

Figure 1b. Finite process of iterated elimination of dominated strategies for $p = 1.3$-mean game (Finite Threshold game). The iteration process starts from 100 upwards. Adjusted from Ho, Camerer, and Weigelt (1998).

believe that all others choose dominated strategies ($E(1)$, or 1-level of iterated dominance). This analysis can be continued. If a player eliminates dominated strategies and believes that all other eliminate dominated strategies and he also believes that all other players believe that nobody uses dominated strategies and so on, he arrives after infinitely many steps to the announcement zero.

A similar process is applied if $p > 1$ (see Figure 1b). The upper bound is the perfect equilibrium and the starting point of the elimination process is the lower (positive) bound of the interval. In this case only finitely many steps are needed to reach equilibrium.

If $p = 1$, the game is similar to a coordination game with any number, chosen by all subjects, forming an equilibrium (see survey of coordination games by Ochs, 1995).

A parameter p different from 1 means that a player wants to distinguish himself from the average, but by not too much. An interior equilibrium is reached if the objective is to be closest to p times the mean plus a constant [see for example 0.7 times (median + 18) in which case the equilibrium is 42]. The advantage is that a deviation from the equilibrium from above and below is possible (see Camerer and Ho, 1998). An economic interpretation could be that the average is exogenously increased by a strong or big outside player who has written down his bid already.

2. Variations on the Beauty Contest Game

For the variations on the beauty contest game, see Table 1. This table states the authors who carried out beauty contest games (column 1), the number of replications of the

Ch. 45: Experimental Beauty Contest Games: Levels of Reasoning and Convergence to Equilibrium

Table 1
Experimental designs and structure of the games by the different authors. Bold text indicates main focus of study

Authors	Subject pool	No. of sessions per treatment	No. of players in one group	Winning no. formular (winner's choice closest to ...)	Parameters p, c	Range of possible choices	Payoffs	No. of periods in a session	Information after each period	No. of iteration steps to reach perfect equilibrium
Nagel (1995)	Undergrads of various faculties Uni-Bonn, Germany	3–4	15–18 (total 166)	$p * \text{mean}$	**$p = 1/2$, $2/3$, $4/3$**	$[0, 100]$, real numbers	20 DM = $10 per period to the winners, 0 to losers, 5 DM show up fee	4	All choices (anonymous), mean $p * \text{mean}$, winning number(s)	Infinite steps for $p < 1$ (equil. 0) n.a. for $p > 1$ (equil. 100)
Stahl (1996, 1998)	Data of Nagel (1995)									
Ho, Camerer, and Weigelt (1998)[a]	Undergrads of business quantitative methods class, Southeast Asia	6–7	**3 or 7** (total 277)	$p * \text{mean}$	$p = 0.7, 0.9, 1.1, 1.3$	$[0, 100]$ for $p < 1$, $[100, 200]$ for $p > 1$ integers	expected $.50 per person and period ($3.50 for $n = 7$) ($1.50 for $n = 3$) losers $0	10	Mean, each subject was privately informed about his payoff (winner > $0, loser $0)	Infinite for $p < 1$ (equil. 100) 8 steps for $p = 1.1$; 3 steps for $p = 1.3$ (equil. 200)
Ho, Camerer (1999)	Data of Ho, Camerer, and Weigelt (1998)									

(continued on next page)

Table 1
(continued)

Authors	Subject pool	No. of sessions per treatment	No. of players in one group	Winning no. formular, (winner's choice closest to ...)	Parameters p, c	Range of possible choices	Payoffs	No. of periods in a session	Information after each period	No. of iteration steps to reach perfect equilibrium
Duffy and Nagel (1997)	Undergrads of various faculties Pittsburgh University	1 or 3	13–16 (total 175)	$p *$ **median** $p *$ **mean** $p *$ **max**	$p = 1/2$	[0, 100] real numbers	$20 per period $5 show-up fee	4, 10	All choices (anonymous), r, $p * r$ (r is mean, med. or max.) winning number (s)	infinite steps (equil. 0)
Camerer and Ho (1998)	Undergrads of UCLA and Penn (Philadelphia)	4, 6–7	7 (total 147)	$\mathbf{p} *$ **(median $+ \mathbf{c}$)**	$p = 0.7, 0.8$ $c = 18$	[0, 100] real numbers	**$5, $7, or $28** for winner, $0 or -2 for others,	10	Median, each subject privately informed about his payoff	Infinite steps above below eq. ($p = .7$, eq. 42) ($p = .8$, eq. 72)
Nagel (1998)	Undergrads of various faculties Caltech, Pasadena	4 (additional sess. with fixed prize)	12–17 (total 59)	$p *$ mean	$p = 2/3$	[0, 100] real numbers	**winner gets x, x is his chosen number**, $5 show-up fee	4	All choices (anonymous), mean $p *$ mean, winning number (s)	Infinite steps (equil. 0)

(continued on next page)

Table 1
(continued)

Authors	Subject pool	No. of sessions per treatment	No. of players in one group	Winning no. formular, (winner's choice closest to …)	Parameters p, c	Range of possible choices	Payoffs	No. of periods in a session	Information after each period	No. of iteration steps to reach perfect equilibrium
Bosch et al. (2002)	**Game theorists, experimenters, classroom**	2–3	32, 27	$p * $ mean	$p = 2/3$	[0, 100] real numbers	Winner gets about $20	1	Winning number	Infinite steps (equil. 0)
Newspaper data of Bosch and Nagel (1997b), Thaler (1997) and Selten and Nagel (1998)										
Bosch and Nagel (1997a)	**Readers of** Expansion	1 (3 weeks to decide)	3696	$p * $ mean	$p = 2/3$	[1, 100] decimals	**Winner gets 100 000 Ptas = $800**	1	Rel. freq of choices, $p * $ mean, winner	12 steps (equil. 1)
Thaler (1997)	**Readers of Financial Times**	1 (1 week to decide)	1460	$p * $ mean, best comment	$p = 2/3$	[0, 100] integers	**Winner gets two tickets to NY**	1	Abs. freq. of choices, $p * $ mean, winner	Infinite steps (equil. 0)
Selten and Nagel (1998)	**Readers of Spektrum der Wissenschaft**	1 (2 weeks to decide)	2728	$p * $ mean	$p = 2/3$	[0, 100] decimals	**Winner gets 1000DM = $800**	1	Rel. frey of choices, $p * $ mean, winner	Infinite steps (equil. 0)

(continued on next page)

Table 1
(*continued*)

Authors	Subject pool	No. of sessions per treatment	No. of players in one group	Winning no. formular, (winner's choice closest to …)	Parameters p, c	Range of possible choices	Payoffs	No. of periods in a session	Information after each period	No. of iteration steps to reach perfect equilibrium
Fehr and Renninger (2000)	**Readers of DIE ZEIT**	1 (2 weeks to decide)		$p * $ mean	$p = 2/3$	[0, 100] decimals	**Winner gets 1000DM = $800**	1	**Open webpage to discuss with others before deciding**	Infinite steps (equil. 0)
Weber (2003)	Caltech undergraduates	3	8–10 (112 in total)	$p * $ mean	$p = 2/3$	[0, 100]		10 periods	**4 treatments: full info**: all choices, $p * $ mean **no info**; **no info + explicit mentioning that average has been calculated**; **no info + asking for beliefs about other players choices**	Infinite steps (equil. 0)

(*continued on next page*)

Table 1
(continued)

Authors	Subject pool	No. of sessions per treatment	No. of players in one group	Winning no. formular, (winner's choice closest to ...)	Parameters p, c	Range of possible choices	Payoffs	No. of periods in a session	Information after each period	No. of iteration steps to reach perfect equilibrium
Grosskopf and Nagel (2001)	Undergraduates of Pompeu Fabra, (Economists in various conferences and seminars)	1 session (3 sessions with economists)	**2** (72 students in total + about 60 economists)	$p *$ mean	$p = 2/3$	[0, 100]	100 pesetas = 0.6 cents	**10 peri with 2 players then 3 periods with 18 players**(1 period for economist sessions)	**4 treatments: full info:** $p *$ mean, own payoff; **partial info:** own payoff; **no info** + **asking for beliefs about other player choices; no info**	For 2 players: **weakly dominant strategy 0 = 1** step
Costa-Gomes and Crawford (2006)	Undergraduates, graduates of UCSD		**2 person matching,** 13–21 in a session (125 students)	$p*$ **other choice**	$p_i =$ 0.5, 0.7, 1.3, or 1.5; might be different for each player, p_i hidden by a "mouselab"	**lower limit** 100 or 300; **upper limit** 500 or 900; maybe be different for each player, limits hidden by a mouselab	$3 for showing up on time, $8 for showing up 5 min. before, $0.04 for each of 0–300 possible points	**16 periods with a different game in each period, random matching**	No feedback	**2 to 51 steps; lower or upper limit** (equilibrium)

(continued on next page)

Table 1
(continued)

Authors	Subject pool	No. of sessions per treatment	No. of players in one group	Winning no. formular, (winner's choice closest to ...)	Parameters p, c	Range of possible choices	Payoffs	No. of periods in a session	Information after each period	No. of iteration steps to reach perfect equilibrium
Slonim (2005)	Ohio undergrads	3 sessions for SAME, 10 sessions for MIX	3 (27 for SAME, 70 for MIX in total)	$p *$ median	2/3	[0, 100]	$3 for each winner	3 supergames with 3 peri: SAME = changing partner in each supergame MIX = 1 pl all periods (insider), 2 changing partners each supergame (outsiders)	$p *$ mean, all choices	Infinite steps (equil. 0)

(continued on next page)

Table 1
(continued)

Authors	Subject pool	No. of sessions per treatment	No. of players in one group	Winning no. formular, (winner's choice closest to...)	Parameters p, c	Range of possible choices	Payoffs	No. of periods in a session	Information after each period	No. of iteration steps to reach perfect equilibrium
Gueth, Kocher, and Sutter (2002)	Undergrads from first micro class in Humbolt University Berlin	5 sessions	4 (40 in total)	$p*(\text{mean}+c)$	$p = 1/2$, $c = 0$; $p = 1/2$, $c = 50$; (heterogen. sessions: 2 pla. $p = 2/3$, 2 players $p = 1/3$ and $c = 50$ or 0 for all players)	[0, 100]	**Payoff dependent on distance to winning number (average payoff about 80 cents per period)**	10 periods	All choices, $p*(\text{mean}+c)$	If $c = 0$, equil. 0, $p = 1/2$, $c = 50$ equil. 50; in heterog. session ($c = 50$): for $p = 1/3$ players: equil. 100/3, for $p = 2/3$ players 200/3
Kocher and Sutter (2005)	First year economic undergrads from Innsbruck	2–3	**Individ. treat:** 17 subjects; **Group treat:** 17 groups of 3 pers.; within group communication. **Heterog. treat: 2 individ. plus one group of 3 persons** (group = 1 pla.) (340 in total)	$p*\text{mean}$	$p = 2/3$	[0, 100]	$6–10 for each winner	4 periods	All choices, $p*\text{mean}$	Infinite steps (equil. 0)

(continued on next page)

Table 1
(continued)

Authors	Subject pool	No. of sessions per treatment	No. of players in one group	Winning no. formular, (winner's choice closest to ...)	Parameters p, c	Range of possible choices	Payoffs	No. of periods in a session	Information after each period	No. of iteration steps to reach perfect equilibrium
Kaplan and Ruffle (2004)	**Economics students, psychology students of Ben Gurion University**	7 (3 with economic students, 4 with psych. students)	30	$p *$ mean	$p = 2/3$	[0, 100]	About $100 for the winner plus **for each odd numbered subject:** mean of all other 29 subjects/4 and for each even numbered subject 100-(mean of all other 29 subjects)/4	1 period	All choices, $p *$ mean	Infinite steps (equil. 0)

[a]Note that in Ho, Camerer, and Weigelt (1998) subjects played within a session and the same group a treatment $p > 1$ and then a treatment with $p < 1$ or vice versa.

same parameter set (called number of sessions per treatment, column 3) and the number of periods within a session (column 6), the number of players interacting (column 4), the parameters (p, c which are the deviation parameters from the average, column 5), information after each period (column 6) and the equilibrium predictions together with the number of reasoning steps (last column). Besides the test of level of reasoning (using different deviation parameters p from the average), the heterogeneity of the subject pool (see column 2, e.g., economists or subjects recruited through newspaper announcements vs students – see Bosch et al., 2002 – or differences in experience with the game – see Slonim, 2005) has become important issues in recent years. Gueth et al. (2002) and Costa-Gomes and Crawford (2006) introduce new asymmetric guessing games in which subjects of the same group may have different parameters p or intervals to choose from in order to separate leading decision rules. Furthermore, in Costa-Gomez and Crawford's experiment subjects need to actively search for information about own or other's parameters (via a so-called mouselab in which information is hidden in boxes). The search pattern is supposed to reveal the thinking process of a subject.

More detailed surveys on the guessing game experiments can be found in Nagel (1995, 1998). How to use the beauty contest game in the classroom is described in Nagel (2000).

3. Bounded Rational Behavior

3.1. Iterated Best Reply Model

Figure 2 shows the relative frequencies of choices for the single treatments in the first period. For example, in the "1/2-median" game, the frequencies of choices around 25 or 12.5 stick out while no one chooses 0 (see Figure 2, 1/2-median game). Or in the 2/3-mean game choices near 33 and 22 are frequently observed (see 2/3-mean game in Figure 2). There are very few choices below numbers 12.5 or 22. In treatments with a small number of players, the midpoint of the interval seems most prominent (see 1.1-mean, 3 players).

How can this behavior be motivated with a common model? Ho, Camerer and Weigelt (1998), Nagel (1995) and Stahl (1996) apply a simple iterated best reply model:
1. Players choose uniformly randomly over the interval with an expected mean as the midpoint of the given interval, say 50, if choices are in interval [0, 100]; or they choose the midpoint as a focal point. This is the lowest level of reasoning (level 0-reasoning), not considering the task of being closest to the winning formula, for example, 1/2 times mean or 2/3 times mean in the particular treatment.
2. A player who thinks that the others just choose randomly might like to choose 1/2 times $50 = 25$ or 2/3 times $50 = 33$, respectively, where 50 is the expected mean of a uniform random distribution (level 1-reasoning).
3. A player might think that others choose 22 or 33, respectively, according to (2), and thus he likes to give best reply resulting in $50 * 1/2 * 1/2 = 12.5$ or $50 * 2/3 * 2/3 = 22$, respectively. This player behaves according to level 2, etc.

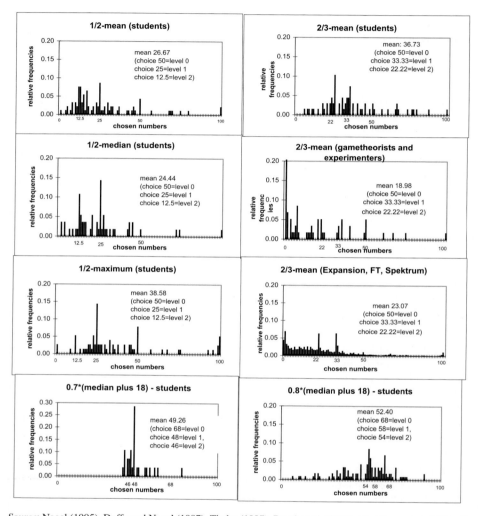

Source: Nagel (1995), Duffy and Nagel (1997), Thaler (1997), Bosch et al. (2002), Ho, Camerer, and Weigelt (1998), Selten and Nagel (1998). *Data*: Camerer and Ho (1999), Nagel (1998).

Figure 2. Relative frequencies of choices in the first period of the different treatments. The numbers on the x-axis indicate the choice related to the reasoning model $(50 + c)p^d$, where 50 is the expected value of an uniform distribution of numbers from [0, 100], p and c are given parameters and d is the depth of reasoning. For example 22 is approximately depth of reasoning 2 in the treatment with $p = 2/3$, $c = 0$ and hence $50 * 2/3^2 = 22.22$. Most choices are concentrated around levels 1–3 in the different graphs.

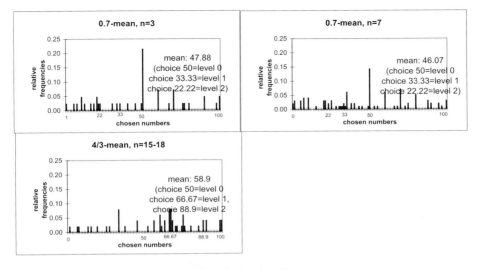

Figure 2. (*continued.*)

The process of iterative elimination of weakly dominated strategies mentioned above does not produce a common explanation for the behavior in the different treatments (see Nagel, 1995, 1998). Given the good fit of the iterated best reply model it is not surprising that less than 10% choose dominated strategies.

Figures 2 also distinguish relative frequencies of choices of the first period of different subject pools. Subjects with training in game theory show much higher level of reasoning and therefore their numbers tend to be closer to equilibrium (see Figure 2, 2/3-mean, game theorists and experimenters) than those choices of students (see Figure 2, 2/3 mean, students). The beauty contest game with $p = 2/3$ has recently been sponsored by three daily business newspapers (*Financial Times* (FT) in Great Britain; Thaler, 1997; *Expansion* in Spain; Bosch and Nagel, 1997a and by *Spektrum der Wissenschaft*; Selten and Nagel, 1998). Prizes were as high as $1000. A rich set of comments from these participants has been gathered (see, for example, the comment in Appendix B). The main results of previous laboratory experiments were confirmed by the newspaper experiments (see Figure 2, 2/3-mean, FT, Expansion and Spektrum). The main difference was the high number of frequencies at or near the equilibrium. The choices closest to the winning number were typically those which came from subjects who did their own pre-experiments with students, friends or even with a newsgroup experiment.

The idea that subjects apply a low degree of iterated dominance has been shown in many other experimental studies, mostly in mixed motive games (see, for example, van Huyck, Wildenthal, and Battalio, 2002; Stahl and Wilson, 1994; McKelvey and Palfrey, 1992; and Nagel and Tang, 1998). The advantage of the beauty contest experiment over these mixed motive games is that the beauty contest game is a constant game, so that non-game-theory features like altruism or reciprocity should not matter. Thus one can

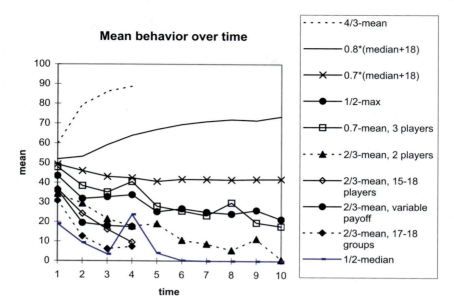

Data source: Nagel (1995), Duffy and Nagel (1997), Camerer and Ho (1999), Ho, Camerer, and Weigelt (1998), Nagel (1998), Grosskopf and Nagel (2001), Kocher and Sutter (2005).

Figure 3. Mean behavior over time from various treatments. In all treatments behavior converges to equilibrium, albeit at different speed.

concentrate on strategic reasoning. Furthermore, one can construct games with a few number of iteration steps to an infinite number of iteration steps to reach an equilibrium (compare Figures 1a and 1b) without complicating the instructions.

3.2. Learning

Figure 3 shows average behavior of some treatments over time. In most of them behavior converges to equilibrium. When p is smaller, the convergence is faster (compare 1/2-median game with 2/3-mean game in Figure 3). If the number of subjects is small, convergence to equilibrium is much slower than with a high number of subjects (see Figure 3, 2/3-mean with 15–18 subjects vs 0.7-mean with 3 subjects, or 2/3 with 2 subjects where a player even has a weakly dominant strategy). If a player's decision is first discussed in a group of three, first period behavior is not different, but convergence over time is faster than if only individuals interact (see Figure 3, 2/3 mean with 15–18 subjects vs 2/3 mean with 17–18 groups, where each group consisted of 3 members).

Note when the size of the prize to the winner is determined by his chosen number (see Nagel, 1998) – i.e., if the winner chooses 5 he gets $5, instead of a fixed prize – the convergence towards equilibrium is slowed down in comparison to the game with fixed

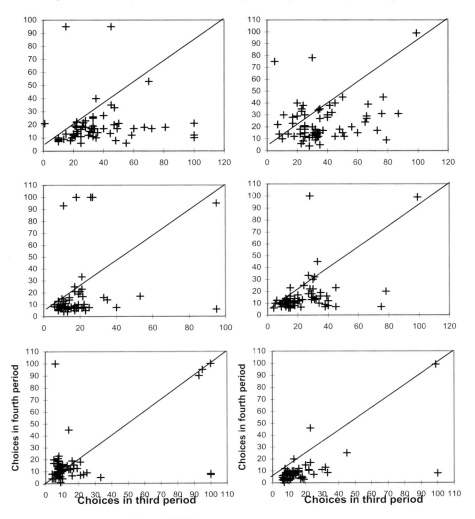

Data source: Nagel (1995) and Nagel (1998).

Figure 4. Transition behavior from period t to period $t+1$ in 2/3-mean variable payoff treatment on the left side and 2/3-mean fixed payoff treatment on the right side. Each cross presents the behavior of one subject. The transition behavior in the rounds 1 to 3 are very similar in the two treatments, however, in the forth period subjects continue to decrease their choices in the right graph, but increase their choices again in the left graph, since otherwise potential gains become too small.

prize (compare 2/3-mean and 2/3-mean variable-payoff in Figure 3). See Figure 4, which shows the transition from period 1 to period 2, period 2 to 3 and period 3 to 4 of these two treatments, respectively. A player's choices in period t and $t+1$ are indicated

Table 2

Classification of choices according to depth of reasoning in 10-round sessions (underlined numbers are modal frequencies); $d < 0$ in $\frac{1}{2}$-median means choices below the median of the previous period, $d = 0$: choices around the median of the previous period, $d = 1$ choices around $\frac{1}{2}^{d=1}*$-median of previous period, etc. $d = 2$ choices around $\left(\frac{1}{2}\right)^{d=2}*$median of previous period, etc. In mean games the reference point is the mean and in maximum game it is the maximum. Only in the $\frac{1}{2}$-median game there is a clear increase of levels of reasoning after 7 periods with more than 50% choosing levels higher than 2. *Source*: Duffy and Nagel (1997)

Period	1	2	3	4	5	6	7	8	9	10
(a) 1/2-median session										
$d > 3$	0	0	0	0.15	0.08	0	0.15	0.23	<u>0.62</u>	1.00
$d = 3$	0.08	0.08	0	0	0.08	0.08	0.31	0.31	0.23	0
$d = 2$	0.38	0.31	<u>0.62</u>	<u>0.46</u>	<u>0.31</u>	<u>0.54</u>	<u>0.54</u>	<u>0.46</u>	0.15	0
$d = 1$	<u>0.54</u>	<u>0.38</u>	0.31	0.15	0.08	0.15	0	0	0	0
$d = 0$	0	0.23	0.08	0	0.08	0.08	0	0	0	0
$d < 0$	0	0	0	0.23	0.38	0.15	0	0	0	0
(b) 1/2-mean session										
$d > 3$	0	0	0	0	0.07	0	0.14	0.07	0.07	0
$d = 3$	0	0.14	0	0	0.07	0.14	0.29	0.14	0.14	0
$d = 2$	0.07	0.14	0.36	0.29	0.14	<u>0.36</u>	<u>0.57</u>	<u>0.29</u>	<u>0.29</u>	<u>0.50</u>
$d = 1$	<u>0.71</u>	<u>0.57</u>	<u>0.43</u>	<u>0.57</u>	<u>0.71</u>	0.29	0	<u>0.29</u>	<u>0.29</u>	0.29
$d = 0$	0.14	0	0.14	0	0	0.14	0	0.14	0	0
$d < 0$	0.07	0.14	0.07	0.14	0	0.07	0	0.07	0.21	0.21
(c) 1/2-maximum session										
$d > 3$	0	0	0	0	0	0	0	0	0	0.07
$d = 3$	0.07	0.13	0	0	0	0	0	0	0	0.07
$d = 2$	<u>0.40</u>	<u>0.53</u>	<u>0.40</u>	0.13	0.07	0.27	0	<u>0.73</u>	0.07	<u>0.80</u>
$d = 1$	0.33	0.33	<u>0.40</u>	<u>0.87</u>	<u>0.67</u>	<u>0.73</u>	<u>0.80</u>	0.27	<u>0.67</u>	0.07
$d = 0$	0.20	0	0.07	0	0.20	0	0.13	0	0.07	0
$d < 0$	0	0	0.13	0	0.07	0	0.07	0	0.20	0

by a cross. In the variable treatment the behavior from period 3 to 4 might resemble the beginning of a bubble (see Sunder, 1995). About 50% of the players increase their choices whereas in the fixed-payoff treatments most subjects choose a number smaller than in period 3 (choices below the diagonal-line). The variable-payoff treatment is a mixed-motive game, in structure similar to a finitely repeated prisoner's dilemma game or the centipede game in which the equilibrium is not Pareto-optimal.

Table 2 shows the relative frequencies of choices classified to the different levels of reasoning, separately for each period and different order statistics with $p = 1/2$. In period 1 the starting point for the level of reasoning is 50 and in the subsequent rounds it is the mean, median or maximum of the previous period, depending on the treatment. Apparently players continue to use low levels of reasoning. Only in the 1/2-median game do more than 50% of the players choose a level of reasoning greater than

2 ($d > 2$) after the 7th period. In all other cases of all treatments the majority plays around level 1 or 2 (the underlined numbers in Table 2 present modal choices).

Various learning models have been applied or developed to study this behavior over time. Nagel (1995) and Duffy and Nagel (1997) apply a learning direction theory á la Selten and Stoecker (1986). Stahl (1996, 1998) developed a rule-learning model which incorporates the level-model described above and elements of learning direction theory and reinforcement learning. Camerer and Ho (1999) apply an experienced-based attraction model for various normal form games such as the beauty contest game. Their model is a generalization of reinforcement (see, for example, Roth and Erev, 1995) and fictitious play models. An iterated best reply model is applied by Ho et al. (1998). These models show that both the order-statistic (e.g., mean or median or maximum choice of all chosen numbers) and the parameter p, which determine the winning number, matter for how quickly players move toward the equilibrium (see Figure 3). The question how the number of subjects influences the convergence over time remains unexplained by the descriptive learning models. In addition, the sudden increase of choices in the variable-payoff-treatment remains unexplained.

In summary, experiments on the beauty contest are easy to perform and are ideal for studying iterated dominance and numbers of levels of reasoning applied by real subjects. In the beginning, behavior is far away from equilibrium but converges to equilibrium over time. A simple bounded rational reasoning model describes the behavior in a consistent way across several treatments, especially in the first period. Convergence over time can be explained by various adaptive learning models and continuous low level of rationality.

Appendix A: Instructions (from Duffy and Nagel, 1997)

A.1. General

You are taking part in an experiment in the economics of decision making. If you have any questions, please feel free to ask. You should have four response cards in front of you, each with a title: first, second, third, or fourth round. You should also have an "explanation sheet."

This experiment will consist of four rounds. The rules, described below, are valid for all four rounds and for all participants.

A.2. The Rules

In each round you will be asked to choose a number between 0 and 100. Write the number you choose on the card of the corresponding round. At the end of each round all cards for that round will be collected, the numbers chosen will be written on the board, and the *median* will be determined. This will be done without identifying any participant. The winner of each round is the person who is closest to 1/2 *times the median* of all chosen numbers for that round.

A.3. What is the Median

The median is found by ranking all chosen numbers from lowest to highest (or from highest to lowest) and picking out the middle number. For example if we have five numbers represented by the letters a, b, c, d, and e, and it is the case that $a < b < c < d < e$, then the middle number, c, is the median. Thus, the median is the number such that half of all numbers lie below it and half of all numbers lie above it.

Remember, however, that you want to choose a number that you believe will be closest to $1/2$ *times the median*.

A.4. Payoffs

1 participant will receive a $5 payment provided that they complete all four rounds of this experimental session. In addition, the winner of each round will get $20. If, in any round, there are several participants at an equal distance to $1/2$ *of the median*, the $20 prize will be divided among them. All payments will be made at the end of the session.

A.5. Explanation Sheet

Briefly describe your decision for each round on the explanation sheet.
  ARE THERE ANY QUESTIONS BEFORE WE BEGIN?

Appendix B

Comment by a school-class (see Bosch et al., 2002), translation from German to English: I would like to submit the proposal of a class grade 8e of the Felix-Klein-Gymnasium Goettingen for your game: 0.228623. How did this value come up? Johanna ... asked in the math-class whether we should not participate in this contest. The idea was accepted with great enthusiasm and lot of suggestions were made immediately. About half of the class wanted to submit their favorite numbers. To send one number for all, maybe one could take the average of all these numbers. A first concern came from Ulfert, who stated that numbers greater than 66 2/3 had no chance to win. Sonja suggested to take 2/3 of the average. At that point it got too complicated to some students and the finding of the decision was postponed. In the next class Helena proposed to multiply 33 1/3 with 2/3 and again with 2/3. However, Ulfert disagreed, because starting like that one could multiply it again with 2/3. Others agreed with him that this process then could be continued. They tried and realized that the numbers became smaller and smaller. A lot of students gave up at that point, thinking that this way a solution could not be found. Other believed to have found the path of the solution: one just has to submit a very small number.

However, one could not agree how many of the people who participate realized this process. Johanna supposed that the people who read this newspaper are quite sophisticated. At the end of the class 7 to 8 students heatedly continued to discuss this problem.

The next day the math teacher received the following message: ... We think it best to submit number 0.228623.

References

Bosch, A., Nagel, R. (1997a). "El juego de adivinar el numero X: Una explicacion y la proclamacion del vencedor". Expansion 16, 42–43.
Bosch, A., Nagel, R. (1997b). "Guess the number: Comparing the FT's and expansion's results". Financial Times, Section Mastering Finance 8, 14.
Bosch, A., Montalvo, Garcia J., Nagel, R., Satorra, A. (2002). "One, two, (three), infinity ... : Newspaper and lab beauty contest experiments". American Economic Review 92 (5), 1687–1701.
Camerer, C., Ho, T. (1998). "The effect of incentives in experimental p-beauty contest". Caltech, Working paper.
Camerer, C., Ho, T. (1999). "Experienced-weighted attraction learning in games". Econometrica 67 (4), 827–874.
Costa-Gomes, M., Crawford, V. (2006). "Cognition and behavior in two-person guessing games: An experimental study". American Economic Review 96 (5), 1737–1768.
Grosskopf, Brit, Nagel, Rosemarie (2001). "Rational reasoning or adaptive behavior? Evidence from two-person beauty contest games". Harvard NOM Research Paper No. 01-09.
Duffy, J., Nagel, R. (1997). "On the robustness of behaviour in experimental 'beauty-contest' games". Economic Journal 107 (445), 1684–1700.
Fehr, Ernst, Renninger, Suzann-Viola (2000). "Gefangen in der Gedankenspirale". Die Zeit 48, 31. November 23.
Gueth, Werner, Kocher, Martin, Sutter, Matthias (2002). "Experimental 'beauty contests' with homogeneous and heterogeneous players and with interior and boundary equilibria". Economics Letters 74 (2), 219–228.
Ho, T., Camerer, C., Weigelt, K. (1998). "Iterated dominance and iterated best–best response in experimental 'p-beauty contests'". American Economic Review 88 (4), 947–969.
Kaplan, Todd, Ruffle, Bradley J. (2004). "Self-serving bias and beliefs about rationality". Economic Inquiry 42 (2), 237–246.
Keynes, J.M. (1936). "The General Theory of Interest, Employment and Money". Macmillan, London.
Kocher, Martin G., Sutter, Matthias (2005). "When the 'decision maker' matters: Individual versus team behavior in experimental 'beauty contest' games". Economic Journal 115 (500), 200–223.
López, Rafael (2002). "On p-beauty contest integer games". Upf, working paper No. 608.
McKelvey, R., Palfrey, T. (1992). "An experimental study of the centipede game". Econometrica 60 (4), 803–836.
Nagel, R. (1995). "Unraveling in guessing games: An experimental study". American Economic Review 85 (5), 1313–1326.
Nagel, R. (1998). "A survey on beauty contest experiments: Bounded rationality and learning". In: Budescu, D., Erev, I., Zwick, R. (Eds.), Games and Human Behavior, Essays in Honor of Amnon Rapoport. Lawrence Erlbaum Associates, Inc., New Jersey.
Nagel, Rosemarie (2000). "A Keynesian beauty contest in the classroom". Classroom Expernomics, http://www.marietta.edu/~delemeeg/expernom/nagel.htm (last accessed June 27, 2007).
Nagel, R., Tang, F.F. (1998). "Experimental results on the centipede game in normal form: An investigation on learning". Journal of Mathematical Psychology 42 (2–3), 356–384.
Ochs, J. (1995). "Coordination problems". In: Kagel, J., Roth, A.E. (Eds.), Handbook of Experimental Economics. Princeton University Press, Princeton.
Roth, A.E., Erev, I. (1995). "Learning in extensive-form games: Experimental data and simple dynamic models in the intermediate term". Games and Economic Behavior 8 (1), 92–100.
Selten, R., Nagel, R. (1998). "Das Zahlenwahlspiel-Ergebnisse und Hintergrund". Spektrum der Wissenschaft (German Edition of Scientific American), Febr., pp. 16–22.

Selten, R., Stoecker, R. (1986). "End behavior in sequences of finite prisoner's dilemma supergames, a learning theory approach". Journal of Economic Behavior and Organization 7 (1), 47–70.

Slonim, Robert (2005). "Competing against experienced and inexperienced players in experimental beauty contest games". Experimental Economics 8 (1), 55–75.

Stahl, D.O. (1996). "Rule learning in a guessing game". Games and Economic Behavior 16 (2), 303–330.

Stahl, D.O. (1998). "Is step-j thinking an arbitrary modeling restriction or a fact of human nature?" Journal of Economic Behavior and Organization 37 (1), 33–51.

Stahl, D.O., Wilson, P.W. (1994). "Experimental evidence on players' models of other players". Journal of Economic Behavior and Organization 25 (3), 309–327.

Sunder, S. (1995). "Experimental asset markets: A survey". In: Kagel, J., Roth, A.E. (Eds.), Handbook of Experimental Economics. Princeton University Press, Princeton.

Thaler, R. (1997). "Giving markets a human dimension". Financial Times, section Mastering Finance 6, June 16.

Van Huyck, J.B., Wildenthal, J.M., Battalio, R.C. (2002). "Tacit cooperation, strategic uncertainty, and coordination failure: Evidence from repeated dominance solvable games". Games and Economic Behavior 38 (2), 156–175.

Weber, R. (2003). "'Learning' with no feedback in a competitive guessing game". Games and Economic Behavior 44 (1), 134–144.

Chapter 46

RECIPROCITY IN ULTIMATUM AND DICTATOR GAMES: AN INTRODUCTION

ELIZABETH HOFFMAN
Iowa State University

KEVIN MCCABE
University of Arizona

VERNON SMITH
University of Arizona

1. Motivation

Social norms of "fairness" have been said to cause the observed deviations from non-cooperative game theoretic predictions in ultimatum and dictator games. But where do social norms and concepts of "fairness" come from? We present data based on treatment manipulations intended to affect subjects' expectations about others' behavior, and degree of social isolation (anonymity) from the experimenter and others who might see the results, holding constant subject anonymity with respect to each other (Hoffman et al., 1994; Hoffman, McCabe, and Smith, 1996a, 1996b). Our manipulations are motivated by the idea that such treatments operate on subject expectations of reciprocity which are hypothesized to underpin putative norms of "fairness." Hence, when people give money away, or otherwise exhibit other-regarding behavior, this need not be contrary to self-interest, but rather an expression of the desire either to avoid punishment or to maintain their reputations (or images) as individuals who reciprocate in ordinary day-to-day social exchange. They expect to be made better off by avoiding punishment and by forming and maintaining such valuable long-term reputations. For certain agent types, such behavior is largely intuitive, unconscious and automatic in social exchange.

This view of social cognition, and evidence consistent with a predisposition to reciprocity, also comes from evolutionary psychology, prominently espoused by Cosmides and Tooby (1992): "the mind should contain organized systems of inference that are specialized for solving various families of problems, such as social exchange, threat, coalitional relations, and mate choice. Advocates of evolutionary views do not deny that humans learn, reason, develop, or acquire culture; however, they do argue that these functions are accomplished at least in part through the operation of cognitive mechanisms that are content specialized – mechanisms that are activated by particular content domains that are designed to process information from those domains" (p. 166).

In contrast, the standard economic/game theoretic model predicts that the (conscious) reasoning process that applies to social exchange – optimization in the self interest against other presumed self-interested protagonists – applies also to coalitional relations, games against nature and other content-specific decision problems. Of course, this paradigm makes provision for cooperative behavior in repeat play interaction, but such outcomes emerge out of reward and threat possibilities, that channel the self-interest into longer term betterment over time. According to game theory, such behavior is strictly ruled out in any one-shot game, unless one postulates a taste (utility) for fairness, a topic to which we shall return after introducing our experimental design and results.

2. Ultimatum and Dictator Games Described

Ultimatum and dictator games are typically two-person games. In an ultimatum game, player 1 makes an offer to player 2 of X from a total of M. If player 2 accepts the offer, then player 1 is paid $(M - X)$ and player 2 is paid X. If player 2 rejects the offer, each gets $0. In the dictator game, player 2 must accept player 1's offer. Hereafter we will refer to player 1 as the proposer, and player 2 as the recipient.

Under the usual rationality assumptions, the non-cooperative equilibrium of the ultimatum game is for the proposer to offer the recipient the smallest $ unit of account, and for the recipient to accept the offer. In the dictator game, the equilibrium is for the proposer to offer the recipient $0. In the ultimatum game, however, the recipient can punish the proposer for "cheating" on an implied social norm of reciprocal sharing across time in social exchange, by rejecting the proposer's offer. That response is a dominated strategy, if viewed in isolation, since both players would be financially better off with even a vanishingly small offer. But, in the absence of common knowledge of self-interested behavior, the possibility of punishment may change the proposer's equilibrium strategy. In the dictator game, the recipient cannot punish the proposer, and therefore the dictator game controls for the strategic property of the ultimatum game. However, if the proposer wishes to maintain a long-term reputation as one who reliably reciprocates in social exchange, that image is threatened if others (such as the experimenter) can observe the proposer not offering a positive amount to the recipient.

3. Experimental Designs and Summary Results

In the next few entries in this *Handbook*, we present our experimental designs and results in some detail. In this entry, we outline the development of the experimental designs and summarize the main results. The design we invoke has its direct origins in a paper by Kahneman, Knetsch, and Thaler (1986) and indirectly in the seminal contribution by Guth, Schmittberger, and Schwartz (1982). Kahneman, Knetsch, and Thaler (1986) describe an ultimatum game in which proposer and recipient are "provisionally allocated" $10 and the proposer is asked to make an initial offer to "divide" the $10 between the two players. The recipient may veto the division, in which case they both get $0. Kahneman, Knetsch, and Thaler (1986) find that most proposers offer $5 to recipients. Offers of less than $5 are sometimes rejected.

Forsythe et al. (1994) replicate Kahneman, Knetsch, and Thaler (1986)'s results from the ultimatum game, and also study the dictator game. They find that about 20% of dictator proposers offer $0 to their recipient counterparts, as non-cooperative game theory would predict, and conclude that fairness alone cannot be an explanation for the generous offers observed in the ultimatum game. However, in the dictator game, Forsythe et al. (1994) find that about 20% of proposers also offer $5, more offer $3 and offers of $1 and $2, are also made.

Recognizing that the desire to maintain reputation might create expectations that change proposers' behaviors, Hoffman et al. (1994) consider experimental treatments explicitly designed to affect subjects' expectations about operating norms of social exchange: equality, equity, and reciprocity. The design of Kahneman, Knetsch, and Thaler (1986) and Forsythe et al. (1994) invoke the equality norm. No distinction is made between the two individuals "provisionally allocated" $10 and they are told to "divide" the money. Hence, deviations from equal division are more likely to be punished as "cheating" on the social "contract." Using the same task description, Hoffman et al. (1994) replicate Forsythe et al. (1994) in a "random/divide $10" treatment.

To invoke equity, Hoffman et al. (1994) explore three variations on their random/divide $10 treatment in a 2×2 experimental design. First (the exchange treatment), without changing the reduced form of the game, Hoffman et al. (1994) describe it as a market, in which the "seller" (proposer) chooses a "price" (division of $10) and the "buyer" (recipient) indicates whether he or she will "buy" or "not buy" (accept or not accept). This treatment follows from Fouraker and Siegel (1963). Second (the contest treatment), following Hoffman and Spitzer (1985), they require each proposer to earn the property right to be a proposer by scoring higher than the recipients on a general knowledge quiz. Winners are told they have "earned the right" to be proposers. Finally, the exchange and contest treatments are combined into a third treatment.

These treatments invoke the norm of equity: sellers in a market are justified in earning a profit and individuals who have earned the right to a higher return are justified in collecting it. With each treatment, Hoffman et al. (1994) find a significant movement in the direction of the game theoretic equilibrium, with no change in the rejection rate, although the actual equilibrium is not observed and infrequent rejections still occur.

Moreover, these results extend to a division of $100 (Hoffman, McCabe, and Smith, 1996a) and to the dictator game (Hoffman, McCabe, and Smith, 1994). In the random/divide $100 experiments, proposers typically offer $50 and offers less than $50 occasionally get rejected; in the contest/exchange $100 experiments, proposers typically offer $30, but offers of $10 are usually rejected. In the dictator game experiments, dictators do offer less to their counterparts than proposers offer recipients in the ultimatum game; but, few offer $0 and the contest/exchange treatment still results in a significant move toward more self-regarding offers.

Interestingly, however, if sellers in the exchange treatment $10 ultimatum game are prompted by the instructions to "...consider what choice you expect the buyer to make," and to "...consider what you think the buyer expects you to choose," they revert to equal division. Therefore, results in both random/exchange and contest/exchange (with the added instructions) are indistinguishable from random/divide (without the added instructions; see Hoffman, McCabe, and Smith, 1997).

But why do these treatments change offers without changing the rejection rate in the ultimatum game? One hypothesis is that both players infer one another's mental states – in this case expectations – from relevant information in the experiment (Baron-Cohen, 1995). "Mind reading" implies the subconscious, intuitive ability to take the perspective of another person who has common information. In the ultimatum experiment, under contest/exchange without the added instructions, proposers expect recipients to find a lower offer acceptable; while recipients expect, and are prepared to accept, a lower offer. When the instructions to proposers to "think" about what recipients will do are added, proposers are alerted to consciously focus on the strategic possibility of rejection and make more generous offers.

Expectations about recipients' willingness to accept cannot, however, explain why dictators offer any money to their counterparts. We hypothesize that, in this case, observability is potentially powerful in the enforcement of social norms, by exposing lapses in one's intended reputational image. Thus, although Forsythe et al. (1994) recruited proposers and recipients to separate rooms, and the players were anonymous with respect to one another, subject decisions were not anonymous with respect to the experimenter. Someone was still "watching"; hence proposers were still not entirely removed from a social exchange setting where reciprocity norms might subconsciously apply.

This led Hoffman et al. (1994) to design a "double blind" dictator experiment, with several features that were later changed two or more at a time, to investigate the role of social isolation in extinguishing behavior reflecting social norms (Hoffman, McCabe, and Smith, 1996b). In the double blind treatment, 64% of proposers take all $10; about 90% take at least $8.

These results are strikingly different from the dictator results in Forsythe et al. (1994), and from the replications in Hoffman et al. (1994). Next, in three stages, Hoffman, McCabe, and Smith (1996b) vary each of the elements of the double blind dictator experiment in ways intended to reduce the "social distance" between the subjects and anyone who might see their choices. The experimental results form a predicted ordered set of distributions. As the social distance between the subjects and others increases, the cumulative distribution of offers to recipients decreases. These results demonstrate the power of isolation from implied observability in the enforcement of norms of equality, equity, and reciprocity.

4. Interpretations and Discussion

Forsythe et al. (1994) showed via the dictator game that "fairness" as a utilitarian ethic could not, by itself, account for the generosity of offers in the ultimatum game. But, dictators still offered anomalously large sums to their counterparts – 62% gave $2 or more

(65% in our replication, Forsythe et al. (1994)–R) – based on standard economic/game theoretic reasoning. Originally, in Hoffman et al. (1994), we hypothesized that this generosity arises from unconscious expectations of reciprocity which we assumed emerged somehow from cultural experience with repeat interaction outside the laboratory. Subsequently, we systematically varied "social distance" in Hoffman, McCabe, and Smith (1996b) and showed that as this distance, or social isolation, increased, subjects made systematically more self-regarding offers.

In Hoffman, McCabe, and Smith (1996b), our interpretation of what we were doing was importantly influenced by the evolutionary psychology perspective (Cosmides and Tooby, 1992). We had come to realize that simply saying that people were culturally conditioned to reciprocity, left unexplained how and why this occurs. Thus, to say it comes from culture ("fairness," "manners," etc.) begs the question of where culture, particularly these elements of it, comes from. Although the forms and norms of reciprocity vary endlessly across cultures, they are functionally equivalent in promoting cooperation, and in moderating the impact of self-interested actions on social cohesiveness. The evolutionary argument is that a predisposition to reciprocity has fitness value, which has promoted its persistence across homo sapien cultures, ancient and modern, over the past 2–3 million years. Hence, culture is not independent of these evolutionary forces, and vice versa.

From the beginning, our perspective sought explanations in terms of expectations rather than other-regarding utility functions, or a taste for fairness, as in Bolton (1991) and Rabin (1993). Bolton's model was born refuted because it violated the known dictator game results, but Rabin's model is more general. We do not rule out utilitarian models as useful place-holders for more general expectational, judgmental and interactive considerations. The problem is that there is a professional tendency to view utility explanations as final – once a result is deemed due to utility, the conversation stops, implying that there is nothing left to explain or test. Also, we have a problem in seeing how the utilitarian approach can handle the many treatment variations we and others have shown to be effective. If utility varies with all these parametric treatment conditions, why is this so, and how can such a perspective, and modeling, motivate new experiments? Which perspective is most useful (neither can be said to be either true or untrue) will ultimately depend upon its capacity to motivate testable new hypotheses and to coherently explain behavior across observational sets. Currently, we are attracted to the comprehensiveness of the evolutionary/reciprocity interpretation, while remaining open to other possibilities. For a fuller examination of these issues see Hoffman, McCabe, and Smith (1998). For a recent articulation of the fine structure of a utility approach, and its testable implications, see Konow (1996).

References

Baron-Cohen, Simon (1995). "Mindblindness: An Essay on Autism and Theory of Mind". MIT Press, Cambridge, MA.

Bolton, G.E. (1991). "A comparative model of bargaining: Theory and evidence". American Economic Review 81, 1096–1136.

Cosmides, Leda, Tooby, John (1992). "Cognitive adaptations for social exchange". In: Barkow, Jerome H., Cosmides, Leda, Tooby, John (Eds.), The Adapted Mind: Evolutionary Psychology and The Generation of Culture. Oxford University Press, New York.

Fouraker, Lawrence, Siegel, Sidney (1963). "Bargaining Behavior". McGraw–Hill, New York.

Guth, Werner, Schmittberger, Rolf, Schwartze, Bernd (1982). "An experimental analysis of ultimatum bargaining". Journal of Economic Behavior and Organization 3, 367–388.

Forsythe, Robert, Horowitz, Joel, Savin, N.E., Sefton, Martin (1994). "Replicability, fairness and pay in experiments with simple bargaining games". Games and Economic Behavior 6 (3), 347–369.

Hoffman, Elizabeth, Spitzer, Matthew (1985). "Entitlements, rights, and fairness: An experimental examination of subjects' concepts of distributive justice". Journal of Legal Studies 15, 254–297.

Hoffman, Elizabeth, McCabe, Kevin, Smith, Vernon (1996a). "On expectations and monetary stakes in ultimatum games". International Journal of Game Theory 25 (3), 289–301.

Hoffman, Elizabeth, McCabe, Kevin, Smith, Vernon (1996b). "Social distance and other regarding behavior in dictator games". American Economic Review 86 (3), 653–660.

Hoffman, Elizabeth, McCabe, Kevin, Smith, Vernon (1997). "Thinking about it doesn't help". Unpublished manuscript.

Hoffman, Elizabeth, McCabe, Kevin, Smith, Vernon (1998). "Behavioral foundations of reciprocity: Experimental economics and evolutionary psychology". Economic Inquiry 36 (3), 335–352.

Hoffman, Elizabeth, McCabe, Kevin, Shachat, Keith, Smith, Vernon (1994). "Preferences, property rights and anonymity in bargaining games". Games and Economic Behavior 7 (3), 346–380.

Kahneman, Daniel, Knetsch, Jack, Thaler, Richard (1986). "Fairness and the assumptions of economics". In: Hogarth, R., Reder, M. (Eds.), Rational Choice. University of Chicago Press, Chicago.

Konow, James (1996). "Fair shares: Accountability and cognitive dissonance in allocation decisions". Department of Economics, Loyola Marymount University.

Rabin, M. (1993). "Incorporating fairness into game theory and economics". American Economic Review 83, 1281–1302.

Chapter 47

PREFERENCES AND PROPERTY RIGHTS IN ULTIMATUM AND DICTATOR GAMES

ELIZABETH HOFFMAN
Iowa State University

KEVIN MCCABE
University of Arizona

VERNON SMITH
University of Arizona

1. Property Rights Defined

A property right is a guarantee allowing action within guidelines defined by the right. The guarantee is against reprisal, in that a property right places restrictions on punishment strategies that might otherwise be used to insure cooperative behavior. Property rights might be viewed as a means by which society legitimizes (makes "fair" or acceptable) the actions of a rights holder. Such rights are taken for granted in private ownership economies.

In bargaining games, such as the ultimatum game, the proposer may be less influenced by the norm of equality, and more inclined to pursue his or her strategic advantage, if endowed with a legitimate property right. Concurrently, subjects' expectations may be more compatible, and the counterpart less inclined to punish, if the proposer is endowed with a legitimate property right. Hoffman and Spitzer (1985) present experimental data which support this view. The ultimatum game experiments summarized in Hoffman et al. (1994) extend Hoffman and Spitzer (1985)'s property rights assignment to ultimatum games.

2. Experimental Design

We begin with a replication of Forsythe et al. (1994)'s $10 ultimatum game experimental design, with subjects at the University of Arizona and with 12 subjects participating at one time in the same room. We maintain the language that the pair has been "provisionally allocated" the $10 and that the task is to "divide" the $10. We refer to this design as the random/divide $10 experimental treatment. Our results are statistically indistinguishable from Forsythe et al. (1994).

We then induce property rights in the position of proposer in two different, and reinforcing ways. First, following Hoffman and Spitzer (1985), we have proposers "earn the

						Seller Chooses PRICE							
			$0	$1	$2	$3	$4	$5	$6	$7	$8	$9	$10	
Buyer Chooses to	BUY		$0	$1	$2	$3	$4	$5	$6	$7	$8	$9	$10	Seller profit
			$10	$9	$8	$7	$6	$5	$4	$3	$2	$1	$0	Buyer profit
	NOT BUY		$0	$0	$0	$0	$0	$0	$0	$0	$0	$0	$0	Seller profit
			$0	$0	$0	$0	$0	$0	$0	$0	$0	$0	$0	Buyer profit

Figure 1. In the Exchange treatment version of the ultimatum game the seller receives a form like the one shown here. The seller chooses a price by circling one of the amounts from $0 to $10. Note that each price represent an offer to split the $10 exactly as in an ultimatum game. This executed form is then transmitted to the matched buyer who circles either "BUY" or "NOT BUY."

right" to be proposers. After the instructions are read, all 12 subjects answer 10 general knowledge quiz questions, selected at random from a large data bank of questions. The subjects are rank ordered on the basis of the number of right answers; ties are decided on the basis of how rapidly subjects complete all 10 questions. The highest scoring subject is made proposer number 1, the second-highest is proposer number 2, ..., the seventh-highest is made recipient number 1, and so on. The highest scoring subject is paired with the seventh highest, the second is paired with the eighth, and so on. When all the positions have been determined, individuals in the proposer role are privately and individually informed that they have "earned the right" to be proposers. It is common information, however, that the purpose of the general knowledge test is to determine which subjects will earn the right to be proposers.

Second, recognizing that the United States' culture affords sellers the "right" to make a profit by moving first to quote a price, we describe the game as a market, with sellers and buyers instead of proposers and recipients. In early experiments with bi-lateral monopoly using the same strategic structure as the ultimatum game, Fouraker and Siegel (1963) generate sub-game perfect equilibrium results using a seller–buyer exchange.

Figure 1 illustrates our task for sellers and buyers. Notice that the reduced form of the game is identical to an ultimatum game. The seller moves first by choosing a price (division of the $10 payoff). A price of $0 implies $0 for the seller, $10 for the buyer; a price of $5 implies $5 for each; and a price of $9 implies $9 for the seller, $1 for the buyer. The buyer moves second and has the task of deciding whether to buy or not buy (accept or reject the offer). If the buyer circles "buy," the seller is paid the price chosen and the buyer is paid $10 − price. If the buyer circles "not buy," both get $0.

Combining the two methods of inducing a property right in being the proposer creates the 2×2 experimental design described in Figure 2. We ran 24 pairs of subjects in each of four experimental treatment cells: random/divide, random/exchange, contest/divide, and contest/exchange.

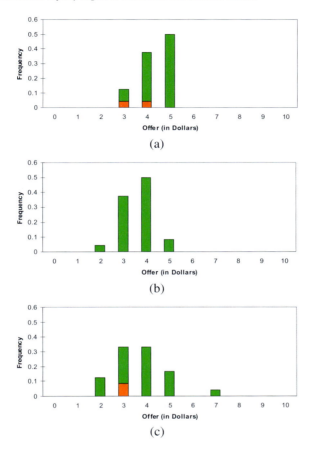

Figure 2. (a) Replication in which 24 pairs use Forsythe et al. (1994) instructions for the $10 ultimatum game with random assignment of the right to propose a division of the $10. (b) Treatment with 24 pairs using Forsythe et al. (1994) instructions, but in each of four sessions with 12 subjects the right to propose a division of the $10 is earned by being among the top 6 scores on a general knowledge quiz. (c) 24 pairs use instructions which formulate the $10 ultimatum game as an exchange between a buyer and a seller (see Figure 1). In each pair the right to be the seller-proposer is assigned at random. (d) 24 pairs use the buyer/seller exchange instructions, but the right to be the seller-proposer is earned by scoring highest on the general knowledge test as above.

3. Ultimatum Results

Figure 2 presents the results for all four experimental treatments. The green bars represent the percentage of accepted offers; the red bars represent the percentage of rejected offers. Where statistical significance is reported, a Wilcoxon rank-sum test is used to compare the sample distributions of all offers across treatments.

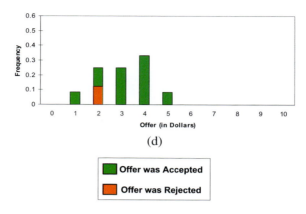

Figure 2. (*continued.*)

Comparing random/divide and contest/divide to determine the independent effect of the general knowledge quiz, we observe a (significant, $p = 0.03$) shift toward lower offers. Comparing random/divide and random/exchange to determine the independent effect of the market frame, we again observe a (significant, $p = 0.03$) shift toward lower offers. Comparing random/exchange and contest/exchange, the latter induces a (significant) shift toward lower offers. Comparing contest/divide and contest/exchange, the latter causes a (insignificant) reduction in offers. Finally, the difference between random/divide and the combined contest/exchange treatment represents a (highly significant, $p = 0.00$) shift toward lower offers.

The recipient results are particularly important in determining the effect of different ways of inducing property rights on shared expectations and the resulting impact on subject behavior. The first thing to note is that the rejection rates are uniformly low: 2/24 (8.3%) in random/divide; 0/24 in contest/divide; 2/24 (8.3%) in random/exchange; and 3/24 (12.5%) in contest/exchange. Moreover, none of these is statistically significantly different, either from one another or from the Forsythe et al. (1994) $10 ultimatum game results. Thus, each treatment is successful in inducing not only a change in proposer behavior, but also in recipient expectations about appropriate proposer behavior.

4. Dictator Games and Results

Hoffman et al. (1994) also report results comparing the random/divide $10 treatment with the contest/exchange $10 treatment in dictator games. In Figure 1, when the form is used for the dictator exchange, the buyer cannot refuse to buy, and must accept whatever is offered. The results are shown in Figure 3. Under the random/divide treatment, 17.9% of the proposers offer nothing to their counterparts, and 25% offer $5. Under the treatment that combines exchange with an earned property right, 41.7% offer nothing

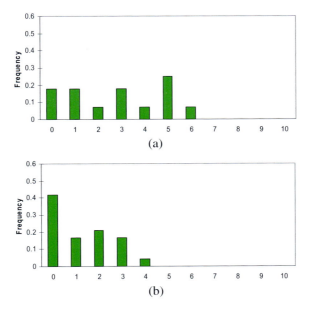

Figure 3. (a) Replication in which 28 pairs use Forsythe et al. (1994) instructions for the $10 dictator game with random assignment of the right to dictate a division of the $10. (b) Treatment in which 24 pairs use instructions that formulate the $10 dictator game as an exchange between a buyer and a seller. In each pair the right to be the seller-dictator is earned by scoring highest on a general knowledge quiz.

and there are no offers of $5. Consequently, the shift in shared expectations, and behavior, with the implied property right treatments in ultimatum games carries over to dictator games.

5. Discussion

These results demonstrate quite clearly the impact of property rights on the shared expectations about appropriate proposer behavior in both ultimatum and dictator games. If the game is presented as division (which by one definition means literally to separate into equal parts by a divisor) and players are randomly assigned to positions, there is no legitimate reason why the proposer should be allowed to exploit his or her strategic advantage. The norm of equality applies and both players assume that is the operating norm. Thus, in the ultimatum game, the proposer knows that deviations from equal division may be punished. In the dictator game, less than 20% of the dictators feel justified in leaving $0 and 25% still feel compelled to give $5.

However, when the game is presented as a market, with the proposer named the seller, the norm of equity allows the seller to earn a "profit" on the exchange. Similarly, when the proposer must "earn the right" to be a proposer, the norm of equity allows the proposer to legitimately offer less than half. When the two procedures for inducing property rights are combined, sellers in the ultimatum game, who have earned the right to be sellers, make the smallest offers, and those smallest offers are accepted by the buyers. Now we observe even a small percentage of subgame perfect outcomes (2 in 24 offer $1). Moreover, in the contest/exchange dictator experiments, nearly 50% of the seller dictators, who have earned the right to be sellers, give $0 (the subgame perfect outcome) to their counterparts, and no sellers give $5.

In the ultimatum game experiments, proposers are engaging in reciprocity in all four property rights treatments. How they decide to exercise reciprocity is affected by the shared expectations about appropriate proposer behavior in each treatment. In the dictator game experiments, the shared change in expectations operates to change the dictators' assessments of what is appropriate behavior in a world in which reputations for reciprocity matter.

References

Forsythe, Robert, Horowitz, Joel, Savin, N.E., Sefton, Martin (1994). "Replicability, fairness and pay in experiments with simple bargaining games". Games and Economic Behavior 6 (3), 347–369.

Fouraker, Lawrence, Siegel, Sidney (1963). "Bargaining Behavior". McGraw–Hill, New York.

Hoffman, Elizabeth, Spitzer, Matthew (1985). "Entitlements, rights, and fairness: An experimental examination of subjects' concepts of distributive justice". Journal of Legal Studies 15, 254–297.

Hoffman, Elizabeth, McCabe, Kevin, Shachat, Keith, Smith, Vernon (1994). "Preferences, property rights and anonymity in bargaining games". Games and Economic Behavior 7 (3), 346–380.

Chapter 48

PROMPTING STRATEGIC REASONING INCREASES OTHER-REGARDING BEHAVIOR

ELIZABETH HOFFMAN
Iowa State University

KEVIN MCCABE
University of Arizona

VERNON SMITH
University of Arizona

1. Introduction

1.1. Previous Results

In two previous papers (Hoffman et al., 1994; Hoffman, McCabe, and Smith, 1996) we document the effects of property rights and monetary stakes on first-mover offers and second-mover responses in an ultimatum game based on the design of Kahneman, Knetsch, and Thaler (1986) and Forsythe et al. (1994). In the Kahneman, Knetsch, and Thaler (1986) and Forsythe et al. (1994) design, two players, are "provisionally allocated" M. Player 1 is asked to propose a "division" of the M, by making a offer of X to player 2. Player 2 then indicates whether he or she accepts or rejects the division. If player 2 accepts the division, player 2 receives X and player 1 receives $M - X. If player 2 rejects the division, both players receive $0. Under the usual rationality conditions, the equilibrium of this game is for player 1 to offer player 2 the smallest $ unit of account, and for player 2 to accept that offer. Hereafter we refer to player 1 as the proposer and player 2 as the recipient.

In the Kahneman, Knetsch, and Thaler (1986) and Forsythe et al. (1994) design, which we replicate in Hoffman et al. (1994), players do not behave as predicted by economic/game theoretic equilibrium theory. Instead, most proposers offer half the pie to recipients and some recipients reject offers of less than half the pie. This has led to considerable discussion in the literature about "fairness" in ultimatum and related two-person interactive games, where use of the word "fairness" implies an other-regarding utilitarian basis for the behavior.

We have taken a different perspective. In Hoffman et al. (1994), we consider the effect of inducing a property right in the proposer position. Our reasoning is that proposers may be more inclined to pursue their self interest when endowed with rights to the proposer position that are deemed legitimate. Similarly, subject expectations may be more compatible, and the recipients less inclined to reject, if the proposer is endowed with a legitimizing property right. Hoffman and Spitzer (1985) present experimental data which support this view.

We use both a general knowledge quiz, reinforced by telling the proposers they have "earned the right" to be proposers (contest), and a seller–buyer market frame (exchange) to induce property rights in being sellers. We refer to the Kahneman, Knetsch, and Thaler (1986) and Forsythe et al. (1994) design as random/divide and compare it to a contest/exchange treatment that combines the two methods of inducing property rights. This combined treatment change significantly lowers proposer/seller offers with no change in the rejection rate.

In Hoffman, McCabe, and Smith (1996), we replicate the above experiments using $100 to divide in $10 increments, instead of $10 to divide in $1 increments. Some might reason that with $100 to divide, subjects would be more likely to play the game "correctly" (i.e., play the equilibrium strategy). On the other hand, if reciprocity norms are important in determining recipient inclinations to reject, then raising the stakes to $100 can also be seen as raising the opportunity cost of making the "wrong" offer.

We find the second explanation more compelling than the first. We compare random/divide $10, random/divide $100, contest/exchange $10, and contest/exchange $100. We find no significant differences in proposer/seller offers as a result of the change in monetary stakes. Random/divide $10 leads to $5 offers and random/divide $100 leads to $50 offers. Contest/exchange $10 and $100 both lead to lower offers that are still above the predicted equilibrium. Moreover, in the random/divide $100 experiments, subjects reject as much as $40, just as $4 is occasionally rejected in $10 ultimatums.

The only difference we detect is that the rejection rate in the contest/exchange $100 experiments is significantly higher than in the other experiments, although it is still quite low. We hypothesize that, with $100 at stake, the property right leads sellers to attempt to exploit their strategic advantage by slightly more than buyers are willing to accept. The offers are slightly lower in contest/exchange $100 than in contest/exchange $10, although the difference is not statistically significant. In the unfamiliar world of $100 ultimatum experiments, the property right treatment is not fully successful in inducing a change in shared expectations about a equitable division of the $100.

The finding that, by changing the allocation rule for assigning the property right to be the proposer we generally change both proposer offers and recipient acceptances, raises interesting questions about how individuals form and change expectations about equitable divisions. We explore the foundations of subject expectations in Hoffman, McCabe, and Smith (1998). In that paper, we hypothesize, based on research in evolutionary psychology that the evolution of the human brain has resulted in the development of specialized mental modules for the solution of complex problems involving cooperation: trust and trustworthy behavior, cheater detection, and reciprocity. These mental modules lead human beings to respond to situations encouraging cooperation with behaviors that cannot be sustained if humans were to make decisions on the basis of the propositional logic. Subjects bring to the lab behaviors and strategies that promote cooperation and they rely upon those known behaviors and strategies when they face decision problems in the unfamiliar world of the experimental laboratory. Certain experimental mechanisms we study in the lab, such as the double auction, successfully extinguish cooperative behavior in a short period of time. Others, such as the asset market (Smith, Suchanek, and Williams, 1988) and the fiat money market (McCabe, 1989), require several periods of "training" before subjects abandon their preconceived notions of cooperation and behave as predicted by standard game theoretic models. Still others, such as the ultimatum game, may simply reinforce cooperative behavior. Our continuing research agenda involves studying the connections between brain function and economic decisionmaking.

1.2. The Current Experiment

One of the questions left unanswered from the results of Hoffman et al. (1994) is the potential effect of calling subjects' attention to the interactive property of the task at hand. In other words, what will happen if proposers are primed, or prompted, to think strategically about the problem before making an offer. This question was partially answered in the $100 experiments reported in Hoffman, McCabe, and Smith (1996). Presumably, raising the stakes to $100 induces at least some subjects to think more carefully about the consequences of their decisions than when the stakes are $10. As we saw, raising the stakes from $10 to $100 had no significant effect on proposer offers; although, it did have a small but significant effect on recipient rejections. This result suggests that making it more salient to be attentive to the task does not, by itself, have the effect of moving subjects closer to a game theoretic equilibrium.

In the experiments reported in this chapter we address this issue more directly. Focusing just on the exchange treatments, we add to both the random/exchange and the contest/exchange designs, outlined in Hoffman et al. (1994), as a suggestion to the seller to consider what the buyer will do. The results are dramatic and in the opposite direction from what might be expected. In both the random/exchange and the contest/exchange treatments, there is a significant increase in seller offers to buyers as a consequence of introducing the added instructions. Moreover, with the added instructions, there is no longer any significant difference between random/exchange and contest/exchange and there is no longer any significant difference between the original random/divide treatment without the added instructions and the contest/exchange and random/exchange treatments with the added instructions. This result suggests that encouraging sellers to be more thoughtful focuses their attention on the strategic interaction with humans who think the way they do, and who may punish them for unacceptable behavior, and not on the logic of the game theoretic structure of the problem.

2. Experimental Design and Subject Recruitment

Subjects are recruited according to the usual recruitment procedures at the University of Arizona Economic Science Laboratory. The experiments without the added instructions

Table 1
Wilcoxon rank-sum test (level of significance)

	Random exchange added instruction	Contest exchange added instruction
Hoffman et al. (1994) random exchange	1.9 (0.06)	
Hoffman et al. (1994) contest exchange		2.7 (0.01)

are the same as the random/exchange and contest/exchange experiments reported in the appendix of Hoffman et al. (1994). In the new experiments, we add the two sentences to the sellers' choice forms. These two sentences are designed to prompt the subjects to think about the strategic aspects of their decisions: "Before making your choice, consider what choice you expect the buyer to make. Also consider what you think the buyer expects you to choose." Otherwise, the instructions and experimental procedures are identical to those reported in Hoffman et al. (1994).

3. Experimental Results

Figure 1 summarizes the experimental results for random/exchange and contest/exchange, with and without the added instructions. Notice that the added instructions, which simply urge sellers to think about buyer responses, shift both the random/exchange and the contest/exchange offers back toward the more equal splits characteristic of Kahneman, Knetsch, and Thaler (1986), Forsythe et al. (1994), and the Hoffman et al. (1994) random/divide treatment. The random/exchange offers shift from a dual mode of $3 and $4 to a strong mode of $5. In the contest/exchange experiments, the added instructions eliminate all offers of $1 or $2, and increase the proportion of offers between $4 and $6. Table 1 shows that these shifts are significant under the Wilcoxon test. These results suggest that, when sellers are reminded of the strategic nature of buyer/seller interaction and the possibility of rejection, sellers are more likely to share their profits equally with buyers.

4. Discussion

As we note in Hoffman et al. (1994) and Hoffman, McCabe, and Smith (1996, 1998), current cultural norms with regard to sharing, cooperation, trust, and punishment are the result of 2–3 million years of evolution and adaptation. During most of those 2–3 million years, humans lived in small interactive groups and developed behaviors and strategies to promote cooperation and social exchange within the group. Within such groups, humans were expected to share with one another and to cooperate to advance the group. This is clear in contemporary studies of extant hunter–gatherer societies.

Ch. 48: Prompting Strategic Reasoning Increases Other-regarding Behavior

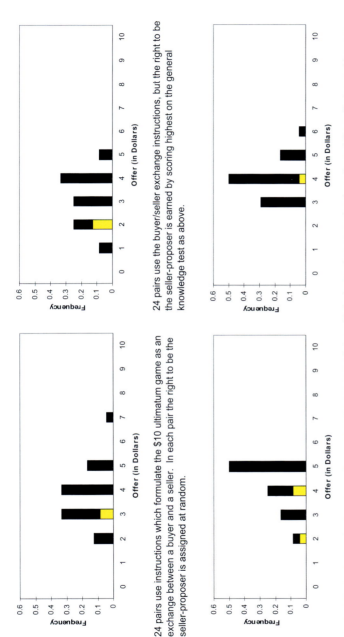

Figure 1. Offers: frequency and rejection rates.

Today, experimental subjects bring many of the same behaviors and strategies to our laboratories. This results in far more cooperative and sharing behavior in first-time decisions than standard game theory would predict. Yet, as we showed in Hoffman et al. (1994) and Hoffman, McCabe, and Smith (1996), we can induce a more game theoretic solution by giving the proposer/sellers a legitimizing property right in their position. Our current results show how fragile is that change. When we draw sellers' attention to considering what the buyer will do, they internalize the potential threat of punishment, not that the buyer prefers more money to less and will thus accept a lower offer. Prompting not only does not help; it makes the results once again like what we observe in the random/divide treatment, the treatment that started so many psychologists and economists wondering about the standard economics rationality assumption.

References

Forsythe, Robert, Horowitz, Joel, Savin, N.E., Sefton, Martin (1994). "Replicability, fairness and pay in experiments with simple bargaining games". Games and Economic Behavior 6 (3), 347–369.

Hoffman, Elizabeth, Spitzer, Matthew (1985). "Entitlements, rights, and fairness: An experimental examination of subjects' concepts of distributive justice". Journal of Legal Studies 15, 254–297.

Hoffman, Elizabeth, McCabe, Kevin, Smith, Vernon (1996). "On expectations and monetary stakes in ultimatum games". International Journal of Game Theory 25 (3), 289–301.

Hoffman, Elizabeth, McCabe, Kevin, Smith, Vernon (1998). "Behavioral foundations of reciprocity: Experimental economics and evolutionary psychology". Economic Inquiry 36 (3), 335–352.

Hoffman, Elizabeth, McCabe, Kevin, Shachat, Keith, Smith, Vernon (1994). "Preferences, property rights and anonymity in bargaining games". Games and Economic Behavior 7 (3), 346–380.

Kahneman, Daniel, Knetsch, Jack, Thaler, Richard (1986). "Fairness and the assumptions of economics". In: Hogarth, R., Reder, M. (Eds.), Rational Choice. University of Chicago Press, Chicago.

McCabe, Kevin (1989). "Fiat money as a store of value in an experimental market". Journal of Economic Behavior and Organization 12 (2), 215–231.

Smith, Vernon L., Suchanek, Gerry L., Williams, Arlington W. (1988). "Bubbles, crashes, and endogenous expectations in experimental spot asset markets". Econometrica 56, 1119–1151.

Chapter 49

SOCIAL DISTANCE AND RECIPROCITY IN DICTATOR GAMES

ELIZABETH HOFFMAN
Iowa State University

KEVIN MCCABE
University of Arizona

VERNON SMITH
University of Arizona

1. Defining Variations on Perceived Social Distance in Dictator Games

We define social distance as the degree of reciprocity that people believe is inherent within a social interaction. The greater the social distance, or isolation, between a person and others, the weaker is the scope for reciprocal relations.

2. Experimental Design

Our examination of this issue begins with the dictator experiments reported by Forsythe et al. (1994). Their motivation was to test the hypothesis that the tendency toward an equal split of the pie in ultimatum games was driven by a desire for fair, or equal, division. The test was effected by comparing dictator game results, where the recipient does not have the power to reject the proposer's offer, with corresponding ultimatum game results. Forsythe et al. (1994) report a significant reduction in dictator game offers, as compared with ultimatum game offers and conclude that "fairness" alone cannot account for the generosity of ultimatum offers.

Yet, 80% of the subjects gave positive amounts of money to their anonymous counterparts in the Forsythe et al. (1994) dictator games. Why should this occur? We conjectured that this was because of two key features of the instructions, used originally by Kahneman, Knetsch, and Thaler (1986, pp. 105–106), and duplicated by Forsythe et al. (1994), whose concern was to replicate the earlier procedures. However, these two features introduced additional treatments: (1) a subject and his or her anonymous counterpart had been "provisionally allocated" $10; and (2) the task is to decide how to "divide" the $10. Since the experimenter provisionally allocated the $10 pie to both members in each pair, the entitlement was shared, which might suggest they are part of a social exchange community where "fairness" norms apply. Similarly, the term "divide" suggests sharing or even equal division (see the definition of "divide" in Webster).

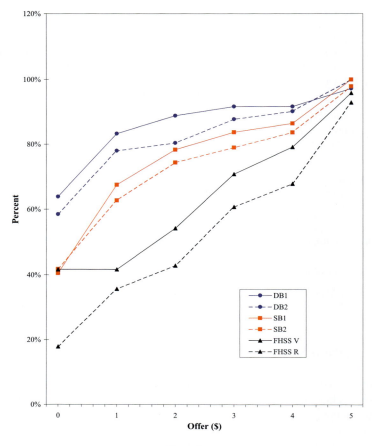

Figure 1.

2.1. Replicating Forsythe et al. (1994)

We begin by noting that we applied these same instructional elements to $N = 28$ pairs of University of Arizona subjects, and found no significant difference between the data reported by Forsythe et al. (1994) and our replication, denoted FHSS-R (see Figure 1) showing that the Forsythe et al. (1994) results extend to different subjects and experimenters. (From this point on, we are referring to data reported in Hoffman, McCabe, and Smith, 1996.)

Figure 1. In DB1, fifteen subjects are recruited to room A and fourteen subjects are recruited to room B. In the following description, (i)–(iv) represent conditions that are altered in subsequent instructional treatments. (i) One subject from room A is chosen to be the monitor. (ii) The subjects are informed that there are fourteen envelopes. Twelve envelopes contain ten one dollar bills and ten blank slips of paper, two envelopes contain 20 blank slips of paper. Subjects in room A are called one at a time, and select an unmarked opaque envelope chosen at random from the box of 14 envelopes. The subject takes the envelope to the back of the room, and sits behind a large cardboard box which maintains his or her privacy. (iii) The subject opens the envelope, and decides how many one dollar bills to keep and how many bills to leave for a person in room B; the bills taken are replaced by blank sheets of paper, so that the envelopes are all the same thickness. (iv) After a subject has made a decision, he or she is asked to seal the envelope and return it to a box near the exit door. The subject then leaves the experiment. This is repeated until all subjects have left room A. The experimenter next takes the box of envelopes to room B. Upon arriving at room B, the monitor and experimenter sit outside the room, and the subjects are called one at a time. In the subject's presence, an envelope is chosen, opened, and the envelope's contents are recorded by the monitor on plain paper containing no names. The subject is then given the envelope's contents, and he or she leaves the experiment. This is repeated until all subjects have left room B. In a second treatment (DB2), we omit (i) the paid monitor and (ii) the two blank envelopes. Complete anonymity is now no longer guaranteed, but is highly likely as long as someone leaves money. In SB1, everything is the same as in DB2, except that we modify (iv), so that the experimenter now learns each decision maker's decision. SB2 is identical to SB1, except that we now modify (iii). The envelope now contains a decision form for making the decision (as in FHHS), instead of money. Money is received when the form is presented to the instructor. FHSS-R is a pure replication of Forsythe et al. (1994). FHSS-V is a treatment variation on the instructions for FHSS-R. We simply omit the phrase: "has been provisionally allocated" $10, and the description that the task is to "divide" the $10 in FHSS-R.

2.2. FHSS-V

Next consider a treatment variation on the instructions for FHSS-R. The object is to subtly increase the social distance between proposer and receiver in the dictator game. We implement this objective very simply by just omitting the phrase: "has been provisionally allocated" $10, and the description that the task is to "divide" the $10. Our instructions simply state that there are 10 one dollar bills, and each person in room A is to decide how many one dollar bills to keep and how many to send to a person in room B. The hypothesis is that the indicated elements together suggest a closeness or community of sharing, and the existence of a social exchange framework, which subtly triggers greater reciprocity (more generous proposal) behavior.

We conjecture that the FHSS-V treatment defines a minimal increase in the social distance between proposer and recipient, as compared with the FHSS-R treatment. At the other pole, which we use to define the maximal social distance (Double Blind 1 below), the experiment is operated "double blind," meaning that the procedures make it evident to all subjects that the experimenter, who makes and retains no record of the data by subject name, and any person who subsequently sees the data, can never know who made what decision. The objective of this procedure is to remove all social context in a manner that is transparent to the subjects.

After implementing the Double Blind 1 (DB1) procedure, which is a large step-out variation on FHSS-R, we use the social distance reasoning to relax one or two elements at a time in the instructional language of DB1 and define three other treatments: Double Blind 2 (DB2), Single Blind 1 (SB1), and Single Blind 2 (SB2), which we predict move the data sequentially closer to the conditions of our FHSS-V treatment, and form an ordered series.

In our original Double Blind Dictator experiments, fifteen subjects are recruited to room A and fourteen subjects are recruited to room B. Subjects are met by an experimenter, paid a $5 show up fee, given a set of instructions, and asked to sit at assigned seats which are positioned so as to keep subjects as separate as possible. Subjects are also reminded that there should be no talking or other attempts to communicate during the experiment. The instructions are reproduced in the Appendix of Hoffman et al. (1994) under "Dictator, Divide $10, Double Blind 1."

In the following description, sentences labeled (i)–(iv) represent conditions that are altered in subsequent instructional treatments. (i) One subject from room A is chosen to be the monitor and will be paid $10. The experimenter than reads aloud the instructions. By reading the instructions aloud, the subjects can verify that they all have the same instructions. After the instructions are read, the decision making part of the experiment begins. (ii) The instructions inform the subjects that there are fourteen envelopes. Twelve envelopes contain ten one dollar bills and ten blank slips of paper, and two envelopes contain 20 blank slips of paper. Subjects in room A are called one at a time and are asked to bring personal belongings with them. This insures a clean exit. Once called, a subject is handed an unmarked opaque envelope chosen at random from the box of 14 envelopes. The subject takes the envelope to the back of the room, and sits behind a large cardboard box which maintains his or her privacy. (iii) The subject opens the envelope, and decides how many one dollar bills to keep and how many bills to leave for a person in room B; all bills taken are replaced by blank sheets of paper, so that the envelopes are all the same thickness. (iv) After a subject has made a decision, he/she is asked to seal the envelope and return it to a box near the exit door. The subject then leaves the experiment. This is repeated until all subjects have left room A. The experimenter next takes the box of envelopes to room B.

Upon arriving at room B, the monitor (and experimenter) sits outside the room, and the subjects are called one at a time. In the subject's presence, an envelope is chosen, opened, and the envelope's contents are recorded by the monitor on plain paper containing no names. The subject is then given the envelope's contents, and he or she leaves the experiment. This is repeated until all subjects have left room B. At this point the monitor is paid and the experiment is over.

In our DB1 experiments, we guarantee complete anonymity by including the two envelopes containing 20 blank slips (ii). Without this precaution, if everyone in room A takes all $10, then each person's decision is clearly known by the experimenter, and perhaps others. However, with the existence of two dummy envelopes, the experimenter and the receivers in room B cannot know whether any one person in room A has left no money, or merely received a dummy envelope. The blank envelopes (ii) are expected to magnify the dictator's sense of isolation, and the existence of a monitor (i) removes the experimenter as an executor of the procedure (although as noted in

2.3. Double Blind 2 (DB2)

We examine these hypotheses in a second treatment that omits (i) the paid monitor and (ii) the two blank envelopes (DB2). Complete anonymity is now no longer guaranteed, but is highly likely as long as someone leaves money. Offers in DB2 are expected to increase, since we have weakened the sense of social isolation. It was in conducting DB2 that we first observed aspects of subject behavior that sensitized us to the subtle features of anonymity and social distance (Hoffman et al., 1994, footnote 9). Not all of the subjects in room A sealed their envelopes as instructed, and both of the experimenters (in this case McCabe and Smith) noted that, most revealingly, there was a pronounced tendency for those leaving no money to seal their envelopes, and for those leaving money to not seal their envelopes. We had not had the opportunity to observe this in DB1 because we used a subject monitor. This experience brought home to us the features of detectability, and reduced privacy, made possible by the presence of an experimenter.

2.4. Single Blind 1 (SB1)

In our next treatment, SB1, everything is the same as in DB2, except that we modify (iv), so that the experimenter now learns each decision maker's decision. The appendix to Hoffman, McCabe, and Smith (1996) contains the instructions for SB1. This is done by (a) having the subject return to the experimenter after deciding what to leave in the envelope; and (b) having his or her unsealed envelope opened behind a large cardboard box at the experimenter's desk. This insures isolation with respect to other subjects, but not with respect to the experimenter. (c) The amount he or she has offered is then recorded on a sheet by the subject's name, (d) the envelope is sealed, and (e) the subject drops it in the return box and leaves. We predict that allowing the experimenter to know the decision makers' decisions reduces their social isolation and increases offers. Except for the use of envelopes containing the money, we have moved closer to the procedures used by Forsythe et al. (1994) and others.

2.5. Single Blind 2 (SB2)

Our last condition, SB2, is identical to SB1, except that we now modify (iii). The envelope now contains a decision form for making the decision (as in FHHS), instead of money, and we use the following procedure. (a) A subject fills out the form in the back of the room behind a cardboard box. (b) The subject returns to the experimenter in the front of the room, where (c) his or her envelope is opened behind a cardboard box, and (d) the subject is paid the amount he or she has decided to keep. This is recorded opposite the subject's name on a data sheet. (e) If the decision gives money to a subject in room B, the money is placed in the envelope, the envelope is sealed, and (f) the subject

Table 1

	Experiment	Number of observations	Anonymity condition	Decision type
1	DB1	36	Double blind and blanks[a]	Dollars
2	DB2	41	Double blind	Dollars
3	SB1	37	Single blind	Dollars
4	SB2	43	Single blind	Form
5	FHSS-V	28	Single blind	No Sharing Language
6	FHSS-R	28	Single	Sharing Language

[a] Includes two envelopes with 20 blank slips and a monitor paid $10.

drops it in the return box as he or she leaves the room. The actual instructions are in the appendix to Hoffman, McCabe, and Smith (1996). This treatment corresponds to the standard way that subjects are paid in experiments, but the use of an intermediate form further socializes the transaction. We ask whether it makes a difference that the envelope contains a credit (or IOU), to be exchanged for money with the experimenter, instead of the actual money to be divided. Since SB2 creates a direct transaction between the subject and the experimenter (in order to get paid) social distance is narrowed, and we predict that offers will increase relative to SB1.

While SB2 is expected to provide the shortest social distance, and yield the most generous offers among the above four treatments, there remain important instructional differences between SB2 and FHSS-V. Particularly important for creating transparency, is that in SB2, as in SB1, DB1, and DB2, all subjects in room A act out, and observe others acting out, the privacy conditions described in the instructions. The decision form is in an envelope, the subject chooses an envelope and carries it to the privacy box, returns it to the experimenter (the monitor in DB1), and so on. Therefore, we expect offers to be less generous in SB2 than in FHSS-V.

3. Experimental Design and Research Hypothesis

The experimental treatments described above are summarized in the design shown in Table 1. Letting $F(\bullet)$ be the population distributions of offers for each of the six treatments, DB1, DB2, SB1, SB2, FHSS-V, and FHSS-R, the hypothesis is:

HR: $F(\text{DB1}) > F(\text{DB2}) > F(\text{SB1}) > F(\text{SB2}) > F(\text{FHSS-V}) > F(\text{FHSS-R})$,

which we test against the null hypothesis that the treatment samples come from population distributions that are identical.

4. Results

Figure 1 plots the cumulative distribution of offers for all six treatments. As the social distance conditions are weakened from DB1, progressively through FHSS-R, we observe, as stated in HR, that the offer probability distributions decrease. Using the Jonchkeere non-parametric order test statistic, as reported in Hoffman, McCabe, and Smith (1996), the null hypothesis that the distributions are indistinguishable across treatments, is rejected in favor of HR. The results for DB1 have been independently replicated by two other researchers: Burnham (2003) and Eckel and Grossman (1996).

References

Burnham, T.C. (2003). "Engineering altruism: An experimental investigation of anonymity and gift giving". Journal of Economic Behavior and Organization 50 (1), 133–144.
Eckel, Catherine, Grossman, Philip (1996). "Altruism in anonymous dictator games". Games and Economic Behavior 16 (2), 181–191.
Forsythe, Robert, Horowitz, Joel, Savin, N.E., Sefton, Martin (1994). "Replicability, fairness and pay in experiments with simple bargaining games". Games and Economic Behavior 6 (3), 347–369.
Hoffman, Elizabeth, McCabe, Kevin, Smith, Vernon (1996). "Social distance and other regarding behavior in dictator games". American Economic Review 86 (3), 653–660.
Hoffman, Elizabeth, McCabe, Kevin, Shachat, Keith, Smith, Vernon (1994). "Preferences, property rights and anonymity in bargaining games". Games and Economic Behavior 7 (3), 346–380.
Kahneman, Daniel, Knetsch, Jack, Thaler, Richard (1986). "Fairness and the assumptions of economics". In: Hogarth, R., Reder, M. (Eds.), Rational Choice. University of Chicago Press, Chicago.

Chapter 50

FAIRNESS IN ULTIMATUM BARGAINING

J. KEITH MURNIGHAN

Northwestern University

When bargaining winds down to its endgame, one party often makes a 'take it or leave it' offer to the other (e.g., Roth, Murnighan, and Schoumaker, 1988). If this offer is a true ultimatum (i.e., it really means 'take it or leave it') and if it provides the recipient with a positive outcome, game theory's models of subgame perfect equilibrium (Selten, 1965) suggest that the recipient should accept it. Since something is better than nothing, the models suggest that rational respondents should accept any positively valued offer, even if it is very small.

Güth, Schmittberger, and Schwarze (1982) tested this prediction with the first experiment on ultimatums. Their ultimatum offerers controlled a specific amount of money and had complete discretion about how much of it to offer to the respondent, who could either accept or reject the offer. Acceptance led to the respondent receiving the amount offered and the offerer receiving the rest; rejection meant that both parties received nothing. Once an offer had been made, it could not be changed, and the respondent could only accept or reject it.

Güth and van Damme's (1998) original experiment had 21 offerers making a single offer to 21 respondents, dividing from 4 to 10 Deutschmarks. Seven people proposed 50–50 agreements, the average was 65–35, and two offers were rejected. The same participants made offers and responses the next week as well, resulting in three 50–50 offers, an average offer of 69–31, and six rejections. The authors concluded that "subjects often rely on what they consider to be a fair result."

Güth and van Damme's (1998) findings have stimulated considerable research on the underlying causes of larger-than-expected ultimatum offers and of ultimatum rejections. Subsequent empirical findings indicate that average offers typically approach 50–50 divisions of the payoff and, as the value of an offer drops, rejections become more frequent (see Roth, 1995 for a more comprehensive summary of this research). Even in games expanded to two or more periods, with offers alternating between the players, there is a strong pull toward 50–50 offers (e.g., Ochs and Roth, 1989). As a result, other authors have also suggested that fairness drives the results (Güth and Tietz, 1990).

Concerns for fairness can lead offerers to increase their offers to be fair to respondents, and it can lead respondents to reject offers that they feel are unfair. Recent research has investigated both possibilities. Several studies (e.g., Croson, 1993; Harrison and McCabe, 1992; Prasnikar and Roth, 1994) have provided data suggesting that larger-than-expected offers are based on offerers' desires to avoid rejection. We present the results of two additional studies here. The first (Straub and Murnighan, 1995) defined fairness for the first time in the context of ultimatum games; the second (Pillutla and Murnighan, 1995) manipulated fairness concerns to more clearly determine their part in the calculation of ultimatum offers.

Several papers have suggested that there may be reasons other than fairness for respondents to reject offers. Binmore, Shaked, and Sutton (1985) suggested that spite might drive rejections; Straub and Murnighan (1995) elaborated on this idea with their wounded pride/spite model. They posited that the receipt of an offer that was less than expected would wound a respondent's pride, make them angry, and generate enough spite to reject positively valued offers. The results of Pillutla and Murnighan's (1996) test of this model are summarized here.

Among the increasing number of experiments on ultimatums, it appears that the strongest evidence for fairness comes from Kahneman, Knetsch, and Thaler (1986): they found that people were willing to sacrifice some of their own outcome (taking $5 rather than $6) to punish someone who had offered an unequal division to another player in a previous game. In sharp contrast, Kravitz and Gunto's (1992) offerers reported that they would make extremely small offers if they knew that respondents would accept any offer. Roth (1995) summarized the research on ultimatums by saying that "the deviations from the equilibrium predictions reflect systematic features of the bargaining environment" (p. 274). As the following data will show, these systematic features seem to have little to do with true concerns for fairness.

1. Defining and Investigating the Impact of Fairness Concerns

Straub and Murnighan's (1995) ultimatum offerers made a series of offers, knowing that only one of them might be put into effect. They also acted as respondents, accepting or rejecting a series of offers, ostensibly from different offerers. Payoffs always depended on the selection of one of their offers or responses in a lottery. Individual payoffs ranged from a matter of cents to as much as $97 for a task that took less than an hour; the expected return, however, tended to be quite small.

Our major addition to ultimatum research methods was the inclusion of a partial information condition, where respondents did not know how much offerers were dividing. Respondents in previous studies almost uniformly knew the amount that the offerer was dividing. By including a condition where respondents did not have this information, we were able to operationally define fairness. That is, we defined identical offers in the partial and complete information conditions as truly fair; we defined consistent 50–50 offers as perfectly fair. Offers that were larger when offerers knew that respondents knew how much they were dividing were operationally defined as strategic. The underlying logic here is that offerers will increase the size of their complete information offers to appear fair to informed respondents; they need not be so careful with uninformed respondents.

The results indicated that complete information offers were significantly larger than partial information offers, indicating that most offerers were strategic rather than truly

Table 1
Frequency of respondents who accepted any offer, and mean and median lowest acceptable offers in complete and partial information conditions; experiment 1; Straub and Murnighan (1993)

Condition	Number (%) accepting any offer	Mean lowest acceptable offer	Median lowest acceptable offer
Partial information	29/45 (64%)	$1.04	$0.01
Complete information:			
$10	11/46 (24%)	$1.92	$1.00
$30	13/49 (27%)	$6.36	$4.00
$50	13/49 (27%)	$10.38	$7.50
$60	13/49 (27%)	$12.94	$9.00
$80	12/49 (24%)	$17.43	$12.00
$100	12/49 (24%)	$20.21	$15.00
$1,000	10/49 (20%)	$166.68	$100.00
$1,000,000	10/49 (20%)	$104,866.50	$5000.00

Table 2
Expected payoffs to offerers in the complete information conditions; experiment 1; Straub and Murnighan (1995)

Amount to be divided	Optimal offer	Expected payoff from $.01 offer	Expected payoff from median offer	Expected payoff from 50% offer	Expected payoff from optimal offer
$10	$3	$2.39	$5.00	$5.00	$5.33
$30	$5	$7.96	$11.76	$14.69	$15.31
$50	$10	$13.26	$24.49	$24.49	$25.31
$60	$20.30	$15.92	$29.39	$29.39	$29.39
$80	$40	$19.59	$38.37	$38.37	$38.37
$100	$20	$24.49	$43.78	$48.98	$50.61

fair. In addition, respondents indicated that they would accept significantly smaller offers in the partial, compared to the complete information conditions (see Figure 1b). In fact, a majority indicated that, when they did not know how much was being divided, they would accept any offer (even one penny; see Figure 1a).

Our results and those of Harrison and McCabe (1992) also showed that 50–50 offers were actually more effective (in an expected value sense, given our samples of respondents) than small offers and, in many cases, provided offerers with their best possible returns (see Figure 2). More generally, Prasnikar and Roth (1992) suggested that unpredicted, non-equilibrium behavior in ultimatum games is more valuable and effective than equilibrium behavior for offerers. Thus, it appears that expectations of rejection and simple attempts to maximize outcomes can explain the unexpectedly large size of ultimatum offers; norms of fairness need not enter the picture.

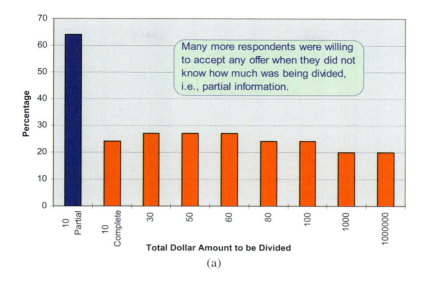

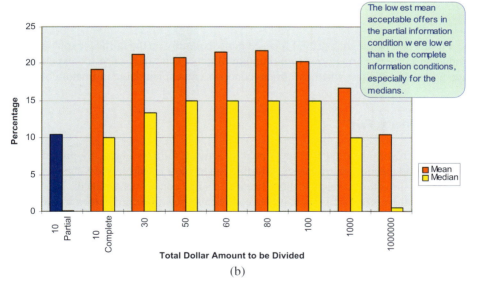

Figure 1. (a) Frequency of respondents who accepted any offer; partial and complete information conditions (Straub and Murnighan, 1995). (b) Mean and median lowest acceptable offers as a percentage of the total amount to be divided; partial and complete information conditions (Straub and Murnighan, 1995)

Table 3
Mean offers and percentage of the total to be divided (in real dollars) for the information and fairness label conditions; experiment 1; Pillutla and Murnighan (1995)

Amount divided	Information		No label	Cheap talk fair label	Third party fair label
$10	Partial	M (%)	3.54 (35%)	2.61 (26%)	4.67 (47%)
	Complete		4.66 (47%)	4.27 (43%)	4.85 (48%)
$30	Partial		7.50 (25%)	5.97 (20%)	13.00 (43%)
	Complete		12.77 (43%)	12.41 (41%)	13.50 (45%)
$50	Partial		10.84 (22%)	8.77 (17%)	21.80 (44%)
	Complete		21.56 (43%)	20.36 (41%)	22.20 (44%)
$70	Partial		14.75 (21%)	12.10 (17%)	29.90 (43%)
	Complete		28.85 (41%)	28.76 (41%)	31.00 (44%)
$100	Partial		19.05 (19%)	14.53 (15%)	41.20 (41%)
	Complete		40.65 (41%)	37.97 (38%)	44.50 (44%)
$1000	Partial		175.72 (18%)	82.20 (8%)	634.80 (63%)
	Complete		498.17 (50%)	353.64 (35%)	652.20 (65%)
$1 m	Partial		63,413 (6%)	61,052 (6%)	240,443 (24%)
	Complete		303,573 (30%)	309,935 (30%)	300,227 (30%)

Note: $n = 66$ in the no labels conditions and 33 in each of the labels conditions.

Pillutla and Murnighan (1995) focused more explicitly on the fairness explanation by inducing fairness norms prior to ultimatum offers. Their study used the experimental method to directly test whether fairness concerns can explain large ultimatum offers.

2. "My Offer is Fair"

Pillutla and Murnighan (1995) attempted to activate fairness norms by providing offerers or independent third parties with the opportunity to add fairness labels prior to presenting the offers to respondents. Offerers in some conditions attached "This is fair" to some of their offers; offerers in others conditions knew that third parties would evaluate their offers and label them fair or unfair before they were transmitted to a respondent. These manipulations were designed to activate offerers' concerns for fairness. They also allowed us to expand Straub and Murnighan's (1995) definition for fairness by suggesting that fair offers should be unaffected by the presence of third parties: offerers who wanted to appear fair rather than be fair would increase their offers when they knew that a third party would be evaluating them.

In the offerer label condition, offerers added a "This is fair" label to a specified half of their offers: they knew which offers would carry the fairness label and which would not. In the third party conditions, offerers were told that an independent third party would evaluate half of their offers and would attach a fair or unfair label (or no label) before

Table 4
Frequencies and percentages of offer rejections (acceptances in parentheses)

Amount divided	Outside options	The offer		Knowledge				
				Partial information		Complete information		
				NotComm Column 1	Common Column 2	NotComm Column 3	Common Column 4	Totals Column 5
$20	$0	$1	Row 1	7 (64) 9.9%	5 (42) 10.6%	12 (59) 16.9%	18 (29) 38.3%	42 (194) 17.8%
		$2	Row 2	4 (67) 5.6%	0 (47) 0%	8 (63) 11.2%	11 (36) 23.4%	23 (213) 9.7%
	$1	$1	Row 3	37 (34) 52.1%	26 (21) 55.3%	50 (21) 70.4%	34 (13) 72.3%	147 (89) 62.3%
		$2	Row 4	10 (61) 14.1%	4 (43) 8.5%	19 (52) 26.8%	18 (29) 38.3%	51 (185) 21.6%
	$2	$1	Row 5	66 (5) 93.0%	44 (3) 93.6%	66 (5) 93.0%	43 (4) 91.5%	219 (17) 92.8%
		$2	Row 6	34 (37) 47.9%	25 (22) 53.2%	47 (24) 66.2%	34 (13) 72.3%	140 (96) 59.3%
$2	$1	$1	Row 7			18 (53) 25.4%	6 (40) 13.1%	24 (93) 20.5%
$4	$2	$2	Row 8			19 (52) 26.8%	5 (41) 10.9%	24 (93) 20.5%
Totals in exptl. conditions (excluding rows 5, 7, +8)				92 (263) 25.9%	60 (175) 25.1%	136 (219) 38.4%	115 (120) 48.9%	403 (777) 34.2%

a respondent received it; they knew which half the third party would see. The other half of their offers would not be evaluated and would have no label. Everyone made four offers (complete or partial information x label/no label) for each of seven amounts: [$10, $30, $50, $70, and $100 (for real), $1000 and $1,000,000 (hypothetically)] in either the offerer or the third party condition. Participants were told that the two high amounts were hypothetical; actual payoffs were always $100 or less.

The design gave strategic offerers the opportunity to not only use the partial information condition strategically; it also gave them the opportunity to be more strategic by using fairness claims to reduce their offers even further. In so doing they could take advantage of information asymmetries and a potentially persuasive message. This strategy is the antithesis of fairness.

The results are shown in Figure 3. The data were remarkably consistent: for each of the amounts, offerers made relatively large offers in the complete information and third party label conditions; they made significantly smaller offers in the no label, partial

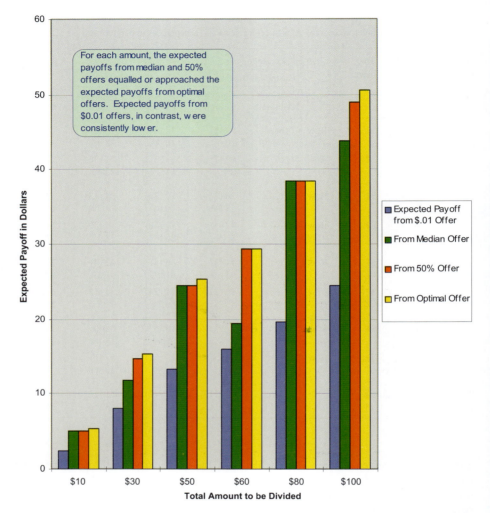

Figure 2. Expected payoffs to offerers in complete information conditions (Straub and Murnighan, 1995).

information conditions; and their offers in the partial information conditions were even smaller (significantly) when they labeled them "This is fair." The same pattern of results surfaced for a frequency count of 50–50 offers.

Only two of 66 offerers made identical offers in the information and/or the third party conditions. When a third party was evaluating offers, almost everyone increased their offers, especially in partial information. When they added their own fairness labels, most offerers took advantage of both the information conditions and the addition of fairness labels: they were about as strategic as possible. Offerers did not treat fairness labels as

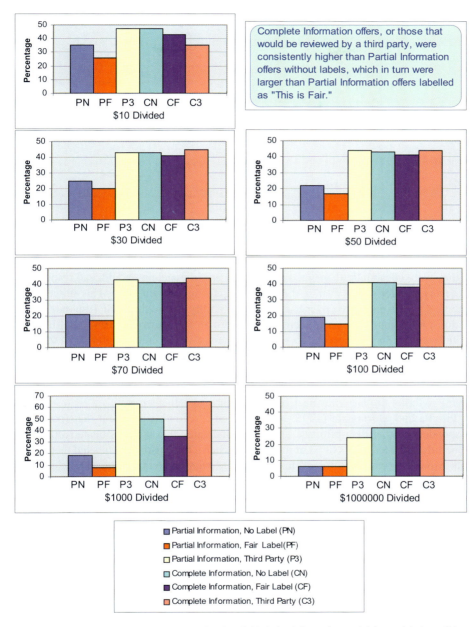

Figure 3. Offers as a percentage of the total to be divided, for information and fairness label conditions (Pillutla and Murnighan, 1995).

Table 5
Monetary offers (in percentages of the amount divided) for the gender and information conditions; Murnighan and Saxon (1994)

Grades	Information			
	Females		Males	
	Partial	Complete	Partial	Complete
3rd/6th[a]				
M	40.4%	42.3%	34.3%	42.2%
Median	50%	50%	42.5%	50%
6th/9th/College[a]				
M	38.3%	42.4%	31.3%	42.6%
Median	42.3%	50%	32.9%	49.1%

[a]Third and sixth grade offerers were dividing $1 in each case, face-to-face; sixth and ninth grade and college offerers were dividing amounts ranging from $1 to $1 million in their responses to a lengthy questionnaire.

if they were cheap talk: they acted as if adding a fairness claim would lead respondents to accept smaller offers, even in the complete information condition. This suggests that people's greed may have overwhelmed their ability to predict their respondents' reactions, a finding that is consistent with Bazerman and Carroll's (1987) and Lawler's (1989) arguments that negotiators rarely put themselves in their counterparts' shoes.

These results go considerably farther than previous studies (e.g., Kahn and Murnighan, 1993; Straub and Murnighan, 1993) by providing almost no basis for thinking that ultimatum offerers are trying to be truly fair. Instead, they seem to be blatantly strategic, trying to look fair when they need to serve their own self-interest.

Pillutla and Murnighan (1995) also included a second experiment that focused on respondents rather than offerers. The results indicated that undergraduate respondents generally accepted offers of $3 or more, even when a third party had labeled them as unfair. More importantly, offerers' fairness claims were essentially ignored; respondents reacted as if an offerer's labels were cheap talk. Finally, the results suggested that fairness did have an impact in respondents' accept/reject decisions: even when they could evaluate their offers in relation to the offerers' likely outcome (i.e., the complete information condition), their choices were still affected by the third party's evaluation.

As in previous studies, respondents invoked fairness as an explanation for rejecting offers. But Straub and Murnighan's (1995) respondents had also acted strategically when they were ultimatum offerers, leading to questions of their consistency if not their honesty. Straub and Murnighan (1995) noted that, in addition to citing fairness, respondents often reacted to small offers emotionally. They proposed that a more complete explanation for the rejection of small ultimatum offers may be wounded pride, and that people invoke fairness as a post hoc, socially acceptable rationalization of their essentially spiteful behavior. The data we report next tested this prediction directly.

3. Fairness, Anger, and Spite

The wounded pride/spite hypothesis states that respondents will look for an offer that they feel is fair; if the offer is smaller than expected, their reaction will be personal (wounded pride and even anger) and they may take personal action (spite) to punish the offerer.

To investigate these phenomena, we needed to create conditions that would generate more than the 15–20% rejections that have been observed in previous research. To do so, this study boosted the amount that offerers were dividing (to $20), gave respondents small offers (either $1 or $2), and gave them an outside option which they allowed them to make clear outcome comparisons. We also gave respondents information about whether offerers knew the value of their outside options. In this way, we created conditions that not only allowed for perceptions of unfairness, but that also gave respondents a reason to be angry.

Surprisingly, many respondents perceive that an offer is unfair even when they do not know how much an offerer is dividing. Croson (1993) reports that a lack of information leads to widely varying expectations: many respondents use the value of the offer to make self-serving but incorrect conclusions about the amount being divided. Respondents who know how much is being divided can use the offerer's outcome as a basis for comparison with their own. We expected that a specific outside option (0, $1, or $2 in this study) would give respondents an even stronger basis for evaluating their offers.

In the common knowledge condition in this study, respondents knew that offerers knew the value of their outside option prior to making offers; with not common knowledge, they knew that offerers did not have this knowledge. We also included two control conditions: offers ($1 or $2) stayed the same but were now 50% of the amount being divided ($2 or $4). The control conditions allowed us to check whether people might reject small offers that were fair (i.e., 50%); rejections would indicate that something other than fairness as the reason for rejecting. In general, we expected that people would accept these offers, even when they had equivalent outside options.

The analyses focused primarily on offers that were identical to a respondent's outside option. In these conditions, we might expect respondents to be most affected by their knowledge of what the offerers knew before making their offers. When offerers did not know the value of their outside option (the not common knowledge condition), respondents might forgive small offers. But when offerers knew their outside option, respondents could then attribute malicious greed to offerers who made small offers, making it easy, at least theoretically, to respond spitefully.

We expected, then, that partial information/not common knowledge would lead most people to accept any offer that was at least as large as their outside option. In contrast, the complete information/common knowledge condition should have generated the most spite and the most rejections. Here, all the blame can be leveled at the offerer. In particular, increased rejections from not common to common knowledge were taken as support for the wounded pride/spite hypothesis.

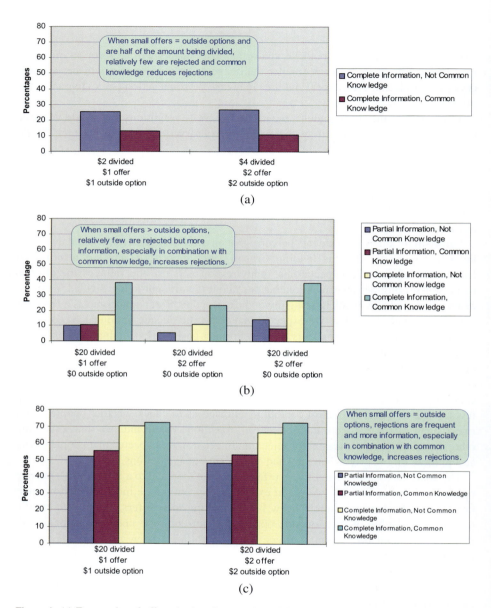

Figure 4. (a) Frequencies of offer rejections in control conditions (complete information); outside option equal to offer. (b) Frequencies of offer rejections in information and knowledge conditions; outside option less than offer. (c) Frequencies of offer rejections in information and knowledge conditions; outside option equal to offer.

Figure 4 displays the results. Less than 20% of the respondents rejected the control condition offers, suggesting that most of the other rejections depended to a great degree on concerns for fairness (see Figure 4a). Acceptances in comparable experimental conditions ($1 offers with outside options of $1 or $2 offers with outside options of $2) dropped to 44% and 22% with partial and complete information, respectively. We attribute this decrease to concerns for fairness and spite.

Respondents without outside options understandably accepted almost all $2 offers in the partial information condition; they rejected only a few $1 offers (accepting 92.4%). With complete information, rejections increased slightly: 83.7% of the $2 and 73.9% of the $1 offers were accepted. Rejections increased further when respondents knew that offerers knew their outside options.

Overall, partial information offers with no common knowledge led to 23% rejections (excluding $1 offers with outside options of $2); adding complete information increased rejections to 37%; adding common knowledge increased them to 52.8% (see Figures 4b and 4c). This larger increase is directly attributable to spite. The effects of common knowledge were strongest in the complete information condition, i.e., increases in rejections occurred most in the common knowledge–complete information conditions, providing additional support for the wounded pride/spite hypothesis. None of these many rejections are predicted by subgame perfect equilibrium models.

A simple unfairness hypothesis can explain the effect for information, i.e., people who know that the offerer is dividing $20 and can easily determine that offerers will do much better than they do if they accept their small offer reject offers that they perceive as unfair. This supports Bolton's (1991) notion that respondents are interested in both their absolute and their relative outcomes. But a simple fairness hypothesis cannot explain the significant knowledge effect: people reject more offers when they know that offerers knew their outside option. This knowledge allows respondents to surmise that the offerer is taking advantage of them.

The results suggest that fairness concerns are a necessary but incomplete explanation of why people reject ultimatum offers. A more complete explanation is that people reject offers when they are angered by the offer and the offerer. In other words, perceptions of unfairness alone led to many rejections; adding anger seemed to cause spiteful reactions that increased rejections even more.

Also, in the control condition, knowledge had no effect on acceptance rates. This strengthens the conclusion that unfair offers are necessary before people make attributions and get angry. In the control condition, there is no reason for respondents to attribute unfairness to offerers, and acceptances actually increased (not significantly) rather than decreased with common knowledge.

In conjunction with the findings on offerers (e.g., Pillutla and Murnighan, 1995), the picture of the two sides of ultimatum bargaining now looks like this: ultimatum offerers in games like these have considerable power; they are the first mover and have considerable discretion in the offers they can choose. They seem to recognize their strength, and their apparently automatic reaction is to be strategic and look for ways to increase their own outcomes. They take advantage of fairness labels when they can, and they guard against unfairness labels (and the greater chance of a rejection) when faced with either a third party or a respondent knowing how much they are dividing.

In contrast, respondents are in a much weaker position: they can only accept or reject the offers they receive; they cannot negotiate a better deal. At the same time, they seem to hope and sometimes expect a fair offer (although not necessarily 50–50). When their offer is not as good as they expected, they perceive it as unfair and may react with anger and spite and reject an offer that is otherwise beneficial.

The asymmetry of the two parties' outlooks is particularly striking. Offerers are strategic: if they calculate well, their offers are accepted and they get at least half of the total; if they calculate badly and appear greedy, respondents may reject them, spitefully. Offerers do have fairness concerns, but only in terms of predicting the fairness concerns of their respondents, because this may determine respondents' reactions. Offerers show little concern for the fairness of the outcomes that respondents actually receive.

In addition to the notion that anger may be necessary to stimulate respondents to reject ultimatum offers, Güth and van Damme's (1994) research suggests that, while they may cite fairness as a reason for rejecting an offer, respondents tend to be concerned for fairness only for themselves rather than for fairness in general. Güth and van Damme round that, when respondents received offers with reasonable outcomes and knew that another recipient, whose outcome depended on their decision, received a small, unfair offer, they tended to accept the offers. They were essentially unaffected by the others' outcomes: whether they accepted or rejected an offer depended on their own outcome rather than others'. In this sense, then, it does not appear that respondents are interested in true fairness either. Instead, they seem to use fairness as a rationale to support their spiteful reactions to small offers.

Although these results suggest that fairness concerns play only a small part in ultimatum behavior, at least as we have observed it in our studies, this research has left out one element that has also been neglected in bargaining research in general: that is the development of bargaining strategies. What this research has not addressed is why ultimatum offerers respond to this game strategically, and why reports of a concern for fairness and feelings of wounded pride, anger, and spite characterize respondents.

To try to address these questions, we used ultimatums – a very simple form of negotiation – to investigate how children bargain (Murnighan and Saxon, 1997). In particular, we gave kindergartners, third, sixth, and ninth graders and college students the opportunity to make and respond to a series of ultimatum offers, with complete and partial information, for money and M&Ms. We hoped to find easily identifiable patterns in the development of their bargaining reactions.

4. Ultimatum Bargaining by Children

Anecdotal evidence (Murnighan, 1991) suggests that young children commonly experience ultimatums and other threats; they often react to negotiations with strong, tenacious stands, leading to either a successful outcome or a disagreement. Older children, in contrast, may be able to handle more complex negotiations, but they also tend to lose the younger child's dogmatic tenacity, possibly due to increasing self-consciousness (Elkind, 1980). To date, the research related to children's bargaining has focused almost exclusively on their allocation norms (e.g., Streater and Chertkoff, 1976) or their competitiveness in a matrix game (e.g., Toda et al., 1978) rather than on their bargaining behavior.

Findings consistently show that younger children are own-gain oriented (e.g., Keil, 1986; McClintock, Moskowitz, and McClintock, 1977) and that they become increasingly fair with age (e.g., Avermaet and McClintock, 1988). Research on generosity suggests that children become more generous as they get older (e.g., Zarbatany, Hartmann, and Gelfand, 1985) and that girls are more generous than boys. Research on children's competitiveness also shows that children become increasingly competitive with age across several cultural groups (e.g., Kagan and Madsen, 1972; Toda et al., 1978). An extrapolation of these results to ultimatum bargaining suggests that younger children will be more selfish, less generous, less fair, but less competitive than older children, and that girls will be more generous than boys.

Ironically, these findings suggest that younger children may be particularly likely to make as well as accept very small offers. In other words, studying younger children not only provides an opportunity to map the development of bargaining strategies and behaviors, but younger children may also provide subgame perfect equilibrium predictions with their strongest support.

5. Ultimatums Dividing Money and M&Ms

The younger children in our experiment made and responded to offers of money and M&Ms to anonymous other children. Older children followed the same questionnaire procedures used in our other research. Restrictions by the children's school administrations made paying them impossible.

Respondents received offers of 1, 2, 3, 5, 10, 25, and 50 cents and from 1 to 10 M&Ms, one at a time, until they had accepted three consecutive offers. (Since many of the kindergartners did not know the difference between a nickel and a quarter, their monetary responses were not analyzed.) As offerers, children made partial information offers, dividing 1 and 4, 5, 10, and 11 M&Ms (small and large amounts of an even and an odd number of M&Ms) before making complete information offers using the same amounts. During the experiment, the complete or partial information nature of the situation was frequently reemphasized. We often asked children why they had chosen a particular action; we tape recorded all of their responses.

The results showed that, first, kindergartners exhibited no guile and no inclination toward strategic behavior. As offerers, they usually separated the coins into two roughly equal piles and pushed one of the two piles across the desk as their offer. As respondents, they rarely refused the offer of one penny; they refused the offer of one M&M even less often.

The most striking result for the kindergartners was that 12% of them gave the other child all of the coins and all of the M&Ms. We did not see this behavior in any of the other children.

Unlike some kindergartners, third graders understood the value of money. They also showed the first signs of strategic behavior. In particular, many shaded their partial information offers.

The most noteworthy results for third graders centered around how they dealt with the issue of equality. When they were asked to make an offer dividing 5 (or 11) M&Ms, many asked if they could cut one in half. When we told them that they could not, girls tended to offer more than half (3 and 6), keeping less than half for themselves, while boys did the reverse. At the same time, more than half of the third graders offered 2, 3, 5, and 6 M&Ms (or some slight variation of this pattern) when they were dividing 4, 5, 10, and 11, in both the complete and partial information conditions.

Even more strikingly, when they responded to M&M offers from another child and knew that 10 M&Ms were being divided (the complete information condition), 13 of 40 third graders (7 girls and 6 boys) rejected 1, 2, 3, and 4 M&Ms, accepted 5, and rejected 6, 7, 8, 9, and 10. A lack of equality, for them or for the other child, was the reason given for the rejections. These third graders exhibited what we have called "extreme fairness."

Overall, younger children offered more but accepted less than older children. Girls' offers were equal to or larger than boys', over all age groups. They were also less strategic than boys: they shaded their offers as often as boys, but less severely (see Figure 5). This dichotomy in the sexes appeared among third graders and continued for all older ages in this sample.

Finally, we observed qualitative differences between money and M&Ms. For every age group, more children accepted offers of 1 M&M than 1 cent, in both the complete and partial information conditions: 41% accepted 1 cent in the partial information conditions; 56% accepted 1 M&M; for complete information, 26% accepted 1 cent; 43% accepted 1 M&M.

The only adults in this sample, college students, offered less and were willing to accept less than younger respondents, suggesting a distinct relaxation of the stringent fairness criteria exercised by the younger children. With increasing age, people may be willing to accept much less than half, especially as amounts increase. Other explanations might include the possibility that college students may be less affected by and less prone to quick emotional reactions. Research by Frank, Gilovich, and Regan (1993) also suggests that college students have had the chance to study economics and, as a result, may have become more consistent in their bargaining strategies.

Like adults, children rejected small complete information offers and offered more than small amounts. A third grade boy explained why. When he made a partial infor-

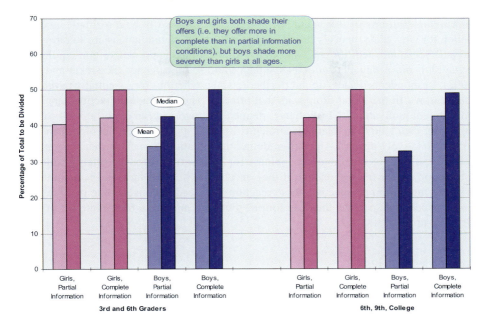

Figure 5. Mean and median offers made by 3rd, 6th, 9th grade and college aged boys and girls (Murnighan and Saxon, 1994).

mation offer dividing $1, he offered 50 cents and explained: "Then it would be 50–50. Both of us would have 50 cents." When he made a similar, complete information offer, he said, "25 cents. No, 60 cents, because sometimes I like to give people some more than I got. Some I let them have all of it, and I just keep what I have. Sometimes money doesn't matter; it depends on what I feel." This quote suggests that young children understand some of the psychological concepts that might be effectively incorporated into economic models. (See Roth and Erev, 1995, for a notable, related example.)

6. Conclusions

Previous ultimatum bargaining researchers tended to conclude that unpredicted outcomes resulted from fairness concerns. In a series of studies, we operationally defined fairness and tested its effects. The accumulated data from our projects document quite clearly that concerns for fairness provide little explanatory value for offerers and only a small part of the explanation for respondents' rejections: the simple cognitive reactions associated with fairness concerns may explain some idiosyncratic rejections; additional, emotional reactions make wounded pride and spite a more compelling explanation for unexpected rejections.

Although fairness concerns may be relevant, they appear to be too simple an explanation for why game theory's strong predictions for ultimatum games are so rarely supported. Self interested offerers want to avoid rejections; unpredicted, non-equilibrium behavior is more valuable and effective than equilibrium behavior (Prasnikar and Roth, 1992). Respondents do not support the theoretical predictions for essentially psychological reasons. In particular, it appears that offerers' and respondents' actions are based on different motivations. Most offerers define the situation as an opportunity for monetary gain; they tend to be blatantly strategic. Many respondents, on the other hand, due to their relatively powerless position, define the situation personally. This asymmetry can lead to disagreement and unhappiness for both parties – for the offerer, following a rejection, or for the respondent, if they accept an offer that they feel is unfair. From a strictly utilitarian perspective, these reactions can lead to considerable inefficiencies. From a social perspective, they can sour negotiations and make future interactions particularly problematic.

Acknowledgements

I sincerely thank my collaborators – Madan Pillutla, Michael Saxon, and Paul Straub – on the projects that I have summarized here. Many colleagues and students have contributed to this work; I am particularly thankful for their comments, suggestions, and support. Much of the work reported here was supported by the Social Science and Humanities Research Council of Canada. A previous summary of much of this work appeared in *Negotiation as a Social Process*, edited by Roderick Kramer and David Messick (Sage, 1995).

References

Bazerman, Max H., Carroll, John S. (1987). "Negotiator cognition". Research in Organizational Behavior 9, 247–288.
Binmore, K., Shaked, A., Sutton, J. (1985). "Testing noncooperative bargaining theory: A preliminary study". American Economic Review 75, 1178–1180.
Bolton, G.E. (1991). "A comparative model of bargaining: Theory and evidence". American Economic Review 81, 1096–1136.
Elkind, D. (1980). "Strategic interactions in early adolescence". In: Adelson, J. (Ed.), Handbook of Adolescent Psychology. Wiley, New York.
Frank, R.H., Gilovich, T., Regan, D.T. (1993). "Does studying economics inhibit cooperation?" Journal of Economic Perspectives 7, 159–171.
Güth, W., Tietz, R. (1990). "Ultimatum bargaining behavior: A survey and comparison of experimental results". Journal of Economic Psychology 11, 417–449.
Güth, W., van Damme, E. (1998). "Information, strategic behavior, and fairness in ultimatum bargaining: An experimental study". Journal of Mathematical Psychology 42, 227–247.
Güth, W., Schmittberger, R., Schwarze, B. (1982). "An experimental analysis of ultimatum bargaining". Journal of Economic Behavior and Organization 3, 367–388.
Kagan, S., Madsen, M. (1972). "Rivalry in Anglo–American and Mexican children of two ages". Journal of Personality and Social Psychology 24, 214–220.

Kahn, L.M., Murnighan, J.K. (1993). "A general experiment on bargaining in demand games with outside options". American Economic Review 83, 1260–1280.

Kahneman, D., Knetsch, J., Thaler, H. (1986). "Fairness and the assumption of economics". Journal of Business 59, S285–S300.

Keil, L.J. (1986). "Rules, reciprocity, and rewards: A developmental study of resource allocation in social interaction". Journal of Experimental Social Psychology 22, 419–435.

Kravitz, D., Gunto, S. (1992). "Decisions and recipients in ultimatum bargaining games". The Journal of Socio-Economics 21, 65–84.

McClintock, C.G., Moskowitz, J.M., McClintock, E. (1977). "Variations in preferences for individualistic, competitive, and cooperative outcomes as a function of age, game class, and task in nursery school children". Child Development 48, 1080–1085.

Murnighan, J.K. (1991). "The Dynamics of Bargaining Games". Prentice Hall, Englewood Cliffs, NJ.

Ochs, J., Roth, A. (1989). "An experimental study of sequential bargaining". American Economic Review 79, 355–384.

Pillutla, M.M., Murnighan, J.K. (1995). "Being fair or appearing fair: Strategic behavior in ultimatum bargaining". Academy of Management Journal 38, 1408–1426.

Pillutla, M.M., Murnighan, J.K. (1996). "Unfairness, anger, and spite: Emotional rejections of ultimatum offers". Organizational Behavior and Human Decision Processes 68, 208–224.

Prasnikar, V., Roth, A.E. (1992). "Considerations of fairness and strategy: Experimental data from sequential games". Quarterly Journal of Economics 107, 865–888.

Roth, A.E., Erev, Ido (1995). "Learning in extensive form games: Experimental data and simple dynamics models in the intermediate term". Games and Economic Behavior 8, 164–212.

Roth, Alvin E., Murnighan, J. Keith., Schoumaker, Francoise (1988). "The deadline effect in bargaining: Some experimental evidence". American Economic Review 78, 806–823.

Selten, Reinhard (1965). "Spieltheoretische behandlung eines Oligopol Modells mit Nachfragetragheit". Zeitschrift für Gesamte Staatswissenschaft 121, 301–324.

Straub, P.G., Murnighan, J.K. (1995). "An experimental investigation of ultimatums: Common knowledge, fairness, expectations, and lowest acceptable offers". Journal of Economic Behavior and Organization 27, 345–364.

Streater, A.L., Chertkoff, J.M. (1976). "Distribution of rewards in a triad: A developmental test of equity theory". Child Development 47, 800–805.

Toda, M., Shinotsuka, H., McClintock, C.G., Stech, F.J. (1978). "Development of competitive behavior as a function of culture, age, and social comparison". Journal of Personality and Social Psychology 36, 825–839.

van Avermaet, E., McClintock, C.G. (1988). "Intergroup fairness and bias in children". European Journal of Social Psychology 18, 407–428.

Zarbatany, L., Hartmann, D.P., Gelfand, D.M. (1985). "Why does children's generosity increase with age: Susceptibility to experimenter influence or altruism?" Child Development 56, 746–756.

Further reading

Croson, R. (1996). "Information in ultimatum games: An experimental study". Journal of Economic Behavior and Organization 30, 197–212.

Harrison, G.W., McCabe, K.A. (1996). "Expectations and fairness in a simple bargaining experiment". International Journal of Game Theory 25, 202–327.

Lawler, E.J. (1986). "Bilateral deterrence and conflict spiral: A theoretical analysis". In: Lawler, E.J. (Ed.), Advances in Group Processes, vol. 3. JAI Press, Greenwich, CT, pp. 107–130.

Murnighan, J.K., Saxon, M.S. (1998). "Ultimatum bargaining by children and adults". Journal of Economic Psychology 19, 415–445.

Roth, A.E. (1995). "Bargaining experiments". In: Kagel, J.H., Roth, A.E. (Eds.), The Handbook of Experimental Economics. Princeton University Press, Princeton, NJ.

Chapter 51

COORDINATION FAILURE IN MARKET STATISTIC GAMES[1]

JOHN VAN HUYCK

e-mail: john.vanhuyck@tamu.edu

RAYMOND BATTALIO

1. Introduction

A central question in economics is how do markets coordinate the behavior of anonymous decision makers in a many person decentralized economy. Economic theory has traditionally addressed the question using the equilibrium method, which abstracts away from an important aspect of the general coordination problem, because it assumes an equilibrium. For abstract games, an equilibrium is defined as an assignment to each player of a strategy that is best for him when the others use the strategies assigned to them. The relevance of this abstract mutual consistency requirement for economic modeling is an open question, see Kreps (1990).

The requirement has two related problems: disequilibrium and coordination failure. First, the mutual consistency requirement of an equilibrium assignment is not an implication of individual rationality, but an additional strong assumption. Individual rationality means internal consistency and internally consistent beliefs and actions of different players may not be mutually consistent. In economies with stable and unique equilibrium points, the influence of inconsistent beliefs and actions would disappear over time, see Lucas (1987). The power of the equilibrium method derives from its ability to abstract from the complicated dynamic process that induces equilibrium and to abstract from the historical accident that initiated the process.

Second, there is often more than one equilibrium assignment. For example, multiple Pareto ranked equilibria arise in both macroeconomic models with production, search, or trading externalities and microeconomic models of monopolistic competition, technology adoption and diffusion, and manufacturing with non-convexities. These superficially dissimilar market and non-market models share the common property that a decision maker's best "level of effort" depends positively upon other decision makers' "level of effort." This property is called strategic complementarity in the coordination failure literature, see Cooper and John (1988). When these equilibria can be Pareto ranked it is possible for historical accident and dynamic process to lead to inefficient equilibria, that is, coordination failure. Consequently, understanding the origin of mutually consistent behavior is an essential complement to the theory of equilibrium points.

---

[1] Related research available at: http://econlab10.tamu.edu/JVH_gtee.

The experimental method provides a tractable and constructive approach to the equilibrium selection problem. This chapter reviews experiments using a class of generic market statistic games with multiple equilibria, which are strictly Pareto ranked, and it reports experiments that provide evidence on how human subjects behave under conditions of strategic uncertainty. Strategic uncertainty exists when the players actions are not mutual knowledge.

A laboratory environment capturing the essential aspects of the mutual consistency problem in a many person decentralized economy must include three features: First, the environment must not assume away the problem by allowing an arbiter – or any other individual – to make common knowledge preplay assignments. Second, the environment must allow individuals little ability to unilaterally alter market outcomes. Finally, the environment must allow repeated interaction amongst the decision makers so that they have a chance to learn to coordinate.

For laboratory research, a tractable class of market processes with these features are market statistic games. Let x_{it} denote the action of player i in period t. An action combination is the vector of actions $x_t = (x_{1t}, \ldots, x_{nt})$ for the n players. A homogeneous action combination occurs when all players take the same action. An abstract market process is a mapping from the action space into a real number, the market outcome $y(x)$.

The market outcome could represent market thickness, industry production, average market price, aggregate demand, or aggregate supply. In the coordination failure literature, the mean of the players' actions is a common example of an abstract market process. As the number of players increases, the influence of an individual player on the mean goes to zero and in the limit an individual player cannot influence the market outcome.

Order statistics are an effective way to capture the anonymity of a many person economy without using enormous group sizes. The jth inclusive order statistic, m_j, is defined by $m_1 \leqslant m_2 \leqslant \cdots \leqslant m_n$, where the m_j are the x_i of action combination x arranged in increasing order. When $y(x) = m_j$ and $1 < j < n$, an actor contemplating defection from a homogeneous action combination cannot influence the market outcome.

Let $OS[n, j]$ denote the stage game of a finitely repeated order statistic game with n subjects and jth order statistic. Let the payoff function be such that an actor's unique best response to the market statistic $y(x)$ in the stage game is simply $x_i^* = y(x)$. This class of order statistic games has the property that any feasible homogeneous action combination is a strict equilibrium and depending on the payoff function these equilibria may or may not be ranked by efficiency.

2. Strategic Uncertainty and Coordination Failure

Van Huyck, Battalio, and Beil (1990) conducted an experiment based on Bryant (1983) Keynesian coordination game that systematically and consistently results in coordination failure. The period game was an OS[14 to 16, 1] defined by the following payoff

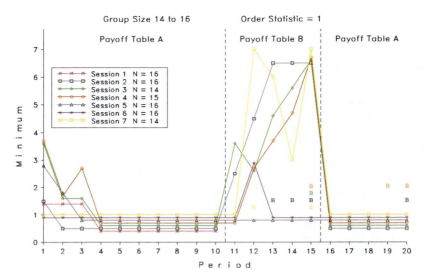

Figure 1. Results from Van Huyck, Battalio, and Beil (1990).

function and action space for each of 14 to 16 players:

$$\pi(x_i, m_1) = \$0.20 m_1 - b x_i + \$0.60, \tag{1}$$

where m_1 is the inclusive minimum and b is a non-negative parameter less than $0.20. Actions are restricted to the set of integers from 1 to 7. The players have complete information about the payoff function and strategy space and know that the payoff function and strategy space are common knowledge.

In treatment A and A', parameter b was set equal to $0.10. Consequently, the payoff-dominant equilibrium $(7, \ldots, 7)$ paid $1.30 while the secure equilibrium $(1, \ldots, 1)$ paid $0.70 per subject per period. In treatment A, the period game was repeated ten times. The number of players varied between 14 and 16 subjects. Treatment A' designates the resumption of these conditions after treatment B.

In period one, the payoff-dominant action, 7, was chosen by 31 percent of the subjects and the secure action, 1, was chosen by 2 percent of the subjects. Neither payoff dominance nor security succeeds in organizing much of the data. The initial play of all seven sessions exhibit both disequilibrium and coordination failure. The minimum action for period one was never greater than 4, see Figure 1.

Repeating the period game does cause actions to converge to a stable outcome, but rather than converging to the payoff-dominant equilibrium or to the initial outcome of the treatment, the most inefficient market statistic obtains in all seven sessions, see Figure 1. By period ten 72 percent of the subjects adopt their secure action, 1, and the minimum for all seven experiments was a 1.

In treatment B, parameter b of Equation (1) was set equal to zero. Because a player's action is no longer penalized, the payoff-dominant action, 7, is a best response to all feasible minimums, that is, action 7 is a dominating strategy. Hence, treatment B tests equilibrium *refinements* based on the elimination of individually unreasonable actions. Strategic uncertainty should now cause an individually rational player to choose the payoff-dominant action, 7.

In period eleven, the payoff-dominant action, 7, was chosen by 84 percent of the subjects. However, the minimum in period eleven was never more than 4 and in sessions four, five, six, and seven it was a 1. Adaptive behavior converges to the efficient market statistic – the payoff-dominant equilibrium – in four of the six experiments. By period fifteen, 96 percent of the subjects chose the dominating and efficient action, 7.

Even in the sessions that obtained the efficient outcome, the B treatment was not sufficient to induce the groups to implement the payoff-dominant equilibrium in treatment A'. Returning to the original payoff table in period sixteen, 25 percent of the subjects chose the payoff-dominant action, 7. However, 37 percent chose the secure action, 1. This bi-modal distribution of actions suggests that play prior to period sixteen influenced subjects' behavior. However, the subjects exhibit a heterogeneous response to this history.

In treatment A', the minimum in all periods of all six experiments was 1. By period twenty, 84 percent of the subjects chose the secure action, 1, and 94 percent chose an action less than or equal to 2. Sessions two and four even satisfy the mutual best response property of an equilibrium by period twenty. Obtaining the efficient outcome in treatment B failed to reverse the observed coordination failure. Like the A treatment, the most inefficient outcome obtained.

This experiment provides an interesting example of coordination failure. The minimum was never above four in period one and all seven experiments converged to a minimum of one within four periods. Since the payoff-dominant equilibrium would have paid all subjects $19.50 in the A and A' treatments and the average earnings were only $8.80, the observed coordination failure cost the average subject $10.70 in lost earnings.

3. The Influence of Out-of-Equilibrium Payoffs

Van Huyck, Battalio, and Beil (1991) report an experiment that replicates the coordination failure result of their large cohort minimum rule paper for smaller cohorts and a best response determined by the median, which they call average opinion games. The aspect of their experiment that we emphasize here is the influence of out-of-equilibrium payoffs on the frequency of observed coordination failure.

The period game was an OS[9, 5] defined by the following payoff function and action space for each of 9 decision makers indexed by i:

$$\pi(x_i, m_5) = \$0.10 m_5 - \$0.05[m_5 - x_i]^2 + \$0.60, \tag{2}$$

where $x_i \in \{1, 2, \ldots, 7\}$. A player's payoff is decreasing in the distance between the player's choice, x_i, and the inclusive median, m_5, and is increasing in the median, m_5.

All symmetric action combinations are equilibria and can be Pareto ranked. Like Van Huyck, Battalio, and Beil (1990), payoffs range from $1.30 in the payoff dominant equilibrium $(7, \ldots, 7)$, to $0.70 in the most inefficient equilibrium $(1, \ldots, 1)$. The secure equilibrium is $(3, \ldots, 3)$, which pays $0.90 in equilibrium and insures a payoff of at least $0.50.

Game Ω differs from Γ only in that disequilibrium outcomes result in a zero payoff. Unlike game, all actions are equally secure in game Ω, because they all insure a payoff of zero. Hence, security cannot be a salient equilibrium selection principle for game Ω, but payoff-dominance uniquely selects $(7, \ldots, 7)$ and, hence, is potentially salient.

Of the six cohorts, three cohorts had an initial median of 4 and three had an initial median of 5. The median never changed over the ten periods of treatment for any cohort. Behavior converged to a mutual best response outcome in five of six cohorts. The historical accident of the initial median selected the equilibrium and this equilibrium was never efficient.

Of the three Ω cohorts, two cohorts had an initial median of 7 and one had an initial median of 5. Again, the historical accident of the initial median selected the equilibrium, but now two of three cohorts coordinate on the payoff-dominant equilibrium. Setting out-of-equilibrium payoffs to zero increased the psychological salience of payoff-dominance.

4. The Influence of Group Size, Grid Size, and Order Statistic

Van Huyck, Battalio, and Rankin (1997) study coordination failure in market statistic games holding the payoff function constant but changing group size, grid size, and order statistic. Group size was 5 or 7. The order statistic was 2 or 4. Crossing these parameters gives four stage games: OS[5, 2], OS[5, 4], OS[7, 2], and OS[7, 4].

Equation (2), the payoff function in Van Huyck, Battalio, and Beil's (1991) Γ treatment, was used in all treatments. Since the sessions were designed to last forty rather than fifteen periods, the constant was reduced to $0.20. The grid size was increased from the 7 actions in treatment Γ to 101 actions. This much finer grid was obtained by using their "blue box" interface, which allows a subject to quickly search the payoff space with a mouse. The action space was $e \in \{0, 1, \ldots, 100\}$ and the map used to determine payoffs was

$$x = 1 + 0.06e. \tag{3}$$

All homogeneous action combinations are strict equilibria and the equilibria can be Pareto ranked. In the payoff dominant equilibrium $(100, \ldots, 100)$ each player earns $0.90 per period. In the secure equilibrium $(33, \ldots, 33)$ each player earns $0.50. And in the least efficient equilibrium $(0, \ldots, 0)$ each player earns $0.30.

The data in period 1 are particularly interesting, because they provide evidence on the salience of payoff-dominance and security. The median choice overall was 55. The median choice overall in VHBB's baseline treatment was 4.5 or 58.3. The mean action overall was 62 in both OS[n, j] and VHBB's baseline treatment. So there exists a sense in which they succeeded in replicating the baseline conditions observed in VHBB despite a much finer action grid, smaller group sizes, and very different experimental methods. However, an analysis of variance conditioned on OS[n, j] rejects the null hypothesis of equal treatment means at conventional levels of statistical significance. The group size and order statistic had a small influence on initial behavior.

Figure 2 reports the order statistic by treatment for periods 1 to 20. A significant number of cohorts converge to the efficient equilibrium, which was never observed using a coarser grid. The most striking examples occur in the average opinion treatment: OS[7, 4]. Using a finer grid reduces the salience of the initial market statistic. Now only half the OS[7, 4] cohorts coordinate on the initial market statistic. Session 8A is remarkable in that subjects coordinate on a time dependent play path. (This phenomena was also observed in four sessions during the crossover treatment.)

Adaptive behavior converges to a mutual best response outcome in 56 percent of the initial cohorts. Comparing terminal outcomes Van Huyck, Battalio, and Rankin (1997) found statistically significant differences in the empirically distribution function between OS[7, 4] and OS[7, 2] at the one percent level, between OS[5, 4] and OS[5, 2] at the five percent level, and between OS[5, 2] and OS[7, 2] at the ten percent level of statistical significance. They conclude that strategic uncertainty interacting with the order statistic had a larger effect on behavior than did group size.

The subjects' inability to solve the strategy coordination problem results in significant inefficiencies. Cohorts in treatment OS[5, 4] realized 85 percent of the efficient earnings, OS[7, 4] realized 76 percent, OS[5, 2] realized 65 percent, and OS[7, 2] realized 58 percent. So it is not true that a much finer approximation of a continuous action space eliminates coordination failure.

5. The Separatrix

All of the cohorts up to this point played in coordination games with the property that any homogeneous action combination was an equilibrium. Van Huyck, Cook, and Battalio (1997) investigate a market statistic game in which there only exist two symmetric equilibria: a high equilibrium (12, ..., 12) and a low equilibrium (3, ..., 3). The group size was 7 and the order statistic was 4. The separatrix between the two symmetric equilibria derived under a best response based dynamic is illustrated in Figure 3.

All ten cohorts started with an initial median contained in the set {7, 8, 9, 10, 11}; after period six none of the observed medians were contained in the set {7, 8, 9, 10, 11}; moreover, the median never crossed the separatrix, that is, subjects trapped in the low equilibrium's basin of attraction never escaped, see Figure 3. While best response based

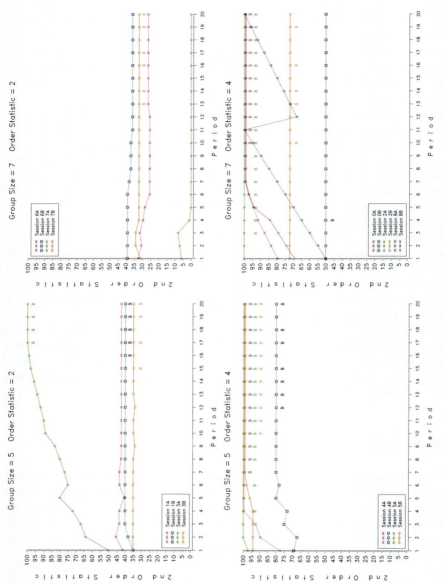

Figure 2. Results from Van Huyck, Battalio, and Rankin (1997).

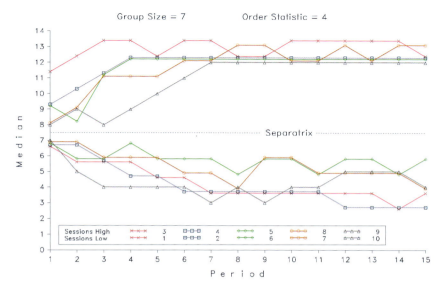

Figure 3. Results from Van Huyck, Cook, and Battalio (1997).

dynamics are symmetric around the separatrix, adaptive behavior is biased towards efficiency, that is, cohorts move to more efficient outcomes quickly, but resist the adaptive dynamics when moving to more inefficient outcomes.

The average subject in the first fifteen periods of the five low sessions earned $9.71. The average subject in the first fifteen periods of the five high sessions earned $15.57. The small differences in the distribution of subjects' period one choices result in large differences in average earnings. Specifically, the average subject in a high session earns about $6 (or 60 percent) more than the average subject in a low session.

Acknowledgements

The National Science Foundation and Texas Advanced Research Program provided financial support. A faculty development leave at the University of Pittsburgh provided time for Van Huyck to write this paper.

References

Bryant, John (1983). "A simple rational expectations Keynes-type model". Quarterly Journal of Economics 98 (3), 525–528.
Cooper, Russell, John, Andrew (1988). "Coordinating coordination failures in Keynesian models". Quarterly Journal of Economics 103 (3), 441–464.

Kreps, David M. (1990). "Game Theory and Economic Modelling". Clarendon Press, Oxford, UK.
Lucas Jr., Robert E. (1987). "Adaptive behavior and economic theory". In: Hogarth, R., Reder, M. (Eds.), Rational Choice. University of Chicago Press, Chicago.
Van Huyck, J.B., Battalio, R.C., Beil, R.O. (1990). "Tacit coordination games, strategic uncertainty, and coordination failure". American Economic Review 80 (1), 234–248.
Van Huyck, J.B., Battalio, R.C., Beil, R.O. (1991). "Strategic uncertainty, equilibrium selection, and coordination failure in average opinion games". Quarterly Journal of Economics 106 (3), 885–911.
Van Huyck, J.B., Cook, J.P., Battalio, R.C. (1997). "Adaptive behavior and coordination failure". Journal of Economic Behavior and Organization 32, 483–503.
Van Huyck, J.B., Battalio, R.C., Rankin, F.W. (1997). "Evidence on learning in coordination games." Texas A&M Research Report No. 7.

Chapter 52

THE PROBLEM OF COMMON CHOICE IN SYMMETRIC
N-PERSON COORDINATION GAMES

CARL M. RHODES

Franklin and Marshall College

RICK K. WILSON

Rice University

National Science Foundation

An apocryphal story is told that in 1897 there were exactly two automobiles (horseless carriages) in the State of Nebraska. Traffic laws regulating these new contraptions were generally lacking and the law was especially silent on how motorized vehicles should pass one another when approaching from opposite directions. Sure enough, as soon as these autos found themselves on the same road, they crashed head-on. The problem confronting these drivers was not that of "chicken" but rather "coordination," in which there were two Pareto-superior equilibria from which to choose. Despite the simplicity of the problem, one or both drivers made the wrong choice.

Coordination problems, such as the one facing our Cornhusker motorists, can be simply and easily solved provided an appropriate institutional remedy is at hand. Markets, for example, with frictionless transaction costs and complete information, constitute one way of quickly coordinating supply and demand. The evolution of social norms constitute another way of coordinating human action. Central to both of these solutions is the presence of a clear, unambiguous signal about what actions individuals should take. Where such a signal is present, the problem of coordination is easily solved; where absent, the problem of coordination can be extraordinarily difficult.

1. The Problem

Table 1 illustrates a simple coordination game with multiple Nash equilibria in pure strategies. In this setting there are three color choices and three individuals. Actors make simultaneous choices and payoffs are symmetric across actors. Payoffs are a function of an actor's choice and the number of others making the same choice. For instance, if only Actor 1 chooses Green, she earns 10 utiles. On the other hand, if everyone chooses Green, Actor 1 earns 100 utiles. Actors 2 and 3 face an identical choice problem. This setting is typical of coordination games in which there are multiple equilibrium. Which color actors choose is irrelevant. What matters is that everyone settles on the same color. Each color constitutes a Nash equilibrium in that once selected, no actor has a unilateral incentive to change.

Handbook of Experimental Economics Results, Volume 1
Copyright © 2008 Elsevier B.V. All rights reserved
DOI: 10.1016/S1574-0722(07)00052-2

Table 1
Three actor coordination game. Symmetric coordination game with three actors and three equilibrium. All actors have the same payoffs and make their choices privately and simultaneously. If everyone chooses the same color (e.g., green) then no one will change their mind and unilaterally choose a different color

Actor 1 chooses	# Others matching the choice		
	0	1	2
Green	10	40	100
Yellow	10	40	100
Brown	10	40	100

The theoretical and empirical literature on coordination games is voluminous (see Ochs, 1995). Schelling (1960) initially suggested that coordination games could be solved with the presence of a "focal point." That is, actors could simply use obvious elements of the game to quickly settle on a single equilibrium where many exist. However, experiments by Van Huyck, Battalio, and Beil (1990) call into question the ease with which actors solve coordination games with the aid of focal points.

A different approach, suggested by Farrell (1987), allows actors to engage in "cheap talk." Farrell shows that if an actor signals her intended action prior to making a choice, she has no reason to lie about that choice in a coordination game. Because the problem is one of equilibrium selection, pre-play signals provide actors a means for committing to a particular play. Cooper et al. (1994) provide evidence that cheap talk can be remarkably effective. In their two-person coordination games, cheap talk allowed subjects to increase their rates of coordination from zero to 51 percent when only one subject signaled and to 91 percent when both subjects signaled.

As the number of actors increases, so too do the problems associated with coordination. While cheap talk remains a powerful solution its impact is attenuated by both problems of learning and path dependence.

2. Experimental Design

Two distinct experiments explore the role of signaling in n-person coordination problems. The first examines only single-stage games while the second examines repeated games. Because both experiments use a similar design (summarized in Table 2), we discuss first their common features.

The experiments involved groups of eight subjects who participated in highly structured decision settings and relied on computer-based instruction and interactions over a local area network. All computer terminals were separated by partitions so that subjects did not have a line of sight to one another's terminals. Subjects were cautioned that they could not speak with one another during the course of the experiment, as doing so would result in its termination. Each experimental session lasted about 60 minutes.

Table 2
Experimental design

- Computer-based instruction and interaction
- Subjects asked to select one color from three choices
- Four subjects per group
- Single stage games:
    Randomize group composition, IDs, and colors before each decision period
- Repeated play games:
    Randomize group composition and IDs once before game
    Randomize colors each period
- Two conditions – no signaling and signaling
- No Signaling:
    Simultaneous color choices without communication
- Signaling
    One subject randomly selected to send cheap-talk signal to others

Prior to each round (either a single decision or a series of decisions, depending on the experiment) subjects were randomly assigned to a four-person group. At the same time each subject was randomly assigned a new identity (consisting of the letters A, B, etc.) in order to minimize reputation effects.

The subject's task was to select a color. Associated with each color was a row payoff indicating that the outcome was contingent on the color choice of one or more other subjects. Throughout the experiment six different colors were used: Brown, Gray, Orange, Green, Yellow, and White. At the outset of each decision three colors were randomly chosen and used. Those colors were randomly ordered at a subject's terminal for each decision period. Subjects were told that the group would see the same colors, but were cautioned that the order of those colors might be very different for other group members. For example, while {Yellow, Green, Brown} might be the order from top row to bottom row for one subject, another might see {Green, Yellow, Brown}. This was done to control for positional norms that could develop in the course of the experiment (e.g., always pick the middle row). Subjects were told that it was the color that mattered, not position.

Subjects made their choice privately and all choices were revealed simultaneously. Once each decision was made, subjects were informed of what the others had chosen and their own earnings for that decision. All earnings were in points and payoffs were based on a lottery conducted at the end of a set of choices (either five decisions in the single-stage experiment or at the end of the repeated game). The more points subjects earned, the more likely they were to win the large prize.

Two conditions were used in both experiments. In the *No Signaling* condition all four members of the group made a color choice and did so without cheap talk. Once everyone made a choice, the choices were revealed, the member's point earnings were displayed and the process resumed. Under the *Signaling* condition a single individual was randomly selected from the group. That member, referred to as a "monitor," was required to send a private signal to each of the other members of this group. The signal was nothing more than a color, was sent via the computer, and each member observed only their own signal. Following the suggestion by the signaler, members made their own choice and when all choices were completed, those choices were revealed, and the member's own point earnings were displayed. The signaler's payoff, like that of the others, was tied to the color choices of others, with the signaler's points increasing with the number of others choosing the same color.

3. Single Stage Results

The first experiment required subjects to participate in 10 distinct decisions. The first 5 decisions were under the *No Signaling* condition and the last 5 decisions were under the *Signaling* condition. Between each decision subjects were randomly reshuffled and randomly reassigned new identities. Consequently subjects were unable to develop expectations about the behavior of any specific participant.

With symmetric equilibrium, randomization across sets of colors and reshuffling row positions for colors, subjects found it extraordinarily difficult to coordinate. Panel A of Figure 1 illustrates this quite well. It compares the percentage of actors choosing the same color across 90 trials with what is expected if all subjects played their mixed strategy Nash equilibrium (see Wilson and Rhodes, 1997). As is clear from the figure, subjects made choices that, in the aggregate, are remarkably similar to random play. They rarely stumbled into coordination, with all four subjects choosing the same color only 17.8 percent of the time.

Once choices were recommended, even though the recommendations were not common knowledge, rates of coordination increased dramatically. Panel B of Figure 1 illustrates what happens once a signaler is introduced. Instead of four subjects seeking to coordinate over the same color, three subjects now had to make a choice. As shown in the figure, all actors selected the same color 78.9 percent of the time. Moreover, their choices are considerably different than if all subjects played a mixed strategy Nash equilibrium. Signaling makes an enormous difference, although it is puzzling that even this simple mechanism does not result in 100 percent rates of coordination.

There are several behavioral deviations in these experiments which account for the imperfect levels of coordination. In order for there to be full coordination the signaler must send the same signal to the other participants and they must follow that signal. Most of the time (95.6 percent) the signaler sent the same signal to all three participants. Likewise, most of the time (93.3 percent) the participants did what the signaler suggested. Most of these deviations occurred early on in the experiment as subjects were learning the design. Only 9 of 18 groups completely coordinated their color choice in the first period. In the second period 14 of 18 groups did so and by the last period all 18 groups coordinated. Presented with a coordinating device, and given sufficient time to learn its value, subjects found full coordination to be an increasingly attainable goal.

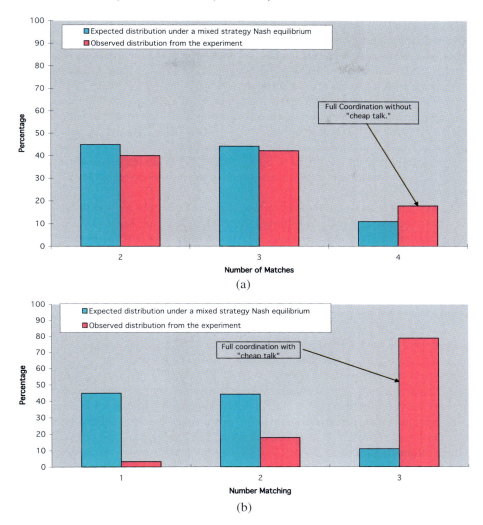

Figure 1. Distribution of coordinated choices in single stage experiments: (a) no signaling condition, (b) signaling condition.

4. Repeated Play Results

The second experiment involves groups participating in five period, repeated play games. Subjects were randomly assigned to a four person group and randomly assigned new identities. For all five periods the same group members were retained (as were their identities) and subjects were reminded they were participating with the same individuals across each decision. The problem remained the same – to choose the same color. In each decision period the set of colors was randomly drawn, and as before, the row position for colors was randomly shuffled for each subject. Again groups were assigned to either the *No Signaling* or *Signaling* condition. If there was a signaler, that individual retained the position across all five decisions.

Figure 2 shows that subjects had a much more difficult time settling on the same color than under the single-shot experimental setting. Not once in 20 decisions, across four groups, did all four subjects settle on the same color. By comparison, as soon as someone was appointed to send private signals, the rate of complete coordination climbed to 46.7 percent (or 14 out of 30 decisions). While an impressive change from the *No Signaling* condition, it lags well behind what was observed in the single-stage experimental conditions.

The differences between the single-stage and repeated trials are due to the varying effects of learning and path dependence. Learning effects are especially clear in the single stage trials. In that experiment, as noted above, only half of the groups fully coordinated in the first period. By the second period, as the groups and signalers were randomly reshuffled, full coordination climbed to 78 percent of the groups. By the final period, subjects fully coordinated 100 percent of the time, learning that the cheap talk signals were useful.

By comparison, the repeated play experiments suggest the presence of path dependence, although the effects of learning are clearly visible as well. Figures 3a–3f depict matching and signaling behavior for all six groups in the repeated games. Each panel constitutes the period by period activity for one of the experimental groups. The series colored in red displays the number of individuals matching the same color. The left (red) vertical axis represents the three ranked possibilities for this game: no one matching, two subjects matching or all three individuals matching their color choice. The series colored in blue represents the type of signal sent. The right (blue) vertical axis notes the signal combination sent: one color signaled to everyone, two colors signaled or three different color signals.

Groups A and B had no problem coordinating. In both cases the signaler always sent subjects the same color signal, the subjects relied on that signal and everyone collected the maximal payoff. Groups C and D began with the signaler sending the same signal to all subjects, but subjects responded differently to those signals. In the second period for Group D subjects began by choosing colors different than those suggested. By the 4th period, the signaler "punished" subjects by sending a different color to each, which they all implemented. In the following period the signaler resumed sending the same signal to everyone. For Group C the experience was slightly different. The signaler began by sending the same signal, but one subject ignored it. The signaler immediately punished everyone by sending two different color signals. Following that move the signaler switched back to sending everyone the same signal and by the 4th period it served as a coordinating mechanism, a pattern that looks like learning with a corrective.

Groups E and F are quite different and are the most "noisy." In both instances at the outset the signaler sent different color signals to everyone. Group F members ignored

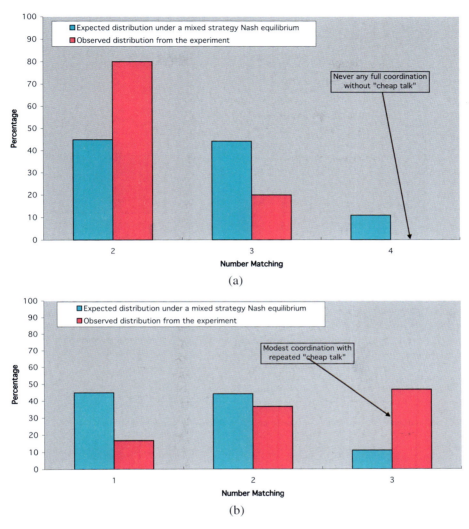

Figure 2. Distribution of coordinated choices in repeated play experiments: (a) no signaling condition, (b) signaling condition.

their signals and they happened to choose the same color. After that, however, the signaler was ignored. Much the same was true for Group E. Even though subjects fully coordinated in the fourth period, only one of the three members followed what the signaler proposed. In the final period every subject chose something different than what was suggested. In these groups, getting off on the wrong foot meant that recovering was very difficult – at least in the short run.

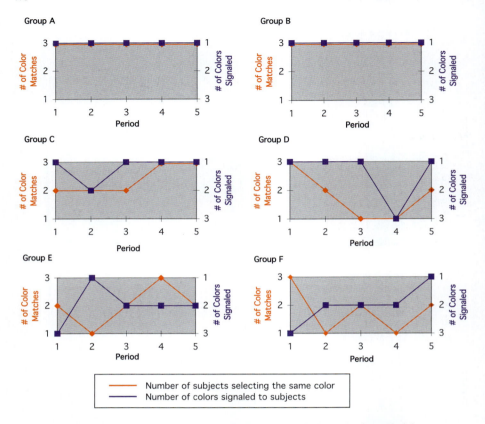

Figure 3. Consistency in signals and choices across periods by experimental trial.

These individual panels, while pointing out that subjects learned the value of cheap talk signals as a coordinating device, they also show that subjects are sensitive to the unfolding history of the trial. Once cheap talk is considered worthless, it is easily ignored.

5. Conclusion

Coordination problems are easily solved when there are clear and unambiguous signals. Institutional mechanisms that enhance the clarity of signals enables even cheap talk to work as a coordinating mechanism. On the other hand, learning about signals, especially if there is path-dependent noise in the environment, complicates the ability of subjects to settle on a common coordinating device.

Acknowledgements

Support by Dirksen Congressional Center and the Caterpillar Foundation is gratefully acknowledged. Neither organization bears any responsibility for the content of this article.

References

Farrell, J. (1987). "Cheap talk, coordination, and entry". RAND Journal of Economics 18, 34–39.
Ochs, Jack (1995). "Coordination problems". In: Kagel, John H., Roth, Alvin (Eds.), The Handbook of Experimental Economics. Princeton University Press, Princeton, NJ, pp. 195–251.
Schelling, Thomas C. (1960). "The Strategy of Conflict". Harvard University Press, Cambridge.
Van Huyck, J., Battalio, R.C., Beil, R.O. (1990). "Tacit coordination games, strategic uncertainty and coordination failure". American Economic Review 80, 234–248.
Wilson, Rick K., Rhodes, Carl M. (1997). "Leadership and credibility in n-person coordination games". Journal of Conflict Resolution 41, 767–791.

Chapter 53

EQUILIBRIUM CONVERGENCE IN NORMAL FORM GAMES

NICOLE BOUCHEZ and DANIEL FRIEDMAN

Economics Department University of California, Santa Cruz

In this chapter we examine convergence behavior in simple bimatrix games. We classify the possible types of simple games, pick interesting examples of each type, and summarize convergence behavior under various information and player matching protocols. See Friedman (1996), Cheung and Friedman (1997) and Bouchez (1997) for more complete descriptions of the experiments.

We begin with normal form games that have only two alternative strategies and a symmetric population of players. These games are defined by a 2×2 matrix $\mathbf{A} = ((a_{ij}))$ specifying the payoff to any player choosing strategy i when the opponent chooses j. Evolutionary game theory predicts that the direction of change in the fraction $p \in (0, 1)$ of players choosing the first strategy is given by the sign of the payoff differential $D(p) = (1, -1)A(p, 1-p)' = (1-p)a - pb$, where $a = a_{12} - a_{22}$ and $b = a_{21} - a_{11}$. When $D(p)$ is positive (the first strategy has the higher payoff) then $p < 1$ increases and the fraction $1 - p$ of players choosing the alternative strategy 2 decreases; the opposite is true when $D(p)$ is negative. The graph of $D(p)$ is a straight line with intercept a at $p = 0$ and value $-b$ at $p = 1$. Thus (apart from the degenerate case $a = b = 0$ in which a player is always indifferent between her two actions) each payoff matrix falls into one of three qualitatively different types as shown in Figure 1. In accordance with this classification scheme, we used single and two population games of all three types.

The next most complicated case is a single population of strategically identical players with three alternative actions. Here the payoff matrix $\mathbf{A}$ is 3×3 and the current state is a point in two-dimensional simplex $S = \{(p, q, 1-p-q) \in \mathbf{R}^3: p, q \geq 0, p+q \leq 1\}$. The classification of matrices becomes more complex as the edges of the simplex retain all three possibilities and the interior can be a sink, source, saddle or center. We use only a version of the "Hawk–Dove–Bourgeois" (HDB) game (see Figure 2 for an illustration).

1. Laboratory Procedures and Treatments

The experiments consist of 60–120 minutes laboratory sessions with 6 to 24 undergraduate subjects. Population size varies from 8 to 16 in the results presented here; Friedman (1996) finds strategic behavior contrary to the evolutionary assumption with population sizes of 6 and smaller. After instruction and a few practice periods, each session consists of 60–200 periods broken up into runs of 10 to 16 periods. Over 90% of the subjects earned between $8 and $32 per session.

Handbook of Experimental Economics Results, Volume 1
Copyright © 2008 Elsevier B.V. All rights reserved
DOI: 10.1016/S1574-0722(07)00053-4

Ch. 53: Equilibrium Convergence in Normal Form Games

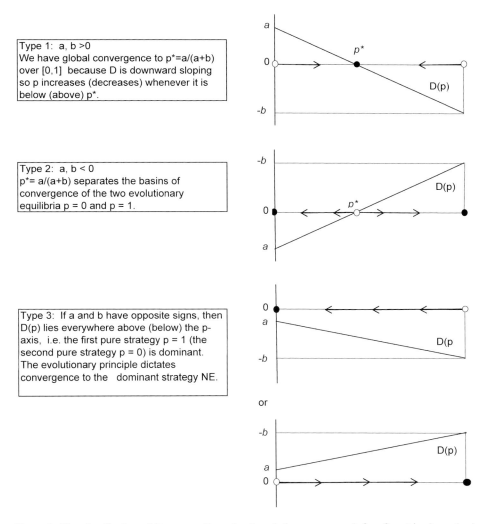

Type 1: a, b >0
We have global convergence to p*=a/(a+b) over [0,1] because D is downward sloping so p increases (decreases) whenever it is below (above) p*.

Type 2: a, b < 0
p*= a/(a+b) separates the basins of convergence of the two evolutionary equilibria p = 0 and p = 1.

Type 3: If a and b have opposite signs, then D(p) lies everywhere above (below) the p-axis, i.e. the first pure strategy p = 1 (the second pure strategy p = 0) is dominant. The evolutionary principle dictates convergence to the dominant strategy NE.

Figure 1. The classification of linear one-dimensional evolutionary games. A 2×2 matrix $A = (a_{ij})$ specifies the payoff to any player choosing strategy i when the opponent chooses j. The direction of change in the fraction p of players choosing the first strategy is the sign of the payoff differential $D(p) = (1, -1)A(p, 1-p)' = (1-p)a - pb$, where $a = a_{12} - a_{22}$ and $b = a_{21} - a_{11}$. The slope of $D(p)$ and location of the root $p^* = a/(a+b)$ of $D(p) = 0$ determine the type of the matrix A.

The treatments used were *random pairwise* (RP) and *mean matching* (MM) matching protocols, and the amount of historical information that appears on each player's screen (Hist/No Hist).

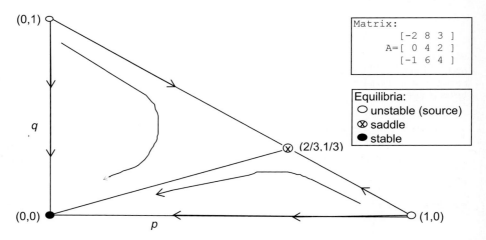

Figure 2. The Hawk–Dove–Bourgeois game. This version of the Hawk–Dome–Bourgeois game has a corner NE at $(p, q) = (0, 0)$ and an edge NE at $(2/3, 1/3)$. Under standard dynamics (e.g., replicator dynamics; see Weibull, 1995, for a simple exposition), the corner NE is an evolutionary equilibrium and the NE is a saddle point. The equations $d\mathbf{p}/dt = (1, 0, 0)'\mathbf{As} - (1/3, 1/3, 1/3)'\mathbf{As}$ and $d\mathbf{q}/dt = (0, 1, 0)'\mathbf{As} - (1/3, 1/3, 1/3)'\mathbf{As}$ characterize the dynamics in the interior of the simplex.

Under *random pairwise* (RP) the player had a single opponent randomly chosen each period. Players view their own (but not the opponent's) payoff matrix, and type "a" or "b" at the keyboard to indicate the choice of the first or second strategy. Under RP matching for payoff matrix **A**, a player's choice of strategy $i = 1$ or 2, gives *expected* payoff $(2 - i, i - 1)\mathbf{A}(p, 1 - p)'$ when the fraction of potential opponents choosing strategy 1 is p. However, his *actual* payoff depends on the action taken by his actual opponent, and so has some variance around its expectation. The variance is eliminated in the alternative matching procedure, called *mean matching* (MM). Here each player is matched once against each possible opponent in each round and receives the average (mean) payoff over all his matches.

The other major treatment in our experiments is the amount of historical information that appears in the upper left box on each player's screen. In the minimum level, *No Hist*, the player receives no historical information other than what she could tabulate herself: her own action and actual payoff in previous periods. In the other level, *Hist*, the box also displays the previous periods' full distribution of choices in the opponent population.

All treatments are held constant within a run to test for convergence. Runs are separated by obvious changes in the player population and/or the payoff matrix, and the history box is erased at the beginning of a new run.

2. Results

We have collected more than 300 such runs and used various statistical tests as well as summary graphs to study convergence properties. Figures 3–5 show some of the summary graphs for both one, two population, and three choice games. The main findings, presented more fully in Friedman (1996), can be summarized as follows.

(1) Some behavioral equilibrium (BE) is typically achieved by the second half of a 10 to 16 period run. The operational definition of BE is that strategy selection is almost constant in each population in a given run (or half-run). "Almost constant" means that the mean absolute deviation from the median number of players choosing a given strategy is less than 1 player ("tight") or less than 2 players ("loose"). Overall we observe tight BE in over 70% of second half-runs and loose BE in over 98% of second half-runs. Tight BE was achieved most reliably in type 3 games (over 95% of all half-runs). By contrast, type 1 games achieved tight BE in only 55% of half runs, but achieved loose BE in 96%.

(2) BE typically coincides with a Nash equilibrium (NE), especially with those (called evolutionary equilibria (EE)) that evolutionary game theory identifies as stable. We operationalize NE by replacing the median number of players by the NE number. In second half-runs, for example, about 79% of the loose BE are loose NE, and 84% of those are loose EE. The only notable exception to this conclusion is that in type 2 runs the BE sometimes coincided with the non-EE mixed NE. A closer look at the graphs suggests that many of these cases actually represent slow divergence from the mixed NE, and many of the half-runs deemed BE but not NE seem to represent slow or incomplete convergence to an EE (a pure NE).

(3) Convergence to BE is faster in the mean-matching (MM) than in the random-pairwise (RP) treatment, and faster in the *Hist* treatment than in the *No Hist* treatment. In particular, the slow and incomplete convergence observed in type-1 games arises mainly in RP matching protocol and *No Hist* runs. The results from type-2, single population games and all two-population games support the same conclusion. There is, however, an interesting exception. The few instances of non-convergence in type-3 games arise more often under MM than under RP.

(4) Individual behavior at a mixed strategy BE is better explained by idiosyncratic "purification" strategies than by identical individual mixed strategies. In particular, in the simplest type 1 game, Hawk–Dove, we see persistent heterogeneity in which some players consistently pick the first ("Hawk") strategy and others consistently pick the other ("Dove") strategy.

(5) "Hawk–Dove–Bourgeois" is a 1-population 3-action game with a triangular state space and with one corner NE (an EE) with target area b^2 and one edge NE (not an EE) with target area $2b^2$. Only one session was explored in Friedman (1996). Additional data has been collected (Bouchez, 1997) and the results discussed here are for the combined data. Loose (tight) convergence was found to some BE in 41 (7) of 46 half-runs, loose (tight) convergence to the EE in 8 (3) half-runs,

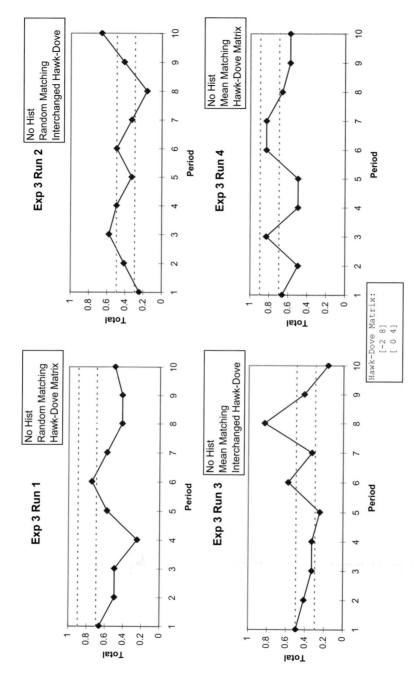

Figure 3. Single population sessions: Exp3 runs 1–4. These graphs chart the time path of p_t in the first four runs of the first usable session. The type 1 payoff matrix here has unique mixed NE $p^* = 2/3 = 8/12$. That is, in NE 8 of 12 players choose the first strategy (or 4 of 12 when the matrix rows and columns are interchanged as in runs 2 and 3). The graphs show a tolerance of 1 player in the band around NE. The time paths in the first four runs suggest that the NE attracts states p_t outside the tolerance band $p^* \pm 1/12$, but there is considerable behavioral noise so hits occur in only about 50% of the periods.

Ch. 53: Equilibrium Convergence in Normal Form Games

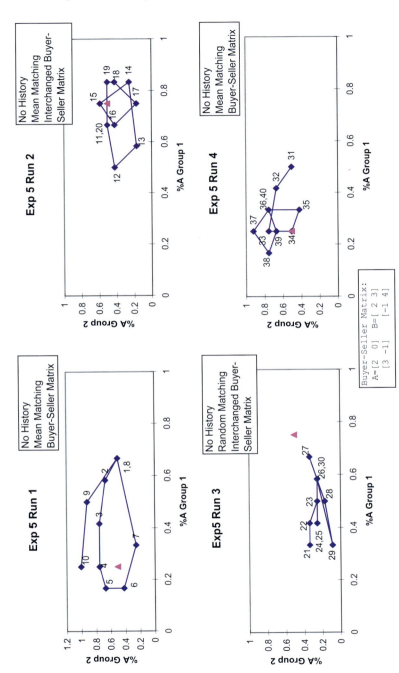

Figure 4. Two population sessions: Exp5 runs 1–4. Graphs of the behavior in the first four runs of exp5, the first 2-population session. All periods use the buyer–seller matrix or its interchange, so the unique NE (denoted by ▲) is at $(p, q) = (.25, .50)$ or, for the interchanged version, at $(.75, .50)$. The graphs show a 2-period moving average of the time path in the unit square. The graph for the first run looks like an unstable counterclockwise spiral diverging from the NE. The second run looks like a tidy counterclockwise double loop around the NE, neither converging nor diverging. The third run uses the RP matching protocol; at best there is a weak tendency to drift towards the NE. The fourth run reverts to MM and looks like a counterclockwise spiral possibly converging to the NE.

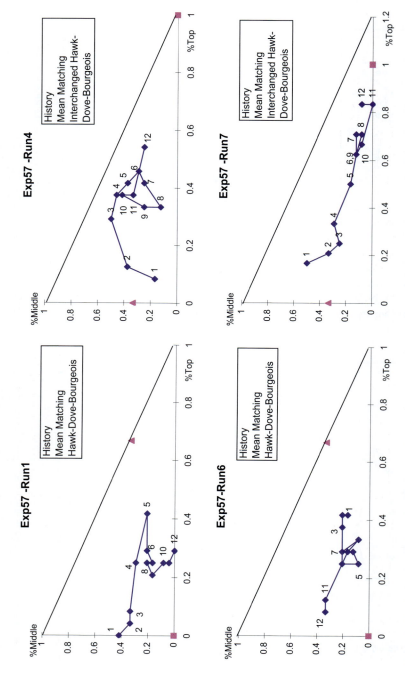

Figure 5. Single population three choice sessions: Exp57 runs 1, 4, 6, 7. Graphs of the behavior in the first four HDB runs of exp57. The two NE are at $(p, q) = (0, 0)$ and $(2/3, 1/3)$ (for the interchanged version, at $(1, 0)$ and $(0, 1/3)$) and are represented by ■ and ▲, respectively. The graphs show a 2-period moving average. The run 1 has loose convergence in the second half of the run as does run 7. Run 4 shows no convergence in either half. Run 6 has loose convergence in both the first and second halves of the experiment.

and no loose or tight convergence was found to the edge NE despite its larger area. The data are sparse but consistent with evolutionary game theory.

3. Discussion

For all three types of one-dimensional games and their two-dimensional analogues, the states reliably achieve a loose behavioral equilibrium (BE) even within the first half-run of 5 periods. Most of the loose BE are also tight BE, the main exceptions occurring in two-dimensional games with unique Nash equilibria (NE). Most BE coincide with NE, and most of the observed NE are indeed evolutionary equilibria (EE). In general, the "evolutionary" treatments of mean-matching (MM) and feedback (Hist) appear to improve convergence to EE. Thus the main tendencies of the data are consistent with evolutionary game theory.

The exceptions or boundaries to these main tendencies may be of special interest. Friedman (1996) shows that when group size is smaller than 6, players much more often appear willing to sacrifice current personal payoffs to increase group payoffs (and perhaps own later payoffs). Cooperative behavior (foregoing the dominant strategy) is sometimes observed in type 3 prisoner's dilemma sessions which have runs splitting the players into groups of size 2 or 4, and it is especially prevalent in the runs with the smaller groups. Such behavior is notably less frequent in sessions where the minimum group size remains above 6.

Perhaps the most surprising finding concerns another boundary for evolutionary game theory. An influential branch of the theory (Kandori, Mailath, and Rob, 1993, and Young, 1993) argues that in simple coordination (type 2) games with two pure strategy (corner) NE = EE and one interior NE, the "risk-dominant" corner EE is most likely to be observed because it has the larger basin of attraction, and indeed that *only* the risk-dominant EE will be observed in the relevant limiting case. Friedman (1996) shows that the data reviewed in this chapter support the contrary theoretical view of Bergin and Lipman (1995) that one can bias convergence towards the other ("payoff-dominant") EE by increasing the potential gains to cooperation. In some applications evolutionary game theory may have to be supplemented by a theory of trembles (or "mutations") that allows for forward-looking attempts to influence others' behavior.

References

Bergin, J., Lipman, B.L. (1995). "Evolution with state-dependent mutations". Draft manuscript, Queen's University Department of Economics.
Bouchez, Nicole (1997). "A study and application of learning in population games". Draft manuscript, University of California, Santa Cruz.
Cheung, Yin-Wong, Friedman, Daniel (1997). "Individual learning in normal form games: Some laboratory results". Games and Economic Behavior 19, 46–76.
Friedman, Daniel (1996). "Equilibrium in evolutionary games: Some experimental results". The Economic Journal 106 (434), 1–25.

Kandori, Michihiro, Mailath, George, Rob, Rafael (1993). "Learning, mutations, and long run equilibria in games". Econometrica 61 (1), 29–56.
Young, H. Peyton (1993). "The evolution of conventions". Econometrica 61 (1), 57–84.
Weibull, Jorgen W. (1995). "Evolutionary Game Theory". MIT Press, Cambridge, MA.

Chapter 54

ANALYZING CHOICE WITH REVEALED PREFERENCE: IS ALTRUISM RATIONAL?

JAMES ANDREONI

Department of Economics, University of Wisconsin, Madison, WI 53706, USA

JOHN H. MILLER

Department of Social and Decision Sciences, Carnegie Mellon University, Pittsburgh, PA 15213, USA

1. Introduction

In consumer theory, a binary preference ordering embodies three axioms of choice: it must be complete, reflexive and transitive. If preferences adhere to these axioms, then they can be characterized by a utility function. If preferences are well-behaved – that is, they are convex and monotonic – then the utility function will generate smooth downward sloping demand curves.

How do we know if our fundamental assumptions are valid? Samuelson (1948) gave us an elegant answer to this question, the theory of revealed preference[1]:

DEFINITION (Directly revealed preferred). An allocation X is directly revealed preferred to a different allocation Y if Y was in the budget set when X was chosen.

Then if a well-behaved utility function could have generated the data, the data will satisfy *WARP*:

WEAK AXIOM OF REVEALED PREFERENCE (WARP). If allocation X is directly revealed preferred to Y, then Y cannot be directly revealed preferred to X.

WARP is a necessary condition on choices to be consistent with utility theory. However, it is not a sufficient condition. For this we need a stronger axiom.

DEFINITION (Revealed preferred). If an allocation A is directly revealed preferred to B, B is directly revealed preferred to C, C is directly revealed preferred ... to Z, and A and Z are not the same bundle, then A is revealed preferred to Z. That is, the revealed preferred relation is the transitive closure of the directly revealed preferred relation.

---

[1] See Varian (1992) for a more detailed discussion of revealed preference.

STRONG AXIOM OF REVEALED PREFERENCE (SARP). *If allocation X is revealed preferred to Y, then Y will never be revealed preferred to X.*

If preferences are strictly convex, then choices will conform to SARP. Moreover, if choices conform to SARP then there exists a well-behaved preference ordering that could have generated the data. That is, utility theory is valid for the data observed.

SARP is a strong tool for economists to use to verify that an individual's behavior is "rational"; that is, it is consistent with neoclassical choice theory. However, SARP is still a bit restrictive in that it requires preferences to be strictly convex. Afriat (1967) and Varian (1982) showed that a fully general axiom that is both necessary and sufficient for the existence of a utility function – even one that has flat spots on indifference curves – is GARP:

GENERALIZED AXIOM OF REVEALED PREFERENCE (GARP). *If an allocation X is revealed preferred to Y, then Y is never strictly directly revealed preferred to X, that is, X is never strictly within the budget set when Y is chosen.*

In this chapter we discuss an application of revealed preference to a common occurrence in experiments – kindness among subjects. In many experiments, including prisoner's dilemma, public goods, and bargaining experiments, subjects are often found to act benevolently toward each other. The immediate reaction when these findings began appearing was that subjects were "irrational" because they did not choose to maximize their own monetary payoffs. Some suggested that neoclassical theory had failed, and others suggested that economics needed to appeal to other behavioral sciences to understand this "non-economic" behavior. But the axioms of choice indicate that what is "rational" is what is consistent, that is, it can be characterized by convex preferences. Hence, whether this benevolent behavior is rational is an empirical question that the experimental economist is perfectly suited to answer.

The hypothesis to explore here is that subjects have consistent preferences for altruism. To address this, we designed an experiment that would measure a subject's simple preferences over allocations between themselves and another subject. Most social dilemma experiments, like prisoner's dilemma, public goods, or alternating offer bargaining, can be decomposed into unilateral allocation problems. Since we see people allocating some of the payoff to themselves and some to the other subject, we pose this question: Can choices over this allocation process be "rational?"

Let π_s be the payoff a subject allocates to "self" and π_o be the payoff the subject allocates to the "other." Then the research question can be restated as, "Can behavior in experiments be characterized by a quasi-concave utility function of the form $U_i = u_i(\pi_s, \pi_o)$?"

Table 1
This table lists the eight allocation decisions presented to the subjects. The decisions were presented in random order to each subject. Each decision can be thought of as choosing a payoff along a budget constraint. For each budget, a subject allocates the token endowment between himself and another subject. Tokens are redeemable for points at different rates for the two subjects. Hence, each allocation problem is a choice of final payoffs for the two subjects, where the price of the other's payoff in terms of self-payoff varies across budgets. We can then check to see that there are no violations of revealed preference, e.g., GARP, in which case the data on the subject is consistent with rational choice

Budget	Token endowment	Points received for each token allocated	
		Self	Other
1	40	3	1
2	40	1	3
3	60	2	1
4	60	1	2
5	75	2	1
6	75	1	2
7	60	1	1
8	100	1	1

2. The Choice Task

The data we describe here is a subset of that used our paper, Andreoni and Miller (2002). Subjects were presented eight different allocation tasks, in random order. Each choice endowed the subject with a budget of tokens which were worth different numbers of points to the two subjects. Points were all worth $0.10 to all subjects. The budget of tokens was 100, 75, 60 or 40 tokens, and tokens were worth 1, 2 or 3 points each. Hence, by varying the endowments and points, we were able to create various budgets of payoffs with different relative prices. The budgets were chosen to intersect often so as to give the strongest test of revealed preference. Table 1 presents the eight choices presented to subjects.

After subjects made allocation decisions in all eight budgets, the experimenter randomly chose one to carry out with another subject chosen at random from the room. We ran four sessions of the experiment, each with 35 or 36 subjects, for a total of 142 subjects, and took great pains to protect the anonymity of all subjects. For details of the experiment and procedures, see Andreoni and Miller (2002).

3. Checking GARP

Table 2 shows the violations of GARP. Over all 142 subjects, fewer than 10 percent had a single violation. For most of these subjects, however, the violations were minor. Altering a single choice by a single unit would eliminate all violations for all but 2 subjects, and

Table 2

Here we list the subjects who showed at least one violation of the revealed preference axioms. Of the 142 subjects, fewer that 10% had any violations. Of those violations, most would disappear if one choice on one budget were moved by one token. Hence, only subject 40 showed serious violations of revealed preference. This implies that virtually all subjects display a rational demand for altruism

Subject	Number of violations		
	WARP	SARP	GARP
3	1	3	3
38	2	4	4
40	3	10	10
41	1	1	1
47	1	1	3
61	1	4	4
72	1	1	1
87	1	1	1
90	1	1	1
104	1	2	2
126	1	3	1
137	1	1	1
139	1	1	1

moving two choices by 1 unit each would eliminate all but 1.[2] The only severe violation of revealed preference was subject 40. His choices are shown in Figure 1. For example, bundles A and B violate WARP, as do bundles A and C. However, bundles B and C also violate SARP and WARP.

Given that virtually everyone's preferences can be rationalized, what do indifference curves look like? It turns out that 22 percent of subjects were perfectly selfish, keeping all of the endowment. Hence preferences of the form $U = x_s$ could characterize these people. Another 16 percent always split the payoffs exactly; hence Leontief utility, $U = \min\{x_s, x_o\}$, could generate this data. Finally, 6 percent always allocated tokens to maximize the total payoff of subjects; that is, they were social maximizers. $U = x_s + x_o$ could represent these people.

This covers over a third of all subjects. The rest of the subjects were similar to these extreme cases but did not fit them exactly. Figure 2 illustrates an example of what we call a weakly selfish person – someone with a bit more price sensitivity than a strong free rider. Figure 3 is a weakly Leontief person. She splits payoffs evenly or nearly evenly on all budgets. Finally, Figure 4 is a weak social maximizer. This person has very flat (but not perfectly flat) indifference curves.

---

[2] We also conducted more sophisticated analysis of violations, including applying Afriat's Critical Cost Efficiency Index, which is a measure of how costly a violation of revealed preference is for the subject. This analysis, which can be found in Andreoni and Miller (2002) yielded a similar interpretation, that is, only subject 40 had severe violations.

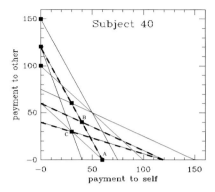

Figure 1. Of the subjects who had any violations of revealed preference axioms, only Subject 40, shown above, had severe violations that could not be eliminated with small adjustments to choices. For instance, A is directly revealed preferred to B, but B is directly revealed preferred to A. Likewise, A and C are directly revealed preferred to each other. Hence, A and B, and A and C violate WARP. Notice C is revealed preferred to B, but since B is directly revealed preferred to C, then B and C violate GARP as well. For this subject, no quasiconcave utility function could rationalize the data.

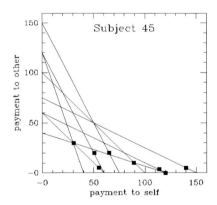

Figure 2. Over all 142 subjects, 22% were perfectly selfish, so $U = x_s$ could rationalize these choices. Another 22% were close to being perfectly selfish. Subject 45 shown here is typical of these. Most of the payoff is kept for himself, but there is still considerable price sensitivity.

Overall we can characterize all individuals as one of these six types.[3] Table 3 shows the distribution of these preferences.

---

[3] This characterization is based on minimizing the Euclidian distance between a subject's choices and those of one of the three exact utility functions, selfish, Leontief, and perfect substitutes. We also categorized people using a Bayesian criterion and by using an adaptive search algorithm. Each produced similar results.

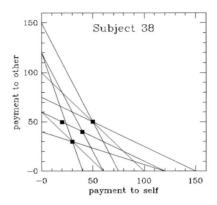

Figure 3. We found that 16% of subjects always divided the payoffs equally, hence $U = \min\{x_s, x_o\}$ could rationalize these choices. Another 18% had preferences that were very near to Leontief preferences but, like Subject 38 in this figure, deviated slightly from perfect Leontief preferences. Note that Subject 38 also violated WARP. However, the deviation (which appears likely to be an honest error) is not severe – moving two of his choices by one token each would remove all violations.

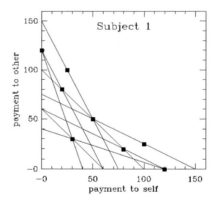

Figure 4. Six percent of subjects always gave all of the endowment to the subject with the highest redemption value, meaning the utility $U = x_s + x_o$ would rationalize this data. Another 15% of subjects had preferences like Subject 1 above. They appear to have very flat indifference curves that generate choices near the socially maximal payoffs.

4. Conclusion

This work illustrates that not all "non-economic" behavior is beyond economic analysis. Our maintained assumption as economists is that individual behavior is consistent with self-interest. At its weakest, self-interest only means that choices conform to some underlying preference ordering that is complete, reflexive and transitive, and, hence, some utility function can be used to describe behavior. However, the assumption of

Table 3
Given that preferences are rational, what utility functions could have generated the observed behavior? By employing several different search algorithms, we found that six categories of utility functions could best characterize the data. There were three utility functions that fit a large fraction of the data precisely. The three other categories of preferences had preferences similar to the exact utility function, but differed some, as is illustrated in Figures 2, 3, and 4

Utility function	Exact fit	Weak fit
Selfish: $U_i = \pi_s$	31	31
Leontief: $U_i = \min\{\pi_s, \pi_o\}$	23	26
Social maximizer: $U_i = \pi_s + \pi_o$	8	22

self-interest does not tell us what variables are in that utility function. What does? Our methodology dictates that people themselves, through their actions, will do so. What we have shown here is that unselfish behavior in experiments can indeed be captured by a model of self-interested agents, but that self-interested agents are not always money-maximizing. When we define the choice set appropriately, unselfish acts can be described and predicted with the standard neoclassical model of choice.

References

Afriat, S. (1967). "The construction of a utility function from expenditure data". Econometrica 6, 67–77.
Andreoni, James, Miller, John H. (2002). "Giving according to GARP: An experimental test of the consistency of preferences for altruism". Econometrica 70, 737–753.
Samuelson, Paul A. (1948). "Consumption theory in terms of revealed preference". Econometrica 15, 243–253.
Varian, Hal R. (1982). "The nonparametric approach to demand analysis". Econometrica 50, 945–972.
Varian, Hal R. (1992). "Microeconomic Analysis", third ed. Norton, New York.

Chapter 55

TESTING THEORIES OF OTHER-REGARDING BEHAVIOR: A SEQUENCE OF FOUR LABORATORY STUDIES

GARY E. BOLTON

310 Beam, Penn State University, University Park, PA 16802, USA
e-mail: geb3@psu.edu

JORDI BRANDTS

Institut d'Anàlisi Econòmica (CSIC), Campus UAB, 08193 Bellaterra, Barcelona, Spain
e-mail: jordi.brandts@uab.es

ELENA KATOK

509H BAB, Smeal College of Business, Penn State University, State College, PA 16870, USA
e-mail: ekatok@psu.edu

AXEL OCKENFELS

Max Planck Institute for Research into Economic Systems, Strategic Interaction Unit, Kahlaische Straße 10, D-07745 Jena, Germany
e-mail: ockenfels@mpiew-jena.mpg.de

RAMI ZWICK

Department of Marketing, The Hong Kong University of Science and Technology, Clear Water Bay, Kowloon, Hong Kong
e-mail: mkzwick@ust.hk

1. Introduction

Behavior that Hoffman et al. (1994) have labeled "other-regarding" often seems incompatible with the standard assumption of payoff maximizing when rationality is common knowledge. Other-regarding behavior includes altruistic action, action motivated out of fairness, and cooperative behavior in the face of incentives to free ride.

These 'anomalies' have given rise to a diverse set of theories. Some explain other-regarding behavior in terms of strategic reputation building, by modifying standard optimization models by introducing a small amount of incomplete information about rationality (e.g., Kreps et al.'s, 1982, tit-for-tat explanation of the finitely repeated prisoner's dilemma), or by taking explicit account of the larger supergame (e.g., Fudenberg and Maskin's, 1986, treatment of the folk theorem). Other theories explicitly introduce bounded rationality (e.g., Sugden's, 1984, reciprocity principle for public good games, Selten's, 1987, theory of equal division payoff bounds for coalition games, and Roth and Erev's, 1995, reinforcement learning model). Both of these classes of theory, strategic reputation building and bounded rationality, are usually based, if only implicitly, on the premise that own material payoff is the sole motivator of behavior. A third class of theory introduces additional motivations, usually by way of interdependent preferences (e.g., Becker's, 1974, theory of social interactions, Andreoni's, 1989, theory of warm glow giving, Bolton's 1991, comparative bargaining model, Rabin's, 1993, fairness equilibrium, and the inequity aversion models by Fehr and Schmidt, 1999, and Bolton and Ockenfels, 2000).[1]

This chapter describes a sequence of four experiments. The hypotheses tested are all informed by one or more of the aforementioned types of models. Each experiment builds on the findings of the previous experiment in the sequence. At the same time, each experiment involves a different game, thereby allowing us to study the phenomenon from a variety of perspectives.

While some of the models we examine get important features of the data correct, none is completely satisfactory. What emerges from this sequence of experiments is a set of empirical regularities that should provide some useful guidance to the construction of more accurate models.

2. Bolton and Zwick (1995): Reputation Building versus Self-centered Fairness in an Ultimatum Game

At first blush, strategic reputation building might not seem to apply to much of the other-regarding behavior we observe in the lab, the reason being that lab games are typically played among anonymous subjects interacting for a single play of the game. Under such conditions, there is little chance for a subject to build a reputation with other subjects. But on reflection, one might conjecture that lab subjects act to build reputations with the person who does usually observe their actions: the experimenter. So for example, subjects might reject a small share of the payoff to avoid looking greedy and unprincipled in the eyes of the experimenter; by rejecting, the subject establishes a reputation with the experimenter that might be profitable to the subject in the future.[2] An alternative explanation, implied by models such as Bolton and Ockenfels (2000) and Rabin (1993), is that subjects reject money because they care about fairness independent of strategic considerations (such as reputation building). Both of these models treat fairness as a matter of individual preference; they imply that those subjects who reject money in the ultimatum game have an aversion to being treated unfairly, much as some people have an aversion to risk.

Bolton and Zwick (1995) report on an experiment that concerns the simplified version of the ultimatum game, called cardinal ultimatum, illustrated in the top panel of

---

[1] Work by Hoffman, McCabe, and Smith (1998) takes an evolutionary psychology approach to these questions. The work we report here has less to say about these sorts of model.
[2] Reputation building with the experimenter was first put forth as an explanation by Hoffman et al. (1994) to explain gift giving in the dictator game.

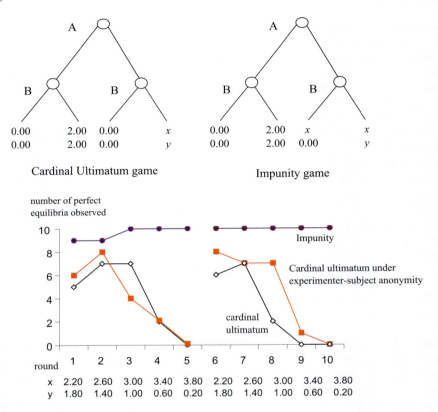

Figure 1. Cardinal ultimatum game and impunity game. In the cardinal ultimatum game, 30% of play is in equilibrium (46% when played under strong experimenter-subject anonymity conditions). When the capacity to punish is removed (impunity game), equilibrium play approaches 100%. Hence, the data provides evidence that unfairness aversion explains much more of the deviation from perfect equilibrium in ultimatum games than does the effects of experimenter observation. Furthermore, Players A respond strategically to the chance of being turned down. They almost never offer the equal split in the impunity game (where no Player B ever rejects), while the equal split is offered in about 40 to 50% of the time in the other games, where, depending on how unequal the division is, the rejection rate ranges from 7 to 100%.

Figure 1. Player A chooses between offering Player B an equal division of the payoff pie, or an unequal division favoring Player A. If Player B rejects the offer then the game ends with both players receiving no money. The payoffs in the unequal division were rotated across rounds as indicated on the horizontal axis of the bottom panel in the figure (each player had a different partner each round). In the standard perfect equilibrium for this game, bargainers settle on the unequal division.

In the base condition of the experiment, known as cardinal ultimatum, the game is played with experimenter observation; that is, the experimenter gathers information in such a way that he can accurately attribute individual actions to individual subjects.

Each of the other two conditions of the experiment features a variation on the base condition. In the experimenter-subject anonymity condition, cardinal ultimatum is played in such a way that the experimenter does not have the information necessary to attribute individual actions to individual subjects (see Bolton and Zwick, 1995, for a description of how this is done). In the impunity condition, the game is modified as shown in the top panel of the figure, so that rejecting an unequal split leaves Player A's share of the payoff in tact; the game is played with experimenter observation, as in the base condition.[3]

Relative to the base condition, the experimenter-subject anonymity condition diminishes the strategic reputation building motive for rejecting the unequal split without changing the unfairness aversion motive, whereas the impunity condition leaves the reputation building motive for rejecting intact but eliminates the unfairness aversion motive, since rejecting in the impunity condition does not avert the unfairness (and arguably makes it worse). Hence the strategic reputation building hypothesis predicts more perfect equilibrium play in the experimenter-subject anonymity condition than in either the cardinal ultimatum or impunity conditions, with no difference for the latter two. In contrast, the unfairness aversion hypothesis predicts the same amount of perfect equilibrium play in cardinal ultimatum and experimenter-subject conditions, but more in the impunity condition.

The bottom panel in Figure 1 summarizes the main results of the experiment. There is a dramatic increase in perfect equilibrium play in the impunity condition over cardinal ultimatum or the experiment-subject anonymity condition. There is little difference between the latter two conditions. Fong and Bolton (1997) analyze the data using a Bayesian bioassay technique. Given the assumptions of the Bayesian model, the analysis identifies some statistical evidence that perfect equilibria are higher in experimenter-subject anonymity than in cardinal ultimatum, but the difference is quite small.

A substantial portion of the deviation from perfect equilibrium in cardinal ultimatum stems from Player B rejections of an offer of the unequal division; the rejection rate ranges from 7 to 100 percent depending on how unequal the division is. In contrast, no Player B rejects the unequal division in the impunity condition. Hence the results of the experiment imply that unfairness aversion is a much stronger motive for rejecting money in the ultimatum game than is building a reputation with the experimenter. Also, Players A in cardinal ultimatum and experimenter-subject anonymity deviate from the unequal division (offer the equal division) about 40 to 50 percent of the time, whereas Players A in impunity deviate only twice in the first two rounds of play and never after that. It appears then that Players A act strategically in the sense that they are far more likely to ask for the unequal division when there is a negligible chance of it being turned down than when the chance is non-negligible.

---

[3] Relative to the original paper, some of the experimental conditions and hypotheses have been renamed to fit the present exposition. The changes are purely semantic.

3. Bolton, Katok, and Zwick (1998): The Nature of Giving Behavior in Dictator Games

The dictator game differs from the ultimatum game solely in that the second mover cannot reject what the first mover offers. If money is the only motive then the dictator should keep the entire pie for himself. But in fact dictator game investigations (e.g., Forsythe et al., 1994; Hoffman et al., 1994) report a wide dispersion of dictator game giving. Some dictators do leave nothing, but others give away as much as 50 percent of the pie. The modal amount left is sometimes as high as 30 percent. What explains this behavior?[4] Bolton, Katok, and Zwick (1998) provides some clues.

The experiment began as a 2 × 2 design and was later extended in response to the initial results. The treatment variables were the number of division choices per game (2 or 6) and the number of games each dictator participated in (1 or 10). Here we focus on two conditions with 6 division choices, one condition featuring 1 game, and another featuring 10 games.[5] In the 1 game condition the game involved a $10 pie, and the dictator could leave $0 to $5 to the recipient in $1 increments. In the 10 games treatments, each game involved a $1 pie, and the dictator could leave $0, 0.1, 0.2, 0.3, 0.4 or 0.5 in each game. So in all cases, the total amount available for division by a single dictator was $10, and up to half of this amount could be given away in gifts.

Figure 2 presents individual dictator giving to 10 recipients. Here, only the 15 dictators (out of 25) who are willing to give a positive total amount are considered. As can be seen from the figure, when distributing a gift among several recipients, individual dictators show little tendency toward equal treatment. Of the 15 subjects who are willing to give a positive total amount, only two subjects gave the same amount to each recipient. In most other cases, the distribution of total gifts appears to be arbitrary.

The haphazard nature of the distribution is puzzling. It is perhaps then all the more striking that we find very consistent behavior when we look at the total sum allocated. The bottom panel of Figure 2 compares frequency distributions for total giving in the 10 games $1 pie and the 1 game $10 pie treatments. While most dictators seem to distribute gifts among multiple recipients in an arbitrary manner, the distribution of *total* gifts is the same whether dividing a pie of $10 with one other or dividing 10 pies of $1 with 10 others. This is what Selten and Ockenfels (1998) call the 'fixed total sacrifice effect.'

Bolton, Katok, and Zwick propose a hypothetical decision procedure (a pre-model model if you will) that posits that dictator giving arises from a concern on the part

---

[4] The preferences in Bolton (1991) imply that a person is concerned exclusively with fairness for himself. The preferences in Rabin (1993) imply that a person gives to another only when he expects the other to give to him. Neither of these characterizations allows giving in the dictator game. However, more recent models by Fehr and Schmidt (1999) and Bolton and Ockenfels (2000) capture both ultimatum and dictator game behavior along with behavior observed in other games.

[5] The experiment included several other treatments, including one designed to look for an experimenter-subject anonymity effect. No effect of this sort was evident. Hoffman et al. (1994) find such an effect in their study. Bolton, Katok, and Zwick provide some discussion towards reconciling these two results.

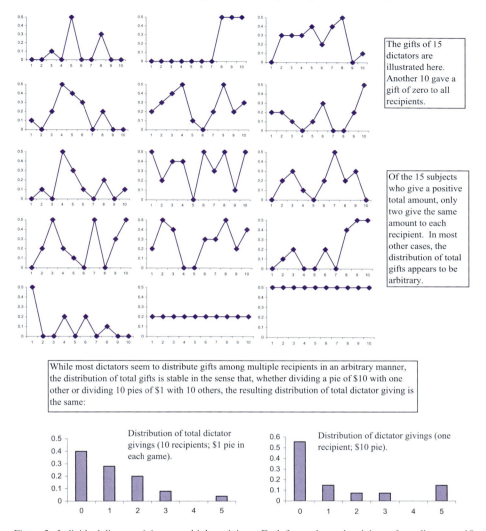

Figure 2. Individual dictator giving to multiple recipients. Each figure shows the givings of one dictator to 10 recipients. In each of the 10 encounters, the dictator could allocate a $1 pie.

of the dictator for a fair distribution between self and the group. In the first step of the decision procedure, dictators decide how much to keep for themselves and how much to give in gifts to the group. Only after deciding the total gift to the group do they decide how to distribute the gift across the group. In the procedure, concerns from fair distribution are posited to originate from personal and social rules that effectively constrain self-interested behavior – although within these constraints dictators behave in a self-interested manner (they act first to secure what they consider to be their own fair share).[6] What purpose these rules might ultimately serve, whether it be to improve others' welfare (altruism) or some other purpose, is not clear from the data in this study.

4. Selten and Ockenfels (1998) and Ockenfels and Weimann (1999): The Fixed Total Sacrifice Effect in the Solidarity Game

The solidarity game was designed by Selten and Ockenfels (1998) to examine the fixed total sacrifice effect in greater detail. The solidarity game is a one-shot, three-person game in which each player independently wins a fixed positive pecuniary amount with probability 2/3 and zero with probability 1/3. Before the dice are rolled, each player is asked how much he is willing to give to a loser if there is only one loser in the group, and how much he is willing to give to each loser if there are two. Let x_1 denote the conditional gift for the case of exactly one loser, and x_2 the conditional gifts given to each of two losers. Of course, no positive gifts should be handed over by payoff maximizing subjects.

The types of conditional gift behavior that were observed are classified in Table 1. The classification is concerned with the question of whether the conditional gifts are positive and how they relate to each other. The corresponding relative frequencies of subjects in the western and eastern part of Germany are based on the data collected by Selten and Ockenfels (1998) and Ockenfels and Weimann (1999), in solidarity experiments which are conducted shortly after the reunification of Germany in Bonn (western Germany) and Magdeburg (eastern Germany), respectively, both under conditions of experimenter-subject anonymity.

In both studies, a majority of subjects choose positive conditional gifts. Among the gift givers, a large majority exhibit fixed total sacrifice behavior, $x_1 = 2x_2 > 0$. The same sort of hypothetical decision procedure as suggested in Bolton et al. fits this data. But in the context of the solidarity game, Selten and Ockenfels (1998) are able to say more: They formally show that fixed total sacrifice behavior cannot easily be interpreted as the result of utility maximization of altruistic subjects (see the paper for the details).

It is natural to wonder whether the rules that govern giving behavior are influenced by culture. Ockenfels and Weimann (1999) examine the solidarity game and repeated public good game experiments in eastern and western Germany in search of potential cross-culture effects. Since the study was conducted in two parts of one nation, it avoided currency, language and related effects which usually cause methodological problems in multinational experimental settings (see Roth et al., 1991). In both subject pools individual behavior exhibits a great deal of heterogeneity. Moreover, as illustrated in Table 1, eastern subjects behave on average in a significantly more self-interested manner than do western subjects. In particular, eastern subjects choose a zero conditional gift in the solidarity game more frequently than do western subjects. Analogously,

---

[6] This line of reasoning is consistent with Bolton and Ockenfels' (2000) model.

Table 1
Types of conditional gift behavior in the solidarity game. Each player in a three-person group independently rolls dice to determine whether they (individually) win a fixed monetary sum. Before the dice are rolled, each player announces how much he wishes to compensate the losers in the case of winning, for both the case where there is one loser (conditional gift $= x_1$), and for the case where there are two (conditional gift for each of two losers $= x_2$). The table shows subjects by type of conditional gift behavior

Types of conditional gift behavior	No gift[a]	Fixed total sacrifice[b] (exact and up to rounding)	Intermediate	Fixed gift to loser
	$x_1 = x_2 = 0$	$x_1 = 2x_2 > 0$	$2x_2 > x_1 > x_2 > 0$	$x_1 = x_2 > 0$
West Germany	21	52	11	16
East Germany	47[c]	35	5	14

[a] Only a minority of subjects leave no gift, even though the experiments are experimenter-subject anonymous.
[b] Among those who are willing to give a gift, a large majority give the same total amount independent of the number of losers. This kind of 'fixed total sacrifice behavior' resembles the gift behavior observed in Bolton, Katok, and Zwick (1998; see Figure 2). It cannot easily be explained as the result of altruistic preferences.
[c] West German students are significantly less inclined to behave selfishly in the solidarity game. The distribution of subjects across non-selfish types of conditional gift behavior, however, is remarkably stable across subject pools.

Ockenfels and Weimann observe that eastern subjects contribute dramatically less than western subjects in all rounds of a repeated linear public good game. A more detailed data analysis suggests the hypothesis that behavioral differences are due to differing social norms that in turn may have resulted from sharply differing economic and social histories in the two parts of Germany.

Despite the differences across cultures, however, the same *qualitative* features of behavior are observed in both subject pools. In the solidarity game, both the distributions of subjects across non-selfish behavioral types of conditional gift behavior and the distributions of quantitative gift levels of non-selfish subjects are very similar in the two parts of Germany (Roth et al., 1991, make similar observations for multinational ultimatum bargaining experiments).

5. Bolton, Brandts, and Ockenfels (1998): Distribution versus Intentions in a 2-person Dilemma Game

Is the other-regarding motive behind rejecting in an ultimatum game or contributing in a dilemma game (e.g., the public goods game by Ockenfels and Weimann discussed in the last section) fundamentally the same as, or fundamentally different than, the giving behavior we see in the dictator game? Rabin's (1993) model suggests they are fundamentally different. In Rabin's model, other-regarding behavior is motivated by a desire to reward or punish the intentions behind another's actions towards oneself. So rejecting in an ultimatum game punishes the poor intentions behind the first mover's poor offer, and contributing rewards the good intentions of those who contribute to oneself. Giving in the dictator game cannot be about the same thing since the recipient can take no action, and hence there are no intentions to reward or punish. Models by Bolton and Ockenfels (1998, 2000) and Fehr and Schmidt (1999), on the other hand, imply that the motive is fundamentally the same for all three types of games. In these models, players act to choose the distribution of payoffs they prefer most among those that are feasible independent of the intentions of other players.

Contrary to Rabin's model, we observe giving in the dictator game, which would seem to suggest that distribution is at least part of the motive in ultimatum and dilemma games. But it is also plausible that there is an additional motive, like the one posited by Rabin's model, involved in other-regarding behavior in dilemma and ultimatum games.

Bolton, Brandts, and Ockenfels (1998) analyze the role of distributional preferences and of intentionality in explaining behavior in two simple sequential dilemma games: treatments I and III in Figure 3. The key insight behind the design is that, in games of this type, the motivation of a second mover who chooses a certain response to a given action by a first mover cannot be assessed correctly without additional information. What needs to be known is what the second mover would choose if faced with the same opportunity set as in the C(ooperation) choice of treatment I and as in the D(efection) choice in treatment III, but without the first mover having had any part in bringing that opportunity set about.

The appropriate control is provided by treatment II, shown in Figure 3, in which the second mover can select a distribution of payoffs for himself and the other player in a "free choice" manner. Choices in treatment II give a measure of what level of contributions is motivated by purely distributional concerns. The relevance of intentionality can be assessed by comparing second movers' choices across treatments. If second movers' responses to C in treatment I were more generous than their choices in treatment II, one could say that second movers' rewarding the first mover's good intentions behind the action. If second movers were more generous in treatment III than in treatment II, then one could speak of punishing bad intentions.

The lower part of Figure 3 compares the cumulative distributions of the second mover's decisions for the three treatments. There are no significant differences between the three distributions. The order of the results of treatments I and II is reversed relative to what corresponds to a reward of good intentions: contributions are lower in treatment I than in treatment II. Although there is no significant difference between treatments II and III, the ordering of contributions is consistent with the punishment of bad intentions. A quantitative comparison, however, shows that the contribution level in treatment II is equal to about nine times the small decrease in contributions that could possibly be attributed to a punishment of bad intentions.[7]

---

[7] Bolton, Brandts, and Katok (2000) present evidence that confirms the comparison of treatments I and II above. Bolton, Brandts, and Ockenfels (1998) and Bolton and Ockenfels (2001) discuss the role of intentionality in variants of the ultimatum game.

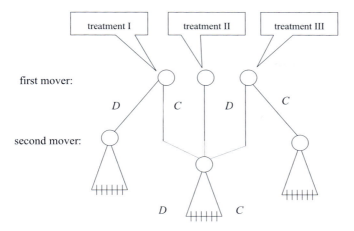

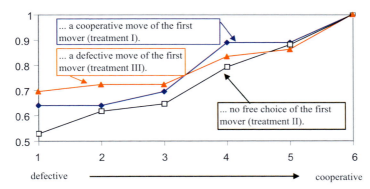

Figure 3. Intentions vs distribution. The following figure shows the structure of three experimental dilemma games. In the treatments I and III a first mover decides whether to cooperate or to defect. In treatment II, he has no choice. In all cases, the second mover can choose from six cooperation levels. The game outcomes associated with each of the cooperation levels are identical after a cooperative or defective choice of the first mover in treatment I and III, respectively, and in treatment II. The three distributions are very similar; no significant effect occurs. Second mover behavior does not seem to depend on first movers' inventions but rather on distributional preferences.

As a whole, we interpret the above results as evidence that behavior in these games can basically be explained on distributional grounds and that the role of intentionality is secondary. At the same time our results suggests that the tendency to punish bad intentions may be a somewhat stronger force than the propensity to reward good intentions, but a firmer conclusion requires additional research.

6. Summary: Regularities for Theory Building

To summarize, three types of regularities of potential importance to theory building emerge from these experiments:

First, there is a strong strategic element to other-regarding behavior. A successful model will therefore be a strategic model. Unfairness-averse second movers reject ultimatum bargaining offers only when doing so makes the resulting division less unequal. And the first mover's proposal is more generous when there is a potential penalty (rejection) for not being generous.

Second, the empirical manifestation of other-regarding behavior – altruism, fairness, and reciprocity – differs in important respects from philosophical and other introspective notions of these concepts. While we do observe a concern for fairness, this concern is in an important sense self-centered (people appear more concerned with whether the agreement is fair to themselves than fair to others; see also Bolton and Ockenfels on this issue). It is difficult for the standard theory of altruism to account for the nature of giving that we observe; specifically, altruism does not easily account for the fixed total sacrifice effect. The Bolton, Brandts, and Ockenfels experiment suggests that instead of being distinctly different motives, altruism, fairness and reciprocity are facets of a common pattern of behavior.

Third, among the factors that do influence other-regarding behavior there is considerable variance in economic significance. Since no model can usefully capture the influence of all factors that influence human behavior, our work has something to say about which factors should be the focus of attention. We found that reputation building with the experimenter does not account for nearly as much of the rejection behavior in ultimatum games as unfairness and aversion do. We found that preferences for distribution, independent of considerations of intentions, are sufficient to explain contributions in a simple dilemma game. The solidarity game and a linear public goods game proved sensitive to East German/West German cultural differences, but not so much so that it changes the qualitative features of giving.

References

Andreoni, James (1989). "Giving with impure altruism: Applications to charity and Ricardian equivalence". Journal of Political Economy 97, 1447–1458.
Becker, Gary S. (1974). "A theory of social interactions". Journal of Political Economy 82, 1063–1093.
Bolton, Gary E. (1991). "A comparative model of bargaining: Theory and evidence". American Economic Review 81, 1096–1136.
Bolton, Gary E., Zwick, Rami (1995). "Anonymity versus punishment in ultimatum bargaining". Games and Economic Behavior 10, 95–121.
Bolton, Gary E., Ockenfels, Axel (1998). "Strategy and equity: An ERC-analysis of the Güth–van Damme game". Journal of Mathematical Psychology 42, 215–226.
Bolton, Gary E., Ockenfels, Axel (2000). "ERC: A theory of equity, reciprocity and competition". American Economic Review 90, 166–193.

Bolton, Gary E., Brandts, Jordi, Katok, Elena (2000). "How strategy sensitive are contributions? A test of six hypotheses in a two-person dilemma game". Economic Theory 15, 367–387.

Bolton, Gary E., Brandts, Jordi, Ockenfels, Axel (1998). "Measuring motivations in the reciprocal responses observed in a dilemma game". Experimental Economics 1, 207–219.

Bolton, Gary E., Katok, Elena, Zwick, Rami (1998). "Dictator game giving: Rules of fairness versus acts of kindness". International Journal of Game Theory 27, 269–299.

Fehr, Ernst, Klaus, Schmidt (1999). "A theory of fairness, competition and cooperation". Quarterly Journal of Economics 114, 817–868.

Fudenberg, Drew, Maskin, Eric (1986). "The Folk theorem in repeated games with discounting or with incomplete information". Econometrica 54, 533–556.

Fong, Duncan, Bolton, Gary E. (1997). "Analyzing ultimatum bargaining: A Bayesian approach to the comparison of two potency curves under shape constraints". Journal of Business and Economics Statistics 15, 335–344.

Forsythe, Robert, Horowitz, Joel L., Savin, N.E., Sefton, Martin (1994). "Fairness in simple bargaining experiments". Games and Economic Behavior 6, 347–369.

Hoffman, Elizabeth, McCabe, Kevin, Smith, Vernon L. (1998). "Behavioral foundations of reciprocity: Experimental economics and evolutionary psychology". Economic Inquiry 36, 335–352.

Hoffman, Elizabeth, McCabe, Kevin, Shachat, Keith, Smith, Vernon L. (1994). "Preferences, property rights and anonymity in bargaining games". Games and Economic Behavior 7, 346–380.

Kreps, David M., Milgrom, Paul, Roberts, John, Wilson, Robert (1982). "Rational cooperation in the finitely repeated prisoners' dilemma". Journal of Economic Theory 27, 245–252.

Ockenfels, Axel, Weimann, Joachim (1999). "Types and patterns – An experimental East–West-German comparison of cooperation and solidarity". Journal of Public Economics 71, 275–287.

Rabin, Matthew (1993). "Incorporating fairness into game theory and economics". American Economic Review 83, 1281–1302.

Roth, Alvin E., Erev, Ido (1995). "Learning in extensive-form games: Experimental data and simple dynamic models in the intermediate term". Games and Economic Behavior 8, 164–212.

Roth, Alvin E., Prasnikar, Vesna, Okuno-Fujiwara, Masahiro, Zamir, Shmuel (1991). "Bargaining and market behavior in Jerusalem, Ljubljana, Pittsburgh, and Tokyo". American Economic Review 81, 1068–1095.

Selten, Reinhard (1987). "Equity and coalition bargaining in experimental three-person games". In: Roth, A.E. (Ed.), Laboratory Experimentation in Economics: Six Points of View. Cambridge University Press, Cambridge, pp. 42–98.

Selten, Reinhard, Ockenfels, Axel (1998). "An experimental solidarity game". Journal of Economic Behavior and Organization 34, 517–539.

Sugden, Robert (1984). "Reciprocity: The supply of public goods through voluntary contributions". Economic Journal 94, 772–787.

Further reading

Bolton, Gary E., Ockenfels, Axel (2005). "A stress test of fairness measures in models of social utility". Economic Theory 25, 957–982.

Bolton, Gary E., Ockenfels, Axel (2008). "Self-centered fairness in games with more than two players". This volume.

Bolton, Gary E., Brandts, Jordi, Ockenfels, Axel (2005). "Fair procedures: Evidence from games involving lotteries". The Economic Journal 115, 1054–1076.

Roth, Alvin E. (1995). "Bargaining experiments". In: Kagel, J., Roth, A.E. (Eds.), The Handbook of Experimental Economics. Princeton University Press, Princeton, pp. 253–348.

Chapter 56

FOCAL POINTS AND BARGAINING

KEN BINMORE
University College London

JOSEPH SWIERZBINSKI
University College London

The idea of a focal point is of great practical importance. However, no consensus exists concerning the manner in which focal points become established or survive after their establishment. At one extreme, some authors emphasize rationality considerations above all else. At the other extreme are authors who argue that social norms are so important that strategic issues can be neglected entirely. Even those who emphasize the importance of social norms are left with unresolved questions. In particular, when several distinct social norms compete for attention, how do people decide which social norm should be followed?

Social norms have played a prominent role in discussions of bargaining, and this paper describes the results of a set of experiments that study the establishment and stability of focal points in the context of a bargaining game. These experiments are described in more detail in the paper by Binmore et al. (1993).

The example of bargaining studied in the experiments is Nash's (1950) bargaining problem. In this problem, two players can achieve any point x in a feasible set X provided that they reach an agreement. Otherwise, the result is a fixed disagreement point ξ in the set X. The feasible set used in the experiments is shown in Figure 1.

There are at least two reasons why the Nash bargaining problem provides a good basis for the experimental study of focal points. First, many candidates have been proposed as focal points for Nash's bargaining problem along with a variety of arguments in support of one or another candidate solution. Proposed solutions include the Nash (1950) bargaining solution, the Kalai–Smorodinsky (1975) bargaining solution, the utilitarian solution associated with Harsanyi (1977), and the equal increments solution associated with Rawls (1972).[1] For the feasible set used in the experiments, these four proposed focal points are shown in Figure 1.

A second attractive feature of the Nash bargaining problem is that it has a continuous strategy space. Cooper et al. (1991) and Van Huyck, Battaglio, and Beill (1991) have studied coordination problems in situations involving discrete choices. But in a discrete

---

[1] The point in X selected by the equal increments solution is the one that would be selected by Rawls' (1972) maximin criterion. It is also a special case of the proportional bargaining solution studied by Raiffa (1953) and others.

Ch. 56: Focal Points and Bargaining

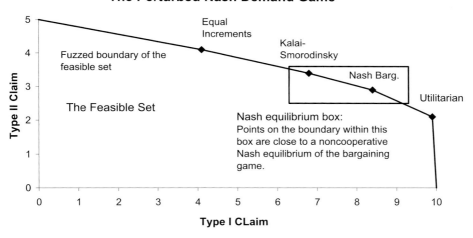

Figure 1. In the Nash demand game, a type I player makes a claim along the horizontal axis of the figure while, simultaneously, a type II player makes a claim along the vertical axis. If the point whose coordinates are determined by this pair of claims falls within the feasible set, then each player receives his claim. If the point falls outside the feasible set, then each player receives the disagreement payoff, which was normalized to 0. The experiments described in this paper involved a perturbed Nash demand game that added a fuzzed boundary to the feasible set. When claims fell on the fuzzed boundary, bargainers received their claims with some probability. In order to control for risk aversion, payoffs were in lottery tickets. After each 10 plays of the game, subjects had the opportunity to win $10 with a probability equal to the number of lottery tickets they had accumulated divided by 100. The horizontal and vertical scales of figures in this paper represent claims to lottery tickets. Focal points that have been proposed to predict the outcome of the Nash demand game include the equal increments solution, the Kalai–Smorodinsky solution, the Nash bargaining solution, and the utilitarian solution. These focal points are all labeled in the figure. The discretized version of the perturbed Nash demand game that was actually played has 12 non-cooperative Nash equilibria which lie along the section of the boundary enclosed by the box shown in the figure.

coordination problem, it may be hard to destabilize an existing focal point. For example, a population cannot drift gradually from driving on the left to driving on the right.

In order to study the Nash bargaining problem, a bargaining protocol must be specified. One of the simplest bargaining protocols is the Nash (1950) demand game, and this is what was used in the experiments. In each experiment, a group of 12 subjects played the same Nash demand game repeatedly, half the time as player I and half the time as player II. At each play, a subject was matched unpredictably with another subject with whom they were to bargain. Subjects interacted anonymously through a computer display like that shown in Figure 2.

A subject assigned the role of player I in the current play registered a demand x_1 by moving a cursor along the horizontal axis of the feasible set as illustrated in Figure 2. Simultaneously, the subject assigned the role of player II registered a demand x_2 by moving a cursor along the vertical axis of his display. Each player made his demand in

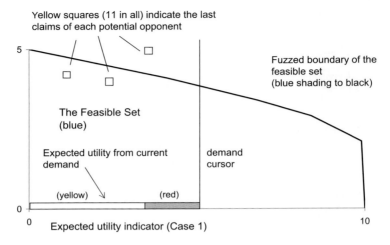

Figure 2. The computer display when a subject is player I.

ignorance of the current demand of the other subject. If the point $x = (x_1, x_2)$ was contained in the feasible set, then each subject received his claim. Otherwise, each player received the disagreement payoff, which was always 0 (i.e., $\xi = 0$).

Risk aversion was controlled using the standard technique of paying the subjects in lottery tickets. Hence, the scales along the vertical and horizontal axes of the figures in this paper represent claims to lottery tickets. After each 10 plays of the game, subjects had the opportunity to win $10 with a probability equal to the number of lottery tickets they had accumulated divided by 100.

Subjects actually played a perturbed Nash demand game in which the boundary of the feasible set was fuzzed along a narrow strip. Whether subjects would receive a pair of claims that fell within this fuzz was uncertain. For example, if the pair of claims fell on a 60% contour running through the fuzzed strip, then subjects would be granted their claims by the computer only 60 percent of the time.

Following a suggestion of Nash (1950), the fuzzing or smoothing was added to reduce the set of non-cooperative Nash equilibria of the Nash demand game. Any Pareto efficient x in X is a Nash equilibrium of the unperturbed Nash demand game. This includes all four of the proposed focal points illustrated in Figure 1. But it would be a much sharper test of the relevance of strategic considerations versus social norms in determining bargaining outcomes if the proposed focal points were not in fact Nash equilibria. With the fuzzed boundary and a continuous strategy space, all the non-cooperative Nash equilibria are close to the Nash bargaining solution. [See papers 4 and 8 of Binmore and Dasgupta (1987).]

As it turned out, the extent to which the set of non-cooperative Nash equilibria could be reduced was limited by technology. The cursor which subjects used to register their claims moved in small but barely perceptible discrete jumps. This changed the strategy space from a continuous set to a set with a large but discrete number of choices. In the discretized version of the perturbed Nash demand game, there were 12 non-trivial Nash equilibria which lie along the section of the boundary enclosed by the box shown in Figure 1.[2] Note that the equal increments solution and the utilitarian solution were not close to Nash equilibria of the discretized, perturbed Nash demand game. However, the Kalai–Smorodinsky solution and, of course, the Nash bargaining solution were close to such equilibria.

After a hands-on interactive session at the computer to learn the mechanics of the program, subjects first played 10 "practice" games "against the computer" followed by 40 games against "real" opponents. Both when playing the computer and playing against real opponents, subjects sometimes occupied the role of player I and sometimes the role of player II.

In both the real and practice games, subjects were provided with considerable information concerning the past plays of the population of potential opponents. On the computer display, 11 small yellow squares were superimposed on the region representing possible demands. The x-coordinate of the center of a given yellow square indicated the demand made by one potential opponent when that opponent last occupied the role of player I. Similarly, the y-coordinate of the center of the square was the last claim made by that opponent as player II. As a type I subject varied his demand by moving his demand cursor horizontally across the computer screen, the squares changed from yellow to red as the demand represented by the current placing of the subject's cursor became incompatible with the last type II demands made by the subjects represented by their respective squares. The display worked analogously for a subject occupying the role of player II.

Subjects in Case 2 were offered only this information about the other subjects. Subjects in the main experiment, Case 1, were given more information by the addition of an "expected utility indicator." This took the form of a second cursor that showed the expected number of lottery tickets that the subject would receive if he made the demand indicated by the current placing of the demand cursor and the other subjects made the demands indicated by the current placing of the yellow squares. Figure 2 shows the expected utility indicator and several yellow squares for a subject occupying the role of player I.

In the practice games, the information display was used in a (successful) attempt to condition the subjects to begin the games against real opponents close to one of the four focal points under consideration. For example, in the treatment designed to study the equal increments solution as a possible focal point, the yellow squares representing simulated potential opponents were designed to converge slowly over the course of the 10 practice games from a fixed initial configuration to a cluster close to the equal increments solution. The convergence was deliberately not total. After being conditioned

---

[2] There were also a large number of trivial Nash equilibria where both players make a claim outside the feasible set and both players receive 0.

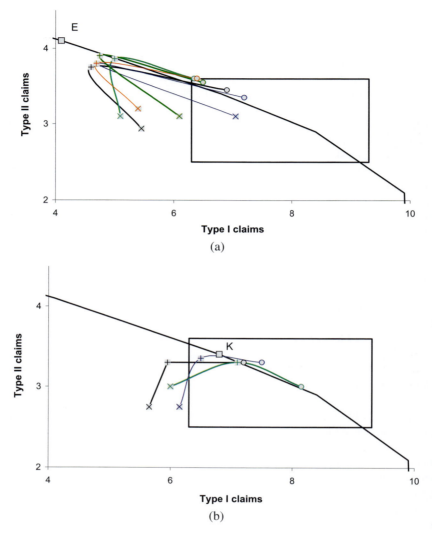

Figure 3. (a) Case 1E. (b) Case 1K. (c) Case 1N. (d) Case 1U.

to begin by making demands close to the equal increments solution, the question was whether subjects would continue to use this focal point once play against real opponents began.

The four panels, 3a through 3d, that comprise Figure 3 illustrate the main results of the experiment. Each of the panels represents a separate treatment used in Case 1. In Case 1E, the yellow squares in the practice games converged toward the equal incre-

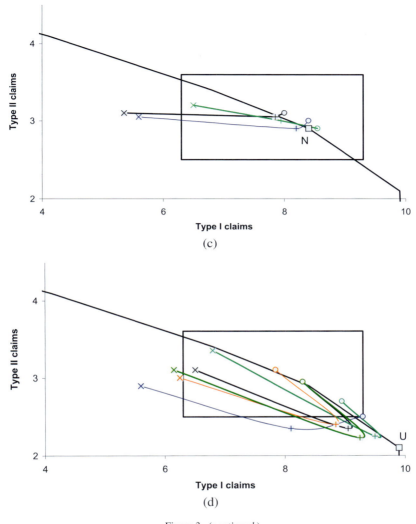

Figure 3. (*continued.*)

ments solution, E. In Case 1K, the squares converged toward the Kalai–Smorodinsky solution, K. In Case 1N, the yellow squares converged toward the Nash bargaining solution, N, and, in Case 1U, convergence was toward the utilitarian solution, U.

The curved lines in Figure 3 do not represent trajectories.[3] Each of the 16 sets of lines corresponds to a different group of 12 subjects and summarizes their experience

---

[3] Trajectories of the median claims made in selected experiments are reproduced in Binmore et al. (1993).

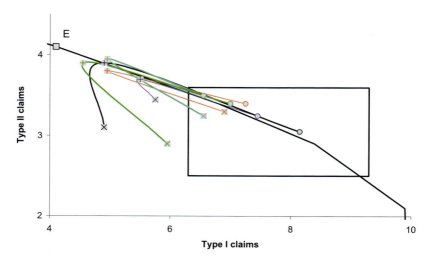

Figure 4. Case 2.

by linking three points. Each point is a pair of median demands. The x-coordinate is the median demand of player I and the y-coordinate is the median demand of the player II. These numbers are plotted for three stages in each experiment. (1) At the very beginning – i.e., in the first and second practice games before any experience had been gained.[4] (2) Immediately after the practice games – i.e., in the 11th and 12th plays that followed the 10 conditioning practice games. (3) At the very end – i.e., in the 49th and 50th plays, after 10 practice games and 40 real games. In Figures 3a through 3d and Figure 4, the points indicating median claims made at the very beginning of each experiment are labeled with an "×." Points indicating the median claims made immediately after the practice games are labeled with a "+." Points indicating the median claims made at the end of each experiment are labeled with a "○."

We draw the following conclusions from the results presented in Figure 3. (1) Whatever social norms the subjects may bring to the experiment are easily displaced. Subjects can be conditioned to begin bargaining against real opponents close to any of the four focal points considered here. (2) The equal increments and utilitarian focal points are not stable. (3) The explanation that groups of subjects converge on an exact Nash equilibrium of the discrete game which they actually played fits the data very well.

One potential criticism of the above experiments is that the graphical display might have made the process of myopic optimization focal. The five experiments in Case 2 were an attempt to investigate the extent to which the results of Case 1 were dependent on the information presented in the computer display. Case 2 was identical to Case 1E

---

[4] The computer updated the information contained in the yellow squares every second play.

except that the subjects were deprived of the expected utility indicator described earlier. The results are illustrated in Figure 4. Perhaps surprisingly, the subjects' behavior was not very different from that in Case 1E.

The results of these experiments clearly do not support the view that strategic considerations in bargaining situations can be ignored in favor of a study of fairness norms. Indeed, we believe that it is a major error to suppose that social norms are commonly so rigid that they are able to sustain behavior in the long run that is not in equilibrium.

References

Binmore, K., Dasgupta, P. (1987). "The Economics of Bargaining". Basil Blackwell, Oxford.
Binmore, K., Swierzbinski, J., Hsu, S., Proulx, C. (1993). "Focal points and bargaining". International Journal of Game Theory 22, 381–409.
Cooper, R., DeJong, D., Forsythe, R., Ross, T. (1991). "Selection criteria in coordination games: Some experimental results". American Economic Review 80, 218–233.
Harsanyi, J. (1977). "Rational Behavior and Bargaining Equilibrium in Games and Social Situations". Cambridge University Press, Cambridge.
Kalai, E., Smorodinsky, M. (1975). "Other solutions to Nash's bargaining problem". Econometrica 45, 1623–1630.
Nash, J. (1950). "The bargaining problem". Econometrica 18, 155–162.
Raiffa, H. (1953). "Arbitration schemes for generalized two-person games". In: Kuhn, H., Tucker, A. (Eds.), Contributions to the Theory of Games II. Princeton University Press, Princeton.
Rawls, J. (1972). "A Theory of Justice". Oxford University Press, Oxford.
Van Huyck, J., Battaglio, R., Beil, R. (1991). "Tacit coordination games, strategic uncertainty, and coordination failure". American Economic Review 80 (1), 234–238.

PART 4.2

ALTERNATIVES TO NASH

Catherine C. Eckel and Philip J. Grossman, "Differences in the Economic Decisions of Men and Women: Experimental Evidence"

John Van Huyck, "Emergent Conventions in Evolutionary Games"

Gary E. Bolton and Axel Ockenfels, "Self-centered Fairness in Games With More Than Two Players"

Richard McKelvey and Thomas Palfrey, "Quantal Response Equilibria: A Brief Synopsis"

Simon P. Anderson, Jacob K. Goeree and Charles A. Holt, "Logit Equilibrium Models of Anomalous Behavior: What to do when the Nash Equilibrium Says One Thing and the Data Say Something Else"

Chapter 57

DIFFERENCES IN THE ECONOMIC DECISIONS OF MEN AND WOMEN: EXPERIMENTAL EVIDENCE

CATHERINE C. ECKEL

School of Social Sciences, University of Texas at Dallas, Richardson, TX 75080, USA

PHILIP J. GROSSMAN

Department of Economics, Saint Cloud State University, St. Cloud, MN 56301, USA

Abstract

This chapter reviews the results from public goods, ultimatum, and dictator experiments for evidence of systematic differences in the behavior of men and women. While the results do not offer consistent evidence of behavioral differences between men and women, there are some intriguing patterns in the data. No significant evidence of systematic differences in the play of men and women is evident in those settings where subjects are exposed to risk. In those settings where risk is absent, systematic differences are revealed. This finding is conditioned by the level of risk.

Do individual decisions vary systematically by the sex of the decision maker? This question has generated considerable debate. Evidence from the other social and behavioral sciences finds substantial differences between the sexes, and tends to support the stereotypes of the more socially-oriented (selfless) woman and the more individually-oriented (selfish) man.[1]

Dating back at least to Rapoport and Chammah (1965), experimenters have tested in the laboratory for differences in behavior between men and women in situations involving salient monetary incentives. The study by Rapoport and Chammah is an early example in a long series of studies that employ variations of the prisoner's dilemma game to test for such differences. The results have been mixed, with some studies finding women more selfless, others finding men more selfless, and still others finding no difference.[2] More recently, researchers have turned to public goods, ultimatum, and dictator experiments, which we survey here. A critical difference among these experimental designs is the extent to which subjects are exposed to a risk of financial loss, exploitation, or the judgment of others. If women and men respond differently to these risks, this may confound underlying differences in the tendency to cooperate, muddying experimental results in some settings and producing behavioral differences in others.

---

[1] See Eckel and Grossman (1998) for a brief review.
[2] Ibid.

1. Public Goods Experiments

Table 1 reports the results from seven recent public goods experiments. Like the prisoner's dilemma experiments before them, these experiments offer no clear evidence of a systematic difference between men and women. Brown-Kruse and Hummels (1993), Sell and Wilson (1991), and Sell, Griffith, and Wilson (1993), find that women contribute less to the public good than do men. Nowell and Tinkler (1994), and Seguino, Stevens, and Lutz (1996) report significantly higher contributions by women than by men.[3] Cadsby and Maynes (1998) and Sell (1997) report mixed results.[4] In same gender groups, women contribute more than men, though this difference is not significant. When men are the minority in mixed gender groups, they contribute at a significantly higher rate than do women when they are the minority in mixed gender groups.

Methodological differences might explain the varying results. In Brown-Kruse and Hummels (1993), Nowell and Tinkler (1994), Sell and Wilson (1991), Sell, Griffith, and Wilson (1993), and Cadsby and Maynes (1998) the game was repeated (6, 13, 10, 18, 18, and 25 periods, respectively), while Seguino, Stevens, and Lutz (1996) was one-shot. Brown-Kruse and Hummels (1993) constrain their subjects to make all-or-nothing allocations of $1 to the public good. The other studies allow subjects to contribute any number of tokens from zero to their full allocation.[5] Cadsby and Maynes (1998) require contributions reach a threshold level (25 percent of all tokens) before a return is earned. Contributions to the public good involve a kind of risk; other group members may not reciprocate. Subjects risk being "exploited," and may feel as if they have been "played for a sucker" (Ingram and Berger, 1977). While a subject may be inclined to contribute something to the public good, the all-or-nothing design of Brown-Kruse and Hummels (1993) precludes such hedging. By requiring subjects to contribute everything, the design increases the vulnerability of subjects to exploitation and the perceived potential return may not justify this exposure. If women are more risk averse or more afraid of the judgment of others (of looking bad by being taken advantage of), they may be less willing to contribute the full dollar.

A second important design difference making comparison of results difficult is the ability of subjects to monitor the behavior of others. The Sell, Griffith, and Wilson (1993) study provides subjects no such information until after all decisions are made.

---

[3] The difference Sell, Griffith, and Wilson (1993) report is not significant. However, Sell, Griffith, and Wilson (1993) also report results from experiments in which the resource subjects earned was "time with an expert." Results from these sessions reveal the same, but now significant, pattern of behavior. On average, men contributed 61.1% of their tokens to the public good, while women contributed 48.7%. They suggest that this may be because men and women value some resources differently.

[4] Cadsby and Maynes (1998) also replicate Brown-Kruse and Hummels's (1993) procedures and report no significant difference.

[5] The number of tokens given to subjects each period varies: Seguino, Stevens, and Lutz (1996) gave their subjects an allocation of 5 tokens, Cadsby and Maynes (1998) gave 10, Sell and Wilson (1991) and Sell, Griffith, and Wilson (1993) gave 30, and Nowell and Tinkler (1994) gave 62.

Table 1
Public goods experiments. Percent of endowment contributed to public good production. Voluntary contribution mechanism experiments

Period[a]	Subjects[c]	Group size[d]	All-male groups				All-female groups				Mixed groups						
											Male subjects			Female subjects		
			# of groups	First (%)	Last (%)	Average (all periods) (%)	# of groups	First (%)	Last (%)	Average (all periods) (%)	# of groups	First (%)	Last (%)	Average (all periods) (%)	First (%)	Last (%)	Average (all periods) (%)
Brown-Kruse and Hummels[b]	64	4	8	93.8[e]	46.9	67.7[e]	8	71.9[e]	40.6	56.3[e]	NA	NA	NA	NA	NA	NA	NA
Nowell and Tinkler	64	4	5	46.1	14.6	29.6[f]	6	50.5	29.5	37.4[f]	5	NA	NA	NA	NA	NA	NA
Cadsby and Maynes	160	10	8	29.3	NR	19.2	8	37.6	NR	18.9	NA	NA	NA	NA	NA	NA	NA
Seguino, Stevens, and Lutz	139	5–52	NA	NA	NA	NA	NA	NA	NA	NA	6	49.2[g]	NA	NA	65.6[g]	NA	NA
Sell and Wilson[b]	92	4	NA	NR	NR	NR	NA	NR	NR	NR		NR	NR	50.6[e]	NR	NR	36.5[e]
Sell, Griffith, and Wilson	99	4		NR	NR	60.4		NR	NR	47.1		NR	NR	63.0	NR	NR	48.0

(continued on next page)

Table 1
(*continued*)

Period[a]	Subjects[c]	Group size[d]	All-male groups				All-female groups				# of groups	Mixed groups					
			# of groups	First (%)	Last (%)	Average (all periods) (%)	# of groups	First (%)	Last (%)	Average (all periods) (%)		Male subjects			Female subjects		
												First (%)	Last (%)	Average (all periods) (%)	First (%)	Last (%)	Average (all periods) (%)
Sell	244	4		NR	NR	43.0		NR	NR	51.8		NR	NR	57.1	NR	NR	46.4

Note. NA – not applicable. NR – not reported.

[a] The number of periods per session varies in each paper: Brown-Kruse and Hummels – six periods; Nowell and Tinkler – thirteen periods; Cadsby and Maynes – twenty-five periods; Seguino, Stevens, and Lutz – one period; Sell, Stevens, and Wilson – ten periods; and Sell, Griffith, and Wilson – eighteen periods. The group fund multiplier also varied across the studies: Brown-Kruse and Hummels – for one-half of the sessions, the multiplier was 1.2 for the first four rounds and 2 for the final two rounds, for the other half the multiplier was 2 for the first rounds and 1.2 for the final two; Nowell and Tinkler – 1.2 for all rounds; Seguino, Stevens, and Lutz – the multiplier was 2; Sell, Sell and Wilson, and Sell, Griffith, and Wilson – the multiplier was 3. Cadsby and Maynes varied the reward (5, 8, 10, or 15 tokens) for meeting the threshold.

[b] Pooling over all treatments. Brown-Kruse and Hummels had two treatments: Anonymity – subjects had no pre-experiment communication and did not know the identity of their fellow group members; Community – subjects had pre-experiment communication and did know the identity of their fellow group members. Sell and Wilson report three information-feedback treatments: no information, aggregate information, and individual information.

[c] In the Sell study, the total number of subjects numbered 254. Ten were excluded from the analysis. The Sell and Wilson study began with 96 subjects; four were excluded from the analysis. The Sell, Griffith, and Wilson study excluded 15 subjects from the original sample pool of 114.

[d] In the Sell and Sell, Griffith, and Wilson studies, subjects played in a group of four where the other three players were simulated.

[e] Hypothesis of like mean contributions rejected at $p \leq 0.05$.

[f] Regression analysis results indicate that contributions by all-female groups were significantly higher than contributions by all-male groups, $p = 0.10$.

[g] Regression analysis results indicate that contributions by female subjects were significantly higher than contributions by male subjects, $p = 0.01$.

The Brown-Kruse and Hummels (1993), Nowell and Tinkler (1994), and Sell studies provide information of average group contributions after each round of play.[6] Sell and Wilson (1991) varies the information conditions, with subjects receiving either no information, group information, or individual information. They find no significant interaction between the sex of the subject and the information treatment.

Finally, the studies vary in what the subjects know about their counterparts. In Sell and Wilson (1991), partners are anonymous; subjects do not know the sex of their counterpart. Sell (1997) and Sell, Griffith, and Wilson (1993) give the subjects only written stimuli (a list of their partners' first names) regarding their partners' sex. In the other three studies, stimuli are visual: all subjects are in the same room. Several of the studies use a computer interface, while others do not. Visual and written stimuli may not elicit the same response from subjects, and the computer interface may raise doubts in the subjects about the identity of their partner.

2. Ultimatum Experiments

Table 2 reports the findings from two ultimatum experiment studies. Solnick (2001) conducts a one-shot game under two treatments. In one treatment, subject anonymity is preserved; in the second, players are told the gender-revealing first name of their partner. Solnick's design employs the "strategy method": players simultaneously propose a division of the pie (if the player is the proposer) and the minimum acceptable division of the pie (if the player is the respondent).

Eckel and Grossman (2001) employ a repeated-play (eight periods) design. In each period subjects play with a different partner. Each subject plays each role (proposer and respondent) four times, though not in the same order. The sex of a subject's partner is made known by having a group of four proposers seated facing a group of four respondents. The design matches players with partners of their own gender (four men face four men, or four women face four women), partners of the opposite gender (four men face four women), or a mixed group (two women and two men face a similar group). Subjects are not told with whom they are matched. The Eckel and Grossman (2001) design employs the "game method": the proposer makes an offer which is presented to the respondent, who then decides whether to accept or reject.

There are considerable similarities in the Solnick (2001) and Eckel and Grossman (2001) results. Both studies find little difference in the overall mean offers made by men and women (46.7 percent of the pie for men versus 46.8 percent for women in the Solnick study and 36.5 versus 38.5 percent in the Eckel and Grossman, 2001, study). Both Solnick (2001) and Eckel and Grossman (2001) report that offers to women are,

---

[6] Sell manipulates the feedback received by subjects. Half of the subjects received feedback suggesting that other group members were playing cooperatively and half received feedback suggesting that other group members were playing non-cooperatively.

Table 2
Ultimatum experiments. Offers made by proposers, and rejection rates by respondents

Offers made by	Eckel and Grossman[a,b]		Solnick[a]	
	Mean offer (% of $5)	Rejection rate (%)	Mean offer (% of $10)	Rejection rate (%)
All subjects to all subjects	37.5	12.8	46.8	12.4
All subjects to men	38.2		48.9[c]	
All subjects to women	37.2		43.7[c]	
Men to all subjects	36.5	17.7	46.7	4.2
Men to men	36.6	18.8	47.3	4.5
Men to women	36.6	17.2	44.3	0.0
Women to all subjects	38.5	7.8	46.8	14.6
Women to men	39.8	9.4	51.3[d]	6.3
Women to women	37.8	3.1	43.1[d]	23.1

[a]Number of subjects: Eckel and Grossman – 96 subjects (each plays four rounds as proposer and four rounds as respondent; 384 proposer/respondent pairings); Solnick – 178 subjects (89 proposer/respondent pairings).
[b]Regression analysis results indicate that: (1) female respondents are significantly more likely to accept a given offer, p-value $= 0.01$; and (2) offers from female proposers are significantly less likely to be rejected than offers from male proposers, p-value $= 0.01$.
[c]Means test p-value $= 0.08$.
[d]Means test p-value $= 0.08$.

on average, lower than those made to men, regardless of the sex of the proposer (43.7 and 37.2 percent versus 48.9 and 38.2 percent, respectively).[7]

Where Solnick's (2001) and Eckel and Grossman's (2001) results differ dramatically is in the behavior of the respondents (see Table 2). While the overall rejection rates are similar (12.4 versus 12.8 percent, respectively), Solnick reports higher rejection rates of offers made by women, while Eckel and Grossman (2001) report higher rejection rates for offers made by men. Both Solnick's (2001) and Eckel and Grossman's (2001) results are significant. One of the most startling differences in the two results is the difference in rejection rates of offers made by women to women. In the Eckel and Grossman (2001) study, these offers were *least* likely to be rejected (3.1%), while in the Solnick (2001) study, these offers were the *most* likely to be rejected (23.1%).

There are two important differences between methodologies of Solnick (2001) and Eckel and Grossman (2001). One is the one-shot design versus repeated-play design. If subjects come to the experiment with no idea of what constitutes an "acceptable offer (minimum acceptable offer)," first-round results may reflect considerable "noise" as subjects experiment.

The second important difference is the risk differences and potential for being "exploited" faced by the respondent in the "strategy" versus "game method" design. In the

---

[7] The difference in the Solnick (2001) study is significant at the 8 percent level.

game method design, the respondent, knowing the proposer's offer, knows the outcome of the game once his decision is made. There is no risk and no potential for exploitation. In the strategy method design, the respondent faces the same risk as the proposer. Both must make a decision without knowing for certain the other's choice. The smaller is a proposer's offer and the higher is a respondent's minimum acceptable offer, the higher is the probability that both will receive nothing. There is both risk and potential for exploitation. Reactions of subjects to these risk differences may vary by sex, and by other characteristics of the subject pool.[8]

3. Dictator Experiments

The contradictory results of the prisoner's dilemma, public goods, and ultimatum experiments may be caused by failure to control for important environmental factors that might confound basic gender differences. The dictator experiment offers a simple design that removes possible confounding factors. The advantage of the dictator environment over others is that it eliminates considerations of strategic risk.

Eckel and Grossman (1996) test for differences in the behavior of men and women in what they called a "punishment" game, a variation on the dictator experiment. In the punishment game, subjects were given a choice of being paired with either, an "ungenerous" person (termed Type A in the experiment), an *unpaid* proposer from a previous experiment who had selected an $18/$2 split, or a "generous" person (Type B), an *unpaid* proposer from a previous experiment who had selected a $10/$10 split. The type of person that a subject chose to be paired with determined their own payoff. Half of the subjects randomly were assigned a "low relative price" payoff (sharing $12 with an ungenerous person or sharing $10 with a generous person), and half randomly were assigned a "high relative price" payoff (sharing $12 with an ungenerous person or sharing $8 with a generous person).

Eckel and Grossman (1996) report a significant difference in the behavior of men and women (see Table 3). Women were more responsive to changes in the parameters of the decision-making environment. In the low relative price treatment, women were about twice as likely as men to sacrifice $1 in earnings in order to choose to reward the generous person. In the high relative price treatment, however, women were slightly less likely than men to sacrifice $2 in earnings in order to choose the generous person. Men's choices did not vary with the price treatment.

Bolton and Katok (1995) and Eckel and Grossman (1998) employ the standard dictator experiment design, though their experimental environments differ. The choice set in one Bolton and Katok (1995) treatment was restricted to giving zero or 50 percent of the pie, and in all Bolton and Katok (1995) treatments the choice set was restricted to

---

[8] In particular, Eckel and Grossman (2001) report substantial differences in play by African–American subjects.

Table 3
Dictator punishment game. Subjects choose to split evenly a large amount with an "ungenerous" recipient or a small amount with a "generous" recipient[a]

	Low relative payoff Percent choosing to		High relative payoff Percent choosing to	
Sex	Split $10 with an ungenerous recipient (# of subjects)	Split $8 with a generous recipient (# of subjects)	Split $12 with an ungenerous recipient (# of subjects)	Split $8 with a generous recipient (# of subjects)
Men	60.7 (37)	39.3 (29)	59.2 (29)	40.8 (20)
Women	36.0 (18)	64.0 (32)	67.3 (35)	32.7 (17)
Total	49.5 (55)	50.5 (56)	63.4 (64)	36.6 (37)

Note. Subjects chose between splitting evenly a smaller amount of money with a recipient who had been a "generous" dictator in a previous game, and splitting evenly a larger amount of money with a recipient who had been an "ungenerous" dictator in a previous game.

[a] Three-way Goodman Placket test of interaction between Sex × Price × Punish: $\chi^2 = 5.64$, p-value $= 0.025$.

contributions of 50 percent of the pie or less. Eckel and Grossman (1998) only restrict the contributions of subjects to whole dollar increments.

Both Bolton and Katok (1995) and Eckel and Grossman (1998) find women donating more to their partners (see Table 4). However, Eckel and Grossman's (1998) difference is highly significant, while Bolton and Katok's (1995) is not. Bolton and Katok's (1995) restricted choice set may be the cause of the difference in results; it may unintentionally signal subjects that smaller donations are expected. If, as Bolton and Katok (1995) argue, '... when confronted with a choice of leaving more or less than they would freely choose, dictators choose less' (p. 290), then this restricted choice set may conceal any sex differences.

Andreoni and Vesterlund (2001) conduct a modified dictator experiment. Instead of making a decision over one choice set, a subject makes allocation decisions for eight different choice sets (a subject's payoff was determined randomly from the decisions made). Each choice set differed in the number of tokens to be divided and the value of a token to each subject.

Overall, women gave away more tokens than men (29.50 versus 25.74, respectively), but this varied considerably with the relative value of tokens to the two subjects (see Table 5; Andreoni and Vesterlund's, 2001, Table 2). Women's token donations varied little with the relative price of giving, while men's donations were more responsive. Increasing the value of a token to the recipient tended to increase men's level of donations. On average, partners of female subjects earned more than partners of male subjects ($2.60

Table 4
Dictator experiments. Women give more than men

	Mean donation as percent of total (# of subjects)	
	Bolton and Katok[a]	Eckel and Grossman[a]
Men	11.3%[b]	8.2%[c]
	(46)	(60)
Women	12.3[b]	16.0[c]
	(31)	(60)

[a]Bolton and Katok employ three treatments: (1) dictator plays with 10 different respondents, dividing $1 in $0.10 increments; (2) dictator plays with 10 different respondents, either taking the whole pie or taking half; and (3) dictator plays with 1 respondent, dividing $10 in $1 increments. In all three treatments, the dictator is restricted to giving away no more than one-half the pie. Eckel and Grossman employ one treatment: the dictator plays with one respondent, dividing $10 in $1 increments. There is no restriction on the amount the dictator may give away. Bolton and Katok did not impose anonymity between subjects and experimenters; Eckel and Grossman did.
[b]Bolton and Katok: means test p-value $= 0.36$.
[c]Eckel and Grossman: means test p-value < 0.01.

Table 5
Dictator games. Percent of endowment given to recipient under different budget constraints

	Token endowment	Relative price[a]	All subjects ($n = 116$)	Male subjects ($n = 84$)	Female subjects ($n = 32$)	Male–female difference
Budget 1	40	1/3	31.83	35.27	22.81	12.46
Budget 2	40	3	24.29	18.51	39.45	20.94
Budget 3	60	1/2	32.37	34.01	28.07	5.94
Budget 4	60	1	26.87	23.51	35.68	−12.17
Budget 5	60	2	25.10	20.08	38.28	−18.20
Budget 6	75	1/2	31.34	33.11	26.71	6.40
Budget 7	75	2	23.99	18.92	37.29	−18.37
Budget 8	100	1	25.15	22.35	32.50	−10.15
Average			27.62	25.72[b]	32.60[b]	−6.88

Source: Andreoni and Vesterlund (1997).
[a]Ratio of the value of a token to the decision maker relative to the value of a token to the recipient.
[b]Means test p-value $= 0.75$.

versus $2.56), and for five of the eight choice sets (budgets 1, 2, 4, 5, and 7) the earnings differential was significant. Only for budget 1 did the partners of male subjects earn significantly more than the partners of female subjects.

Andreoni and Vesterlund's (2001) outcomes for budgets 4 and 8 are directly comparable to the Eckel and Grossman (1998) and Bolton and Katok (1995) sessions. These two choice sets offer the same choice options as a simple dictator experiment. In both cases, the results are consistent with Eckel and Grossman's (1998) findings; women are significantly more generous than men, giving approximately 41% more than men for budget 4 and 26% more than men for budget 8.

4. Conclusions

While the results from public goods, ultimatum, and dictator experiments do not offer consistent evidence of behavioral differences between men and women, there are some intriguing patterns in the data. In those settings where subjects are exposed to risk – i.e., public goods experiments, as proposer in ultimatum experiments, and as respondent in ultimatum experiments employing the "strategy method" design – there is no significant evidence of systematic differences in the play of men and women. Results seem to depend on the details of the payoff structure and experimental procedure. In those settings where subjects are not exposed to risk – i.e., as respondent in ultimatum experiments employing the "game method" design and dictator games – systematic differences are revealed. The choices women make are less individually-oriented and more socially-oriented. This finding is conditioned by the level of risk, which points to an important avenue for future research. If men and women systematically differ in their responses to risk, then this has important implications for behavior.

References

Andreoni, J., Vesterlund, L. (2001). "Which is the fair sex? Gender differences in altruism". Quarterly Journal of Economics 116, 293–312.
Bolton, G.E., Katok, E. (1995). "An experimental test for gender differences in beneficent behavior". Economics Letters 48, 287–292.
Brown-Kruse, J., Hummels, D. (1993). "Gender effects in laboratory public goods contributions: Do individuals put their money where their mouth is?" Journal of Economic Behavior and Organization 22, 255–267.
Cadsby, C.B., Maynes, E. (1998). "Gender and free riding in a threshold public goods game: Experimental evidence". Journal of Economic Behavior and Organization 34, 603–620.
Eckel, C.C., Grossman, P.J. (1996). "The relative price of fairness: Gender differences in a punishment game". Journal of Economic Behavior and Organization 30, 143–158.
Eckel, C.C., Grossman, P.J. (1998). "Are women less selfish than men: Evidence from dictator experiments". Economic Journal 108, 726–735.
Eckel, C.C., Grossman, P.J. (2001). "Chivalry and solidarity in ultimatum games". Economic Inquiry 39, 171–188.
Ingram, B.L., Berger, S.E. (1977). "Sex-role orientation, defensiveness, and competitiveness in women". Journal of Conflict Resolution 21, 501–518.
Nowell, C., Tinkler, S. (1994). "The influence of gender on the provision of a public good". Journal of Economic Behavior and Organization 25, 25–36.
Rapoport, A., Chammah, A.M. (1965). "Sex differences in factors contributing to the level of cooperation in the prisoner's dilemma game". Journal of Personality and Social Psychology 2, 831–838.

Seguino, S., Stevens, T., Lutz, M. (1996). "Gender and cooperative behaviour: Economic man rides alone". Feminist Economics 2, 1–21.
Sell, J. (1997). "Gender, strategies, and contributions to public goods". Social Psychology Quarterly 60, 252–265.
Sell, J., Wilson, R.K. (1991). "Levels of information and contributions to public goods". Social Forces 70, 107–124.
Sell, J., Griffith, W.I., Wilson, R.K. (1993). "Are women more cooperative than men in social dilemmas?" Social Psychology Quarterly 56, 211–222.
Solnick, S. (2001). "Gender differences in the ultimatum game". Economic Inquiry 39, 189–200.

Chapter 58

EMERGENT CONVENTIONS IN EVOLUTIONARY GAMES[1]

JOHN VAN HUYCK
e-mail: john.vanhuyck@tamu.edu

1. Introduction

A stranger in a foreign land often finds those around him incomprehensible. He may not understand what they say. They laugh or frown at what he does. Above all it is difficult for a stranger to give or receive help from the people he meets. Conventions make those around us comprehensible and allow us to work together productively.

Lewis (1969) demonstrated that it is useful to model people using sounds, gestures, or symbols to communicate things to one another as a coordination game and he used game theory to explain what it means to say that language is a convention. Roughly speaking a convention is a regularity in behavior amongst members of a community in a recurrent situation that is customary, expected, and mutually consistent.[2]

An example of a mutual consistency condition for an abstract game is Nash equilibrium. A Nash equilibrium is an assignment to each player a strategy that is optimal for him when the others use the strategies assigned to them. The mutual consistency condition is important because it insures that members of the community have a good reason to conform to the regularity in behavior.

Understanding the origin of convention requires us to understand how people learn mutually consistent behavior, which then becomes customary and expected. This chapter reports experimental results on the emergence of conventions in evolutionary games. In an evolutionary game, a stage game is played repeatedly by random subsets of the cohort. Laboratory communities or cohorts are usually chosen to be large enough to make repeated game strategies unrewarding, but small enough to allow a convention to emerge quickly.[3]

A cohort is likely to bring customary and expected behavior into the laboratory that is not mutually consistent given the incentives of the experiment. Widely discussed examples are the salience of efficiency in games with inefficient dominant strategies and the salience of equal division in games with unequal bargaining power. The emergent convention approach to the origin of mutually consistent behavior explains such facts

---

[1] Related research available at http://econlab10.tamu.edu/JVH_gtee.
[2] Roughly speaking because Lewis (1969) actually gives seven different definitions none of which suit our purposes exactly. See also Schotter (1982), Sugden (1986, 1989) and Young (1993a, 1993b, 1998).
[3] Experience suggests that one population with eight randomly paired subjects or two populations with seven subjects in each achieves these design parameters for the class of games reviewed here.

Handbook of Experimental Economics Results, Volume 1
Copyright © 2008 Elsevier B.V. All rights reserved
DOI: 10.1016/S1574-0722(07)00058-3

Table 1
2 × 2 symmetric stag hunt game

	X	Y
X	A, A	C, B
Y	B, C	D, D

Note. $A > B$, $D > C$, $A > D$, $B > C$.

as due to the ambient convention into which the experiment is placed. Moreover, if the emergent convention approach is correct, one can design experiments in which inefficient or unequal division conventions emerge, because while each individual member of a community has an incentive to conform to the community's convention by definition, it is possible for the community as a whole to coordinate on a behavioral regularity that is not efficient or fair.

The chapter begins by reviewing the evolutionary stag hunt game literature in which inefficient conventions emerge systematically. It then focuses on two papers. Van Huyck, Battalio, and Rankin (1997) reported observing emergent conventions based on labels and populations in evolutionary pure coordination (collaboration) games. Van Huyck et al. (1995) reported observing the emergence of unequal division conventions in cohorts of symmetrically endowed subjects.

2. Inefficient Conventions

Evolutionary stag hunt games have been widely studied both theoretically and experimentally. The stag hunt game poses the potential conflict between efficiency and security in a simple setting. The 2 × 2 symmetric stag hunt game is given in Table 1. The game has two strict Nash equilibria, which can be Pareto ranked, and one mixed-strategy equilibrium in which X is played with probability $(D - C)/(A + D - B - C) \equiv k^*$. When $k^* > 1/2$ (X, X) is the payoff dominant equilibrium and (Y, Y) is the risk-dominant equilibrium.[4]

The recent shift from models based on substantive rationality to models of boundedly rational agents has directed attention to learning based theories of equilibrium selection. Deterministic dynamics predict history dependent equilibrium selection. For example, if the frequency of action X in the initial state is less k^* then both the replicator or the myopic best response dynamic predict that (Y, Y) will emerge as the conventional way to play and if the frequency is more than k^* then (X, X) will emerge as the convention. Such deterministic dynamics divide the state space into two basins of attraction, where k^* is the separatrix between the two basins.

---

[4] The concepts of payoff dominance and risk dominance are taken from Harsanyi and Selten (1988). The risk-dominance equilibrium in a 2 × 2 symmetric game is the one with the larger basin of attraction under best-response dynamics.

Battalio, Samuelson, and Van Huyck (1997) summarize recent evidence on human behavior in evolutionary stag hunt games in a table reproduced here as Table 2. Each row represents a cohort. The cohorts are ordered first by value of the separatrix, k^*, so that the basin of attraction of the risk-dominant equilibrium shrinks as one moves down the table, and second by the size of the scaled earnings difference. The initial and terminal outcomes are reported as the ratio of subjects using the payoff-dominant action to the total number of subjects active in the cohort. The last two columns report the number of periods and the source. The experiments differ in many details such as matching protocol, induced value technique, and the cohort's experience as a group with pretrial games. We do not focus on these differences because we think the results in the literature tell a fairly consistent story.

First, subjects do not bring risk dominance into the laboratory. The payoff dominant action is usually the modal initial choice even when k^* takes on extreme values. Changing the scaled earnings difference has little discernable influence on initial conditions. Efficiency seems to be the ambient equilibrium selection convention for this sort of coordination problem.[5]

Second, the experimental subjects typically approach a mutual best response outcome, that is, the cohort converges to a customary way to solve their strategy coordination problem that is based on their experience within the cohort. The emergent convention is usually the inefficient, risk-dominant equilibrium when $k^* > 0.75$ and the efficient, payoff-dominant equilibrium when $k^* < 0.5$. For $0.5 < k^* < 0.75$, results are mixed.

Third, in most cases the terminal outcome is accurately predicted by the location of the initial outcome in the respective equilibrium's basin of attraction. The kind of separatrix crossings predicted by stochastic dynamics occur, but are rare.

Finally, the earnings difference between the two actions influences the frequency of observed separatrix crossings. Battalio, Samuelson, and Van Huyck (1997) observed separatrix crossings as they varied the relative earnings difference holding k^* equal to 0.8. This phenomena is predicted by probabilistic choice learning models.

3. Coordination Conventions: Labels and Populations

Van Huyck, Battalio, and Rankin (1997) investigate the influence of labels and populations on the ability of subjects in an evolutionary coordination game to adopt a conventional way to play. Van Huyck, Battalio, and Rankin's labels treatments investigate the abstraction assumptions that underlie the concept of a strategy, while their

---

[5] Rankin, Van Huyck, and Battalio (1997) report an experiment in which payoff dominance emerges as a deductive selection principle in sequences of similar but not identical stag hunt stage games. Payoff dominance salient even when some stage games have extreme values for k^*, such as 0.97. So in some cohorts players can become very confident in the mutual salience of payoff dominance. Studying the emergence of conventions in payoff perturbed games may eventually explain why efficiency and equal division are ambient convention.

Table 2
Recent evidence on human behavior in evolutionary stag hunt games

N	Game = {A, C} {B, D}	R(k)	k^*	Initial outcome	Terminal outcome	Periods	Source
1	{45, 0}, {35, 40}	$(10k - 8)/9$	0.80	5/8	1/8	75	Battalio, Samuelson, and Van Huyck (1997)
2	{45, 0}, {35, 40}	$(10k - 8)/9$	0.80	4/8	0/8	75	Battalio, Samuelson, and Van Huyck (1997)
3	{45, 0}, {35, 40}	$(10k - 8)/9$	0.80	5/8	0/8	75	Battalio, Samuelson, and Van Huyck (1997)
4	{45, 0}, {35, 40}	$(10k - 8)/9$	0.80	3/8	0/8	75	Battalio, Samuelson, and Van Huyck (1997)
5	{100, 0}, {80, 80}^{T}	$(5k - 4)/5$	0.80	6/10	0/10	22	Cooper et al. (1992)
6	{100, 0}, {80, 80}^{T}	$(5k - 4)/5$	0.80	6/10	0/10	22	Cooper et al. (1992)
7	{100, 0}, {80, 80}^{T}	$(5k - 4)/5$	0.80	5/10	1/10	22	Cooper et al. (1992)
8	{100, 0}, {80, 80}^{T}	$(5k - 4)/5$	0.80	7/20	4/20	10	Clark, Kay, and Sefton (2001)
9	{100, 0}, {80, 80}^{T}	$(5k - 4)/5$	0.80	5/20	2/20	10	Clark, Kay, and Sefton (2001)
10	{100, 0}, {80, 80}^{T}	$(5k - 4)/5$	0.80	4/10	0/10	9	Straub (1995)
11	{45, 0}, {40, 20}	$(5k - 4)/9$	0.80	6/8	1/8	75	Battalio, Samuelson, and Van Huyck (1997)
12	{45, 0}, {40, 20}	$(5k - 4)/9$	0.80	5/8	0/8	75	Battalio, Samuelson, and Van Huyck (1997)
13	{45, 0}, {40, 20}	$(5k - 4)/9$	0.80	6/8	5/8	75	Battalio, Samuelson, and Van Huyck (1997)
14	{45, 0}, {40, 20}	$(5k - 4)/9$	0.80	6/8	0/8	75	Battalio, Samuelson, and Van Huyck (1997)
15	{45, 0}, {42, 12}	$(5k - 4)/15$	0.80	4/8	3/8	75	Battalio, Samuelson, and Van Huyck (1997)
16	{45, 0}, {42, 12}	$(5k - 4)/15$	0.80	6/8	8/8*	75	Battalio, Samuelson, and Van Huyck (1997)
17	{45, 0}, {42, 12}	$(5k - 4)/15$	0.80	6/8	8/8*	75	Battalio, Samuelson, and Van Huyck (1997)
18	{45, 0}, {42, 12}	$(5k - 4)/15$	0.80	6/8	2/8	75	Battalio, Samuelson, and Van Huyck (1997)
19	{100, 20}, {80, 80}^{T}	$(4k - 3)/5$	0.75	2/10	0/10	9	Straub (1995)

(continued on next page)

Table 2
(continued)

N	Game = {A, C} {B, D}	R(k)	k*	Initial outcome	Terminal outcome	Periods	Source
20	{5, −1}, {3, 3}	(6k − 4)/5	0.67	5/12	3/12	10	Friedman (1996)
21	{5, −1}, {4, 1}	(3k − 2)/5	0.67	7/12	3/12	10	Friedman (1996)
22	{5, −1}, {4, 1}	(3k − 2)/5	0.67	7/12	3/12	16	Friedman (1996)
23	{5, −1}, {4, 1}	(3k − 2)/5	0.67	6/10	3/10	16	Friedman (1996)
24	{5, −1}, {4, 1}	(3k − 2)/5	0.67	2/12	3/12	10	Friedman (1996)
25	{5, −1}, {4, 1}	(3k − 2)/5	0.67	3/12	2/12	10	Friedman (1996)
26	{80, 10}, {70, 30}^{T}	(3k − 2)/8	0.67	9/10	9/10	9	Straub (1995)
27	{100, 20}, {60, 60}^{T}	(4k − 2)/5	0.50	7/10	10/10	9	Straub (1995)
28	{5, 0}, {4, 1}	(2k − 1)/5	0.50	6/12	9/12	10	Friedman (1996)
29	{55, 25}, {35, 35}^{T}	(6k − 2)/11	0.33	9/10	10/10	9	Straub (1995)

$R(k)$ – scaled earnings difference given k, the probability of X: $R(k) = (\{kA + (1 − k)C\} − \{kB + (1 − k)D\})/A$.
k^* – separatrix, zero earnings difference, mixed strategy equilibrium.
^{T} – payoff dominant equilibrium in the lower right cell of subjects earnings table.
* – separatrix crossings between initial and terminal outcome.

Ch. 58: *Emergent Conventions in Evolutionary Games* 525

Table 3
Earnings table for no labels and labels treatments: game CO

		No labels Earnings table Other participant's choice				Labels Earnings table Column choice	
		1	2			1	2
Your	1	0	40	Row	1	0, 0	40, 40
choice	2	40	0	choice	2	40, 40	0, 0

population treatments investigate the attraction of alternative mutually consistent ways to play under adaptive behavior. They observed conventions emerging in communities with one population and labels and with two populations and no labels, but the most effective treatment was two labeled populations.

Table 3 reports the earnings tables used in the experiment. The main difference between the two earnings tables is how they are labeled. In the no labels treatment, the rows are labeled "your choice" and the columns are labeled "other participant's choice." In the labels treatment, subjects were labeled either row or column and the earnings table described their potential earnings according to "row choice" and "column choice."

Making the usual abstraction assumptions gives a 2×2 game, call it CO, with two efficient but asymmetric pure strategy equilibria, (1, 2) and (2, 1), and an inefficient but symmetric mixed strategy equilibrium.

Labels may serve as a focal point that solves the strategy coordination problem, if their significance is established and recognized by members of the community, see Sugden (1995). Alternatively, changing the matching protocol from one to two populations changes the state space of models of population dynamics and for many population dynamics this change has the implication that only strict equilibria are asymptotically stable, see Weibull (1995). Consequently, inefficient but symmetric mixed strategy equilibria are no longer asymptotically stable.

Figure 1a graphs the vector field under the continuous time limit of the two population logit response dynamic with the noise parameter, set equal to 1. The axes measure the frequency of action 1 in the first and second population, respectively. The points (1, 0) and (0, 1) represent pure strategy equilibria in which everyone in one population takes the action opposite to the action taken by everyone in the second population. The mixed equilibrium in the center of the space is unstable, but vectors forcing the populations away from the center are small. (As the vector's color goes from black to red it represents smaller values. The tail of the vector is also proportional to size, but the head is not.) Note also that the logit equilibria with equal 1, denoted by red dots, are shifted slightly towards the center of the space. The shift will be more dramatic in the

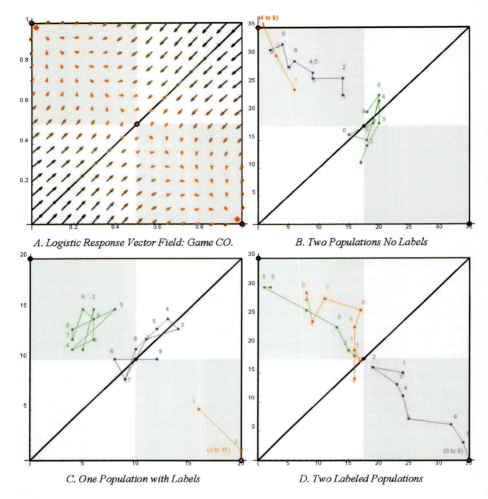

Figure 1. Evolutionary game CO; numbers order five period sums or states, sessions denoted by color.

bargaining game reviewed next. The gray shading represents states in which all players have a pecuniary incentive to conform to the emerging convention.[6]

Figure 1b graphs results of three sessions under a no labels two population treatment, which is the same case as the vector field although with seven subjects per population. The data points, denoted *states* below, are five period sums of action 1 in the two respec-

---

[6] See McKelvey and Palfrey (1995) for an introduction to logistic equilibria and Fudenberg and Levine (1997) for an introduction to the continuous time logistic response dynamic.

Table 4
Game form DS

	1	2	3
1	3, 3	3, 0	6, 4
2	0, 3	5, 5	0, 0
3	4, 6	0, 0	0, 0

tive populations and can sum to at most 35 (seven subjects playing 1 in all five periods of a state). State 1 is the sum for periods 1 to 5 and so on.

The "red" session in Figure 1b converges to perfect conformity with the convention everyone in the row population plays 2 and everyone in the column population plays 1. The same convention is emerging in the "blue" session. No convention emerges in the "green" session, which results in subjects losing half their potential earnings.

Figure 1d graphs the results of three sessions under a two labeled population treatment. The "blue" session in Figure 1d converges to perfect conformity with the convention everyone in the row population play 1 and everyone in the column population play 2. The alternative convention is emerging in the "red" and "green" sessions. Conventions emerged most consistently with two labeled populations.

Figure 1c graphs the results of three sessions under a one population with labels treatment, that is, eight subjects are randomly labeled either row or column and then randomly paired each period. Hence, a state denotes the sum of action 1 played by four subjects for five periods and ranges from 0 to 20. No convention appears to be emerging in the "blue" session. The "green" session is in an area where all subjects have a pecuniary incentive to conform to the emergent convention, but a high degree of conformity with the convention does not emerge within the 45 periods of the session. The "red" session in Figure 1c converges to perfect conformity with the following convention: when labeled row play 1 and when labeled column play 2.

4. Unequal Division Bargaining Conventions

Van Huyck et al. (1995) discovered an evolutionary bargaining game in which unequal division conventions emerge amongst symmetrically endowed subjects. They call it *DS*.

DS is symmetric. Units denote dimes. If both players choose 2 they divide a dollar equally. If one player chooses action 1 and the other chooses action 3, the first earns \$0.60 and the other earns \$0.40. Game *DS* is unusual in that the aggressive demand is also the secure demand. Using action 1 insures earning \$0.30. While the stage game is symmetric, Van Huyck et al. (1995) used a two labeled population protocol, which as we have just seen, allows some cohorts to use labels and populations to break the symmetry of the stage game in the evolutionary game.

Figure 2a graphs the logistic response vector field for the game that results when action 2 becomes extinct in game *DS*, which will be denoted *BOS*. The black dots denote Nash equilibria and the red dots denote logistic equilibria (again with equal 1). The gray

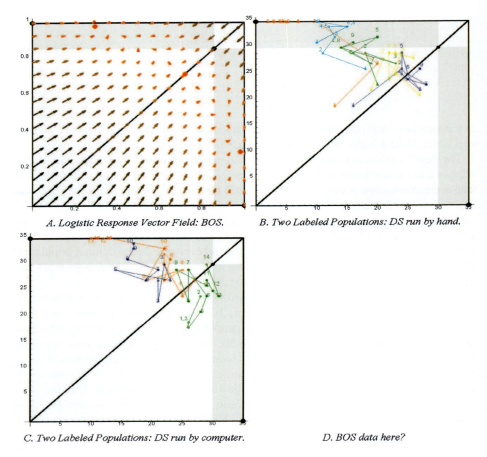

Figure 2. Evolutionary game DS; numbers order five period sums, color denote sessions.

shaded regions indicate states in which everyone has a pecuniary incentive to conform to the emerging convention.

It is not obvious from the figure or from logistic response theory why action 2 goes extinct, but one expects it to depend on the initial condition. Once action 2 is extinct, however, the vector field implies that one of the two unequal division conventions emerge. Van Huyck et al. (1995) discovered that the equal division action always goes extinct. Security was a more salient and convincing selection principle than equal division.

Figure 2b graphs the results for five sessions run by hand and Figure 2c graphs the results for three sessions run by computer. Again the points denote five period sums of action 1 for the row and column population. The sums can range from 0 to 35 (seven subjects choosing action 1 for five periods). Dots denote states in which the equal division action is extinct and circles denote states in which it is not. Numbers sequence the states by the time order they were observed.

An unequal division convention emerges in five of eight sessions. The "red," "light blue," and "green" sessions in Figure 2b and the "red" and "blue" session in Figure 2c. In these five sessions, the average favored subject earned between 6 and 14 cents per period or between $2.70 and $6.30 per session more than the average disadvantaged subject.

Van Huyck et al. (1995) used the replicator dynamic to inform their behavioral predictions. It provides a formal way to show that the symmetric mixed equilibrium is unstable and to check that unequal division equilibria have large basins of attraction. The fixed points of the replicator dynamic are the Nash equilibrium illustrated in Figure 2a. The logistic response dynamic can be calibrated to fit the data better. Specifically, the logistic response dynamic with the noise parameter set to 1 makes more accurate predictions of the regions of the state space with little motion (especially around the shifted equilibria) and the direction of the expected motion than the replicator dynamic.

Acknowledgements

The National Science Foundation and Texas Advanced Research Program provided financial support. A faculty development leave at the University of Pittsburgh provided time to write this paper.

References

Battalio, Raymond, Samuelson, Larry, Van Huyck, John (1997). "Risk dominance, payoff dominance, and probabilistic choice learning". Laser-script, http://econlab10.tamu.edu/JVH_gtee/c4.htm.

Clark, Kenneth, Kay, Stephen, Sefton, Martin (2001). "When are Nash equilibria self-enforcing? An experimental analysis". International Journal of Game Theory 29, 495–515.

Cooper, Russell, DeJong, Douglas V., Forsythe, Robert, Ross, Thomas W. (1992). "Communication in coordination games". Quarterly Journal of Economics 107, 739–773.

Friedman, Daniel (1996). "Equilibrium in evolutionary games: Some experimental results". Economic Journal 106, 1–25.

Harsanyi, John C., Selten, Reinhard (1988). "A General Theory of Equilibrium Selection in Games". MIT Press, Cambridge, MA.

Lewis, David (1969). "Convention: A Philosophical Study". Harvard University Press, Cambridge, MA.

McKelvey, Richard D., Palfrey, Thomas R. (1995). "Quantal response equilibria for normal form games". Games and Economic Behavior 10 (1), 6–38. http://www.hss.caltech.edu/~rdm/qrew.html.

Straub, Paul (1995). "Risk dominance and coordination failure in static games". The Quarterly Review of Economics and Finance 35 (4), 339–363.

Sugden, Robert (1986). "The Economics of Rights, Co-operation, and Welfare". Basil Blackwell, Oxford, UK.

Sugden, Robert (1995). "A theory of focal points". The Economic Journal 105 (430), 533–550.

Van Huyck, John B., Battalio, Raymond C., Rankin, Frederick (1997). "On the origin of convention: Evidence from coordination games". Economic Journal 107 (442), 576–597.

Van Huyck, J.B., Battalio, R.C., Mathur, S., Ortmann, A., Van Huyck, P.P. (1995). "On the origin of convention: Evidence from symmetricbargaining games". International Journal of Game Theory 24 (2), 187–212.
Young, Peyton (1998). "Individual Strategy and Social Structure: An Evolutionary Theory of Institutions". Princeton University Press, Princeton, NJ.
Weibull, Jorgen W. (1995). "Evolutionary Game Theory". MIT Press, Cambridge, MA.

Further reading

Binmore, Ken, Gale, John, Samuelson, Larry (1995). "Learning to be imperfect: The ultimatum game". Games and Economic Behavior 8, 56–90.
Fudenberg, Drew, Levine, David K. (1996). "Theory of learning in games". Laser-script, http://levine.sscnet.ucla.edu/Papers/book1.pdf (last accessed on 14 January, 1998).
Rankin, Frederick, Van Huyck, John, Battalio, Raymond (2000). "Strategic similarity and emergent conventions: Evidence from scrambled payoff perturbed stag hunt games". Games and Economic Behavior 32, 315–337.
Roth, A.E., Erev, I. (1995). "Learning in extensive-form games: Experimental data and simple dynamic models in the intermediate term". Games and Economic Behavior 8, 164–212. http://www.pitt.edu/~alroth/lowgame.html.
Young, Peyton (1993). "The evolution of conventions". Econometrica 61, 57–84.

Chapter 59

SELF-CENTERED FAIRNESS IN GAMES WITH MORE THAN TWO PLAYERS

GARY E. BOLTON

Smeal College of Business, 310 Beam, Penn State University, University Park, PA 16802, USA
e-mail: geb3@psu.edu

AXEL OCKENFELS

Max Planck Institute for Research into Economic Systems, Strategic Interaction Unit,
Kahlaische Str. 10, D-07745 Jena, Germany
e-mail: ockenfels@mpiew-jena.mpg.de

1. Introduction

What we now label as 'fair behavior' in the lab often differs from philosophical notions of the concept. Establishing a clear understanding of the empirical nature of fairness is important if we are to gauge the impact fairness has on economic and political institutions.

Most experiments that aim to reveal the nature of fairness examine two-player games. Among these, the ultimatum game and the dictator game are probably the most prominent. In the ultimatum game, a proposer offers a division of a monetary cake, which the responder can either accept or reject; rejection leaves both players with a zero payoff. The dictator game differs from the ultimatum game only in that the responder has no choice but to accept. In both games, we observe outcomes that deviate from standard perfect equilibrium in the direction of the *egalitarian solution*, the outcome in which both subjects receive half the cake. In ultimatum games, the egalitarian solution is typically the modal outcome and in dictator games it is typically the second most frequent outcome (cf. Roth, 1995).

Recent experiments show that adding players to ultimatum and dictator games in certain ways tends to invalidate the attraction of the egalitarian solution. In some of these games, egalitarianism does not seem to guide individual behavior at all, even though people still deviate from standard predictions of selfish payoff maximization. In other games, behavior conforms nearly perfectly to selfish payoff maximization, even though the corresponding outcomes are far from egalitarian. Hence games with more than two players challenge our understanding of the two-player games.

In the next section, we describe a class of preferences that characterize 'self-centered fairness.' In Section 3, we outline how these preferences can reconcile seemingly incompatible behavior from selected games. Except for the number of players, all of these games are closely related to either the two-person ultimatum or dictator game.

2. Sketch of ERC Preferences

'ERC' is short for equity, reciprocity and competition, the patterns of behavior that ERC preferences attempt to reconcile. Bolton and Ockenfels (1998, 2000) provide a full account of the model. An earlier model, Bolton's (1991) comparative model, posited preferences consistent with ultimatum game behavior. According to this model a player cares not only about her material or *absolute payoff*, but also about her share of the cake or *relative payoff*. Ultimatum game second movers turn down money – sacrifice own pecuniary payoff – in order to gain relative payoff (all receiving nothing is an equal split). Beyond ultimatum games, the comparative model is consistent with a variety of phenomena observed in laboratory play of two-period alternating offer bargaining games. But the comparative model fails with the dictator game. The reason for the failure is straightforward: Comparative model utility functions are non-decreasing in both own pecuniary and relative payoffs. Consequently, no one should be inclined to give a gift to another.

ERC posits that people behave in a self-centered way, but different from the comparative model, as well as from the standard assumption of selfish behavior. Specifically, in an n-player game, player i maximizes the expected value of her *motivation function*:

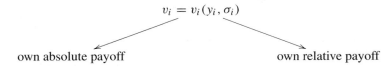

$$v_i = v_i(y_i, \sigma_i)$$

own absolute payoff　　　　　　　　own relative payoff

where

$$\sigma_i = \sigma_i(y_i, c, n) = \begin{cases} y_i/c, & \text{if } c > 0, \\ 1/n, & \text{if } c = 0, \end{cases} \quad \text{and} \quad c = \sum_{j=1}^{n} y_j$$

is the total payoff distributed.

Preferences over the relative payoff are interpreted as preferences over the fairness of the payoff allocation. Note that players care only about own absolute and own relative payoffs, but that the payoff (or welfare) of other individuals does not enter directly into the motivation function. In this sense, the concern for fairness is self-centered.[1]

---

[1] Self-centered fairness must be distinguished from the "self-serving bias" in assessments of fairness. We define the former as a property of individual motivations while the latter describes a tendency of human beings "[...] to conflate what is fair with what benefits oneself"; see Babcock and Loewenstein (1997, p. 110) and the references cited therein for empirical studies of the self-serving bias. Fehr and Schmidt (1999) propose a model of "self-centered inequity aversion." The model differs from our notion of self-centered fairness in that absolute payoffs of all other players directly enter into the utility function. In the domain of 'advantageous inequality,' individuals are assumed to have standard altruistic preferences.

We assume the motivation function increases in the absolute payoff y_i, and decreases as the relative payoff σ_i moves away from the *social reference share* $1/n$, the average proportion of the cake.[2] Furthermore, we assume that each player i prefers a distribution in which i receives more than the social reference share to an allocation in which all players receive nothing.[3]

The assumptions imply that, *fixing the absolute payoff*, all players prefer their relative payoff to be the social reference share; in this sense the egalitarian solution is of collective prominence. In most situations, however, the relative payoff is not easily separated from the absolute payoff, and in fact the two are usually positively correlated (for instance, if the cake size is fixed). For this reason, some, perhaps most people will strive for more than their social reference share – how much more depends on the marginal rate of substitution between absolute and relative payoffs.

We obtain a visual representation by observing that $c\sigma_i = y_i$, and writing $v_i(y_i, \sigma_i)$ as $v_i(c\sigma_i, \sigma_i)$. Holding c fixed, a typical motivation function looks like Figure 1. The peak of the function at 0.75 indicates that, as a dictator in the dictator game, i keeps 75 percent of the cake, and gives the rest to the other player. The function taking the value zero at 0.2 indicates that, as a second mover in the ultimatum game, i is indifferent between accepting 20 percent of the cake or rejecting, in which case $v_i(0, 0.5) = 0$.

The marginal rate of substitution between absolute and relative payoffs will differ from person-to-person, and so too the ultimatum and dictator game thresholds. There are, however, some general bounds: The model implies that all dictators will choose to keep at least the social reference share. The rejection threshold of a responder in the ultimatum game is always an offer between half the cake and nothing. Hence when making an offer to a randomly chosen responder, the probability of acceptance increases as the offer increases from zero to half the cake. Therefore the proposer in the ultimatum game should never offer more than half the cake. These bounds are in basic accord with what we see in the lab (cf. Roth, 1995).[4]

---

[2] In Bolton and Ockenfels (2000) we demonstrate that our simple definition of the social reference share organizes a wide range of behaviors observed in experimental fairness games. But, of course, the definition can be modified for games that allow for competing fairness norms. For instance, what is perceived as fair may depend on the payoff menu (see Bolton and Ockenfels, 2001, and the references cited therein) as well as on the fairness of the procedure by which the allocation is reached (see Bolton, Brandts and Ockenfels, 2001).

[3] Our statement of the assumptions is rough. See Bolton and Ockenfels (2000) for a detailed depiction.

[4] In Bolton and Ockenfels (2000) we model the heterogeneity in marginal rates of substitution in terms of the proportion a person takes when in the role of dictator in the dictator game, together with the rejection threshold when in the role of ultimatum game responder. The model is then solved by applying perfect Bayesian equilibrium under the assumption that individual motivation functions are private information. We derive predictions for a variety of experimental games, including variations on dictator and ultimatum games, the gift-exchange game, the prisoner's dilemma, Bertrand markets, and the guessing game.

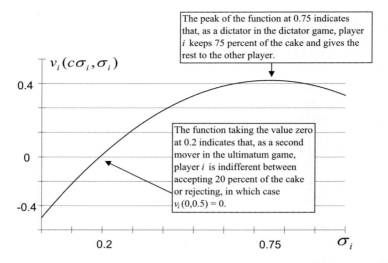

Figure 1. A typical motivation function $v_i(y_i, \sigma_i)$, $y_i = $ 'absolute payoff,' $\sigma_i = $ 'relative' payoff. We obtain a visual representation by holding the cake size c fixed, observing that $c\sigma_i = y_i$, and writing $v_i(y_i, \sigma_i)$ as $v_i(c\sigma_i, \sigma_i)$. The motivation function in the figure provides an example of ERC preferences. These are based on the assumption that people are motivated by their own absolute (pecuniary) payoff as well as their own relative share of the payoff cake. The payoffs of other individuals do not enter directly into the motivation function. In this sense, the concern for fairness is self-centered.

3. Evidence in Games with More Than Two Players

3.1. The Güth–van Damme Bargaining Game

Güth and van Damme (1998) present a three-person bargaining game, which is closely related to the standard two-person ultimatum game. The only difference is a third player, the 'dummy.' The proposer proposes a division of 120 points among herself, the responder and the dummy. A minimal amount, 5 points, must be allocated to each player, but otherwise the proposer is free to allocate as she chooses. The responder either accepts or rejects the proposal. If accepted, the money is distributed accordingly. If rejected, all receive nothing. The dummy has no say in the negotiation, and no choice but to accept any agreement set by the other two.

The game was played under three information conditions. We restrict attention to two. In the *full information* condition, the responder knows the full proposal at the time of accepting or rejecting. In the *irrelevant information* condition, the responder knows only the dummy's share.[5]

---

[5] In the information condition not described, the responder knows only his own allocation. Güth and van Damme (1998) examined all three information conditions in two modes. In the constant mode, all games had

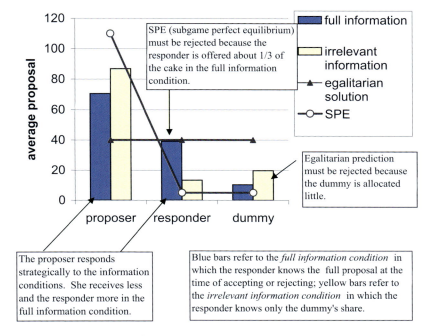

Figure 2. Average proposals in the Güth–van Damme game: The proposer proposes a division of 120 points among herself, the responder and the dummy. The responder either accepts or rejects the proposal. If rejected, all receive nothing. The dummy has no say in the negotiation. ERC preferences, like those described in Figure 1, can organize the proposer's behavior. First, since the risk of rejection is decreasing in the offer to the responder, proposers offer more to the responder than predicted by the standard subgame perfect equilibrium. Second, since ERC-players are self-centered, and do not strive for egalitarian allocations, the dummy – who has no veto-power – is allocated little (see Table 1 for more on this point). Third, since there is no evidence in the data that the responders could ascertain their own share from what is offered to the dummy, ERC-proposers strategically exploit the incomplete information condition.

The subgame perfect equilibrium under the standard self-interest assumption (henceforth SPE) is invariant to the information condition: every feasible proposal gives each bargainer a positive amount, so the responder always makes more money accepting than rejecting. The proposer should therefore ask for the maximum allowable. The egalitarian solution is also invariant to the information condition: each bargainer gets a one-third share. Figure 2 shows the average proposals.

The figure illustrates that neither SPE nor egalitarianism fits the data particularly well. In both information conditions, the proposer receives more than the responder and the dummy combined but still significantly less than in the SPE allocation. While the

the same information condition, and in the cycle mode, games were rotated through all conditions. We confine ourselves to the constant mode. See Bolton and Ockenfels' (1998) analysis.

Table 1

Rejection behavior in the full information condition in the Güth–van Damme game. Self-centered ERC-responders care neither about the absolute nor the relative payoffs of the other individual players, which explains why the responders reject only when they personally receive less than the social reference share (40) regardless of the dummy's payoff. Second, offering something to the responder decreases the risk of rejection and improves the proposer's relative position while giving to the dummy can only improve the relative position. Consequently, responders are 'served first' by ERC-proposers. Third, from the point of view of self-centered players, the three-person Güth–van Damme game creates more room to agree on a distribution of relative payoffs than a standard two-person ultimatum game. Therefore, ERC predicts a smaller rejection rate in the three-person game than in the two-person game

Number of proposals in the full information condition in the Güth–van Damme game	Dummy's payoff = 5 (minimum value allowed)		Dummy's payoff > 5	
	Responder's payoff <40	Responder's payoff ≥40	Responder's payoff <40	Responder's payoff ≥40
Accepted	23	18	0	26
Rejected[a]	5[b]	0[c]	0[d]	0[d]

[a] The overall rejection rate (7%) is remarkably small.

[b] Rejections only occur if the offer to the responder is smaller than the 'social reference share' 1/3 of 120 = 40.

[c] In particular, none of the proposals that give the minimum value to the dummy are rejected if the responder's payoff is at least 40.

[d] The proposer is 'served first': The dummy is never allocated more than the minimum as long as the proposer is offered less than the 'social reference share.'

responder is, on average, offered about the social reference payoff (1/3 of 120) in the full information condition, the dummy is allocated little in both conditions.[6] In contrast with what we observe in the dictator game, there is nothing here to make us think that the proposer cares about the dummy's payoff.

Table 1 suggests that the responder too cares little about the dummy's payoff. Rejections only occur if the offer to the responder is smaller than the social reference share. Note in particular that if the responder's allocation is at least 40, none of the proposals that give the minimum value to the dummy are rejected.

ERC preferences can organize the behavior of both the proposer and the responder. ERC-players care neither about the absolute nor about the relative payoffs of other individuals, which immediately explains why the responder rejects only when he personally receives less than the social reference.

Offering something to the responder has, from the proposer's point of view, two positive effects: First, the risk of rejection decreases, at least up to the point that the offer is equal to the social reference share. Second, giving something may improve the proposer's relative position (see Figure 1). In contrast, giving to the dummy can only

---

[6] Keep in mind that the rules of the game require that a minimum of 5 be allocated to each player.

improve the relative position. Therefore, ERC predicts that the responder is 'served first,' at least up to the social reference share. Table 1 is in line with this prediction: only in those cases in which the responder receives at least the social reference share is the dummy allocated more than the minimum.

Figure 2 and Table 1 capture two other phenomena.

First, observe from Figure 2 that, compared to the full information condition, the proposer receives more, and the responder less, in the irrelevant information condition. It turns out that the data shows no evidence of signaling behavior in the irrelevant information condition; that is, no evidence that the responder could ascertain her own share from what is offered the dummy. As we would expect if the responder cares only about her own share of the payoff, proposers strategically exploit the situation by allocating smaller amounts for the responder in the irrelevant information condition than they would in the full information condition.[7]

Second, observe in Table 1 that the overall rejection rate is small, 7 percent, compared to rates in the two-person ultimatum game, which typically run in the neighborhood of 15 to 20 percent (see Roth, 1995). ERC offers an explanation. The underlying idea is that the three-person game creates more room to agree on a distribution of relative payoffs between the proposer and the responder than a two-person game: A proposer in the three-person game can demand up to 2/3 of the cake for herself with no risk of rejection, but not generally so in the two-person game. It can be shown that (risk-averse) proposers who want more than 2/3 of the cake will use some of the extra resources in the three-person game to lower the probability of rejection relative to the risk they would assume in the two-person game (cf. Bolton and Ockenfels, 1998).

3.2. Market Game

Roth et al. (1991) report an experiment on the 'market game' similar to the ultimatum game: Nine proposers simultaneously submit offers on the cake. One responder is given the opportunity to accept or reject the highest offer. In the case of a tie, one offer is chosen at random. All SPE imply a highly unequal payoff distribution: the responder receives virtually the entire cake, namely 995 or 1000. Roth et al. ran the market game in each of four countries. In each country, there were four markets, each market iterated for 10 rounds. Figure 3 shows the minimum of the four winning offers per round by country. We see that, after a few rounds, outcomes are remarkably consistent with the SPE prediction, with the best offer rising to the SPE offer no later than round seven.

Competing in this market game is consistent with ERC preferences. For simplicity, let us restrict attention to pure strategies. Suppose that all proposers but i are offering 995. If i offers less than 995 his offer will not get to the responder and he receives

---

[7] That proposers exploit their private information about the share offered to the responder has also been observed in the two-person ultimatum game; cf. Mitzkewitz and Nagel (1993), Kagel, Kim, and Moser (1996), and Rapoport, Sundali, and Potter (1992).

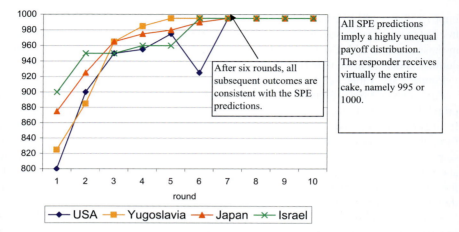

Figure 3. Winning offers in the market game (Roth et al., 1991): Nine proposers simultaneously submit offers on the cake (=1000). One responder is given the opportunity to accept or reject the highest offer. The game was run in each of four countries. In each country there were four markets, each market iterated for 10 rounds. We show the minimum of the four winning offers per round by country. Typical market environments interact with ERC-preferences in a way that aligns absolute and relative motives: Self-centered proposers can improve both their absolute and relative position by overbidding offers that are smaller than SPE-offers. Consequently, competing in the market game is consistent with self-centered fairness.

nothing; if he offers the entire cake, 1000, it comes to the same: $v_i(0, 0)$, a very poor payoff. If i offers 995, then he has a 1/9 chance of receiving $v_i(5, 5/1000)$, which is better. So all proposers offering 995 is stable.[8] Suppose, however, that everybody else is offering something less than 995, say 980. Now if i offers just a bit more, 985, the offer goes to the responder for sure, and i receives $v_i(15, 15/1000)$ instead of a 1/9 chance of $v_i(20, 20/1000)$. So long as the difference between $v_i(15, 15/1000)$ and $v_i(20, 20/1000)$ is small, i has an incentive to overbid the others, and hence a winning offer of less than 995 cannot be stable.

3.3. The Fixed Total Sacrifice Effect

Bolton, Katok, and Zwick (1998) study a dictator game in which the dictator divides the cake among himself and 10 recipients. They found no difference between the distribution of the total gift that dictators leave the multiple recipients and the distribution for the game where there is but one recipient.

Selten and Ockenfels (1998) observe the same sort of fixed total sacrifice effect in the solidarity game: Each player in a three-person group independently throws dice

---

[8] By our assumptions, the responder will accept the offer with probability one. A positive acceptance probability, however, would be enough. A similar argument shows that a winning offer of 1000 can also be stable.

to determine whether they (individually) win a fixed monetary sum. Before the dice are rolled, each player announces how much he wishes to compensate the losers, for both the case where there is one loser, and for the case where there are two. Most subjects give the same total (positive) amount independent of the number of losers. Selten and Ockenfels formally demonstrate that the behavioral pattern is not easy to justify if subjects have standard altruistic preferences (a class that includes egalitarian preferences).[9]

4. Summary

The concept of self-centered fairness, as embodied in ERC preferences, organizes the data from the two-person ultimatum and dictator game, as well as the Güth–van Damme game, the market game, the dictator game with multiple recipients, and the fixed total sacrifice effect as observed by Bolton, Katok, and Zwick (1998).

There are also some clear limitations to the approach. Specifically, a more comprehensive decision theory need incorporate learning and bounded rationality:

Subjects in the market game require experience before playing SPE. Likewise, Güth and van Damme (1998) report an experience effect for their game. While the dynamics in both games are consistent with the idea that behavior converges towards equilibrium play of self-centered subjects, the dynamics themselves cannot be explained in the framework of a static model.

The solidarity game by Selten and Ockenfels (1998) poses a different challenge. There, dictator behavior together with the expectations they report sometimes imply that a recipient may receive more than the dictator which contradicts ERC-predictions. Selten and Ockenfels (1998) propose a model of boundedly rational decision making in order to capture the phenomenon.

An interesting theme for future empirical and theoretical research, particularly in games with more than two players, is the identification of the 'appropriate' reference group. While this task is rather obvious in the simple games considered here, this need not to be true in more complex social environments. A nice example of an environment with competing reference groups can be found in European parliaments. The income distribution of the Europe-parliamentarians in Brussels is highly unequal. Since Europe-parliamentarians of all European countries basically have the same tasks and work load, this was regarded as unfair, and a proposal was made to equalize incomes. However, German European-parliamentarians (among others) objected to the proposal, on the grounds that, under the proposal, they would earn much less than their colleagues in the German parliament in Bonn. Likewise, a Spanish European-parliamentarian voted

---

[9] The "embedding effect" in the contingent valuation literature is a related phenomenon. It suggests that the willingness-to-pay does not vary substantially with the number of projects to be valued. Kahneman and Knetsch (1992) and Desvousges et al. (1993) find empirical support. See Hanemann (1994) for a skeptical assessment.

against the proposal, stating that he would earn much more than his colleagues in Spain. Due to the conflicting reference groups and given the differing incomes of the parliamentarians across nations, it is far from obvious what constitutes a 'fair' income distribution within the European parliament.

References

Babcock, Lind, Loewenstein, George (1997). "Explaining bargaining impasse: The role of self-serving biases". Journal of Economic Perspectives 11, 109–126.
Bolton, Gary E. (1991). "A comparative model of bargaining: Theory and evidence". American Economic Review 81, 1096–1136.
Bolton, Gary E., Ockenfels, Axel (1998). "Strategy and equity: An ERC-analysis of the Güth–van Damme game". Journal of Mathematical Psychology 42, 215–226.
Bolton, Gary E., Ockenfels, Axel (2000). "ERC: A theory of equity, reciprocity and competition". American Economic Review 90 (1), 166–193.
Bolton, Gary E., Ockenfels, Axel (2001). "A stress test of fairness measures in models of social utility". Working paper, Penn State University.
Bolton, Gary E., Brandts, Jordi, Ockenfels, Axel (2001). "Fair procedures: Evidence from games involving lotteries". Working paper, Max Planck Institute, Jena.
Bolton, Gary E., Katok, Elena, Zwick, Rami (1998). "Dictator game giving: Rules of fairness versus acts of kindness". International Journal of Game Theory 27, 269–299.
Desvousges, W.H., Johnson, F.R., Dunford, R.W., Boyle, K.J., Hudson, S.P., Wilson, K.N. (1993). "Measuring natural resource damages using contingent valuation: Tests of validity and reliability". In: Hausman, J. (Ed.), Contingent Valuation: A Critical Assessment. North-Holland Press, Amsterdam, pp. 91–164.
Fehr, Ernst, Schmidt, Klaus (1999). "A theory of fairness, competition and cooperation". Quarterly Journal of Economics 114, 817–868.
Güth, Werner, van Damme, Eric (1998). "Information, strategic behavior and fairness in ultimatum bargaining: An experimental study". Journal of Mathematical Psychology 42, 227–247.
Hanemann, W. Michael (1994). "Valuing the environment through contingent valuation". Journal of Economic Perspectives 8, 19–43.
Kagel, John, Kim, Chung, Moser, Donald (1996). "Fairness in ultimatum games with asymmetric information and asymmetric payoffs". Games and Economic Behavior 13, 100–110.
Kahneman, Daniel, Knetsch, Jack L. (1992). "Valuing public goods: The purchase of moral satisfaction". Journal of Environmental Economics and Management 22, 57–70.
Mitzkewitz, Michael, Nagel, Rosemarie (1993). "Envy, greed and anticipation in ultimatum games with incomplete information". International Journal of Game Theory 22, 171–198.
Rapoport, Amnon, Sundali, James A., Potter, Richard E. (1992). "Ultimatum games with incomplete information: Effects of the variability of the pie size". Mimeo, University of Arizona.
Roth, Alvin E. (1995). "Bargaining experiments". In: Kagel, J., Roth, A.E. (Eds.), Handbook of Experimental Economics. Princeton University Press, Princeton.
Roth, Alvin E., Prasnikar, Vesna, Okuno-Fujiwara, Masahiro, Zamir, Shmuel (1991). "Bargaining and market behavior in Jerusalem, Ljubljana, Pittsburgh, and Tokyo". American Economic Review 81, 1068–1095.
Selten, Reinhard, Ockenfels, Axel (1998). "An experimental solidarity game". Journal of Economic Behavior and Organization 34, 517–539.

Chapter 60

QUANTAL RESPONSE EQUILIBRIA: A BRIEF SYNOPSIS

RICHARD D. MCKELVEY and THOMAS R. PALFREY

Division of the Humanities and Social Sciences, California Institute of Technology, Pasadena, CA 91125, USA

1. Introduction

The quantal response equilibrium (QRE) is an extension of the standard model of Nash equilibrium which allows for errors in choice. The QRE can be viewed as a generalization of statistical models of discrete choice behavior of individuals to a game theoretic setting. Just like in discrete choice models of individual behavior, individuals are assumed to have an observed and unobserved component of their utility function. However, unlike in models of individual choice, the unobserved part of an individual's utility is unobserved not just to the econometrician, but also to the other players in the game. Thus, the game becomes a game of incomplete information. A QRE is simply a Bayesian equilibrium to this game.

In a QRE, individuals do not choose the strategy with the highest (observed) utility for sure, but rather choose it with a probability that is a function of the utility difference between that strategy and other strategies. Specifically, given a set of alternative choices, individuals choose probabilistically, choosing better alternatives more often than worse alternatives. The Nash equilibrium model corresponds to an extreme special case of this model, in which the probability of choosing an optimal alternative is equal to one and the probability of making a suboptimal choice is zero.

2. The Model

We begin by defining a game in its normal form in the standard way. Let $I = \{1, \ldots, n\}$ be the set of *players*. For each $i \in I$ there is a strategy set A_i, which we assume to be finite, with J_i elements. Each player has a payoff function $u_i : A \to \mathcal{R}$, where $A = \prod_{i \in I} A_i$. Let S_i be the set of probability distributions over A_i and an element $s_i \in S_i$ is a *mixed strategy*. Given a strategy profile $s \in S = \prod_{i \in I} S_i$ player i's expected payoff is $v_i(s) = \sum_{a \in A} p(a) u_i(a)$, where $p(a) = \prod_{i \in I} s_i(a_i)$. A (mixed) strategy profile $s \in S$ is a *Nash equilibrium* if, for all $i \in I$ and for all $t_i \in S_i$, $v_i(s) \geq v_i(t_i, s_{-i})$.

For each i and each $j \in \{1, \ldots, J_i\}$, and for any $s \in S$, denote by $v_{ij}(s)$ the expected utility to i of adopting the pure strategy a_{ij} when the other players use s_{-i}. For a quantal response equilibrium, it is assumed that for each pure strategy a_{ij}, player i receives an additional privately observed disturbance to their payoff, ε_{ij}. Thus i's payoff from adopting strategy a_{ij} under the strategy profile s is not $v_{ij}(s)$ but instead:

$$\hat{v}_{ij} = v_{ij}(s) + \varepsilon_{ij}.$$

Player i's profile of payoff disturbances, $\varepsilon_i = (\varepsilon_{i1}, \ldots, \varepsilon_{iJ_i})$, is distributed according to a joint distribution with density function $f_i(\varepsilon_i)$. Assume that the marginal distribution of f_i exists for each ε_{ij} and $E(\varepsilon_i) = 0$. McKelvey and Palfrey (1995) call $f = (f_1, \ldots, f_n)$ *admissible* if f_i satisfies the above properties for all i. The assumed choice behavior is that each player chooses strategy a_{ij} such that $\hat{v}_{ij} \geq \hat{v}_{ik}$ $\forall k = 1, \ldots, J_i$. Given this choice behavior, v and f together induce a distribution over the actual choices by each player. To be more specific, for any v, define $B_{ij(v)}$ as the set of realizations of ε_i such that strategy a_{ij} has the highest disturbed expected payoff. So

$$P_{ij}(v) = \int_{B_{ij}(v)} f(\varepsilon)\,d\varepsilon$$

is the induced probability that player i will select strategy j given v. Since $P(v) \in S$ and $v = v(s)$ is defined for any $s \in S$, $P \circ v(s) = P(v(s))$ defines a mapping from S into itself. Any fixed point s^* such that $s^* = P(v(s^*))$ is called a *quantal response equilibrium* of the game (I, A, u).

3. Properties of the QRE

The above definitions for normal form games can be extended to extensive form games. In the case of extensive form games, each for each information set of a player, there is assumed to be an independent payoff disturbance for each action. In the case where the payoff disturbance is known only to the "agent" in charge of each information set, the QRE can be defined in a similar fashion to the definitions for the normal form game, where instead one uses the agent normal form (see McKelvey and Palfrey, 1998). McKelvey and Palfrey (1995, 1998) prove the following results for the QRE and it's modification for extensive form games, the agent quantal response equilibrium (AQRE):

THEOREM 1. *For any admissible f, a QRE (AQRE) exists.*

In the remainder of the paper, we focus mainly on a specialized version of the model, where each ε_{ij} is independently and identically distributed according to the type I extreme value (or log Weibull) distribution with cumulative density $F(\varepsilon_{ij}) = e^{-e^{-\lambda \varepsilon_{ij}}}$.

This distribution of the disturbances leads to choice probabilities following a multinomial logit distribution (see, e.g., McFadden, 1975). We call the resulting equilibrium a logit QRE (AQRE), or just a logit equilibrium.

THEOREM 2. *For every finite normal (extensive) form game, every limit point of a sequence of logit QREs (AQREs) with λ going to infinity corresponds to the strategy of a Nash (sequential) equilibrium of the game.*

THEOREM 3. *For almost all finite normal (extensive) form games*:
1. *The logit QRE (AQRE) correspondence, Q is a one-dimensional manifold.*
2. *For almost all λ there are an odd number of logit QRE (AQRE).*
3. *There is a unique branch, $\mathcal{B}$ (the principal branch) of the logit QRE (AQRE) selection connected to the centroid of the game at $\lambda = 0$.*
4. *The principal branch of the logit QRE (AQRE) correspondence selects a unique Nash equilibrium (sequential equilibrium component) of the game as $\lambda \to \infty$.*

4. Fit to Experimental Data

We illustrate with three examples some features of experimental data that the QRE can help explain. These examples are presented in more detail in McKelvey and Palfrey (1995, 1998).

4.1. Learning to Play Nash Over Time

In some experiments, individuals take time to learn how to play the Nash equilibrium. Lieberman (1960) conducted experiments on the following two person zero sum game (the payoffs are to the row player):

	B_1	B_2	B_3
A_1	15	0	-2
A_2	0	-15	-1
A_3	1	2	0

The fit of the QRE to the data from this experiment illustrates a pattern of learning that is seen in some experiments. In Figure 1, the QRE correspondence is shown along with the aggregate data, broken down by time period. In this figure, the curved line represents the logistic QRE correspondence. For low values of λ (which is the precision of the error term) the QRE starts at the centroid, and then as λ increases, the QRE approaches a Nash equilibrium. The learning is be captured by the QRE through the estimation of decreasing variance (increasing precision) of the payoff disturbances as subjects become more experienced. Also, in this case, the QRE captures the fact that subjects learn fairly quickly to eliminate the dominated strategy, but more slowly to eliminate the iterated dominated strategy.

4.2. Systematic Bias Away from the Nash Equilibrium

In games with mixed strategy equilibria, the subjects are indifferent between their strategies, and hence there is no reason, in equilibrium, for them to adopt the pure strategies with the correct probabilities. In such experiments, one frequently sees systematic deviations away from the Nash predictions.

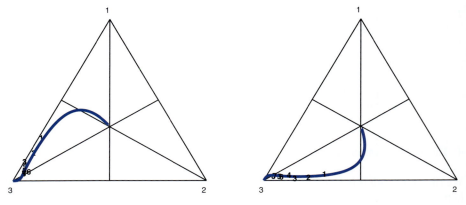

Figure 1. QRE as a function of λ for Lieberman experiment.

O'Neill (1987) conducted experiments on the following two person zero sum normal form game:

	B_1	B_2	B_3	B_4
A_1	5	−5	−5	−5
A_2	−5	−5	5	5
A_3	−5	5	−5	5
A_4	−5	5	5	−5

The data from this experiment illustrate the systematic bias away from equilibrium that is predicted by the QRE. In these experiments, the row players underplayed the first strategy, while the column players overplayed their first strategy. The QRE correspondence for this game is plotted in Figure 2. Here, the value of λ, which is the precision of the error, is on the horizontal axis, and the corresponding probabilities of selected strategies is on the vertical axis. The data is broken down by time periods, and the aggregate data for each time period is plotted at the value of λ that maximizes the likelihood function of the data. Each time period thus corresponds to four points on the graph, one for each of the selected probabilities.

As is evident from the figure, the QRE predicts that when there is error, player 1 will systematically (i.e., for all values of λ), underplay his first strategy, while player 2 will systematically overplay her first strategy except for very low values of λ. This clearly is borne out in data of Figure 2.

4.3. Nash Equilibrium Selection

A third feature of the QRE, which follows from Theorem 3, is that it can be used to select a unique Nash, or sequential equilibrium in a game. This is illustrated by an

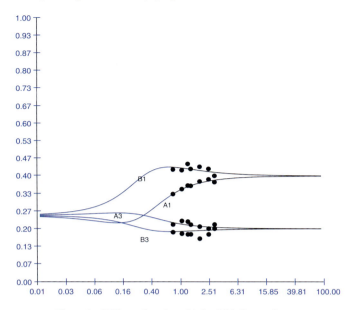

Figure 2. QRE as a function of λ for O'Neill experiment.

Table 1

BH #3 (sequential vs intuitive)							
Sequential (S, D, C)				Intuitive (I, C, D)			
$m = I$	C	D^n	E	$m = S$	C	D	E
A	45, 30	15, 0	30, 15	A	30, 90	0, 15	45, 15
B	30, 30	0, 45	30, 15	B	45, 0	15, 30	30, 15
BH #4 (sequential vs intuitive)							
Sequential (S, D, C)				Intuitive (I, C, D)			
$m = I$	C	D^n	E	$m = S$	C	D	E
A	30, 30	0, 0	50, 35	A	45, 90	15, 15	100, 30
B	30, 30	30, 45	30, 0	B	45, 0	0, 30	0, 15

experiment of Brandts and Holt (1993) who ran a pair of signaling experiments each of which contained a sequential and intuitive equilibrium.

The intuitive equilibrium is a more refined equilibrium concept than sequential equilibrium. Signaling games studied by Banks, Camerer, and Porter (1994) suggested that subjects go to the more refined equilibrium. The objective of Brandts and Holt was to

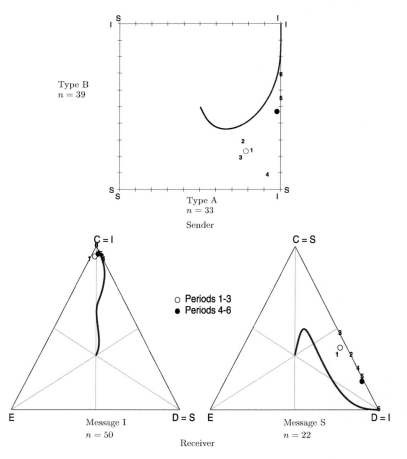

Figure 3. Brandts and Holt (1993) game 3. Sequential vs intuitive.

see if they could take a game with two equilibria, one sequential, and one intuitive, and by changing the payoffs (without affecting the properties of the equilibria), get subjects to choose a different equilibrium in the different games. In particular, could a game be designed where the subjects would choose a less refined (sequential) equilibrium over a more refined (intuitive) one.

The games that Brandts and Holt studied are given in Table 1. Each has a sequential and an intuitive equilibrium. The experiment was successful in achieving its objective – in the first game, subjects tended to select the intuitive equilibrium. and in the second, subjects tended to select the sequential equilibrium. However, standard refinement theory can not be used in general to predict which equilibrium would be selected. The AQRE offers an explanation of this failure. Figures 3 and 4 illustrate that the principal

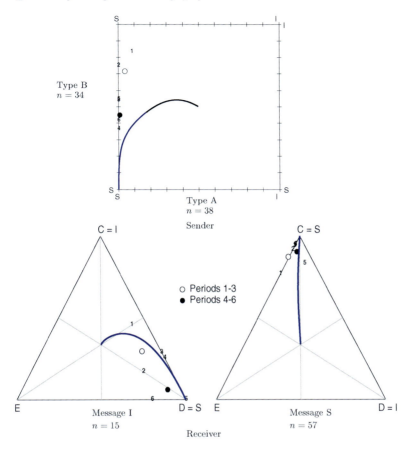

Figure 4. Brandts and Holt (1993) game 4. Sequential vs intuitive.

branch of the AQRE selects the non-intuitive sequential equilibrium in the first game, and the intuitive equilibrium in the second, and that it compares favorably with the experimental data.

Acknowledgement

The financial support of the National Science Foundation (Grant #SBR-9631627) is gratefully acknowledged.

References

Banks, J., Camerer, C., Porter, D. (1994). "Experimental tests of Nash refinements in signaling games". Games and Economic Behavior 6, 1–31.

Brandts, J., Holt, C.A. (1993). "Adjustment patterns and equilibrium selection in experimental signaling games". International Journal of Game Theory 22, 279–302.

Lieberman, B. (1960). "Human behavior in a strictly determined 3×3 matrix game". Behavioral Science 5, 317–322.

McKelvey, R.D., Palfrey, T.R. (1995). "Quantal response equilibria in normal form games". Games and Economic Behavior 7, 6–38.

McKelvey, R.D., Palfrey, T.R. (1998). "Quantal response equilibria in extensive form games". Experimental Economics 1, 9–41.

O'Neill, B. (1987). "Nonmetric test of the minimax theory of two person zero sum games". Proceedings of the National Academy of Science, USA 84, 2106–2109.

Chapter 61

LOGIT EQUILIBRIUM MODELS OF ANOMALOUS BEHAVIOR: WHAT TO DO WHEN THE NASH EQUILIBRIUM SAYS ONE THING AND THE DATA SAY SOMETHING ELSE

SIMON P. ANDERSON, JACOB K. GOEREE, and CHARLES A. HOLT

Department of Economics, 114 Rouss Hall, University of Virginia, Charlottesville, VA 22903-3328, USA

Every experimentalist will sooner or later come across a situation in which results from initial "baseline" treatments conform nicely to the Nash equilibrium, but subsequent changes in parameters push the data in ways not predicted by Nash. This may happen when one begins by giving theory its "best shot," reserving stress tests for later. Such tests often involve changing a parameter that, on the basis of intuition, is likely to alter behavior, but which has no effect on the Nash equilibrium. For example, behavior in a symmetric matching-pennies game conforms to the Nash prediction of mixing with equal probabilities. However, changing a player's own payoff parameters will typically change that player's choice probabilities (Ochs, 1995; Goeree, Holt, and Palfrey, 2003), in spite of the fact that in a Nash equilibrium a player's mixed strategy only depends on the *other* players' payoffs. In "Ten Little Treasures of Game Theory and Ten Intuitive Contradictions," Goeree and Holt (2001) report a variety of games in which behavior conforms nicely to Nash predictions in one treatment (the "treasures") but deviates sharply from Nash predictions in the other treatment (the "contradictions").

A particularly striking example of the contrast between economic intuition and the cold logic of game theory is the "traveler's dilemma" described by Basu (1994). The dilemma is based on a situation in which two vacationers have purchased identical objects, which are then lost on the flight home. The airline tells them to fill out claim forms independently, with the promise that both claims will be paid if they match. Otherwise, both travelers are only reimbursed at the lower of the claims, with a small penalty for the high claimant and an equally small reward for the low claimant. Even with a very low penalty and reward, each person has an incentive to "undercut" any anticipated common claim amount, and so the only Nash equilibrium (in pure or mixed strategies) is at the lowest possible claim. The implausibility of this prediction becomes apparent when one considers very low values of the penalty and reward parameter.

Capra et al. (1999) report a traveler's dilemma experiment in which claims are required to be between 80 and 200 cents, so the Nash equilibrium involves claims of 80 cents.[1] With the penalty for the high claimant and the reward for the low claimant set at 50 cents, claims converged to near-Nash levels, as indicated by the blue bars in Figure 1.

---

[1] See also Capra et al. (2002) for experiments that involve a similar game based on a model of imperfect price competition.

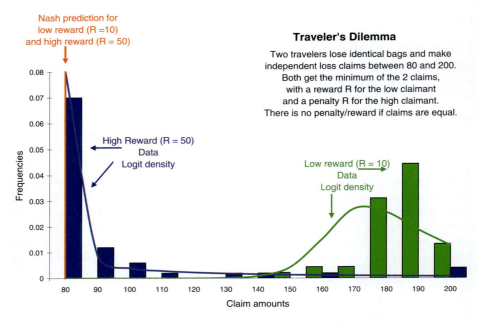

Figure 1. Data and theoretical predictions for the traveler's dilemma game.

But with a relatively low penalty-reward level of 10 cents, the frequency distribution of claims (represented by the green bars) is much higher. Note that this distribution is concentrated at the *opposite* side of the feasible set from the Nash equilibrium (indicated by the red bar at 80 cents). What is needed is a theory that explains Nash-like behavior in some contexts and deviations in others, i.e., a generalization of the Nash solution concept.

This chapter describes such a generalization and how it can be used to generate testable predictions for a variety of economic games. This approach involves introducing random elements, interpreted as either bounded rationality or unobserved preference shocks, into an equilibrium analysis. Individuals' choices are assumed to be positively, but not perfectly, related to expected payoffs, in that decisions with higher expected payoffs are more likely to be selected. With repeated (random) matchings, the choice probabilities of one player will affect the beliefs, and hence the expected payoffs, of others. The *equilibrium* is a fixed point: the choice probabilities that determine expected payoffs correspond to the probabilities determined by expected payoffs via a probabilistic choice rule (Rosenthal, 1989; McKelvey and Palfrey, 1995). The degree of bounded rationality is described by an error parameter, and the equilibrium probabilities converge to a Nash equilibrium as this parameter goes to zero.

We use this approach to explain stylized facts emerging from laboratory tests of game theory. The focus is on games with continuous strategy spaces: e.g., voluntary contributions games, all-pay auctions, continuous coordination games, and the traveler's dilemma game. The goal is to establish comparative-statics properties that are consistent with patterns in laboratory data, especially when these patterns are intuitive but not explained by Nash predictions. See Anderson, Goeree, and Holt (2002), for a formal derivation of existence, uniqueness, and comparative statics results for the logit quantal response equilibrium in games with continuous strategies.

1. Background: The Logit Approach

The idea of bounded rationality – that agents are limited in their ability to evaluate their environments – has been around for decades (the term was coined by Nobel-prize-winner Herbert Simon). Little attempt, however, has been made to use the idea to generate formal equilibrium predictions until recently, when Rosenthal (1989) and McKelvey and Palfrey (1995) incorporated decision error into an analysis of non-cooperative games. To see how this is done, suppose that there are two decisions, D_1 and D_2, with associated expected payoffs π_1^e and π_2^e. Under perfect rationality, the decision with the higher expected payoff is always chosen. Bounded rationality can be modeled by adding a random element in the expected-payoff comparison. In particular, suppose that the probability of choosing D_1 is:

$$\Pr(D_1) = \Pr(\pi_1^e - \pi_2^e > \mu\varepsilon), \tag{1}$$

where ε is a random variable with mean zero, and μ is an error parameter that determines the importance of the error term. If μ is small enough, the effects of errors vanish and the decision with the highest payoff is always chosen. If μ is large enough, decisions are equally likely to be selected, irrespective of their expected payoffs. The particular characteristics of the model depend on the distribution of the random component. If ε is uniform on $[-.5, .5]$, for example, $\Pr(D_1) = .5 + (\pi_1^e - \pi_2^e)/2\mu$, unless the expected payoff difference is so great as to push the probability to 0 or 1. This is known as a linear probability model because choice probabilities are linear in payoff differences, which is the assumption made in Rosenthal (1989).

McKelvey and Palfrey (1995) propose a more general *quantal-response* equilibrium model, in which choice probabilities are increasing, but possibly non-linear functions of expected-payoff differences. Using an exponential function, which corresponds to a logistic distribution of ε in (1), yields the familiar logit form that is widely used in empirical work. In this case, the choice probabilities are:

$$\Pr(D_1) = \frac{\exp(\pi_i^e/\mu)}{\exp(\pi_1^e/\mu) + \exp(\pi_2^e/\mu)}, \quad i = 1, 2, \tag{2}$$

where the denominator ensures that the probabilities sum to one. The continuous analogue to (2) applies when there is a continuum of alternatives, with the probabilities in (2) replaced by a probability density for choosing an action x from a feasible set $[0, \omega]$:

$$f_i(x) = \frac{\exp(\pi_i^e(x)/\mu)}{\int_0^\omega \exp(\pi_i^e(s)/\mu)\,ds}, \qquad (3)$$

where the denominator is a constant of integration that is independent of x. The continuous formulation was first used by Lopez (1995). Equation (3) does not provide explicit solutions since the expected payoff on the right side of (3) depends on the choice densities of the other players. Rather, it gives *equilibrium consistency* conditions: the choice densities that determine expected payoffs should match the choice densities determined by expected payoffs via the logit choice rule.

Differentiating both sides of (3) with respect to x establishes that the equilibrium densities satisfy the *logit differential equation*:

$$\mu f_i'(x) = f_i(x)\pi_i^{e'}(x), \qquad (4)$$

where the prime denotes the derivative with respect to x. When μ goes to zero, Equation (4) dictates that $\pi_i^{e'}(x) f_i(x) = 0$, which is the condition needed for an interior Nash equilibrium: either the necessary condition for payoff maximization is satisfied at x, or else the density of decisions is zero. As μ goes to infinity in (4), the noise effect dominates and the equilibrium density is uniform with $f_i' = 0$. In the next section we will use (4) to derive the logit equilibrium densities for specific games.

The focus above has been on the equilibrium, and not on some learning process that presumably leads to it. This analysis can be supported by dynamic adjustment models that explain convergence to a quantal response equilibrium, e.g., the fictitious play learning model in Chen, Friedman, and Thisse (1997) and the noisy evolution model in Anderson, Goeree, and Holt (1999). The equilibrium analysis presented here, however, applies to the long-run situation in which players are familiar with the distributions of others' decisions, e.g., when behavior has stabilized in the later rounds of an experiment.

2. How to Find a Logit Equilibrium

In this section we will sketch how the differential equation (4) can be used to derive the logit equilibrium densities for specific games. One starts by writing down the expression for a player's expected payoff as a function of that player's own decision and of the other players' densities. Substituting this expected payoff into (4) yields a differential equation for the equilibrium density. For a number of games, this equation admits a closed-form solution.

EXAMPLE 1 (*linear payoffs*). Consider a linear public goods game in which individuals are given an endowment, ω. When player i contributes an amount x_i to the public good, the player earns $\omega - x_i$ for the part of the endowment that is kept. In addition, every player receives a constant (positive) fraction m of the total amount contributed to the public good. So the payoff to player i is: $\pi_i = \omega - x_i + mX$, where X is the sum of all contributions including those of player i. Since the derivative of expected payoff with respect to x_i is $(m-1)$, Equation (4) reduces to $\mu f_i'(x) = (m-1) f_i(x)$ for $x \in [0, \omega]$. Therefore, f_i'/f_i equals a constant, $(m-1)/\mu$, and the equilibrium density is simply a (truncated) exponential: $f_i(x) = K \exp(\alpha x/\mu)$, where K is a constant of integration and $\alpha = (m-1)$. Indeed, the logit equilibrium density is exponential with parameter α for any game in which players' payoffs are linear in own decisions with constant slope α.

EXAMPLE 2 (*quadratic payoffs*). When the expected payoff function is quadratic in one's own decision, the solution to (4) is proportional to an exponential of a quadratic function, i.e., a (truncated) normal density. We use this observation to characterize the equilibrium for public goods games with quadratic payoffs (Anderson, Goeree, and Holt, 1998a). The logit equilibrium density for other quadratic models, such as Cournot competition with linear demand, is also given by a truncated normal. This normality result is important, given the pervasiveness of quadratic payoffs both in theoretical models and experimental work.

EXAMPLE 3 (*all-pay auction*). In this game, a prize is awarded to the person making the highest effort or "bid," but all competitors incur the costs of their own bids, whether or not they are successful. Consider a symmetric two-person auction in which the prize is worth V dollars. If $F(x)$ denotes the equilibrium distribution of bids, then the expected payoff for a bid of x is given by $VF(x) - cx$, where c is an effort cost parameter. Hence, $\pi^{e'}(x) = Vf(x) - c$, and it follows from (4) that the logit equilibrium density satisfies $\mu f'(x) = Vf(x)^2 - cf(x)$. It is straightforward to verify that the solution to this differential equation is: $f(x) = 1/[1 - K \exp(x/\mu)]$, where K is a constant of integration. In Anderson, Goeree, and Holt (1998b) we extend this analysis to cover asymmetric, n-player all-pay auctions.

EXAMPLE 4 (*minimum-effort coordination game*). A player's payoff in this game is the minimum of all efforts minus the cost of that player's effort: $\pi_i = \min_{j=1...n}\{x_j\} - cx_i$, where the cost parameter c is less than one and $x_i \in [0, \omega]$. Given the linear payoff structure, the Pareto-dominant equilibrium is for each player to provide the maximum effort, ω, but *any* other common effort level is also a Nash equilibrium.

Consider the symmetric two-player case, in which each player is characterized by a distribution of efforts, $F(x)$. The probability that the other's effort is below x is then given by $F(x)$ with density $f(x)$. Recall that a player's payoff is the minimum effort minus the cost of the player's own effort:

$$\pi^e(x) = \int_0^x yf(y)\,dy + x(1 - F(x)) - cx, \tag{5}$$

where the first term is the benefit when another player's effort is below the player's own effort, x, and the second term is the benefit when the player's own decision determines the minimum effort. Differentiation of (5) establishes that $\pi^{e'}(x) = (1 - F(x)) - c$, which together with (4) results in the logit differential equation: $\mu f'(x) = f(x)(1 - F(x) - c)$. In Anderson, Goeree, and Holt (2001), we show that the solution is a truncated logistic distribution of the type used in epidemiological models of the transmission of disease over time.

EXAMPLE 5 (*traveler's dilemma*). The expected payoff for this game consists of two terms, depending on whether or not the person's claim is lower:

$$\pi^e(x) = \int_0^x (y - R) f(y) \, dy + (x + R)(1 - F(x)),$$

where the first term on the right corresponds to the case where the penalty R is paid, and the second term corresponds to the case where the reward R is obtained. The derivative of expected payoff is thus: $\pi^{e'}(x) = 1 - F(x) - 2Rf(x)$, so it follows from (4) that $\mu f'(x) = f(x)(1 - F(x) - 2Rf(x))$. In this case there is no closed-form solution, although numerical methods can be used to plot the equilibrium density. For instance, the curved blue and green lines in Figure 1 are plots of the logit density for an error parameter $\mu = 6$ (see Capra et al., 1999).

These examples demonstrate that the logit equilibrium approach can be applied to a wide variety of interesting economic contexts. Closed-form solutions are available in some cases, but even when they are not, it is often possible to derive comparative static properties of the logit equilibrium. This is the topic of the next section.

3. Comparative Static Properties

Our research is motivated by experimental evidence that cannot be explained by a standard Nash equilibrium analysis. We are particularly interested in deviations from Nash predictions that are consistent with economic intuition. This section summarizes intuitive comparative statics results from a number of specific applications of the logit equilibrium to games with a continuum of feasible decisions.

EXAMPLE 1 (*linear payoffs*). Suppose the expected payoff is linear in one's own contribution. In the standard public goods game, the slope equals $m - 1$. This slope is negative when the marginal value of the public good, m, is less than the cost of contribution, 1, and the Nash equilibrium involves zero contributions (free riding). Some contributions are observed in laboratory experiments, however, even after repetition. These deviations from the Nash prediction are often consistent with loose economic intuition. For instance, average contribution levels in public goods experiments increase with the marginal value of the public good, even though the Nash prediction is unaffected by (non-critical) changes in this parameter. The logit equilibrium provides one explanation of this effect: since $\pi^{e'}(x) = m - 1$, an increase in m will increase the slope of the density in (4), which in equilibrium, raises the average level of contributions. This result is derived formally in Anderson, Goeree, and Holt (1998a).

Of course, there are many other possible explanations of the positive relationship between m and average contributions, e.g., altruism. These explanations need not be mutually exclusive: altruistic concerns for others' earnings can be added to the payoff functions, in which case the total benefit to others from one's own contribution increases with the number of people who enjoy the public good. An increase in the number of participants is then predicted to increase average contributions, a prediction that is also roughly consistent with laboratory evidence, at least for low values of m.

EXAMPLE 2 (*quadratic payoffs*). Quadratic payoffs have been introduced in public goods games by using either a declining marginal value of the public good or an increasing marginal cost of contribution. The purpose of introducing non-linear payoffs was to move the Nash equilibrium away from the boundary of the feasible set. Experiments with interior Nash equilibria have yielded average contribution levels that are between the Nash prediction and the midpoint of the feasible set. Recall that the logit equilibrium density for the quadratic case is a truncated normal on $[0, \omega]$. When the mode of this density is to left or to the right of the midpoint of the feasible set, the symmetry of the normal implies that the mean is between the mode and the midpoint. This is the intuition behind the logit equilibrium prediction that the average contribution is "sandwiched" between Nash and the midpoint of the feasible set (Anderson, Goeree, and Holt, 1998a).

EXAMPLE 3 (*all-pay auction*). The winner-take-all nature of these contests makes the outcome sensitive to decision errors. When the bids represent costly efforts (e.g., lobbying) to obtain the prize, rent dissipation is determined by comparing the value of the prize with the expected effort costs. The logit equilibrium model predicts that the extent of rent dissipation increases with the number of players and the cost of bidding, which is not the case for the Nash equilibrium (Anderson, Goeree, and Holt, 1998b). To evaluate comparative statics, consider the form of the expected-payoff function for the case of two players: $VF(x) - cx$. Thus an increase in c lowers the slope of expected payoff and thus the slope of the equilibrium density by (4). This is why an increase in the bid cost causes stochastically lower bids.

Over-dissipation of rents is impossible with fully rational players, since it implies negative expected payoffs, which can be avoided by non-participation. However, over-dissipation is observed in some laboratory experiments (e.g., Davis and Reilly, 1998). Such over-dissipation is predicted for high enough values of n and c in our model with endogenous decision errors.

EXAMPLE 4 (*minimum-effort coordination game*). The classic dilemma in coordination games is that better outcomes require higher effort and more risk of coordination failure. Uncertainty about others' actions is a central element of such situations. The coordination game has a continuum of pure-strategy Nash equilibria, which means that the Nash equilibrium has no predictive power. In contrast, the logit model can be used to

Table 1
Comparative statics results and experimental evidence

Game	Treatment variable	Nash prediction	Logit prediction	Laboratory evidence
Linear public goods (effect on contributions)	MPCR	0	+	+
	number of players	0	+	+
Minimum effort coordination (effect on effort levels)	Effort costs	0	−	−
	number of players	0	−	−
All-pay auction (effect on rent dissipation)	Effort cost	0	−	na
	number of players	0	−	na
Traveler's dilemma (effect on claims)	Penalty/reward	0	−	−

determine a unique probability distribution of effort decisions, and so generates testable hypotheses (Anderson, Goeree, and Holt, 2001). For example, increases in c and n result in lower average efforts. The proof is by contradiction, but the underlying intuition is again that increases in these parameters will lower the slope of the expected payoff, and therefore the slope of the equilibrium density determined by (4). These comparative static results are consistent with some experimental findings of Van Huyck, Battalio, and Beil (1990). These authors conducted laboratory experiments with a minimum-effort structure, with seven effort levels and seven corresponding Pareto-ranked pure-strategy Nash equilibria. The intuition that coordination is more difficult with more players is apparent in the data: behavior approaches the "best" equilibrium with two players, but the "worst" Nash outcome has more drawing power with large numbers of players. Similarly, the experiments confirm that higher effort costs reduce the level of effort.

EXAMPLE 5 (*traveler's dilemma*). Recall that the slope of the expected payoff in the symmetric logit equilibrium is: $\pi^{e\prime}(x) = 1 - F(x) - 2Rf(x)$. Hence, an increase in the penalty and reward parameter, R, decreases this slope and therefore the slope of the equilibrium density by (4). This provides the intuition behind the comparative-static result that increases in R result in a stochastic decrease in claims (see Capra et al., 1999).

The main comparative results discussed in this paper are summarized in Table 1. In each of the models listed on the left, the Nash equilibrium predicts no effect of the exogenous treatment variables, as shown by the zeros in the Nash column. In all cases, the logit equilibrium makes a prediction, positive or negative, that is qualitatively consistent with the laboratory data. (In the case of the all-pay auction, the logit equilibrium can explain observed over-dissipation of rents, but there is no direct evidence on the relationship between the amount of dissipation and effort costs or the number of rent seekers.) The logit equilibrium also explains some data patterns that are not summarized in the table, e.g., the "sandwich" result for quadratic games.

Other explanations have been offered for some, but by no means all, of these empirical anomalies, but the ability of the logit equilibrium to track these patterns is striking. Many aspects of the data do not correspond to the predictions of any one-parameter family of models, but the logit equilibrium predictions are superior to those of the Nash equilibrium that is the workhorse of standard game theory, and indeed, of much of economic theory.

Acknowledgement

This research was supported by a grant from the National Science Foundation (SES-0094800).

References

Anderson, S.P., Goeree, J.K., Holt, C.A. (1998a). "A theoretical analysis of altruism and decision error in public goods games". Journal of Public Economics 70 (2), 297–323.

Anderson, S.P., Goeree, J.K., Holt, C.A. (1998b). "Rent seeking with bounded rationality: An analysis of the all-pay auction". Journal of Political Economy 106 (4), 828–853.

Anderson, S.P., Goeree, J.K., Holt, C.A. (1999). "Stochastic game theory: Adjustment to equilibrium under noisy directional learning". Working paper, University of Virginia.

Anderson, S.P., Goeree, J.K., Holt, C.A. (2001). "Minimum-effort coordination games: Stochastic potential and logit equilibrium". Games and Economic Behavior 34 (2), 177–199.

Anderson, S.P., Goeree, J.K., Holt, C.A. (2002). "The logit equilibrium: A perspective on intuitive behavioral anomalies". Southern Economic Journal 69 (1), 21–47.

Basu, K. (1994). "The traveler's dilemma: Paradoxes of rationality in game theory". American Economic Review 84 (2), 391–395.

Capra, C.M., Goeree, J.K., Gomez, R., Holt, C.A. (1999). "Anomalous behavior in a traveler's dilemma?" American Economic Review 89 (3), 678–690.

Chen, H.C., Friedman, J.W., Thisse, J.F. (1997). "Boundedly rational Nash equilibrium: A probabilistic choice approach". Games and Economic Behavior 18 (1), 32–54.

Davis, D.D., Reilly, R.J. (1998). "Do too many cooks always spoil the stew? An experimental analysis of rent-seeking and the role of a strategic buyer". Public Choice 95 (1–2), 89–115.

Goeree, J.K., Holt, C.A. (2001). "Ten little treasures of game theory and ten intuitive contradictions". American Economic Review 91 (5), 1402–1422.

Goeree, J.K., Holt, C.A., Palfrey, T.R. (2003). "Risk averse behavior in generalized matching pennies games". Games and Economic Behavior 45 (1), 97–113.

Lopez, G. (1995). "Quantal response equilibria for models of price competition". Unpublished Ph.D. dissertation, University of Virginia.

McKelvey, R.D., Palfrey, T.R. (1995). "Quantal response equilibria for normal form games". Games and Economic Behavior 10 (1), 6–38.

Ochs, J. (1995). "Games with unique mixed strategy equilibria: An experimental study". Games and Economic Behavior 10 (1), 202–217.

Rosenthal, R.W. (1989). "A bounded rationality approach to the study of noncooperative games". International Journal of Game Theory 18, 273–292.
Van Huyck, J.B., Battalio, R.C., Beil, R.O. (1990). "Tacit coordination games, strategic uncertainty, and coordination failure". American Economic Review 80 (1), 234–248.

PART 4.3

LEARNING IN GAMES

Amnon Rapoport, Terry E. Daniel and Darryl A. Seale, "Asymmetric Two-person Bargaining Under Incomplete Information: Strategic Play and Adaptive Learning"

Andreas Blume, Douglas V. DeJong and Geoffrey B. Sprinkle, "The Effect of Message Space Size on Learning and Outcomes in Sender–Receiver Games"

David J. Cooper, "Learning in Entry Limit Pricing Games"

Lawrence M. Kahn and J. Keith Murnighan, "Payoff Uncertainty and Cooperation in Finitely-repeated Prisoner's Dilemma Games"

Colin F. Camerer, Teck H. Ho and Juin-Kuan Chong, "Learning in Games"

Chapter 62

ASYMMETRIC TWO-PERSON BARGAINING UNDER INCOMPLETE INFORMATION: STRATEGIC PLAY AND ADAPTIVE LEARNING

AMNON RAPOPORT

University of Arizona

TERRY E. DANIEL

Department of Finance and Management Science, Faculty of Business, University of Alberta, Edmonton, Alberta, Canada T6G2R6
e-mail: tdaniel@gpu.srv.ualberta.ca

DARRYL A. SEALE

Kent State University

The present chapter focuses on a series of experiments investigating decision behavior in single-stage, two-person bargaining over the exchange of a single commodity, where neither trader knows with precision the reservation value that the other places on the good or service being bought or sold. Uncertainty about the other trader's reservation value is represented by a commonly known probability distribution. We summarize the major behavioral regularities that have been observed in two computer-controlled bargaining experiments using the sealed-bid double auction mechanism (Daniel, Seale, and Rapoport, 1998; Rapoport, Daniel, and Seale, 1998). Under this mechanism, the buyer submits a bid anonymously over a computer network, and the seller submits an offer for the good she possesses. Bids and offers are submitted simultaneously. If the buyer's bid is at least as high as the seller's offer, then a transaction takes place at a price halfway between the offer and the bid. If not, then no trade occurs. Considerable theoretical progress has been made in analyzing these bilateral bargaining situations with two-sided incomplete information within the general framework of the Bayesian–Nash equilibrium (Chatterjee and Samuelson, 1983; Leininger, Linhart, and Radner, 1989; Linhart, Radner, and Satterthwaite, 1992). When both parties to the bargaining are assumed to be active, this theory typically permits a wide range of equilibrium bargaining behavior. Replicable behavioral regularities, to the extent that they can be found in the laboratory, can be combined with the theoretical results to choose between the multiple equilibria and, more importantly, construct a viable, descriptive theory of two-person bargaining under incomplete information. The following behavioral regularities appear to be particularly significant.

Handbook of Experimental Economics Results, Volume 1
Copyright © 2008 Elsevier B.V. All rights reserved
DOI: 10.1016/S1574-0722(07)00062-5

1. Most Participants Behave Strategically in General Accordance with the Linear Equilibrium Strategy

The results of our experiments leave little doubt that most participants in the sealed-bid two-person bargaining game behave strategically. By this we mean that traders make offers and bids which are systematically different from their reservation values for the item being traded, and that these offers and bids are accounted for (with some systematic departures discussed below) by the linear equilibrium strategy (LES) constructed by Chatterjee and Samuelson (1983). Earlier experiments using the same mechanism iterated over time suggested this result (Radner and Schotter, 1989; Linhart, Radner and Schotter, 1990; Rapoport and Fuller, 1995), but were in varying degrees inconclusive either because the predictions of the LES and an alternative theory postulating truth telling (honest disclosure of the reservation values, which maximizes joint profit) made close predictions over large ranges of the reservation values, or because they used fixed pairs, thereby allowing for dependencies between successive iterations of the game and reputation building.

Figure 1 portrays the LES functions of the buyer and seller for two different cases. The upper panel pertains to the case where the buyer's reservation values are commonly known to be randomly drawn from a uniform distribution defined over the interval [0, 200], and the seller's reservation values are commonly known to be drawn from a uniform distribution defined over the interval [0, 100]. In the lower panel, the buyer's distribution is the same, whereas the seller's uniform distribution is now defined over a considerably narrower interval [0, 20]. Truthful disclosure of the reservation values is depicted by the straight line with a slope of one. In both cases, the seller's LES function has an intercept of 50 and slope of 2/3. The buyer's LES is a piecewise linear function with three connected segments. In both cases, the difference between truth telling and equilibrium play is seen to be substantial.

Figure 2 shows a representative sample of all fifty bids of three buyers from each of two independent experiments in which ten buyers were randomly paired, trial by trial, with ten sellers for a set of fifty periods (bargains). The reservation values in the first experiment by Daniel et al. were randomly selected from commonly known uniform distributions with a range of 0 to 200 for the buyer and 0 to 100 for the seller (see the LES functions for this case in the upper panel of Figure 1). The reservation values in the second experiment by Rapoport et al. were randomly selected from commonly known distributions with the same range of 0 to 200 for the buyer and a considerably smaller range from 0 to 20 for the seller (see the LES functions for this case in the bottom panel of Figure 1). In both experiments the payoff was contingent on performance. In both of them the buyer has an information advantage over the seller in the sense that the buyer's uncertainty about the seller's reservation value is smaller than the seller's uncertainty about the buyer's reservation value. This information advantage increases as the distribution of reservation values of one of the traders become narrower. One-sided uncertainty is obtained when the distribution of reservation values of one of the traders shrinks to a single point.

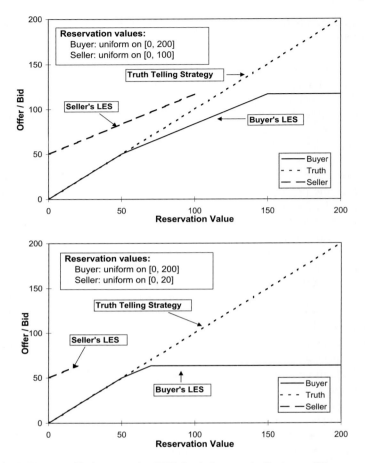

Figure 1. Linear equilibrium strategies (LES) for the buyer and seller in two different games.

Figure 2 displays all the fifty bids of each of the six buyers as a function of the corresponding reservation values. All the six panels exhibit bidding patterns very suggestive of the LES (Figure 1). See, in particular, the non-linear, piecewise-like behavior of the bids. No compelling case can be made for competing models predicting that buyers bid their reservation values or even some constant fraction of those values. To the extent that the results of both buyers and sellers depart from LES, they do so primarily in three ways. First, high bids which are closer to the reservation values than to the LES values typically occur early in the experiment and seldom after ten trials, indicating a learning process. Second, buyers bid slightly more aggressively (lower bids) than the theory would predict. Third, most of the sellers make less aggressive offers than predicted; their offers (not displayed here) typically fall on a straight line between the LES and

Ch. 62: Asymmetric Two-person Bargaining Under Incomplete Information 563

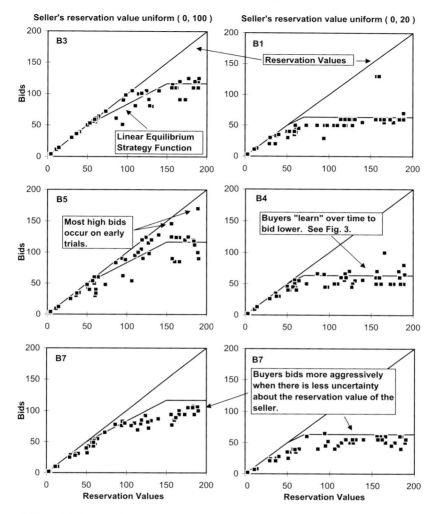

Figure 2. Buyer's bids vs their reservation values for two groups of sellers (for a sample of three buyers facing each type of seller). Over 50 trails, all buyers bid strategically (much closer to the linear equilibrium strategy values than to their reservation values).

truth telling linear functions. These small but systematic departures from the LES and their implications for the two traders are discussed below.

2. There is an Information Advantage Exceeding the Predictions of the LES

The two experiments manipulated the information structure by using a 2 by 2 between-subjects design to compare fixed vs random pairing of subjects and wide vs narrow

Table 1

Actual and potential profits of buyers and sellers (in experimental money units over 50 trials). Because of the information disparity, buyers should do a little better than sellers, if both played their equilibrium strategies (LES–LES). In actual play (A–A), buyers do much better than this and the sellers do much worse. If both revealed their true reservation values, both would profit (RV–RV). With fixed pairing over the 50 trials, the buyer's profit is higher than under random pairing of buyers and sellers

Reservation values				Sellers – uniform (0, 100) Buyers – uniform (0, 200)		
Random partners				Fixed partners		
Strategy	A–A	LES–LES	RV–RV	A–A	LES–LES	RV–RV
Buyer 1	1693	1519	1693	1199	1549	1582
Buyer 2	1262	1422	1442	971	1412	1546
Buyer 3	1779	1534	1737	1641	1463	1543
Buyer 4	1385	1395	1529	2064	1491	1624
Buyer 5	1589	1426	1526	1894	1409	1569
Buyer 6	1398	1345	1405	1749	1542	1604
Buyer 7	1437	1385	1476	1417	1416	1543
Buyer 8	1102	1389	1442	1088	1426	1553
Buyer 9	1394	1490	1524	2229	1474	1535
Buyer 10	1536	1488	1591	1501	1454	1564
Total buyers	14,573	14,392	15,363	15,751	14,635	15,662
Seller 1	1074	1256	1531	985	1309	1569
Seller 2	1074	1214	1381	1173	1389	1624
Seller 3	989	1502	1654	730	1388	1535
Seller 4	1274	1420	1728	346	1545	1604
Seller 5	827	1216	1367	864	1481	1582
Seller 6	961	1187	1472	1055	1234	1546
Seller 7	1177	1433	1640	1028	1345	1553
Seller 8	714	1074	1314	1248	1270	1543
Seller 9	1278	1554	1827	1316	1395	1564
Seller 10	909	1294	1451	1066	1319	1543
Total sellers	10,276	13,149	15,363	9811	13,675	15,663
Total all	24,849	27,541	30,725	25,559	28,310	31,325
% deals made	52%	53%	77%	52%	52%	76%

ranges of the seller's reservation values. This information structure was chosen so that the predictions of the LES would differ markedly from those that would have been obtained if the buyers bid and the sellers offered a fixed proportion of their reservation values. This information structure provided the buyers with an advantage which, if both traders bid their LES values, would have led to only modestly larger profits. Table 1 presents three sets of payoffs for each buyer and each seller in each of our two experiments, one (left panel) where pair members changed randomly from trial to trial (random pairing), and another (right panel) in which a fixed pairing of the buyer and seller was preserved for all fifty trials (fixed pairing). The payoffs in the column labeled A–A are those actually observed in the experiments; the ones in the column labeled LES–LES would have been obtained (with the reservation values actually generated in the experiments), if each trader had played according to the LES; and the payoffs in the column labeled RV–RV would have been obtained if each trader had simply reported his/her true reservation values. The LES–LES column illustrates the point made above – profits for the buyers were expected to be from 7 to 10 percent higher than those of the sellers. However, the actual payoffs (A–A) are strikingly different. The buyers made between 40 percent (under random pairing) and 60 percent (under fixed pairing) more profit. These results are mostly due to the aggressive behavior of the buyers who "pushed down" the sellers' offers particularly in the second half of the experiment. Experiments are currently under way to see if the mirror image of these results holds – 'Do sellers achieve equal or even higher profits when they hold a corresponding information advantage?'

3. Repeated Play with a Fixed Partner Enhances Strategic Advantages

A comparison of the left- and right-hand panels of Table 1 shows that any strategic advantage that a buyer has in a bargaining situation can be enhanced by being able to deal with the same seller over a relatively long sequence of transactions. The operative word in the preceding sentence is 'can.' Whereas the average buyer did eight percent better dealing with a fixed partner and the average seller did five percent worse, the standard deviation of the buyers' profits with fixed pairing of traders (not presented here) is more than twice that when bargaining under random pairing. Our results suggest that most of the gain accorded to the buyers when dealing with fixed partners comes from the ability of a few buyers to discover and then exploit weaknesses on the part of a few sellers. In general, the bidding behavior of both buyers and sellers in the fixed pairing case shows more commonality than difference with the bargaining behavior in the randomly matched design.

4. Explanation of the Findings in Terms of Adaptive Learning

The LES bids and offers for the sealed-bid double auction mechanism are obtained by a solution of a pair of differential equations, which is clearly beyond the capability of our inexperienced subjects; yet the actual bids of such subjects (particularly the buyers), as seen in Figure 2, are in close agreement with the theory. As alluded to above, this correspondence is even closer if bids in the first few trials are discarded. Figure 3 illustrates the strong trend in the bidding behavior of the buyers in the experiment of Rapoport et al. (the one where the sellers' reservation values are uniformly distributed between 0 and 20 and the buyers' reservation values between 0 to 200). The results for the second

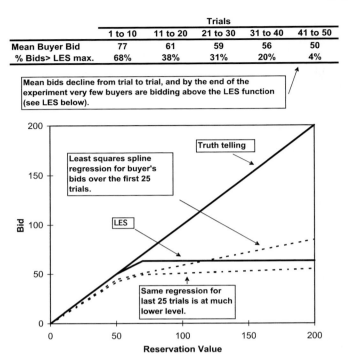

Figure 3. Learning trend exhibited by all the buyers over 50 trials.

half (trials 26–50) of the experiment are significantly different than those for the first half (trials 1–25). After the first few trials, there are very few high bids and the buyers learn to bid at or below the LES values.

Our results suggest that inexperienced subjects discover by some process of trial and error the most profitable bidding level for each reservation price. To account for changes in decisions across iterations (see Daniel, Seale, and Rapoport, 1998 for preliminary results, and Rapoport et al., 1997 for a more extensive test of the reinforcement-based learning model with a different set of data), we proposed and tested a reinforcement-based learning model based on two fundamental observations from the vast psychology literature on this topic: subjects tend to repeat what works well for them and discard that which does not, and consequences have more impact early in the learning process, with that impact diminishing with experience (see Roth and Erev, 1995 for a related approach). In the learning model that we have proposed, profitable trades on the immediately previous trial lead to more aggressive bids or offers on the next trial and missed trades lead to more conservative bids or offers, with the model being more sensitive to these profit and loss outcomes in the early phase of the experiment.

The learning model was tested with the data from the experiment of Daniel et al. in which the buyer's reservation values were randomly distributed between 0 and 200 and

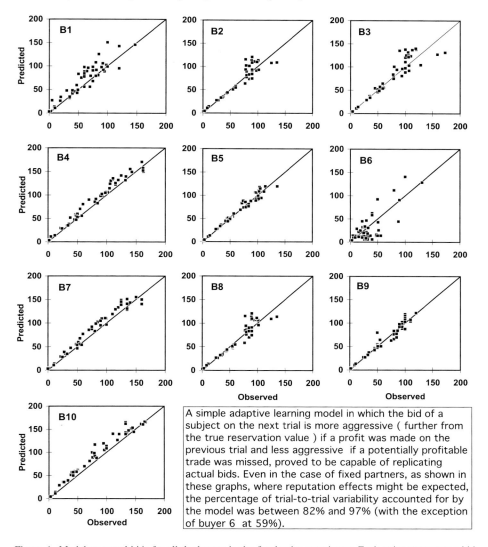

Figure 4. Model vs actual bids for all the buyers in the fixed pairs experiment. Each point represents a bid predicted by the learning model (vertical axis) corresponding to an actual bid made by the subject (horizontal axis). The diagonal lines represent perfect correspondence between model and actual bids.

A simple adaptive learning model in which the bid of a subject on the next trial is more aggressive (further from the true reservation value) if a profit was made on the previous trial and less aggressive if a potentially profitable trade was missed, proved to be capable of replicating actual bids. Even in the case of fixed partners, as shown in these graphs, where reputation effects might be expected, the percentage of trial-to-trial variability accounted for by the model was between 82% and 97% (with the exception of buyer 6 at 59%).

the seller's values were distributed between 0 and 100. We used an extensive search procedure to estimate the best fitting parameter values for each subject separately. When the trial-to-trial decisions of each of the ten buyers and ten sellers in the fixed pairing condition were simulated by this model (using the same reservation values as were pre-

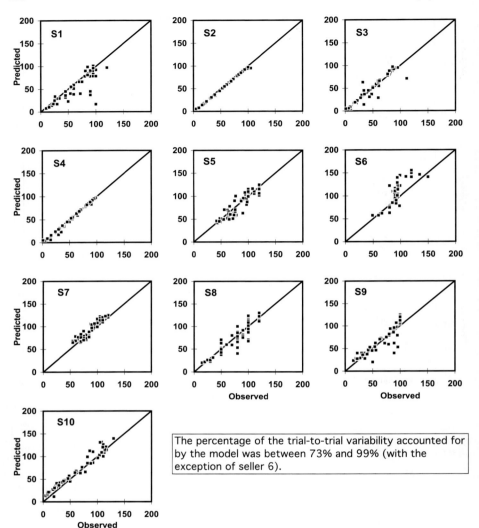

Figure 5. Model vs actual offers for all the sellers in the fixed pairs experiment.

sented in the actual experiments and only considering the outcome of the previous trial when generating a prediction for the next trial), the correspondence with the observed decisions was close. Figure 4 displays the predicted vs actual bids for each of the ten buyers in the fixed pairing condition, whereas Figure 5 compares the predicted and observed offers, again trial-by-trial, for all the ten sellers in the same condition. Each plot in both Figures 4 and 5 includes fifty points, one for each trial. The numbering of the

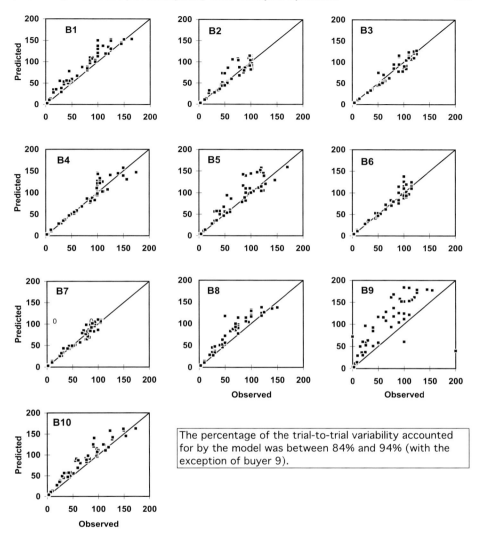

Figure 6. Model vs actual bids for all the buyers in the random pairs experiment.

buyers (1–10) corresponds to the numbering of the sellers. Perfect prediction would have resulted in all the fifty points for each subject falling on the 45 degree line. Figures 4 and 5 show that, with a few exceptions (e.g., Buyer 6, Seller 6, and Seller 9), the learning model accounts for the trial-to-trial bids and offers of our subjects remarkably well.

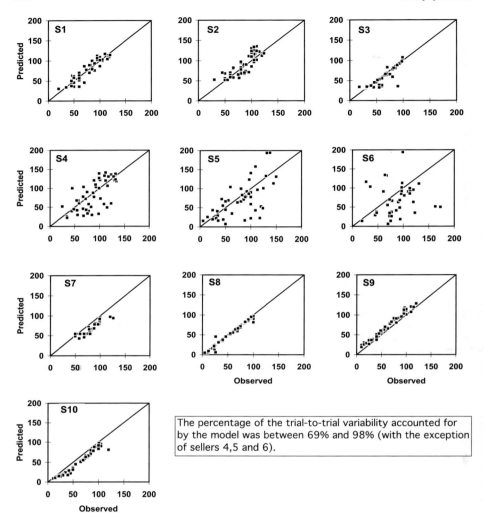

Figure 7. Model vs actual offers for all the sellers in the random pairs experiment.

Figures 6 and 7 exhibit corresponding results for a different study (Daniel, Seale, and Rapoport, 1998) with random rather than fixed pairing of buyers and sellers and same distributions of reservation values. Comparing predicted and observed bids trial by trial for buyers in the fixed pairing condition, the model accounts for (with a single exception) 82%–97% of the variability in the individual bids. Similar results hold for most of the buyers and sellers in each of the other conditions. Although we regard these results as impressive, we contend that the appropriate way of assessing the performance of our reinforcement-based learning model – and, for this matter, any other adaptive learning model – is not through hypothesis testing but rather through a competitive test against alternative models (Bush, 1963).

References

Bush, R.R. (1963). "Estimation and evaluation". In: Luce, R.D., Bush, R.R., Galanter, E. (Eds.), Handbook of Mathematical Psychology, vol. I. Wiley, New York, pp. 429–469.

Chatterjee, K., Samuelson, W. (1983). "Bargaining under incomplete information". Operations Research 31, 835–851.

Daniel, T.E., Seale, D.A., Rapoport, A. (1998). "Strategic play and adaptive learning in the sealed-bid bargaining mechanism". Journal of Mathematical Psychology 42, 133–166.

Leininger, W., Linhart, P.B., Radner, R. (1989). "Equilibria of the sealed-bid mechanism for bargaining with incomplete information". Journal of Economic Theory 48, 63–106.

Linhart, R., Radner, R., Satterthwaite, M.A. (Eds.) (1992). Bargaining with Incomplete Information. Academic Press, San Diego.

Linhart, P., Radner, R., Schotter, A. (1990). "Behavior and efficiency in the sealed-bid mechanism". C.V. Starr Center for Applied Economics, New York University Working Paper No. 90-51.

Rapoport, A., Fuller, M. (1995). "Bidding strategies in a bilateral monopoly with two-sided incomplete information". Journal of Mathematical Psychology 39, 179–196.

Rapoport, A., Daniel, T.E., Seale, D.A. (1998). "Reinforcement-based adaptive learning in asymmetric two-person bargaining with incomplete information". Experimental Economics 1, 221–253.

Roth, A.E., Erev, I. (1995). "Learning in extensive-form games: Experimental data and simple dynamic models in the intermediate term". Games and Economic Behavior 8, 164–212.

Chapter 63

THE EFFECT OF MESSAGE SPACE SIZE ON LEARNING AND OUTCOMES IN SENDER–RECEIVER GAMES

ANDREAS BLUME

University of Pittsburgh, Pittsburgh, PA 15260, USA

DOUGLAS V. DEJONG

University of Iowa, Iowa City, IA 52242, USA

GEOFFREY B. SPRINKLE

Indiana University, Bloomington, IN 47405, USA

1. Introduction

This chapter uses experiments to investigate learning and outcomes in sender–receiver games with imperfect incentive alignment. In sender–receiver games, the sender sends a message to a receiver who then takes an action that affects the payoffs of both players. Payoffs depend only on the sender's private information, represented by his type, and the receiver's action. We say that these games are of "partial common interest" if the sender wants to reveal some but not all of his private information. Using "a priori" meaningless messages in such games, we are interested in how agents attach meaning to these messages. Specifically, we ask: What are the outcomes? What is the learning process? Do outcomes and learning vary with the size of the message space?

Recent advances in evolutionary game theory allow us to address the interplay between private information, the size of the message space, and outcomes in sender–receiver games. In games with "a priori" meaningless messages, learning is necessary to reach those outcomes. We consider games of partial common interest because of the saliency of the message space size in such games.

2. The Games

Evolutionary game theory focuses on an environment in which there are repeated interactions among a population of agents. An individual game is played between a randomly paired informed sender and an uninformed receiver. The sender's private information is his type, t, where each type is equally likely. The sender sends a message m to the receiver, who responds with an action, a. Payoffs to both players depend on the sender's private information and the receiver's action, but not on the message sent. Repeated interactions occur by randomly pairing the sender and receiver populations to play an individual game in each iteration.

Handbook of Experimental Economics Results, Volume 1
Copyright © 2008 Elsevier B.V. All rights reserved
DOI: 10.1016/S1574-0722(07)00063-7

	a_1	a_2
t_1	0, 0	700, 700
t_2	700, 700	0, 0

Figure 1. Game 1.

	a_1	a_2	a_3	a_4
t_1	0, 0	200, 700	400, 400	0, 0
t_2	200, 700	0, 0	400, 400	0, 0
t_3	0, 0	0, 0	0, 0	400, 400

Figure 2. Game 2.

A strategy for the sender maps types into messages; for the receiver, a strategy maps messages into actions. A strategy pair is a Nash equilibrium if the strategies are mutual best replies. An equilibrium is called "separating" if each sender type is identified through his message. In a pooling equilibrium, the equilibrium action does not depend on the sender's type. Such an equilibrium exists in every sender–receiver game.

Figure 1 presents the payoffs (sender, receiver) for a simple common interest game, Game 1, that is played by all agents in our experiments. The payoffs are a function of the sender's type and the receiver's action. An example of a separating equilibrium in this game is one where the sender sends m_1 if he is type t_1 and m_2 otherwise, and where the receiver takes action a_2 after message m_1 and a_1 otherwise. An example of a pooling equilibrium is one in which the sender, regardless of type, sends m_1 and the receiver always takes action a_1.

In Game 1, both senders and receivers prefer that all information be revealed. Thus, if players are repeatedly and randomly matched to play Game 1 with a message space of size two, #(M) = 2, observed play should converge to an efficient separating equilibrium. This prediction is based on the intuition contained in the evolutionary approaches of Canning (1992), Nöldeke and Samuelson (1993), Wärneryd (1993), and Blume, Kim, and Sobel (1993).

In games where the sender wants to reveal some but not all of his information the size of the message space may affect the predicted equilibrium outcome. Consider the partial common interest game, Game 2, with payoffs shown in Figure 2.

While there is a fully separating equilibrium (with at least three messages), the sender prefers an equilibrium in which two of his types (t_1 and t_2) send a common message and the third type, t_3, separates. The treatment variable, "message space size," systematically changes the nature of the game as it varies from smaller, to equal to, and to greater than the size of the type space. With two messages there is a strict equilibrium; two types, t_1 and t_2, send a common message and the third type, t_3, separates. There is also another equilibrium component that is essentially strict; only the sender is indifferent in this equilibrium component and only for one of his types. Specifically, either t_1 or t_2 separates from the other two types, t_2 and t_3 or t_1 and t_3, in the game. With three messages there is a unique strict equilibrium; this equilibrium is fully separating. Finally, with four (or more) messages there is a plethora of equilibria and none are strict.

We appeal to the intuition from evolutionary game theory (e.g., Nöldeke and Samuelson, 1993; Wärneryd, 1993; and Blume, Kim, and Sobel, 1993) to hypothesize the following outcomes in Game 2: observed play will converge to the strict equilibrium with a message space of size two; observed play will converge to the unique strict, fully separating equilibrium with a message space of size 3; and, with a message space of size 4, observed play will converge to the partial pooling equilibrium with types t_1 and t_2 sending a common message and separating from type t_3.

To ensure that initially there is no common understanding of messages among agents, each agent is endowed with his own representation of the message space. At the end of each iteration of the game, all agents receive information about sender types and all messages sent by the respective sender types. This information is displayed in terms of each agent's representation of the message space. From evolutionary theory, this is the population history needed by agents to assign meaning to the "a priori" meaningless messages.

We conduct three treatments, and each treatment consists of three replications. Further, each replication involves twelve players, six senders and six receivers. Players are randomly designated as either a sender or a receiver at the start of the experiment and keep their designation throughout. In each period of a game, senders and receivers are paired using a random matching procedure. Sender types are equally likely and independently and identically drawn in every period for each sender. Senders and receivers participate in two sessions. Session I is common to all treatments and replications; it consists of playing Game 1 for 20 periods with a message space of size two. Session II varies across the three treatments; it consists of playing Game 2 for 40 periods with a message space size of either two, three, or four.

3. Results

3.1. Game 1

Prior to playing Game 2, all participants play 20 periods of Game 1. Game 1 is included as part of the experimental design to familiarize participants with sender–receiver games and the learning environment. Our intention is to make the learning task more manageable in Game 2, where both the incentive structure and message space structure are more complex.

The essential properties of the Game 1 outcomes (type–action associations) are shown in Table 1. Notice from this table that for each of the nine replications of Game 1, the outcome is very close to full separation, and in four out of nine replications play over the final five periods is consistent with a fully separating equilibrium. Across the nine replications of Game 1, 89% of the type–action pairs in the last five periods are consistent with the separating equilibrium. In the final period alone this coordination proportion increases to 93%, and in six of the nine replications play in the final period is consistent with a fully separating equilibrium.

Figure 3 provides some insight about the dynamic (learning) process that led to the outcomes presented in Table 1. Notice from this figure that convergence to the efficient separating equilibrium is gradual, suggesting that it takes time for senders to learn to fully reveal their type through the message sent and receivers to respond to the information contained in senders' messages (see, e.g., Blume et al., 1998, 2001). This result is of particular interest because rational players could, in most instances, use play in the first period as a precedent that would allow them to perfectly coordinate in period 2. More specifically, the gradual adjustment process presented in Figure 3 is incompatible with Cournot adjustment and fictitious play (examples of adaptive dynamics) as well as optimal learning as in Crawford and Haller (1990) (an example of rational learning).

3.2. Game 2

We conduct three treatments of Game 2 where each treatment consists of three replications. The treatments involve having participants play Game 2 for 40 periods where the sender's message space is either of size two, $\#(M) = 2$, three, $\#(M) = 3$, or four, $\#(M) = 4$.

The essential properties of the Game 2 outcomes (type–action associations) are presented in Table 2. Notice from this table that for each of the three replications of Game 2 with $\#(M) = 2$, the outcome is most closely aligned with a partial pooling equilibrium (where t_1 and t_2 separate from t_3), and across the three replications, 73% of the type–action pairs in the last five periods are consistent with the partial pooling equilibrium. For both Game 2 with $\#(M) = 3$ and $\#(M) = 4$, the outcome is most closely aligned with a fully separating equilibrium, and across the three replications of each treatment, 59% and 60% of the type–action pairs in the last five periods are consistent with a fully separating equilibrium, respectively. However, notice that there is also a significant incidence of partial pooling play in both treatments; 46% (36%) for the four (three) message treatment. Finally, notice that in all three treatments of Game 2 there is a non-trivial proportion of non-equilibrium play in the final five periods.

Table 3 reports the messages that were sent by the various sender types over the last five periods for each replication of each treatment of Game 2. Consistent with the outcomes presented in Table 2, notice from Table 3 that across the three replications of Game 2 with $\#(M) = 2$, sender types 1 and 2 essentially send a common message and sender type 3 separates by using the other message. Further notice that for both Game 2 with $\#(M) = 3$ and $\#(M) = 4$, 79% of senders are fully identified through the messages they send by the end of the game. This latter result, combined with the outcomes presented in Table 2, suggest that in the three and four message space treatments of Game 2, receivers had not fully responded to (or learned) the information contained in senders' messages.

Table 1

This table reports, aggregated over the final five periods, which actions were taken by receivers conditional on sender type for each of the nine replications of Game 1. For example, under "Rep 2" we learn that in the final five periods of the second replication of Game 1, type t_1 was drawn 14 times and received the preferred action a_1 12 times. Notice that for each of the nine replications of Game 1 the outcome is very close to full separation, and in four of the nine replications play over the final five periods is consistent with a fully separating equilibrium

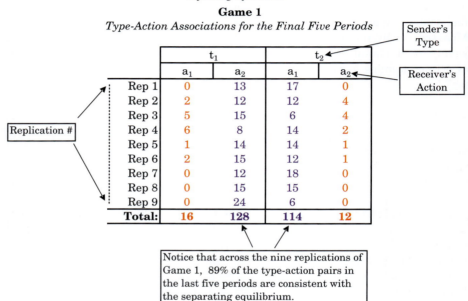

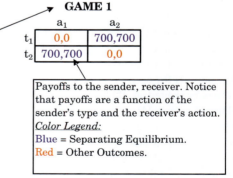

This common interest game, Game 1, is played by all participants in our experiments (prior to playing Game 2). Notice that both senders and receivers prefer that all information be revealed. Thus, if players are repeatedly and randomly matched to play this game where the sender's message space is of size two, #(M)=2, play should converge to an efficient separating equilibrium.

Payoffs to the sender, receiver. Notice that payoffs are a function of the sender's type and the receiver's action.
Color Legend:
Blue = Separating Equilibrium.
Red = Other Outcomes.

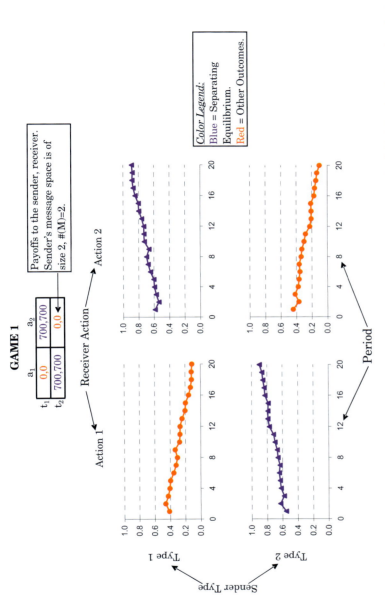

Figure 3. For the nine replications of Game 1 this figure presents the time paths that led to the outcomes presented in Table 1. Specifically, for each replication of Game 1 we first measure, over five-period intervals, the frequency of play (i.e., the # of a_i, t_i's) in each of the four cells of Game 1. Next, we divide each of these frequencies by their respective frequency of t_i's over these five-period intervals to measure, for each sender type, the proportion of play of each action. Finally, for purposes of parsimony and given the similarity of outcomes over replications, these proportions are averaged across replications. Notice from this figure that convergence to the final separating outcome is a gradual process. This is particularly interesting because rational players could, in most instances, use play in the first period as a precedent that would allow them to perfectly coordinate in period 2.

Table 2

This table reports, aggregated over the final five periods, which actions were taken by receivers conditional on sender type for each replication of each Game 2 treatment. For example, under '#(M) = 2: Rep 1' we learn that in the final five periods of the first replication of Game 2 with two messages, type t_1 was drawn 6 times and received action a_3 4 times; type t_2 was drawn 11 times and received action a_3 7 times; and, type t_3 was drawn 13 times and received action a_4 13 times. Notice that for each of the three replications of Game 2 with #(M) = 2, the outcome is most closely aligned with a partial pooling equilibrium (where t_1 and t_2 separate from t_3). For Game 2 with #(M) = 3 and #(M) = 4, terminal play across the three replications of each treatment is most consistent with a separating outcome, 59% and 60%, respectively. However, also notice that the incidence of partial pooling play is 36% and 46% in the three and four message space treatments, respectively. Finally, notice that in all three treatments there is a non-trivial proportion of non-equilibrium play in the final five periods

Game 2
Type-Action Associations for the Final Five Periods

		t_1				t_2				t_3			
		a_1	a_2	a_3	a_4	a_1	a_2	a_3	a_4	a_1	a_2	a_3	a_4
#(M)=2	Rep 1	1	1	4	0	1	3	7	0	0	0	0	13
	Rep 2	0	0	8	0	1	1	8	1	0	1	2	8
	Rep 3	0	1	6	1	2	0	6	2	1	0	5	6
	Total:	**1**	**2**	**18**	**1**	**4**	**4**	**21**	**3**	**1**	**1**	**7**	**27**
#(M)=3	Rep 1	4	3	0	2	5	2	0	2	1	4	2	5
	Rep 2	1	6	2	1	1	1	5	1	0	1	4	7
	Rep 3	0	7	1	0	10	0	3	0	0	0	0	9
	Total:	**5**	**16**	**3**	**3**	**16**	**3**	**8**	**3**	**1**	**5**	**6**	**21**
#(M)=4	Rep 1	4	5	2	0	4	4	2	0	0	0	0	9
	Rep 2	3	6	5	0	3	4	1	0	0	0	1	7
	Rep 3	1	3	3	0	9	2	4	0	0	0	0	8
	Total:	**8**	**14**	**10**	**0**	**16**	**10**	**7**	**0**	**0**	**0**	**1**	**24**

GAME 2

This partial common interest game, *Game 2*, is played by all participants in our experiments (after playing Game 1). We conduct three treatments of Game 2 where the sender's message space is either of size 2, 3, or 4. Predictions regarding equilibrium outcomes vary depending on the size of the sender's message space.

	a_1	a_2	a_3	a_4
t_1	0,0	200,700	400,400	0,0
t_2	200,700	0,0	400,400	0,0
t_3	0,0	0,0	0,0	400,400

Payoffs to the sender, receiver. Notice that payoffs are a function of the sender's type and the receiver's action.
Color Legend:
Blue + Purple = Separating Equilibrium.
Green + Purple = Partial Pooling Equilibrium.
Red = Other Outcomes.

Table 3

This table reports, aggregated over the final five periods, which messages were sent by various sender types for each replication of each Game 2 treatment. Messages are presented in terms of the underlying message space used to construct each player's representation of the message space. For example, under '#(M) = 2: Rep 1' we learn that in the final five periods of the first replication of Game 2 with two messages, type t_1 was drawn 6 times and sent the message 'B' 6 times; type t_2 was drawn 11 times and sent the message 'B' 11 times; and, type t_3 was drawn 13 times and sent the message 'A' 13 times. Notice that for each of the three replications of Game 2 with #(M) = 2, t_1 and t_2 separate from t_3 by using a common message distinct from sender type 3's message. For Game 2 with #(M) = 3 and #(M) = 4, notice that across the three replications of each treatment, 79% of senders are fully identified through the messages they send

Game 2
Type-Message Associations for the Final Five Periods

		t_1				t_2				t_3			
		A	B	C	D	A	B	C	D	A	B	C	D
#(M)=2	Rep 1	0	6	*	*	0	11	*	*	13	0	*	*
	Rep 2	0	8	*	*	1	10	*	*	8	3	*	*
	Rep 3	6	2	*	*	5	5	*	*	3	9	*	*
#(M)=3	Rep 1	5	1	3	*	0	4	5	*	2	0	10	*
	Rep 2	6	2	2	*	1	5	2	*	2	0	10	*
	Rep 3	8	0	0	*	0	13	0	*	0	0	9	*
#(M)=4	Rep 1	7	3	0	1	4	3	0	3	0	0	9	0
	Rep 2	0	0	2	12	4	0	2	2	0	8	0	0
	Rep 3	1	0	0	6	14	0	0	1	0	8	0	0

* = Message not available in this treatment of Game 2

Messages are colored according to the receiver's best response to the posterior distribution derived from the message frequencies over the last five periods.

This partial common interest game, Game 2, is played by all participants in our experiments (after playing Game 1). We conduct three treatments of Game 2 where the sender's message space is either of size 2, 3, or 4.

GAME 2

	a_1	a_2	a_3	a_4
t_1	0,0	200,700	400,400	0,0
t_2	200,700	0,0	400,400	0,0
t_3	0,0	0,0	0,0	400,400

Payoffs to the sender, receiver. Notice that payoffs are a function of the sender's type and the receiver's action.

Color Legend:
Blue + Purple = Separating Equilibrium.
Green + Purple = Partial Pooling Equilibrium.
Red = Other Outcomes.

Figures 4, 5, and 6 provide some insight about the learning process that led to the outcomes presented in Table 2. Notice from these figures that convergence to the observed equilibrium, across each treatment of Game 2, is both gradual and incomplete. For example, in Game 2 with #(M) = 3 and #(M) = 4, one might suspect that t_3, a_4 coordination would be quick because incentives are aligned for this type and because the cardinality of the message space is at least as large as the cardinality of the type space. Accordingly, senders could use one available message to identify t_3 and receivers, knowing this, should respond optimally with a_4. However, as the figures show, this convergence is by no means instantaneous. Second, notice from Figures 4–6 that, compared to Game 1, there is more noise in the Game 2 data, particularly with regard to play involving sender types 1 and 2, suggesting that resolving the conflict between senders and receivers in this part of the game is not a trivial matter.

To summarize, our Game 2 results provide some evidence that the size of the message space influences equilibrium selection. Specifically, we find that with a message space of size two, observed play is most closely aligned with a partial pooling equilibrium (where t_1 and t_2 separate from t_3), but with a message space size of three or four, observed play is most closely aligned with a fully separating equilibrium. Further, in both the three and four message treatments of Game 2, we observe a substantial amount of partial pooling play, with the four message treatment exhibiting a higher frequency of partial pooling play than the three message treatment (as suggested by theory).

Thus, while our results suggest that, at least for the message space sizes considered, the equilibrium most frequently selected is not affected by the size of the message space (as long as the size of the message space is at least as large as the size of the type space), this finding should be interpreted with some caution for a number of reasons. First, the presence of Game 1 may have prodded players towards a higher frequency of separation in Game 2 with #(M) = 3 and #(M) = 4. Specifically, because players experienced separation in Game 1, they may have carried over their efforts to separate in Game 2 when the size of the message space allowed them to do so. Second, in another paper, Blume et al. (1998) find that in games of divergent interest, the size of the message space influences whether the final outcome is pooling or separating. Essentially, they show that when the size of the message space equals (exceeds) the size of the type space, the final outcome is more likely to be separating (pooling). Accordingly, the current results may only generalize to games of partial common interest. In other words, because senders in our partial common interest game, Game 2, want to experience separation for one of their types (type 3), experiencing separation with this type may prod players to pursue separation with the other types as long as the size of the message space allows them to fully separate. Finally, compared to the divergent interest games considered by Blume et al. (1998), the partial common interest game we consider is more complex (i.e., there are more types and actions as well as equilibria) and, in addition, because both games were conducted over the same number of periods, we have fewer observations per type than they had. As a result, it is possible that extending the number of periods participants play might affect equilibrium selection in the direction suggested by theory.

Ch. 63: *The Effect of Message Space Size on Learning and Outcomes in Sender–Receiver Games* 581

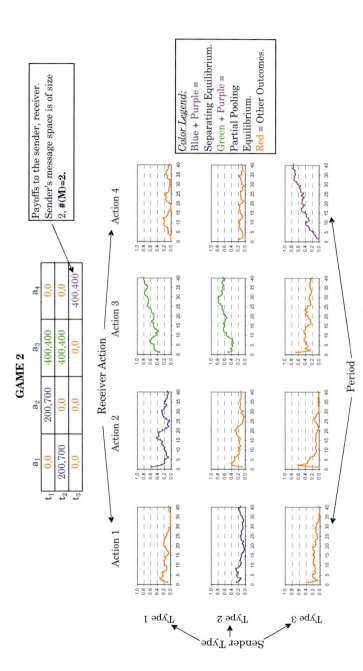

Figure 4. For the three replications of Game 2 with a message space of size 2, this figure presents the time paths that led to the outcomes presented in Table 2. Specifically, for each replication of Game 2 with #(M) = 2, we first measure, over five-period intervals, the frequency of play (i.e., the # of a_i, t_i's) in each of the twelve cells of Game 2. Next, we divide each of these frequencies by their respective frequency of t_i's over these five-period intervals to measure, for each sender type, the proportion of play of each action. Finally, for purposes of parsimony and given the general similarity of the outcomes over replications, these proportions are averaged across replications. Notice from this figure that while behavior is most consistent with partial pooling (where types t_1 and t_2 separate from t_3) there is persistent non-equilibrium play (i.e., convergence to this equilibrium is not complete). Further notice that convergence to the partial pooling equilibrium is gradual.

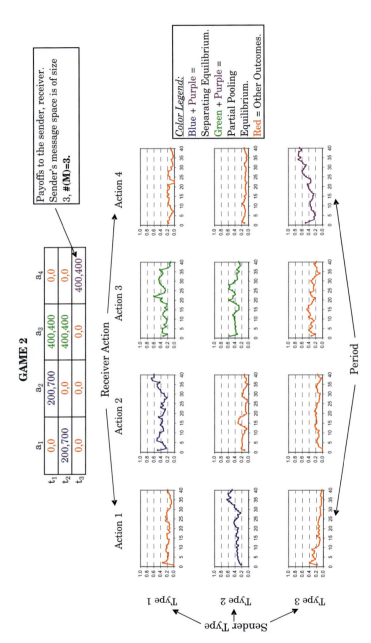

Figure 5. For the three replications of Game 2 with a message space of size 3, this figure presents the time paths that led to the outcomes presented in Table 2. Specifically, for each replication of Game 2 with #(M) = 3, we first measure, over five-period intervals, the frequency of play (i.e, the # of a_i, t_i's) in each of the twelve cells of Game 2. Next, we divide each of these frequencies by their respective frequency of t_i's over these five-period intervals to measure, for each sender type, the proportion of play of each action. Finally, for purposes of parsimony and given the rough similarity of the outcomes over replications, these proportions are averaged across replications. Notice from this figure that while terminal behavior is most consistent with separation, there is both a fairly high incidence of partial pooling play and some persistent non-equilibrium play. Compared to Game 2 with #(M) = 2, however, observed separating (partial pooling) play is significantly higher (lower) in Game 2 with #(M) = 3.

Ch. 63: *The Effect of Message Space Size on Learning and Outcomes in Sender–Receiver Games* 583

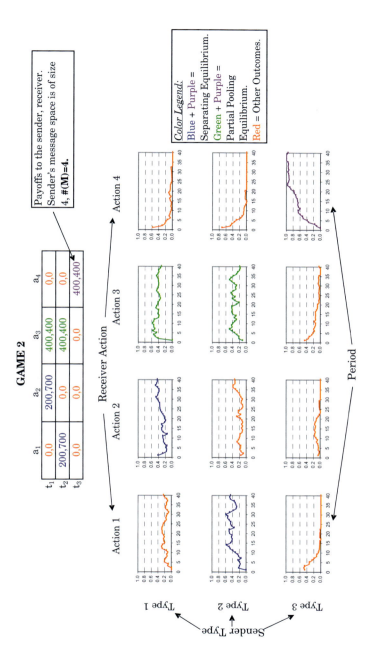

Figure 6. For the three replications of Game 2 with a message space of size 4, this figure presents the time paths that led to the outcomes presented in Table 2. Specifically, for each replication of Game 2 with #(M) = 4, we first measure, over five-period intervals, the frequency of play (i.e., the # of a_i, t_i's) in each of the twelve cells of Game 2. Next, we divide each of these frequencies by their respective frequency of t_i's over these five-period intervals to measure, for each sender type, the proportion of play of each action. Finally, for purposes of parsimony and given the rough similarity of the outcomes over replications, these proportions are averaged across replications. Notice from this figure that the frequency of terminal play is higher for separation than partial pooling, but the frequency of partial pooling play is high. Compared to Game 2 with #(M) = 3, the separating (partial pooling) tendencies appear to be slightly lower (higher) in Game 2 with #(M) = 4.

4. Summary

As documented in the dynamics (figures) and outcomes (tables), agents learn to attach meaning to "a priori" meaningless messages. For the common interest game, Game 1, we observe the efficient separating outcome, although the learning process is gradual. For the partial common interest game, Game 2, the outcomes and dynamics vary with the size of the message space. With two messages, we observe a partial pooling outcome with a minimal amount of non-equilibrium play. Again, the dynamic adjustment (learning) process is gradual. For three and four messages, the highest frequency of play is the fully separating equilibrium, although there is a significant amount of partial pooling play in both treatments and, consistent with theory, there is more partial pooling play in the four message treatment than in the three message treatment. Finally, while there is less non-equilibrium play in the four message treatment than in the three message treatment, the dynamic adjustment (learning) process in both treatments is gradual and incomplete.

References

Blume, A., Kim, Y., Sobel, J. (1993). "Evolutionary stability in games of communication". Games and Economic Behavior 5, 547–575.

Blume, A., DeJong, D.V., Kim, Y., Sprinkle, G.B. (1998). "Experimental evidence on the evolution of meaning of messages in sender–receiver games". The American Economic Review 88, 1323–1340.

Blume, A., DeJong, D.V., Kim, Y., Sprinkle, G.B. (2001). "Evolution of communication with partial common interest". Games and Economic Behavior 37, 79–120.

Canning, D. (1992). "Learning language conventions in common interest signaling games". Working paper, Columbia University.

Crawford, V., Haller, H. (1990). "Learning how to cooperate: Optimal play in repeated coordination games". Econometrica 58, 581–596.

Nöldeke, G., Samuelson, L. (1993). "An evolutionary analysis of backward and forward induction". Games and Economic Behavior 5, 425–454.

Wärneryd, K. (1993). "Cheap talk, coordination, and evolutionary stability". Games and Economic Behavior 5, 532–546.

Chapter 64

LEARNING IN ENTRY LIMIT PRICING GAMES

DAVID J. COOPER

1. Introduction

Signaling games play a central role for many models in economic theory and information economics. Applications of signaling games include education (Spence, 1974; Riley, 1979), market entry games (Milgrom and Roberts, 1982; Cho, 1987; Bagwell and Ramey, 1988), and advertising (Milgrom and Roberts, 1982). For all of these applications, the conclusions depend on what outcomes are considered likely for signaling games.

When signaling games admit a large number of sequential equilibria, as is typical, game theory cannot provide a definitive answer as to which is most likely. Theorists have attempted to narrow down the set of possible equilibria via various processes of forward induction (see Fudenberg and Levine, 1998, pp. 446–460). This approach has not been entirely satisfactory; to reach fairly specific predictions, strong assumptions about the reasoning ability of players must be employed. Brandts and Holt (1992) demonstrate experimentally that violations can be generated of even the relatively weak Cho–Kreps intuitive criterion. As an alternative, attention has recently turned to models of learning in which boundedly rational players gradually learn to play a game through an adaptive process. While equilibrium may eventually emerge in these models, it reflects a steady-state of the dynamic process rather than the culmination of some reasoning process.

Cooper, Garvin, and Kagel (1997a, 1997b) examine whether refinements based on forward induction or simple adaptive learning models are better able to capture behavior in signaling game experiments. We find that observed behavior is inconsistent with either the equilibrium refinements literature or pure belief-based adaptive learning models. An augmented adaptive learning model in which some players recognize the existence of dominated strategies and their consequences successfully captures the major qualitative features of the data.

2. The Limit-pricing Game

Our research program has focused on Milgrom and Roberts' (1982) entry limit-pricing game which serves as a rich vehicle for investigating a number of properties of signaling games. In the Milgrom–Roberts model an incumbent monopolist (M) faces a potential entrant (E). There is asymmetric information as Es are uncertain whether they are facing a high (M_H) or low (M_L) cost M; ex ante, each type is equally likely. Entry is profitable against an M_H but not against an M_L. Before E decides to play IN or OUT it observes M's output which plays the role of a signal.

Table 1
(Monopolist.) A player's payoffs as a function of B player's choice

Your Choice	A1 (High cost)		A2 (Low cost)		Your choice
	X (IN)	Y (OUT)	X (IN)	Y (OUT)	
1	150	426	250	542	1
2	168	444	276	568	2
3	150	426	330	606	3
4	132	408	352	628	4
5	56	182	334	610	5
6	−188	−38	316	592	6
	38	*162*			
7	−292	−126	213	486	7
	20	*144*	**298**	**574**	

Note. Terms in ( ) not included in experiment. Payoffs are in "francs." Francs converted to dollars at 1 franc = $0.001.

Table 2a
(Entrant.) B's payoffs

Your action choice	A1 (High cost)	A2 (Low cost)	Expected value[a]
A player's type			
X (IN)	300	74	187
Y (OUT)	250	250	250

Notes. Terms in ( ) and expected values not included in experiments. Payoffs are in "francs." Francs converted to dollars at 1 franc = $0.001.
[a] Based on prior distribution (50% M_H, 50% M_L) of M types.

Table 1 shows the payoffs employed for Ms in our original sessions, referred to as SP (for standard payoff) sessions, in regular print. Modifications to these payoffs for a later set of sessions, referred to as ZA (for zero anticipation) sessions and MR (for mixed recognition), are shown in italics and boldface, respectively. Table 2a gives payoffs for "high cost" Es, and Table 2b gives payoffs for "low cost" Es.

Several features of the Ms' payoff tables are noteworthy. First, Ms are always better off, ceterus paribus, if the Es choose OUT. Second, M_Ls have more incentive to choose high output levels than M_Hs. In particular, suppose that Ms maximize their payoffs ignoring any effect their output has on Es' responses. The resulting "myopic" maxima are 2 for M_Hs and 4 for M_Ls. Finally, output levels 6 and 7 are strictly dominated strategies for M_Hs in all treatments.

Table 2b
(Entrant.) B's payoffs

Your action choice	A1 (High cost)	A2 (Low cost)	Expected value[a]
A player's type			
X (IN)	500	200	350
Y (OUT)	250	250	250

Notes. Terms in ( ) and expected values not included in experiments. Payoffs are in "francs." Francs converted to dollars at 1 franc = $0.001.
[a] Based on prior distribution (50% M_H, 50% M_L) of M types.

Turning to the Es' payoff tables, note that in either case an E should play IN if it knows it is facing an M_H and OUT if it knows it is facing an M_L. The two tables differ in the optimal response versus the prior distribution over types; the best response versus a 50–50 distribution over types is OUT with Table 2a and IN with Table 2b.

In analyzing the sequential equilibria of the limit-pricing game, we concentrate on the SP payoff table; the set of equilibria is unaffected by using the other payoff tables. With Es using Table 2a, there are pure strategy-pooling equilibria at output levels 1–5. For all of these equilibria, choice of the pooling outcome is followed by OUT; all other output levels induce choice of IN. There also exist two pure strategy separating equilibria. In both of these equilibria, M_Hs choose 2. M_Ls choose 6 in one separating equilibrium and 7 in the other. The M_Ls' equilibrium output generates a response of OUT in both equilibria, while all other output levels induce choice of IN.

With Es using Table 2b, no pure strategy equilibria exist. The same two pure strategy-separating equilibria exist as were described for Table 2a. This treatment also has several partial pooling (mixed strategy) equilibria. One of these is especially noteworthy, as it arises in a significant number of simulations. In this equilibrium, M_Ls always select 5 while M_Hs mix between 2 (probability .80) and 5 (probability .20). Es always enter on output levels other than 5, and enter on 5 with probability .11.

To reduce the set of equilibria, we follow the approach of the signaling game refinements literature by restricting the set of possible beliefs. One of the weakest equilibrium refinements is (non-iterated) elimination of dominated strategies. Applying a single round of deletion of dominated strategies to Table 1 removes play of 6 or 7 by M_Hs. This eliminates the separating equilibrium with M_Ls choosing 7, since this equilibrium depends on Es believing that M_Hs will play a strictly dominated strategy (choose 6 with sufficiently high probability to justify entry). The partial pooling (mixed strategy) equilibrium is likewise eliminated. A more demanding requirement is that beliefs are intuitive in the sense of Cho and Kreps (1987). The Cho and Kreps intuitive criterion eliminates the pooling equilibria at 1, 2, and 3 with Table 2a, as well as the inefficient separating equilibrium and the partial pooling equilibrium.

3. Experimental Procedures

Experimental sessions employed between 12 and 16 subjects who participated in 36 plays of the game (announced in advance). Ms' types were randomly determined in each play of the game. Subjects switched roles after every 6 games with Ms becoming Es and vice versa. Ms were randomly paired with a different E in each play of the game. Neutral terms were used throughout, with Ms called A players (type A1 for M_H, type A2 for M_L) and Es called B players. A players chose first, after which the B players decided between X (IN) and Y (OUT).

Following each play of the game subjects learned the outcome of their own choices and the type of M player they were paired with (but not the other player's identity). In addition, subjects' screens displayed the results for all pairings (Ms' choices, Es' responses, and Ms' type) with subjects' identification numbers suppressed and pairings presented in random order.

Sessions varied along several dimensions which are summarized in Table 3. While most of the treatment variables are self-explanatory, a few require additional explanation. Recall that the dominated strategies play a crucial role in picking out an equilibrium for the games with Table 2b. The treatments differed in how obvious it was to Es that M_Hs should never play these strategies. With the SP treatment, M_Hs had negative earnings from both of the dominated strategies, making it relatively obvious that these would not be used. In the ZA treatment, these strategies had positive earnings. While play of 6 or 7 was still dominated for M_Hs, this was less transparent in the ZA treatment than in the SP treatment. In some of the sessions, we restricted the choices available to M_Hs by not allowing them to choose either 6 and 7 or just 7. By forbidding use of 6 or 7 by M_Hs, we made it trivial for Es to realize that play of these strategies must come from an M_L. Combining the MR payoff table with forbidding use of 7 by M_Hs establishes perfect recognition that 7 is dominated for M_Hs and little recognition that 6 is, while increasing the returns to M_Ls choosing 7. This treatment was designed to induce the inefficient separating equilibrium.[1]

4. Adaptive Learning

We simulated an adaptive learning model to predict the outcomes for our experiments. In this model, players learn to play the game through a relatively simple process of trial and error loosely based on fictitious play (Brown, 1951). Players are rational in the limited sense that they maximize payoffs subject to their beliefs and update their beliefs in accordance with observed outcomes. However, they do not account for the changing distribution of opponents' strategies.

In our model Ms begin with initial beliefs regarding the probability of Es choosing IN or OUT in response to each of their possible choices. Es start with initial beliefs

---

[1] Cooper, Garvin, and Kagel (1997a) also reports results from an earlier version of Treatment V.

Table 3
Experimental treatments

Treatment	Number of experimental sessions	Payoff tables	Strategies eliminated for $M_H s$	Subject experience	Cho–Kreps intuitive criterion prediction	Remarks
I	2 inexperienced 1 experienced	SP & 2A	None	None or same game	Pooling at 4 or 5 or separating with M_L at 6	Stronger equilibrium refinements predict pooling at 4
IB	2 experienced	SP & 2A	None	Prior experience with treatment II	Same as treatment I	Prior experience has no effect within equilibrium refinements approach
II	2 inexperienced 1 experienced	SP & 2B	None	None or same game	Separating with M_L at 6	Partial pooling equilibrium at 5 is a frequent outcome in simulations
III	2 inexperienced 1 experienced	ZA & 2B	None	None or same game	Same as treatment II	Positive payoffs on 6 and 7 for $M_H s$ to make recognition of dominated strategies more difficult
IV	2 inexperienced 1 experienced	SP & 2B	6 & 7	None or same game	Same as treatment II	$M_H s$ explicitly forbidden to use dominated strategies
V	2 inexperienced 1 experienced	MR & 2B	7	None or same game	Same as treatment II	Mixture of treatment III and IV with payoffs on 7 increased for $M_L s$

about the probability of an M_H or M_L choosing a particular output. The distributions of initial beliefs for Ms and Es in the simulations are fitted from first period data. After initial beliefs are randomly generated from these distributions, simulated Ms and Es are randomly matched to play sixty rounds of the entry limit pricing game. In each round, Ms' choices and Es' responses maximize their payoffs, conditional on beliefs. Following play of the game, beliefs are updated based on observed outcomes from own play and others' play in the previous period. The updating rule averages each players' initial beliefs and historical experience, where all prior experience receives equal weight (see Cooper, Garvin, and Kagel, 1997b for details). Augmented versions of the model permit some Es to recognize that M_Hs have dominated strategies. In this case these Es attach zero prior probability to M_H choosing 6 or 7 and never enter on 6 or 7.

Although this model does not converge to a steady state for all games, simulations consistently converge to a steady state for the limit-pricing game. In the limit-pricing game, observed steady state strategies must correspond to the outcomes induced by some sequential equilibrium. Figure 1 provides two typical examples of the simulation results. Play follows a distinctive pattern. Initially, choices by Ms are clustered around the myopic maxima, and Es do not distinguish strongly between output levels. Over time, entry rates rise on 2, the myopic maximum for M_Hs. In response, M_Hs move to pooling with M_Ls at 4. In simulations with high cost Es (Table 2a), play consistently converges to the pooling equilibrium at 4 with entry rates on 4 dropping to zero. With low cost Es (Table 2b), entry rates rise on 4, causing the M_Ls to separate to higher output levels. The results with low cost Es are sensitive to the percentage of Es who recognize the existence of dominated strategies. The larger this percentage becomes (i) the more rapidly M_Ls learn to limit price and (ii) the more likely play is to converge to the undominated separating equilibrium with M_Ls choosing 6 rather than the partial pooling equilibrium with M_Ls choosing 5. We hypothesize that increasing this proportion is equivalent to moving from Treatment III to Treatment II and then Treatment IV.

Simulations of our adaptive learning model with 0% of Es recognizing that 6 is dominated and 100% recognizing that 7 is, converge to the dominated separating equilibrium (M_Ls choose 7) 60% of the time. Further, permitting a few (15%) Ms to recognize that the 100% elimination of a dominated strategy by Es will result in zero entry when M_Ls choose 7 (these Ms attach zero prior probability to entry at 7), results in 95% of the simulations converging to the *dominated* separating equilibrium. We hypothesize that patterns of play in these simulations should be similar to behavior in Treatment V.

The adaptive learning model does not discard sequential equilibrium, but is an alternative way of characterizing how equilibria emerge; not by the careful reasoning through of the motives behind opponents strategies as in the refinements literature, but by a trial and error learning process in which subjects have some limited intelligence/perceptiveness.

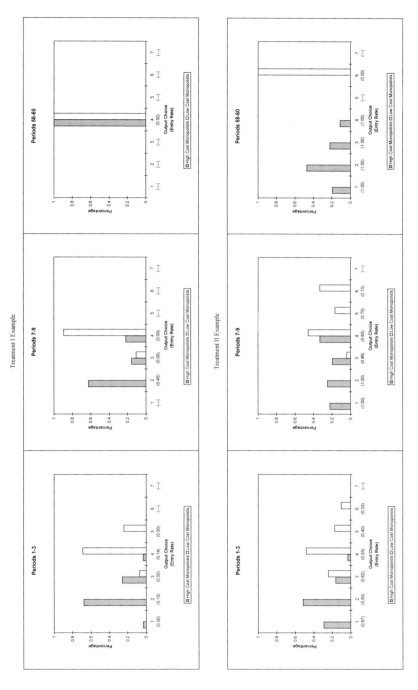

Figure 1. Sample simulation results.

5. Experimental Results

Figure 2 summarizes data from typical inexperienced subject sessions for Treatment I and Treatment II, respectively.[2] Figure 3 reproduces the corresponding experienced subject sessions. For all treatments, play starts with Ms clustered around the myopic maxima. As entry on 2 increases, $M_H s$ attempt to pool with $M_L s$. In Treatment I sessions, the entry rate falls on 4, leading to pooling at 4. In Treatment II sessions, the entry rate rise on 4. This is followed by the $M_L s$ separating to 6. A clear separating equilibrium only emerges for experienced subjects. Although sequential equilibria which fulfill the intuitive criterion emerge in both treatments, the pattern of play in the experiments bears a striking resemblance to that predicted by the simulations of the adaptive learning model.

This conclusion is reinforced by considering the results of Treatment Ib (reported in Figure 4). Here, rather than converging to the pooling equilibrium at 4, play flirts with pooling at 4 and then returns to the separating equilibrium. The refinements literature has nothing to say about this result, but the adaptive learning model is easily able to capture this result as an effect of accumulated beliefs.

Figure 5 compares results from Treatments II, III, and IV. Limit pricing develops progressively faster as we move from Treatment III to Treatment II and then Treatment IV. Comparing Treatment II with Treatment III, play tends more toward the partial pooling equilibrium rather than the undominated separating equilibrium. In Treatment IV, entry on 6 and 7 is close to zero and play converges much more rapidly to the undominated separating equilibrium than in Treatment II. These results are consistent with simulation results for the adaptive learning model.

Like Treatment IV, Treatment V leads to rapid emergence of a separating equilibrium. However, virtually all limit pricing takes place at 7 rather than 6. By the end of the experienced subject session, extremely strong convergence to the dominated separating equilibrium is observed. Output level 6 is chosen only 3 times in the inexperienced subject sessions and never in the experienced subject session. This outcome is a strong violation of all existing refinements to sequential equilibrium, but is consistent with simulations of the adaptive learning model.

6. Conclusions

Equilibrium refinements do quite poorly in capturing our results. The refinements say nothing about the observed dynamics of play and cannot predict observed differences between Treatments I and IB and between Treatments II, III, and IV. The results of Treatment V are completely inconsistent with any refinement to sequential equilibrium. All of these results can be characterized by a simple belief-based learning model augmented to allow for some limited reasoning ability by players.

---

[2] See Cooper, Garvin, and Kagel (1997b) for a full accounting of all sessions run. For replication of these results, see Cooper and Kagel (2002).

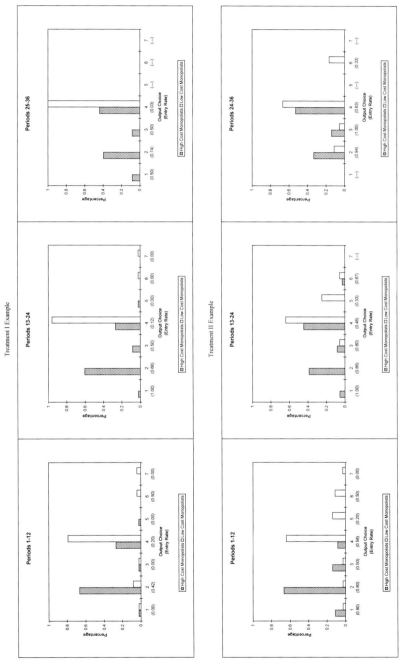

Figure 2. Sample inexperienced session results from Cooper, Garvin, and Kagel (1997b).

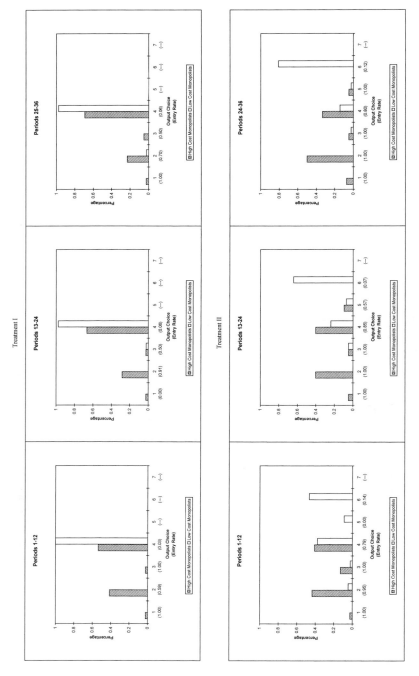

Figure 3. Experienced session results from Cooper, Garvin, and Kagel (1997b).

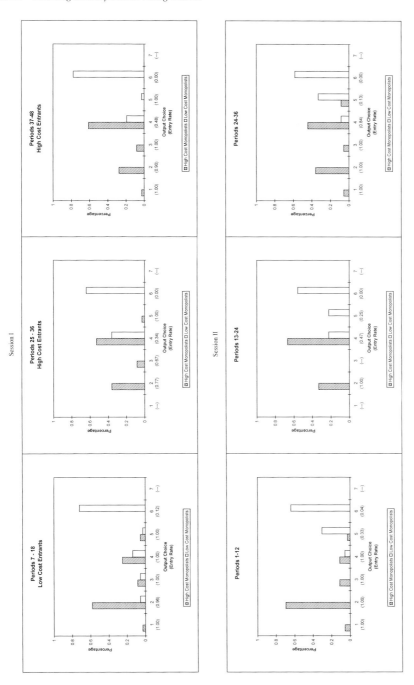

Figure 4. Treatment IB, crossover from low cost entrants to high cost entrants (Cooper, Garvin, and Kagel, 1997b).

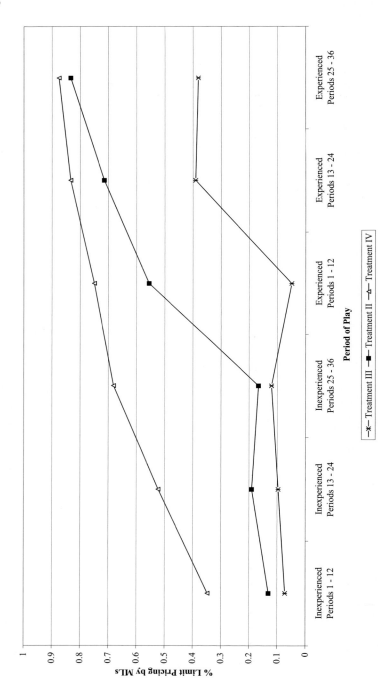

Figure 5. Comparison of limit pricing by M_Ls across Treatments II, III, and IV from Cooper, Garvin, and Kagel (1997a).

References

Bagwell, Kyle, Ramey, G. (1988). "Advertising and limit pricing". RAND Journal of Economics 19, 59–71.
Brandts, J., Holt, C.A. (1992). "An experimental test of equilibrium dominance in signaling games". American Economic Review 82, 1350–1365.
Brown, G.W. (1951). "Iterative solutions of games by fictitious play". In: Koopmans, T.J. (Ed.), Activity Analysis of Production and Allocation. Wiley, New York.
Cho, I., Kreps, D. (1987). "Signaling games and stable equilibria". Quarterly Journal of Economics 102, 179–221.
Cooper, David J., Garvin, Susan, Kagel, John (1997a). "Adaptive learning vs. equilibrium refinements in an entry limit pricing game". Economic Journal 107, 553–575.
Cooper, David J., Garvin, Susan, Kagel, John (1997b). "Signaling and adaptive learning in an entry limit pricing game". RAND Journal of Economics 28, 662–683.
Fudenberg, Drew, Levine, David (1998). "The Theory of Learning in Games". MIT Press, Cambridge, MA.
Milgrom, P., Roberts, J. (1982). "Limit pricing and entry under incomplete information: An equilibrium analysis". Econometrica 50, 443–459.
Riley, John (1979). "Informational equilibrium". Econometrica 48, 331–359.
Spence, A.M. (1974). "Market Signaling". Harvard University Press, Cambridge, MA.

Chapter 65

PAYOFF UNCERTAINTY AND COOPERATION IN FINITELY-REPEATED PRISONER'S DILEMMA GAMES[1]

LAWRENCE M. KAHN

Cornell University, 264 Ives Hall, Ithaca, NY 14853, USA

J. KEITH MURNIGHAN

Northwestern University

It is well known that for the finitely repeated prisoner's dilemma game, the unique Nash equilibrium strategy for rational players is non-cooperation at each stage of the game. The argument rests on the backwards induction argument described by Luce and Raiffa (1957): neither player should be motivated to choose cooperatively on the last trial. If neither expects the other to choose cooperatively on the last trial, the next to last trial becomes important. And so on, back to the current trial. The logic of the last trial motivates non-cooperative choices back to the point when the players believe that the game is finite; after that point, rational players should never choose cooperatively (Friedman, 1986).

This expectation, however, does not fit the behavior observed in many experiments including those by Rapoport and Chammah (1965), Axelrod (1984), Selten and Stoecker (1986), Roth (1988), and Andreoni and Miller (1993), among others.[2]

Kreps et al. (1982) suggested that uncertainty might be a factor that contributes to this disparity in theoretical predictions and observed behavior. They formulated two different models: Model 1 assumes that each player thinks that his/her opponent might play tit-for-tat instead of persistent non-cooperation; Model 2 assumes that players may be uncertain about their opponent's payoffs, particularly whether they have a dominant strategy and what that strategy is. The central feature of their analysis is that players' uncertainties about their counterparts' strategies or payoffs leads to uncertainty in their expectations about their opponents' likely strategies, which in turn influences their own strategic choices and may lead to cooperation when it would not otherwise be theoretically expected. In this chapter, we summarize the part of our previous research

---

[1] Portions of this chapter were written while the second author was a Fellow at the Center for Advanced Study in the Behavioral Sciences.

[2] In contrast to finitely repeated PD, cooperative equilibria may exist in games with low probabilities of termination when the future gains from current cooperation (i.e., future Pareto-optimal outcomes) outweigh the gains from current defection. Roth and Murnighan (1983) have shown that a PD with a given probability p of continuation to at least the next round is analytically equivalent to an infinitely repeated game with p as discount factor. Murnighan and Roth (1983) presented data from a dozen different games that supported the basic predictions of their theory.

(Kahn and Murnighan, 1993) that investigates their second model, testing whether payoff uncertainty can lead to cooperation in finitely-repeated games,[3] one of which was a prisoner's dilemma.

The players in our experiment were either certain or uncertain about their counterpart's payoffs in a finitely-repeated game; theoretically, this uncertainty provided the basis for cooperative equilibria during the game's early play in some conditions but not in others. For all of the games, even for those with a cooperative equilibrium, the non-cooperative outcome was also an equilibrium. Thus, cooperative behavior was frequently not predicted, even given the players' uncertainties about their counterparts' outcomes.

1. Methods

The participants were 154 undergraduate volunteers, primarily enrolled in a management class, at the University of Illinois at Urbana-Champaign. Participating gave them a small amount of extra credit in one of their courses (a common practice) and the chance for one of four monetary prizes (of $200, $100, $100, and $100).

2. The Experimental Design

We manipulated two basic factors: the strength of the players' roles and their uncertainty about their counterpart's payoffs. We labeled players Strong if they had a dominant strategy; we labeled them Weak if they did not.

Players played one of two games, either Game 1 or Game 2 in Table 1a. In some conditions, they were completely uncertain (i.e., chances were 50–50) whether they were playing one of these two games or one of Games 3 and 4 (also shown in Table 1a). The uncertainty conditions included neither or both players being uncertain of the game they were playing, or one or the other of the Row and Column players being uncertain. As noted in Table 1b, uncertainty for Row was essentially immaterial in a one shot game since they always had a dominant single-period strategy, even when they were uncertain about which game their counterpart was playing. Of course, in the repeated games we study here, even players with a dominant one-period strategy may gain by cooperating

---

[3] While not based on PD, Camerer and Weigelt's (1988) experiments also bear on the rationales for cooperation identified by Kreps et al. They established a lending game in which a "banker" (B) chooses whether to "lend" to an entrepreneur (E). B is uncertain about E's preferences to repay the loan or renege. Each E played eight rounds of this game against a series of lenders. The results suggested that lenders had "homemade" prior beliefs of the probability that E would prefer to repay the loan even when E gained more by reneging. Specifically, the E players repaid the loan more often and later in the game than predicted by a rational model. Also, see Kahn and Murnighan (1993) for some results on Model 1 and further detail on the findings we report here.

Table 1

(a) The four possible games

Game 1

		Column	
		A	B
Row	A	(18, 18)	(5, 20)
	B	(24, 5)	(12, 12)

Both players have dominant, non-cooperative strategies; a prisoner's dilemma game

Game 2

		Column	
		A	B
Row	A	(18, 18)	(5, 10)
	B	(24, 5)	(12, 12)

Row has a dominant, non-cooperative strategy; Column has no dominant strategy

Game 3

		Column	
		A	B
Row	A	(24, 18)	(15, 20)
	B	(18, 5)	(12, 12)

Both players have dominant strategies: cooperation for Row and non-cooperation for Column

Game 4

		Column	
		A	B
Row	A	(24, 18)	(15, 10)
	B	(18, 5)	(12, 12)

Row has a dominant, cooperative strategy; Column has no dominant strategy

(b) Uncertainty conditions: The game the players felt they were playing with one-shot game predicted outcomes

	Strong–Strong	Predicted Outcome(s)	Strong–Weak	Predicted Outcome(s)
Neither Uncertain				
For Row:	Game 1	(12, 12)	Game 2	(12, 12)
For Column:	Game 1	(12, 12)	Game 2	(12, 12)
Row Uncertain				
For Row:	Game 1 or 2	(12, 12)	Game 2 or 1	(12, 12)
For Column:	Game 1	(12, 12)	Game 2	(12, 12)
Column Uncertain				
For Row:	Game 1	(12, 12)	Game 2	(12, 12)
For Column:	Game 1 or 3	(12, 12) or (15, 20)	Game 2 or 4	(12, 12) or (24, 18)
Both Uncertain:				
For Row:	Game 1 or 2	(12, 12)	Game 2 or 1	(12, 12)
For Column:	Game 1 or 3	(12, 12) or (15, 20)	Game 2 or 4	(12, 12) or (24, 18)

(c) Predicted periods of mutual cooperation, 20 trial repeated game

	Strong–Strong	Strong–Weak
Neither Uncertain	0	0
Row Uncertain	0	0
Column Uncertain	0	19
Both Uncertain	≥ 2	≥ 14

over portions of the repeated game. Column players, on the other hand, often had no dominant single-period strategy (they were Weak in our terms) and they therefore were considerably affected by their uncertainty even in the one-shot game.

We refer to Game 1 as Strong–Strong since both players have dominant strategies, in this case non-cooperative (Game 1 is a prisoner's dilemma). Game 2 is Strong–Weak since only the Row player has a dominant strategy; this is not a prisoner's dilemma game. Uncertain players were told that one of two of the games were equally likely (see Table 1b). Certainty or uncertainty was common knowledge: both players knew who was certain or uncertain and what they were certain or uncertain about.

The design resulted in eight cells (Table 1b) created by crossing the four possible uncertainty combinations with the two actual payoff matrices. With player rationality, only three of the eight cells in the design admitted cooperative equilibria for some portion of the 20-round game: Strong–Weak (SW), Column Uncertain; Strong–Strong (SS), Both Uncertain; and SW, Both Uncertain (Table 1c). The proof is available from the authors upon request.

Intuitively, the clearest case for a cooperative equilibrium is the Strong–Weak, Column Uncertain condition. Here, Column perceives a 50% chance that Row's dominant strategy is A, to cooperate. Since Column does not gain even temporarily by playing B in response to Row's A play, Column has a strong motivation to cooperate. Row's motivation to cooperate comes from the idea that cooperation may build Row's reputation for having a dominant cooperative strategy, inducing Column to choose A rather than B. Further, Row knows that Column does not gain by playing B in response to Row's A play – Column's only temptation to choose B and defect is to protect against the chance that they are playing Game 2. The theory, then, suggests that Column should cooperate for all 20 periods and Row should cooperate until the last period. These strategies provide Row with clearly preferable payoffs of 18 each trial and 24 on the last trial rather than payoffs of 12 on every trial after the first.

The two other conditions with cooperative equilibria are less compelling. In SW, Both Uncertain, both parties have an incentive to build a cooperative reputation. However, Row no longer knows whether Column can achieve single-period gains by choosing B. If Row acts defensively to protect against such behavior, cooperation should theoretically break down some time after 14 periods. In SS, Both Uncertain, reputation building for part of the repeated game is again a sequential equilibrium. However, Row may realize that Column may be able to reap a single-period gain by playing B in response to Row's A play. This should lead to an earlier breakdown in cooperation, theoretically after 2 periods.

The five other conditions in Table 1 do not admit any cooperative sequential equilibria: if Column knows that Row is Strong, then cooperation should unravel from the last period to the first. Thus, there are no cooperative equilibria for any game in which Column is certain about Row's payoffs. In the one remaining condition, SS, Column Uncertain, Row knows that Column has a dominant, non-cooperative strategy; therefore, the backwards induction argument applies here as well.

Theoretically, then, the uncertainty in three of the eight conditions provided an opportunity for the players to make cooperative choices, if only to suggest to their counterparts that their payoffs favor cooperative action. Uncertainty in the other games still did not create cooperative equilibria.

Each game was played for 20 rounds; following each round, players received feedback on the results of the prior round. Everyone participated in two sessions: each pair's first bargaining session was randomly chosen from among the eight cells in the design; the second session either duplicated the first, with a different opponent, or switched to either the Both or Neither Uncertain Conditions, also with a different opponent. Data analysis indicated that order had no significant impact on the results.

3. Results

This large experiment produced several results. In particular:
1. The two conditions that generated theoretical cooperative equilibria for many trials of the game (SW, Column Uncertain and SW, Both Uncertain) led to significantly more cooperative choices than the other conditions. Participants in these conditions made an average of 13.8 cooperative choices, compared to 9.5 cooperative choices in all of the other conditions. These data suggest that the theoretical analysis of Kreps et al. (1982) has behavioral consequences.
2. The five conditions that did not provide the conditions for a cooperative equilibrium nevertheless led to considerable cooperative behavior. Without a cooperative equilibrium, participants still chose cooperatively almost half the time. This suggests a serious problem for the theory.
3. People seemed to pay no attention to the fact that the games were finite – there was no end game play – until the 17th trial. Figure 1 shows the pattern of cooperative choices across the 20 trials: after the first few trials, cooperative choices were relatively stable for much of the game, even though all of the players knew that the game was finite.
4. The Strong–Weak conditions generated more cooperative choices (average = 13.5) than the Strong–Strong (average = 7.7).
5. When both parties were certain about the payoffs, whether they were SS or SW, they tended to make more cooperative choices (on average, 12.7 versus 9.6). In addition, for both the Strong–Strong and the Strong–Weak game, there was more first round cooperation when both parties were certain about their payoffs than when either or both parties were uncertain about them.

The figure provides an important picture of all of the data; it displays the mean frequency of cooperative choices in each condition across trials, pooled over Row and Column players, who behaved similarly in each condition. After a primarily cooperative first round, the data reveal an almost immediate and substantial drop in cooperation, particularly in the conditions that were less cooperative on the first round. Then, cooperation rates leveled off for most of the rest of the game. Over most of the 20 trials, the

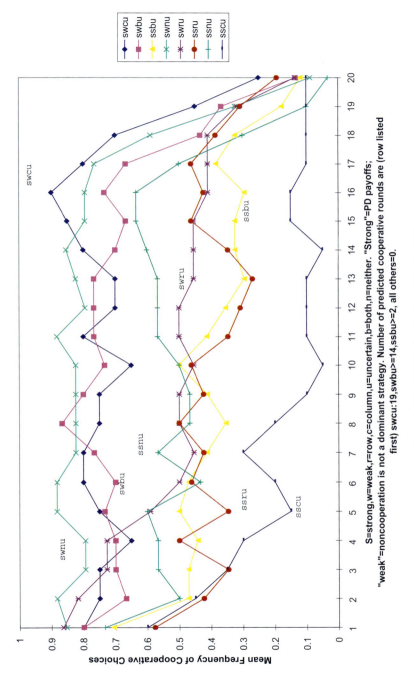

Figure 1. Mean frequencies of cooperation over trials.

eight conditions seemed to fall into three distinct sets: the three cooperative SW conditions, a set of four moderately cooperative conditions, and the primarily non-cooperative SS, Column Uncertain condition. Among the moderately cooperative group, the SS, Neither Uncertain condition was the most cooperative and, after the early plunge in cooperation rates, seemed to evidence a gradual increase in cooperation from trials 8 to 16. This is particularly surprising given the fact that non-cooperation is a dominant strategy for both players and they have no uncertainty about it.

Finally, the data reveal a huge drop in cooperation rates in all of the conditions starting on the 17th of the 20 trials. We liken the image to a ball falling off a table. In this case, however, the ball falls a few trials before the end of the game rather than at the very end. This steep drop in cooperation shows awareness of the impending end game among players who had otherwise displayed high levels of cooperation.

Further, Figure 1 again illustrates that the conditions when neither of the two parties had any uncertainty about each others' payoffs generally led to more cooperation throughout the repeated trials than any of the Row, Column, or Both Uncertain conditions within a Strong–Strong or Strong–Weak game.

Needless to say, these data provide only minimal evidence to suggest that uncertainty about a counterpart's payoffs explains why they are cooperative in finite prisoner's dilemma games. Other models are clearly necessary to explain these anomalies. The extensive nature of the data in this study, however, provide some clues.

4. Discussion and Conclusions

Several of the results reported here broadly support theories of sequential equilibria. In particular, at least four pieces of data indicate that game theory's structurally-oriented models predict some of the reasons for individuals' play in the prisoner's dilemma game: (1) more cooperation resulted when a cooperative equilibrium existed; (2) players cooperated more overall and more in the first round in SW than in SS; (3) Column was more cooperative than Row on the first trial; and (4) the SW Column Uncertain condition produced the most end game cooperation.

Unfortunately, these effects only explain part of the picture. In essence, even after considering the effects of uncertainty, the original issue still remains: considerable cooperation resulted when no cooperative equilibria exist. It is our impression that the most important findings in these data are that: (1) the players were more cooperative when they were certain of each other's payoffs; and (2) they only began to react to the presence of the endgame with four of the 20 trials remaining. Rather than being best explained by rational models, it appears that what seems to be unexpected cooperation may depend on psychological factors, including: (1) the personal discomfort of uncertainty; (2) myopia with respect to the endgame; (3) the desire to avoid losses; and (4) the fact that only two choices are available in these games. Points 1, 3, and 4 combine to suggest that, because the non-cooperative equilibrium exists in all conditions of both games, players may have reacted to uncertainty by choosing non-cooperatively. A systematic psychological discontinuity between the certain and uncertain conditions may have driven them to choose non-cooperatively without non-cooperative, anti-opponent intent. Indeed, this reflects a criticism of PD games, that the person choosing non-cooperation may perceive it as defensive rather than offensive (see, for example, Apfelbaum, 1974 or Nemeth, 1972]. In economic terms, the existence of payoff uncertainty may raise the transaction costs involved in reaching a cooperative outcome: with payoff uncertainty, it may be difficult for players to identify the efficiency gains from cooperating. Thus, the net effect of payoff uncertainty may be negative – the negative effects on the ability of parties to negotiate cooperative agreements may outweigh the positive effects of the existence of additional cooperative equilibria.

Points 1, 2, and 3, above, may have led people to depend more on their counterparts' previous choices than on any calculation of the underlying structural contingencies of the game. In particular, participants may have focused on reaping as many mutually cooperative outcomes as they could but, as the end approached, tried to avoid being the last person to shift to non-cooperation. This compounds a player's uncertainty. Yet, almost all of the conditions, regardless of their structural uncertainty, show that cooperation starts to break down on trial 17. This suggests that payoff uncertainty and the uncertainty of one's counterpart's reactions to the endgame are qualitatively different, one requiring a wait-and-see strategy and the other requiring a preemptive strategy. This suggests that further modeling of the play in prisoner's dilemma games may need to be even more complex.

Acknowledgements

We are grateful for the financial support provided by the National Science Foundation (#BNS87-00864 and SES88-15566) and the Russell Sage Foundation. The authors thank Patty DeForrest and Felice Herbin for serving as experimenters.

References

Andreoni, J., Miller, J. (1993). "Rational cooperation in the finitely repeated prisoner's dilemma: Experimental evidence". Economic Journal 103, 570–585.
Apfelbaum, E. (1974). "On conflicts and bargaining". Advances in Experimental Social Psychology 7, 103–156.
Axelrod, R. (1984). "The Evolution of Cooperation". Free Press, New York.
Camerer, C., Weigelt, K. (1988). "Experimental tests of a sequential equilibrium reputation model". Econometrica 56, 1–36.
Friedman, J.W. (1986). "Game Theory with Applications to Economics". Oxford University Press, New York.
Kahn, L.M., Murnighan, J.K. (1993). "Conjecture, uncertainty, and cooperation in prisoner's dilemma games". Journal of Economic Behavior and Organization 22, 91–117.
Kreps, D., Milgrom, P., Roberts, J., Wilson, R. (1982). "Rational cooperation in the finitely repeated prisoner's dilemma". Journal of Economic Theory 27, 245–252.

Luce, R.D., Raiffa, H. (1957). "Games and Decisions; Introduction and Critical Survey". Wiley, New York.

Murnighan, J.K., Roth, A.E. (1983). "Expecting continued play in prisoner's dilemma games". Journal of Conflict Resolution 27, 279–300.

Nemeth, C. (1972). "A critical analysis of research utilizing the prisoner's dilemma paradigm for the study of bargaining". In: Berkowitz, L. (Ed.), Advances in Experimental Social Psychology, vol. 6. Academic Press, New York.

Rapoport, A., Chammah, A. (1965). "Prisoner's Dilemma". University of Michigan Press, Ann Arbor.

Roth, A.E. (1988). "Laboratory experimentation in economics: A methodological overview". Economic Journal 98, 974–1031.

Roth, A.E., Murnighan, J.K. (1983). "Equilibrium behavior and repeated play of the prisoner's dilemma". Journal of Mathematical Psychology 17, 189–198.

Selten, R., Stoecker, R. (1986). "End behavior in sequences of finite prisoner's dilemma supergames". Journal of Economic Behavior and Organization 7, 47–70.

Chapter 66

LEARNING AND EQUILIBRIUM IN GAMES

COLIN F. CAMERER

Division of Humanities and Social Sciences, California Institute of Technology, Pasadena, CA 91125, USA
e-mail: camerer@hss.caltech.edu

TECK H. HO

The Wharton School, University of Pennsylvania, Philadelphia, PA 19104-6366, USA
e-mail: hoteck@wharton.upenn.edu

JUIN-KUAN CHONG

National University of Singapore, Lower Kent Ridge Road, Singapore 192610

1. Introduction

In the last ten years theory (e.g., Fudenberg and Levine, 1998) and empirical data fitting have provided many ideas about how equilibria arise in games or markets. This short chapter describes a very general approach to learning in games: "experience-weighted attraction" (EWA) learning. This approach strives to explain, for every choice in an experiment, how that choice arose from players' previous behavior and experience, using a general model which can be applied to most games with minimal customization and which predicts well out of sample. Sophisticated EWA includes important equilibrium concepts and many other learning models (simple reinforcement, Cournot, fictitious play, weighted fictitious play) as special cases (see Camerer and Ho, 1999; Ho, Camerer and Chong, 2001, and cited references for details). The model therefore allows "one-stop shopping" for learning about the latest statistical comparisons of many different learning and equilibrium models (see Camerer, 2002, Chapter 6 for more details). The model can also be adapted to field applications in which strategies and payoffs are often poorly-specified (e.g., it has been used successfully to predict actual consumer choices of products like ice cream, see Ho and Chong, 1999).

2. Adaptive EWA and Other Learning Models

Notation: Denote player i's jth strategy by s_i^j and the other player(s)' strategy by s_{-i}^k. The strategy actually chosen in period t is $s_i(t)$. Player i's payoff for choosing s_i^j in period t is $\pi(s_i^j, s_{-i}^k(t))$. Like most learning theories, EWA assumes each strategy has a numerical measure, called an attraction $A_i^j(t)$. The model also has an experience weight, $N(t)$. The variables $N(t)$ and $A(a,t)$ begin with prior values (estimated from the data or specified from a model of first-period play) and are updated each period. The rule for updating attraction sets $A_i^j(a, t)$ to be the sum of a depreciated, experience-weighted previous attraction $A_i^j(a, t - 1)$ plus the (weighted) payoff from period t, normalized by the updated experience weight (argument a stands for adaptive learning):

$$A_i^j(a, t) = \frac{\phi \cdot N(t - 1) \cdot A_i^j(a, t - 1) + [\delta + (1 - \delta)I(s_i^j, s_i(t))] \cdot \pi_i(s_i^j, s_{-i}(t))}{N(t)}$$

(2.1)

where indicator variable $I(x, y)$ is 1 if $x = y$ and 0 otherwise. The experience weight is updated by $N(t) = \phi(1 - \kappa)N(t - 1) + 1$. In Bayesian models (belief special cases with Dirichlet priors), $N(0)$ is the strength of prior beliefs, in terms of units of observation. In general, $N(t)$ approaches the steady-state value $\frac{1}{1-\phi \cdot (1-\kappa)}$ value, it steadily rises, capturing an increase in the weight placed on previous attractions and a (relative) decrease in the impact of recent observations, so that learning slows down. [In practice, assuming $N(0) = 1$ or imposing the restriction $N(t) \frac{1}{1-\phi \cdot (1-\kappa)}$ save degrees of freedom and impair fit very little.]

Attractions are mapped into choice probabilities using an exponential logit rule (other functional forms fit about equally well; Camerer and Ho, 1998):

$$P_i^j(a, t + 1) = \frac{e^{\lambda \cdot A_i^j(a,t)}}{\sum_{k=1}^{m_i} e^{\lambda \cdot A_i^k(a,t)}}.$$

(2.2)

The key parameters are δ, ϕ, and κ (which are generally assumed to be in the [0, 1] interval). When $\kappa = 0$, the attractions are weighted averages of lagged attractions and payoff reinforcements (with weights $\phi \cdot N(t-1)/(\phi \cdot N(t-1)+1)$ and $1/(\phi \cdot N(t-1)+1)$). When $\kappa = 1$, $N(t) = 1$, the attractions are accumulations of previous reinforcements rather than averages (i.e., $A_i^j(a, t) = \phi \cdot A_i^j(a, t-1) + [\delta + (1-\delta) \cdot I(s_i^j, s_i(t))] \cdot \pi_i(s_i^j, s_{-i}(t))$). In the logit model, the *differences* in strategy attractions entirely determine their choice probabilities. When κ is high, the attractions can grow furthest apart over time, making choice probabilities closer to zero and one. We therefore interpret k as an index of "commitment" or cumulation. It seems related to a distinction in machine learning between exploration (trying different strategies to see which is best) and exploitation (locking in to the strategy which has worked best). High values of κ correspond to quicker exploitation. The parameter ϕ represents the rate at which old experience is discounted relative to new, a measure of sensitivity to change. The most important parameter, δ, is the weight on foregone payoffs relative to realized payoffs, "consideration" or imagination.

Triples of parameter values δ, ϕ, κ represent specific learning rules, which can be shown in a three-dimensional cube (see Figure 1). Simple algebra shows that certain corners and vertices of the cube correspond to extreme special cases which are historically significant. The vertex $\delta = 1$, $\kappa = 0$ corresponds, surprisingly, to weighted fictitious play models in which players form beliefs based on past observation of others, and

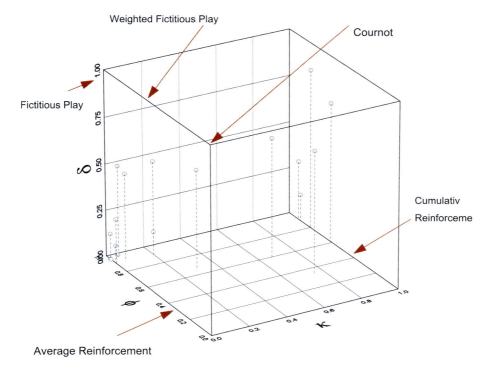

Figure 1.

choose best responses given their beliefs. The corners $\phi = 0$ and $\phi = 1$ correspond to Cournot best-response dynamics and fictitious play, respectively. Reinforcement models in which only chosen strategies are reinforced according to their payoffs correspond to vertices in which $\delta = 0$, and $\kappa = 1$ (cumulative reinforcement) or $\kappa = 0$ (averaged reinforcement). Interior configurations of parameter values incorporate both the intuition behind reinforcement learning, that realized payoffs weigh most heavily ($\delta < 1$), and the intuition implicit in belief learning, that foregone payoffs matter too ($\delta > 0$). The vertex $\delta = 1$, $\kappa = 0$ represents "cumulative" best-response learning. Though that vertex has never been studied, its parameter restrictions fit best in three coordination games (Ho, Camerer and Chong, 2001), which shows the advantage of hybridizing the responsiveness of belief learning (high δ) with the cumulation of some reinforcement models (high κ).

The cube shows that contrary to popular belief for many decades, reinforcement and belief learning are not fundamentally different approaches to learning. Instead, they are simply two extreme configurations on opposite edges of a three-dimensional cube. That is, belief learning (of the fictitious play variety) is a kind of generalized reinforcement in which unchosen strategies are reinforced as strongly as chosen ones. Parameter estimates in a wide variety of experimental data sets also show the empirical advantages of hybridizing the three features of learning. Figure 1 also shows estimates of the three parameters in 20 different studies (Ho, Camerer and Chong, 2001). The estimation maximizes the likelihood function using each data point (there is no averaging across individuals or blocks of trials). About 70% of the data are used to estimate best-fitting parameter values, and those values are used to forecast data in the remaining 30% of the data to be sure the model is not fitting well by overfitting. While this procedure is different than fixing a set of parameter values and simulating a priori an entire sample path, there is no evidence that in explaining data from games the maximum-likelihood and simulated-path methods yield different results on relative fit of models (see Camerer, 2002, Chapter 6).

Each point in Figure 1 is a triple of estimates. Most points are sprinkled throughout the cube, rather than at the extreme vertices mentioned in the previous paragraph, although some (generally from games with mixed-strategy equilibria) are near the averaged reinforcement corner $\delta = 0, \kappa = \phi = 1$.

Parameter estimates are generally significantly inside the interior of the cube, rather than near the vertices. That means the general EWA specification fits better than cumulative reinforcement (with $\kappa = 1$) in 27 of 31 cases, and better than belief learning in 25 of 27 data sets (penalizing for free parameters or predicting out-of-sample). Given the plausibility of the hybrid EWA model, the psychological interpretability of its parameters, the efficiency of searching for optimal parameters in the entire cube rather than along a single vertex or corner, and its demonstrated superiority in more than 90% of comparisons in 25–30 data sets, it is hard to think of a good reason to continue to focus only on extreme special cases rather than EWA.

One concern about a model like EWA is that it has "too many" parameters, and the parameters vary across games (so it might be difficult to guess what values would be in a new game). In Ho, Camerer and Chong (2001) both problems are solved by substituting functions of experience for free parameters. (For example, ϕ is a "change-detection" function which dips down below zero, discarding old information, if an opponent's strategies change dramatically.) This "functional EWA" (or fEWA) model has only one free parameter (λ) and is hence more parsimonious than most reinforcement and belief learning models. Furthermore, the functional values which fEWA generates tend to be close to estimated values across games, reducing cross-game unpredicted variation. Finally, Ho et al. propose a measure of the theory's "economic value" – if players followed theory recommendations, by best-responding to theory forecasts of others' behavior rather than making the choices they did, how much more money would they have earned? Across seven data sets, EWA and fEWA add the most economic value by this measure, compared to general belief, reinforcement, and QRE models. To guard against the possibility that the original model was overfit, Ho et al also collected three more data sets after their first draft was written and found that performance on those new data was comparable to the earlier ones.

3. Sophisticated EWA and Equilibrium Models

The EWA model presented is a simplification (as are all the other adaptive models) because it does not permit players to anticipate learning by others (cf. Selten, 1986). Omitting anticipation logically implies that players do not use information about the payoffs of other players, and that whether players are matched together repeatedly or randomly re-matched should not matter. Both of the latter implications are unintuitive and have proved false in experiments, and there is direct evidence for anticipatory learning also.

In Camerer, Ho, and Chong (2002a, 2002b) we propose a simple way to include "sophisticated anticipation" by some players that others are learning, using two parameters. We assume a fraction of players are sophisticated. Sophisticated players think that a fraction $(1 - \alpha')$ of players are adaptive and the remaining fraction α' of players are sophisticated like themselves. They use the adaptive EWA model to forecast what the adaptive players will do, and choose strategies with high expected payoffs given their forecast.

All the adaptive models discussed above (EWA, reinforcement, weighted fictitious play) are special cases of sophisticated EWA with $\alpha = 0$. The assumption that sophisticated players think some others are sophisticated, creates a small whirlpool of recursive thinking which implies that quantal response equilibrium (QRE; McKelvey and Palfrey, 1998) and hyperresponsive QRE (Nash) equilibrium, are special cases of sophisticated EWA. Our specification also shows that equilibrium concepts combine two features which are empirically and psychologically separable: "social calibration" (accurate guesses about the fraction of players who are sophisticated, $(\alpha > \alpha')$ and full sophistication ($\alpha = 1$)). Psychologists have identified systematic departures from social calibration called "false" uniqueness or overconfidence ($\alpha > \alpha'$) and "false" consensus or curse of knowledge ($\alpha > \alpha'$).

Formally, adaptive EWA learners follow the updating equations above. Sophisticated players have attractions and choice probabilities specified as follows (where arguments a and s denote adaptive and sophisticated, respectively):

$$A_i^j(s,t) = \sum_k \left[(1-\alpha') \cdot P_{-i}^k(a, t+1) + \alpha' P_{-i}^k(s, t+1)\right] \cdot \pi_i(s_i^j, s_{-i}^k), \quad (3.1)$$

$$P_i^j(s, t+1) = \frac{e^{\lambda \cdot A_i^j(s,t)}}{\sum_{k=1}^{m_i} e^{\lambda \cdot A_i^k(s,t)}}. \quad (3.2)$$

The sophisticated model has been applied to experimental data from 10-period p-beauty contest games (Ho, Camerer, and Weigelt, 1998). In these games, seven subjects choose numbers in [0, 100] simultaneously. The subject whose number is closest to p times the average (where $p = .7$ or $.9$) wins a fixed prize. Subjects playing for the first time are called "inexperienced"; those playing another 10-period game (with a different p) are called "experienced."

Table 1
Parameter estimates for p-beauty contest game

	Inexperienced subjects		Experienced subjects	
	Sophisticated EWA	Adaptive EWA	Sophisticated EWA	Adaptive EWA
ϕ	0.436	0.000	0.287	0.220
δ	0.781	0.900	0.672	0.991
κ	1.000	1.000	0.927	1.000
$N(0)$	0.253	0.000	0.000	0.887
α	0.236	*0.000*	0.752	*0.000*
α'	0.000	*0.000*	0.412	*0.000*
LL (in sample)	−2095.32	−2155.09	−1908.48	−2128.88
LL (out of sample)	−968.24	−992.47	−710.28	−925.09

Table 1 reports results and parameter estimates. For inexperienced subjects, adding sophistication to adaptive EWA improves log likelihood (LL) substantially both in- and out-of-sample. The estimated fraction of sophisticated players is $\hat{\alpha} = .236$ and their estimated perception $\hat{\alpha}' = 0$. The consideration parameter δ is estimated to be .781.

Experienced subjects show a larger improved fit from adding sophistication, and a larger estimated proportion, $\hat{\alpha} = .752$. (Their perceptions are again too low, $\hat{\alpha}' = .413$, showing a degree of overconfidence.) The increase in sophistication due to experience reflects a kind of "cross-period" learning which is similar to rule learning (Stahl, 2003).

Figure 2a shows actual choice frequencies for experienced subjects across the ten periods. Figures 2b–2d show predicted frequencies for choice reinforcement, weighted fictitious play, and sophisticated EWA. Figure 2b shows that reinforcement learns far too slowly because only one player wins each period and the losers get no reinforcement. [The reinforcement model in Roth and Erev (1995) has a simpler problem in games with proposer competition, which they circumvent by reinforcing ex post winning strategies in a way much like EWA updating.] Figure 2c shows that belief models with low values of ϕ, update beliefs very quickly but do not capture anticipatory learning, in which subjects anticipate that others will best-respond and leapfrog ahead. As a result, the frequency of low choices (1–10) predicted by belief learning only grows from 20% in period 5 to 35% in period 10, while the actual frequencies grow from 40% to 55%. Adding sophistication (Figure 2d) captures those actual frequencies quite closely.

An important implication of sophistication we are exploring in current research is "strategic teaching" (Camerer, Ho, and Chong, 2002a, 2002b): Sophisticated players who are matched with the same players repeatedly may have an incentive to "teach" adaptive players, choosing strategies with poor short-run payoffs which will change what adaptive players do, in a way that benefits the sophisticated player (e.g., Fudenberg and Levine, 1989; Watson, 1993). Strategic teaching provides a learning-based foundation to theories of reputation formation and appears to fit better than type-based equilibrium approaches (even allowing for quantal response) in experimental data on

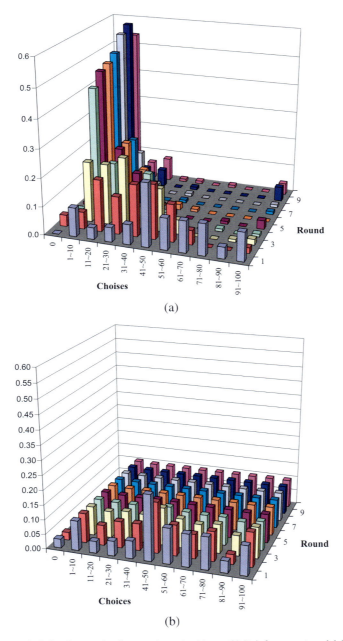

Figure 2. (a) Actual choice frequencies for experienced subjects. (b) Reinforcement model frequencies for experienced subjects. (c) Belief learning model frequencies for experienced subjects. (d) Sophisticated EWA model frequencies for experienced subjects.

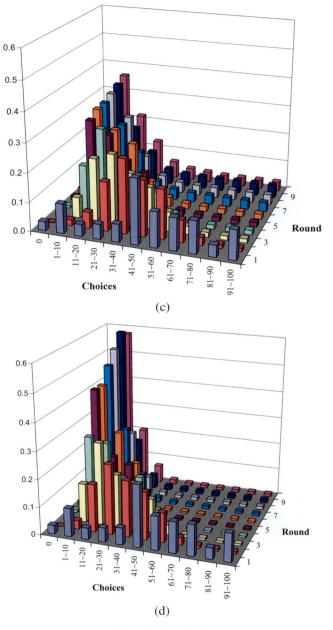

Figure 2. (*continued*)

repeated entry deterrence (chain-store; Jung, Kagel, and Levin, 1994) and trust games (Camerer and Weigelt, 1988).

References

Camerer, Colin.F. (2002). "Behavioral Game Theory: Experiments on Strategic Interaction". Princeton University Press, Princeton.
Camerer, Colin F., Ho, Teck-Hua (1998). "EWA learning in normal-form games: Probability rules, heterogeneity and time-variation". Journal of Mathematical Psychology 42, 305–326.
Camerer, Colin F., Ho, Teck-Hua (1999). "Experience-weighted attraction learning in normal-form games". Econometrica 67, 827–874.
Camerer, Colin F., Weigelt, Keith (1988). "An experimental test of a sequential equilibrium reputation model". Econometrica 56, 1–36.
Camerer, Colin F., Ho, Teck-Hua, Chong, Juin-Kuan (2002a). "Sophisticated experience-weighted attraction learning and strategic teaching in repeated games". Journal of Economic Theory 104, 137–188.
Camerer, Colin F., Ho, Teck-Hua, Chong, Juin-Kuan (2002b). "Strategic teaching and equilibrium models of repeated trust and entry games". Caltech working paper, http://www.hss.caltech.edu/camerer/camerer.html.
Fudenberg, Drew, Levine, David (1998). "The Theory of Learning in Games". MIT Press, Cambridge.
Fudenberg, Drew, Levine, David (1989). "Reputation and equilibrium selection in games with a patient player". Econometrica 57, 759–778.
Ho, Teck-Hua, Chong, Juin-Kuan (1999). "A parsimonious model of SKU choice: Familiarity-based reinforcement and response sensitivity". Wharton Department of Marketing.
Ho, Teck-Hua, Camerer, Colin, Chong, Juin Kuan. (2001). "Economic value of EWA Lite: A functional theory of learning in games". Unpublished, http://www.hss.caltech.edu/camerer/camerer.html.
Ho, Teck-Hua, Camerer, Colin, Weigelt, Keith (1998). "Iterated dominance and iterated best-response in p-beauty contests". American Economic Review 88 (4), 947–969.
Jung, Yun Joo, Kagel, John H., Levin, Dan (1994). "On the existence of predatory pricing: An experimental study of reputation and entry deterrence in the chain-store game". RAND Journal of Economics 25, 72–93.
McKelvey, Richard D., Palfrey, Thomas R. (1998). "Quantal response equilibria for extensive form games". Experimental Economics 1, 9–41.
Roth, Alvin E., Erev, I. (1995). "Learning in extensive-form games: Experimental data and simple dynamic models in the intermediate term". Games and Economic Behavior, 164–212.
Selten, Reinhard (1986). "Anticipatory learning in 2-person games". University of Bonn Discussion Paper Series B.
Stahl, Dale (2003). "Sophisticated learning and learning sophistication". Working paper, University of Texas at Austin.
Watson, Joel (1993). "A 'reputation' refinement without equilibrium". Econometrica 61, 199–205.

PART 5

MECHANISM DESIGN AND POLICY APPLICATIONS

5. MECHANISM DESIGN AND POLICY APPLICATIONS

Early in the development of experimental economics interest emerged in using the lab as a test bed for mechanism design and the examination of public policy questions. Thus, a long standing debate as to the procedures used by the US Treasury in the primary auction of treasury bills and notes led Smith (1967) to compare the uniform price with the "as bid" price discrimination mechanism in a laboratory market environment like that faced by dealers in the Treasury's primary auction. This helped to motivate the US Treasury under George Schultz to conduct a series of 16 bond issues – 10 uniform price competitive and 6 discriminative – all conducted in the early to mid 1970s. This was a nice example of a substantive change in policy that was assisted by first by laboratory and then by field experiments, but many examples emerged during the 35-year debate.

The public policy issue of posted pricing versus negotiated pricing in rail and barge competition led Hong and Plott (1977) to examine it in the laboratory, and this led to a reexamination of rail-barge regulatory policy.

5.1. Abstract, Theory Driven

Public goods theory going back to Wicksell, Lindahl and Samuelson had long called attention to the incentive problem in the provision of goods with a common outcome for many or all agents. Hence there was adequate motivation in the theory literature to fuel interest in studying these incentive issues in the laboratory. Further impetus was provided by the path breaking work of Vickery, independently reexamined in the innovations by Clark, Groves and Ledyard a decade or so later.

In this section, Chen provides a survey of the theoretical literature on incentive compatible mechanisms and a large number of experiments designed to test the ability of these mechanisms to solve the free rider problem and predict the outcomes achieved by groups of cash motivated subjects in the laboratory. He also points out the many gaps in this literature – not all mechanisms have been tested, and equilibrium selection issues have not been examined.

Rassenti and Smith summarize their early published work introducing the concept of the combinatorial auction based on Rassenti's 1981 PhD dissertation at the University of Arizona. The combinatorial auction allows products, consisting of packages of elemental items, or characteristics, to be defined by the buyers who bid for the combinations they prefer, allowing the market to define the composition of the products in final demand. Although this was a contribution to basic auction design, theory, and testing, it was motivated by the move to deregulate airline routes in the late 1970s. Landing and take-off rights provide an excellent example of a product packaging problem in which all the relevant information for assembling optimal packages is dispersed among the buyers. For these cases a mechanism that better aggregates that widely dispersed and heterogeneous information is of paramount importance.

The combinatorial auction is a special case of the more general concept of the smart, computer-assisted electricity market now widely applied in liberalized electrical power systems. It is also making inroads in a great variety of other applications.

5.2. Applied, Problem Driven

In the control of air and other forms of pollution in the economic theory literature, the traditional approach has been to recommend an optimal per-unit tax on those emissions creating the pollution. An equivalence theorem shows that an optimal pollution quota system is associated with the optimal tax. This classical approach is not useful because it is based on an institution-free static analysis that begs all the important questions of how to implement a control system; it represents one of the many examples of how experimental economics changes the way one thinks about economic theory and policy.

A tax arbitrarily, and therefore unfairly, impacts firms with higher abatement costs who need time to adapt, and any given tax may be too high or too low to incentivize the target reduction in carbon, sulfur, nitrogen oxides, or other emissions. Knowing how much to reduce emissions does not tell regulators the tax level needed to target that reduction. Failing to understand this principle invites government policy makers to favor taxes as a means of collecting revenue rather than an indirect control device. Information on abatement cost is dispersed among all emitters and is not given to any one individual, including in particular the regulator who is most in need of the required information. It is far better to set the aggregate target directly – however hazardous this is in the absence of a mechanism for determining the willingness-to-pay for clean air – and adjust it marginally over time as needed based on continuous observation. The tightening schedule of allowable emissions over time motivates the exchange of permits from those whose permits can fetch a price higher than their abatement cost to those for whom abatement costs are greater than the permit price. The market price that emerges for the emission rights enables emitters to plan ahead for introducing abatement technologies. Simultaneously, it allows those emitters who face higher cleanup costs to buy time before facing bankruptcy, and perhaps avoid it, in the event that technical innovations induced by the price of the permits lowers the cost of clean up.

Many technical issues arise in the design of a practical pollution control system. Mestleman and Muller discuss the problem that firms do not have perfect advance information on their emission levels, and Cason provides a survey spotlighting the importance of the institution in pollution abatement. If no allowance is made for the lack of perfect information on a firm's emissions, end period spikes in permit prices cause inefficiencies to occur as well as random and unnecessary redistributions of income. Mestleman and Muller explore the option of allowing permits to be "banked" in advance to cover this uncertainty. Another device, such as staggered permit expiration dates, is part of Cason's discussion of the many important institutional details in practical emissions control. Cason also discusses the EPA acid rain auction as an example of poor auction design, spotlighting the importance of thorough laboratory testing of any proposed design and comparison to alternatives before it is introduced into the field. The kinds of design errors commonly discovered during laboratory experiments are easily exposed and corrected because the issues are grouped around the problem of whether or not incentives are compatible with the desired public outcome.

Cox and Isaac use a model of cost information asymmetry in procurement contracting to derive hypotheses for experimental testing. They treat two objectives that government is likely to have in procurement contracting: (1) minimization of the budgetary cost of making the purchases; (2) the promotion of efficient allocations. Among other results, they find that budgetary cost minimization and the maximization of economic efficiency can be conflicting objectives when there is a cost information asymmetry between the parties to a procurement contract.

Rassenti and Smith offer three entries dealing with some of the many issues they have investigated in the smart, computer-assisted economic design and testing of electric power markets. The reports they summarize and many other studies they cite provided an important basis for the liberalization of electricity in New Zealand and Australia, and served to explicitly inform – alas to no political avail – the management requirements for effective deregulation in California. Their first entry provides an introduction to the issues that arise in electric market design, and to an elementary treatment of network power engineering and the resulting constraints on network prices that must be honored by an efficient smart market design.

The next entry uses experimental methods to study what should be the rules governing the bidding process in the spot market, and how transmission should be priced for short run efficiency in network allocations. These two questions are examined in a regime in which the number of independent generators is not systematically varied, and in which extensive interruptible demand side bidding is postulated. Moreover the network is an elementary radial system approximating those used in small countries such as the United Kingdom, New Zealand and Australia.

The last Rassenti–Smith entry studies how the existence of large must-serve inelastic loads impact market performance, and how markets can be used to provide both energy reserves and energy supplies in complex multi-node networks. In this case, a complex, nine-node network is used in a distributed power supply system consisting of 144 generators. Both the network and the generator parameters were those characterizing the south-east region of the United States.

The two experimental studies summarized illustrate contrasting degrees of complexity in laboratory experiments: a simple system in which certain kinds of behavioral questions can be answered with a minimum of confounding elements; a complex system to examine issues of feasibility, proof of concept and interactive behavior not addressable in smaller designs.

Chao and Plott examine a simple three node electric network in which inadvertent so called "loop flows" can occur as in any alternating current (AC) network where flows are famously controlled by the physics of the network. (There exists nothing comparable to "valves" in AC networks, as in pipeline networks.) As in previous experimental studies of gas pipeline networks, suppliers submit location-specific asks, demanders submit location-specific bids, and transmission rights holders submit arc-specific asking prices for capacity. Again, as in previous gas pipeline experiments, smart optimization support is provided by linear programming algorithms, except that transmission prices are zero if none of the line constraints are binding. This is because the experiments assume no energy loss in transmission; otherwise, nodal transmission prices would reflect the marginal cost of lost power in each line as in the entries by Rassenti and Smith.

5.3. From the Lab to the Field

Camerer asks whether asset markets can be manipulated by making purchases that are observed by others, inducing them to enter and buy more, thus driving up the price. The context is horse race betting where the rules of the track allow bets to be canceled at the last minute. His field experiment involved heavy betting on long shots, e.g., 50 to 1, then canceling them at no cost to his temporary experimental purse budget. A matched long-odds control horse was not bet on for comparison. Betting is very thin on these horses so that by placing many $500 and $1000 bets there exists a good chance of influencing the market odds. The results suggest that it may be possible to weakly manipulate asset market prices, but it proved hard to move the market by much, making it plain that those who believe that such markets are readily manipulated will find little comfort in this study, a finding reminiscent of the historical demise of the Hunt fortune in his attempt to manipulate the price of silver.

Bohn provides three entries reporting on field experiments: the diverse topics include pollution permit trading, the demand for each of two public goods, and the evaluation of employment subsidies. In the emissions study, the first test investigated the cost effectiveness of international emissions trading within a group of four small countries using negotiating teams from their energy ministries. The second examined the acceptability of a tradable-quota proposal, using Swedish diplomats from the study countries.

In his second entry, Bohm reports two path-breaking public good field experiments conducted in 1969 and 1982. In the first, a random sample of Stockholm residents were asked to participate in a new type of TV rating. The test was designed by Bohm, and conducted by the Swedish public TV company. Various procedures for sharing the cost were then applied to different groups who could watch the program if and only if their total WTP covered the program cost. Under all the cost sharing procedures the public good was chosen with no significant difference in the WTP for the different groups. In a control treatment group hypothetical responses were solicited and, consistent with more recent contingent valuation methodologies, they significantly overstated WTP compared to the other treatment groups.

In the second test, the public good was a statistical data package that could only be made available by the government while the decision to produce the package was to be determined by the 279 local governments who might use the package. Total willingness-to-pay exceeded cost in each of two treatments.

These and a series of laboratory public good experiments in the 1970s consistently established the finding that various simple practical cost allocation mechanisms enabled small and even large groups to overcome the free rider problem in the case where a public good could be provided if and only if sufficient funds were forthcoming – the group excludability principle.

Berg, Forsythe, Nelson and Reitz report results from a unique innovation by experimental economists: the Iowa Presidential Market (IPM). This market was the best known in the class of futures markets that have been designed to predict public events ranging from election outcomes to a corporation's sales. Whereas election polls ask people who they will vote for, traders in the IPM and other election markets must ask who all the voters will vote for, and take positions in candidate shares based on their answer. Similar candidate elections have been run in many states and countries throughout the world. Compared with the polls, election markets average somewhat lower final prediction error (1.5% versus 1.9%), are closer to the final outcome over their history and are less volatile over that history.

The contingent valuation method (CVM) is a hypothetical survey instrument that has been widely used and promoted in the assessment of environmental resource damages. Harrison and Rutström discuss the crucial issue of whether there is bias in CVM instruments arising from the fact that both the policy being evaluated and its damage prevention value are hypothetical with weak and distorted private incentives for respondents to accurately reveal their preferences. In these settings the question is whether people overstate their true evaluations. They provide a comprehensive review of a wide range of experiments allowing the existence of hypothetical bias to be determined, concluding that the existence of such bias, while highly variable, is persistent and cannot be ignored in the use of CVM instruments.

References

Hong, James T., Plott, Charles R. (1977). "Implications of rate filing for domestic dry bulk transportation on inland waters: An experimental approach". Social Science Working Paper No. 164, California Institute of Technology, Pasadena.

Smith, Vernon L. (1967). "Experimental studies of discrimination versus competition in sealed-bid auction markets". Journal of Business 40 (1), 56–84.

PART 5.1

ABSTRACT, THEORY DRIVEN

Yan Chen, "Incentive-compatible Mechanisms for Pure Public Goods: A Survey of Experimental Research"

Stephen J. Rassenti and Vernon L. Smith, "The Combinatorial Auction"

Chapter 67

INCENTIVE-COMPATIBLE MECHANISMS FOR PURE PUBLIC GOODS: A SURVEY OF EXPERIMENTAL RESEARCH

YAN CHEN

School of Information, The University of Michigan, Ann Arbor, MI 48109-1092, USA
e-mail: yanchen@umich.edu

1. Introduction

The presence of public goods seriously challenges traditional or "natural" solutions for the allocation of private goods. Important policy questions, of whether we can rely on the market to provide optimal amounts of public goods such as air pollution, and how much we can rely on "natural" processes such as voluntary contribution to solve environmental problems, boil down to fundamental issues about human nature, i.e., about whether people are selfish or cooperative. There has been an extensive experimental literature that tried to answer this question and to evaluate the extent of the free-rider problem in environments with public goods. Ledyard (1995) concluded in his survey that

> "although inexperienced subjects can be led to provide large contributions in one-time decisions with the use of relevant discussions, one cannot rely on these approaches as a permanent organizing feature without expecting an eventual decline to self-interested behavior.[1] ... Since 90 percent of subjects seem to be responsive to private incentives, it is possible to create new mechanisms which focus that self-interest toward the group interest." (p. 173, "Public Goods: A Survey of Experimental Research." In: *The Handbook of Experimental Economics*, 1995.)

This article surveys experimental research on these "new mechanisms," i.e., incentive-compatible mechanisms for pure public goods.

1.1. Theoretical Results and Unresolved Issues

Hurwicz (1972) formally introduced the concept of incentive compatibility, which captures the forces for individual self-interested behavior. The theory of mechanism design treats incentive compatibility as a constraint on the choice of procedures used to make group allocation decisions in various economic contexts. The task of the mechanism

---

[1] Mark and Matthews (2000) consider the dynamic private provision of a public project. They show that under certain conditions perfect Bayesian equilibria exist that essentially complete the project.

designer, therefore, is to find a mechanism such that the performance of the mechanism under an *assumed behavioral rule* is consistent with some normative performance criterion (e.g., Pareto-efficiency) given a class of environments. Experiments confront theory in these assumed behavioral rules.

"A fundamental, but generally unstated axiom of non-cooperative behavior is that if an individual has a dominant strategy available, he will use it" (Groves and Ledyard, 1987, p. 56) Therefore, theoretically it is desirable to design dominant strategy mechanisms, i.e., mechanisms which are non-manipulable. However, by now it is well known that it is impossible to design a mechanism for making collective allocation decisions, which is informationally decentralized, non-manipulable and Pareto optimal. This impossibility has been demonstrated in the work of Green and Laffont (1977), Hurwicz (1975), Roberts (1979), Walker (1980) and Mailath and Postlewaite (1990) in the context of resource allocation with public goods. The Vickrey–Clarke–Groves mechanism (Vickrey, 1961; Clarke, 1971; Groves, 1973; Groves and Loeb, 1975) admits dominant strategies but the allocation is not fully Pareto-efficient.

There are many "next-best" mechanisms which preserve Pareto optimality at the cost of non-manipulability, some of which preserve "some degree" of non-manipulability. Some mechanisms have been discovered which have the property that Nash equilibria are Pareto optimal. These can be found in the work of Groves and Ledyard (1977), Hurwicz (1979), Walker (1981), Tian (1989), Kim (1993), Peleg (1996), Falkinger (1996) and Chen (2002). Other implementation concepts include perfect Nash equilibrium (Bagnoli and Lipman, 1989), undominated Nash equilibrium (Jackson and Moulin, 1992), subgame perfect equilibrium (Varian, 1994b), strong equilibrium (Corchon and Wilkie, 1996), and the core (Kaneko, 1977), etc. Apart from the above non-Bayesian mechanisms, Ledyard and Palfrey (1994) propose a class of Bayesian Nash mechanisms for public goods provision.

To make any of these mechanisms operational and put it to use as an actual economic process that solves fundamental social problems, it is important to observe and evaluate the performance of the mechanism in the context of actual decision problems faced by real people with real incentives. These situations can be created and carefully controlled in a laboratory. When a mechanism is put to test in a laboratory, behavioral assumptions made in theory are most seriously challenged. More specifically,

1. Perfect vs Bounded Rationality: theory assumes that people are perfectly rational. As a result they can reach the equilibrium instantaneously through introspection. Since real people are boundedly rational, they need to learn by trial and error. This leads to an important aspect of mechanism design that has not received much attention: does a mechanism provide incentives for agents to learn?
2. Static vs Dynamic Games: since perfectly rational agents can reach equilibrium instantaneously, it is sufficient to restrict attention to static games. When a mechanism is implemented among boundedly rational agents, we expect the actual implementation to be a dynamic process, starting somewhere off the equilibrium path. This raises two questions:

(a) Can the learning dynamics lead to convergence to one of the equilibria promised by theory?
(b) What learning algorithms should be used to study the dynamic stability of a mechanism? This question can only be answered by estimating a rich repertoire of learning algorithms across a wide variety of experiments.
3. The Dominant Strategy Axiom: will agents use dominant strategies? If not, what other aspects might be important?
4. Learnability: what aspects of a mechanism might help agents to learn to play their Nash equilibrium strategies?
5. Refinement Criteria: do people learn to follow certain refinements of Nash equilibrium?

Despite the proliferation of theoretical literature on incentive-compatible mechanisms there have not been many experimental studies of these mechanisms. The existing experimental research on incentive-compatible mechanisms provides some data on the dynamic paths of these mechanisms when they are implemented among boundedly rational individuals. Some of these data have been used to investigate new theories on the dynamic stability of these mechanisms, incorporating bounded rationality and learning. The combination of theory and experimental results is likely to provide a fresh perspective on the mostly static implementation theory. They also raise many interesting questions, which call for further experimental as well as theoretical investigations.

1.2. Economic Environments in Experiments

Before reviewing the experimental results, we first introduce notation and the economic environment. Most of the experimental implementations of incentive-compatible mechanisms use a simple environment. Usually there is one private good x, one public good y, and $n \geqslant 3$ players, indexed by subscript i. Production technology for the public good exhibits constant returns to scale, i.e., the production function, $f(\cdot)$, is given by $y = f(x) = x/b$, for some $b > 0$. Preferences are largely restricted to the class of quasilinear preferences.[2] Let E represent the set of transitive, complete and convex individual preference orderings, $\geqslant_i$, and initial endowments, w_i^x. We formally define E^Q as follows.

DEFINITION 1. $E^Q = \{(\geqslant_i, w_i^x) \in E : \geqslant_i$ is representable by a C^2 utility function of the form $v_i(y) + x_i$ such that $Dv_i(y) > 0$ for all $y > 0$, and $w_i^x > 0\}$, where D^k is the kth order derivative.

The chapter is organized as follows. Section 2 reviews experimental studies of dominant strategy mechanisms. Section 3 reviews experiments on Nash-efficient mechanisms and introduces theoretical results on the convergence of these mechanisms. Section 4

---

[2] Smith (1980), Harstad and Marrese (1982) and Falkinger et al. (2000) are exceptions.

reviews experiments on mechanisms, which use refinements of Nash as implementation concepts. Section 5 reviews experiments on the Smith Auction. Section 6 concludes the chapter.

2. Dominant Strategy Mechanisms

When preferences are quasi-linear, the Vickrey–Clarke–Groves (VCG) mechanism is strategy-proof, where reporting one's preferences truthfully is always a dominant strategy. It has also been shown that any strategy-proof mechanism selecting an efficient public decision at every profile must be of this type (Green and Laffont, 1977). A special case of the Vickrey–Clarke–Groves mechanism is known as the pivotal mechanism. The pivotal mechanism has been tested in the field and laboratory by various groups of researchers.

Scherr and Babb (1975) compare the pivotal mechanism with the Loehman–Whinston mechanism in the laboratory, where human subjects played robots programmed to reveal their preferences. Preferences of subjects were not controlled by using the induced value method. They used two types of public goods, which were of no clear value to the subjects. Furthermore, the subjects were deceived about the situation. Therefore, it is not possible to draw conclusions about the performance of the pivotal mechanism based on this experiment.

Tideman (1983) reports field experiments in college fraternities, using the pivotal mechanism for real collective decisions. First, as in field experiments it is impossible to control the subjects' preferences. Second, dominant strategies were explained to the subjects, in which case we do not know whether the mechanism itself can induce the subjects to reveal their true preferences without prompting. Third, some of the initial endowments went to the fraternity, which redistributed the money afterwards. This clearly distorted the incentives of the mechanism. In the questionnaire, 21% of the subjects reported overstating their preferences, while 46% reported understating their preferences. Without induced value, it is difficult to evaluate the performance of the pivotal mechanism, such as the extent and magnitude of misrevelation.

Attiyeh, Franciosi and Isaac (forthcoming) report the first well-controlled laboratory experiments on the pivotal mechanism. They reported results from eight independent sessions under two different designs. Design I consisted of a group of five subjects. Design II consisted of a group of ten subjects by replicating the economy of Design I. In each of ten periods the subjects participated in a public goods provision decision-making task. It cost zero to produce the public good, which was of a fixed size. The collective decision was binary, to produce the good or not. The pivotal mechanism was compared to that of a majority rule. Individual values for the public good were sometimes negative and sometimes positive, redrawn each period from the same uniform distribution. Four striking results came from Attiyeh, Franciosi and Isaac (forthcoming):

1. Misrevelation: very few subjects reveal their true valuations. About 10% of the separate bids in Design I and 8% of the separate bids in Design II were truthfully revealing their values.
2. Pattern of misrevelation:
   (a) Positive values: overbid on low values and underbid on high values;
   (b) Negative values: underbid on low values and overbid on high values;
   (c) Bids are closest to value for medium high and medium low draws.
3. Efficiency: 70% of the decisions were efficient. This did not exceed the efficiency of majority rule (also 70%).
4. No-Learning: there was no convergence tendency towards value revelation. This result is similar to the experimental results on second-price auctions, where learning to bid one's true valuation shows little evidence of occurring with experience (e.g., Kagel, 1995, p. 511).

These results raise many questions that should lead to further study of the VCG mechanisms in the public goods context. The failure of most subjects to reveal their true values suggests that the dominant strategy is not transparent.

A recent study by Kawagoe and Mori (2001) analyzes the weakness of incentive compatibility of the pivotal mechanism as a cause for misrevelation. As in Attiyeh, Franciosi, and Isaac (2000), they study the pivotal mechanism in the context of a binary decision-making task to determine whether or not to produce a public project of a fixed size. They conjecture that misrevelation might be due to the fact that the pivotal mechanism is only weakly dominant strategy incentive-compatible. That is, within certain ranges of the strategy space an agent can be indifferent between truth-telling and other strategies. Therefore, an agent might not be able to find the unique dominant strategy without comprehensive understanding of the entire payoff structure. They suggest that one could overcome the problem of weak incentive compatibility by giving the subjects more information about the payoff structure.

Their design has three information treatments. In the Non-Enforcement treatment, each subject was assigned a fixed value and the mechanism was explained without a payoff table. In the Wide Enforcement treatment, each subject was randomly assigned values each round and the mechanism was explained without a payoff table, which is very similar to Attiyeh, Franciosi, and Isaac (2000). In the Deep Enforcement treatment, each subject was assigned a fixed value and given a detailed payoff table. The percentage of truthfully revealing bids was 17% in the Non-Enforcement treatment, 14% in the Wide Enforcement treatment and 47% in the Deep Enforcement treatment. The percentage of public project realized (i.e., efficient decisions) was 40% in the Non-Enforcement treatment, 70% in the Wide Enforcement treatment and 90% in the Deep Enforcement treatment. Overall, more detailed information about the payoff structure significantly improved the rate of dominant strategy play.

Kawagoe and Mori (2001) identified one aspect of the pivotal mechanism, which might have lead to misrevelation. Apart from the weakness of incentive compatibility, the pivotal mechanism provides very little incentives for the subjects to learn their dominant strategies over time. The incentives to learn are provided by connecting non-equilibrium behavior with the resulting losses. In the binary version of the pivotal mechanism, an agent is rarely pivotal in a relatively large economy. Therefore, even if an agent submitted non-equilibrium strategies, her payoff is hardly affected. Note that in the non-binary version of the VCG mechanisms, i.e., when the public goods level is continuous, an agent's message is much more likely to affect the total level of production. Therefore, a non-equilibrium message will result in tax that affects an agent's payoff. Furthermore, strictly convex preferences and continuous levels of public goods are necessary and sufficient for strict incentive compatibility (Kawagoe and Mori, 1998). It would be very interesting to see whether the continuous VCG mechanism has better performance in the laboratory.

3. Nash-efficient Mechanisms

The Groves–Ledyard mechanism Groves and Ledyard (1977) is the first mechanism in a general equilibrium setting, whose Nash equilibrium is Pareto optimal. The mechanism balances the budget both on and off the equilibrium path, but it does not implement Lindahl allocations. Later on, more game forms have been discovered, which implement Lindahl allocations in Nash equilibrium. These include Hurwicz (1979), Walker (1981), Tian (1989), Kim (1993), Peleg (1996), and Chen (2002). Falkinger (1996) presents a mechanism whose Nash equilibrium is Pareto optimal when a parameter is chosen appropriately, however, it does not implement Lindahl allocations and the existence of equilibrium can be delicate.

Most of the experimental studies of Nash-efficient mechanisms focus on the Groves–Ledyard mechanism. Chen and Tang (1998) also compare the Walker mechanism with the Groves–Ledyard mechanism. Falkinger et al. (2000) study the Falkinger mechanism. In all studies except Harstad and Marrese (1982) and Falkinger et al. (2000) quasilinear preferences were used to get a unique Nash equilibrium.[3]

Smith (1979a) reports the first sets of experiments studying various public goods mechanisms. He compared the performance of a voluntary contribution mechanism, a simplified version of the Groves–Ledyard mechanism,[4] and the Smith Auction. The process used in the simplified Groves–Ledyard mechanism was the Smith process, where all the subjects have the opportunity to simultaneously reconsider their messages and to repeat the same choices three times in a row to finalize the production of public goods, and they were paid when agreement was reached. The simplified Groves–Ledyard mechanism provided significantly more public goods than the voluntary contribution mechanism. In the five-subject treatment (R1), one out of three

---

[3] Bergstrom, Simon, and Titus (1983) show that the Groves–Ledyard mechanism can have a large number of Nash equilibria messages in a general environment. Each will yield an efficient allocation. So far there has been no experimental or theoretical work addressing the equilibrium selection problem in the Groves–Ledyard mechanism.

[4] This simplified version only balanced the budget in equilibrium.

sessions converged to the stage game Nash equilibrium. In the eight-subject replication with different parameters (R2), neither session converged to the Nash equilibrium prediction.

Harstad and Marrese (1981) compare the simplified version of the Groves–Ledyard mechanism under two different processes: the Smith process and the Seriatim process. The Seriatim process also requires unanimity of the subjects to produce the public good, but it differs from the Smith process in that subjects reconsider messages sequentially and only need to repeat their messages once for an iteration to end. They found that only three out of twelve sessions attained approximately Nash equilibrium outcomes.

Harstad and Marrese (1982) study the complete version of the Groves–Ledyard mechanism in Cobb–Douglas economies with the Seriatim process. In the three-subject treatment, one out of five sessions converged to the Nash equilibrium. In the four-subject treatment, one out of four sessions converged to one of the Nash equilibria. This is the only experiment which studied the Groves–Ledyard mechanism in an environment with multiple equilibria, but the equilibrium selection problem was not addressed.

Mori (1989) compares the performance of a Lindahl process with the Groves–Ledyard mechanism.[5] He used a dynamic process similar to the Smith process except that the process stops when each subject repeats her messages once. He ran five sessions for each mechanism, with five subjects in each session. The aggregate levels of public goods provided in each of the Groves–Ledyard sessions were much closer to the Pareto optimal level than those provided using a Lindahl process. On the individual level, each of the five sessions stopped within ten rounds when every subject repeated the same messages. However, since individual messages must be in multiples of .25 while the equilibrium messages were not on the grid, convergence to Nash equilibrium messages was approximate.

None of the above experiments study the effects of the punishment parameter,[6] γ, on the performance of the mechanism. It turns out that this punishment parameter plays an important role in the convergence and stability of the mechanism.

Chen and Plott (1996) first assessed the performance of the Groves–Ledyard mechanism under different punishment parameters. They found that by varying the punishment parameter the dynamics and stability changed dramatically. For a large enough γ, the system converged to its stage game Nash equilibrium very quickly and remained stable; while under a small γ, the system did not converge to its stage game Nash equilibrium. This finding was replicated by Chen and Tang (1998) with more independent sessions (twenty-one sessions: seven for each mechanism) and a longer time series (100 rounds) in an experiment designed to study the learning dynamics. Chen and Tang (1998) also studied the Walker mechanism in the same economic environment.

---

[5] I thank Toru Mori for providing the data and payoff tables for his experiments, Toshiji Kawagoe and Yo Nagai for the English translation.

[6] Roughly speaking, the punishment parameter in the Groves–Ledyard mechanism determines the magnitude of punishment if a player's contribution deviates from the mean of other players' contributions.

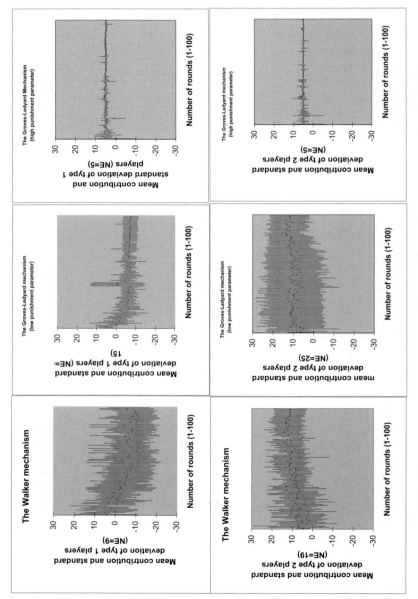

Figure 1. Each column presents the time series data under each mechanism from Chen and Tang (1998). Neither the Walker mechanism nor the Groves–Ledyard mechanism under a low punishment parameter converged to their stage game Nash equilibrium. The Groves–Ledyard mechanism under a high punishment parameter converged very quickly to its stage game Nash equilibrium and remained stable.

Figure 1 presents the time series data from Chen and Tang (1998) for two out of five types of players.[7] Each graph presents the mean (the black dots) and standard deviation (the error bars) for each of the two different types averaged over seven independent sessions for each mechanism – the Walker mechanism, the Groves–Ledyard mechanism under a low punishment parameter (hereafter GL1), and the Groves–Ledyard mechanism under a high punishment parameter (hereafter GL100). From these graphs, it is apparent that the Groves–Ledyard mechanism under a high punishment parameter converged very quickly to its stage game Nash equilibrium and remained stable, while the same mechanism did not converge under a low punishment parameter; the Walker mechanism did not converge to its stage game Nash equilibrium either.

Because of its good dynamic properties, GL100 had far better performance than GL1 and Walker, evaluated in terms of system efficiency, close to Pareto optimal level of public goods provision, less violations of individual rationality constraints and convergence to its stage game equilibrium. All these results are statistically highly significant.

These results illustrate the importance to design mechanisms, which not only have desirable static properties but also good dynamic stability properties. Only when the dynamics lead to the convergence to the static equilibrium, can all the nice static properties be realized.

Muench and Walker (1983) provide a sufficient condition for the Groves–Ledyard mechanism to converge under the Cournot best response dynamics with parameterized quasi-linear utility functions. Chen (1997) provides a necessary and sufficient condition for the GL mechanism to be a supermodular game given quasilinear preferences. Supermodular games are games in which each player's marginal utility of increasing her strategy rises with increases in her rival's strategies, so that (roughly) the player's strategies are "strategic complements." Supermodular games have very robust stability properties, in the sense that a large class of interesting learning dynamics converges to the set bounded by the largest and the smallest Nash equilibrium strategy profiles. This includes Bayesian learning, fictitious play, adaptive learning, Cournot best response and many others (Milgrom and Roberts, 1990). Therefore, Chen (1997) generalizes Muench and Walker's (1983) results to a more general class of preferences and a much wider class of learning dynamics.

OBSERVATION 1 (Chen, 1997). *The Groves–Ledyard mechanism is a supermodular game for any* $e \in E^Q$ *if and only if* $\gamma \in [-\min_{i \in N}\{\frac{\partial^2 v_i}{\partial y^2}\}n, +\infty)$.

Therefore, when the punishment parameter is above the threshold, a large class of interesting learning dynamics converge, which is consistent with the experimental results.

Falkinger et al. (2000) study the Falkinger mechanism in a quasilinear as well as a quadratic environment. In the quasilinear environment, the mean contributions moved

---

[7] The data for the remaining three types of players are not displayed due to limited space, but are available from the author upon request. They display very similar patterns.

towards the Nash equilibrium level but did not quite reach the equilibrium. In the quadratic environment the mean contribution level hovered around the Nash equilibrium, even though none of the 23 sessions had a mean contribution level exactly equal to the Nash equilibrium level in the last five rounds. Therefore, Nash equilibrium was a good description of the average contribution pattern, although individual players did not necessarily play the equilibrium. It is interesting to note that in the quadratic environment the game is *very close* to being a supermodular game: the threshold subsidy coefficient for the mechanism to be supermodular is one, while in the experiment it was set to 2/3. This is the only experimental study of Nash efficient public goods mechanisms that I am aware of, where parameters were set so close to the threshold.

The following observation organizes all experimental results on Nash-efficient mechanisms with available parameters, by looking at whether they are supermodular games.

OBSERVATION 2 (Chen, 1997). (1) None of the following experiments is a supermodular game: the Groves–Ledyard mechanism studied in Smith's (1979a) R2 treatment, Harstad and Marrese (1982), Mori (1989), Chen and Plott's (1996) low γ treatment, and Chen and Tang's (1998) low γ treatment, the Walker mechanism in Chen and Tang (1998) and Falkinger et al. (2000).

(2) The Groves–Ledyard mechanism under the high γ in Chen and Plott (1996) and Chen and Tang (1998) are both supermodular games.

These past experiments serendipitously studied supermodular mechanisms. The parameters were set either far away from the supermodular threshold (e.g., Chen and Plott, 1996; Chen and Tang, 1998) or very close to the threshold (e.g., Falkinger et al., 2000). None of the experiments systematically varies the parameters from below, close to, at and above the threshold to assess the effects of supermodularity on learning dynamics.

Two recent papers systematically study supermodular mechanisms. Arifovic and Ledyard (2003) conduct computer simulations of an individual learning model in the context of a class of the Groves–Ledyard mechanisms. They vary the punishment parameter systematically, from extremely small to extremely high. They find that their model converges to Nash equilibrium for all values of γ. However, the speed of convergence does depend on the value of the parameter. The speed of convergence is U-shaped: very low and very high values of γ require long periods for convergence, while a range of intermediate values requires the minimum time. In fact, the optimal punishment parameter identified in the simulation is much lower than the supermodularity threshold proposed in Observation 1. Since these results rely on the particular learning model used for the simulation, a natural next step would be to test the prediction in the laboratory with human subjects.

Chen and Gazzale (2002) is the first systematic experimental study of supermodular mechanisms, in the context of the compensation mechanisms. Results of this study is reviewed in Section 4.2.

Four specific game forms[8] implementing Lindahl allocations in Nash equilibrium have been introduced, Hurwicz (1979), Walker (1981), Kim (1993) and Chen (2002). All four improve on the Groves–Ledyard mechanism in the sense that they all satisfy the individual rationality constraint in equilibrium. While Hurwicz (1979) and Walker (1981) can be shown to be unstable for any decentralized adjustment process in certain quadratic environments,[9] the Kim mechanism is stable under a gradient adjustment process given quasilinear utility functions, which is a continuous time version of the Cournot–Nash tatônnement adjustment process. Whether the Kim mechanism is stable under other decentralized learning processes is still an open question.

OBSERVATION 3 (Chen, 1997). None of the Hurwicz (1979), Walker (1981) and Kim (1993) mechanisms is a supermodular game for any $e \in E^Q$. Chen (2002) provides a family of mechanisms, which are supermodular games for $e \in E^Q$.

Since supermodularity is sufficient but not necessary for convergence, this implies that:
1. supermodular mechanisms ought to converge to Nash equilibrium predictions fairly robustly, such as the Groves–Ledyard mechanism under a high punishment parameter;
2. mechanisms which are not supermodular could also converge to its equilibrium under some learning algorithms.

The open question is what learning rules are reasonable and descriptively accurate. Supermodularity provides a sufficient but not necessary condition for convergence under a wide range of learning dynamics. For a complete characterization of the stability of incentive compatible mechanisms, we need a sufficient and necessary condition for convergence under a wide range of learning dynamics, which remains to be found.

4. Mechanisms Using Refinements of Nash as Implementation Concepts

Mechanisms in this category use refinements of Nash equilibrium as the prediction of outcomes. Since there are multiple Nash equilibria, the convergence question is more complex. The behavioral question is whether individuals adopt strategies which support particular refinements of Nash equilibria.

4.1. Perfect Nash Mechanisms

Bagnoli and Lipman (1989) propose a very natural and simple mechanism, which fully implements the core in undominated perfect equilibria in an environment with one private good and a single unit of public good. In a complete information economy agents

---

[8] Since Tian (1989) and Peleg (1996) do not have specific mechanisms, we will only investigate the supermodularity of these four mechanisms.
[9] See Kim (1986).

voluntarily contribute any non-negative amount of the private good they choose and the social decision is to provide the public good if and only if contributions are sufficient to pay for it. The contributions are refunded otherwise. This result is extended to a public good with finitely many values, where a sequential game with several rounds of contributions implements the core in successively undominated perfect equilibria.

The mechanism in the single unit case is also called the provision-point mechanism in the experimental literature. (See Davis and Holt, 1993 and Ledyard, 1995 for a description of the mechanism and review of related public goods experiments.)

Bagnoli and McKee (1991) test the theoretical predictions of the one unit case in the laboratory. They reported results from seven five-person groups and two ten-person groups. All sessions were implemented as repeated games of 14 periods. Three different treatments were implemented among the five-subject groups: (1) a baseline treatment with homogeneous endowments and homogeneous valuations of the public good (one group), (2) homogeneous endowments and heterogeneous valuations (three groups), and (3) homogeneous endowments and homogeneous valuations (three groups). The two ten-person groups explored only treatments (1) and (2). The results of the Bagnoli and McKee (1991) study provide strong support for the hypothesis that groups will voluntarily contribute sufficient resources to provide the public good, and that group contributions will exactly equal the provision point. Pooling all five-person groups, the public good was provided in 86.7% of the rounds; the Pareto efficient outcome of contributions equal the provision point was observed 54.1% of the cases.

Note, however, there were very few independent sessions in each treatment of the Bagnoli and McKee (1991) study, which raised the question of the robustness of their results. Mysker, Olson, and Williams (1996) report a set of experiments designed to check the robustness of the Bagnoli and McKee (1991) results. They note that Bagnoli and McKee (1991) ran several independent groups simultaneously in the same room and publicly posted contributions for all groups. Bagnoli and McKee (1991) did not use a personal record sheet on which subjects logged their personal contributions and payoffs in each round. Mysker, Olson, and Williams (1996) used a design identical to the Bagnoli and McKee (1991) treatment (1) with homogeneous endowments and homogeneous public good valuation, which also addressed the behavioral effects of the two procedural modification – multiple, simultaneous groups vs single, isolated groups, and the use of a personal record sheet. The Mysker, Olson, and Williams (1996) data challenged the robustness of the Bagnoli and McKee (1991) results. In the Bagnoli and McKee (1991) study the efficient equilibrium contribution is a modal distribution, while in the Mysker, Olson, and Williams (1996) study contributions are evenly distributed along the strategy space.

Both studies have relatively few independent observations (at most three groups) for each treatment. We cannot conclude from the small body of data whether the provision-point mechanism studied in Bagnoli and Lipman works in a laboratory.

Bagnoli, Ben-David, and McKee (1992) report an experiment designed to test the provision-point mechanism for the multiple unit case. The design repeated the single unit case in Bagnoli and McKee (1991) over a sequence. They conducted two treatments: (1) subjects were reassigned to different groups between periods for 6–8 periods, and (2) subjects remained in the same group for the entire session of 15 periods. They found limited support for the prediction that subjects will play equilibrium strategies that achieve a core allocation. This result challenges the strong refinement criterion used in the theory paper. It could also result from the inability of the subjects to coordinate among the multiple equilibria.

Apart from the laboratory experiments, there have also been field experiments using variants of the provision-point mechanism, e.g., the Green Choice Program in upstate New York (Schulze, 1995). In field experiments the complete information assumption in Bagnoli and Lipman (1989) does not hold anymore. Properties of the mechanism under incomplete information are unclear. Other details of the mechanism have been studied as well, for example the effect of refund rules (Isaac, Schmidtz, and Walker, 1989), of rebate rules (Marks and Croson, 1998), of subject pool (Cadsby and Maynes, 1998a, 1998b), of identifiability of the contributors (Croson and Marks, 1998), of incomplete information about valuations (Marks and Croson, 1999), of incomplete information about the number of players or cost of the public good (Rondeau, Schulze, and Poe, 1999), of recommending contributions (Croson and Marks, 1999a), of valuations for the public good (Croson and Marks, 1999b), and of sequentiality of contribution (Coats and Gronberg, 1996). The simplicity of the provision-point mechanism justifies future research into the properties of the mechanism.

4.2. Subgame Perfect Mechanisms

Varian (1994a, 1994b) introduces a class of simple two-stage mechanisms, known as the compensation mechanisms, which implement efficient allocations as subgame-perfect equilibria for economic environments involving externalities and public goods. The basic idea is that each player offers to compensate the other for the "costs" incurred by making the efficient choice.

Andreoni and Varian (1999) report a series of experiments on a variation of the compensation mechanisms. In a particularly simple and elegant design, they considered a modified Prisoners' Dilemma game in which each agent can offer to pay the other agent to cooperate. The mechanism was implemented as card games. Each session consisted of two phases. The first phase was a baseline Prisoners' Dilemma game, called the "Push–Pull" game, which was run for 15 rounds with each subject playing against a different subject each round. The second phase added a contracting stage to the Prisoners' Dilemma, called the "Pay for Push" game, which was run for 25 rounds. They conducted a total of six independent sessions, with eight players per session.

The data show that the mechanism is largely successful at inducing cooperation. The amount of cooperation doubled (from 25.8% to 50.5%) during the second phase when the mechanism was implemented. Players made offers of side payments that should induce cooperation about 63.5% of the time. When such offers were received, subjects responded with cooperation nearly 70% of the time. Full efficient equilibrium was achieved in about 60% of the time. Interestingly, they also found subjects' tastes for cooperation and equity interact significantly with the incentives of the mechanism.[10]

Cheng (1998) studies the dynamic stability of the compensation mechanisms. He proved that the original mechanism is globally stable under the Cournot best response dynamics, but is not supermodular. He also proposed a generalized version of the compensation mechanism, which is supermodular. This generalized version is an excellent playground for studying supermodular mechanisms, as it has two free parameters, one for each type of players. One parameter "determines" whether the mechanism is supermodular, while the other does not play a role in this distinction. This gives the experimenter more freedom in choosing "varying degrees of supermodularity."

Chen and Gazzale (2002) experimentally study the generalized version of the compensation mechanism. They systematically vary the free parameter from below, close to, at and beyond the threshold of supermodularity to assess the effects of supermodularity on the performance of the mechanism. They have three main findings. First, in terms of proportion of equilibrium play and efficiency, they find that supermodular and "near supermodular" mechanisms perform significantly better than those far below the threshold. This finding is consistent with previous experimental findings. Second, they find that from a little below the threshold to the threshold, the improvement in performance is statistically insignificant. This result is important, as theory is silent on this issue. This implies that the performance of "near supermodular" mechanisms, such as the Falkinger mechanism, ought to be comparable to supermodular mechanisms. Therefore, the mechanism designer need not be overly concerned with setting parameters that are firmly above the supermodular threshold – close is just as good. This enlarges the set of robustly stable mechanisms. The third finding concerns the selection of mechanisms within the class of supermodular mechanisms. Again, theory is silent on this issue. Chen and Gazzale find that within the class of supermodular mechanisms, increasing the parameter far beyond the threshold does not significantly improve the performance of the mechanism. Furthermore, increasing another free parameter, which is not related to whether or not the mechanism is supermodular, does improve convergence. Simulation shows that these experimental results persist in the long run.

5. Other Mechanisms

The "Smith Auction" (1979a, 1979b, 1980) was a dynamic process designed for public goods provision. In this mechanism each agent first submit a bid and a proposed quantity of the public good. Each agent's tentative share of the unit cost is the unit cost minus the sum of other agents' bid. The tentative quantity of public good is the average of all agents' proposed quantities. Then each agent is given the right to veto or agree to his/her tentative share of the unit cost and the tentative quantity of the public goods.

---

[10] For a related theoretical analysis of altruism on the efficiency of public good mechanisms, see Clark (1999).

Group agreement prevails if and only if all players unanimously agree on accepting all the offers. The theoretical properties of this mechanism are not completely understood. However, leaving aside the equilibria of the supergame, the Smith Auction implements the Lindahl allocations in perfect Nash equilibrium in a "one-shot" static game (Banks, Plott, and Porter, 1988).

Smith (1979a) reports 12 sessions of auction experiments in three different environments, where valuation functions were quasilinear, with parameters such that zero contribution would be a dominant strategy for some but not all subjects in a voluntary contribution mechanism. In most sessions average proposals and bid sums were posted on every trial. Nine out of twelve sessions converged to the Pareto optimal quantity of public goods. However, only a small fraction of subjects (11 out of 67) converged to their Lindahl equilibrium bids.

Smith (1980) examines the Smith Auction in environments with income effects. Out of a total of 29 sessions only two sessions failed to reach agreement to provide units of the public good. All sessions that reached agreement provided much larger quantities of public goods than the free-rider quantity. The quantities were not predicted exactly by the Lindahl equilibrium quantity. In fact, the mean quantity is slightly larger than the Lindahl quantity. Compared to the results of Smith (1979a), with income effects, "the LE quantity of the public good is a fair predictor, and the LE bids a very poor predictor of experimental outcomes." (Smith, 1980, p. 597)

Banks, Plott, and Porter (1988) study the Smith Auction and a voluntary contribution mechanism both with and without an additional unanimity feature. They used quasilinear utility functions, where it was a strictly dominant strategy for each agent to contribute zero in a voluntary contribution mechanism. This experiment confirmed that the Smith Auction generated higher levels of public goods provision than the voluntary contribution mechanisms. Aggregate quantity of public goods was near the Pareto optimum. Interestingly, they also found that the inclusion of unanimity reduced the overall efficiency of the process, as well as the success rate of the mechanism. A puzzling result is that overall provision level (efficiency) fell with repetition for the Smith Auction without unanimity, while repetition did not significantly affect the efficiency of the Smith Auction with unanimity. This "no-learning" or decay result could be due to the fact that each session only lasts between three and nine periods.

6. Concluding Remarks

From the existing experimental studies of incentive-compatible mechanisms we can draw several conclusions:
1. Mechanisms with the same static properties can have dramatically different dynamic stability performances.
2. Under the pivotal mechanism it is possible to provide environments where misrevelation is prevalent. More information about the payoff structure help reduce the degree of misrevelation.

3. Available data show that supermodular mechanisms, such as the Groves–Ledyard mechanism under a high punishment parameter, converge robustly well to the Nash equilibrium. Mechanism close to the threshold of being supermodular converges reasonably well. Existing experiments on non-supermodular Nash mechanisms suggest that they did not converge well to the Nash equilibrium predictions.
4. Experiments and simulation show that the performance of "near supermodular" mechanisms ought to be comparable to supermodular mechanisms. Furthermore, within the class of supermodular mechanisms, increasing the parameter far beyond the threshold does not significantly improve the performance of the mechanism.
5. Performance of mechanisms using refinements of Nash as solution concepts is ambiguous. Experimental results could be sensitive to procedural specifications.

Existing experiments on incentive-compatible mechanisms have focused on a few mechanisms. The data, combined with theoretical investigation, give us a fresh perspective on implementation among real people. For these mechanisms that have been studied in the laboratory, we need more replications and robustness tests. Meanwhile, many mechanisms have never been tested in the laboratory. Equilibrium selection problem is almost untouched in this context. Therefore, more experiments should be conducted in this exciting field.

Acknowledgements

I thank Charles Plott for extensive comments on an earlier version, Mark Bagnoli, Rachel Croson, Robert Gazzale, John Kagel, John Ledyard, Bart Lipman, John Morgan, Vernon Smith, James Walker, Arlington Williams for helpful comments.

References

Andreoni, J., Varian, H. (1999). "Pre-play contracting in the prisoners' dilemma". Proceedings of the National Academy of Science 96, 10933–10938.
Arifovic, J. Ledyard, J. (2003). "Computer testbeds and mechanism design: Application to the class of Groves–Ledyard mechanisms for provision of public goods". Working paper, Computing in Economics and Finance 244.
Attiyeh, G., Franciosi, R., Isaac, M. (2000). "Experiments with the pivot process for providing public goods". Public Choice 102, 93–112.
Bagnoli, M., Lipman, B. (1989). "Provision of public goods: Fully implementing the core through private contributions". Review of Economic Studies 56, 583–602.
Bagnoli, M., McKee, M. (1991). "Voluntary contribution games: Efficient provision of public goods". Economic Inquiry 29, 351–366.
Bagnoli, M., Ben-David, S., McKee, M. (1992). "Voluntary provision of public goods: The multiple unit case". Journal of Public Economics 47, 85–106.
Banks, J., Plott, C., Porter, D. (1988). "An experimental analysis of unanimity in public goods provision mechanisms". Review of Economic Studies 55 (2), 301–322.
Bergstrom, Theodore, Simon, Carl P., Titus, Charles J. (1983). "Counting Groves–Ledyard equilibria via degree theory". Journal of Mathematical Economics 12 (2), 167–184.

Cadsby, C., Maynes, E. (1998a). "Choosing between a socially efficient and free-riding equilibrium: Nurses versus economics and business students". Journal of Economic Behavior and Organization 37, 183–192.

Cadsby, C., Maynes, E. (1998b). "Gender and free riding in a threshold public goods game: Experimental evidence". Journal of Economic Behavior and Organization 34, 603–620.

Chen, Y. (1997). "Supermodularity of Nash-efficient public goods mechanisms". University of Bonn SFB303 working paper. (Later circulated under the title, "Dynamic stability of Nash-efficient public goods mechanisms: Reconciling theory and experiments.").

Chen, Y. (2002). "A family of supermodular Nash mechanisms implementing Lindahl allocations". Economic Theory 19, 773–790.

Chen, Y., Gazzale, R. (2002). "Supermodularity and convergence: An experimental study of the compensation mechanism". Manuscript, University of Michigan.

Chen, Y., Plott, C.R. (1996). "The Groves–Ledyard mechanism: An experimental study of institutional design". Journal of Public Economics 59, 335–364.

Chen, Y., Tang, F.-F. (1998). "Learning and incentive compatible mechanisms for public goods provision: An experimental study". Journal of Political Economy 106 (3), 633–662.

Cheng, J. (1998). "Essays on designing economic mechanisms". Ph.D. thesis, University of Michigan.

Clark, J. (1999). "The effects of altruism on the efficiency of public good mechanisms". Working paper, University of Canterbury.

Clarke, Edward H. (1971). "Multipart pricing of public goods". Public Choice 11 (1), 17–33.

Coats, J., Gronberg, T. (1996). "Provision of discrete public goods: An experimental investigation of alternative institutions". Working paper, Texas A&M University.

Corchon, Luis, Wilkie, Simon (1996). "Double implementation of the ratio correspondence by a market mechanism". Review of Economic Design 2 (1), 325–337.

Croson, R., Marks, M. (1998). "Identifiability of individual contributions in a threshold public goods experiment". Journal of Mathematical Psychology 42, 167–190.

Croson, R., Marks, M. (1999a). "Equilibrium selection: Preplay communication and learning". Working paper, OPIM, The Wharton School, University of Pennsylvania.

Croson, R., Marks, M. (1999b). "Step returns in threshold public goods: A meta- and experimental analysis". Working paper, OPIM, The Wharton School, University of Pennsylvania.

Davis, D., Holt, C. (1993). "Experimental Economics". Princeton University Press, Princeton, NJ.

Falkinger, J. (1996). "Efficient private provision of public goods by rewarding deviations from average". Journal of Public Economics 62, 413–422.

Falkinger, J., Fehr, E., Gächter, S., Winter-Ebmer, R. (2000). "A simple mechanism for the efficient provision of public goods – Experimental evidence". American Economic Review 90, 247–264.

Green, J., Laffont, J.-J. (1977). "Characterization of satisfactory mechanisms for the revelation of the preferences for public goods". Econometrica 45, 427–438.

Groves, Theodore (1973). "Incentives in teams". Econometrica 41 (40), 617–631.

Groves, T., Ledyard, J. (1977). "Optimal allocation of public goods: A solution to the 'free rider' problem". Econometrica 45 (4), 783–809.

Groves, T., Ledyard, J. (1987). "Incentive compatibility since 1972". In: Groves, T., Radner, R., Reiter, S. (Eds.), Information, Incentives and Economic Mechanisms: Essays in Honor of Leonid Hurwicz. University of Minnesota Press, Minneapolis.

Groves, Theodore, Loeb, Martin (1975). "Incentives and public inputs". Journal of Public Economics 4 (3), 211–226.

Harstad, R.M., Marrese, M. (1981). "Implementation of mechanism by processes: Public good allocation experiments". Journal of Economic Behavior and Organization 2, 129–151.

Harstad, R.M., Marrese, M. (1982). "Behavioral explanations of efficient public good allocations". Journal of Public Economics 19, 367–383.

Hurwicz, L. (1972). "On informationally decentralized systems". In: McGuire, C., Radner, R. (Eds.), Decision and Organization. North-Holland, Amsterdam, pp. 297–336.

Hurwicz, Leonid (1975). "On the existence of allocation systems whose manipulative Nash equilibria are Pareto optimal". Presented at the Third World Congress of the Econometric Society, Toronto.

Hurwicz, L. (1979). "Outcome functions yielding Walrasian and Lindahl allocations at Nash equilibrium points". Review of Economic Studies, 217–225.

Isaac, R. Mark, Schmidtz, David, Walker, James M. (1989). "The assurance problem in a laboratory market". Public Choice 62 (3), 217–236.

Jackson, Matthew O., Moulin, Herve (1992). "Implementing a public project and distributing its cost". Journal of Economic Theory 57, 125–140.

Kagel, J. (1995). "Auctions: A survey of experimental research". In: Kagel, J., Roth, A. (Eds.), Handbook of Experimental Economics. Princeton University Press.

Kaneko, Mamoru (1977). "The ratio equilibrium and a voting game in a public goods economy". Journal of Economic Theory 16 (2), 123–136.

Kawagoe, T., Mori, T. (2001). "Can the pivotal mechanism induce truth-telling? An experimental study". Public Choice 108, 331–354.

Kawagoe, T., Mori, T. (1998). "A short report on pivotal mechanism experiment". Mimeo, Nagoya City University.

Kim, T. (1986). "On the nonexistence of a stable Nash mechanism implementing Lindahl allocations". Mimeo, University of Minnesota.

Kim, T. (1993). "A stable Nash mechanism implementing Lindahl allocations for quasi-linear environments". Journal of Mathematical Economics 22, 359–371.

Ledyard, J. (1995). "Public goods: A survey of experimental research". In: Kagel, J., Roth, A. (Eds.), Handbook of Experimental Economics. Princeton University Press.

Ledyard, John O., Palfrey, Thomas R. (1994). "Voting and lottery drafts as efficient public goods mechanisms". Review of Economic Studies 61, 327–355.

Mailath, G., Postlewaite, A. (1990). "Asymmetric information bargaining problems with many agents". Review of Economic Studies 57, 351–367.

Mark, L., Matthews, S. (2000). "Dynamic voluntary contribution to a public project". Review of Economic Studies 67, 327–358.

Marks, M., Croson, R. (1998). "Alternative rebate rules in the provision of a threshold public good: An experimental investigation". Journal of Public Economics 67, 195–220.

Marks, Melanie B., Croson, Rachel T.A. (1999). "The effect of incomplete information and heterogeneity in the provision point mechanism of voluntary contributions: An experimental investigation". Public Choice 99 (1–2), 103–118.

Milgrom, P., Roberts, J. (1990). "Rationalizability, learning and equilibrium in games with strategic complementarities". Econometrica 58 (6), 1255–1277.

Mori, T. (1989). "Effectiveness of mechanisms for public goods provision: An experimental study". Economic Studies 40 (3), 234–246.

Muench, T., Walker, M. (1983). "Are Groves–Ledyard equilibria attainable?" Review of Economic Studies 50, 393–396.

Mysker, M., Olson, P., Williams, A. (1996). "The voluntary provision of a threshold public good: Further experimental results". Research in Experimental Economics 6, 149–163.

Peleg, B. (1996). "Double implementation of the Lindahl equilibrium by a continuous mechanism". Economic Design 2, 311–324.

Roberts, J. (1979). "Incentives and planning procedures for the provision of public goods". Review of Economic Studies 46, 283–292.

Rondeau, Daniel, Schulze, William D., Poe, Gregory L. (1999). "Voluntary revelation of the demand for public goods using a provision point mechanism". Journal of Public Economics 72 (3), 455–470.

Scherr, B., Babb, E. (1975). "Pricing public goods: An experiment with two proposed pricing systems". Public Choice 21, 35–53.

Schulze, W. (1995). "Green pricing: Solutions for the potential free-rider problem". Mimeo, University of Colorado.

Smith, V. (1979a). "Incentive compatible experimental processes for the provision of public goods". In: Smith, V. (Ed.), Research in Experimental Economics, vol. 1. JAI Press Inc., Greenwich, CT.

Smith, V. (1979b). "An experimental comparison of three public goods decision mechanisms". Scandinavian Journal of Economics 81, 198–251.
Smith, V. (1980). "Experiments with a decentralized mechanism for public goods decision". American Economic Review 70, 584–599.
Tian, G. (1989). "Implementation of the Lindahl correspondence by a single-valued, feasible, and continuous mechanism". Review of Economic Studies 56, 613–621.
Tideman, T.N. (1983). "An experiments in the demand revealing process". Public Choice 41, 387–402.
Varian, Hal R. (1994a). "Sequential contributions to public goods". Journal of Public Economics 53 (2), 165–186.
Varian, Hal (1994b). "A solution to the problems of externalities when agents are well-informed". American Economic Review 84 (5), 1278–1293.
Vickrey, William S. (1961). "Counterspeculation, auctions, and competitive sealed tenders". Journal of Finance 16, 8–37.
Walker, M. (1980). "On the impossibility of a dominant strategy mechanism to optimally decide public questions". Econometrica 48, 1521–1540.
Walker, M. (1981). "A simple incentive compatible scheme for attaining Lindahl allocations". Econometrica 49, 65–71.

Chapter 68

THE COMBINATORIAL AUCTION

STEPHEN J. RASSENTI and VERNON L. SMITH

In the 1970s the airline industry was scheduled for deregulation. This meant that routes, flight schedules, and fares were to be freely chosen by individual airlines who were to be free to enter or exit any market for city pair service. Deregulating fares and the free movement of equipment among routes left open an important policy question: how should airport runway rights (time slots for the take-off or landing of aircraft to support airline flight schedules) be allocated? These rights have an important, and novel (but far from unique) characteristic: an airline's demand (willingness-to-pay) for a take-off slot is zero unless it is packaged with a landing slot at the flight destination airport. Moreover, a given flight may take off and land in a sequence of connected demand-interdependent segments that are required as a package to support a particular flight schedule.

Grether, Isaac, and Plott (1979, 1989) proposed a sequential procedure for using a primary sealed-bid auction, followed by an after-market, to achieve the allocation of slots. Under their proposal an independent primary market for slots at each airport would be organized as a sealed-bid competitive auction at timely intervals. Since this auction would allocate the primary resources, but did not make provision for package demand interdependence, a computerized version of the oral double auction, with block transaction capabilities, was proposed as an after market to allow the allocations to be adjusted for interdependent demand.

In this entry, we summarize a market mechanism for a "combinatorial" sealed-bid auction that was motivated by the airport slot problem under which bidders would submit bids for packages of slots that support their schedules. A more complete report is provided in Rassenti, Smith, and Bulfin (1982). Under this scheme, the elemental resources would be allocated only in the form of those combinations desired by the bidders. Under this scenario, the purpose of an after market would be to adjust for allocation errors in the primary market (the objective in the experiments reported below), or to adjust for post-primary market changes in demand. Although this form of combinatorial auction was never applied to airport runway rights, the issue of pricing runway slots has arisen in the new century as a means of managing airport congestion.

The combinatorial procedure below is not generally incentive compatible; i.e., if any bidder desires multiple units of either packages or elements, or multiple units of any element, then it may be to a bidder's advantage to strategically underbid the true value of a package. This has been known since Vickrey's (1961) remarkable paper, which provides the correct dominant strategy mechanism solution in which each bidder pays an amount equal to the opportunity cost(s) of the bidder(s) he/she displaces. Vickrey's solution is widely believed to be impractical for two reasons: (1) different agents pay different prices and it is thought that this creates a procedure too inscrutable to be acceptable to users; (2) in general, in two-sided versions, the budget is not balanced – sellers receive more than buyers pay.

The solution below, however, was simple and practical enough to be implemented in the laboratory, and yielded 98.5 to 99.3 percent of the maximum gains from exchange.

1. The Environment

We report experiments using both an "easy" and a "difficult" environment. Table 1 defines the "easy" combinatorial environment. (See Rassenti, Smith, and Bulfin, 1982, Appendix B.)

There are six agent bidders: 1, 2, ..., 6, and six elemental resource items, A, B, ..., F. Each row lists a package desired by some agent, with value to that agent listed in column 3 (1978 values in cents), and the composition of the package that consists of two or more of the elements. A package contains each element for which the integer, 1, appears in the column for that element. Thus, package 5, demanded by agent 2, has value 663, and consists of one each of the elements B and C. At the bottom of the table in the row for "# Units Demanded" appears the sum, across all 25 packages, of the maximum number of units of each resource item that are required to service the total package demand of all agents. Thus 15 units of item B would satisfy the maximum demand for item B from the 25 packages. The last row for "# Units Available" lists the total available supply of each resource item. Each item is scarce in the sense that more units are demanded than are in supply.

Table 1 is described as an "easy" combinatorial environment because (1) there is considerable replication of the demand for each package across subject agents; (2) there is considerable replication of the demand for the same elemental item across the packages of any one agent. Thus, only seven outlying '1s' are dispersed among items D, E. and F. Here Rassenti, Smith, and Bulfin (1982) followed Grether, Isaac, and Plott (1979, 1989) in introducing only a slight variation on an environment with a traditional non-combinatorial structure. The motivation is to create an environment that is favorable to the independent auction described below. Thus, a combinatorial auction may do worse (or at least no better) than an independent auction when applied to an environment with little combinatorial structure.

A more difficult combinatorial environment is shown in Table 2. In particular note that there is relatively little replication of the same package across agents, or of the same elemental item across the packages of any one agent; i.e., the pattern of '1s' are well dispersed across rows and columns. This environment is conjectured to be challenging to both the independent and combinatorial auction, but one for which the latter is more clearly suited.

Table 1
Easy resource utilization design

Agent	Package	Value	Item A	Item B	Item C	Item D	Item E	Item F
1	1	598	1	1				
1	2	946	1	1	1			
1	3	517		1	1			
2	4	632	1			1		
2	5	663		1	1			
2	6	951	1	1	1			
3	7	877	1	1				1
3	8	595	1		1			
3	9	515		1	1			
3	10	885	1	1	1			
4	11	546	1		1			
4	12	983	1		1			1
4	13	569	1	1				
4	14	603		1	1			
5	15	642	1	1				
5	16	450	1				1	
5	17	498		1	1			
5	18	913	1		1		1	
5	19	476	1		1			
6	20	576	1		1			
6	21	802		1	1	1		
6	22	439		1	1			
6	23	945	1		1			1
6	24	617	1		1			
6	25	520	1	1				
Units demanded			18	15	18	2	2	3
Units available			13	11	15	1	2	3

1.1. Two Market Mechanisms: The Independent Auction and the Combinatorial Auction

We compare two market mechanisms.

An Independent Auction (IA). The first, introduced by Grether, Isaac, and Plott (1979, 1989), begins with a primary market consisting of six uniform price sealed-bid auctions run simultaneously, one for each of the six elemental resources with induced combinatorial values as shown in Tables 1 and 2. Thus, in Table 1, 13 units of A are offered for sale and the 13 units are allocated to the 13 highest bidders at the 13th highest bid price. Similarly for B, C, ..., F. Individual allocations are private. The clearing prices for each resource are made public.

Table 2
Difficult resource utilization design

Agent	Package	Value	Item A	Item B	Item C	Item D	Item E	Item F
1	1	627	1	1				
1	2	577			1	1		
1	3	506	1				1	
1	4	825	1		1			1
1	5	834		1	1		1	
2	6	531	1	1				
2	7	556			1	1		
2	8	576	1		1			
2	9	644		1			1	
2	10	584			1		1	
2	11	886	1				1	1
3	12	517	1	1				
3	13	576			1	1		
3	14	887	1		1		1	
3	15	940		1	1			1
4	16	598	1	1				
4	17	627			1	1		
4	18	578	1					1
4	19	578		1		1		
4	20	556				1		1
4	21	861		1			1	1
5	22	560	1	1				
5	23	582			1	1		
5	24	565		1				1
5	25	834		1		1	1	
5	26	782	1			1		1
6	27	507	1	1				
6	28	565			1	1		
6	29	833		1		1		1
6	30	959	1			1	1	
# Units demanded			14	14	12	12	9	9
# Units available			7	7	7	7	7	7

A Combinatorial Auction (CA). Each agent submits bids of the form $(c_j; x_j)$ one for each package, j that is desired, where c_j is the bid price to be paid for package j, and $x_j = (a_{1j}, a_{2j}, \ldots, a_{mj})$, $a_{ij}\varepsilon\{0, 1\}$, where m is the number of resources. Thus, in Table 1, bidder 1 might submit $(c_1; a_1, \ldots, a_6) = (\$5; 1, 1, 0, 0, 0, 0)$: a bid of \$5 for one unit each of A and B for package 1.

All such agent bids are then processed using algorithms that solve the following integer programming problem, P:

$$\text{Maximize} \quad \sum_j c_j x_j$$

$$\text{Subject to} \quad \begin{aligned} \sum_j a_{ij} x_j &\leq b_i \quad \forall i \\ \sum_j d_{kj} x_j &\leq e_k \quad \forall k \\ x_j &\in \{0, 1\}, \end{aligned}$$

where $i = 1, \ldots, m$, subscripts an elemental resource item ($m = 6$ in Tables 1 and 2) $j = 1, \ldots, n$, subscripts a package of resource items ($n = 30$ in Table 2), $k = 1, \ldots, \ell$, subscripts a logical constraint imposed on a set of packages by some bidder (see below).

$$a_{ij} = \begin{cases} 1 & \text{if package } j \text{ includes item } i, \\ 0 & \text{otherwise;} \end{cases}$$

$$d_{kj} = \begin{cases} 1 & \text{if package } j \text{ is in logical constraint } k \\ 0 & \text{otherwise;} \end{cases}$$

$e_k = $ some integer ≥ 1,

$c_j = $ the bid for package j by some buyer.

The logical constraints indicated above are included to illustrate the generality of the combinatorial process; they were not implemented in the experiments reported here. The logical constraints represent any restriction on an agent's bids that can be expressed in linear form. One class of examples is "accept no more than p of the following packages." Thus, suppose an agent bids for C_a on package a, and C_b on b, and specifies either a, or b, but not both. Then the added logical constraint is $x_a + x_b \leq 1$.

Another class of logical constraints is of the form "b only if a." This is satisfied by creating a new package as defined, $C_{ab} = C_a + C_b$, which replaces package b in the submission set, and the logical constraint is $x_a + x_{ab} \leq 1$. Another logical constraint could be "accept any or all of the following packages but do not spend more than e_1 dollars."

Having solved P at the end of a bidding period, what information does the mechanism report back to the agents in preparation for the next bid period? In the experiments reported below, we used the following procedure:

1. Each subject was informed as to his/her submitted bids that were accepted, and which were rejected.

In addition two pseudo-dual programs of problem P were solved to determined two sets, low and high, of elemental resource prices that would allow each package to be priced as follows:

2. Each accepted bid represents the purchase of one package at a price equal to the sum of its low item resource values. The purchase price is always less than or equal

to the bid price of an accepted bid, because any bid less than the sum of its low item prices is definitely rejected. Any bid greater than the sum of its high item prices is definitely accepted. Bids in between these low and high prices may or may not be accepted depending upon whether they provide an integer fit with other package bids in satisfying all constraints. The resulting low and high package prices are reported to each subject and provides a set of best, worst and problematic replies to all other bids.

Here is an example. Assume an agent has values, and submits bids, for three packages as follows: $(A, F) = 72$; $(A, F) = 48$; $(A, C) = 37$. Let the set of low and high computed dual prices for A, C, and F be $(A, C, F)_L = (25, 10, 32)$; $(A, C, F)_H = (25, 16, 34)$. Then the bid $(A, F) = 72$ is definitely accepted, since $72 > 25 + 34 = 59$, and the market price paid is $25 + 32 = 57$. The package bid $(A, F) = 48$ is definitely rejected since $48 < 57$. But the bid $(A, C) = 37$ might be rejected or accepted since $25 + 10 = 35 < 37 < 25 + 16 = 41$. Note that it is hazardous to bid less than one's value for a package, while bidding above value risks winning the package but paying more than it is worth and losing money on it.

2. The After Market

In each experiment after the completion of the primary market, whether run as an IA or as a CA, an open book two-sided auction was conducted. Any subject was free to announce a price and corresponding element or set of elements at which the subject was willing to either buy or sell the indicated element(s). The announcement was posted on the blackboard and remained standing until modified or accepted. Thus, a bid to buy might be Bid ($5; 1, 1, 0, 0, 0, 1): buy one unit each of A, B, and F for $5. A seller might post Ask ($6; 0, 0, 1, 1, 0, 0): asking $6 for one C and one D. This allowed missing elements in packages that were bid in the primary auction to be obtained in an open two-sided bid/ask auction. The secondary market was essential if efficient combinations were to be had in the IA, and allowed missed packages in the CA to have a second chance to be filled.

3. Results

We report data on market efficiency and agent profitability in eight experiments comparing: (i) inexperienced with experienced subjects, (ii) IA with CA, and (iii) easy with difficult environment.

In Figure 1 market efficiency is plotted in each trading period for four different experiments using the easy environment. Efficiency following the primary market is plotted in red, while efficiency achieved following the after market is plotted in green. Of course the after market can only improve on the primary market if agents prefer more money to less. The top panel, for inexperienced subjects, illustrates a problem that surfaced with inexperience: a tendency to use the primary market to acquire resources or packages beyond what is demanded by the agent in an attempt to profit from resale to others in the after market. Thus in IA, upper left panel of Figure 1, the primary market efficiency in periods, 2, 3, 4 and 5 was actually less than it was in period 1, but generally recovered in the after market as subjects found buyers. In the CA such speculative attempts were largely absent except in the final period, when efficiency was not improved by the after market. Generally, in the easy environment of Figure 1, efficiency was higher in the after market under CA than IA in 4 of 5 periods with inexperienced subjects, and in 2 of 4 periods with experienced subjects. In the easy environment CA provided most of its advantage over IA when subjects were inexperienced. Experienced subjects handle the easy environment quite well without combinatorial aid.

In contrast, as shown in Figure 2 for the difficult environment, CA dominates IA in both the primary and after markets in every period. In complex combinatorial environments, IA causes severe coordination problems even with experienced subjects. In fact the CA does so well in achieving high efficiencies in the primary market (85% to over 99% across experience levels) that improvements in the after market are almost impossible to discover in the open auction.

The efficiency comparisons in Figures 1 and 2 provide no insight as to the profit consequences of the coordination properties of the two auction mechanisms. Data on the percentage of agents across all periods who ended with a deficit (profit loss) in a period is plotted in the bar charts of Figure 3 for each experimental condition. Hence, in the upper left panel, corresponding to the IA primary market in the easy environment using inexperienced subjects, there were a total of 30 observations on agent-period profits (5 subjects × 6 periods each); in 14 of these cases (46.7%) a subject ended the period with a deficit, as indicated by the red bar. This deficit rate for agents declines to 36.7% (11 of 30) following the after market as shown by the red bar in the upper right panel for inexperienced subjects. The corresponding results for experienced subjects are 37.5% and 8.3%, respectively. For the CA the agent deficit rate is never over 6.7% and is zero for experienced subjects following the after market shown plotted as green bars. The deficit rate contrast between CA and IA is much more pronounced in the difficult environment shown in the lower panel. For experienced subjects there are no deficits following the primary market, for CA, and hence none following the after market. But 22.2% of the IA cases show a deficit for experienced subjects following the after market.

Profitable, efficient allocation is just not achievable in difficult environments using IA. But why is efficiency for the CA mechanism higher in the difficult than in the easy environment? Our explanation is that the greater replication of elements and packages across agents in the easy environment invites speculative purchases in the primary market for resale in the after market, introducing some deficits in the primary market, and reducing efficiency. Thus, easy environments appear to invite manipulations that are avoided in difficult environments because they are perplexing to subjects and hazardous to manipulate.

Ch. 68: *The Combinatorial Auction* 651

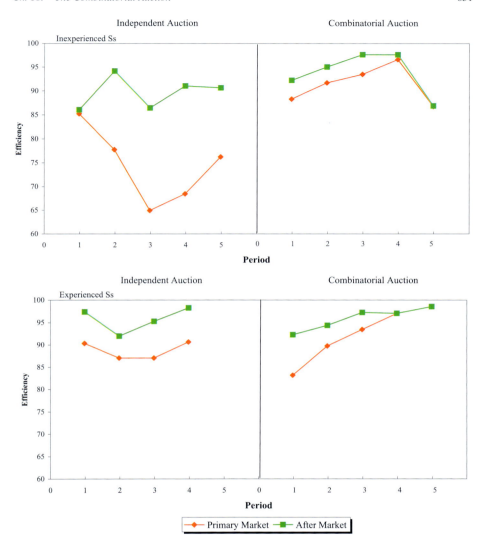

Figure 1. For the easy combinatorial environment, each of the four panels plots efficiency by period in the primary market (red), and efficiency for each period following the after market (green). For inexperienced subjects in the top panels, the declines shown in periods 1 to 3 for the independent auction (IA), and in period 5 for the combinatorial auction (CA) are the result of speculation: subjects purchase items in excess of their own demands in an attempt to profit from resale in the after market. These speculations caused losses (see Figure 3) and use of this behavioral strategy was much reduced when subjects become experienced. Overall the CA provided only slightly improved after market efficiency relative to IA in this simple environment. With inexperienced subjects, CA efficiency was higher in periods 1 to 4 than in IA, but below it is period 5. With experienced subjects in periods 1 and 4 IA efficiency was higher than CA, while in periods 2 and 3 this ranking was reversed.

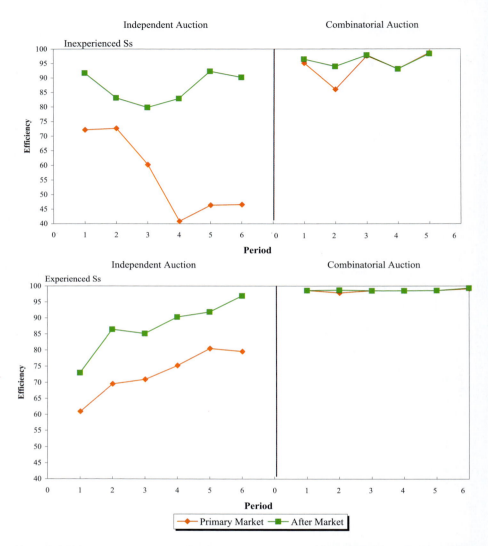

Figure 2. Efficiency is plotted by period for each treatment using the difficult combinatorial environment: primary market efficiency is in red, the after market in green. Note that the improvement in efficiency going from the primary market to the after market is much more pronounced in IA than CA. Even for inexperienced subjects the primary market CA easily solves the coordination problem in a complex environment, leaving little room for efficiency improvement in an after market. In IA the low primary market efficiencies were a consequence of speculative attempts by subjects to buy elements in excess of their individual demand needs in the hope of reselling at a profit in the after market. This was a much less severe problem in CA where the complexity of the environment led subjects to reply on the support of computer coordination in the primary market and to avoid using the after market to piece together valuable packages.

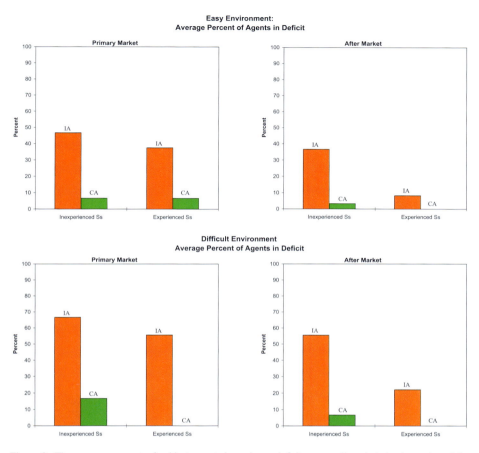

Figure 3. The average percent of subject agents incurring a deficit across all periods is shown in red for the independent auctions (IA) and green for the combinatorial auction (CA). Deficits are common in the IA primary market, even with experienced subjects, and persist into the after market, especially in the difficult combinatorial environment shown in the lower panels. Thus over 20% of agent periods end in deficit with experienced subjects in the IA. (Lower right panel.) Such deficit problems are minor in the CA with inexperienced subjects, and disappear entirely with experience in both the easy and difficult environments.

References

Grether, David, Isaac, R. Mark, Plott, Charles (1979). "Alternative methods of allocating airport slots: Performance and evaluation". CAB Report, Polynomics Research Laboratories, Inc., Pasadena, CA.

Grether, David, Isaac, R. Mark, Plott, Charles (1989). "The Allocation of Scarce Resources". Westview Press, Boulder, CO.

Rassenti, Stephen J., Smith, Vernon L., Bulfin, Robert L. (1982). "A combinatorial auction mechanism for airport time slot allocation". Bell Journal of Economics 13, 402–417.

Vickrey, William (1961). "Counterspeculation, auctions, and competitive sealed tenders". Journal of Finance, 8–37.

PART 5.2

APPLIED, PROBLEM DRIVEN

Stuart Mestelman and R. Andrew Muller, "Share Trading and Coupon Banking Interact to Improve Performance in Emission Trading Markets"

Timothy N. Cason, "Trading Institutions and Emission Allowances"

James C. Cox and R. Mark Isaac, "Procurement Contracting"

Stephen Rassenti and Vernon L. Smith, "Electric Power Market Design Issues and Laboratory Experiments"

Mark A. Olson, Stephen Rassenti and Vernon L. Smith, "Energy Reserve and Adjustment Market Behavior with Industry Network, Demand and Generator Partners"

Steven Backerman, Stephen Rassenti and Vernon L. Smith, "Transmission Constraints, Incentive Auction Rules and Trader Experience in an Electric Power Market"

Hung-Po Chao and Charles R. Plott, "A Smart Market for the Spot Pricing and Pricing of Transmission Through a Power Grid"

Chapter 69

SHARE TRADING AND COUPON BANKING INTERACT TO IMPROVE PERFORMANCE IN EMISSION TRADING MARKETS

STUART MESTELMAN and R. ANDREW MULLER

McMaster University

Emissions trading refers to the exchange of permits conveying the legal right to discharge specified quantities of waste. Unlike naturally occurring markets for many commodities and services, emissions trading markets are the product of deliberate choices by regulatory authorities. Frequently these choices must be made without practical experience or clear guidance from theory. Laboratory experiments are well suited to investigating such choices without the high economic and political cost of field trials.

Under a typical emissions trading plan the regulatory authority sets a quota on the total allowable discharge of a specified waste during each control period. This quota is distributed among eligible firms in the form of permits which we shall call coupons. Some rule is required to determine the allocation of coupons among firms. Normally firms' initial shares of coupons will be proportional to their shares of pre-regulatory emissions, perhaps adjusted to reflect some standard of best practice. Firms are then free to trade coupons among themselves.

The demand for coupons is derived from firms' discharge of wastes, which is determined in turn by their technological choices and volume of production. Firms may or may not be able to control their production processes and volumes precisely. If not, at the beginning of the control period they will be uncertain about the exact quantity of coupons they will require by the end. This uncertainty may lead to unstable coupon prices, since firms may arrive at the end of a control period having discharged more or less waste than expected. They must attempt to clear their surplus or deficit of coupons in what may be termed a "reconciliation" market. Both the supply of, and demand for, coupons will be highly price inelastic and small variations in excess demand for reconciliation coupons may cause great variation in coupon prices. This may be avoided if firms are permitted to carry forward ("bank") unused permits from one period to the next because firms can then meet unexpected demand from their coupon inventories.

Emissions trading plans can vary in many potentially important details. One of these is banking, which is important in facilitating intertemporal reallocation of coupons as well as mitigating the effects of production uncertainty on coupon prices. A second is the manner in which trading in future coupons is to be organized. For example, one proposal advanced in the early 1990s provided for simultaneous trading in coupons (dated and potentially bankable permits to discharge a specific quantity of waste) and in shares (time streams of coupons defined as a fraction of each year's total allowable discharge). In this chapter we focus on the interaction of banking and share trading under varying conditions of uncertainty in the production of emissions.

Several studies have addressed aspects of this issue. Franciosi, Isaac, and Reynolds (1999) and Cronshaw and Kruse (1999) investigated banking in the context of proposed trading rules for the US EPA sulfur dioxide allowances market. Both found relatively low efficiencies. Subjects in the Franciosi et al. experiment underbanked while Cronshaw's and Kruse's overbanked coupons relative to the efficient time path. Muller and Mestelman (1994), reported in more detail in Mestelman, Moir, and Muller (1999), showed that open outcry markets with shares and coupons outperformed the environments tested both by Franciosi et al. and by Cronshaw and Kruse. Carlson et al. (1993) report two experimental sessions which show that a limited form of intertemporal substitution of coupons eliminates price spikes in the reconciliation market under uncertainty. The only systematic investigation of the interactions of banking, share trading and uncertainty, however, is that reported by Godby et al. (1997).

Godby et al. created a laboratory environment in which coupons were distributed to subjects through shares bearing two coupons in each of the first four periods and one coupon in each of the remaining eight periods. Trade was conducted through a computer-mediated double-auction. In the most complex treatment (with banking, share trading and uncertainty in the control of discharges) subjects first traded shares and then received coupon dividends. Next, they traded coupons and then chose how much waste they planned to discharge in the current period and the corresponding use of coupons. Actual discharges were then computed by adding a random element which was previously determined but unknown to the participants. Finally, subjects were informed of their actual coupon requirements and allowed to participate in a reconciliation market. Subjects were provided with computerized assistance in valuing coupons and shares: a *planner* allowed experimentation with the probable consequences of holding varying numbers of coupons and shares and a *wizard* advised on the increment or decrement in expected profit which would be caused by a unit change in holdings of coupons or shares, assuming these were efficiently allocated. The individual effects of coupon banking, share trading and uncertain control of discharges were investigated through a complete $2 \times 2 \times 2$ factorial design replicated three times.

Figure 1 compares a baseline session in which there is neither banking of coupons, nor trading of shares with a session in which coupon banking and share trading were both permitted. There was uncertainly in the control of emissions in both sessions. In the baseline session, prices generally follow the competitive market prediction, being low in periods 1 to 4 when the coupon dividend is high and high in periods 5 to 12 when the coupon dividend is low. The adjustment to the higher price is relatively slow for a double auction experiment. Reconciliation trades are highly variable and lie distinctly off the path of regular coupon prices. These confirm the price spikes found by Carlson et al. (1993).

Introducing banking and share trading leads to dramatic changes. Banking is predicted to smooth coupon prices over time; indeed the competitive equilibrium price band is constant, despite the reduction of coupon dividend from two to one per share in period five. Figure 1 shows that coupon prices stay very close to this band. Moreover the frequency and amplitude of price spikes in the reconciliation market is greatly

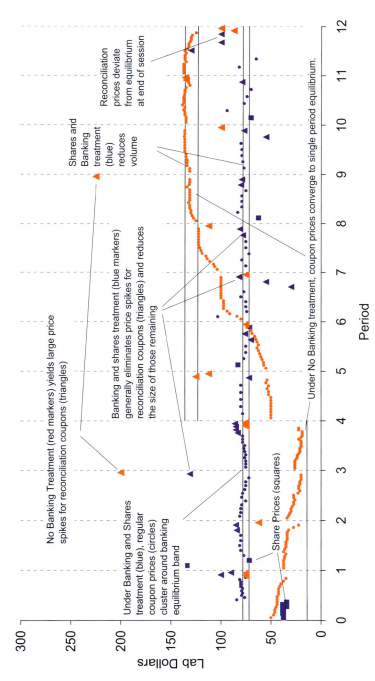

Figure 1. Share trading and banking markedly improve price performance. Without shares or banking (red markers), trading volume is high and reconciliation prices (triangles) exhibit large spikes. With banking and share trading, trading volume is reduced. Regular coupon prices (circles) and most reconciliation prices lie close to the equilibrium band. After period 1, share prices (squares; expressed as coupon equivalents) are also close to the equilibrium band. Data are from a typical session for each treatment.

reduced and many reconciliation trades lie close to or in the competitive equilibrium band. The introduction of share trading substantially reduces coupon trading volume. Early share prices lie outside the equilibrium band but quickly converge to it and stay near it until the end of the session. Other sessions (not illustrated) show that share trading accelerates the adjustment to the change of dividend in period 5 in treatments with no banking.

Coupon banking and share trading affect the efficiency as well as the price behavior of emissions markets. Efficiency can be measured by the percentage of available reduction in system abatement cost, i.e., gains from trade, that are realized under a trading institution. Godby et al. (1997) considered a wide variety of efficiency measures differentiated chiefly by the definition of potential gain from trade.

Figure 2 plots net efficiency by treatment. In this measure, the potential gains from trade are defined to take into account the slight reduction in aggregate coupon availability caused by the realization of the random error term uncertainty treatments. Figure 2 reveals three particularly interesting results. First, banking substantially increases efficiency in both the shares and no shares conditions. This is chiefly due to the fact that banking allows the market to reallocate coupons over time. The initial distribution of coupons (two per share in periods one to four and one per share in periods five through twelve) is not efficient given the abatement cost schedules built into subjects' payoff functions. Provided the pollution damage function is linear in period by period emissions, reallocating coupons from early to late periods via banking is both privately and socially efficient. Second, share trading always increases efficiency, as shown by the positive slope of the lines in Figure 2. The effect is noticeably greater in the case of banking. Third, banking *as a market institution* can actually reduce efficiency. The topmost line in Figure 2 reports the net efficiency of the no banking treatments expressed as a percentage of the maximum achievable gains from trade given that coupons simply could not be reallocated over time. This *adjusted net efficiency* measure coincides with the standard measure in the banking treatments. The adjusted net efficiency of no-banking sessions lies above the adjusted net efficiency of the banking sessions, indicating that subjects achieved a larger fraction of the potential gains from trade in the no-banking condition. This effect, however, is very much reduced when share trading is permitted.

The results are significant for both environmental policy and the study of markets. Proposals for explicit trading in shares, prominent in Canadian policy discussions five years ago, are now less frequently heard. The laboratory results suggest this is unfortunate. At a broader level, the results raise two questions about auction markets generally.

First, what explanation is to be offered for the apparent reduction in market efficiency induced by banking? One conjecture is that banking provides agents a degree of flexibility in production planning without a corresponding market to guide it. If so, a complete series of future markets might provide the market signals required for improved intertemporal efficiency.

Second, what explanation is to be offered for the role of shares in improving price performance and reducing the efficiency losses due to banking? On the one hand, shares

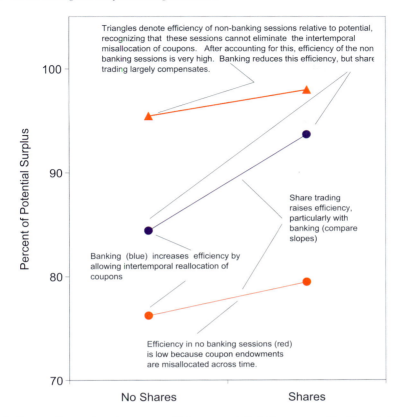

Figure 2. Share trading consistently promotes efficiency, especially in the presence of banking. Banking raises gross efficiency by allowing intertemporal redistribution of initially misallocated coupons. Abstracting from this, banking without shares reduces the efficiency of the market institution. Share trading largely compensates for this effect. Data points are means for uncertainty treatments.

seem to be a substitute for organized trading in future coupons. If this is the case, performance should be enhanced even more by instituting such futures markets. On the other hand, trading in shares may represent a way of reducing the complexity of futures markets, in which case a market restricted to trading current coupons and shares might actually outperform a more complete set of futures markets.

References

Carlson, D., Olmstead, N., Forman, C., Ledyard, J., Plott, C., Porter, D., Sholtz, A. (1993). "An analysis and recommendation for the terms of the RECLAIM trading credit". Report submitted to the South Coast Air Quality Management District, Contract No. R-C93074.

Cronshaw, M.B., Kruse, J.B. (1999). "An experimental analysis of emission permits with banking and the clean air act amendments of 1990". Research in Experimental Economics 7, 1–24.

Franciosi, R., Isaac, R.M., Reynolds, S.S. (1999). "Experimental research on the EPA's "two-tier" system for marketable emissions permits". Research in Experimental Economics 7, 25–44.

Godby, R.W., Mestelman, S., Muller, R.A., Welland, J.D. (1997). "Emissions trading with shares and coupons when control over discharges is uncertain". Journal of Environmental Economics and Management 32, 359–381.

Mestelman, S., Moir, R., Muller, R.A. (1999). "A laboratory test of a Canadian proposal for an emissions trading program". Research in Experimental Economics 7, 45–91.

Muller, R.A., Mestelman, S. (1994). "Emission trading with shares and coupons: A laboratory test". Energy Journal 15, 185–211.

Chapter 70

TRADING INSTITUTIONS AND EMISSION ALLOWANCES

TIMOTHY N. CASON
Purdue University

Nearly 30 years ago economists first proposed tradable emission allowances as a regulatory tool to achieve environmental goals at lower costs than command and control regulation (Dales, 1968; Montgomery, 1972). Policy-makers experimented with tradable emissions during the 1980s with limited success (Hahn, 1989), but this approach was not implemented on a wide scale until in the 1990s. There are now numerous emission allowance trading programs being implemented or designed in the U.S. and abroad at both the federal and local levels. Unfortunately, most policy-makers and many economists fail to appreciate the importance of trading institution and instrument design when translating the (institution-free) theoretical properties of emission allowance trading to practical applications. Consequently, the development of several trading programs has been handicapped when regulators have not adequately accounted for the incentive and efficiency properties of trading mechanisms and instruments. Experimental economics provides a valuable tool to inform and guide the development of these new market-based approaches, because laboratory results can help determine the relative performance of alternative trading institutions and other rules that govern trading.

Plott (1983) was the first to use laboratory methods to evaluate the potential performance of emission allowance trading. He employed the oral double auction institution, and found that overall efficiency levels (after the first two periods) increased from 34.4 percent for a command and control "standards" policy to 98.3 percent for a tradable emission allowance policy. His study was not motivated by a specific emissions trading program, and this impressive performance of allowance trading is probably due in part to his use of the highly efficient double auction institution. More recent laboratory studies have evaluated features of the trading institutions implemented or planned for specific emissions trading programs, beginning with the sulfur dioxide emissions allowance market created by the Clean Air Act Amendments of 1990 ("the Act").

1. The Federal Sulfur Dioxide Allowance Program and the EPA Emissions Trading Auction

The Act instructed the U.S. Environmental Protection Agency (EPA) to conduct annual sealed-bid/sealed-offer auctions to ensure the availability of allowances and to provide clear price signals to the evolving allowance market. The first auction was conducted in March of 1993 at the Chicago Board of Trade. Franciosi et al. (1993) conducted an experiment during the development of the EPA auction rules that captures an important revenue neutral feature of the EPA auction proposed by Hahn and Noll (1982). EPA withholds between two and three percent of the available allowances from firms and sells them in the annual auctions. These auctions are revenue neutral because EPA distributes the sales proceeds to the firms who had ownership rights to these withheld allowances. Franciosi et al. compare the performance of the revenue neutral sealed-bid auction to an alternative no-rebate version, and find little difference in either prices or market efficiency. However, because it was conducted before the EPA auction rules were finalized, their study did not capture an important feature of the EPA auction. In particular, all of the experiments in Franciosi et al. (1993) used a uniform pricing (also known as "competitive") rule, in that all successful bidders paid a common market-clearing price; by contrast, the EPA auction in the field employs a discriminative price rule, in which all successful bidders pay their bid price.

Vickrey (1961) first identified the importance of these differing rules, and Cox, Roberson, and Smith (1982) studied these differences in the laboratory. The discriminative price rule creates an incentive for buyers to submit bids below their opportunity cost of emission control so that they receive gains from trade. The EPA auction has an additional odd feature that creates strong misrepresentation incentives on the seller side as well: Sellers who offer units voluntarily to the EPA auction receive the bid price of a specific buyer. Sellers with the lowest asking prices receive the highest bids, which Cason (1993, 1995) shows creates an incentive for sellers to submit offer prices below their true cost of emission control. Theoretical analysis indicates that since both buyers and sellers have an incentive to submit bids and offers below true abatement cost, equilibrium prices in this EPA auction are biased downward.

Cason and Plott (1996) compare the performance of this EPA auction to an alternative uniform price sealed-bid/sealed-offer auction. This uniform price auction is used, for example, by specialists on the New York Stock Exchange to set daily opening prices based on limit orders submitted by traders prior to the opening. It has superior theoretical incentive properties relative to the EPA auction because only the marginal traders affect the uniform price (Rustichini, Satterthwaite, and Williams, 1994), and it performs well in the laboratory even in "thin" markets with constantly changing supply and demand conditions (Cason and Friedman, 1997).

Unfortunately for the EPA, the Cason and Plott (1996) experiment indicates that human subjects understand the differing incentives of these two institutions. In the EPA auction treatment, buyers and especially sellers grossly underreveal their true valuations for emission allowances in their submitted bids and offers. By contrast, in the uniform price auction, the marginal buyers and sellers submit bids and offers that more accurately reveal their values and costs. Figure 1 illustrates the resulting difference in transaction prices in the two treatments due to the differing revelation incentives. This figure presents average market clearing prices in a "constant aggregate" environment in which aggregate demand and supply remain constant across periods, except for one unannounced shift before period 17. Uniform price auction transactions occur very near the competitive equilibrium (CE) midpoint in nearly all periods, while the EPA auction

Ch. 70: *Trading Institutions and Emission Allowances* 663

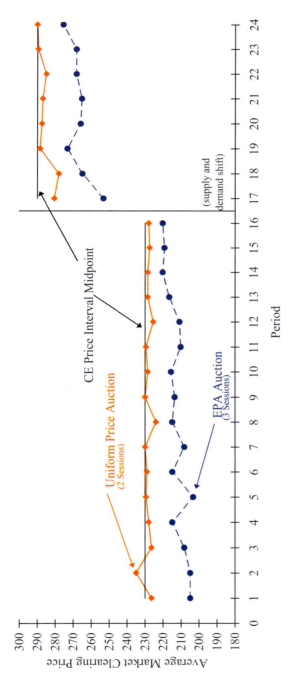

Source: Cason and Plott (1996).

Figure 1. In the EPA auction buyers pay their bid price, and the lowest seller asks receive the highest buyer bids; this results in a downward bias in market clearing prices, compared to the uniform price auction in which all trades occur at one price.

prices remain below the CE price interval in most periods.[1] Price performance results are similar in a "random draws" environment in which supply and demand shift randomly each period due to independent and identically distributed draws of values and costs from announced distributions. Although market efficiency differences for the two institutions are not as pronounced as the price differences, efficiency of the uniform price auction exceeds that of the EPA auction except in the initial periods in the constant aggregate environment.

When confronted with these findings, officials in the Acid Rain Division of EPA emphasized that the wording of Act required use of a discriminative price auction. The Act states that "allowances shall be *sold on the basis of bid price*, starting with the highest-price bid and continuing until all allowances for sale at such auction have been allocated" (emphasis added).[2] However, in late 1994 the General Accounting Office (GAO) issued a report critical of the EPA auction based on the surprisingly low observed auction prices as well as these laboratory findings (GAO, 1994). Attorneys at the GAO concluded that this wording is sufficiently vague to permit the EPA to modify the auction rules, and they recommended that EPA should "change the design of the auction so that it is a single-price auction" (GAO, 1994, p. 59). In response, in June 1996 the EPA formally proposed changing the rules of their auction to a uniform price auction, and this change is likely to take effect beginning in 1998 (Federal Register, 1996). While this positive impact of laboratory results on public policy is refreshing, it is unfortunate that the EPA – unlike the Federal Communications Commission prior to the broadcast spectrum auctions – did not consult auction theorists and experimental economists prior to conducting many auctions with an inferior design.

Fortunately, this EPA auction is only one mechanism through which firms can trade emission allowances. Firms can also trade allowances on alternative, private markets, and recent evaluations suggest that non-auction trading is growing significantly (Joskow, Schmalensee, and Bailey, 1998). At present these alternative trading opportunities occur through decentralized "search" or "brokered" markets, with substantially higher transaction costs than centralized auctions. Nevertheless, these markets may evolve into centralized exchange markets. Franciosi, Isaac, and Reynolds (1999) use laboratory methods to study the interaction of the EPA auction (but without voluntary units offered for sale) with a computerized double auction market. They find that double auction prices consistently exceed the EPA auction prices, a puzzling result replicated by Cason, Elliott, and Van Boening (1999).

Both the Franciosi et al. and Cason et al. studies allow for allowance "banking" across periods which is permitted in the sulfur dioxide allowance trading program. Banking allows firms to carry forward unused allowances for use in future years, which can help mitigate allowance price volatility due to emissions uncertainty. Cronshaw and

---

[1] The CE "interval" (not shown) extends ten experimental francs above and ten francs below the CE midpoint on the figure, since a range of prices can clear the market.

[2] Clean Air Act Amendments of 1990 (Public Law 101-549), Sec. 416(d)(2). See Hausker (1992) for an analysis of the political economy of this decision by Congress.

Brown-Kruse (1999) focus on the role of allowance banking, and they find that the combination of banking and allowance trading allows subjects to improve efficiency relative to baseline sessions with only banking permitted.

2. Other Emission Allowance Trading Assessments: China, Ontario and Los Angeles

Rich and Friedman (1998) also use laboratory methods to evaluate the performance of a new auction designed for trading emission allowances, compared to the uniform price auction. They study the matching market institution, which is used by the Chinese environmental protection agency for allowance trading. In this institution, like the U.S. EPA auction, buyers and sellers submit sealed bids and offers and successful buyers pay their bid price. The key difference is that the matching market institution matches the highest bid to the highest offer less than that bid, and then matches the second highest bid to the second highest remaining offer less than that bid, etc., until no further trades are possible. Depending on the exact incentives these rules generate (which have not been fully worked out in theory), this institution could increase transaction volume relative to the competitive equilibrium volume. This institution has been implemented on a pilot basis for five cities, and is being considered for widespread allowance trading throughout China.[3]

Rich and Friedman find that this new institution is significantly less efficient than the uniform price auction, and leads to bids and offers that reveal less of the underlying values and costs compared to the uniform price auction. The matching market auction also generates greater price and transaction volume variation. On all of these performance measures, it appears to be an inferior trading institution to the uniform price auction.

Researchers at McMaster University have conducted a series of laboratory experiments that evaluate proposals for a nitrous oxide allowance trading program in southern Ontario. Their research introduces new trading institutions and tradable allowance instruments not present in the U.S. sulfur dioxide allowance trading program. Muller and Mestelman (1994) permit the simultaneous trading of coupons (the right to emit a certain quantity of emissions in a specific year) and shares (a claim to stream coupons for future years). Their coupon is equivalent to the allowance traded in the U.S. They employ a market institution that differs from other research because the Canadian proposals do not specify specific institution rules. In Muller and Mestelman (1994) trading occurs in an open outcry market similar to pit trading on commodities exchanges, and transaction prices were not revealed publicly in a systematic fashion.[4] They observe

---

[3] Rich and Friedman also note that a variant of this matching market institution is used by the Australian Stock Exchange to open trading, and has been proposed to open trading on Nasdaq.

[4] It should be emphasized, however, that this trading institution differs from a decentralized search market because subjects in the open outcry "pit" can obtain transaction price information indirectly by overhearing others' negotiations, and can observe others' willingness to pay and accept as they search for transaction partners. This information is not available if traders are not centralized.

improved trading efficiency relative to the Cronshaw and Brown-Kruse (1999) and Franciosi, Isaac, and Reynolds (1999) studies, which used the same parameters. They also find little opportunity for arbitrage in the relative share and coupon prices.

Godby et al. (1997) also allow for trading in shares and coupons, but they employ a computerized double auction for trading. This study also introduces uncertainty in emissions control as a treatment variable. Carlson and Sholtz (1994) point out that this uncertainty can occur in the field because facilities' knowledge of their future emissions is imprecise, and because information on present emissions often arrives with a lag. Godby et al. (1997) find that this uncertainty leads to significant price instability when allowance banking is not permitted. This instability arises because the market must clear each period, and the uncertainty is resolved only after some transactions take place. Their experiment demonstrates that allowance banking is effective in eliminating this price instability, since it allows traders to reallocate allowances across periods.[5]

Emissions uncertainty was also considered in the design of the Regional Clean Air Incentives Market (RECLAIM), an allowance trading program in the Los Angeles Basin intended to reduce the emissions of sulfur oxides and nitrogen oxides. In this case, the local Air Quality Management District (AQMD) wisely solicited assistance from experimental researchers at Caltech prior to implementing their proposals, and laboratory experiments were used directly to improve several aspects of the allowance instrument. For example, the AQMD ruled out bankable allowances, because of fear that banked allowances could permit emissions to exceed federal standards in future years. This eliminated one possible regulatory strategy that could help reduce allowance price instability in the presence of emissions uncertainty.

In experiments reported in Carlson et al. (1993), the Caltech team demonstrated that allowances with staggered issue and expiration dates avoided the need for banking and were effective in smoothing out price instability due to emissions uncertainty. This proposal was adopted in the final design of the RECLAIM program, and consists of Cycle 1 allowances (which could cover emissions between January 1 and December 31) and Cycle 2 allowances (which could cover emissions between July 1 and June 30). This dual set of trading instruments does not reduce uncertainty, but it accommodates it better. The availability of two substitutable allowances to cover emissions eliminates end-of-year shortages or surpluses of allowances, which are the cause of the price instability.

The RECLAIM program began in January of 1994, and trading occurs through brokers or directly between firms. In order to facilitate trading directly between firms,

---

[5] Godby, Elliott, and Brown-Kruse (1997) investigate the potential impact of market power on allowance trading, which can arise when a small number of firms represent a large share of the total emissions in a region. For example, in the proposed Ontario market for nitrogen oxide allowances, Ontario Hydro accounts for over one-half of the total emissions. Godby, Elliott, and Brown-Kruse (1997) find that this power can affect market outcomes in the presence of asymmetric information (i.e., when the dominant firm knows the competitive fringe valuations). They also show that this problem is exacerbated by the potential use of market power in downstream product markets, because the dominant firm can manipulate the allowance market to raise rivals' costs.

the AQMD designed an "electronic bulletin board" where potential traders can post proposed terms of trade and find other interested transaction parties.[6] To date, this bulletin board market has seen limited activity. Cason and Gangadharan (1998) conduct an experiment to compare the performance of the bulletin board market institution to a computerized double auction, and find that prices reflect underlying market conditions equally well in both trading institutions. This experiment also examines the impact of trading restrictions imposed across two zones of the Los Angeles Basin to avoid trades that lead to emissions migration that could harm air quality. The results suggest that properly-designed restrictions that permit some trading across zones can improve efficiency, relative to more severe restrictions that prohibit any trading across zones.

3. Summary

In the frictionless world of theory without transaction costs, allowance trading offers the potential of billions of dollars in savings when compared to traditional command and control regulation. It is therefore not surprising that regulators have embraced this approach in recent years to reduce the pain of achieving specific environmental objectives. This short review highlights the fact that policy-makers must recognize that "the devil is in the details," and that several intermediate steps are necessary when translating these plans and schemes from the theorist's blackboard to the field. For example, regulators need to carefully consider the design of any new trading institutions and allowance characteristics. Failure to consider these details can lead to poorly designed trading institutions – such as the EPA auction – which can slow the development of the market and require redesign after only several years of operation. By contrast, sufficient consideration of incentives and sponsoring laboratory experiments when appropriate can lead to a better design of allowance characteristics – such as in the RECLAIM program.

References

Carlson, Dale, Sholtz, Anne (1994). "Designing pollution market instruments: Cases of uncertainty". Contemporary Economic Policy 12, 114–125.

Carlson, Dale, Forman, Charles, Ledyard, John, Olmstead, Nancy, Plott, Charles, Porter, David, Sholtz, Anne (1993). "An analysis and recommendation for the terms of the RECLAIM trading credit". Pacific Stock Exchange Incorporated and California Institute of Technology.

Cason, Timothy (1993). "Seller incentive properties of EPA's emission trading auction". Journal of Environmental Economics and Management 25, 177–195.

Cason, Timothy (1995). "An experimental investigation of the seller incentives in the EPA's emission trading auction". American Economic Review 85, 905–922.

---

[6] Recently, several other assets have traded through bulletin board markets, such as small stocks, foreign stocks, and limited partnerships on Nasdaq.

Cason, Timothy, Friedman, Daniel (1997). "Price formation in single call markets". Econometrica 65, 311–345.
Cason, Timothy, Gangadharan, Lata (1998). "An experimental study of electronic bulletin board trading for emission permits". Journal of Regulatory Economics 14, 55–73.
Cason, Timothy, Plott, Charles (1996). "EPA's new emissions trading mechanism: A laboratory evaluation". Journal of Environmental Economics and Management 30, 133–160.
Cason, Timothy, Elliott, Steven, Van Boening, Mark (1999). "Speculation in experimental markets for emission permits". In: Holt, C., Isaac, R.M. (Eds.), Research in Experimental Economics, vol. 7. JAI Press, Greenwich, CT, pp. 93–119.
Cronshaw, Mark, Brown-Kruse, Jamie (1999). "An experimental analysis of emission permits with banking and the clean air act amendments of 1990". In: Holt, C., Isaac, R.M. (Eds.), Research in Experimental Economics, vol. 7. JAI Press, Greenwich, CT, pp. 1–24.
Cox, James, Roberson, Bruce, Smith, Vernon (1982). "Theory and behavior of single object auctions". In: Smith, V. (Ed.), Research in Experimental Economics, vol. 2. JAI Press, Greenwich, CT, pp. 1–43.
Dales, John (1968). "Pollution, Property and Prices". University of Toronto Press, Toronto.
Federal Register, Environmental Protection Agency (40 CFR) Part 73 (1996). "Acid rain program, SO_2 allowance auction and electronic allowance transfer". Advance Notice of Proposed Rulemaking, pp. 28995–28998 (June 6).
Franciosi, Robert, Isaac, R. Mark, Reynolds, Stanley (1999). "Experimental research on the EPA's "two-tier" system for marketable emissions permits". In: Holt, C., Isaac, R.M. (Eds.), Research in Experimental Economics, vol. 7. JAI Press, Greenwich, CT, pp. 25–44.
Franciosi, Robert, Isaac, R. Mark, Pingry, David, Reynolds, Stanley (1993). "An experimental investigation of the Hahn–Noll revenue neutral auction for emissions licenses". Journal of Environmental Economics and Management 24, 1–24.
General Accounting Office (1994). "Air pollution: Allowance trading offers an opportunity to reduce emissions at less cost". GAO/RCED-95-30, December.
Godby, Rob, Elliott, Steven, Brown-Kruse, Jamie (1997). "Market power in pollution permit markets: An experimental investigation". McMaster University Working Paper.
Godby, Rob, Mestelman, Stuart, Muller, R. Andrew, Welland, J. Douglas (1997). "Emissions trading with shares and coupons when control over discharges is uncertain". Journal of Environmental Economics and Management 32, 359–381.
Hahn, Robert (1989). "Economic prescriptions for environmental problems: How the patient followed the doctor's orders". Journal of Economic Perspectives 3, 95–114.
Hahn, Robert, Noll, Roger (1982). "Designing a market for tradable emissions permits". In: Magat, W.A. (Ed.), Reform of Environmental Regulation. Ballinger Press, Cambridge, MA, pp. 119–146.
Hausker, Karl (1992). "The politics and economics of auction design in the market for sulfur dioxide pollution". Journal of Policy Analysis and Management 11, 553–572.
Joskow, Paul, Schmalensee, Richard, Bailey, Elizabeth (1998). "The market for sulfur dioxide emissions". American Economic Review 88, 669–685.
Montgomery, W. David (1972). "Markets in licenses and efficient pollution control programs". Journal of Economic Theory 5, 395–418.
Muller, R. Andrew, Mestelman, Stuart (1994). "Emission trading with shares and coupons: A laboratory experiment". The Energy Journal 15, 185–211.
Plott, Charles (1983). "Externalities and corrective policies in experimental markets". The Economic Journal 93, 106–127.
Rich, Changhua Sun, Friedman, Daniel (1998). "The matching market institution: A laboratory investigation". American Economic Review 88, 1311–1322.
Rustichini, Aldo, Satterthwaite, Mark, Williams, Steven (1994). "Convergence to efficiency in a simple market with incomplete information". Econometrica 62, 1041–1063.
Vickrey, William (1961). "Counterspeculation, auctions, and competitive sealed tenders". Journal of Finance 16, 8–37.

Chapter 71

PROCUREMENT CONTRACTING

JAMES C. COX and R. MARK ISAAC

University of Arizona

Purchases by government agencies from private sector firms are often initiated by solicitation of bids to supply the desired items. Payment to the firm that is awarded the supply contract may be determined by (a) the bid price or (b) bid price plus a share of the difference between observable production cost and the bid price or (c) observable production cost plus an additional fee that may be a function of costs. Interest in the theory and behavior of procurement contracting stems mainly from two features of the political economy: (a) government may have multiple, possibility-conflicting objectives in procurement; and (b) there may be an asymmetry in knowledge of some components of firms' production costs.

One objective that government is likely to have in procurement contracting is minimization of the budgetary cost of making the purchases. Another objective that the government may have in conducting its economic activities, including procurement, may be the promotion of allocative efficiency. As we shall see, budgetary cost minimization and economic efficiency maximization can be conflicting objectives when there is a cost information asymmetry.

Potential suppliers may not all have the same production costs. In addition, government typically cannot observe firms' expected production costs before awarding the contract; hence, the government may not award the contract to the lowest cost producer even if it is attempting to promote allocative efficiency. Accepting the bid of an inefficient producer is known as "adverse selection." Other inefficiencies can occur when a firm's realized cost of supplying the desired items to the government agency are not predetermined but, rather, depend on the effort that the firm's employees make to hold down production costs. Such efforts are costly to the employees and, furthermore, some elements of effort costs are typically not observable by others. When a firm's effort costs are not observable by others, they cannot be reimbursable under the enforceable terms of a procurement contract and profit-maximizing behavior can result in inefficiently low effort to reduce costs. If this occurs, costs are inefficiently too high because of "moral hazard."

1. A Model of Cost Information Asymmetry

Let n denote the number of potential suppliers that bid on the procurement contract. If firm i is granted the contract, its production cost can be assumed to have three distinct components,

$$c_i = c_i^* + w_i - \xi_i, \tag{1}$$

where c_i^* is certain base cost, w_i is a random variable that represents the part of production cost that is uncertain at the time of contracting, and ξ_i is the amount of discretionary cost reduction. Total production cost, c_i, is observable by both the buyer and the seller after delivery of the contracted product. But the separate components of cost, c_i^*, w_i and ξ_i, are observable only by the selling firm (and the experimenter in a controlled experiment).

The discretionary cost reduction comes at the expense of an effort cost, $h(\xi_i)$, such that zero effort has zero cost and marginal effort cost is positive and increasing for all positive effort levels.

2. Linear Contracts

The contract is awarded to the firm that submits the lowest bid. If the contracting market institution is a first (lowest) price sealed bid auction then the "bid price" of the contract is the amount of the lowest bid. If the market is a second price sealed bid auction then the bid price is the second lowest bid.

Let b denote the bid price of the contract and let α be the cost-sharing rate. Then payment to the contracting firm with total cost, c_i, is

$$p_i = b + \alpha(c_i - b). \tag{2}$$

A "fixed price contract" is one in which $\alpha = 0$. A "cost-sharing contract" is one in which $0 < \alpha < 1$. Finally, a "cost plus contract" with zero economic profit is one in which $\alpha = 1$. The form of the payment equation (2) makes it clear that fixed price, cost-sharing, and cost plus contracts are all linear contracts.

If firm i is awarded the contract then its profit, π_i, equals the difference between the contract payment given by Equation (2) and the sum of observable cost, c_i, and unobservable cost, $h(\xi_i)$; hence, Equations (1) and (2) imply:

$$\pi_i = p_i - c_i - h(\xi_i) = (1 - \alpha)(b - c_i) - h(\xi_i). \tag{3}$$

3. Testable Hypotheses

Given that corner solutions are ruled out by the assumption that $h'(0) < 1 - \alpha$, expected utility maximization by the low bidder on the contract implies that the chosen cost-reducing effort level, ξ_i^0, satisfies the equation (McAfee and McMillan, 1986),

$$h'(\xi_i^0) = 1 - \alpha. \tag{4}$$

Since marginal effort cost is positive and increasing, Equation (4) implies that the amount of discretionary cost reduction varies inversely with the cost-sharing rate.

Given some additional assumptions, several other testable hypotheses can be derived from the theoretical model (Cox et al., 1996). Thus, if each bidder's base cost is independently drawn from the uniform distribution on an interval, and all bidders are either risk neutral or have the same constant relative risk averse preferences, then Nash equilibrium bid functions can be derived for bidding in first-price and second-price auctions of contracts. These bid functions, together with Equation (4), imply several hypotheses. These hypotheses involve the predicted effects on performance of the procurement contracting market of varying the cost-sharing rate, of the presence or absence of post-auction cost uncertainty (w_i in Equation (1)), and of the form of the auction market used to award the contract.

Hypotheses: (1) Discretionary cost reduction varies inversely with the cost-sharing rate. (2) With post-auction cost uncertainty, expected procurement payments for first-price auctions of contracts vary inversely with the cost-sharing rate. (3) Expected procurement payments for second-price auctions of contracts vary inversely with the cost-sharing rate for either post-auction cost certainty or uncertainty. (4) Expected procurement payments are not higher for first-price auctions than for second-price auctions of contracts.

4. Experimental Results

The figures show some of the experimental results reported in Cox et al. (1996). Figure 1 shows the incidence of moral hazard costs in the experiments in which contracts were awarded with first-price auctions. Results are reported for experiments with post-auction cost uncertainty and for experiments with post-auction cost certainty. The moral hazard costs are measured by calculating the average actual discretionary cost reduction in the experiments with a given value of the cost-sharing parameter (α), dividing by the efficient (or optimal) level of discretionary cost reduction, and multiplying the result by 100 to get a percentage. As shown in Figure 1, these percentages vary inversely with α; thus, the actual efficiency cost due to moral hazard increases with the cost-sharing rate in the procurement contract. This result is predicted by the theory.

Figure 2 reports pairwise treatment comparisons for both experiments with post-auction cost uncertainty and experiments with post-auction cost certainty. The green bars report the differences between mean procurement payments for fixed-price ($\alpha = 0$) contracts awarded with second-price auctions and those awarded with first-price auctions. These differences are positive as predicted by the theory for risk averse bidders. The theory predicts zero difference for risk neutral bidders. For the certain cost environment, the difference is significantly different from zero by both the difference of means t-test that assumes independence across experiments and the test that assumes independence across periods. For the uncertain cost environment, the difference is significant only for the test that assumes independence across periods.

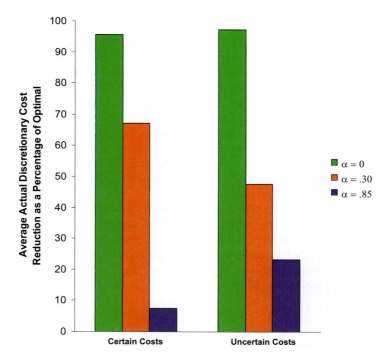

Figure 1. α is the cost-sharing rate in a contract awarded with a first-price sealed-bid auction. The figure shows the average actual discretionary cost reduction as a percentage of the optimal discretionary cost reduction for three values of the cost-sharing rate for experiments with and without post-auction cost uncertainty. Moral hazard costs increase with the cost-sharing rate, as predicted by the theory.

The red bars in Figure 2 show the positive differences between mean procurement payments for contracts with $\alpha = 0$ and $\alpha = .30$ cost-sharing rates, both awarded with first-price auctions. For the certain cost environment, the theory yields no prediction for risk averse bidders but it predicts a positive difference for risk neutral bidders. Theory predicts a positive difference for the uncertain cost environment. These differences are significantly different from zero by both types of t-test for both cost environments.

The blue bars in Figure 2 report positive differences between mean procurement payments for contracts awarded with first-price auctions and having cost-sharing rates of $\alpha = 0$ and $\alpha = .85$. Theoretical predictions are the same as for the red bar comparisons. For the certain cost environment, the difference is significantly different from zero by the t-test that assumes independence across experiments but not by the test that assumes independence across periods. The difference is significant for both types of t-test with data for the uncertain cost environment.

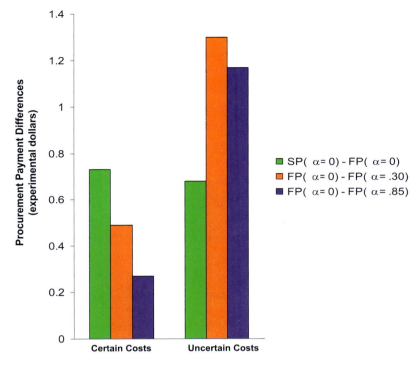

Figure 2. The figure shows procurement payment pair-wise treatment comparisons. SP denotes contracts awarded with the second-price auction. FP denotes contracts awarded with the first-price auction. α is the cost-sharing rate in a contract. The mean difference, $SP(\alpha = 0) - FP(\alpha = 0)$, is predicted to be positive for risk averse bidders. With certain costs, the theory yields no prediction for the mean differences, $FP(\alpha = 0) - FP(\alpha = .30)$ and $FP(\alpha = 0) - FP(\alpha = .85)$, for risk averse bidders. With post-auction uncertain costs the mean differences, $FP(\alpha = 0) - FP(\alpha = .30)$ and $FP(\alpha = 0) - FP(\alpha = .85)$, are predicted to be positive for risk averse or risk neutral bidders. All of the positive differences are significantly different from zero by either a t-test that assumes independence across experiments or one that assumes independence across periods.

Figure 3 portrays the relationship between the rank of the contracts based on their procurement payments and the rank based on their overall allocative efficiencies. The lower the total procurement payment in an experiment, the higher the procurement payment rank (because the assumed objective is budgetary cost minimization). Overall efficiency in an experiment is measured by the ratio of the lowest possible cost of fulfilling the contract to the actual cost of the low bidder. An efficiency number less than 1 can include inefficiencies from both moral hazard costs and adverse selection costs. The higher the efficiency in an experiment, the higher the efficiency rank (because the assumed objective is allocative efficiency maximization). Observe in Figure 3 that there is a predominantly inverse relation between the efficiency rank and the procurement payment rank of the experiments. In other words, lower procurement payments are as-

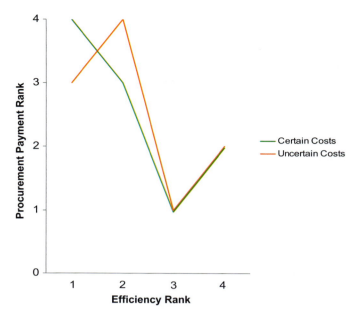

Figure 3. This figure shows that lower procurement payments are associated with lower production efficiencies. There are four experiments with post-auction cost uncertainty and four with post-auction cost certainty. Within each cost environment, the experiments are ranked in terms of their average procurement payment and their overall efficiency, as measured by the ratio of the lowest possible cost of fulfilling the contract to the actual cost of the low bidder. The lower the total procurement payment in an experiment, the higher the procurement payment rank (because the assumed objective is budgetary cost minimization). The higher the efficiency in an experiment, the higher the efficiency rank (because the assumed objective is allocative efficiency maximization). For the most part, cost-sharing contracts have both lower procurement payments and lower efficiencies than do fixed price contracts.

sociated with lower efficiencies. The effects of positive cost-sharing rates stands out in the rankings: for both certain and uncertain cost environments, the efficiency ranks of the $\alpha = .30$ and $\alpha = .85$ contracts are 3 and 4 and their procurement payment ranks are 1 and 2. Thus, cost-sharing contracts have both lower procurement payments and lower efficiencies than do fixed price contracts.

Acknowledgements

This paper was written while the first author (Cox) was visiting the Center for Research in Experimental Economics and Political Decision Making, University of Amsterdam and The Netherlands Agricultural Economics Research Institute. Todd Swarthout provided valuable assistance by preparing the figures.

References

Cox, James C., Isaac, R. Mark, Cech, Paula-Ann, Conn, David (1996). "Moral hazard and adverse selection in procurement contracting". Games and Economic Behavior 17, 147–176.

McAfee, R. Preston, McMillan, John (1986). "Bidding for contracts: A principal–agent analysis". RAND Journal of Economics 17, 326–338.

Chapter 72

ELECTRIC POWER MARKET DESIGN ISSUES AND LABORATORY EXPERIMENTS

STEPHEN RASSENTI and VERNON SMITH

The incentive failure of government ownership of public utility industries has helped to motivate the worldwide privatization of these industries (Smith, 1996). Similar shortcomings of rate-of-return regulation in the United States has led to major changes in the way in which the gas, telephone and cable TV industries are regulated, as public policy has leaned toward, if not fully embraced, the substitution of markets for direct regulation of these industries. Radical technological changes in long distance communication and transmission have also contributed to this accelerating trend. The United Kingdom prominently denationalized electric power in 1991, providing a model for other countries in deciding how (and how not) to create a competitive electric power industry. Since the UK was among the first, the effort was marred by shortcomings, which largely represented political compromises that were most likely unavoidable. Littlechild (1995) provides a recent review of the UK experience. New Zealand, Australia and many other countries initiated the process of privatizing/deregulating their electric power industries. Australia began trading spot power on an interstate grid in the southeast region of the continent in the autumn of 1998. The Energy Policy Act of 1992 set the stage for deregulating the industry in the United States, and major reforms in the current regulatory system are well underway, California's being among the most prominent.

Here are only a few of the many economic design questions that dependably arise in the typical country's debate on competition in producing electrical energy: (1) What should be the rules governing the bidding process in the spot market? (2) How many independent generator companies are required for competition? (3) How should transmission be structured and priced? (4) Should there be demand side as well as supply side bidding in the spot market? (5) How does excess base load capacity (inflexible must-run generators) affect market performance? (From Australia to California off-peak spot prices are sometimes near or equal to zero.) (6) How does the existence of large must-serve inelastic loads impact market performance? (7) How can markets be used to provide both energy reserves and energy supplies in complex multi-node networks?

In the first entry below we use experimental methods to study (1) and (3) in a regime in which the number of independent generators is not systematically varied and in which extensive interruptible demand side bidding is considered (based on Backerman, Rassenti, and Smith, 2000). The spot auction mechanism we use is the Uniform Price Double Auction (UPDA) studied in a simple one-node supply and demand environment by McCabe, Rassenti, and Smith (1993), and implemented by the Arizona Stock Exchange. Initially we examine transmission pricing and income shares on the basis of short-run marginal cost (energy loss) in transmission lines, with a residual congestion price, based on network opportunity costs, when a line is loaded to capacity. This allows us to focus entirely on the technical and behavioral question: Who receives the congestion rents when a line is capacity constrained? Based on engineering optimization models, it has been assumed that congestion rents will be collected by the line owners (Bohn, Caramanis, and Schweppe, 1984). But such analysis does not deal with the question of how bidding behavior may be affected by line constraints; nor does it ask if optimization is supported by an equilibrium model. We also inquire as to how market efficiency and the income shares of producers, wholesale buyers, and transmission line owners are altered with a variation on the auction market bidding rules. The effects of a line constraint and of changing the auction market rules are both examined under different levels of experience on the part of the subjects.

The second entry examines questions (6) and (7) in the above list within a six-period repetitive demand cycle environment in a nine node network with eight demand/supply centers (based on Olson et al., 1999). An experimental study of (2), (5) and (6) is reported by Denton, Rassenti, and Smith (2001).

1. Nodal Price Theory for Lossy Lines

In this section we provide a very brief introduction to the engineering economics of electric power supply and transmission that are used in the experimental designs underlying the two essays to follow.

Energy flows in transmission lines are subject to resistance that causes energy loss in the sense that energy is dissipated in the form of heat in the transmission conductor, and is therefore unavailable to do work at the delivery end of the line. For simplicity we derive the optimal pricing rules using a two-node network. The principles, however, apply to multinode, multiple generator and multiple buyer networks.

If X megawatts (one thousand kilowatts or one million watts) of power per unit of time (power is a time rate of energy flow) are injected into the input buss on the line, then $Y < X$ megawatts per unit of time are withdrawn from the output buss. Since the line loss, $L(X)$ is approximately a quadratic function of injected power, we have

$$Y = X - L(X), \quad L(X) \cong aX^2. \tag{1}$$

If $B(Y)$ is the benefit function for Y units of power delivered to buyers, and $G(X)$ is the supply cost of generators injecting power into the line, the standard engineering optimization problem for an interior maximum is

$$\max_{X,Y>0} B(Y) - G(X) - \lambda(Y - X + L(X)), \tag{2}$$

where λ is a Lagrange multiplier. The marginal conditions for an interior maximum point (X^0, Y^0) in (2) are

$$\lambda = B'(Y^0) = \frac{G'(X^0)}{1 - L'(X^0)}, \tag{3}$$

where $L'(X)$ is the marginal transmission loss (MTL), and $1/(1 - L'(X))$ is the transmission 'loss factor' used to adjust the marginal cost of generation, $G'(X)$, for line losses.[1] The 'system lambda' (λ) measures the marginal cost of generation, after adjustment for transmission loss, at the delivery buss where marginal value is $B'(Y)$. Henceforth we drop the superscript zero, but it will be understood that we are dealing with optimal quantities.

Letting $P_B = B'(Y)$ be the delivered price of power, and $P_G = G'(X)$ be the price of generated power, then from (3)

$$\frac{P_B - P_G}{P_B} = \frac{B' - G'}{B'} = L' \cong \frac{2L}{X} = 2ATL, \qquad (4)$$

where $ATL = L/X$ is the average unit transmission loss of power. The percentage decrease in price from the delivery to the injection node is simply the percentage marginal power loss in the line, which is approximately twice the average percentage loss. Thus, if the average loss in the line is 5%, and the price at the delivery node is normalized to unity, $P_B = 1$, then the generator node price $P_G = 1 - 2(.05) = 0.9$, 90% of the delivery price. These principles generalize to any network with losses $L_{ij}(X_i)$ on line ij with power X_i injected at i and power Y_j extracted at j (see Bohn, Caramanis, and Schweppe, 1984). At peak loads long lines – for example in New Zealand from the South Island to the top of the North Island – can dissipate 15% or more of the injected power.

Note that buyer expenditures total $P_B Y$, while generator revenues total $P_G X$. The revenue imputed to the transmission line is the difference, which by substitution from (1), (3) and (4) can be written

$$\begin{aligned} R_T = P_B Y - P_G X &= \left[P_B(X - L) - P_B(1 - L')X\right] \\ &= P_B\left[(XL' - L)\right] \cong P_B L. \end{aligned} \qquad (5)$$

The line receives optimal revenue equal in value to the losses (it does not "receive" the losses) evaluated at the delivered price. The imputed "price" of the transmission line (per unit of injected power) is then

$$P_T = \frac{R_T}{X} = \frac{P_B L}{X} \cong P_B ATL. \qquad (6)$$

---

[1] More precisely, with multiple wholesale buyers, $B_i(y_i)$, $i = 1, \ldots, n$ and multiple generators, $G_j(x_j)$, $j = 1, \ldots, m$, we have in place of (2)

$$\max_{x_i, y_i > 0} \sum_{i=1}^{n} B_i(y_i) - \sum_{j=1}^{m} G_j(x_j) - \lambda \left(\sum_{i=1}^{n} y_i - \sum_{j=1}^{m} x_j + L \left(\sum_{j=1}^{m} x_j \right) \right).$$

Then for an interior maximum (3) becomes

$$\lambda = B'_1(y_1) = \cdots = B'_n(y_n) = \frac{G'_1(x_1)}{1 - L'(X)} = \cdots = \frac{G'_m(x_m)}{1 - L'(X)}.$$

If any buyer, i, is inactive, then $B'_i(0) < \lambda$ for that buyer; if any generator, j, is inactive then $G'_j(0) > \lambda(1 - L'(X))$ for that generator.

If the transmission line has a capacity constraint, K, then the criterion (2) becomes

$$\max_{X,Y>0} B(Y) - G(X) - \lambda\bigl(Y - X + L(X)\bigr) - \mu(X - K). \tag{2'}$$

The last term expresses the opportunity cost caused by congestion when the capacity constraint is binding.

For a maximum point (X^0, Y^0),

$$\lambda = B'(Y^0) = \frac{G'(X^0) + \mu}{1 - L'(X^0)}, \quad X^0 = K, \ Y^0 = K - L(K). \tag{3'}$$

Transmission revenue corresponding to (5) is then

$$R_T = P_B Y - P_G X = P_B\bigl(KL'(K) - L(K)\bigr) - \mu K \cong P_B L(K) + \mu K. \tag{5'}$$

The imputed price of transmission is therefore

$$P_T = P_B ATL(K) + \mu, \tag{6'}$$

which is the value of the average energy lost plus the unit opportunity cost incurred because of congestion.

Acknowledgements

Partial support from the National Science Foundation, Grant #SBR9223267, 1993–1996 and Grant #INT9312030, 1993–1997, to the University of Arizona, Economic Science Laboratory, to principal investigators, Stephen Rassenti and Vernon Smith is gratefully acknowledged. We also want to acknowledge the early support of the Arizona Corporation Commission in a research grant entitled "Alternatives to Rate of Return Regulation," 1984–1985. It was this grant and a report issued under the same title, dated February 1985, which launched our subsequent research into electric power, and natural gas pipeline network markets.

References

Backerman, Steven, Rassenti, Stephen J., Smith, Vernon L. (2000). "Efficiency and income shares in high demand energy networks: Who receives the congestion rents when a line is constrained?" Pacific Economic Review 5 (3), 331–347.

Bohn, Roger E., Caramanis, Michael C., Schweppe, Fred (1984). "Optimal pricing in electrical networks over space and time". RAND Journal of Economics 15, 360–376.

Denton, M., Rassenti, S., Smith, V. (2001). "Spot market mechanism design and competitivity issues in electric power". Journal of Economic Behavior and Organization 44, 435–453.

Littlechild, Stephen (1995). "Competition in electricity: Retrospect and prospect". In: Beesley, M.E. (Ed.), Utility Regulation: Challenge and Response. Institute of Economic Affairs, London, pp. 101–114.

McCabe, Kevin A., Rassenti, Stephen J., Smith, Vernon L. (1993). "Designing a uniform-price double auction". In: Friedman, D., Rust, J. (Eds.), The Double Auction Market Institutions, Theories, and Evidence. Proceedings, vol. XIV, Santa Fe Institute. Addison–Wesley, Reading, MA, pp. 307–332.

Olson, M., Rassenti, S., Smith, V., Rigdon, M., Ziegler, M. (1999). "Market design and motivated human trading behavior in electricity markets". In: Proceedings of the Thirty-Second Annual Hawaii International Conference on System Sciences, vol. 3. IEEE Computer Society Press, Washington, DC, pp. 3022–3039.

Smith, Vernon L. (1996). "Regulatory reform in the electric power industry". Regulation 1, 33–46.

Chapter 73

ENERGY, RESERVE AND ADJUSTMENT MARKET BEHAVIOR WITH INDUSTRY NETWORK, DEMAND AND GENERATOR PARAMETERS

MARK A. OLSON, STEPHEN RASSENTI and VERNON L. SMITH

In this chapter we report results from experiments using a complex 9-node network market with parameters supplied by the electric utility industry (see Olson et al., 1999).

1. Modeling Generators

Generator companies (Gencos) consist of portfolios of generator units of various types (coal, oil, gas, hydro, nuclear), including portfolios of identical units. Parameters of each type and companies that own portfolios, are shown in Table 1. Large coal and nuclear units are represented by high capacity, low marginal costs, large start-up costs, large minimum loads (50% and 100% of maximum capacity, respectively), large fixed costs per hour, and long start-up times (10 and 60 hours, respectively). Gas and oil fired turbines vary considerably in capacity and cost, but generally have high marginal costs, low fixed cost, and low minimum loads (5% of maximum capacity or less), but represent quick-start sources of reserve power in the event of unscheduled outages (see Figure 1 in Olson et al., 1999 for the supply schedule implied by Table 1).

A portion of the screen display for the Genco at node 7 is shown in Figure 1. (The screen also displays the network and the Genco's location in the network, but this is shown separately in Figure 2). Genco 7 controls seven classes of generator units designated A7, B7, ..., G7. Each class consists of one or more individual units, each unit represented by its own lightning icon. By clicking on the icon, the essential data for that generator is displayed in the box titled "A Costs." For example, the 5th unit in A7 is highlighted in the upper panel, and the data for that unit is indicated in the left lower panel. (The data are identical for all other class A units in Genco 7's A portfolio). The first box displays the startup cost of this unit, 1500 (measured in ¶ units of experimental "pesos"). Then the ramp (start up) time, 10 h, followed by the fixed (sunk) cost 389 ¶/H, pesos per hour. Under Fuel Cost, the first box lists the fuel cost, 15 (¶/MWH), for the unit's minimum loaded capacity step, 80 MW. Subsequent capacity steps, up to the maximum loaded capacity, are listed next. In this example, there is one additional step at the same fuel cost and capacity, the unit having a capacity of 160 MW at a constant fuel cost up to capacity.

Table 1

Eight Gencos each own a portfolio of generator units listed in the rows with parameters shown in the columns. Reading from the left, company 1, row 3, owns large coal facilities consisting of 4 generators, each with maximum capacity of 530 MW, with variable operating cost of 12.9 ¶/MWH, minimum load capacity 265 MW, start up cost 1500, requiring 10 hours to ramp up to its minimum capacity. One of these units is precontracted for full capacity at low off peak demand, 2 for 620 MWH at shoulder demand, and 2 for 820 MWH on peak demand

Company	Type of unit	# units	Max capacity (MW/unit)	Var. op. costs (¶/MWH)	Min load (MW)	Start cost (¶)	Ramp time (hours)	Precontracted supply		
								Low MWH (# units)	Shoulder MWH (# units)	Peak MWH (# units)
1	Hydro	1	70	2.500	3	10	0			
1	Nuclear	1	180	7.825	180	25,000	60	180 MWH (1)	180 MWH (1)	180 MWH (1)
1	Large coal	4	530	12.900	265	1500	10	530 MWH (1)	620 MWH (2)	820 MWH (2)
1	Small coal	2	10	17.100	3	400	3			
1	ct/ic/je	1	10	46.400	1	40	0			
Totals		9	2400					710 MWH (2)	800 MWH (3)	*1000 MWH (3)*
2	Hydro	1	270	1.830	5	10	0			
2	Nuclear	1	550	11.520	550	25,000	60	550 MWH (1)	550 MWH (1)	550 MWH (1)
2	Large coal	1	620	16.350	310	1500	10			
2	Small coal	1	80	20.110	10	400	3	10 MWH (1)	10 MWH (1)	80 MWH (1)
2	Oil ct	10	20	37.300	1	40	0			
Totals		*14*	*1720*					*560 MWH (2)*	*560 MWH (2)*	*630 MWH (2)*
3	Hydro	1	90	7.900	3	10	0			
3	Large coal	3	210	13.230	105	1500	10	105 MWH (1)	105 MWH (1)	105 MWH (1)
3	Small coal	1	40	19.230	3	400	3			
3	Steam turbines oil/gas	1	20	40.000	3	400	3			
Totals		*6*	*780*					*105 MWH (1)*	*105 MWH (1)*	*105 MWH (1)*

(continued on next page)

Table 1
(continued)

Company	Type of unit	# units	Max capacity (MW/unit)	Var. op. costs (¶/MWH)	Min load (MW)	Start cost (¶)	Ramp time (hours)	Precontracted supply Low MWH (# units)	Shoulder MWH (# units)	Peak MWH (# units)
4	Nuclear	1	60	11.520	60	25,000	60	60 MWH (1)	60 MWH (1)	60 MWH (1)
4	Large coal	1	160	14.700	80	1500	10			
4	Small coal	1	30	20.100	10	400	3			
4	ct/ic/je	1	10	87.900	1	40	0			
Totals		4	260					60 MWH (1)	60 MWH (1)	60 MWH (1)
5	Hydro	1	30	0.000	5	10	0			
5	Large coal	4	190	12.900	95	1500	10	95 MWH (1)	95 MWH (1)	190 MWH (1)
5	Nuclear	1	260	14.550	260	25,000	60	260 MWH (1)	260 MWH (1)	260 MWH (1)
5	Small coal	2	30	17.100	3	400	3			
5	Steam turb	1	10	26.000	3	400	3			
5	ct/ic/je	2	20	105.000	1	40	0			
Totals		11	1160					355 MWH (2)	355 MWH (2)	450 MWH (2)
6	Hydro	1	150	3.040	5	10	0			
6	Nuclear	1	290	12.230	290	25,000	60	290 MWH (1)	290 MWH (1)	290 MWH (1)
6	Large coal	10	60	14.500	30	1500	10	240 MWH (8)	360 MWH (8)	480 MWH (8)
6	Small coal	1	10	16.400	10	400	3			
6	Steam turb	10	10	18.660	3	400	3			
6	ct/ic/je	10	20	33.220	1	40	0			
Totals		33	1350					530 MWH (9)	650 MWH (9)	770 MWH (9)

(continued on next page)

Table 1
(continued)

Company	Type of unit	# units	Max capacity (MW/unit)	Var. op. costs (¶/MWH)	Min load (MW)	Start cost (¶)	Ramp time (hours)	Precontracted supply		
								Low MWH (# units)	Shoulder MWH (# units)	Peak MWH (# units)
7	Hydro	1	190	2.010	5	10	0			
7	Nuclear	1	1010	12.230	1010	25.000	60	1010 MWH (1)	1010 MWH (1)	1010 MWH (1)
7	Large coal	10	160	15.400	80	1500	10	1000 MWH (10)	1600 MWH (10)	1600 MWH (10)
7	Small coal	1	170	18.870	10	400	3	10 MWH (1)	155 MWH (1)	150 MWH (1)
7	Combined	1	100	24.135	40	1000	1	40 MWH (1)	40 MWH (1)	100 MWH (1)
7	ct/ic/je	10	90	52.100	1	40	0			
7	Steam turb	10	90	55.000	3	400	3	15 MWH (5)	15 MWH (5)	15 MWH (5)
Totals		34	4870					2075 MWH (18)	2820 MWH (18)	3310 MWH (18)
8	Hydro	1	300	1.830	5	10	0			
8	Nuclear	1	480	12.230	480	25.000	60	480 MWH (1)	480 MWH (1)	480 MWH (1)
8	Large coal	10	230	17.400	115	1500	10	1150 MWH (10)	1620 MWH (10)	2260 MWH (10)
8	Small coal	1	90	22.600	10	400	3			
8	ct/ic/je	10	30	49.500	1	40	0			
8	Steam oil/gas	10	10	64.940	3	400	3			
Totals		33	3570					1630 MWH (11)	2100 MWH (11)	2740 MWH (11)

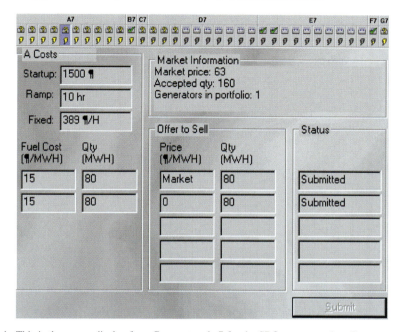

Figure 1. This is the screen display for a Genco at node 7 for the SBO energy market. Generator units are represented by the lightening icons for power generator classes: A7, B7, ..., G7. Multiple units are indicated by the number of icons in each class. A green icon indicated the generator was turned on the previous period; blue it was off; red (not shown) it is out of commission. The parameters for a generator in class A are shown: startup cost; 1500 ¶ ("pesos"); Ramp time 10 h from startup to minimum loaded capacity; fuel cost 15 ¶/MWH for the minimum capacity, 80 MWH; and 15 MWH for the next 80 MWH (capacity, 160 MWH). The minimum loaded capacity (80) is offered automatically "at market" (0 price). Up to four additional (price, quantity) steps may be used to offer the remaining capacity (shown all offered at 0 price).

All loaded generators are assigned forced outage rates based on industry-supplied data for units of different types. If an outage is realized, its duration is then specified, and during such periods that unit cannot be offered to the market.

2. Modeling Demand

Demand cycles from a low off-peak period, through a middle level shoulder period to a peak period, and back to a shoulder period. The four periods are repeated in a series of 5 market days during each experiment, for a total of 20 energy trading periods. Each period each wholesale buyer is assigned a large spike of "must serve" demand that he can resell at a fixed regulated price. In these experiments no portion of the demand can be interrupted voluntarily. The must-serve spike in demand is uncertain. There was a "day-ahead" forecast with + or -8% confidence interval error, then a new forecast at + or -2% error an "hour ahead" of spot market execution.

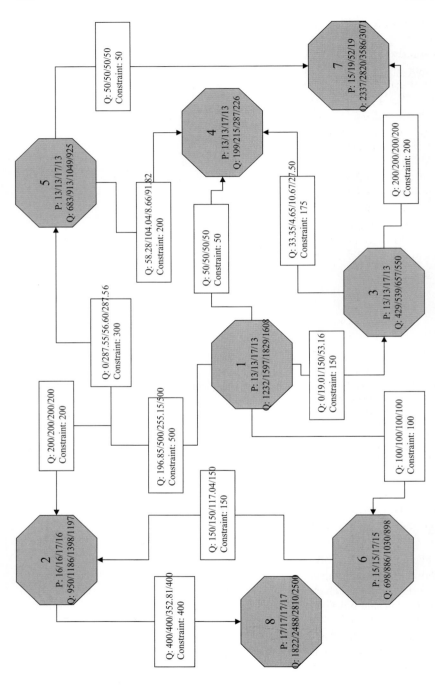

Figure 2. The eight demand and generator supply nodes are represented by the numbered octagons. The average CE prices are indicated after (P:) for the off peak, shoulder, peak and shoulder demands; The average corresponding CE quantities of energy consumed are indicated after (Q:). Similarly the CE flow quantities, are indicated on the power lines (first row of each box) connecting the nodes after (Q:). The maximum flow constraint is shown on the second line in each box.

3. Market Design

The power market consists of three sequential auction submarkets: (1) an energy market for generator supply commitment, which either employs sealed bids to buy and offers to sell based on day-ahead demand forecasts, or continuous bilateral double auction trading up until the hour-ahead forecast is delivered; (2) a market for spinning and quick start reserves conducted after the results of auction (1) are completed; (3) a load adjustment (often called the increment/decrement) market, based on hour-ahead forecasts, under which the terms of (1) are to be incrementally or decrementally adjusted based on the deviation of realized demand from the forecast demand. This market allows Gencos to make marginal adjustment after learning the commitment outcome of (1). Also, to the extent that bilateral contracts have been entered into, (privately, or) in the continuous double auction public version of the energy market, such Gencos could supply their adjustment terms to the Center to enable priorities to be established among all Gencos in the event of line congestion. Such congestion requires the higher cost generators upstream from a constraint to be throttled back and the lowest cost available downstream units to be ramped up.

4. Sealed Bid Day-Ahead Energy Market

The objective of this market is to marshal generator commitment in advance of more exact information on demand. The baseline mechanism for this market is the two-sided sealed bid-offer (SBO) auction. Generator commitment means that any Genco unit with a must-run minimum load requirement is offered as follows: the minimum loaded capacity is offered as the first quantity step at a zero price to the auction; subsequent steps are offered at any prices selected at the discretion of the Genco's owner, except that the center ranks the steps in increasing order of price, whether or not they are submitted in that form.

Buyers submit bids for all their demand, which consists of all must-serve loads, none of which can be voluntarily interrupted. All demand and supply are channeled through a central exchange market. To the extent that Gencos contract directly with buyers, those contracted amounts are subtracted off of both the demand and the supply, but such contracts are simulated and are not a treatment variable in the experiments reported here. For example, we assume that all nuclear units are completely contracted, and that something between minimum and maximum capacity of several of the large coal units are also contracted. The columns on the far right of Table 1 show the number of contracted generators from each Genco, and total contracted capacity of those generators for off, shoulder and peak periods are indicated in summary rows for each seller. Such contracted amounts are subtracted from demand at each local distribution node, and are never under threat of being constrained off. Capacity not contracted is comparable in magnitude to the export capacity of each node. This still creates congestion due to stochastic and cyclical demand variation, and the variance in the marginal prices for generating additional power at various nodes in the system.

As the experiment proceeds from period to period, the status of each generator is indicated by the color of its lightning icon (see Figure 1): green indicates that the generator was providing power in the previous period; blue indicates that it was off; and red indicates that it was unavailable (due to an outage). If a generator was off, offered into the market, and the offer accepted, then the Genco incurred the start-up cost in addition to the fixed and fuel costs. If it was on, and the offer accepted in the market, only the fixed cost and fuel cost are incurred.

The sealed bid procedure for entering energy offers for a generator is illustrated in Figure 1. On his computer monitor in the window entitled "Offer to Sell," each generator's capacity can be offered to the market in up to five asking price steps. In the illustration for a unit in class A, Genco 7, there is automatic entry of the first minimum loaded capacity step (80 MWH) "at market." This is defined as commitment. This can be viewed as an expert system local control over the offer entered, not necessarily a rule of the Exchange Center. In the example, Genco 7 chose to offer the remaining capacity, 80 MWH, at zero. This assures that all the capacity of the unit will be accepted at the ruling market price, unless there is excess minimum base load capacity in the system, as can occur, and the price is zero. (The California PX has produced zero prices in portions of the 1–3 AM interval.) Having entered the offer prices, the subject clicks on the submit button at the bottom right of Figure 2, and each offer step under Status is marked as Submitted. At the close of the market, if the offer is accepted, the Status changes to Accepted.

By clicking one generator and then dragging the mouse across several icons in a class while depressing the mouse button, a portfolio of identical generators is combined into a single offer, i.e., the one representative offer was cloned for all the like units in the portfolio. If the offer was only partially accepted, a local expert system algorithm managed the generators by turning on the minimum cost subset needed to meet the output requirement. Consequently, units must be offered individually if the subject wants to force any unit to be kept on when the offer would not be fully accepted. This algorithm freed the subject to give thought to the intertemporal management problem.

Sellers whose generator offers to the energy market were accepted at less than full capacity are free to offer that capacity, or any surplus capacity, either to the reserve market or the load adjustment market. Only generators with a zero ramp time, or already minimum loaded in the energy market, are eligible.

5. Reserve Market

The reserve market accepted seller offers of capacity as spinning or quick start reserves in the event of an unscheduled outage, or in the event that a buyer falls short of purchasing his forecast requirements in the energy market. Each offer from a generator owner has two parts: (i) the first is a capacity supply price representing the Genco's minimum required payment for maintaining the capacity's readiness to supply temporary reserves; (ii) the second is an energy charge in megawatt hours for drawing upon the capacity until the reserve was no longer needed.

The buyers and sellers are told that the probability of unscheduled outage is about .06 for any generator. Required reserve capacity is always set at 12% of the forecast load in the entire system. In addition to the required reserve, RR, for outages, we treat individual buyers as imposing a buyer reserve requirement, BR, on the system if they did not purchase enough power to cover their forecast demand in the primary energy market. A sudden large increase in load above the energy market allocation is viewed as economically equivalent to a generator going down.

Allocations were made as follows: the capacity supply prices (i) were ordered from lowest to highest; if RR + BR was the total required reserve capacity in megawatts, the lowest RR + BR units of capacity offered were accepted at the lowest rejected offer. Buyers pay for the first RR units in proportion to their forecast demand. Individual buyers, who had fallen short in the energy market, pay for BR, since (in this study) they had no interruptible demand.

The set of RR + BR accepted reserve offers were then sorted from lowest to highest energy asking prices (ii) at which each unit was offered. Now suppose a stochastic failure occurred, requiring OC_i units of reserves to be drawn to replace a failed generator owned by seller i. Then i paid the reserve energy price to all those Gencos supplying the reserve energy, until the next energy market period. However, an expert system automatically substituted any ready but uncommitted capacity owned by i for the reserve market supply, if the fuel cost of that capacity was less than the energy reserve market price. Thus, quick start units not committed to any of the three markets, still served the Genco by placing an upper bound on the cost of replacement power due to an outage.

In similar fashion buyers who failed to purchase enough power through the energy market, were obligated to pay the second tier of energy prices supplied in the reserve market. The buyer's residual demand was automatically satisfied by recourse to the reserve market to incentivize buyers to cover their must-serve demand.

6. Load Adjustment Market

Quick responding generator capacity not accepted (or offered) in either the energy or the reserve market can be offered for load adjustment to realized demand (load following). At this point we model demand as known with a confidence interval of + or -2%. Realized demand may have been either above or below the total capacity of generators accepted in the energy market.

In the load adjustment market, Gencos submit their supply price for providing additional energy above that accepted in the energy market; also the price they are willing to pay to supply less power. Contractually they will be paid their supply price in the energy market based on the day-ahead forecast (hence, generating less than this saves fuel). This information, when supplied after the energy and reserve markets have been run and demand becomes better known, allows substitutions between downstream and upstream generators on either end of a constrained line for congestion management. All Gencos in the energy market are free to supply this information for congestion management, and as a tertiary source of supply for forecast load not yet contracted in the energy or reserve markets.

7. Continuous Double Auction Energy Market

We executed a single major experimental treatment variation on the day-ahead sealed bid energy market described above, keeping constant our treatment of the auction procedures for the reserve market and the load adjustment market. This was the continuous double auction (CDA) energy market.

In this variation we followed the proposal in California under which all buyers and sellers are free to contract via a double auction market that runs continuously down to the hour-ahead spot market. There was no day-ahead energy market, only a day ahead forecast with $+$ or -8% confidence. (Other demand related events could be publicized at any time.) Shortly before the double auction energy market closed, a new forecast was publicized with $+$ or -2% confidence. Following the energy market, we ran the reserve and load adjustment markets as above.

The convention employed was that the acceptor of a CDA bid (offer) agreed to deliver (or take) power from the submitter's location. If the energy could not ultimately be delivered or taken because of line constraints, the acceptor suffered the cost of rectifying the situation. The acceptor had to purchase locally available energy to satisfy the buyer's load and avoid the constrained line, and he could attempt to unload his previously contracted remote energy source in the adjustment market.

A time line for the energy, reserve, and load adjustment markets is provided in Olson et al. (1999, Figure 8).

8. The Network

A chart of the 8-node network we used for the experiments is shown in Figure 2. Each node is a control area connected to other nodes so as to correspond to an aggregated version of a portion of the grid in the Mid-Atlantic, South and Midwest. In this figure are presented the set of surplus maximizing competitive equilibrium allocations based on the demand in the four periods on the final day of trading. These allocations are based only on marginal costs of energy, assuming all the right generators are available to inject power into the system. The competitive equilibrium line flows and sector costs and profits are computed by applying the optimization to simulated fully revealing bids/offers; i.e., each simulated buyer bids his resale value schedule, and each seller her marginal cost schedule for each generator unit as if it is currently running. The equilibrium allocations are shown for periods 17–20 (Day 5). On other days the realization of demand was different, though of the same pattern, so the corresponding equilibrium allocations were somewhat different.

Under each node name is a vector of prices ($P:$) above a vector of quantities ($Q:$). These represent the equilibrium prices for power (rounded to the nearest peso) in the Off-peak, Shoulder, Peak, and Shoulder average demand periods, and the corresponding quantities buyers would consume. Each transmission line, which shows a direction of flow and a maximum flow constraint, also shows a vector of quantities indicating the amount of flow that would occur in each of the four periods if the competitive equilibrium allocation were achieved.

Each control area (node) had demand and supply capacity that was large relative to the transfer capacity of the lines connecting it with other control areas. This meant that the control areas were sealed off from substantial inter-connect contestability. We imposed local bilateral contracts in sufficient quantity to allow contestability through imports and exports loosely matched in volume to the capacity of the transmission lines. This allowed us to study a reasonably competitive market structure, but public policy must ultimately address the issue of creating more competitive conditions within each control area. The transmission system is inadequate to rely on export–import contestability.

9. Optimization

In the experiments conducted, we used a DC model with quadratic line losses to compute the real power flows in the aggregated network.

10. Subjects

More than 100 undergraduate students were recruited from business, engineering and economics classes. Subjects received a fixed fee of $15 for arriving on time for each experiment, and their accumulated earnings in the experiment after they have finished. Where subjects were recruited for several experiments, including training sessions, all payments were withheld until they completed the series. All trading was denominated in experimental "pesos," and each agent was provided a private exchange rate that was used to convert pesos earned to American dollars at the end of the experiment. The exchange rates were calibrated to provide each subject with competitive equilibrium earnings of approximately $25 for his two hours of effort, depending on how well he and other members of his group traded. Subject earnings varied from $0 to $180 during various individual trading sessions.

Each subject was originally recruited for a series of four 2-hour training experiments. The first session consisted of the delivery of written and oral instructions, followed by a question and answer period concerning the experimental environment in which they would trade. That was followed by a training session in which subjects traded in a symmetric star network with no losses, line constraints or reserve and adjustment markets. Losses and line constraints were added in session three, and the auxiliary markets in session four. Across the four sessions subjects earned up to several hundred dollars.

Through self and experimenter selection for the best traders, the original 100 were reduced to 44 who participated in the series of three experiments reported here. Therefore, all subjects had participated in at least four previous trading sessions.

11. Data Analysis: Questions and Answers

Running an SBO versus CDA variation in the energy market allowed us to compare the two different auction institutions in terms of efficiency, the distribution of surplus between buyers and sellers, the effect of location on prices and profitability, and the effect on profitability of Gencos with varying mixes of generators who can offer portfolios of like units to the market. In this comparison we note that the CDA provides continuous feedback of information, and permits Gencos to lock in some individual generators in advance, while others are committed later when more information is available. These advantages, relative to the day-ahead SBO, must be weighed against the latter's optimization support advantages.

For the sake of conciseness and clarity in reporting the experiment results, we chose four representative measurement nodes in the network. In equilibrium, they represented the major sources: Node 1, one transhipment point, Node 5, and the major sinks at opposite ends of the stylized trading network, Node 7 and Node 8. Results are reported separately for each of four super-experienced groups in each environment, and then summarized with averages.

11.1. What is the Competitive Efficiency of the Two Markets Based on Marginal Energy Costs?

The primary measure of market performance will be efficiency measured as the realized proportion of total competitive equilibrium surplus per period; i.e., the ratio of actual to equilibrium earnings attributable to producers, wholesale buyers and transmission. Table 2 gives a summary of Total Efficiency for the SBO and CDA environments. Overall efficiencies are high (well above 90%) in both markets, but the results here indicate that post energy market efficiencies of the day ahead SBO markets are on average 2.5% more efficient than those of the CDA markets.

Moreover the difference grows to 3.4% in the post adjustment market. These differences can only be due to the lack of coordination in the CDA, and the consequent reduced potential to fix inefficiencies in the auxiliary markets.

How effective are buyers in meeting their energy requirements? How cost effective is generation? Consider the fact that in equilibrium we know which is the most economical set of generators to supply the power and which buyers should buy. We observed:

Table 2

The results realized for sellers' % equilibrium costs, buyers' % equilibrium quantity of power delivered (post energy and post adjustment markets) are shown for each of four distinct super experienced subject groups, under both the SBO and CDA trading rules. The average across the four groups is listed at the bottom of each column for SBO and CDA. Observe that on average sellers incur costs of 112.56% of the equilibrium cost following the adjustment market in SBO, but 122.56% in CDA. Buyers fill 98.76% of their demand quantity, post adjustment, in SBO and 97.03% in CDA. Similarly total efficiency is 97.01% in SBO, 93.79% in CDA

Auction	Group	Sellers' % equilibrium costs		Buyers' % equilibrium quantities		Total efficiency	
		Post energy Mkt	Post adjustment Mkt	Post energy Mkt	Post adjustment Mkt	Post energy Mkt	Post adjustment Mkt
SBO	1	106.63%	109.72%	97.39%	98.87%	96.21%	97.49%
	2	104.04%	112.15%	95.78%	98.96%	94.73%	97.28%
	3	103.10%	118.45%	94.07%	98.61%	92.92%	96.09%
	4	104.90%	109.93%	96.50%	98.61%	95.43%	97.19%
	Ave.	104.67%	112.56%	95.94%	98.76%	94.82%	97.01%
CDA	1	120.80%	125.25%	95.00%	96.89%	91.72%	93.29%
	2	124.04%	126.91%	97.80%	98.85%	94.46%	95.28%
	3	118.95%	125.46%	93.55%	96.66%	90.32%	93.02%
	4	110.55%	112.60%	94.79%	95.71%	92.78%	93.56%
	Ave.	118.59%	122.56%	95.29%	97.03%	92.32%	93.79%

(1) the proportion of expected energy consumption that was actually realized by buyers (% Equilibrium Quantities), and (2) the cost of producing that energy for the sellers (% Equilibrium Costs). This information, also contained in Table 2, indicates that the major cost of inefficiency was due to a higher than expected total average cost of producing energy, and not so much due to buyers missing consumption. But again, the CDA environment produced seller costs that averaged 10% in excess of the SBO.

11.2. Do SBO Prices and CDA Weighted Average Prices Converge to Comparable Levels?

CDA prices are maintained at a higher level than SBO prices. This is borne out by Table 3 that provides absolute energy trading prices observed at the four measurement nodes at the four demand levels. The average CDA prices dominate the uniform SBO prices in 14 of 16 cases, usually by a factor between 1.5 and 2. Moreover SBO prices dominate the competitive equilibrium price prediction in 14 of 16 cases (cf. the competitive equilibrium prices at the bottom of each average price column). Table 3 also provides quantities consumed, which varies little by group and treatment, and quantities imported or exported which reinforces the notion of high group variance and the unpredictability of flow patterns in a network where similar marginal costs are distributed well throughout the network.

11.3. What are the Profitability Levels for the Various Agents in the System?

If generation costs and trading prices are systematically higher, and quantity traded systematically lower in CDA than SB, then the consequence can only be that buyers suffer lower profitability: they paid 1.5 times as much for 4% less energy. However, the potential for increased seller profitability is contingent on whether sellers negotiate price increases that more than cover the cost of their increased inefficiencies, and whether sellers gather enough demand and value information during the double auction feedback to behave more strategically in the reserve and adjustment markets.

Comparing CDA with SBO, the energy prices recorded (Tables 3a–3b) indicate that sellers' CDA prices tend to be much above SBO prices, while power deliveries are reduced only modestly. But from Table 2 we have seller costs in the energy market increasing by only 10%. Sellers are able therefore to capture some of the buyers' surplus in the CDA energy market where there is more opportunity to explore the "willingness to pay" and less risk to bear in having an offer refused. In some sense they are blessed by the fact that higher priced inefficient generators trade to bolster the prices, and buyers are more cautious in buying close to home to avoid the risks of congestion.

11.4. Do Nodal Prices Reflect Distance Sensitivity and Line Constraints?

For the sake of clarity, because buyers and sellers were quoting prices in integers, nodal prices were always displayed as rounded integers on the network diagram that agents

Table 3

Average prices at nodes 1 and 5 (3a) and nodes 7 and 8 (3b), are listed by subject group in columns 3, 6, 9 and 12 for four sequential demand levels: off peak, shoulder, peak and shoulder. Average prices are followed by the quantity of power consumed (QC), followed by the quantity imported (+) or exported (−) under QIE. The top 5 rows are for SB, the last 5 rows for CDA. Observe that for most nodes and demand condition, the average price is higher in CDA trading than SBO. In parentheses below the average price column for each node is contained the competitive price (Figure 2)

(a) Energy market prices and quantities (price, quantity consumed, quantity imported (+) or exported (−))

Node 1

Auction	Group	Off peak			Shoulder			Peak			Shoulder		
		Price	QC	QIE	Price	QC	QIE	Price	QC	QIE	Price	QC	QIE
SB	1	16.8	1209.0	150.3	19.2	1606.0	−259.4	36.6	1618.4	140.4	32.8	1606.0	314.7
	2	13.8	967.0	84.7	19.8	1551.0	215.0	19.8	1621.0	−64.6	20.0	1574.8	30.5
	3	14.8	1209.0	−128.4	20.4	1562.0	−220.5	30.8	1419.2	147.2	32.8	1505.8	325.8
	4	15.4	1209.0	226.8	24.0	1606.0	26.5	30.2	1803.0	−13.9	28.8	1606.0	75.6
	Ave.	15.2	1148.5	83.4	20.9	1581.3	−59.6	29.4	1615.4	52.3	28.6	1573.2	186.7
CDA	1	19.7	1176.8	91.8	44.2	1587.8	−106.6	81.9	1608.4	178.2	47.9	1485.8	129.2
	2	23.1	1209.0	158.4	39.6	1606.0	−20.4	47.0	1756.8	−172.1	45.1	1546.2	−42.0
	3	39.3	1170.8	307.4	27.1	1606.0	223.2	41.2	1694.6	214.0	22.5	1476.9	500.7
	4	55.8	1164.2	13.8	46.4	1606.0	−256.8	33.6	1803.0	−55.7	42.6	1601.8	18.3
	Ave.	34.5	1180.2	142.9	39.3	1601.5	−40.2	50.9	1715.7	41.1	39.5	1527.7	151.6
		(13)			(13)			(17)			(13)		

Table 3
(continued)

Node 5

Auction	Group	Off peak			Shoulder			Peak			Shoulder		
		Price	QC	QIE	Price	QC	QIE	Price	QC	QIE	Price	QC	QIE
SB	1	16.8	658.0	56.4	19.6	923.0	181.0	38.6	909.3	120.9	32.8	923.0	113.8
	2	14.0	658.0	−79.3	19.8	920.0	−90.6	19.8	946.4	−147.2	20.0	883.0	−193.7
	4	15.4	658.0	120.2	24.8	920.3	321.2	30.2	1023.0	214.3	28.8	923.0	249.8
	Ave.	15.3	658.0	21.8	21.2	920.1	130.6	29.9	904.8	36.1	28.6	885.0	45.5
		(13)			(13)			(17)			(13)		
CDA	1	27.0	653.6	33.0	38.1	865.3	58.5	47.6	892.6	41.9	48.2	785.3	45.4
	2	53.8	658.0	−69.8	39.4	915.3	53.6	41.9	963.6	56.8	45.4	901.8	−11.4
	3	15.9	550.1	92.3	31.1	915.7	24.9	59.3	977.8	56.6	39.9	852.9	93.9
	4	15.7	615.0	−101.4	29.5	923.0	154.1	30.3	1023.0	38.4	27.4	923.0	102.2
	Ave.	28.1	619.2	−11.5	34.5	904.8	72.8	44.8	964.3	48.4	40.2	865.8	57.5
		(13)			(13)			(17)			(13)		

Table 3
(continued)

(b) Energy market prices and quantities (price, quantity consumed, quantity imported (+) or exported (−))

Node 7

Auction	Group	Off peak			Shoulder			Peak			Shoulder		
		Price	QC	QIE	Price	QC	QIE	Price	QC	QIE	Price	QC	QIE
SB	1	17.2	2310.8	199.8	30.8	3064.1	223.3	60.0	3376.2	238.3	53.0	3042.4	149.7
	2	15.2	2311.0	167.1	20.0	3069.0	94.7	48.0	3559.0	238.3	29.0	3069.0	238.3
	3	18.6	2308.9	123.9	24.6	2923.3	28.0	35.0	3143.3	−104.5	31.0	2745.7	−147.7
	4	15.4	2311.0	98.2	26.2	3066.7	157.0	43.0	3407.1	158.2	30.8	2979.7	104.8
	Ave.	16.6	2310.4	147.3	25.4	3030.8	125.8	46.5	3371.4	132.6	36.0	2959.2	86.3
CDA	1	19.5	2307.6	−210.7	40.4	2991.2	−115.1	51.2	3354.1	−183.8	48.3	2919.5	−139.4
	2	4.0	2286.3	167.3	33.7	3016.2	20.2	47.9	3362.1	109.0	37.4	3058.5	77.8
	3	23.3	2311.0	−112.2	30.2	3009.6	15.8	47.6	3455.9	197.1	42.3	2884.9	91.9
	4	16.2	2280.6	−187.3	27.7	3015.2	−10.2	32.6	3465.3	125.3	29.5	3019.0	−7.9
	Ave.	15.8	2296.4	−85.7	33.0	3008.1	−22.3	44.8	3409.4	61.9	39.4	2970.5	5.6
		(15)			(19)			(52)			(19)		

Table 3
(continued)

Node 8

Auction	Group	Off peak			Shoulder			Peak			Shoulder		
		Price	QC	QIE	Price	QC	QIE	Price	QC	QIE	Price	QC	QIE
SB	1	13.2	1797.0	−133.0	18.4	2498.0	−264.8	20.0	2784.0	−287.2	18.8	2498.0	−384.2
	2	12.8	1797.0	−133.0	19.2	2498.0	−0.7	20.0	2784.0	−214.5	21.4	2498.0	40.4
	3	14.4	1797.0	167.0	22.6	2493.7	324.7	21.4	2783.0	−66.2	27.4	2493.7	−274.3
	4	13.6	1797.0	−127.4	23.8	2498.0	127.3	24.8	2784.0	−196.2	37.4	2495.7	185.0
	Ave.	13.5	1797.0	−56.6	21.0	2496.9	46.6	21.6	2783.8	−191.0	26.3	2496.4	28.9
CDA	1	20.2	1756.0	−3.0	39.4	2462.6	154.4	52.2	2753.0	−116.0	49.2	2395.0	−35.8
	2	26.3	1787.7	−64.1	35.9	2467.8	49.4	66.9	2758.4	−147.3	51.7	2356.7	11.9
	3	16.0	1670.2	−66.0	30.3	2201.6	−118.8	47.7	2718.1	−129.9	40.6	2185.2	−122.1
	4	6.9	1746.1	33.1	27.4	2454.3	80.1	30.5	2768.1	−157.7	31.3	2453.4	3.2
	Ave.	17.4	1740.0	−25.0	33.3	2396.6	41.3	49.3	2749.4	−137.7	43.2	2347.6	−35.7
		(17)			(17)			(17)			(17)		

could observe. This meant that minor price differences were frequently undetectable. However, the exact nodal prices, taking into account the marginal losses along network transmission lines, were always used to count realized profits.

Since average line loss on every line was scaled from 2.5% at maximum capacity, the largest price difference due to losses could be 5%. (Marginal loss price differences are approximately twice the average loss.) Whenever the upstream and downstream prices differed by at least 5%, there was line congestion. Genco production cost differences between control areas yielded lines often loaded to constraint in our calculated competitive equilibria (see Figure 2). Notice, however, that even though several lines are frequently up to constraint, there is just one large equilibrium congestion price difference in this network, which occurs at Node 7 during peak demand. In equilibrium the constraints are just barely binding.

Larger price differences due to congestion were frequently realized during the trading, and the observed flow was often the reverse of the equilibrium direction. These price differences really did not reflect the physical reality of the production cost differences, but are artifacts of strategic bidding in a very delicately balanced system. Generators with similar cost characteristics were disbursed throughout the system, and only the offers determined which direction the power flowed.

We conclude that with intensive training and screening subjects can handle very complex and demanding environments when assisted by local expert system algorithms similar to the support needed by practitioners in the field. Moreover they engage in extensive, successful manipulation attempts to take advantage of the regulatory "must-serve" restrictions on the ability of the local distribution monopoly to interrupt demand to discipline seller withholding of supply. Sellers, however, are much more consistently successful in this respect under the CDA trading rule condition. These findings contrast sharply with those of other experimental studies in which modest proportions of peak consumer demand could be interrupted by wholesale buyers, enabling the latter to discipline seller attempts to raise clearing prices.

Reference

Olson, Mark A., Rassenti, Stephen J., Smith, Vernon L., Rigdon, Mary L., Ziegler, Michael J. (1999). "Market design and motivated human trading behavior in electricity markets". In: Sprague, Ralph H. (Ed.), System Sciences, HICSS-32. Proceedings of the 32nd Annual Hawaii International Conference on System Sciences. Track 3. IEEE Computer Society, Los Alamitos, CA.

Chapter 74

TRANSMISSION CONSTRAINTS, INCENTIVE AUCTION RULES AND TRADER EXPERIENCE IN AN ELECTRIC POWER MARKET

STEVEN BACKERMAN, STEPHEN RASSENTI and VERNON L. SMITH

1. Experimental Network Environment

The lower panel in Figure 1 displays a simple 3-node radial network underlying the experiments we report herein. Wholesale buyers, B(4), with the number of independent buyers denoted in parenthesis, are located at the center node. Three generators are at the left node, G1(3), and three at the right node, G2(3). Each generator node is connected to the buyer node by a single transmission line, T1(1) and T2(1). In this case T1 and T2 have no active agents quoting transmission prices which are computed using (6) or (6′) from Backerman, Rassenti, and Smith (2000). The transmission function is served passively; i.e., revenue accruing to a line is a residual rent. This network provides a very simplified, aggregated, representation of the United Kingdom grid. London is at the center, and is by far the dominant buyer node. The major generation complex is to the north of London with the power lines bringing power into the London metropolitan region subject to constraint when winter peak demand is heavy. A smaller generation complex is to the south of London where there are controversial proposals to locate new generation capacity on the coast.[1]

The last line printed in Figure 1, labeled Eq., states a competitive equilibrium for a particular parameterization of this network (see below). The right-hand side (hereafter RHS) displays the equilibrium with 49 units of power (e.g., 490 megawatts) being injected at a price of 202.2 at node G2 by three generators. At the buyers' node B, four wholesale buyers receive 42.5 units delivered by T2 from G2 at price 275.

Applying the principles of section I on the RHS line we have $ATL_2 = L(X_2)/X_2 = (49 - 42.5)/49 = 0.13235$, and therefore $MTL_2 = L'(X_2) \cong 2ATL_2 = 0.2647$. With price 202.2 at G2, we verify that $P_B = P_{G2}/[1 - L'(X_2)] = 202.2/(1 - 0.2647) = 275$. From (6) the equilibrium price imputed to T2 is $P_{T2} = P_B ATL_2 = 36.3$. (All calculations are subject to rounding errors.)

On the LHS, the calculations must take into account that T1 is constrained with capacity $K = 29$, so that $X_1 \leqslant 29$. The three generators at G1 inject 29 units into T1 and 24.1 units arrive at B from the LHS. The average loss of power on T1 is therefore $ATL_1 = L(X_1)/X_1 = (29 - 24.1)/29 = 0.1689$, with marginal

---

[1] This sketch is based on conversations between Rassenti and Smith and the UK Office of Electricity Regulation (OFFER) in 1994.

Handbook of Experimental Economics Results, Volume 1
Copyright © 2008 Elsevier B.V. All rights reserved
DOI: 10.1016/S1574-0722(07)00074-1

```
Electric Net Loss Experiment Monitor V1.00                    9/30/94
─────────── MENU ───────────      #  Time Agent Loc. Order Unit Price
About this software              67   22    3    B     3    15  240
Retrieve Existing Parameter File 68   18    3    B     3    15  244
View/Edit Current Parameters     69   16   11   G2     1     4  195
Save Current Parameters to a File 70  16    1    B     2     8  290
Subject Screen Demonstration     71    9    7   G1     3     2  175
View/Print Subjects/Network Status 72  9    9   G1     1     6  177
Experiment Data Menu             73    8    4    B     1    15  246
Save Experiment Data to a File   74    7    1    B     3    15  275
Retrieve Experiment Data File    75    7   11   G2     2    11  190
Terminate Subject Programs       76    5   11   G2     1     4  190
Exit to DOS                      77    4    4    B     1    15  290
                                 78    2    2    B     3    15  259
Current period: 27        | Countdown clock:  1 |
```

```
   ASK: 180.0              ASK: 262.1             ASK: 203.0
   BID: 177.9              BID: 259.0             BID: 194.7

    G1(3)    →T1 (1)→     B(4)     ←T2 (1)←       G2(3)

Re. 26.0 @ 177.4   26.0@38.3   22.1+39.5@254.0   45.0@30.9    45.0@192.3
Eq. 29.0 @ 125.0   29.0@103.8  24.1+42.5@275.0   49.0@36.3    49.0@202.2
```

Figure 1. The monitor screen for the three-node radial network, used in the electric power experiments reported below, has two remote generator nodes G1 and G2 (shown as ovals) each with three generation companies, and a central load center at node B (shown as a rectangle), with 4 wholesale buyers. The line labeled Eq. on the bottom left shows a competitive equilibrium: 29 units of power at price 125 is injected at G1. The constrained (flow ⩽ 29) transmission line T1 accepts the 29 units for transfer at price 103.5 to B. At B, 24.1 units arrive (loss = 29.0 − 24.1 = 4.9) from G1. Reading from the right, at G2, 49 units are injected at price 202.2. The unconstrained line T2 accepts the 49 units at transfer price 36.3. At B, 42.5 units arrive from G2, where buyers pay the delivery price 275. The line labeled Re shows the actual flows and prices for period 27 (middle left) for one experiment with 1 second shown remaining on the countdown clock (center of figure). Immediately above the network is displayed the standing bid and ask at each node. In the experiments reported below subjects see only the bid and ask at their own node. The upper right display exhibits the most recent order flow items #67–#78 in period 27. Thus at time 22 (seconds remaining) agent 3 at location B submits her 3rd order to buy, 15 units at limit price 240, which is subsequently improved (displaced) at time 18 by the higher bid price 244.

loss $MTL_1 = L'(X) \cong 2ATL_1 = 0.3379$, where $X_1 = K$ is optimal under constraint. $P_B = B'(K - L(K)) = 275$, and $P_G = G'(K) = 125$ we have $275 = (125 + \mu)/(1 - .3379)$ and therefore $\mu = 57.1$. Consequently, from (6′) in Backerman, Rassenti, and Smith (2000), $P_{T1} = P_B ATL_1 + \mu = 275(.1698) + 57.1 = 103.8$, showing how $P_B ATL_1 + \mu$, the congestion rental price of a constrained line, can soar relative to marginal loss. This also suggests why the regulation, or ownership, of electrical utilities by political entities does not use opportunity cost principles in pricing transmission networks. In this case the unit opportunity congestion cost is over two times the marginal loss price. Of course the economic function of these congestion rents is to signal the need for investment – investment to increase the transmission capacity of T1, to increase low cost generation capacity at node G2, or to introduce demand side management technologies that will conserve energy consumed by buyers at B.

In the top right panel of Figure 1, column 1 shows messages (orders to buy or sell) 67 through 78 sent by agents to the control center. Column 2 shows the time remaining, in seconds, when each message arrived. Columns 3–5 identify respectively the agent, his/her location, and the order number for that agent. The last two columns show the quantity in units and unit price specified in the order. On the first line below the top panels is shown the current period number (27), and the seconds remaining (1) on the countdown clock for that period. Immediately above the G1, B and G2 nodes is the standing bid/ask state of the market at each node. It is important to note that each agent sees only the bid/ask spread at his/her own node. This is primarily because the subjects have enough to do without trying to observe bids and asks at all nodes. We expect, however, to run experienced subject experiments with all this information displayed on each subject's monitor screen. All the nodal bids and asks do appear on the experimenter's monitor screen, but not the bid/ask state of the two transmission lines. We have added these for the display in Figure 1. Since the transmission price is given by Equation (6), we apply (6) (see Backerman, Rassenti, and Smith, 2000) to the ask at B to get the ask for T1 (T2) and to the bid at B to get the bid at T1 (T2).

The equilibrium price and quantity calculations, illustrated above, are based on marginal losses $L'(X^0)$ where X^0 is the last unit injected at a generator node. But the bid and ask prices at each node are computed for an additional unit added to the flow if a new trade occurs at the quoted bid or ask. For example consider the G1 node where the best unaccepted current ask price by one of the G1 generators is 180. What asking price does this translate into at the buyer's node, after correction for losses? To determine this look at the data for the current realizations appearing on the second line from the bottom in Figure 1, labeled "Re." Note that 26 units of power will be the injection at G1 based on the current state of the market. The ask of 180 is for one additional unit, which would make the injection rate 27 units of power. Since the coefficient of loss is 0.0058 on the left (not shown) we have a marginal loss of $L'(27) = 2(0.0058)27 = 0.3132$. Therefore the marginal transmission factor is $1 - L'(27) = 0.6868$. It follows that the asking price at B corresponding to an ask of 180 at G1 is $180/0.6868 = 262.1$ as shown.

Now look at G2 where the best ask by a generator is 203. The coefficient of loss on T2 is 0.0027 (not shown). Since the current tentative injection rate at G2 is 45, we have $1 - L'(46) = 0.7516$ and the ask at B corresponding to an ask at G2 of 203 is $203/.7516 = 270.1$. This is higher than the asking price at B for power coming from G1 which, as computed above, was 262.1. The optimization algorithm requires the ask at B to equal $\min(262.1, 270.1) = 262.1$, as shown in Figure 1.

In like manner we can compute the bid at G1 which corresponds to the standing bid of 259 at B. As above the marginal transmission factor on line 1 is 0.6868 and from (3) the bid at G1 is $.6868(259) = 177.9$. Similarly the bid at G2 is $.7516(259) = 194.7$. If some generator lowers an unaccepted offer to less than this locational adjusted bid, he/she is guaranteed to increase his/her volume of trade.

Table 1
The experimental design uses a 2 (auction rule variations) by 2 (LHS constrained or not) by 2 (experience level, once, ×, or twice, ××) design. Ten inexperienced training sessions are not included. The entries n (m) under the × and ×× columns indicated the number of experiments (n) and periods (m). Under the Other-side rule, as soon as at least one bid and offer has been provisionally accepted in the supply/demand cross a new bid (offer) arriving in real time cannot displace any inferior bid (offer) standing in the cross until it first meets the terms of an offer (bid) on the other side of the market. Consequently, at any time t, all bids and offers in the (provisionally accepted) cross earn conditional time priority. In the Both-sides rule, any bid (offer) that is higher (lower) than a bid (offer) in the cross immediately replaces the latter. Note that the left-hand side (LHS) transmission line is constrained at 29 units in nine experiments, unconstrained in 9 experiments

Auction rule	Left-hand side (LHS) constrained	Experiment ×	Experiment ××
Both-sides	Yes	2(27)	1(28)
			1(25)
Both-sides	No	2(28)	2(28)
Other-side	Yes	1(23)	1(28)
		2(28)	1(29)
Other-side	No	1(23)	2(29)
		1(24)	
		1(27)	

2. Experimental Design

Our experimental design is summarized in Table 1. We report 18 experiments (10 experienced, and 8 twice experienced subjects) using 100 subjects in total. Subject payout averaged $34 per subject per experiment. The supply, demand and transmission loss environment is illustrated in Figure 2 for our two treatments: when neither T1 nor T2 is constrained and when only T1 is constrained. All subjects were first run in initial "training" sessions to familiarize them with the environment and the spot market trading procedures. This data is not reported and has not been examined. When subjects returned for the second (experienced) sessions, and for the third (twice experienced) sessions from 23 to 29 trading periods were completed. In these sessions subjects were free to review the instructions again but most of the two-hour sessions were devoted to trading.

3. The Mechanism: A Continuously Updated Nodal Uniform Price Auction

We employ a 3-node version of the Uniform Price Double Auction (UPDA) studied in McCabe, Rassenti, and Smith (1993). In fact the mechanism used here is identical to the one cited if the asking prices at G1 and G2 are all adjusted for marginal transmission losses, and thus represent delivered prices at the reference buyers' node. We use the following UPDA rules that, under test, were favored among the many alternatives discussed and studied in McCabe, Rassenti, and Smith (1993, pp. 309–316).

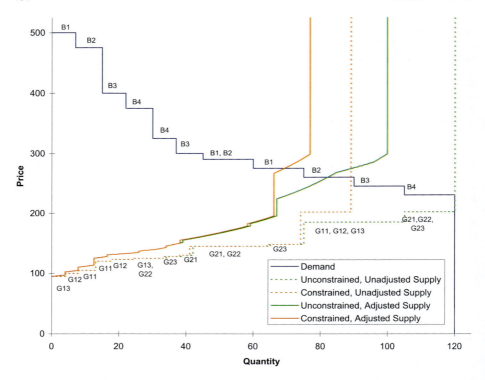

Figure 2. The generator supply schedule, and load demand schedule illustrate the induced supply-demand environment. All prices are computed (loss adjusted) at the B (buyer) reference node. Each of four buyers have three demand steps; interruptible at the price levels shown or lower at the buyer's discretion who is contractually bound to receive no higher resale price. Each generator step, denoted G_{ij}, refers to generator node $i(=1,2)$ and generation owner $j(=1,2,3)$. At each node, each generation company has three generators whose marginal cost is indicated by the vertical level of the step. The unadjusted generation cost schedules are shown dashed, while the supply, adjusted for transmission loss to node B, is shown as a solid line. In each case the smaller supply (higher cost) schedule applies when the LHS line is constrained, the larger supply schedule is for the LHS unconstrained.

1. Call Rule. The market is called at the end of a preannounced period of time. Each period in these experiments closed after 4 minutes.
2. Message Rule. An agent's order is acceptable if it is a new order or improves the price terms of the last order submitted: bids must be at a higher price, or demand more units, while offers must be at a lower price, or supply more units. The price improvement requirement captures one important feature of the continuous double auction rules used widely in financial markets.
3. Update rules (for explicit details see McCabe, Rassenti, and Smith, 1993, pp. 312–315);

(i) The Both-sides rule: allows any agent to beat the terms of accepted orders (displace them) on his/her own side of the market (buying or selling), or meet the terms of an unaccepted order on the other side, whichever is best for the agent submitting the order. For example if the highest accepted offer is $9, and a new order to sell at $8 is entered it replaces the accepted offer at $9.

(ii) The Other-side rule: agents must meet the terms of unaccepted bids or asks on the other side of the market to become accepted. This rule assigns temporary time priority to orders tentatively accepted; i.e., an accepted bid (ask) cannot be displaced by an unaccepted bid (ask) until that order has met the terms of an unaccepted order on the other side of the market. In the previous example the new offer at $8 does not automatically replace the accepted offer at $9. It will do so only when the standing unaccepted bid by a buyer exceeds $8, but does not exceed $9. If it exceeds $9, then both the bid and the offer are accepted.

(iii) The tentative price at each node, or for transmission capacity, is uniform for all agents at that location (or on that line), and represents a clearing price for all accepted bids and asks at that point in time.

McCabe, Rassenti, and Smith (1993, p. 320) report that the other-side rule increases efficiency relative to the both-sides rule. Why? A buyer (seller) can enter the demand and supply (bid/ask) cross with an accepted bid (offer) only by meeting the terms of a seller (buyer) unit that is currently unaccepted. This provides an incentive for buyers and sellers outside the cross to meet each other's terms, increasing the chance that there will be an increase in volume traded and therefore in efficiency. It also undercuts the incentive to wait until near the period's end to enter bids (offers). The other-side rule recognizes a form of temporary time priority; i.e., a bid (offer) that is accepted has priority over later ones – even those that provide better terms – unless such orders yield new trades with the other-side. The other-side rule is especially efficient at overcoming price inertia when initial trades are off equilibrium: it accelerates price discovery. Figure 1 provides a snapshot of the price pressure the other-side rule provides. Notice the standing bid (259) is above the current trading price (254) but below the standing ask (262.1), so the owner of this bid is not trading because lower accepted bids have higher priority. This puts strong upwards price pressure on this buyer that will tend to move the market-clearing price toward the competitive equilibrium (275).

4. Hypotheses and Tests

We use the following regression equations to measure the effect of the experimental treatment variables on efficiency and the income share of each agent class:

$$Y_{i,t} = \alpha + \beta Y_{i,t-1} + \beta_1 D_1 + \beta_2 D_2 + \beta_3 D_3 + \varepsilon_{it}, \\ i = 1, 2, 3, 4; \; t = 1, 2, \ldots, T; \tag{1}$$

where T = number of trading periods; $D_1 = 1$, if subjects are twice previously experienced and $D_1 = 0$, if subjects are once experienced; $D_2 = 1$ if the LHS transmission line is constrained, $D_2 = 0$ if the LHS is unconstrained; $D_3 = 1$, when the other-side auction rule applies, and $D_3 = 0$, when the both-sides rule applies. The dependent variables, Y_{it}, include total market efficiency, G1 profit share, B profit share and G2 profit share, respectively in each of four different regression equations, $i = 1, 2, 3, 4$. The lagged dependent variable, $Y_{i,t-1}$, is included to correct for expected significant auto correlation in each time series. The profit shares are all normalized with respect to the competitive equilibrium predicted share. Thus, if the buyer's share is 1.1 this indicates that they are receiving 110% of their competitive equilibrium share.

We test three a priori hypotheses.

HYPOTHESIS 1. Increased subject experience will increase efficiency.

This prediction is based on previous experimental findings in which experience is sometimes found to significantly increase total subject earnings. The null alternative argues that in some contexts attempts at manipulation may emerge with experience, which may yield a negative impact on efficiency, but increased profit for some subjects.

HYPOTHESIS 2. The effect of the constraint on line T1 will be to increase the share of income accruing to the upstream generators, G1.

When a line is constrained the demand for energy injected at the upstream node becomes perfectly inelastic for all generator node price increases from $P_G = G'(X^0)$ up to $P_G = G'(X^0) + \mu$ as in Equation (3′) in Backerman, Rassenti, and Smith (2000). The supply also becomes perfectly inelastic for all price decreases from $P_B = G'(X^0) + \mu$ down to $G'(X^0)$. In between there are a great many non-cooperative equilibria depending upon the configuration of extra marginal generation and demand steps. Since in the present design we have no generator agent excluded at prices above $G'(X^0)$, we expect G1 subjects to effect a substantial increase in the G1 node price. There is nothing insidious (or collusive) about this expected increase in generator prices. To control for this the subjects are not informed at any time that T1 is constrained at 29 units.

HYPOTHESIS 3. Efficiency, using the other-side rule, will be greater than under the both-sides rule.

As noted in Section 4 this is because the other-side rule provides better incentives for those buyers and sellers, who are outside the cross at any time, to agree on their respective terms of trade. Such agreement is a precondition for subverting the temporary time priority afforded those units which currently have acceptance status. This also provides incentives to enter into contracts early in the period to gain some time priority.

Table 2

A regression analysis of measures of market performance on experience level (once or twice previously experienced), whether the LHS transmission line is constrained or not, and the Other-side versus Both-sides auction rule, yields the indicated results. Thus efficiency increases (not significantly) with experience level, decreases (significantly) when the LHS line is constrained and increases (significantly) with the Other-side rule

Performance measure	Effect of treatment on performance measure		
	Experience	LHS line constraint	Other-side auction rule
Efficiency	Increases	Decreases[a]	Increases[a]
G1 profit share	Decreases[a]	Increases[a]	Increases[b]
B profit share	Increases[a]	Decreases	Increases
G2 profit share	Decreases	Increases	Increases[a]

[a]Significant, $p < 0.001$.
[b]Significant, $p < 0.01$.

5. Regression Results

Table 2 summarizes the regression results using all the experiments listed in Table 1. The results support Hypothesis 1 but it is not significant, while Hypothesis 3 is strongly supported; i.e., efficiency is increased significantly by the other-side rule. Hypothesis 2 is also supported: under the T1 line constraint the upstream generators at G1 raise their offers and gain an increase in their share of the surplus. We also observe the prior unpredicted result that the T1 constraint significantly lowers efficiency. It would appear that strategic behavior by the generators on the left, when they face a line constraint, also interferes with the achievement of efficiency. Also as expected from Hypothesis 3 is the observation that the G1 (also G2) generators gain a significant increase in surplus under the other-side rule. The buyers also gain, but the increase is not significant. All these classes of agents enjoy an increased (Pareto improving) share of surplus (relative to the competitive equilibrium prediction) because the other-side rule increases efficiency by 5.5 percentage points (not shown). More surplus is available and all agents receive an increase in earnings.

6. Further Results

In this section we report charts for one experiment which illustrate the regression results, and provides the reader with a visual representation of the dynamics of an experiment, which is imperfectly captured in the regression report of the previous section.

Figure 3 plots the period-by-period results for an experiment with twice-experienced subjects, operating under a T1 line constraint. In this figure an observation of 1 means 100% of the competitive equilibrium share of the surplus for some class of agents –

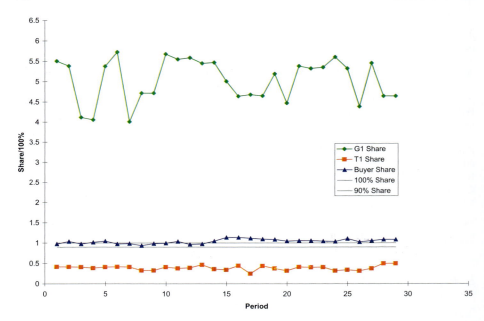

Figure 3. The share of realized surplus obtained by buyers, all generators at G1, and imputed to the constrained line T1, are plotted in the chart for each trading period 1 through 29. (Experiment 9283CXX.) Each observation on share is charted as a proportion of the benchmark competitive equilibrium imputation to each agent class. Thus the buyers' share hovers around 100% of the CE prediction until period 15, then rises slightly. The T1 transmission share is 50% or less than the CE prediction. This leads to a greatly enlarged share for the three generators at node G1, who receive some 400–500% of the CE imputation. Consequently, much of the congestion rent that would accrue to the constrained line, T1, if the generator and buyer node prices were competitive, is transferred to the upstream generators at G1, who raise their offer prices, increasing the price at G1 much above the CE bench mark.

buyers, generators, transmission lines. Not shown is total efficiency which is very high: 95 to 100%.

Figure 3 shows very clearly that: (1) buyers capture very little of the congestion rents from the LHS constraint; (2) generators at G1 capture much of these congestion rents; (3) these shares are extracted directly from the transmission share. Thus, G1 agents average about 500% of their predicted equilibrium share of the surplus while transmission line T1 receives less than half of the rents imputed to it at the competitive equilibrium.

7. Conclusions

Our conclusions can be summarized as follows:
1. The assumption that under optimal nodal pricing passive transmission line owners collect all the congestion rents on a constrained line, as well as incremental loss

rents, is not supported by the experimental results in a three-node radial network system with four buyers and six generators at two dispersed locations.
2. Market efficiency results:
   (i) Efficiency is increased with more (twice) experienced subjects by only 0.6 percentage points, which is not statistically significant.
   (ii) Efficiency is reduced by a line constraint, and this is statistically significant.
   (iii) The other-side auction rule, giving temporary time priority to accepted bids and offers, increases efficiency (by 5.5 percentage points which is highly significant).
3. Profit share results for generators (G1) upstream from the line that is constrained under some treatments:
   (i) More experience reduces generator share of profits significantly (3.6 percentage points).
   (ii) The effect of the line constraint is to increase generator profit share (by 165 percentage points which is highly significant), as upstream generators raise their offers and capture much of the transmission share of the congestion rents.
   (iii) The other-side auction rule increases the G1 share of profits (by 4.9 percentage points which is significant).
4. Profit share of wholesale buyers:
   (i) Increased experience improves the profit share of buyers. This is because, as seen in Figure 2, seller surplus exceeds buyer surplus at the competitive equilibrium, and convergence is relatively slow from below as sellers learn over successive sessions to bargain more effectively in the auction.
   (ii) The line constraint has an infinitesimal effect on buyer profits.
   (iii) Buyer profits are increased 1.4 percentage points by the other-side rule, but this could be due to sampling error.
5. Profit share of generators (G2) served by the line which is never constrained:
   (i) Increased experience has no important effect on the G2 share.
   (ii) When the other line is constrained this increases G2 share of profit by 1 percentage point. Hence generators extract some of the incremental loss revenue of a transmission line, but we cannot rule out that this is due to sampling variation.
   (iii) The other-side rule increases the G2 share of profit (by 5.8 percentage points and this is significant).

References

Backerman, Steven R., Rassenti, Stephen J., Smith, Vernon L. (2000). "Efficiency and income shares in high-demand energy networks: Who receives the congestion rents when a line is constrained?" Pacific Economic Review 5, 331–347.

McCabe, Kevin A., Rassenti, Stephen J., Smith, Vernon L. (1993). "Designing a uniform-price double auction". In: Friedman, D., Rust, J. (Eds.), The Double Auction Market Institutions, Theories, and Evidence. Proceedings, vol. XIV, Santa Fe Institute. Addison–Wesley, Reading, MA, pp. 307–332.

Chapter 75

A SMART MARKET FOR THE SPOT PRICING AND PRICING OF TRANSMISSION THROUGH A POWER GRID

HUNG-PO CHAO and CHARLES R. PLOTT

This chapter illustrates a mechanism capable of competitively allocating power through an electricity network in which "loop flow" and the unusual economic phenomenon caused by loop flow are anticipated and integrated into the competitive process. At the base of the complexity is Kirchoff's law governing electricity flow through power grids. This physical law creates a form of externalities throughout a power transmission network and these externalities must be incorporated into any efficient and decentralized pricing mechanism. The mechanism developed here is a special, continuous double auction in which buyers and sellers are in essence buying and selling differentiated products in the sense that they wish to purchase and sell power at different locations, but the purchasing and selling activities are technically related through resource limitations and the physical law of electricity flow.

1. Kirchoff's Law and Resource Constraints

The easiest way to explain the process is by reference to the experiments that were actually conducted. Figure 1 represents a power grid with consumers and producers located at the nodes and the arcs connecting the nodes representing power transmissions lines with limited capacity. Consumers are located at Nodes 2 and 3, while producers are located at Nodes 1 and 2. In the example to be explored the consumers and producers located at Node 2 are marginal in the sense of low values and high marginal costs and would be excluded from the market if there are no transmission constraints. Kirchoff's law requires power to travel through all paths between the node of injection and the node of extraction in such as way that is (roughly speaking) inversely proportion to the impedance of the path. The power that can be transmitted across a line is limited by the capacity of the line. So, a single line with limited capacity can constrain the power that flows through the entire network even though that line connects no two nodes on a direct path between the source of injection and the location of extraction. In Figure 1 all lines have the same impedance so the impedance of a path is proportional to the sum of the lengths along a path. That is, if a megawatt is injected at Node 1 and extracted at Node 3, 2/3 megawatts will travel along the line 1-3 and 1/3 megawatt will travel along the lines 1-2 and 2-3. Constrained capacities along any line can thus constrain the transmission of power along all lines. Or, putting another way, in order to make the nature of the externality clear, transmission along any line has an influence on the feasible transmission along all other lines.

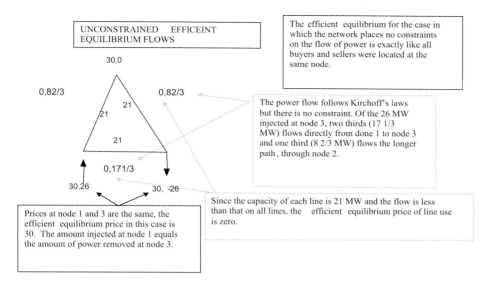

Figure 1. The unconstrained network and Kirchoff's laws as applied to the network.

2. The Mechanism

Power buyers submit bids for quantities of power demanded at a node. These bids are in the form of a price and a quantity that a bidder demands at that price or lower. The bidder can submit as many bids as desired. Sellers of power submit asks for power to be injected at a node. The asks are in the form of a price and a quantity that the seller is willing to sell at that price or higher. Sellers can submit as many bids as desired. Transmission line owners can submit asks for the capacity of the line that they will supply. Like suppliers of power, the asks are in the form of a price per megawatt that will travel through the line and a capacity quantity that the line owner is willing to supply at that price.

As bids and asks are tendered, the mechanism computes winning bids and prices in either real time or in rounds and publicly announces them. That is, the mechanism computes the allocations and payments that will take place and publicly announces them. The allocation and prices are called the "provisional winners" in the sense that if the mechanism stops, the provisional winners are those that have the contracts as specified by the provisional winning allocation and prices. If the process does not stop, bids and asks not involved as provisional winners can be revised but provisional winners cannot be revised. The system stops if no new bids or asks are submitted but if the process is taking "too long" a random stopping process is employed with an increasing probability that the mechanism will stop.

The computation of the provisional winners and prices takes place in a "smart market" optimization technique. The allocation problem is formulated as a linear (integer) programming problem and the multipliers of the problem (the dual) are the prices. The objective function of the problem reflects "consumer's surplus" as embodied in bids and the constraints of the problem are those imposed by the physical properties of the network and the capacities supplied by those who own the lines. The prices themselves become the competitive equilibrium prices if there were no externalities in the system so the general behavioral postulate, since there are no monopolists in the study, is captured by the same principles of competitive behavior that exist in the competitive equilibrium model.

Technically, the mechanism works as follows. We apply an algorithm to compute provisional allocations and prices in either a continuous or a multiple round auction of electricity and transmission rights. Tender orders can be submitted during each round or instant of time. Each eligible tender will be indexed by l. Suppose that there are n nodes in an electric network and T trading periods in a day. There are potentially $n(n-1)$ directed links, each of which is associated with a set of transmission capacity rights. Each tender is represented generically as an $n^2 + 1$ vector, (V_l, q_l, T_l), where $V_l \in R$ represents the value of an offer (+) or bid (−), $q_{il} \in R^n$ represents the quantities of power injected (+) or extracted (−) at node $i (= 1, \ldots, n)$, and $T \in R^{n \times n-1}$ represents the quantities of transmission capacity rights offered (+) or demanded (−).

The components of a tender offer can take on either positive or negative values. We adopt the convention that a positive value of V_l signifies payment (for a purchase) and a negative value signifies receipt (from a sale). Similarly, a positive value of q_{lk} signifies power injection, whereas a negative value signifies power extraction. This vector representation is flexible. For instance, we allow a portfolio tender which involves simultaneous trades at multiple nodes over multiple periods.

For simplicity, we assume that each tender can be accepted fractionally, and the net trade vector will therefore be scaled in proportion to the accepted fraction. When the tendered quantities take on integer values, the algorithm could always yield integer solutions. The following linear program is solved each round.

2.1. Notation

V_l: the value of the lth tender
x_l: the fraction of tender l accepted
q_{lkt}: the amount of electricity traded at node k in period t by tender l
Q_{kt}: net power injection at node k in period t
β_{ij}^k: the loading factor of power flow on link (i, j) for injection at node k
K_{ij}: the transmission capacity on link (i, j)

$$\underset{x,Q}{\text{Maximize}} \sum_l V_l x_l \tag{1}$$

subject to:

$$Q_{kt} - \sum_l x_l q_{lkt} = 0, \quad \text{for } k = 1, \ldots, n \text{ and } t = 1, \ldots, T, \qquad (2)$$

$$\sum_{k=1}^n Q_{kt} = 0, \quad \text{for } t = 1, \ldots, T, \qquad (3)$$

$$\sum_{k=1}^{n-1} \beta_{ij}^k Q_{kt} \leq \sum_l x_l T_{ij}^l, \quad \text{for all } i, j, \quad 0 \leq x_l \leq 1 \quad \text{for all } l. \qquad (4)$$

Tender orders that are accepted with positive fractions, $x_l > 0$, will be accepted. The above problem will be solved repeatedly during each round. The condition in (4) requires that the power flows associated with each trade must be covered by an adequate amount of transmission capacity rights.

Since no trade (i.e., $x \equiv 0$) is always a feasible solution to (2)–(4), and thus the objective value should always be nonnegative. In other words, the trade surplus is always nonnegative. When multiple solutions exist, the convention adopted as an equitable way to resolve the indeterminacy is to set a priority of acceptance based on the chorological order of tender submission.

For reference, the corresponding dual linear program that calculates the prices is described as follows.

2.2. Notation

p_{kt}: Shadow price of electricity at node k in period t
π_{ij}^t: Shadow price of transmission link (i, j) in period t
μ_l: Shadow price of the constraint $x_l \leq 1$, which measures the benefit of the bid

2.3. Dual Linear Program for Continuous-time Double Auction

$$\underset{\pi,\mu,p}{\text{Minimize}} \sum_l \mu_l \qquad (5)$$

Subject to:

$$\sum_{ij} \pi_{ij}^t \beta_{ij}^k + p_{kt} - p_{nt} = 0, \qquad (6)$$

$$-\sum_{k=1}^n p_{kt} q_{lkt} - \sum_{i,j} \pi_{ij}^t T_{ij}^l + \mu_l \geq V_l, \quad \mu_l \geq 0. \qquad (7)$$

Equation (6) indicates that the sum of the transmission prices weighted by the loading factors equals to the nodal price difference between the injection node and the hub. Condition (7) implies that the shadow price of each accepted tender minus the energy and transmission costs must exceed the value of the tender.

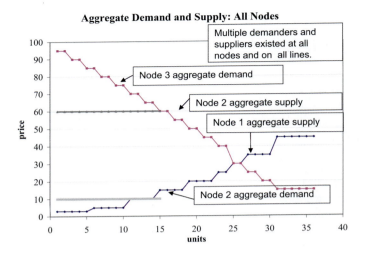

Figure 2. Demand and supplies of power at nodes. The costs of lines to line suppliers are not shown.

3. Parameter and the Testbed

Figure 2 contains the demand and supply for power at the various nodes. If the transmission system places no constraints on deliveries, as is the case as represented in Figure 1, then electricity would have one price that is the same at all nodes and the price of transmission would be zero. The electricity price would simply be that which equates demand and supply in Figure 2.

Figures 1, 3 and 4 illustrate the configuration of power flows and the capacities of the lines at the efficient allocation. The figure also contains the competitive equilibrium prices that are predicted by the behavioral model employed. The testing strategy was as follows. The first experiments were conducted in an unconstrained system with the parameters of Figure 1. This helped train subjects in the operation of the system and also provided an "easy test" of the system performance. The test then moved to more difficult environments in which economically surprising phenomena might emerge. These cases are the "must produce" and "must take" cases illustrated in Figure 3. The final test parameters represented in Figure 4, had multiple constraints satisfied or similar difficulties that had multiple prices as possible equilibria. The issue was whether or not the multiple prices would themselves be a source of difficulty in the allocation process.

Three experiments were conducted under each condition except the unconstrained case, for which four were conducted. The subjects and general circumstances were the same for all experiments.

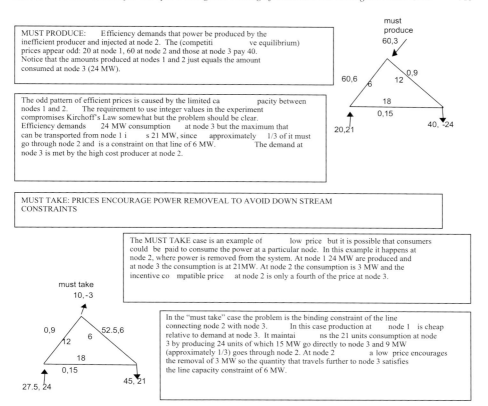

Figure 3. Parameters for the must produce case-inefficient producers supply the demand not met by efficient producers due to transmission constraints.

4. Performance

How one might evaluate the performance of a new mechanism are outlined in Plott (1994) as: (1) Does the mechanism do what it is supposed to do? (2) Does it do it for understandable (the correct) reasons? In the context of this mechanism the objective is to achieve an efficient allocation of resources in light of the fact that no economic features, costs or benefits, are known to the mechanism except as might be reflected by behavior. So, if the system achieves near 100% efficiency as calculated from information known only to the experimenter but not the mechanism, it is doing what it is supposed to do. In addition it should do that job in a "smooth" and "rapid" manner. The second criterion is captured by the prices. Are the prices the "competitive equilibrium" prices as based on the information unknown to the mechanism but are known to the experimenter?

As an auction process the mechanism worked quickly, with many auctions taking place in a two hour period. Prices developed smoothly and while termination of the

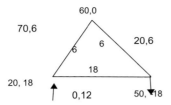
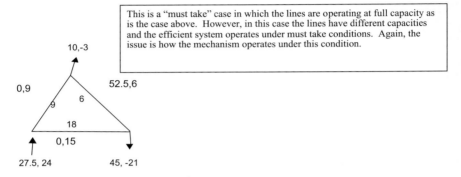

Figure 4. Non-unique price examples – extreme cases to test the system operation.

process sometimes required the use of the random stopping rule, it generally converged in an asymptotic manner. More modern versions of this mechanism employ the use of various types of clocks that force the bidding process. The general impression is that continuous processes work much better than processes that employ rounds.

Does the mechanism do what it is supposed to do? In almost all cases the efficiency levels are in the high 90% and close to 100%. From an efficiency point of view the mechanism works exceedingly well.

Does it perform well-understandable (the right) reasons? Prices and allocations are near the predicted competitive equilibrium levels as shown in Figures 5 and 6, respectively. As shown in Figure 5, prices tend to be slightly higher than the competitive equilibrium, especially when the equilibrium prices are zero. This upward tendency is most pronounced in the unconstrained case, perhaps reflecting the tendency of prices to converge from above when the consumer surplus exceeds producer surplus as it does in these parameters. Thus, there is a bias in the incomes away from the competitive model but at this point there is no reason to assume that the bias is pronounced relative to what is ordinarily observed in experimental markets. In general, the prices are highly correlated with the competitive equilibrium.

The allocations are illustrated in Figure 6. Allocations tend to be distributed around the competitive equilibrium quantities. The figure contains the frequency with which the allocations deviated from the efficient allocations that are predicted by the competitive model. As is clear from the figure, the mass of data are centered around zero deviations.

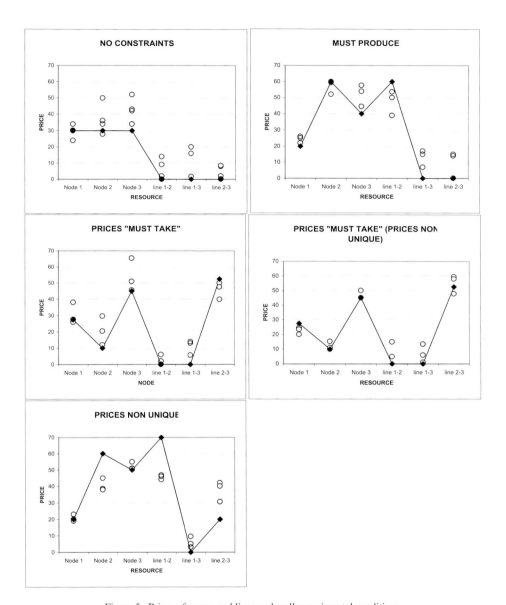

Figure 5. Prices of power and lines under all experimental conditions.

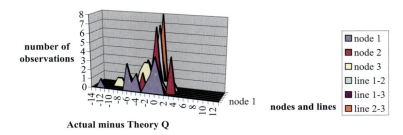

Figure 6. Actual Q minus competitive equilibrium Q.

Reference

Plott, Charles (1994). "Market architectures, institutional landscapes and testbed experiments". Economic Theory 4 (1), 3–10.

Further reading

Chao, H., Peck, S. (1996). "A market mechanism for electric power transmission". Journal of Regulatory Economics 10 (1), 25–59.
Chao, H., Peck, S., Oren, S., Wilson, R. (2000). "Flow-based transmission rights and congestion management". Electricity Journal.
McCabe, K., Rassenti, S., Smith, V. (1993). "Designing an uniform price double auction: An experimental evaluation". In: Friedman, D., Rust, J. (Eds.), The Double Auction Market Institutions, Theories, and Evidence. Santa Fe Institute Studies, Addison–Wiley Publishing Company, Santa Fe.
Plott, Charles (1997). "Laboratory experimental testbeds: Application to the PCS auction". Journal of Economics and Management Strategy 6 (3), 605–638.
Wilson, Robert (1997). "Activity rules for the power exchange". Report to the California PX and ISO Trusts for Power Industry Restructuring.

PART 5.3

FROM THE LAB TO THE FIELD

Colin F. Camerer, "Asset Market Manipulation: A Field Experiment with Racetrack Betting"

Peter Bohm, "Pre-testing International Climate Change Policies: Methods and Results"

Peter Bohm, "Quasi-experimental Evaluation of Regional Employment Subsidies"

Peter Bohm, "Field-test Elicitation of Demand for Public Goods"

Joyce Berg, Robert Forsythe, Forrest Nelson and Thomas Rietz, "Results from a Dozen Years of Election Futures Market Research"

Glen W. Harrison and E. Elisabet Rutström, "Experimental Evidence on the Existence of Hypothetical Bias in Value Elicitation Methods"

Chapter 76

ASSET MARKET MANIPULATION: A FIELD EXPERIMENT WITH RACETRACK BETTING

COLIN F. CAMERER

Division of Humanities and Social Sciences 228-77, California Institute of Technology, Pasadena, CA 91125, USA
e-mail: camerer@hss.caltech.edu

The possibility that asset markets could be strategically manipulated by large informed traders has fascinated social scientists and market observers for years. There is a well-known story of minions of Nathan Rothschild, who was thought to have the fastest carrier pigeons in London, selling shares during the Battle of Waterloo to drive the price down artificially (the news was actually good for British share prices) so others trading on his behalf could quietly buy up shares cheaply. This kind of attempt by informed speculators to fool markets by trading against their information, luring others to trade in the same way in order to profit later, was also observed in laboratory markets by Noth and Weber (1996), and Plott, Wit, and Yang (1996). More recently (in the late 1990s and 2000) the fact that intraday volatility of many NASDAQ is so extremely high has been attributed to speculators pushing up prices of thinly-traded stocks, knowing that "day traders" will often chase trends so the speculators can sell later at higher prices to the day traders.

Inspired by these observations, I conducted an experiment at horse racing tracks which allow bettors to cancel bets before a race is run (see Camerer, 1998 for details). The possibility of cancellation means that large bets can be made for free, to see whether observable movements in 'prices' (betting odds) manipulate markets as Rothschild is alleged to have done, and as the laboratory subjects tried to do. I have also been told that bettors in New Zealand and Australia have done this, with some success (see Auckland Sunday News, 1997).

Experimental manipulations of this sort can also reveal something about the microstructure of how diverse information is aggregated. If bettors bet more when they see that a large bet is made, this suggests they learn from observable prices, laying the foundation for fully-revealing rational expectations equilibrium. On the other hand, if bettors bet less when a large bet is made, this means they do not learn anything from prices and bet according to private information or opinions instead.

1. Experimental Design

American racetrack betting is 'parimutuel,' which means that bettors who bet on a horse and win share the money bet by everyone (after the track takes out a 15–20% share). The experiment used only win betting, which means that players earn money only if their horse wins. Notice that in the parimutuel system, bettors are essentially betting against each other. Beginning about thirty minutes before a race, the track displays the cumulative amount of money bet so far on that race, every minute or so. The track also computes the 'odds,' the net payoff per dollar for each horse, if that horse wins. In the parimutuel system, when more money is bet on a horse the odds fall because the winning bettors have to share the losers' bets (minus track take) with more winners.

My experiment used a within-race matched-pair design. In order to maximize the impact of a $500 bet, I bet on longshot horses with odds of 20-1 or more. (Relatively less is bet on these horses, by definition, so the absolute movements in the odds is larger than it would be for more favored horses.) I chose races in which there were two or more horses with the same 'morning-line' (beginning) odds, and which had similar bet totals when the totals were first displayed, about thirty minutes before 'post time' (the projected starting time of the race; usually races start 2–3 minutes later than this). This procedure generated races with a pair of horses who are matched on pre-bet features. A temporary $500 bet is made on one horse, chosen at random by flipping a coin, and movements in betting on that horse and on the unbet (control) horse were recorded. The unbet horse serves as a control for shocks which are idiosyncratic to a race but mostly common to two longshots within the race. Intuitively, the behavior of betting on the control horse provides an approximate answer to the question, 'What would have happened if the temporary bet was not made?' While this kind of matched-pair design is rarely used in experimental economics, it is extremely efficient for some purposes. (For example, identical twins are used as a pair that are matched on genes to separate environmental and genetic influences; in this experiment, the two horses are like 'race-twins'.)

The temporary bets were made 18–20 minutes before post time and were canceled about five minutes before post time. Fifty $500 bets were made. An important feature of betting at these tracks is that bettors have little incentive to bet early, because the final odds are not determined until the race starts. Indeed, half the bets are made in the three minutes before post time.

Theory implies that the bets will have some effect if several assumptions hold: Bettors do not realize bets can be canceled (most do not); bets affect the odds visibly; bettors react to changes in odds in some way; and there is an asymmetry between their initial reaction when the bet is made and their reaction when the bet is canceled. (The asymmetry could result because the $500 bet moves the odds more when it is made, and the total win pool is smaller, than when it is canceled because the total pool grows as the race approaches.)

The direction of the effect will depend on whether bettors think there is information in odds movements or not. If bettors have private information or opinions, and do not think price movements contain information they need to know, they will bet less on the temporary-bet horse (relative to the control) because the bet simply lowers the odds and makes the potential payoff unattractive. As a result, the odds on the temporary-bet horse should drift up over time while the bet is still live (before it is canceled), as the flow of money into that horse is inhibited. Oppositely, if bettors have rational expectations then they believe the post-bet odds are correct and will bet accordingly (betting more on the temporary-bet horse than on the control), maintaining a steady path of odds over time. If the asymmetry assumption holds – these reactions are stronger when the bet is first made than when it is canceled – then the final odds will be higher on temporary-bet horses (compared to the control) if opinion bettors are influential, and lower if rational-expectations bettors are influential.

2. Experimental Results

One way to look at the data is to treat the bets as events and use the kind of 'event study' popular in financial economics. An event study looks at a time series of price anticipations and reactions to an event, defines time at which the event occurs as zero, and lines up all the time series relative to event time. Each slice of time – say, time -5 – then gives a cross-section of data showing what tends to happen five time units before an event.

Figure 1 shows such a time series. The graph displays the geometric mean odds, across fifty temporary bets, for temporary-bet horses and control horses. The thinner lines at the bottom of the graph show the frequency distribution of the times at which bets were made ('number of INs') and canceled ('number of OUTs'). Both horses start at about 20-1 odds. As the bets are made, between 21 and 16 minutes before post time, the temporary-bet horse odds fall, because of the experimental bet. After the bets are in, the temporary-bet horse odds are about half as large as the matched-pair control, so the effect is large and visible. (A couple of times people at the track commented, within earshot of us, on the drop in odds.) While the bets are on, between times -16 and -5 or so, the temporary-bet horse odds drift upward. This shows that bettors do not all infer information from odds movements (otherwise the odds would stay flat). After the bet is canceled, from five to three minutes before post, the control and temporary-bet horse odds are almost exactly the same.

A more powerful test exploits the matched-pair control. To do this, we compute the change in the percentage of the pool bet on a horse, from two minutes before the bet is made to two minutes after the bet is canceled. Then we take the difference in these changes between the control horse and the temporary-bet horse. This difference has a mean of 0.00211 ($t(48) = .74$, insignificant), so there is a very slight tendency for the temporary-bet horse to attract more money over time than the control horse, but the tendency is nowhere near significantly different from chance.

Perhaps the $500 bets are too small, or were made too early or canceled too early to appear informative. To measure the effect of larger, later bets a second sample of 33 bets were made at smaller racetracks with substantially smaller amounts of betting. The bets were $1000 and were made in two $500 waves, about 13 and nine minutes before post time. (These bets are 7% of the entire win pool when they are placed.) Bets were canceled later as well, three and one minutes before post.

The results from this second sample are much like the first. After both waves of betting are done, around 8 minutes before post time, the temporary-bet horse odds are

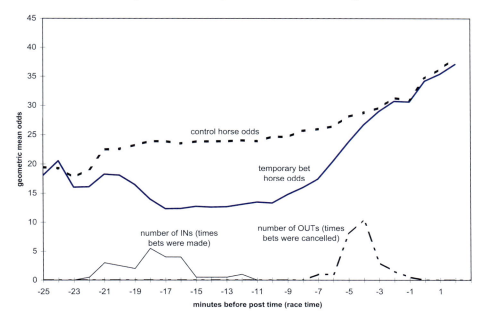

Figure 1. Geometric mean odds on temporary-bet horses vs control horses (Camerer, 1998).

less than half of the control horse odds. While the bets are live, between -8 and -3, the odds drift upward substantially, indicating the presence of some opinion bettors who are betting against a horse they think is 'overbet.' After the bets are all canceled, two minutes after post time, the temporary-bet horse odds are visibly lower than the control horse odds. The within-pair test described above gives a difference in post-bet minus pre-bet percentage changes of 0.006734 ($t(31) = 1.23$, $p = .24$ one-tailed).

Pooling these results with the first sample gives an overall percentage change difference of .00395 ($t(81) = 1.43$, $p = .16$). A conservative sign test shows that 50 of 83 differences are positive (i.e., 50 times there was a larger change toward the temporary-bet horse than toward the control horse, and 33 times the opposite), which is marginally significantly different from chance ($z = 1.91$, $p = .06$). Thus there, is very modest evidence that the temporary bet tends to draw money toward the horse which is bet (consistent with rational expectations) rather than pushing money away from the temporarily-bet horse. But the effect is small and only marginally significant.

3. Conclusion

My studies were designed to test whether active naturally-occurring markets could be manipulated experimentally in a way that permitted statistically powerful identification of whether manipulation generally works (rather than anecdotal evidence). The studies also serve as a reminder that true experiments can sometimes be conducted in the field, cheaply; we should seize those opportunities when they arise, or create them.[1]

The answer to the primary research question seems to be that these markets can be very weakly manipulated. I made temporary $500 or $1000 bets on longshot horses, roughly cutting the posted odds on the temporary-bet horse in half. About 60% of the time more money was eventually bet on the temporary-bet horse, relative to a similar control horse in the same race, and 40% of the time more was bet on the control horse. This result indicates a slight tendency toward rational expectations, in which bettors infer information from price movements about a horse's chance of winning. (This rational-expectations tendency is only a mistake here, of course, because our bets were not informative, but most bettors do not know that large bets can be canceled costlessly.) However, the effect is very small in magnitude (one could not profit from it) and only marginally significant, even with two large samples of 50 and 33 bets.

More generally, the inability of these large bets to move the market systematically is a blow to the beliefs of those who think markets are easily and routinely manipulated by large investors. For those who do not believe manipulation is common, and instead are inclined to marvel at the mysterious collective intelligence of centralized markets populated by self-interested traders, the general immunity of these markets to substantial, systematic attempts at manipulation may represent something new to explain, or at least marvel at.

References

Auckland Sunday News (1997). "New rules hit pro punters". August 17, p. 43.
Camerer, Colin F. (1998). "Can asset markets be manipulated? A field experiment with racetrack betting". Journal of Political Economy, 457–482.
Lucking-Reiley, David H. (1999). "Using field experiments to test equivalence between auction formats: Magic on the Internet". American Economic Review 89 (5), 1063–1080.
Nöth, Markus, Weber, Martin (1996). "Insider detection in experimental asset markets". Manuscript, Mannheim, Lehrstühle für Finanzwirtschaft.
Plott, Charles R., Wit, Jörgen, Yang, C. Winston (1996). "Parimutuel betting markets as information aggregation devices: Experimental results". Manuscript, Pasadena, California Institute of Technology.

---

[1] In one ingenious example, Lucking-Reiley (1999) created internet auction markets to sell trading cards, in order to test theories of the effects of reserve prices on bids, which are hard to test with naturally-occurring data. Opportunities to conduct field experiments like his and mine are now more limited by imagination and energy than by technology or research funds.

Chapter 77

PRE-TESTING INTERNATIONAL CLIMATE CHANGE POLICIES: METHODS AND RESULTS

PETER BOHM

Stockholm University

Under certain circumstances, experimental methods can be used to evaluate public policies. Laboratory tests may be designed to check various properties of a specific policy (see, e.g., Plott, 1987; Cason and Plott, 1996). Field testing of new policies is conceivable when policymakers actually want to have such tests carried out before a policy change is made permanent and when relevant, e.g., regional, control groups can be formed. (For an example, see 'Quasi-experimental Evaluation of Regional Employment Subsidies' in this volume or Bohm and Lind, 1993).

For obvious reasons, field tests with real decision makers are particularly hard to carry out concerning international policy options. Here, where international climate change policy is the object of study, there is one particular policy option – internationally tradable (carbon) emission quotas – which, although efficient and capable of addressing distributional concerns in theory, has met with strong opposition from several countries, in particular in the developing world. The policy amounts to (1) allocating, by international agreement, acceptable emission quotas to individual countries and (2) attaining cost effectiveness by allowing trade of quota units among the signatories. (The opposition seems to stem mainly from a lack of understanding of the flexibility in the design of this policy.)

Since there are no real precedents to this type of international agreement and since arguments based on theory or lab tests alone are unlikely to convince suspicious governments, the question is, what could provide them with relevant and possibly convincing information? For example, can field-like tests, capable of improving the level of information, be designed for subjects who could respond in a relevant fashion? The principal results and, in particular, the designs of two such tests are reported here. In the first test, the purpose was to identify and use a field-like experimental design to investigate the cost effectiveness of international emissions trade within a small group of countries. In the second test, which examined the international acceptability of a specific take-it-or-leave-it tradable-quota proposal, the primary task was to identify, and solicit the participation of, subjects who had the information required and could be furnished with incentives to respond in a relevant fashion to the question of what position a given country could be expected to take.

In both tests, the crucial points were to solicit relevant subjects and to provide them with incentives to respond in a well-considered fashion to the, unavoidably hypothetical, questions posed. Monetary incentives were not relevant to use here since the recruited subjects participated in their capacity as public officials.

1. Testing Gains from Emissions Quota Trade among a Few Countries (Bohm, 1997a)

A subset of the world's countries may wish to commit themselves to stringent emission targets in an attempt to influence other countries to follow suit, thereby bringing about a significant reduction in the threat to the global climate. Moreover, if the pioneering countries were to connect a tradable quota system to these commitments, they would be in a position to provide information not only about the practicability and efficiency properties of this policy instrument but also about the general economic implications of the commitments made. If the set of countries were small, which seems quite likely in the case of pioneering agreements, this action could reveal, in particular, how efficient a small market for quota trade would be. Furthermore, it could also show, for a set of similarly *developed* countries as the only participants, whether the common presumption that their costs would be too similar for any significant amount of trade gains to arise were in fact correct.

Second best to this approach could be to let such a set of countries conduct a hypothetical quota-trade experiment with real-world government traders provided that incentives similar to those of a real trade environment could be created. Such a test was carried out in 1996 for Denmark, Finland, Norway and Sweden, four countries that already had implemented unilateral carbon emission reduction policies by introducing significant domestic carbon taxes, and also had been advocating a more stringent international climate change policy.

1.1. Test Design

The energy ministries of the four countries agreed to appoint negotiating teams of experienced public officials or experts, who would act *as if* each country
- had committed itself to keeping its year 2000 emissions at its 1990 level (in line with the 1992 Framework Convention on Climate Change, FCCC), and
- could exceed its target emissions level to the extent that another country among them had (hypothetically) committed itself to an additional reduction of its emissions, which amounts to a tradable-quota arrangement.

In the real world, this kind of intergovernmental trade would most likely be guided by relative emissions abatement costs, politically adjusted for unwanted employment and income distribution effects. Earlier cooperation among the four countries had made them familiar with their partners' estimated technical emissions abatement costs and business-as-usual (BAU) emission levels, as would be likely before any international agreement of this type could be implemented. Thus, such information could be taken to be more or less common knowledge, whereas the additional political considerations and hence, the directly negotiation-relevant 'social' abatement costs would more likely be private information.

Furthermore, in the real world, incentives could be expected to be provided by the fact that the negotiators' performance – e.g., cost savings achieved as compared to po-

Table 1
Gains from hypothetical carbon emissions trading involving four countries represented by realistic negotiating teams. Emission reductions in million tons and carbon emission abatement costs in million U.S. dollars; net gains are net of trade payments, at prices that differ between trades, but all close to a perfectly competitive price; fully efficient trade in parentheses

Country	Unilateral		Trade	Ex post TQ trade		
	Em. red. (Mton)	Cost (M$)	Exp./Imp. (−) (Mton)	Em. red. (Mton)	Cost (M$)	Net gain M($)
Denmark	1.7	61	0.5 (1.19)	2.2 (2.9)	83 (116)	6.7 (5.1)
Finland	6.0	94	5 (5.76)	11 (11.8)	212 (251)	136 (132.2)
Norway	5.4	456	−3.5 (−4.4)	1.9 (1.0)	91 (40)	178 (194.5)
Sweden	1.6	102	−2 (−2.55)	−0.4 (−1.0)	−22 (−51)	24.4 (25.1)
Total	14.7	713	Gross 5.5 (6.95)	14.7	368 (356)	345 (357)

Implications:
1. Quota trade reduced aggregate abatement costs by 50%, realizing 97% of potential maximum cost savings.
2. Net gain relative to unilateral costs: 11% (DK), 145% (SF), 39% (N), and 24% (S).
3. All four negotiating teams attained similar percentages of potential cost savings (= cost savings under perfect competition).

tential cost savings – could be evaluated by their peers in their respective countries. In the test, these incentives were mimicked by an agreement among the negotiating teams to disclose, prior to the negotiations, their negotiation-relevant marginal social cost schedules to an evaluation group of non-Nordic economic experts. After the bilateral trade negotiations were completed (by fax over a four-day period), a report where this group evaluated the performance of each country would be published (see Appendix 1 in Bohm, 1997a).

1.2. Test Results

The results are shown in Figures 1, 2 and Table 1. The required emission reductions, if unilateral, are shown in Figure 1 as the distance between the estimated BAU level and the target level for each country. In that figure, the negotiation-relevant cost curves are drawn with the target level at the origin. *Ex post* quota trade, the required emission levels for year 2000 were shifted from the origin to the levels (Em_i) indicated in Figure 2. As is suggested in that figure and more clearly shown in Table 1, quota trade reduced the four countries' aggregate abatement costs by 50%. Although there were only four countries trading bilaterally, trade achieved 97% of the trade gains that would have been attained had market behaved as if perfectly competitive; see Figure 2 and Table 1. (Similar efficiency rates were obtained in eleven pilot tests, using monetary incentives and graduate students in economics as subjects; see Bohm and Carlén, 1999.) The performance of the negotiating teams, defined as the individual country's attained

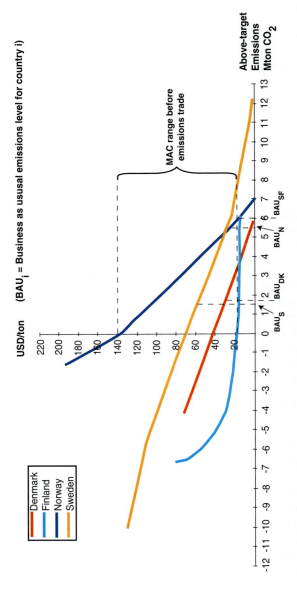

Figure 1. Marginal social carbon emissions abatement costs (MAC) for four Nordic countries. Cost curves centered at quota levels in year 2000 = FCCC target levels (1990 emissions); business-as-usual (BAU) emissions for year 2000 estimated at present domestic carbon tax levels; abatement costs to unilaterally reach target = the area below cost curves from BAU to target (at origin).

Ch. 77: Pre-testing International Climate Change Policies: Methods and Results

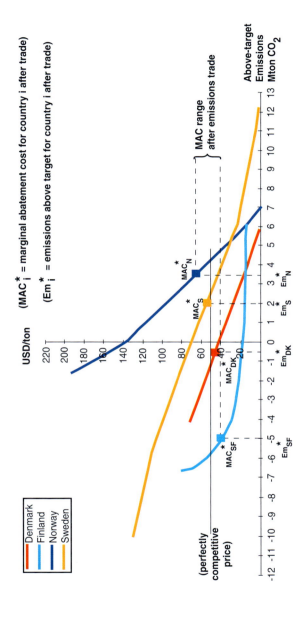

Figure 2. Emissions and marginal abatement cost range after emissions quota trade. Quota imports given by emissions (Em_i^*) in excess of target (at origin) where total imports (by Norway and Sweden) equal total exports (by Denmark and Finland); perfectly competitive equilibrium price inserted for comparison.

share of potential gains under perfect competition, was quite similar. Still, quota trade gains deviated considerably among the countries (see implication 2 in Table 1).

These results could provide politicians with the insights (1) that differences in abatement costs may be large even between seemingly similar developed countries, hence that potential gains from emissions trade among such countries may be significant, and (2) that these trade gains may be considerable even when only a few countries participate.

2. Testing International Acceptability of a 'Global' Tradable-quota Treaty with Diplomats as Subjects (Bohm, 1997b)

The topic of the second test was to investigate how subjects, knowledgeable about the general policies of the government in each of a selected set of 29 countries, would respond to a proposed, allegedly 'fair,' global tradable-quota treaty. (In this test, the world was taken to consist of only this selection of 29 countries covering 90% of the true global carbon emissions.) Would the responses to this particular proposal be as negative as the initial reactions of most countries (except the U.S.) have been? If not, an implication could be that more effort should be devoted to analyzing and evaluating the potentially cost-effective tradable-quota solution than had so far (1996) seemed called for. Here, as well as in the test reported above, the relevance of the results hinges on the qualifications of the experimental subjects and the incentives presented to them.

Recruiting real country representatives or country experts of an international organization like the World Bank as test subjects is hardly feasible, nor would it seem possible to present such subjects with relevant incentives. Instead, the subjects chosen were high-level diplomats in the service of one country (Sweden), each of whom had recently been stationed in a selected country, which they had now left, and which they were asked to represent. In the test, the world was assumed to consist of 29 countries (see the list in Table 2).The test was sanctioned by the Swedish State Department, where a chief official (No. 3 in command) asked the 29 diplomats (24 of whom were ambassadors) to invest a maximum of four hours and respond in two rounds to the set of questions posed to them. The subjects' identity was not revealed to anyone outside the Department. But since the responses were available for scrutiny by the chief official and others inside the Department, the responses could be peer reviewed. This was taken to provide an incentive for the subjects to consider the questions carefully before responding. All subjects responded (by fax) to the two rounds of questions within a period of four months.

In the first round, subjects were given 15 single-spaced pages of background information and instructions:
- presenting the policy issue, a review of common *pro* and *con* arguments regarding the type of treaty proposed and the information asked for;
- asking them to suggest how 'their' government would respond to a take-it-or-leave-it tradable-quota proposal to a world of 29 countries, where carbon emission quotas for 2010-14 were allocated so that, *ex post* quota trade, non-rich countries would

Table 2
How experienced diplomats, each knowledgeable of a country's policies, think 'their' country would respond to a 'fair' tradable carbon emissions quota treaty proposal

OECD countries (8 Yes, 4 No)		
Australia	Yes	
EU: Denmark		No
Belgium	Yes	
Finland		No
France	Yes	
Germany	Yes	
Spain		No
Italy	Yes	
United Kingdom	Yes	
Japan		No
Norway	Yes	
United States	Yes	
(Old) Non-OECD countries (9 Yes, 8 No)		
Brazil	Yes	
Chile	Yes	
Mexico		No
China		No
India		No
Indonesia	Yes	
Israel	Yes	
Republic of Korea	Yes	
Malaysia		No
Pakistan		No
Czech Republic		No
Poland		No
Russia		No
Ukraine	Yes	
Egypt	Yes	
Kenya	Yes	
Zambia	Yes	

remain economically unharmed and rich (OECD) countries would share the net costs of the treaty in the same proportion as their respective GDPs;

- asking them to consider 2005 as a 'realistic' date when this proposal would be made and to take for granted that at that time all the countries' marginal abatement cost curves would in essence be common knowledge (which provided the basis for reliable estimates of the economic implications of the treaty, see the preceding point); and

- emphasizing that the basis for the responses would be the respondents' *present* knowledge of 'their' governments' policy attitudes.

The last two points implied that the time between 1996 (when the study was undertaken) and 2005 collapsed into a single point in time.

In the second round (not reported here), the No respondents were asked to explain why their government would say no.

As can be seen from the results of the first round listed in Table 2:
- 17 of the 29 respondents said that their countries' governments would accept the proposal, which was
- true for 8 of the 12 rich countries, with all major countries (except Japan) saying yes, and
- true for 9 of the 17 non-rich countries, with the major countries – China, India and Russia – saying no.

Thus, according to this test and contrary to the views expressed by a large part of the global community, a considerable number of countries appear to find a tradable-quota treaty potentially acceptable. This seems to call for much more extensive analysis and evaluation of this policy option among climate-change policy negotiators than has so far taken place.

References

Bohm, P. (1997a). "Joint Implementation as Emission Quota Trade: An Experiment Among Four Nordic Countries, Nord 1997:4". Nordic Council of Ministers, Copenhagen.

Bohm, P. (1997b). "Are Tradable Carbon Emission Quota Internationally Acceptable? An Inquiry with Diplomats as Country Representatives, Nord 1997:8". Nordic Council of Ministers, Copenhagen.

Bohm, P., Carlén, B. (1999). "Emission quota trade among the few: Laboratory evidence of joint implementation among committed countries". Resource and Energy Economics 21 (1).

Bohm, P., Lind, H. (1993). "Policy evaluation quality: A quasi-experimental study of regional employment subsidies in Sweden". Regional Science and Urban Economics 23, 51–65.

Cason, T., Plott, C. (1996). "EPA's new emissions trading mechanism: A laboratory evaluation". Journal of Environmental Economics and Management 30 (2), 133–160.

Plott, C. (1987). "Dimensions of parallelism: Some policy applications of experimental methods". In: Roth, A. (Ed.), Laboratory Experimentation in Economics. Cambridge University Press, Cambridge, UK.

Chapter 78

QUASI-EXPERIMENTAL EVALUATION OF REGIONAL EMPLOYMENT SUBSIDIES

PETER BOHM

Stockholm University

Although certain government policies might be tested in controlled experiments during a pilot phase, such tests are rarely undertaken. Ideally, a policy could be tried, when feasible and meaningful, on a random subset of areas, firms or consumers exposed to the policy and be compared with the remaining subset over a significant period of time. The results reported here are from a test where the Swedish government introduced a regional employment policy in a limited part of a fairly homogeneous area with high chronic unemployment, hence creating a non-random division into an experiment region and a control region. Once the decision was made to introduce the policy, a quasi-experimental evaluation of the policy was proposed to the government; and, as a result, the government agreed to leave the two regions intact for a period of three years to allow this evaluation to take place and cover a non-trivial period of time – a quite unusual, perhaps unprecedented, step for a government to take.

The policy involved a significant reduction in payroll taxes from January 1984 – lowering labor costs by seven percent – for manufacturing firms in the county of Norrbotten, the northernmost part of a set of similarly depressed areas in Northern Sweden. Hence, a non-random control region was created, consisting of certain municipalities, some of which were adjacent to the experiment region. One implication of this division was that, if employment became significantly higher in the experiment region than in the control region, part of the difference could be attributed to business activity and hence employment having moved a short distance into the experiment region, reducing employment in the control region as much as it increased employment in the experiment region. If so, this would tend to exaggerate the policy effect. Fortunately, from the point of view of policy evaluation, but unfortunately from the point of view of the policy advocates, it turned out that employment in the experiment region did not improve relative to that of the control region, an unexpected result given the significant budgetary costs of this subsidy program.

1. Experimental Design

Careful checks were made to safeguard that the two regions were indeed similar, especially with respect to other, pre-existing forms of policy support. However, since the industrial structure was not identical in the two regions, the development of their unemployment rates might differ over the business cycle. Hence, when the policy evaluation was designed in early 1984, i.e., prior to access to any post-treatment results, it was deemed important that employment in the two regions should be compared with their relative development in the relevant phase of the most recent business cycle. Thus, it was documented in an evaluation plan, published in mid-1984, that the three-year test period should be compared with that of three pre-specified historical three-year periods of a downturn, an upturn or a stable period in Swedish GNP, which *ex post* (1987) would best fit GNP development over the test period 1984–1986. (The relevant period turned out to be 1979–1981.)

The evaluation design was prespecified in other respects as well, to avoid any unwarranted influence from access to test data. Should a change in the evaluation approach be called for later on, an explicit reason for doing so would be required (but no such change was called for in this particular case). Furthermore, the fact that the study was carried out concurrently with the study period allowed an important continuous check of incoming data errors. Thus, the policy evaluation approach differed in several respects from the traditional approach of determining evaluation design *ex post* concurrently with data evaluation which, if nothing else, typically makes it easier for those policy advocates who prefer not to take the evaluation results seriously.

Employment in the two regions was compared for manufacturing as a whole as well as for areas disaggregated with respect to the degree of unemployment and for major sub-sectors of the manufacturing industry. In addition, given that not even these sub-sectors were truly homogeneous, a 'twin study' was conducted for 44 pairs of similar firms in the two regions. The selection of these firms, made in 1985 when data for 1983 were available, was based on size, age, type of ownership and line of production. The question in this – the most ambitious – attempt to attain homogeneity between the objects of comparison was whether or not the firms in the experiment region would undergo a systematically more favorable development in employment than their twins in the control region.

2. Results

The results summarized in the table below indicate that it was difficult to see any positive effect of the significant support given to the experiment region. Growth in employment in manufacturing from the pre-policy year 1983 to the end-year 1986 was almost the same. When corrected for the historical (1978–1981) asymmetric development in the two regions, the change in employment was actually worse in the experiment region. This pattern essentially remained when data were disaggregated with respect to areas of different degrees of chronic unemployment and with respect to different sub-sectors of the manufacturing industry. The twin study showed similar results in that, for a majority of the pairs of firms, the control region performed better than the experiment region. These results were checked for the influence of chance events, indicating as the major finding of the study that it was highly unlikely that such events could have hidden any significant employment effect of the labor subsidies.

It should be noted that, if subsidy effects on employment appeared only after the 3½ years covered by this study, this lag would have meant that the subsidy cost per unit of new employment had been very high, given the high subsidy costs during the years when no significant effects occurred.

Seven percent employment subsidies introduced in 1984 in an area with chronic unemployment in Northern Sweden revealed no significant employment effects during an observation period of three years.

Employment changes in percent for experiment vs control region 1983–1986, corrected for systematic differences between the regions as revealed by the preceding similar business cycle phase (1978–1981)

	1978–1981	1983–1986
E(xperiment) region, change in employment	0	5.6
C(ontrol) region, change in employment	−2.6	5.3
Difference E − C region, change in employment	2.6	0.3
'Subsidy effects,' difference 83–86 *minus* difference 78–81		−2.3
'Subsidy effects' wrt different degrees of unemployment		
Areas with severe unemployment (1)		0.4
Areas with less severe unemployment (2)		−4.5
'Subsidy effects' in different manufacturing subsectors ranging from/to		
Wood in area 1		−0.4
Paper in area 2		−30.8
'Subsidy effects' on 44 pairs of 'twin firms' where		
E firm had a positive change relative to C firm		18 pairs
" " " " negative " " " " "		26 pairs

Note. Possible explanation of missing effects:
 1. Incidence: subsidies spill over to wages? (observed only to a minor extent).
 2. Response exhaustion: subsidies introduced on top of a series of pre-existing employment stimuli.

Further reading

Bohm, P., Lind, H. (1993). "Policy evaluation quality: A quasi-experimental study of regional employment subsidies in Sweden". Regional Science and Urban Economics 23, 51–65.

Chapter 79

FIELD-TEST ELICITATIONS OF DEMAND FOR PUBLIC GOODS

PETER BOHM

Stockholm University

Market economies would be more capable of establishing consumer sovereignty if the provision of public goods could be based on consumer demand. Ever since Wicksell (1896), as restated in Samuelson (1954), it has been noted that free-rider incentives seem to preclude such an outcome. Theory has suggested an ingenious method for neutralizing these incentives (see, e.g., Clarke, 1971; Groves and Ledyard, 1975; Green and Laffont, 1979). However, since this method is difficult for ordinary people to understand, governments may hesitate to use it in actual decision making (see, e.g., Bohm, 1984; see also experimentation with the method reported in Davis and Holt, 1993). Some economists have suggested that the best approach available is to ask well-structured hypothetical questions about the willingness to pay (WTP) for public goods and rely on the responses as good enough approximations, in spite of incentives to distort, or not carefully consider, responses to hypothetical questions.

A large group of experimentalists have analyzed the nature of free riding in the context of so-called public exchanges, a laboratory device for investigating the consequences of various aspects of non-rivalry in consumption related to voluntary public goods (for references, see Davis and Holt, 1993). However, there have been few attempts to identify and test practicable mechanisms for implementing consumer power over public-good decision making in real-world settings as a means of observing the extent of free riding in such contexts. A couple of exceptions to this rule are reported here.

The following pair of issues are in focus in two field tests of public-good decision making (Bohm, 1972, 1984):

Do incentives to misrepresent WTP produce significant distortions (strong free-rider behavior) when WTP for public goods is elicited in the field?

If not, can combinations of simple, not incentive-compatible, mechanisms be used to attain verifiable approximations useful for demand estimation in practice?

In test case 1, a random sample of the inhabitants in Stockholm was asked to participate in a new type of TV rating. The test was carried out by the Swedish public TV company (although it was the experimentalist who took the initiative and was responsible for the experimental design). Subjects were asked to assign a money value to a new program they could watch if their aggregate WTP were high enough to cover costs. (This was in 1969, when TV was still exciting in Sweden; in addition, the new program offered could be expected to attract wide interest.) In test case 2, the public good was an information package that could only be made available by the government, while the decision to produce the package was to be determined by the actual consumers.

The two field tests were designed to reflect the elicitation instrument selected, if used for decision making in actual practice concerning a non-trivial public good. In particular, consumers were told that:
- their collective decision would determine whether the public good in question would be produced or not, specified as whether or not their aggregate WTP exceeded production costs;
- if the good were to be produced, the consumers actually had to pay according to the rules for payment given to them; and
- there were incentives for misrepresentation of preferences for the public good; in addition, the participants were informed about various arguments likely to appear in a public WTP elicitation process.

The last point is particularly important since the ambition was to mimic a public decision making process where people would have had time to discuss the issues with others and would be likely to have heard – directly or indirectly – the media analyze the issues and possibly argue in favor of a particular kind of 'voting' behavior. Given this objective, attempts were made in the tests to lay bare the principal arguments likely to be exposed in such a process and their implications for information about the incentives confronting the respondents. Although it is difficult to speculate on the nature of an equilibrium state of such information, it was presumed that certain incentives to misrepresent WTP would be widely known and talked about, and that the organizers of the 'referendum' would try to counter these incentives by referring to the 'duties' of citizens participating in this kind of public process and/or the meaninglessness of conducting 'referenda' of this type if voters simply gave in to such incentives.

TEST 1. WTP for closed-circuit preview of a popular TV show (Bohm, 1972).

Subjects summoned to the test rating of a TV program, not previously shown but with well-known features and quality, were divided into six groups. Subjects in the first five groups were told that if their aggregate stated WTP exceeded a certain cost of showing them the program, they would be given the opportunity to watch the program, and prior to which each person would have to pay in group:
  I. the WTP stated,
  II. a percentage (as explained) of the WTP stated,
  III. the WTP stated or a percentage (as explained) of the amount stated or 5 *kronor* or nothing, all four with equal probability,
  IV. 5 *kronor*, the current average price of a cinema ticket,
  V. nothing; taxpayers would foot the bill.

This means that the first two groups, and those in group IV whose WTP fell short of 5 *kronor*, were exposed to incentives to understate WTP, while group V, and those in group IV whose WTP exceeded 5 *kronor*, were exposed to incentives to overstate WTP. With a dominating number of WTP statements above 5 *kronor* in group IV (as turned out to be the case), this group can be taken to offer an overstated mean WTP. There were no clear misrepresentation incentives for group III. Accordingly, in Figure 1, the groups

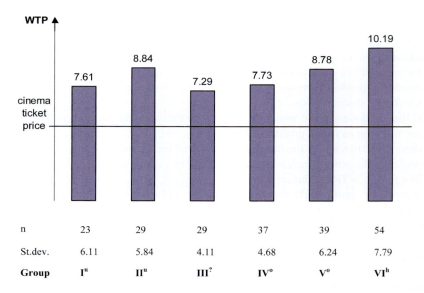

Figure 1. Mean WTP for a closed-circuit preview of a coming TV highlight, shown if (a) aggregate WTP exceeded 'production' costs and (b) subjects pay according to pre-specified rules for groups I–V, all non-hypothetical – two with incentives to understate WTP (u), two with incentives to overstate WTP (o), and one of unknown incentive effects (?); group VI faced a hypothetical question (h). Subjects: A representative sample of 211 inhabitants of Stockholm randomly allocated to the groups. *Results*: No significant differences in mean WTP among the non-hypothetical groups I–V, in spite of the diverging incentives to misrepresent WTP. Hypothetical WTP (VI^h) significantly different from non-hypothetical WTP (aggregate for groups I–V).

are presented as I^u, II^u, III$^?$, IV°, and V^o, where u (o) stands for incentives to understate (overstate) WTP. *Result 1*: There were no significant differences between mean WTP in these five groups. Thus, in the particular setting used here there were no signs of strong free-rider behavior; in other words, the same order of magnitude of true aggregate WTP could have been elicited using any of the five approaches.

Subjects in the sixth group (VI^h, h for hypothetical) were simply asked to "estimate in money how much you think watching this program would be worth to you" without indicating whether or not the program would be shown or whether or not their responses could have an effect on such a decision. Comparing mean WTP responses to this hypothetical question with the pool of the responses to the five non-hypothetical questions (Bohm, 1994), a Kolmogoroff–Smirnov test showed a difference at the five percent level of significance, i.e., that *result 2*: the hypothetical version, nowadays called a 'contingent valuation,' tended to give an overstatement of the WTP.

TEST 2. WTP elicited for actual decision making concerning a government-provided public good (Bohm, 1984).

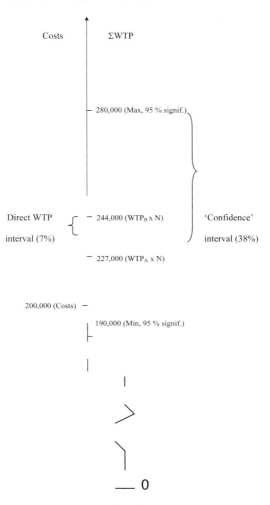

Figure 2. Aggregate effects of misrepresentation incentives using the interval method. Random fifty percent of a population (or sample) exposed to an incentive to understate (Group A) and the rest to en incentive to overstate (Group B) public good demand. Mean stated WTP_i (i = A, B) by consumers, the N (= 274) Swedish local governments, for a real-world public good (statistics) multiplied by N; WTP_A = SEK 827 and WTP_B = SEK 889; in SEK. *Results*: Interval between WTP means equals 7 percent of average WTP and exceeds costs. Correction for sampling error: 95 percent confidence interval equals 38 percent of average WTP; 8/9 of interval exceeds costs; central government interpretation: true aggregate WTP likely to exceed costs; therefore, the good was produced and respondents paid according to pre-specified rules.

In 1982, a Swedish government committee investigating potential operational demand criteria for deciding whether or not to produce costly statistics allowed one particular statistical investment project (providing access to information about certain attributes of housing in Sweden) to be determined by the following "interval method."

Potential consumers were identified as the 279 local governments in Sweden. About half of them were randomly allocated to group A, whose members were asked to report their WTP for access to this type of service according to the principle of group II^u in the test reported above. The remainder of the population (group B) was asked to report their WTP in a way similar to the principle of group IV° above, but excluding those who did not want to pay the stated price (an excludable public good). More specifically, if the good were to be provided, those in group A would have to pay a percentage of the WTP stated so that the average payment in this group equaled per capita costs of the project, and group B would have to pay a fixed fee of SEK 500 (in 1982, about $100) if they had stated a WTP of at least SEK 500, while those stating a WTP below SEK 500 would be excluded from access to the service.

The average responses from these two groups gave an estimate of a lower and an upper bound to the true average WTP, since there were incentives to underreport but not overreport (overreport but not underreport) WTP in group A (B). The method could then be used so that the relation between the resulting (average or aggregate) WTP interval and the (average or total) project cost would determine the outcome as follows: If the WTP interval exceeded (fell short of) the cost, the project would (would not) be carried out. If the interval overlapped the costs and (a) the interval was small, i.e., responses to incentives to misrepresent WTP were weak, the project would not have any significant net benefit of the project; hence, it would not be carried out. If instead (b) the interval was large, the government would have to make the decision.

If the government would prefer to use the method only after observing the influence of sampling errors when randomly allocating the population to the two groups, the direct WTP interval just mentioned could be replaced by one including one-sided confidence intervals, as illustrated in Figure 2. The resulting larger interval would then be used instead of the interval directly observed, but in a manner similar to that reported above.

The results from the actual test carried out indicate, as shown in the figure, that regardless of the two alternative designs of the WTP interval, the natural decision was to have the public good produced. (And that was the way the government interpreted the results.) Of the 279 local governments, 274 responded and all of the 130 respondents who qualified for consumption of the good paid the charges. The results reveal a very small direct WTP interval (some 7% of the interval mid-point) and a "95% confidence interval" of 38%, 8/9 of which exceeded the cost figure.

References

Bohm, P. (1972). "Estimating demand for public goods: An experiment". European Economic Review 3, 11–130.
Bohm, P. (1984). "Revealing demand for an actual public good". Journal of Public Economics 24, 135–152.
Bohm, P. (1994). "CVM spells responses to *hypothetical* questions". Natural Resources Journal 34, 37–50.
Clarke, E. (1971). "Multipart pricing of public goods". Public Choice 11, 19–33.

Davis, D., Holt, C. (1993). "Experimental Economics". Princeton University Press, Princeton, NJ.
Green, J., Laffont, J.-J. (1979). "Incentives in Public Decision-Making". North-Holland, Amsterdam.
Groves, T., Ledyard, J., 1975. "An incentive mechanism for efficient resource allocation in general equilibrium with public goods". Center for Mathematical Studies in Economics and Management Sciences, Northwestern University.
Samuelson, P. (1954). "The pure theory of public expenditures". Review of Economics and Statistics 36, 387–389.
Wicksell, K. (1896). "Finanzteoretische Untersuchungen". Jena; English translation in: Musgrave, R., Peacock, A., "Classics in the Theory of Public Finance". Macmillan, London, 1958.

Chapter 80

RESULTS FROM A DOZEN YEARS OF ELECTION FUTURES MARKETS RESEARCH

JOYCE BERG, ROBERT FORSYTHE, FORREST NELSON and THOMAS RIETZ

Department of Accounting, Henry B. Tippie College of Business, University of Iowa, Iowa City, IA 52242, USA

1. Introduction and Description of Election Futures Markets

The Iowa Electronic Markets (IEM) are small-scale,[1] real-money futures markets conducted by the University of Iowa Henry B. Tippie College of Business. In this review, we focus on the best known of these markets, The Iowa Political Markets.[2] Contracts in these markets are designed so that prices should predict election outcomes. The data set contains the results of 49 markets covering 41 elections in 13 countries.

The Iowa Electronic Markets operate 24-hours a day, using a continuous, double-auction trading mechanism. Traders invest their own funds, make their own trades, and conduct their own information searches. The markets occupy a niche between the stylized, tightly controlled markets conducted in the laboratory and the information-rich environments of naturally occurring markets. By virtue of this design, the Iowa Markets provide data to researchers that is not otherwise available.

In addition to examining the accuracy of prices in these markets, we also compare the results of the national elections to a natural benchmark, polls, when available. Relative to polls, the markets rely on very different mechanisms for data collection and aggregation. Polls ask the question, "If the election were being held today, would you vote for the Democratic candidate or for the Republican candidate?" They rely on a representative sample of likely voters, truthful responses to the poll questions and classical statistics to arrive at their predictions of election outcomes. In the Iowa Markets, traders receive an explicit financial reward tied to correctly answering the question, "Who will everyone vote for on election day?" Traders are not a representative sample of likely voters; they are overwhelmingly male, well-educated, high income, and young (the average age is close to 30). In fact, we do not require our traders to be eligible to vote in the election.

---

[1] Investments are typically limited to a $500 maximum per trader and generally average less than a tenth of this. Vote share markets have ranged in size from a dozen or so active traders to more than 500. Dollar and quantity volumes range up to $21,445 and 78,007 contracts in the 1992 U.S. Presidential Vote Share market (see Berg, Nelson, and Rietz, 2001).

[2] The Iowa Electronic Markets offer vote-share, seat-share and winner-takes-all election markets and markets based on other political outcomes, economic indicators and corporate earnings and returns. Here we focus on vote-share and seat-share election markets because, unlike other IEM offerings, they have both an accuracy criterion (election outcome) and recognizable performance benchmarks (polls).

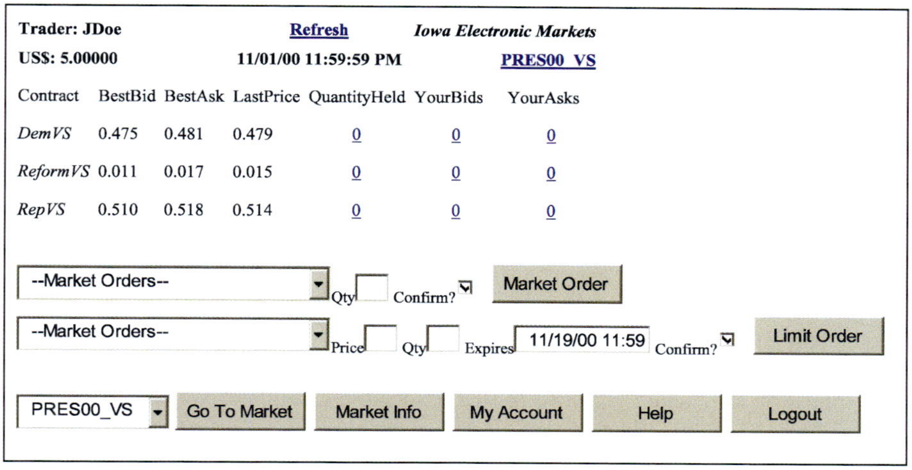
Trader: JDoe
Refresh
Iowa Electronic Markets
US$: 5.00000
11/01/00 11:59:59 PM
PRES00_VS
Contract BestBid BestAsk LastPrice QuantityHeld YourBids YourAsks
DemVS 0.475 0.481 0.479 0 0 0
ReformVS 0.011 0.017 0.015 0 0 0
RepVS 0.510 0.518 0.514 0 0 0
--Market Orders--
Qty
Confirm?
Market Order
--Market Orders--
Price
Qty
Expires
11/19/00 11:59
Confirm?
Limit Order
PRES00_VS
Go To Market
Market Info
My Account
Help
Logout

Figure 1. IEM Market trading screen. The top table displays the current market, contracts, bids, asks and last trade prices along with the current trader's portfolio, number of outstanding bids and number of outstanding asks. The menu in the middle section allows the trader to place orders and make trades. The menu bar at the bottom allows the trader to undertake other activities.

2. Market Mechanism[3]

Each market is related to a specific future event, for instance a presidential election, and contains a set of contracts with liquidation values pegged to the outcome of the future event. Contracts enter into circulation by the voluntary purchase from the IEM trading system of bundles of contracts that we call "unit portfolios," or they are removed from circulation by sales of unit portfolios back to the system. These unit portfolios consist of one of each contract available in the market, and they are purchased from and sold to the system for a fixed price, which is the predetermined aggregate payoff to that portfolio. This use of unit portfolios ensures that the market operates as a zero-sum game and it permits the supply of contracts to be determined endogenously by the net number of unit portfolios that have been purchased by traders. Unit portfolios are employed only to place contracts in circulation; transactions among traders occur with individual contracts at prices determined by the participants.

Traders in these markets can place market orders (requests for immediate execution of a trade at current market prices) and limit orders (offers to buy (bid) or sell (ask) specified quantities at specified prices within some specified period of time). Limit orders are kept in queues ordered by price and time. Traders can withdraw their own outstanding limit orders at any time before they trade or expire. The market information set available

[3] Here, we highlight the important features of the markets. For more detailed descriptions, see Berg, Forsythe, and Rietz (1996, 1997) and Forsythe et al. (1992).

to traders consists of current best bid and ask prices and the last trade price. Traders do not know the quantity available at the best bid and ask. Nor do they know other entries in the bid and ask queues, except for their own bids and asks. This information appears on the trading screen as depicted in Figure 1. In addition, traders can access historical daily price information consisting of the quantity and dollar volume and the high, low, average and last trade prices.[4]

3. Results from Share Markets

In vote-share markets, the relative vote shares that candidates receive determine contract liquidation values. Typically, a particular contract will have a liquidating payoff equal to $1 times the vote share received by the associated candidate. We insure that vote shares sum to 100% by either (1) including a single contract associated with all minor-party vote shares (a "rest-of-the-field" contract) or (2) calculating vote shares based on fractions of the major-party vote (e.g., the Democratic vote divided by the summed Democratic and Republican votes).[5] Simple arbitrage arguments imply that contracts should trade at the expected liquidation values.[6] Thus, in these markets, prices should equal expected vote shares.

In seat-share markets, contracts liquidate at values determined by the congressional or parliamentary seats allocated to parties in an election. Typically, a particular contract will have a liquidating payoff equal to $1 times the seat share allocated to the associated party. We insure that seat shares sum to 100% by either (1) including a single contract associated with all minor parties (a "rest-of-the-field" contract) or (2) calculating seat shares based on fractions of one party versus the all the other parties (e.g., the Republican share of seats versus seats held by non-Republicans).[7] In these markets, prices should equal expected seat shares.

3.1. Absolute Market Accuracy

Efficiency evaluations are simple in vote share markets because they can be compared directly to the election outcome. To evaluate the ultimate predictive efficiency of the

---

[4] While our markets are continuous, we report price information by 24-hour daily periods.

[5] A prospectus details the particular method used in each market.

[6] This arises because there is no aggregate risk in the markets. Thus, all agents can hold the well-diversified, "market" portfolio consisting purely of unit portfolios. Individual contracts can be priced from this portfolio and the risk/return tradeoff inherent in it. The return to holding unit portfolios is the same as the risk free rate (zero here). Thus, there is no risk premium in these markets. Because the risk premium is zero, the expected return for each risky asset must also be zero. This can only be true if all contracts are priced at their expected values. See Rietz (1998) for a more detailed explanation of how these results can be derived from general equilibrium arguments, from the capital asset pricing model and from arbitrage pricing theory.

[7] Again, a prospectus details the particular method used in each market.

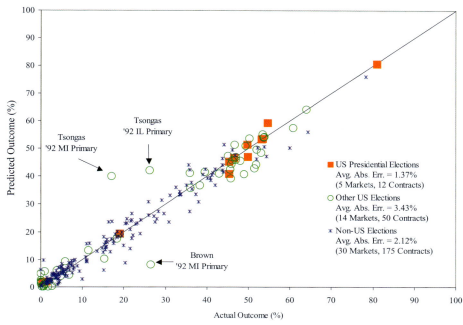

Vote Share
Austria (Fed. Par. '95, Styrian Region '95; Vienna City '95, EU Par. '96)
Canada (Par. '93, '96)
Denmark (Par. '91)
Finland (Pres. '94 (×2 mkts.))
France (Pres. '95)
Korea (Pres. '92)

Germany (Par. '90 (×3 mkts. in Bonn, Frankfurt and Leipzig), '91, '94, '98 Fed, '98 State)
The Netherlands (Par. '91, '94 (2nd Chamber); EU Par. '94; Muni. Council '94)
Norway (Par. '95)
Sweden (EU Mbrshp. '94)
Turkey (Par. '91)

Vote Share (Continued)
U.S. Pres. ('88, '92, '96 (×2 mkts.), '00)
U.S. Pres. Primaries (IL '92, MI '92)
U.S. Sen. (IL '90, IA '90, AZ '94, NJ '94, PA '94, TX '94, VA '94)
U.S. Gov. (NY '94, TX '94)
U.S. House (UT '94)

Seat Share & Other
Australia (Par. '93)
Canada (Par. '93, '96)
The Netherlands (Par. (2nd Chamber) Turnout '94, EU Par. Turnout '94)
U.S. House ('94)
U.S. Senate ('94)

Figure 2. Political futures market predicted versus actual outcomes for vote-share and seat-share markets. Vote-share market predictions are for percentages of votes received by parties or candidates. Seat-share market predictions are for percentages of seats in congress or parliament held by parties. Predictions are based on normalized (to sum to 100%), last-trade prices as of midnight the night before each election. The 45-degree line represents perfect accuracy. Markets included in the figure.

market, we compare the market predictions at midnight the evening before the election to the actual election outcome.[8] Figure 2 extends a similar figure in Forsythe, Rietz, and Ross (1999). It shows the absolute accuracy of 237 contract predictions in 49 markets run in 13 countries. In this figure, the bottom axis shows actual outcomes while the left axis shows market predictions. If all predictions lined up on the 45-degree line, the market would be perfectly accurate. Over-prediction errors lie above the line and under-prediction errors below.

Figure 2 shows no obvious biases in the market forecasts and, on average, considerable accuracy, especially for large U.S. election markets.[9] Berg, Forsythe, and Rietz (1996) study how aggregate market characteristics affect accuracy in U.S. markets. Three factors explain most of the variance in accuracy. Presidential election markets perform better than (typically lower profile) congressional, state and local election markets. Markets with more volume near the election perform better than those with less. Finally, markets with fewer contracts (i.e., fewer candidates or parties) predict better than those with more.

3.2. Accuracy Relative to Polls

Figure 3 shows how the market compares to polls for the subset of national elections in which we have poll data for comparison.[10] Since market prices vary continuously, the question arises of which price to take as the prediction from the market. We include two measures: (1) the market price as of midnight on election eve and (2) the volume weighted average price of all transactions over the week before the election. The former incorporates all information available to traders as of that point in time but often reflects a great deal of volatility which results from the thinning out of queues on the last day of trading. The latter involves trades that are largely contemporaneous to the polls against which the market prices are being compared. Each error measure is the average (across candidates) of the absolute prediction error. Polling data in the figure represents the absolute errors of the final pre-election polls averaged across all candidates and across all of the major polling organizations for which data was available. The market outperformed polls in 9 of 15 cases according to each measure (election eve closing prices and last week average prices). Across all elections, the average poll error was 1.91% while the average market error was 1.49% and 1.58% by the two measures. In a few cases (e.g., the 1988 and 1992 U.S. Presidential elections) the market dramatically outperformed polls. The worst outcome, the 1996 U.S. Presidential election, is a peculiar

---

[8] The clock on the market's host computer determines "Midnight." For markets run from the University of Iowa, this is U.S. Central Time. We choose midnight because expiring orders are removed from the queues just after midnight. This may cause substantial increases in the bid/ask spread and, in turn, the price volatility associated with a bid/ask bounce.

[9] Biases might be predicted by arguments along the lines of Kahneman and Tversky (1979) or Jacobsen et al. (2000). The obvious outliers are associated with Tsongas's and Brown's showing in 1992 Primary elections.

[10] Typically, polls are designed to evaluate current opinions and not to predict future election outcomes. However, they serve as the obvious basis of comparison for the market predictions.

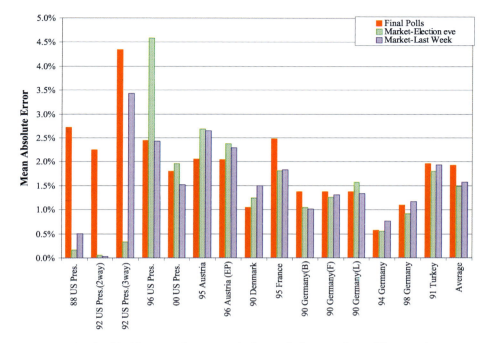

Figure 3. National political futures market average absolute prediction errors for candidate vote shares versus errors from polls in the week before the election. Final week market errors are calculated from the normalized (to sum to 100%) average trade prices from the last week before each election. Election eve market errors are calculated from normalized (to sum to 100%), last-trade prices as of midnight the night before each election. Errors for each poll are calculated from the normalized (to sum to 100% and allocate undecided voters) poll responses. Then, poll errors are averaged across known major polls from the last week before the election.

one that gets additional attention below. In the majority of other cases, the market does about as well as the average poll, sometimes worse but often better, even if by a small margin.

Election eve outcomes are to some extent less interesting than predictions over the full course of the campaign. We notice a general tendency for the market to be both closer to eventual election outcomes and more stable than polls over the course of election campaigns. We illustrate this point in Figure 4 using the *worst* performing U.S. Presidential market as indicated by the election eve outcome relative to polls. This graph shows the relative stability of the market compared to polls over time, a feature typical of markets run to date. In the previous presidential elections, the market changed little or became slightly more accurate near the end of the election. However, in 1996, the market diverged from the correct outcome in the final days to close at midnight on the eve of the election with prices further from the election outcome than they had been since the Super Tuesday primaries in March. Apparently a large cash influx by new traders late in the campaign drove the price movement. Nevertheless, over the majority of the time

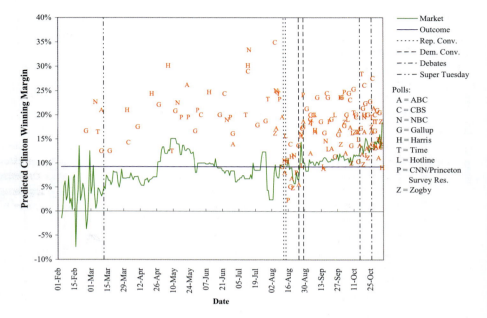

Figure 4. Performance of the 1996 Presidential Election Market and contemporaneous opinion polls over the full course of the campaign. The vertical axis is the normalized margin of victory for Clinton (Clinton outcome minus Dole outcome divided by the sum of the two). Time is along the horizontal axis, the solid horizontal straight line indicates the outcome of the election on November 5, and the vertical lines represent important events – the Republican and Democratic conventions, two debates and Super Tuesday. The right-most limit of the graph is the election. The solid jagged line represents market prices, and the letters indicate the outcome of various polls.

this market ran, its predictions were dramatically more accurate and stable than polls. This shows the value of the markets as longer run forecasting devices.

4. How and why do Election Futures Markets "Work?"

For the markets to work in theory, two features must be present. First, there must be enough traders so that the aggregate of their knowledge can forecast correctly the outcome of the election. Second, the market mechanism must facilitate aggregation of their disparate information so that the prevailing market price becomes a sufficient statistic for the traders' collective information. Whether real markets can accomplish these two tasks is a behavioral question best answered by observing market dynamics and individual trader actions.

The markets appear to work efficiently in practice. Studying IEM Presidential markets run to date, Berg, Nelson, and Rietz (2001) show that these markets are efficient in four senses. First, they predict well on election eve. Second, weeks or months before the election, prices are much better forecasts than polls. Third, the prices appear to follow a random walk as predicted by efficient market theory. Fourth, efficient inter-market pricing relationships hold.

What drives this market efficiency? At the market level, Berg, Forsythe, and Rietz (1996) show that larger, more active markets with fewer contracts are more accurate. Forsythe et al. (1992), discuss the relationship between polls and market prices. They conclude that, while pre-election polls are obvious sources of information for market traders, market prices do not follow poll results. If anything, market prices predict changes in polls. Forsythe et al. (1992), Oliven and Rietz (2004) and Forsythe, Rietz, and Ross (1999) all show that individual traders display considerable biases and often make mistakes in the largest and most accurate of the IEM markets. All three papers reconcile these observations with apparently high levels of market efficiency in a similar way. Specifically, the core group of traders that tend to set market prices appears less biased and error prone than typical traders. Forsythe et al. (1992) show that typical traders have unrealistically optimistic beliefs for their preferred candidates (see Granberg and Brent, 1983 for a historical discussion of this bias). However, "marginal traders" (those who regularly trade or place bids and asks near the top of the queues) are much less prone to this bias. Oliven and Rietz (2004) show that typical traders often trade at a price that is not the most advantageous price for the trader or that violates arbitrage restrictions. Such "mistakes" are "irrational" because they decrease the trader's payoff regardless of expectations or outcomes. However, "market makers" (those who actually set market prices by placing the best bids and asks) make mistakes much less often. Forsythe, Rietz, and Ross (1999) study these issues further, relating the biases to psychological foundations. These results are what distinguish much of economics from the other social sciences. Marginal traders, not average traders, drive market prices and, therefore, predictions.

We also believe that the differences between election markets and polls give the markets an edge in prediction. Not only are the traders paid for correct decisions about the eventual election outcomes, but the market information set also includes previous market outcomes, poll results and any other information deemed relevant by traders.

5. Other Issues Studied and Future Research Potential

In addition to share markets, the IEM runs political "winner-takes-all" markets. Contracts in "winner-takes-all" markets liquidate at $1 if an associated event occurs. For example, if a particular candidate wins an election, the associated winner-takes-all contract will pay $1.[11] Because of how we specify contracts and the event space, a full portfolio of all contracts in a market will always liquidate at $1. Again, prices should equal expected values. Because of the $0/$1 payoff structure, prices should equal the

---

[11] Typically, we define "win" as taking the majority of the popular vote in an election.

probability of the $1 liquidation. Thus, prices can be used to evaluate a candidate's chances of winning an election, assess the relative viability of candidates and measure the impact of specific events on elections. In addition to winner-takes-all election markets, we have run such markets on various other political events. These include markets designed to predict: who party nominees will be in elections, who will control the houses of congress, whether particular bills or treaties will pass (e.g., NAFTA), whether countries will join the EMU, etc.[12] These markets respond quickly to some events, but often appear unaffected by events that one might otherwise think should affect a campaign. This allows us to separate "surprises" from "news" that is anticipated. (For examples of using the markets to evaluate news events, see Forsythe et al., 1991, 1992).

In addition to predicting outcomes and evaluating accuracy relative to polls, the IEM has been used to study a variety of other market related research topics. Forsythe et al. (1992) and Oliven and Rietz (2004) study relationships between individual trader characteristics and actions. Oliven and Rietz (2004) also study arbitrage restrictions and violations. Forsythe, Rietz, and Ross (1999) study price formation and psychological biases. Berg and Rietz (2003a) study predictive accuracy of winner-takes-all contracts in markets based on returns and price levels in the computer industry. Bondarenko and Bossarts (2000) study price dynamics and Bayesian updating. Beckmann and Werding (1996) compare call and continuous markets. Slemrod and Greimel (1999) study the relationship between IEM forecasts and bond markets. Plott (2000) and Ortner (1997, 1998) use similar markets to predict corporate events. Berg and Rietz (2003b) show how such markets can serve for decision support.

Thus, the IEM and similar markets have been used to study a variety of interesting topics. We believe that, by filling the gap between traditional experimental markets and the "real world," markets such as the IEM have great research potential. The IEM includes more data than available from typical financial markets. This data includes transaction and order flow data associated with individual traders, complete queue information, portfolio positions of each trader and trader demographics. The IEM can also be used to survey traders at any time, recording survey responses and associating them with other data. Thus, they provide an excellent complement to other existing research techniques.

Acknowledgements

For many helpful comments and discussions during the course of research summarized here, we thank Tom Gruca, George Neumann, Kent Oliven, Tom Ross and Jack Wright.

---

[12] Since 1993, the IEM has conducted markets based on economic indicators and corporate earnings and returns. These markets are limited to participants from academic communities and, along with the political markets, are used in many classes. Examples of the "earnings and returns" include: monthly contracts based on future market returns in the computer industry and Microsoft's stock price level, periodic markets designed to predict earnings announcements of companies and periodic markets designed to predict box-office earnings for movies. For an example of research using earnings and returns markets, see Bondarenko and Bossarts (2000).

References

Beckmann, K., Werding, M. (1996). "'Passauer Wahlbörse': Information processing in a political market experiment". Kyklos 49, 171–204.

Berg, J.E., Rietz, T.A. (2003a). "Longshots, overconfidence and efficiency on the Iowa Electronic Market". Mimeo, Department of Finance, University of Iowa.

Berg, J.E., Rietz, T.A. (2003b). "Prediction markets as decision support systems". Information Systems Frontiers 5, 79–93.

Berg, J.E., Forsythe, R., Rietz, T.A. (1996). "What makes markets predict well? Evidence from the Iowa Electronic Markets". In: Albers, W., Güth, W., Hammerstein, P., Moldovanu, B., van Damme, E. (Eds.), Understanding Strategic Interaction: Essays in Honor of Reinhard Selten. Springer, New York, pp. 444–463.

Berg, J.E., Forsythe, R., Rietz, T.A. (1997). "The Iowa Electronic Market". In: Paxson, D., Wood, D. (Eds.), Blackwell Encyclopedic Dictionary of Finance. Blackwell, Oxford, UK.

Berg, J.E., Nelson, F.D., Rietz, T.A. (2001). "Accuracy and forecast standard error of prediction markets". Mimeo, Department of Finance, University of Iowa.

Bondarenko, O., Bossarts, P. (2000). "Expectations and learning in Iowa". Journal of Banking and Finance 24, 1535–1555.

Forsythe, R., Rietz, T.A., Ross, T.W. (1999). "Wishes, expectations and actions: Price formation in election stock markets". Journal of Economic Behavior and Organization 39, 83–110.

Forsythe, R., Nelson, F.D., Neumann, G.R., Wright, J. (1991). "Forecasting elections: A market alternative to polls". In: Palfrey, T.R. (Ed.), Contemporary Laboratory Experiments in Political Economy. University of Michigan Press, Ann Arbor, pp. 69–111.

Forsythe, R., Nelson, F.D., Neumann, G.R., Wright, J. (1992). "Anatomy of an experimental political stock market". American Economic Review 82, 1142–1161.

Granberg, D., Brent, E. (1983). "When prophecy bends: The preference-expectation link in U.S. Presidential elections". Journal of Personality and Social Psychology 45, 477–491.

Jacobsen, B., Potters, J., Schram, A., van Winden, F., Wit, J. (2000). "(In)accuracy of a European political stock market: The influence of common value structures". European Economic Review 44, 205–230.

Kahneman, D., Tversky, A. (1979). "Prospect theory: An analysis of decision under risk". Econometrica 47, 263–291.

Oliven, K., Rietz, T.A. (2004). "Suckers are born but markets are made: Individual rationality, arbitrage and market efficiency on an electronic futures market". Management Science 50, 336–351.

Ortner, G. (1997). "Forecasting markets: An industrial application: Part I". Mimeo, Technical University of Vienna.

Ortner, G. (1998). "Forecasting markets: An industrial application: Part II". Mimeo, Technical University of Vienna.

Plott, C.R. (2000). "Markets as information gathering tools". Southern Economic Journal 67, 2–15.

Rietz, T.A. (1998). "Enforcing arbitrage restrictions in experimental asset markets". Mimeo, Department of Finance, University of Iowa.

Slemrod, J., Greimel, T. (1999). "Did Steve Forbes scare the municipal bond market?" Journal of Public Economics 74, 81–96.

Chapter 81

EXPERIMENTAL EVIDENCE ON THE EXISTENCE OF HYPOTHETICAL BIAS IN VALUE ELICITATION METHODS

GLENN W. HARRISON and E. ELISABET RUTSTRÖM

Hypothetical bias is said to exist when values that are elicited in a hypothetical context, such as a survey, differ from those elicited in a real context, such as a market. Although reported experimental results are mixed, we claim that the evidence strongly favor the conclusion that hypothetical bias exists. Nevertheless, some optimism is called for with respect to the ability to calibrate either the hypothetical survey instrument itself, or the responses from it. Calibration could be performed in such a way that elicited values are unbiased estimates of actual valuations.

The usual concern with hypothetical bias is that people will overstate their true valuation in hypothetical settings. Why? As a matter of logic, if you do not have to pay for the good but a higher *verbal* willingness to pay (WTP) response increases the chance of it's provision, then verbalize away to increase your expected utility! Similarly, if your verbal statement of a higher willingness to accept (WTA) compensation might reduce the risk that the commodity will be taken away from you, verbalize as high an amount as you want. This seems like such a simple logic, so why even bother testing if the problem arises behaviorally with experiments? The rationale for these tests arises from debates over the validity of the Contingent Valuation Method (CVM) for valuing environmental damages. The CVM is a survey instrument commonly used in environmental resource valuations, which is hypothetical in both the payment for and the provision of the good being valued. Proponents of the CVM have often claimed that hypothetical bias simply does not exist or that it is quantitatively unimportant even if it does exist.[1] Given the importance that such claims about the validity of the CVM have for environmental policy, and the confidence that some proponents of the CVM place in their *a priori* claims, testing the existence of hypothetical bias has been necessary. Moreover, tests that establish the existence of the behavioral problem invariably provide information to help one quantify how important it is. That can also be useful when measuring the efficacy of attempts to mitigate the problem.

Some simple experimental tests have managed to shift the burden of proof back on those making claims that hypothetical bias is not a problem. In addition, several experimental results point the way to a more complete understanding of the process of eliciting values, as well as constructive means of mitigating the effects of hypothetical bias. The usual scenario in experiments has been the exchange of a commodity, although for policy purposes the scenario is often some change in policy. The use of a commodity

---

[1] See Cummings and Harrison (1994) for a literature review of the CVM debates over hypothetical bias.

instead of some general policy change simplifies the problem of detecting and dealing with hypothetical bias. The reason is that the description of the scenario itself may entail hypothetical or incredible features (e.g., "are you willing to pay $5 to eradicate the risk of global warming"). In this case one might easily confound the perception of a non-credible policy with the hypothetical nature of the payment itself. Thus the use of simple commodities in experiments should be seen as an instance of the experimenter gaining more control over the behavior under study.

The experimental literature on the existence of hypothetical bias falls into three groups. The first group of studies examined open ended elicitation methods in which the object to be valued is presented to subjects and a dollar value solicited. The typical institution used in these studies is the sealed-bid, second-price (Vickrey) auction. The second group of studies examined closed ended elicitation methods (often called dichotomous choice) in which the object to be valued and an offer price is presented to subjects, and a purchase decision solicited. The typical institution used in these studies is the posted offer institution. The third group of studies examined binary choice in a referendum context. A group of subjects is offered a public good at a given price and asked to vote yes or no.

In all cases the results are quite clear: there is a hypothetical bias problem to be solved. We review the basic experimental results that support this conclusion. Table 1 summarizes these results. The conclusion is that the weight of the evidence supports the claim that hypothetical valuations exceed real valuations.

The literature of experimental results falls into two waves. The first consists of a series of relatively disconnected studies in the 1980's using innovative experimental designs in an attempt to shed light on the general validity of the CVM. These are briefly reviewed in Sections 1 and 2. More recently there has been a series of experimental studies using extremely simple designs that are more narrowly focused on the issue of hypothetical bias and how it interacts with the elicitation mechanism. These are reviewed in Sections 3 through 4.

1. The CVM Literature and Tests with Private Goods

We begin with a study that claims not to have found any significant hypothetical bias, although the difference in responses between hypothetical and actual contexts is large. Dickie, Fisher, and Gerking (1987) obtained values for a pint of strawberries by using CVM, and also by actually selling the strawberries to households. They concluded (p. 73) that they could not reject the null hypothesis of structurally identical demand equations estimated from actual sales and CVM data. However, their results are mixed if one examines them in further detail. Specifically, they found that there were large differences in the estimated actual and hypothetical demand schedules (p. 74, in their Tables 3 and 4, and Figure 1). Depending on the price one uses, the hypothetical demand curve can overstate the quantity demanded from 351.4% to 68.6% if all interview team results are included. The average hypothetical bias, calculated from the raw responses,

Table 1
Summary of findings of hypothetical bias

Study	Key features of bias comparison	Hypothetical bias	Statistically significant?
BH		−46%	no
JLJ	Conservative interpretation of CVM responses vs real; largest bias reported.	−43%	no
MSC	Smallest bias found at highest risk treatment.	−25%	?
Bohm	Comparison with auction institution.	0%	no
JLJ	Conservative interpretation of CVM responses vs real; smallest bias reported.	0%	no
SM		3%	no
DFG	Excluding team 2 and outlier identified in study.	8%	no
Bohm	Comparison of means; smallest bias reported.	16%	yes
JLJ	Standard interpretation of CVM responses vs real; smallest bias for lowest price.	19%	yes
Bohm	Comparison of medians; smallest bias reported.	25%	?
Griffin et al.	Comparison of proportion of "yes" responses.	29%	?
KMD	Private good.	30%	yes
DP	Means, excluding non-respondents.	35%	?
Bohm	Comparison of means; highest bias reported.	40%	yes
Frykblom	Dichotomous choice responses.	56%	yes
DFG	Comparison of "raw" means.	58%	no
BHK	Comparison of means.	60%	yes
Frykblom	Open-ended responses.	60%	yes
CEHM		67%	yes
DFG	Estimated demand functions; comparison of means; smallest bias reported.	69%	no
KMP	Public good.	100%	yes
Bohm	Comparison of medians; largest bias reported.	100%	?
MSC	Largest bias reported at lowest risk.	120%	?
CHR	Juicers; within-subjects.	163%	yes
CHR	Calculators; between-subjects.	163%	yes
BHK	Comparison of medians.	176%	?
DP	Comparison of means, assuming non-respondents have WTP = $0.	203%	?
Neill et al.	Painting; comparison of means.	290%	yes
DFG	Estimated demand functions; comparison of means; largest bias reported.	351%	no
Neill et al.	Painting; comparison of medians.	400%	?
JLJ	Standard interpretation of CVM responses vs real; highest bias reported.	701%	yes
CHR	Chocolates; within-subjects comparisons.	873%	yes
SS	Comparison of means.	2017%	?

(*continued on next page*)

Table 1
(continued)

Study	Key features of bias comparison	Hypothetical bias	Statistically significant?
Neill et al.	Map; HVA vs RVA; comparison of means.	2400%	yes
Neill et al.	Map; CVM vs RVA; comparison of means.	2600%	yes

Notes: The acronym for each study is provided in the References; bias measured as hypothetical minus real over real when positive, and real minus hypothetical over hypothetical when negative; statistical significance is determined at a one-sided 10% level, and a question mark indicates that there was insufficient information in the study to allow a simple determination.

is about 58%.[2] We include this number in Table 1 that compiles the results from all the studies we survey. We conclude that there is hardly unequivocal support in this study for the view that hypothetical and actual questions generate the same demand schedules.

Furthermore, a number of other studies demonstrate that there may be significant differences between CVM values and market values.

Bishop and Heberlein (1979) and Bishop, Heberlein, and Kealy (1983) found significant differences between CVM estimates for subjects' WTA for returning their goose hunting permits and WTA values based upon actual cash payments. The expected value based on actual cash payments was $63 and that based on the CVM was $101, implying a bias of about 60%, as shown in Table 1. Median values were $29 and $80 for the actual and hypothetical valuations, respectively, a bias of 176%. Mitchell and Carson (1989, pp. 195–199) dispute these conclusions. Hanemann (1984) also re-evaluates the results of Bishop and Heberlein, demonstrating the extreme sensitivity of their conclusions to alternative statistical assumptions.

In a later study, Bishop and Heberlein (1986) obtained CVM and actual cash values for deer hunting permits, and found that WTP values were significantly overstated in the CVM relative to the cash market. In three different valuation institutions they found that the average hypothetical values exceeded the real ones by 33%, 68%, and 79%. In one institution did they find that the real valuations exceeded the hypothetical by 46%, but this was not significant.

2. The CVM Literature and Tests with Public Goods

We next turn to a series of studies from the older CVM literature that attempted to test for hypothetical bias in the more complicated setting of public goods valuation in the field.

---

[2] We generally calculate the hypothetical bias as the excess of the hypothetical to real WTP as a percentage of the real. The exception is when the real WTP is higher than the hypothetical, in which case we report the bias as the excess of the real over the hypothetical as a percentage of the hypothetical.

Bohm (1972) is a landmark study that has had a great impact on many researchers, primarily with respect to the design of field experiments of public goods provision and tests of the extent of free riding and strategic bias. The commodity used in Bohm's experiments was a closed-circuit broadcast of a new Swedish TV program. Six elicitation procedures were used. In each case except one, the TV program was made available and subjects in each group allowed to see it, if aggregate WTP equaled or exceeded a known total cost. Every subject received 50 Swedish Kroner (SEK) when arriving at the experiment.

The question of free riding behavior in public goods provision is relevant to hypothetical bias because part of the latter can be claimed to derive from strategic behavior. In particular, as we discussed in our introductory remarks, hypothetical bias arises from a strategic over-bidding when no actual payment is expected.

Bohm employed five basic procedures for valuing his commodity to capture different degrees and directions of strategic bias. In Procedure I, the subject paid according to his stated WTP. In Procedure II, the subject paid some fraction ($\leqslant 1$) of stated WTP, with the fraction determined equally for all in the group such that total costs are just covered. In Procedure III, subjects did not know the specific payment scheme at the time of their bid, but did know that it was a lottery with equal probability attached to the payment schemes of Procedures I, II, IV, and V. In Procedure IV, each subject paid a fixed amount (SEK 5). In Procedure V, the subject paid nothing. No formal theory was provided to generate free-riding hypotheses for these procedures, and all predictions should be interpreted as making weak inequality predictions. Procedure I was deemed the most likely to generate strategic *under*-bidding, and procedure V the most likely to generate strategic *over*-bidding. The other procedures, with the exception of VI, lay somewhere between these two extremes. Procedure VI was introduced in two stages. The first stage, denoted VI:1, approximates a CVM since nothing was said to the subject about actually being offered the opportunity to watch the program (i.e., it was purely hypothetical). The second stage, VI:2, involved subjects bidding for the right to see the program against what they thought was a group of 100. This was a discriminative auction, with the 10 highest bidders actually paying their bid and being able to see the program.

The major result cited from Bohm's study was that bids were virtually identical for all institutions, averaging between SEK 7.29 and SEK 10.33. Unfortunately, these conclusions are based on parametric test procedures, which are unreliable given the non-Gaussian nature of the samples. The mean contributions for Procedures I–V, VI:1 and VI:2, respectively, were 7.6, 8.8, 7.3, 7.7, 8.4, 10.2, and 10.3 (all in SEK), implying a hypothetical bias that ranges from 16% to 40% (not including VI:2). The respective medians, 5, 8, 5, 5, 7, 10, and 10, in these cases suggest an even larger disparity between the hypothetical institution and the first five procedures: the hypothetical bias ranges from 25% to 100%. Using a non-parametric Kolmogorov–Smirnov test procedure, Cummings and Harrison (1994) derived critical probabilities that Procedure VI:1 elicited the same values as Procedures I–V and VI:2. With the exception of institution VI:2 they conclude that there is a clear presence of hypothetical bias for all institutions.

This means that not all of the hypothetical bias can be explained as strategic bias. These values are included in Table 1.

Kealy, Montgomery, and Dovidio (1990) examine the predictive validity of CVM values for actual cash payment for both a private good (a chocolate bar) and a public good (a de-acidification program for lakes in the Adirondack region). Each subject was first asked for their WTP, and two weeks later the same subjects were asked for an actual payment. 52 out of the 72 respondents to the private good valuation question answered yes, but then given a chance to make an actual purchase only 40 did so. This corresponds to a hypothetical bias of 30%.[3] For the public good, 56 of the 107 respondents said yes hypothetically, but only 28 said yes when given an actual opportunity to contribute. The hypothetical bias is calculated as 100%. Both of these biases are significant.

Another experiment with a public-like good is reported by Seip and Strand (1992). A sample of 101 Norwegians were asked in personal interviews whether they would pay 200 Norwegian Kroner for membership in the Norwegian Association for the Protection of Nature (Norges Naturvernforbund, NNV), which is the largest and best established private environmental organization in Norway. Sixty-four subjects responded "yes." A short time later, the 64 subjects that answered yes in the CVM study were sent letters encouraging them to join the NNV at a membership cost of 200 Kroner. There was no reference in these letters to the earlier CVM study. One month later a second mailing was sent to subjects that had not joined the NNV as a result of the first letter. Again, reference was not made to the initial CVM study. At the end of the second mailing only *six* of the original 64 "yes" respondents in the CVM had actually paid the 200 Kroner to join the NNV. Moreover, all of the hypothetical "no" respondents in the CVM could be reasonably expected to say "no" again if asked for real. Since the expected hypothetical WTP from this sample is 127 Kroner (= 200 Kroner × 64 yes responses ÷ 101 possible responses) and the expected real WTP is only 6 Kroner (= 200 Kroner × 6 yes responses ÷ 101 possible responses), we conclude that there was a hypothetical bias of 2017%.

Duffield and Patterson (1992) used mail surveys to obtain three sets of values for a fund to be established for the purpose of leasing water rights to be used for the preservation of in-stream flows in a set of Montana rivers. They asked one set of subjects (Cash-TNC) to *actually* make a tax deductible contribution to an *actual* fund, the "Montana Water Leasing Trust Fund," that had been established by the Montana Nature Conservancy. They asked a second group (Hypo-TNC) a hypothetical question: if contacted in the next month with a request to make a tax deductible contribution to the Montana Water Leasing Trust Fund, how much *would* they be willing to contribute?

Apart from finding that the average WTP among respondents was significantly different across the two groups, they also found a very different response rate. The average WTP among respondents to the hypothetical questionnaire was $12.70 and among

---

[3] Responses are not reported for each price response, so we have calculated this bias based on the average offer price of $0.90.

respondents to the actual cash request was $9.40, amounting to a bias of 35%. If non-respondents are included as expressing a zero WTP, the numbers change to $2.97 for the hypothetical and $0.98 for the actual cash and a bias of 203%. In a field study of the introduction of new water systems in India, Griffin et al. (1995) also found some evidence of hypothetical bias. Based on an initial survey in 1988 that asked respondents for their willingness to connect to a potential new system at different rates, they found when re-visiting the respondents in 1991 that 91% of the respondents had, indeed, acted as they claimed they would. Nevertheless, the responses from 1988 over-predicted actual behavior. Among those who claimed in 1988 that they would connect at the relevant rate, 29% never did.

This brief review of results from experiments concerned with the validity of the CVM show us that there is some evidence of hypothetical bias in valuation tasks. Nevertheless, results are sometimes difficult to interpret due to statistical complexities necessitated by the experimental design and the field context in which many of the experiments were conducted. For example, Dickie, Fisher, and Gerking (1987) found that the responses to one of their survey teams was significantly different from the others and that deleting these responses changes the conclusions about hypothetical bias in important ways. Likewise, deleting one respondent who expressed an extremely high demand affects the bias estimate. The interpretation of the results in Bohm (1972) depends on which institution that is selected to represent the true WTP. If institution VI:2 gives the true value, rather than any one of I–V, there is no hypothetical bias. In fact, it could be argued that values in an institution such as VI:2 are underestimates of true WTP, in which case the CVM response is also below the true WTP. The study by Seip and Strand (1992), finally, did a follow-up interview which indicated that responses in the original CVM might not have reflected the question the investigators had posed. Many subjects indicated that the hypothetical value expressed was their WTP for environmental goods in general, and not just for membership in NNV.

Two themes emerge from this brief review:
- There does appear to be some evidence for hypothetical bias in valuation tasks;
- The results can be difficult to interpret and sensitive to variations in experimental design and field conditions.

In partial reaction to these complications and difficulties of interpretation, a series of laboratory experiments were undertaken to identify more directly the extent of hypothetical bias in valuation tasks.

3. Open-ended Elicitation in the Lab

Neill et al. (1994) opened the recent debate on the existence of hypothetical bias by conducting experiments with Vickrey auctions for private, deliverable commodities. Their auctions were "one shot," and the instructions contained language explaining in simple terms the dominant strategy property of the institution. Each subject was asked to bid on a small oil painting by an unknown Navajo artist, or a reprint of a medieval map.

The most interesting design feature of these experiments is the attempt to differentiate a generic CVM elicitation from a hypothetical Vickrey auction (HVA). The former amounted to a relatively unstructured request for the subject to just state the maximum amount of money they would be willing to pay for the painting. No allocation or provision rules were discussed, although the instructions made it clear that the question was hypothetical. The latter was identical to the real Vickrey auction (RVA) treatment except that the instructions were minimally changed to reflect the hypothetical nature of the transaction. The goal of this intermediate design was to see how much of the hypothetical bias might be due to the hypothetical nature of the economic commitment, as revealed by the difference between HVA and RVA, and how much might be due to the absence of a structured institution in a CVM, as revealed by the difference between HVA and the generic CVM.

Their results were clear: the culprit was the lack of a real economic commitment in either of the two hypothetical institutions. Average hypothetical bids for the map were $301 and average real bids were $12, implying a bias of over 2400% between the HVA and the RVA. Between the CVM and the RVA, for the same good, the bias found was 2600%, but for the painting it was less: 290%. This is shown in Table 1. Omitting some outliers, which is common in much of the CVM literature, reduces the bias but does not eliminate it.

McClelland, Schulze, and Coursey (1993) created an interesting hybrid of "induced" and "homegrown" values by generating a market for insurance. Subjects could bid for insurance policies to avoid some low-probability bad outcome that was generated by the experimenters according to a specified probability distribution. To the extent that the risk attitudes of subjects were homegrown, the fact that the underlying risk was induced does not change the fact that the experimenters were eliciting homegrown values. They employed uniform-price auctions in which the top 4 bidders out of 8 would receive the insurance policy at the bid-price of the 5th highest bidder. The uniform-price auction is the multiple-unit analogue of the single-unit Vickrey auction, and shares the same properties in terms of incentives for truth-telling by bidders.

Subjects bid for 10 rounds on each of either 4 or 2 different underlying probability functions, for a total of 40 or 20 bidding rounds. In each case the reigning bids were displayed after each round. In addition, experimenters elicited open-ended hypothetical responses to valuation questions posed both before the session started (referred to as inexperienced responses) and between initializations of new probability functions (referred to as experienced responses). They find that the hypothetical bias changes with the probability function such that at low probabilities hypothetical WTP is about twice that of actual bids, but this bias is reduced, then eliminated, and in some cases reversed, as the probability of a loss increases. The highest bias (120%) was found for inexperienced responses to the lowest risk event. For the two highest risk events the inexperienced responses show that real bids exceed hypothetical by about 25%.

4. Dichotomous Choice Elicitation in the Lab

In response to Neill et al. (1994), many CVM proponents commented that this type of hypothetical bias was "well-known" in open-ended elicitation procedures, and that it was precisely this type of unreliability which had prompted the use of dichotomous choice (DC) methods. Incentive-compatibility is apparent in DC, at least in the usual partial-equilibrium settings in which such things are discussed.

However, the fact that an institution is incentive compatible when the consequences are real says nothing about the incentive compatibility of the institution when the consequences are not real. Cummings, Harrison, and Rutström (1995) designed some simple experiments, to expose the boldness of the claims that hypothetical DC institutions would be incentive compatible.

Subjects were randomly assigned to one of two treatments, the only difference being the use of hypothetical or real language in the instructions. Both student and non-student adults (drawn from church groups) were employed in this study and both within and between subject treatments were explored. An electric juicer was displayed, and passed around the room with the price tag removed or blacked-out. The display box for the juicer had some informative blurb about the product, as well as pictures of it "in action." In other sessions subjects valued a box of gourmet chocolate truffles or a small solar-powered calculator. Subjects were asked simply to say whether or not they would be willing to pay some stated amount for the good.

Hypothetical subjects responded much more positively than the real subjects, allowing Cummings, Harrison, and Rutström to reject incentive compatibility. The same qualitative results were obtained with both the student and non-student subjects. Table 1 displays the hypothetical bias found as 163%, 873%, and 163%, for the juicers, chocolates, and calculators, respectively.

Johannesson, Liljas, and Johansson (1998) provide an attempt at understanding the degree to which interpretation lies at the root of the hypothetical bias problem, in replications of the Cummings, Harrison, and Rutström (1995) experimental design. Interpretation was an issue brought up in discussions of the "here and now" wording of the Cummings, Harrison, and Rutström instructions, and also reflected in the follow-up interviews in the Seip and Strand study, discussed above. Apart from some wording changes to try to make the hypothetical subjects aware that they are being asked if they would buy the good here and now, they followed-up all hypothetical "yes" responses by asking subjects to state if they were "fairly sure" or "absolutely sure" they would buy the good. By taking *only* the *latter* responses as indicating a "yes," they conclude that hypothetical bias disappears. Their results are displayed in Table 1, denoted JLJ.

Smith and Mansfield (1998) employ a DC design in which subjects, who have just participated in a survey, are asked if they would be willing to participate in another, future survey for a given compensation. Five different compensation amounts are used in the design, ranging from $5 up to $50. The primary treatment was whether the compensation was offered in a "real context" or a "hypothetical context." The "hypothetical context" was as follows:

Researchers at Duke University are considering establishing a sample of households that would be contacted once a year to ask their opinions on programs like the ones I described. This is one of several plans. If this approach were taken and if they could pay you [$ amount] for your continued involvement in two more interviews like the two we have done, would you participate?

The "real context," on the other hand, asked the question as follows:

Researchers at Duke University are establishing a sample of households that would be contacted again to ask their opinions on programs like the ones I described. They can pay you [$ amount] for your continued involvement in two more interviews like the two we have done. They would send a check for [$ amount] to you when the next two interviews are finished. Will you participate in this new program?

Out of a total sample of 540, roughly split across treatments, 83% of those in the hypothetical context said "yes" to the offer and 82% of those in the real context said "yes" to the offer (their Table III, p. 215). This is not a significant difference.[4] The spread of subjects across DC prices in the two treatments was statistically random (fn. 4, p. 210), so this appears to be strong evidence of the absence of hypothetical bias. Simple statistical models of the DC response provide evidence in support of the hypothesis that the subjects in each treatment used the same choice function when responding.

Two aspects of the experimental design appear as candidates for explaining the lack of a hypothetical bias: the fact that subjects were familiar with the good being valued, having just completed one survey, and the possibility that subjects did not perceive a difference between the hypothetical and the real treatment, given the instructions quoted above.

Frykblom (1997) provides a test of hypothetical bias that involves both open- and closed-ended valuations. The good is a private good, selected because its possible preference relationship to environmental values: an environmental atlas that retails for SEK 200. The real institution is a Vickrey auction. This study found no significant difference between the two hypothetical survey formats. The hypothetical bias based on the open-ended survey is 60%, and it is 56% based on the dichotomous choice survey. Both are significant.

5. Social Elicitation in the Lab

In response to the experimental results of Cummings, Harrison, and Rutström (1995), some CVM proponents argued that their claims for the incentive-compatibility of the DC approach actually pertained to simple majority rule settings in which there was

---

[4] Lacking information on responses by DC price, we assume the same response rate across all to calculate the hypothetical bias of 3.2% that is reported in Table 1.

some referendum over just two social choices. Somehow that setting would provide the context that subjects need to spot the incentive compatibility, or so it was argued.

In response to these arguments, Cummings et al. (1997) undertook simple majority rule experiments for an actual public good. After earning some income, in addition to their show-up fee, subjects were asked to vote on a proposition that would have each of them contribute a specified amount towards this public good. If the majority said "yes," all had to pay.

The key treatment in their simple experimental design was again the use of hypothetical or real payments, and again there was significant evidence of hypothetical bias. The hypothetical bias found is 67%, and it is significant. Table 1 shows this.

6. Constructive Solutions

There have been two broad, constructive responses to the evidence of the existence of hypothetical bias. Each entails an effort to use experimental methods to calibrate the extent and the correlates of hypothetical bias. We refer to these as "instrument calibration" and "statistical calibration."

6.1. Instrument Calibration

Much of the debate and controversy over "specifications" in the CVM literature concerns the choice of words. The problem of "choosing the right words" in CVM studies has assumed some importance through the result of judicial decisions. In 1989, the U.S. District Court of Appeals, in *State of Ohio v. U.S. Department of the Interior* (880 F. 2nd. at 474), asserted that the "... simple and obvious safeguard against overstatement [of WTP], however, is more sophisticated questioning" (p. 497). While disagreeing that this process is "simple and obvious," it is apparent that one can only assess the improvement from different CV questionnaires if one has a way of knowing if any bias is being reduced. This mandates the use of some measure of the real economic commitment that a subject would make in the same setting as the hypothetical question.

The laboratory is clearly one place where such measures can be readily generated. It can provide a simple metric by which one can test, in meaningful ways, the importance of different presentations of valuation questions. Because controlled laboratory experiments may be used to enforce real economic commitments, they provide "benchmarks" to which alternative scenario designs, or wording choices, may be evaluated in their effectiveness of reducing hypothetical bias. Thus, using laboratory experiments is likely to be more informative than the casual introspective nature of the literature on wording choice in survey design. The problem of deciding which set of words is "best" might, in some instances, be easily and directly tested using controlled laboratory experiments. Unfortunately, to our knowledge no published experimental results are available that test the notion of instrument calibration. Several unpublished studies have been circulated, however, such as Cummings, Harrison, and Osborne (1995) and Cummings and Taylor (1999).

6.2. Statistical Calibration

The word "calibrate" is defined in *The Oxford Dictionary* as to "determine or correct the calibre or scale of a thermometer/gauge or other graduated instrument." Can a decision maker *calibrate* the responses obtained by a hypothetical survey so that they more closely match the real economic commitments that the subjects would have been expected to make? A constructive answer to this question has been offered by Blackburn, Harrison, and Rutström (1994), Fox et al. (1998) and Harrison et al. (1996). The essential idea underlying this approach is that the hypothetical survey provides an informative, but statistically biased, indicator of the subject's true willingness to pay for the environmental good. Blackburn, Harrison, and Rutström (1994) offer the analogy of a watch that is always 10 minutes slow to introduce the idea of a statistical bias function for hypothetical surveys. The point of the analogy is that hypothetical responses can still be informative about real responses if the bias between the two is systematic and predictable. The watch that is always 10 minutes slow can be informative, but only if the error is *known* to the decision maker and if it is *transferable* to other instances (i.e., the watch does not get further behind the times over time). The trick is how to estimate and apply such bias functions. This is done with the *complementary* use of field elicitation procedures that use hypothetical surveys, laboratory elicitation procedures that use hypothetical and non-hypothetical surveys, and laboratory elicitation procedures that use incentive-compatible institutions.

The upshot of the statistical calibration approach is a simple comparison of the original responses to the hypothetical survey and a set of calibrated responses that the same subjects *would be predicted to have made* if asked to make a real economic commitment in the context of an incentive-compatible procedure. This approach does not predetermine the conclusion that the hypothetical survey is "wrong." If the hypothetical survey is actually eliciting what its proponents say that it is, then the calibration procedure should say so. In this sense, calibration can be seen as a way of validating "good hypothetical surveys" and correcting for the biases of "bad hypothetical surveys."[5]

The statistical calibration approach can do more than simply point out the possible bias of a hypothetical survey. It can also evaluate the confidence with which one can infer statistics such as the population mean from a given survey. In other words, a decision maker is often interested in the bounds for a damage assessment that fall within prescribed confidence intervals. Existing hypothetical surveys often convey a false sense of accuracy in this respect. A calibration approach might well indicate that the population mean inferred from a hypothetical survey is reliable in the sense of being unbiased, but that the standard deviation was much larger than the hypothetical survey would directly suggest. This type of extra information can be valuable to a risk-averse decision maker.

---

[5] Mitchell and Carson (1989) provide a popular and detailed review of many of the traits of "bad hypothetical surveys."

Blackburn, Harrison, and Rutström (1994) define a "known bias function" as one that is a systematic statistical function of the socio-economic characteristics of the sample. If this bias is not mere noise then one can say that it is "knowable" to a decision maker. They then test if the bias function is transferable to a distinct sample valuing a distinct good, and conclude that it is. In other words, they show that one can use the bias function estimated from one instance to calibrate the hypothetical responses in another instance, and that the calibrated hypothetical responses statistically match those observed in a paired *real* elicitation procedure.

This simple test was encouraging, but was limited by design to deliverable private goods such as juicers and chocolates. Harrison et al. (1998) attempted to generalize their procedures to the case of greater interest in field applications of hypothetical surveys to assess environmental damages. They undertook five surveys, each one designed to provide information that would allow for the calibration of a field public good. One survey was for a deliverable private good, and used a Vickrey auction with real payment required. The next survey varied this by allowing for public provision of the private good, albeit with real payment required. Comparison of the results of the two surveys, after correcting for socioeconomic differences in the sample, was intended to provide a statistical measure of the propensity for free-riding bias. Similarly paired surveys provided a measure of the propensity for hypothetical bias in the provision of a deliverable public good. Arguing that the propensity to engage in hypothetical bias would be independent of the propensity to engage in free-riding bias, the results from the initial two surveys were then used to adjust the results in the latter two surveys used to elicit hypothetical bias. The end-result was a statistical measure of the propensity of subjects to engage in both types of bias. This measure was used to adjust hypothetical responses to a survey asking for valuation of a non-deliverable public good.

Although the statistical procedures employed by Harrison et al. (1998) were illustrative, their design demonstrates the potential complementarity between lab and field experiments. Their results were surprisingly encouraging. The most important result is that they cannot reject the hypothesis that true WTP is equal to the raw WTP elicited by a hypothetical survey in the case of national wetlands preservation (their non-deliverable field public good). However, they can reject this hypothesis in the case of local wetlands preservation (their deliverable field public good). These results illustrate well the view that one can validate *or* calibrate the results from CVM surveys in a constructive manner. If the CVM result is a valid reflection of true WTP, calibration methods can show that it is (as in the case of national wetlands preservation). However, if the CVM result is not a valid reflection of true WTP, calibration methods not only show that, but are able to provide some guide as to how serious the bias is.

Fox et al. (1998) discuss and apply a calibration approach to hypothetical survey values that uses experiments to ascertain the possible hypothetical bias. Their approach differs from BHR and Harrison et al. (1998) by using experiments to calibrate hypothetical to real values for the same good, rather than using experiments to determine some calibration function that can be used to calibrate across different goods. One setting in which it could be practically useful is in which one conducts a large-scale hypothetical survey and seeks to calibrate it with smaller-scale real experiments.

The commodity used was health risk reduction in a food product. Telephone interviews with 174 pork-eating respondents selected at random in Story County, Iowa, resulted in a series of hypothetical valuations. Of these, 75% indicated a preference for an irradiated food product over the "raw" food product. Each subject was also asked to state an open-ended hypothetical valuation for their preferred product.

From these subjects, 78 agreed to participate further in some lab experiments in return for a payment of $30. Those subjects were endowed with their less-preferred food product from the hypothetical telephone survey, and then a series of auctions were undertaken to see what they would be willing to pay to "upgrade" to their preferred food product. Each subject was reminded, before bidding, of their previous hypothetical valuation and that this bid would be used as their initial bid in round 1. After 5 rounds of bidding, subjects were given information on the difference between the two products, and allowed to bid for 5 more rounds. One of the rounds was chosen at random, and the transactions effected. In one treatment group there was only one bidding round, and in some treatments the standard single-unit Vickrey auction rules were modified to allow a random nth price auction.[6] The potentially winning bids and the ID numbers of the winning bidders was announced after each round.

The results suggest calibration factors of roughly two-thirds if one compares hypothetical survey values and the round 2 auction values. The auction values in the final round are generally higher than those in round 2, so the calibration factors are higher as well (between 60% and 83%).

7. Conclusions

There seems to be little doubt that the presumptive absence of hypothetical bias in CVM surveys is invalid. It is invalid as a general proposition, since the experiments surveyed here provide special cases when it is demonstrably false. The importance of these experimental results is that they change the tenor of the debate on the validity of the CVM. The variety of elicitation formats, the variety of subject pools, and the variety of private and public goods all serve to show that one cannot ignore the problem. Of course, it is possible that hypothetical bias may be absent or swamped by other biases in *particular* settings. But one cannot make sweeping and unqualified claims as to its absence, as has been common in the CVM literature.

There is some experimental evidence that comparing simple "yes" responses in real settings to "definitely yes" responses in hypothetical settings indicates less hypothetical bias than when simple "yes" responses in hypothetical settings are used. Although these

---

[6] If N is the number of bidders, then a number n between 1 and $N-1$ is chosen by the auctioneer. Everyone who bids greater than the bid of the nth bidder wins and pays the bid of the nth highest bidder.

results provide some promise for generating hypothetical responses that better match real responses, no theory underlies these results and no guarantees can be made that hypothetical bias is removed in all settings with this change in interpretation.

There is some evidence that the extent of hypothetical bias varies from setting to setting, but the sample sizes and design employed thus far are too slight for one to draw any broad conclusions from that. Hence it is particularly inappropriate to try to claim that hypothetical bias is any more of a problem in open ended formats as compared to closed ended formats, or that referendum formats are "less inaccurate" than DC formats.

Attempts at calibrating responses of hypothetical surveys have been reasonably successful. This implies that experimental methods may well have an important role to play in improving the reliability of hypothetical survey methods.

References

Bishop, Richard, Heberlein, Thomas (1979). "Measuring values of extra market goods: Are indirect measures biased?" American Journal of Agricultural Economics 61, 926–930. [BH].

Bishop, Richard, Heberlein, Thomas (1986). "Does contingent valuation work?" In: Cummings, R., Brookshire, D., Schulze, W. (Eds.), Valuing Environmental Goods: A State of the Arts Assessment of the Contingent Valuation Method. Rowman & Allenheld, Totowa, NJ.

Bishop, Richard C., Heberlein, Thomas A., Kealy, Mary Jo (1983). "Contingent valuation of environmental assets: Comparisons with a simulated market". Natural Resources Journal 23, 619–633. [BHK].

Blackburn, McKinley, Harrison, Glenn W., Rutström, E. Elisabet (1994). "Statistical bias functions and informative hypothetical surveys". American Journal of Agricultural Economics 76 (5), 1084–1088.

Bohm, Peter (1972). "Estimating the demand for public goods: An experiment". European Economic Review 3, 111–130.

Cummings, Ronald G., Harrison, Glenn W. (1994). "Was the *Ohio* Court well informed in their assessment of the accuracy of the contingent valuation method?" Natural Resources Journal 34 (1), 1–36.

Cummings, Ronald G., Taylor, Laura O. (1999). "Unbiased value estimates for environmental goods: A cheap talk design for the contingent valuation method". American Economic Review 89, 649–665.

Cummings, Ronald G., Harrison, Glenn W., Osborne, Laura L. (1995). "Can the bias of contingent valuation be reduced? Evidence from the laboratory". Economics Working Paper B-95-03, Division of Research, College of Business Administration, University of South Carolina.

Cummings, Ronald G., Harrison, Glenn W., Rutström, E. Elisabet (1995). "Homegrown values and hypothetical surveys: Is the dichotomous choice approach incentive compatible?" American Economic Review 85 (1), 260–266. [CHR].

Cummings, Ronald G., Elliott, Steven, Harrison, Glenn W., Murphy, James (1997). "Are hypothetical referenda incentive compatible?" Journal of Political Economy 105 (3), 609–621. [CEHM].

Dickie, M., Fisher, A., Gerking, S. (1987). "Market transactions and hypothetical demand data: A comparative study". Journal of the American Statistical Association 82, 69–75. [DFG].

Duffield, John, Patterson, David A. (1992). "Field testing existence values: An instream flow trust fund for Montana rivers". National Center for Environmental Economics Report EE-0282.

Fox, John A., Shogren, Jason F., Hayes, Dermot J., Kliebenstein, James B. (1998). "CVM-X: Calibrating contingent values with experimental auction markets". American Journal of Agricultural Economics 80, 455–465.

Frykblom, Peter (1997). "Hypothetical question modes and real willingness to pay". Journal of Environmental Economics and Management 34 (3), 275–287.

Griffin, Charles C., Briscoe, John, Singh, Bhanwar, Ramasubban, Radhika, Bhatia, Ramesh (1995). "Contingent valuation and actual behavior: Predicting connections to new water systems in the state of Kerala, India". The World Bank Economic Review 9 (3), 373–395.

Hanemann, W. Michael (1984). "Welfare evaluations in contingent valuation experiments with discrete responses". American Journal of Agricultural Economics 66, 332–341.
Harrison, Glenn W., Beekman, Robert L., Brown, Lloyd B., Clements, Leianne A., McDaniel, Tanga M., Odom, Sherry L., Williams, Melonie (1998). "Environmental damage assessment with hypothetical surveys: The calibration approach". In: Boman, M., Brännlund, R., Kriström, B. (Eds.), Topics in Environmental Economics. Kluwer Academic Press, Amsterdam.
Johannesson, Magnus, Liljas, Bengt, Johansson, Per-Olov (1998). "An experimental comparison of dichotomous choice contingent valuation questions and real purchase decisions". Applied Economics 30, 643–647. [JLJ].
Kealy, M.J., Montgomery, M., Dovidio, J.F. (1990). "Reliability and predictive validity of contingent values: Does the nature of the good matter?" Journal of Environmental Economics and Management 19, 244–263. [KMD].
McClelland, Gary H., Schulze, William D., Coursey, Don L. (1993). "Insurance for low-probability hazards: A bimodal response to unlikely events". Journal of Risk and Uncertainty 7, 95–116. [MSC].
Mitchell, Robert C., Carson, Richard T. (1989). "Using Surveys to Value Public Goods: The Contingent Valuation Method". Johns Hopkins Press, Baltimore.
Neill, Helen R., Cummings, Ronald G., Ganderton, Philip T., Harrison, Glenn W., McGuckin, Thomas (1994). "Hypothetical surveys and real economic commitments". Land Economics 70 (2), 145–154.
Seip, K., Strand, J. (1992). "Willingness to pay for environmental goods in Norway: A contingent valuation study with real payment". Environmental and Resource Economics 2, 91–106. [SS].
Smith, V. Kerry, Mansfield, Carol (1998). "Buying time: Real and hypothetical offers". Journal of Environmental Economics and Management 36, 209–224. [SM].

PART 6

NON-MARKET AND ORGANIZATIONAL RESEARCH

6. NON-MARKET AND ORGANIZATIONAL RESEARCH

Introduction

Modern laboratory experimental methods were heavily influenced by research in the worlds of non-market, public choice and political science. In the early 1970s these areas held much new theory and the conflicts among theories, including conflicts across disciplinary boundaries were visible. The public economics and political science worlds are worlds without prices, property rights and exchanges other than through voting. Multiple agents are involved as opposed to the two, typical of game theory experiments and preferences do not depend upon your own actions but instead could depend on the action of others. So, an individual could become benefited or harmed while taking no actions at all. The first subpart of Part 6 contains research papers (nine) on externalities and public goods and the second subpart contains five papers on committees and voting processes. The final subpart is a single entry that is focused on broad organizations.

6.1. Public Goods and Externalities

Early experiments demonstrated that the group makes contributions to the public good early in an experiment but contributions decay over time (first demonstrated by Isaac, McCue, and Plott, 1985). The subsequent challenge was to discover why any contribution took place at all and why it tended to change over time.

Many of the traditional public goods experiments placed the equilibrium on the boundary. This is important because if the equilibrium is on the boundary of zero contribution then any error at all appears as a purposefully cooperative act. By contrast Laury and Holt look at interior equilibrium. A large number of studies reviewed demonstrate that moving the equilibrium within the interior can change the pattern of contributions relative to the equilibrium. However, it is not the case that having an equilibrium on the interior is sufficient to produce equilibrium levels of contributions. Thus, other factors are at work.

Those "other factors" began to emerge with surprising dimensions with a discovery by Saijo that the attitudes might not be positively inclined toward others at all. Through experiments with public goods with an interior equilibrium he discovered the existence of spiteful behavior, those who fail to invest when the private value is above the marginal cost. It is as though they view the benefits that they provide to others from the public investment as a cost to themselves. This behavior seems to be prevalent among Japanese and in more complex games it has an effect on the path to an equilibrium.

Andreoni and Croson study public goods provision environments in which one has experience with those in the group as opposed to an environment in which the public goods problem must be solved by people who are thrown together for the first time – strangers. The striking result is the difference in provision that depends on the whether the group consists of partners or strangers and the challenge is to determine why. The paper reviews experiments that search confusion, a taste for cooperation (warm glow), altruism and reputation formation as the reasons. The issue is pursued further by Croson who becomes focused on beliefs about what others will contribute. Beliefs that others will contribute enhances contribution. The conjecture is that reciprocity is the driving attitude.

The matter of fundamental attitudes is addressed by Brandts and Schram by using a different methodology. Rather than a single decision they as subjects for a contribution function for multiple situations, which is then analyzed and applied for group decisions. They conjecture that the phenomena of contribution is driven by attitudes of reciprocal altruism and note that a tension between dominant strategy equilibrium and efficiency suggest that the central driving attitude is not the warm glow of giving in general. And their theme is echoed by Chan, Mestelman and Muller, whose voluntary provision of public goods experiments are used to test equity theory with positive results. They also focus on the effects of redistributing endowments and income to determine the effect on provision. And, the issue of differing attitudes is explored further by Holt and Laury in an examination of a series of models based on different motivations. The performance of the models is compared in the sense of their ability to capture observed comparative statics. No firm resolution among the models emerges.

The question of fundamental types is raised in still another context by Schram, Offerman and Sonnemans. The step level goods they study are fundamentally different from the continuous versions of public goods provision problems. A threshold of contributions must be reached before any benefits are provided. It is a non convexity of special magnitude and it has the consequence of changing the nature of the equilibrium in that beliefs about the contributions of others are central to the concept. In this context a test to see if personality type had an effect on contributions suggested that the variable is not important. Group size as a variable decreases average contribution but increases the instances of successful provision. This influence is explained by the difference in beliefs about being marginal (or crucial) contributor whose contribution makes the total cross the threshold. Whether the group consists of partners or strangers makes no difference but the framing of the problem is important as people will contribute more to a public good than to a public bad.

The focus on the characteristics of the individual was pursued by Von Winden. He uses a social value orientation measure from social psychology to classify subjects as individualists or cooperators. Positive social orientation leads to greater contributions to the public good and contributions to the public good facilitates group ties. The success or failure of the public good provision has an influence on the attitudes that the members of the group have toward each other. Thus, his result suggests that the issues of the role of individual attitudes in the provision of public goods might be addressed through direct measurements of individual personality types.

6.2. Committees and Voting Groups

The basic model presented by Bottom, Handlin, King and Miller rests on a primitive concept of a decisive coalition from which a dominance relation is derived and solution concepts applied. This abstraction permits the modeling of institutions that are far more complex than can be accommodated by game trees and the non-cooperative game model. The focus of the research is on institutions and in particular agendas, super majorities, divided houses and other institutional structures that induce the existence of a core in a world in which majority rule cores do not otherwise exist. The evidence of institutional influence on the group decision is overwhelming and the power of the underlying model to predict the results of the experiments is astounding. The model and data expose an underlying tendency of the data to gravitate to the core of the underlying model.

The same type of theoretical analysis is used in two contexts by Wilson. Five-person committees operating under majority rule such as Roberts Rules are known to converge to near the core. Wilson demonstrates that this is through a process of agenda proposals that move toward the core when it exists. He then studies committees in which the core does not exist and demonstrates that the pattern of outcomes is sensitive to the locations of preferences but the outcomes themselves are dispersed, suggesting that the instability suggested by the theory is a fact of life.

Wilson's second paper is focused on institutional structures that induce equilibria in the context of a committee process. In particular, a monopoly agenda setter is studied as is a special set of rules requiring the "backward" consideration of proposals and amendments. While the decision rule is majority rule, a rule that gives an individual the monopoly authority to call for a vote is extremely powerful. The outcomes gravitate to the area of the agenda setter's ideal point. The backward consideration procedures are remarkable in that they create several equilibria in a world in which equilibria do not ordinarily exist. The result is a well contained pattern of outcomes that can be compared with the "scattered" outcomes that result in the absence of the "backward" agenda.

The two final papers of the section draw the discussion back to traditional non cooperative game theory. In the first Reitz demonstrates that Duverger's law operates in three candidate elections. Consider a three candidate race in which candidates are preferred by a majority in the order A > B > C. Yet in a three way race the vote can be split between A and B with the result that C wins. Duverger's law says that strategic voting will prevent that from happening. Those who prefer B but sense that it will loose will switch to A thereby defeating C. Of course this requires certain configurations of preferences but the idea is that such avoidance of choosing a majority loser can surface through the natural and uncoordinated strategic behavior of voters. The data clear demonstrate the operation of the law.

A second application of non cooperative theory is found in Sonnemans and Schram. In a majority rule election system a single person's vote becomes important only if the election is a dead heat and otherwise, it makes no difference on the outcome. If it makes no difference and it is at all costly, then there is no incentive to vote. Thus voter turnout becomes a challenge to theory. Sonnemans and Schram explore the turnout in the light of equilibrium theory and in the context of two different election systems. While the quantitative features of the data depart from theory the comparative statics resulting form non-cooperative game theory are correct.

Reference

Isaac, R. Mark, McCue, Kenneth F., Plott, Charles R. (1985). "Public goods provision in an experimental environment". Journal of Public Economics 26, 51–74.

PART 6.1

PUBLIC GOODS, EXTERNALITIES AND COMMON POOLS

James Andreoni and Rachel Croson, "Partners versus Strangers: Random Rematching in Public Goods Experiments"

Rachel T.A. Croson, "Differentiating Altruism and Reciprocity"

Susan K. Laury and Charles A. Holt, "Voluntary Provision of Public Goods: Experimental Results with Interior Nash Equilibria"

Tatsuyoshi Saijo, "Spiteful Behavior in Voluntary Contribution Mechanism Experiments"

Arthur Schram, Theo Offerman and Joep Sonnemans, "Explaining the Comparative Statics in Step-Level Public Goods Games"

Jordi Brandts and Arthur Schram, "Cooperation in VCM Experiments: Results Using the Contribution Function Approach"

Kenneth S. Chan, Stuart Mestelman and R. Andrew Muller, "Voluntary Provision of Public Goods"

Frans van Winden, Frans van Dijk and Joep Sonnemans, "Intrinsic Motivation in a Public Good Environment"

Charles A. Holt and Susan K. Laury, "Theoretical Explanations of Treatment Effects in Voluntary Contributions Experiments"

Chapter 82

PARTNERS VERSUS STRANGERS: RANDOM REMATCHING IN PUBLIC GOODS EXPERIMENTS

JAMES ANDREONI

Department of Economics, University of Wisconsin–Madison, Madison, Wisconsin 53711, USA

RACHEL CROSON

University of Texas at Dallas, 2601 N. Floyd Road, P.O. Box 830688, GR 31, Richardson, TX 75083-0688, USA
e-mail: crosonr@utdallas.edu

1. Introduction

How can an experimenter balance the desire to test a single-shot Nash equilibrium prediction with the need for repeated experience by subjects? Simply repeating the game with the same set of subjects may change the nature of equilibrium, since incomplete information about "types" can lead to reputation effects of the sort described by Kreps et al. (1982). A common way to deal with this has been to rematch subjects randomly into groups for each iteration of the game, hence forming a repeated single-shot design and avoiding the repeated-game effects. This raises the natural question: what is the effect of random rematching?

The rematching of subjects in linear public goods experiments was introduced by Andreoni (1988). The first linear public goods experiments, by Marwell and Ames (1981), were single-shot games and produced little of the dominant strategy Nash equilibrium free riding they predicted. Subjects, it was argued, needed experience to learn the dominant strategy. Isaac and Walker (1988) replicated these games, but used a 10-period, finitely repeated game. However, free riding was still not chosen, and repetition had only a small effect in increasing free riding. Was it reputation effects that kept subjects from adopting the single-shot dominant strategy?

Andreoni (1988) tested this question by comparing a set of subjects who played in finitely repeated games with another set who played in a repeated single-shot. Players in the repeated game were called "Partners," while those in the repeated single-shot game were called "Strangers." If reputations matter, then Partners should cooperate more than Strangers. Surprisingly, Andreoni found just the opposite – Strangers cooperated significantly more than Partners.

Since this time, many researchers have explored this anomalous result. This chapter will attempt to synthesize the various replications and studies that have addressed this puzzle.

Handbook of Experimental Economics Results, Volume 1
Copyright © 2008 Elsevier B.V. All rights reserved
DOI: 10.1016/S1574-0722(07)00082-0

2. Partners versus Strangers

Linear public goods experiments can be described simply. Individuals are given a budget m of tokens which they can "invest" in a public good, g, or a private good, x, hence $x + g = m$. Payoffs to any subject i are determined by $P_i = x_i + \alpha \sum_j^n g_j$, where n is the number of group members. The parameter α is chosen such that $0 < \alpha < 1$, hence free riding, $g = 0$, is a single-shot dominant strategy, and such that $n\alpha > 1$, so that $g = m$ for all i is the symmetric Pareto efficient outcome.

Andreoni examined groups of five players, with $\alpha = 0.5$, in ten-period games. In each session of the Strangers treatment, 20 subjects were randomly rematched into groups of five after each play of the game, while a comparable set of Partners played in an adjacent room.[1] Andreoni also included another design twist intended to test learning effects. After ten periods subjects were told they would "restart" the experiment for another ten rounds – if no learning effects are present, the restart should have no effect. Due to budget constraints, the restart ended after three periods. Andreoni's results are plotted in Figure 1A.

The nearest replication to Andreoni's experiment was performed by Croson (1996). Again using $\alpha = 0.5$, ten periods, and a surprise ten-period restart, Croson considered four person groups.[2] A plot of the data by Croson is shown in Figure 1B.

We can see that Andreoni and Croson get different results for the first ten periods – Croson finds Partners are significantly more cooperative, while Andreoni finds it is Strangers. Looking at the restart, however, both find similar results. For Partners the effect of the restart is far more pronounced, indicating that for both experiments there is some effect of repeated play. Given the contradictory effects of the first ten periods, however, one must ask whether the effect of repeated play is on reputations or something else.

Several other authors have also compared Partners to Strangers in experiments. A summary of these results is given in Table 1. All of these experiments differ in sundry ways from either Andreoni or Croson's studies, so the comparisons to these results are not precise. Nonetheless, this summary of results does little to clear up the picture. In all, four studies find more cooperation among Strangers, five find more by Partners, and four fail to find any difference at all.

3. A Closer Look

The discussion of Partners versus Strangers thus far has been predicated on the assumption that the incentives of individuals are consistent with money-maximization in the

---

[1] In each replication of the game there were 15 Partners and 20 Strangers. The experiment was run twice, hence the total experiment includes 70 subjects. The restart was only added in the second run.
[2] In the Partners session, Croson (1996) used 24 subjects, broken out into groups of four. For Strangers, she ran two separate sessions of 12 subjects each, randomly rematched into groups of four.

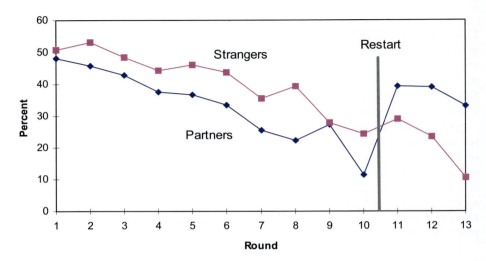

A. Andreoni (1988): Percent of endowment in the public good

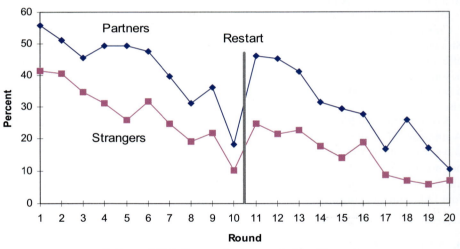

B. Croson (1996): Percent of endowment in the public good

Figure 1. This illustrates the differing results of Andreoni and Croson in linear public goods experiments. Partners means subjects face the same opponents in a finitely repeated linear public goods game, and Strangers means groups are randomly rematched after each iteration. Both experiments are 10 periods, have a marginal return from the public good of 0.5, and both had a surprise "Restart" after the first 10 periods. Andreoni (panel A) had groups of 5 matched from a room of 20, while Croson (panel B) had groups of 4 matched from a room of 12. The two experiments differ on whether Partners or Strangers contribute more, but agree that the restart has a bigger effect on Partners.

Table 1

Below we summarize the studies that have compared Partners and Strangers. Many studies have made the comparison under a variety of conditions and parameter values, with is no consistent finding about which group contributes more. Plus, there is only slight evidence that random rematching controls for repeated-game effects, as intended. Palfrey and Prisbrey (1996) provide unifying evidence that Strangers are more variable, indicating that there is more unexplainable behavior among Strangers than Partners. Hence, random rematching simply appears to diminish the predictive power of a model of money-maximizing subjects

Study		Which group gives more?		
		Partners	Strangers	Neither
Andreoni (1988)			•	
Croson (1996)		•		
Palfrey and Prisbey (1996)			•	
Weiman (1994)				•
Keser and van Winden (2000)		•		
Burlando and Hey (1997),	UK:		•	
	Italy:	•		
Brandts and Schram (2001)				•
Brandts, Saijo and Schram (1997),	US:	•		
	Spain:		•	
	Japan:			•
	The Netherlands:			•
Sonnemans, Schram and Offerman (1999)		•		

experiment. What if there is some other model of preferences that captures the behavior of subjects better than money maximization? Could Partners and Strangers generate different predictions under an alternative model?

Three recent studies — by Andreoni (1995), Croson (1998) and Palfrey and Prisbrey (1997) — have attempted a closer look at preferences of subjects in public goods games. All have explored the hypothesis that subjects have some preferences other than money maximization. Andreoni suggests that subjects are altruistic toward other subjects or possibly that they get a warm-glow from giving to the public good (Andreoni, 1989, 1990). Croson (1998) suggests that a part of subjects' preferences may be to reciprocate or match the contributions of others in their groups.[3] Palfrey and Prisbrey (1997) suggest that subjects may be confused about the incentives of the game and/or make errors in their play.

Andreoni (1995), looking only at Strangers, compared a group in a standard public goods game, called the Regular condition, with subjects who played the same game but whose monetary earnings were determined on the basis of their rank in the standard

---

[3] Other researchers have proposed evolutionary reasons why reciprocity might be observed in experimental games in general. In particular, Amden, Gunnthorsdottir, and McCabe (1998) suggest that subjects in experiments are accustomed to (or have evolved to) playing infinitely repeated games. This suggests they may act as Partners even when matched as Strangers.

game – those with higher experimental earnings also got higher monetary earnings.[4] This rank condition was intended to remove much of the effect of tastes for cooperation while maintaining the money-maximizing equilibrium. This is because mutual cooperation, while increasing one's own experimental earnings, will only lower one's rank among other subjects. Hence, cooperation in the rank condition can only be consistent with the hypothesis of confusion.

The results of Andreoni's study indicate that indeed confusion is very important, accounting for at least a third of all cooperation. However, tastes for cooperation were even more important, accounting for at least 43 percent of giving. The data indicate, in fact, that many subjects learn the dominant strategy incentives well before they implement them; they try first to engender cooperation, and only after being frustrated at this do they adopt free riding.

Croson (1998) looks at the relationship among Partners between an individual's contribution and their belief of the contributions of others in their group. Subjects exhibit a significant and positive relationship, consistent with the idea that subjects try to match the contributions of others. In both Partners and Strangers designs, a similar positive relationship is observed between subjects' contributions and the contributions of others in their group. These results suggest that one motivation for the differences between the Partners and Strangers settings are the expectations subjects bring with them to the laboratory about the contributions of others, combined with their desire to match those contributions.

Palfrey and Prisbrey (1997) present an elaborate and ingenious experiment designed to identify altruism separately from warm-glow. All subjects in a group of partners face the same marginal return from investments in a public good, V, but have different privately known costs of giving, r_i, which change randomly each round. If $r_i > V$, then there is a dominant strategy to free ride, but if $r_i < V$ then there is a dominant strategy to give to the public good. The parameter V affects the social benefits of giving, hence affects altruism, while $r_i - V$ affects the private cost of giving, hence influences the warm-glow. By allowing independent variation between r_i and V, Palfrey and Prisbrey are able to identify the strength of altruism relative to warm-glow. Behavior that they are not able to capture, that is, the econometrician's error term, they attribute to some behavior other than warm-glow or altruism, such as subjects' confusion.

With their model, Palfrey and Prisbrey make the surprising observation that warm-glow is highly significant and that altruism, while present, is insignificant. Moreover, there is a great deal of heterogeneity among subjects. Warm-glow varied from slightly negative (i.e., spite) but insignificant, to highly positive and significant. There was also a large portion of the data (the error term) that could not be explained. As the experiment progressed, however, the magnitude of the errors decreased as did the level of cooperation. Hence, reduced confusion, rather than reputations, could explain patterns of giving in standard public goods experiments.

---

[4] The rank payoffs were determined by a predetermined table. The payoffs were designed to minimize differences in incentives and income effects across conditions.

4. Partners, Strangers, Warm-glow and Confusion

Palfrey and Prisbrey (1996) next applied their methodology to compare Partners to Strangers. In each session 12 subjects played four ten-period games as either Partners or Strangers.[5] The V was either 6 or 10, and the r_i varied from 1 to 20 randomly and independently for each subject each round. Half the subjects were Partners and half were Strangers. Palfrey and Prisbrey centered their analysis around the assumption that individual preferences are linear, and hence individuals will choose a "cut-point" decision rule like the following: Contribute everything if $V - r_i + W_i > 0$, and contribute 0 otherwise. W_i is interpreted as an individual "warm-glow parameter." For each subject they find the W_i that leads to the fewest violations of the decision rule.

As in Andreoni (1988), these authors find that the Strangers cooperate more than Partners. Moreover, both groups are characterized by the same optimal W_i, hence they exhibit equal amounts of warm-glow – this is true at either the aggregate or individual levels. Rather, the main finding of Palfrey and Prisbrey is that the Partners conformed to the cut-point decision rule much better than the Strangers. That is, the behavior of the Strangers was significantly less predictable by linear preferences.

Palfrey and Prisbrey (1997) thus provide the most compelling explanation for the differences between Partners and Strangers yet. They find that the estimated preferences of Partners and Strangers are the same, hence, there is no interaction affect between Partners/Strangers and warm-glow. However, that part of the data that does not fit the model, what we have been calling confusion, does interact with Partners/Strangers; the behavior of Strangers becomes more variable. This result, that Strangers exhibit more variance in their contributions, is also reported in Croson (1996).

Notice how this evidence can capture all of the disparate findings in Table 1. If Partners versus Strangers does not affect preferences but only makes Strangers more variable, then we might not be surprised the array of results listed in Table 1.

5. What is Next?

The evidence on Partners versus Strangers suggests that repeated play is quite different from repeated single-shot play, but it is unlikely that much of that difference is due to game-theoretic reputation effects.[6] What is the effect? Thus far the answer is rather

---

[5] Partners formed new groups every ten periods, while Strangers were rematched after every decision. A total of 48 subjects was used in this experiment.

[6] Note several other authors have examined reputation effects directly. These include Camerer and Weigelt (1988), McKelvey and Palfrey (1992), and Andreoni and Miller (1993). These experiments reveal that indeed reputation effects do matter, but it appears that these effects themselves must be learned. That is, with plenty of experience in a number of finitely repeated games, subjects will learn the benefits of reputation building. In a single finitely repeated game, such as these public goods experiments, these results indicate that subjects are unlikely to have learned the sophisticated strategy of reputation building.

unsatisfying: Putting subjects in a Strangers treatment increases the fraction of the data that we cannot explain. The next step in research should look to putting more substance into this statement.

One option is that the simple behavioral models of warm-glow, altruism, and linear utility cannot capture the important aspects of the choice. For instance, one could develop some behavioral theory of reciprocity, anonymity, or morality that would provide an explanation grounded in a neoclassical utility maximizing framework. Alternatively, perhaps preferences are strictly convex, rather than linear (Andreoni and Miller, 2002), and this may affect the variance of choices. A second approach may be to examine how Partners and Strangers conditions affect learning. Is there something about a Partners condition that makes learning easier? Third, it is possible that the current specifications of preferences and learning are adequate, but that the choice mechanism may be misunderstood. Hence, something could be gained from a decision-theoretic framework that examines how the Partners versus Strangers treatments affect the process of choosing an action.

Finally, can one conclude from this that random rematching of subjects in order to avoid reputation effects is unnecessary? People will, of course, read the data differently. Perhaps the evidence presented suggests that there may be less to fear than had been thought. However, without knowing more about what causes the difference between Partners and Strangers, it is impossible to say which condition is the most natural and which will give us the best insights into our models and into human behavior. Until that time, it seems only prudent that if a prediction is based on a single-shot equilibrium, then a Strangers condition will be most appropriate.

References

Andreoni, James (1988). "Why free ride? Strategies and learning in public goods experiments". Journal of Public Economics 37, 291–304.
Andreoni, James (1989). "Giving with impure altruism: Applications to charity and Ricardian equivalence". Journal of Political Economy 97, 1447–1458.
Andreoni, James (1990). "Impure altruism and donations to public goods: A theory of warm glow giving". Economic Journal 100, 464–477.
Andreoni, James (1995). "Cooperation in public goods experiments: Kindness or confusion?" American Economic Review 85, 891–904.
Andreoni, James, Miller, John H. (1993). "Rational cooperation in the finitely repeated prisoner's dilemma: Experimental evidence". Economic Journal 103, 570–585.
Andreoni, James, Miller, John H. (2002). "Giving according to GARP: An experimental test of the consistency of preferences for altruism". Econometrica 70, 737–753.
Amden, Holly, Gunnthorsdottir, Anna, McCabe, Kevin (1998). "When does reciprocity sustain cooperation in the linear VCM?" Working paper, University of Arizona.
Brandts, Jordi, Schram, Arthur (2001). "Cooperation and noise in public goods experiments: Applying the contribution function approach". Journal of Public Economics 79, 399–427.
Burlando, Roberto, Hey, John D. (1997). "Do Anglo–Saxons free-ride more?" Journal of Public Economics 64, 41–60.
Camerer, Colin, Weigelt, Keith (1988). "Experimental tests of the sequential equilibrium reputation model". Econometrica 56, 1–36.

Croson, Rachel T.A. (1996). "Partners and strangers revisited". Economics Letters 53, 25–32.
Croson, Rachel T.A. (1998). "Theories of altruism and reciprocity: Evidence from linear public goods games". Working paper, The Wharton School.
Isaac, R. Mark, Walker, James M. (1988). "Group size effects in public goods provision: The voluntary contributions mechanism". Quarterly Journal of Economics 53, 179–200.
Keser, Claudia, van Winden, Frans (2000). "Conditional cooperators and voluntary contributions to public goods". Scandinavian Journal of Economics 102, 23–39.
Kreps, David, Milgrom, Paul, Roberts, John, Wilson, Robert (1982). "Rational cooperation in the finitely repeated prisoners' dilemma". Journal of Economic Theory 27, 245–252.
Marwell, Gerald, Ames, Ruth E. (1981). "Economists free ride, does anyone else?" Journal of Public Economics 15, 295–310.
McKelvey, Richard D., Palfrey, Thomas R. (1992). "An experimental study of the centipede game". Econometrica 60, 803–836.
Palfrey, Thomas R., Prisbrey, Jeffrey E. (1996). "Altruism, reputation, and noise in linear public goods experiments". Journal of Public Economics 61, 409–427.
Palfrey, Thomas R., Prisbrey, Jeffrey E. (1997). "Anomalous behavior in public goods experiments: How much and why?" American Economic Review 87, 829–846.
Sonnemans, Joep, Schram, Arthur, Offerman, Theo (1999). "Strategic behavior in public good games: When partners drift apart". Economic Letters 62, 35–41.
Weimann, Joachim (1994). "Individual behavior in a free riding experiment". Journal of Public Economics 54, 185–200.

Chapter 83

DIFFERENTIATING ALTRUISM AND RECIPROCITY

RACHEL T.A. CROSON

University of Texas at Dallas, 2601 N. Floyd Road, P.O. Box 830688, GR 31,
Richardson, TX 75083-0688, USA
e-mail: crosonr@utdallas.edu

1. Introduction

U.S. individuals made over 100 billion dollars of philanthropic contributions in 1997 (*Giving USA*, 1998).[1] This behavior is inconsistent with traditional utility theory in which individuals care only for their own consumption. A number of alternative theories have been invoked to explain such behavior in this and other settings, including altruism and reciprocity. This chapter describes a set of experiments which distinguish between these theories of altruism and reciprocity, by testing their comparative statics predictions in a linear public goods setting.

In altruism theories of public goods provision (either pure or impure), the consumption of others appears positively as an argument in an individual's utility function (e.g., Becker, 1974; Andreoni, 1989, 1990), causing individuals to contribute to the public good to ensure others' consumption. In contrast, Sugden (1984) proposes a theory in which the *principle of reciprocity* acts as a constraint on traditional individual utility maximization in public goods provision. The principle says (roughly) that an individual must contribute when others are contributing, thus no cheap or free riding is permitted.

Although both theories have been used in economic analysis, they generate some conflicting predictions. In particular, altruism theories predict a negative relationship between the contributions of others and the contributions of an individual; as others give more to the public good, the group's consumption from the public good increases and the individual substitutes away from providing it. In contrast, reciprocity theories predict a positive relationship between the contributions of others and the contributions of an individual; as others give more to the public good, an individual's contribution increases to avoid cheap-riding.

The paper on which this chapter is based (Croson, 2007) was the first to distinguish between these two theories. We use a traditional linear public goods game (finitely repeated, voluntary contribution mechanism with four person groups and an MPCR of .5) reviewed elsewhere in this book and in Davis and Holt (1994) and Ledyard (1995). Details about the experimental parameters, implementation and instructions can be found in Croson (2007).

---

[1] The actual amount contributed by individuals in 1997 was approximately $109,260,000,000. This number excludes charitable giving by corporations, foundations and bequests.

2. Hypotheses

We differentiate between theories of altruism and reciprocity by distinguishing their comparative statics predictions. In addition to these, however, we would like to retain the traditional theory of pure self-interest as a benchmark. When individuals care only about their own payoffs, a pure public goods problem like the one our subjects face generates a unique equilibrium in which all players contribute zero (fully free ride). In this equilibrium, an individual's contribution is independent of what others in the group contribute. Thus our benchmark *self-interest hypothesis* is that subjects will always contribute zero to the public good and (the comparative static prediction) there will be no correlation between what an individual contributes and what others in his group contribute.[2]

In contrast, theories of altruism assume that individuals care directly about the consumption or utility of others. These theories then go on to generate behavior which involves positive levels of contributions to public goods, but also contributions which are *negatively* related to the contributions of others, when personal consumption and altruistic consumption are normal goods with decreasing returns (Sugden, 1984, p. 346, presents a proof in the case of altruism and Andreoni, 1989, p. 1451 in the case of warm-glow altruism). Thus our comparative static prediction from both of these types of theories of altruism (the *altruism hypothesis*) is that there will be a negative relationship between an individual's own contribution and (his beliefs about) the contributions of others in his group.

A final set of theories of giving behavior assume that individuals reciprocate or match the contributions of others. These theories then go on to generate behavior which involves positive levels of contributions to public goods, but also contributions which are positively related to the contributions of others (see Sugden, 1984, p. 780, for a proof).

The experiments reported in this chapter and in greater detail in Croson (2007) separate these theories by distinguishing their comparative statics predictions in two ways. First, we compare an individual's contributions with his beliefs of the contributions of others in his group. Next, we compare an individual's contributions with the actual contributions of others in his group.

3. The Experiments and Results

The first set of data compares an individual's contributions with his beliefs about the contributions of others in his group. Before making their contribution decision in each

---

[2] Other theories might also predict this comparative static prediction. For example, theories of *commitment* in which an individual contributes a fixed amount also predicts no relationship between an individual's contribution and the contribution of others in this setting (Sugden, 1984 provides a discussion of such theories). Similarly, pure warm-glow without altruism as discussed by Palfrey and Prisbrey (1997) predicts no relationship.

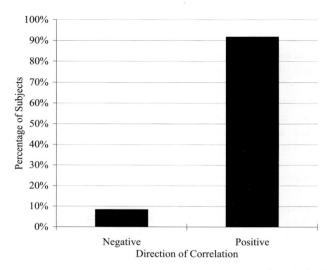

Figure 1. For each subject we find the correlation of own contribution and expectations of the contributions of others in the group of the 24 subjects in the Guess experiment, 22 had a positive correlation, consistent with models of reciprocity and only 2 a negative correlation, consistent with models of altruism. This distribution is significantly different than the null hypothesis of equal frequencies, $p < .01$

period, subjects are asked to estimate the contributions of the three other members of their group. They are paid for accurate estimates.

Twenty-four subjects arranged in six groups of four participated in this experiment. Subjects were undergraduate students at the University of Arizona summer session. They were paid a five dollar show-up fee along with their earnings in the experiment. Average earnings were $14.69, plus the $5 fee, for less than an hour of experimental time. The entire experiment was computerized; instructions were given through the computer screen, subjects entered their contributions via the keyboard and, at the end of each period, feedback about the outcome was displayed on the screen. Subjects could also access a "history" of past outcomes of their group at any time.

We characterize the behavior of individual subjects in the experiment. For each of the 24 subjects, we calculate the correlation between their contribution and their belief of the contribution of others in their group over time. In this way, we can identify individual subjects whose behavior is consistent with comparative statics of self-interest, altruism or reciprocity models. Figure 1 depicts the results from this analysis.

Twenty-two out of 24 subjects (almost 92%) exhibit a positive correlation between their own contribution and their estimates of the contributions of others, consistent with models of reciprocity. Only two subjects exhibit a negative correlation, consistent with models of altruism.

These results represent a statistically significant difference from random behavior. A chi-squared test comparing the actual categorization of subjects against a null hypothesis of equal probability of positive and negative correlations, rejects the null at $p < .01$. Croson (2007) presents a more comprehensive statistical analysis with similar support for reciprocity.

Although these results appear encouraging for reciprocity models, a few questions remain. First, it may be that asking subjects for their estimates of others' actions leads them to think reciprocally where they would not otherwise (an elicitation explanation). Second, it may be that the repeated game nature of this experiment is yielding the positive correlation and not reciprocity *per se* (a reputation explanation).

To answer these questions and test the robustness of our results, three more experiments were run and the comparative static predictions of our models re-analyzed. None involved the elicitation of beliefs of others' actions. Instead, we compare an individual's contribution with the actual contribution of the other members of his group.

To test the first explanation, we ran a new experiment, identical to the first but excluding the estimation stage (No Guess). Twenty-four subjects, different from the previous subjects but from the same subject pool, participated in this experiment, arranged in six groups of four. To test the second explanation, we ran a new experiment, excluding the estimation stage in which subjects were re-randomized into groups after each round (a Strangers treatment as described in the Andreoni and Croson chapter of this volume). A different 24 subjects participated in the strangers experiment, run in two separate sessions of 12 subjects each. Finally, a further robustness check is presented in a new experiment where subjects remained in the same groups through time, but were given information at the end of each round on not only the total amount contributed by their group members, but the distribution of those contributions (full information as in Sell and Wilson, 1991; Croson, 2001). A different 24 subjects participated in this experiment from the same subject pool, again in six groups of four subjects.[3]

Figure 2 provides the correlations between subjects' contributions and the actual contributions of the others in their group for all four treatments (the original Guess, and the No Guess, Strangers and Full variations).

In all four treatments, subjects overwhelmingly exhibited positive correlations between their own contribution and the actual contributions of others in their group, consistent with reciprocity theories (remember that the previous comparison was between individual contributions and beliefs of the contributions of others; this is between individual contributions and the actual contributions of others).

These results represent a statistically significant difference from random behavior. A chi-squared test comparing the actual categorization of subjects against a null hypothesis of equal probability of positive and negative correlations rejects the null at $p < .01$ for each treatment (excluding the zero correlation subjects). More detailed analysis in Croson (2007) presents further support of models of reciprocity. We conclude that reciprocity in this setting is robust.

---

[3] Croson (1996, 1998, 2001) compares absolute contribution levels between these different treatments; for purposes of this chapter we focus on the comparative static predictions of the competing models of altruism and reciprocity in the four treatments.

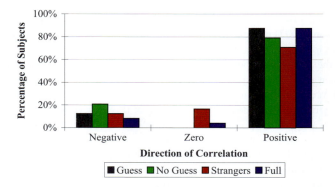

Figure 2. For each subject we find the correlation of own contribution and actual contributions of others in the group for the four experiments, Guess (where beliefs of others' contributions are elicited), No Guess (where they are not), Strangers (where subjects are randomly assigned to new groups after each period of the game) and Full (where subjects remain in the same group but are given feedback of the full distribution of individual contributions). In all four experiments, the overwhelming majority of subjects exhibit a positive relationship, consistent with models of reciprocity. Few subjects exhibit a negative correlation, consistent with models of altruism. In addition, a small number of subjects in the Strangers and Full conditions fully free-ride, leading to zero correlations between their contributions and the contributions of others. These distributions are significantly different than the null hypothesis of equal frequencies of the two types, $p < .01$ for each experiment, excluding free riders.

4. Types of Reciprocity

Additionally, we can use the data from the final experiment (Full) to characterize the *type* of reciprocity used by subjects. In Sugden's (1984) model of reciprocity, he suggests that actors will match the *minimum* contribution of others. In contrast, however, we can imagine different types of reciprocity in which subjects try to match the median or the maximum contribution of others. The full experiment allows us to distinguish between these different types of reciprocity.

In maximum reciprocity, subjects would attempt to match the maximum contribution of the other three members of their group. In minimum reciprocity, subjects would attempt to match the minimum contribution of the other three members of their group (this is essentially what Sugden proposed). Finally, in median reciprocity, subjects would attempt to match the contributions of the median contributor of the other three members of their group.

Our goal is to determine which of these three models of reciprocity best fits the data: whether the minimum, maximum or median contribution of an individual's partners better predicts an individual's own contribution.[4] We estimate four weighted fixed effects

---

[4] Notice it is quite possible for an individual's contribution to be above the maximum (or below the minimum) of the other three members of his group. In fact, the contributions of one person in each group in each period will have this characteristic.

regressions, correcting for both period and individual heteroscedasticity, as below

$$\text{CONT}_{it} = \alpha_0 + \alpha_1 \text{MINIMUM}_t$$
$$+ \sum_{t \neq 10} \beta_t \text{PERIOD} + \sum_{i \neq 1} \gamma_i \text{INDIVIDUAL} + \varepsilon, \quad (1)$$

$$\text{CONT}_{it} = \alpha_0 + \alpha_1 \text{MAXIMUM}_t$$
$$+ \sum_{t \neq 10} \beta_t \text{PERIOD} + \sum_{i \neq 1} \gamma_i \text{INDIVIDUAL} + \varepsilon, \quad (2)$$

$$\text{CONT}_{it} = \alpha_0 + \alpha_1 \text{MEDIAN}_t + \sum_{t \neq 10} \beta_t \text{PERIOD} + \sum_{i \neq 1} \gamma_i \text{INDIVIDUAL} + \varepsilon, \quad (3)$$

$$\text{CONT}_{it} = \alpha_0 + \alpha_1 \text{MINIMUM}_t + \alpha_2 \text{MAXIMUM}_t + \alpha_3 \text{MEDIAN}_t$$
$$+ \sum_{t \neq 10} \beta_t \text{PERIOD} + \sum_{i \neq 1} \gamma_i \text{INDIVIDUAL} + \varepsilon. \quad (4)$$

Results from these regressions are shown in Table 1.

Evidence from these regressions suggests that median reciprocity is a better predictor than either minimum or maximum reciprocity. First, in the individual regressions (1), (2) and (3), the t-statistic is higher for the median contribution than for either of the others. In addition, in the regression which includes all measures (4), only median is significantly different than zero ($p = .0134$). This suggests that the median contribution of the others in a subject's group is a better predictor of that subject's own contribution than either the maximum or the minimum.

This analysis sheds light on exactly what subjects in this experiment might be trying to reciprocate. We find significant evidence for median reciprocity, suggesting that subjects try to match the median contributions of others, rather than the minimum (as suggested by Sugden's theory of reciprocity) or the maximum.

5. Discussion and Conclusion

The experiments reported in this chapter test comparative statics predictions of models of reciprocity and altruism. The results support the reciprocity model in which individual contributions are positively related to the contributions of others, or to their beliefs about those contributions.

In the studies presented here, contributions decrease over time. However, when subjects are organized into groups based on their level of contributions, other authors have observed upward trends in linear public goods games with similar parameters. This phenomenon has also been attributed to reciprocity (Amden, Gunnthorsdottir, and McCabe, 1998). Reciprocity can also explain why communication increases contributions in similar games, by changing the expectations of what others will contribute (Isaac and Walker, 1991). Finally, one can imagine situations in which reciprocity is optimal, for

Table 1
Weighted regressions of individual contributions in full experiment on minimum, maximum and median contributions of others in group, including indicator variables for each individual (subject 1 is excluded) and each period (period 10 is excluded). The weights correct for heteroscedasticity of periods and individuals. The median contribution of others in the group is a better predictor of an individual's own contribution than either the minimum (as suggested by Sugden, 1984) or the maximum. In regressions (1) through (3), the coefficient on median is the largest and most significant. In regression (4), only the median remains a significant predictor of individual contributions. This result suggests that players try to match the contribution of the middle contributor, rather than the maximum or the minimum

Individual contributions	(1)	(2)	(3)	(4)
Intercept (α_0)	10.289[a]	8.182[a]	9.029[a]	8.320[a]
	(0.499)	(0.898)	(0.597)	(0.878)
MINIMUM (α_1)	0.115			0.019
	(0.070)			(0.079)
MAXIMUM (α_2)		0.156[b]		0.055
		(0.047)		(0.049)
MEDIAN (α_3)			0.180[a]	0.145[b]
			(0.048)	(0.048)
PERIOD ($\beta_t, t = 1, \ldots, 9$) (suppressed)				
INDIVIDUAL ($\gamma_i, i = 2, \ldots, 24$) (suppressed)				
Sum weights	74.854	79.666	74.325	75.885
R^2 adjusted	0.5981	0.5920	0.5676	0.5713

[a] $p < .001$.
[b] $p < .05$.

example, when the contributions of others provide valuable signals of the quality of the public good being funded, as in Vesterlund (2003).

This study examines the factors that motivate individuals to make voluntary contributions in social dilemma situations. In particular, it finds support for reciprocity theories over altruistic theories and traditional self-interest theories. We find a significant and positive relationship between an individual's contribution and his belief about the contributions of others in his group, as well as between an individual's contribution and the actual contributions of the others in his group. This result does not imply, however, that altruistic motives do not exist. In other settings altruism may indeed play a role in an individual's decision. However, in the public goods provision setting discussed here, comparative statics of individual's decisions are more consistent with theories of reciprocity than of altruism.

References

Amden, Holly, Gunnthorsdottir, Anna, McCabe, Kevin (1998). "When does reciprocity sustain cooperation in the linear VCM?" Working paper, University of Arizona.
Andreoni, James (1989). "Giving with impure altruism: Applications to charity and Ricardian equivalence". Journal of Political Economy 97, 1447–1458.
Andreoni, James (1990). "Impure altruism and donations to public goods: A theory of warm-glow giving". Economic Journal 100, 464–477.
Becker, Gary (1974). "A theory of social interaction". Journal of Political Economy 82, 1063–1093.
Croson, Rachel (1996). "Partners and strangers revisited". Economics Letters 53, 25–32.
Croson, Rachel (1998). "Effects of eliciting beliefs in a linear public goods game". OPIM working paper, The Wharton School of the University of Pennsylvania.
Croson, Rachel (2001). "Feedback in voluntary contribution mechanisms: An experiment in team production". In: Isaac, R.M. (Ed.), Research in Experimental Economics, vol. 8. Elsevier Science, New York, pp. 85–97.
Croson, Rachel (2007). "Theories of commitment, altruism and reciprocity: Evidence from linear public goods games". Economic Inquiry 45, 199–216.
Davis, Douglas, Holt, Charles (1994). "Experimental Economics". Princeton University Press, Princeton, NJ.
Davis, Douglas, Holt, Charles (1998). In: Kaplan, Ann E. (Ed.), Giving USA. American Association of Funding Counsel, New York.
Isaac, R. Mark, Walker, James (1991). "Costly Communication: An experiment in a nested public goods problem". In: Palfrey (Ed.), Laboratory Research in Political Economy. University of Michigan Press, Ann Arbor, MI.
Ledyard, John (1995). "Public goods: A survey of experimental research". In: Roth, Kagel (Eds.), The Handbook of Experimental Economics. Princeton University Press, Princeton, NJ.
Palfrey, Thomas, Prisbrey, Jeffrey (1997). "Anomalous behavior in public goods experiments: How much and why?" American Economic Review 87, 829–846.
Sell, Jane, Wilson, Rick (1991). "Levels of information and contributions to public goods". Social Forces 70, 107–124.
Sugden, Robert (1984). "Reciprocity: The supply of public goods through voluntary contributions". Economic Journal 94, 772–787.
Vesterlund, Lise (2003). "The informational value of sequential fundraising". Journal of Public Economics 87, 627–657.

Chapter 84

VOLUNTARY PROVISION OF PUBLIC GOODS: EXPERIMENTAL RESULTS WITH INTERIOR NASH EQUILIBRIA

SUSAN K. LAURY and CHARLES A. HOLT

1. Introduction

The standard public goods experiment involves linear payoffs in which the unique Nash equilibrium is at the lower boundary, i.e., full free riding. Contributions in these experiments tend to decline toward the Nash equilibrium in most treatments, but contributions persist even after as many as 60 rounds. This observation raises the question of whether the persistence of contributions is merely a boundary condition, with residual noise keeping contributions from reaching the Nash equilibrium. In other experimental environments, behavior shows a tendency to differ from boundary equilibria, but is reasonably close to interior predictions (see Smith and Walker, 1993 for examples). One way to address this issue in public goods experiments is to modify the standard linear payoff structure so that the Nash equilibrium is located in the interior of the set of feasible contributions. This paper surveys the evidence from interior-Nash public goods experiments. In some papers, the internal equilibrium is a dominant strategy and in others it is not. The designs also differ in terms of where the equilibrium is located relative to the upper and lower boundaries of the decision space. These relatively new designs are important because they can be used to evaluate the effects of treatment variables (for example, endowments, group size, and information) when the data are not being pulled toward the boundary. In addition, moving the equilibria to the center of the set of feasible contributions tends to reduce or neutralize any bias due to decision errors.

Before considering the interior Nash designs, it is useful to review the standard linear structure that produces a boundary equilibrium. An individual i who contributes x_i to the public good out of an endowment of E units, thereby consumes $E - x_i$ units of the private good. If the marginal value of the private good is a constant, v, and the individual's marginal value of total contributions to the public good is also a constant, m, then the individual's earnings are given by

$$\pi_i = v(E - x_i) + mX, \tag{1}$$

where X is the sum of all individuals' contributions to the public good. Notice that the constant marginal value of both the public and private goods produces a linear earnings function that is maximized at either the upper or lower boundary (unless v is exactly equal to m, in which case any level of contribution is optimal).[1] In a more realistic

---

[1] These calculations are based on the assumption that individuals maximize their own monetary earnings; the presence of altruism and fairness considerations may lead to different equilibrium outcomes.

Handbook of Experimental Economics Results, Volume 1
Copyright © 2008 Elsevier B.V. All rights reserved
DOI: 10.1016/S1574-0722(07)00084-4

setting, it is natural to think that both the public and private goods are subject to diminishing marginal values after some point. This feature requires the earnings function to be non-linear in private and/or public consumption.

The most common approach used to implement non-linearities is to think of (1) as additively separable with two possibly non-linear components: $V(E - x_i)$ and $M(X)$, where the capitalized notation indicates that $V()$ and $M()$ are functions. In the linear public goods environment described by (1), both of these functions are linear in contributions to the public good, and a dominant strategy at one of the boundaries results. Non-linearities have typically been introduced in only one of the components of the earnings function. Either of these two quasi-linear approaches can result in interior Nash equilibria, but they have different implications for the nature of these equilibria, as described below.[2] We begin with the simpler (although less common) setup: a non-linear value of private consumption. This yields a unique Nash equilibrium in dominant strategies.

2. Dominant Strategy Designs

The simplest way to introduce a non-linearity in the value of the private good is by using a quadratic function:

$$\pi_i = a(E - x_i) - b(E - x_i)^2 + mX, \qquad (2)$$

where $a, b > 0$, mX is the value of the public good, and $(E - x_i)$ is the consumption of the private good. Thus private consumption has diminishing marginal value. Maximizing earnings results in a unique equilibrium level of individual contributions where the marginal cost of contributing $[a - 2b(E - x_i)]$ is equated with the marginal benefit (m). For an appropriately specified earnings function and endowment, this yields an internal equilibrium, given by

$$x_i = \frac{m - a}{2b} + E. \qquad (3)$$

Notice that the equilibrium contribution depends only on the parameters of the experiment and not on others' contributions. Thus the equilibrium contribution is a dominant strategy, as in the linear public goods experiments.

Keser (1996) implemented this design in an experiment that tested whether moving the equilibrium away from the boundary would result in more dominant-strategy behavior. The equilibrium contribution to the public good was 7 tokens (35 percent of

---

[2] The focus of this paper is on *continuous* public goods experiments, where the earnings function from the public good is a continuous function of contributions. Other studies, not surveyed here, have implemented an interior equilibrium in a provision point setting, where the public good yields no return (or a comparatively low return) until contributions reach a specified threshold level. For examples of this research, see Marwell and Ames (1979, 1980) and Bagnoli and McKee (1991).

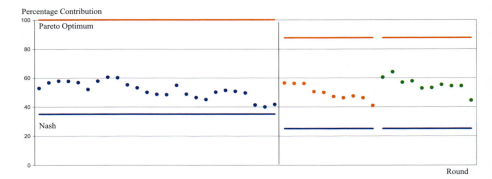

Figure 1. Percentage of endowment contributed. Keser (1996), shown with blue dots, implemented an interior Nash equilibrium in which each subject had a dominant strategy to contribute a portion of their resource endowment. Although contributions decline over the experiment, in every round average contributions are above the Nash equilibrium. Sefton and Steinberg (1996) compared a dominant strategy interior Nash equilibrium environment (red dots) with a non-dominant strategy environment (green dots). Average contributions are also above the Nash equilibrium in every round of the Sefton and Steinberg study. Contributions are somewhat lower than the equilibrium when this is a dominant strategy, shown by the red dots, than when there is no dominant strategy, shown by the green dots.

each individual's endowment), while full contribution was the Pareto optimal outcome. Although the dominant-strategy Nash equilibrium was the modal contribution (overall, 25 percent of all observations were at this level), average contributions were greater than this level in each round. This may be seen on the left side of Figure 1. Average contributions declined over the 25-round sessions, from about 33 percent greater than the equilibrium in the first five rounds, to about 15 percent greater in the last five rounds. More dominant-strategy behavior was observed in the final rounds of the sessions.[3]

Additional studies using the dominant strategy earnings structure described by (2) have yielded contribution patterns similar to Keser's. In van Dijk, Sonnemans, and van Winden (2002), the equilibrium contribution for each subject was three of ten tokens, with full contribution again the Pareto optimal outcome. Average contributions were about 35 percent higher than the equilibrium in early rounds, however there was less decay in contributions than observed in Keser's sessions, and a larger end-round drop in contributions. Sefton and Steinberg (1996) provided further evidence that equilibrium contributions are not, on average, attained by moving the dominant-strategy equilibrium into the interior of the decision space. As shown by the red dots on the right side of

---

[3] Ortmann, Hansberry, and Fitzgerald (1997) found behavior more consistent with the dominant-strategy Nash equilibrium in a study intended to replicate Keser's. There were, however, several changes relative to her study: the introduction of a conversion factor resulted in three dominant strategy equilibria, subjects were reassigned between two groups after every round, the sessions lasted only eight rounds, greater controls for anonymity were implemented, and individual earnings were publicly posted after each round. It is not clear which of these changes may account for the difference in results.

Figure 1, contributions in their study were about mid-way between the Nash equilibrium (set at 25 percent of the endowment) and the Pareto optimal outcome (set at 87.5 percent of the endowment).[4]

Considered together, these results indicate that moving the equilibrium away from the boundary is not sufficient in itself to induce Nash behavior in public goods experiments, even when the Nash equilibrium involves dominant strategies. Moreover, a systematic upward bias in contributions persists. The following section considers a number of other studies that have induced an interior equilibrium in a different way: by specifying a declining marginal value for the *public* good. They examine not only whether moving the equilibrium away from the boundary matters, but also how the location of the equilibrium in the set of feasible decisions affects contribution behavior.

3. Non-dominant Strategy Designs

A second source of non-linearity is to introduce a diminishing marginal value of the public good, while maintaining the constant marginal cost of contributing (the marginal value of the private good). A simple quadratic specification of this quasi-linear environment is

$$\pi_i = v(E - x_i) + aX - bX^2, \tag{4}$$

where $a, b > 0$. Maximizing earnings results in an equilibrium contribution in which the marginal cost of contributing (v) is equated with the marginal benefit ($a - 2bX$). In equilibrium, the aggregate contribution is given by

$$X = \frac{a - v}{2b}. \tag{5}$$

Thus, for appropriately specified parameters, there is a unique equilibrium for *aggregate* contributions in the interior of the decision space.[5] However, there are multiple individual equilibria, each depending on the level of others' contributions, and there is no longer a dominant strategy. This adds a layer of complexity not present in the dominant-strategy design. In order to attain an equilibrium outcome, subjects must not only determine the optimal allocation (as in the dominant-strategy specification), but also correctly anticipate others' contribution decisions.

---

[4] Like Keser's design, the dominant strategy in Sefton and Steinberg's study was induced via a declining marginal value of the private good. However, the marginal value of the private good was not generated using an algebraic payoff function. This was done in order to hold constant the cost of a 1-unit deviation from equilibrium play between this treatment and a non-dominant-strategy treatment, described in the next section.

[5] Two studies (Isaac, McCue, and Plott, 1985; Isaac and Walker, 1991) used the quadratic earnings structure in (4), but with the marginal cost set to be higher than the individual's marginal benefit at any level of contributions. Thus, zero contributions remained the dominant-strategy equilibrium.

Given this additional coordination problem, it is perhaps not surprising that Sefton and Steinberg (1996) found that contributions had a higher variance in such a non-dominant-strategy environment than in a parallel, dominant-strategy treatment. Under both treatments, subjects were given the same endowment, faced the same aggregate Nash equilibrium and Pareto-optimal outcomes, and faced the same monetary loss from a one-unit deviation from equilibrium play. In addition to the higher variance in the non-dominant-strategy design, contributions were somewhat higher than in the dominant-strategy sessions (see the green dots on the right side of Figure 1). This difference, however, was not significant.

In each of the cases reviewed so far, the Nash equilibrium has been less than half of the feasible contribution amount, and average contributions remained above the Nash prediction, as can be seen in Figure 1. In a path-breaking paper, Isaac and Walker (1998) considered how the location of the aggregate Nash equilibrium, relative to the group's aggregate endowment, affected contributions to the public good. They considered treatments in which the aggregate Nash equilibrium was low relative to the group's endowment (19.4 percent), in the middle of the endowment space (50 percent) and high relative to the group's endowment (80.6 percent). As shown in Figure 2, the "low-Nash" and "high-Nash" treatments were mirror images of each other. Overall, only a small percentage of actual contributions were close to the aggregate Nash prediction. Like the studies discussed above, contributions in the low-Nash treatment were significantly greater than the aggregate equilibrium. When the equilibrium was in the middle of the decision-space, contributions tracked the equilibrium initially, but declined below Nash by the final rounds of the sessions. Contributions in the high-Nash treatment were significantly below the Nash equilibrium.[6] However, the upward bias in low-Nash sessions was found to be significantly greater than the downward bias in high-Nash sessions, perhaps suggesting a greater tendency toward cooperative behavior.

A different approach toward exploring boundary effects is to hold the Nash equilibrium contribution constant, while moving the lower boundary closer to this level. Andreoni (1993) implemented such a design by imposing a minimum required contribution for each individual. Moving the boundary toward the equilibrium resulted in increased contributions, but by less than the amount of the "tax." Thus, some crowding out of voluntary contributions occurs, although the crowding out is incomplete. Chan et al. (2002) report a similar finding. They also examine how the size of the required transfer affects contributions. When the transfer is small relative to the equilibrium contribution, incomplete crowding out occurs. For a larger transfer, however, crowding out is complete.

It is also interesting to consider the level of contributions in the control treatments, i.e., in the absence of a required transfer. Average contributions in both studies were

---

[6] This downward bias is consistent with below-Nash contributions reported by Saijo and Nakamura (1995) in a linear public goods experiment where the dominant-strategy Nash equilibrium was located at the Pareto optimal upper boundary.

Ch. 84: *Voluntary Provision of Public Goods*

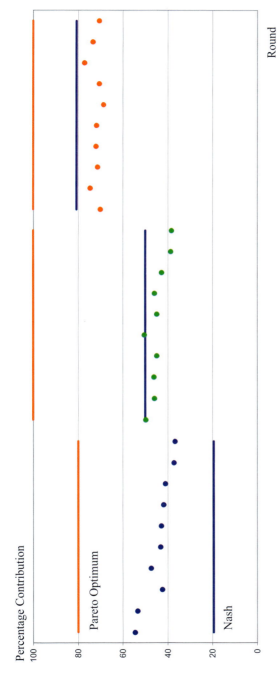

Figure 2. Percentage of endowment contributed. Isaac and Walker (1996) studied how the location of the Nash equilibrium, within the range of feasible outcomes, affected the level of contributions to the public good in an environment without a dominant strategy. Contributions below Nash are observed when the Nash equilibrium is high relative to total token endowment (see the red dots in the third treatment). The first and third treatments are mirror images of one another. However, in the "low Nash" treatment (blue dots, shown on the left) deviations from the Nash prediction are larger than in the "high Nash" treatment (red dots, shown on the right). The Nash equilibrium does relatively well when it is in the middle of the decision space, as in the second treatment (green dots, shown in the center).

less than the Nash prediction, although this difference was not significant. While the equilibrium in Andreoni's study was close to half of the endowment (43 percent), the equilibrium in Chan et al. was considerably lower in the decision space (27 percent of the endowment). The clearest differences between these experiments and those reported earlier was in the payoff structure. Andreoni used an integer-approximation to a Cobb–Douglas payoff function, and Chan et al. added a Cobb–Douglas specification, $(E - x_i)X$, to the standard linear earnings function in (1). In the studies discussed so far, earnings from the private and public goods were additively separable, and hence were presented in *separate* tables that showed earnings from each good at various contribution levels. In contrast, subjects in the Andreoni and Chan et al. experiments were presented with a complete payoff matrix that showed total earnings as a function of both own and others' contributions to the public good.[7] We conjecture that subjects may have a hard time noticing and responding to the positive externality from the public good when the payoff structure is highly non-linear, as in the Cobb–Douglas case, and earnings are presented in matrix form. This matrix presentation of earnings may make the outcome that maximizes individual earnings more apparent than that which maximizes group earnings, resulting in lower contributions than when earnings from the public and private goods are presented separately.

These observations suggest that the way in which subjects perceive the tradeoff between the private and public goods, and hence their contributions, could depend upon the way in which the earnings structure is presented. Laury, Walker, and Williams (1999) tested this by providing subjects with a table that explicitly showed the declining marginal benefit of the public good and the constant marginal benefit of the private good. In other sessions, without this information, there was evidence that subjects focused on the outcome that maximized earnings from the public good, ignoring the marginal cost of contributing. Providing subjects with additional earnings information was associated with a decrease in contributions to the public good. Although contributions remained above the Nash equilibrium level, complete free-riding was the modal contribution in these sessions.

While contributions in excess of the Nash equilibrium level are typical, these experiments have demonstrated that contributions may fall below the Nash level when this equilibrium is near the upper boundary or when the payoff structure is not separable and therefore must be presented in matrix form. Deviations from the predicted level are small when the equilibrium is near the middle of the set of feasible decisions. Providing subjects with detailed earnings information may also reduce the size of these deviations. The next session examines how two other treatments, individual endowment and group size, affect contributions in a non-dominant strategy interior Nash environment.

---

[7] Cason, Saijo, and Yamato (2003) also used a Cobb–Douglas earnings function and presented earnings to subjects in a payoff matrix. Contributions were not significantly different than the Nash equilibrium prediction for U.S. subjects, but were significantly less than this level for Japanese subjects.

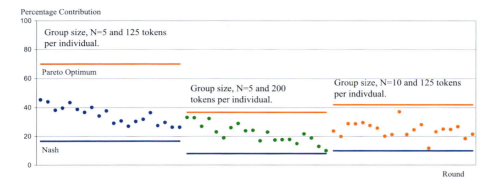

Figure 3. Percentage of endowment contributed. Laury, Walker, and Williams (1997) examined the effect of group size and individual token endowment on contributions in a non-dominant strategy environment. In each treatment, 100 tokens contributed to the public good was the aggregate Nash equilibrium. However, the Nash equilibrium varied as a percentage of total group resource endowment between treatments. For groups of size five, the percentage contribution is lower when each participant is given 200 tokens (green dots) than when each is given 125 tokens (blue dots), although the total number of tokens contributed is quite close between these two treatments. The percentage contribution is lower for groups of size ten (red dots) than for groups of size five (blue dots), although the total number of tokens contributed by groups of size ten is higher.

4. Treatment Effects

It is possible that contributions to the public good are a positive function of "wealth," defined in the lab as subjects' resource endowment. As a special case of this, one can test whether subjects contribute a fixed percentage of their endowment. Laury, Walker, and Williams (1999) studied the effect of a change in individual endowments, from 125 to 200 tokens, holding constant the aggregate Nash prediction of 100 tokens. Contributions exceeded the Nash level in both treatments. When subjects were provided only with rough payoff tables, the *level* of contributions increased when the individual endowment was increased. However, the *percentage* of endowment contributed declined. When subjects were provided with additional earnings information, as described above, an increase in token endowment had almost no effect on the level of contributions. The results of these sessions (in terms of the percentage of endowment contributed to the public good) are shown on the left side of Figure 3.

Chan et al. (1996) instead examined the effect of changing the distribution of endowments among subjects, holding constant the three-person group's aggregate endowment. They found that small changes in the endowment distribution did not have a significant effect on contributions. However, a large inequality in endowment distribution led to a significant increase in contributions. On average, those subjects with relatively high endowments tended to under-contribute relative to the theoretical prediction, while subjects with relatively low endowments tended to over-contribute. A heterogeneous distribution of endowments was also implemented by van Dijk, Sonnemans, and van Winden (2002) in a dominant-strategy environment. In two-person groups, both the low-endowment and high-endowment subjects over-contributed relative to the Nash prediction. However, the extent of this over-contribution was greater for those with a low endowment, for whom the predicted contribution was lower (one of eight tokens for low-endowment subjects, compared with five of 12 tokens for high-endowment subjects).

The effect of changing group size, holding constant the aggregate Nash equilibrium level of contributions, has also been examined. Both Guttman (1986) and Laury, Walker, and Williams (1999) report similar group-size effects. Doubling group size (from three to six in Guttman's study and from five to ten in Laury, Walker, and Williams) results in an increase in aggregate contributions to the public good, but a decrease in individual contributions. Contributions are higher than the Nash equilibrium prediction in all of these sessions, however. Results from the Laury, Walker, and Williams experiments are shown in Figure 3.

5. Final Observations

The majority of evidence from internal Nash public goods experiments shows that simply moving the equilibrium into the interior of the decision space is not sufficient to produce contributions that are, on average, close to the equilibrium prediction. When the Nash equilibrium falls between the lower boundary and the mid-point of the decision space, average contributions typically exceed the equilibrium level. This is true both in dominant-strategy and non-dominant-strategy environments. There is less variance in contribution decisions, however, when the interior Nash equilibrium is a dominant strategy. The most important determinant of the size and direction of these deviations appears to be the equilibrium's location relative to the group's aggregate endowment. For example, significant *under-contribution* is observed when the equilibrium is relatively close to the upper boundary. Other treatments have been shown to impact contributions as well. While a uniform change in individual endowment may not affect the *level* of contributions, a change in the distribution of endowments may. An increase in group size increases aggregate contributions, while individual contributions fall. There is also some evidence that the way in which the earnings function is presented to subjects may affect contributions, although a controlled study of this has not been conducted.

Acknowledgements

This work was funded in part by the National Science Foundation (SBR-9617784 and SBR-9753125).

References

Andreoni, J. (1993). "An experimental test of the public goods crowding-out hypothesis". American Economic Review 83, 1317–1327.

Bagnoli, M., McKee, M. (1991). "Voluntary contribution games: Efficient private provision of public goods". Economic Inquiry 29, 351–366.
Cason, T., Saijo, T., Yamato, T. (2003). "Voluntary participation and spite in public good provision experiments: An international comparison". Experimental Economics 5, 133–153.
Chan, K., Mestelman, S., Moir, R., Muller, R.A. (1996). "The voluntary provision of public goods under varying income distributions". Canadian Journal of Economics 29, 54–69.
Chan, K., Godby, R., Mestelman, S., Muller, R.A. (2002). "Crowding out voluntary contributions to public goods". Working paper, McMaster University.
Guttman, J.M. (1986). "Matching behavior in collective action: Some experimental evidence". Journal of Economic Behavior and Organization 7, 171–198.
Isaac, R.M., Walker, J. (1991). "On the suboptimality of voluntary public goods provision: Further experimental evidence". Research in Experimental Economics 4, 211–221.
Isaac, R.M., Walker, J. (1998). "Nash as an organizing principle in the voluntary provision of public goods: Experimental evidence". Experimental Economics 1 (3), 191–206.
Isaac, R.M., McCue, K., Plott, C. (1985). "Public goods provision in an experimental environment". Journal of Public Economics 26, 51–74.
Keser, C. (1996). "Voluntary contributions to a public good when partial contribution is a dominant strategy". Economics Letters 50, 359–366.
Laury, S., Walker, J., Williams, A. (1999). "The voluntary contribution mechanism: Provision of a pure public good with diminishing marginal returns". Public Choice 99 (1–2), 139–160.
Marwell, G., Ames, R.E. (1979). "Experiments on the provision of public goods. I. Resources, interest, group size, and the free-rider problem". American Journal of Sociology 84, 1335–1360.
Marwell, G., Ames, R.E. (1980). "Experiments on the provision of public goods. II. Provision points, stakes, experience, and the free-rider problem". American Journal of Sociology 85, 926–937.
Ortmann, A., Hansberry, K.M., Fitzgerald, J. (1997). "Voluntary contributions to a public good when partial contribution is a dominant strategy". Working paper, Bowdoin College.
Saijo, T., Nakamura, H. (1995). "The 'spite' dilemma in voluntary contribution mechanism experiments". Journal of Conflict Resolution 39, 535–560.
Sefton, M., Steinberg, R. (1996). "Reward structures in public good experiments". Journal of Public Economics 61, 263–287.
Smith, V., Walker, J. (1993). "Monetary rewards and decision cost in experimental economics". Economic Inquiry 31, 245–261.
van Dijk, F., Sonnemans, J., van Winden, F. (2002). "Social ties in a public good experiment". Journal of Public Economics 85 (2), 275–299.

Chapter 85

SPITEFUL BEHAVIOR IN VOLUNTARY CONTRIBUTION MECHANISM EXPERIMENTS

TATSUYOSHI SAIJO

Institute of Social and Economic Research, Osaka University, and Research Institute of Economy, Trade and Industry, Tokyo

One of the basic findings in public good provision experiments via the voluntary contribution mechanism is that subjects contribute a considerable amount of their initial holdings to the provision of a public good even when no contribution is the dominant strategy [see Ledyard's survey article (1995)]. This seemingly non-rational behavior has been interpreted as resulting from confusion, kindness or fairness. For example, Andreoni (1995) developed a method to distinguish between confusion and kindness, and concluded that a relatively large part of positive contributions is interpreted as kindness.

On the other hand, there are three fundamental criticisms of voluntary contribution mechanism experiments. First, most experiments to date have used a linear utility function where the marginal return of a public good out of one unit of contribution of a private good is less than one. Therefore, no contribution is the best strategy. Since the solution is a corner solution, the experimental results were biased in favor of contribution. In order to answer this criticism, Saijo and Nakamura (1995) conducted experiments where the marginal return of a public good is greater than one (high marginal return). That is, all contribution is the dominant strategy. They compared the results to experiments where the marginal benefit of a public good is less than one (low marginal return) and found that the deviation from the dominant strategy in the case of high marginal return is larger than that in the case of low marginal return. They also found subjects who did not contribute cared about their relative ranking as well as monetary reward. In the case of high marginal return, if they cared about relative ranking among subjects, they would contribute nothing out of their initial holdings, but if they cared about the monetary reward, they would contribute everything. They termed this ambivalence the *spite* dilemma.

The second criticism is on the linearity of a utility function. In usual theoretical analyses, economists use a non-linear utility function such as the Cobb–Douglas utility function, Saijo, Yamato, and Yokotani (2004) conducted two-subject voluntary contribution mechanism experiments using the Cobb–Douglas utility function. They found that most subjects employed an interior Nash equilibrium strategy, but not quite: assuming that the other subject would choose his Nash contribution, some subjects chose slightly lower contributions than the Nash contribution.[1] The reason for choosing slightly lower con-

---

[1] This observation is compatible with the data in Andreoni (1993), who studied the crowding out hypothesis in public good experiments with non-linear payoff functions, though he did not refer to spiteful behavior.

Handbook of Experimental Economics Results, Volume 1
Copyright © 2008 Elsevier B.V. All rights reserved
DOI: 10.1016/S1574-0722(07)00085-6

tributions than the Nash contribution was because it did not change their own payoffs (since the first order condition of a utility maximization problem is satisfied), however, the other subject's payoff would be lowered considerably.

The third criticism comes from mechanism design theory (Saijo and Yamato, 1999). Mechanism designers implicitly assumed that agents in their mechanisms must participate in the mechanisms. As Olson (1965) noticed, any non-participant can obtain benefit of a public good that is provided by others. This is due to the nature of a public good called *non-excludability*. In other words, almost all mechanism designers after Groves and Ledyard (1977) designed mechanisms for the free-rider problem where every participant decided to participate in the mechanisms, but not mechanisms for the problem whether or not they have incentives to participant in them. This criticism is also valid to the voluntary contribution mechanism. Cason et al. (2004) designed a two-stage game where the first stage is for participation decision and the second is for contribution decision and found that the public good provision game with the voluntary contribution mechanism became a hawk–dove game, but not a prisoner's dilemma game. Although participation is not an equilibrium strategy, in a hawk–dove game experiment with an evolutionary setting, Saijo et al. (2003) observed that among Japanese subjects evolutionarily stable strategies did not appear, but high participation emerged through a transmutation from a hawk–dove game to a game where participation to the mechanism is the dominant strategy. They also found that this transmutation is not due to kindness, but to *spitefulness* among subjects. On the other hand, in Cason, Saijo, and Yamato (2002) these results among Japanese subjects were compared with results among American subjects and found that American subjects followed relatively to evolutionarily stable strategies.

1. Saijo–Nakamura Experiments

Saijo and Nakamura (1995) conducted voluntary contribution mechanism experiments with no communication. Each of seven subjects has ten units of initial holdings for each period, and the total number of periods is ten. There are two parameters in the experiments: the marginal return from the contribution or investment [high marginal return ($a = 1/0.7$) and low marginal return ($a = 0.7$)] and the payoff information (detailed and rough tables). As for the payoff information effect, they found that results with detailed payoff tables are closer to theoretical predictions than those with rough payoff tables. In a detailed payoff table, each column represents the subject's own investment and each row represents the sum of other subjects' investment. That is, a subject can see every payoff from his strategy given the other subjects' strategies, and hence this table is exactly the same as the payoff matrix usually used in game theory. Since the difference of results between rough and detailed payoff tables may be attributed to confusion of the subjects, results with detailed payoff tables are the main concern here. Each subject participated in two marginal return experiments consecutively. For example, a subject attended a ten period experiment with high marginal return and then a ten period experiment with low marginal return. Let us denote this experiment (H, L). (H, L) experiments were repeated four times and (L, H) experiments were repeated four times.

Figure 1 shows the patterns of mean investment for (H, L) and (L, H). The horizontal axis denotes periods and the vertical axis expresses the ratio of the observed amount of investments to the sum of all subjects' initial holdings. No investment for all periods is a unique subgame perfect Nash equilibrium with $a = 0.7$ and all investments for all periods are the unique dominant strategy equilibrium with $a = 1/0.7$. Therefore, the difference between the actual investment and the equilibrium investment provides a method of measuring how far subjects are away from theoretical behavior. Figure 1 shows that the difference in high marginal return is larger than that with low marginal return. There are two basic findings with low marginal return. First, the mean investments for all low marginal return experiments are lower than those in experiments by Isaac and Walker (1988) and others. Second, although the decay effect is one of the major findings in the voluntary contribution mechanism experiments, no specific decay toward the end period is observed. These are due to the detailed payoff table effect.

Why did not subjects invest their full initial holdings in the high marginal return case? Consider the voluntary contribution mechanism with two subjects and two strategies. Each subject invests zero or ten. Table 1 shows the payoff tables with high marginal return and low marginal return where $*$ indicates the dominant strategy. Using these tables, we can construct payoff tables where the payoff for each cell is the difference between your payoff and your opponent's payoff. In fact, as Table 2 shows, these two payoff tables become the same.

If $a = 0.7$, as in the prisoner's dilemma case, no investment is still the dominant strategy in Table 2. On the other hand, if $a = 1/0.7$, all investments are the dominant strategy in Table 1 while no investment is the dominant strategy in Table 2. That is, the subject's mind wavers between investment and no investment depending on the relative strengths of the "profit" and "spite" motives. Saijo and Nakamura have named this dilemma the spite dilemma.

Since each subject participated in both high and low marginal return experiments, two mean investments can be plotted in Figure 2. The horizontal axis represents investment with $a = 0.7$ and the vertical axis represents investment with $a = 1/0.7$. When $a = 0.7$, zero investment corresponds to the free-riding side in Figure 2, and 10 corresponds to the altruism side. Similarly, when $a = 1/0.7$, 10 corresponds to the non-spite side, which is called the pay-riding side, and zero investment corresponds to the spite side. The box in the figure is divided into four although this division is arbitrary. Since the "theoretical" solution that is predicted by the dominant strategy is the upper-left corner of the box, i.e., $(0, 10)$, the FP region represents the theoretical prediction. It is less likely to find subjects in the AS region since this region denotes subjects who invest a lot in the free-riding situation and act spitefully toward others when she can receive more than her investment. The focal point is the distribution of subjects among FP, AP, and FS regions. As Figure 3 shows, almost no subjects are found in the AP region, and

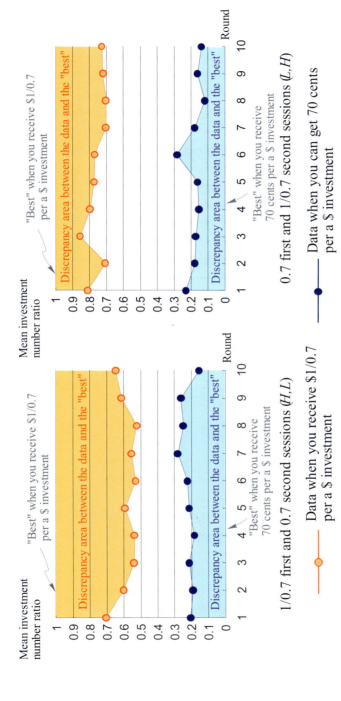

Figure 1. The discrepancies from the "best" and the mean investments.

Table 1
Two simplified payoff tables

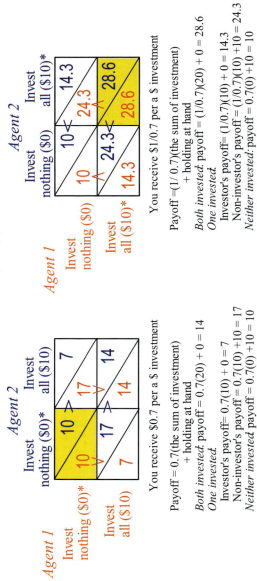

Table 2
An illustration of the spite dilemma

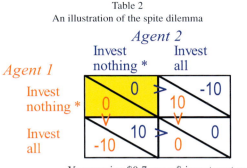

You receive $0.7 per a $ investemnt and
You receive $1/0.7 per a $ investemnt
(* indicates the dominant strategy)

The number of each cell = Your payoff in either table in Table 1 – the other subject's payoff. When you receive $0.7 per a $ investment, "investment nothing" is the dominant strategy in Tables 1 and 2. However, when you receive $1/0.7, "Invest all" is the dominant strategy in Table 1, but "invest nothing" is. A conflict between "going for money" and the "winning" is called the spite dilemma.

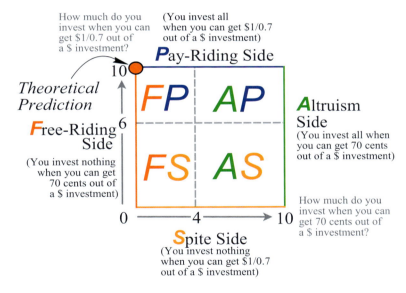

Figure 2. The mean investment distribution box.

most subjects are distributed in the FP and FS regions. That is, pay-riding subjects are "theoretical" and spiteful subjects free-ride.

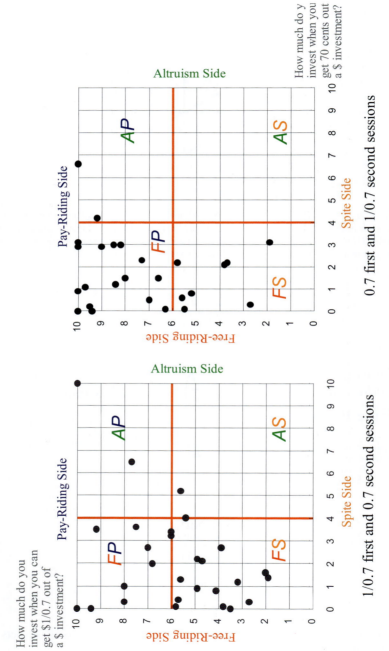

Figure 3. The data of mean investment distribution of all subjects.

Ch. 85: *Spiteful Behavior in Voluntary Contribution Mechanism Experiments*　　809

Table 3

A part of the detailed payoff table used in sessions A and B (no circles or shades are marked in the real experimental payoff table)

Your Investment Number

Your Payoff	0	1	2	3	4	5	6	7	8	9	10	11	12	13	14	... 24
0	706	871	1072	1297	1536	1775	2003	(2210)	2386	2523	2615	(2658)	2648	2585	2470	
1	905					2183	2427	2641	2816	2944	3019	3039	3001	2905	2755	
2	1186	*Spiteful Strategy Region*				2658	2913	3129	3297	3411	3465	3456	3385	3252	3061	
3	1554	(you reduce your own				3202	3463	3675	3831							
4	2017	payoff to reduce your opponent's payoff more)				3817	4078	4281	4420	44						
5	2578	3010	3432	3831	4193	4507	4762	4950	5064	51						
6	3244	3718	4171	4590	4960	5272	5515	5681	5766	57						
7	(4018)	4529	5008	5440	5812	6115	6339	6478	(6526)	64						
8	4904	5447	5944	6383	6751	7038	7237	(7340)	(7345)	72						
9	5907	6475	6984	7422	7779	8043	8209	8271	8225	8073	7816	7458	7007	6472	5867	
10	7031	7616	8130	8561	8897	9132	9257	9270	9168	8951	8624	8193	7664	7051	6367	
11	(8278)	8873	9384	9800	10109	10330							35		*Altruistic Strategy*	
12	9653	10250	10750	11142	11416	11156							09		*Region* (you reduce	
13	11158	11749	12229	12589	12820	12910							86		your own payoff to increase the other	
14	12796	13372	13824	14144	14323	14350							66		subject's payoff)	
... 24																

Your Opponent's Investment Number

← *Nash Best Response Region*

The Voluntary Participation Case: The best response when the other subject does not participate is 11. However, if you choose 7 rather than 11, your own payoff is reduced from 2658 to 2210 (448 units), but the other subject's payoff is reduced from 8278 to 4018 (4260 units).

The Mandatory Participation Case: assume that the other player chooses 8. If you choose 7 rather than 8, your own payoff is reduced from 7345 to 7340 (5 units), but the other subject's payoff is reduced from 7345 to 6526 (819).

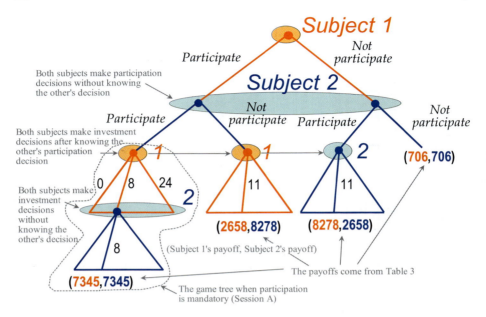

Figure 4. The two stage game tree when subjects can choose their participation in the voluntary contribution mechanism.

2. Non-excludable Public Good Experiments

Cason et al. (2004) and Cason, Saijo, and Yamato (2002) conducted voluntary contribution mechanism experiments with two subjects who had the same Cobb–Douglas utility function,

$$u_i(x_i, y) = \frac{(x_i^{0.47} y^{1-0.47})^{4.45}}{50} + 500,$$

where x_i is subject i's consumption of a private good and y is the consumption of a public good. They assumed that the sum of contribution of two subjects becomes the level of the public good and each subject has 24 units of initial holdings; see Figure 4. Both subjects are required to participate in the mechanism in Session A. On the other hand, each subject can choose her participation decision before her contribution decision in Session B. That is, in the first stage, subjects choose whether or not they participate in the mechanism at the same time, and in the second stage, knowing the other subject's participation decision, subjects who selected participation in the first stage choose contributions to the public good. Therefore, Session A includes the second stage while Session B includes both stages. Each session has twenty subjects and each subject is randomly paired with the other subject. The same game was repeated 19 periods, 4 for practice and 15 for monetary reward, so as not to pair the same two subjects more than once. They used detailed payoff tables in both sessions (see Table 3).

Table 4
The payoff table becomes a hawk–dove game

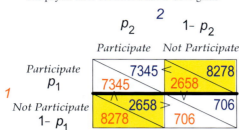

(7345, 7345) are based on the Nash equilibrium second stage investments of (8, 8) when both participate in the first stage (see Table 3 and Figure 4). (2658, 8278) is based on the equilibrium investments of (11, 0) when only subject 1 participates. The subgame perfect Nash equilibria are participation probabilities for subjects 1 and 2 ($p1, p2$) of (1, 0) (0, 1), and (0.68, 0.68). The unique evolutionary stable strategy (ESS) is ($p1, p2$) = (0.68, 0.68).

Transforming this two-stage game in Session B to a normal form game, they show that the game becomes a hawk–dove game, but not a prisoner's dilemma game introducing participation as a decision variable (see Table 4). This game has two pure strategy Nash equilibria and one mixed strategy Nash equilibrium that is the unique evolutionarily stable strategy (ESS) equilibrium. Therefore, Session B can be considered as a test of the ESS prediction.

Cason et al. (2004) used Japanese subjects and Cason, Saijo, and Yamato (2002) compared the results with American subjects. Both used students in several universities in each country, but the following are summaries of results from University of Tsukuba in Japan and University of Southern California in the United States.

In Session A, as Table 3 shows, the Nash equilibrium investment pair is (8, 8). Since each period had 10 pairs and 15 periods were conducted, each session generated 150 pairs of data. Figure 5 shows the frequency distributions of investment data rearranging each pair (a, b) with $a \geqslant b$ since the order of investment numbers does not matter. The maximum frequency pair is (8, 8) with 36 pairs at Tsukuba and with 29 pairs at USC. Both are similar, but Tsukuba rarely has data such as (a, b) with $a, b \geqslant 8$ and USC has data such as (9, 8) with 14 pairs and (12, 8) with 5 pairs.

Figure 6 shows the average investment pattern of Session A. In Tsukuba's case, the average investment is less than the Nash equilibrium level of investment in all periods except for one. In order to understand the subjects' behavior throughout the experiment, each subject was asked to write her reason for the investment decision in each period. According to this information, there are four subjects who explicitly stated the following: they estimated that their opponent would choose 8, and then they chose 6 or 7 because this would make their opponent's payoff much lower than their own payoff. For example, suppose that your opponent chooses 8 in Table 3. If you choose 8, you and your opponent obtain 7345. If you choose 7, you obtain 7340, but your opponent obtains 6526. By choosing 7, you can make the reduction of your opponent's payoff

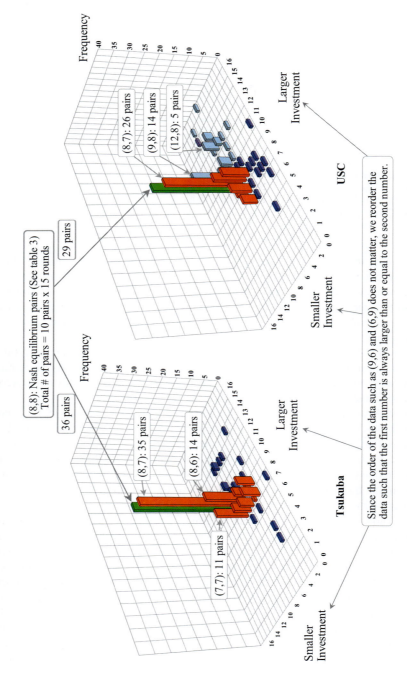

Figure 5. The distribution of investment pairs when two subjects must participate in the mechanism.

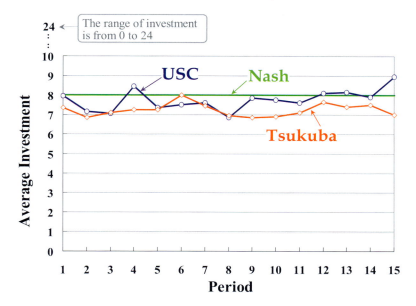

Figure 6. Average investments when subjects must participate in the mechanism.

(819 = 7345 − 6526) much larger than your own reduction (5 = 7345 − 7340). Employing a random effects error specification, Cason, Saijo, and Yamato (2002) found that the pooled data strongly reject the Nash equilibrium, even when these four spiteful subjects and their opponents' data are excluded. The average USC sequence, however, is close to the Nash equilibrium contribution.

Figure 7 shows that the distributions of investment pairs in Session B are very different from those of Session A. In Tsukuba, the maximum frequency pair is (8, 7) with 28 pairs, and the second is (8, 8) and (0, 0) with 18 pairs, and the fourth is (7, 0) with 15 pairs. At USC, the maximum frequency pair is (11, 0) with 36 pairs, and the second is (0, 0) with 25 pairs, the fourth is (8, 7) with 11 pairs, and the fifth is (7, 0) with 10 pairs.

Figure 8 shows the participation ratio pattern of Session B. In Tsukuba, although the participation ratio starts with 40% in period 1, it gradually increases and is more than 85% in the last 4 periods. On the other hand, the USC data is close to the ESS prediction where the participation ratio should be 68%. Due to the participation ratio difference between the two schools, Tsukuba's average investments toward the end period are higher than those at USC. As a result, Tsukuba provides the public good more than USC does.

In order to understand these rather high participation ratios, consider the case where only one subject participates in the mechanism. As Table 3 shows, the participant should invest 11 to maximize her own payoff. In this case, the maximum frequency investment number is 7, and no participant invested more than 11. If the participant invests 11,

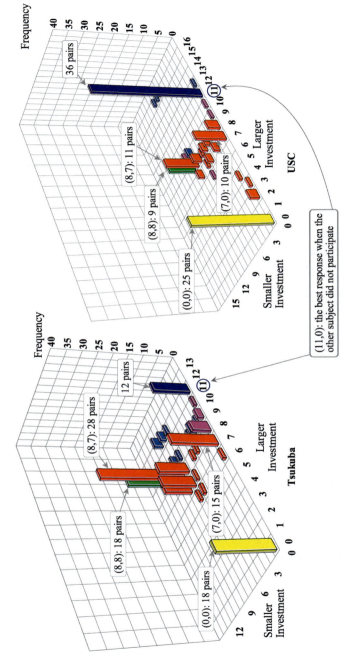

Figure 7. The distribution of investment pairs when two subjects can choose to participate in the mechanism.

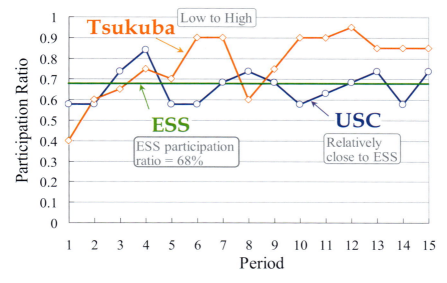

Figure 8. Participation pattern.

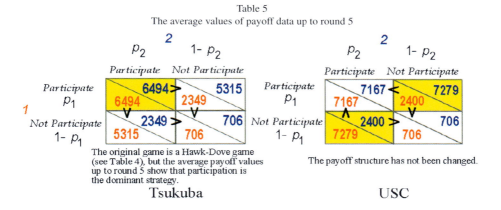

Table 5
The average values of payoff data up to round 5

then she earns 2658 and her opponent earns 8278. On the hand, by investing 7 in this situation, the non-participant obtains 4018 while the participant earns 2210. Thus, the reduction of the participant's payoff ($448 = 2658 - 2210$) is relatively small, while the reduction of the non-participant's payoff ($4269 = 8278 - 4018$) is relatively large. That is, subjects seemed to punish (or behave spitefully toward) the non-participant choosing 7 although no subjects are paired twice or more. On the other hand, it is hard to interpret the "spiteful" behavior as punishment in Session A since the game in this session has just one stage.

Table 5 illustrates the average values of payoff data up to period 5. In Tsukuba, although no dominant strategy exists in Table 4 representing a theoretically predicted payoff table, Table 5 shows that participation is the dominant strategy. In other words, after non-participants have experienced spiteful behavior from participants, non-participants realize that non-participation is not a good strategy and then find that participation is the dominant strategy. That is, evolutionarily stable strategies do not appear, and participation emerges through a transmutation from a hawk–dove game (Table 4) to a game where a dominant strategy outcome is Pareto efficient (Table 5). On the other hand, in the USC experiments, the basic structure of the game is not changed as the rounds proceeded.

Acknowledgement

This research was partially supported by a grant from the Aid for Scientific Research 08453001 of the Ministry of Education, Science and Culture in Japan.

References

Andreoni, J. (1993). "An experimental test of the public-goods crowding-out hypothesis". American Economic Review 83 (5), 1317–1327.

Andreoni, J. (1995). "Cooperation in public-goods experiments: Kindness or confusion?" American Economic Review 85 (4), 891–904.

Cason, T.N., Saijo, T., Yamato, T. (2002). "Voluntary participation and spite in public good provision experiments: An international comparison". Experimental Economics 5, 133–153.

Cason, T.N., Saijo, T., Yamato, T., Yokotani, K. (2004). "Non-excludable public good experiments". Games and Economic Behavior 49, 81–102.

Groves, T., Ledyard, J.O. (1977). "Optimal allocation of public goods: A solution to the 'free rider' problem". Econometrica 45, 783–811.

Isaac, R., Walker, J. (1988). "Group size effects in public goods provision: The voluntary contribution mechanism". Quarterly Journal of Economics 103, 179–200.

Ledyard, J.O. (1995). "Public goods: A survey of experimental research". In: Kagel, J.H., Roth, A.E. (Eds.), The Handbook of Experimental Economics. Princeton University Press, Princeton, pp. 111–194.

Olson, M. (1965). "The Logic of Collective Action: Public Goods and the Theory of Groups". Harvard University Press, Cambridge.

Saijo, T., Nakamura, H. (1995). "The 'spite' dilemma in voluntary contribution mechanism experiments". Journal of Conflict Resolution 39, 535–560.

Saijo, T., Yamato, T. (1999). "A voluntary participation game with a non-excludable public good". Journal of Economic Theory 84 (2), 227–242.

Chapter 86

EXPLAINING THE COMPARATIVE STATICS IN STEP-LEVEL PUBLIC GOOD GAMES

ARTHUR SCHRAM, THEO OFFERMAN and JOEP SONNEMANS

University of Amsterdam, Faculty of Economics and Econometrics, Department of Economics/CREED, Roetersstraat 11, 1018 WB Amsterdam, The Netherlands

1. Introduction

In step-level (a.k.a. provision point) public goods a funding threshold has to be reached before the good can be provided. Large scale examples of these goods are dikes, lighthouses and bridges. Many small scale example exist at the organizational level: some initial investments in organizing the fundraising have to be made before any voluntary provision of a public good is possible (Olson, 1971, p. 22).

We consider the case where contributions exceeding the threshold do not affect the level of provision (i.e., further contributions are redundant once the threshold is reached) and where the contribution decision is reduced to a binary choice. In our set-up n group-members repeatedly face the binary decision whether or not to contribute an endowment c. If s or more of the n players contribute, a public good is provided (i.e., the contribution threshold is reached), yielding a payoff $f(s)$ to each player. Futile and redundant contributions are not refunded. In all of our experiments, we use $c = 0.60$ Dutch guilder ($\approx$ \$0.42) and $s = 3$. Hence if the contribution threshold is reached, the earnings are $f(3) - 60$ for subjects who contributed and $f(3)$ for subjects who did not. If the threshold is not reached, these earnings are 0 and 0.60, respectively.

The step-level public good game differs strategically from the linear public good game. In the one-shot linear public good game the dominant strategy is not to contribute. In the one-shot step-level public good game multiple Nash equilibria exist. An inefficient Nash equilibrium involves nobody contributing. There are efficient Nash equilibria in pure strategies where 3 of the n players contribute (i.e., there are exactly enough contributions to reach the threshold). A rational player maximizing expected value will contribute if and only if she estimates the probability that her contribution will be critical for the provision of the public good to be sufficiently high. To be more precise, she will contribute if and only if she estimates the probability that 2 of the $n - 1$ other group-members will contribute to be higher than $0.60/(f(3) - 60)$.

In various papers, we have studied different aspects of behavior in these games; for references, see Offerman (1997). In this project, we distinguish individual preferences (allowing them to be non-selfish) and individual beliefs about the behavior of others. Both beliefs and preferences are important building blocks for most theories explaining behavior in games. This note provides an overview of the results we have obtained in the project and an interpretation in terms of preferences and beliefs.

Handbook of Experimental Economics Results, Volume 1
Copyright © 2008 Elsevier B.V. All rights reserved
DOI: 10.1016/S1574-0722(07)00086-8

2. Basic Experimental Tools

To enable a direct evaluation of the role of beliefs and preferences in the contribution decisions, we obtain independent measures on both in our experiments. This makes a more detailed testing of theories possible. Measures on beliefs and preferences allow us to attribute experimental treatment effects either to changes in preferences or to changes in beliefs or to both.

According to many social psychologists, different people pursue distinct goals when making decisions that affect others. A preference regarding one's own payoff relative to the payoffs of others is represented by a *value orientation*. An often used classification distinguishes the following value orientations. *Competitors* strive to be better off than others; *individualists* pursue the best for themselves and *cooperators* try to achieve outcomes that are best for both themselves and others. Social psychologists have developed a decomposed game technique that allows one to classify subjects according to their value orientation (Griesinger and Livingston, 1973; Liebrand, 1984). We measured subjects' value orientations before the start of the public good experiment, using the so-called ring test.

In every experimental period, after a subject had made the decision whether or not to contribute to the step-level public good, we measured her beliefs about how many of the other group members would contribute. Truthful and serious reporting was encouraged by using an incentive compatible quadratic scoring rule that rewards accurate expectations (Murphy and Winkler, 1970).

These experimental tools for obtaining measures on preferences and beliefs are discussed and evaluated in more detail in Offerman, Sonnemans, and Schram (1996) and Offerman (1997).

3. Treatments

We consider four changes in the institutions and environment that may affect contribution decisions.
1. We focus on *the value* $f(3)$ of the public good. Do subjects contribute more when $f(3)$ is higher, as often observed in linear public good games (Ledyard, 1995)?
2. We investigate whether individuals contribute less when *group size n* is large, as suggested by Olson (1971).
3. We address the question whether *partners* (fixed groups in a repeated game) contribute more than *strangers* (rematching in each period).
4. We test whether the *framing* of the problem matters. The problem can be posed in the usual 'positive' frame, where individuals decide whether or not to contribute and the public good is provided if and only if sufficient contributions are made. It can also be posed in a 'negative' frame, where individuals decide whether or not to withdraw their contribution and where a 'public bad' occurs (i.e., the public good is not provided) if and only if more than $n - 3$ subjects withdraw. This

Table 1
Summary of treatments

Treatment	Low7s+	High7s+	High5s+	High5p+	High5p−
f	180	245	245	245	245
n	7	7	5	5	5
Mode	Strangers	Strangers	Strangers	Partners	Partners
Frame	Public good	Public good	Public good	Public good	Public bad

Notes. The name of a treatment is mnemonic for its properties: the first part refers to the value of the public good, the number refers to group size, the subsequent letter refers to *s*trangers or *p*artners, a final + indicates that the public good frame was used, a—that the public bad frame was used. The value of the public good f is denoted in Dutch cents.

public bad game is strategically equivalent to the public good game (Sonnemans, Schram, and Offerman, 1998). Uncontrolled evidence suggests that people are more cooperative in games with a positive externality than in games with a negative externality.

Five treatments allow us to evaluate these four issues. Table 1 summarizes their features. In each treatment the game was played for 20 periods.

Figure 1 illustrates the treatment effects by showing the average contribution levels per period for each treatment. The following results are obtained.

1. The effect of a change in *the value* $f(3)$ of the public good can be evaluated by comparing treatments high7s+ and low7s+. Subjects contribute substantially and significantly more when the value of the public good is high than when it is low. The difference between the treatments increases over time, because there is an end-period effect in low7s+ but not in high7s+.

2. Increasing *group size n* while keeping all other parameters constant decreases the average contribution level per individual: subjects contribute consistently and significantly more in high5s+ than in high7s+. Nevertheless, the public good is provided more often when groups are large, because it is easier to reach the threshold with more people (cf. Table 2).

3. Whether subjects play in the *partners* mode or in the *strangers* mode does not systematically affect behavior in our experiments: the difference between high5s+ and high5p+ is negligible and not significant.

4. The *framing* of the problem matters: subjects contribute significantly more in the public good frame (high5p+) than in the public bad frame (high5p−). The difference is negligible in early periods but increases substantially.[1]

---

[1] For a linear public good game, Andreoni (1995) also finds that subjects contribute more in a positive frame than in a negative one. In his experiments, the difference is more or less stable across periods.

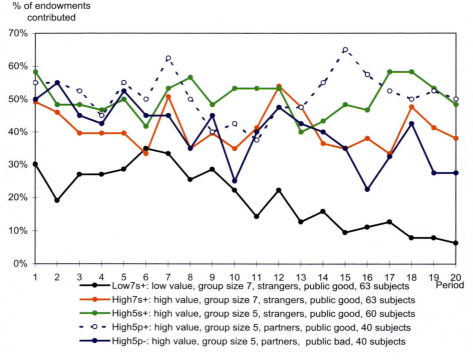

Figure 1. Percentage of contributions per period.

Table 2
Mean contribution per treatment

Subjects	Individualists	Cooperators	All	% periods in which the threshold is reached
Low7s+	16.5% ($n = 49$)	28.5% ($n = 10$)	19.8% ($n = 63$)	18.3%
High7s+	38.7% ($n = 38$)	48.1% ($n = 21$)	41.0% ($n = 63$)	61.7%
High5s+	46.2% ($n = 34$)	60.0% ($n = 19$)	50.4% ($n = 60$)	51.3%
High5p+	43.3% ($n = 18$)	54.1% ($n = 17$)	51.1% ($n = 40$)	50.6%
High5p−	33.9% ($n = 23$)	50.0% ($n = 12$)	39.9% ($n = 40$)	31.3%

Note. The number of individuals is given in parentheses. Low7s+: low value, group size 7, strangers, public good; High7s+: high value, group size 7, strangers, public good; High5s+: high value, group size 5, strangers, public good; High5p+: high value, group size 5, partners, public good; High5p−: high value, group size 5, partners, public bad.

4. Interpreting the Results

How can these treatment effects be explained? A first possibility is that they are an artifact caused by subject types (which we measured through their value orientation). It may be that cooperators contribute more than individualists and that treatment effects are due to different mixtures of these types in different sessions.[2] In fact, in all treatments subjects that are classified as cooperators on the basis of the ring test contribute consistently and significantly more than subjects classified as individualists. Nevertheless, differences between cooperators and individualists cannot account for any of the treatment effects, because the effects carry over to both types of subjects. For example, both cooperators and individualists contribute more when the value of the public good is high than when it is low. Table 2 gives the mean contributions (across 20 periods) per treatment for these two types.

The treatment effects we observed in Figure 1 may be due either to differences in preferences or to differences in beliefs. Subjects may contribute more in a particular treatment because they attribute higher utility to contributing (or more utility to achieving the public good) or because they estimate the probability of being critical higher than in other treatments. Figure 2 focuses on these explanations: it presents logit regression results per treatment.[3] The choice whether or not to contribute is explained by the estimated probability of being critical. In addition, Figure 2 presents the average estimated probabilities of being critical per treatment.

Note that in all treatments a clear positive relationship exists between the estimated probability of being critical and the inclination to contribute. Rational choice theory predicts a step function. If utility is given by expected value, the probability of contributing should go from 0 to 1 when the probability of being critical is estimated to be 0.324 (0.5 for low7s+).[4]

The logit results and the average probabilities presented in Figure 2 allow us to analyze whether observed treatment effects are due to differences in beliefs or in preferences (in the latter case, different contribution decisions are made for the same belief). We do so for the various effects we observed.

1. For any estimated probability of being critical, subjects are more likely to contribute to the public good in high7s+ than in low7s+, while their estimates of being critical are more or less the same on average. Hence, the effect that subjects contribute more when the *value* is high is not a consequence of differences in beliefs but can be attributed to differences in preferences.

---

[2] Overall 61% of our subjects were classified as individualists and 30% as cooperators. The remaining subjects were classified as competitors or could not be classified because their consistency in the ring test was too low.

[3] The exact estimates of the logit equations are presented in Offerman (1997).

[4] Our data show an unexpected result w.r.t. the estimated probabilities of being redundant (the case where the good is provided irrespective of an individual's contribution). Like Caporael et al. (1989), we find that contributions increase with a rise in this probability.

1. For given probability of being critical, the contribution probability is higher if the payoff is higher.
2. The effect of group size is mainly due to a difference in mpc.
3. The mpc is lower in partners than in strangers. For given probability of being critical, the probability of contributing is higher in partners, however.
4. For given probability of being critical, the contribution probability is higher for a public good than for a bad.

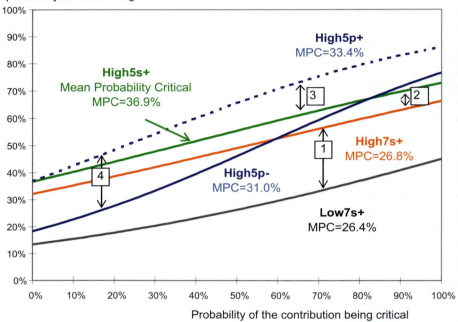

Figure 2. Logit regressions.

2. We observed a decrease in contributions with an increase in *group size*. Figure 2 shows that the estimated probability of being critical is much higher in high5s+ than in high7s+. For any given probability of being critical, subjects are only slightly more likely to contribute in small groups than in large groups, however. We conclude that this effect is better explained by a difference in beliefs than by a difference in preferences.
3. We did not observe an effect of *partners* versus *strangers*. Figure 2 shows that the estimated probability of being critical is lower in the partners condition (high5p+) than in the strangers condition (high5s+). On the other hand, given a probability of being critical, partners are more likely to contribute. These two effects are small and compensate each other.

4. Finally, the difference in contribution level between the *public good* frame and the *public bad* frame seems to be largely due to a difference in preferences. The difference in average beliefs is small and the logit function of high5p+ lies well above that of high5p−.

These experimental results show that both preferences and beliefs play an important role in determining behavior in step-level public good games. Elsewhere, we have studied in more detail how value orientations might affect decision rules and how the interaction between players may affect beliefs in a way consistent with our findings. The following summarizes the results obtained.

For preferences, we consider the subjects with a cooperative value orientation. Their 'other regarding' preferences can be modeled by specific mappings from payoff to utility. We distinguish the following three. First, *material cooperators* attach extra utility to the provision of the public good. Second, *warm-glow cooperators* acquire extra utility from the act of contributing (Andreoni, 1990).[5] Third, *in-group cooperators* obtain additional utility if the good is provided, but only if they contributed. Maximum likelihood results, allowing for differences between individualists and cooperators, favor the warm glow interpretation (Offerman, 1997, pp. 100–103). Moreover, the warm-glow interpretation can explain the result that subjects' preferences in high7s+ and high5s+ are more or less equal, which is hard to rationalize with the material cooperators interpretation (if individuals care for the material welfare of others, they should be more inclined to contribute when the public good accrues to more individuals).

When analyzing the interaction between players, one may follow either a learning (disequilibrium) route or a rational (equilibrium) route. Belief learning models are in the former group of studies. They assume that players update a prior belief about the behavior of others on the basis of observed behavior. In these models, players assume that the distribution of others' behavior is constant in some probabilistic sense. Given their beliefs, they myopically maximize expected utility. On the other hand, equilibrium models assume that players have rational expectations, i.e., their beliefs are consistent with the actual play of the others. One could judge theories on their ability to predict comparative statics, like the ones described above. Unfortunately, the treatment effects can be rationalized by both learning and equilibrium models and can therefore not be used to discriminate between them. (For a discussion, see Offerman, 1997, chapter 2.) Nevertheless, Offerman, Schram, and Sonnemans (1998) compare a quantal response naive Bayesian model (where players update beliefs naively and give noisy best responses) with a quantal response equilibrium model (where players have rational expectations and give noisy best responses). Maximum likelihood results reveal that the naive Bayesian model describes actual choices better than the equilibrium model. Moreover, an analysis of reported beliefs makes clear that there is a systematic updating

---

[5] For linear public goods games Anderson, Goeree, and Holt (1998) show theoretically that evidence of group size effects can be rationalized by allowing for (linear) altruism. This corresponds to our material cooperators. On the other hand, Palfrey and Prisbrey (1998) find no evidence of linear altruism but do find warm glow.

pattern in subjects' beliefs, a pattern that is consistent with belief learning models but not with existing game theoretic models (Offerman, 1997, pp. 132–139).

References

Anderson, S.P., Goeree, J.K., Holt, C.A. (1998). "A theoretical analysis of altruism and decision error in public good games". Journal of Public Economics 70, 297–323.

Andreoni, J. (1990). "Impure altruism and donations to public goods: A theory of warm-glow giving". Economic Journal 100, 464–477.

Andreoni, J. (1995). "Warm-glow versus cold-prickle: The effects of positive and negative framing on cooperation in experiments". Quarterly Journal of Economics 110, 1–22.

Caporael, L.R., Dawes, R.M., Orbell, J.M., van der Kragt, A.J.C. (1989). "Selfishness examined: Cooperation in the absence of egoistic incentives". Behavioral and Brain Sciences 12, 683–739.

Griesinger, D.W., Livingston, J.W. (1973). "Toward a model of interpersonal motivation in experimental games". Behavioral Science 18, 173–188.

Ledyard, J.O. (1995). "Public goods: A survey of experimental research". In: Kagel, J.H., Roth, A.E. (Eds.), The Handbook of Experimental Economics. Princeton University Press, New Jersey.

Liebrand, W.B.G. (1984). "The effect of social motives, communication and group size on behaviour in an N-person multi stage mixed motive game". European Journal of Social Psychology 14, 239–264.

Murphy, A.H., Winkler, R.L. (1970). "Scoring rules in probability assessment and evaluation". Acta Psychologica 34, 273–386.

Offerman, T. (1997). "Beliefs and Decision Rules in Public Good Games – Theory and Experiments". Kluwer, Dordrecht.

Offerman, T., Schram, A., Sonnemans, J. (1998). "Quantal response models in step-level public good games". European Journal of Political Economy 14, 89–100.

Offerman, T., Sonnemans, J., Schram, A. (1996). "Value orientations, expectations and voluntary contributions in public goods". Economic Journal 106, 817–845.

Olson, M. (1971). "The Logic of Collective Action". Harvard University Press, Cambridge, MA.

Palfrey, T.R., Prisbrey, J.E. (1998). "Anomalous behavior in public good experiments; how much and why?" American Economic Review 87, 829–846.

Sonnemans, J., Schram, A., Offerman, T. (1998). "Public good provision and public bad prevention: The effect of framing". Journal of Economic Behavior and Organization 34, 143–161.

Chapter 87

COOPERATION IN VCM EXPERIMENTS: RESULTS USING THE CONTRIBUTION FUNCTION APPROACH

JORDI BRANDTS

Institut d'Analisi Econòmica (CSIC), Barcelona

ARTHUR SCHRAM

CREED, Universiteit van Amsterdam, The Netherlands

1. Introduction

The results we present below stem from a series of experiments we conducted using a new method for collecting data from voluntary contributions mechanism environments. The main virtue of our design is that it makes it possible to collect a very rich set of data. Our results are inconsistent with the hypothesis that contributions are made only by mistake (cf. Palfrey and Prisbrey, 1996) and with simple linear altruism and warm glow models. The type of motivation that our evidence favors is one involving some kind of reciprocal altruism.

2. Description of the Design

The economic model we used in our experiments is most standard in experimental economics; it is the well-known voluntary contributions mechanism (hereafter, VCM) with a linear payoff function, which has been previously used in experiments by, e.g., Isaac and Walker (1988), Isaac, Walker, and Williams (1994), Andreoni (1995), Palfrey and Prisbrey (1996) and Saijo and Nakamura (1996). The VCM has been one of the main tools for analyzing people's motivation in situations in which the behavior consistent with the unique equilibrium leads necessarily to an inefficient outcome.

For a complete description of our design and our procedures see Brandts and Schram (2001). The idea for our design comes from two rather elementary insights. First, richer data may be the key to understanding subjects' behavior more fully. Second, in previous VCM experiments, any subject's decision in any single period has always been for one, given, value of the marginal rate of substitution (MRS) between a public and a private good. For different values of the MRS, subjects' motivations and choices may vary. Hence, one might prefer to obtain information about individual choices for a variety of MRS values.

In our experiments we ask subjects for their contribution to the public good for each of 10 different situations, which correspond to different values of the MRS. We call this set of contribution levels a contribution function. After every subject has reported a contribution function for a period, one MRS is selected to be 'played.' This procedure is closely related to the strategy method, introduced by Selten (1967). Though subjects are not reporting strategies in response to possible moves by other players, they are reporting strategies in response to possible moves by nature (i.e., the selection of an MRS).

The difference between the situations is not only quantitative but also qualitative. For some situations contributing the whole endowment (which is 9 tokens per situation) will be a dominant choice and it will be efficient for all to contribute. This is the case when MRS < 1. For some situations the dominant choice will consist in contributing nothing although it will be efficient to contribute everything. Because we use group size 4, this occurs when $1 <$ MRS < 4. For a third type of situations (MRS > 4) contributing nothing will be both the dominant and the efficient choice. A contribution function will, therefore, give quite a complete picture of subjects' behavior. It will reveal each subject's deviations from the game-theoretic prediction in various circumstances.

We used two variations of our basic design which involved two different configurations of situations. The first of these configurations, called 'asymmetric,' gives a more complete view of behavior while the second, called 'symmetric,' will better reveal a conceptually important feature of our data. In asymmetric the MRS of situation 1 was 0.25. Each situation had an MRS that was 0.5 higher than the previous one. Hence, situation 10 was characterized by MRS $= 4.75$. This design is asymmetric because for only 2 of the 10 situations the dominant strategy prescribes contributing the whole endowment, while for the remaining 8 situations, the dominant strategy behavior consists in contributing nothing. In symmetric configuration, the MRS of situation 1 was 0.1. Each situation had an MRS that was 0.2 higher than the previous one. Hence, situation 10 was characterized by MRS $= 1.9$. Note that the MRS's are symmetric around MRS $= 1$; in this case there are no situations in which contributing nothing is the efficient choice.

3. Results

Figure 1 shows the results aggregated over sixteen experimental sessions with asymmetric run in Amsterdam, Barcelona, Osaka, and Tucson. These data were first reported on in Brandts, Saijo, and Schram (2004). This figure is based on 1920 complete contribution functions, which are the result of the decisions of 192 subjects over ten periods.

The main conclusions presented in the figure are:
1. when a dominant strategy yields efficiency (MRS < 1 or MRS > 4), most subjects follow it;
2. when a dominant strategy yields inefficiency ($1 <$ MRS < 4), many subjects deviate from it by contributing;
3. when a dominant strategy yields inefficiency ($1 <$ MRS < 4), contributions (hence, deviations from the dominant strategy) decline strongly with the MRS.

Ch. 87: Cooperation in VCM Experiments: Results Using the Contribution Function Approach

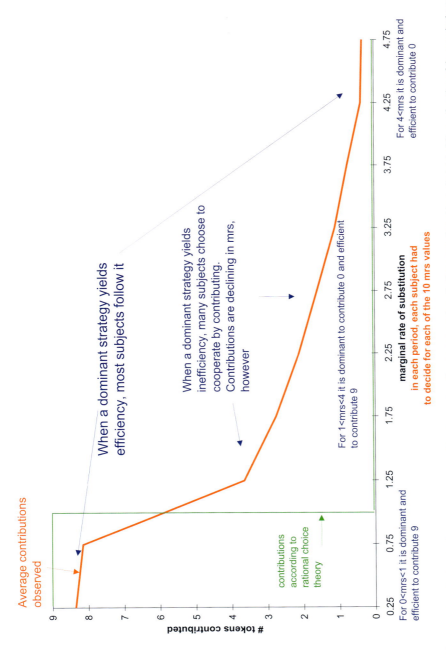

Figure 1. Contributions in the asymmetric cases. This figure gives the average number of tokens contributed (out of a total of 9) as a function of the marginal rate of substitution (mrs). The mrs varies between 0.25 and 4.75. Group size is 4. The data are based on 16 sessions with 3 groups in each session. Data for partners and strangers (8 sessions each) and countries (4 each in Japan, the Netherlands, Spain, and the United States) are aggregated.

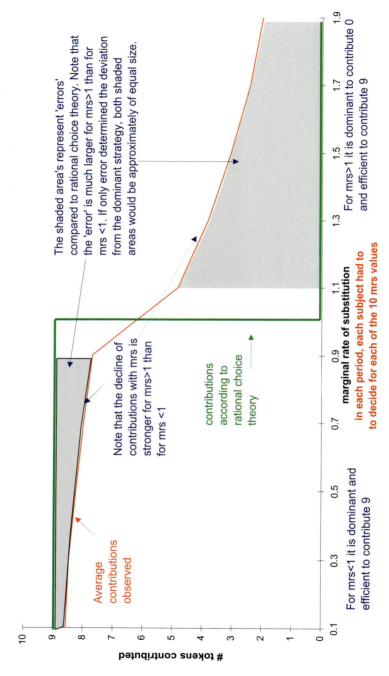

Figure 2. Contributions in the symmetric cases. This figure gives the average number of tokens contributed (out of a total of 9) as a function of the marginal rate of substitution (mrs). The mrs varies between 0.1 and 1.9 and is symmetric around mrs = 1. Group size is 4. The data are based on 4 (partners) sessions with 3 groups in each session. 2 sessions were run in Japan, and 2 in the Netherlands.

Figure 2 presents the aggregate data from experiments with our symmetric design, carried out in Amsterdam and Osaka; it is based on 480 contribution functions from 48 subjects. These data also first appeared in Brandts, Saijo, and Schram (2004). The results from this section can be used to evaluate the notion that subjects' errors depend on the cost of making them. In Figure 2 the payoff cost of an error is the same for situations 5 and 6, for situations 4 and 7, etc. Hence, in Figure 2 the situations to the right of MRS $= 1$ correspond exactly to the same set of costs of errors than those on the right. The main conclusions of our analysis revealed by Figure 2 are that:
1. the error against rational choice theory is much larger for MRS > 1 than for MRS < 1, even though the cost of error is the same on both sides of the MRS $= 1$;
2. the decline of contributions with MRS is stronger for MRS > 1 than for MRS < 1.

Both figures also reveal that when the dominant strategy yields inefficiency, subjects tend to split their endowment between the public and the private good.

4. Some Insights

The main feature of our results, shown in Figures 1 and 2, is that deviations are not symmetric around the MRS of 1, as a simple error hypothesis would predict. This evidence is reinforced by our results about individual behavior which are not reported here. It turns out that a large fraction of individuals contributes substantial amounts over the 10 periods of our experiments, while others contribute almost nothing from the beginning, i.e., both contributing and not contributing reflects subjects' intended behavior to a large extent. We believe that these results show that contributions in the standard VCM environment are not exclusively the results of errors but involve purposive behavior. The generation of solid evidence showing that decision errors cannot be the whole story is, in our view, an important first step towards understanding behavior in environments like this.

Overall, cooperation declines over time. However, in period 10, contributions are still about 16% of endowments in asymmetric and 20% in symmetric. In Brandts and Schram (2001), we present an adaptive interpretation of this behavior in terms of the interaction between individualists and cooperators.

Together, our results suggest that simple warm glow or linear altruism models are unsatisfactory from the empirical point of view. Some kind of reciprocal motivation – which makes people condition their behavior on that of others – is needed to explain our data. Schram (2000) discusses some of the recent models and their ability to explain the relevant evidence.

References

Andreoni, J. (1995). "Cooperation in public-goods experiments: Kindness or confusion?" American Economic Review 85, 891–904.

Brandts, J., Schram, A. (2001). "Cooperation and noise in public goods experiments: Applying the contribution function approach". Journal of Public Economics 79, 399–427.

Brandts, J., Saijo, T., Schram, A. (2004). "How universal is behavior? A four country comparison of spite, cooperation and errors in voluntary contribution mechanisms". Public Choice 119, 381–424.

Isaac, R.M., Walker, J. (1988). "Group size effects in public goods provision: The voluntary contributions mechanism". Quarterly Journal of Economics 103, 179–199.

Isaac, R.M., Walker, J., Williams, A. (1994). "Group size and the voluntary provision of public goods: Experimental evidence utilizing large groups". Journal of Public Economics 54, 1–36.

Palfrey, T.R., Prisbrey, J.E. (1996). "Altruism, reputation and noise in linear public goods experiments". Journal of Public Economics 61, 409–427.

Saijo, T., Nakamura, H. (1996). "The 'spite dilemma' in voluntary contribution mechanism experiments". Journal of Conflict Resolution 39, 535–560.

Schram, A. (2000). "Sorting out the seeking: Rents and individual motivation". Public Choice 103, 231–258.

Selten, R. (1967). "Die Strategiemethode zur Erforschung des eingeschraenkt rationalen Verhaltens im Rahmen eines Oligopolexperiments". In: Sauermann, H. (Ed.), Beiträge zur experimentellen Wirtschatsforschung. J.C.B. Mohr, Tübingen, pp. 136–168.

Chapter 88

VOLUNTARY PROVISION OF PUBLIC GOODS

KENNETH S. CHAN, STUART MESTELMAN and R. ANDREW MULLER

McMaster University

This research addresses the predictions of the conventional model of voluntary public goods provision presented by Bergstrom, Blume, and Varian (1986) which extends the work of Warr (1983). Bergstrom et al. argue that redistributing resource endowments from people who contribute to public goods to other people who contribute to public goods will have no effect on the aggregate contributions to public goods. However, redistribution from non-contributors to contributors will result in an increase in the provision of public goods. A model which incorporates equity theory is used to generate alternative hypotheses for the behavior of individual contributors.

Tests of the predictions of the conventional voluntary contribution model are reported in Chan et al. (1996a). Aggregate contribution data from three-person public goods environments support the neutrality theorem originally presented by Warr when endowments were redistributed among contributors. When endowments are redistributed from non-contributors to contributors, the predictions of Bergstrom et al. that public good provision would increase were observed. The individual contribution data, however, did not support the predictions of the conventional model. Individuals with relatively high endowments tended to under-contribute, relative to the conventional predictions, while individuals with relatively low endowments over-contributed.

Chan et al. suggest that participants in contribution games may bring notions of fairness into the laboratory, which augment the induced payoffs provided by the experimenters. They propose that the average contribution by the group is the measure of the fair contribution. Deviations from this value will induce feelings of guilt or spite and will result in payoffs lower than the induced payoffs reflect. If the induced payoffs are augmented in this way, there is a unique individual Nash equilibrium in which individuals with lower endowments will overcontribute (relative to the predicted Nash equilibrium contribution when the payoff is not augmented) and individuals with higher endowments will under-contribute. Tests of these predictions are reported in Chan et al. (1996a) and later integrated with the psychology literature on equity theory (see Walster, Walster, and Berscheid, 1978) in Chan et al. (1997). If the induced payoffs are augmented as suggested by equity theory, the neutrality theorem generally will not hold and the effect of endowment redistribution on the aggregate level of voluntary contributions to public good provision is indeterminate.

The experimental design used by Chan et al. keeps subjects in the same three-person groups for fifteen decision periods. Chan et al. (1996b, 1997) scramble the membership in the three-person groups after each decision period. The former treatment is called a *partners* treatment, while the latter is a *strangers* treatment. The strangers treatment is

Table 1
Individual and total endowments (and Nash equilibrium contributions)

	Treatment				
	A	B	C	D	E
Low individual endowment	20 (5)	18 (3)	15 (0)	12 (0)	9 (0)
High individual endowment	20 (5)	24 (9)	30 (15)	36 (18)	42 (21)
Total endowment	60 (15)	60 (15)	60 (15)	60 (18)	60 (21)

Note. Numbers in parentheses are the Nash equilibrium contributions for each treatment and individual and total endowments. In all cases the Pareto optimal allocation of tokens to the public good is 31 tokens.

used to keep reputation effects and signaling from influencing the decisions of subjects. Furthermore, the Chan et al. design provides an across-subject effect of endowment redistribution, while the Chan et al. design provides a within-subject effect.

The payoffs induced in these environments result in an interior Nash equilibrium and an interior Pareto optimal allocation. There is no Nash equilibrium consistent with all participants contributing nothing to the public good. The payoffs are consistent with those in Bergstrom et al. and are represented as

$$U = (e - g) + G + (e - g)G,$$

where U is the payoff to an individual, e is the individual's endowment, g is the contribution made to the group good and G is the sum of the contributions to the group good made by all individuals in the group. The endowment distributions and Nash equilibria are presented in Table 1. This is a very different environment than that developed by Isaac, McCue, and Plott (1985) and Isaac and Walker (1988) in which each participant's dominant strategy is to contribute none of his endowment to the public good. The Pareto optimal allocation, however, is for all of his endowment to be contributed to public good provision. In this environment both the Nash equilibrium contributions and the Pareto optimal contributions are in the interior of the endowment set.

Figure 1 shows the mean individual contributions over the fifteen periods when each individual has an endowment of twenty tokens and when two individuals each have endowments of 15 tokens and one has an endowment of 30 tokens. This is a partners treatment. The strong pattern of tight fluctuation around the Nash equilibrium contribution of five tokens in the equal endowment environment is very different from the pronounced decay towards the Nash equilibrium contribution displayed in the linear public goods environments (e.g., see Isaac and Walker, 1988). Regardless of whether the treatment is a partners or a strangers treatment (not illustrated), the aggregate group contributions to public good provision is very close to fifteen tokens. This is consistent with both the conventional behavioral model and the model augmented by the attitudes of fairness which are reflected in equity theory.

Also shown in Figure 1 is the time series of mean contributions by individuals with endowments of 30 tokens and 15 tokens in partners sessions. These show a clear con-

Ch. 88: *Voluntary Provision of Public Goods* 833

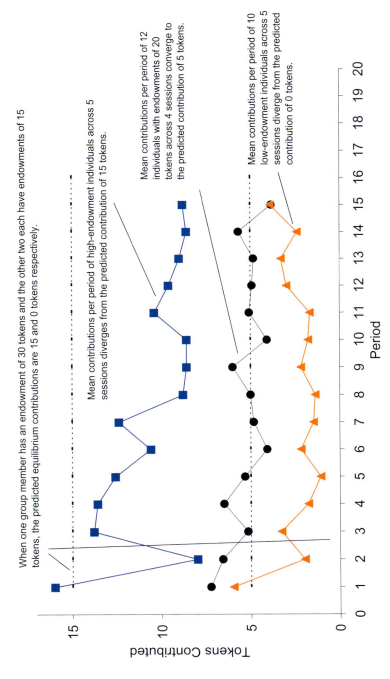

Figure 1. Time series of individual voluntary contributions for public good provision by members of 3-person groups show stability around the predicted contribution when individual endowments are equal but diverge from predicted contributions as endowments are redistributed (for partners treatment).

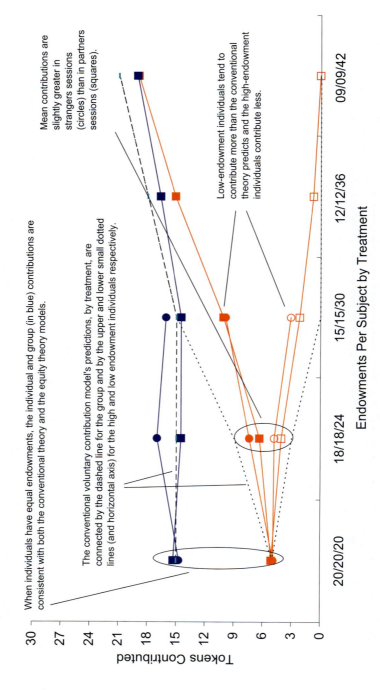

Figure 2. As endowments are redistributed, low-endowment individuals contribute more than predicted by the conventional model and high-endowment individuals contribute less. This behavior is consistent with psychology's theory of equity.

vergence below the Nash equilibrium contribution of 15 tokens and above the Nash equilibrium contribution of 0 tokens predicted by the conventional model for the high and low endowment individuals respectively.

Figure 2 summarizes data from approximately 60 periods for each of five different endowment distributions in the partners treatment and 48 periods for each of the three distributions in the strangers treatment. As the endowment distributions go from 20 tokens to each participant to 9 tokens to two participants and 42 tokens to the third participant in a group, the endowment distributions are becoming increasingly skewed. Regardless of whether participants were interacting with partners or strangers, the average individual contribution in the equal endowment environment supported both the conventional and alternative behavioral models.

As income distribution becomes slightly skewed, some differences in the aggregate contributions across partners and strangers treatments emerge. Individual contributions by high endowment individuals consistently fall short of that predicted by the conventional model while contributions by low endowment individuals exceed the prediction of the conventional model. This pattern persists as the endowment distribution becomes more and more skewed.

Aggregate data from sessions using the partners treatment suggest that the predictions of the conventional model of the voluntary contribution mechanism may be supported. Redistributing endowments among contributors leads to no change in the provision of the public good, but redistributing income from non-contributors to contributors leads to an increase in public good provision. Individual data from these laboratory environments and the strangers environments, however, suggest that some notion of fairness may be brought into the laboratory by subjects. Equity theory leads to Nash equilibrium predictions which are supported by data from these laboratory public goods experiments.

References

Bergstrom, Ted, Blume, Lawrence, Varian, Hal (1986). "On the private provision of public goods". Journal of Public Economics 29, 25–49.
Chan, Kenneth S., Godby, Rob, Mestelman, Stuart, Muller, R. Andrew (1996a). "Spite, guilt and the voluntary provision of public goods when income is not distributed equally". Canadian Journal of Economics 29, S605–S609.
Chan, Kenneth S., Mestelman, Stuart, Moir, Rob, Muller, R. Andrew (1996b). "The voluntary provision of public goods under varying income distributions". Canadian Journal of Economics 29, 54–69.
Chan, Kenneth S., Godby, Rob, Mestelman, Stuart, Muller, R. Andrew (1997). "Equity theory and the voluntary provision of public goods". Journal of Economic Behavior and Organization 32, 349–364.
Isaac, R. Mark, McCue, Kenneth F., Plott, Charles R. (1985). "Public good provision in an experimental environment". Journal of Public Economics 26, 653–670.
Isaac, R. Mark, Walker, James M. (1988). "Group size effects in public goods provision: The voluntary contribution mechanism". Quarterly Journal of Economics 103, 179–200.
Walster, Elaine, Walster, G. William, Berscheid, Ellen (1978). "Equity: Theory and Research". Allyn and Bacon, Boston.
Warr, Peter (1983). "The private provision of a public good is independent of the distribution of income". Economics Letters 13, 207–211.

Chapter 89

INTRINSIC MOTIVATION IN A PUBLIC GOOD ENVIRONMENT

FRANS VAN WINDEN, FRANS VAN DIJK and JOEP SONNEMANS

CREED, University of Amsterdam, Roetersstraat 11, 1018 WB Amsterdam, The Netherlands

1. Introduction

One of the stylized facts of public good experiments is the existence of different types of individuals. Some appear to be more cooperative than others, even though the extrinsic incentives are the same (see Ledyard, 1995). It seems that the reason should, therefore, be searched in variations in the cognitive (beliefs), motivational (interests) and/or emotional (feelings) determinants of behavior. Here, we report on a series of experiments that were designed to shed some light on the impact of the latter two determinants in a public good environment (see van Dijk, Sonnemans, and van Winden, 1997; Sonnemans, van Dijk, and van Winden, 1998). The basic idea driving this research is that individuals may have different intrinsic motivation for contributing to the public good, and that this motivation may be affected by sentiments triggered by the success of the interaction between the individuals involved. Two important socio-psychological concepts are used for the investigation. The first is that of a "social value orientation," which refers to stable preferences of individuals with respect to allocations of payoffs to themselves and an arbitrary other individual. Using the so-called decomposed game technique, psychologists have offered substantial experimental evidence that individuals typically fall into one of the following three categories: "individualists," maximizing payoffs to self; "cooperators," maximizing joint payoffs; or "competitors," maximizing the difference in payoffs to self and other (see, e.g., van Lange et al., 1997). Value orientations have been shown to be predictive for among others, helping behavior. They provide an intrinsic motivation for such behavior, which is of obvious relevance for the private provision of public goods. This was shown by Offerman, Sonnemans, and Schram (1996) for a step-level public good game, where a funding threshold has to be reached for the provision of the good. Using a so-called ring-test to measure social value orientation (Liebrand, 1984), they found that in all treatments subjects classified as cooperators contributed consistently and significantly more than individualists. In the experiments discussed below a similar test is employed. The second concept focused on in these experiments is that of a "social tie." This concept refers to the willingness of individuals to foresake narrowly defined self-interest to support specific others. Key element in the development of ties are the sentiments that individuals have regarding these specific others, which refers to the extent to which they care about the well-being of those others (suggesting a formalization in terms of utility interdependence; see Coleman, 1984). Positive or negative sentiments are formed dependent on whether social interaction is valued positively or negatively (cf. Homans, 1950, 1961;

Handbook of Experimental Economics Results, Volume 1
Copyright © 2008 Elsevier B.V. All rights reserved
DOI: 10.1016/S1574-0722(07)00089-3

Feld, 1981; Fararo, 1989). In a public good game, ties should therefore be expected to depend on the success of the interaction, as measured (for instance) in monetary terms. To establish the existence of a social tie, two orientations need to be measured: the orientation of an individual towards the interests of an arbitrary (generalized) other, and the orientation towards the interests of a specific other. In the experiments this is done by applying the ring-test twice, before the multiperiod public good game (where the other is a randomly selected subject) and at some point during or after the game (where the other was a subject interacted with in all periods of the game). The difference between the two tests is a measure of the tie that has developed. Stability of the value orientation measure was shown by using an individual decision-making experiment instead of the public good game for a control group. Note that the establishment of social ties would suggest that intrinsic motivation is affected by social interaction. By investigating the impact of value orientation on (initial) contributions in the public good game, and the influence of ties on the further interaction with subjects that participants are matched with in that game, these experiments are informative on the important issue of the role played by intrinsic motivation and its dynamics (cf. Kreps, 1997; see also Becker, 1993).

2. Experimental Design

In a ring-test each subject is randomly coupled with an unknown other subject and has to make a number of computerized choices (32 in the experiments) between two "self/other" payoff combinations. Each combination allocates a (positive or negative) amount of money to the decision maker her- or himself and the other subject. All combinations lie on a circle, with the origin as center and the $x(y)$-axis representing the payoffs to self (other), which explains the name of the test. Each allocation of money can be considered a vector. If the preferred allocations for each subject are added, the angle of the resulting vector is a measure of the extent to which the individual cares about other, reflecting the marginal rate of substitution (MRS) between the other's payoff and own payoff; see Figure 1. This test was used to measure a subject's social value orientation – orientation towards an arbitrary other – before the public good game ("pre-test"), and to measure the subject's orientation to her or his partner in the two-person games that were studied ("post-test"). The difference between the post-test and pre-test angles represents the social tie for this subject. For the four-person game investigated in one of the experiments, this form of the ring-test is not practical, as it would result in too many questions and would cost too much time. Therefore, the circle-test was developed. In this computerized test the orientation of a subject towards another subject is measured by only one decision, that is, by having the subject directly choose the preferred point on a circle shown on the computer screen (see Figure 1). In this case the post-test comprised three separate test, one for each of the other group members.

In all experiments subjects were, at the end of each period, informed about the contribution of the other group member(s). When doing the post-test, these individual results

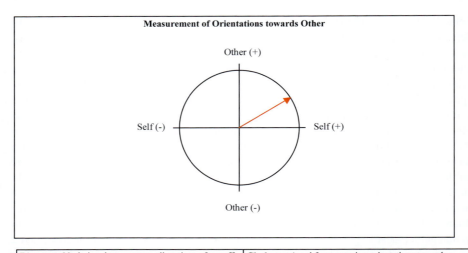

Figure 1.

could still be looked up. No feedback on the choices of others in either the pre-test or the post-test was given during the experiment.

The following public good game was part of all the experiments. Subjects were randomly allocated to groups, which stayed the same for all periods of the game (so-called partners condition). In each period, a subject had to distribute 10 markers over two activities, X and Y. Activity X generated a payoff exclusively for the subject her/himself (private account), whereas activity Y generated a payoff to all group members (public account). For rational subjects that are only interested in their own earnings, the game had an internal subgame-perfect Nash equilibrium where it was a dominant strategy to put 3 (7) markers in the public (private) account, while the Pareto-optimal solution was to put all markers in the public account. Each of the experiments consisted of three parts: (1) pre-test, (2) public good game, and (3) post-test. Subjects got only instructions for the part at hand. Two experiments concerned a two-person public good game: one with 25 and one with 32 periods (to check for the impact of the so-called end-effect).

Ch. 89: Intrinsic Motivation in a Public Good Environment

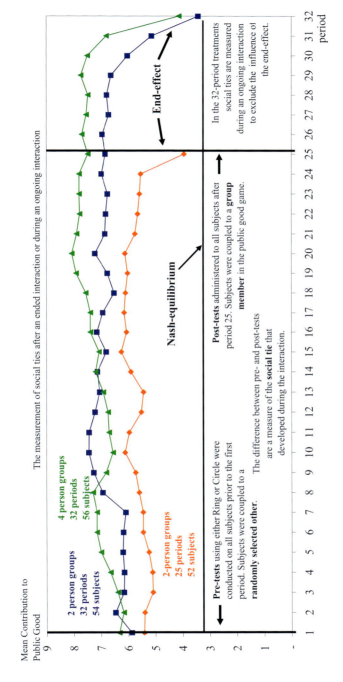

Figure 2.

Table 1
Pre-test and post-test orientation, and correlations of orientation with own contributions to the public good

experiment	Social value orientation (pre-test)			Orientation towards specific other (post-test)			Mean change of orientation	Mean absolute change of orientation
	Negative <-5°	Neutral between -5° and +5°	**Positive** >+5°	Negative <-5°	Neutral between -5° and +5°	Positive >+5°		
2 persons 25 periods	24%	28%	48%	26%	33%	41%	-3.7°	11.4°
2 persons 32 periods	10%	54%	36%	10%	50%	40%	3.3°	9.4°
4 persons 32 periods	2%	51%	47%	8%	44%	48%	-2°	13°

About 50% of subjects are not neutral in orientation, most of them showing a positive orientation towards interest of others

Mean changes in orientations are small, but there are large differences: absolute changes are considerable

Experiment	Correlation pre-test with own contribution in period(s)		Correlation post-test with own contribution in period(s)	
	1	1-5	26	26-32
2 persons 25 periods	.14	.28*	n.a.	n.a.
2 persons 32 periods	.44***	.41***	.27*	.35**

Social value orientation is positively correlated with contributions in first periods

Social tie is positively correlated with contributions after period 25

Note: * significant p<0.10 ** significant p<0.05 *** significant p<0.01

A third experiment concerned a four-person public good game of 32 periods. The post-test (third part) was always after 25 periods. In case of a 32 periods game subjects did not know exactly when the third part would take place. Figure 2 summarizes the design of the three experiments. This figure also shows the development of the average contribution level. We only note here that this level does not show the continuously declining trend that has been regarded as typical for this type of public good game. After an initial increase, contributions stay at a relatively high level, and only decline in the direction of the Nash equilibrium (the dominant strategy for self-interested individuals) in the last two or three periods (end-effect).

3. Main Observations

3.1. Different Intrinsic Motivation for Contributing

As shown by the first three columns in the top-panel of Table 1, on average, around half of the subjects appear to be non-neutral towards the interests of the other in the pre-test (testing social value orientation). The great majority of these subjects show a positive orientation, in the sense that they are willing to sacrifice money to the benefit of an arbitrary other, implying a positive MRS between the other's payoff and own payoff. But, there are also subjects who show a negative orientation (MRS). The predictive nature of these orientations is manifested by the (significant) correlation between the angle in the pre-test and the contribution in the first (five) period(s); see the first two columns in the bottom-panel of the table. Thus, it turns out that the aforementioned findings of Offerman, Sonnemans, and Schram (1996) for a step-level public good game carry over to a continuous public good game. It seems that individuals with different social value orientations, as measured by the ring-test, enter the public good game with a different intrinsic motivation for contributing to the public good.

3.2. Intrinsic Motivation Changes with Social Interaction

On average, the orientation towards the specific other(s) that subjects were matched with in the public good game, as measured by the post-test, does not differ much from the pre-test orientation towards an arbitrary (generalized) other. Orientations appear to be somewhat less neutral, but the mean change of angle is small (circa 3 degrees); see the one but last column in the top-panel of Table 1. This slight drift in orientations obscures developments at the individual level, however. As the last column shows, absolute changes of angle are much larger (about 11 degrees on average). The last two columns of the bottom-panel show that also the post-test angles are (strongly) correlated with the respective subjects' contributions in periods following the test (for the four-person experiment the average of the three post-test angles per subject is taken). These results suggest that intrinsic motivation may change under the influence of the interaction with the specific other(s) in the public good game. The next observation addresses this issue.

3.3. Effect of Success of Social Interaction (Social Ties)

As argued above, differences between the angles in the post-test and pre-test are a measure of social ties. It is expected that the development of ties depends on the success of the interaction in the public good game. For the two-person games, own earnings are selected as indicator of success, whereas for the four-person game, we take the contributions by each of the other group members. Table 2 presents the outcomes of a statistical analysis where the post-test angle is regressed on the pre-test angle and the success indicator. Not surprisingly, social value orientation (the pre-test score) has a substantial impact on the post-test score. However, the success indicator has a significant additional

Table 2
Regressions with orientation towards specific group member after the public good game (post-test) as dependent variable and the social value orientation (pre-test) and own earnings (2-person game) and contributions of specific group members (4-person game) as independent variables

2 person game 25 periods: orientation towards specific other					
Independent variables	B	SE B	Beta	t	Sign. t
Social value orientation	0.832	0.110	0.752	7.574	0.000
Own Earnings periods 21-25	0.039	0.020	0.200	2.013	**0.051**
Constant	-30.127	13.593		-2.216	0.033
Adjusted R-square =0.597					

2 person game 32 periods: orientation towards specific other					
Independent variables	B	SE B	Beta	t	Sign. t
Social value orientation	0.715	0.141	0.564	5.056	0.000
Own Earnings periods 21-25	0.048	0.018	0.283	2.536	**0.015**
Constant	-33.074	14.661		-2.256	0.029
Adjusted R-square =0.484					

4 person game 32 periods: orientation towards specific groupmember					
Independent variables	B	SE B	Beta	t	Sign. t
Social value orientation	0.366	0.086	0.298	4.279	0.000
Contributions by other periods 1-25	0.126	0.025	0.355	5.099	**0.000**
Constant	-15.118	4.536		-3.333	0.001
Adjusted R-square =0.207					

We find a robust positive relation between the success of interaction and the orientation towards specific groupmember

positive effect, suggesting that individuals having experienced an (un)satisfactory interaction with a partner show a tendency to (dis)like this specific other individual. The previous result showed that such changes are predictive of subsequent behavior. Interestingly, whereas in the two-person games the interaction during the last five periods turns out to be particularly important for the success indicator, earlier periods are more important for the four-person game. This stands to reason because subjects may realize that the behavior of a partner is partly a reaction to the behavior of the other group members. Earlier periods are then more indicative of true intentions. Finally, it is noted that changes in orientation are typically not the same for the different partners in the four-person game, since they are dependent on their contributions. This shows that the orientation uncovered by a post-test differs from a social value orientation. Of course, experiences with (many) specific others may affect an individual's social value orientation.

Table 3
Orientations and social ties after a 4-person public good game

type	sign	orientation towards specific others (percentage of pairs)	social ties (percentage of pairs)
symmetric	+ +	29%	10%
	~ ~	0%	5%
asymmetric	+ 0	37%	22%
	+ ~	4%	10%
	0 ~	8%	34%
mutually neutral	0 0	22%	19%

Examples of networks of social ties in 4-person groups after a public good game.

Group for which the provision level of the public good is low: mean contribution per period and subject of 3.7.

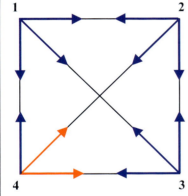

Group for which the provision level of the public good is high: mean contribution per period and subject of 9.9.

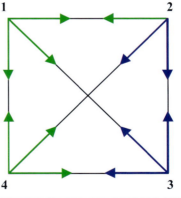

→ Negative tie   → Neutral tie   → Positive tie

Orientations and social ties do not develop harmoniously; even with highly successful interaction mutually positive ties are not guaranteed.

3.4. Group Formation

An important question that can be addressed with our experimental results is whether orientations (measured by the angles in the post-test) and social ties (measured by the difference in the post- and pre-test angles) develop harmoniously among group members. Table 3 presents the observed frequencies of different types of orientations and social ties characterizing pairs of subjects in the four-person game experiment. In only about 20% of the cases, orientations are mutually neutral and social ties are absent. Symmetry is most frequent among orientations (29% of the pairs, all mutually positive), whereas asymmetry is much more common among social ties (66% of the pairs). Apparently, even with equal endowments and payoff functions, individual differences in social value orientation and reaction patterns lead to complex dynamics resulting in very different types of groups in terms of the mutual attractiveness of group members, a major determinant of group cohesiveness. This is illustrated by the figures in Table 3. The left (right) figure shows the social ties network of the worst (best) performing group in terms of mean contributions to the public good (respectively, 3.7 and 9.9 markers). Even with highly successful interaction mutually positive social ties are not guaranteed. These results tone down the suggestion in the literature that bonds (via identification) form easily and lead to cooperative behavior towards group members (see, e.g., Baumeister and Leary, 1995).

4. Conclusions

- Subjects differ in social value orientation as measured in the pre-test. The contributions in the first periods of the public good game are positively correlated to the value orientation.
- The success of social interaction in the public good game influences the orientation towards group members (social ties).
- Subjects in 4-person groups discriminate between group members: a social tie is positively correlated with the contributions of the other. However, most relations are not symmetric. Apparently individual differences in social value orientation and reaction patterns can lead to complex group-dynamics.

References

Baumeister, R.F., Leary, M.R. (1995). "The need to belong: Desire for interpersonal attachments as a fundamental human motivation". Psychological Bulletin 117, 497–529.
Becker, G.S. (1993). "Nobel lecture: The economic way of looking at behavior". Journal of Political Economy 101, 385–409.
Coleman, J.S. (1984). "Foundations of Social Theory". Harvard University Press, Cambridge.
Fararo, T.J. (1989). "The Meaning of General Theoretical Sociology". Cambridge University Press, Cambridge.

Feld, S.L. (1981). "The focused organization of social ties". American Journal of Sociology 86, 1015–1035.
Homans, G.C. (1950). "The Human Group". Harcourt, Brace and World, New York.
Homans, G.C. (1961). "Social Behavior: Its Elementary Forms". Routledge & Kegan Paul, London.
Kreps, D.M. (1997). "Intrinsic motivation and extrinsic incentives". American Economic Review, Papers and Proceedings 87, 359–364.
Ledyard, J. (1995). "Public goods: A survey of experimental research". In: Roth, A., Kagel, J. (Eds.), The Handbook of Experimental Economics. Princeton University Press, Princeton, pp. 11–181.
Offerman, T., Sonnemans, J., Schram, A. (1996). "Value orientations, expectations and voluntary contributions in public goods". Economic Journal 106, 817–845.
Sonnemans, J., van Dijk, F., van Winden, F. (1998). "Group formation in a four-person public good experiment". CREED, University of Amsterdam.
van Dijk, F., Sonnemans, J., van Winden, F. (1997). "Social ties in a public good experiment". CREED, University of Amsterdam.
van Lange, P.A.M., Otten, W., de Bruin, E.M.N., Joireman, J.A. (1997). "Development of prosocial, individualistic, and competitive orientations: Theory and preliminary evidence". Journal of Personality and Social Psychology 73, 733–746.

Chapter 90

THEORETICAL EXPLANATIONS OF TREATMENT EFFECTS IN VOLUNTARY CONTRIBUTIONS EXPERIMENTS

CHARLES A. HOLT

Economics, University of Virginia, Charlottesville, VA 22904-4182, USA

SUSAN K. LAURY

Andrew Young School of Policy Studies, Georgia State University, University Plaza, Atlanta, GA 30303-3083, USA
e-mail: slaury@gsu.edu

1. Introduction

Public goods experiments are notable in that they produce an array of systematic treatment effects that are inconsistent with the predictions of standard game theory. In response, theorists have proposed alternative models designed to explain these interesting (and often intuitive) patterns in the data. This paper surveys several of these models, and compares their predictions with some of the stylized facts that have emerged from laboratory experiments. In these experiments, a fixed number of individuals decide simultaneously how to divide a resource endowment between private consumption and contribution toward a public good that benefits all individuals equally.

Our focus will be on the most common type of experiment, where the value of the public good is a *linear* function of total contributions. The marginal value of the public good relative to that of the private good is often called the MPCR, which refers to the "marginal per-capita return" from investing in the public good. The MPCR is usually specified to be low enough so that it is individually optimal to contribute nothing, but high enough so that it is socially optimal to contribute fully. Therefore, the Nash equilibrium involves no contributions. The prediction of complete free riding is irrespective of (non-critical) changes in the marginal value of the public good, the number of participants, and the number of rounds, as long as this number is finite and known in advance.

The broad data patterns that have motivated the theoretical work are[1]:

(1) On average, contributions to the public good are a significant fraction of total endowment. In most treatments, more than half of all contribution decisions involve "splitting" the endowment between private consumption and contributions to the public good.

---

[1] The evidence for many of these patterns is surveyed in Ledyard (1995). In particular, these patterns may be observed in the results reported in Isaac, Walker, and Williams (1994) and Saijo and Nakamura (1995).

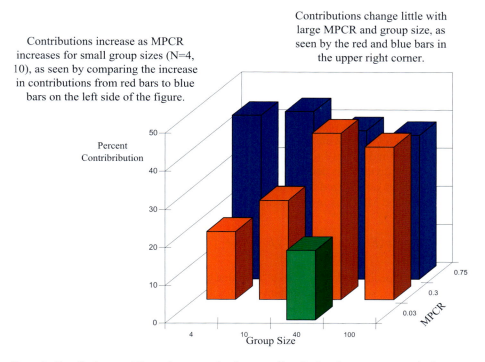

Figure 1. Contribution to public good: percent of endowment. Contributions increase as group size increases for low MPCR and moderate group sizes ($N = 4, 10, 40$), as seen by looking from left to right along the row of red bars.

(2) Increases in the MPCR are associated with higher contributions, especially for small groups (see the increases from corresponding red to blue bars in Figure 1).
(3) An increase in group size is associated with higher contributions, at least for low values of the MPCR and low-to-moderate group sizes (see the left-to-right increases in bar heights on the left side of Figure 1). The group size effect is dominated by the MPCR effect in situations where the product of MPCR and group size is constant. For example, compare the contributions for (MPCR = .75, $N = 4$) shown in the far left blue bar with those for (MPCR = .3, $N = 10$) shown in the second red bar in Figure 1.
(4) In most treatments, average contributions begin at about 50 percent of the endowment, and typically decline over time, although not always monotonically. However, contributions do not disappear, even after as many as 60 rounds.
(5) As the total number of rounds in a session is varied, contributions toward the end of the session are no lower in long time horizon experiments (40 or 60 rounds) than in short time horizon experiments (10 or 20 rounds).

These observations indicate the Nash equilibrium prediction fails in two respects: the level of contributions deviates from the prediction, and average contributions respond to treatments that have no predicted effect in a Nash equilibrium. A number of explanations for these treatment effects have been proposed; these explanations include altruism, error, reciprocity, fairness, adaptive evolutionary responses, and tacit cooperation (perhaps combined with signals). Before discussing these modeling approaches, it is useful to review the Nash predictions.

In the standard linear voluntary contributions game, there are n individuals, each endowed with E tokens that must be divided between private and public consumption. The contribution of individual i to the public good is denoted by x_i, and the total contribution from all individuals is denoted by X. The value of private consumption is $v(E-x_i)$, where v is often normalized to be one. The value of the public good to each individual is mX. Thus the MPCR is m/v. The individual's monetary earnings, π_i, are calculated as:

$$\pi_i(x_i) = v(E - x_i) + mX = vE + (m-v)x_i + m\sum_{j\neq i} x_j. \tag{1}$$

The standard specification is for $mn > v$, so that the social optimum is full contribution, and for $v > m$, so that the dominant-strategy Nash equilibrium is zero contribution when this game is only played once. Notice that the equilibrium level of contributions is independent of non-critical changes in the MPCR and group size. When this game is repeated a finite number of times, the usual backward-induction arguments imply that zero contributions should be expected in all rounds.

The theoretical work to be surveyed is motivated by the dramatic difference between the Nash prediction and the empirical regularities described above. We will consider families of models that incorporate:

(1) generalized preferences to allow for factors such as altruism, spite, and fairness,
(2) noisy decisions caused by unobserved preference shocks or calculation errors,
(3) evolutionary adaptation toward decisions with desirable outcomes, and
(4) cooperative responses to acceptable earnings or to others' contributions.

For each family of models we will present a representative specification and its empirical implications.

2. Generalized Preferences

Perhaps the most obvious (and most often explored) explanation for non-zero contributions is that individuals are willing to give up some of their own earnings to raise others' earnings.[2] This is usually modeled as a utility function that depends on one's

---

[2] Andreoni and Miller (2002) report data for situations in which a subject could unilaterally give up some money in order to increase the earnings of another randomly selected subject. They report that the amount of such giving depends on the price of helping others.

own earnings and the sum (or average) of other's earnings:

$$u_i = U\left(\pi_i, \sum_{j \neq i} x_j\right), \qquad (2)$$

where U is assumed to be increasing in both arguments. This is an old idea in economics that dates back to Edgeworth's (1881) notion of a "coefficient of sympathy." Following Ledyard (1995), most researchers have used a simple, linear specification for the study of voluntary contributions[3]:

$$u_i = \pi_i + \alpha \sum_{j \neq i} \pi_j = C + \bigl(m - v + \alpha(n-1)\bigr)x_i, \qquad (3)$$

where α is an altruism parameter. The constant, C, on the right side of (3) includes all terms that are independent of the person's own contribution, x_i. Notice that the effect of this altruistic concern for the $(n-1)$ others is to introduce the $\alpha(n-1)$ term in (3).

With linear altruism, the utility function in (3) is linear in the decisions, x_i, so that the optimal choice is to contribute all or nothing, depending on the relative size of the altruism parameter. In particular, full contribution is optimal if $\alpha > (v-m)/(n-1)$. Given a distribution of α parameters across individuals, increases in MPCR and group size would tend to increase the probability of full contribution. Heterogeneous linear altruism models explain how the proportion of individuals who contribute responds to these treatment variables, but they cannot explain "splitting."

Levine (1998), for example, uses the results of ultimatum games to estimate a distribution of linear altruism parameters. Unlike public goods games, ultimatum bargaining is a zero-sum game; this may be one reason that Levine concludes that a majority of individuals are characterized by a *negative* altruism parameter, which corresponds to "spite" (Saijo and Nakamura, 1995). Casari and Plott (2003) also find evidence of heterogeneous, linear other-regarding preferences, including altruism and spite as special cases.

Another possible modification of the basic model is to allow individuals to care about the size of their earnings relative to others. Typically these models are framed in terms of reciprocity or fairness. In the altruism model shown in Equation (3), contributions do not depend on the amount that others contribute. However, reciprocity (positive or negative) suggests that contributions are made as an "in-kind response to beneficial or harmful acts" (Fehr and Gachter, 2000a). For example, Croson (2007) reports a strong correlation between contributions and one's expectation of others' contributions, and Fehr and Gachter (2000b) show that cooperators are willing to punish free riders, even when it is costly to do so.

Related models propose that individuals have a taste for fair (or equitable) outcomes. The easiest way to incorporate these preferences is to subtract an inequality measure

---

[3] See, for example, Laury (1996), Anderson, Goeree, and Holt (1998), Goeree, Holt, and Laury (2002b). A non-linear Cobb–Douglas specification is tested in Goeree, Holt, and Laury (2002a).

from the earnings function. For example, Ledyard (1995) uses the squared deviation of one's own payoff from average earnings as a measure of inequality. This type of fairness is symmetric: it is just as bad to be above the average as below. Bolton and Ockenfels (2000) model utility as depending one's own payoff and one's payoff relative to others. This relative payoff function reaches a maximum when earnings are equally divided among all players. Fehr and Schmidt (1999) present a similar model, but incorporate *asymmetric* inequality aversion. The idea is that an equal division is the preferred outcome, however individuals "suffer more from inequity that is to their material disadvantage than from inequity that is to their material advantage" (p. 822).

3. Noisy Decision Making

In a Nash equilibrium, individuals are assumed to choose the decision with the highest expected utility, even if the utility difference is arbitrarily small. Deviations from this ideal can be caused by transitory (unobserved) random shocks to preferences or by random calculation and recording errors. Note that a random shock to preferences could be something like a change in altruistic attitudes, whereas a calculation or recording error corresponds to a type of bounded rationality. In either case, the effects of these random shocks should be less important when earnings differences are great. Indeed, scaling up payoffs in a variety of laboratory experiments tends to reduce the variance of observed decisions, and to move behavior away from the boundaries (Smith and Walker, 1993, 1997).[4]

The effects of random shocks can be captured with probabilistic choice models in which decisions with higher expected earnings are more likely. The most common probabilistic choice model is the logit specification, in which the probability density of choosing decision i is an exponential function of expected earnings, π_i:

$$f(x_i) = K \exp(\pi_i(x_i)/\mu), \tag{4}$$

where K is a constant of integration and μ is an error parameter that determines the degree of rationality. In the limit as μ goes to zero, payoff differences get magnified and probability is concentrated around the decisions with the highest expected payoff.

Anderson, Goeree, and Holt (1998) use this kind of specification to evaluate contributions to the public good.[5] When the earnings are linear in x_i as in (1), then the choice density in (4) is an exponential function of x_i. This combination yields an exponential distribution of contributions (truncated if a maximum contribution is specified). The MPCR determines the effect of one's contribution on one's own payoff, either without

---

[4] To our knowledge, there are no public goods experiments that directly consider the effects of independent changes in the scale of payoffs on the variability of decisions.

[5] This model is an application of McKelvey and Palfrey's (1995) notion of a quantal response equilibrium to the public goods game with a continuum of possible decisions.

altruism, as in (1), or with altruism, as in (3). Hence, the MPCR determines the parameter of the exponential distribution. First consider the intuition for the case of no altruism, where it is an error to contribute anything. The magnitude of the "observed" error is determined by the difference between the marginal values of the private and public goods, $v - m$, which goes down with an increase in the MPCR. As the cost of this "error" decreases, random preference shocks and/or calculation errors are more likely to dominate and result in contribution. A small amount of altruism further reduces the magnitude of the utility cost associated with contributions, and enough altruism may make contributions more likely than not. Goeree, Holt, and Laury (2002a, 2002b) estimate this model, and find that both the altruism and error parameters are significant.

This is an equilibrium model, however, and therefore does not explain the declining time patterns of contributions in early rounds. This brings us to dynamic models of evolution and adjustment.

4. Evolution and Adaptation

Like the error models discussed above, models of noisy evolutionary adjustment involve probability distributions over the set of possible contribution decisions. One difference, however, is that the probabilities change over time in evolutionary models, with high-payoff decisions generally becoming more likely. There are many ways to specify such processes. Miller and Andreoni (1991) propose a particularly simple specification, in which the probability, p_i^t, of making contribution level x_i, is assumed to change in a manner that depends on earnings relative to the average for some population. Let X^t denote the average contribution calculated using the probabilities at time t: $X^t = \sum_j p_j^t x_j$. Then the expected contribution to the public good is nX^t, and the average earnings level for the population is $v(E - X^t) + mnX^t$. The idea behind the replicator dynamic is that any specific contribution, x_i, with an expected payoff above the population average should increase in frequency. Similarly, any contribution below this average should decrease in frequency. The ratio form of the replicator dynamic used by Miller and Andreoni (1991) is:

$$p_i^{t+1} = p_i^t \frac{v(E - x_i) + mnX^t}{v(E - X^t) + mnX^t}. \tag{5}$$

The term on the right is just the previous probability of making contribution x_i times the ratio of the expected payoff for that contribution to the payoff averaged over all contributions.[6]

As long as the process starts out with some dispersion (some positive probability of at least two distinct contribution levels), then the contributions below the average will have

---

[6] The formula used by Miller and Andreoni ignores the effect of the contribution decision on the average itself, and hence, on the mnX^t in the numerator. This simplifying assumption has little effect on the simulations they carried out.

higher expected payoffs than those above the average. Hence, the lower contributions will increase in frequency and the higher contributions will decrease in frequency. This process will eventually drive the average contribution down to the Nash level of zero. An interesting feature of this model is that decay can be quite slow, and the rate of decay in contributions is influenced by MPCR and group size. To see this, note that sufficiently high values of each will result in a high value of the term, mnX^t that appears in both the numerator and denominator on the right side of (5). When the numerator and denominator increase in this manner, the ratio gets closer to 1, which translates into a slow decay of the probabilities. In addition, a high value of either MPCR or group size will reduce the impact of changes in the other parameter on decay rates, which is consistent with the average contribution patterns shown in Figure 1.[7] As Miller and Andreoni note, however, the predictions of their model only depend on the product of group size and MPCR, which contradicts the observation that the MPCR effect tends to dominate the group size effect (stylized fact 3, above).

Anderson, Goeree, and Holt (1997) present a gradient-based model of noisy evolutionary adjustment that can explain a declining pattern of contributions when the Nash equilibrium involves full free riding. Unlike the predictions of Miller and Andreoni's model, the decision-making noise keeps the contributions from falling all the way to zero. They prove that their model is stable for a class of games that includes public goods games, and that the steady-state distribution of decisions is a logit equilibrium determined by (4). When the logit equilibrium distribution is concentrated in the range of relatively low contributions, the average contributions will decline over time.

4.1. Cooperation and Signaling

There are a number of other models that capture some of the dynamic properties of contribution behavior, positing that subjects recognize the potential gains from cooperation. Those models that involve backward-looking behavior typically specify that expectations or preferences are endogenous and evolve based upon observed behavior. In contrast, other models allow more forward-looking behavior, i.e., that individuals consider the effects of their decisions on others' contributions in future rounds.

Some empirical evidence supports the notion that preferences or expectations may evolve over time. Contributions tend to be lower in late rounds of a session than in early rounds, and contributions by experienced participants are typically lower than by inexperienced participants. One explanation for these patterns is that subjects are learning, but the issue is what is being learned. One possibility is that they are learning to use

---

[7] The implications of the Miller and Andreoni model are quite specific to the ratio structure that they use. It is straightforward to specify evolutionary models, even with a replicator dynamic, that do not produce such nice predictions. For example, in a "difference form" of the replicator model, the change in the probability associated with a specific contribution would be proportional to the difference between the expected payoff for that contribution and the average contribution. Notice that the mnX^t terms would cancel in taking the difference, so that the rate of decay would not depend on MPCR or group size.

a dominant strategy. Another possibility is that they are learning what to expect from others, which may affect their attitudes toward others' earnings.[8] In a post-experiment questionnaire performed by Laury, Walker, and Williams (1995) several subjects expressed frustration over the lack of cooperation by other group members. A study by van Dijk, Sonnemans, and van Winden (2002) tested attitudes toward others both before and after a 25-round public goods game. They found that attitudes changed, and the direction of this change depended upon the results of the public goods game.

Brandts and Schram (1996) propose a model in which a subset of the subjects is "cooperative gain seekers." These subjects contribute (and forego the benefit of private consumption) if they believe total contributions to the public good (by all "cooperative" subjects, including themselves) will be high enough so that earnings will be higher than if no cooperative players contribute. These cooperative gain seekers will contribute only if they expect enough others to do so as well. Their model is backward-looking in that the cooperative gain seekers have prior beliefs about the number of others of this type. These beliefs evolve over time, based up observed contributions. Declining contributions throughout the experiment would be observed if cooperative gain seekers systematically over-estimate the number of others of this type in their group and reduce contributions in response to observed (lower-than-expected) contributions.

From this type of model in which expectations evolve based on past behavior, it is a small logical step to a forward-looking model. If subjects believe that others' future decisions are based in part upon observed contributions in previous rounds, it may be worthwhile to contribute in early rounds to lessen the decline or to encourage others to contribute. This is the basis of an earlier model put forth by Isaac, Walker, and Williams (1994). The flavor of their model is very similar to that of Brandts and Schram (1996), but it includes a forward-looking component. Subjects are willing to forego current private consumption in order to signal a willingness to contribute to the public good in the upcoming round. They will undertake this signal if future earnings are at least as great as if no one contributes anything to the public good (the Nash equilibrium). However, because subjects consider the impact of their decisions only one round in the future, the time-horizon of the experiment is predicted to have no impact on decisions. Laury (1996) generalizes this model so that subjects consider the impact of their contributions over all remaining rounds of the experiment. In this setting, contributing is more attractive with a longer time horizon, so contributions are expected to be lower late in an experimental session, when there are fewer rounds remaining.

In each of these models, the net cost of contributing in the current round, $(v - m)x_i$, is lower with an increase in MPCR, thus contributions are expected to increase with an increase in MPCR.

---

[8] Rabin (1993) argues that preferences in games are affected by others' prior actions.

Table 1
Predicted treatment effects from classes of models

	MPCR	Group size	Time	Splitting
Nash	0	0	0	No
Heterogeneous linear altruism[a,b]	+	+	0	No
Decision error[c]	+	0	0	Yes
Decision error (with altruism)[c]	+	+	0	Yes
Evolutionary (ratio-replicator) dynamic[d]	+	+	−	Yes
Forward-looking signaling[a]	+	0	−	Yes
Cooperative gain seeking[e]	+	0	−	Yes

[a]From Laury (1996).
[b]From Ledyard (1995).
[c]From Anderson, Goeree, and Holt (1998).
[d]From Miller and Andreoni (1991).
[e]From Brandts and Schram (1996).

5. Final Observations

Aart-3pt The main qualitative predictions of the alternatives to the Nash model are summarized in Table 1. All of these capture the most prominent feature of the data, the MPCR effect. One way to pick up the group size effect is to add altruism. In addition, Miller and Andreoni's ratio-replicator dynamic predicts some interesting non-linearities (a high value of either group size or MPCR will reduce the effect of changing the other). The typically observed pattern of declining contributions can be explained by dynamic models, for example, evolution, evolving preferences and expectations, or signaling in an attempt to alter others' behavior.

The various approaches listed in Table 1 are not necessarily mutually exclusive. It is likely that many of the key elements (for example, altruism, error, learning, endogenous preferences, and signaling) are present in the laboratory. A good model will select the most important of these factors and ignore the others (or include them in a noise terms). The best such models can only be determined from carefully designed experiments coupled with econometric work that estimates parameters representing components of alternative models.

Acknowledgement

This work was funded in part by the National Science Foundation (SBR-9617784 and SBR-9753125).

References

Anderson, S., Goeree, J., Holt, C. (1997). "Stochastic game theory: Adjustment to equilibrium under bounded rationality". Working paper, University of Virginia.

Anderson, S., Goeree, J., Holt, C. (1998). "A theoretical analysis of altruism and decision error in public goods games". Journal of Public Economics 70 (2), 297–323.
Andreoni, J., Miller, J. (2002). "Giving according to GARP: An experimental test of the consistency of preferences for altruism". Econometrica 70 (2), 737–753.
Bolton, G.E., Ockenfels, A. (2000). "ERC: A theory of equity, reciprocity, and competition". American Economic Review 90 (1), 166–193.
Brandts, J., Schram, A. (1996). "Cooperative gains or noise in public goods experiments: Applying the contribution function approach". Working paper, University of Amsterdam.
Casari, M., Plott, C. (2003). "Decentralized management of common property resources: Experiments with a centuries-old institution". Journal of Economic Behavior and Organization 51 (2), 217–247.
Croson, Rachel (2007). "Theories of commitment, altruism and reciprocity: Evidence from linear public goods games". Economic Inquiry 45, 199–216.
Edgeworth, F.Y. (1881). "Mathematical Psychics". C. Kegan Paul and Co., London.
Fehr, E., Gachter, S. (2000a). "Fairness and retaliation: The economics of reciprocity". Journal of Economic Perspectives 14 (3), 159–181.
Fehr, E., Gachter, S. (2000b). "Cooperation and punishment in public goods experiments". American Economic Review 90 (4), 980–994.
Fehr, E., Schmidt, K. (1999). "A theory of fairness, competition, and cooperation". Quarterly Journal of Economics August, 817–868.
Goeree, J., Holt, C., Laury, S. (2002a). "Private costs and public benefits: Unraveling the effects of altruism and noisy behavior". Journal of Public Economics 83 (2), 255–276.
Goeree, J., Holt, C., Laury, S. (2002b). "Incentives in public goods experiments: Implications for the environment". In: List John, de Zeeuw Aart, (Eds.). Recent Advances in Environmental Economics, in press.
Isaac, R.M., Walker, J., Williams, A. (1994). "Group size and the voluntary provision of public goods: Experimental evidence utilizing large groups". Journal of Public Economics 54, 1–36.
Laury, S. (1996). "Experimental studies on the voluntary provision of public goods". Unpublished doctoral dissertation, Indiana University.
Laury, S., Walker, J., Williams, A. (1995). "Anonymity and the voluntary provision of public goods". Journal of Economic Behavior and Organization 27, 365–380.
Ledyard, J. (1995). "Public goods: A survey of experimental research". In: Kagel, J., Roth, A. (Eds.), The Handbook of Experimental Economics. Princeton University Press, Princeton, NJ.
Levine, D. (1998). "Modeling altruism and spitefulness in experiments". Review of Economic Dynamics 1 (3), 593–622.
McKelvey, R., Palfrey, R. (1995). "Quantal response equilibria for normal form games". Games and Economic Behavior 10, 6–38.
Miller, J., Andreoni, J. (1991). "Can evolutionary dynamics explain free riding in experiments?" Economics Letters 36, 9–15.
Rabin, M. (1993). "Endogenous preferences in games". American Economic Review 83, 1281–1302.
Saijo, T., Nakamura, H. (1995). "The 'spite' dilemma in voluntary contribution mechanism experiments". Journal of Conflict Resolution 39 (3), 535–560.
Smith, V., Walker, J. (1993). "Monetary rewards and decision costs in experimental economics". Economic Inquiry 31, 245–261.
Smith, V., Walker, J. (1997). "Monetary rewards and decision costs in experimental economics: An extension". Working paper, Indiana University.
van Dijk, F., Sonnemans, J., van Winden, F. (2002). "Social ties in a public good experiment". Journal of Public Economics 85 (2), 275–299.

PART 6.2

COMMITTEES AND VOTING GROUPS

William P. Bottom, Ronald A. King, Larry Handlin and Gary J. Miller, "Institutional Modifications of Majority Rule"

Rick K. Wilson, "Endogenous Properties of Equilibrium and Disequilibrium in Spatial Committee Games"

Rick K. Wilson, "Structure Induced Equilibrium in Spatial Committee Games"

Thomas Rietz, "Three-way Experimental Election Results: Strategic Voting, Coordinated Outcomes and Duverger's Law"

Joep Sonnemans and Arthur Schram, "Participation Game Experiments: Explaining Voter Turnout"

Chapter 91

INSTITUTIONAL MODIFICATIONS OF MAJORITY RULE

WILLIAM P. BOTTOM and RONALD A. KING

John M. Olin School of Business, Washington University in St. Louis

LARRY HANDLIN and GARY J. MILLER

Department of Political Science, Washington University in St. Louis

1. General Introduction

Because institutions impact policy choices, people have preferences about institutions. Institutions are themselves the result of past negotiations among players who anticipate (to various degrees) the impacts of their institutional choices on policies (Knight, 1992).

For that reason, institutions and preferences are hopelessly confounded with the world of politics. Starting with data about institutional variation and variation in policy outcomes, it is impossible to make any hard and fast inferences about the impact of institutional features on policy outcomes. Do the states with a line-item veto spend less on certain budget categories because of the line-item veto, or because those states have electorates that prefer both the line-item veto and those expenditure patterns? Disentangling cause, effect, and spurious correlation can be virtually impossible with natural data.

Experiments are uniquely suited for examining institutional effects.[1] The experimenter can hold preferences constant and randomly assign subjects to treatments distinguished only by variations in institutional rules; resulting differences in behavior may be ascribed to the institutional differences with a degree of confidence that would be impossible in natural political settings.

This is especially true of legislative institutions. Legislatures are few in number, and each legislature's combination of institutional rules tends to be the unique result of a long path-dependent history of conflict and negotiation.

In analyzing majority rule legislatures, the problem of instability is fundamental. The instability of simple majority rule springs from the superfluity of decisive coalitions. Following Plott (1976), we can say that a coalition is decisive for alternatives **x** and **y** if $xP_i y$ for every member of the coalition implies $xP_s y$, where P_i is the normal preference ranking for individuals and P_s is the social preference. Simple majority rule can be defined as a social choice mechanism in which every simple majority is decisive for every pair of choices; any time every member of any simple majority prefers x to y,

---

[1] For an analysis of experiments testing various solution concepts for simple majority rule, see Eavey (1991).

society must rank x over y. Instability exists when some majority prefers some y to any possible x.

Many democratic institutions have reduced instability by limiting the number of decisive coalitions. In every legislature that we are aware of, there are institutional rules (which we will shortly illustrate) that deny certain majority coalitions the ability to enforce some (or any) of their preferences. That is, there are some majority coalitions that cannot enforce a social preference of x over y, even when every member of the coalition prefers x over y. This may have the effect of increasing the stability of the institution; if a majority prefer y to x, but cannot enforce that preference, then x will be undominated – i.e., an element of the core (Hammond and Miller, 1987). Stability is created by limiting the number of coalitions that can enforce change.

This paper will present experimental evidence of the effect of institutional rules that limit the number and range of decisive majority coalitions.[2] The first institutional feature having this effect is agenda control. Others include supermajority requirements, a veto, and bicameralism. All have the potential to create a core in a setting where simple majority rule – operating on the same profile of preferences – would be unstable.

The results presented in this paper suggest that legislative rules do matter. Holding preferences constant, outcomes vary based on allocation of agenda control, supermajority rules, executive veto and bicameralism. Typically, the impact of these rules is due to their effect on dominance relations: by making some majority coalitions non-decisive, they tend to create undominated outcomes that guide the process of coalition formation in experimental committees.

2. Agenda Control

Rules that limit the ability of voters to bring proposals forward for a vote may have the effect of disempowering some majority coalitions.[3] If legislation dealing with taxes must originate in the House Ways and Means Committee in order to proceed to the floor of the House of Representatives for a vote, then a simple majority coalition that does not include a majority of the Committee is not decisive. The majority of House members may be willing to vote to eliminate the oil and gas depletion allowance, but unable to bring the proposal to the floor to enforce their wishes. Do these limits on agenda control have an impact on outcomes?

2.1. One-dimensional Agenda Control

Romer and Rosenthal (1977) concerned themselves with the effect of an agenda setter on the decisions of a group of voters having single-peaked preferences in a single di-

---

[2] In response to Tullock's (1981) query, "why so much stability?," a large literature on institutional sources of majority rule stability emerged, often building from Shepsle (1979).

[3] Early literature on agenda control was influenced by Levine and Plott (1977) and Romer and Rosenthal (1977).

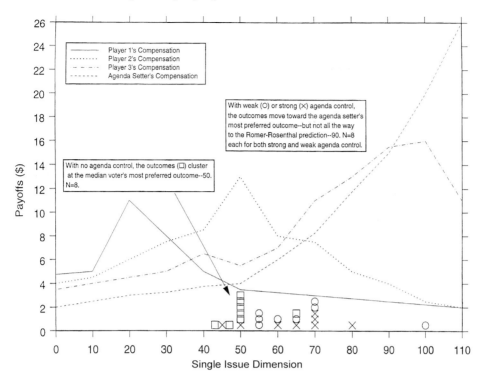

Figure 1. One-dimensional agenda control with monopolistic agenda setting (Eavey and Miller, 1984).

mension. Given a status quo not at the median voter's most preferred outcome, there would be a set of alternatives that was majority-preferred to the status quo. They predicted that the agenda setter will impose his most preferred outcome from the set of alternatives that beat the status quo.

Technically, however, in this same setting, every alternative lying in the policy space between the median voter's most preferred alternative and the agenda setter's most preferred alternative would be a core alternative. The median voter would prefer to move toward her most preferred alternative, but would lack the agenda power to make the proposal. The agenda setter would prefer to move toward his most preferred alternative, but would lack the votes to enforce such a move if offered.

Eavey and Miller (1984) tested the influence of monopolistic agenda setting in three-voter committees. The single-peaked payoffs for Players 1, 2, and 3 are shown in Figure 1.

A fourth player, the agenda setter, had no vote, but had differing degrees of influence over the agenda. Since the agenda setter's payoff increased monotonically to the right, the agenda setter's most preferred alternative from among the set that dominate the status quo is just to the left of 90.

With no agenda control, the agenda setter could make informal suggestions, but any voter was allowed to bring any number of proposals to the floor for a vote. With weak agenda control, the agenda setter was allowed to bring multiple proposals for a vote until one succeeded; only the agenda setter could bring proposals to the floor.

With strong agenda control, only the agenda setter was allowed to introduce alternatives for a vote against the status quo, and the agenda setter was allowed to make exactly one such proposal. In this case, the agenda-control game is essentially an ultimatum game between the agenda setter and the median voter. The median voter has no credible threat to vote against a proposal to the left of 90; so outcome 90 was the unique subgame perfect equilibrium of the game. With strong agenda control, that outcome is the only subgame perfect equilibrium.

However, Eavey and Miller found that the outcomes covered the entire range from the median voter's most preferred outcome to the agenda setter's most preferred outcome. The outcomes were not clustered toward the agenda setter's preferred end of the core, contrary to Romer and Rosenthal's prediction. Even with strong agenda control, median voters were able to negotiate outcomes that were likely to be halfway between the Romer–Rosenthal prediction and the median voter's preferred outcome.

Miller and Stengel, in previously unpublished experiments, replicated the Eavey and Miller experiments using sophisticated, experienced "stooges" as either the median voter or the monopolistic agenda setter. They found, once again, that the entire range of outcomes in the core were accessible, depending on the relative bargaining ability and experience of the agenda setter and the median voter. They tended toward the agenda-setter's preferred outcome when the sophisticated player was the agenda setter, and toward the median voter's most preferred outcome when the sophisticated player was the median voter.

The first experiments on agenda control in two-dimensional majority rule voting were done by Kormendi and Plott (1982). The experiments were replications of the five-person open agenda experiments used in Fiorina and Plott (1978). In this setting, Player 2 is at the intersection of the contract curves between two other pairs of players, making Player 2's most preferred alternative the core (Plott, 1967). Fiorina and Plott (1978) had demonstrated that, with these preferences, the core was an excellent predictor of simple majority rule committee decision-making. In particular, Players 3 and 4, at some distance from the core, did not do well at all.

Kormendi and Plott then made the same disadvantaged Players 3 and 4 the monopolistic agenda setters in subsequent replications. Any committee decision had to be proposed by the agenda setter before being voted on by the committee, as in the Eavey–Miller experiments. This has the effect of expanding the core to a line segment extending from Player 2's ideal point to the monopolistic agenda setter's most preferred outcome.

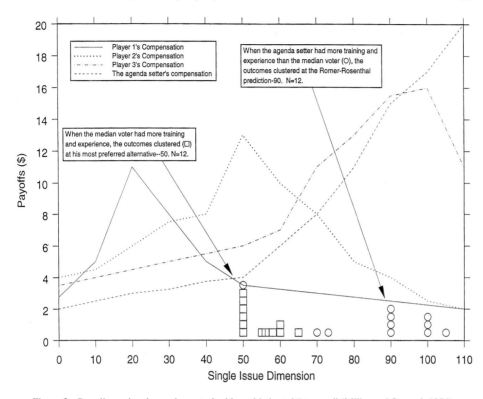

Figure 2. One-dimensional agenda control with sophisticated "stooges" (Miller and Stengel, 1986).

As Figure 3 shows, the effect of this rule was striking. The outcomes were no longer clustered around Player 2's most preferred outcome, but roughly matched the core, in each case.

2.2. Decentralized Agenda Control

In the case of the one-dimensional experiments and the Kormendi–Plott experiments, the design was one for which there was already a core, even with simple majority rule. In the Kormendi and Plott experiments, for example, Player 2's ideal point was a core, even in the simple majority rule game with no agenda control. The effect of agenda control was to expand the core. In Figure 4, on the other hand, there is no simple majority rule core. Every possible outcome is dominated by some other outcome which preferred by some majority coalition.

Using these preferences, Eavey and Miller (1995) examine the effect of limited, or decentralized agenda control. That is, one actor is given monopolistic agenda control over one dimension, while a different actor is given monopolistic agenda control over

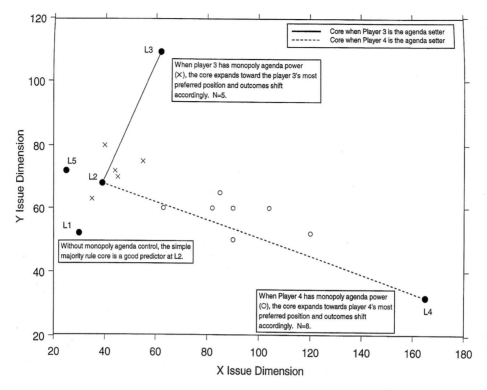

Figure 3. Two-dimensional agenda control (Kormendi and Plott, 1982).

a second dimension. If alternatives **a** and **b** differ on their values in the X dimension, then $\mathbf{a}P_s\mathbf{b}$ only if there is a majority coalition that includes the agenda setter in X. Otherwise, a majority coalition is not decisive for the ranking of the two alternatives. Similarly, a coalition can only be decisive for alternatives that differ in their Y values if it is a majority coalition that includes the Y agenda setter.

In general, then, this kind of decentralized agenda control will induce a core whenever the agenda setters have preferences in the dimensions that are sufficiently removed from the preferences of the median voters in their dimensions (Miller and Hammond, 1990). That is, it is the opposition between agenda setters and median voters that creates undominated regions.

In Figure 4, for example, when Player 2 is the agenda setter for the Y dimension and Player 3 is the agenda setter for the X dimension, then the triangular region given by their ideal points and the point Z is the core. These two agenda setters have unrepresentative preferences in the dimensions they control.

The alternatives shown by ∗ indicate the outcomes selected when the agenda is controlled in this way. Figure 4 reveals that the outcomes chosen were almost entirely

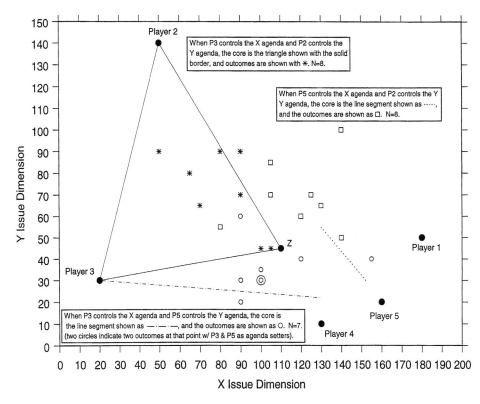

Figure 4. Decentralized two-dimensional agenda control (Eavey and Miller, 1995).

undominated while the coalition of Players 1, 4, and 5 might prefer to move to the south-east, their preferences were blocked by the agenda setters wanting to move to the north and west, respectively.

By shifting agenda-setters, the set of undominated outcomes is altered. When Player 5 is given agenda control for the Y dimension, while Player 3 retains agenda control for the X dimension, the core shifts to a portion of the contract curve between Players 3 and 5 (as shown in Figure 4). Because the contract curve between the agenda setters is a median line, any point not on the contract curve can be upset by a logrolling coalition that includes both agenda setters. The core consists of that portion of the 35 contract curve to the left of Player 4's ideal X-coordinate ($X = 130$) because Player 4 is the median voter along the X dimension. As Figure 4 reveals, the eight outcomes selected by the experimental committees in this case moved on average to the south and east, compared to those in the previous treatment.

The final treatment made Player 2 the Y agenda setter and gave Player 5 agenda control in the X dimension. Once again, the contract curve between the agenda setters was a median line, and the core consisted of a portion of that contract curve. Here again, the outcomes shifted, this time to the right. While outcomes approached the 25 contract curve in this case, they did not move particularly close to that portion of the contract curve that defined of the core. Subsequent experiments (Bottom, Eavey, and Miller, 1996) with this design kept Players 2 and 5 as the agenda setters but varied the status quo. This research indicated that committees were reluctant to form and reform coalitions in the way that would be required to arrive at the core from some status quo points; consequently, the location of the status quo influenced which section of the 25 contract curve was reached in one coalitional negotiation.

Overall, the outcomes shifted significantly from one assignment of agenda control to another. Shifting the location of agenda control from a member with extreme to one with moderate preferences altered the core, and experimentally achieved outcomes tracked the core. While agenda control had policy implications, it also had distributional implications. Players assigned a certain player number received significantly higher payoffs if they had agenda control than those who were assigned the same role without agenda control (Eavey and Miller, 1995). Even when agenda control was limited to only one of two policy dimensions, agenda control was definitely a prize worth having.

3. Extraordinary Majorities and the Veto

Other institutional features, besides agenda control, may create undominated outcomes by limiting the number of decisive coalitions. The most obvious case is the executive veto. This was investigated by King (1994).

The potential influence of a veto player is shown in Figure 5. The point E indicates the executive's ideal point; the other seven points are legislators' ideal points. Each of the actors has a payoff function that falls off as a function of Euclidean distance from the ideal point. This implies that the contract curves between each pair of voters is a straight line. A contract curve that has a majority of voters on or to either side of the line is called a median line. In a simple majority rule game, some majority would always prefer to move to a median line from any point off the median line. Since the median lines do not all cross at a single point in Figure 5, there is no majority rule core in this game.

In the same setting, when the executive has the right to veto a decision (with no possibility of a veto-override) the core consists of the darkened line segment extending southwest from E. Any point off of this contract curve can be upset by a coalition that consists of the executive, Player L4, and three more legislators that would prefer to be on the contract curve rather than at any point off of it. The core stops at the median line between L1 and L5 because there exists an executive-led coalition of four voters that would prefer some point on the line to anything to the southwest of it. The exec-

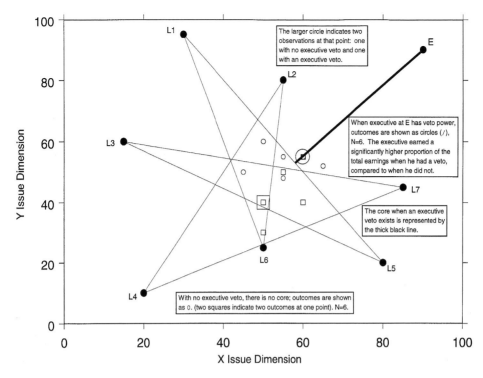

Figure 5. Simple majority with and without executive veto (King, 1994).

utive's ideal point is part of the core because there is no possibility of a veto-override coalition.[4]

Figure 5 shows the outcomes for the simple majority rule games with and without a veto. The results show that the executive earned a significantly higher proportion of the total earnings when he had a veto.

Requiring an extraordinary majority may also create undominated outcomes, once again by limiting the decisive majority coalitions. Greenberg (1979) has shown that in two-dimensional space, there will always be a core if the only decisive coalitions are majority coalitions greater than 2/3 of the voting population. For example, with seven voters, there must always be undominated outcomes when only coalitions of five voters or more are decisive – i.e., when all four-person coalitions are judged non-decisive.

---

[4] If the executive's ideal point is centrally located with regard to the legislature's ideal points, then it may well be a unique core. If the executive's ideal point is not centrally located, then other points may be in the core, as in Figure 5. See Hammond and Miller (1987).

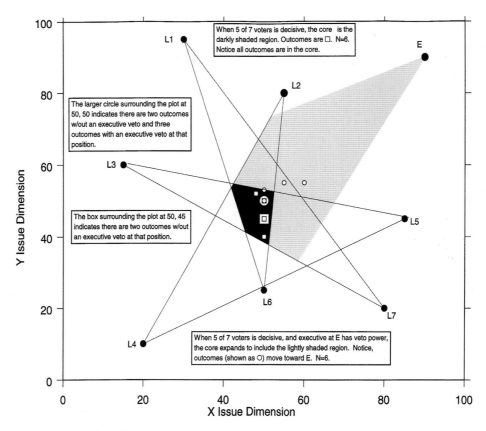

Figure 6. Super majority with and without executive veto (King, 1994).

With this supermajority requirement, the core of the seven-person game is shown as the heavily darkened region in Figure 6, as shown in King (1994). This region is the intersection of the Pareto optimal sets for all five-legislator coalitions.

The interaction of the executive veto with the supermajority rule expands the size of the core considerably, as shown by the lighter shaded region in Figure 6. In this case, the core is the intersection of the Pareto optimal sets for all coalitions that consist of five legislators and the executive.

The core as a solution concept works very well for the supermajority rule experiments, as shown by the squares in Figure 6. The bargaining position of the veto-empowered executive once again tugs the outcomes slightly toward the executive's ideal point in those experiments in which the executive has a veto (shown with a small circle). While the spatial clusters of the two sets of experiments are not far apart, they are distinct enough that once again the executive was able to command a higher proportion of the total committee payoffs in those experiments in which he wielded the veto.

As in experiments with agenda power, the executive veto power makes some simple majority coalitions non-decisive. These institutional rules do not make either the veto-empowered executive or the agenda setter a dictator; but it does give them a significant degree of bargaining power that is reflected in the distribution of payoffs. No coalition that does not include the executive has the authority to enforce its choices.

4. Bicameralism

The executive veto is an example of divided government; affirmation by two institutions is required for action instead of one. Bicameralism resembles the executive veto, except that both institutions operate on the basis of majority rule.

While each chamber of a bicameral legislature operates with majority rule, the membership of the legislature taken as a whole does not operate by majority rule. In the U.S. Congress, for example, a majority of 300 members of Congress is not decisive if it does not include both 218 members of the House and 51 members of the Senate. As a result, any legislature divided into two mutually exclusive and collectively exhaustive chambers is much more likely to have a core than the identical legislature operating with simple majority rule (Hammond and Miller, 1990).

For example, examine Figure 7, which shows the preferences for six actors over five alternatives. The status quo alternative is E. With simple majority rule, there is no undominated alternative. In particular, outcome A loses to alternative D by the coalition of Players 3, 4, 5, and 6. Outcome D loses to alternative C by a coalition of Player 1, 2, 3, and 5.

Consequently, if either of these majority coalitions is deprived of the authority to enforce their preferred alternatives, there would be a core – either alternative A or D. Various divisions of the six voters into two bicameral chambers would have this effect. For example, when the legislature is divided into one chamber with players (1, 2, and 4) and another chamber with players (3, 5, and 6), then the coalition of 3, 4, 5, and 6 is not decisive because it includes only one member of the first chamber. Consequently, this bicameral composition is called DESIGN A.

Similarly, when the legislature is divided into two chambers composed of (1, 3, and 5) and (2, 4, and 6), then the coalition of 1, 2, 3, and 5 is no longer decisive, because it includes only one member of the second chamber. As a result, outcome C no longer dominates outcome D, and outcome D is the predicted core under DESIGN D.

Groups of six subjects were randomly assigned to Design A and Design D, and individuals were randomly assigned to particular roles (Miller, Hammond, and Kile, 1996). The results are shown in Figure 8. The outcomes selected were statistically different between the two groups, and in each case the core outcome was by far the predominant outcome in each case.

	Players and Their Preferences					
Choices	1	2	3	4	5	6
1st Choice	A	A	B	B	C	D
2ND Choice	B	C	C	D	D	A
3RD Choice	C	D	D	A	A	B
4th Choice	E	E	E	E	E	E
5th Choice	D	B	A	C	B	C

Map of Dominance Relationships

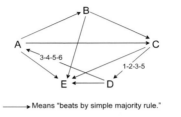

⎯⎯→ Means "beats by simple majority rule."

Result: A simple majority rule core (the unicameral core) does not exist.

Figure 7. Preference profile for six legislators, no simple majority rule core exists (Miller, Hammond, and Kile, 1996).

Calculating the core is slightly more complex in a two-dimensional setting. In Figure 9, there are six voters with widely scattered ideal points. The three median lines (contract curves with two ideal points on each side of the line) are shown. The status quo is as shown at (100, 20). Again, with simple majority rule, there is no majority rule core. Any policy choice off of any of the three contract curves can be upset by some majority that would prefer a policy on one of the contract curves. Since the three median lines do not intersect at a common point, every point is dominated.

However, imagine that voters 1, 3, and 6 are in one chamber, while the other voters are in a different chamber. Again, only coalitions that include a majority of both chambers are decisive. A coalition that includes voters 1, 4, 5, and 6 would prefer to move to a subset of the 14 contract curve. Furthermore, they have the power to make such a move, since they include a majority of both chambers. Furthermore, any point in that line segment is stable, since the coalitions preferring moves to the other two contract curves are not decisive. Although Players 1, 2, 3, and 6 would prefer to move to the 36 contract curve, Player 2 is the only member of that coalition in the second chamber. A bicameral composition in which Players 1, 3, and 6 are in the same chamber is called Treatment 136, and results in the core prediction shown on the 14 contract curve.

		Design	
		Design A	Design D
Outcome	A	6	1
	B	1	1
	C	0	0
	D	0	9
	E	0	0

		Design A	Design D
Outcome	A,B,C	7	2
	D	0	9

Fisher's Exact Test
One-Tail: .00113
Two-Tail: .00226

		Design A	Design D
Outcome	A	6	1
	D,B,C	1	10

Fisher's Exact Test
One-Tail: .00123
Two-Tail: .00245

Result: The null hypothesis of no impact by the design variable can be rejected with a high level of confidence, given either treatment of the two intermediate cases.

Figure 8. Discrete bicameral results (Miller, Hammond, and Kile, 1996).

Similarly, Treatment 146 consists of an identical set-up, except that Players 1, 4, and 6 are in one chamber. This results in a core prediction along the 36 contract curve, as shown.[5]

Treatment 135 is one in which members 1, 3, and 5 are in the same chamber. In this case, there is no core, because any point on any of the three contract curves may be upset by some bicameral coalition.

Results for the three treatments are shown in Figure 9. While there were some variations, there was a tendency for outcomes to cluster near the cores for their respective treatments in treatments 136 and 146. Variance was greater for treatment 135. Bicameralism seemed to create an inter-chamber negotiating dimension along the predicted contract curve.

---

[5] The bicameral treatments were crossed with differences in cardinal preferences, to examine the robustness of the core to differences in cardinal preferences. Since the core does not vary with cardinal preferences, the predictions should not change with changes in cardinal preferences; however, outcomes were somewhat sensitive to cardinal payoffs. Even though the range of payoffs was large across the entire space of alternatives, the difference between particular pairs of payoffs under discussion might well be rather small, allowing subjects to vote in ways that seemed inconsistent with ordinal preferences. See Bottom et al. (1998) for data and discussion.

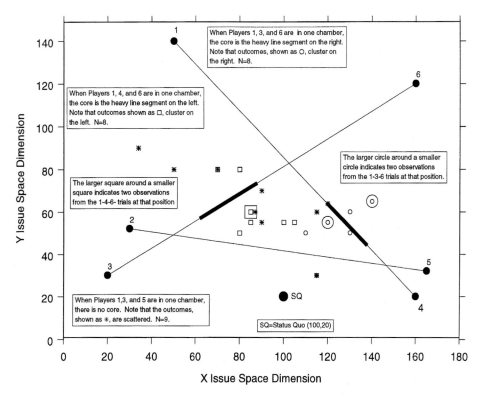

Figure 9. Spatial bicameral results (Bottom, Eavey, and Miller, 1996).

Acknowledgements

The authors would like to acknowledge an intellectual debt to Cheryl Eavey for her long-term contribution to the research agenda which resulted in the data reported in this chapter. Some of the research reported in this chapter was originally supported by a grant from the National Science Foundation SES-9210114 to Cheryl Eavey and to the first and fourth authors.

References

Bottom, William, Eavey, Cheryl, Miller, Gary (1996). "Getting to the core: Coalitional integrity as a constraint on the power of agenda setters". Journal of Conflict Resolution 40, 298–319.
Bottom, William, Eavey, Cheryl, Nicoll, Jennifer, Miller, Gary (1998). "The institutional effect on majority rule instability: Bicameralism in spatial policy decisions". Working paper, Washington University in St. Louis.
Eavey, Cheryl L. (1991). "Patterns of distribution in spatial games". Rationality and Society 3 (4), 450–474.

Eavey, Cheryl L., Miller, Gary J. (1984). "Bureaucratic agenda control: Imposition or bargaining?" American Political Science Review 78, 719–733.
Eavey, Cheryl L., Miller, Gary J. (1995). "Subcommittee agenda control". Journal of Theoretical Politics 7 (2), 125–156.
Fiorina, Morris P., Plott, Charles R. (1978). "Committee decisions under majority rule: An experimental study". American Political Science Review 72 (2), 575–598.
Greenberg, Joseph (1979). "Consistent majority rules over compact sets of alternatives". Econometrica 41 (3), 627–636.
Hammond, Thomas H., Miller, Gary J. (1987). "The core of the constitution". American Political Science Review 81, 1155–1174.
Hammond, Thomas H., Miller, Gary J. (1990). "Committees and the core of the constitution". Public Choice 66, 201–227.
King, Ron (1994). "An experimental investigation of supermajority voting rules: Implications for the financial accounting standards board". Journal of Economic Behavior and Organization 25, 197–217.
Knight, Jack (1992). "Institutions and Social Conflict". Cambridge University Press, Cambridge.
Kormendi, Roger C., Plott, Charles R. (1982). "Committee decisions under alternative procedural rules". Journal of Economic Behavior and Organization 3, 175–195.
Levine, Michael, Plott, Charles R. (1977). "Agenda influence and its implications". Virginia Law Review 63, 561–604.
Miller, Gary J., Hammond, Thomas H. (1990). "Committees and the core of the constitution". Public Choice 66 (3), 201–227.
Miller, Gary J., Hammond, Thomas H., Kile, Charles (1996). "Bicameralism and the core". Legal Studies Quarterly 21 (1), 83–103.
Miller, Gary J., Stengel, Daniel (1986). "Agenda control with sophisticated agenda setters and median voters". Unpublished manuscript.
Plott, Charles R. (1967). "A notion of equilibrium and its possibility under majority rule". American Economic Review 57 (4), 787–806.
Plott, Charles R. (1976). "Axiomatic social choice theory: An overview and interpretation". American Journal of Political Science 20 (Aug), 511–596.
Romer, Thomas, Rosenthal, Howard (1977). "Political resource allocation, controlled agendas, and the status quo". Public Choice 33, 27–45.
Shepsle, Kenneth (1979). "Institutional arrangements and equilibrium in multidimensional voting models". American Journal of Political Science 23, 27–59.
Tullock, Gordon (1981). "Why so much stability?" Public Choice 37, 189–202.

Chapter 92

ENDOGENOUS PROPERTIES OF EQUILIBRIUM AND DISEQUILIBRIUM IN SPATIAL COMMITTEE GAMES

RICK K. WILSON

Rice University

Unlike a market in which the combination of individual actions yields Pareto optimal outcomes, a political setting generally involves collective choices over Pareto suboptimal reallocations. Whereas the combination of private interests in a market leads to the efficient allocation of resources, in politics coalitions decide how to reallocate resources, oftentimes taking from some to give to others. Political decisions are often made under a process in which everyone agrees to abide by a choice made by some (e.g., a majority). Models of social choice point out that such processes are hardly neutral and need not reflect the general will of those participating in the decision (Arrow, 1963; Plott, 1967; McKelvey, 1976; Riker, 1980; Austen-Smith and Banks, 1998).

Within many political institutions, collective choices are sensitive to the endogenous preferences of actors. One such archetypal institution is the spatial committee game. In it there are a set of actors, each of whom hold equivalent powers. An initial status quo is arbitrarily imposed on the committee and any actor is free to propose an amendment to the status quo. Once an amendment is brought to the floor it is voted on under simple majority rule. If a majority prefers the amendment, it replaces the status quo, otherwise the status quo remains unchanged. The process of amending the current status quo continues until a motion to adjourn passes with a simple majority. At that point the current status quo is declared the final outcome for the committee process. In this sense the process is an idealized version of democratic practice in which any proposal can be considered, each proposal is compared under a binary choice procedure to the current status quo, and the final outcome is that which is preferred by the majority.

1. Theoretical Background

The collective choice setting discussed here relies on standard assumptions tied to spatial modeling and some of that notation is developed here. Let $N = \{1, 2, \ldots, n\}$ be the n-membered set of decision makers charged with selecting a single alternative, x, from a convex policy space $X \subset \mathbf{R}^m$. Each member $i \in N$ has a strictly quasi-concave binary preference relation over all $x \in X$ (such that $u_i(\bullet): \mathbf{R}^m \to \mathbf{R}^1$). Taking a strong set of preference relations, for any pair of alternatives, $x, x^o \in X$, if $u_i(x) > u_i(x^o)$, then an individual's preference ordering is represented as $x P_i x^o$. In the case that $u_i(x) = u_i(x^o)$, actors are indifferent among alternatives, or $x I_i x^o$. While an actor's utility function can take on many forms, in the experiments presented here an individual's utility declines as a function of distance away from her ideal point. Indifference contours can be represented as circles around that ideal point. For the ith actor with an ideal point located at x_i and for $x^i, x^o \in X$ the set of alternatives preferred to x^o by actor i is defined as $P_i(x^o) = \{x \in X | \|x^i - x\| < \|x^i - x^o\|\}$.

For simple majority rule games the set of winning coalitions is given as $\mathbf{S} = \{S_1, S_2, \ldots, S_k\}$ where $S_j \in \mathbf{S}$ if and only if $|S_j| > n/2$ (if n is odd) or $|S_j| > (n+1)/2$ if n is even. In a spatial committee setting, alternatives can only be implemented by a majority coalition. In the same fashion that the set of alternatives preferred by an individual to some x^o was defined, a set of alternatives preferred by the coalition S_j to x^o can be defined. Keeping with common usage the existing policy is referred to as the status quo (x^o). The set of alternatives preferred by a winning coalition is made up of the intersection of those alternatives preferred by members of the coalition to the status quo, or $\mathbf{P}(x^o) = \bigcap_{i \in S_j} P_i(x^o)$. Borrowing liberally from Shepsle and Weingast (1984) the set of *all* socially preferred alternatives is called the win set of x^o or $W(x^o) = \bigcup_{S_j \in \mathbf{S}} \mathbf{P}_{S_j}(x^o)$. The standard finding in social choice is that $W(x^o) \neq \emptyset$. That is, for any status quo, there exists at least one alternative (and usually many) that defeats it under simple majority rule. It is only when the preferences of actors satisfy very specific conditions (e.g., pairwise symmetry) that $W(x^o) \neq \emptyset$ and therefore an equilibrium exists.

2. Experimental Design

The experimental design uses a computer-controlled setting in which 5 subjects are brought together as a committee to make a decision. Each subject is assigned a different ideal point in a two-dimensional alternative space. That space is 300 by 300 units and has 90,000 unique points. Payoffs to subjects, for any point, are a non-linear decreasing function of distance from their ideal point. Sample indifference contours are provided for a subject and by moving a pointer in the alternative space the computer provides an exact dollar value for any point in the space. The locations of other subject's ideal points are common knowledge, while other's payoffs are not.

Subjects are able to place a motion on the floor at any time. No motion is brought to a vote unless "seconded" by another. At that time the status quo and the amendment are highlighted and subjects notified that a vote is forthcoming. After a 20 second delay subjects are transferred to a voting screen in which the status quo and its value are posted against the same information for the amendment. Subjects are then asked to vote for one or the other and their vote is cast privately. Once voting ends the results are revealed. If the amendment gains at least three of five votes, it becomes the new status quo, otherwise the status quo is retained. The committee process then continues with all previous proposals on the floor and subjects are invited to make additional proposals. The committee ends its deliberations when a motion to adjourn is brought to the floor and a majority votes to end the experiment. At that point subjects earn the value of the current status quo (for detailed discussion of this procedure, see Haney, Herzberg, and Wilson, 1992 or Fiorina and Plott, 1978).

3. Endogenous Preferences

The experiment reported here manipulates only the distribution of subject ideal points. Three manipulations are used: the Core, the Star and the Skew Star. Each of these manipulations has unique characteristics (see Plott, 1967 for a more general discussion). The Core is a unique equilibrium located at the ideal point of member 5 and it has the property that it defeats any other alternative in a pairwise contest. In the language used above, if x^5 is member 5's ideal point, then $W(x^5) \neq \emptyset$. By contrast the Star distribution has no unique equilibrium prediction. Indeed, any point in the alternative space can be selected via some agenda. In the language used above, for any x^o, $W(x^o) \neq \emptyset$. Likewise there exists no unique equilibrium under the Skew Star distribution. However, in this setting there is a natural simple majority coalition of members 2, 3 and 4. These three actors are located relatively close to one another and at some distance from members 1 and 5.

3.1. The Core

A large number of experiments have been run with the Core as a prediction (see McKelvey and Ordeshook, 1990 for a survey). Those results demonstrate two things. First, outcomes converge on the Core. Second, those outcomes seldom end up at the unique point prediction of the Core. The results reported here are consistent with a large number of experiments run by others. Figure 1 plots the outcomes from seven experimental trials using the Core preference configuration. Several things are worth noting on the figure. The ideal points for subjects are given by red squares and member 5's position lies at the Core (it is almost obscured by outcomes). The initial status quo is denoted by "Initial Status Quo" and its location is given as a small circle. Amendments passed by a majority at some point in the experimental trials are plotted in green. Finally, the outcome from each trial is plotted in blue.

The first thing to note from the figure is that no outcome falls at the equilibrium – member 5's ideal point. As a point prediction the Core fails. However, taking the Core as *the* prediction assumes that it is included in the agenda. It is important to remember that subjects had 90,000 distinct alternatives to pick from, on average put 27 on the floor and, on average, voted on only 2.9 different alternatives. Moreover, the point prediction, (120, 125) was bound to fail because it was *never* proposed in *any* of the experimental trials. However, in five of seven trials the final outcome is the Condorcet winner. It could defeat all other alternatives on the floor when subjects adjourned the experiment. That a Condorcet winner existed is due to the structure of preferences. In the remaining two cases subjects at x^5 voted against their self interest to move the status quo away from their ideal point. Although they subsequently amended the agenda to move back to the Core, the trial ended before they reached the Condorcet winner.

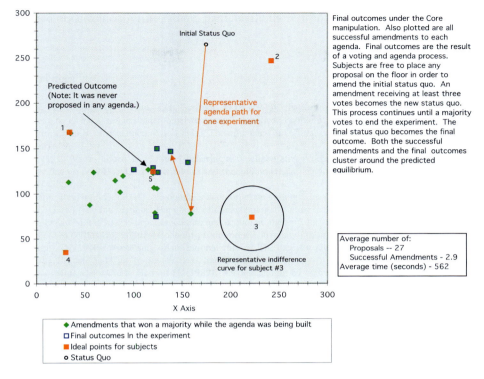

Figure 1. Outcomes under an experiment with a Core.

A more important feature of this agenda process is that outcomes are convergent. Plotted in Figure 1 are the successful amending steps to the agenda. These points are more broadly distributed in the alternative space than the outcomes. What is not readily apparent is the manner in which an agenda converged toward the Core. However, this can be shown by noting that in five of the seven trials *every* successful amendment was closer to the Core than its predecessor. Moreover, the agenda process rapidly converged. While, on average, it took under 10 minutes of floor discussion to adjourn the experiment, it took very little time to reach the final outcome for the trial. On average the final outcome was selected within 41.6 seconds of beginning the trial. This meant that the final outcome was quickly selected, was chosen from a handful of proposals on the floor, and was reached via a short agenda.

3.2. Star Preferences

By comparison under the Star preference manipulation there is no endogenous equilibrium. The outcomes from 18 trials under this configuration are plotted in Figure 2. While many of these outcomes fall in the central portion of the alternative space, they

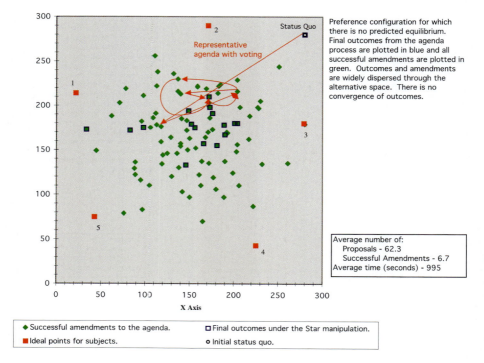

Figure 2. Outcomes under an experiment with symmetrically distributed preferences and no equilibrium.

are located in a very different area of the alternative space than outcomes under the Core configuration and they are more widely dispersed.

Several things are worth noting in these trials. First, given that there is no equilibrium, outcomes do not converge on any particular point. Instead the agenda wanders across the alternative space. This is especially pronounced in 6 of 12 trials with long agendas. In those 6 trials voting cycles were observed in the sense that an alternative A was defeated by an alternative B which was defeated by an alternative C which was then defeated by alternative A. While predicted by theory (Arrow, 1961), voting cycles are almost impossible to observe, yet here they occurred at least half of the time.

Second, because outcomes fail to converge, there are far more proposals placed on the floor, far more votes taken, and far more changes to the status quo than under the Core preference trials. For instance in these trials subjects averaged 62.3 proposals on the floor, called just under 21 amendment votes on average, and changed the status quo more often (6.7 times versus 2.9 times, on average). Some sense of this can be gained by comparing the dispersion of successful amendments (noted in green) in Figures 1 and 2. Under the Star configuration the agenda was much more likely to wander in the alternative space. All of this proposing, voting, and amending activity is a hallmark of disequilibrium behavior predicted by standard models of collective choice. There is

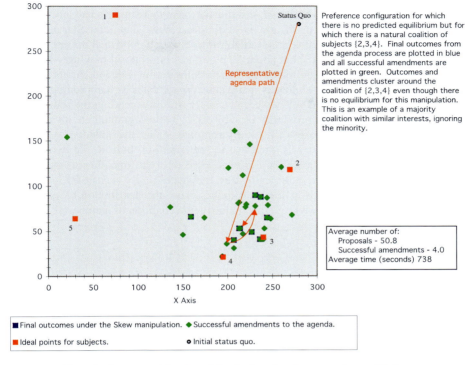

Figure 3. Outcomes with a skewed distribution of preferences and no equilibrium.

substantial instability in choice, the dynamics of the agenda path appear chaotic and the outcomes are shifted to a different part of the alternative space than outcomes under the Core.

3.3. Skew Star Preferences

The Skew Star preference configuration, like the Star configuration, has no majority rule equilibrium. It is introduced to show that outcomes are sensitive to the endogenous preferences of actors, independent of any equilibrium prediction. Figure 3 plots the outcomes from nine trials using this preference configuration. Those outcomes are clustered around the coalition {2, 3, 4}, even though no equilibrium prediction exists. This clustering represents two remarkable features about this voting process. First, outcomes are clearly dependent on the distribution of preferences. Second, the presence of a specific majority rule coalition, defined by its proximity, exerts enormous influence over the decision process. In this design no subject is granted the right to control the agenda. However these outcomes reflect the ease with which a majority coalition can impose outcomes – especially when its members share common interests.

Even though outcomes are clustered, this did not mean that subjects had an easy time settling on them. The agenda process in these trials resembled that in the Star manipulation. First, under the Skew Star configuration, subjects took a good deal of time to reach an outcome. On average they spent about 12.5 minutes in proposal making – less than under the Star but greater than under the Core configuration. Second, subjects in the Skew Star manipulation cast almost as many amendment votes as their counterparts in the Star manipulation (although they were less successful in amending the status quo).

As noted above, the close proximity of subjects 2, 3 and 4 granted an advantage to that coalition. The agenda process did not discriminate against the outside players, they simply had little to offer that was attractive to the coalition. Indeed, the two outside players, 1 and 5, were responsible for almost 82 percent of the amendments that failed. Although they could, and often did, call votes, they were rarely successful in pushing an amendment. Consequently, as Figure 3 makes clear, the distribution of successful amendments is focused around the simple majority rule coalition of members 2, 3 and 4.

4. Discussion

These experiments demonstrate the extent to which outcomes are responsive to the structure of preferences. Where a preference-induced equilibrium exists, outcomes converge toward that equilibrium. Where a natural majority coalition exists, outcomes cluster around it. Where preferences are widely distributed, so too are outcomes.

In a different vein Eavey (1991) suggests that subjects eschew their own private concerns and pay attention to relative payoffs among the group. In small groups, with face-to-face interaction, this is an interesting possibility worth further study. Grelak and Koford (1997) re-analyze Eavey's data and compare them with the Fiorina and Plott (1978) data. Grelak and Koford (1997) do not reach the same conclusion about fairness, but they cannot dismiss the fact that subjects may hold other-regarding preferences and that such preferences have an impact on spatial committee games. By and large, the fact that outcomes are sensitive to endogenous preferences comes as some relief. These results indicate that there is a clear patterning to outcomes and they are dependent on the preferences of actors. Rather than throwing up our hands in frustration over the "impossibility" of understanding basic collective choice processes, these results point to the possibility of predicting outcomes. Work on the "Uncovered Set" (McKelvey, 1986) and extensions by Austen-Smith and Banks (1998) provide insight into the results reported here. Those theoretical constructs aim at capturing the complex relationships between preference and choices.

Acknowledgements

Support by the National Science Foundation (SES 87-21250) is gratefully acknowledged as is support by the Workshop in Political Theory and Policy Analysis at Indiana University. Neither organization bears any responsibility for the content of this article.

References

Arrow, K.J. (1963). "Social Choice and Individual Values". Yale University Press, New Haven.
Austen-Smith, D., Banks, J.S. (1998). "Positive Political Theory I: Collective Preference". University of Michigan Press, Ann Arbor.
Eavey, C.L. (1991). "Patterns of distribution in spatial games". Rationality and Society 3, 450–474
Fiorina, M.P., Plott, C.R. (1978). "Committee decisions under majority rule: An experimental study". American Political Science Review 72, 575–598.
Grelak, E., Koford, K. (1997). "A re-examination of the Fiorina–Plott and Eavey voting experiments: How much do cardinal payoffs influence outcomes?" Journal of Economic Behavior and Organization 32, 571–589.
Haney, P., Herzberg, R., Wilson, R.K. (1992). "Advice and consent: Unitary actors, advisory models and experimental tests". Journal of Conflict Resolution 36, 603–633.
McKelvey, R.D. (1976). "Intransitivities in multidimensional voting models and some implications for agenda control". Journal of Economic Theory 12, 472–482.
McKelvey, R.D. (1986). "Covering, dominance, and institution free properties of social choice". American Journal of Political Science 30, 283–314.
McKelvey, R.D., Ordeshook, P.C. (1990). "A decade of experimental research on spatial models of elections and committees". In: Enelow, J.M., Hinich, M.J. (Eds.), Advances in the Spatial Theory of Voting. Cambridge University Press, Cambridge.
Plott, C.R. (1967). "A notion of equilibrium and its possibility under majority rule". American Economic Review 57, 787–806.
Riker, W.R. (1980). "Implications from the disequilibrium of majority rule for the study of institutions". American Political Science Review 74, 432–446.
Shepsle, K.A., Weingast, B.R. (1984). "Uncovered sets and sophisticated voting outcomes with implications for agenda institutions". American Journal of Political Science 28, 49–74.

Chapter 93

STRUCTURE INDUCED EQUILIBRIUM IN SPATIAL COMMITTEE GAMES

RICK K. WILSON

Rice University

Political economists have long recognized that collective choice processes are inherently unstable. Work by Arrow (1963), Plott (1967) and McKelvey (1976) illustrate just how sensitive collective choices are to the structure of preference. Absent distinct distributions of preferences for decision makers, outcomes are predicted to be unpatterned. These findings led at least one social scientist to declare that political science, rather than economics, ought to assume the mantle of the "dismal science" because if political scientists cannot predict outcomes from common forms of democratic practice, then political science has little to offer (Riker, 1980).

This view first was challenged by Shepsle (1979) who claimed that while disequilibrium was the logical outcome of much social choice theorizing, disequilibrium in empirical settings was surprisingly rare. Decisions are often made in predictable ways. Shepsle argued that collective choices are seldom made under the minimal institutional mechanisms proposed by social choice theory, but instead take place within a richer institutional structure. Institutional rules are viewed as producing a "structure induced equilibrium" (SIE) in which preferences combined with institutions yield predictable, equilibrium outcomes.

The experimental results discussed here illustrate two examples of SIE. The first develops a point raised by McKelvey (1976) in which a single individual is granted monopoly agenda power. This simple change to the ordinary rules leads to a unique equilibrium prediction where previously none existed. The second example reopens agenda setting to all members of the committee. However, instead of a forward moving agenda, in which any proposal can be brought against the current status quo, a backward agenda process is used. In this process the status quo is voted last, with the sequence of votes fully specified, the last proposal voted on first, and the first proposal is voted next-to-last. Some variant of this mechanism is common in many collective choice institutions, including many legislatures.

1. Theoretical Basics

The basic notation for this discussion is in a previous entry (see the article entitled "Endogenous Properties of Equilibrium and Disequilibrium in Spatial Committee Games"). It is important to note that sets of individually preferred alternatives can be characterized as $P_i(x^o)$, which are those $x \in X$ that the ith actor prefers to the status quo under binary comparisons. Likewise, for a particular coalition S_j that is able to implement a choice, the set of preferred elements from the alternative space is given as $\mathbf{P}(x^o) = \bigcap_{i \in S_j} P_i(x^o)$. Those alternatives preferred to the status quo by all winning coalitions is given as $W(x^o) = \bigcup_{S_j \in \mathbf{S}} \mathbf{P}_{S_j}(x^o)$.

There are two distinct settings investigated here. The first is a social choice setting in which $W(x^o) \neq \emptyset, \forall x \in X$. This is the standard social choice problem in which there is no preference-induced equilibrium under a standard open agenda procedure. Suppose this procedure is changed such that a single individual, given by $\ell \in N$, whose ideal point is located at x^ℓ and who is the only actor allowed to bring amendments to a vote. Such a case implies that no alternative is called to a vote unless ℓ prefers the amendment. This fundamentally changes the set of alternatives preferred by a coalition, requiring $\mathbf{P}(x^o) = \bigcap_{i \in S_j} P_i(x^o) \cap P_\ell(x^o)$ such that the agenda setter is always a pivotal member of any winning coalition. With this qualification in mind at a minimum this yields $W(x^\ell) = \emptyset$ such that there exists a unique equilibrium at the agenda setter's ideal point. In other words a simple, albeit important, change in the structural rules yields stability where none previously existed.

In the second case suppose that an agenda must be announced and is voted backwards. First consider the usual case under a forward moving agenda with two steps. Suppose the agenda begins from the status quo, x^o. At the first step it must be that $x_1 \in W(x^o)$ for the amendment to succeed. Depending on the specific x_1, then the only constraint on the second element of the agenda is that $x_2 \in W(x_1)$. Conceivably this could cover a very large portion of the alternative space. It may well be the case that $x^o \in W(x_2)$. In such a case there is an intransitive social choice in which x_1 defeats x^o, x_2 defeats x_1, and finally x^o defeats x_2. Now consider the case where specific amendments must be chosen and the agenda is ordered backward (x_2, x_1, x^o), with x_2 and x_1 first paired and the winner of that pairing voted against x^o. At a minimum for x_2 to win it must be that $x_2 \in W(x_1) \cup W(x^o)$ (see Shepsle and Weingast, 1984).

This places a powerful constraint on the choice of amendments – especially if they are expected to win. Of course the strategic problems of what to select are compounded by "sophisticated" choices and voting by actors (see McKelvey and Niemi, 1978). Regardless of the case this change in the agenda process results in a structure induced equilibrium.

2. Experimental Design

The experimental design uses a computer-controlled setting in which 5 subjects are brought together as a committee to make a decision. Each subject is assigned a different ideal point in a two-dimensional alternative space. That space is quite dense, made up of either 300 × 300 or 350 × 350 points, depending on the experimental design. Payoffs to subjects, for any point, are a non-linear decreasing function of distance from their ideal point. Sample indifference contours are provided for a subject and by moving a pointer in the alternative space the computer provides an exact dollar value for any point in the space. The location of other subject's ideal points are common knowledge, while other's payoffs are not.

In the baseline condition subjects are able to place a motion on the floor at any time. No motion is brought to a vote unless "seconded" by another. At that time the status quo and the amendment are highlighted and subjects notified that a vote is forthcoming. After a 20 second delay subjects are transferred to a voting screen in which the status quo and its value are posted against the same information for the amendment. Subjects are then asked to vote for one or the other and their vote is cast privately. Once voting ends the results are revealed. If the amendment gains at least three of five votes, it becomes the new status quo, otherwise the status quo is retained. The committee process continues leaving all previous proposals on the floor and inviting subjects to make additional proposals. The committee ends its deliberations when a motion to adjourn is brought to the floor and a majority votes to end the experiment. At that point subjects earn the value of the current status quo (for detailed discussion of this procedure, see Haney, Herzberg, and Wilson, 1992).

Two distinct manipulations are introduced to the baseline condition. Under the first, an *Agenda Setter* manipulation, any subject can put a proposal on the floor. The agenda setter, who is randomly assigned to that position, is granted exclusive power to bring an alternative to a vote. The agenda setter is also given sole power to call a vote to adjourn. A simple majority is needed to either change the status quo or end the trial.

In the second manipulation, a *Backward Voting Agenda*, any subject may place proposals on the floor. Subjects are required to build a list of proposals over which they will vote in reverse order. A proposal requires a "second" to be added to the list and subjects are given a fixed period of time to add proposals to the list. When the agenda building period ends subjects vote, in reverse order, over pairs of alternatives. The winning alternative is that proposal receiving a majority at the last pairing.

3. Monopoly Agenda Setting

Outcomes from an open agenda baseline experiment and from a monopoly agenda setter experiment are displayed in Figure 1. Actors' ideal points are given in red. Under the agenda setting manipulation the subject at member 5's position was *always* assigned to be the agenda setter. Outcomes under this manipulation are given in blue. Outcomes under the baseline condition are green. Two points are clear from the figure. First, even though the structure of preference remains the same for both experiments, the pattern of outcomes is quite different. Under the baseline condition outcomes are more scattered in the alternative space and more centrally located. Outcomes under the agenda setter condition are more compact and they are anchored to the agenda setter's ideal point.

Second, outcomes under the agenda setting manipulation do not all fall at the equilibrium. Instead, outcomes range from the agenda setter's ideal point to the central portion of the alternative space. At one level this might call into question the predictive capacity of this SIE concept. However, only focusing on a point prediction is misleading.

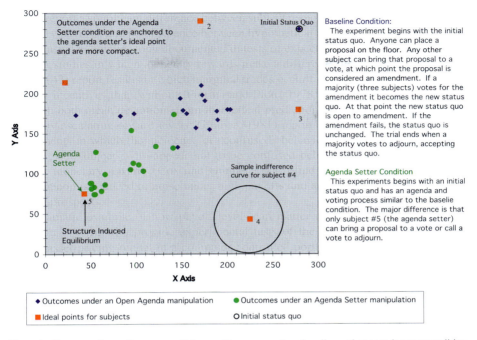

Figure 1. Outcomes from a 5-person spatial committee game under a baseline and an agenda setter condition.

Given the alternatives placed on the floor, 13 of the 21 final outcomes under the agenda setting manipulation were Condorcet winners; that is the outcome could have defeated any other proposal that was placed on the floor in the trial. Moreover, the power to set the agenda is extremely important.

Both points are illustrated by the agenda plotted in Figure 2. The figure details the ideal points of the players, all of the proposals that were on the floor at the end of the trial and the agenda path chosen by the agenda setter. Interestingly, even though the agenda setter's very first proposal was at the equilibrium (and made within 8 seconds of beginning the round), the agenda setter chose alternative (145, 73) as the first amendment to the status quo. It handily defeated the status quo, (280, 280), via the coalition {1, 4, 5} and constituted the first agenda step. The second vote was over amendment (43, 152) which won via the coalition {1, 2, 5}. By this point the agenda setter had enjoyed complete success and steadily moved the status quo closer to the equilibrium. The agenda setter misjudged with the third vote that she called. The proposed amendment, (49, 97), left members 4 and 5 better off, while 1, 2 and 3 were left worse off. That proposal was defeated so the agenda setter brought the fourth vote on alternative (92, 62) which improved member 3 who joined with 4 and 5 to effect passage. Finally, on the fifth vote, alternative (50, 88) was brought forward and voted for by the coalition {1, 2, 5}. As is clear from the figure the agenda setter chose amendments that played off members 1

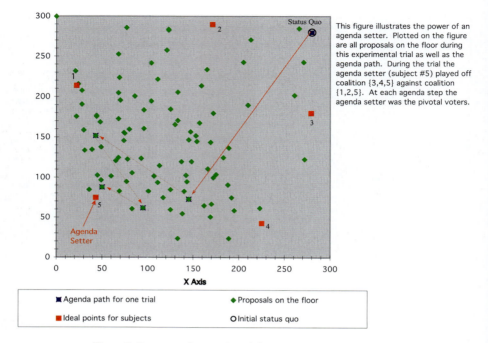

Figure 2. Representative agenda path for an agenda setter experiment.

and 2 against members 3 and 4. In building the agenda the agenda setter did not have to rely on her own proposals, but rather used alternatives placed on the floor by others.

Following the successful 5th vote the agenda setter called for adjournment. That vote failed 1-4, with only the agenda setter voting in favor. The agenda setter paused for a considerable amount of time studying the proposals on the floor. Building an agenda leading to her ideal point would have involved a series of minute steps. Instead of taking such action the agenda setter amended (50, 88) with itself and in this way signaled her commitment to the status quo. Immediately afterward she proposed that the trial end and that vote was successful under a 4-1 vote.

4. Backward Voting Agenda

This experiment changes the form of the agenda. Figure 3 displays the outcomes for both a forward moving agenda and a backward constructed agenda. Under the former there exists no equilibrium. Under the later there exist several equilibrium. If subjects are assumed to be myopic (and the evidence supports this point) then the initial status quo is one equilibrium. The others are those points contained in the petals on the figure which are those $x \in W(x^o)$ – or the proposals that can defeat the initial status quo.

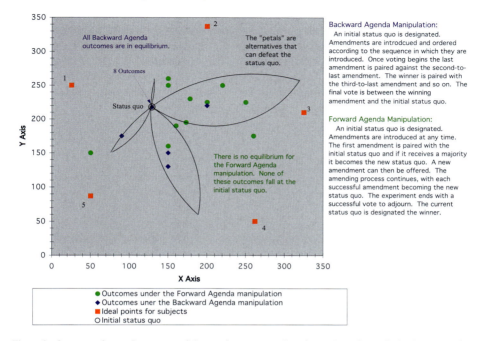

Figure 3. Outcomes from a 5-person spatial committee game under a forward moving and a backward moving agenda condition.

Under a backward voting agenda mechanism, the penultimate winner is paired with the status quo. In this experiment, under both a forward and backward agenda, the initial status quo was placed at (129, 218).

Simply eye-balling the figure it is clear that this form of an agenda mechanism has an important effect on outcomes. Fully 8 of 12 final outcomes were at the initial status quo, while the remaining 4 were in the win set of that status quo. By comparison, outcomes under the forward voting mechanism are scattered across the alternative space. Although 7 of 12 outcomes fall in the win set of the initial status quo, it does not constitute a prediction for the forward moving agenda manipulation. Also striking is that no outcomes appear at the initial status quo. The pattern of outcomes across the two manipulations differs considerably and so too does the process by which outcomes were selected.

To get a sense of how these different manipulations affected the voting process, two sample agenda are illustrated in Figure 4. In each case the arrows indicate the direction of changes to the agenda. Each agenda "step" represents a majority agreeing to an amendment and is given by an arrow pointing from the previous winner. The processes are different in that the backward agenda mechanism *ends* with a vote over the status quo, while the forward agenda mechanism *begins* with a vote over the status quo.

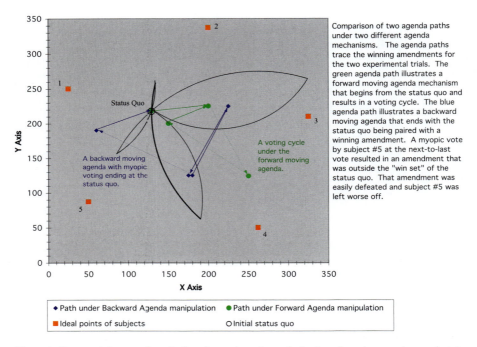

Figure 4. Representative agenda paths for a forward moving and a backward moving agenda experiment.

Under the backward voting agenda process (given by the blue diamonds) the first three amendments had the property that any of them could have defeated the final outcome. This is easily seen because each was an element of the win set of the initial status quo. On the fourth vote, an alternative outside of $W(x^o)$ won a majority. In this sequence the myopic vote by member 5 came back to haunt him. On the fifth vote x^o easily defeated the fourth amendment and member 5 was left worse off than if he had voted strategically. In doing so, member 5 would have voted against the fourth amendment (the move outside of the win set) anticipating that at the last vote the third amendment would have become the final outcome and he would have been left better off. Myopic voting by subjects was common in these experimental trials and points to why outcomes so often ended up at the initial status quo, x^o. Of course, strategic voting is only possible when the agenda is completely known. While the full agenda was known under this backward voting process, subjects did not anticipate the consequences of their votes, picking when to strategically vote against their short-run interests in order to gain long-term benefits. Instead, this agenda process, combined with myopic voting, exercised a powerful constraint on outcomes.

By contrast the agenda under a forward moving process (given by the green circles) is common to these experimental trials. The first move is to a point in the win set of the initial status quo. Subsequent amendments illustrate a property that occurred over 30 percent of the time in these experimental trials: subjects built an agenda incorporating a voting cycle. While theorists commonly warn against the possibility of voting cycles they are seldom observed. This is largely a function of the types of agenda mechanisms used in natural settings (which often limit the number of amendments that can be posed). Here voting cycles, rather than being rare events, are common. This is especially the case under an unconstrained forward agenda process in which earlier alternatives can be revisited.

5. Conclusion

Preferences matter, but so too do institutions. Markets, auction mechanisms and political institutions all affect outcomes. For students of collective choice, minimal decision making institutions provide a baseline by which we expect outcomes that best can be characterized as chaotic. Such outcomes are rarely predictable and the processes by which they are selected are marked by voting cycles and drifting through the alternative space. More interesting for collective choice theorists are those mechanisms introduced into a minimal institutional setting that in turn brings predictability to outcomes.

Almost all institutions charged with making collective choices are richly layered with rules. The United States House of Representatives is one of the more rule-bound institutions that has been studied extensively and empirical scholars take for granted that its outcomes will be predictable and patterned. However, disentangling *which* structural features matter and *when* they matter remains a task for theorists. Experimentalists continue to offer examples as to when institutions matter. Recent work includes bargaining between multiple institutions by Bottom et al. (2000); levels of communication by Endersby (1993); and the endogenous choice of allocation rules by Walker et al. (2000).

The experiments discussed here illustrate two distinct structural changes to an agenda and note the impact of a rules change for the pattern of outcomes. Changing the collective choice mechanism so that a single individual controls the agenda does two things. First it results in predictions about which outcomes will be chosen. Second it has a predictable effect on the distribution of resources – the agenda setter gains benefits to the detriment of others. This happens even though everyone has an equal vote over outcomes. Changing the collective choice mechanism so that amendments are ordered and the initial status quo is voted last also enables precise predictions about which outcomes will be chosen.

Paying attention to institutional structure is important. Knowing which institutional structures matter and assessing their impact is an important part of building our social science knowledge. Experiments, working hand-in-hand with theory, provide a useful means for testing and assessing institutional change.

Acknowledgements

Support by the National Science Foundation (SES 87-21250) is gratefully acknowledged as is support by the Workshop in Political Theory and Policy Analysis at Indiana University. Neither organization bears any responsibility for the content of this article.

References

Arrow, K.J. (1963). "Social Choice and Individual Values". Yale University Press, New Haven.
Bottom, W.P., Eavey, C.L., Miller, G.J., Nicoll, J. (2000). "The institutional effect on majority rule instability: Bicameralism in spatial policy decisions". American Journal of Political Science 44, 523–540.
Endersby, J.W. (1993). "Rules of method and rules of conduct: An experimental study on 2 types of procedure and committee behavior". Journal of Politics 55, 218–236.
Haney, P., Herzberg, R., Wilson, R.K. (1992). "Advice and consent: Unitary actors, advisory models and experimental tests". Journal of Conflict Resolution 36, 603–633.
McKelvey, R.D. (1976). "Intransitivities in multidimensional voting models and some implications for agenda control". Journal of Economic Theory 12, 472–482.
McKelvey, R.D., Niemi, R.G. (1978). "A multistage game representation of sophisticated voting for binary procedures". Journal of Economic Theory 18, 1–22.
Plott, C.R. (1967). "A notion of equilibrium and its possibility under majority rule". American Economic Review 57, 787–806.
Riker, W.R. (1980). "Implications from the disequilibrium of majority rule for the study of institutions". American Political Science Review 74, 432–446.
Shepsle, K.A. (1979). "Institutional arrangements and equilibrium in multidimensional voting models". American Journal of Political Science 23, 27–59.
Shepsle, K.A., Weingast, B.R. (1984). "Uncovered sets and sophisticated voting outcomes with implications for agenda institutions". American Journal of Political Science 28, 49–74.
Walker, J.M., Gardner, R., Hess, A., Ostrom, E. (2000). "Collective choice in the commons: Experimental results on proposed allocation rules and votes". Economic Journal 110, 212–234.

Chapter 94

THREE-WAY EXPERIMENTAL ELECTION RESULTS: STRATEGIC VOTING, COORDINATED OUTCOMES AND DUVERGER'S LAW

THOMAS RIETZ

Department of Finance, Henry B. Tippie College of Business, University of Iowa, Iowa City, IA 52242-1000, USA

1. Introduction

When a majority is split between two majority-preferred candidates in an election, a minority-preferred candidate can win a three-way race. The winner would lose the two-way race with each other candidate and, therefore, is known as a Condorcet Loser (see Condorcet, 1785, and discussions in Black, 1958). Here, I discuss recent experimental work that shows (1) when a split-majority results in a minority-preferred (Condorcet Loser) candidate winning an election, (2) when a split-majority can coordinate using a pre-election signal to defeat the Condorcet Loser and (3) what kind of signals work best in coordinating the majority.

To see what causes the Condorcet Loser problem and how strategic voting can overcome it, consider the electorate profile given in Figure 1. Type "O" and "G" voters form the split majority. When they can coordinate and concentrate their votes on one of their preferred candidates (essentially ignoring the other), they can defeat the Condorcet Loser (candidate "B"). Then, the election becomes a two-way race with one majority-preferred candidate and the minority-preferred candidate as the remaining viable candidates. This is the outcome predicted by Duverger (1967) for plurality voting elections.[1]

Felsenthal, Rapoport, and Maoz (1988), Felsenthal (1990) and Rapoport, Felsenthal, and Maoz (1991) present a series of bloc voting models that allow tacit cooperation between voting blocs in elections among three alternatives. They find that majority voters can often find means of tacit coordination to overcome the Condorcet Loser problem under a variety of payoffs. The papers discussed below build on this research by allowing individual voting models (which have more appealing continuity properties, see Rietz, 1993) and comparing several types of public coordinating signals that may allow immediate coordination. McKelvey and Ordeshook (1985a, 1985b, 1990) show that non-binding pre-election polls can transmit information between voters and between candidates and voters. Plott (1991) also studies polls and finds that they can both

---

[1] See any of the papers cited in Figure 1 for a discussion of the roots and importance of the split-majority/ Condorcet Loser problem and Duverger's Law.

Payoff Schedule Group:

Voter Type	Election Winner			Total Number of Each Type
	Orange (O)	Green (G)	Blue (B)	
1 (O)	$1.20	$0.90	$0.20	4
2 (G)	$0.90	$1.20	$0.20	4
3 (B)	$0.40	$0.40	$1.40	6

Figure 1. Split-majority, "symmetric" payoff schedule used to induce voter preferences in: (1) Forsythe et al. (1993) in single-shot and initial elections without pre-election, coordinating signals. (2) Forsythe et al. (1993, 1996) in repeated elections with previous election results as coordinating signals. (3) Forsythe et al. (1993, 1996) in single-shot and repeated elections with pre-election polls as coordinating signals. (4) Rietz, Myerson, and Weber (1998) in single-shot elections with campaign finance levels as coordinating signals. (5) Gerber, Morton, and Rietz (1996) in single-shot elections with a majority requirement/runoff rule. Preferences were induced by paying voters of each type (row) the amount listed under the winning candidate in each election (regardless of who they voted for). Voter types are labeled by first preference here for convenience. (They were not in the experiments.) Type O and G voters constitute the split majority, while type B voters form the minority. Actual payoff tables were randomly scrambled and labeled for each voting group. They are unscrambled here for reporting purposes so that O always represents the first listed (on the ballot) of the majority-preferred candidates, G represents the second listed, majority preferred candidate and B represents the minority candidate.

transmit information and help voters coordinate in multi-candidate elections. The papers discussed below build on this research by focusing exclusively on the coordination effect of polls (isolated from the information transmission role) and by comparing polls with other coordination mechanisms.

Here, I discuss a series of papers with common electorate profiles (from Figure 1) and common experimental design elements. Forsythe et al. (1993, 1996) begin this research with baselines documenting that, without coordinating signals, the Condorcet Loser problem is very real in experimental elections. Then, they show that both polls and repeated elections can overcome the problem, leading to Duverger-type effects. Rietz, Myerson, and Weber (1998) discuss how campaign finance levels can coordinate voters and discuss the efficiency and rationality of campaigns. Gerber, Morton, and Rietz (1996) study the effects of runoff elections in these split-majority electorates. Each paper analyzes a series of elections with the same electorate profile. Here, I discuss the equilibria to the voting game (Figure 2) and summarize how subjects use strategic coordination based on pre-election signals to overcome the Condorcet Loser problem (Figure 3).

2. The Experiments

2.1. Common Procedures

Each experiment used subjects recruited from university populations as voters in a series of laboratory elections. For each session, subjects received instructional information and any questions were answered. (See Forsythe et al., 1993, for basic instructions.) Each subject participated as a member of several "voting groups" in 24 elections. With two voting groups each period, this gives 48 total elections in each session. Except for the study of repeated elections in Forsythe et al. (1996), each voting group participated in one election before random re-assignment to new groups.[2] In each election, the voting group was divided into voters of three "types," differing by their payoffs as given in Figure 1. Voters received complete information about their groups in the sense that they knew these induced preferences exactly. At the end of the sessions, subjects received cash payments based on the election winners for the voting groups in which they participated.

The results I discuss here all used plurality voting (with an additional majority requirement in Gerber, Morton, and Rietz, 1996). Thus, subjects could cast the vote vectors $(1, 0, 0)$, $(0, 1, 0)$, $(0, 0, 1)$ and $(0, 0, 0)$ for the candidates "O," "G" and "B," respectively. After each election, the candidate with the most votes was declared the winner and subjects were paid accordingly. If a tie occurred between two or more candidates, the winner was selected randomly with the tied candidates having equal probabilities of being selected. After each election, subjects were informed of the number of votes received by each candidate, the election winner and their payoffs.

2.2. Equilibria

Each paper focuses on the stage-game voting equilibria for each election using Myerson and Weber's (1993) definition. Figure 2 shows equilibria for plurality voting and the electorate profile of Figure 1. The equilibria are based on expectations about (1) which candidates will be in contention in a close race (conditional tie probabilities) and (2) the values voters place on breaking ties in their favor. For these payoffs, only the relative strengths of candidates O and G matter in selecting the equilibrium. When O is perceived strong while G is weak, all majority voters vote for O. This justifies the expectations. O wins with 8 votes to B's 6 and G's 0. Similarly, if G is perceived as strong, G wins. When neither O nor G is perceived as significantly stronger, no majority voters "cross over" and B wins with 6 votes to O's 4 and G's 4. Thus, there are two "coordinated" equilibria (right and left ends of the relative strength continuum).

---

[2] In Forsythe et al. (1996), each subject participated as a member of three voting groups and in eight elections in each group, for 24 elections total. Again, there were two voting groups at any given time resulting in 48 elections in 6 repeated election series.

In each, the majority voters cast all their votes on a single majority-preferred candidate, that candidate wins and the other majority-preferred candidate receives zero votes. These equilibria are Duverger-like in that one majority preferred candidate receives zero votes. However, they require both strategic voting and coordination on a specific equilibrium. In the other equilibrium, the majority voters are unable to coordinate and split their vote across the majority-preferred candidates. This results in the Condorcet Loser winning and the non-Duverger property that all three candidates remain in the race.

2.3. Specific Treatments

Forsythe et al. (1993) ran a series of single-shot elections under the electorate profile given in Figure 1. After each election, subjects were randomly re-assigned to two new voting groups with randomly rearranged and re-labeled payoff tables. (They have been unscrambled to correspond to Figure 1 for reporting purposes.) This allowed subjects to gain experience while preserving independence across elections. In effect, there were no coordinating signals in these elections. While Forsythe et al. (1996) run repeated elections, the first election in each series is similar in the sense that there are no coordinating signals. I group these elections as "elections without coordinating signals" for reporting.

Forsythe et al. (1993) run a series of single-shot elections each preceded by a non-binding pre-election poll. Poll results were reported to subjects before the election. Forsythe et al. (1996) run pre-election polls in repeated elections. They find a similar poll/outcome relationship. I report these outcomes with the "preceding poll" as the coordinating signal.

Forsythe et al. (1996) also run repeated elections without intervening polls. I report these outcomes with the "preceding election" as the coordinating signal.

Rietz, Myerson, and Weber (1998) have subjects contribute to candidates in a pre-election campaign and report the finance levels garnered by each candidate before each election.[3] I report these outcomes with the "preceding campaign" as the coordinating signal.

Gerber, Morton, and Rietz (1996) impose a majority requirement rule. Under this rule, if a candidate receives an absolute majority in the three-way race, that candidate is declared the winner. If not, the two leading candidates compete in a two-way runoff election to determine the winner. I report these outcomes with "runoff" as the coordinating signal.

Notice that each coordinating signal can result in three rankings between the majority-preferred candidates. The first-listed ("O" for reporting purposes) can lead, the second-listed ("G" for reporting purposes) can lead, or they can tie. One might expect that these differences lead to different behaviors among the majority voters. Thus, I report the results split across these three cases.

---

[3] The campaign contributions were subtracted from each subject's election payoffs. The funds were used to buy "commercials" which consisted of randomly tiled "Vote for X" statements that appeared on each subject's terminal over a 10-second period.

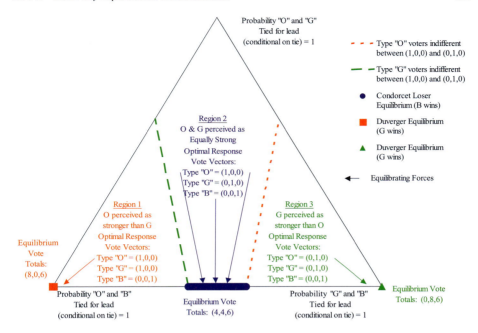

Figure 2. Perceived relative strength continuum representing equilibria for the electorate profile in Figure 1 according to Myerson and Weber's (1993) model. Vote vectors are given in the order of votes for O, G and B. Here, optimal vote responses depend only on the perceived relative strengths of O and G. If O seems much stronger than G, all majority voters vote for O. O wins with 8 votes, followed by B with 6 votes and G with 0 votes. If G seems much stronger than O, all majority voters vote for G. G wins with 8 votes, followed by B with 6 votes and O with 0 votes. These are Duverger equilibria because only two candidates receive positive vote totals. The other equilibrium results when neither O nor G seems strong enough to "swing" one majority voter type or the other and the majority splits. Then B wins the election with 6 votes, followed by O and G with 4 votes each. This coordination failure results in the Condorcet Loser (B) winning the election. This is also not a Duverger-type equilibrium since all three candidates received a significant number of votes.

3. Results

3.1. Candidate Winning Frequencies

Figure 3 shows the candidate winning frequencies (on a simplex) for each type of election. Major tendencies in the data are discussed there. Briefly, without a coordinating signal that distinguishes between majority-preferred candidates, the majority voters are unable to coordinate effectively. In contrast, when a coordinating signal distinguishes between the majority-preferred candidates, the leading majority-preferred candidate generally wins the ensuing election. The outcome is typically Duverger-like in the sense that the trailing majority-preferred candidate receives few, if any, votes. However, notice that the coordination is not perfect. The Condorcet Loser still wins a considerable

894 T. Rietz

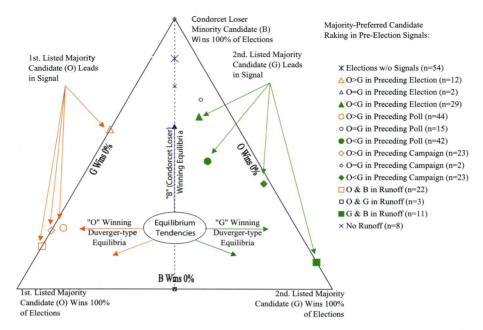

Figure 3. Candidate winning frequency simplex in three-way experimental elections with electorate profiles corresponding to Figure 1. The following pre-election signal type/election outcome relationships hold: (1) No coordinating signals ("no talk" in context, large ∗) result in frequent Condorcet Loser wins. (2) Previous election results ("common history" in context, large △ and large ▲ and small △ at the bottom center) are the least effective coordinating signal in defeating the Condorcet Loser. (3) Non-binding pre-election polls ("cheap talk" in context, large ○, large ● and small ○) are more effective in defeating Condorcet Losers. (4) Costly campaign contributions ("costly talk" in context, large ◊, large ♦ and small ◊ at the apex) are still more effective in defeating Condorcet Losers. (5) A majority requirement/runoff structure ("binding talk" in context, large □, large ■, small □ at the bottom center and small X) is the most effective in defeating Condorcet Losers. The following pre-election signal result/election outcome relationships hold: (1) No co-ordinating signals (large ∗) and coordinating signals that do not distinguish between the majority-preferred candidates (small △ at bottom center, small ○, small ◊ at the apex, small □ at the bottom center and small X) result in frequent Condorcet Loser wins. (Note the small numbers in most of the latter cases.) (2) No coordinating signals (large ∗) and non-distinguishing signals (small △ at bottom center, small ○, small ◊ at the apex, small □ at the bottom center and small X) result in relatively even majority candidate splits when the Condorcet Loser does not win. (3) When "O" leads "G" in the coordinating signal (large △, large ○, large ◊ and large □), "O" generally wins with Duverger-like outcomes (low "G" vote totals). (4) When "G" leads "O" in the coordinating signal (large ▲, large ●, large ♦ and large ■), "G" generally wins with Duverger-like outcomes (low "O" vote totals).

fraction of the time. Thus, coordinating signals aid in overcoming Condorcet Losers and the coordination seems intuitive (on the leader in the signal). However, the coordination is far from perfect. Types of signals are ranked in the following order according to their ability to aid coordination and defeat the Condorcet Loser. Previous election results prove least effective in aiding coordination and defeating the Condorcet Loser. This is followed by non-binding pre-election polls, costly campaign contributions and elections with majority requirement/runoff structures, in order of increasing effectiveness.

3.2. Other Results

The papers discussed here contain a variety of other results that may interest readers. In particular, all discuss individual voter behavior and the degree of and rationality of strategic voting. Voters differ in their strategies, but strategies generally appear rational in the sense that voters cast few dominated votes and, further, strategies appear consistent with "perfect" equilibria (in the sense of Myerson and Weber, 1993). Rietz (1993) discusses in detail what underlying model best fits observed behavior in Felsenthal, Rapoport, and Maoz (1988), Felsenthal (1990), Rapoport, Felsenthal, and Maoz (1991) and Forsythe et al. (1993, 1996). In contrast to what bloc voting models might predict, voters with the same preferences often seem to vote according to different strategies. Thus, the individual voting models explain the data better because voters are allowed to act as individuals.

Each paper discusses the degree to which elections obey Duverger's Law. Typically, when the majority voters can coordinate, they do so quite well and the equilibria appear quite Duverger-like. However, the results show two necessary conditions for Duverger's law to hold under plurality voting. First, split-majority voters must have a signal that allows them to focus on a particular candidate. Second, this signal must separate the two majority-preferred candidates sufficiently for one to become focal in order for coordination to occur.

In addition, Forsythe et al. (1993, 1996) look at election dynamics across series of repeated elections. They find that only the most recent signal seems relevant in coordination. Forsythe et al. (1996) study approval voting and the Borda rule as well. Rietz, Myerson, and Weber (1998) also discuss approval voting briefly. They find that all three voting rules are subject to Condorcet Losers winning elections. In contrast to the Duverger-like outcomes under plurality voting, results under approval voting and the Borda rule tend to close three-way races. (We would not expect Duverger's Law to hold under these voting rules and, in the experiments, it does not.) Rietz, Myerson, and Weber (1998) also discuss the rationality of campaign contribution levels. Using a variety of measures, they find that finance levels appear quite rational.

4. Conclusions and Other Issues Studied with Similar Experiments

The results from these papers clearly show that subjects are aware of the Condorcet Loser problem and act strategically to avoid it. Depending on the signals they use to coordinate their vote, they are more or less successful. The results show how Duverger's law arises from this strategic interaction, highlighting the conditions necessary for it to arise. The results also accord well with Myerson and Weber's (1993) concept of voting equilibria. Few voters cast non-equilibrium votes and, given a coordinating signal, most voters in a cohort cast votes consistent with a single equilibrium.

In closing, I note that several other papers use similar experimental designs to study different topics related to election systems. For example, Gerber, Morton, and Rietz (1998) compare voting rules in a somewhat different election system. They extend Myerson and Weber's (1993) theory to analyze straight voting and cumulative voting in multi-member districts (i.e., those in which two candidates each win a seat in a two-seat, three-way election). Again, in the experimental tests, voters' actions appear largely rational and equilibria appear consistent with rational modeling. Using a similar design, Forsythe, Rietz, and Weber (1994) study behavior in two-way elections when voting is costly. They find that candidates who would surely lose elections without costs sometimes win under costly voting because voters frequently abstain. Turnouts vary with cost levels and electorate sizes. Finally, also using a similar design, Peterson (1998) explores the "California effect" (the supposed reduction in turnout on the West Coast that results from early projections of East Coast outcomes). He finds support for the idea that knowing early election returns depresses turnout among those who vote later in the laboratory. Thus, the basic experimental design and theory behind the papers discussed here can be extended to study a variety of other interesting issues surrounding elections and voting systems.

Acknowledgements

For many helpful discussions, I think Robert Forsythe, Rebecca Morton, Roger Myerson and Robert Weber.

References

Black, D. (1958). "The Theory of Committees and Elections". Cambridge University Press, Cambridge.
Condorcet, Marquis de M.J.A.N.C. (1785). "Essai sur l'Application de l'Aalyse à la Probabilité des Decisions Rendues à la Pluralité des Vcix". L'Imprimerie Royale, Paris.
Duverger, M. (1967). "Political Parties: Their Organization and Activity in the Modern State". B. North and R. North, trans. Methuen and Company, London.
Felsenthal, D.S. (1990). "Topics in Social Choice: Sophisticated Voting, Efficacy, and Proportional Representation". Praeger Publishers, New York.
Felsenthal, D.S., Rapoport, A., Maoz, Z. (1988). "Tacit cooperation in three alternative noncooperative voting games: A new model of sophisticated behavior under the plurality procedure". Electoral Studies 7, 143–161.
Forsythe, R., Rietz, T.A., Weber, R.J. (1994). "Theory, outcomes and individual voter behavior in two candidate elections with voting costs". Mimeo, University of Iowa.
Forsythe, R., Myerson, R.B., Rietz, T.A., Weber, R.J. (1993). "An experiment on coordination in multi-candidate elections: The importance of polls and election histories". Social Choice and Welfare 10, 223–247.
Forsythe, R., Myerson, R.B., Rietz, T.A., Weber, R.J. (1996). "An experimental study of voting rules and polls in three-way elections". The International Journal of Game Theory 25, 355–383.

Gerber, E.R., Morton, R.B., Rietz, T.A. (1996). "Majority requirements and minority representation". Mimeo, University of Iowa.

Gerber, E.R., Morton, R.B., Rietz, T.A. (1998). "Minority representation in multi-member districts". The American Political Science Review 92, 127–144.

McKelvey, R.D., Ordeshook, P.C. (1985a). "Elections with limited information: A fulfilled expectations model using contemporaneous poll and endorsement data as information sources". Journal of Economic Theory 36, 55–85.

McKelvey, R.D., Ordeshook, P.C. (1985b). "Rational expectations in elections: Some experimental results based on a multidimensional model". Public Choice 44, 61–102.

McKelvey, R.D., Ordeshook, P.C. (1990). "A decade of experimental research on spatial models of elections and committees". In: Hinich, M.J., Enelow, J. (Eds.), Government, Democracy, and Social Choice. Cambridge University Press, Cambridge.

Myerson, R.B., Weber, R.J. (1993). "A theory of voting equilibria". American Political Science Review 87, 102–114.

Peterson, G. (1998). "East Coast information and West Coast elections: How the release of early election results can alter election outcome". Ph.D. thesis, University of Iowa, Department of Political Science.

Plott, C.R. (1991). "A comparative analysis of direct democracy, two-candidate elections and three-candidate elections in an experimental environment". In: Palfrey, T.R. (Ed.), Laboratory Research in Political Economy. University of Michigan Press, Ann Arbor.

Rapoport, A., Felsenthal, D.S., Maoz, Z. (1991). "Sincere versus strategic behavior in small groups". In: Palfrey, T.R. (Ed.), Laboratory Research in Political Economy. University of Michigan Press, Ann Arbor.

Rietz, T.A. (1993). "Comportamiento estratégico en elecciones con múltiples alternativas: Una revisión de alguna evidencia experimental". Cuadernos Economicos de ICE 54, 129–170.

Rietz, T.A., Myerson, R.B., Weber, R.J. (1998). "Campaign finance levels as coordinating signals in three-way, experimental elections". Economics and Politics 10, 185–217.

Chapter 95

PARTICIPATION GAME EXPERIMENTS: EXPLAINING VOTER TURNOUT

JOEP SONNEMANS and ARTHUR SCHRAM

CREED, University of Amsterdam, Roetersstraat 11, 1018 WB Amsterdam, The Netherlands

The paradox of voter turnout has been the subject of academic debate for decades (for an early survey, see Schram, 1991). The debate probably started with Downs' (1957) formulation of the problem. He noted that the expected benefits from voting in a large-scale election are generally outweighed by the cost of the act. Nevertheless a very large number of voters actually turns out to vote in general elections. Many theoretical and empirical papers have been published trying to explain the paradox, but only in the last 20 years or so have rational choice models been developed that show that turning out to vote might sometimes be rational in an instrumental sense (see Ledyard, 1984, or Schram, 1991, and the references given there).

Palfrey and Rosenthal (1983) model the turnout problem as a participation game and study it game-theoretically. In this game, there are two or more teams. Everyone has to make a private decision that is beneficial to every member in one's own team and harmful to members of other teams. The decision is whether or not to 'participate' in an action, where participation is costly. Palfrey and Rosenthal show that, in many cases, Nash equilibria with positive levels of participation exist.

It is difficult to study voter turnout using field data. Participation games provide a structure to study this decision experimentally, however. This has been done by Bornstein (1992) and Schram and Sonnemans (1996a, 1996b). Here, we shall present some of the results reported in the latter two papers. We are particularly interested in testing the game-theoretic predictions. We begin with a brief description of the experiments. More details about the design and procedures are given in our two 1996 papers.

In the experiments, subjects were split in two groups of 6 individuals, named yellow and blue. Each subject had to decide whether or not to buy a token. The price of a token (i.e., the cost of participation) was common knowledge and equal for everyone. The number of tokens bought in each group determined the payoffs. The payoff was equal for everyone within a group. The earnings of a subject in a period equaled this payoff minus the cost of a token if one was bought by that subject. This was repeated for 20 periods.

There were two payoff schedules, representing a winner-takes-all election (WIN) and proportional representation (PR). In WIN, each member of the group that bought the most tokens (won the elections) received a payoff of 2.50 Dutch Guilders and the payoff for the other group was zero. A tie was broken randomly with equal probability for both teams. In PR the payoff to any group-member was proportional to the relative turnout of the groups. More precisely, the number of tokens bought in one's own group was divided by the total number of tokens bought and the result was multiplied by 2.22 Dutch Guilders. The price of a token was 1.00 Dutch Guilders in WIN and 0.75 Dutch Guilders in PR. These payoff schedules were presented to the subjects in matrix form. Nash equilibria of the static (one-shot) game in pure strategies are 1–1 (in both groups 1 token is purchased) in PR and 6–6 in WIN. One quasi-symmetric mixed strategies equilibrium (all subjects in one group buy a token with the same probability) exists in PR: all subjects buy a token with probability 0.098. In WIN two quasi-symmetric mixed strategies equilibria exist in which all subjects buy either with probability 0.051 or 0.949.

Besides the distinction in WIN and PR, in some sessions we used a partners (fixed group) design and others a strangers (groups rematched in every period) design. This gives four different kinds of sessions: WIN-partners, WIN-strangers, PR-partners, and PR-strangers. Each kind was run in two sessions. In addition, we ran two additional WIN-partners and two additional PR-partners sessions. In these, we added a surprise 5 extra periods. Before these were run (with the same groups and same conditions), subjects were allowed to talk freely within the own group, for five minutes.

Before presenting the results for these sessions, we briefly describe the results of some related participation game experiments we ran. To investigate the effect of group size, we ran two WIN-partners sessions with groups of 14 subjects and two WIN-partners sessions where one group consisted of 8 and the other of 6 participants. On average, subjects bought 7.36, 7.63, and 8.67 tokens in 20 periods when in a group of 14, 8 (facing a group of 6), and 6 (facing a group of 8), respectively. In comparison, on average 8.40 tokens were bought when in a group of 6 (facing a group of 6). None of the differences was statistically significant, however.

The results of the 12 sessions are presented in Figure 1. The hypothesis (point prediction) that subjects play a Nash equilibrium in pure or quasi-symmetric mixed strategies is rejected. Details of the tests are presented in Schram and Sonnemans (1996a), where we also show that the choices observed do not constitute an asymmetric Nash equilibrium. However, we find interesting differences in behavior across treatments. Though these differences decrease towards the end of the 20 periods, two effects that appear to be present in the data are that:

(1) participation is higher in winner-takes-all than in proportional representation (in spite of the lower costs of participation in the latter case). This is in line with the comparative statics of the pure strategy equilibria.
(2) participation is higher in partners than in strangers (especially in winner-takes-all).

Both effects are statistically significant. In addition, the restart shows that:

(3) participation increases substantially (and statistically significantly) after five minutes of free communication. This is in line with the results of Bornstein (1992).

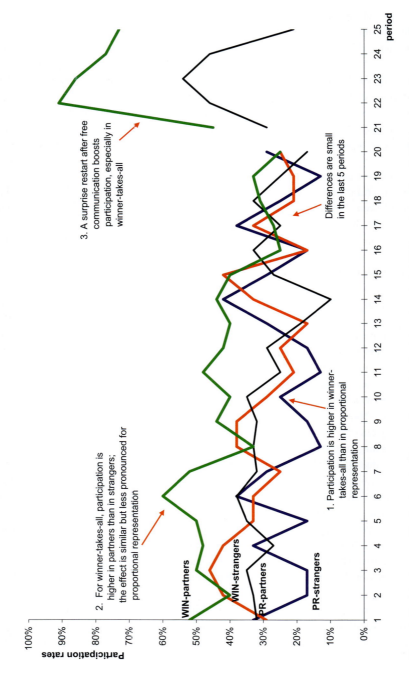

Figure 1. Participation rates. The fraction of subjects that buys a token (participates) per period. WIN = winner-takes-all; PR = proportional representation.

References

Bornstein, G. (1992). "The free-rider problem in intergroup conflicts over step-level and continuous public goods". Journal of Personality and Social Psychology 62, 597–606.
Downs, A. (1957). "An Economic Theory of Democracy". Harper and Row, New York.
Ledyard, J.O. (1984). "The pure theory of large two-candidate elections". Public Choice 44, 7–41.
Palfrey, Th.R., Rosenthal, H. (1983). "A strategic calculus of voting". Public Choice 41, 7–53.
Schram, A.J.H.C. (1991). "Voter Behavior in Economic Perspective". Springer Verlag, Heidelberg.
Schram, A., Sonnemans, J. (1996a). "Voter turnout as a participation game: An experimental investigation". International Journal of Game Theory 25, 385–406.
Schram, A., Sonnemans, J. (1996b). "Why people vote: Experimental evidence". Journal of Economic Psychology 17, 417–442.

PART 6.3

BEHAVIOR AND ORGANIZATIONS

Colin F. Camerer and Roberto Weber, "Growing Organizational Culture in the Laboratory"

Chapter 96

GROWING ORGANIZATIONAL CULTURE IN THE LABORATORY

COLIN F. CAMERER
Caltech

ROBERTO WEBER
Carnegie-Mellon

An organization's culture is its system of values, symbols, rituals, heroes and villains, slang – or more simply, 'how business is done.' To an economist, it is irresistible to take an approach to culture that anthropologists call "functionalist" – viz., try to understand a culture and its persistence by asking whether it enhances economic efficiency or worker satisfaction, or resolves coordination problems by telling workers what they should do when contracts are incomplete (Camerer and Vepsalainen, 1988; Kreps, 1990; Cremer, 1993; Hermalin, 2001). Despite the apparent importance of culture, little systematic empirical research has been about organizational cultures and their economic impact. This is partly due to the difficulty associated with measuring culture precisely in the field (e.g., Rousseau, 1990).

One way to study organizational culture is to create it in the laboratory and explore its properties. In Weber and Camerer (2003) we studied how experimental subjects create specialized homemade languages – like "slang" or codes which are used to rapidly communicate what to do in organizations. Examples which spring to mind are the slang of teenagers, mobsters, and rappers ("whatever," "fuggedaboutit," "benjamins" = money), government acronyms, academic jargon, and phrases ("Does he drink the Kool-Aid?" is used at Microsoft as a measure of corporate loyalty, alluding to the use of Kool-Aid to dispense cyanide in the Jonestown Massacre). Codes are obviously one facet of culture. Codes are also a metaphor for others aspects of culture, but they are easier to synthesize and measure in the laboratory in short time-frames (compared to other cultural features like values and "creation myths").

In our experiment, groups of subjects are shown pictures and must develop a common "homemade" language to refer to the pictures (cf. linguistics experiments by Clark and Wilkes-Gibbs, 1986; and Schober and Clark, 1989; and cf. Blume et al., 1998 on evolution of meaning in sender–receiver games). In the task, one subject (the "manager") is aware of which of many possible states of the world is true and has to communicate this to the other subject (the "employee"). The states of the world are possible sequences of pictures that both the manager and employee have in front of them. The pictures are of complex office environments, in which there are several people, objects, and activities (see Figure 1). The pictures all overlap substantially in content, but also all have several unique elements.

Figure 1. An example of a picture subjects had to identify with code (Weber and Camerer, 2003).

In each round of the experiment, the manager is told which sequence of pictures is the correct one. The manager must communicate this information to the employee(s) by only describing features of the pictures (with a financial penalty for finishing slowly). While performing the task, subjects in a group can freely talk back and forth with each other, but are not allowed any other communication. Since the pictures are displayed in different orders to different subjects, they cannot refer to them by numbers or physical location on a computer screen. To perform well, subjects therefore need to develop a common language to refer to the pictures as rapidly as possible. This results in a tacit, shared understanding that is similar to corporate culture in a simple form. Like cultural practices, the internal language is an important source of the "firm's" efficiency (the ability to communicate which pictures to select rapidly) and also a source of potential cultural conflict (players using different codes choose more slowly). Like culture, the homemade language arises endogenously through shared experience, so it is likely to be idiosyncratic and differ between firms – even though each firm's language may be equally efficient. "Good" cultural codes pick out the special features of each picture, are brief, and are often memorable (because they are funny or tap other kinds of affect). For example, subjects described Figure 1 office scene as "cubicles," "headphones," or "telemarketers." In another picture a businessman is gesturing at a meeting with his hands outstretched. One group called this picture "Macarena" because the outstretched hand gesture resembled one move in the faddish dance of the same name from the 1990s.

In the experiments, culture can be measured precisely as the agreed-upon code which subjects develop. Efficiency of culture can be measured by how rapidly subjects are able to locate the correct pictures using the code. Differences in culture can be measured by using linguistic measures of word similarity (or by having subjects in one group try to locate pictures using another group's code).

Weber and Camerer (2003) used this experimental procedure to address how conflicting cultures may cause inefficiencies in corporate mergers. In the experiments, two pairs of subjects independently repeated the task for 20 rounds. Each subject alternated between the roles of manager and employee, resulting in 10 rounds as manager for each participant. The left part of Figure 2 shows the amount of time it took groups of subjects to complete the task. Note that while initially the completion time was high (average time = 249 seconds), the time decreased considerably by round 20 (average time = 48 seconds).

After allowing the groups 20 rounds of experience with the task so that they could develop a shorthand language, the two groups were merged. One of the firms was randomly selected to take over the other firm. After the merger, subjects' roles (manager or employee) were fixed. The "merged" firm consisted of one manager and two employees (one form the "acquiring firm" and one from the "acquired firm"). Thus, the manager and one employee were both from the acquiring firm and the other employee was from the acquired firm. The acquiring manager then participated in the same task as before – now communicating simultaneously with two employees – for 10 rounds.[1] In this second part of the experiment, each employee was timed separately and could therefore complete the task individually of the other employee and could receive a different amount in each round for completing the task. As before, the manager and employees could freely talk back and forth. The manager received the average of the earnings of both employees for the 10 rounds multiplied by 1.5.

As the right-hand side of Figure 2 shows, "merging" two laboratory firms led to persistent decreases in efficiency due to the difficulty of establishing a common language. The average completion time increased from 48 s in the last pre-merger round to 130 s in the first-post merger round. This is purely because of the differences in "cultures."

More interestingly, perhaps, subjects underestimated the difficulty of integrating these very simple forms of culture. Prior to the merger, we elicited estimates from all subjects about the average performance of the merged "firm" in the 10 post-merger rounds. One subject (the subject who was excluded from the merged firm) would receive a monetary reward for making a more accurate prediction. This produces a situation where it is incentive compatible for subjects to state their true belief of the post-merger firm's performance. The results clearly indicate that subjects overestimate the value of a merged firm.

Finally, using survey questionnaires eliciting beliefs about the competence of other subjects in the experiment, we also found that subjects blamed other members of the

---

[1] There is not a pure "group-size" effect on the completion time. That is, a control group in which subjects performed the task in three-person groups for 20 rounds performed identically to the two-person groups.

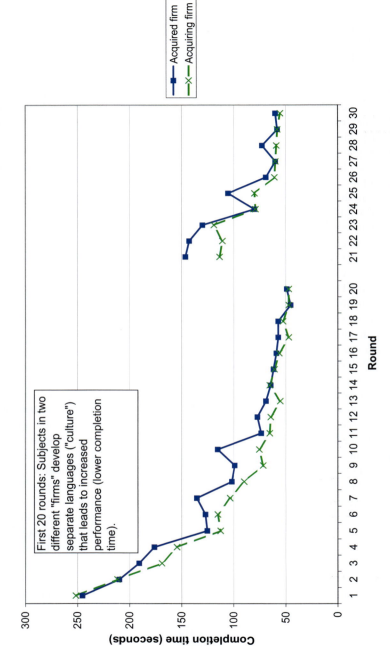

Figure 2. Average completion times in organizational culture experiments ($n = 11$ sessions) (Weber and Camerer, 2003).

merged organization for its failure, particularly those who were originally in the other firm.

References

Blume, A., DeJong, D.V., Kim, Y.G., Sprinkle, G.B. (1998). "Experimental evidence on the evolution of meaning of messages in sender–receiver games". American Economic Review 88 (5), 1323–1340.
Camerer, Colin F., Vepsalainen, Ari (1988). "The efficiency of cultural contracting". Strategic Management Journal 9, 77–94.
Clark, H.H., Wilkes-Gibbs, D. (1986). "Referring as a collaborative process". Cognition 22 (1), 1–39.
Cremer, Jacques (1993). "Corporate culture and shared knowledge". Industrial and Corporate Change 2 (3), 351–386.
Hermalin, Benjamin E. (2001). "Economics and corporate culture". In: Cooper, C., Cartwright, S., Earley, P.C. (Eds.), The International Handbook of Organizational Culture and Climate. Wiley, New York.
Kreps, David M. (1990). "Corporate culture and economic theory". In: Alt, J.E., Shepsle, K.A. (Eds.), Perspectives on Positive Political Economy. Cambridge University Press, Cambridge, UK.
Rousseau, D. (1990). "Assessing organizational culture: The case for multiple methods". In: Schneider, B. (Ed.), Climate and Culture. Jossey-Bass, San Francisco.
Schober, Michael F., Clark, Herbert H. (1989). "Understanding by addressees and overhearers". Cognitive Psychology 21 (2), 211–232.
Weber, Roberto A., Camerer, Colin F. (2003). "Cultural conflict and merger failure: An experimental approach". Management Science 49 (Special Issue), 400–415.

PART 7

INDIVIDUAL CHOICE, BELIEFS AND BEHAVIOR

7. INDIVIDUAL CHOICE, BELIEFS AND BEHAVIOR

Risk: Effect of Stakes and Sex

In many experimental studies it has been found that increasing the level of rewards, while not always significantly improving average support for the predictive hypothesis, nevertheless reduces the variance of the observations around the predicted outcome. Smith and Walker model the decision as maximizing the expected utility of the reward where the subjective cognitive cost of effort is increasing in the accuracy of the decision. Consequently, increasing payoffs induces more costly effort, and reduces the error variance relative to the prediction.

In a second entry, they apply this model to the first price auction decision format to examine the effect of payoff levels and experience on bidding behavior. The payoffs vary from zero to 20 times the normal amounts paid to subjects in first price auction experiments. Both payoff level and experience reduce the volatility of bids relative to assigned value: the standard error around the fitted bid function decreases with these two treatment control variables. The slopes of the individual bid functions – theoretically determined entirely by the individual attitudes toward risk – do not change significantly with these treatments. This is consistent with constant relative risk aversion. But contrary to this result, compare the study of payoff scale and risk attitude by Laury and Holt using choice between lotteries showing that people are more risk averse at larger payoffs. The payoffs are varied by factors of 20, 50 and 90 times the baseline reward.

Eckel and Grossman offer a comprehensive survey of field and laboratory comparisons of risk aversion in men and women. Although the field studies conclude that women are more risk averse than men, the results from laboratory experiments are less conclusive. Most of the laboratory evidence is consistent with the field evidence, but the counter-evidence raises questions of the stability of measures across different contexts and instruments used for the measurement. Thus they report studies showing very low correlations in the measure of risk aversion across different valuation tasks for similar gambles.

This is reminiscent of a study by Berg, Dickhaut, and McCabe (2005) showing large variations in measures of risk aversion (including a sign change to risk preferring behavior) with systematic variation in the instruments used. Measures of risk attitude are clearly not independent of the institutional measurement procedure. This raises fundamental questions as to the validity of expected utility theory as a context independent universal means of characterizing behavior under risk. Consistent with these findings, new theoretical models based on the economics of survival have charted an alternative path to classical utility maximization models (Radner, 1998).

Endowment effects

The entry by Kahneman, Knetsch and Thaler (KKT) summarizes their work, and related literatures examining the following question: in consumer choice does an individual's (Marshallian) inverse demand have a discontinuity at zero where – as the price increases – the individual shifts from being a buyer of additional units of an item in his inventory to a seller of units? The traditional theory of consumer behavior assumed smooth preferences and deduced no discontinuity. Why is this question interesting if final demand by consumers is defined only in the positive domain, except for yard sales and flea markets? KKT themselves have argued that their claims have no valid application to goods purchased for resale by a firm – only to the final consumer. It is a question of the consistency and generality of demand theory.

Also, the KKT hypothesis that there is a discontinuity at zero – with the selling price much in excess of the buying price – is related to a much more general phenomenon: the hypothesized asymmetry between losses and gains that has been studied in entirely different contexts with important applications to behavior under uncertainty. This important proposition, however, has much older origins and was succinctly stated by Adam Smith in the *Theory of Moral Sentiments* (first published in 1759): "We suffer more ...when we fall from a better to a worse situation, than we ever enjoy when we rise from a worse to a better ...It is averse to expose our health, our fortune, our rank, or reputation, to any sort of hazard. It is rather cautious than enterprising, and more anxious to preserve the advantages which we already possess, than forward to prompt us to the acquisition of still greater advantages" (p. 213).

KKT examines the endowment effect with two methodologically distinct approaches: individual choice, and market exchange. The former approach directly measures an individual's buying and selling price at zero demand; the latter indirectly tests the prediction that an endowment effect implies a reduce volume of trade.

Briefly, the KKT entry shows that with certain consumer goods people's selling price averages about 2.5 times their buying price, and in a trading environment in which conventional theory predicts that 11 units will trade in fact only 1–4 units trade.

Kujal and Smith (KJ) modify the KKT experiments based on a critique of their procedures. Thus, in their choice experiments KKT ask subjects to bring their own money for purchases, but endow the sellers each with a free unit of the consumer good used. KJ eliminate this asymmetric income effect by endowing all subjects with money or goods of similar value; also they convert the KKT experiments into pure choice among options with no reference to "buying" and "selling." The KJ results show that substituting a choice task for the buying and selling tasks narrows the KKT reported discrepancy. But the qualitative differences persist and are significant.

The KJ test of the market trading prediction shows much less under trading than the KKT experiments, and in three of the eleven experiments half of the mugs trade as predicted by standard theory. Moreover, they show why there is under trading: the natural tendencies toward under revelation of intra marginal units leads to very flat reported inverse supply and demand so that in mechanisms that all but eliminate the discrepancy between selling and buying prices small deviations can lead to magnified under trading.

It is important to note that the efficacy of market trading institutions is conditional on preferences and therefore quite independent of how preferences may be affected by an endowment effect: markets do their thing subject to individual tastes, however the latter might be most appropriately modeled.

References

Berg, J., Dickhaut, J., McCabe, K. (2005). "Risk preference instability across institutions: A dilemma". Proceedings of the National Academy of Sciences 102, 4209–4214.

Radner, Roy (1998). "Economic survival". In: Jacobs, D.P., Kalai, E., Kamien, M. (Eds.), Frontiers of Research in Economic Theory: The Nancy L. Schwartz Memorial Lectures, 1983–1997. Cambridge University Press, Cambridge, UK.

Chapter 97

MOTIVATION THEORY AND EXPERIMENTAL BEHAVIOR UNDER THE DECISION COST HYPOTHESIS[1]

VERNON L. SMITH and JAMES M. WALKER

1. Payoffs and Behavior

There is a long experimental literature, going back at least to Siegel (1959, 1961), Siegel and Fouraker (1960) and Fouraker and Siegel (1963), in which monetary payments affecting subject opportunity cost is varied as a treatment variable, and their controlled effects on performance are measured. Most of the psychology literature reports the results of experiments conducted without monetary reinforcement, but in which the "subject is instructed to do his best." (See Siegel, 1961, p. 767.) Psychologists defend such hypothetical choice procedures on the grounds that money either does not matter or matters insignificantly. Thus Dawes, 1988, pp. 122, 124, 131, 259) cites several examples of decision making experiments in which the use of monetary rewards yields results "the same" or "nearly" the same as when choices were hypothetical: Slovic, Fischoff, and Lichtenstein (1982), Grether and Plott (1979), Tversky and Kahneman (1983) and Tversky and Edwards (1966). But some contrary citations in the psychology literature showing that monetary incentives do matter are as follows: Goodman et al. (1979), who conclude, "These data, though far from conclusive, should not enhance the confidence of those who use elicitation methods based on obtaining certainty equivalents of imaginary bets" (p. 398); Siegel, Siegel, and Andrews (1964) ... "we have little confidence in experiments in which the 'payoffs' are points, credits[2] or tokens" (p. 148); Messick and Brayfield (1964), passim, and Kroll, Levy, and Rapoport (1988).

In the economics literature there is the study of 240 farmers in India by Binswanger (1980, 1981) comparing hypothetical choice among gambles with choices whose real payoffs ranged to levels exceeding the subjects' monthly incomes; the hypothetical results were not consistent with the motivated measures of risk aversion; because payoffs varied across three levels, subjects tended to show increased risk aversion at higher payoffs. Similarly, Wolf and Pohlman (1983) compare hypothetical with actual bids of a Treasury bill dealer, and find that the dealer's measure of constant relative risk aversion using actual bid data is four times larger than under hypothetical assessment. In a study of risk preferences under high monetary incentives in China, Kachelmeier and Shehata

---

[1] In this essay we have updated, but drawn freely from the literature survey in Smith and Walker (1993a), and the strategic interaction model in Smith and Szidarovszky (1999).

[2] It is now well documented that grade credits compare well with monetary rewards when the payments are salient as in Isaac, Walker, and Williams (1991); and in Kormendi and Plott (1982).

(1991) report a significant difference between subject responses under low and very high monetary payoffs, and no difference between hypothetical and low monetary payments, but the usual anomalies long documented in tests of expected utility theory remain.

Other studies in which monetary rewards make a difference include: Plott and Smith (1978, 142) report results in which marginal trades occur far more frequently with commission incentives than without; Fiorina and Plott (1978) report committee decisions in which both mean deviations from theoretical predictions and standard errors are reduced by escalating reward levels; Grether (1981) reports individual decision making experiments in which the incidence of "confused" behavior is reduced with monetary rewards, but subjects who appear not to be confused behave about the same with or without monetary rewards. Cox and Grether (1996) find that the preference reversal phenomenon is reduced to noise under high payoffs and an English Clock Auction for valuing prospects.

A dramatic example of how payoff levels can matter is found in Kroll, Levy, and Rapoport (1988), who provide experimental tests of the separation theorem and the capital asset pricing model in a computer controlled portfolio selection task. Two experiments are reported: experiment 1 (30 subjects) and experiment 2 (12 subjects). The payoffs in experiment 2 were ten times greater than the payoffs in experiment 1, averaging $165 per subject, or about $44 per hour (30 times the prevailing student hourly wage in Israel). The authors find that performance is significantly improved, relative to the capital asset pricing model, by the tenfold increase in stakes, and suggest that "This finding casts some doubt on the validity of the results of many experiments on decision making which involve trivial amounts of money or no money at all" Kroll, Levy, and Rapoport (1988, p. 514).

Forsythe et al. (1994) find that results in the dictator game are affected significantly by monetary incentives and that under no-pay conditions the results in ultimatum games are inconclusive because they fail to be replicable. With monetary incentives, the authors strongly reject the fairness hypothesis. Hoffman, McCabe, and Smith (1996) compare $10 with $100 ultimatum games and find that although the lower offer distributions for $100 payoffs are statistically equivalent to the offers for $10 payoffs, the rejection frequencies increase significantly in the $100 games.

Finally, McClelland et al. (1991) directly manipulate foregone expected profit in incentive decision mechanisms with treatments making the payoff optimum more or less peaked. They find that where the mechanism is "transparently" simple (which we interpret as low decision cost) flat maxima do as well as peaked maxima, but where the mechanism is "opaque," requiring search, the absolute deviation of subjects' bids from the optimal is significantly reduced when the payoff function is more peaked.

1.1. Decision Making and Decision Cost Under Uncertainty

The study by Tversky and Edwards (1966) is of particular interest since they found that paying (charging) 5 cents (as compared with no salient reward) when a subject makes a correct (incorrect) prediction, yields outcomes closer to "the optimal" outcome. The task is the standard binary choice prediction experiment: two lights illuminate by an "independent trials" Bernoulli process with fixed probabilities, p and $1 - p$, unknown to the subjects. The standard result is for subjects to reach a stable asymptote in which the pooled proportion of times the more frequent event is predicted is $\hat{x} \cong p$. Since the expected number of correct predictions is $xp + (1 - x)(1 - p)$, when the more frequent event is chosen with frequency x, the "optimal" response is to set $x^* = 1$ ($p > 1/2$). Tversky and Edwards report higher (than matching) pooled total frequencies for 1000 trials: $\hat{x} = 0.705$ when $p = 0.60$ and $\hat{x} = 0.76$ when $p = 0.70$; the asymptotic levels (not reported) can be presumed to be somewhat higher. Their conclusion: "Though most differences between the treatment groups were in the direction predicted by a normative model, Ss were far indeed from what one would expect on the basis of such a model" (Tversky and Edwards, 1966, p. 682). They conjecture that: "A formal model for the obtained data might incorporate a notion such as cost associated with making a decision" (p. 683).

Such a formal model attempting to do this was published and tested somewhat earlier by Siegel (1959), Siegel and Goldstein (1959), Siegel (1961), Siegel and Andrews (1962), and Siegel, Siegel, and Andrews (1964). Instead of rejecting the utility theory of choice, Siegel elected to explore the possibility that the theory was essentially correct but incomplete. In particular, citing Simon (1956), he argued that one should keep in mind the distinction between objective rationality, as viewed by the experimenter, and subjective rationality as viewed by the subject, given his perceptual and evaluational premises. Siegel postulated that (i) in the absence of monetary reinforcement, the only reward would be the satisfaction (dissatisfaction) of a correct (incorrect) prediction, and (ii) the task is incredibly boring, since it involves both cognitive and kinesthetic monotony, and in this context there was a utility from varying one's prediction.

Subsequently, Smith (1976) generalized Siegel's work for experimental economics, and Smith and Walker (1993a) reformulated the problem in terms of decision cost and provided some direct tests of the model (1993b). In what follows this formulation is further expanded to include interactive decision making.

We interpret Siegel's formal model as one in which boredom is a decision cost to be weighed against the payoff value of the decision. As such it is embedded in the general class of environments in which utility value is achieved only by incurring subjective decision cost. His model predicted that an increase in rewards would move subjects closer to the optimum with $x^* = 1$, and in fact, the data testing the model strongly support this prediction. The Bernoulli trials environment and Siegel's results exhibit three key properties:

(1) The optimal response is a boundary solution on the set $(X: 0 \leqslant x \leqslant 1)$ with $x^* = 1$.
(2) As the payoff reward from an optimal response increases the observed frequency, moves closer to 1.
(3) Since the environment is a Bernoulli process, the mean varies directly with x, for a fixed number of trials, n, while the variance varies as $x(1 - x)$. Therefore if

x increases with the reward level the variance necessarily declines with reward level.

In Smith and Walker (1993a) we inquire as to whether and how these empirical findings by Siegel generalized across other experimental environments, and found that they did in the following sense:

(i) When the theoretical optimum, or equilibrium in strategic interactions, was at an interior point, and the observations supported this prediction, then increased rewards tended to reduce the variance of the observations around the prediction.

(ii) When the predicted equilibrium was on the boundary of the constraint set, then increasing rewards tended to move the central tendency of the data closer to the theoretical prediction, and reduced the variance of the observations.

We derived a decision cost, or effort, model that is consistent with these empirical results.[3] In what follows we generalize that model to include strategic non-cooperative equilibria.

1.2. Two-person Interactive Model of Decision Cost

Consider a 2-person experimental game with outcome π^i ($i = 1, 2$), which is converted into a monetary reward using the conversion constant λ ($\lambda \geqslant 0$). Let $C_i(z_i)$ be the subjective or mental cost of cognitive effort z_i. The utility of player i can therefore be written as

$$U^i = (1 + \lambda)\pi^i(y_1, y_2) - C_i(z_i), \tag{1}$$

where y_1 and y_2 are the decision variables of an interactive Nash game. When no cash reward is offered, then $\lambda = 0$, and the formulation (1) allows that there is some self satisfaction in maximizing the paper profit $\pi^i - C_i$. This is indicated by the common observation that subjects make reasonably good decisions – they do not choose arbitrarily or randomly – when there is no monetary reward.

Let (x_1^*, x_2^*) denote the Nash equilibrium computed by the theorist when net payoffs are π^i, and the cost term in Equation (1) is ignored.

Now write each subject's decision in the error deviation form

$$y_i = x_i^* - s_i \xi_i(z_i), \tag{2}$$

where s_i is a random variable and ξ_i is some function of i's effort, z_i. Thus, $\xi_i(z_i)$ is i's production function for reducing error by application of cognitive or physiological resource effort. Neither z_i nor $\xi_i(z_i)$ is observable, but we do observe their effect on y_i

---

[3] The model serves to explicate the argument in Harrison (1989) that when the theory fails it is a consequence of low opportunity cost for deviations from the prediction. Since standard theory predicts optimal decision, however flat the payoff hill is, it follows that the theory is misspecified. When the theory is adequately specified there should be nothing left to be explained by low opportunity cost – the benefit margin is weighed against cost and there is nothing left to forgo.

and the deviation error, $x_i^* - y_i$. Under this assumption the utility of player i can be rewritten as follows:

$$U^i = (1+\lambda)\pi^i\left(x_1^* - s_1\xi_1(z_1), x_2^* - s_2\xi_2(z_2)\right) - C_i(z_i). \tag{3}$$

Let a pair (z_1, z_2) be an interior equilibrium of the 2-person game with payoff functions (3). Then it satisfies relations

$$(1+\lambda)\frac{\partial \pi^i}{\partial y_i}\left(x_1^* - s_1\xi_1(z_1), x_2^* - s_2\xi_2(z_2)\right)\left(-s_i\xi_i'(z_i)\right) - C_i'(z_i) = 0 \tag{4}$$

for $i = 1, 2$. Assuming that the operations of expectation and differentiation are interchangeable we have

$$\frac{\partial E(\pi^i)}{\partial z_i} - \frac{C_i'(z_i)}{1+\lambda} = 0 \quad (i = 1, 2). \tag{5}$$

In addition assume that Equations (5) have a unique solution (z_1, z_2) with arbitrary $\lambda > 0$. Then z_1 and z_2 are functions of λ. Differentiate both sides of Equation (5) with respect to λ to see that

$$\begin{pmatrix} \frac{\partial^2 E(\pi^1)}{\partial z_1^2} - \frac{C_1''(z_1)}{1+\lambda} & \frac{\partial^2 E(\pi^1)}{\partial z_1 \partial z_2} \\ \frac{\partial^2 E(\pi^2)}{\partial z_1 \partial z_2} & \frac{\partial^2 E(\pi^2)}{\partial z_2^2} - \frac{C_2''(z_2)}{1+\lambda} \end{pmatrix} \begin{pmatrix} \frac{dz_1}{d\lambda} \\ \frac{dz_2}{d\lambda} \end{pmatrix} = \frac{1}{(1+\lambda)^2} \begin{pmatrix} C_1'(z_1) \\ C_2'(z_2) \end{pmatrix}. \tag{6}$$

We make now the following additional assumptions:
(i) $\xi_i(z_i) > 0$, $\xi_i'(z_i) < 0$;
(ii) $C_i'(z_i) > 0$, $C_i''(z_i) \geq 0$;
(iii) $\frac{\partial^2 E(\pi^i)}{\partial z_i^2} < 0$, $\frac{\partial^2 E(\pi^i)}{\partial z_1 \partial z_2} \geq 0$, and

$$\frac{\partial^2 E(\pi^1)}{\partial z_1^2} \cdot \frac{\partial^2 E(\pi^2)}{\partial z_2^2} - \frac{\partial^2 E(\pi^1)}{\partial z_1 \partial z_2} \cdot \frac{\partial^2 E(\pi^2)}{\partial z_1 \partial z_2} > 0.$$

Under assumption (iii), matrix

$$\begin{pmatrix} -\frac{\partial^2 E(\pi^1)}{\partial z_1^2} & -\frac{\partial^2 E(\pi^1)}{\partial z_1 \partial z_2} \\ -\frac{\partial^2 E(\pi^2)}{\partial z_1 \partial z_2} & -\frac{\partial^2 E(\pi^2)}{\partial z_2^2} \end{pmatrix}$$

is an M-matrix with nonnegative inverse; furthermore, assumption (ii) implies that the negative of the coefficient matrix of Equation (6) is also an M-matrix. Since the right-hand side components are negative, from Equation (6) we conclude that both derivatives $\frac{dz_1}{d\lambda}$ and $\frac{dz_2}{d\lambda}$ are positive. The discrepancy between the actual equilibrium (y_1, y_2) of the subject's experience, and the equilibrium (x_1^*, x_2^*) of the theorist is characterized by the component-wise discrepancies

$$\varepsilon_i = x_i^* - y_i = s_i\xi_i(z_i). \tag{7}$$

Simple calculation shows that

$$E(\varepsilon_i) = E(s_i)\xi_i(z_i) \quad \text{and} \quad \text{Var}(\varepsilon_i) = \text{Var}(s_i)\xi_i^2(z_i), \tag{8}$$

therefore

$$\frac{dE(\varepsilon_i)}{d\lambda} = E(s_i)\xi_i'(z_i) \cdot \frac{dz_i}{d\lambda}, \tag{9}$$

which is positive if $E(s_i) < 0$, negative if $E(s_i) > 0$, and vanishes if $E(s_i) = 0$. In the latter case the subject's error in cognition is unbiased. Notice that $E(s_i) < 0$ indicates that y_i is above x_i^* in the average and since $\frac{dE(\varepsilon_i)}{d\lambda}$ becomes positive, in the expectation, the discrepancy ε_i becomes smaller as λ increases. Similarly, if $E(s_i) > 0$, then y_i is below x_1^* in the average, and since $\frac{dE(\varepsilon_i)}{d\lambda}$ becomes negative, the discrepancy decreases again, in the average, if λ increases. These conditions open a rich theory of biased cognition error, its effect on expected observational error, and its interaction with payoff levels, issues that will not be explored here. Similarly,

$$\frac{d\text{Var}(\varepsilon_i)}{d\lambda} = \text{Var}(s_i)2\xi_i(z_i)\xi_i'(z_i) \cdot \frac{dz_i}{d\lambda_i} < 0, \tag{10}$$

showing that the variance of the discrepancy in the average must decrease if λ increases. This result corresponds to a principal characteristic of the data reported in Smith and Walker (1993a, 1993b). Note that to get this empirical prediction, the multiplicative form of the error equation (2) is needed.

The model easily extends to the n-person case (Smith and Szidarovszky, 1999).

In Cournot duopoly, y_i is output by firm i. With linear demand and zero costs, profit is $\pi^i = [a - b(y_1 + y_2)]y_i$, $i = 1, 2$, where $a > 0$, and $b > 0$ are the linear demand parameters. Another example, shown in Figure 1, compares baseline payoffs with a tripled payoff treatment in two-stage, two-person, sequential move bilateral bargaining between a buyer and a seller.

Using data from Fouraker and Siegel (1963) for linear Cournot duopoly experiments, Smith and Walker (1993a) report mean square deviations from the optimum of 7.2 under low payoffs, and 5.5 under high payoffs. Using data from various versions of bilateral bargaining (simultaneous move versus sequential move and private versus complete information on cash payoffs), the mean square deviations vary from 2 to 27 times greater under low compared with high payoffs (see Smith and Walker, 1993a, p. 257). Double auction supply and demand experiments with perfectly elastic supply, and perfectly inelastic demand (yielding a competitive equilibrium at the supply price boundary) exhibit large differences, period by period in both the mean deviation, and the mean square deviation from equilibrium, when comparing weak with strong payoff motivation (Smith and Walker, 1993a, p. 259). Finally, Smith and Walker (1993b) published new first price auction experiments that varied rewards, setting $\lambda = 0, 1, 5, 10$, and 20 times the normal amounts paid to individual subjects, and reported a significant reduction in the mean square error for linear bid function regressions as λ was increased. They also report a large reduction in the mean square error linear bid function when subject experience is

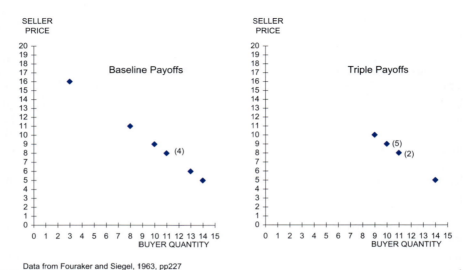

Figure 1. In bilateral monopoly Fouraker and Siegel (1963, pp. 14–17) analyze the case in which the seller with linear cost, $C = a + bX$, moves first and chooses price, P; then the buyer, facing a linear resale demand, $P = A - BX$, chooses quantity. X. Applying the decision cost model in the text to this two-stage game, using backward induction, solving first for the buyer's choice of X, given P, then solving for the seller's choice of P given the buyer's choice of X as a function of P, defines the Nash equilibrium (P^*, X^*). This allows one to show that any increase in λ will reduce the variance of decision error in the choice of P^* by the seller and X^* by the buyer. Each data point plotted in the left panel of the figure is the choice of (P, X) by some buyer–seller pair using a baseline payoff level. In the right panel is a second set of data points for a parallel experiment in which each buyer–seller pair chose (P, X) with the payoffs to each person three times larger than for the data on the left. Comparing the two panels it can be seen that both the price and quantity variances are smaller on the right than they are on the left.

increased. Experience is interpreted in the above model as lowering decision cost. As familiarity with a task increases, decisions become routine requiring reduced attention from higher cognitive resources. This is the brain's way of conserving scarce attentional resources.

References

Binswanger, Hans P. (1980). "Attitudes toward risk: Experimental measurement in rural India". American Journal of Agricultural Economics 62 (3), 395–407.
Binswanger, Hans P. (1981). "Attitudes toward risk: Theoretical implications of an experiment in rural India". Economic Journal 91 (364), 867–890.

Cox, James C., Grether, David M. (1996). "The preference reversal phenomenon: Response mode, markets and incentives". Economic Theory 7 (3), 381–405.
Dawes, Robyn M. (1988). "Rational Choice in an Uncertain World". Harcourt Brace Jonanovich, New York.
Fiorina, Morris P., Plott, Charles R. (1978). "Committee decisions under majority rule". American Political Science Review 72 (2), 575–598.
Fouraker, Lawrence, Siegel, Sidney (1963). "Bargaining Behavior". McGraw–Hill, New York.
Forsythe, Robert, Horowitz, Joel L., Savin, N.E., Sefton, Martin (1994). "Replicability, fairness and pay in experiments with simple bargaining games". Games and Economic Behavior 6, 347–369.
Goodman, Barbara, Saltzman, Mark, Edwards, Ward, Krantz, David H. (1979). "Prediction of bids for two-outcome gambles in a casino setting". Organizational Behavior and Human Performance 24, 382–399.
Grether, David M. (1981). "Financial incentive effects and individual decision making". Social Science Working Paper No. 401, California Institute of Technology.
Grether, David M., Plott, Charles (1979). "Economic theory of choice and the preference reversal phenomenon". American Economic Review 72 (3), 623–638.
Harrison, Glenn (1989). "Theory and misbehavior of first price auctions". American Economic Review 79, 749–762.
Hoffman, Elizabeth, McCabe, Kevin A., Smith, Vernon L. (1996). "On expectations and the monetary stakes in ultimatum games". International Journal of Game Theory 25, 289–301.
Isaac, R. Mark, Walker, James M., Williams, Arlington W. (1991). "Group size and the voluntary provision of public goods: Experimental evidence utilizing large groups". Indiana University Working Paper.
Kachelmeier, Steven J., Shehata, Mohamed (1991). "Examining risk preferences under high monetary incentives: Experimental evidence from the People's Republic of China". Draft, Graduate School of Business, University of Texas at Austin.
Kormendi, Roger C., Plott, Charles R. (1982). "Committee decisions under alternative procedural rules: An experimental study applying a new non-monetary methods of payment". Journal of Economic Behavior and Organization 3 (2–3), 175–195.
Kroll, Yoram, Levy, Haim, Rapoport, Amnon (1988). "Experimental tests of the separation theorem and the capital asset pricing model". American Economic Review 78 (3), 500–519.
McClelland, Gary, McKee, Michael, Schulze, William, Beckett, Elizabeth, Irwin, Julie (1991). "Task transparency versus payoff dominance in mechanism design: An analysis of the BDM." Laboratory for Economics and Psychology, University of Colorado.
Messick, Samuel, Brayfield, Arthur H. (1964). "Decision and Choice". McGraw–Hill, New York.
Plott, Charles R., Smith, Vernon L. (1978). "An experimental examination of two exchange institutions". Review of Economic Studies 45 (1), 133–153.
Siegel, Sidney (1959). "Theoretical models of choice and strategy behavior: Stable state behavior in the two-choice uncertain outcome situation". Psychometrika 24, 303–316.
Siegel, Sidney (1961). "Decision making and learning under varying conditions of reinforcement". Annals of the New York Academy of Science 89, 766–783.
Siegel, Sidney, Andrews, Julia (1962). "Magnitude of reinforcement and choice behavior in children". Journal of Experimental Psychology 63, 337–341.
Siegel, Sidney, Goldstein, D.A. (1959). "Decision-making behavior in a two-choice uncertain outcome situation". Journal of Experimental Psychology 57, 37–42.
Siegel, Sidney, Fouraker, Lawrence (1960). "Bargaining and Group Decision Making: Experiments in Bilateral Monopoly". McGraw–Hill, New York.
Siegel, Sidney, Siegel, Alberta, Andrews, Julia (1964). "Choice, Strategy, and Utility". McGraw–Hill, New York.
Simon, Herbert A. (1956). "A comparison of game theory and learning theory". Psychometrika 21, 267–272.
Slovic, Paul, Fischoff, Baruch, Lichtenstein, Sarah (1982). "New Directions for Methodology of Social and Behavioral Science: Question Framing and Response Consistency (No. 11)". Jossey-Bass, San Francisco.
Smith, Vernon L. (1976). "Experimental economics: Induced value theory". American Economic Review 66 (2), 274–279.

Smith, Vernon L., Szidarovszky, Ferenc (1999). "Monetary rewards and decision cost in strategic interactions". University of Arizona, Economic Science Laboratory.

Smith, Vernon L., Walker, James M. (1993a). "Monetary rewards and decision costs in experimental economics". Economic Inquiry 31 (2), 245–261.

Smith, Vernon L., Walker, James M. (1993b). "Rewards, experience and decision costs in first price auctions". Economic Inquiry 31 (2), 237–245.

Tversky, Amos, Edwards, Ward (1966). "Information versus reward in binary choice". Journal of Experimental Psychology 71, 680–683.

Tversky, Amos, Kahneman, Daniel (1983). "Extensional versus intuitive reasoning: The conjunction fallacy in probability judgement". Psychological Bulletin 90, 293–315.

Wolf, Charles, Pohlman, Larry (1983). "The recovery of risk preferences from actual choice". Econometrica 51, 843–850.

Chapter 98

INTERTEMPORAL CHOICE UNDER HABIT FORMATION

ERNST FEHR

Institute for Empirical Economic Research, University of Zürich, Blümlisalpstr. 10, CH-8006 Zürich, Switzerland
e-mail: efehr@iew.unizh.ch

PETER K. ZYCH

Institute of Economics, University of Technology, Vienna, Argentinierstr. 8, A-1040 Vienna, Austria
e-mail: pkzych@pop.tuwien.ac.at

1. Introduction

The fundamental question addressed in this research is the degree to which models of optimal intertemporal choice are good descriptions of non-interactive individual intertemporal behavior in the presence of habit formation. The papers by Fehr and Zych (1995, 1998) provide the first laboratory examination of this question.

Many decisions in real life have an intertemporal dimension because they involve flows of future costs and benefits. Moreover, many important activities are habit forming in the sense that past activity levels affect present and future tastes for this or related activities. Most work in the economics of intertemporal choice assumes that agents behave as if they solve the intertemporal problem optimally (e.g., Deaton, 1992; Browning and Lusardi, 1996; Romer, 1996). For a broad class of intertemporal decision problems, optimal behavior has to satisfy Bellman's principle of optimality. Unfortunately, Bellman's principle per se has no empirically testable content unless one is willing to impose strong a priori identifying restrictions on the functional forms of agents' preferences and beliefs (Rust, 1994). Outside the laboratory, the researcher does not, in general, know agents' preferences or agents' beliefs about random variables. However, in the laboratory, the researcher has control over preferences and beliefs which allows for rigorous tests of intertemporal models. This renders experimental methods very useful in this area of research.

2. Experimental Design

For our experiment we used a perfectly isomorphic implementation of the "Model of Rational Addiction" by Becker and Murphy (1988) with a time horizon of 30 periods. The experimental instructions were framed in neutral terms to avoid associations with addictive goods, which would have led to a loss of control over the subjects' preferences. Subjects' task in the experiment was to transform the endowment ("points";

Table 1
The experimental implementation of the Becker–Murphy theory of rational addiction

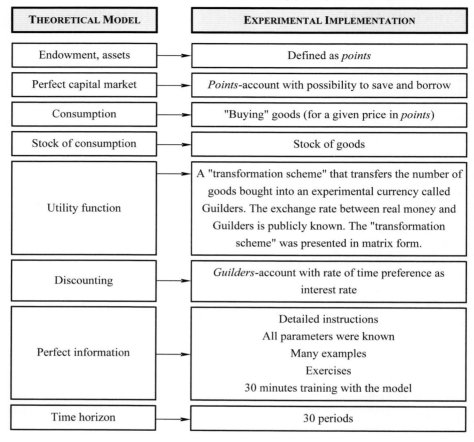

these points were of no value after the experiment) into utility ("Guilders") by buying "goods." Table 1 summarizes the implementation and the design.

Figure 1 shows the optimal consumption path for the parameters used. By comparing the optimal consumption path with subjects actual choices we can directly test the predictions of the model.

3. Results

25 undergraduate students of business administration from the University of Vienna participated in this experiment. Since there were no statistically significant differences in the results of the two experimental sessions we pooled the data.

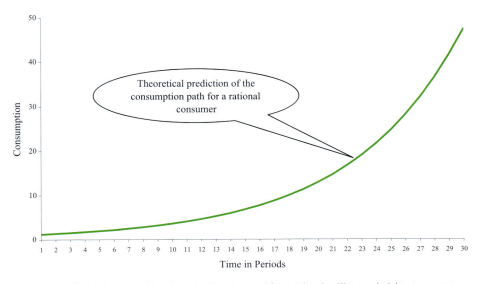

Figure 1. Optimal consumption of a habit forming good for a rational, utility-maximizing consumer.

RESULT 1. The experimental data do not support the "Theory of Rational Addiction." In fact, mean consumption is characterized by significant and stable overconsumption during the first 20 periods. Thereafter, overconsumption declines gradually and vanishes towards the end.

Support: Figure 2 shows the difference between the actual consumption and the conditionally optimal consumption (i.e., the optimal consumption decision conditional on the previous consumption history) together with the 95% confidence band. The figure reveals that the deviations from optimality are not randomly distributed around zero but very systematic. We can observe stable overconsumption that vanishes only towards the end of the experiment.

RESULT 2. Not only the aggregate data but also the individual data show that only a small number of individual consumption decisions can be labeled as "optimal". The majority of individual decisions is characterized by overconsumption.

Support: From a total of 1500 decisions[1] only 13% (193 decisions) are optimal, 18% (271) are characterized by underconsumption, and in 69% (1036) of the cases overconsumption occurs. In Figure 3 we have split individual decisions into three groups: overconsumption, optimal consumption, and underconsumption. As one can see, except

---

[1] 25 participants à 2 sessions à 30 periods.

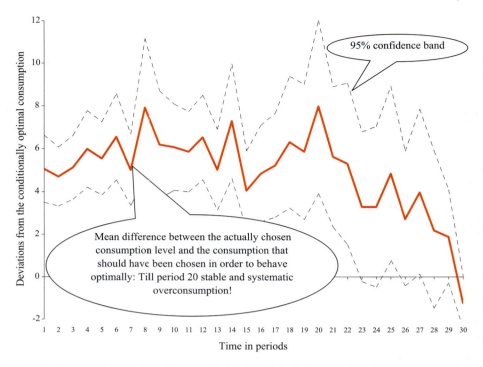

Figure 2. Experimental test of the "Theory of Rational Addiction": The model can be rejected as a correct representation of the experimental data. Actual mean consumption is characterized by significant and stable overconsumption during the first 20 periods. Thereafter, overconsumption declines gradually and vanishes towards the end.

for the last period, about 70% of individual decisions are characterized by overconsumption whereas the share of optimal decisions is rather small and diminishes over time. This high and stable overconsumption corroborates the presumption that deviations from the conditionally optimal path are driven by systematic forces. In our experiment past overconsumption may well lead to a situation in which the conditionally optimal decision involves a temporary loss. From many experiments (e.g., Tversky and Kahneman, 1992) it is well known that loss aversion is a behaviorally relevant phenomenon. Here, loss aversion implies that subjects whose optimal decision requires to incur a loss tend to avoid or reduce this loss by consuming too much. This conjecture is confirmed by

RESULT 3. *If the optimal consumption decision implies a temporary loss nearly all decisions are characterized by overconsumption.*

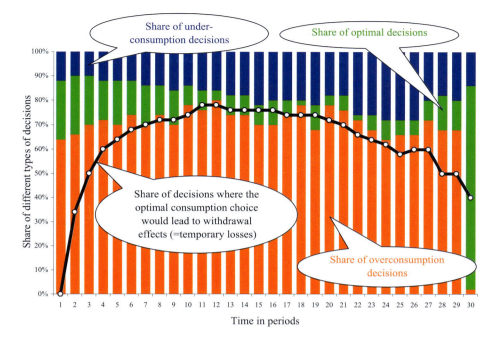

Figure 3. This graph shows for each period the share of the consumption decisions that exhibit over-, under-, or optimal consumption. The overwhelming share of decisions is characterized by overconsumption (around 70%). This overconsumption is driven by loss avoidance: If the optimal choice would imply a temporary utility loss, 98.8% of the non-optimal decisions exhibit overconsumption. The black line indicates the share of optimal decisions that would result in temporary losses ("withdrawal effects").

Support: If the utility in period t gained from an optimal consumption decision in period t were positive, underconsumption (260 decisions) was slightly more frequent than overconsumption (180 decisions). In contrast, there are huge differences in case that the optimal choice is associated with temporary losses: If the conditionally optimal choice implies a loss 98.8% of the non-optimal decisions are characterized by overconsumption (856 decisions) whereas only 1.2% of individual decisions exhibit underconsumption (11 decisions). For roughly 75 percent of the overconsumption decisions, consumption was sufficiently high to render the temporary utility positive. This suggests that loss avoidance was an important determinant of individual decisions that stabilized overconsumption at high levels.

4. Conclusions

We have shown that in the presence of habit-forming goods intertemporal choices deviate systematically from individually optimal decisions in the direction of overconsumption. This overconsumption was partly driven by loss avoidance, comparable to a real life situation in which addicted people consume addictive substances only in order to overpower withdrawal symptoms.

The existence of loss avoidance does, however, not explain why subjects consume too much in the first few periods. We conjecture that overconsumption during the first periods is driven by cognitive limitations. If subjects are unable to compute the aggregate present value of future costs which is associated with each level of consumption, they face a form of subjective uncertainty. Hence, psychologically relevant features of the decision problem play an important role. In our context, the fact that the present benefits of consumption are relatively large, immediately available, and thus unambiguously given is likely to be of psychological relevance because it renders present benefits highly salient. In contrast, the fact that future costs per period are relatively small, distributed over time and, thus, subjectively of ambiguous size renders them much less salient. It may well be that this creates a biased perception, that is, an cognitive undervaluation of the aggregate present value of future costs relative to present benefits that gives rise to overconsumption.

References

Becker, Gary S., Murphy, Kevin M. (1988). "A theory of rational addiction". Journal of Political Economy 96, 675–700.
Browning, Martin, Lusardi, Annamaria (1996). "Household saving: Micro theories and micro facts". Journal of Economic Literature 34 (4), 1797–1855.
Deaton, Angus (1992). "Understanding Consumption". Clarendon Press, Oxford.
Fehr, Ernst, Zych, Peter K. (1995). "Die Macht der Versuchung – Irrationaler Überkonsum in einem Suchtexperiment". Zeitschrift für Wirtschafts und Sozialwissenschaften 115 (4), 569–604.
Fehr, Ernst, Zych, Peter K. (1998). "Do addicts behave rationally?" The Scandinavian Journal of Economics 100, 643–662.
Romer, David (1996). "Advanced Macroeconomics". McGraw–Hill Companies, New York.
Rust, John (1994). "Do people behave according to Bellman's principle of optimality?" Manuscript, University of Wisconsin.
Tversky, Amos, Kahneman, Daniel (1992). "Loss aversion in riskless choice: A reference dependent model". Quarterly Journal of Economics 106, 1039–1062.

Chapter 99

PREFERENCE REVERSAL:
NOW YOU SEE IT, NOW YOU DO NOT!

PETER BOHM

Preference reversal (PR) means that an individual's choice – a direct reflection of his preferences – between two options is inconsistent with the ranking of his (selling) reservation prices – an indirect reflection of his preferences. Such choice/reservation-price inconsistency is potential dynamite. If it existed to a significant extent, it could blow standard economic theory to pieces. And if reservation prices did not reflect preferences, market behavior is unlikely to have the welfare-economic implications normally ascribed to market economies.

Psychologists were the first to observe the PR phenomenon using experiments with simple lotteries, for which choices and reservation prices were elicited either at low incentive levels or only hypothetically (e.g., Lichtenstein and Slovic, 1971; Lindman, 1971). These results began to worry economists after Grether and Plott (1979) failed in their attempt to disprove the psychologists' findings. (Grether and Plott summarized their findings by stating that the inconsistency implied by preference reversal "is deeper than the mere lack of transitivity ... It suggests that no optimization principles of any sort lie behind even the simplest of human choices and that the uniformities in human choice behavior may result from principles which are of a completely different sort from those generally accepted," p. 623.) Subsequent studies of the same type showed that these results were robust (for a listing, see, e.g., Tversky, Slovic, and Kahneman, 1990). Several economists tried to identify what changes in the standard economic theory of decision making would have to be made to account for these findings (see, e.g., Karni and Safra, 1987; Segal, 1988; Loomes and Sugden, 1983; and Loomes, Starmer, and Sugden, 1989).

Ever since Lichtenstein and Slovic (1971) tests of preference reversal frequently use pairs of lotteries such as:

Pbet: 35/36 chances to win $4 and 1/36 chance to lose $1 (expected value $3.86)
$bet: 11/36   "   "   " $16 " 25/36 chances "   " $1.50 ("   " $3.85)

where Pbet ($bet) stands for a lottery with a high (low) probability of winning a small (large) amount. The results for these and similar pairs of lotteries have typically indicated high rates of PR for those who chose the Pbet, up to some 70 percent, whereas those who chose the $bet rarely stated the highest price for the other lottery, perhaps only in some 5–15 percent of the cases. This, in combination with a particular "anchoring and adjustment" theory advanced by psychologists, gave rise to the labels "predicted" vs "unpredicted" preference reversal, respectively.

On the basis of these findings, it has been argued that PR is characteristic of decision making under uncertainty in general and hence that it could also be observed outside the context of a specific type of lottery. For example, psychologists claimed that the PR phenomenon pervaded vast areas of decision making (e.g., Slovic and Lichtenstein, 1983; Tversky, Slovic, and Kahneman, 1990). Specifically, Tversky and Thaler (1990) argued that the "findings indicate that the preference reversal phenomenon is an example of a general pattern, rather than a peculiar characteristic of choice between bets" (p. 208).

Given such generalizations, an agenda for further testing of the prevalence of PR should respond to at least three points, all governed by the requirement that theory should be valid in particular for non-trivial issues. That is, does PR remain to an extent significantly larger than can be explained by pure mistakes also when:
- the maximum payoffs to the experimental subjects and/or the expected values of the options are significant?
- there are more than two outcomes for each option?
- the issues are real and relevant to the experimental subjects?

More specifically, it may be questioned whether the test results can be taken as relevant for decisions concerning real-world lotteries; i.e., are real-world lotteries well represented by the lotteries used in the tests? Furthermore, do the experimental lotteries well represent objects central to the theory of decision making under uncertainty, such as financial assets, insurance policies and commodities with uncertain service prospects, where there are typically more than two outcomes and, in addition, no objective probabilities? And, how should the test results be interpreted when subjects are to an unknown extent historically unfamiliar with making lottery decisions or even opposed, morally or otherwise, to making such decisions?

Results from three tests designed to address some of these research needs are summarized here. Characteristic of all three is that attempts were made:
- to use choice objects of non-trivial values,
- to elicit bids or asks for real auctions or other market transactions, and
- to identify and engage subjects for whom the issue tested could be relevant.

The first two tests refer to choice between objects with uncertain outcomes. Test no. 1 used non-trivial real choice objects which the test subjects had revealed an interest in buying, and where uncertainty was characterized by subjective probabilities and more than two outcomes. Test no. 2 used real-world lotteries where there were more than two (7–12) levels of prizes and where lottery consumer subjects could be separated from those who did not want to buy lottery tickets. Test no. 3 investigated choice/reservation-price consistency with respect to another case where high (hypothetical) PR rates have been observed, i.e., claims redeemed at different future dates; here, the alleged inconsistency was tested non-hypothetically and with subjects qualified to make decisions on these kinds of issues. The main results of the three tests are summarized in Table 1.

Before proceeding, it should be noted that lotteries of the Pbet and $bet types exemplified above have hardly been taken to mirror solely that particular type of choice objects. Instead it has become a doctrine among some experimental economists that tests

Table 1
Frequency of preference reversal (or choice/reservation-price inconsistency)[a] in different environments; results from three tests with objects of non-trivial value or real-world lotteries; percent of subjects

	Subjects preferring Pbets (high probability winning low prize) or – in test #3 – short-term claims[b]	Subjects preferring $bets (low probability winning high prize) or – in test #3 – long-term claims[b]
Earlier observations (tests reported in the literature 1971–1990): Lab lotteries with two outcomes; mostly low incentive levels; elicited asks not used for market transactions; robust results from many tests	40–80	0–15
Test #1: Consumer-durable choice objects with subjective probabilities over many outcomes (used cars); motivated subjects (see further Figure 1)	0[c]	0[c]
Test #2: Real-world lotteries with at least seven outcomes[d] (see further Table 2)	23	5
Test #3: Claims with different redemption values; 'expert' subjects, real choices/bids[c] (see further Table 3)	15	18

[a]The term preference reversal has been used for instances where a decision maker prefers A to B but places a higher (seller) reservation price on B than on A, hence making preferences revealed by choice and by relative reservation prices inconsistent.
[b]Examples of a Pbet, 35/36 chances to win $4 and 1/36 chance to lose $1, and a $bet, 11/36 chances to win $16 and 25/36 chances to lose $1.50. The short-term claim, SEK 1000 in 3 months, and the long-term claim, SEK 1200 in 15 months, were used in Test #3.
[c]Ranking of asks assumed to be revealed by the ranking of elicited bids (bids elicited for reasons of experimental costs); bids used in the real auction.
[d]Elicited bids and asks used for real market transactions.

of a particular 'kind' of decision making should be removed from the particular context where it appears. According to this approach, only the 'bare bones' or principles of the issue should remain to influence the subjects and the results can reflect the implication of the principles in all contexts. Regardless of whether robustness of a result concerning principles can best be obtained from a large number of artificial 'bare bones' tests or from a large number of tests using different contexts, there is a 'parallelism precept' (Smith, 1982) which requires that robust laboratory test results eventually be subjected

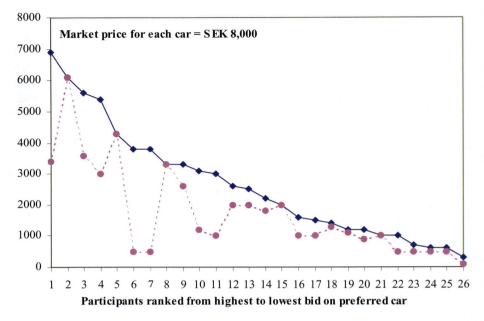

Figure 1. Used cars, no preference reversal – i.e., bid on preferred car (solid line) did not fall short of bid on other car (dashed line) for any of 26 subjects. (Participant no. 21 stated indifference.) 26 subjects interested in buying a used car were invited to place bids on two cars in a second-price auction. After having agreed to participate, subjects were informed that they stood a chance to win one of the cars in a lottery: his/her preferred car with a probability twice that of winning the other car. Hence, incentives were provided for bids = reservation prices (the incentive-compatibility property of the auction type used) and for stating which car is preferred.

to tests in the field. The three tests highlighted here, and the first one in particular, are designed in an attempt to comply with such an ambition.

TEST 1. Non-trivial real choice objects, demanded by test subjects; subjective probabilities and more than two outcomes (Bohm, 1994a).

In the first test, used cars were selected as an example of 'non-lottery' objects whose performance (outcome) is uncertain. Two cars were bought – both priced at SEK (Swedish kronor) 8000 or $1200 1990 U.S. dollars – to be sold at an auction, offered to some 2000 students at Stockholm University. Twenty-six of them showed up, test drove the cars, checked inspection reports, and participated in a hypothetical second-price auction (of two bicycles) to make them more familiar with this type of auction. In a final meeting, subjects were asked to state, which of the two cars each of them preferred as well as their bids on the two cars in a second-price auction as follows.

In order to obtain meaningful responses to the question of which car each individual preferred, the subjects – before they stated their bids – were given the good news that one of the two cars, or a money value of this car, would be given away in a lottery. The winner of the lottery would have a 2/3 chance of winning the preferred car, or money equal to his/her bid on that car, and a 1/3 chance of winning (money equal to his/her bid on) the other car, thus providing incentives for the subjects to probe and reveal their true preferences. After the winner and the prize car had been identified, the toss of a coin would determine whether the winner got the car or money equal to the winner's bid on this car. (This experimental design, where the winner could get money equal to the stated bid on one of the two cars, was chosen so as to create enough interest in the car which a subject did not particularly fancy, in order to ensure that he or she would also pay some attention to his/her bid on that car.) The rest was a regular auction of one or – as the case might be – two cars.

It was assumed that the ranking of actual bids could be used as a proxy for the ranking of actual asks. Asks were found unfeasible to elicit in practice, given the type and costs of the objects used.

Given the reputations of the two types of cars used in the test, one of them would have a high probability of delivering the performance it could provide (a Volvo), whereas the other one had fancier equipment but lower performance reliability (an Opel). Hence, the Volvo bore some resemblance to a Pbet and the Opel to a $bet. Since inconsistency between choices and reservation prices is 'predicted' for Pbets, it is worth noting that twenty subjects preferred the Volvo and five the Opel (one indifferent).

The main results are summarized in Table 1 (Test #1) and in Figure 1. In the figure, the 26 subjects are ranked according to the bid on their preferred car, from high to low (see the bold line). The dashed line shows the corresponding bids on the other car. (Example: bidder no. 3, who gave his highest bid, SEK 5600, on the car he preferred, bid SEK 3600 on the other car.) As illustrated by the fact that the price lines for the preferred car and the other car, respectively, do not cross, bids on the preferred car never fell short of bids on the other car. In other words, no PR was observed here.

Identical bids on the two cars were made by five subjects, one of whom (no. 21) stated indifference between the cars. Thus, some of the subjects who stated preference did not differentiate their bids. A likely reason is that specifying exact reservation prices is a more difficult task than making choices, especially if a subject does not come out strongly in favor of one of the options. Under such circumstances, rough estimates, e.g., to avoid 'petty' calculations, can end up in statements of identical prices.

TEST 2. Real-world lotteries and subjects identified as lottery consumers (Bohm and Lind, 1993).

Real-world lotteries typically have more than two outcomes or prize levels, and are aimed at raising revenue, with expected prizes typically around 50% of ticket prices. The lotteries tested in the PR literature are rarely of a type that would qualify as a real-world lottery in which anyone would like to participate. Given a 50% net revenue requirement, a typical lab Pbet with a 9/10 chance of winning $5 and a 1/10 of winning nothing would cost around $9, which no one would be willing to pay. The question addressed here concerns the extent to which PR can be observed in the case of real-world lotteries, which all have more exciting prizes, and in a setting where it is possible to distinguish between subjects who prefer lotteries to money and those who have the opposite preference.

Here, 86 student subjects were presented with a choice among the following three options:
- SEK 40 ($7 U.S. dollars in 1991) in cash,
- an SEK 40 share of a package of $bet-type Swedish state lottery tickets, and
- an SEK 40 share of a package of Pbet-type Swedish state lottery tickets.

Both lottery options have expected payoffs of SEK 20 and at least seven prize levels. In the first lottery, where one ticket out of seven wins, the highest prize was SEK 1,000,000. The second lottery, where one ticket out of five wins, had a highest prize of only SEK100,000. The choice options were formed as packages of shares of lottery tickets, one package type for each type of lottery, instead of individual tickets. The reason was to avoid making the pricing task trivial, since the lottery tickets are for sale 'everywhere.' The packages formed were such that the probabilities of winning anything were 0.4 and 0.8, respectively.

To replicate typical PR tests, but now with probabilities of winning resembling those in the state lottery experiment (I), a second experiment (II) was arranged where the lotteries used had only two outcomes, some positive prize and zero. For reasons already indicated, it is not easy to make such lotteries interesting, if they are also required to yield a 50% net revenue. In experiment II, 57 student subjects got the following options to choose from:
- SEK 40 in cash,
- a 1/7 chance of winning SEK 210 ($bet; expected value = SEK 30),
- a 2/5 chance of winning SEK 75 (Pbet; expected value = SEK 30).

In a trial test with lotteries of this type but with expected values of SEK 20 as in experiment I, it became obvious that very few subjects would be interested in such lotteries and hence that all might take the cash offered. Therefore, the prizes were raised to make the expected values equal to SEK 30, as shown above.

In both experiments, the following procedure was used. After the subjects had chosen one of the three options, offered for keeps, they were informed that a choice should now be made between the remaining two options. After that task was completed, they were also given the remaining item. In a second stage, two markets, one for Pbet packages and another for $bet packages, were opened where subjects could sell their packages. Also, a random 50% of the subjects were allocated to each of the two markets as buyers of one more package each. To implement the two markets, subjects were asked to state minimum selling prices and maximum buying prices. Transactions were carried out at equilibrium prices.

Table 2
Frequency of preference reversal with lottery − vs not lottery-interested subjects and real-world lotteries vs two-outcome lab lotteries[a] (percent), $N_I = 86$, $N_{II} = 57$

Participants' preferences (as revealed by choice)	Real-world lotteries (I)		Two-outcome lab lotteries (II)	
Pbet ≻ $bet, total thereof	23		73	
$\quad M ≻ P ≻ \$$ ('not lottery-interested')		29		77
$\quad P ≻ \$ ≻ M$ ('lottery-interested')		26		80
$bet ≻ Pbet, total thereof	5		4	
$\quad M ≻ \$ ≻ P$ ('not lottery-interested')		0		11
$\quad \$ ≻ P ≻ M$ ('lottery-interested')		6		0
Weighted average PR	12		44	

[a] In experiment I, subjects could first choose for keeps one of the three options, cash (M), Pbet lottery tickets (P) and $bet lottery tickets ($), where the real-world market prices of P and M, two different kinds of Swedish state lotteries, were the same and equal to the offered cash amount M. In a next step, subjects could choose the preferred one of the remaining two options, hence establishing the preference order for all three options. Finally, having also been given the remaining option, subjects were asked to enter asks for the tickets in their possession and bids for more tickets in real market transactions. In experiment II, the two real-world lotteries with 7–12 prize levels were replaced by typical PR lab lotteries with two outcomes, here with expected values similar to those of the real-world lotteries.

In this fashion, it was known how the subjects ranked the lotteries as well as whether or not they preferred lotteries to money, as would lottery consumers. In addition, selling reservation prices had been obtained.

As shown in Table 2, a much larger share of the participants preferred the $bet to the Pbet in experiment I (the real-world lotteries) than in experiment II, 65% vs 42%. For those who preferred the $bet, PR was insignificant in both experiments. For those who made the opposite choices, i.e., those for whom PR is 'predicted,' PR in experiment II (73%) was as high as in the tests this experiment was designed to mimic. By contrast, PR was only 23% in experiment I where real-world lotteries were used.

Interestingly, there was almost no difference at all between subjects who preferred money to both lotteries and those who consistently preferred lotteries to money (a clearly 'lottery-interested' group).

Moreover, market equilibrium prices as well as average buying and selling prices were considerably higher for the lotteries in experiment I than those in experiment II. Fifty percent of the subjects in experiment I had buying reservation prices of at least SEK 40 as compared to 12% in experiment II. Even more telling is the fact that 15% vs only 1%, respectively, had buying reservation prices exceeding SEK 40, the market price for standard tickets of the two lotteries.

The results may be interpreted as saying that when a lottery with some high prizes (as in experiment I) is replaced by a lottery with only low prizes (as in experiment II), but with a similar expected value, the lottery loses much of its attraction. In fact, it comes as no surprise that, as the data suggest, few would be interested in any of the lotteries in the PR test mimicking experiment (II), either the Pbet or the $bet. So, the types of lotteries for which there have been robust findings of PR either do not exist as marketable lotteries or are interesting only in their possible capacity to represent something else. What this could be does not seem to have been made clear in the PR literature.

TEST 3. Choice/reservation-price inconsistency for claims redeemed at different future dates, using expert subjects and real vs hypothetical claims (Bohm, 1994b).

Tversky, Slovic, and Kahneman (1990) argued that PR is a general phenomenon, arising not only in connection with risk or uncertainty but also, e.g., when decision makers are confronted with claims of different maturity. As a typical example of the claims analyzed by Tversky, Slovic, and Kahneman (1990), hypothetical choices between $1600 a year and a half from now and $2500 five years from now revealed an inconsistency with hypothetical selling prices for such claims, especially for those subjects who chose the short-term claim. Thus, short-term claims and long-term claims were said to play a role similar to that of Pbets and $bets, respectively, i.e., with similar functions of how soon claims would be redeemed and how large the probabilities of winning were.

These results were checked in a test using subjects who could be expected to be confronted with decisions of this type, here mid-level bank employees and third-year students in Finance. In one subgroup, offered real payments, subjects were asked to choose between (A) SEK 1000 ($200 in 1992) in three months and (B) SEK 1200 in fifteen months. (Longer periods might not have been credible when payments were real.) Thus, waiting had a rate of return of 20%, similar to the rates used in Tversky, Slovic, and Kahneman (1990). This rather special choice problem was accompanied by a story, suggesting that the subject was a member of a group of 10 people considering two business options, where the subject would be casting the decisive vote on which option to choose and where a randomly selected member of the group would get the claim. Thus, in this real payment test, each respondent would have 1/10 chance of getting the claim preferred.

Before winners were drawn in each of three subgroups of 10–11 subjects, they were asked to state (i) their choices between A and B, as well as (ii) bids on both claims in a real second-price auction within each subgroup. Again, it was deemed too expensive to design the experiment so that real selling prices could be elicited. Thus, the test relied on the ranking of selling reservation prices being at least approximately revealed by a ranking of real buying reservation prices. The other two subgroups were asked hypothetical versions of the two questions, (i) and (ii).

As shown in Table 3, PR rates were low (4–15%) for those who hypothetically chose the B claim. The rates of hypothetical PR were high (62–63%) for those who preferred the short-term claim A. These rates were similar to those observed by Tversky, Slovic, and Kahneman (1990), using undergraduate students as subjects. Thus, the level of expertise did not seem to have much impact, at least not on hypothetical behavior.

Table 3
Preference reversal for claims with different redemption dates (claim A = SEK 1000 in three months; claim B = SEK 1200 in 15 months)

Subjects	Percent of choices inconsistent with ranking of bids when	
	Short-term claim (A) chosen	Long-term claim (B) chosen
Mid-level bank employees ($n = 54$, 48% choosing A) hypothetical	62	15
Third-year Finance students ($n = 41$, 39% choosing A) hypothetical	63	4
Third-year Finance students ($n = 32$, 63% choosing A) real bids and payments	15	18

By contrast, in the subgroup where claims and auctions were real, choice/reservation-price inconsistency was observed for only 15–18% of the subjects. Interestingly, the inconsistency rates were approximately the same regardless of which claim was preferred. Since PR is 'predicted' only for those who prefer the short-term claim, with PR among those who prefer the long-term claim to be explained by errors, it is tempting to conclude that also the 'predicted' reversals here might be given a similar explanation. But, even if the error rate in this subgroup were lower, the resulting rate of intentional preference reversals would still be low and hardly demonstrate the asserted threat to economic theory.

Concluding remarks

Earlier studies have indicated that the rate of PR is robustly significant in cases with low incentive levels and options with at most two, two-dimensional (e.g., prize and probability) outcomes. Hence, proof of choice/reservation-price inconsistency may be said to exist for such cases. High rates of PR, which are estimated to significantly and robustly exceed likely error rates, have not been observed for other, more general and "more important" instances of decision making. In fact, given the set of such "other" issues in all three tests presented here, where, among other things, salient incentives were provided and care was taken to use decision makers relevant for the issue in question, it becomes reasonable to presume that PR is not valid for anything more than it has been proven to be valid for (cf. Table 1).

Estimating one's own reservation prices with precision can be quite difficult. Moreover, efforts invested in such estimations are likely to decrease with the decision maker's general valuation (or approximate reservation price) of the objects. So, with trivial objects specified in two dimensions for at most two outcomes only, one of which is a conditional money value (e.g., a prize), a task of reporting reservation prices is not likely to be attended to with much care and, if so, the response can end up being highly influenced by the ranking of the only money amounts stated in connection with the objects. Then, reported reservation prices may be lowest for the object connected with the lowest amounts, even for those subjects who do not prefer/choose this object. This is exactly what psychologists' theory of "anchoring an adjustment" predicts, although now we may limit the relevance of this theory to cases in which inconsistency between choice and reservation price has been shown to exist. Such inconsistencies may have a still more limited role to play, since – at least, so far – they have been clearly documented to exist for trivial objects only. Such objects are normally transacted at posted prices, so that the individual seller/buyer does not have to calculate any reservation prices. In cases where such calculations are needed, e.g., in auctions and bilateral bargaining, the objects are rarely insignificant. But for objects of significant value there is little or no evidence of preference reversal.

References

Bohm, P. (1994a). "Behavior under uncertainty without preference reversal: A field experiment". Empirical Economics, Special issue on Experimental Economics 19, 185–200.
Bohm, P. (1994b). "Time preference and preference reversal among experienced subjects: The effect of real payments". Economic Journal 104, 1370–1378.
Bohm, P., Lind, H. (1993). "Preference reversal, real-world lotteries, and lottery-interested subjects". Journal of Economic Behavior and Organization 22, 327–348.
Grether, D., Plott, C. (1979). "Economic theory of choice and the preference reversal phenomenon". American Economic Review 69, 623–638.
Karni, E., Safra, Z. (1987). "Preference reversals and the observability of preferences by experimental methods". Econometrica 55, 675–685.
Lichtenstein, S., Slovic, P. (1971). "Reversals of preferences between bids and choices in gambling decisions". Journal of Experimental Psychology 89, 46–55.
Lindman, H. (1971). "Inconsistent preferences among gambles". Journal of Experimental Psychology 89, 390–397.
Loomes, G., Sugden, R. (1983). "A rationale for preference reversal". American Economic Review 73, 428–432.
Loomes, G., Starmer, C., Sugden, R. (1989). "Preference reversal: Information – Processing effect or rational non-transitive choice?" Economic Journal 99, 140–151.
Segal, U. (1988). "Does the preference reversal phenomenon necessarily contradict the independence axiom?" American Economic Review 78, 233–236.
Slovic, P., Lichtenstein, S. (1983). "Preference reversals: A broader perspective". American Economic Review 73, 596–605.
Smith, V. (1982). "Microeconomic systems as an experimental science". American Economic Review 72, 923–955.
Tversky, A., Thaler, R. (1990). "Anomalies: Preference reversal". Journal of Economic Perspectives 4 (2), 201–211.
Tversky, A., Slovic, P., Kahneman, D. (1990). "The causes of preference reversal". American Economic Review 80, 204–218.

Chapter 100

THE ENDOWMENT EFFECT:
EVIDENCE OF LOSSES VALUED MORE THAN GAINS

DANIEL KAHNEMAN
Princeton University

JACK L. KNETSCH
Simon Fraser University

RICHARD H. THALER
University of Chicago

It has long been assumed that an individual's valuations of a good are independent of his or her entitlement to the good. In the absence of a wealth (or income) effect, the maximum sum a person would agree to pay to obtain the good should be equal to the minimum amount the person would demand to give it up. The traditional view that, "...we shall normally expect the results to be so close together that it would not matter which we choose" (Henderson, 1941, p. 121) (when the usual income effects are allowed for) is central to conventional economic theory. This view also provides the working assumption of economic practice in such diverse situations as predicting market responses, assessing damages for environmental harms, and the design of public policies.

There is, however, little or no empirical support for the empirical assertion of people's symmetrical valuations of gains and losses and the presumed economic choices and behavior that results from them. Instead, tests consistently indicate that people value the loss of an entitlement more, and usually far more, than a fully commensurate gain and make choices accordingly.

The early empirical evidence of a wide disparity between people's valuations of gains and losses appeared in results of contingent valuation studies in which respondents were asked both how much they would be willing to pay to prevent a loss of an environmental or other amenity, and what sum they would demand to accept its loss. In perhaps the first of these, duck hunters were reported to be willing to pay an average of $247 to prevent the loss of an area of duck habitat but demanded $1044 to accept its loss (Hammack and Brown, 1974). Many similar results were subsequently reported of people's valuations of environmental as well as other goods. Thaler (1980), for example, found that the minimum compensation people demanded to accept a .001 risk of death was one or two orders of magnitude greater than the maximum amount they would pay to avoid the same risk.

Table 1
Results of a random price market for coffee mugs. Subjects given a mug demanded more to give up the entitlement than others were willing to pay to gain a mug

	Mean	Median
Selling price	$5.78	$5.75
Buying price	2.21	2.25

1. Experimental Verification

The findings of large asymmetries in valuations of gains and losses in responses to hypothetical survey questions, prompted a further series of experimental tests involving real exchanges of goods and money. In the first of these real money experiments, one half of the participants were asked to pay varied sums to obtain a lottery ticket and the other half of the subjects were given a ticket and then offered different amounts of money to give it up (Knetsch and Sinden, 1984). When real good and actual cash payments motivate the valuations, the subjects having a lottery ticket demanded four times more to give it up than the others were willing to pay to obtain one.

The large disparity between buy and sell valuations has repeatedly also been evident in the results of a large number of market experiments. These include more persuasive random price tests in which subjects know that their bids to buy and offers to sell can have no conceivable effect on the eventual ruling price – as this is known to be determined randomly – and therefore know that there is no strategic reason to nominate any price other than one representing the true value. In one such experiment, mugs were given to one half of the participants and, after extensive explanations and two hypothetical trials, they were asked their minimum selling price; with the other half asked their maximum buying price (Kahneman, Knetsch, and Thaler, 1990). The results are given in Table 1, which show that the minimum sum needed to compensate losers was about two and a half times the maximum amount that others were willing to pay for the same mugs.

Similar findings of large differences have been found in between-subject real exchange experiments (in which participants in one group are offered an opportunity to acquire a good and those in another group an opportunity to give up the same good) but in within subject experiments, in which the same individuals can both acquire and give up a good. In one such test, the same twenty-eight individuals were given the opportunity to value a gain (loss) of a fifty percent chance to win $20 by offering to both buy (sell) such a prospect (Kachelmeier and Shehata, 1992). The experiment controlled for order effects by having half of the subjects buy first and the other sell first. Table 2 gives the results of this experiment. The value of this simple prospect was much larger in the domain of losses than in the domain of gains, which is consistent with essentially all experimental tests for an endowment effect. In this case, individuals on average de-

Table 2
Same subjects' valued losing a 50 percent chance to win $20 more than
they valued gaining the same entitlement

Mean willingness to pay to acquire	$5.43
Mean compensation demanded to give up	10.50

manded about twice as much to lose the prospect than they were willing to pay to gain it.

2. Exchanges

Many experimental studies have demonstrated a large asymmetry between the value of a loss and a gain of an otherwise fully commensurate entitlement in the context of a market exchange in which opportunities to exchange money and goods are offered to subjects. Such differences have also been shown in exchange experiments in which individuals exhibit reluctance to made simple trades: the value of the loss of a good looms larger than the value of the gain.

One straightforward exchange experiment was conducted with three groups in which all participates were given the opportunity to obtain one of two goods – a 400 gram chocolate bar or a coffee mug (Knetsch, 1989). The first group ($N = 55$) was given a simple choice between receiving a mug or a chocolate bar. The second group ($N = 76$) was given a mug, and then offered the opportunity to exchange (costlessly) it for a chocolate bar. The third group ($N = 87$) was provided with the opposite choice of first receiving a chocolate bar and then given the chance to give it up and obtain a mug in exchange. Given the absence of any possible income effects or wealth constraints, and minimum, if any, transaction costs necessary to make an exchange, traditional economic theory provides the strong prediction that the proportions of subjects indicating a preference for mugs over chocolate bars, and the proportions with the opposite preferences, should be roughly the same for each of the three groups.

The results, indicating a very different pattern from the one predicted by conventional views of valuation symmetry, are given in Table 3. With a reference of having neither good, slightly more than half (56%) of subjects in the first group selected a mug over a chocolate bar. However, after having been given a mug, the reference state for subjects in the second group is one of having a mug. Therefore, the exchange offer is seen to be a loss of the mug and a gain of the chocolate bar. Nearly nine of ten (89%) refused to make this trade. The reference position for subjects in the third group is one of having a chocolate bar and a full ninety percent of them turned down the opportunity to give up their chocolate bar to gain a mug. The very wide differences between the proportions of individuals taking home mugs and chocolate bars were consistent with their reference positions and with losses from this state being valued much more than gains to it.

Table 3
Results of choices between coffee mug and chocolate bar. No strong preference in group without reference of an initial entitlement, but random initial distribution of either good induced strong reluctance to exchange for other good

Group	Prefer mug over chocolate	Prefer chocolate over mug
No initial entitlement	56%	44%
Mug, chocolate offered	89%	11%
Chocolate, mug offered	10%	90%

Table 4
Results of offers to exchange an initial randomly distributed entitlement of either of two goods or money with one of the other entitlements. Participants were very reluctant to lose their entitlement to gain either of the alternatives, regardless of the nature of the initial or offered entitlement

Initial entitlement	Exchange offer	Prefer (percent)	
		Mug	Pen
Mug	Pen	88	12
Pen	Mug	10	90
		Mug	$2
Mug	$2	97	12
$2	Mug	18	82
		Pen	$2
Pen	$2	82	18
$2	Pen	14	86

The results from another exchange experiment demonstrated that asymmetries in the value of gains and losses can be as evident in exchanges of money and goods as they are in trades of one good for another (Knetsch, 1995). Approximately 50 individuals in each of six groups were given an initial entitlement of either a coffee mug, a pen in a sealed box, or $2. They were then all offered one of the other two goods in exchange for their reference entitlement in a way that covered all six possible entitlement-exchange possibilities (mug for a pen, mug for $2, pen for a mug, pen for $2, $2 for a mug, and $2 for a pen). Again, the assumption that valuations are independent of entitlements is greatly at variance with the outcome of the experiment. Rather than preferences between any pair being invariant to the direction of trade, the results presented in Table 4 show a strong contrary pattern of an overwhelming majority of subjects refusing to lose their initial entitlement to gain an alternative. (The pattern also shows widespread violations of common preference axioms as, for example, in the lack of transitivity of participants indicating a preference for pens over money, money over mugs, but also mugs over pens.)

3. Repeated Trials

Several endowment effect experiments have also been carried out over repeated iterations to test for possible impacts of learning, about the trading institutions or about values. For the most part, little change in the asymmetric valuation of gains and losses has resulted from the repetitions. While a few tests have shown convergence of the gain and loss values over the repeated trials (for example, Shogren et al., 1994), these have occurred in experiments using some variant of Vickrey auction institutions whereby the potential buyer making the highest bid buys at the next highest bid, and the potential seller offering to sell at the lowest price sells at the second lowest price. Given the absence of reports of converging buy and sell values over repeated trials using any other trading institution, the narrowing of values using the Vickrey auction appears to be an artifact of this particular institution.

The usual pattern of wide disparities continuing over repeated iterations is illustrated by the results of a market experiment in which 22 buyers and 22 sellers engaged in three induced-value markets, and then four actual exchange markets for each of two consumption goods (Kahneman, Knetsch, and Thaler, 1990). The same trading rules were used for all of the eleven iterations, with the market clearing price determined by the bids and offers of the participants in each market. On completion of the four rounds for each consumption good – a mug and a boxed pen – one of the real goods market rounds was randomly selected as the trial that "counted," and trades actually took place at the market price for that particular round.

The results showed little change over the repeated markets. The median sell prices ranged from 1.9 to 3.3 times larger than the median buy prices with no trend toward convergence of gain and loss values over the repetitions. There was in this, as in other studies, no evidence that participants learned anything over the repeated trials that would lead them to adopt equal buying and selling prices. A further indication of this result is given in Figure 1, which shows very little change in either the demand or the supply curve for the first and the fourth, and last, market for mugs in this experiment.

4. Buy, Sell, and Choose

Exchanges of either money and a good, or one good for another, offer the possibility of four comparisons or valuations of a good. In the case of money and good exchanges, the first is giving up money to gain a good: a purchase or buy valuation measured by the willingness of the individual to pay for the good. The second is a choice between either a good or money: a choice of two gains. The third is a giving up a good for a gain of money: a sell or loss valuation measured by the willingness of the individual to accept compensation for the good. The fourth is a choice between giving up money or a good: a choice of two losses.

The four values can be illustrated as comparisons in the four quadrants of Figure 2, with the vertical axis indicating a gain or loss of a good, and the horizontal axis indicating a gain or loss of money. The exchange and valuation, indicated in Quadrant I

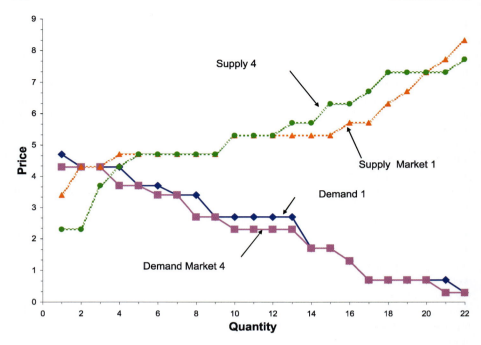

Figure 1. Supply and demand curves, markets 1 and 4. Markets were repeated four times, with little change evident in either supply or demand functions over the four iterations.

("Buy"), shows that this is in the domain of gains for the good and in the domain of losses for money. As gains are expected to be worth less than losses – the endowment effect – the value of the good, in terms of the sum of money willingly given up, would be expected to be less in this than in other quadrants. The opposite would be expected of values in Quadrant III ("Sell") where money is in the domain of gains and the good in the domain of losses: individuals would therefore be likely to demand the greatest monetary compensation to give up a good, indicating the highest valuation of the good among the four possibilities.

The valuations in Quadrants II and IV would normally be expected to be intermediate between those of Quadrant I and Quadrant III, depending on the relative extent of the gain and loss asymmetry between money and the good. The valuation in Quadrant III is in terms of both money and the good being in the domain of gains, and an indifference between receiving the good and a sum of money closer to the value in buy rather than to the value in the sell Quadrant would indicate that the disparity between the gain and loss valuations was likely due more to the reluctance of individuals to give up the good than to give up money. The valuation in Quadrant IV is in terms of money and the good being in the domain of losses, and a sum of money nearer to that of the buy value would

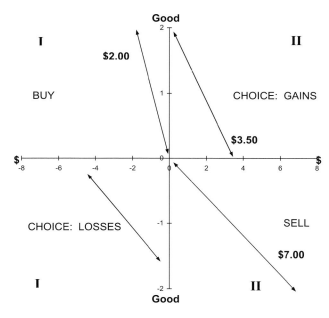

Figure 2. Comparisons of valuation of a good in domains of gains and losses of good and money. Smaller willingness to give up money to gain good; larger demand for compensation to give up good. Intermediate values of choices in same domains.

also indicate more of the difference between the gain and loss valuation being due to the welfare loss associated with giving up the good.

The results of a real exchange experiment involving three groups of participants who either were asked how much they would pay to gain a mug, how much they would demand to give up a mug, or how much they would need to receive rather than receive a mug are indicative of the expected pattern of valuations (Kahneman, Knetsch, and Thaler, 1990). The medians of the three values are given in Figure 2 in the corresponding buy, sell, and choice of gains quadrants. The $3.50 that these individuals indicated that they would accept rather than gain a mug is much closer to the buy value of $2.00 than to the sell value of $7.00, suggesting that the large difference between the gain and loss value is likely mostly due to a greater aversion to giving up a mug than giving up money.

The interpretation of the results in terms of the four valuations indicates the importance of the reference in distinguishing between gains and reductions of losses, and between losses and foregone gains. It also indicates the need to distinguish between valuations in the different quadrants. It is not uncommon, for example, to estimate time preference rates for a future gain by asking respondents if they would rather have X now or $X + Y$ later, a choice between two gains (Quadrant II). Comparisons of such results with analogous ones from choices between two losses, would likely give differing interpretations of time preferences for gains and losses, than a comparison between paying and compensation (Quadrants I and III).

5. Market Transactions

The endowment effect may also have significant implications for voluntary market exchanges, as the greater value of losses over gains and consequent reluctance to pay as much as demanded to part with goods will lead to fewer mutually advantageous transactions than would be the case if values were indeed independent of entitlement. This shortfall is illustrated in the demand and supply curves of Figure 1. Given the random distribution of the mugs in that experiment, half of the 22 subjects receiving this good would likely value it less than half of the 22 who did not. This would imply 11 mutually advantageous exchanges. However, the actual markets based on the participants' real valuations of gains and losses yielded only from one to four trades.

The reluctance to trade is, of course, due to the diminished real gains from trade available in the presence of the valuation disparity, relative to the gains presumed to be available if valuations were independent of entitlement. The extent of this possible difference in the gains was illustrated by the results of two market simulations of the buy and sell valuations of the individual participants in the Kachelmeier and Shehata experiment involving the entitlement to a 50 percent chance to win $20 referred to earlier (Borges and Knetsch, 1998). In the first simulations, the average gains from trade available to market participants from repeated distributions of 10 entitlements, assuming that each individual's sell value was equal to their buy value was $34.02, in accord with conventional theory. In the second simulations, the average gains from trade that were available from repeated distributions of the same entitlements, but using the individuals' actual buy and sell values, was only $7.71. In this case the actual available gains were only 23 percent of those traditionally assumed to be available to motivate trades.

The extent of the difference in the gains from trade that can be realized given the presence of endowment effects, relative to those normally assumed to be available, is illustrated in the Edgeworth box diagram of Figure 3, which is drawn with the difference in the areas of mutual gain roughly proportional to the difference found in the simulations of the markets for the prospect of a $20 win. It is such shortfalls from the expected gains that lead directly to the fewer market transactions observed in experimental markets. On current evidence, such shortfalls – or perhaps more accurately, the exaggerations of the extent of available gains inherent in the accounts of traditional theory – are likely to lead to the same result in actual markets.

6. Summary

The results of experiments testing people's valuations of gains and losses have been consistent in showing that individuals value losses far more than otherwise fully com-

Ch. 100: The Endowment Effect: Evidence of Losses Valued More than Gains

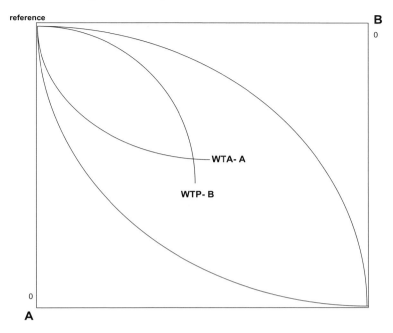

Figure 3. Illustrative representation of the smaller area of gains from trade resulting from the endowment effect, compared to the area of gains with assumed valuation equivalence.

mensurate gains. This leads to smaller gains from trade and fewer voluntary market transactions than would be the case with valuation equivalence. The valuation disparity also suggests greater caution in assessing welfare losses, predicting market outcomes, and may well imply different policy designs.

References

Borges, Bernhard F.J., Knetsch, Jack L. (1998). "Tests of market outcomes with asymmetric valuations of gains and losses: Smaller gains, fewer trades, and less value". Journal of Economic Behavior and Organization 33, 185–193.

Hammack, Judd, Brown, Gardner M. (1974). "Waterfowl and Wetlands: Toward Bioeconomic Analysis". Johns Hopkins Press, Baltimore.

Henderson, A.M. (1941). "Consumer's surplus and the compensation variation". Review of Economic Studies 8, 117.

Kachelmeier, S.J., Shehata, M. (1992). "Examining risk preferences under high monetary incentives: Experimental evidence from the People's Republic of China". The American Economic Review 82, 1120–1141.

Kahneman, Daniel, Knetsch, Jack L., Thaler, Richard H. (1990). "Experimental tests of the endowment effect and the coase theorem". Journal of Political Economy 98, 1325–1348.

Knetsch, Jack L. (1989). "The endowment effect and evidence of nonreversible indifference curves". The American Economic Review 79, 1277–1284.

Knetsch, Jack L. (1995). "Asymmetric valuation of gains and losses and preference order assumptions". Economic Inquiry 38, 138–141.
Knetsch, Jack L., Sinden, J.A. (1984). "Willingness to pay and compensation demanded: Experimental evidence of an unexpected disparity in measures of value". The Quarterly Journal of Economics 99, 507–521.
Shogren, Jason F., Shin, S.Y., Hayes, D.J., Kliebenstein, J.B. (1994). "Resolving differences in willingness to pay and willingness to accept". The American Economic Review 84, 255–270.
Thaler, Richard H. (1980). "Toward a positive theory of consumer choice". Journal of Economic Behavior and Organization 1, 39–60.

Chapter 101

THE ENDOWMENT EFFECT

PRAVEEN KUJAL
Universidad Carlos III

VERNON L. SMITH
University of Arizona

1. The Background

The emergence of empirical evidence suggesting divergence between the willingness-to-accept (WTA), for the sale of an object, and the willingness-to-pay (WTP), for the purchase of an object, has resulted in two explanations. One of the explanations was proposed by Kahneman, Knetsch, and Thaler (1991), that the discrepancy between the WTP and the WTA may be a manifestation of the endowment effect. Thus, "...endowment effects will almost certainly occur when owners are faced with an opportunity to sell an item purchased for use that is not easily replaceable" (p. 1344). Further they argue that the endowment effect will not apply when the goods are purchased for resale and not for use; there is no endowment effect for the retail firm, only for the consumer purchasing the firm's good. Similarly, they argue that the endowment effect does not apply to the exchange of tokens (or rights) to which private redemption values, or induced values have been assigned by the experimenter (Smith, 1976).

The second explanation came from Hanemann (1991) who showed that when close substitutes exist for the good in question (and given positive income elasticity) WTA and WTP can be shown to be very close, and vice versa.

Given the explanations for the divergence between the average WTA and WTP the experimental literature focused on direct choice tests of these (theoretical) explanations, and there examination in market contexts.

The first choice, and exchange, experiments were run by Kahneman, Knetsch, and Thaler (1991) establishing the endowment effect for Cornell and other (emblem) coffee mugs but not for induced value tokens. These were followed by experiments from Shogren et al. (1994) and Franciosi et al. (1996). Shogren et al. establish that the Hanneman hypothesis under repeat play is robust and that the divergence between the WTA and WTP disappears with repeat interaction for close substitutes but not for imperfect substitutes. Further, in their experimental setting (distinct from that of Kahneman, Knetsch, and Thaler, 1991) they show that under repeat interaction the endowment effect disappears. Franciosi et al. show that we can observe undertrading in markets even if the WTA-WTP discrepancy is negligible. This is the result of underrevelation of intramarginal units leading to very flat reported inverse supply and demand so that very small deviations in reported WTA and WTP can lead to undertrading.

2. The Experiments

2.1. Kahneman–Knetsch–Thaler Choice Experiments

In the typical experiment of Kahneman, Knetsch, and Thaler (1991) an undergraduate class is divided into equal parts. Half the subjects were randomly assigned to the role of buyers and the other half sellers. University emblem coffee mugs (Cornell, Simon Fraser, or University of British Columbia), costing around $6 in the local University bookstore, were then distributed to the sellers, and all the buyers were given the opportunity to examine the mug. The following forms were then executed.

	I Will Sell [Buy]	I Will Keep [Not Buy] the Mug
If the price is $0	_____	_____
If the price is $0.50	_____	_____
⋮		
If the price is $9.50	_____	_____

Next, a random price (Kahneman, Knetsch, and Thaler (1991) used the BDM procedure, in Becker, DeGroot, and Marschak, 1964) was drawn from the list between $0 and $9.50, and exchanges were conducted by the experimenter on the basis of this price. The typical result was a median selling price that was double the median buying price, an observation that is consistent with the endowment effect. Kahneman, Knetsch, and Thaler (1991), however, recognized that this procedure did not control for any income effect. This problem was exacerbated by the fact that buyers in their experiments were required to use their own funds while the sellers were given the coffee mugs.

To address the need to control for income effects Kahneman, Knetsch, and Thaler (1991, pp. 179–180) developed an ingenious variation on the above experiments. Instead of two groups they used three: sellers, buyers and choosers. The sellers/buyers made the same choices as before, while the choosers were asked to choose at each prospective price between the mug, or cash. Thus, sellers were given a mug, and choosers were given the right to either a mug or cash as they chose; any income effect on sellers as distinct from buyers, should then also apply to the choosers. The difference according to the Kahneman, Knetsch, and Thaler (1991) implementation of the endowment effect is that sellers own the mug, choosers do not.

Their results were clear: choosers behave more like buyers than like sellers, although choosers value mugs sixty percent more highly than buyers. (See Kahneman, Knetsch, and Thaler, 1991, pp. 178–180.)

2.2. Franciosi et al. Choice Experiments

Franciosi et al. conducted four experiments each with 24 subjects (8 in each group; $N = 96$ subjects in total) motivated by the three-group design which controlled for

Table 1
Row 2 lists the mean WTA and WTP prices obtained from experiments 6 and 7 reported by Kahneman, Knetsch, and Thaler (1991) for mugs and other objects at Simon Fraser and UBC. Row 4 lists the corresponding means from the University of Arizona experiments. In the latter all subjects make choices: Group 1 endowed with a mug; Group 2 endowed with money earned in a pre experiment in the same session; Group 3 endowed with the right to choose either a mug or additional money. The U of A procedures yield lower seller WTA, higher buyer WTP and higher chooser WTA than the Kahneman, Knetsch, and Thaler (1991) procedures. But the qualitative relationship among the treatment measures of value are preserved as in Kahneman, Knetsch, and Thaler (1991)

Experiment	WTA sellers	WTP buyers	WTA choosers	WTA-S/ WTP-B	WTA-S/ WTA-C	Sample size, N
Kahneman, Knetsch, and Thaler (1991) 6 and 7	$6.89	$1.91	$3.05	$3.61	$1.60	194
	WTA Group 1	WTP Group 2	WTA Group 3	WTA-1/ WTP-2	WTA-1/ WTA-3	
U of A	$5.36	$2.19	$3.88	2.45	1.38	120

any income effects. However, they made several instructional changes which might be important in the context of the choice experiments due to their framing effects. Because the use of emotive terms such as "buying," and "selling" may alter the strategic behavior of market participants, Franciosi et al. (1996) neutralized their instructions and removed all mention of "buying" or "selling." Instead they use expressions that did not suggest any specific role behavior on the part of market participants. First, the three groups were simply called Group 1, Group 2 and Group 3. The subjects were told that each member of Group 1 is an owner of an Arizona Wildcat Mug, and their task is to choose, for each amount of money (no mention of "price"), between retaining their mug or accepting the additional amount of money. Each member of Group 2 was designated as having the right to choose between accepting a mug or retaining an amount of money out of their earnings in a previous unrelated experiment in the same session. Finally, each person in Group 3 is designated as having the right to choose between a accepting a mug or accepting an additional amount of money. Thus, all subjects were symmetrically described as choosers, but under different initial conditions.

All their choice experiments were run at the end of two simultaneous posted offer market experiments (6 buyers, 6 sellers in each), reported in Franciosi et al. (1996). Subjects were assigned to the three groups randomly, and were paid their earnings in cash at the end of the market experiments. Earnings ranged from $8.75–$62.50 providing all Group 2 subjects with sufficient funds to obtain a mug based on the experimental prices. The mugs were priced at $9.95 (price tags removed) in the campus bookstore.

From Table 1 it can be seen that the subjects report substantially lower Group 1 WTA, a somewhat higher WTP, and a higher Group 3 WTA, than did the Kahneman, Knetsch, and Thaler (1991) subjects. Substituting a choice task for the buying and selling tasks appears to narrow the WTA-WTP discrepancy. Pairwise statistical tests, however, show

Table 2

Part 1 in each of two series of experiments used induced value supply and demand schedules to train subjects in the Uniform Price Double Auction (McCabe, Rassenti, and Smith, 1993). The environment was one in which the random equilibrium prices and volumes were comparable to what would be expected, theoretically, in the subsequent mug trading experiments. In Part 2 buyers were endowed with $9.99 as in Part 1, but sellers were endowed with University of Arizona emblem mugs and cash was traded for mugs. A total of 4 experiments were run in series 1, and 7 in series 2

	Series 1	Series 2
Part 1	Induced values [0, $9.99]; random equilibrium; 4 min periods	Induced values [0, $9.99]; constant equilibrium; 4 min periods
Part 2	Buyers: $9.99 Sellers: one mug each 4 min periods	Buyers: $9.99 Sellers: one mug each 4 and 6 min periods $9.95 price tag left on mug
Number of experiments (subjects)	4(96)	7(144)

that the data from all three groups come from different distributions (Franciosi et al., 1996). Hence, the qualitative differences among the three groups, as postulated by Kahneman, Knetsch, and Thaler (1991), were supported as is evident in the last row of Table 1.

2.3. Kahneman, Knetsch, and Thaler (1991) Exchange Experiments

In addition to their BDM choice experiments Kahneman, Knetsch, and Thaler (1991) report the results of several exchange experiments. Half the subjects were randomly assigned the role of buyers, the others sellers. Sellers were each endowed with a mug, while the former used money they had been asked to bring to class. Buyers each submitted a bid price to buy a mug and sellers each submitted an offer price to sell the mug. Their 'bids' and 'offers' were solicited by asking each subject to choose between a price and a mug for a series of prices as in the BDM procedure except that the range starts at $0.25 and goes up in increments of $0.50. The intersection of the descending bids and ascending offers determines the price and quantity exchanged. If there are no endowment or income effects, then due to the random allocation of subjects to the buy or sell condition, the supply schedule of those given the mugs should be a mirror image of the demand schedule for those not given the mugs. This leads to the prediction that one-half of the mugs should trade. Consequently, in their experiments with 22 buyers and 22 sellers, 11 mugs were predicted to trade. They observe that between 1 and 4 trade at prices between $4.25 and $4.75. As before only one bid/offer trial is chosen at random.

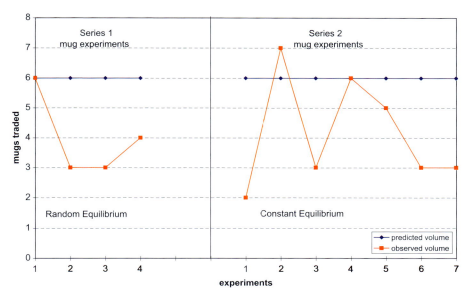

Figure 1. See Table 2 for a description of the series 1 and series 2 experiments. The mugs traded in Part 2 of each of the two series of experiments are shown plotted in red in the figure. Plotted in blue are the predicted volumes of trade (6). Note that in three of the eleven total experiments six or more of the mugs trade; in eight less than 6 mugs trade. Generally we observed much more trading volume than obtained by Kahneman, Knetsch, and Thaler (1991), but still substantially below the prediction, tending to confirm the undertrading hypothesis. UPDA Exchange experiments: Volume of mugs traded in constant and random equilibrium experiments. Two series of experiments, constant and random equilibrium, were run. In each experiment 24 different subjects were randomly assigned to groups of 12 buyers and 12 sellers. Each series was divided into two parts. The first part was a market experiment while the second part was the mug exchange experiment. In the first part each buyer was assigned a value and each seller a cost from the distribution [$0, $ 9.99] at the beginning of each experiment. In Part 1 of series 1 each period lasted for 4 minutes. In Part 2 of series 1 and 2 each buyer was endowed with a $9.99 cash balance which was theirs to keep if the mug was not purchased; each seller was endowed with a University of Arizona emblem mug which was theirs to keep if not sold. In series 2, Part 1 used the constant equilibrium environment, but in each period a random constant was added to each value, and the values randomly assigned to individuals. Part of series 2 was like that of series 1 except that the price tag was left on the mug, and this was pointed out to all the subjects. This was done to reduce the uncertainty regarding the market or cash value of the mug. The trading time for the mug exchange experiment in series 2 was increased from 4 to 6 minutes in four of the six experiments. This was done as it appeared that the subjects were still expecting their bids when the period ended after 4 minutes.

2.4. Mug Exchange Experiments using Uniform Price Double Auction

Franciosi et al. (1996) used the uniform price double auction (UPDA) mechanism to study mug exchange due to its strong equilibrating properties. (See McCabe, Rassenti, and Smith, 1993.) The authors felt that using an efficient auction market mechanism may be crucial to testing the undertrading hypothesis.

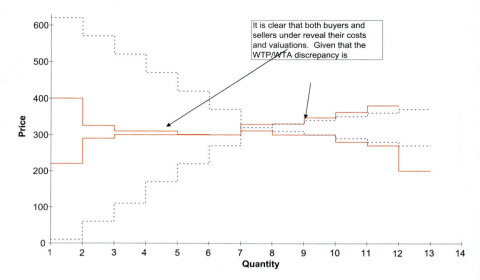

Figure 2. Two series of experiments were run. Each series was divided into Part 1 and 2. In each experiments 24 different subjects were assigned randomly to groups of 12 buyers and 12 sellers. In Part 1 of series 1 each buyer was assigned a value and each seller a cost by a random draw with replacement from the uniform distribution [$0, $9.99] at the beginning of each of the 10 (12) trading periods. This baseline served as a training session. All periods lasted 4 minutes. In Part 2, series 1 and 2, each buyer was endowed with a $9.99 cash balance which was theirs to keep if no mug was purchased; each seller was endowed with a University of Arizona emblem mug priced at $9.95 in the University bookstore and was theirs to keep if not sold. Each subject was paid their earnings in cash from the induced value training experiments in Part 1 of each of the sessions. In series 2, Part 1 used the constant volume environment shown in the figure, but in each period a random constant was added to each value, and the values randomly assigned to individuals. Part 2 of series 2 was like that of series 1 except that the price tag ($9.95) was left on each mug, and this was pointed out to the subjects. This was done to reduce uncertainty concerning the cash or market value of the mug in each group. Also in series 2 the trading time was increased from 4 to 6 minutes in four of the six experiments. This was done because it appeared that the subjects were still adjusting their bids and offers when the period ended (see the figure: several subjects are within 10–30 cents of a trade). Most mug experiments in series 1 and 2 were characterized by under revelation on the part of both Buyers and Sellers. Conclusion: The WTA/WTP discrepancy can be negligible, but one can still get undertrading from under revelation.

Two series of experiments were run. In each experiment 24 different subjects were randomly assigned to groups of 12 buyers and 12 sellers. Each series was divided into parts 1 and 2. In Part 1 of series 1 each buyer was assigned a value and each seller a cost from the uniform distribution on [$0, $9.99] at the beginning of each of 10 (or 12) trading periods. This baseline served as a training session. All periods lasted 4 minutes. In Part 2, series 1 and 2, each buyer was endowed with a $9.99 cash balance which was theirs to keep if no mug was purchased; each seller was endowed with a University of Arizona emblem mug priced at $9.95 which was theirs to keep if not sold. Each subject was paid cash for all of his or her earnings from the induced value training experiments in Part 1 of each of the sessions. In series 2, Part 1 used the constant volume equilibrium environment, but in each period a random constant was added to each value, and the values randomly assigned to each individual. Part 2 of series 2 was like that of series 1 except that the price tag ($9.95) was left on each mug, and this was pointed out to the subjects. This was a treatment to reduce uncertainty concerning the cash or market value of the mug in each group. Also in series 2 the trading time for mug exchange was increased from 4 to 6 minutes in four of the six experiments. This was done because it seemed that subjects were still adjusting their bids and offers when the period ended after 4 minutes. The experimental designs are summarized in Table 2.

The trading volume in the two series of experiments is plotted in Figure 1. Comparing the results with the Kahneman, Knetsch, and Thaler (1991) experiments it is clear that in these experiments there was much less undertrading. In three of the eleven experiments half of the mugs trade as predicted by standard theory. In the Kahneman, Knetsch, and Thaler (1991) exchanges no more than one-third of the mugs ever trade. But undertrading still occurs. How can undertrading be reconciled with the Shogren et al. (1994) finding that the WTP–WTA discrepancy converges to miniscule levels? The answer is as follows: Francioso et al. observe that the reported supply and demand schedules using UPDA are very flat, with many bids to buy and offers to sell very near the market clearing price. Hence, undertrading can result from very slight underrevelation, although there is little discrepancy between WTA and WTP.

References

Becker, G.M., DeGroot, M.H., Marschak, J. (1964). "Measuring utility by a single sequential method". Behavioral Science 9, 226–232.
Franciosi, R., Kujal, P., Michelitsch, R., Smith, V., Deng, G. (1996). "Experimental tests of the endowment effect". Journal of Economic Behavior and Organization 30, 213–226.
Hanemann, Michael W. (1991). "Willingness to pay and willingness to accept: How much can they differ?" American Economic Review 81, 635–647.
Kahneman, D., Knetsch, J., Thaler, R. (1991). "Experimental tests of the endowment effect and the coase theorem". Journal of Political Economy 98, 1325–1348; Reprinted in Richard Thaler, Quasi Rational Economics, Russell Sage Foundation, New York, pp. 167–188.
McCabe, K., Rassenti, S., Smith, V. (1993). "Designing a uniform price double auction: An experimental evaluation". In: Friedman, D., Rust, J. (Eds.), The Double Auction Market Institution, Theories, and Evidence. Addison Wesley, Reading, MA.
Shogren, J.F., Shin, S.Y., Hayes, D.J., Kliebenstein, J.B. (1994). "Resolving differences in willingness to pay and willingness to accept". American Economic Review 66, 274–279.
Smith, V.L. (1976). "Experimental economics: Induced value theory". American Economic Review 66, 274–279.

Chapter 102

THE BECKER–DEGROOT–MARSCHAK MECHANISM IS NOT GENERALLY INCENTIVE-COMPATIBLE IN PRACTICE

PETER BOHM

Stockholm University

The Becker, DeGroot, and Marschak (1964) (BDM) mechanism is widely used in experimental economics as an instrument to elicit non-distorted buyer or seller prices. As shown here, although incentive compatible in theory, the mechanism is not robustly so in actual practice.

When applied to elicit seller reservation prices, the BDM mechanism works as follows. (1) Subjects, who each have an object to sell, are asked to state their seller reservation prices. (2) The subjects are confronted with a buyout price randomly selected within a range that is taken to cover their true reservation prices. (3) Only subjects whose stated reservation prices are at most equal to the buyout price receive this price and part with the item for sale. Consequently, subjects have an incentive to state their true reservation prices.

Experimentalists have been so sure of the incentive compatibility of this mechanism in practice that they often explicitly inform their subjects that it is in the respondents' interest to report their true reservation prices, or words to that effect. However, as is reported here, it turns out that behavior is not fully determined by these incentives alone and that, contrary to the incentives provided, the choice of upper bound of the buyout price range tends to influence the seller prices that subjects state.

1. Experimental design

To test the BDM mechanism with respect to the effect of the choice of the upper bound of the buyout price range, it helps to have an experimental commodity that has a rather obvious lowest maximum price above which no real buyers would consider purchasing the commodity. The commodity used in Bohm, Lindén, and Sonnegård (1997) was a card entitling the bearer to 30 liters of gasoline at a nearby gas station. A realistic price at which a real buyer would accept to purchase such a card could hardly exceed the market price of gasoline, which equaled SEK 225 (approx. $30).

Every subject in four groups, each consisting of 20–22 undergraduate students in Economics, was given a gasoline card and offered the chance to sell it according to the rules of the BDM mechanism. The transaction design and the resulting mean asks in the four groups are reported below.

Handbook of Experimental Economics Results, Volume 1
Copyright © 2008 Elsevier B.V. All rights reserved
DOI: 10.1016/S1574-0722(07)00102-3

Testing the BDM mechanism for variations of the upper bound of buyout prices

The four groups of seller subjects:
Group "BDM225": BDM buyout prices known to be drawn from 0 to SEK 225
Group "BDM300":   "   "   "   "   "   "   "   " "   "   300
Group "BDMU": the upper bound (SEK 225) not announced but said "to equal what we believe is the maximum price any real buyer would be willing to pay"
Group "MARKET": the sellers met a group of 23 buyers to form a market for the experimental commodity (cards entitling the bearer to 30 liters of gasoline).

Test results:
Pairwise Wilcoxon–Mann–Whitney rank sum tests and a regression, respectively, showed that
  (1) BDM300 asks were significantly higher than BDM225 asks (p-values $= 0.0003$ and 0.00004, respectively), even when the BDM300 ask distribution was truncated at SEK 225
  (2) BDM225 and BDMU asks did not differ to any significant extent (p-values $= 0.84$ and 0.77, respectively)
  (3) Nor did BDM225 asks differ from asks in the MARKET test (p-values $= 0.63$ and 0.21).

2. Conclusions

If the MARKET arrangement produced an unbiased estimate of seller reservation prices, these results indicate that:
- neither BDM225 nor BDMU biased seller reservation prices, implying in turn that
- BDMU might be used when a clear lowest maximum price such as that in the tests reported here (SEK 225) cannot be identified, and
- an upper bound clearly exceeding what any real buyer would be willing to pay (such as in BDM300) leads to upward biases in reported seller reservation prices.

Thus, studies which have used upper bounds clearly exceeding what real buyers could consider paying may have produced biased estimates of seller reservation prices. (For reference to examples in the literature where such upper bounds were used, as well as a detailed report on the above tests, see Bohm, Lindén, and Sonnegård, 1997).

References

Becker, G., DeGroot, M., Marschak, J. (1964). "Measuring utility by a single-response sequential method". Behavioral Science 9, 226–232.
Bohm, P., Lindén, J., Sonnegård, J. (1997). "Eliciting reservation prices: Becker–DeGroot–Marschak mechanisms vs markets". Economic Journal 107, 1079–1089.

Chapter 103

UTILITY MAXIMIZATION

JAMES C. COX

University of Arizona

The model of the utility-maximizing agent is central to theoretical and applied economics and to economics education. But how can one test for the presence of utility maximization? More specifically, how can one test "the utility hypothesis," defined as the hypothesis that real economic agents behave as if they maximize utility functions subject to binding budget constraints?

1. The Utility Hypothesis

A testable form of the utility hypothesis results from identifying necessary condition(s) for the existence of a utility function that "rationalizes" the price and quantity data, meaning a utility function that correctly predicts choices that do not violate an agent's budget constraint. Consider the traditional model of a "consumer" that chooses only consumption good quantities. Let the data consist of price vectors, p^t, and quantity vectors, q^t, for observations, $t = 1, 2, \ldots, T$. The consumer has been observed to choose q^t, which therefore did not violate her budget constraint. The cost of q^t was $p^t \cdot q^t$; hence any q such that

$$p^t \cdot q \leqslant p^t \cdot q^t \tag{1}$$

would also not violate the situation t budget constraint. Thus the utility function $u(\cdot)$ rationalizes the (p^t, q^t) observations if and only if $u(q^t) \geqslant u(q)$ for all q such that $p^t \cdot q^t \geqslant p^t \cdot q$. Thus we have:

STATEMENT 1. *If there exists a utility function, $u(\cdot)$, that rationalizes data for a consumer then that agent behaves as if he maximizes $u(\cdot)$; that is, his behavior is consistent with the utility hypothesis.*

Possible inconsistencies with utility-maximizing choices are of no clear economic interest unless the objects of choice are scarce. In order for the chosen commodities to be scarce, the agent's budget constraint must be binding. Hence, a specific testable form of the utility hypothesis must incorporate scarcity. There are various ways to incorporate scarcity in the model of the utility-maximizing agent. (Sufficient conditions include assumptions that the agent's preferences are: (a) strictly monotonic; or (b) globally non-satiated and strictly convex; or (c) locally non-satiated.) I shall assume that the agent's preferences are locally non-satiated, meaning that for any admissible commodity vector, q, and any neighborhood around q, there exists an admissible q^* in the neighborhood that is strictly preferred to q.

A key theoretical result is derived in Varian (1982). He demonstrated that the necessary and sufficient condition for the existence of a locally non-satiated utility function that rationalizes consumption good price and quantity observations is the generalized axiom of revealed preference (GARP).

GARP: if $p^i \cdot q^i \geq p^i \cdot q^j$, $p^j \cdot q^j \geq p^j \cdot q^r$, ..., $p^s \cdot q^s \geq p^s \cdot q^k$
then $p^k \cdot q^k \leq p^k \cdot q^i$.

Thus, in principle, a test of the utility hypothesis can be based on GARP.

But how, in practice, can one actually test the utility hypothesis with data for real economic agents? The utility hypothesis has no testable implication for aggregate data (Sonnenschein, 1973a, 1973b) nor for proper subsets of the variables ("incomplete" data) that enter an agent's budget constraint (Varian, 1988). The utility hypothesis and the hypothesis that preferences are homogeneous across consumers together place testable restrictions on aggregate data (Shafer and Sonnenschein, 1982). Therefore, if one conducts a test with aggregate data he is doing a joint test of a compound hypothesis consisting of the (core) utility hypothesis and the (subsidiary) hypothesis that preferences are homogeneous across agents. The utility hypothesis and the hypothesis that preferences are weakly separable together place testable restrictions (Varian, 1983) on both the incomplete data (one set of inequalities) and the complete data (another set of inequalities). Therefore, if one conducts a test with incomplete data, he is doing an incomplete (one of two sets of inequalities) joint test of the compound hypothesis consisting of the utility and separability hypotheses. But the homogeneity and separability hypotheses are not central to economics while the utility hypothesis is central. The key test is one that is capable of yielding results that would be known to be inconsistent with the utility hypothesis: a "simple" test of the core hypothesis, not a (complete or incomplete) joint test involving one or more subsidiary hypotheses. Thus we have:

STATEMENT 2. *In order to conduct a simple test of the utility hypothesis, one must use data that are "disaggregated" (i.e., are for individual decision-makers) and "complete" (i.e., include observations of all of the choice variable that enter budget constraints).*

The choice variables that enter the budget constraints of economic agents in national economies typically include labor supplies and asset net demands in addition to consumption good demands. Thus we have:

STATEMENT 3. *In most economies, a data set must include observations of consumption good demands, labor supplies, and asset (net) demands in order for it to be complete.*

This statement implies that we need to identify necessary condition(s) for utility-maximizing choice of consumption goods, labor supplies, and assets. Cox (1997) reports the extended form of GARP that includes labor supplies and asset net demands. Let the asset price vector observed in situation t be v^t and the observed asset quantity vector be a^t. Let the observed wage rate vector be w^t and the observed labor supply vector be h^t. Let I^t be the maximum possible labor income that the agent can earn in situation t. The agent spends $p^t \cdot q^t$ of I^t on consumption goods and "spends" $I^t - w^t \cdot h^t$ of I^t on leisure. The consumption, labor supply, and asset net demand quantities (q^t, h^t, a^t) were observed to have been chosen in situation t; hence they are known to have been affordable. Thus any (q, h, a) such that

$$p^t \cdot q + I^t - w^t \cdot h + v^t \cdot a \leqslant p^t \cdot q^t + I^t - w^t \cdot h^t + v^t \cdot a^t \qquad (2)$$

is also known to have been affordable in situation t. The utility function, $u(q, h, a)$ rationalizes the observations if $u(q^t, h^t, a^t) \geqslant u(q, h, a)$, for all (q, h, a) that satisfy (2), for all observations $t = 1, 2, \ldots, T$. Hence the necessary and sufficient condition for the existence of a such a utility function is the following extended form of the generalized axiom of revealed preference that incorporates labor supply and asset (net) demand.

$$\text{GARP}_{\text{LA}}: \quad \text{if } p^i \cdot q^i + I^i - w^i \cdot h^i + v^i \cdot a^i \geqslant p^i \cdot q^j + I^i - w^i \cdot h^j + v^i \cdot a^j,$$
$$p^j \cdot q^j + I^j - w^j \cdot h^j + v^j \cdot a^j$$
$$\geqslant p^j \cdot q^r + I^j - w^j \cdot h^r + v^j \cdot a^r,$$
$$\ldots,$$
$$p^s \cdot q^s + I^s - w^s \cdot h^s + v^s \cdot a^s$$
$$\geqslant p^s \cdot q^k + I^s - w^s \cdot h^k + v^s \cdot a^k,$$
$$\text{then } p^k \cdot q^k + I^k - w^k \cdot h^k + v^k \cdot a^k$$
$$\leqslant p^k \cdot q^i + I^k - w^k \cdot h^i + v^k \cdot a^i.$$

Thus we have:

STATEMENT 4. With data from most economies, conducting a simple test of the utility hypothesis is equivalent to testing GARP$_{\text{LA}}$ with data for individual economic agents.

2. A Complete, Disaggregated Data Set

Since conducting a simple test of the utility hypothesis requires the use of data that are disaggregated and complete, one must attempt to find such data. It appears that the only disaggregated and complete data that exist are the data from the token economy experiment reported in Battalio et al. (1973) and Kagel (1972). The experiment was conducted with 38 female patients that were part of the ongoing token economy in the Central Islip State Hospital. This was an essentially closed economy in which residents could earn tokens by performing various tasks. The tokens could be used to purchase

Table 1
Experimental price treatments. The experimental treatments were large changes in the prices of Group 1 and Group 2 consumption goods

Week 1	Group 1	Group 2	Group 3
1	Baseline	Baseline	Baseline
2	0.5 × Baseline	2 × Baseline	Baseline
3	Baseline	Baseline	Baseline
4	2 × Baseline	0.5 × Baseline	Baseline
5	2 × Baseline	0.5 × Baseline	Baseline
6	Baseline	Baseline	Baseline
7	Baseline	Baseline	Baseline

consumption goods available within the hospital economy and could be carried over for indefinite periods. Thus the choice variables in the token economy were consumption good quantities, labor hours for various tasks, and token money balance.

The economics experimenters obtained permission to conduct an experiment with the token economy that involved introducing the large changes in relative prices of three groups of consumption goods reported in Table 1. The experiment was conducted over a seven week period. The data consist of individual subjects' weekly earnings, weekly expenditures on each of the three groups of consumption goods, and end-of-week token balances. Although the labor hours supplied to various tasks were not recorded, one can still test $GARP_{LA}$ because nominal wage rates were not changed; that is, since $w^t = w$, for all t, one can substitute week t labor income, y^t, for $w^t \cdot h^t$ and $w^s \cdot h^t$ in all revealed preference statements. Furthermore, since the one asset in the experiment (tokens) was the numeraire, its price was always equal to one and therefore one can substitute the token money balance at the end of week t, m^t, for $v^t \cdot a^t$ and $v^s \cdot a^t$ in all revealed preference statements.

3. Test Results and Power

Figure 1 (right scale) shows the number of observed violations of $GARP_{LA}$ by each of the 38 subjects reported in Cox (1997). (No results are reported for subject 3 because she left the token economy shortly after the economics experiment began.) Data for 24 out of the 38 subjects contain no observed inconsistencies with $GARP_{LA}$. Data for the other 14 subjects contain 54 observed inconsistencies with $GARP_{LA}$, with subject 29 accounting for 17 of them.

Counting the number of inconsistencies with revealed preference inequalities is not informative unless one can assess the power of the test. For example, if none of the budget hyperplanes intersected then we would necessarily count zero inconsistencies with all revealed preference inequalities but the test would be completely uninformative. Figure 1 shows a measure of the power of the test for the data for each subject that

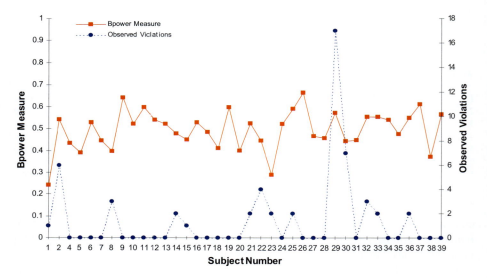

Figure 1. In order to test the hypothesis that consumers' behavior is consistent with utility maximization, one must use data that are disaggregated (are for individual decision-makers) and complete (include all of the choice variables that enter budget constraints). In order for data from most economies to be complete, it must include observations of consumption goods, labor supplies, and asset net demands. The necessary and sufficient condition for utility maximizing choices is an extended form of the generalized axiom of revealed preference that includes labor supplies and asset net demands. This figure reports the number of observed inconsistencies with this extended form of the axiom (right scale) for 38 consumers in a token economy. Data for 24 consumers contain zero observed violations of the axiom's inequalities. Data for the other 14 subjects contain 54 violations. The figure also reports a measure of the power of the test (left scale) based on a random choice model for which all budget shares (for individual commodities) are equally likely to occur. Zero or low numbers of violations cannot be attributed to low test power for data for those consumers. The number of violations and the test power measure have a $-.034$ rank correlation.

is reported in Cox (1997). The test power is measured with a randomization procedure based on Becker's (1962) random choice model. First, a computer algorithm generates all possible combinations of budget shares for the n commodities that sum to 1 on a 0.01 unit of divisibility. Then a sample of 1000 random budget shares is drawn (with replacement) from a discrete uniform distribution on the generated set of possible budget shares for each subject for each data observation week. Let $\tilde{S}^t_j$, $j = 1, 2, \ldots, n$, be one element of the sample of budget shares drawn for a subject; then the random quantities, $\tilde{q}^t_j$, are calculated as

$$\tilde{q}^t_j = \tilde{S}^t_j p^t \cdot q^t / p^t_j, \qquad (3)$$

where p^t_j and $p^t \cdot q^t$ are in the actual data. The random quantities, $\tilde{q}^t_j$, and actual prices, p^t_j, are then used as data in tests of $GARP_{LA}$. The frequencies with which this random choice model produces one or more violations of the relevant revealed preference inequalities are reported in Figure 1 (left scale).

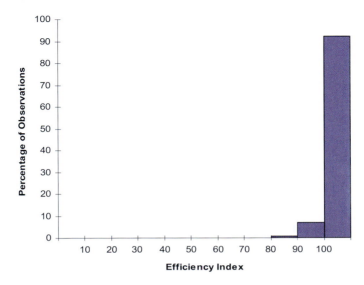

Figure 2. Simply counting the number of inconsistencies with revealed preference inequalities does not inform us about the significance of these observed inconsistencies with utility maximization. A non-parametric measure (partial efficiency) of the significance of the observed inconsistencies is reported in this figure. 243 out of 263 (or 92.4%) of the bundles chosen by consumers in the token economy are 100% efficient in maximizing utility. 18 (or 6.8%) of the chosen bundles are 90–99% efficient and 2 (or 0.8%) of the chosen bundles are 80–89% efficient. 99.2% of the chosen bundles pass a non-parametric "10% test" for consistency with utility maximization.

For the 24 subjects with zero violations using actual data, the power measure has an average value of .507 and it varies from a low of .371 for subject 38 to a high of .664 for subject 26. Therefore, the absence of violations in the data for 24 subjects cannot be attributed to non-intersecting budget hyperplanes. The power measure for the 14 subjects with one or more violations has an average value of .474 and it varies from a low of .243 for subject 1 to a high of .591 for subject 25. It seems clear that the different test results for the 24 subjects with no violations and the 14 subjects with violations cannot be attributed to lower test power for the no-violations group. This conclusion is supported by the *negative* rank correlation of −.034 between the number of observed violations and the power measure.

4. Are the Inconsistencies with Utility Maximization Significant?

Simply counting the 54 violations of $GARP_{LA}$ committed by 14 out of the 38 subjects does not inform us about the significance of these inconsistencies with utility maximization. Do these 14 subjects "almost maximize" utility functions or are their choices "far from" utility-maximizing choices? A non-parametric approach to assessing the sig-

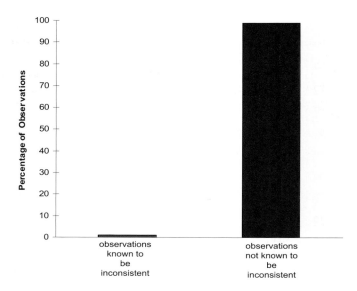

Figure 3. Data for the token economy contain observation errors similar to the observation errors in data for national economies and consumer panel studies. But data for the token economy contain an independent measure of consumer expenditure that makes it possible to discriminate between those observed inconsistencies with utility maximization that can be attributed to observation errors and those that are known to be inconsistencies. This figure reports the results from comparing the partial efficiency measures with the proportional reporting errors for the data. After correcting the tests for these observation errors, only 3 out of 263 (or 1.1%) of the chosen commodity bundles are known to be inconsistent with utility maximization. 260 out of 263 (or 98.9%) of the chosen bundles are either fully consistent with utility maximization or contain deviations that can be attributed to errors in observations.

nificance of deviations from utility maximization was introduced by Afriat (1972) and further developed by Afriat (1987) and Varian (1993).

This approach can be most easily explained using the conventional revealed preference model in which consumption goods are the only choice variables (Cox, 1997). Let q^t be the observed n-vector of commodities chosen in situation t and let p^t be the corresponding observed price vector. Varian's (1993) efficiency index approach can be explained as follows. For some numbers $e^t \in [0, 1]$, redefine GARP as

$$\text{GARP}(e^t): \text{ if } e^i p^i \cdot q^i \geq p^i \cdot q^j, \ e^j p^j \cdot q^j \geq p^j \cdot q^r, \ \ldots, \ e^s p^s \cdot q^s \geq p^s \cdot q^k$$

$$\text{then } e^k p^k \cdot q^k \leq p^k \cdot q^i.$$

Then solve for the *minimal* perturbations of the budget hyperplanes, $e_*^t, t = 1, 2, \ldots, T$, such that the data satisfy $\text{GARP}(e_*^t)$. The number, $1 - e_*^t$, can be interpreted as the proportion of expenditure that the consumer is allowed to "waste" in situation t and still be considered a utility maximizer. Alternatively, the number, e_*^t, measures the efficiency of a consumer in realizing utility-maximizing purchases in situation t. This approach can be adapted in a straightforward way to apply to the extended form of the revealed preference axiom, $GARP_{LA}$ (Cox, 1997).

Figure 2 shows results from calculation of Varian's minimal perturbation efficiency index for the consumption good, labor supply, and token balance data (Cox, 1997). There were 263 bundles chosen in the experiment: 243 (or 92.4%) of the chosen bundles were 100% efficient in maximizing utility; 18 (or 6.8%) of the chosen bundles were 90–99% efficient; and 2 (or 0.8%) of the chosen bundles were 80–89% efficient. Thus 99.2% of the chosen bundles pass a non-parametric "10% test" for consistency with utility maximization.

A conservative test of the utility hypothesis will not count any inconsistency with revealed preference axioms that can be attributed to reporting errors in the data. It is known (Battalio et al., 1973) that the token economy data is like data from national accounts and consumer panel studies in that it includes reporting errors. The token economy data include both under-reporting and over-reporting of quantities. But the token economy data also include an independent measure of the size of the reporting errors that can be used to adjust tests for the reporting errors. Results from Cox (1997), comparing the partial efficiency measures with the proportional reporting errors for the data are reported in Figure 3. Note that 260 (or 98.9) of the chosen bundles were either fully consistent with utility maximization or contained deviations from full maximization that can be attributed to errors in observations. Only 3 (or 1.1%) of the chosen bundles are known to be inconsistent with utility maximization.

Acknowledgement

Todd Swarthout provided valuable assistance by preparing the table and graphs.

References

Afriat, Sidney (1972). "Efficiency measures of production functions". International Economic Review 8, 568–598.
Afriat, Sidney (1987). "Logic of Choice and Economic Theory". Clarendon Press, Oxford.
Battalio, Raymond C., Kagel, John H., Winkler, Robin C., Fisher Jr., Edwin B., Basmann, Robert L., Krasner, Leonard (1973). "A test of consumer demand theory using observations of individual consumer purchases". Western Economic Journal XI, 411–428.
Becker, Gary S. (1962). "Irrational behavior and economic theory". Journal of Political Economy 70, 1–13.
Cox, James C. (1997). "On testing the utility hypothesis". Economic Journal 107, 1054–1078.
Kagel, John H. (1972). "Token economies and experimental economics". Journal of Political Economy 80 (4), 779–785.
Shafer, Wayne, Sonnenschein, Hugo (1982). "Market demand and excess demand functions". In: Arrow, Kenneth J., Intriligator, Michael D. (Eds.), Handbook of Mathematical Economics, vol. II. North-Holland, New York.
Sonnenschein, Hugo (1973a). "Do Walras' identity and continuity characterize the class of community excess demand functions?" Journal of Economic Theory 6, 345–354.

Sonnenschein, Hugo (1973b). "The utility hypothesis and market demand theory". Western Economic Journal XI, 404–410.
Varian, Hal R. (1982). "The nonparametric approach to demand analysis". Econometrica 50, 945–973.
Varian, Hal R. (1983). "Non-parametric tests of consumer behaviour". Review of Economic Studies 50, 99–110.
Varian, Hal R. (1988). "Revealed preference with a subset of goods". Journal of Economic Theory 46, 179–185.
Varian, Hal R. (1993). "Goodness of fit for revealed preference tests". Unpublished paper, University of Michigan.

Chapter 104

PREFERENCE REVERSALS

JAMES C. COX

University of Arizona

Study of preference reversals originated with cognitive psychologists and has spread to experimental economics because it is directly relevant to the empirical validity of economic theories of decision-making under uncertainty. A preference reversal experiment involves paired choice and valuation responses, usually over simple two-outcome gambles. Subjects are asked to choose which of a pair of gambles they want to play. They are also asked to place minimum selling prices on the gambles in an experimental context in which telling the truth is a dominant strategy. A preference reversal occurs when a subject places a lower selling price on the gamble that he/she chooses than on the other gamble in a pair.

Preference reversals call into question the empirical validity of economic theory because they provide support for the conclusion that the preferences that subjects reveal vary with the response mode (choice or valuation) that is used to elicit the preferences. If the preference reversal phenomenon is robust, then standard economic decision theory is on shaky ground as an empirically useful positive theory of decision-making. Robust preference reversals would be even more of a problem for normative economics: consider the implications for cost-benefit analysis of preferences over alternatives that reverse with a change in the response mode used to elicit the preferences.

Binary lotteries that were used in the early experiments by Lichtenstein and Slovic (1971) and many subsequent papers are reported in Table 1. There are six pairs of lotteries. Each pair consists of a probability (or P) bet with a relatively large probability of a relatively small win state payoff and a dollar (or $ bet) with a relatively small probability of a relatively large win state payoff. Psychologists explain preference reversals as response mode effects on decisions. For example, when asked to place a value (minimum selling price) on a bet, a subject may first "anchor" on the values of the win state payoffs in two bets and then make an insufficient "adjustment" for the difference in probability of winning. In contrast, when asked to choose between two bets a subject may first anchor on the probabilities of the win state payoffs and then make an insufficient adjustment for the difference in dollar values of the win state payoffs. This explanation implies that preference reversals will be asymmetric: it will be much more frequent that subjects will (a) place a higher value on the $ bet and choose the paired P bet, than (b) place a higher value on the P bet and choose the paired $ bet. Hence, preference reversals of type (a) are called "predicted reversals" and those of type (b) are called "unpredicted reversals."

Table 1
Typical pairs of binary lotteries used in experiments. A preference reversal experiment involves choice and valuation responses, usually over pairs of simple two-outcome lotteries such as the ones in this table. Each lottery pair contains a "P bet," with a relatively high probability of a relatively low win state payoff, and a "$ bet," with a relatively low probability of a relatively high win state payoff

Pairs	Type	Probability of winning	Amount if win	Amount if lose	Expected value
1	P	35/36	$4.00	−$1.00	3.86
	$	11/36	$16.00	−$1.50	3.85
2	P	29/36	$2.00	−$1.00	1.42
	$	7/36	$9.00	−$0.50	1.35
3	P	34/36	$3.00	−$2.00	2.72
	$	18/36	$6.50	−$1.00	2.75
4	P	32/36	$4.00	−$0.50	3.50
	$	4/36	$40.00	−$1.00	3.56
5	P	34/36	$2.50	−$0.50	2.33
	$	14/36	$8.50	−$1.50	2.39
6	P	33/36	$2.00	−$2.00	1.67
	$	18/36	$5.00	−$1.50	1.75

1. Seminal Experiments

Grether and Plott (1979) explained several design features of earlier preference reversal experiments that called into question their implications for economics. They developed an experimental design that was more appropriate for economics and were surprised that the results confirmed the earlier findings. Figure 1 presents results from experiments by Lichtenstein and Slovic (1971, 1973) and Grether and Plott (1979). The reported experiments have the following characteristics: (a) Lichtenstein and Slovic III is a monetary payoff experiment with psychology students as subjects; (b) Lichtenstein and Slovic P is a monetary payoff experiment with positive expected payoff gambles run on the floor of a Las Vegas casino with adult gamblers as subjects; (c) Grether and Plott 1H is a hypothetical payoff experiment with undergraduate students as subjects; and (d) Grether and Plott 1M is a monetary payoff experiment with undergraduate students as subjects. Results from all of these experiments are similar. About 1/3 of all decisions involve preference reversals and predicted reversals are much more common than unpredicted reversals. Furthermore, there is no notable difference between the results from Grether and Plott's hypothetical payoff and monetary payoff experiments.

Thus the preference reversal phenomenon was robust to the changes in experimental procedures introduced by Grether and Plott. They attributed preference reversals to subjects' violations of transitivity.

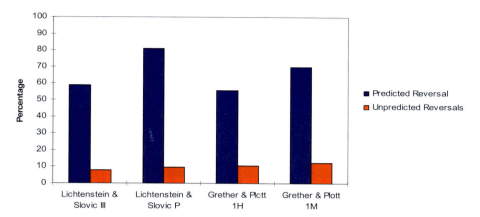

Figure 1. A preference reversal occurs when a subject places a lower selling price on the lottery that he/she chooses than on the other lottery in the pair. Using data from the seminal experiments, this figure shows the percentage of choices of P bets for which the paired $ bets had higher selling prices ("predicted reversals," shown in blue) and the percentage of choices of $ bets for which the paired P bets had higher selling prices ("unpredicted reversals," shown in red). Lichtenstein and Slovic III is a monetary payoff experiment with psychology students as subjects. Lichtenstein and Slovic P is a monetary payoff experiment with positive expected payoff gambles run on the floor of a Las Vegas casino with adult gamblers as subjects. Grether and Plott 1H is a hypothetical payoff experiment with undergraduate students as subjects. Grether and Plott 1M is a monetary payoff experiment with undergraduate students as subjects.

2. Independence Axiom Treatments

Grether and Plott's paper motivated several authors to critique their design and question how robust were their results. However the experiments reported by these other authors produced results similar to those reported by Grether and Plott.

Holt (1986) and Karni and Safra (1987) questioned Grether and Plott's interpretation of their results and offered alternative interpretations as follows. In order to eliminate changes in subjects' wealth during an experiment, and thus remove a "wealth effects" easy explanation of preference reversals, Grether and Plott randomly selected a single decision of each subject for monetary payoff at the end of the experiment. Holt explained that this procedure requires the independence axiom of expected utility theory in order for the experimental results to be interpreted as preference reversals. Thus, Grether and Plott's conclusion that the preference reversals in their experiments were violations of transitivity was called into question. Karni and Safra examined another feature of the preference reversal experiments reported by Grether and Plott and most others, the use of the Becker, DeGroot, and Marshak (1964) procedure for eliciting selling prices. They explained that this procedure requires the independence axiom in order for the results to be interpreted as preference reversals.

Cox and Epstein (1989) and Tversky, Slovic, and Kahneman (1990) designed experiments that did not use either the Becker–DeGroot–Marshak (BDM) or the random

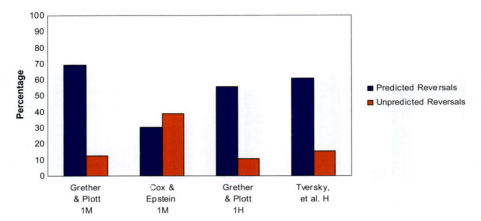

Figure 2. This figure compares results from Grether and Plott's experiments that require the independence axiom for interpretation, with results from the ordinal pricing experiments of Cox and Epstein and Tversky et al. that do not require this axiom to interpret the data as preference reversals. The Cox and Epstein experiment produced about the same rate of reversals as the Grether and Plott experiment (1M) with monetary payoffs but the latter did not replicate the asymmetry of reversals. The Tversky et al. experiment with hypothetical payoffs replicated both the rate and asymmetry of the preference reversals in the Grether and Plott experiment (1H) with hypothetical payoffs. Thus preference reversals cannot be attributed to violations of the independence axiom of expected utility theory.

decision selection procedure. They both used price elicitation procedures ("ordinal pricing tasks") that gave subjects an incentive to reveal sales prices with the correct relative values, but not the true values, and that did not require the independence axiom. Cox and Epstein paid their subjects after every decision in order to avoid the random decision selection procedure. They then used econometric analysis of the data to check for any significant wealth effects on decisions and found none. The experiments of Tversky et al. used hypothetical payoffs (except in one treatment in which 15% of the subjects were randomly selected for small monetary payoffs at the end of the experiment).

Results from the experiments by Cox and Epstein and Tversky et al. are reported in Figure 2, along with those from Grether and Plott's experiments 1M (with monetary payoffs) and 1H (with hypothetical payoffs) for comparison. The overall reversal rate in Cox and Epstein 1 is almost as high as in Grether and Plott 1M, but the former does not exhibit the asymmetric pattern of the latter. The different reversal pattern in Cox and Epstein 1 may be evidence that it was transparent to the subjects in their experiment that an ordinal pricing task is, in fact, a choice task framed as valuation.

Tversky et al. 1 has a higher overall reversal rate than Grether and Plott 1H and both exhibit the asymmetric pattern. The asymmetry of reversals in Tversky et al. 1 may be evidence that in their experiment, which is more complicated than Cox and Epstein's, the subjects did not realize that the ordinal pricing task is a choice task framed as valuation. Alternatively, it may instead be the case that the asymmetry resulted from subjects' lack of motivation in the complicated experiment. (See the next section.)

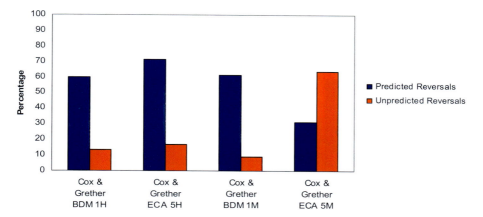

Figure 3. Results from some preference reversal experiments have been robust to use of hypothetical or monetary payoffs. This figure reports results from an experiment in which monetary payoffs produced fundamentally different preference reversals than did hypothetical payoffs. BDM 1H (respectively, M) shows the preference reversals that occurred with selling prices produced by the first repetition of the Becker–DeGroot–Marshak mechanism with hypothetical (respectively, monetary) incentives. ECA 5H (respectively, M) shows the preference reversals that occurred with selling prices produced by the fifth repetition of a sequential choice task using the English clock auction with hypothetical (respectively, monetary) payoffs.

Together, the Cox and Epstein and Tversky et al. experiments make clear that preference reversals cannot simply be attributed to violations of the independence axiom of expected utility theory.

3. Incentive Treatment

As noted above, Grether and Plott (1979) found that the use of monetary payoffs did not affect their conclusions about preference reversals. The results reported by Cox and Grether (1996) were also invariant to cash versus hypothetical payoffs with one striking exception, the English clock auction treatments. The English clock auction is a market sequential choice task that can be used to elicit selling prices. Figure 3 reports some results that make clear the pattern found. The results for the hypothetical payoff treatments, BDM 1H and ECA 5H, are quite similar. This would suggest the conclusion that after five replications in the market environment of the English clock auction the frequency and asymmetry of preference reversals are essentially the same as for the BDM mechanism. But now consider the results for the monetary payoff experiments, BDM 1M and ECA 5M. Results for BDM 1M are very similar to BDM 1H. In contrast, results for ECA 5M are very different than those for all other experiments in Figure 3; in particular, the asymmetry of reversals is strikingly reversed.

The effects of financial incentives in this market environment are quite intuitive if one considers the decision procedure that it is involved. The sooner the subject chooses

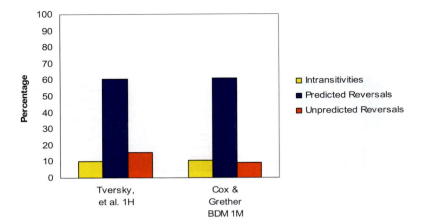

Figure 4. Tversky et al. and Cox and Grether report results from experiments with designs that can discriminate between violations of transitivity and other causes of preference reversals. This figure reports the rates of intransitivity (IT), predicted reversals (PR), and unpredicted reversals (UR) from some of the experiments in these two papers. Note that the rates of intransitivity are far lower than the overall rates of preference reversal. These experiments support the interpretation of the preference reversal phenomenon as a response mode effect, not a result of preference intransitivity.

to play the bet rather than remain in the market, and thus remain eligible to sell it, the less time and effort that is expended watching the computer screen and making decisions. This effect is quite pronounced for $ bets with their high win state payoffs and high starting prices for the clock. A subject could spend less time watching the computer screen by pressing the key for choosing the bet and dropping out early. This is exactly what many subjects did when no money was at stake in the hypothetical payoff experiments.

Together, the Grether–Plott and Cox–Grether papers make clear that many results from preference reversal experiments are the same for hypothetical and monetary payoffs but that some results differ dramatically.

4. Transitivity Treatments

Tversky, Slovic, and Kahneman (1990) designed their hypothetical payoff experiments to be able to discriminate between violations of transitivity and other causes of preference reversals. Cox and Grether (1996) adopted this design feature in their monetary payoff experiments. Figure 4 reports the rates of intransitivity (IT), predicted reversals (PR), and unpredicted reversals (UR) from some of the experiments in these two papers. Note that the rates of intransitivity are far lower than the overall rates of preference reversal.

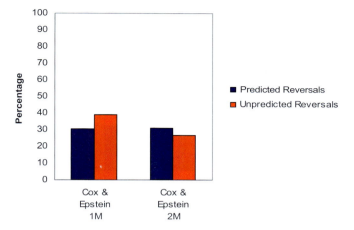

Figure 5. Most preference reversal experiments used pairs of P and $ bets with approximately equal expected values. Thus it is necessary to ascertain whether preference "reversals" simply reflect some convenient rule used by risk neutral subjects to resolve indifference. This figure reports results from Cox and Epstein's experiment, 1M using the gambles in Table 1, and results from their experiment 2M, using bet pairs with a 50% difference in expected payoff. The ordinal pricing task used in these experiments did not produce the asymmetric pattern of reversals characteristic of preference reversal experiments; hence the results are called choice reversals. The observed choice reversals in the two experiments are similar; therefore these results indicate that such reversals do not result from the resolution of indifference by risk neutral subjects.

These experiments support the interpretation of the preference reversal phenomenon as a response mode effect, not a result of preference intransitivity.

5. Risk Neutrality Treatment

Most of the preference reversal experiments used gambles like those in Table 1 that involve pairs in which the P bet has essentially the same expected value as its paired $ bet. If the subjects were risk neutral then they would be essentially indifferent between the two bets in any such pair; in that case, preference "reversals" might simply reflect some convenient rule for resolving indifference. To check on this possibility, Cox and Epstein ran a second experiment in which there was a 50% difference between the expected payoffs of the two bets in each pair. In addition, in one-half the pairs the P bet had the higher expected payoff and in the other one-half the $ bet did. Figure 5 reports results from Cox and Epstein's experiment 1M using some of the P bets and $ bets in Table 1 and results from their experiment 2M using bet pairs with the 50% difference in expected payoff. The ordinal pricing task used in these experiments did not produce the asymmetric pattern of reversals characteristic of preference reversal experiments; hence the results are called choice reversals.

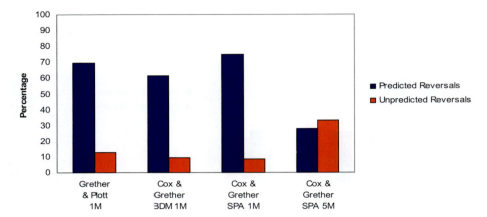

Figure 6. This figure presents comparisons of preference reversals from Grether and Plott's monetary payoff experiment, using the BDM mechanism, with Cox and Grether's monetary payoff experiments using the BDM mechanism and the second price auction. The first round of responses in the second price auction experiment, SPA 1M, produce about the same level and asymmetric pattern of reversals as in both BDM experiments. But by the fifth round of responses in the second price auction experiment, SPA 5M, the frequency of reversals has markedly decreased and, more importantly, the asymmetry of reversals has disappeared. Thus the preference reversal phenomenon is not robust to five repetitions in the second-price sealed-bid auction market environment with monetary incentives for the subjects.

The observed choice reversals in the two experiments are similar; hence these results indicate that such reversals do not result from the resolution of indifference by risk neutral subjects.

6. Market Treatment

The preference reversal phenomenon has troubling implications for the applicability of expected utility theory to non-market, non-repetitive choice and valuation decisions. But the central concern of economics is market behavior, much of which is repetitive decision-making. Cox and Grether (1996) examined preference reversals in paired market and non-market environments with choice and valuation response modes. Results from some of their treatments are reported in Figure 6 for comparison with those of Grether and Plott. First note that the results from Cox and Grether BDM 1M are quite similar to those for Grether and Plott 1M. Thus, Cox and Grether's computerized experiments with the BDM mechanism involving monetary payoffs after each decision replicated Grether and Plott's manual experiments with BDM involving random selection of one decision for monetary payoff. Cox and Grether SPA 1M is the first round of market experiments in which the second-price sealed-bid auction is the valuation task used to elicit selling prices rather than the BDM mechanism. The preference reversals for SPA 1M are comparable to BDM 1M; hence the preference reversal phenomenon is robust to the market environment. Cox and Grether SPA 5M is the fifth round of experiments with the second-price auction. Here, the results are very different from those for BPA 1M and SPA 1M. In SPA 5M, the frequency of reversals has markedly decreased and, more importantly, the asymmetry of reversals has disappeared.

The preference reversal phenomenon is not robust to five repetitions in the second-price sealed-bid auction market environment with monetary incentives for the subjects.

Acknowledgement

Todd Swarthout provided valuable assistance by preparing the table and figures.

References

Becker, G.M., DeGroot, Morris H., Marshak, Jacob (1964). "Measuring utility by a single-response sequential method". Behavioral Science 9, 226–232.
Cox, James C., Epstein, Seth (1989). "Preference reversals without the independence axiom". American Economic Review 79, 408–426.
Cox, James C., Grether, David M. (1996). "The preference reversal phenomenon: Response mode, markets, and incentives". Economic Theory 7 (3), 381–405.
Grether, David M., Plott, Charles R. (1979). "Economic theory of choice and the preference reversal phenomenon". American Economic Review 69, 623–638.
Holt, Charles (1986). "Preference reversals and the independence axiom". American Economic Review 76, 508–515.
Karni, Edi, Safra, Zvi (1987). "'Preference reversal' and the observability of preferences by experimental methods". Econometrica 55, 675–685.
Lichtenstein, Sarah, Slovic, Paul (1971). "Reversals of preference between bids and choices in gambling situations". Journal of Experimental Psychology 89, 46–55.
Lichtenstein, Sarah, Slovic, Paul (1973). "Response-induced reversals of preference in gambling: An extended replication in Las Vegas". Journal of Experimental Psychology 101, 16–20.
Tversky, Amos, Slovic, Paul, Kahneman, Daniel (1990). "The causes of preference reversal". American Economic Review 80, 204–217.

Chapter 105

RATIONALITY THE FAST AND FRUGAL WAY: INTRODUCTION

GERD GIGERENZER

PETER M. TODD

Max Planck Institute for Human Development, Berlin, Germany

What is bounded rationality? The neoclassical answer is optimization under constraints such as information costs (e.g., Sargent, 1993). For behavioral economists, however, bounded rationality is the study of cognitive illusions and decision anomalies (e.g., Camerer, 1998; Rabin, 1998). These two interpretations make an odd couple, one promoting rationality, the other irrationality. Behavioral economists report that human behavior deviates from optimization models and reject these as descriptively inadequate. Proponents of optimization respond with Milton Friedman's (1953) "as if" defense: Our models may incorrectly depict people as if they had the statistical sophistication of econometricians, but this does not matter, because our "as if" models are not intended to portray the process of decision making, but only to predict its outcome. One might think that behavioral economists focus on process, but that is not so either. Prospect theory (Kahneman and Tversky, 1979), for instance, predicts outcomes, not processes. Its equations are not meant to describe the steps of decision making, nor is there experimental evidence that people would actually go through these calculations. The same holds for other models that leave the Bernoullian framework of probability-times-utility untouched but tinker with the functions or add a single variable such as "regret" or "disappointment." If one is interested in how decisions are actually made, and in using this knowledge to design prescriptive models for improving decision making, one must go back to the blackboard and risk a more radical step.

This step is inherent in a third interpretation of bounded rationality that focuses on process: the study of the fast and frugal heuristics people use to make decisions with limited time and knowledge (Gigerenzer and Selten, 2001a; Gigerenzer, Todd, and the ABC Research Group, 1999). This third interpretation is an elaboration of Simon's (1955, 1990) analogy between bounded rationality and a pair of scissors: one blade is cognition and its limitations, the other the environment and its structure. To focus on bounded rationality as the study of heuristics that can exploit structures of their environments, we use the term "ecological rationality." If one focuses only on cognitive limitations, one can hardly understand why cognition works as well as it does – just as looking at one blade alone does not explain how scissors cut. Simon's use of the term "cognitive limitations" (as opposed to neutral terms such as "cognitive heuristics") is unfortunate because it has been taken to imply poor performance. However, equating limits with failure, and lack of limits with success, may underlie a deep misunderstanding about the consequences of omniscience. An unlimited memory, for instance, could be disastrous: The sheer mass of details stored could critically slow down and inhibit the retrieval of the few important experiences when they are needed. And too much information would impair the mind's ability to abstract, infer, and learn. A human brain or an artificial neural network that starts with an overabundant memory capacity may never be able to learn a language, whereas having a working memory that starts small (and then grows) can act as a filter of environmental input, enabling learning of important linguistic scaffolding first (Elman, 1993; Hertwig and Todd, 2003). Less can be more.

1. Heuristics

The term "heuristic" is of Greek origin, meaning "serving to find out or discover." Heuristics are a useful instrument in science as well as in everyday decision making (Payne, Bettman, and Johnson, 1993; Polya, 1954). Einstein (1905 taken from Holton, 1988) used the term "heuristic" to label an idea that he considered incomplete, given the limits of our knowledge, but useful. Behavioral economists, in contrast, have been using the term "heuristics" to account for errors of judgment and biased behavior that should be avoided. The positive power of heuristics has been replaced by a bad reputation. Moreover – or perhaps as a consequence – there are rather few concrete models of heuristics, and instead a preponderance of vague labels such as "availability" that can be applied post hoc to explain everything and nothing (see the exchange between Gigerenzer, 1996 and Kahneman and Tversky, 1996).

In this chapter, we give an introduction to the study of fast and frugal heuristics as specific models of decision mechanisms; the chapters that follow focus on particular heuristics. Fast and frugal heuristics do not try to optimize, that is, to compute the maximum or minimum of some function, nor, for the most part, do they calculate probabilities or utilities. Rather, they rely on simple building blocks for searching for information, stopping search, and finally making a decision. The goal of studying such heuristics is both descriptive and prescriptive. First, understanding how people make decisions enables us to predict when they will succeed and fail, typically more effectively than an outcome-oriented "as if" model would allow. Second, knowing which heuristics work in which environments allows us to design appropriate heuristic decision procedures for use by institutions, individuals, and artificial systems, and to teach people how to decide in an uncertain world when time is pressing and resources are scarce.

2. A Fast and Frugal Heuristic

We illustrate the mesh between the descriptive and prescriptive goals with an example from sports. Imagine a company that wants to design a robot that can catch balls, as in cricket and baseball. For the sake of simplicity, we will only consider the case where a ball comes in high, behind or in front of a player. (This is a thought experiment, as no such robot exists yet; see Gigerenzer and Selten, 2001b.)

One team of engineers, taking an optimizing approach, attempts to provide the robot with expensive computing and sensory equipment and a full representation of its environment (omniscience), including knowledge of possible parabolic flight paths and the ball's initial distance, velocity, and projection angle. But in a real game, due to air resistance, wind, and spin, balls do not fly in parabolas. Hence, the robot would need more instruments that can measure the speed and direction of the wind at each point of the ball's flight in order to compute the resulting path and ultimately the spot where the ball will land.

A second team, the cognitive illusion team, contends that the optimization equation is descriptively wrong. Real players are bounded in their rationality, and so make systematic errors. They show that when experienced players are asked to predict where a fly ball will land, they consistently underestimate the distance to the landing spot. They call this the "optimistic bias" – because underestimating the distance suggests to players that they might actually get the ball even when they cannot. The optimization team responds that they will nevertheless maintain their "as if" model; a model that can approximately predict the point to which players run is better than no model. Furthermore, they argue, even if the story about the optimistic bias were true, it would not help to understand how actual players catch a ball, nor how to build the robot.

A third group of engineers, the heuristics team, agrees that humans may not be able to compute the point where the ball will land. However, they point out, that may not be the interesting question. Players, after all, typically can catch high fly balls, so the proposed optimism bias is not holding them back. Instead, the question is: how do players catch a ball, if they do not perform the measurements that the optimization team proposes? Experiments and observation have shown that experienced players use a fast and frugal heuristic (McLeod and Dienes, 1996). When a ball comes in high, the player visually fixates the ball and starts running. The heuristic is to adjust the running speed so that the angle of gaze (between the ball and the horizon) remains roughly constant. In our thought experiment, a robot that uses this heuristic does not need to measure wind, air resistance, spin, or any other causal variables. It can get away with ignoring this information. All the relevant information is contained in one variable: the gaze angle. The gaze heuristic thus uses one-reason decision making. Note that this robot is not able to compute the point at which the ball will land. But it will be there when the ball comes low enough to catch. What looks like a serious mental flaw in need of de-biasing turns out to be irrelevant for good ball catching.

How is such a simple solution possible? The gaze heuristic makes use of an environmental feature that the player can easily exploit. In place of the complicated true trajectory of the ball's flight – which the optimization team was trying to work out – the gaze heuristic uses (and, through the action it dictates, creates) a simple relation between the player's eye and the ball. This solution is an instance of ecological rationality; that is, exploiting a match between cognition and its environment.

This thought experiment illustrates that a good model of the decision process (here the gaze heuristic) can supersede "as if" optimization models, both descriptively and prescriptively. First, the heuristic can predict behavior that the "as if" model cannot, such as that the player will catch the ball while running because he has to move to keep the angle of gaze constant. This is an experimentally testable prediction, and in fact, players do not run to a spot and wait there – they catch the ball while running. Second, a good process model can predict what the person relying on a heuristic cannot do, such as computing the point where the ball will land. This will help behavioral economists to predict what decision failures can occur and why. Third, a heuristic can aid in achieving prescriptive goals. For instance, the gaze heuristic can be used to make a robot good at ball catching, or to instruct inexperienced players. An optimizing "as if" model, however, may lead to computational explosion that makes it impossible to implement in any hardware, whether human or computer.

3. The Adaptive Toolbox

The vision of rationality embodied in the first team of robot builders matches that held by many economists: rationality as optimization, with or without constraints, assuming that economic agents act as if they are omniscient (at least approximately) and have the ability to make sophisticated statistical calculations. The Bayesian approach and subjective expected utility maximization are examples of this vision. In contrast, the vision of ecological (bounded) rationality takes into account the realistic psychological abilities of agents and the structures of the environments they face. Instead of relying on one all-powerful decision mechanism, ecological rationality arises through the use of a collection of fast and frugal heuristics in the mind's adaptive toolbox. The gaze heuristic is one such tool in this box. Like hammers and wrenches, heuristics are designed for specific classes of problems. The gaze heuristic, for instance, works for a class of problems that involve the interception of moving objects. If you learn to fly an airplane, you will be taught a version of it for *avoiding* interception of another moving plane. In other domains, such as choosing what to eat, this heuristic would not be sensible to use.

We call the heuristics "fast" because they process information in a relatively simple way, and "frugal" because they search for little information. To study these heuristics, they are formulated as computational models, making them amenable to mathematical analysis and simulation as well as experimentation. (This is one major difference from the heuristics-and-biases program – e.g., Kahneman and Tversky, 1996 – which did not specify precise mechanisms.) Each heuristic is composed of building blocks, or heuristic principles, that serve three functions: They give search a direction, stop search, and make a decision.

3.1. Heuristic Principles for Guiding Search

Alternatives and cues must be sought in a particular order. For instance, search for cues can be simply random or in order of cue validity.

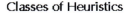

Figure 1. Four classes of simple heuristics distinguished by the problem settings in which they are applied, along with examples of each that can be constructed with different combinations of building blocks for searching, stopping, and deciding.

3.2. Heuristic Principles for Stopping Search

Search for alternatives or cues must be stopped at some point. Fast and frugal heuristics employ stopping rules that do not try to compute an optimal cost-benefit trade-off as in optimization under constraints. Rather, heuristic principles for stopping involve simple criteria that are easily ascertained, such as halting information search as soon as the first cue or reason that favors one decision alternative is found.

3.3. Heuristic Principles for Decision Making

Once search has been stopped, a decision or inference must be made. Many models of judgment and decision making ignore search and stopping rules and focus exclusively on decision: Are predictor values combined in a Bayesian way, linearly as in multiple regression, or in some other fashion? Instead, we focus on simple principles for decisions (such as one-reason decision making) that avoid expensive computations and extensive knowledge by working hand in hand with equally simple search and stopping rules.

Figure 1 shows four (non-exhaustive) classes of heuristics in the adaptive toolbox that can be built from these building blocks. Ignorance-based decision making refers to heuristics that can exploit the fact that one does not know everything. For instance, consumer behavior is guided by brand name recognition, a necessary precondition for reputation. When consumers choose between two brands, one they recognize by name, the other not, they tend to select the recognized one. This recognition heuristic works in environments where name recognition is correlated with product quality, but can be exploited by firms who put their money into promoting name recognition through advertisement rather than increasing the quality of the product. The next two chapters introduce the recognition heuristic, the less-is-more effect, and studies in which the heuristic guides investment decisions in the stock market. Heuristics falling into the second class, one-reason decision making, are introduced in Chapter 108. The heuristics in this class either pay attention only to one reason or cue, such as the gaze heuristic, or they search through several reasons but at the end only use one to reach their decision. The third class of elimination heuristics contains mechanisms that start with a set of alternatives and go through a sequence of cues to successively eliminate alternatives until only one remains (Berretty, Todd, and Martignon, 1999; Tversky, 1972). Finally, satisficing heuristics in the fourth class go through alternatives (rather than cues) sequentially – for example in looking for a new home – and choose the first one that satisfies an aspiration level, which may change with time spent on search (Selten, 2001; Simon, 1990). The heuristics in these four classes are described in more detail in Gigerenzer and Selten (2001a), Gigerenzer, Czerlinski, and Martignon (1999), and Todd and Gigerenzer (2000).

4. Emergency Room Decisions

In the following chapters we present examples of various heuristics from the adaptive toolbox. Here we begin with an example of how a heuristic for a particular, very important application can be constructed from the three types of building blocks described above, illustrating the prescriptive use of simple decision mechanisms.

A man is rushed to the hospital with serious chest pains. The doctors suspect acute ischemic heart disease and need to make a decision – quickly: Should the patient be assigned to the coronary care unit or to a regular nursing bed for monitoring? How do doctors make such a decision, and how should they? In a study conducted at a Michigan hospital, doctors relied on their intuition and sent some 90% of the patients to the coronary care unit (Green and Mehr, 1997). This defensive decision making led to unnecessary costs (too many people in the expensive coronary care unit), decreased the quality of care provided (the unit was overcrowded), and became a health risk for patients who should not be in the unit (it is one of the most dangerous places in a hospital due to the risk of secondary infections, which can be fatal). Other researchers tried to solve this overcrowding problem by training physicians to use the Heart Disease Predictive Instrument (Pozen et al., 1984). This decision support system consists of a chart with some 50 probabilities and a logistic regression formula – programmed into a pocket calculator – with which the physician can compute the probability that a patient has acute ischemic heart disease and therefore requires the coronary care unit. Physicians, however, typically do not understand logistic regression and are not happy using this and similar complicated systems (Pearson et al., 1994). The dilemma the hospital now faced was as follows: Should patients in life-and-death situations be classified by intuitions that are natural but sub-optimal, or by complex calculations that are alien but possibly more accurate? This dilemma arises in many contexts, from financial advising to personnel recruiting: Should we rely on experts' intuition or on a fancy statistical model?

Once again there is another alternative: smart heuristics. Green and Mehr (1997) designed a fast and frugal tree by using three building blocks for ordered search, a fast

A "Fast and Frugal" Decision Tree

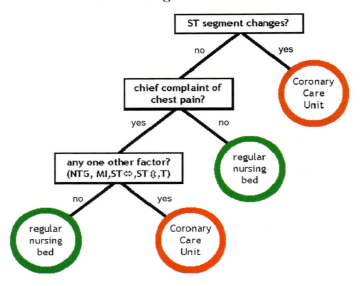

Figure 2. A fast and frugal tree for deciding whether a patient should be placed in a coronary care unit or a regular nursing bed, depending on as few cues as possible. At each stage in the tree, a single cue (in the rectangular boxes) determines whether an immediate decision (in the circles) can be made or if more information must be checked.

stopping rule, and one-reason decision making. The resulting heuristic is shown in Figure 2. It ignores all 50 probabilities and asks only a few yes-or-no questions. If a patient has a certain anomaly in his electrocardiogram (the so-called ST segment change), he is immediately admitted to the coronary care unit. No other information is searched for. If that is not the case, a second variable is considered: whether the patient's primary complaint is chest pain. If not, he is immediately classified as low risk and assigned to a regular nursing bed. No further information is considered. If the answer is yes, then a third and final question comprising additional cues is asked to classify the patient.

This decision tree employs fast and frugal rules of search, stopping, and decision. First, the predictors are looked up in an order determined simply by their sensitivity and specificity. No attempt is made to compute an "optimal" order, such as using conditional probabilities or beta weights, and dependencies between cues are disregarded. Second, search can stop after each predictor; the rest will be ignored. Third, only one predictor determines each decision. The heuristic does not combine – weight and add – the predictors; for instance, a change in the ST segment cannot be compensated for by any of the other predictors. This decision rule is thus an instance of one-reason decision making. The entire heart disease tree is a realization of a fast and frugal tree, which is defined as a decision tree with a small number of binary predictors that allows for a final decision at each branch of the tree.

The simple tree can be evaluated by multiple performance criteria. A good decision strategy (a) has a high sensitivity, that is, sends most of the patients who will actually have a serious heart problem into the coronary care unit; (b) has a low false alarm rate, that is, sends few patients into the care unit who will not need it; (c) is fast in situations where slow decision making can cost a life; (d) is frugal, that is, able to make good decisions with only limited information; and (e) is transparent, so that it will be accepted by physicians and actually be used. The fast and frugal tree is, by design, superior in speed, frugality, and transparency to the decision-support system with its logistic regression and 50 probabilities. But how accurate is it? The counterintuitive result is that the fast and frugal tree was more accurate in classifying actual heart attack patients than both the physicians' intuition and the Heart Disease Predictive Instrument. It correctly assigned the largest proportion of patients who subsequently had a myocardial infarction into the coronary care unit. At the same time, it had a comparatively low false alarm rate. Note that the expert system had more information than the smart heuristic, and could make use of sophisticated statistical calculations. Nevertheless, in this complex situation, less is more. Simplicity can pay off.

5. Ecological Rationality

How can heuristics that ignore information nevertheless be accurate? First, heuristics can exploit environmental structure. As shown by the gaze heuristic, their rationality is ecological. In the following chapters, we give examples of two classes of heuristics that exploit different ways that information can be structured in an environment to help them make accurate decisions. Heuristics that employ ignorance-based decision making (Chapters 106 and 107) exploit environments in which missing data (in particular, lack of name recognition) occur not randomly but systematically. The use of these heuristics is ecologically rational when lack of recognition (e.g., of brand names, stocks, sports teams) is correlated with the criterion (e.g., quality, market performance, winning a game). Heuristics that employ one-reason decision making (Chapter 108) can exploit environments in which the importance (e.g., beta weights in regression) of the cues available are exponentially decreasing, that is, non-compensatory. If this is the case, one can prove that a simple heuristic called Take The Best can perform as well as any "optimal" linear combination of binary cues.

The second reason why simplicity can be smart is its robustness, that is, the ability to generalize well to new environments – specifically to those whose structure is not known in advance. The important distinction here is between data fitting and prediction. In the first case, one fits a model to the empirical data, that is, the training set is the same as the test set. In prediction, the model is based on a training set, but tested on new data. A good fit may be deceptive because of overfitting. In general, a model A overfits the training data if there exists an alternative model B, such that A has higher or equal accuracy than B in the training set, but lower accuracy in the test set. Models with many free parameters, such as multiple regression or Bayesian methods, tend to overfit in environments where information is noisy or fluctuating, particularly when forced to make predictions from small samples.

As an illustration, consider again the coronary care unit allocation problem. The decision-support system using logistic regression was validated on several thousand patients in a large hospital. But it was subsequently applied in different hospitals to new groups of patients who deviated in unknown ways from the original sample. As a result, the model that was best in the original population was no longer guaranteed to be the best in those new situations. There are statistical techniques that expend considerable computational power and time to try to determine the point at which a model maximizes its predictive accuracy without overfitting. Fast and frugal heuristics sidestep this expenditure – their simplicity alone helps them avoid overfitting and perform robustly. For instance, in Chapter 108 we will see that the Take The Best heuristic generalized robustly across 20 predictive tasks, outperforming multiple regression, which overfitted the data.

To summarize, the reasonableness of fast and frugal heuristics derives from their ecological rationality, not from following the classical definitions of rationality in terms of coherence or internal consistency of choices. Indeed, some of the heuristics can produce intransitive inferences in direct violation of standard rationality norms, but they can still be quite accurate (Gigerenzer, Czerlinski, and Martignon, 1999). A heuristic is ecologically rational to the degree it is adapted to the structure of information in an environment, whether the environment is physical or social.

6. What is to Come

The heuristics presented in the coming chapters of this Handbook are examples drawn from a larger group of fast and frugal mental mechanisms that various researchers have begun to explore, both analytically and experimentally. All of these heuristics are process models, allowing for stronger experimental tests than the outcome models that are more typically studied in economics. A variety of experimental set-ups are being developed to test the search, stopping, and decision rules of heuristics, including information-board displays (e.g., Mouselab; Payne, Bettman, and Johnson, 1993) and Internet web sites designed for electronic commerce (Jedetski, Adelman, and Yeo, 2002). The empirical studies typically reveal that there are multiple heuristics (often up to four) that people use in any given task, with some being much more commonly used than others. This variation in the tools drawn from the adaptive toolbox is most pronounced when people are unfamiliar with a task or in environments with flat maxima (where several strategies perform equally well). Given this observed variation, it is necessary to test multiple models of heuristics against one another in a competitive way (rather than performing null hypothesis testing), and to analyze experimental data on an individual rather than aggregate level to discover which heuristic each person is using.

In the next chapter, we introduce the simplest heuristic in the adaptive toolbox, the recognition heuristic, which is an instance of ignorance-based decision making that gives rise to the counterintuitive less-is-more effect. In Chapter 107 we apply the recognition heuristic to a chaotic, unpredictable environment – the stock market – and show how it can guide profitable investment decisions. Chapter 108 introduces one-reason decision heuristics and describes how they fare in comparison with other more traditional inference mechanisms across a variety of environments. In Chapter 109 we discuss the importance of considering environment structure for making cognitive illusions appear or disappear. Finally, in Chapter 110 we present a variety of social heuristics that are designed to promote rapid and appropriate decisions in encounters with other social agents.

These chapters are meant to encourage a vision of economic agents that is anchored in the psychological possibilities of actual humans rather than in the fictional construction of economic optimizers. The widespread opposition between the psychological and the rational is, in our view, an unnecessary fiction. The real human mind can be ecologically rational – its heuristics can be fast, frugal, and accurate at the same time.

References

Berretty, P.M., Todd, P.M., Martignon, L. (1999). "Categorization by elimination: Using few cues to choose". In: Gigerenzer, G., Todd, P.M., the ABC Research Group (Eds.), Simple Heuristics that Make Us Smart. Oxford University Press, New York, pp. 235–254.
Camerer, C. (1998). "Bounded rationality in individual decision making". Experimental Economics 1, 163–183.
Elman, J. (1993). "Learning and development in neural networks: The importance of starting small". Cognition 48, 71–99.
Friedman, M. (1953). "Essays in Positive Economics". University of Chicago Press, Chicago.
Gigerenzer, G. (1996). "On narrow norms and vague heuristics: A reply to Kahneman and Tversky". Psychological Review 103, 592–596.
Gigerenzer, G., Selten, R. (Eds.) (2001a). Bounded Rationality: The Adaptive Toolbox. MIT Press, Cambridge, MA.
Gigerenzer, G., Selten, R. (2001b). "Rethinking rationality". In: Gigerenzer, G., Selten, R. (Eds.), Bounded Rationality: The Adaptive Toolbox. MIT Press, Cambridge, MA, pp. 1–12.
Gigerenzer, G., Czerlinski, J., Martignon, L. (1999). "How good are fast and frugal heuristics?" In: Shanteau, J., Mellers, B., Schum, D. (Eds.), Decision Research from Bayesian Approaches to Normative Systems: Reflections on the Contributions of Ward Edwards. Kluwer, Norwell, MA, pp. 81–103.
Gigerenzer, G., Todd, P.M., the ABC Research Group (1999). "Simple Heuristics that Make Us Smart". Oxford University Press, New York.
Green, L., Mehr, D.R. (1997). "What alters physicians' decisions to admit to the coronary care unit?" The Journal of Family Practice 45, 219–226.
Hertwig, R., Todd, P.M. (2003). "More is not always better: The benefits of cognitive limits". In: Macchi, L., Hardman, D. (Eds.), Thinking: Psychological Perspectives on Reasoning, Judgement and Decision Making. Wiley, Chichester, UK.
Holton, G. (1988). "Thematic Origins of Scientific Thought", second ed. Harvard University Press, Cambridge, MA.
Jedetski, J., Adelman, L., Yeo, C. (2002). "How web site decision technology affects consumers". IEEE Internet Computing 6, 72–79.
Kahneman, D., Tversky, A. (1979). "Prospect theory: An analysis of decision under risk". Econometrica 47, 263–291.

Kahneman, D., Tversky, A. (1996). "On the reality of cognitive illusions". Psychological Review 103, 582–591.

McLeod, P., Dienes, Z. (1996). "Do fielders know where to go to catch the ball, or only how to get there?" Journal of Experimental Psychology: Human Perception and Performance 22, 531–543.

Payne, J.W., Bettman, J.R., Johnson, E.J. (1993). "The Adaptive Decision Maker". Cambridge University Press, New York.

Pearson, S.D., Goldman, L., Garcia, T.B., Cook, E.F., Lee, T.H. (1994). "Physician response to a prediction rule for the triage of emergency department patients with chest pain". Journal of General Internal Medicine 9, 241–247.

Polya, G. (1954). "Mathematics and Plausible Reasoning: Induction and Analogy in Mathematics", vol. 1. Princeton University Press, Princeton.

Pozen, M.W., D'Agostino, R.B., Selker, H.P., Sytkowski, P.A., Hood, W.B. (1984). "A predictive instrument to improve coronary-care-unit admission practices in acute ischemic heart disease". The New England Journal of Medicine 310, 1273–1278.

Rabin, M. (1998). "Psychology and economics". Journal of Economic Literature 36, 11–46.

Sargent, T.J. (1993). "Bounded Rationality in Macroeconomics". Oxford University Press, Oxford, UK.

Selten, R. (2001). "What is bounded rationality?" In: Gigerenzer, G., Selten, R. (Eds.), Bounded Rationality: The Adaptive Toolbox. MIT Press, Cambridge, MA, pp. 13–37.

Simon, H.A. (1955). "A behavioral model of rational choice". Quarterly Journal of Economics 69, 99–118.

Simon, H.A. (1990). "Invariants of human behavior". Annual Review of Psychology 41, 1–19.

Todd, P.M., Gigerenzer, G. (2000). "Précis of 'Simple heuristics that make us smart'". Behavioral and Brain Sciences 23, 727–741.

Tversky, A. (1972). "Elimination by aspects: A theory of choice". Psychological Review 79, 281–299.

Chapter 106

THE RECOGNITION HEURISTIC AND THE LESS-IS-MORE EFFECT

DANIEL G. GOLDSTEIN

London Business School

GERD GIGERENZER

Max Planck Institute for Human Development, Berlin

Missing data are often considered an annoyance. However, a fast and frugal heuristic can turn missing knowledge into predictive information. Consider the outcomes of the following two cross-cultural experiments. We asked Americans and Germans, "Which city has a larger population: Milwaukee or Detroit?" Forty percent of Americans correctly responded that Detroit is larger. Compared to the Americans, the Germans knew very little about Detroit, and many had not even heard of Milwaukee. Yet 90% of the Germans answered the question correctly. In another study, Turkish students and British students made forecasts for all 32 English F.A. Cup third round soccer matches (Ayton and Önkal, 1997). The Turkish participants had very little knowledge about English soccer teams while the British participants knew quite a bit. Nevertheless, the Turkish predictions were nearly as accurate as the English ones (63% versus 66% correct).

Can a lack of knowledge be useful for making accurate inferences? It can be when using the recognition heuristic, a simple rule that exploits not abundant information, but rather a lack of knowledge (Goldstein and Gigerenzer, 1999, 2002; Gigerenzer and Goldstein, 1996). Following the heuristic, a person who has heard of Detroit but not Milwaukee would infer that Detroit is larger. For inferring which of two objects is greater on some criterion, the recognition heuristic is simply stated:

If only one of a pair of objects is recognized, then infer that the recognized object has the higher value on the criterion.

As opposed to an all-purpose tool like a linear model, the recognition heuristic is domain specific. Instead of being unboundedly rational, it is ecologically rational, that is, reasonable with respect to some environments but not others. There are domains in which the recognition heuristic will not work. A wise organism will only apply the rule in domains where recognition is strongly correlated with the criterion. (If this correlation is negative, then the rule should be reversed, and the unrecognized object should be chosen.) There are situations in which the recognition heuristic cannot be applied, for instance, when all objects are recognized. There are domains in which people will not apply it, for example, when they suspect that they are being asked a trick question. And there will be individual differences: different people use different heuristics at different times. Nonetheless, the very simple rule can make very accurate predictions from very little information, as we shall see.

1. Accuracy of the Recognition Heuristic

Here we derive the proportion of correct answers one would expect to achieve using the recognition heuristic on two-alternative inference tasks (Goldstein and Gigerenzer, 1999, 2002). Suppose there is a reference class of N objects and a test consisting of pairs of randomly-drawn objects. When randomly drawing pairs of objects, there are three ways they can turn out: one recognized and one unrecognized, both unrecognized, or both recognized. Suppose there are n recognized objects and thus $N-n$ unrecognized objects in the reference class. This means that there are $n(N-n)$ pairs in which one object is recognized and the other is unrecognized. A similar calculation shows that there are $(N-n)(N-n-1)/2$ pairs in which neither object is recognized. Finally, there are $n(n-1)/2$ pairs in which both objects are recognized. To transform each of these absolute numbers into a proportion of cases, it is necessary to divide each of them by the total number of possible pairs, $N(N-1)/2$.

To compute the proportion correct on such a test, it is necessary to know the probability of a correct answer for each type of pair. Let the recognition validity α be the probability of getting a correct answer when one object is recognized and the other is not. The probability of getting a correct answer when neither object is recognized (and a guess must be made) is .5. Finally, let β be the knowledge validity, the probability of getting a correct answer when both objects are recognized. We shall make the simplifying assumption that α and β stay constant as n varies. Combining all these terms together, the expected proportion of correct inferences, $f(n)$, on an exhaustive pairing of objects is:

$$f(n) = 2\left(\frac{n}{N}\right)\left(\frac{N-n}{N-1}\right)\alpha + \left(\frac{N-n}{N}\right)\left(\frac{N-n-1}{N-1}\right)\frac{1}{2} + \left(\frac{n}{N}\right)\left(\frac{n-1}{N-1}\right)\beta. \tag{1}$$

The right side of the equation breaks into three parts: the leftmost term equals the proportion of correct inferences made by the recognition heuristic; the middle term equals the proportion of correct inferences resulting from guessing; and the rightmost term equals the proportion of correct inferences made when knowledge beyond mere recognition can be used. Inspecting this equation, we see that if the number of objects recognized, n, is 0, then all questions will lead to guesses and the proportion correct will be .5. If $n = N$, then the leftmost two terms become zero and the proportion correct will be β. We can see that the recognition heuristic will come into play most when an organism is operating under "partial ignorance." Based on the recognition validity α, the knowledge validity β, and the degree of ignorance, that is, n compared to N, Equation (1) specifies the proportion of correct inferences made by the recognition heuristic.

2. The Less-is-More Effect

Equation (1) lets us make exact predictions, for instance, about how accurate American students should be making inferences about cities in Germany. We surveyed University

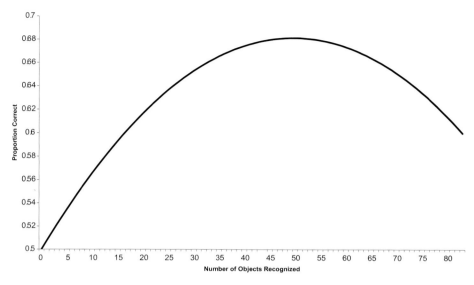

Figure 1. Plot showing how use of the recognition heuristic can lead to a less-is-more effect. The recognition validity α is 80%, the knowledge validity β is 60%, the total number N of objects is 83, and the number n of objects recognized varies. When over 50 objects are recognized, learning to recognize more only causes inferential accuracy to decrease. When all objects are recognized, accuracy equals the knowledge validity. Figure adapted from Goldstein and Gigerenzer (1999).

of Chicago students on all cities in Germany with more than 100,000 inhabitants (83 cities in 1994). We found that the cities they recognized had larger populations than those they did not recognize in about 80% of all possible pairs. This figure corresponds to a recognition validity α of .8. Interestingly, this value of 80% seemed largely independent of the number of cities recognized, giving support to the assumption that α is constant. Americans differ greatly on the knowledge validity β. Assume for illustration that it is around .6. Inserting these two values into Equation (1) we see the relationship between the accuracy and the number of objects recognized in Figure 1 (Goldstein and Gigerenzer, 1999, 2002).

The striking aspect of the accuracy curve is its non-monotonicity. Accuracy increases until a certain point (around 50 objects recognized), after which learning to recognize objects causes accuracy to decrease. This state of affairs, where less recognition knowledge leads to greater inferential accuracy, is what we call the less-is-more effect.

When will the less-is-more effect appear? A proof shows that, under assumptions, Equation (1) leads to a non-monotonic curve whenever $\alpha > \beta$ (Goldstein and Gigerenzer, 1999, 2002). The intuition for this is simple. When all objects are recognized, accuracy is equal to β. When just one object is unrecognized, accuracy equals some combination of α and β. If $\alpha > \beta$ this combination will be greater than β alone, and the condition for a less-is-more effect is met.

The surprising results cited at the beginning of this paper could be due to less-is-more effects resulting from the recognition heuristic. In addition to predicting people's inferences, recognition even helped out in forecasting the outcomes of soccer matches. Often, the name of an English soccer team includes a city name within it, such as "Manchester United." It happens that teams from well-recognized cities tend to be good ones. The Turkish students could use city-name or team-name recognition to inform their forecasts. In cases where the Turkish students rated one team as unfamiliar and the other as familiar to some degree, they chose the more-familiar team in 627 out of 662 (95%) of the forecasts (Ayton and Önkal, 1997). In the sections that follow, we present experiments that test whether people apply the recognition heuristic in their judgments, and if we can evoke a less-is-more effect in the laboratory.

3. Do People Use the Recognition Heuristic?

This simple test asks how often unprompted people will use the recognition heuristic (Goldstein and Gigerenzer, 1999, 2002). We quizzed people on pairs of cities drawn from the largest in Germany and asked them to choose the more populous city in each case. We had the participants check off from a list which of these cities they recognized either before or after the test. From this recognition information, we could calculate how often participants had an opportunity to choose in accordance with the recognition heuristic, and compare it to how often they actually did. Figure 2 shows the results for 22 individual participants.

For each participant, two bars are shown. The left-hand bars show how many opportunities the person had to apply the recognition heuristic, and the right-hand bars show how often their judgments agreed with the heuristic. For example, the person represented by the leftmost pair of bars had 156 opportunities to choose according to the recognition heuristic, and did so every time. The next person did so 216 out of 221 times, and so on. The proportions of recognition heuristic adherence ranged between 100% and 73%. The median proportion of inferences following the recognition heuristic was 93% (mean 90%).

People may follow the recognition heuristic when they have no better strategy to rely on. But what about those who have access to more reliable information? In a companion experiment, we taught Americans facts about which German cities have major league soccer teams (Goldstein and Gigerenzer, 1999, 2002). The presence of a major league soccer team is an excellent predictor of city population in Germany. We wanted to see which they would choose as larger: a city they had never heard of before, or one that they recognized but just learned, has *no* soccer team. The result was that they chose the recognized cities as often as in the previous experiment, despite the knowledge that these recognized cities are likely to be small (that is, that they lack soccer teams).

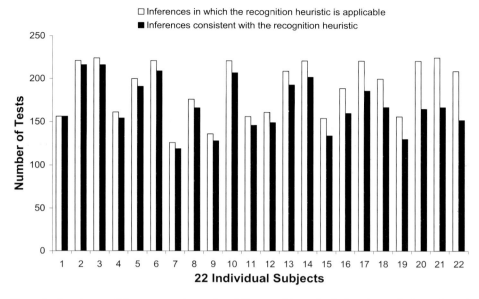

Figure 2. American participants were given pairs of German cities and asked to choose the larger in each case. Before or after this task, they were asked which cities they had heard of before the experiment. The left-hand bars show for each subject how many pairs they were presented in which one city was recognized and the other not. The right-hand bars show in how many of these cases the recognized city was chosen. Figure adapted from Goldstein and Gigerenzer (1999).

4. Does the Less-is-More Effect Occur in Human Reasoning?

We asked 52 University of Chicago students to take two tests each. One was on the 22 largest cities in the United States. The other was on the 22 largest cities in Germany: cities about which they knew little or nothing beyond mere recognition (Goldstein and Gigerenzer, 1999, 2002). Each question consisted of two randomly drawn cities, and the participants' task was to pick the larger. One would expect participants in this experiment to score somewhat higher on the American cities than the German ones. For instance, many Americans can name the three largest American cities in order, and this alone would give them the correct answer in 26% of all possible questions. For those who know the top five cities in order, this figure climbs up to a definite 41% correct.

When tested on their own cities, the Americans scored a median 71% (mean 71.1%) correct. On the German cities, the median was 73% (mean 71.4%) correct – roughly the same accuracy despite great differences in knowledge. For half of the subjects, we kept track of which German cities they recognized. In this group, the mean proportion of inferences in accordance with the recognition heuristic was 88.5% (median 90.5%). Participants recognized a mean of 12 cities, roughly half of the total, which would allow them to apply the rule about as often as possible. In a study that is somewhat the reverse of this one, the less-is-more effect was demonstrated with German and Austrian students who scored more accurate inferences on American cities than on German ones (Hoffrage, 1995; see also Gigerenzer, 1993).

5. The Underpinnings of the Recognition Heuristic

Name recognition can be a good predictor, as it is often correlated with wealth, resources, quality, and power. This correlation can arise from people being interested in, and thus talking and publishing about, highly-ranking people, places, and things. Top athletes and star lawyers make the headlines more than average ones do. If people prefer recognized products, these preferences can be manipulated by advertisers paying great sums for a place in the recognition memory of potential customers.

Much modeling of choice uses linear models that can be applied to domains from meterology to marketing. In contrast, the recognition heuristic is rooted in a fundamental and well-studied part of the cognitive architecture: recognition memory. It proves capable of making accurate inferences in the real world where recognition is often correlated with various important criteria. This heuristic exploits a quantity that is readily available to all organisms: missing knowledge.

References

Ayton, P., Önkal, D. (1997). "Forecasting futball fixtures: Confidence and judged proportion correct". Unpublished manuscript, City University, London.
Gigerenzer, G. (1993). "The bounded rationality of probabilistic mental models". In: Manktelow, K.I., Over, D.E. (Eds.), Rationality: Psychological and Philosophical Perspectives. Routledge, London.
Gigerenzer, G., Goldstein, D.G. (1996). "Reasoning the fast and frugal way: Models of bounded rationality". Psychological Review 104, 650–669.
Goldstein, D.G., Gigerenzer, G. (1999). "The recognition heuristic: How ignorance makes us smart". In: Gigerenzer, G., Todd, P.M., the ABC Group (Eds.), Simple Heuristics that Make Us Smart. Oxford University Press, New York, pp. 37–58.
Goldstein, D.G., Gigerenzer, G. (2002). "Models of ecological rationality: The recognition heuristic". Psychological Review 109, 75–90.
Hoffrage, U. (1995). "The adequacy of subjective confidence judgments: Studies concerning the theory of probabilistic mental models". Doctoral thesis, University of Salzburg.

Chapter 107

THE RECOGNITION HEURISTIC: A FAST AND FRUGAL WAY TO INVESTMENT CHOICE?

ANDREAS ORTMANN
CERGE-EI, Prague, Czech Republic

GERD GIGERENZER
Max Planck Institute for Human Development, Berlin, Germany

BERNHARD BORGES
Coopers and Lybrand, Westport, CT, USA

DANIEL G. GOLDSTEIN
Columbia University, NY, USA

Picking a portfolio of stocks that will beat the market is notoriously difficult. Empirical evidence suggests that on average it is not possible. In fact, the majority of professional stock pickers consistently underperform market averages. It is therefore an interesting question without an obvious answer as to how a simple heuristic like the recognition heuristic performs in such a turbulent real world domain. Here we report how stock portfolios that employed recognition heuristics fared relative to market indices, mutual funds, chance or "dartboard" portfolios, individual investment decisions, portfolios of unrecognized stocks and other benchmarks proposed by third parties.

1. Investment Theory and Practice

Some academics have concluded that it is impossible to beat the market in the long run. This stance is captured in the efficient market hypothesis (EMH), which maintains that agents cannot attain above average returns indefinitely (e.g., Muth, 1961; Cootner, 1967; Lucas, 1980). Despite early empirical challenges (e.g., Rozef and Kinney, 1976), the EMH has been fully incorporated into the leading normative models, such as the widespread Capital Asset Pricing Model (e.g., Sharpe, 1964) – itself constituting the basis for modern portfolio management theory.

Outside the ivory tower, professional investors such as Soros (1994) have doubted the realism and relevance of the EMH and have turned instead to technical trading rules based on sophisticated analytical measures that lie beyond the layperson's reach. The effectiveness of such measures, however, is questionable. The empirical evidence suggests that, while top-decile mutual funds earn back their investment costs, most other funds underperform performance benchmarks such as the Standard and Poor 500 by about the magnitude of their investment expenses (Carhart, 1997). Those in the bottom deciles do even worse.

2. Recognition-based Investment Decisions

Since knowledge and expertise seem to be of less use in predicting the stock market than commonly presumed and asserted, we wondered how an investment heuristic based on ignorance would fare. Putting the recognition heuristic to work in the stock market requires some degree of ignorance (i.e., a lack of recognition). For example, financial experts who recognize the names of all stocks cannot use the recognition heuristic to choose among them. Nor can people who have not heard of any stocks. Between these two extremes, a large number of people display what we call a "beneficial degree of ignorance."

Originally, Gigerenzer and Goldstein (1996, 2002) formulated the recognition heuristic as follows: When choosing between two objects, of which only one is recognized, choose the recognized object. The following generalization of the recognition heuristic is useful when picking stocks for investment:

2.1. When Choosing a Subset from a Larger Set, Choose Those Objects in the Larger Set That are Highly Recognized

Thus, there are two versions of the recognition heuristic, one for individual and one for group recognition. In the individual case, the recognition heuristic dictates choosing only those stocks recognized by the person. In the group case, the recognition heuristic dictates choosing "highly" recognized stocks, that is, those with names that are recognized by a high percentage (e.g., 90%) of the group.

3. Study 1

3.1. Study Design

Germans and Americans were asked to indicate which companies they recognized from those that constituted the Standard and Poor 500 and a German analogue of 298 stocks trading on German stock exchanges in December 1996 (Borges et al., 1999). The interviewees were randomly selected and belonged to one of four categories: American laypeople, American experts, German laypeople and German experts. The laypersons were 360 pedestrians surveyed in downtown Chicago and Munich; the experts were 120 graduate students in finance or economics interviewed at the University of Chicago and the University of Munich. Every participant was paid a token of appreciation (e.g., the

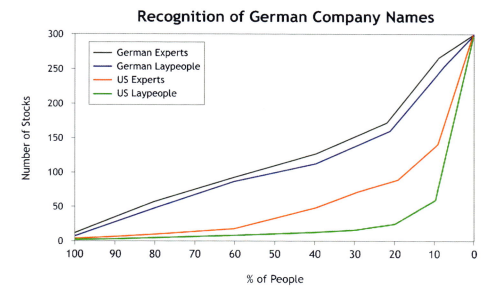

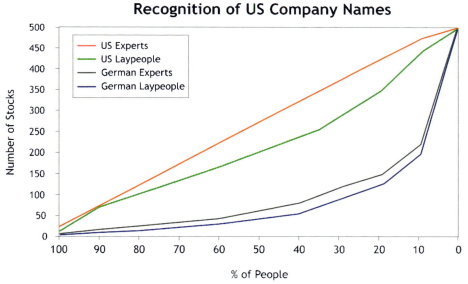

Figure 1. Number of company names recognized by % of people, for four groups of people and German and U.S. companies. For instance, 14 German company names were recognized by 100% of German experts, 33 company names were recognized by 90% or more of German experts and so on. The international recognition rates were the lowest: The American pedestrians surveyed, for instance, did not unanimously recognize a single German firm (Borges et al., 1999).

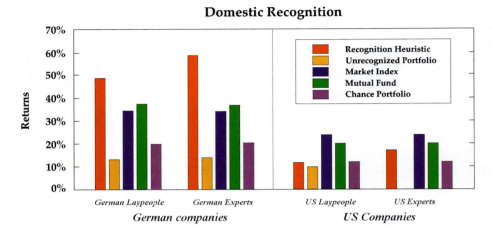
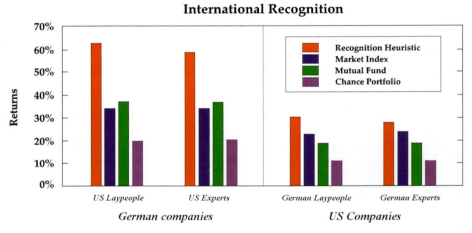

Figure 2. Performance of the recognition heuristic for companies with the highest recognition rates by German laypeople, German experts, U.S. laypeople and U.S. experts. Results are for the six months following the date of the recognition test, December 1996 to June 1997. For comparison, the performances of unrecognized stocks (0% to 10% recognition rates), the market (Dow or Dax), managed mutual funds (Fidelity Growth Fund or Hypobank Investment Capital Fund) and chance portfolios (average returns of 5000 portfolio combinations) are given. The recognition-based portfolio for the German experts, for example, reached a return of 57% compared to 14% for the unrecognized stocks and outperformed the market, that is, the Dax 30 (Borges et al., 1999).

German pedestrians were paid DM 5 for about 5 minutes of their time). Figure 1 shows the number of companies recognized by a given percentage or more of the population.

To test the performance of the recognition heuristic on the stock market for each of the four groups, we constructed two investment portfolios consisting of highly recognized companies. One portfolio type consisted of companies within the group's home country ("domestic recognition") recognized by 90% or more of the participants in a group. The other portfolio type contained the top ten most-recognized foreign companies for each group ("international recognition"). Thus, there were a total of eight recognition-based portfolios, as shown in Figure 2. All portfolios were "bought" and held (i.e., we did not change their composition after purchase).[1]

We analyzed the performance of recognition-based portfolios for six months from the completion date of the recognition test, December 13, 1996. The returns of the high recognition portfolios were compared with the performance of (a) the stocks of essentially unrecognized companies ("low recognition portfolios"), defined as companies recognized by fewer than 10% of the participants, (b) market indices, (c) mutual funds, (d) chance portfolios and (e) individuals' investment choices.[2]

3.2. How Did High Recognition Portfolios Perform Relative to Low Recognition Portfolios?

Figure 2a shows that the returns associated with each of the four recognition-based portfolios based on domestic recognition were favorable compared to portfolios comprised of stocks from unrecognized companies. The average return of the portfolios built using the recognition heuristic was more than triple that of portfolios built from unrecognized stocks.

As a control, we calculated the performance of portfolios based on the top 20 and top 30 recognized stocks for the four international tests. The result was similar: Figure 3 shows that portfolios comprised of stocks with higher rates of recognition led to higher returns in seven of eight cases.

3.3. How Did High Recognition Portfolios Perform Relative to Market Indices?

Recognized stocks outperformed unrecognized ones, but this may be of little interest to professional stock pickers whose main interest is beating the market. Can the

---

[1] One of the authors decided to put his money where his heuristic was and in a bid for early retirement he invested a nontrivial amount of money on German stocks recognized by Munich pedestrians. While not yet retired, he was not disappointed by the ignorance of the laypeople.

[2] Our performance analysis is based on price data only. The data were collected from the *Wall Street Journal*, the *New York Times* and the *Amtliches Kursblatt* and do not adjust for stock splits. It turns out that about 8% of the companies in our U.S. sample underwent such splits – three out of four of the splits being 2-for-1 and most of the remaining ones being 3-for-2 splits. (We have not been able to assert to what extent this problem also affects the German data.) We note that the comparisons reported below are therefore systematically biased against the recognition heuristic wherever performance measures included such adjustments for those splits, as is the case for market indices and mutual funds. In other words, in comparisons with market indices and mutual funds, the recognition heuristic actually did better than our results suggest. We are in the process of computing a comprehensive follow-up study of Borges et al. (1999); the extension study will employ data from CRSP and KKMDB.

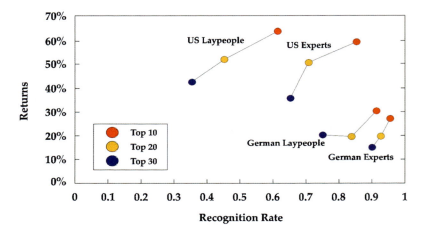

Figure 3. There is a direct relationship between the recognition rate and the returns of international portfolios for each of the four groups. The Top 10 portfolio, for example, contains the ten most recognized non-domestic stocks. The performance of the four Top 10 portfolios were shown in Figure 2 (international recognition). When portfolios were expanded to include the 20 or 30 most recognized stocks, recognition rates decreased, as did returns (Borges et al., 1999).

recognition-based portfolios perform close to the Dow and Dax market indices? Figure 2a shows that for domestic recognition, the result was divided. Investment portfolios based on recognition by German experts and laypeople outperformed the Dax 30 for the period of investigation. The portfolios of highly recognized American stocks, based on recognition by American laypeople and experts, made money but failed to outperform the Dow 30 benchmark.

Did international recognition, with its greater degree of ignorance, lead to greater returns? It did. Figure 2b shows that in all four cases of international recognition, the recognition heuristic beat the relevant market index. Furthermore, in all four cases, international recognition led to higher returns than did domestic recognition and the ignorance of laypeople led to slightly more profitable portfolios than did that of experts. This result suggests that the greater the degree of a group's ignorance, the better it is for picking stocks using the recognition heuristic.

3.4. How Did High Recognition Perform Relative to Managed Funds?

How did the recognition heuristic perform when compared to the tools and knowledge of professional portfolio managers? We selected two major mutual funds, the American-based Fidelity Blue Chip Growth Fund and the German Hypobank Investment Capital Fund, as benchmarks for the performance of the recognition heuristic.

As evident from Figure 2 and confirming Carhart's (1997) results, portfolios based on the recognition heuristic beat managed funds in six of the eight possible tests. The

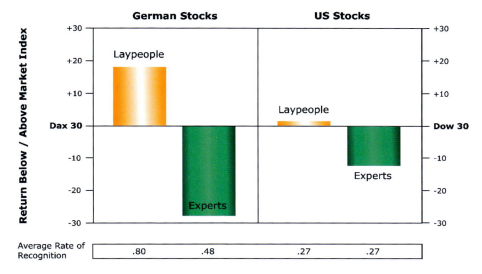

Figure 4. The performance of stocks picked by German laypeople and experts for both domestic and international portfolios followed the trend set by "beneficial ignorance." Laypeople tended to pick highly recognized German stocks for investment, whereas experts opted for less recognized stocks. Laypeople's stock picks achieved a staggering return, whereas the experts' picks actually lost money. For the Germans' picks of ten American stocks, the average recognition rate was low (.27) and did not differ between experts and laypeople. Consequently, both portfolios of international picks performed worse than the portfolios of recognized stocks in Figure 2 (Borges et al., 1999).

collective ignorance of pedestrians in Munich, for instance, led to higher returns than the knowledge and expertise of American and German fund managers. Moreover, international ignorance led to higher returns than domestic ignorance: The two most ignorant groups, German laypeople and experts (as measured by the total number of stocks recognized), gained the most from their lack of knowledge.

3.5. How Did High Recognition Portfolios Perform Relative to Random Stock Picks?

The *Wall Street Journal*'s renowned investment column has demonstrated that random stock picks, determined by throwing darts at scrambled lists of stocks, often outperform expert picks. We constructed 5000 random portfolios, each consisting of ten stocks from both the American and German markets and evaluated them for the period of our study. The recognition heuristic beat the average returns of the random portfolios in seven of the eight possible tests and matched it in the remaining one. The recognition heuristic turned out to be a far better stock-selection tool than random stock picks.

3.6. How Did High Recognition Portfolios Perform Relative to Individuals' Investment Choices?

German experts and laypeople were asked to identify up to ten stocks that they would choose for investment purposes from the lists of companies used for the recognition test. Did they pick highly recognized stocks? As measured by the average recognition in their group, the German laypeople tended to pick highly recognized stocks for investment while the experts chose more esoteric ones. As evident from Figure 4, the laypeople outperformed the experts by a wide margin. Note that the stocks which laypeople picked performed above the market and about as well as the recognition heuristic based on their recognition data (Figure 2), In contrast, the stocks which experts picked performed below the market; had they instead relied on mere recognition, they would have outperformed the market, for both German and U.S. stocks.

4. From Recognition to Riches?

Can a fast and frugal heuristic that exploits patterns of ignorance rather than substantial knowledge make money on the stock market? For the period investigated, stock portfolios that employed the recognition heuristic outperformed in the overwhelming number of cases and often clearly, market indices, mutual funds, chance or "dartboard" portfolios, individual investment decisions and portfolios of unrecognized stocks.

5. Study 2

Our initial results prompted plenty of press coverage and a bimodal pattern of response. There were those who said, "We knew it all along." Then there were those who suggested that our results were flawed for various reasons and that, in any case, we would not be able to replicate our results – especially in a down market. We are currently following up on the original study (Borges et al., 1999). In the meantime, we decided to put the recognition heuristic to a test in two slightly different environments: two stock-picking contests in Germany organized by nationally distributed magazines in the spring and summer of 2000.

The timing of these contests was the six-week period from February 28, 2000 to April 7, 2000 for the first competition and the eight-week period from May 29, 2000 to July 21, 2000 for the second. The timing of the competitions could not have been better: it gave us the opportunity to evaluate the performance of the recognition heuristic in exceptionally turbulent and contracting market environments. In fact, in early March of 2000, the NASDAQ finished above 5000 (as things look at the writing of this contribution, its all-time high for a long time to come) and started to decline for the remainder of the first contest period.

The two competitions also gave us the opportunity to test our fast and frugal way of investing under parsimonious conditions and thus respond to the objection that our collection of the recognition data in the earlier study (Borges et al., 1999) was rather elaborate. Lastly, we were given the chance to explore to what extent the widespread coverage of our original experiment had invalidated the recognition heuristic as a successful investment strategy.

5.1. Study Design

The two sets of stocks on which the stock-picking contests were based had been respectively determined by two German magazines that aspire to be specialist journals for financial markets, namely *Capital* and *Boerse Online*. (For the contest, the latter joined forces with the well-known national magazine *Stern*.) Both contests followed essentially the same format: moderate sign-up fees, no trading fees, no restriction on portfolios, significant prizes. The *Capital* stock-picking contest was based on 50 "international internet equities"; the *Stern–Boerse Online* stock-picking contest was based on a broader set of 100 international internet equities and more traditional firms such as Adidas, American Express, Coca-Cola, Daimler Chrysler rand the like (for details see Ortmann and Gigerenzer, 2002).

In the week preceding the *Capital* (and, respectively, the *Stern–Boerse Online*) contest, we asked 50 (30) female and 50 (30) male pedestrians randomly selected in Berlin to identify the companies that they recognized from lists they were presented. We offered all participants DM 5 as a token of appreciation. As in our earlier study, we compiled the recognition data from the questionnaires and constructed separate portfolios of high and low recognition stocks. These portfolios were submitted to the respective stock-picking contest in a buy-and-hold pattern (i.e., we did not change the composition of our portfolios once purchased).

In the *Capital* stock-picking contest, we entered portfolios that contained the ten most and ten least recognized stocks. For the *Stern–Boerse Online* contest, we followed Borges et al. (1999) and identified those companies that 90% of the female and 90% of the male study participants recognized (7 and 14, respectively). Since we were concerned about a reasonable degree of diversification and since seven seemed to give any one outlier too much influence, we also identified those companies that 80% of the female and male study participants recognized (20 and 23, respectively). Finally, we compiled a portfolio of those stocks that were recognized by no more than 10% of all participants. These five portfolios were then entered in the *Stern–Boerse Online* stock-picking contest.

5.2. How Did High Recognition Portfolios Perform Relative to Low Recognition Portfolios?

In the *Capital* stock-picking contest, the 10-stock, high recognition portfolio gained 2.53% and ranked 2085 (out of about 17,600 portfolios submitted by 11,400 participants), placing it safely in the top 15% of portfolios. The 10-stock low recognition portfolio lost 16.97% and ranked 12,976. In the *Stern–Boerse Online* stock-picking contest, all four high recognition portfolios (7.38%, rank 9029; 4.80%, 13,975; 3.32%; 17,325; 2.32%, 19,664; out of about 43,000 portfolios submitted by 31,000 participants) outdid the low recognition portfolio (−1.69%, rank 29,348).

5.3. How Did High Recognition Portfolios Perform Relative to Various Benchmarks?

The recognition heuristic beat various *Capital* stock-picking contest indices, such as buying equal amounts of all stocks, by more than 6% to 8%. It also beat the benchmark proposed by *Capital* – its editor-in-chief, whose portfolio lost 18.55%. In the *Stern–Boerse Online* contest, all four high recognition portfolios outperformed the median portfolio decisively. Each of them also proved better than the benchmark that *Stern–Boerse Online* had proposed – a TV show master and former trader, whose portfolio gained less than 1%.

5.4. What About Gender Effects?

Recall that we entered four high recognition portfolios in the *Stern–Boerse Online* competition, two of which drew on recognition data from female pedestrians and two of which drew on portfolios from male pedestrians. We compiled these portfolios because there is tantalizing evidence (Barber and Odean, 2001) that women are less confident about their financial savvy, yet perform better.

We found that in both stock-picking contests, female participants reported to recognize fewer stocks. Yet the performance of the two portfolios based on women's recognition data (7.28% and 4.80%) was better than the two portfolios based on men's recognition data (3.32% and 2.32%).

5.5. From Recognition to Riches?

Stock-picking competitions have their own laws. Since the entry fees are low and since there are no trading fees, people are likely to buy multiple portfolios and to engage in riskier strategies. These idiosyncrasies induce a mean preserving spread of returns, which in turn handicaps the performance of the recognition heuristic.

The results reported here provide evidence for the surprising viability of the recognition heuristic in the notoriously difficult environment of financial markets – and down markets, for that matter.[3] Once again, high recognition portfolios outperformed

---

[3] After finishing the manuscript, we learned about Boyd (2001), who reports somewhat different results. His results seem to be mainly due to a different subject pool (college students rather than pedestrians), whose recognition of stocks was idiosyncratic and resulted in disproportionate losses (e.g., Yahoo!, Xerox, Bausch and Lomb, Texas Instruments, ATandT) or disproportionate gains (e.g., nursing home operator Manor Care, energy provider Central and South West, forest products company Willamette Industries). In fact, these companies accounted for roughly all gains in Boyd's high recognition portfolio and all losses in his low recognition portfolio.

both low recognition portfolios and various reasonable benchmarks. The results of the stock-picking contests show that the recognition heuristic can be implemented with a minimum of effort. The results also suggest that the publication of earlier research has not yet invalidated the success of the recognition heuristic.

6. Conclusion

The surprising performance of recognition-based portfolios in both studies provides further evidence that simple heuristics can make accurate inferences about real-world domains. The stock market is a complex real-world environment in which lack of recognition is not completely random but systematic and simple heuristics such as recognition can exploit these regularities to make accurate inferences at little cost. The recognition heuristic does not rely on a sophisticated analysis of financial markets, the Capital Asset Pricing Model and the like. It is imperative to understand why and under what conditions this simple heuristic can survive in markets that are far removed from those situations where it served some evolutionary purpose.

References

Barber, B., Odean, T. (2001). "Boys will be boys: Gender. overconfidence and common stock investment". Quarterly Journal of Economics 116, 261–292.
Borges, B., Goldstein, D.G., Ortmann, A., Gigerenzer, G. (1999). "Can ignorance beat the stock market?" In: Gigerenzer, G., Todd, P.M., the ABC Research Group (Eds.), Simple Heuristics that Make Us Smart. Oxford University Press, Oxford, UK, pp. 59–72.
Boyd, M. (2001). "On ignorance, intuition and investing: A bear market test of the recognition heuristic". Journal of Psychology and Financial Markets 2, 150–156.
Carhart, M.M. (1997). "On persistence in mutual fund performance". Journal of Finance 52, 57–82.
Cootner, P. (1967). "The Random Character of Stock Market Prices". MIT Press, Cambridge, MA.
Gigerenzer, G., Goldstein, D.G. (1996). "Reasoning the fast and frugal way". Psychological Review 103, 650–669.
Goldstein, D.G., Gigerenzer, G. (2002). "Models of ecological rationality: The recognition heuristic". Psychological Review 109, 75–90.
Lucas Jr., R.E. (1980). "Studies in Business Cycle Theory". MIT Press, Cambridge, MA.
Muth, J.F. (1961). "Rational expectations and the theory of price movement". Econometrica 29, 315–335.
Ortmann, A., Gigerenzer, G. (2002). "The recognition heuristic in financial markets: Results from two stock-picking contests". Discussion paper, CERGE-EI, Prague.
Rozef, M.S., Kinney, W.R. (1976). "Capital market seasonality: The case of stock returns". Journal of Financial Economics 3, 379–402.
Sharpe, W.F. (1964). "Capital asset prices: A theory of market equilibrium under conditions of risk". Journal of Finance 19, 425–442.
Soros, G. (1994). "The Theory of Reflexivity". Soros Fund Management, New York.

Chapter 108

ONE-REASON DECISION MAKING

GERD GIGERENZER, LAURA MARTIGNON, ULRICH HOFFRAGE, JÖRG RIESKAMP and JEAN CZERLINSKI

Max Planck Institute for Human Development, Berlin, Germany

DANIEL G. GOLDSTEIN

Columbia University, New York USA

"One-reason decision making" is a label for a class of fast and frugal heuristics that base decisions on only one reason. These heuristics do not attempt to optimally fit parameters to a given environment; rather, they have simple structural features and "bet" that the environment will fit them. By not attempting to optimize, these heuristics can save time and computations, and demand only little knowledge concerning a situation. Models of one-reason decision making have been designed for various tasks, including choice, numerical estimation, and classification (Gigerenzer, Todd, and the ABC Research Group, 1999). In this chapter, we focus on two of these heuristics, "Take The Best" and Minimalist, and compare their performance with that of standard statistical strategies that weigh and combine many reasons, such as multiple regression. Contrary to common intuition, more reasons are not always better.

1. "Take The Best" and Minimalist

We deal with two-alternative prediction tasks, such as which of two American cities will have the higher homelessness rate, or which of two stocks will yield a higher return. In general terms, the task is to predict which object, a or b, has the higher value on a criterion. There is a set of N objects and a set of M cues. In the case of binary cues, cue values "1" and "0" indicate higher and lower criterion values, respectively. Take The Best can be characterized by the following building blocks (see also Gigerenzer and Goldstein, 1996):

(0) Recognition heuristic: If only one object is recognized, and recognition is positively correlated with the criterion, predict that this object has the higher value on the criterion. If neither is recognized, then guess. If both are recognized, go on to Step 1.
(1) Search rule: Choose the cue with the highest validity and look up the cue values of the two objects.
(2) Stopping rule: If one object has a cue value of one ("1") and the other does not (i.e., "0" or unknown), then stop search and go on to Step 3. Otherwise exclude this cue and go back to Step 1. If no cues are left, guess.

Handbook of Experimental Economics Results, Volume 1
Copyright © 2008 Elsevier B.V. All rights reserved
DOI: 10.1016/S1574-0722(07)00108-4

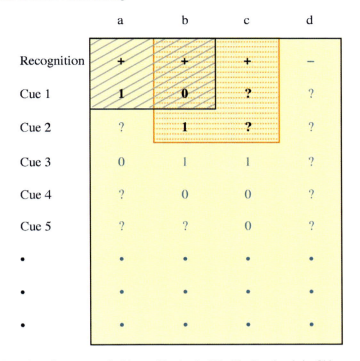

Figure 1. Illustration of one-reason decision making by the Take The Best heuristic. Objects a, b, and c are recognized (+), d is not (−), Cue values are binary, "1" and "0" indicate higher and lower criterion values, respectively. Missing knowledge, that is, unknown cue values are denoted by a question mark. For instance, to infer whether $a > b$, Take The Best looks up only the values in the gray-striped space. To infer whether $b > c$, search is bounded to the dotted space. In each case, the decision is based on only one cue; the cue values of less important cues are not even looked up.

(3) Decision rule: Predict that the object with the cue value of one ("1") has the higher value on the criterion.

The recognition heuristic (Step 0) only plays a role in situations of partial ignorance: when some of the N objects are unknown, such as when one recognizes only a subset of brand names (Goldstein and Gigerenzer, 2002). The validity v_i of a cue i (Step 1) is defined as

$$v_i = \frac{R_i}{R_i + W_i},$$

where R_i is the number of right (correct) inferences, and W_i is the number of wrong (incorrect) inferences based on cue i alone. $R_i + W_i$ equals the number of cases where one object has the value "1" and the other does not.

Figure 1 illustrates the logic of Take The Best. Search for information is stopped when the first cue is found on which the two alternatives differ. This stopping rule does

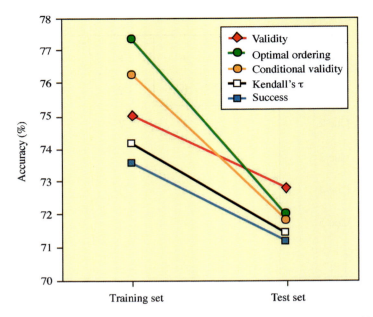

Figure 2. How robust is Take The Best's search rule? Five search rules (for establishing the cue hierarchy of a lexicographic strategy) were tested in a task to infer which of two German cities has a larger population, based on $M = 9$ cues. The reference class consisted of all cities with more than 100,000 inhabitants (83 in all), half of the cities in the training set, and the other half in the test set, yielding about 800 pair comparisons in each set. Performance is averaged across 100 random assignments of cities to training and test sets. Each search rule was used to establish an order in the training set, and a lexicographic strategy with this order was then tested in the test set. Take The Best's search rule orders cues by validity v_i. The optimal ordering is obtained empirically by determining which of all possible orderings of M cues results in the highest accuracy in the training set. The conditional validity of a cue is computed conditionally on the cues that have been looked up before the cue, taking account of the dependencies between cues. Kendall's τ is a rank correlation, which is used here to order cues. Finally, success orders cues according to their probabilistic success. The simple search rule of Take The Best proves to be robust (Martignon and Hoffrage, 2002).

not attempt to compute an optimal stopping point, that is, when the costs of further search exceed its benefits. Rather, the motto of the heuristic is "Take The Best, ignore the rest." The term "one-reason decision making" refers to decision rules that do not weigh and integrate information, but rely on one cue only.

2. Simple Rules for Search

Take The Best orders cues according to their validities, which can be estimated from previous experience (e.g., on a training set). Like the stopping rule, the search rule does not employ optimization calculations either. To order cues according to v_i is fast and

Table 1
Six cues for predicting homelessness in U.S. cities. Cues are ordered by validity, with rent control having the highest (.90) validity (from Tucker, 1987)

	Los Angeles	Chicago	New York	New Orleans
Homeless per million	10,526	6618	5024	2671
Rent control (1 is yes)	1	0	1	0
Vacancy rate (1 is below median)	1	1	1	0
Temperature (1 is above median)	1	0	1	1
Unemployment (1 is above median)	1	1	1	1
Poverty (1 is above median)	1	1	1	1
Public housing (1 is below median)	1	1	0	0

frugal, but not optimal, because this order ignores dependencies between cues. How much more accurate would the optimal order be? Figure 2 shows two unexpected results. First, in a noisy real-world environment, Take The Best actually comes close to the optimal ordering when the task is to fit given data (i.e., training set). Second, and most important, when the task is to predict new data, the simple ordering used by Take The Best is actually more robust and makes more accurate predictions (on the test set) than the ordering that was optimal on the training set. Thus, the simple ordering, which ignores dependencies between cues, turns out to be the better one when generalizing to new objects. The simple search rule of Take The Best strikes a balance between the dangers of overfitting (i.e., extracting too much information from the training set, as optimal ordering and conditional validity do) and underfitting (extracting too little information, which Kendall's τ and success do). In general, a model A overfits the training data if there exists an alternative model B, such that A has higher or equal accuracy than B in the training set, but lower accuracy in the test set.

Minimalist is another heuristic that embodies one-reason decision making. It does not try to order cues by validity, but chooses cues in random order. The only difference from Take The Best is the search rule, which now reads:

STEP 1. Search rule: Pick a cue randomly (without replacement) and look up the cue values of the two objects.

What price does one-reason decision making have to pay for being fast and frugal? How much more accurate are strategies that use all cues and combine them? We first answer these questions for one specific example – homelessness rates – in order to explain the logic of the tests. Thereafter, we report the results of 20 studies, including economic, demographic, environmental, and other prediction tasks.

3. Predicting Homelessness

The task is to predict which of two cities has a higher homelessness rate, using the data on 50 U.S. cities from Tucker (1987). An excerpt from the data, including the values for Los Angeles, Chicago, New York, and New Orleans on six relevant cues, and the homelessness rates, is shown in Table 1. Here, and in subsequent studies reported, there are no unknown objects; thus the recognition heuristic is of no use. One cue (rent control) is binary, and the other five have been dichotomized at the median. For example, cities with rent control more often have a higher homelessness rate than cities without rent control; therefore cities that have rent control are marked with a cue value of "1" for this cue.

In the tests, half of the cities were randomly drawn. From all possible pairs within this training set, the order of cues according to validity v_i was determined. Thereafter, performance was tested on the other half of the cities. Minimalist used the training set only to determine whether a cue is positively or negatively correlated with the criterion (e.g., whether rent control indicates higher or lower homelessness rates). In the test set, it picked the cues in a random order. Two linear models were introduced as competitors: multiple regression and a simple unit-weight linear model (Dawes, 1979). To determine which of two cities has the higher rate, multiple regression estimated the homelessness rates of each city, and the unit-weight model simply added up the number of 1's.

Figure 3, left panel, shows the frugality (average number of cues looked up) and the accuracy of the two fast and frugal heuristics and the two linear models. The two heuristics looked up on average only 2.1 and 2.4 cues, as opposed to 6 cues used by the linear models that have no search and stopping rules. In data fitting (training set), multiple regression fits the data best. The striking result is that Take The Best is more accurate in prediction (test set) than multiple regression and the other competitors. Minimalist also does surprisingly well given the little information it uses.

4. Fast and Frugal Heuristics Versus Linear Models: A Competition

How well do these results generalize to making predictions in other domains? Czerlinski, Gigerenzer, and Goldstein (1999) tested one-reason decision making on 20 prediction problems. These data sets contained real-world structures rather than convenient multivariate normal structures; they ranged from having 11 to 395 objects, and from 3 to 19 cues. The predicted criteria included economic variables, such as selling prices of houses and professors' salaries; demographic variables, such as mortality rates in U.S. cities and population sizes of German cities; environmental variables, such as the amount of rainfall, ozone, and oxidants; health variables, such as obesity at age 18; and sociological variables, such as drop-out rates in Chicago public high schools.

Figure 3, right panel, shows that the counterintuitive results obtained for predicting homelessness held up on average across these 20 different prediction problems. The two fast and frugal heuristics looked up fewer than a third of the cues. Minimalist was most

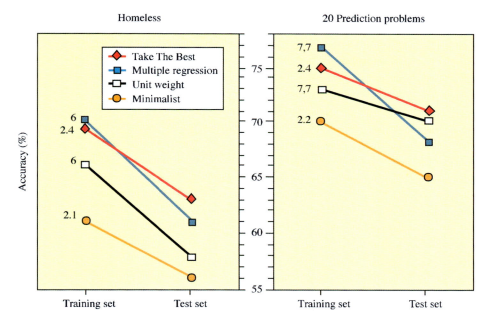

Figure 3. A competition between two heuristics and two linear models. The left panel shows the accuracy and frugality of the four strategies in predicting homelessness in U.S. cities, and the right panel shows the results for 20 real-world problems (Czerlinski, Gigerenzer, and Goldstein, 1999). Accuracy is measured for data fitting (performance in the training set) and prediction (performance in the test set), Take The Best and Minimalist are heuristics that practice one-reason decision making, whereas the unit-weight model and multiple regression use all information available and combine all cues. The numbers next to the graphs denote the average number of cues that have been used by this strategy.

frugal and performed not too far behind the two linear strategies in predictive accuracy (test set). Take The Best was both more frugal and more accurate than the two linear strategies. This result may sound paradoxical because multiple regression processed all the information that Take The Best did and more (we resolve this apparent paradox below).

5. Fast and Frugal Heuristics Versus Bayesian Methods

How does Take The Best compare to Bayesian methods? With large numbers of cues, as with many of the 20 predictive problems studied, Bayes' rule can no longer be used, because it quickly leads to computational explosion. Martignon and Laskey (1999) used two approximations, one simple and one that used days of computing time. The simple Bayesian model was naive Bayes, which assumes that all cues are independent of each other, given the criterion. The computationally expensive model was a Bayesian net-

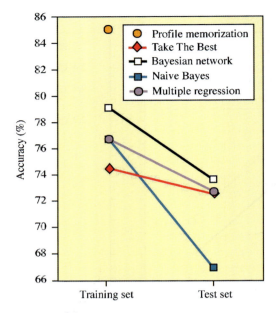

Figure 4. The accuracy of Take The Best compared to a Bayesian network, naive Bayes, and multiple linear regression across 20 predictive problems. The profile memorization method specifies the upper limit of accuracy in the case of fitting given data (Martignon and Laskey, 1999).

work that estimates relevant dependencies between cues from the data. Figure 4 shows that the predictive accuracy of Take The Best came, on average, within three percentage points of the complex Bayesian network, with naive Bayes in-between.

What would be the maximum accuracy a strategy could reach? We can answer this question for fitting known data (i.e., performance in the training set). The optimal Bayesian method for fitting known data – we call it the profile memorization method – memorizes the corresponding criterion value for each cue profile. When comparing two profiles, it chooses the one for which the memorized criterion is larger. If there are several pairs of objects with the same pair of cue profiles, the method determines the proportion of pairs for which the first object scores higher and makes an inference based on whether this proportion is larger than 0.5. For the 20 problems, profile memorization results in a fit of 85% on average. However, this method cannot be used for generalization (test set) because, in new data, unknown profiles may appear.

6. Why is Take The Best so Robust?

The answer lies in its simplicity: Take The Best uses few cues. The first cues tend to be highly valid and, in general, they will remain so across different subsets of the same class of objects. The stability of highly valid cues is a main factor for the robustness of Take The Best, that is, its low danger of overfitting in cross-validation as well as in other forms of incremental learning. In contrast, strategies that use all cues must estimate a number of parameters larger than or equal to the number of cues. Some, like multiple regression, are sensitive to many features of the data, for instance, by taking correlations between cues into account. As a consequence, they suffer from overfitting, especially with small data sets.

The result that simple heuristics can match strategies that use more information is reminiscent of the phenomenon of flat maxima. If many sets of weights, even unit weights, can perform about as well as the optimal set of weights in a linear model, this is called a flat maximum (e.g., Dawes and Corrigan, 1974). The performance of Take The Best indicates that flat maxima can extend beyond weights: Inferences based solely on the best cue can be as accurate as those based on any other weighted linear combination of all cues. The theorems presented below, in particular the theorem on non-compensatory information, identify conditions under which we can predict flat maxima.

7. Ecological Rationality: Which Environmental Structures Can Take The Best Exploit

What are the characteristics of information in real-world environments that make Take The Best a better predictor than other strategies, and where will it fail? To answer these questions, we need to examine properties of information, that is, the information about an environment known to a decision maker. Here we discuss three properties. The first two characterize many real-world situations, at least approximately: When the information structure is non-compensatory, or the available information is scarce, Take The Best is smarter than its competitors. The third property is abundance of information: When information is abundant, a simple unit-weight linear rule will be more accurate.

8. Non-compensatory Information

Among the 20 environments in Figure 3, we found 4 in which the weights for the linear models were non-compensatory (i.e., each weight is larger than the sum of all other weights to come, such as $1/2, 1/4, 1/8, \ldots$). In short, we refer to an environment with such a structure as a non-compensatory environment. Figure 5 shows examples of non-compensatory and compensatory environments. The following theorem states a property of non-compensatory environments and is easily proved (Martignon and Hoffrage, 2002):

THEOREM 1. *Take The Best is equivalent – in performance – to a linear model whose weights form a non-compensatory set* (*and decay in the same order as that of Take The Best*).

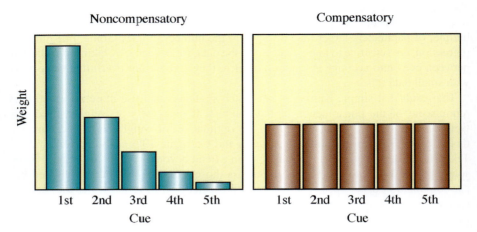

Figure 5. Heuristics can exploit structures of environments. The left side shows an environment which consists of binary cues whose weights are non-compensatory (e.g., 1/2, 1/4, 1/8, and so on). In this environment, no weighted linear model can outperform the faster and more frugal Take The Best. The right side shows a compensatory environment, where linear models will have an advantage (Martignon and Hoffrage, 2002).

Therefore, if an environment consists of cues that are non-compensatory, then no linear model can have higher predictive accuracy than Take The Best.

9. Scarce Information

To illustrate the concept of scarce information, let us recall a fact from information theory: A class of N objects contains $\log_2 N$ bits of information. This means that if we were to encode each object in the class by means of binary cue profiles of the same length, this length should be at least $\log_2 N$ if each object is to have a unique profile. For instance, to encode eight objects, it is sufficient to use three ($\log_2 8 = 3$) binary variables. If there were only two, these eight objects could not be perfectly distinguished, and for some pairs there would be identical cue profiles.

THEOREM 2. *If the number of cues is fewer than $\log_2 N$, profile memorization method will never achieve 100% correct inferences. Thus, no other strategy will do so either.*

This theorem motivates the following:

DEFINITION 1. *A set of M cues provides scarce information for a reference class of N objects if $M \leq \log_2 N$.*

We can now formulate a theorem that relates the performance of Take The Best to that of a unit-weight linear model in small environments, that is, in environments with fewer than 1000 objects.

THEOREM 3. *In the majority of small environments with scarce information, Take The Best is more accurate than a unit-weight linear model.*

This result was obtained by exhaustive counting. The intuition underlying the theorem is the following: In scarce environments, a unit-weight linear model can take little advantage of its strongest property, namely compensation.

10. Abundant Information

Adding cues to a scarce environment will do little for Take The Best if the best cues in the original environment already have high validity. For a unit-weight linear model, however, adding cues may help because they can compensate for various mistakes this rule would have made if restricted to using only the first cues. In fact, by continually adding cues, we can make a unit-weight linear model achieve perfection. This is true even if all cues are uncertain, that is, if all cues have a validity of less than 1.

THEOREM 4. *If an environment consists of all possible uncertain cues, a unit-weight linear model will discriminate among all objects and make only correct inferences.*

The proof is given in Martignon and Hoffrage (2002). Note that in the context of Theorem 4, we are using the term "cue" to denote a binary-valued function in the reference class. Therefore, the number of different cues in a finite reference class is finite. The theorem can be generalized from the simple linear model with unit weights to linear models that use cue validities as weights.

11. Do People Intuitively Adapt Heuristics to Environmental Structures?

How do people know when to apply which heuristic? Can mere feedback select heuristics? In an experiment by Rieskamp and Otto (2002), participants took the role of bank consultants with the task of evaluating which of two companies applying for a loan was more creditworthy. Six cues such as qualification of employees and profitability were provided for each company. For the first 24 pairs of companies, no feedback was provided as to the correctness of the participants' inferences. Thereafter, feedback was given. For one group of participants, the correct answer was determined in about 90% of the cases by Take The Best, that is, feedback was obtained from the cues in a non-compensatory way. For the second group, the more creditworthy company was determined in about 90% of the cases by a weighted additive rule, that is, the feedback

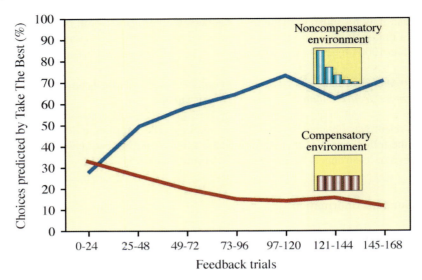

Figure 6. Do people intuitively learn when to use Take The Best? When the participants were in an experimental environment in which feedback was generated in a non-compensatory way, the frequency of choices consistent with Take The Best increased over time; when the feedback was compensatory, this frequency decreased (Rieskamp and Otto, 2002).

was generated in a compensatory way. Did people intuitively adapt their heuristics to the feedback structure of the environments? As can be seen from Figure 6, this was the case: Feedback changed the frequency of responses consistent with Take The Best. Note that in this experiment, participants could acquire information without paying for it. This fosters compensatory strategies, as can be seen from the low initial frequency of around 30% for Take The Best. People learned – without instruction – that different heuristics are successful in different environments.

12. Does the Use of Lexicographic Strategies Depend on Time Pressure?

Empirical evidence for lexicographic strategies (e.g., Payne, Bettman, and Johnson, 1988, 1993; Edland, 1994) and Take The Best (e.g., Bröder, 2000; Newell and Shanks, 2003) has been frequently reported in the literature. Take The Best (but not Minimalist) is a variant of a lexicographic strategy, although it has additional features, including the recognition heuristic as its initial step and an asymmetric stopping rule for unknown values. Rieskamp and Hoffrage (1999) tested how well eight strategies proposed in the literature predicted people's decisions under low and high time pressure. The participants' task was to predict which of four companies had the highest yearly profit. They could look up, sequentially, the information from six cues (e.g., amount of investments, the number of employees, etc.). Two strategies modeled participants' choices

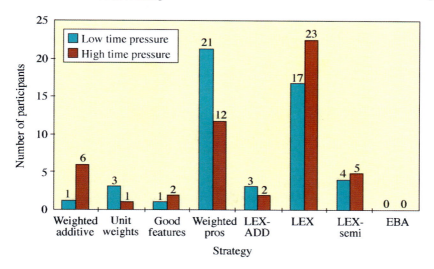

Figure 7. A test of how well eight strategies predict people's choices under low (50-second) and high (20-second) time pressure (Rieskamp and Hoffrage, 1999). Participants had to infer which of four companies had the highest profit. Two strategies, Weighted Pros and LEX, best predicted participants' behavior for low and high time pressure, respectively. LEX, the most simple heuristic among the candidates, is a generalization of Take The Best from binary choices to choices among several alternatives, whereas Weighted Pros is a simple compensatory strategy. The Weighted Additive Model weights cues by their validities and adds all weighted cue values; the Unit-Weight Model attaches the same weight to each cue; Good Features (Alba and Marmorstein, 1987) selects the alternative with the highest number of good features, that is, cue values that exceed a specified threshold. Weighted Pros (Huber, 1979) considers only the highest value on each cue (i.e., ignores all other values) and computes the sum of the validities of these cues for each alternative. LEX-ADD is a two-step strategy: It first uses LEX-Semi to choose two alternatives as favorites, then evaluates them by a unit-weight model, and finally selects the one with the highest score. LEX-Semi (Luce, 1956) works like LEX, except that negligible differences between cue values are disregarded. LEX and LEX-Semi are the only strategies in this set of eight which employ one-reason decision making. Elimination By Aspects (EBA; Tversky, 1972) eliminates all alternatives that do not exceed a specified value on the first cue examined. If more than one alternative remains, another cue is selected.

best: a generalization of Take The Best from binary choices to choices among several alternatives (lexicographic heuristic or LEX) and Weighted Pros (Huber, 1979). Weighted Pros considers only the highest value on each cue (i.e., ignores all other values). Under time pressure, participants' choices conformed better to LEX, which is also the computationally less expensive strategy. Only a low number of participants could be best described by any of the other six models.

13. An Intelligent System Must Ignore Information

This section illustrates both the descriptive validity and the prescriptive power of simple heuristics that employ one-reason decision making. It has long been known that people often base their decisions on only one, or a few, reasons. However, in the behavioral economics literature, ignoring information is all too quickly labeled a judgmental bias, or an act of irrationality. Sometimes this is true, but often it is not, as the performance of Take The Best demonstrates. For instance, in the 1960s, conservatism – that is, the overweighting of base rates in Bayesian problems – was reported, whereas in the 1970s and 1980s, the base rate fallacy – that is, the underweighting or ignoring of base rates – was considered to be an established fact. Both phenomena appeared to contradict each other, and researchers puzzled as to why (Gigerenzer, 2000). It is now easy to see how heuristics such as Take The Best can produce both phenomena. If one of the predictors refers to the base rates of events, then either base rate neglect or conservatism will result, depending on where this base rate cue is in the cue hierarchy. There is no puzzling empirical contradiction, nor is there necessarily irrationality. Rather, by means of precise models of heuristics – unlike merely verbal labels such as availability – we can understand how phenomena and anomalies are created.

References

Alba, J.W., Marmorstein, H. (1987). "The effects of frequency knowledge on consumer decision making". Journal of Consumer Research 14, 14–26.

Bröder, A. (2000). "Assessing the empirical validity of the 'Take-the-best' heuristic as a model of human probabilistic inference". Journal of Experimental Psychology: Learning, Memory, and Cognition 26, 1332–1346.

Czerlinski, J., Gigerenzer, G., Goldstein, D.G. (1999). "How good are simple heuristics?" In: Gigerenzer, G., Todd, P.M., the ABC Research Group (Eds.), Simple Heuristics that Make Us Smart. Oxford University Press, New York, pp. 97–118.

Dawes, R.M. (1979). "The robust beauty of improper linear models in decision making". American Psychologist 34, 571–582.

Dawes, R.M., Corrigan, B. (1974). "Linear models in decision making". Psychological Bulletin 81, 95–106.

Edland, A. (1994). "Time pressure and the application of decision rules: Choices and judgments among multiattribute alternatives". Scandinavian Journal of Psychology 35, 281–291.

Gigerenzer, G. (2000). "Adaptive Thinking: Rationality in the Real World". Oxford University Press, New York.

Gigerenzer, G., Goldstein, D.G. (1996). "Reasoning the fast and frugal way: Models of bounded rationality". Psychological Review 103, 650–669.

Gigerenzer, G., Todd, P.M., the ABC Research Group (1999). "Simple Heuristics that Make Us Smart". Oxford University Press, New York.

Goldstein, D.G., Gigerenzer, G. (2002). "Models of ecological rationality: The recognition heuristic". Psychological Review 109, 75–90.

Huber, O. (1979). "Nontransitive multidimensional preferences: Theoretical analysis of a model". Theory and Decision 10, 147–165.

Luce, R.D. (1956). "Semiorders and a theory of utility discrimination". Econometrica 24, 178–191.

Martignon, L., Hoffrage, U. (2002). "Fast, frugal, and fit: Simple heuristics for paired comparisons". Theory and Decision 52, 29–71.

Martignon, L., Laskey, K. (1999). "Bayesian benchmarks for fast and frugal heuristics". In: Gigerenzer, G., Todd, P.M., the ABC Research Group (Eds.), Simple Heuristics that Make Us Smart. Oxford University Press, New York, pp. 169–188.

Newell, B., Shanks, D. (2003). "Take the best or look at the rest? Factors influencing 'one-reason' decision-making". Journal of Experimental Psychology: Learning, Memory, and Cognition 29, 53–65.

Payne, J.W., Bettman, J.R., Johnson, E.J. (1988). "Adaptive strategy selection in decision making". Journal of Experimental Psychology: Learning, Memory, and Cognition 14, 534–552.

Payne, J.W., Bettman, J.R., Johnson, E.J. (1993). "The Adaptive Decision Maker". Cambridge University Press, New York.

Rieskamp, J., Hoffrage, U. (1999). "When do people use simple heuristics, and how can we tell?" In: Gigerenzer, G., Todd, P.M., the ABC Research Group (Eds.), Simple Heuristics that Make Us Smart. Oxford University Press, New York, pp. 141–167.

Rieskamp, J., Otto, P. (2002). "Adaptive strategy selection in decision making: A learning perspective". Manuscript in preparation.

Tucker, W. (1987). "Where do the homeless come from?" National Review 25, 34–44.

Tversky, A. (1972). "Elimination by aspects: A theory of choice". Psychological Review 79, 281–299.

Chapter 109

COGNITIVE ILLUSIONS RECONSIDERED

GERD GIGERENZER, RALPH HERTWIG and ULRICH HOFFRAGE
Max Planck Institute for Human Development, Berlin, Germany

PETER SEDLMEIER
University of Chemnitz, Germany

Behavioral economists have done a great service in connecting psychology and economics. Up to now, however, most have focused on cognitive illusions and anomalies, in order to prove the descriptive failure of neoclassical economic models. Some conjectured that "mental illusions should be considered the rule rather than the exception" (Thaler, 1991, p. 4), thus questioning the assumption that probabilistic judgments are consistent and unbiased. In an influential article, Rabin (1998) concluded: "Because these biases lead people to make errors when attempting to maximize $U(x)$, this research poses a more radical challenge to the economics model" (p. 11).

Not everything that looks like a fallacy, however, is one. Economists have been presented a lopsided view of research in psychology (e.g., by Rabin, 1998). Here we explain three of the factors producing the phenomena labeled cognitive illusions: inefficient representations (in the context of base rate fallacy), selected sampling of problems (in the context of overconfidence and availability), and narrow norms (in the context of conjunction fallacy). Understanding these factors allows us to gain theoretical insight into the processes underlying judgment and decision making and to design effective tools to help people reason under uncertainty.

We begin with the power of representations. The argument is that the human mind does not work on information, but on representations of information. Many cognitive illusions disappear if one pays attention to this fundamental property of human thinking. For instance, evolved representations of information, such as natural frequencies, promote probabilistic reasoning, whereas conditional probabilities tend to create cognitive illusions. We illustrate the power of representations by demonstrating how one can foster Bayesian reasoning in laypeople and experts.

1. Base Rate Fallacy Reconsidered

Optimal allocation decisions in markets involve updating probabilities. When probabilities need to be updated to reflect new information, people are assumed to reason in a Bayesian way. In other words, people are assumed to be rational Bayesian EU maximizers. But are they really? Many experimenters have concluded that people lack the ability to make Bayesian inferences, even in simple situations involving a binary predictor and criterion: "Man is Apparently not a Conservative Bayesian: He Is not Bayesian at All" (Kahneman and Tversky, 1972, p. 450). Consider breast cancer screening with mammography, which incurs costs of about $2 billion every year in the U.S. Given how much money is spent for this technology, physicians and patients should understand what its outcome means.

A woman tests positive and asks her physician how likely it is that she has breast cancer. The relevant statistical information for the woman's age group is:

The probability of breast cancer is 1% [base rate]; the probability of a positive test given breast cancer is 90% [sensitivity]; and the probability of a positive test given no breast cancer is 10% [false positive rate].

The posterior probability $p(H \mid D)$ that a woman who tests positive actually has breast cancer can be calculated by Bayes' rule. Here, H stands for hypothesis, such as cancer, and D for data, such as a positive test result:

$$p(H \mid D) = \frac{p(H)p(D \mid H)}{p(H)p(D \mid H) + p(\text{not-}H)p(D \mid \text{not-}H)}$$
$$= \frac{(.01)(.90)}{(.01)(.90) + (.99)(.10)} \approx .08. \qquad (1)$$

That is, roughly 9 out of every 10 women who test positive do not have breast cancer. Radiologists, gynecologists, and other physicians, however, tend to overestimate this probability by an order of magnitude (Gigerenzer, 2002). For instance, some physicians believe this probability to be 90% – and for two different reasons. They either mistake the sensitivity for the posterior probability, or alternatively, they subtract the false positive rate from 100%, which results in the same estimate. In both cases, the base rate is ignored – an instance of the "base-rate fallacy." Overestimating the chance of breast cancer after a positive screening test exacts unnecessary physical, psychological, and monetary costs. For instance, every year more than 300,000 American women who do not have breast cancer undergo a biopsy as a consequence of false positives, and for every $100 spent on screening, an additional $33 is spent on following up on false positive results (Gigerenzer, 2002). We will now show how to improve laypeople's and experts' reasoning by selecting a more efficient representation of the statistical information.

2. The Ecological Argument

To understand and evaluate the performance of the human mind, one needs to look at its environment, in particular at the external representation of information. Mathematical probabilities are representations of uncertainty that were first devised in the 17th century (Gigerenzer et al., 1989). For most of the time during which the human mind evolved, information was encountered in the form of natural frequencies, that is, counts that have not been normalized with respect to base rates. Representation matters because Bayesian reasoning is relatively simple with natural frequencies, but becomes cumbersome the moment conditional probabilities (or normalized frequencies) are introduced.

An example of a representation in terms of natural frequencies is:

Ten of every 1000 women have breast cancer; 9 of those 10 women with breast cancer will test positive and 99 of the 990 women without breast cancer will also test positive.

How many of those who test positive actually have breast cancer? Natural frequencies help people to see the answer: Nine out of the 108 women who tested positive actually have cancer. Natural frequencies facilitate Bayesian computations because they carry information about base rates, whereas normalized frequencies and probabilities do not. If a is the frequency of D and H (e.g., positive test and disease), and b the frequency of D and not-H, then the posterior probability can be calculated as follows:

$$p(H \mid D) = \frac{a}{a+b} = \frac{9}{9+99} \approx .08. \qquad (2)$$

Note that with natural frequencies, base rates need not be directly attended to. In contrast, if natural frequencies have been normalized with respect to the base rates, resulting in conditional probabilities or relative frequencies, one has to multiply the normalized values by the base rates in order to bring the base rates "back in" [compare Equations (1) and (2)]. Unlike conditional probabilities, natural frequencies are an efficient representation for Bayesian reasoning because the representation does part of the computation.

This insight provides a powerful tool for improving probabilistic reasoning, in laypeople as well as physicians and other professionals.

3. Helping John Q. Public

The majority of demonstrations of the base rate fallacy involved people with no specific competence in probabilistic reasoning. In almost all of these demonstrations, they encountered the statistical information in the form of probabilities. Would natural frequencies help? As Figure 1 shows, in each of 15 problems, including the breast cancer problem, the cab problem, and other standard problems in the literature, natural frequencies increased the proportion of Bayesian inferences substantially (Gigerenzer and Hoffrage, 1995). On average, people reasoned the Bayesian way with probabilities in only about 1 out of 6 cases, whereas in 1 out of 2 cases they did so with natural frequencies.

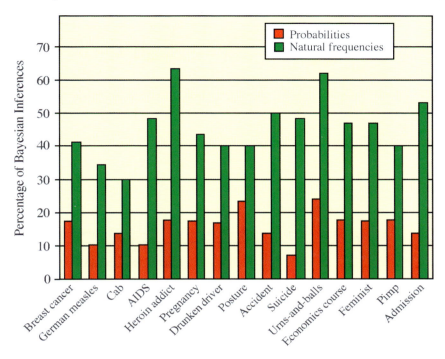

Figure 1. How an efficient representation – natural frequencies – improves probabilistic reasoning in laypeople. Sixty participants were tested on 15 problems each. They had to infer, for instance, the probability of breast cancer given a positive mammogram (see text), or the probability of severe prenatal damage of a newborn given the mother suffered from German measles during pregnancy. To qualify as a Bayesian inference, the participant had to respond with the exact Bayesian estimate, and the written protocol had to confirm that the response was derived from actual Bayesian reasoning. The statistical information was either presented in conditional probabilities or in natural frequencies. In each problem, probabilistic reasoning improved when statistical information was communicated in natural frequencies (Gigerenzer and Hoffrage, 1995).

4. Helping Physicians

Would the same simple method work with physicians who make diagnostic inferences in daily practice? Figure 2 (left) shows the answers of 48 physicians to the mammography problem. When the statistical information was presented in probabilities, as it is common in medical textbooks, then their estimates of the probability that a woman has breast cancer given a positive mammogram varied between 1% and 90%. If women knew about this disturbing variability, they would be rightly alarmed. When the same information was presented in natural frequencies, the physicians' estimates clustered around the correct answer. Figure 2 (right) shows the same positive effect of an efficient representation for colorectal cancer screening, that is, estimating the chance that a patient has colorectal cancer given a positive hemoccult test.

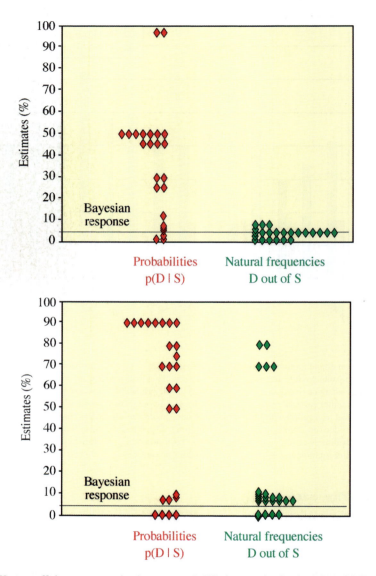

Figure 2. How an efficient representation improves probabilistic reasoning in physicians. Of 48 physicians with an average of 14 years of professional experience, half received the statistical information in conditional probabilities, the other in natural frequencies. Each point represents one physician. The ordinate shows their estimates of the probability or frequency of breast cancer (colorectal cancer) after a positive screening test. With conditional probabilities, the physicians were highly inconsistent; with natural frequencies, this inconsistency largely disappeared and the physicians' estimates clustered around the correct estimate (from Gigerenzer, 2002; Hoffrage and Gigerenzer, 1998).

5. Helping AIDS Counselors

Between 1986 and 1996, U.S. federal spending for AIDS research, educational programs, counselor training, testing, and prevention programs increased from $300,000 to $9 billion. In the U.S., some 50 million blood and plasma samples are tested every year. Most HIV tests are performed on low-risk clients, for whom the base rate of infection is very small. Though HIV tests are excellent, they are occasionally in error, which makes probabilistic thinking indispensable. Do professional AIDS counselors know what a positive test result means?

In a study by Gigerenzer, Hoffrage, and Ebert (1998), one of the authors went undercover to 20 public health centers to take 20 HIV tests. He used the mandatory pretest counseling session to ask questions about base rates for low-risk clients, sensitivity, false positive rate, and his chances of having HIV were he to test positive. None of the 20 counselors communicated information in natural frequencies; all used conditional probabilities and got confused without noticing. Fifteen of the 20 counselors estimated the chances that the client has HIV were he to test positive (in both the Elisa and Western blot tests) as 99.9% or higher. Natural frequencies, in contrast, help to replace confusion by insight. Out of every 10,000 men with no risky behavior, about one will be infected by HIV, and he will test positive with practical certainty. Of the other 9999, one will falsely test positive. Thus, we can expect that out of two men who test positive, only one has the virus. Again, the best technology does not suffice when people do not understand their products. In the case of HIV testing, efficient representations can help to avoid psychological and physical costs, ranging from losing one's job to contemplating suicide.

6. Helping Lawyers and Judges

In the counseling room as well as in the courtroom, choosing an efficient representation can make the difference between life and death. Like medical tests, DNA fingerprinting requires reasoning about base rates, false positives, and false negatives. Notwithstanding this fact, out of some 175 accredited law schools in the U.S., only one requires a course in basic statistics. Lindsey, Hertwig, and Gigerenzer (2003) asked advanced law students and legal professionals (including law school professors) to evaluate two criminal case files based upon two actual rape and murder cases. In both cases, a match was reported between the DNA of the defendant and a trace on the victim. When the statistical information was expressed as conditional probabilities, only 13% of the professionals and less than 1% of the law students correctly inferred the probability that the defendant was actually the source of the trace given a match (Figure 3, left). When the identical information was stated in terms of natural frequencies, the correct inferences increased to 68% and 44%, respectively. Did the representation also matter for the verdict? Yes. More professionals and students voted "guilty" when the evidence was presented in terms of probabilities, that is, when their minds were clouded (Figure 3, right).

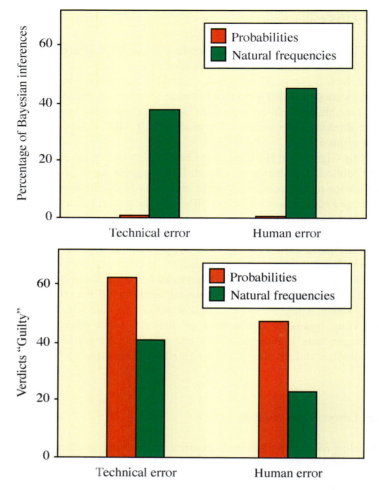

Figure 3. How an efficient representation improves probabilistic reasoning and influences verdicts in legal professionals and law students. When 27 professionals and 127 law students responded to DNA evidence presented in terms of conditional probabilities, few could correctly infer the probability that the defendant was actually the source of the trace, given a DNA match. With natural frequencies, more than 40% of the students and the majority of the professionals "saw" the correct answer (a). Representation also influenced participants' ultimate verdict (b). With conditional probabilities, more students and professionals voted "guilty" (from Hoffrage et al., 2000; Lindsey, Hertwig, and Gigerenzer, 2003).

7. How to Teach Bayesian Reasoning

In the studies reported so far, probabilistic reasoning improved without instruction. The effects observed can be boosted by explicitly teaching people to translate probabilities

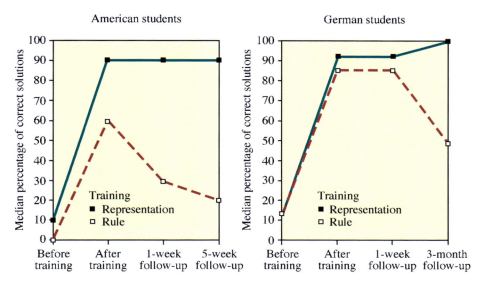

Figure 4. How to learn and not forget after the exam. With the traditional method of teaching how to insert probabilities into Bayes' rule (rule training), American and German students tend to forget what they have learned. However, when they have been taught to translate probabilities into natural frequencies (representation training), performance remains high (from Gigerenzer, 2002; Sedlmeier and Gigerenzer, 2001).

into natural frequencies. Sedlmeier and Gigerenzer (2001) (Sedlmeier, 1999) designed a tutorial computer program that teaches people to translate probabilities into natural frequencies (representation training) or, alternatively, to insert probabilities into Bayes' rule (rule training). As every teacher knows, the problem is not so much to get statistical knowledge into students' minds, but to keep it there after the exam. Figure 4 shows, that for both for American and German students, rule training leads to the typical forgetting curve, whereas representation training results in robust probabilistic thinking lasting over the entire time examined.

To conclude: The base rate fallacy, or more generally, the difficulties people have in reasoning with conditional probabilities, is often presented as if it were the natural consequence of flawed mental software. This view, however, overlooks the fundamental fact that the human mind processes information through external representations, and that how representations are selected can improve or impair our performance in statistical reasoning.

8. Overconfidence Bias Reconsidered

Overconfidence bias has become one of the stock-in-trade examples of research on cognitive illusions. Many kinds of economic disasters, from the large proportion of start-ups that quickly go out of business to the exaggerated confidence of financial investors, have been attributed to this alleged cognitive illusion. "[S]ome basic tendency toward overconfidence appears to be a robust human character trait" (Shiller, 2000, p. 142). These conjectures have been justified by reference to experiments in which confidence is studied with general knowledge questions of the following kind:

Which city has more inhabitants?
(a) Hyderabad (b) Islamabad
How confident are you that your answer is correct?
50%, 60%, 70%, 80%, 90%, 100%.

The typical finding is that when people say they are 100% confident, the relative frequency of correct answers is only about 80%. When they are 90% confident, the proportion correct is about 75%, and so on. This systematic discrepancy has been interpreted as a cognitive illusion and labeled overconfidence bias (e.g., Lichtenstein, Fischhoff, and Phillips, 1982). Quantitatively, overconfidence bias is defined as the difference between mean confidence and mean percentage of correct answers. Like many other cognitive illusions, overconfidence bias has been claimed to be a stable fallacy: "...can anything be done? Not much" (Edwards and von Winterfeldt, 1986, p. 656).

We know now that much can be done. Overconfidence is nothing like a robust character trait but a consequence of three determinants that can be manipulated outside people's minds: the question researchers ask, the sampling technique researchers employ, and the regression phenomenon. Challenging the view that "overconfidence bias" reflects a shortcoming of the human mind, Erev, Wallsten, and Budescu (1994) showed that regression to the mean is a sufficient condition for the systematic discrepancy (imperfect calibration) called overconfidence bias to arise. That is, an ideal statistical device would generate a similar discrepancy, namely estimates that regress towards the mean. Concerning the first determinants, one can ask a frequency question after a series of items: How many of the last 50 questions did you answer correctly?

If overconfidence were indeed a stable character trait, asking a frequency question rather than the typical confidence question should not affect overconfidence. Yet the question makes overconfidence disappear. Moreover, Figure 5 shows that overconfidence bias can be made to appear, disappear, or even reverse into underconfidence by using random samples of questions rather than selected samples. In random samples, pairs such as Hyderabad–Islamabad, where a cue with high ecological validity (Islamabad is a capital, and capitals tend to have a large number of inhabitants) is misleading, are no longer overrepresented. The effects of frequency questions and random sampling were first shown by Gigerenzer, Hoffrage, and Kleinbölting (1991). In a subsequent study, Griffin and Tversky (1992) replicated the effect of frequency questions, but disputed the effect of sampling. However, a meta-analysis of 135 studies finally showed that overconfidence consistently disappears when questions are randomly sampled, and that this finding cannot be attributed to a hard-easy effect (Juslin, Winman, and Olsson, 2000).

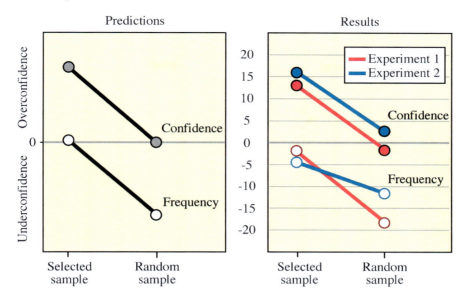

Figure 5. How to make overconfidence disappear – or even reverse to underconfidence. The predictions (left panel) are derived from the theory of probabilistic mental models (Gigerenzer, Offrage, and Kleinbölting, 1991), which specifies the processes underlying confidence and frequency judgments. The results of two experiments (right panel) show that when questions were randomly sampled from a natural environment (here: all German cities with more than 100,000 inhabitants), then overconfidence bias disappeared in confidence judgments. Frequency judgments (How many questions did you answer correctly?) showed no overconfidence in selected samples, and exhibited underconfidence in random samples. This simultaneous demonstration of over- and underconfidence indicates that overconfidence is nothing like a stable mental trait. Rather, this result is consistent with a heuristic process that is adapted to specific environmental structures but can be let astray in others.

To summarize, the experimental phenomenon that has been (mis)labeled overconfidence bias can be fully explained by three determinants in a person's environment: the question researchers ask, the sampling technique researchers employ, and the regression phenomenon. There is no reason to attribute the experimental results to robust shortcomings of the human mind. To understand how overconfidence and underconfidence are generated, one has to look outside the individual mind – such as to the sampling process (Figure 5). The theory of probabilistic mental models specifies how cognitive heuristics lead to these phenomena as a function of the environments in which they operate (Gigerenzer, Hoffrage, and Kleinbölting, 1991).

9. Conjunction Fallacy Reconsidered

A most elementary rule of probability is the conjunction rule, which states that the conjoint probability $p(A \wedge B)$ cannot exceed $p(A)$. "[A] system of judgments that does not obey the conjunction rule cannot be expected to obey more complicated principles that presuppose this rule, such as Bayesian updating, external calibration, and the maximization of expected utility" (Tversky and Kahneman, 1983, p. 313). Not surprisingly, following these authors' report that most people commit the "conjunction fallacy," this cognitive illusion has since been invoked to explain various economic and societal problems. These include John Q. Public's unreasonable fear of technological risks such as nuclear reactor failures (Stich, 1985), his questionable spending on insurance (Johnson et al., 1993), and even major blunders in U.S. security policy (Kanwisher, 1989).

The classic problem designed to demonstrate violations of the conjunction rule is the Linda problem (Tversky and Kahneman, 1983):

Linda is 31 years old, single, outspoken, and very bright. She majored in philosophy. As a student, she was deeply concerned with issues of discrimination and social justice, and also participated in anti-nuclear demonstrations.

Rank the following statements by their probability:
    Linda is a bank teller (T).
    Linda is active in the feminist movement (F).
    Linda is a bank teller and is active in the feminist movement (T&F).

The typical result was that 80 to 90% of participants judged T&F to be more probable than T, a judgment inconsistent with the conjunction rule. This judgment was labeled the "conjunction fallacy" and soon became the primal sin of human rationality. However, one ought to be cautious of labeling these judgments a fallacy. With Tversky and Kahneman's norm for rational reasoning, the content of the Linda problem is irrelevant; one does not even need to read the description of Linda. All that counts are the terms "probability" and "and," which they assume must be interpreted as the mathematical probability and logical AND, respectively. However, as the Oxford English Dictionary shows, this is far from true: These words have multiple legitimate meanings in natural language; only few of them correspond to the mathematical probability and logical AND, and therefore need not obey the conjunction rule. To reveal the various ways people understand the natural language word "probability" in the Linda problem, Hertwig and Gigerenzer (1999) asked participants to paraphrase it. Bearing testimony to the polysemy of "probability," participants responded with 18 different interpretations (Figure 6). Across all their responses, only 18% were mathematical, a number that corresponds to the usual 80 to 90% violations found.

To test this polysemy argument, Hertwig and Gigerenzer (1999) used the same description of Linda but asked participants a frequency question:

Imagine 200 women who fit the description of Linda. How many of the 200 women are:
    Bank tellers (T).
    Active in the feminist movement (F).
    Bank tellers and are active in the feminist movement (T&F).

Figure 6 shows that the paraphrases switched towards mathematical probability, and Figure 7 shows that the violations of the conjunction rule largely disappeared when the frequency question clarified what the task is about (see also Fiedler, 1988; Mellers, Her-

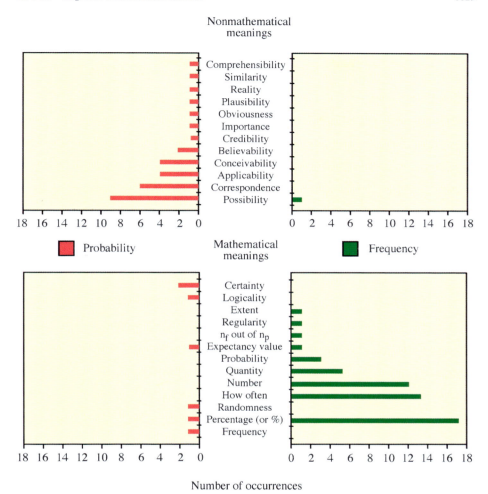

Figure 6. The word "probability" is interpreted non-mathematically and the word "frequency" is interpreted mathematically in the Linda problem, making the conjunction rule irrelevant and relevant, respectively. Participants were first presented with either the probability or the frequency version of the Linda problem. Then they were asked to imagine themselves in the role of an experimenter who must describe the Linda problem verbally to a participant who is not a native speaker, and for whom the term "probability" or "frequency" must be paraphrased. The bars show the frequency of participants' paraphrases for the terms "probability" (red bars) and "frequency" (green bars). For details see Hertwig and Gigerenzer (1999).

twig, and Kahneman, 2001; Tversky and Kahneman, 1983). This effect is moderated by response mode (people are more likely to violate the conjunction rule when instructed to give ranks rather than estimates; Hertwig and Chase, 1998).

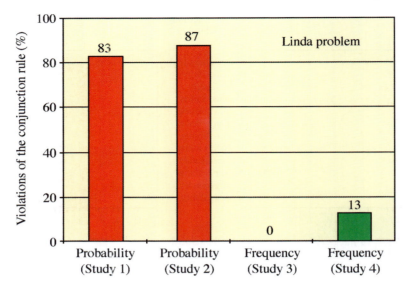

Figure 7. Frequency judgments can make the "conjunction fallacy" disappear. Hertwig and Gigerenzer (1999, Studies 1–4) asked participants to judge either the probability or the frequency of statements T, F, and T&F (see text). The bars show the percentages of violations of the conjunction rule for probabilities (red bars) and frequencies (green bars).

To summarize, when the polysemy of the English term "probability" is eliminated, the phenomenon dubbed the "conjunction fallacy" largely disappears, too. Any computer can mechanically apply the conjunction rule. In contrast, the ability to infer the meaning of polysemous terms from the context they are embedded in is an impressive human capability unmatched by any computer. In the present case, the relevant context is the fact that the experimenter provided a description of Linda, which suggests legitimate non-mathematical meanings of probability such as possibility and conceivability. By interpreting people's semantic inferences as a conjunction fallacy, human social intelligence has been mistaken for irrationality.

10. Availability Reconsidered

Behavioral economics is often criticized for merely listing anomalies without providing a theory. Whether or not this is true in general, the attempt to explain human behavior in terms of "availability," "representativeness," and "anchoring and adjustment" is a case in point. These labels are too vague to count as explanations and, post hoc, one of them can account for almost any phenomenon. Representativeness, for instance, refers to some form of similarity judgment. However, psychological research has since long proposed and tested precise models of similarity, including Euclidean distance, City

Block distance, and likelihood ratios. In light of these models, the new preference for vague terms such as representativeness reflects a step backwards, which is in itself an interesting phenomenon. The danger is that these one-word explanations account for everything and nothing.

The term availability has been used to explain distorted frequency or probability judgments. Beginning with the original work (Tversky and Kahneman, 1973), this term has been attributed various ambiguous meanings, such as the number of instances that come to mind and the ease with which the operations of retrieval can be performed. Despite, or possibly because of its vagueness, availability has repeatedly been invoked to explain various phenomena – for instance, why the purchase of earthquake insurance rises after a quake, why personal experience distorts crime risk perception, or more generally why "people disproportionately weigh salient, memorable, or vivid evidence even when they have better sources of information" (Rabin, 1998, p. 30).

Given how little theory there is, the weight of the argument rests on the experimental evidence. In a widely cited study designed to demonstrate how people's judgments are biased due to availability, Tversky and Kahneman (1973) had people estimate whether each of five consonants (K, L, N, R, V) appears more frequently in the first or the third position in English words. Each of these five selected consonants actually occurs more frequently in the third position, which is untypical because the majority of consonants occur more frequently in the first position. Thus, the test sample was deliberately unrepresentative. Two-thirds of participants judged the first position as being more likely for a majority of the five consonants. This result was interpreted as a demonstration of a cognitive illusion and attributed to the availability heuristic: Words with a particular letter in the first position come to mind more easily. While this latter assertion may be true, there was no independent measure of availability in this study, nor has there been a successful replication in the literature.

Sedlmeier, Hertwig, and Gigerenzer (1998) defined the two most common meanings of availability. Thus they were able to measure them independently of people's frequency judgments, and test whether availability can actually predict them. The number of instances that come to mind was measured by the number of retrieved words within a constant time period (availability-by-number), and ease of retrieval was measured by the speed of the retrieval of the first word for each letter (availability-by-speed). Figure 8 shows the predictions of both versions of the availability heuristic and people's actual estimates. The test involved a large sample of letters rather than the five consonants, which, as described above, were untypical. Neither of the two versions of availability predicted people's actual frequency judgments. Rather, the judgments were roughly a monotonic function of the actual proportions, with a regression toward the mean, that is, an overestimation of low and an underestimation of high proportions.

To summarize, vague notions such as availability have been used as surrogates for theory. For a classic "demonstration" of availability, we showed that when one independently defines and measures it, availability does not account for people's frequency judgments. It is understandable that when availability and similar notions were first proposed in the early 1970s, they were only loosely characterized. Yet, more than

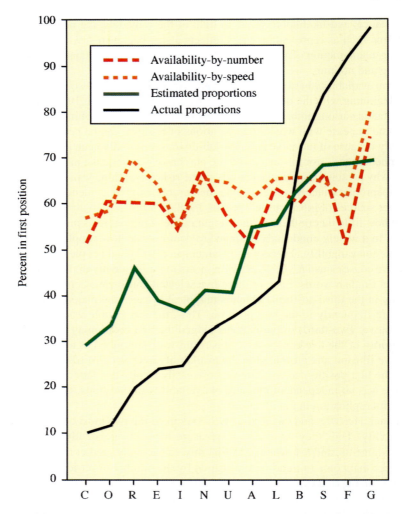

Figure 8. Participants were presented with either one or several vowels and consonants. They were asked to estimate the relative frequency with which each letter occurs in the first position compared to the second position in German. The red lines show the empirically derived predictions of two versions of the availability heuristic. The means of participants' relative frequency estimates in three subsequent studies are plotted against these predictions. The green line shows these estimated proportions transformed into percent in the first position (where the sum of the frequencies with which a particular letter occurs in the first and second position equals 100%). The black line shows the actual relative proportions with which the letters appear in the first position (calculated from an extensive German text corpus), with the rank ordered from left to right.

three decades later, the reluctance to define precise models has become a burden to the progress in connecting psychology and economics.

11. Conclusion

The key problems in the cognitive illusions literature can be summarized in two terms: narrow norms and vague heuristics (Gigerenzer, 1996). The fact that the cognitive illusions we have dealt with can be reduced by efficient representations, or turn out to be no illusions at all, should not lead to the conclusion that people make no errors. By definition, any intelligent system that can operate in an uncertain world will make errors. When one defines precise models of heuristics, one can predict in which tasks people who use them will fail and where they will succeed. For instance, the hindsight bias is a memory distortion that corresponds to the feeling "I knew it all along." The "Take The Best" heuristic, as part of an adaptive memory updating mechanism that has the hindsight bias as its by-product, can predict in which task hindsight bias will and will not occur (Hoffrage, Hertwig, and Gigerenzer, 2000). The task ahead is to model the cognitive processes underlying judgment and decision making. Once we understand them, we will be able to both predict when judgments are likely to go astray and help people make reasonable decisions in an uncertain world.

References

Edwards, W., von Winterfeldt, D. (1986). "On cognitive illusions and their implications". In: Arkes, H.R., Hammond, K.R. (Eds.), Judgment and Decision Making. Cambridge University Press, Cambridge, UK, pp. 642–679.

Erev, I., Wallsten, T.S., Budescu, D.V. (1994). "Simultaneous over- and underconfidence: The role of error in judgment processes". Psychological Review 101, 519–527.

Fiedler, K. (1988). "The dependence of the conjunction fallacy on subtle linguistic factors". Psychological Research 50, 123–129.

Gigerenzer, G. (1996). "On narrow norms and vague heuristics: A reply to Kahneman and Tversky". Psychological Review 103, 592–596.

Gigerenzer, G. (2002). "Calculated Risks: How to Know When Numbers Deceive You". Simon & Schuster, New York.

Gigerenzer, G., Hoffrage, U. (1995). "How to improve Bayesian reasoning without instruction: Frequency formats". Psychological Review 102, 684–704.

Gigerenzer, G., Hoffrage, U., Ebert, A. (1998). "AIDS counselling for low-risk clients". AIDS Care 10, 197–211.

Gigerenzer, G., Hoffrage, U., Kleinbölting, H. (1991). "Probabilistic mental models: A Brunswikian theory of confidence". Psychological Review 98, 506–528.

Gigerenzer, G., Swijtink, Z., Porter, T., Daston, L., Beatty, J., Krüger, L. (1989). "The Empire of Chance: How Probability Changed Science and Everyday Life". Cambridge University Press, Cambridge, UK.

Griffin, D., Tversky, A. (1992). "The weighing of evidence and the determinants of confidence". Cognitive Psychology 24, 411–435.

Hertwig, R., Chase, V.M. (1998). "Many reasons or just one: How response mode affects reasoning in the conjunction problem". Thinking and Reasoning 4, 319–352.

Hertwig, R., Gigerenzer, G. (1999). "The 'conjunction fallacy' revisited: How intelligent inferences look like reasoning errors". Journal of Behavioral Decision Making 12, 275–305.

Hoffrage, U., Gigerenzer, G. (1998). "Using natural frequencies to improve diagnostic inferences". Academic Medicine 73, 538–540.

Hoffrage, U., Hertwig, R., Gigerenzer, G. (2000). "Hindsight bias: A by-product of knowledge updating?" Journal of Experimental Psychology: Learning, Memory, and Cognition 26, 566–581.

Hoffrage, U., Lindsey, S., Hertwig, R., Gigerenzer, G. (2000). "Communicating statistical information". Science 290, 2261–2262.

Johnson, E.J., Hershey, J., Meszaros, J., Kunreuther, H. (1993). "Framing, probability distortions, and insurance decisions". Journal of Risk and Uncertainty 7, 35–51.

Juslin, P., Winman, A., Olsson, H. (2000). "Naive empiricism and dogmatism in confidence research: A critical examination of the hard–easy effect". Psychological Review 107, 384–396.

Kahneman, D., Tversky, A. (1972). "Subjective probability: A judgment of representativeness". Cognitive Psychology 3, 430–454.

Kanwisher, N. (1989). "Cognitive heuristics and American security policy". Journal of Conflict Resolution 33, 652–675.

Lichtenstein, S., Fischhoff, B., Phillips, L.D. (1982). "Calibration of probabilities: The state of the art to 1980". In: Kahneman, D., Slovic, P., Tversky, A. (Eds.), Judgment under Uncertainty: Heuristics and Biases. Cambridge University Press, Cambridge, UK, pp. 306–334.

Lindsey, S., Hertwig, R., Gigerenzer, G. (2003). "Communicating statistical evidence". Jurimetrics 43, 147–163.

Mellers, B., Hertwig, R., Kahneman, D. (2001). "Do frequency representations eliminate conjunction effects? An exercise in adversarial collaboration". Psychological Science 12, 269–275.

Rabin, M. (1998). "Psychology and economics". Journal of Economic Literature 36, 11–46.

Sedlmeier, P. (1999). "Improving Statistical Thinking: Theoretical Models and Practical Implications". Erlbaum, Mahwah, NJ.

Sedlmeier, P., Gigerenzer, G. (2001). "Teaching Bayesian reasoning in less than two hours". Journal of Experimental Psychology: General 130, 380–400.

Sedlmeier, P., Hertwig, R., Gigerenzer, G. (1998). "Are judgments of the positional frequencies of letters systematically biased due to availability?" Journal of Experimental Psychology: Learning, Memory, and Cognition 24, 754–770.

Shiller, R.J. (2000). "Irrational Exuberance". Princeton University Press, Princeton, NJ.

Stich, S.P. (1985). "Could man be an irrational animal? Some notes on the epistemology of rationality". Synthese 64, 115–135.

Thaler, R.H. (1991). "Quasi Rational Economics". Sage, New York.

Tversky, A., Kahneman, D. (1973). "Availability: A heuristic for judging frequency and probability". Cognitive Psychology 5, 207–232.

Tversky, A., Kahneman, D. (1983). "Extensional versus intuitive reasoning: The conjunction fallacy in probability judgment". Psychological Review 90, 293–315.

Chapter 110

SOCIAL HEURISTICS

PETER M. TODD, JÖRG RIESKAMP and GERD GIGERENZER

Center for Adaptive Behavior and Cognition, Max Planck Institute for Human Development, Berlin, Germany

Some of the most challenging decisions faced by humans and other social species are those arising from an environment comprising the decisions of conspecifics. The particular demands of social environments – such as the necessity of responding quickly to decisions made by others, coordinating mutual decisions, and detecting cheaters – call for heuristics that make rapid decisions rather than spend time gathering and processing information over a long period during which a fleeter-minded competitor could leap forward and gain an edge. Moreover, heuristics that handle social situations must address specifically social goals such as making decisions that can be justified and defended to others, that are transparent and understandable by the peer group, and that do not violate the fairness expectations held by people in the group (Tetlock, 1983). Thus, social heuristics must be judged by standards of effectiveness, adaptive advantage, and social intelligence, rather than by the traditional norms of optimality and consistency. Here we describe two types of social heuristics, for social exchange (including cheater detection) and sequential mate choice, and show how they perform from the standpoint of ecological rationality.

1. Social Heuristics for Cooperation

Ever since Darwin, altruism has caused a problem for the view of humans as selfish. In evolutionary biology, Hamilton's (1964) inclusive fitness theory provided an answer to why genetically related conspecifics would cooperate. *Homo sapiens* is one of the very few species that exhibits cooperation between genetically unrelated individuals, an ability that underlies the development of trade, negotiation, and markets. How can cooperation between unrelated individuals be explained? Repeated interactions enable cooperation because it offers the opportunity to reciprocate cooperative behavior and punish uncooperative behavior. Trivers (1971) was one of the first researchers to emphasize the role of such repetition, a perspective that has inspired most of the research since then that tries to explain cooperation between unrelated, self-interested individuals (e.g., Axelrod, 1984; Schelling, 1960).

To study how people decide whether or not to cooperate in repeated interactions, we can look at possible decision mechanisms used in simple economic games. The Iterated Prisoner's Dilemma (Luce and Raiffa, 1957) is often used to explore cooperation in symmetric situations where both players have equivalent roles. Less work has been done on the interesting case of asymmetric settings, where the two players have different actions available to them – a condition often encountered in the real world (e.g., between doctors and patients or auto mechanics and customers). The investment game is a two-person sequential bargaining game (Berg, Dickhaut, and McCabe, 1995) that has been used to study cooperation and trust in such asymmetric situations. Two players, A and B, both receive an initial endowment, for instance $10. Player A can invest any amount of the endowment, which is then tripled, producing some surplus before it is delivered to player B. Player B decides how much of the then tripled amount she wishes to return to player A. The game provides the opportunity of a surplus for both players. If player A trusts player B and invests the entire endowment, an efficient outcome that maximizes the mutual payoffs is produced. However, according to the subgame-perfect equilibrium player B will return nothing to player A to maximize his monetary payoff, which is anticipated by player A; hence, no amount is sent to player B. However, again, if the game is repeated indefinitely, substantial investments and returns are reasonable. Player B will hesitate to exploit player A, as A might then not invest in the following periods. With this threat, it becomes reasonable for player A to invest.

Rieskamp and Gigerenzer (2002) studied how well simple social heuristics could predict people's decisions in the indefinitely repeated investment game. In their experiment, participants played several indefinitely repeated investment games against different opponents. After each period of the game a new period followed with a continuation probability of 87.5%. The participants in the role of player A invested 100% of their endowment in 47% of all periods. The most frequent outcome (19% of all periods) led to an equal split of the final payoff for both players, consistent with the equity principle (Walster, Berscheid, and Walster, 1973), defining fair outcomes. However, participants often did not reach an agreement – one participant exploited the other or payoff allocations contrary to the equity principle were obtained. This large variance cannot be explained by a static fairness principle. In contrast, as the different outcomes result from dynamic decision processes, it is necessary to describe this process.

To explore the decision mechanisms used by people playing the investment game, Rieskamp and Gigerenzer (2002) modeled social heuristics with finite state automata. Heuristics for both player roles were developed and fitted to the observed data and then cross-validated for an independent data set. Two heuristics describing participants' decisions in the role of player A outperformed competing models including a simple learning mechanism in predicting participants decisions. The best heuristic for player A, Moderately–Grim, predicted 65% of the decisions for the validation sample by using three states (see Figure 1). The heuristic starts with an investment of 100% and if player B returns an amount greater than or equal to 34% it moves to state 2, in which it repeats the investment of 100% as long as player B makes a substantial return. However, if in the first period player B makes a return lower than 34%, Moderately–Grim advances to the third state, in which it will make no investment in the next and in all following periods. After the first period, if the opponent ever returns less than 34% two times consecutively, the heuristic always ends in the third (terminal) state. Moderately–

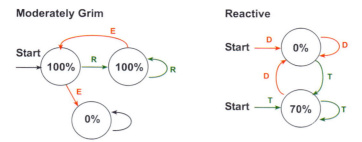

Figure 1. The figure shows the best heuristics developed to predict individual's behavior in the indefinitely repeated investment game. Moderately–Grim, the heuristic for player A, starts with an investment of 100% as long as the other player makes a reciprocal return (R) of at least 34%. If player B exploits (E) player A twice in succession, the heuristic moves to the third state with no investment from that point on. Reactive, the social heuristic for player B, returns 70% when player A trusts (T) player B by making a substantial investment, which leads to an equal final payoff for both players. If player A distrusts (D) player B by making investments lower than 17%, no return is made.

Grim is mostly trusting, even if it is occasionally exploited, but it turns to distrust if it is exploited repeatedly.

Two heuristics developed for player B also outperformed competing models. The better of these heuristics, Reactive, predicted 52% of the decisions for the validation sample using two states (see Figure 1). Depending on player A's decision in the first period, Reactive either returns nothing if the investment is lower than 17% or returns 70% given a higher investment, which leads to final equal payoffs for both players. The combination of the simple social heuristics Reactive and Moderately–Grim demonstrate how people can make good cooperative decisions in asymmetric interactions with a minimum of memory and computation.

2. Detecting Cheaters

Cooperation demands specific cognitive mechanisms in humans, and their study can further our understanding of when cooperation succeeds and when it fails. In contrast to experimental games where behavior can easily be interpreted as trust, cooperation, defection etc., in the real world outside the laboratory, cognitive mechanisms are necessary to interpret the behavior and figure out the intentions of others. One such cognitive adaptation is a cheater detection heuristic, which can be formulated as follows: If an agent is engaged in a social contract with another party, then the agent's attention is directed to information that could reveal that he or she is being cheated. A social contract is an agreement of the type "if you take the benefit, then you pay the costs," and cheating means that one party took the benefit but did not pay the costs. Cosmides (1989) looked for evidence of such a social heuristic in human cognition by employing the "selection

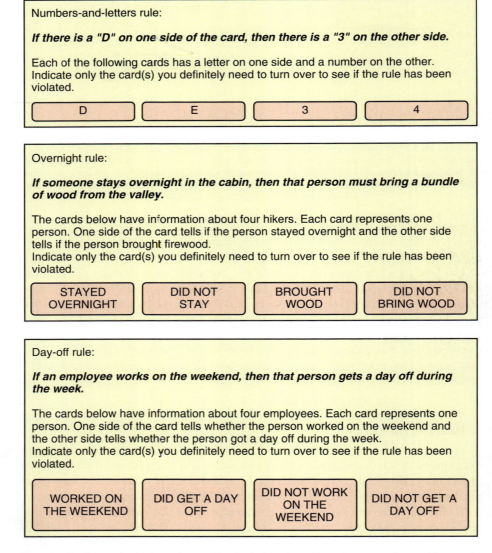

Figure 2. The four-card selection task. Top: The classical version with an abstract numbers-and-letters rule. Middle: A social contract (overnight rule) comprising two possible perspectives, one with and one without the possibility of being cheated. Bottom: A social contract (day-off rule) with two possible perspectives and cheating options for *both* parties.

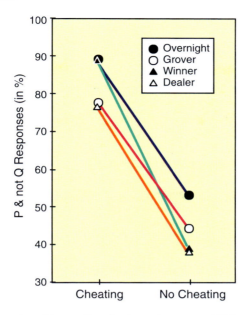

Figure 3. Search for information of the type "benefit taken and costs not paid" depends on whether or not the agent can be cheated in a social contract. The overnight rule is shown in the figure; the Grover rule is "If a student is to be assigned to Grover High School, then that student must live in Grover City"; the winner rule is "If a player wins a game, then he will have to treat the others to a round of drinks at the club's restaurant"; the dealer rule is "If a small-time drug dealer confesses, then he will have to be released" (see Gigerenzer and Hug, 1992).

task" (Wason, 1966), which is widely used in cognitive psychology to study rational reasoning.

The classical version of the selection task involves four two-sided cards and a conditional statement in the form "if P then Q" – for example, "if there is a 'D' on one side of the card, then there is a '3' on the other side." The four cards are placed on a table so that the participant can read only the information on the side facing upward. For instance, the four cards may read "D," "E," "3," and "4" (Figure 3). The participant's task is to indicate which of the four cards need(s) to be turned over to find out whether the conditional statement has been violated.

According to propositional logic, the "P" and "not-Q" cards (here, "D" and "4"), and no others, must be selected to test for rule violations. However, only about 10% of the participants in numerous experiments gave this answer. This result has been taken as evidence that human reasoning is "irrational" due to cognitive fallacies (see Gigerenzer and Hug, 1992). Further experiments showed that, depending on the content of the P's and Q's, the proportion of people giving the logical answer could go up or down. But the sources of this "content effect" remained elusive after it became clear that it is not simply "availability" or "familiarity" with the content or the rule (as proposed by Griggs and Cox, 1982; see Gigerenzer, 1996). Finally, Cosmides (1989) reported that if the conditional statement is coded as a social contract, then people's attention is directed to information that can reveal being cheated. Participants in this case then tend to select those cards that correspond to "benefit taken" and "cost not paid." There are competing views about what these results signify: Do they indicate that people have a specific cognitive adaptation for checking for cheaters, or just that people are better at reasoning about social contracts than about abstract numbers-and-letters problems?

3. Cheater Detection Versus Social Contracts

Gigerenzer and Hug (1992) experimentally disentangled reasoning about social contracts from cheater detection by varying whether the search for violations constitutes looking for cheaters or not. Consider the following social contract: "If someone stays overnight in the cabin, then that person must bring along a bundle of firewood from the valley" (Figure 3). This was presented in one of two context stories, as follows.

The "cheating" version explained that a cabin high in the Swiss Alps serves as an overnight shelter for hikers. Because it is cold and firewood is not otherwise available at this altitude, the Swiss Alpine Club has made the rule that each hiker who stays overnight in the cabin must bring along a bundle of firewood from the valley. The participants were cued to the perspective of a guard who checks whether any of four hikers has violated the rule. The four hikers were represented by four cards that read "stays overnight in the cabin," "does not stay overnight," "carried wood," and "carried no wood." The instruction was to indicate only the card(s) you definitely need to turn over to see if any of these hikers have violated the rule (Figure 3).

In the "no-cheating" version, the participants were cued to the perspective of a member of the German Alpine Association, visiting the same cabin in the Swiss Alps to find out how it is managed by the local Alpine Club. He observes people carrying firewood into the cabin, and a friend accompanying him suggests that the Swiss may have the same overnight rule as the Germans, namely "If someone stays overnight in the cabin, then that person must bring along a bundle of firewood from the valley." That this is also the Swiss Alpine Club's rule is not the only possible explanation; alternatively, only its members (who do not stay overnight in the cabin), and not the hikers, might bring firewood. Participants were now in the position of an observer who checks information to find out whether the social contract suggested by his friend actually holds. This observer does not represent a party in a social contract. The participants' instructions were the same as in the "cheating" version.

Thus, in the "cheating" scenario, the observation "stayed overnight and did not bring wood" means that the party represented by the guard is being cheated; in the "no-cheating" scenario, the same observation suggests only that the Swiss Alpine Club never made the supposed rule in the first place.

Suppose that what matters to human reasoners is only whether a rule is a social contract and therefore somehow easier to process – in this case, a cheater-detection

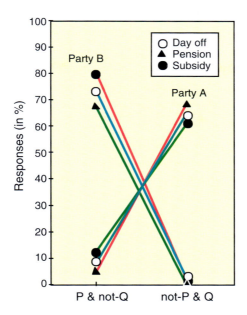

Figure 4. Responses to social contract rules become "illogical" when perspective is switched. When participants' perspective is switched from Party A to Party B in three social contract rules, the cards chosen to be checked when looking for cheaters in the selection task switch from the logical choices P and not-Q to the opposite choices, not-P and Q, indicating that cheater detection is not the same as logical reasoning. The day-off rule is specified in Figure 3; the pension rule is "If a previous employee gets a pension from the firm, then that person must have worked for the firm for at least 10 years"; and the subsidy rule is "If a home owner gets a subsidy, then that person must have installed a modern heating system" (see Gigerenzer and Hug, 1992).

mechanism becomes irrelevant. Because the rule to check is the same social contract in both versions of the alpine cabin story, this conjecture implies that there should be no difference in the selections observed. In the overnight problem, however, 89% of the participants selected "benefit taken" and "cost not paid" when cheating was at stake, compared to 53% in the no-cheating version, as shown in Figure 4. Similarly, the averages across four test problems were 83% and 45%, respectively (Gigerenzer and Hug, 1992). This evidence supports the presence of a specific cheater-detection heuristic used when processing social contracts.

4. Cheater Detection Versus Logical Reasoning

The experiment just reported, however, does not rule out the possibility that social contracts with cheating options somehow merely facilitate logical reasoning rather than invoke an additional psychological adaptation specifically designed for cheater detection. The reason for this is that the cheater-relevant "benefit taken" and "cost not paid" choices coincide with the logically implied "P" and "not-Q" choices. Gigerenzer and Hug (1992) tested this conjecture by using social contracts in which both sides can cheat and inducing participants to switch perspectives. For instance, one of the social contracts was the Day-off rule: "If an employee works on the weekend, then that person gets a day off during the week" (Figure 3). If social contracts merely facilitate logical reasoning, then the perspective of the participant should not matter (nor the content of the contract), because logical reasoning is by definition independent of perspective and content.

Figure 5 shows that perspective does matter in social contracts. When participants were assigned the role of the employee in this scenario, 75% checked "worked on the weekend" and "did not get a day off," that is, the "benefit taken" and "cost not paid" information from the employee's perspective, which coincide with the logically implied answers. Only 2% of participants checked the "did not work on the weekend" and "did get a day off" cases. When participants were assigned the role of the employer, the choices reversed. Now the majority checked "did not work on the weekend" and "did get a day off," which are the "benefit taken" and "cost not paid" cases from the employer's point of view. But these do not correspond with the logical "P" and "not-Q" cases. Two other social contracts gave essentially the same results (Figure 5). Thus, humans do indeed appear to have cognitive adaptations specifically designed to look for cues to being cheated in social exchanges – content does not simply facilitate logical reasoning about social contracts. (See Ortmann and Gigerenzer, 1997, for more on the economic implications of these results.)

5. Searching for Mates

When choosing which offspring to feed (as we have explored in Hertwig, Davis, and Sulloway, 2002 and Davis and Todd, 1999), or which stock to purchase (see Ortmann et al., this handbook), all of the alternatives are currently available to the decision maker, so it is only necessary to search for cues to base a choice upon. But a different strategy is called for when alternatives themselves (as opposed to cue values) take time to find, appearing sequentially over an extended period or spatial region. In this type of choice task, a fast and frugal reasoner need not (only) limit information search, but must (also) have a stopping rule for ending the search for alternatives themselves. One instance of this type of problem is the challenge that faces individuals searching for a mate from a stream of potential candidates met at different points in time. Mate choice is thus a process of sequential search rather than selection from a set of known options. What strategies are appropriate for sequential search such as this?

Models of optimal search behavior have been developed for decades in statistics (e.g., Ferguson, 1989) and economics (particularly in job search and consumer shopping behavior; see, e.g., Stigler, 1961 and Rapoport and Tversky, 1970, for early work). Classical search theory indicates that in the realm of mate choice one should look for a new mate until the costs of further search outweigh the benefits that could be gained by

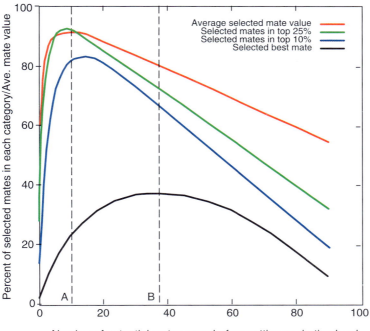

Figure 5. Basing an aspiration level on a small sample (rather than a large one) can be advantageous if the goal is to find a good mate rather than the best mate. Performance on four different criteria is plotted as a function of number of individuals sampled initially (assuming one-sided, non-mutual search), with the highest value individual from that initial sample used as the aspiration level for future search. These smoothed results are based on simulations with a total mating population of 100, each individual having a mate value between 1 and 100. If the initial sample comprises 10 individuals ($x = 10$, marked A), the average mate value obtained given the resulting aspiration level will be 92 (red curve); the chance that the selected mate will be in the top 25% of the population is 92% (green curve); the chance that the selected mate will be in the top 10% is 82% (blue curve); and the chance that the very highest value mate will be selected is 23% (black curve). "Sampling about 10 individuals is also a fast way to form a useful aspiration level for population sizes larger than 100." In contrast, the "37% rule" ($x = 37$, marked B) does better at maximizing the chance of obtaining the very highest valued mate (to 37%) but has a much higher search cost and does worse on the other three criteria – average mate value of 81 (red); only a 72% chance of getting a mate in the top 25% (green); only a 67% chance of getting a mate in the top 10% of the population (blue) (reprinted from Miller and Todd, 1998).

leaving the current candidate (see Roth and Sotomayor, 1990, for a different approach when search and choices are both mutual). But in practice, not only is performing a rational cost-benefit analysis for optimal mate search intractable, it also makes a bad impression on a would-be partner. As a consequence, some economists (e.g., Frey and Eichenberger, 1996) have proposed that human mate choice is not performed in a rational manner, and in particular that individuals search far too little before deciding on a marriage partner. In contrast, the results reported below indicate that relatively fast search heuristics can yield adaptive decisions in this domain.

We have focused on the applicability of Herbert Simon's (1955, 1990) notion of a satisficing heuristic for mate search, in which an aspiration level is set for the selection criterion being used (e.g., mate value, defined somehow on a unidimensional scale), and search proceeds until a prospect is encountered who meets that aspiration. How should that aspiration level be set? One well-known approach is the "37% rule" derived for the "Secretary Problem" from statistics (Ferguson, 1989): Estimate the number of prospects one is likely to meet in life, let the first 37% of them pass by without picking any of them, but use the highest mate value observed in that initial sample as the aspiration level for searching through the rest, until one is found who exceeds that threshold. This is the optimal method for setting an aspiration level, provided the search situation meets the following restrictive characteristics: The searcher receives positive payoff solely for picking the very highest value prospect, from a random sequence of prospects with an unknown distribution of values, without any backtracking to previously encountered prospects, without any search or courtship costs, and without any possibility of being rejected by the prospect. Different heuristic approaches become appropriate when these characteristics are changed, particularly when the payoff criterion is relaxed so that other choices are also rewarded to some degree.

We have investigated satisficing heuristics for mate search by simulating their performance in various settings (Miller and Todd, 1998; Todd and Miller, 1999), focusing on simple methods for setting the aspiration level. The goal was to find satisficing heuristics that would limit both the time needed to determine a good aspiration level and the average number of potential mates that had to be considered before one was found exceeding the aspiration level. By sampling a much smaller number of prospects initially, say a dozen, one can actually attain a higher expected mate value than the 37% rule delivers (although a somewhat lower chance of finding the very highest valued prospect) and a higher chance of picking a mate in the top 10% of the population (see Figure 2) while greatly lowering the search time required and the risk of picking a low-quality mate; moreover, people put in such a situation seem to take this into account in their searching behavior (see Dudey and Todd, in press; see also Seale and Rapoport, 1997, for related experimental results). However, this only works in the one-sided search setting of the Secretary Problem. When two-sided search is introduced, so that both sexes are searching for appropriate mates simultaneously, an aspiration level set near to one's own mate value can quickly lead to assortative mating in a population. A further class of simple heuristics can enable individuals to learn their own value or rank in the mating population on the basis of mating proposals and refusals (Todd and Miller, 1999). Additionally, these search rules can account for demographic data on patterns of mate choice: When an entire population of individuals searches for mates according to these rules, they get paired up over time at rates that mirror the distribution for age at first marriage observed in many cultures (Todd and Billari, in press).

6. Conclusion

The results presented in this section illustrate how a concept of social rationality that differs from traditional definitions of domain-independent rationality can be built. Socially rational agents can solve the adaptive challenges that face them in their interactions with conspecifics without amassing all available information and combining it optimally (as shown by the single-cue parental investment heuristics) and without calculating costs and benefits to guide search (as shown by the satisficing heuristics for mate search). They need not even follow the laws of propositional logic (as shown by the domain-specific cheater-detection reasoning results). Instead, simple rules that apply to specific situations can give social agents an adaptive – and, often, economic – advantage.

References

Axelrod, R. (1984). "The Evolution of Cooperation". Basic Books, New York.
Berg, J., Dickhaut, J.W., McCabe, K.A. (1995). "Trust, reciprocity, and social history". Games and Economic Behavior 10, 122–142.
Cosmides, L. (1989). "The logic of social exchange: Has natural selection shaped how humans reason?" Cognition 31, 187–276.
Davis, J.N., Todd, P.M. (1999). "Simple decision rules for parental investment". In: Gigerenzer, G., Todd, P.M., the ABC Research Group (Eds.), Simple Heuristics that Make Us Smart. Oxford University Press, New York, pp. 309–324.
Ferguson, T.S. (1989). "Who solved the secretary problem?" Statistical Sciences 4, 282–296.
Frey, B.S., Eichenberger, R. (1996). "Marriage paradoxes". Rationality and Society 8, 187–206.
Gigerenzer, G. (1996). "Rationality: Why social context matters". In: Baltes, P.B., Staudinger, U.M. (Eds.), Interactive Minds: Life-span Perspectives on the Social Foundation of Cognition. Cambridge University Press, Cambridge, UK, pp. 319–346.
Gigerenzer, G., Hug, K. (1992). "Domain-specific reasoning: Social contracts, cheating, and perspective change". Cognition 43, 127–171.
Griggs, R.A., Cox, J.R. (1982). "The elusive thematic-materials effect in Wason's selection task". British Journal of Psychology 73, 407–420.
Hamilton, W.D. (1964). "The genetic evolution of social behavior, Parts I, II". Journal of Theoretical Biology 7, 1–52.
Hertwig, R., Davis, J.N., Sulloway, F.J. (2002). "Parental investment: How an equity motive can produce inequality". Psychological Bulletin 128, 728–745.
Luce, R.D., Raiffa, H. (1957). "Games and Decision". Wiley, New York.
Miller, G.F., Todd, P.M. (1998). "Mate choice turns cognitive". Trends in Cognitive Sciences 2, 190–198.
Ortmann, A., Gigerenzer, G. (1997). " Reasoning in economics and psychology: Why social context matters". Journal of Institutional and Theoretical Economics 153, 700–710.
Rapoport, A., Tversky, A. (1970). "Choice behavior in an optional stopping task". Organizational Behavior and Human Performance 5, 105–120.
Rieskamp, J., Gigerenzer, G. (2002). "Heuristics for social interactions: How to generate trust and fairness". Manuscript submitted for publication.
Roth, A.E., Sotomayor, M. (1990). "Two-sided Matching: A Study in Game-theoretic Modeling and Analysis". Cambridge University Press, Cambridge, UK.
Seale, Darryl A., Rapoport, Amnon (1997). "Sequential decision making with relative ranks: An experimental investigation of the 'secretary problem'". Organizational Behavior and Human Decision Processes 69 (3), 221–236.

Schelling, T.C. (1960). "The Strategy of Conflict". Harvard University, Press Cambridge, MA.
Simon, H.A. (1955). "A behavioral model of rational choice". Quarterly Journal of Economics 69, 99–118.
Simon, H.A. (1990). "Invariants of human behavior". Annual Review of Psychology 41, 1–19.
Stigler, G.J. (1961). "The economics of information". Journal of Political Economy 69, 213–225.
Tetlock, P.E. (1983). "Accountability and complexity of thought". Journal of Personality and Social Psychology 45, 74–83.
Todd, P.M., Miller, G.F. (1999). "From pride and prejudice to persuasion: Satisficing in mate search". In: Gigerenzer, G., Todd, P.M., the ABC Research Group (Eds.), Simple Heuristics that Make Us Smart. Oxford University Press, New York, pp. 287–308.
Trivers, R.L. (1971). "The evolution of reciprocal altruism". Quarterly Review of Biology 46, 35–57.
Walster, E., Berscheid, E., Walster, G.W. (1973). "New directions in equity research". Journal of Personality and Social Psychology 25, 151–176.
Wason, P.C. (1966). "Reasoning". In: Foss, B.M. (Ed.), New Horizons in Psychology. Penguin, Harmondsworth, UK, pp. 135–151.

Chapter 111

PAYOFF SCALE EFFECTS AND RISK PREFERENCE UNDER REAL AND HYPOTHETICAL CONDITIONS

SUSAN K. LAURY and CHARLES A. HOLT

1. Introduction

Economists are primarily concerned with decisions that involve monetary consequences, and therefore, laboratory economics experiments almost always use financial incentives. The psychologist Sidney Siegel established the importance of using real (instead of hypothetical) payments. For example, Siegel and Goldstein (1959) report a "probability matching" experiment in which subjects had to predict which of two light bulbs would be illuminated in a sequence of trials. For at least 20 years, psychologists had conducted probability-matching experiments, concluding that subjects consistently violated rationality assumptions. However, when Siegel and Goldstein (1959) paid subjects a small reward for correct choices, optimal behavior was observed more than 90 percent of the time.

Of course, when more interesting tasks are used, incentives may not matter as much. For example, subjects may enjoy playing out choices among risky prospects, regardless of whether they are paid based on the outcome. If using real incentives does not matter, conducting experiments with hypothetical payments is an attractive, inexpensive alternative. There is an additional (frequently cited) motive for using hypothetical payments. If the naturally occurring decisions of interest involve substantial sums of money (for example, purchasing insurance against large losses), it is not feasible to pay experimental subjects comparable sums of hundreds or thousands of dollars. If "people often know how they would behave in actual situations of choice, and ... the subjects have no special reason to disguise their true preferences" (Kahneman and Tversky, 1979, p. 265) then it may be preferable to use high hypothetical payments over the low real payments typically used in the lab.

The effect of using hypothetical payments is not yet settled. Smith and Walker (1993) report that mean bidding behavior in auctions is little affected by the choice of payment method, but that noise is reduced when payments are real. In a follow-up paper, Tversky and Kahneman (1992) state that none of their conclusions are contradicted when real payoffs are used.

These are important procedural issues, and it is natural to use experiments to evaluate them. This chapter summarizes some recent evidence on the effects of payoffs on risk attitudes. In particular we compare choices under real and hypothetical incentives, and look at the effect of payoff scale (up to several hundred dollars) under both real and hypothetical conditions, for gains and losses.

Table 1
Menu of lottery choices

	Option A	Option B	Your choice
Decision 1	$2.00 with probability = 0.1 $1.60 with probability = 0.9	$3.85 with probability = 0.1 $0.10 with probability = 0.9	
Decision 2	$2.00 with probability = 0.2 $1.60 with probability = 0.8	$3.85 with probability = 0.2 $0.10 with probability = 0.8	
⋮	⋮	⋮	⋮
Decision 9	$2.00 with probability = 0.9 $1.60 with probability = 0.1	$3.85 with probability = 0.9 $0.10 with probability = 0.1	
Decision 10	$2.00 with probability = 1.0	$3.85 with probability = 1.0	

2. Incentive Effects for Choices Involving Gains

Holt and Laury (2001) examined the effects of payoff magnitudes in an experiment where people were asked to choose between matched pairs of safe and risky lotteries. These pairs were arranged in a menu of the type shown in Table 1. In all rows, the payoffs are $1.60 and $2.00 for Option A, the safe lottery, and $3.85 and $0.10 for the Option B, the risky lottery. The probability of the higher payoff in each pair is 0.1 in the top row, and then increases by 0.1 in each subsequent choice. The choice in Decision 10, listed in the bottom row, is between a sure $2.00 and a sure $3.85.

Earnings were determined on the basis of one decision, selected at random after all choices had been made. In total, 93 subjects made the choices in Table 1, followed by a hypothetical choice menu for payoffs scaled up by a factor of 20 ($40 or $32 for the safe option, and $77 or $2 for the risky option). After the hypothetical earnings were determined, these same subjects were given an identical payoff menu with a clear statement that all earnings would be paid in cash. (See Holt and Laury, 2001, for complete procedural details and instructions.)

Figure 1 shows the results, with the Decision (1 through 10) on the horizontal axis and the percentage of safe choices shown on the vertical axis. The dashed black line represents the risk neutral choice pattern: choose safe with probability 1.0 in Decisions 1–4, then choose risky (0% safe choices) for all remaining decisions. More than four safe choices indicate risk aversion, and fewer safe choices indicate risk preference.

The colored lines show actual choice frequencies in each of our treatments, where real payoffs are shown with thick lines and hypothetical payoffs with thin lines. The percentages for the low payoff trial, the yellow line, generally lie to the right of the risk neutral prediction, indicating some risk aversion even for low payoffs. Choices under scaled up hypothetical payoffs (see the thin red line), are quite close to the 1× real line. It became apparent to us, however, that subjects were *not* able to predict how risk averse they would be when actually faced with these choices. The thick red line shows

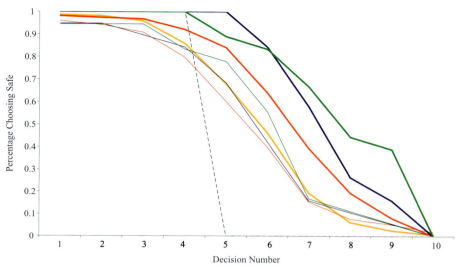

(1x, 20x, 50x, and 90x Payoff Scale)

Key: Real Payoffs (thick lines), Hypothetical Payoffs (thin lines), Risk Neutral Precition (thin, dashed line)

Figure 1. Percentage of safe choices under real and hypothetical conditions.

observed choices when these high payoffs were actually paid; it lies significantly to the right, indicating a greater degree of risk aversion.

We ran an additional 19 subjects through the same sequence, but with hypothetical and real payoffs scaled up by a factor of 50 (blue lines), and another group of 18 had payoffs scaled up by 90 (green lines). In the 90× payoff treatment, the safe lottery earned $180 or $144, and the risky lottery earned $346.50 or $9. It is clear from the thin lines in Figure 1, scaling up of hypothetical payoffs had little effect on choice frequencies. In contrast, the thick lines show that each successive increase in real payoffs resulted in higher risk aversion. In the 90× real condition, one-third of the subjects chose the safe option in Decisions 1–9, only switching on Decision 10 where the highest payoff was a certainty. The safe option in this condition ensured earnings of at least $144; this minimum was sufficiently attractive that a large fraction of people did not take *any* risk of receiving the low ($9) payoff from the risky lottery. A similar tendency to observe more risk aversion as payoffs are scaled up was reported by Binswanger (1980), who ran experiments with farmers in rural Bangladesh with some payoffs equivalent to the average monthly income.

These results indicate the danger of comparing low real payoffs with high hypothetical payoffs, and concluding that payoff effects may not be present (as has been done in some widely cited papers). They also suggest that high hypothetical payments may not yield good predictions of behavior under high real payoffs. The next section considers these issues when lottery choices involve losses.

3. Choices in the Loss Domain, and the Reflection Effect

In a second paper, Laury and Holt (2002) consider the effect of reflecting all payoffs around zero to obtain lotteries over losses. The choice menu was like that shown in Table 1, with two exceptions. The top row involved a sure thing (a probability of 0 for the higher payoff); as before, the probability of the high payoff increased by 0.1 in each successive row, so the probability of the high payoff was 0.9 in Decision 10. Also, the choices in the low-payoff gain treatment were twice the level shown in Table 1 ($4 or $3.20 for the safe option and $7.70 or $0.20 for the risky option). When these numbers were reflected, the payoffs were −$4 or −$3.20 for the safe option and −$7.70 or −$0.20 for the risky option. The structure of the menu was such that a risk-neutral person would choose exactly 5 safe choices, and a risk-averse person would choose more safe choices, whether the payoffs were in terms of gains or losses.

Each subject completed the menu of lottery choices for both gains and losses. Typically when losses are possible, subjects are given an initial stake by the experimenter. In these experiments, subjects first participated in another decision-making experiment during which they built up their initial stake. We hoped to minimize any "found money" effects by having subjects earn this money. After the initial experiment, subjects were given the menu of lottery choices, first for gains (losses), and then for losses (gains). The order in which gains and losses were presented was varied between sessions. Results from the first lottery choice treatment were not revealed until choices in the second treatment had been made. We separated the two lottery choice experiments by a neutral matching pennies experiment. See Laury and Holt (2002) for a complete description of the procedures.

Figure 2 shows the relationship between an individual's choices in the gain and loss conditions in our hypothetical payoff sessions (81 subjects). The blue bar in the back right corner of the graph (labeled "Reflection") represents subjects who made choices consistent with risk aversion in the lottery over gains, and risk preference in the lottery over losses. This choice pattern is the well known "reflection effect," which is one component of Prospect Theory, as described by Kahneman and Tversky (1979) and Tversky and Kahneman (1992). Although the rate of reflection observed in our experiment (26 percent) is lower than that obtained in Kahneman and Tversky's pair-wise lotteries (with hypothetical payments), this is the modal choice pattern in these sessions. Figure 3 presents the same information when payoffs are real (76 subjects). The difference is dramatic. The rate of reflection (13 percent) is half that observed when hypothetical payments are used. Moreover, the modal choice pattern involves risk aversion under both gains and losses (29 percent). The rate of reflection is even lower when payoffs (real and hypothetical) are increased by a factor of 15 (to 30 times the levels shown in Table 1; earnings from the initial experiment were similarly increased). Only about

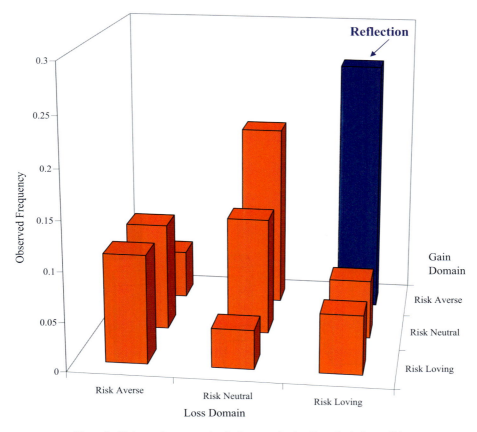

Figure 2. Risk aversion categories for losses and gains (hypothetical payoffs).

19 percent of subjects reflect under high hypothetical payoffs, compared with 9 percent of subjects who faced high real payoffs.

Considering the average number of safe choices made under gains and losses, subjects are less risk averse under losses, which is consistent with Prospect Theory's directional prediction. However, people tend to be risk averse for gains and approximately risk neutral for losses (not risk preferring for losses as Prospect Theory predicts), regardless of whether incentives are real or hypothetical, low or high.

Harbaugh, Krause, and Vesterlund (2001) similarly find that support for reflection depends on how the choice problem is presented. Specifically, they report that risk attitudes are consistent with Prospect Theory when subjects price gambles, but not when they choose between the gamble and its expected value. Others have found evidence of reflection when cash payments are used (Myagkov and Plott, 1997; Camerer, 1989; Battalio, Kagel, and Jiranyakul, 1990). However, taken together, these studies suggest

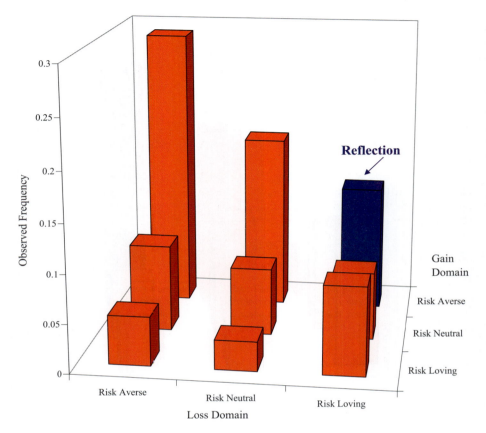

Figure 3. Risk aversion categories for losses and gains (real payoffs).

that the degree of observed reflection may be context-specific (for example, whether real payments are used, how the choice problem is presented, market context, and initial stake in the loss treatment).

4. Conclusion

The use of monetary incentives may not affect behavior much in some contexts, or it may simply reduce the dispersion of data around some theoretical prediction. But our experiments indicate that incentive effects may be large and systematic in other contexts. In the absence of a widely accepted theory of when incentives matter, it is probably not advisable to derive scientific conclusions from laboratory studies that do not provide clear, salient motivation.

While hypothetical choice studies are not common in economics, and are rarely published in the top journals, this is not the case in other disciplines. Al Roth (1995, p. 86) comments that "the question of actual versus hypothetical choices has become one of the fault lines that have come to distinguish experiments published in the economics journals from those published in psychology journals." In a recent paper, Hertwig and Ortmann (2001) reviewed all papers published in the *Journal of Behavioral Decision Making* for a recent 10-year period. In 186 experimental studies, financial incentives were only used in 26% of those. In a second survey of about 100 papers on Bayesian inference tasks in a variety of psychology journals, only about 2–3 papers used financial incentives.

The evidence surveyed here shows that relying on hypothetical payments can yield misleading results in some circumstances. Moreover, social scientists do not have a good feel for when to believe hypothetical choice patterns. Given this, we believe that performance-based incentives should be used in economics experiments, and results motivated by hypothetical incentives should be interpreted with caution.

References

Battalio, R.C., Kagel, J.H., Jiranyakul, Komain (1990). "Testing between alternative models of choice under uncertainty: Some initial results". Journal of Risk and Uncertainty 3 (1), 25–50.

Binswanger, H.P. (1980). "Attitude toward risk: Experimental measurement in rural India". American Journal of Agricultural Economics 62, 395–407.

Camerer, C.F. (1989). "An experimental test of several generalized utility theories". Journal of Risk and Uncertainty 2, 61–104.

Harbaugh, W., Krause, K., Vesterlund, L. (2001). "Prospect theory in choice and pricing tasks". Working paper 268, University of Pittsburgh, Department of Economics.

Hertwig, R., Ortmann, A. (2001). "Experimental practices in economics: A challenge for psychologists?" Behavioral and Brain Sciences 24 (4), 383–451.

Holt, C.A., Laury, S.K. (2001). "Risk aversion and incentive effects". Working paper, Department of Economics, University of Virginia.

Kahneman, D., Tversky, A. (1979). "Prospect theory: An analysis of choice under risk". Econometrica 47 (2), 263–291.

Laury, S.K., Holt, C.A. (2002). "Further reflections on prospect theory". Working paper, Department of Economics, Georgia State University.

Myagkov, M., Plott, C.R. (1997). "Exchange economies and loss exposure: Experiments exploring prospect theory and competitive equilibria in market environments". American Economic Review 87 (5), 801–828.

Roth, A.E. (1995). "Introduction to experimental economics". In: Kagel, J., Roth, A. (Eds.), Handbook of Experimental Economics. Princeton University Press, Princeton.

Siegel, S., Goldstein, D.A. (1959). "Decision making behavior in a two-choice uncertain outcome situation". Journal of Experimental Psychology 57, 37–42.

Smith, V.L., Walker, J.M. (1993). "Monetary rewards and decision costs in experimental economics". Economic Inquiry 31 (2), 245–261.

Tversky, A., Kahneman, D. (1992). "Advances in prospect theory: Cumulative representation of uncertainty". Journal of Risk and Uncertainty 5, 297–323.

Chapter 112

REWARDS AND BEHAVIOR IN FIRST PRICE AUCTIONS

VERNON L. SMITH

University of Arizona

JAMES M. WALKER

Indiana University

We examine the impact on subjects' behavior of substantial increases in the size of expected laboratory payoffs and experience in the context of a first price auction. Bidding behavior in this institution has been investigated by experimental economists for over 20 years. Virtually all studies reveal behavior in which: (1) bidding behavior across subjects is heterogeneous; and (2) subjects consistently bid above the level predicted for risk-neutral agents, behavior which is consistent with "as if risk averse."

1. The First Price Auction

The trading rules for the first price auction can be summarized as follows. A single object is offered in perfectly inelastic supply to $N > 2$ bidders. Each bidder submits a single bid for the commodity with the understanding that the commodity will be awarded to the highest bidder at a price equal to the highest bid.

In Nash–Harsanyi incomplete information models of the first price auction as in Cox, Smith, and Walker (1988) each bidder $i = 1, 2, \ldots, N$ is characterized by an M tuple $(v_i(t), \delta_i)$, where $v_i(t) \in [0, \bar{v}]$ is the value of the auctioned item to i in auction $t = 1, 2, \ldots, T$, and $\delta_i \in \Delta$ is an $M - 1$ tuple of parameters defining the characteristics of bidder i. The values $v_i(t)$ are realizations drawn with replacement from the rectangular density $f(\theta) = 1/\bar{v}$, and the probability density function for the δ_i in the population of bidders is assumed to be $\Phi(\delta)$, integrable on the convex set Δ. The utility of outcome plus monetary reward to i is $u[(\mu_i + \lambda)\pi_i(t), \delta_i]$. $\pi_i(t)$ is the outcome if i wins auction t. (μ_i, λ) are defined as in Smith and Walker (1993). $\mu_i > 0$, is a scalar characteristic of the subject which measures the monetary equivalent of the subjective value of outcome π_i on the assumption that there is self-satisfaction, weak or strong, in achieving any outcome π_i. This parameter is assumed to be additive with the reward scalar, $\lambda \geq 0$, and allows the model to account for observed systematic behavior when the salient exogenous reward is $\lambda = 0$. The utility of outcome is $u_i = u(\mu_i \pi_i(t), \delta_i)$. If i's bid in auction t is $b_i(t) \in [0, \bar{v}]$, then:

$$\pi_i(t) = v_i(t) - b_i(t). \tag{1}$$

If i believes that each of his/her rivals will bid according to the strictly increasing differentiable bid function, $b(v(t), \delta)$, with inverse $v(b(t), \delta)$, then the probability that any one rival will bid less than (or equal to) $b_i(t)$ is:

$$J(b_i(t)) = \Delta_0 v(b_i(t), \delta) f(\theta) \, d\theta \, d\Phi(\delta) = \Delta F[v(b_i(t)), \delta] \, d\Phi(\delta). \quad (2)$$

Therefore, the probability that a bid $b_i(t)$ will win is given by the probability that all $N - 1$ rivals will bid less than $b_i(t)$,

$$G[b_i(t) \mid N] = [J(b_i(t))]^{N-1}. \quad (3)$$

Then expected utility as modeled by the experimenter/theorist is

$$U(b_i(t) \mid v_i(t), \delta_i) = u[(\mu_i + \lambda)(v_i(t) - b_i(t)), \delta_i] G[b_i(t) \mid N]. \quad (4)$$

If u is log-concave in the reward (u_1/u is strictly decreasing in its first argument), then it can be shown (see Cox, Smith, and Walker, 1988, pp. 64–65) that there exists a unique $b_i^*(t) = b(v_i(t), \delta_i) = \arg\max U(b_i(t) \mid v_i(t), \delta_i)$, and therefore that $b(v_i(t), \delta_i)$ is the equilibrium bid function for the auction with N bidders. It can also be shown that if δ^N, δ^A and δ^P are characteristic vectors for bidders that are respectively risk neutral, risk averse and risk preferring so that u is respectively linear, strictly concave and strictly convex in its first argument, then $b(v_i(t), \delta^A) > b(v_i(t), \delta^N) > b(v_i(t), \delta^P)$.

A class of special cases of the log-concave model is the constant relative risk averse model (CRRAM), first reported in Cox, Roberson, and Smith (1982). In this case δ_i is the scalar r_i, where $u[(\mu_i + \lambda)\pi_i(t), \delta_i] = [(\mu_i + \lambda)\pi_i(t)]^{r_i}$. The equilibrium bid function is now:

$$b_i^*(t) = \begin{cases} \frac{N-1}{N-1+r_i} v_i(t), & \text{if } v_i(t) \leq \frac{N-1+r_i}{N} \bar{v}, \ 0 < r_i \leq 1, \\ B(v_i(t), r_i), & \text{if } v_i(t) > \frac{N-1+r_i}{N} \bar{v}, \ 0 < r_i < 1, \end{cases} \quad (5)$$

where $B(v_i(t), r_i)$ is non-linear with no closed form. By numerical integration $B(v_i(t), r_i)$ can be computed (see Rassenti, Smith, and Van Boening, 1992) for given values of r_i and estimates of $\Phi(r)$. When $r_i = 1$ (5) reduces to the Vickrey risk neutral bid function: $b_i^*(t) = ((N-1)/N))v_i(t) V - v_i(t) \in [0, \bar{v}]$.

2. The Experimental Environment

The complete instructions and detailed experimental procedures can be found in Cox, Smith, and Walker (1985, 1988). Key characteristics of the experiments can be summarized as follows. Each subject was informed that for any winning bid the bidder would receive a profit equal to his or her "resale value" minus the bid. Resale values were announced privately for each auction in advance of bids for that auction. Each bidder was informed that in each auction his or her resale value (and that of each his/her rivals) would be: (a) drawn by the computer from a finite set contained in the interval $(0, \bar{v})$;

and (b) drawn randomly (with replacement), with each value having an equal probability of being chosen. Subjects were informed there would be numerous auctions but did not know the actual number.

The subjects in these experiments were informed that they were bidding against 3 computerized rivals ($N = 4$). They were informed that each rival would bid a fixed proportion of their value R_i, where $R_i \leqslant .75$. Implicitly, the subjects were informed that their rivals were computerized heterogeneous Nash bidders. In previous controlled comparisons using the above procedures, no significant difference was found in the estimated bid functions of individuals facing human rivals and humans facing computerized rivals in Walker, Smith, and Cox (1987).

The experiments reported here focus on two treatment variables: experience and the conversion rate of computer dollars into cash dollars. The level of subject experience was varied with $E = 0, 1, 2, 3$ corresponding to no experience, once, twice and thrice experienced. Experience levels were varied by running subjects in multiple auction series (2 or 4). A series consisted of 20 or 25 auctions. The payoff conversion rate of experimental "dollars" into money was varied across series with $\lambda = 0, 1, 5, 10$ and 20. For example, one specific four series experiment consisted of 100 auctions with $\lambda = 20$, 0, 1, 10 respectively across series. In all experiments, $\bar{v}- = \$10.00$. (If all bidders were risk neutral, $r_i = 1$, $\forall i$, expected earnings per subject would be $\$0.50$ per auction or $\$12.50$ for 25 auctions when $\lambda = 1$, $\$62.50$ when $\lambda = 5$, $\$125$ when $\lambda = 10$, and $\$250$ when $\lambda = 20$.) An experiment with four series of 25 auctions took two to three hours to complete. Instructions were used to motivate subjects in the no payoff condition. Specifically, subjects were told that "it would be wise to bid seriously since the practice could be helpful in later experiments where you will earn money." As demonstrated in Cox, Smith, and Walker (1988), the multiplicative payoff treatment has three related effects. Increasing λ provides a scale increase in payoffs, increases the curvature of the expected "utility" functions, and addresses the "flat maximum" property discussed by Harrison (1989).

3. Behavior

The summary results reported below are based on behavior in 1020 auctions from seventeen individual experiments, with sixty-five distinct subjects. As in (5) above, and using OLS, the following linear bid function is estimated for each subject: $b_i(t) = \alpha_i + \beta_i(v_i(t)) + \varepsilon_i(t)$, $t = 1, 2, \ldots, 20$ or 25. The value of β_i estimated for each subject's bid equation, is used as that subject's measure of risk aversion. The standard error (RMSE) of individual bid deviations from the estimated bid function provides a measure of decision error.

For illustrative purposes, Figure 1 shows the bidding behavior of one of our subjects who participated in an experiment with 4 auction series. In this particular experiment, series 1 computer dollar payoffs were multiplied by a factor of 5, series 2 by a factor of 0, series 3 by a factor of 10, and series 4 by a factor of 1. Moves between series

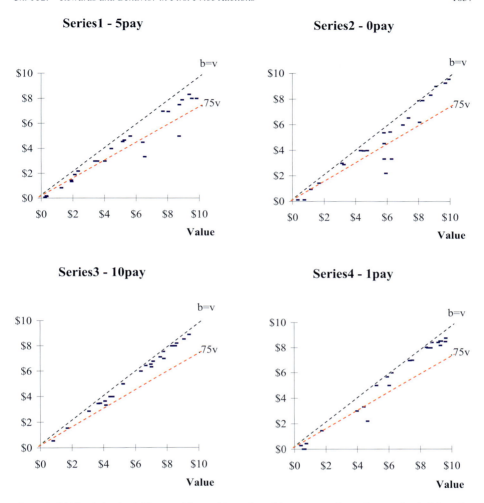

Figure 1. Bidding behavior is illustrated for a subject selected from an experiment that consisted of 4 auction series. Plotted are bids as a function of resale value. The ".75v" line depicts the theoretical bid function for a risk neutral bidder. In this particular series, dollar payoffs from winning the auction are multiplied by factors of 5, 0, 10, and 1, respectively. This subject was selected to illustrate the overall tendencies observed. Bids as a function of value tended to become "tighter" with higher payoff levels and with experience. That is, decision error around the estimated bid function decreased with higher payoff levels and with experience.

are interpreted as an increase in experience, $E = 0, 1, 2, 3$. As can be seen, bids as a function of value systematically follow a linear relationship and lie above the bid function for a risk-neutral agent ($.75v$). Further, beginning with the upper left hand panel of Figure 1, and moving across series, one can see the effect on bidding behavior as payoff levels are changed and experience increases. More specifically, the data show

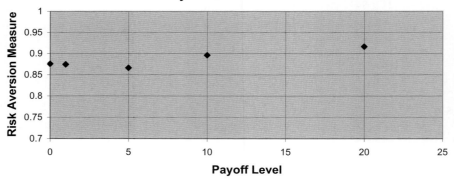

Figure 2. Summary based on 1020 first price auction experiments, from 17 experimental sessions using 65 distinct subjects. Each subject faced 3 computerized competitors. Subjects participated in 2 or 4 sequential series of 20 or 25 auctions, yielding up to 4 different "levels of experience," for a given subject. Further, cash payoffs for a series were varied by multiplying dollar payoffs by a factor of 0, 5, 10, or 20. A linear regression was estimated for each subject, regressing bids against resale value. The slope coefficient from this regression can be interpreted as a "measure of risk aversion." The root mean square error of deviations from the estimated regression line can be interpreted as "decision error." Pooling data across subjects and controlling for level of experience, this figure shows the relationship between payoff level and decision error (risk aversion). The top chart plots the mean decision error as a function of payoff level. The bottom chart plots the mean measure of risk aversion. The decline in decision error with increase in payoff levels was statistically significant, but the increase in the measure of risk aversion was not, as reported in Smith and Walker (1993).

the tendency for the bidding relationship to become "tighter" with increases in payoff levels and experience; RMSE falls.

Pooling across subjects and series, we have 154 distinct measures of risk aversion and decision error. These measures are regressed against level of experience, E (modeled as a dummy variable) and the payoff level, λ (modeled as a continuous variable). The results from this analysis are summarized in Figures 2 and 3. As predicted by the decision cost model of Smith and Walker (1993), the regression for decision error shows a

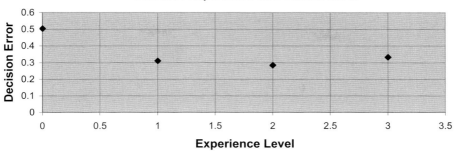

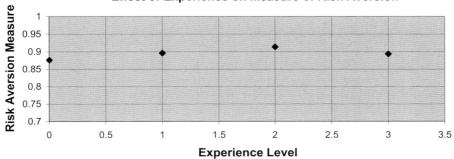

Figure 3. See Figure 2 for a summary description. Pooling data across subjects and controlling for level of payoff, this figure shows the relationship between level of experience and decision error (risk aversion). Experience was modeled using dummy variables for each level of experience, with the zero payoff condition as the base condition. The top chart plots the mean decision error as a function of experience. The bottom chart plots the mean measure of risk aversion. The decline in decision error, relative to the base condition, with increase in experience levels was statistically significant for all levels of experience. The increase in the measure of risk aversion was not generally significant, as reported in Smith and Walker (1993).

significant decline in bid variability with payoff level and with experience. In general, the regressions for risk aversion show that there is some small insignificant tendency for individuals to bid higher (more risk averse) as payoff level is increased after correcting for the effect of experience. Since increases in λ create an increase in the opportunity cost of deviations from the optimal bid, these results contradict Harrison's (1989) hypothesis that subjects bid as if risk averse because of low opportunity cost, and that rejection of the risk neutral model is therefore not warranted. Furthermore, we do not observe diffuse random bidding when $\lambda = 0$, as implied by Harrison's argument; no standard model can account for decision behavior when $\lambda = 0$.

These decision error results are consistent with the previous experiments surveyed in Smith and Walker (1993). Further, the results are consistent with an effort theory of decision making in which decision error decreases with increases in payoffs (and expected foregone payoffs from non-optimal bidding). They are also consistent with the error-incentive model and data reported by Berg and Dickhaut (1990) for preference reversal phenomena.

References

Berg, Joyce E., Dickhaut, John W. (1990). "Preference reversals: Incentives do matter". Working paper, University of Chicago.

Cox, James C., Roberson, Bruce, Smith, Vernon L. (1982). "Theory and behavior of single object auctions". In: Smith, V.L. (Ed.), Research in Experimental Economics, vol. 2. JAI Press, Greenwich, CT, pp. 1–43.

Cox, James C., Smith, Vernon L., Walker, James M. (1985). "Expected revenue in discriminative and uniform price sealed bid auctions". In: Smith, V.L. (Ed.), Research in Experimental Economics, vol. 3. JAI Press, Greenwich, CT, pp. 183–232.

Cox, James C., Smith, Vernon L., Walker, James M. (1988). "Theory and individual behavior in first price auctions". Journal of Risk and Uncertainty, 63–99.

Harrison, Glenn (1989). "Theory and misbehavior in first price auctions". American Economic Review, 749–762.

Rassenti, Stephen J., Smith, Vernon L., Van Boening, Mark (1992). "Numerical estimation of first price equilibrium bid functions". Working paper, University of Arizona.

Smith, Vernon L., Walker, James M. (1993). "Monetary rewards and decision costs". Economic Inquiry, 245–261.

Walker, James M., Smith, Vernon L., Cox, James C. (1987). "Bidding behavior in first price sealed bid auctions, use of computerized competitors". Economics Letters 23, 239–244.

Chapter 113

MEN, WOMEN AND RISK AVERSION: EXPERIMENTAL EVIDENCE

CATHERINE C. ECKEL

School of Economic, Political and Policy Sciences, University of Texas at Dallas, Richardson, TX 765080, USA
e-mail: eckelc@utdallas.edu

PHILIP J. GROSSMAN

Department of Economics, Saint Cloud State University, St. Cloud, MN 56301, USA

This paper reviews the results from experimental measures of risk aversion for evidence of systematic differences in the behavior of men and women. In most studies, women are found to be more averse to risk than men. Studies with contextual frames show less consistent results.

Whether men and women systematically differ in their responses to risk is an important economic question. If women are more sensitive to risk than men, this will be reflected in all aspects of their decision making, including choice of profession (and so earnings), investment decisions, and what products to buy. Several recent studies investigate this difference directly.

Most experiments that investigate preferences over risky choices deal with the question of whether people make choices that are consistent with expected utility maximization. (See, for example, Starmer, 2000.) This contribution focuses instead on the narrower issue of differences between women and men in attitudes towards risk in the context of experiments involving valuation of gambles and/or choices among gambles.

By way of background, numerous studies in sociology and psychology support the hypothesis that women and men respond to risk differently. Studies have found sex differences in: the perception of risk associated with alcohol and drug use (Spigner, Hawkins, and Loren, 1993); the perception of the catastrophic potential of nuclear war, technology, radioactive waste, industrial hazards, and environmental degradation (Silverman and Kumka, 1987; Cutter, Tiefenbacher, and Solecki, 1992; MacGregor et al., 1994; McStay and Dunlap, 1983; Stallen and Tomas, 1988; Flynn, Slovic, and Mertz, 1994); and the perceived risk associated with various recreational and social activities (Boverie, Scheuffele, and Raymond, 1995). Evidence also indicates that women are less likely than men to engage in risky behavior such as illicit drug use and criminal activities.[1] However, it is important to note that risk attitudes tend to

---

[1] See, for example, Cooperstock and Parnell (1982), Daly and Wilson (1988), Gottfredson and Hirschi (1990), Kandel and Logan (1984), and Wilson and Herrnstein (1985).

vary over environments, with low levels of correlation across tasks, measures, and context.[2]

Laboratory tests of differences in behavior under risk are relatively recent. Studies have employed a variety of instruments, including both abstract gambling experiments and experiments involving risky decisions within contextual environments such as investment and insurance. Must have significant financial stakes. Our discussion below focuses on experiments (with hypothetical or real stakes) that measure differences between men and women in risk attitudes using either choices among financially risky alternatives, or valuations of risky payoffs.[3] We divide the following discussion into abstract gamble experiments and experiments with context, incorporating studies of both risk aversion and (weak) ambiguity aversion.

1. Abstract Gamble Experiments

In general, most results from abstract gamble experiments indicate that women are more risk averse than men. Levin, Snyder, and Chapman (1988) and Hartog, Ferrer-i-Carbonell, and Jonker (2002) present their subjects with hypothetical gambles. Brinig (1995) conducts experiments with low-stake gambles (candy). Schubert et al. (1999), Moore and Eckel (2003), Holt and Laury (2002), Eckel and Grossman (2002, 2008), and Harbaugh, Krause, and Vesterlund (2002) incorporate gambles with salient stakes. The gambles in Levin, Snyder, and Chapman (1988), Hartog, Ferrer-i-Carbonell, and Jonker (2002), Brinig (1995), Holt and Laury (2002), and Eckel and Grossman (2002, 2008) all fall in the gain domain; Schubert et al. (1999), Moore and Eckel (2003), and Harbaugh, Krause, and Vesterlund (2002) have gambles in both the gain and the loss domain. See Table 1 for a summary of results.

Levin, Snyder, and Chapman (1988) asked subjects (110 college students) to indicate whether or not they were willing to take each of 18 different gambles. The gambles varied in initial investment, amount to be won, level of probability, and gain/loss framing. They used, as their primary dependent variable, the proportion of gambles a subject was willing to play. They report a significant difference in the mean proportion of "yes" responses for men and women. Consistent with other evidence, both men and women were more willing to accept gambles the greater was the amount spent on gambling during the past year. Finally, the Levin, Snyder, and Chapman (1988) study finds that framing significantly affects men's choices, but not women's.

---

[2] See Slovic (1964) for an early study that makes this point, and Weber, Blais, and Betz (2002) for a recent study which develops and tests survey measures of risk attitudes across environments.

[3] Note we do not address the issue of risk perception, but rather focus on behavioral measures of risk aversion. A person may be more risk averse because he perceives that a particular situation is "riskier," or because he prefers less risk given a level of perceived risk. See Blais and Weber (2001) for a discussion of gender differences in risk perceptions across domains.

Table 1
Summary table of findings of sex differences in risk behavior

Experimental studies	Significantly more risk averse sex[a]			
	Abstract environment		Contextual environment	
	Gain domain	Loss domain	Gain domain	Loss domain
Brinig	Female	NA	NA	NA
Eckel and Grossman (2008)	Female	NA	Female	NA
Harbaugh, Krause, Vesterlund	Neither	Neither	NA	NA
Gysler, Brown Kruse, Schubert	NA	NA	Neither	NA
Harrison et al.	Neither	NA	NA	NA
Holt and Laury – low payoff	Female	NA	NA	NA
Holt and Laury – high payoff	Neither	NA	NA	NA
Kruse and Thompson	NA	NA	NA	Neither
Levy, Elron, and Cohen	NA	NA	Female	NA
Levin, Snyder, and Chapman	Female	Female	NA	NA
Moore and Eckel	Neither	Male	Female	Neither
Powell and Ansic	NA	NA	Female	Female
Schubert et al. (1999)	Female	Male	Neither	Neither
Schubert et al. (2000)	NA	NA	Neither	Neither
Field Studies			Gambling	Investment
Jianakoplos and Bernasek			NA	Female
Johnson and Powell			Female	NA
Sundén and Surette			NA	Female

[a]Significant at the 10 percent level or higher.

In three separate surveys, Hartog, Ferrer-i-Carbonell, and Jonker (2002) elicit hypothetical willingness to pay for a series of high-stakes lotteries. The number of respondents to the surveys is large: 2011, 1599, and 17097 persons. From the answers, they estimate the risk aversion parameter of a utility function for each respondent. This parameter is then regressed on a number of individual characteristics. In all three studies, they find a significant (and substantial) coefficient on sex, with women's estimated parameter 10 to 30 percent larger than men's.

Brinig gave her subjects (300 volunteers from an elementary school, a high school, and a center for legal and graduate education) a choice of one of three gambles, all of which consisted of drawing a winning ball from one of three urns. One urn provided a 90 percent chance of winning a "very small" prize; a second urn provided a 20 percent chance of winning a "slightly larger" prize, and a third urn provided a 5 percent chance of winning a "very large" prize (in all three cases, the prize to be won consisted of candy). Although Brinig finds no evidence of a sex difference in choice, when sex is interacted with age, it becomes a significant predictor of risk-taking behavior. Males exhibit a greater preference for risk from the onset of adolescence to approximately the mid-forties. In her study, the difference in risk preferences reached its peak at about age 30. As Brinig notes, this finding is "consistent with the sociobiologists' hypothesis that men are relatively more risk-loving during the period in which they are trying to attract mates; while women tend to be more risk-averse during their child-bearing years."

The Harbaugh, Krause, and Vesterlund (2002) study also considers both sex and age differences in risk aversion. They present subjects (234 total participants including children, teenagers, college students, and adults) with 14 different choices between a certain outcome and a lottery. Their procedure is designed to be especially user-friendly for children, and uses images of stacks of coins compared to spinners with colored areas representing different probabilities. Potential earnings vary directly with age. One of the 14 choices is selected at random to determine a subject's earnings. Seven of the choices are in the gain domain and seven were in the loss domain. To measure risk aversion, sets of three choices are presented that contain the same gamble, but the certainty option is varied to be less than, equal to, or more than the gamble's expected value. Contrary to Brinig, Harbaugh, Krause, and Vesterlund (2002) find neither consistent nor significant evidence of a sex difference in risk aversion. The sex variable, either by itself or interacted with age, is consistently insignificant.

Subjects in the Schubert et al. (1999) study (73 college students) are presented with four choices between certain payoffs and risky lotteries. Like Hartog, Ferrer-i-Carbonell, and Jonker (2002), Schubert et al. (1999) elicits certainty equivalents for each of four lotteries. However, she uses a Becker–Degroot–Marshcak incentive-compatible procedure. This procedure has come to be a standard for eliciting preferences, though its difficulty may confuse subjects (e.g., see Kachelmeier and Shehata, 1992; Plott and Zeiler, 2002). In addition, this procedure has been criticized by Harrison (1992) and Harrison and Rutstrom (2008) because of distortions introduced by the low cost of making mistakes in valuing gambles, especially those with a low probability of paying off.

Two of the lotteries are presented as potential gains from an initial endowment, while the other two lotteries are presented as potential losses from an initial endowment. Consistent with the other abstract gamble studies, Schubert et al. (1999) find women more risk averse in the gain-domain frame, though only marginally so (the regression coefficient for the female dummy variable is negative and significant at the 10 percent level). For the loss-domain gambles, however, this result is reversed; women are significantly more risk-prone than men (the regression coefficient for the female dummy variable is negative and significant at the 5 percent level).

Schubert et al. (1999) also elicit subjects' (73 college students) certainty equivalents for a series of lotteries and frame the lotteries as both gains and losses. Moore and Eckel (2003) introduce an added complexity by incorporating into the lotteries "weak ambiguity" in the level of risk, the payoff, and both the level of risk and payoff.[4] A given lottery

---

[4] Weak ambiguity consists of giving subjects a range of probabilities or payoffs instead of a known probability or payoff. For example, instead of a 10 percent probability of winning $10, subjects might be presented with a 5–15 percent chance of winning $10, or a 10 percent chance of winning $0–$20. These gambles are just compound lotteries.

Table 2
Summary table of findings of sex differences in ambiguity aversion

Experimental studies	Ambiguity	Significantly more ambiguity averse sex[a]			
		Abstract environment		Contextual environment	
		Gain domain	Loss domain	Gain domain	Loss domain
Moore and Eckel	In probability	Neither	Male	Female	Neither
	In payoff	Neither	Male	Female	Neither
	In both	Neither	Neither	Female	Male
Schubert et al. (2000)	Weak	NA	NA	Female	Neither
	Strong	NA	NA	Female	Male

[a]Significant at the 10 percent level or higher.

might encompass a known risk and a known payoff; ambiguous risk and known payoff; known risk and ambiguous payoff; ambiguous risk and payoff. Moore and Eckel (2003) report regression results that indicate no significant sex difference in aversion to risk and/or ambiguity in the gain-domain gambles. However, consistent with Schubert et al. (1999), they report that women subjects are significantly more risk prone than men for the loss-domain gambles. Women are also more ambiguity seeking than men for gambles involving losses. See Table 2 and the discussion below for further ambiguity results.

Holt and Laury (2002) ask their subjects (212 college students) to make ten choices between paired lotteries (i.e., paired in terms of the probabilities of two possible outcomes occurring). For the low-risk lottery the potential payoffs differ only slightly; for the higher-risk lottery the potential payoffs differ more widely. A subject's degree of risk aversion was inferred from the point at which he switched from preferring the low-risk lottery to preferring the high-risk lottery. Finally, to test if a subject's level of risk aversion changed as the lottery stakes increased, subjects made choices for both low-payoff and high-payoff paired lottery treatments.[5] Holt and Laury (2002) report mixed results regarding a sex difference in risk aversion. Considering only the low-payoff decisions, Holt and Laury (2002) find that women are slightly, but significantly, more risk averse than men. When considering the high-payoff decisions, however, Holt and Laury (2002) find no sex difference. Faced with the higher potential payoffs, men's relative taste for risk disappears. Harrison et al. (2005) replicate their finding correcting for order effects and find no significant sex difference.

Eckel and Grossman (2002) present subjects (148 college students) with five gambles and ask them to choose which of the five they wish to play. All decisions are framed as simple gambles with two alternative, equally probable, payoffs. The gambles include

---

[5] To ensure that the earnings from the low-payoff lottery treatment (for which subjects first made decisions) did not bias the decisions in the high-payoff lottery treatment, subjects had to agree to forgo their earnings from the low-payoff lottery to be permitted to participate in the high-payoff lottery.

one sure thing with the remaining four increasing (linearly) in expected payoff and risk (measured by the standard deviation of expected payoff). Their design includes a baseline Abstract Gamble with losses and a No-Loss treatment: in the treatment with losses, subjects are paid $6 for completing a survey, and the $6 is then subject to loss; in the No-Loss treatment all payoffs are increased by $6 so that the lowest possible payoff is zero.

Eckel and Grossman (2002) report that for both environments there is a significant sex difference in risk aversion. The mean choice by men exceeds the mean choice by women: men's overall mean gamble choice was 3.76 versus 3.14 for women in the abstract frame with losses; scaling up the payoff produces mean gamble choices of 3.63 and 2.95. A means test rejects the null hypothesis of no differences in mean gamble choice by sex for the combined data ($t = 3.90$, p-value < 0.001). They find no significant treatment effects; men are significantly more risk prone than women in both treatments (Abstract $t = 3.32$, p-value < 0.001, and No-Loss $t = 1.94$, p-value < 0.03). Ordered Probit regression analysis confirmed these results.[6]

2. Contextual Environment Experiments

While the evidence from abstract gamble experiments suggests greater risk aversion by women, the evidence from experiments with a contextual environment is less conclusive. This heterogeneity in results is consistent with results from psychology, which tend to show differences in risk attitudes across environments for a given subject (Weber, Blais, and Betz, 2002). Moore and Eckel (2003), Eckel and Grossman (2002, 2008), Powell and Ansic (1997), and Levy, Elron, and Cohen (1999) offer results suggestive of differential attitudes towards risk. Gysler, Kruse, and Schubert (2002) report results suggesting a complex relationship between financial risk and gender. Schubert et al. (1999) report results indicating no difference in risk attitudes, as do Kruse and Thompson (2003).

In addition to their abstract gamble treatments, Schubert et al. (1999), Moore and Eckel (2003), and Eckel and Grossman (2002, 2008) conducted contextual environment experiments. Schubert et al. (1999) and Moore and Eckel (2003) framed their lotteries as investment decisions (gain domain) and as insurance decisions (loss domain).

---

[6] In addition to the issue of sex differences in risk preferences, Eckel and Grossman (2002, 2008) consider whether sex is taken to be a signal of risk preference. Each subject is asked to predict the gamble choice of each of the other players in her session. The only information a subject has on which to base a prediction is the set of visual clues provided by observing another. To encourage subjects to make their best predictions, subjects received $1 for every correct prediction they made. Consistent with actual gamble choices, in Eckel and Grossman (2008) we show that men were predicted to be less risk-averse than women by both women and men. The mean prediction by men for men of 3.33 is significantly greater than their mean prediction of 2.48 for women ($t = 13.73$, p-value < 0.001). Women predicted a mean gamble of 3.26 for men but only 2.61 for women, also a significant difference ($t = 11.17$, p-value < 0.001).

Placed in a contextual environment, Schubert et al.'s (1999) subjects (68 college students) exhibited no evidence of systematic or significant differences in risk attitudes. The coefficients for the female dummy variables in the regression analysis, while negative (indicating greater female risk aversion), are insignificantly different from zero.

Moore and Eckel (2003), on the other hand, report mixed evidence of significant differences in risk attitudes between their male and female subjects (76). For the investment (gain domain) gambles, women are significantly more risk averse than men, as well as significantly more averse to weak ambiguity. This difference reverses in the loss domain, when the gambles are framed as insurance decisions, with women more risk-seeking than men. Moore and Eckel (2003) report no significant differences in ambiguity aversion in the insurance frame.

Schubert et al. (2000), in a follow up to their 1999 study, test for sex differences in ambiguity aversion (see Table 2). Schubert et al. (2000) modified their investment and insurance lotteries to introduce ambiguity. In addition to the original, no-ambiguity frame, they included a weak ambiguity frame – lottery comprised of a low and a high-risk gamble, each with 0.5 probability – and a "strong" ambiguity frame – no probability information on lottery outcomes provided. Consistent with Moore and Eckel (2003), Schubert et al. (2000) find women to be more ambiguity averse in the investment (gain domain) frame; and the degree of aversion increased with the degree of ambiguity. Schubert et al.'s (2000) findings for their insurance (loss domain) frame are mixed. Neither sex was significantly more averse to weak ambiguity, but men were significantly more averse to strong ambiguity.

Gysler, Kruse, and Schubert (2002) conducted a two-part study of risk preferences and how preferences are influenced by ambiguity, a subject's knowledge of financial markets, and the subject's level of overconfidence in financial decision-making. In the first part of their study, subjects (50 university students) are evaluated on their knowledge of financial markets, and their confidence in their judgments.[7] The responses in this part of the experiment were used to generate measures of a subject's knowledge and overconfidence.

In the second part of the experiment, Gysler, Kruse, and Schubert (2002) elicit subjects' certainty equivalents for twelve lotteries. Four of the lotteries are based on the performance of mutual funds issued by a Swiss bank. Four additional lotteries are based on the performance of four simulated, virtual mutual funds. Times series from real mutual fund prices were used to create the virtual fund simulations. The final four lotteries, the pure risk cases, were standard lotteries with the probabilities known to both subjects and experimenters. For the 12 lotteries, subjects bet on whether or not the funds would post a daily market price increase of 0.5%.

---

[7] Subjects answer twenty questions concerning financial markets, of which 15 were used to asses their knowledge. Subjects are also asked to state the probability that their answers are correct. The stated probabilities for each question were used to construct corresponding lotteries. Subjects then decided whether to bet that their answer was correct or to accept the corresponding lottery. The expected payoffs in both cases were the same.

Gysler, Kruse, and Schubert (2002) find no evidence of a sex difference in risk preferences in the absence of controls for competence, knowledge, and overconfidence. Controlling for these factors does, however, reveal signs of a sex difference. Women are shown to be significantly more risk-averse, with their risk aversion decreasing with competence, overconfidence, and knowledge: women's risk-aversion diminishes as their expertise increases. The interactions have just the opposite effect for men, with risk aversion increasing in expertise and confidence.

In Eckel and Grossman's (2008) Investment treatment, subjects (57 college students) face the same choices as the baseline Abstract Gamble treatment, but the decision is framed as investing in a share of stock of one of five different companies. The payoff value of the stock is stated to be determined by the company's performance. The possible payoff values (performance) of the shares are the same as the payoffs for the abstract gambles. In contrast to Schubert et al. (1999), Eckel and Grossman (2002, 2008) do not find that sex differences disappear in the richer, investment-based decision making context. As in their abstract gamble experiments, Eckel and Grossman's (2002, 2008) results indicate that men are significantly more risk prone than women ($t = 3.96$, p-value < 0.001). This result is confirmed in their regression analysis.[8]

Powell and Ansic (1997) consider risk attitude differences in two contexts: insurance and a currency trading market. In the insurance treatment, subjects (126 college students) make 12 separate insurance decisions.[9] They are given an initial endowment before each decision. Subjects are told that one of three events will occur: no loss; lose half of the endowment (damage); lose all of the endowment (disaster). Subjects are given the opportunity to purchase one of five insurance options – no insurance, damage insurance, disaster insurance, both damage and disaster insurance, or to "pass" and permit the computer to select at random one of the other four options. Either the prices of the different insurance options, their endowment, or the level of risk differ across the 12 decisions.

In their currency market experiment, Powell and Ansic's (1997) subjects (101 college students) play a computer-based simulated trading game. There are four treatments with each treatment distinguished by the cost to enter the market. Given an initial endowment, subjects trade one currency for another in a risky market in order to make gains. Subjects can avoid the risk by exiting the market and holding their wealth. To reenter the market requires payment of an entry fee. In both experiments, Powell and Ansic (1997) find evidence of greater risk aversion on the part of their female subjects. In the insurance experiment, women more often purchase insurance and purchase more extensive insurance than men. These results are significant at the traditional levels. Powell and Ansic (1997) find that, in their currency market experiment, women are, on

---

[8] As in the abstract gamble treatments, men were predicted to be more risk prone than women by both women and men. The mean prediction by men and women for men was of 3.47 and for women it was 2.93; a significant difference ($t = 5.80$, p-value < 0.001).

[9] A subject's earnings were determined by his choice and the outcome for only one randomly chosen decision.

average, less in the market than men, also suggesting greater risk aversion. This finding is also significant at traditional levels.

Kruse and Thompson (2003) elicit values for 93 student subjects for risk mitigation using three different methods: one experiment and two surveys. In the experiment, subjects are given the opportunity to purchase a reduction in the probability of loss at various prices; their measure is the minimum accepted price. The higher this measure, the more risk averse are the subjects. While women are willing to pay more, the difference is not statistically significant. This pattern is repeated in the survey instruments.

Finally, Levy, Elron, and Cohen (1999) conduct an elaborate simulated stock market game to analyze investment decisions. An interesting difference between this study and the others cited is that subjects in this study can actually suffer out-of-pocket losses. Subjects (64 MBA students) are provided an initial endowment with which they can purchase shares in any, some or all, of 20 pure equity "firms." These securities are constructed by the experimenters to have particular properties. Firms differ in their mean (and standard deviation) return to equity (per trading period). The design of the experiment is such that the higher the risk chosen, the higher the expected return, reflecting properties of a real stock market. Subjects can avoid risk by lending their endowment at a risk-free interest rate of 2 percent; subjects may also borrow at this interest rate if they wish to leverage their investments in risky assets. Levy, Elron, and Cohen (1999) find that the average wealth of men is significantly higher than that of women from the third trading period on, and the difference increases with each subsequent period.

Levy, Elron, and Cohen's (1999) study is able to consider separately two components of sex differences in risk attitudes: the percent of wealth held in riskless assets, and the variance of return on the stock portfolio. In all but one of the ten trading periods, women hold a higher percentage of their wealth in riskless assets; however, the difference never reaches a level of significance. Comparing the average "simple," average "Book to Market," and average "Book to End" variances of portfolios held, Levy, Elron, and Cohen (1999) find greater variance in men's portfolios in seven of ten, eight of ten, and nine of ten market periods, respectively. In only two of the market periods (for each measure of variance) were the differences significant. Levy, Elron, and Cohen (1999) also find no consistent pattern of greater efficiency of investment on the part of men relative to women.

The authors do, however, find that the combined effect of these three factors explains the differences in the cumulative wealth of men and women. They conclude that men tend to: (1) hold more of their wealth in risky assets; (2) hold risky stocks in their portfolio; (3) hold more stock; and (4) make more efficient investments. Though, there is no significant difference for each alone, the combined effect is highly significant.

3. Evidence From Field Studies

The evidence from both abstract gambling and contextual environment experiments of greater risk aversion by women is consistent with non-laboratory studies of behavioral differences between men and women. Johnson and Powell (1994) studied actual betting decisions on horse and dog races made at 50 betting offices throughout the United Kingdom over a one-week period. While they discovered no significant sex difference in decision quality (measured by the propensity to win), they did find that men were significantly more risk prone than women in their betting habits. Men: (1) made bigger bets on average; (2) made more and bigger higher-risk "win" bets, and fewer and smaller lower-risk "each-way" bets; (3) made more and bigger higher-risk "straight forecast" bets, and fewer and smaller lower-risk "reverse forecast" bets; and (4) made fewer and smaller "multiple bets."[10]

Bajtelsmit and VanDerhei (1997) provide further evidence consistent with the hypothesis of greater risk aversion by women. They studied the defined contribution pension allocation decisions of 20,000 management employees of a large U.S. employer. All employees were provided the same investment alternatives. They report that, relative to men, women held a significantly greater share of their account balances in relatively low-risk fixed income investments and a significantly smaller share in higher-risk employer stock. The same pattern of behavior held true for allocations of current contributions. Bajtelsmit and VanDerhei (1997) find no sex difference in either holdings of, or current allocations to, diversified equities. The results must be applied cautiously as the authors had no information on marital status or other measures of household wealth and income.

Jianakoplos and Bernasek (1998), using data from the 1989 Survey of Consumer Finances, examined investment behavior of single men, single women, and married couples. As their dependent variable they employed the ratio of risky assets held to wealth. Controlling for factors such as age, education, children, and home ownership, Jianakoplos and Bernasek (1998) find that single women are significantly more risk averse (i.e., hold a smaller percentage of their wealth in the form of risky assets) than single men.

Using data from the 1992 and 1995 Surveys of Consumer Finances, Sundén and Surette (1998) examine sex differences in the allocation of defined contribution plan assets. Investment choices were defined as: (1) invest mostly in stocks; (2) invest mostly in interest earning assets (bonds); or (3) investments split between stocks and bonds. Using a multinomial logit model, Sundén and Surette (1998) find that sex and marital status are significantly related to asset allocation. Married men and married women were less risk prone than their single counterparts (i.e., married men were less likely than single men to choose investment choice 1; and married women were less likely

---

[10] Win bets only pay if the selection wins. An each-way bet pay if the selection finishes first, second, or third, and therefore, is a form of hedging. Straight forecast bets pay if the first and second place finishers were selected and the exact order of finish was predicted. Reverse forecast bets pay if the first and second place finishers were selected, the order of finish need not be predicted. Multiple bets require combinations of bets on runners in different races. Payoffs may occur even if only one of the selected runners wins. Reverse forecast and multiple bets have elements of diversification to them, indicating less willingness to accept risk.

than single women to choose investment choice 3). Single women were less risk prone than single men (i.e., less likely to choose investment choice 1).[11]

4. Discussion

The findings from field studies conclude that women are more risk averse than men. The findings of laboratory experiments are, however, somewhat less conclusive. While the preponderance of laboratory evidence is consistent with field evidence, there is enough counter-evidence to warrant caution. For example, both field and lab studies typically fail to control for knowledge, wealth, marital status and other demographic factors that might bias measures of male/female differences in risky choices.

Another difficulty with drawing conclusions from the existing experimental evidence is the lack of comparability across studies. Studies differ in the form the risk takes (i.e., the structure of the gamble), the potential payoffs, and the degree of risk as variance. Studies also differ in the nature of the decision that subjects are required to make. Elicitation methods and frames also differ in their transparency and in the cost of mistakes. In some experiments, subjects must state a value for a gamble; in others they must state a minimum selling or buying price, with or without an incentive compatible mechanism. In others subjects choose between certain amounts and gambles; and in still others, subjects choose between or among gambles. Sometimes gambles are ordered in a transparent way, from high to low probabilities, say; in others they are randomly ordered. One possibility, only just beginning to be investigated, is that subjects make "errors" in these tasks, and that there are systematic differences in the types of errors made in each that may be correlated with the gender of the decision makers. At any rate, each study is sufficiently unique as to make comparisons of results across studies problematic.

Another issue that has rarely been addressed in gamble-based laboratory experiments is the consistency of measures of risk aversion across tasks. Eckel, Grossman, and Lutz (2002) present data that shows very low correlations across different valuation tasks for similar gambles. For example, in one task subjects must name a minimum selling price for a 10 percent chance of $10 using a BDM procedure. In another, the same subjects indicate a willingness to sell or not sell an "egg" that pays of $10 with probability .10. The correlation between these two measures is .04. This result is quite consistent with results published in the psychology journals beginning with Slovic (1964), and confirmed by many others since (see Weber, Blais, and Betz, 2002). While more research is clearly necessary, the findings thus far shed serious doubt on the existence of risk attitude as a measurable, stable personality trait, or as a domain-general property of a utility function in wealth or income.

---

[11] Relative performance of male and female mutual fund managers is examined in Atkinson, Baird, and Frye (2003). Their findings suggest that differences in male and female investment patterns may be due to differences in knowledge and wealth.

References

Atkinson, S.M., Baird, S.B., Frye, M.B. (2003). "Do female fund managers manage differently". Journal of Financial Research 26, 1–18.

Bajtelsmit, V.L., VanDerhei, J.L. (1997). "Risk aversion and pension investment choices". In: Gordon, Michael S. (Ed.), Positioning Pensions for the Twenty-First Century. University of Pennsylvania Press, Philadelphia, pp. 45–66.

Blais, A.-R., Weber, E.U. (2001). "Domain-specificity and gender differences in decision making". Risk Decision and Policy 6, 47–69.

Boverie, P.E., Scheuffele, D.J., Raymond, E.L. (1995). "Multimethodological approach to examining risk-taking". Current Psychology 13, 289–302.

Brinig, M.F. (1995). "Does mediation systematically disadvantage women?" William and Mary Journal of Women and the Law 2, 1–34.

Cooperstock, R., Parnell, P. (1982). "Research on psychotropic drug use: A review of findings and methods". Social Science and Medicine 16, 1179–1196.

Cutter, S.L., Tiefenbacher, J., Solecki, W.D. (1992). "En-gendered fears: Femininity and technological risk perception". Industrial Crisis Quarterly 6, 5–22.

Daly, M., Wilson, M. (1988). "Homicide". Aldine de Gruyter, Hawthorne, NY.

Eckel, C.C., Grossman, P.J. (2002). "Sex differences and statistical stereotyping in attitudes toward financial risk". Evolution and Human Behavior 23 (4), 281–295.

Eckel, C.C., Grossman, P.J. (2008). "Forecasting risk attitudes: An experimental study using actual and forecast gamble choices". Journal of Economic Behavior and Organization, in press.

Eckel, C.C., Grossman, P.J., Lutz, N.A. (2002). "Risk aversion, risky behavior, and insurance". Unpublished manuscript, Department of Economics, Virginia Tech.

Flynn, J., Slovic, P., Mertz, C.K. (1994). "Gender, race, and perception of environmental health risks". Risk Analysis 14, 1101–1108.

Gottfredson, M.R., Hirschi, T. (1990). "A General Theory of Crime". Stanford University Press, Stanford.

Gysler, M., Kruse, J.B., Schubert, R. (2002). "Ambiguity and gender differences in financial decision making: An experimental examination of competence and confidence effects". Working paper, Center for Economic Research, Swiss Federal Institute of Technology.

Harbaugh, W.T., Krause, K., Vesterlund, L. (2002). "Risk attitudes of children and adults: Choices over small and large probability gains and losses". Experimental Economics 5 (1), 53–84.

Harrison, G.W. (1992). "Theory and misbehavior of first-price auctions: Reply". American Economic Review 82, 1426–1443.

Harrison, G.W., Rutström, E.E. (2008). "Risk aversion in the laboratory". In: Cox, J.C., Harrison, G.W. (Eds.), Risk Aversion in Experiments, Research in Experimental Economics, vol. 12. Emerald, Bingley, UK, in press.

Harrison, G.W., Johnson, E., McInnes, M.M., Rutström, E.E. (2005). "Risk aversion and incentive effects: Comment". American Economic Review 95, 897–901.

Hartog, J., Ferrer-i-Carbonell, A., Jonker, N. (2002). "Linking measured risk aversion to individual characteristics". Kyklos 55 (1), 3–26.

Holt, C.A., Laury, S.K. (2002). "Risk aversion and incentive effects". American Economic Review 92 (5), 1644–1655.

Jianakoplos, N.A., Bernasek, A. (1998). "Are women more risk averse?" Economic Inquiry 36, 620–630.

Johnson, J.E.V., Powell, P.L. (1994). "Decision making, risk and gender: Are managers different?" British Journal of Management 5, 123–138.

Kachelmeier, S.J., Shehata, M. (1992). "Examining risk preferences under high monetary incentives: Experimental evidence from the Peoples Republic of China". American Economic Review 82, 1120–1141.

Kandel, D.B., Logan, J.A. (1984). "Patterns of drug use from adolescence to young adulthood. 1. Periods of risk for initiation, continued use, and discontinuation". American Journal of Public Health 74, 660–666.

Kruse, J.B., Thompson, M.A. (2003). "Valuing low probability risk: Survey and experimental evidence". Journal of Economic Behavior and Organization 50, 495–505.

Levin, I.P., Snyder, M.A., Chapman, D.P. (1988). "The interaction of experiential and situational factors and gender in a simulated risky decision-making task". The Journal of Psychology 122, 173–181.

Levy, H., Elron, E., Cohen, A. (1999). "Gender differences in risk taking and investment behavior: An experimental analysis". Unpublished manuscript, The Hebrew University.

MacGregor, D., Slovic, P., Mason, R.G., Detweiler, J., Binney, S.E., Dodd, B. (1994). "Perceived risks of radioactive waste transport through Oregon: Results of a statewide survey". Risk Analysis 14, 5–14.

McStay, J.R., Dunlap, R.E. (1983). "Male–female differences in concern for environmental quality". International Journal of Women's Studies 6, 291–301.

Moore, E., Eckel, C.C. (2003). "Measuring ambiguity aversion". Unpublished manuscript, Department of Economics, Virginia Tech.

Plott, C.R., Zeiler, K. (2002). "The willingness to pay/willingness to accept gap, the 'endowment effect' and experimental procedures for eliciting valuations". HSS Working Paper 1132, California Institute of Technology.

Powell, M., Ansic, D. (1997). "Gender differences in risk behaviour in financial decision-making: An experimental analysis". Journal of Economic Psychology 18, 605–628.

Schubert, R., Gysler, M., Brown, M., Brachinger, H.W. (1999). "Financial decision-making: Are women really more risk averse?" American Economic Review Papers and Proceedings 89, 381–385.

Schubert, R., Gysler, M., Brown, M., Brachinger, H.W. (2000). "Gender specific attitudes towards risk and ambiguity: An experimental investigation". Working paper, Center for Economic Research, Swiss Federal Institute of Technology.

Slovic, P. (1964). "Assessment of risk-taking behavior". Psychological Bulletin 61, 330–333.

Silverman, J.M., Kumka, D.S. (1987). "Gender differences in attitudes toward nuclear war and disarmament". Sex Roles 16, 189–203.

Spigner, C., Hawkins, W., Lorens, W. (1993). "Gender differences in perception of risk associated with alcohol and drug use among college students". Women and Health 20, 87–97.

Stallen, P.J.M., Tomas, A. (1988). "Public concern about industrial hazards". Risk Analysis 8, 237–245.

Starmer, C. (2000). "Developments in non-expected utility theory: The search for a descriptive theory of choice under risk". Journal of Economic Literature 38, 332–382.

Sundén, A.E., Surette, B.J. (1998). "Gender differences in the allocation of assets in retirement savings plans". American Economic Review Papers and Proceedings 88, 207–211.

Weber, E.U., Blais, A.-R., Betz, N.E. (2002). "A domain-specific risk-attitude scale: Measuring risk perceptions and risk behaviors". Journal of Behavioral Decision Making 15, 1–28.

Wilson, J.Q., Herrnstein, R.J. (1985). "Crime and Human Nature". Simon and Schuster, New York.

PART 8

METHODS

8. METHODS

The two entries in this part provide examples of the use of experiments to calibrate or evaluate standard methodologies used in field or experimental economic analysis. The first arises from a standard econometric method used in the analysis of empirical field data; the second arises from the need in some experimental contexts to control for risk aversion, particularly when it is desired to test the predictions of decision models that assume risk neutral decision making agents.

One of the most elementary theorems in econometrics is that ordinary least squares estimators are inconsistent, while two stage least squares estimates are consistent estimators of simultaneous equation parameters. The canonical problem is to estimate the unknown parameters of supply and demand from market observations. The theorem is derived from the assumption that the data are generated by observations on a competitive equilibrium with zero-mean random error.

Cox and Oaxaca test this methodology in an experimental environment in which the supply and demand parameters are known to the experimenter using standard induced value rewards for the subjects, then ask if they can accurately recover these parameters from the market observations alone using econometric estimation procedures. They find that it depends on the trading institution: the standard estimators perform well with closing price data from the double auction institution, but they are dominated by ordinary least squares estimation when applied to data from the posted offer market suggesting the need to condition the choice of an estimator on the market institution that generated the data?

Berg, Dickhaut and Reitz test a procedure for inducing known risk preferences on experimental subjects, and thus controlling for such preferences in experiments that confound such preferences with other objectives of interest. Preference induction relies on the result that, independent of the shape of the utility function or the size of the prizes, expected utility is linear in the probability of winning the higher of two prizes in a two-prize lottery. By making the probability functions linear, convex, or concave the experimenter can then induce risk neutral, risk seeking or risk averse behavior. They find that in auctions the risk neutral procedures approximate observed decisions better as subjects gain experience in auctions run with the induction mechanism. For the nonlinear cases, subjects who are induced to be risk seeking nearly always choose the riskier gamble, while those induced to be risk averse choose the less risky one.

Chapter 114

EXPERIMETRICS: THE USE OF MARKET EXPERIMENTS TO EVALUATE THE PERFORMANCE OF ECONOMETRIC ESTIMATORS

JAMES C. COX and RONALD L. OAXACA

University of Arizona

Experiments with human subjects have been widely used to test hypotheses derived from economic theory and to provide stylized facts about empirical regularities in economics. One of the clear implications of experimental economics is that the efficiency and distributional properties of market allocations are dependent on the market institutions through which exchange takes place (Plott, 1982; Smith, 1982). This makes clear the limitations of economic theories of markets that are institution-free.

Econometric theory, as conventionally taught in graduate schools and applied by many economists, is largely institution-free. Properties of econometric estimators are derived from assumptions about the data generating process (DGP) and the error distribution. A clear example is provided by the most central simultaneous equations in economics, supply and demand equations. The basic results in econometric textbooks, that ordinary least squares is an inconsistent estimator and two stage least squares is a consistent estimator, are derived from the assumption that the DGP is competitive equilibrium with zero-mean random error. Can it be demonstrated that these results provide reliable guidance to applied econometricians wanting to estimate the parameters of supply and demand equations using *market* price and quantity data? Or may there be a demonstrable need to condition the choice of an estimator on the market institution that generated the data?

Experiments with human subjects are just beginning to be used to generate data for evaluation of econometric methods. Cox and Oaxaca (1999) presents results from estimating the known (to the experimenter) parameters of supply and demand equations with data from paired double auction and posted offer experiments. Double auctions are the form of market typically used on organized (stock, bond, and commodity) exchanges. Most retail trade in highly-developed economies is conducted with the posted offer market institution.

Cox and Oaxaca's analysis of the experimental data indicates that the standard simultaneous equations estimators perform quite well with closing price data from the double auction institution but that they perform very poorly, and are dominated by ordinary least squares estimation, when applied to data from the posted offer market. Thus, at least for their experimental market data, the market institution that generated the data is a critical factor in determining the performance of the estimators.

Handbook of Experimental Economics Results, Volume 1
Copyright © 2008 Elsevier B.V. All rights reserved
DOI: 10.1016/S1574-0722(07)00114-X

1. Designing Experiments to Study the Properties of Estimators

In designing the first experiments to evaluate the performance of econometric estimators, Cox and Oaxaca used control parameters that produce competitive equilibrium data with the properties assumed by econometric theory. The design principles are as follows.

(a) Use of demand and supply shifts variables that identify the supply and demand equations and are independently distributed.

In order *not* to design an inconsistency into the experiments with econometric theory, the controlled market demand and supply equations should each include a variable that is not in the other equation and these variables should be independently distributed. This can be accomplished by including a demand shift variable (X_d) and a supply shift variable (X_s), respectively, in the market inverse demand and supply equations and drawing their values independently.

(b) Use of controlled error variables, one for demand and one for supply, which are independently distributed.

Including induced error terms, u_d and u_s, in the market inverse demand and supply equations permits analysis of the data such that the estimators are either over-identified or exactly identified, depending on whether u_d and u_s are or are not included as right hand variables in the estimating equations. Again, in order *not* to design into the experiments an inconsistency with econometric theory, the values of u_d and u_s should be independently drawn.

(c) Use of sets of values for the demand and supply shift and random error variables such that any possible combination of values yields a horizontal overlap of the controlled market supply and demand step functions and payment of a commission to both the buyer and seller for each trade of a unit of the abstract commodity.

This design feature implies that, in each market period, there is a unique competitive equilibrium price and quantity that lie at the intersection of the demand and supply step functions for the discrete units traded in the experiment. This unique price and quantity will also lie at the intersection of the continuous linear demand and supply curves that pass through the "outside of the steps" of the step functions. Standard econometric estimators are designed to recover the parameters of the equations of such continuous demand and supply curves. Any other design would have competitive equilibrium prices and quantities that would *not* lie at the intersection of the continuous demand and supply curves; this would artifactually "throw off" the estimators in a way that had little relation to the inherent properties of the double auction and posted offer market institutions, with human buyers and sellers, as data generating processes.

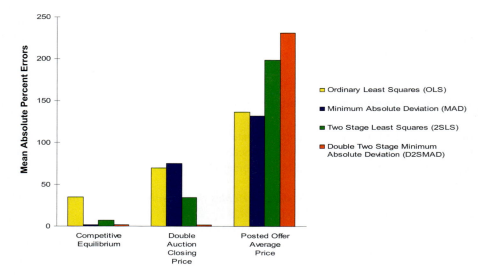

Figure 1. The figure reports the demand intercept and slope parameter estimation error rates for four estimators with both (theoretical) competitive equilibrium data and data from experiments with market institutions. Consistent with asymptotic econometric theory, simultaneous equations estimators (2SLS and D2SMAD) dominate OLS with competitive equilibrium (CE) quantities and prices. MAD does as well or better than 2SLS and D2SMAD with CE data. 2SLS and D2SMAD dominate OLS and MAD with double auction market quantity and closing price data. In contrast, OLS and MAD dominate 2SLS and D2SMAD with posted offer quantity and average price data.

(d) Random re-initialization of the market demand and supply curves each market period so that the competitive equilibrium price and quantity vary over a wide range.

Market experiments often repeat the parameter values for several periods. This can cause experimental market prices and quantities to "lock on" to their competitive equilibrium values, especially in double auction markets. This type of design can produce data with a scatter diagram that is a "tight clump." Such data cannot be used to estimate demand and supply parameters with any precision. In order to generate data that is more appropriate to estimation, the demand and supply parameters should be randomly varied over values that yield a wide range of prices and quantities. Since competitive equilibrium prices and quantities can be observed during experimental design, it is natural to use their variability as the design guideline.

The principles of design of experiments for evaluating the performance of econometric estimators is more fully explained in Cox and Oaxaca (1999).

2. Performance of the Estimators

Figures 1–4 present results from Cox and Oaxaca (1999) on the performance of four estimators, two single equation estimators (ordinary least squares and minimum ab-

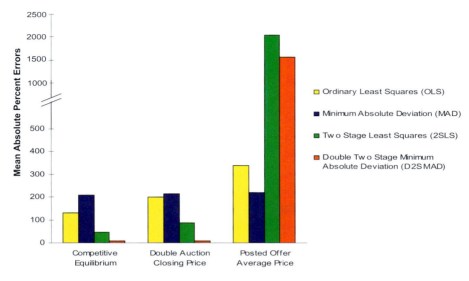

Figure 2. This figure reports supply intercept and slope parameter estimation error rates for four estimators with both (theoretical) competitive equilibrium data and data from experiments with market institutions. Consistent with asymptotic econometric theory, simultaneous equations estimators (2SLS and D2SMAD) dominate single equation estimators (OLS and MAD) with competitive equilibrium quantities and prices. Similarly, 2SLS and D2SMAD dominate OLS and MAD with double auction market quantity and closing price data. In contrast, OLS and MAD dominate 2SLS and D2SMAD with posted offer market quantity and average price data.

solute deviation) and two simultaneous equations estimators (two stage least squares and double two stage minimum absolute deviation). The results presented here are for the exactly identified model; results for over-identified models are similar. Performance of the estimators is measured by their mean absolute percent errors (MAPES) in recovering the true parameters. The estimators are applied to competitive equilibrium prices and quantities, double auction market data, and posted offer market data. The price measure that is used for each market institution is the one used in field versions of these institutions, closing price for the double auction and average price for the posted offer market. Closing prices are the ones usually reported for organized exchanges. The national income and product accounts report price data for retail trade that are average price indexes.

First consider Figure 1, which reports the MAPES for estimates of the demand equation's intercept and slope parameters. The four left-side bars present results from applying the estimators to competitive equilibrium prices and quantities from the experiments. This analysis is a Monte Carlo study of the small sample properties of the estimators using the same induced random errors used in the market experiments. Consistent with asymptotic econometric theory, the simultaneous equations estimators, two stage least squares (2SLS) and double two stage minimum absolute deviation (D2SMAD), are

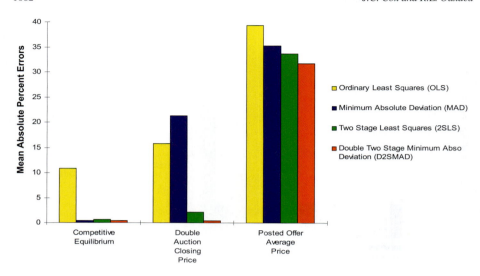

Figure 3. This figure reports demand slope parameter estimation error rates. Consistent with asymptotic econometric theory, simultaneous equations estimators (2SLS and D2SMAD) dominate OLS with competitive equilibrium (CE) quantities and prices. MAD does as well or better than 2SLS and D2SMAD with CE data. 2SLS and D2SMAD dominate OLS and MAD with double auction market quantity and closing price data. In contrast, 2SLS and D2SMAD are only slightly better than OLS and MAD, and all four estimators perform poorly with posted offer quantity and average price data.

more accurate than ordinary least squares (OLS) in recovering the true demand intercept and slope parameters from the competitive equilibrium prices and quantities for this experimental design. The single equation minimum absolute deviation estimator (MAD) does as well as D2SMAD, with both estimators having a 0.0 MAPE. The middle bars show the performance of the estimators with double auction quantity and closing price data. 2SLS and D2SMAD dominate OLS and MAD with double auction data, with D2SMAD having a 0.0 MAPE. The right-most four bars report the results from estimation with posted offer quantity and average price data. The single equation estimators dominate the simultaneous equations estimators when estimation is done with posted offer data.

Figure 2 reports results for estimates of the supply equation's intercept and slope parameters. 2SLS and D2SMAD dominate OLS and MAD with both competitive equilibrium and double auction data, with D2SMAD having a 0.0 MAPE with both data sets. The results are vastly different with posted offer data: OLS and MAD have large MAPES of 340 and 221, but 2SLS and D2SMAD have astronomical MAPES of 2100 and 1663.

Figure 3 shows the MAPES for only the demand slope parameters. Consistent with asymptotic theory, 2SLS and D2SMAD once again dominate OLS and MAD with both competitive equilibrium and double auction data, with D2SMAD having a 0.0 MAPE

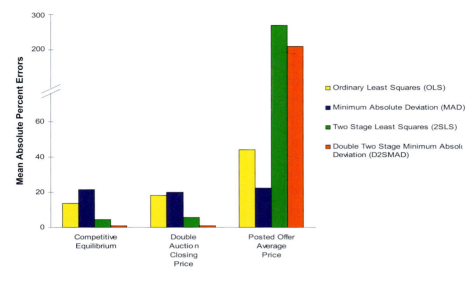

Figure 4. This figure reports supply slope parameter estimation error rates. Consistent with asymptotic econometric theory, simultaneous equations estimators (2SLS and D2SMAD) dominate single equation estimators (OLS and MAD) with competitive equilibrium quantities and prices. Similarly, 2SLS and D2SMAD dominate OLS and MAD with double auction market quantity and closing price data. In contrast, OLS and MAD dominate 2SLS and D2SMAD with posted offer market quantity and average price data.

with both data sets. In contrast 2SLS and D2SMAD are only slightly better than OLS and MAD with posted offer data, and all four estimators perform poorly.

Figure 4 reports the results for estimates of the supply slope parameters. The simultaneous equations estimators dominate the single equation estimators with competitive equilibrium and double auction data, with D2SMAD once again turning in a perfect performance. In stark contrast, OLS and MAD dominate 2SLS and D2SMAD with posted offer data, with the simultaneous equations estimators having MAPES of 271 and 214.

3. Explanation of the Posted Offer Results

The inaccuracy of simultaneous equations estimators in recovering demand and, more especially, supply parameters from posted offer market data can be explained by the inherent properties of this market institution. In contrast with the double auction, the pricing decision lies exclusively with the sellers in posted offer markets. The buyers cannot make price bids; they can only choose quantities after the sellers post their prices. This does not mean that the buyers have to be textbook "price-takers"; they can withhold demand to attempt to get lower prices. But prices are "posted" in a market period; hence buyers wanting to counter-speculate against sellers must forgo gains from exchange in an earlier market period in the hope of obtaining lower prices in later periods. The strategic disadvantage of buyers is exacerbated by a "public goods" problem: if one buyer withholds demand in a market period, in the hope of getting lower prices later, she will incur all of the cost of forgone gains from exchange but any benefit of lower prices will be shared by all of the buyers. Presumably as a consequence of this strategic disadvantage, almost all buyers in posted offer experiments do fully reveal their demands at the prices posted by the sellers. But the sellers do not know the market demand; instead, they just learn what they can sell at the prices that they post. These features of the posted offer market institution with human buyers and sellers mean that it is a DGP with properties that cause 2SLS and D2SMAD to perform very badly. The problem is that this DGP produces error terms in estimating equations that are not independent of the supply and demand shift variables. The evidence for this is as follows.

Cox and Oaxaca (1999) reports results from a series of OLS regressions in which the actual reduced form errors were regressed on the demand and supply shift variables. Figure 5 shows some of the results from the reduced form error regressions. The quantity error regressions produce generally insignificant results with both double auction and posted offer data: the R^2s are tiny (0.003 and 0.005) and all of the absolute values of the t-ratios are less than 1.5 except the one for the constant with posted offer data, which is -4.61. This significantly negative constant reflects the fact that posted offer quantities are more often less than, instead of greater than, competitive equilibrium quantities. The regression for the price error with double auction data yields constant and demand shift t-ratios of -2.96 and 2.80 but the R^2 is only 0.03. Results for the price error with posted offer data are very different: the R^2 is 0.62 and the constant, demand shift, and supply shift t-ratios are 16.97, -19.74, and 8.95. Here is the explanation of the huge MAPES that result from applying the simultaneous equations estimators to posted offer data: the reduced form price errors are highly dependent on the demand and supply shift variables whereas the estimators require the errors to be independent of the shift variables in order to perform well.

The dependence of the reduced form price errors on the demand and supply shift variables with posted offer data is a predictable consequence of the operation of this institution with human buyers and sellers. An increase in the supply shift variable is experienced by the sellers as marginal cost increases before they post their prices. The sellers are not able to observe demand before posting their prices and tend to react to their cost increases by posting prices that are above market-clearing prices, resulting in a significantly positive coefficient on the supply shift variable in the reduced form price error regression. In contrast, when there is an increase in demand that is unobserved by sellers before prices are posted, the sellers often post prices that are below market-clearing prices, resulting in a significantly negative coefficient on the demand shift variable in the reduced form price error regression.

In order for an estimator to have acceptable performance with the posted offer experiment data, it would have to be designed to accommodate the inherent properties of this DGP, not designed for the properties of the competitive equilibrium DGP. These

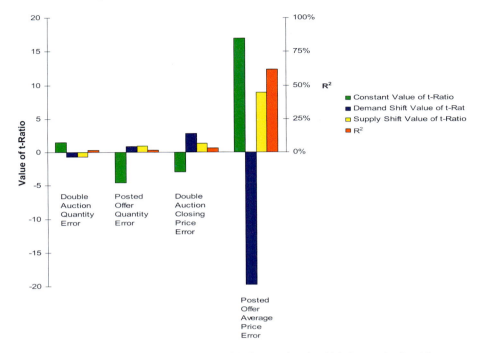

Figure 5. This figure reports results from a series of OLS regressions in which the actual reduced form errors were regressed on the demand and supply shift variables in order to learn why the simultaneous equations estimators perform as they do with market data. The quantity error regressions produce generally insignificant results with both double auction and posted offer data. The regression for the price error with double auction data yields constant and demand shift t-ratios of -2.96 and 2.80 but the R^2 is only 0.03. The price error regression with posted offer data has an R^2 of 0.62 and the constant, demand shift, and supply shift t-ratios are 16.97, -19.74, and 8.95. This explains the huge mean absolute percent errors that result from applying the simultaneous equations estimators to posted offer data.

results do not "prove" that 2SLS and D2SMAD would perform unacceptably with non-experimental posted offer market data such as retail trade data. It may be that there are differences between laboratory and non-laboratory posted offer markets, as DGP's, that would affect estimator performance. But the poor performance of the simultaneous equations estimators with the posted offer experimental data are deserving of further consideration because they can be easily explained by the inherent properties of the posted offer market institution.

Acknowledgement

Todd Swarthout provided valuable assistance by preparing the figures.

References

Cox, James C., Oaxaca, Ronald L. (1999). "Can supply and demand parameters be recovered from data generated by market institutions?" Journal of Business and Economic Statistics 17 (3), 285–297.
Plott, Charles R. (1982). "Industrial organization theory and experimental economics". Journal of Economic Literature XX (4), 1485–1527.
Smith, Vernon L. (1982). "Microeconomic systems as an experimental science". American Economic Review 72 (5), 923–955.

Chapter 115

ON THE PERFORMANCE OF THE LOTTERY PROCEDURE FOR CONTROLLING RISK PREFERENCES

JOYCE E. BERG and THOMAS A. RIETZ

Henry B. Tippie College of Business, University of Iowa, Iowa City, IA 52242-1000, USA

JOHN W. DICKHAUT

Carlson School of Management, University of Minnesota, 321 19th Avenue South, Minneapolis, MN 55455, USA

1. Introduction

In theory, the lottery-based induction procedure for controlling risk preferences (Roth and Malouf, 1979; Berg et al., 1986) allows experimenters to induce subjects to display pre-specified risk preferences. Thus, like induced value theory (Smith, 1976), it extends experimenters' ability to perform controlled laboratory tests by controlling parameters, such as preferences, that are exogenous to the theory being tested. Theoretically, the procedure is incontrovertible. However, the empirical performance of the procedure is an open issue. In this paper, we present the theoretical basis for the induction procedure and examine how it works in practice, using two example sets of data.

2. Inducing Risk Preferences in Theory

Often, experiments are conducted with explicit dollar payoffs or with units of exchange (e.g., "francs") that later convert to dollars at a fixed rate. Subjects' preferences over wealth can be concave (risk averse), convex (risk seeking), linear (risk neutral) or a combination of these in different regions. Thus, such payment mechanisms leave risk preferences uncontrolled. To see how this can affect choice, consider the utility function depicted by the heavy, curved line in the left panel of Figure 1, where the horizontal axis is denominated in dollars (or francs converted directly into dollars). The utility function depicted represents a person who is risk averse in his choices among monetary gambles: the person strictly prefers the expected value of the gamble to the gamble itself. If the graph were convex instead, the person would be risk loving and strictly prefer the gamble to the expected value of the gamble. That is, depending on their risk preferences, subjects may make different choices among risky alternatives. This is problematic in an experiment when we wish to determine whether behavior is in accordance with a particular theory and the predictions of the theory depend on risk preferences. Deviations can occur because risk preferences differ from those assumed

Handbook of Experimental Economics Results, Volume 1
Copyright © 2008 Elsevier B.V. All rights reserved
DOI: 10.1016/S1574-0722(07)00115-1

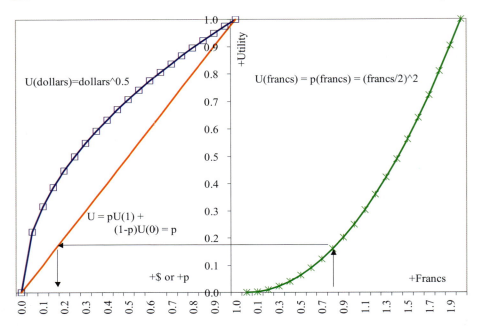

Figure 1. A graphical depiction of inducing a risk averse subject to have risk seeking preferences. The left panel shows the utility function for a subject with the risk averse utility function: $U(\text{dollars}) = \text{dollars}^{0.5}$. The straight line gives the expected utility function for a gamble with a \$1 payoff with probability p. The utility function is normalized so that $U(1) = 1$ and $U(0) = 0$. (This can be done with any utility function since expected utility is unique up to a positive affine transformation.) Then, the expected utility equals p. The right panel shows the desired, risk seeking utility function $U(\text{francs}) = (\text{francs}/2)^2$. This function maps francs into the probability of winning the \$1 prize. Since the expected utility is p, the subject's utility for francs is given by the transformation from francs into p. In this case, $U(\text{francs}) = (\text{francs}/2)^2$.

in theory or because the theory does not explain behavior. Without a reliable method of controlling for risk preferences, we cannot untangle these two possibilities.[1]

In theory, the lottery-based induction procedure allows the experimenter to control risk preferences. By using a unit of reward tied to the probability of winning the higher prize in a two-prize gamble, the lottery procedure induces expected utility maximizing subjects to behave as if they have pre-specified risk preferences relative to this unit of reward regardless of their native preferences over monetary gambles. Thus, subjects can be induced to act as if they are risk averse, risk loving, or risk neutral.

Risk preference induction depends on expected utility maximization as depicted by the lighter straight line in the left panel of Figure 1. This line shows the expected utility of a two-prize gamble with payoffs of \$0 and \$1 (following Varian, 1984, p. 159). We

---

[1] Alternatively, the experimenter could choose to measure native risk preferences and use that information in analyzing experimental results. Which choice is better depends on the experiment and its design.

have normalized utility so that the utility of $0 is 0 and the utility of $1 is 1. Thus, the bottom axis can also be interpreted as the probability of winning the $1 prize. (We can always normalize in this way since expected utility functions are unique up to a positive affine transformation.)

Preference induction relies on the result that, independent of the shape of the utility function or the size of the prizes, expected utility is linear in the probability of winning the higher of two prizes in a two-prize lottery.[2] Graphically, expected utility as a function of probability is a straight line (as shown in Figure 1) independent of the original utility function. That is,

$$E(U) = pU(M_h, \mathbf{X}) + (1-p)U(M_l, \mathbf{X}),$$

where p = probability of winning the higher valued prize, M_h = higher valued prize, M_l = lower valued prize, and $\mathbf{X}$ = is a vector of all other components in the utility function.

When $U(M_h, \mathbf{X})$ and $U(M_l, \mathbf{X})$ are normalized to 1 and 0 respectively, we have:

$$E(U) = pU(M_h, \mathbf{X}) + (1-p)U(M_l, \mathbf{X}) = p.$$

Preferences are induced by using an experimental unit of exchange (say, "francs") that is later converted into the probability of winning the higher of two monetary prizes (instead of converting directly into dollars).[3] The conversion function determines how subjects should behave relative to francs. If the conversion function is $p = V(\text{francs})$ then, expected utility maximizing subjects will maximize $V(\text{francs})$ because they maximize the probability of winning the higher valued prize. Thus, they act as if they each have the utility function $V(\text{francs})$ regardless of their preferences over dollars!

Figure 1 shows how this works graphically. Suppose you would like to investigate the effect of risk-seeking behavior on market prices and want to induce the utility function, $V(\text{francs}) = (\text{francs}/2)^2$, shown in the right panel. To do this, undertake the following procedures:

(1) Have subjects trade in francs in a market with a maximum possible payoff (normalized here to 1) and a minimum possible payoff (normalized here to 0).
(2) Translate francs into the probability of winning the higher of a two-prize lottery according to the function $p = V(\text{francs}) = (\text{francs}/2)^2$.
(3) At the end of trading, run an induction lottery to determine the prize won, thus determining the ultimate payoffs to subjects.

The translation of francs to probability can be read from Figure 1. Start with the level of francs earned by the subject in the right panel. The desired level of utility for this level of francs is $(\text{francs}/2)^2$. Taking this desired level of utility into the left panel to the

---

[2] Technically, induction does not depend specifically on expected utility maximization. It works for any preference function that gives preferences that are linear in probabilities.
[3] Note that the prize does not need to be monetary. However, we discuss monetary prizes so that the lottery technique is more easily compared to induced value theory.

expected utility function (the straight line) shows the probability that must correspond to this level of francs to induce the desired preferences in francs (here, $p = (\text{francs}/2)^2$).

This procedure has been implemented in a number of different ways. Berg et al. (1986), Berg, Dickhaut, and Rietz (2003) use "spinners" where the probability of winning (chances the spinner lands in the "win area") is determined by the number of points the subject earns in a choice or pricing task and the desired induced utility function. If the spinner stops in the win area, the subject wins the higher monetary prize. Rietz (1992) uses a box of lottery tickets numbered 1 to 1000. A ticket is drawn randomly from the box. If the ticket number is less than or equal to the number of points earned by the subject, the subject wins the high monetary prize.

3. Evidence

3.1. Inducing Risk Neutrality: Evidence from Sealed Bid Auctions

We will begin with evidence from attempts to induce risk neutral preferences in sealed bid auctions. Harrison (1989), Walker, Smith, and Cox (1990), Rietz (1992) all attempt to induce risk neutral preferences in similar sealed bid auction experiments. All run series of four-person, private-value, first-price sealed bid auctions with values drawn from a uniform distribution (over a range which we will normalize to 0 to 1000). Some use dollar payoffs and some use a lottery procedure designed to induce risk neutral preferences.[4] All compare the dollar payoff results to the induced results.

Vickrey (1961) derives the symmetric Nash equilibrium bid functions for traders with risk neutral preferences as:

$$\text{Bid} = \big[(n-1)/n\big] \times \text{Value},$$

where n is the number of bidders in the auction. Thus, in these 4 person auctions, bids should be 3/4 of value for risk neutral traders. Cox, Smith, and Walker (1984) show that risk averse bidders will use a bid function with a higher slope than that of risk neutral traders. Intuitively, bidders trade off expected value for a higher probability of winning the auction. Thus, risk aversion is one possible explanation for the commonly observed "over-bidding" relative to the risk neutral bid function in sealed bid auctions (see Cox, Roberson, and Smith, 1982, 1984, 1985, 1988; Harrison, 1989; Walker, Smith, and Cox, 1990; Rietz, 1992). Alternatively, over-bidding could result from a positive intercept. Intuitively, this results from a utility of winning the auction that is independent of the profit received.

The red line in Figure 2 shows the average level of overbidding (bidding greater than the predicted risk neutral bid) as a function of value. This is measured as the difference

---

[4] Rietz (1992) also runs second-price sealed bid auctions and attempts to induce risk averse preferences in some treatments.

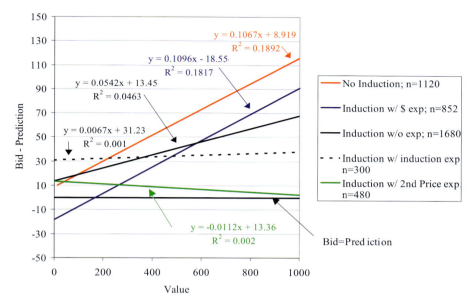

Figure 2. Least-squares trend lines for deviations in bids from the risk neutral prediction using data from Harrison (1989), Walker, Cox, and Smith (1990), and Rietz (1993). A trend line slope of "0" would indicate on-average, risk-neutral bidding behavior. Within each treatment, data is aggregated across sources. The treatments are as follows. "No Induction" includes data from dollar-valued auctions. "Induction w/$ exp" includes data from auctions in which risk neutral preferences were induced on subjects who had previously participated in dollar-valued auctions. "Induction w/o exp" includes data from auctions in which risk neutral preferences were induced on subjects without previous auction experience. "Induction w/induction exp" includes data from auctions in which risk neutral preferences were induced on subjects who had previously participated in auctions with risk neutral, induced preferences. "Induction w/2nd Price exp" includes data from auctions in which risk neutral preferences were induced on subjects who had previously participated in second-price auctions under risk neutral, induced preferences.

between the bid and the predicted bid, aggregating the data from all the dollar payoff auctions in Harrison (1989), Walker, Smith, and Cox (1990), and Rietz (1992) using a least-squares trend line. Subjects with low values bid higher than the risk neutral prediction and the amount of "over-bidding" increases with value.[5] Thus, the slope (0.1067) is greater than the risk neutral bid function prediction (0), as risk-averse preferences would predict. Inducing risk neutral preferences should flatten the slope of the bidding line. We classify the value of winning the auction as one of the "other" factors in the utility function, a factor unaffected by induction, so we do not predict that the positive intercept will decrease with induction.

---

[5] We note that, in addition to being true in aggregate, this in nearly universally true for each individual subject.

The rest of the lines in Figure 2 show, the average level of overbidding for various risk-neutral preference-induction treatments, aggregating the data from all similar-treatment auctions in Harrison (1989), Walker, Smith, and Cox (1990), and Rietz (1992) using least-squares trend lines.

When induction is attempted on subjects who have already been in dollar payoff auctions (shown as the blue line), the intercept drops but the slope (0.1096) changes little. Apparently it is difficult to break the over-bidding behavior in subjects who have had experience in dollar-payoff auctions. Rietz (1992) refers to this as hysteresis. Induction on inexperienced subjects or subjects experienced with induction in the same or similar environments meets with more success.

When induction is attempted on subjects who have no previous experience in sealed bid auctions (shown as the solid black line), there is a significant reduction in the slope of the bid function (down to 0.0542). The slope falls further (to 0.0067) when subjects return for a second set of induced-preference auctions, as shown by the dashed black line. In fact, this treatment results in a slope closest to the risk neutral prediction of 0.

Finally, when subjects are given the opportunity to learn about the induction mechanism in second-price sealed bid auctions before using it in first-price sealed bid auctions (the green line), bids conform quite closely to the risk-neutral predictions. Rietz (1992) suggests that, because there is a dominant strategy in second-price sealed-bid auctions, subjects are able to learn about the induction mechanism without having to learn about optimal strategies at the same time. Note also that, as values increase, the slight negative slope (-0.0114) results in bids becoming even closer to predictions. This is consistent with the importance of saliency in experimental payoffs. The chances of winning the auction increase and the rewards become more salient as the value increases.

Overall, the evidence from sealed bid auctions suggests that:
(1) It is more difficult to induce preferences when subjects have already formed strategies under dollar payoffs.
(2) Under induction, the behavior of inexperienced subjects conforms more closely to the risk-neutral predictions than the behavior of inexperienced subjects under dollar payoffs.
(3) Experience with the induction mechanism, especially in a similar, but less complex context, increases the correspondence between the actual outcomes and the risk neutral prediction.

Finally, Rietz (1992) also shows that risk averse preference induction results in bid functions that closely track the appropriate risk averse predictions. We will address the ability to induce risk seeking and risk averse preferences in more detail in the next two sections.

3.2. Inducing Risk Aversion and Risk Seeking: Evidence from Paired Choice Tasks

Berg et al. (1986) attempt to induce both risk averse and risk seeking preferences. Across these treatments, they compare the choices that subjects make over paired bets. The bets in a pair differ only in variance. Each bet has the same expected value, but one

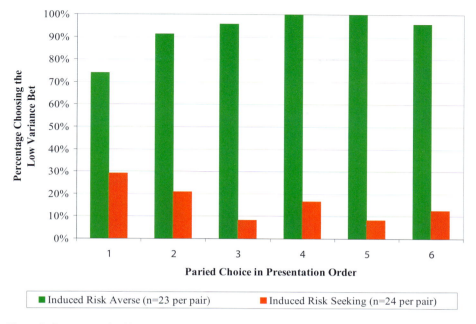

Figure 3. Percentage of subjects choosing the low-variance bet in paired choice tasks in Berg et al. (1986). The green bars are choices made by subjects with induced risk averse preferences. The red bars are choices made by subjects with induced risk seeking preferences.

is a relatively high variance bet while the other is a relatively low variance bet. Figure 3 shows the percentage of subjects who chose the low variance bet of each pair. Subjects with induced risk aversion chose the low variance bet the majority of the time (100% in some cases) and they chose it significantly more often than subjects with induced risk seeking preferences. The evidence here suggests that inducing different risk preferences results in a significant change in behavior as predicted.[6]

3.3. Inducing Risk Aversion and Risk Seeking: Evidence from the Becker–DeGroot–Marshak Procedure

Berg et al. (1986) also study induced risk averse and risk seeking preferences using a pricing task. Valuations for gambles are elicited as prices for the gambles using the Becker, DeGroot, and Marschak (1964) procedure. In this incentive-compatible procedure, subjects submit a minimum acceptable sales price for each gamble. Then,

---

[6] Prasnikar (1998) demonstrates that the comparative static results hold for a much larger set of gambles. She also builds a method of calibrating the degree of error in induction enabling her to demonstrate more precisely the relationship between saliency and the performance of the lottery method.

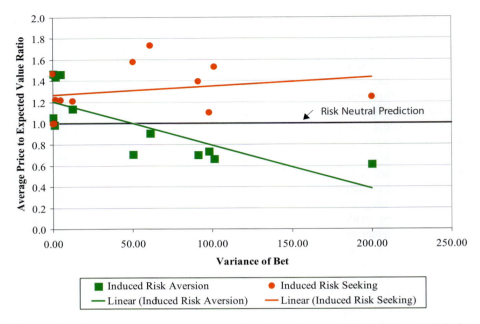

Figure 4. Ratio of average prices to expected values of gambles in Berg et al. (1986). Prices are elicited using the incentive compatible mechanism of Becker, DeGroot, and Marschak (1964). The lines "Linear (Induced Risk Aversion)" and "Linear (Induced Risk Seeking)" represent linear least-squares trend lines.

a random draw from a known distribution determines an "offer" price. If the offer price exceeds the minimum acceptable sales price, the subject sells the bet at the offer price. If not, the subject plays the bet. The dominant strategy for this pricing task is to reveal one's true value as the minimum acceptable sales price.

Figure 4 shows the ratios of average stated prices to expected values for the gambles as a function of variance. The risk neutral prediction is that prices will equal expected values, making the ratio one. Risk averse subjects should price gambles at less than expected values, with the discount increasing with risk. Risk seeking subjects should price gambles at more than expected values, with the premium increasing with risk. This pattern is clearly shown in Figure 4. The evidence suggests that inducing different risk preferences results in shifts in valuations as predicted.

4. Summary

In this chapter, we describe the lottery procedure for inducing preferences over units of experimental exchange and show how it is supported by several experiments on behavior in simple contexts.

We consider the evidence from several papers by different researchers that attempt to induce risk neutral preferences in first-price sealed bid auctions. The evidence is quite clear in these auction experiments: The experiences of subjects affect how the inducing technique performs. Experience with monetary payoffs appears to dampen the effect of the induction technique so much that results differ little from those observed under monetary payoffs. This appears to be a hysteresis effect resulting from the prior monetary payoff auctions because the results come significantly closer to the risk neutral prediction when subjects have no previous auction experience. Results come even closer to the risk neutral prediction as subjects gain experience in auctions run with the induction mechanism. Finally, the results point to the importance of simple settings as learning tasks. Convergence toward the risk neutral prediction appears to be accelerated by experience with the induction mechanism in second-price sealed bid auctions (where there is a dominant strategy for bidding).

We also review evidence from a set of paired choice and pricing tasks designed to determine whether subjects' revealed preferences over gambles are consistent with attempted risk preference induction. There is strong support for the performance of inducing when subjects choose between paired gambles. Subjects induced to be risk seeking nearly always choose the riskier gamble, while those induced to be risk averse choose the less risky one. There is similar support for pricing gambles, but the strength of the effect is a function of the variance of the gambles. This is consistent with other experimental evidence about the importance of saliency. Risk preferences matter little when there is little risk! As risk increases, risk preferences should become more important and, in fact, we see this in the experiments. Subjects appear to price gambles more consistently with their induced risk preferences as variance increases.

The lottery technique can be a powerful experimental tool. Theoretically it depends on very few assumptions and is therefore robust to many conditions. We note several of interest to experimenters:

(1) Preferences can be induced in single person or multiple person settings.
(2) The ability to induce preferences is independent of an equilibrium concept.
(3) The technique is immune to wealth changes during the experiment.[7]
(4) There is no limitation on the form of the induced preference function, $V(.)$, with the caveat that the range of V must be mapped in a 0 to 1 probability range.[8]
(5) There is no limitation on the dimensionality of the induced preference function, $V(.)$, so that $V(.)$ could be used to induce a multi-period utility function. Thus, if

---

[7] Suppose we had the subject make two choices and between choices we used the lottery technique to pay the subject. Using the technique after choice 1 would in no way alter our ability to induce using exactly the same procedure on choice two. Preferences are still linear in probability even after the wealth change and the function used to transform units of experimental exchange to probability will determine the utility function that is induced.

[8] Frequently, given the structure of economic theory (e.g., portfolio and agency theory) monotonic functions (e.g., linear or risk averse utility functions) are necessary to test the predictions of theory. However, V(francs) could be much more general and in fact non-monotonic or non-differentiable.

francs$_1$ and francs$_2$ represented the amount of francs received at the end of each of two periods then a multi-period utility function can be defined by:

$$V(\text{francs}_1, \text{francs}_2) = p.$$

(6) Preferences can be induced even when subjects are not expected utility maximizers, provided that (i) it is possible to reduce the payoffs in the setting to be one of two prizes, and (ii) preferences are linear in probability. Thus, induction should "work" for some of the proposed replacements of expected utility theory such as rank dependent utility theory and regret theory.[9]

Finally, because the lottery technique of inducing risk preferences relies on a strict subset of the axioms of expected utility theory, to reject induction is to reject expected utility theory.

Acknowledgements

We thank James Cox, Glenn Harrison, Vernon Smith and James Walker for their data.

References

Becker, G.M., DeGroot, M.H., Marschak, J. (1964). "Measuring utility by a single-response sequential method". Behavioral Science 9, 226–232.
Berg, J.E., Dickhaut, J.W., Rietz, T.A. (2003). "Preference reversals and induced risk preferences: Evidence for noisy maximization". Journal of Risk and Uncertainty 27, 139–170.
Berg, J.E., Daley, L.A., Dickhaut, J.W., O'Brien, J.R. (1986). "Controlling preferences for lotteries on units of experimental exchange". Quarterly Journal of Economics 101, 281–306.
Cox, J.C., Roberson, B., Smith, V.L. (1982). "Theory and behavior of single object auctions". Research in Experimental Economics 2, 1–43.
Cox, J.C., Smith, V.L., Walker, J.M. (1984). "Theory and behavior of multiple unit discriminative auctions". Journal of Finance 39, 983–1010.
Cox, J.C., Smith, V.L., Walker, J.M. (1985). "Experimental development of sealed-bid auction theory: Calibrating controls for risk aversion". AEA Papers and Proceedings 75, 160–165.
Cox, J.C., Smith, V.L., Walker, J.M. (1988). "Theory and behavior of first price auctions". Journal of Risk and Uncertainty 1, 61–99.
Harrison, G.W. (1989). "Theory and misbehavior of first-price auctions". The American Economic Review 79, 749–762.
Prasnikar, V. (1998). "How well does utility maximization approximate subjects' behavior? An experimental study". Mimeo.

---

[9] Even for prospect theory when probabilities are bounded away from the endpoints, the valuations of outcomes are weighted by a monotonic function, $\varphi(p)$, of the probability of the preferred outcome. Thus, in principle, if we could determine $\varphi(p)$, we would be able to induce an arbitrary function under prospect theory by mapping francs into the probability of winning the larger prize using $p = \varphi^{-1}(V(\text{francs}))$. Then, subjects would act as if maximizing $V(\text{francs})$.

Rietz, T.A. (1993). "Implementing and testing risk preference induction mechanisms in experimental sealed bid auctions". Journal of Risk and Uncertainty 7, 199–213.

Roth, A.E., Malouf, M.W.K. (1979). "Game-theoretic models and the role of bargaining". Psychological Review 86, 574–594.

Smith, V.L. (1976). "Experimental economics: Induced value theory". American Economic Review 66, 274–279.

Vickrey, W. (1961). "Counterspeculation, auctions, and competitive sealed tenders". The Journal of Finance 16, 8–27.

Walker, J.M., Smith, V.L., Cox, J.C. (1990). "Inducing risk neutral preferences: An examination in a controlled market environment". Journal of Risk and Uncertainty 3, 5–24.

AUTHOR INDEX OF VOLUME 1

n indicates citation in a footnote.

Adelman, L., *see* Jedetski, J.   984
Afriat, Sidney   482, 964
Akerlof, George   121, 325
Alba, J.W.   1015
Alger, Dan   63
Aliprantis, C.D.   17
Allsopp, Louise   340
Alsemgeest, P.   187
Amden, Holly   779n, 789
Ames, Ruth E., *see* Marwell, Gerald   776, 793n
Anderson, C.   377–380
Anderson, Lisa R.   335, 336, 336n, 337n, 338–340, 344
Anderson, Lisa R., *see* Holt, Charles A.   337n
Anderson, Simon P.   68n, 551–556, 823n, 849n, 850, 852, 854
Andreoni, James   483, 484n, 489, 516, 518, 598, 637, 776, 779, 781, 781n, 782, 784, 785, 796, 802, 802n, 819n, 823, 825, 848n
Andreoni, James, *see* Miller, John H.   851, 854
Andrews, Julia, *see* Siegel, Sidney   914, 916
Ansic, D., *see* Powell, M.   1066, 1068
Apfelbaum, E.   605
Archibald, Glen   195n, 211
Arifovic, J.   634
Arrow, K.J.   872, 880
Asparouhova, Elena   24, 376
Atkinson, S.M.   1071n
Attiyeh, G.   629
Austen-Smith, D.   872, 878
Ausubel, L.M.   186, 188
Axelrod, R.   598, 1035
Ayton, P.   987, 990

Babb, E., *see* Scherr, B.   628
Babcock, Lind   532n
Bachelier, M.L.   364
Backerman, Steven R.   676, 700–702, 706
Bagnoli, M.   626, 635–637, 793n
Bagwell, Kyle   585
Bailey, Elizabeth, *see* Joskow, Paul   664

Baird, S.B., *see* Atkinson, S.M.   1071n
Bajtelsmit, V.L.   1070
Banerjee, A.V.   335, 340
Banks, J.   196n, 545, 639
Banks, J.S., *see* Austen-Smith, D.   872, 878
Barber, B.   1002
Baron-Cohen, Simon   414
Basmann, Robert L., *see* Battalio, Raymond C.   960, 965
Basu, K.   549
Battalio, Raymond C.   521–523, 960, 965, 1051
Battalio, Raymond C., *see* Van Huyck, John B.   293, 403, 455–461, 464, 500, 521, 522, 527–529, 556
Baumeister, R.F.   844
Baumol, William J.   71, 155
Bazerman, Max H.   444
Beatty, J., *see* Gigerenzer, G.   1019
Becker, G.M.   950, 956, 969, 1093, 1094
Becker, Gary S.   37, 109n, 489, 784, 837, 923, 962
Beckett, Elizabeth, *see* McClelland, Gary H.   915
Beckmann, K.   750
Beekman, Robert L., *see* Harrison, Glenn W.   764
Beil, R.O., *see* Van Huyck, John B.   293, 455–458, 464, 500, 556
Ben-David, S., *see* Bagnoli, M.   636
Berg, E., *see* Kitzis, S.   303, 305
Berg, Joyce E.   742n, 743n, 746, 748–750, 911, 1036, 1060, 1087, 1090, 1092–1094
Berger, S.E., *see* Ingram, B.L.   510
Bergin, J.   479
Bergstrom, Theodore   630n, 831
Bernasek, A., *see* Jianakoplos, N.A.   1070
Bernheim, B. Douglas   165
Berretty, P.M.   981
Berscheid, Ellen, *see* Walster, Elaine   831, 1036
Bettman, J.R., *see* Payne, J.W.   977, 984, 1014
Betz, N.E., *see* Weber, E.U.   1062n, 1066, 1071

Bhatia, Ramesh, *see* Griffin, Charles C. 758
Bikhchandani, Sushil 335
Binmore, K. 60, 437, 500, 502, 505n
Binney, S.E., *see* MacGregor, D. 1061
Binswanger, Hans P. 914, 1049
Bishop, Richard C. 755
Black, D. 889
Blackburn, McKinley 763, 764
Blais, A.-R. 1062n
Blais, A.-R., *see* Weber, E.U. 1062n, 1066, 1071
Blume, A. 573–575, 580, 903
Blume, Lawrence, *see* Bergstrom, Theodore 831
Boening, M., *see* Archibald, Glen 195n
Bohm, Peter 725–727, 730, 736–738, 755, 756, 758, 932, 933, 936, 956, 957
Bohn, Roger E. 677, 678
Bolton, Gary E. 415, 447, 489, 491, 492, 492n, 494n, 495, 496, 496n, 515, 516, 518, 532, 533n, 535n, 537–539, 850
Bolton, Gary E., *see* Fong, Duncan 491
Bondarenko, O. 750, 750n
Borges, Bernhard F.J. 946, 994–996, 997n, 998–1001
Bornstein, G. 898, 899
Bosch-Domenech, Antoni 370n, 395, 401, 403, 408
Bossaerts, Peter L. 367, 376
Bossaerts, Peter L., *see* Asparouhova, Elena 24, 376
Bossaerts, Peter L., *see* Bondarenko, O. 750, 750n
Bottom, William 864, 869n, 870, 887
Bouchez, Nicole 472, 475
Bounmy, Kene 341
Boverie, P.E. 1061
Bower, G.H., *see* Gluck, M.A. 303
Bowles, Samuel 123
Bowman, L.B., *see* Dolbear, F.T. 63
Boyd, M. 1002n
Boyle, K.J., *see* Desvousges, W.H 539n
Brachinger, H.W., *see* Schubert, R. 1062–1068
Brandts, Jordi 545–547, 585, 779, 825, 826, 829, 853, 854
Brandts, Jordi, *see* Bolton, Gary E. 495, 496, 496n, 533n
Bratton, Kenneth, *see* Smith, Vernon L. 85, 112, 266
Brayfield, Arthur H., *see* Messick, Samuel 914
Brent, E., *see* Granberg, D. 749

Brewer, Paul J. 44
Brinig, M.F. 1062
Briscoe, John, *see* Griffin, Charles C. 758
Bröder, A. 1014
Brown, G.W. 588
Brown, Gardner M., *see* Hammack, Judd 939
Brown, Lloyd B., *see* Harrison, Glenn W. 764
Brown, M., *see* Schubert, R. 1062–1068
Brown-Kruse, Jamie L. 71, 72, 74, 155, 510, 510n, 513
Brown-Kruse, Jamie, *see* Cronshaw, Mark B. 664–666
Brown-Kruse, Jamie, *see* Godby, Robert 666n
Browning, Edgar F. 127
Browning, Jacquelene M., *see* Browning, Edgar F. 127
Browning, Martin 923
Brusco, S. 186, 193
Bryant, John 455
Budescu, D.V., *see* Erev, Ido 1026
Bulfin, Robert L., *see* Rassenti, Stephen J. 644, 645
Burlando, Roberto 779
Burnham, T.C. 435
Burns, Penny 192
Bush, R.R. 571

Cadsby, C.B. 510, 510n, 637
Caginalp, Gunduz 256
Camerer, Colin F. 303, 341, 344, 392–394, 407, 599n, 607, 608, 610–612, 615, 720, 723, 781n, 903, 976, 1051
Camerer, Colin F., *see* Banks, J. 545
Camerer, Colin F., *see* Ho, Teck-Hua 392, 393, 400, 401, 407, 607, 609–611
Camerer, Colin F., *see* Weber, Roberto A. 903–906
Campbell, Joseph 27, 102, 228, 229
Canning, D. 573
Caporael, L.R. 821n
Capra, C.M. 181, 549, 554, 556
Caramanis, Michael C., *see* Bohn, Roger E. 677, 678
Carhart, M.M. 994, 998
Carlén, B., *see* Bohm, Peter 727
Carlson, Dale 656, 666
Carlson, John A. 217
Carroll, John S., *see* Bazerman, Max H. 444
Carson, Richard T., *see* Mitchell, Robert C. 755, 763n
Casari, M. 849

Cason, Timothy N.   19n, 20, 36, 39, 39n, 88, 164, 165, 166n, 167, 175, 176, 265, 267, 269, 271, 662, 664, 667, 725, 798n, 803, 810, 811, 813
Cech, Paula-Ann, *see* Cox, James C.   671
Chammah, A.M., *see* Rapoport, Amnon   509, 598
Chan, Kenneth S.   796, 799, 831
Chapman, D.P., *see* Levin, I.P.   1062
Chase, V.M., *see* Hertwig, R.   1029
Chatterjee, K.   560, 561
Chen, H.C.   552
Chen, Kay-Yut   349, 626, 630–635, 638
Cheng, J.   638
Chertkoff, J.M., *see* Streater, A.L.   449
Cheung, Yin-Wong   472
Cho, I.   587
Chong, Juin-Kuan, *see* Camerer, Colin F.   611, 612
Chong, Juin-Kuan, *see* Ho, Teck-Hua   607, 609, 610
Christie, William   175
Clark, H.H.   903
Clark, Herbert H., *see* Schober, Michael F.   903
Clark, J.B.   11, 638n
Clark, Kenneth   523
Clarke, Edward H.   626, 736
Clauser, Laura   170, 185
Clements, Leianne A., *see* Harrison, Glenn W.   764
Coatney, K., *see* Menkhaus, D.   196n
Coatney, K., *see* Phillips, O.   196
Coats, J.   637
Cohen, A., *see* Levy, H.   1066, 1069
Cohen, Kalman J.   25
Coleman, J.S.   836
Condorcet, Marquis de M.J.A.N.C.   889
Conn, David, *see* Cox, James C.   671
Constantine, Greg, *see* Caginalp, Gunduz   256
Cook, E.F., *see* Pearson, S.D.   981
Cook, J.P., *see* Van Huyck, John B.   459, 461
Cooper, David J.   585, 588n, 590, 592n, 593–596
Cooper, Russell   164n, 454, 500, 523
Cooperstock, R.   1061n
Cootner, P.   993
Copeland, Thomas E.   25, 344
Corchon, Luis   626
Corrigan, B., *see* Dawes, Robyn M.   1011
Cosmides, Leda   411, 415, 1037, 1040
Costa-Gomes, M.   397, 401

Coursey, Don L.   71, 72, 74, 155, 156, 200, 235, 239
Coursey, Don L., *see* McClelland, Gary H.   759
Cox, J.R., *see* Griggs, R.A.   1039, 1040
Cox, James C.   92, 93, 95–97, 157–161, 186n, 311, 313–316, 318, 662, 671, 915, 960–962, 964, 965, 969, 971, 972, 974, 1054–1056, 1078, 1080, 1084, 1090
Cox, James C., *see* Walker, James M.   1056, 1090–1092
Cramton, P.   185
Cramton, P.C., *see* Ausubel, L.M.   186
Crawford, V.   575
Crawford, V., *see* Costa-Gomes, M.   397, 401
Cremer, Jacques   903
Cronshaw, Mark B.   656, 664–666
Croson, Rachel T.A.   637, 777, 777n, 779–781, 784, 785, 787, 787n, 849
Croson, Rachel T.A., *see* Marks, Melanie B.   637
Cummings, Ronald G.   752n, 756, 760–762
Cummings, Ronald G., *see* Neill, Helen R.   758, 760
Cutter, S.L.   1061
Czerlinski, J.   1008, 1009
Czerlinski, J., *see* Gigerenzer, G.   981, 984

D'Agostino, R.B., *see* Pozen, M.W.   981
Dales, John   661
Daley, L.A., *see* Berg, Joyce E.   1087, 1090, 1092–1094
Daly, M.   1061n
Daniel, T.E.   294, 560, 566, 570
Daniel, T.E., *see* Rapoport, Amnon   560
Dasgupta, P., *see* Binmore, K.   502
Daston, L., *see* Gigerenzer, G.   1019
Davis, Douglas D.   63, 64, 64n, 66, 66n, 68, 68n, 69, 72, 74, 84, 138–143, 145, 171, 174, 175, 185, 186n, 555, 636, 736, 784
Davis, Douglas D., *see* Cason, Timothy N.   164, 165, 166n, 167, 176
Davis, Douglas D., *see* Holt, Charles A.   165, 167, 176
Davis, J.N.   1042
Davis, J.N., *see* Hertwig, R.   1042
Dawes, Robyn M.   914, 1008, 1011
Dawes, Robyn M., *see* Caporael, L.R.   821n
de Bruin, E.M.N., *see* van Lange, P.A.M.   836
Deaton, Angus   923
Debondt, W.   365
DeGroot, Morris H., *see* Becker, G.M.   950, 956, 969, 1093, 1094

DeJong, Douglas V., *see* Blume, A.   575, 580, 903
DeJong, Douglas V., *see* Cooper, Russell   164n, 500, 523
Demsetz, Harold   25
Deng, G., *see* Franciosi, Robert   57, 949, 951–953
Denton, M.   677
Desvousges, W.H.   539n
Detweiler, J., *see* MacGregor, D.   1061
Dickens, William   120
Dickhaut, John W., *see* Berg, Joyce E.   911, 1036, 1060, 1087, 1090, 1092–1094
Dickie, M.   753, 758
Dienes, Z., *see* McLeod, P.   978
Dodd, B., *see* MacGregor, D.   1061
Dolbear, F.T.   63
Dovidio, J.F., *see* Kealy, Mary Jo   757
Downs, A.   898
Duffield, John   757
Duffy, J.   394, 406, 407
Dulatre, J., *see* Sherstyuk, K.   194, 195
Dunford, R.W., *see* Desvousges, W.H.   539n
Dunlap, R.E., *see* McStay, J.R.   1061
Durham, Yvonne   136, 206, 209
Duverger, M.   889

Easley, D.   20
Eavey, Cheryl L.   857n, 859, 861, 863, 864, 878
Eavey, Cheryl L., *see* Bottom, William   864, 869n, 870, 887
Ebert, A., *see* Gigerenzer, G.   1023
Eckel, Catherine C.   435, 509n, 513–515, 515n, 516, 518, 1062, 1063, 1065, 1066, 1066n, 1068, 1071
Eckel, Catherine C., *see* Moore, E.   1062, 1064–1067
Edgeworth, Francis Y.   69, 849
Edland, A.   1014
Edwards, Corwin   165
Edwards, W.   1026
Edwards, Ward, *see* Goodman, Barbara   914
Edwards, Ward, *see* Tversky, Amos   914–916
Eichenberger, R., *see* Frey, B.S.   1043
Elbaz, Gilad., *see* Plott, Charles R.   200
Elder, H.W., *see* Misiolek, W.S.   144
Elkind, D.   449
Elliott, Steven, *see* Cason, Timothy N.   664
Elliott, Steven, *see* Cummings, Ronald G.   762
Elliott, Steven, *see* Godby, Robert   666n

Elman, J.   977
Elron, E., *see* Levy, H.   1066, 1069
Endersby, J.W.   887
Engelbert-Wiggans, R.   186
Engelmann, Dirk, *see* Grimm, Veronica   190, 191
Epstein, Seth, *see* Cox, James C.   969
Erev, Ido   273, 274, 1026
Erev, Ido, *see* Rapoport, Amnon   273, 274, 281–286
Erev, Ido, *see* Roth, Alvin E.   294, 407, 436, 437, 451, 488, 566, 612

Falk, Armin, *see* Fehr, Ernst   319, 320, 325, 327, 329
Falk, Armin, *see* Gächter, Simon   322n
Falkinger, J.   626, 627n, 630, 633, 634
Fama, Eugene   364, 365
Fararo, T.J.   837
Farrell, J.   464
Federal Register   664
Fehr, Ernst   121–124, 319–321, 322n, 323–325, 326n, 327–329, 396, 489, 492n, 496, 532n, 849, 850, 923
Fehr, Ernst, *see* Falkinger, J.   627n, 630, 633, 634
Feld, S.L.   837
Felsenthal, D.S.   889, 895
Felsenthal, D.S., *see* Rapoport, Amnon   889, 895
Ferguson, T.S.   1042, 1044
Ferrer-i-Carbonell, A., *see* Hartog, J.   1062–1064
Fiedler, K.   1028
Finsinger, Jörg   157
Fiorina, Morris P.   860, 874, 878, 915
Fischhoff, B., *see* Lichtenstein, Sarah   1026
Fischoff, Baruch, *see* Slovic, Paul   914
Fisher, A., *see* Dickie, M.   753, 758
Fisher, Eric O'N.   256–258
Fisher Jr., Edwin B., *see* Battalio, Raymond C.   960, 965
Fitzgerald, J., *see* Ortmann, A.   794n
Flynn, J.   1061
Fong, Duncan   491
Forman, Charles, *see* Carlson, Dale   656, 666
Forsythe, Robert   344, 376, 413–415, 417, 419–421, 423, 424, 426, 429–431, 433, 492, 743n, 746, 749, 750, 890, 891, 891n, 892, 895, 896, 915

Forsythe, Robert, *see* Berg, Joyce E.   743n, 746, 749
Forsythe, Robert, *see* Cooper, Russell   164n, 500, 523
Fouraker, Lawrence   66n, 146, 148–151, 413, 418, 914, 919, 920
Fouraker, Lawrence, *see* Siegel, Sidney   914
Fox, John A.   763, 764
Franciosi, Robert   57, 656, 661, 662, 664, 666, 949, 951–953
Franciosi, Robert, *see* Attiyeh, G.   629
Frank, R.H.   450
French, K., *see* Fama, Eugene   365
Frey, B.S.   1043
Friedman, Daniel   85, 88, 94, 112, 206, 264, 266, 267, 344, 472, 475, 479, 524
Friedman, Daniel, *see* Cason, Timothy N.   19n, 20, 36, 39, 39n, 88, 265, 267, 269, 271, 662
Friedman, Daniel, *see* Cheung, Yin-Wong   472
Friedman, Daniel, *see* Copeland, Thomas E.   344
Friedman, Daniel, *see* Kelley, H.   306
Friedman, Daniel, *see* Kitzis, S.   303, 305
Friedman, Daniel, *see* Rich, Changhua Sun   109, 114, 665
Friedman, J.W.   598
Friedman, J.W., *see* Chen, H.C.   552
Friedman, M.   553–976
Frye, M.B., *see* Atkinson, S.M.   1071n
Frykblom, Peter   761
Fudenberg, Drew   488, 585, 607, 612
Fuller, M., *see* Rapoport, Amnon   561

Gächter, Simon   322n
Gächter, Simon, *see* Falkinger, J.   627n, 630, 633, 634
Gächter, Simon, *see* Fehr, Ernst   121, 122, 319–321, 322n, 323–325, 326n, 328, 329, 849
Galai, Dan, *see* Copeland, Thomas E.   25
Gale, David   109n
Ganderton, Philip T., *see* Neill, Helen R.   758, 760
Gangadharan, Lata, *see* Cason, Timothy N.   667
Garcia, T.B., *see* Pearson, S.D.   981
Gardner, R., *see* Walker, James M.   887
Garvin, Susan, *see* Cooper, David J.   585, 588n, 590, 592n, 593–596
Gazzale, R., *see* Chen, Kay-Yut   634, 638
Gelfand, D.M., *see* Zarbatany, L.   449
General Accounting Office   664

George, Glen, *see* Plott, Charles R.   115, 116, 223
Gerber, E.R.   890–892, 896
Gerking, S., *see* Dickie, M.   753, 758
Gibbard, A.   84
Gigerenzer, G.   976, 977, 981, 984, 987, 992, 994, 1004, 1016, 1019–1023, 1025–1027, 1033, 1039–1042
Gigerenzer, G., *see* Borges, Bernhard F.J.   994–996, 997n, 998–1001
Gigerenzer, G., *see* Czerlinski, J.   1008, 1009
Gigerenzer, G., *see* Goldstein, D.G.   987–991, 994, 1005
Gigerenzer, G., *see* Hertwig, R.   1028–1030
Gigerenzer, G., *see* Hoffrage, U.   1022, 1024, 1033
Gigerenzer, G., *see* Lindsey, S.   1023, 1024
Gigerenzer, G., *see* Ortmann, A.   1001, 1042
Gigerenzer, G., *see* Rieskamp, J.   1036
Gigerenzer, G., *see* Sedlmeier, P.   1025, 1031
Gigerenzer, G., *see* Todd, P.M.   981
Gilovich, T., *see* Frank, R.H.   450
Gjerstad, S., *see* Williams, Arlington W.   376
Glosten, Lawrence R.   25
Gluck, M.A.   303
Godby, Robert   144, 656, 658, 666, 666n
Godby, Robert, *see* Chan, Kenneth S.   796, 831
Gode, Dhananjay K.   31, 37, 39, 44
Goeree, Jacob K.   181, 183, 549, 849n, 851
Goeree, Jacob K., *see* Anderson, Simon P.   68n, 551–556, 823n, 849n, 850, 852, 854
Goeree, Jacob K., *see* Capra, C.M.   181, 549, 554, 556
Goldman, L., *see* Pearson, S.D.   981
Goldstein, D.A., *see* Siegel, Sidney   916, 1047
Goldstein, D.G.   987–991, 994, 1005
Goldstein, D.G., *see* Borges, Bernhard F.J.   994–996, 997n, 998–1001
Goldstein, D.G., *see* Czerlinski, J.   1008, 1009
Goldstein, D.G., *see* Gigerenzer, G.   987, 994, 1004
Golladay, K. Brett   341
Gomez, R., *see* Capra, C.M.   181, 549, 554, 556
Gomez, R., *see* Goeree, Jacob K.   181, 183
Goodfellow, J.   376
Goodman, Barbara   914
Gottfredson, M.R.   1061n
Granat, S., *see* Anderson, C.   377–380
Granberg, D.   749
Green, J.   626, 628, 736
Green, L.   981

Greenberg, Joseph   865
Greimel, T., *see* Slemrod, J.   750
Grelak, E.   878
Grether, David M.   165, 175, 303, 644–646, 914, 915, 929, 968, 971
Grether, David M., *see* Cox, James C.   915, 971, 972, 974
Griesinger, D.W.   818
Griffin, Charles C.   758
Griffin, D.   1026
Griffith, W.I., *see* Sell, Jane   510, 510n, 513
Griggs, R.A.   1039, 1040
Grimm, Veronica   190, 191
Gronberg, T., *see* Coats, J.   637
Grosskopf, Brit   397
Grossman, Herschel   127
Grossman, Philip, *see* Eckel, Catherine C.   435, 509n, 513–515, 515n, 516, 518, 1062, 1063, 1065, 1066, 1066n, 1068, 1071
Groves, Theodore   156, 626, 630, 736, 803
Guarnaschelli, Serena   341, 344
Gueth, Werner   399, 401
Gunnthorsdottir, Anna, *see* Amden, Holly   779n, 789
Gunto, S., *see* Kravitz, D.   437
Güth, Werner   412, 436, 534, 534n, 539
Güth, Werner, *see* Selten, Reinhard   273
Guttman, J.M.   800
Gysler, M.   1066–1068
Gysler, M., *see* Schubert, R.   1062–1068

Haavelmo, Trygve   127
Hahn, Robert W.   144, 661, 662
Haller, H., *see* Crawford, V.   575
Hamilton, W.D.   1035
Hammack, Judd   939
Hammond, Thomas H.   858, 865n, 867
Hammond, Thomas H., *see* Miller, Gary J.   862, 867–869
Hanemann, W. Michael   539n, 755, 949
Haney, P.   874, 882
Hansberry, K.M., *see* Ortmann, A.   794n
Harbaugh, W.T.   1051, 1062, 1064
Harrison, Glenn W.   94, 155, 157, 180, 181, 183, 318, 764, 917n, 1056, 1059, 1064, 1065, 1090–1092
Harrison, Glenn W., *see* Blackburn, McKinley   763, 764
Harrison, Glenn W., *see* Cummings, Ronald G.   752n, 756, 760–762

Harrison, Glenn W., *see* Neill, Helen R.   758, 760
Harsanyi, John C.   500, 521n
Harstad, Ronald   164, 167, 627n, 630, 631, 634
Hartmann, D.P., *see* Zarbatany, L.   449
Hartog, J.   1062–1064
Hastard, R., *see* Kagel, John H.   188
Hausker, Karl   664n
Hawkins, W., *see* Spigner, C.   1061
Hayes, D.J., *see* Shogren, Jason F.   949, 955
Hayes, Dermot J., *see* Fox, John A.   763, 764
Heberlein, Thomas A., *see* Bishop, Richard C.   755
Henderson, A.M.   939
Hermalin, Benjamin E.   903
Herrnstein, R.J., *see* Wilson, J.Q.   1061n
Hershey, J., *see* Johnson, E.J.   1028
Hertwig, R.   977, 1028–1030, 1042, 1053
Hertwig, R., *see* Hoffrage, U.   1024, 1033
Hertwig, R., *see* Lindsey, S.   1023, 1024
Hertwig, R., *see* Mellers, B.   1028, 1029
Hertwig, R., *see* Sedlmeier, P.   1031
Herzberg, R., *see* Haney, P.   874, 882
Hess, A., *see* Walker, James M.   887
Hey, John D., *see* Allsopp, Louise   340
Hey, John D., *see* Burlando, Roberto   779
Hirota, Masayoshi   376
Hirschi, T., *see* Gottfredson, M.R.   1061n
Hirshleifer, David, *see* Bikhchandani, Sushil   335
Hirshleifer, Jack   127
Hirshleifer, Jack, *see* Durham, Yvonne   136
Ho, Teck-Hua   392, 393, 400, 401, 407, 607, 609–611
Ho, Teck-Hua, *see* Camerer, Colin F.   392–394, 407, 607, 608, 611, 612
Hoffman, Elizabeth   411, 413–415, 417, 420, 423–426, 428, 430, 432–435, 488, 489n, 492, 492n, 915
Hoffrage, U.   992, 1022, 1024, 1033
Hoffrage, U., *see* Gigerenzer, G.   1020, 1021, 1023, 1026, 1027
Hoffrage, U., *see* Martignon, L.   1006, 1011–1013
Hoffrage, U., *see* Rieskamp, J.   1014, 1015
Hoggatt, A.C.   146–148, 151
Holt, Charles A.   62, 63, 84, 138–140, 165, 167, 176, 181, 185, 337n, 969, 1048, 1062, 1065
Holt, Charles A., *see* Anderson, Lisa R.   335, 336, 336n, 337n, 338, 344

Holt, Charles A., *see* Anderson, Simon P.   68n, 551–556, 823n, 849n, 850, 852, 854
Holt, Charles A., *see* Brandts, Jordi   545–547, 585
Holt, Charles A., *see* Capra, C.M.   181, 549, 554, 556
Holt, Charles A., *see* Davis, Douglas D.   63, 64, 64n, 66, 66n, 68, 69, 72, 139–143, 171, 174, 186n, 636, 736, 784
Holt, Charles A., *see* Goeree, Jacob K.   549, 849n, 851
Holt, Charles A., *see* Laury, S.K.   1050
Holton, G.   977
Homans, G.C.   836
Hong, James T.   619
Hood, W.B., *see* Pozen, M.W.   981
Horowitz, Joel L., *see* Forsythe, Robert   413–415, 417, 419–421, 423, 424, 426, 429–431, 433, 492, 915
Hsu, S., *see* Binmore, K.   60, 500, 505n
Huang, Maria, *see* Brewer, Paul J.   44
Huber, O.   1015
Huck, Steffen   337n
Hudson, S.P., *see* Desvousges, W.H.   539n
Hug, K., *see* Gigerenzer, G.   1039–1042
Hume, David   256
Hummels, D., *see* Brown-Kruse, Jamie L.   510, 510n, 513
Hung, Angela A.   337n, 340, 341, 344
Hurwicz, L.   31n, 37, 101, 625, 626, 630, 635

Ibn Khaldoun   256
Ingram, B.L.   510
Irwin, Julie, *see* McClelland, Gary H.   915
Isaac, R. Mark   44, 46, 63, 153, 156, 164, 170, 175n, 178, 180, 183, 185, 186n, 223n, 235, 239, 241, 244, 637, 771, 776, 789, 795n, 796, 804, 825, 832, 846n, 853, 914n
Isaac, R. Mark, *see* Attiyeh, G.   629
Isaac, R. Mark, *see* Coursey, Don L.   71, 72, 74, 155, 156, 200
Isaac, R. Mark, *see* Cox, James C.   157–161, 671
Isaac, R. Mark, *see* Franciosi, Robert   656, 661, 662, 664, 666
Isaac, R. Mark, *see* Grether, David M.   644–646

Jackson, Matthew O.   626
Jacobsen, B.   746n
James, Duncan, *see* Isaac, R. Mark   186n
Jamison, Julian C.   20

Jedetski, J.   984
Jevons, W.S.   4
Jianakoplos, N.A.   1070
Jiranyakul, Komain, *see* Battalio, Raymond C.   1051
Johannesson, Magnus   760
Johansson, Per-Olov, *see* Johannesson, Magnus   760
John, Andrew, *see* Cooper, Russell   454
Johnson, E., *see* Harrison, Glenn W.   1065
Johnson, E.J.   1028
Johnson, E.J., *see* Payne, J.W.   977, 984, 1014
Johnson, F.R., *see* Desvousges, W.H.   539n
Johnson, J.E.V.   1070
Johnson, Michael D.   217
Joireman, J.A., *see* van Lange, P.A.M.   836
Jonker, N., *see* Hartog, J.   1062–1064
Joskow, Paul   664
Joyce, P.   100
Jung, Yun Joo   180, 615
Juslin, P.   1026

Kachelmeier, Steven J.   55–58, 914, 915, 940, 1064
Kagan, S.   449
Kagel, John H.   185, 186n, 187, 188, 190–192, 344, 537n, 629, 960
Kagel, John H., *see* Battalio, Raymond C.   960, 965, 1051
Kagel, John H., *see* Cooper, David J.   585, 588n, 590, 592n, 593–596
Kagel, John H., *see* Jung, Yun Joo   180, 615
Kahn, C.M., *see* Engelbert-Wiggans, R.   186
Kahn, L.M.   444, 599, 599n
Kahneman, Daniel   55–58, 61, 273, 281, 412, 413, 423, 424, 426, 429, 437, 539n, 746n, 940, 943, 945, 949–953, 955, 976, 977, 979, 1019, 1047, 1050
Kahneman, Daniel, *see* Mellers, B.   1028, 1029
Kahneman, Daniel, *see* Tversky, Amos   326n, 914, 926, 929, 930, 936, 969, 972, 1028, 1029, 1031, 1047, 1050
Kalai, E.   500
Kandel, D.B.   1061n
Kandori, Michihiro   479
Kaneko, Mamoru   626
Kanwisher, N.   1028
Kaplan, Todd   400
Karni, Edi   929, 969
Katok, Elena, *see* Bolton, Gary E.   492, 495, 496n, 515, 516, 518, 538, 539

Katz, Lawrence   120
Katz, Lawrence, *see* Dickens, William   120
Kawagoe, T.   629, 630
Kay, Stephen, *see* Clark, Kenneth   523
Kealy, Mary Jo   757
Kealy, Mary Jo, *see* Bishop, Richard C.   755
Keil, L.J.   449
Kelley, H.   303, 305, 306, 308
Kelley, H., *see* Kitzis, S.   303, 305
Kelly, Frank S., *see* Fisher, Eric O'N.   256
Keser, Claudia   779, 793, 794
Ketcham, Jon   56, 63, 66n, 72, 139, 236n
Keynes, John Maynard   341, 391
Kile, Charles, *see* Miller, Gary J.   867–869
Kim, Chung, *see* Kagel, John H.   537n
Kim, Minseong, *see* Grossman, Herschel   127
Kim, T.   626, 630, 635, 635n
Kim, Y., *see* Blume, A.   573–575, 580
Kim, Y.G., *see* Blume, A.   903
King, Ronald R.   242, 247, 254, 864–866
Kinney, W.R., *see* Rozef, M.S.   993
Kinross, S., *see* Kagel, John H.   191
Kirchler, E., *see* Fehr, Ernst   325, 328, 329
Kirchsteiger, Georg, *see* Fehr, Ernst   121–124, 323–325, 326n, 327, 329
Kitzis, S.   303, 305
Klaus, Schmidt, *see* Fehr, Ernst   489, 492n, 496
Kleinbölting, H., *see* Gigerenzer, G.   1026, 1027
Kleinman, Daniel, *see* Bossaerts, Peter L.   376
Kliebenstein, James B., *see* Fox, John A.   763, 764
Kliebenstein, James B., *see* Shogren, Jason F.   943, 949, 955
Knetsch, Jack L.   940–942
Knetsch, Jack L., *see* Borges, Bernhard F.J.   946
Knetsch, Jack L., *see* Kahneman, Daniel   55–58, 61, 412, 413, 423, 424, 426, 429, 437, 539n, 940, 943, 945, 949–953, 955
Knight, Jack   857
Kocher, Martin G.   399
Kocher, Martin G., *see* Gueth, Werner   399, 401
Koford, K., *see* Grelak, E.   878
Konow, James   415
Kormendi, Roger C.   860, 862, 914n
Kraemer, Carlo   337n
Krantz, David H., *see* Goodman, Barbara   914

Krasner, Leonard, *see* Battalio, Raymond C.   960, 965
Krause, K., *see* Harbaugh, W.T.   1051, 1062, 1064
Kravitz, D.   437
Kreps, David M.   180, 454, 488, 598, 602, 776, 837, 903
Kreps, David M., *see* Cho, I.   587
Kroll, Yoram   914, 915
Krueger, Alan   120, 122
Krüger, L., *see* Gigerenzer, G.   1019
Kruse, Jamie Brown   63, 63n, 66–69, 139, 1066, 1069
Kruse, Jamie Brown, *see* Cronshaw, Mark B.   656
Kruse, Jamie Brown, *see* Gysler, M.   1066–1068
Kujal, P., *see* Franciosi, Robert   57, 949, 951–953
Kujal, Praveen   235, 239
Kumka, D.S., *see* Silverman, J.M.   1061
Kunreuther, H., *see* Johnson, E.J.   1028
Kvasnica, Anthony M., *see* Guarnaschelli, Serena   344
Kwasnica, A.   192n, 193

Labys, W.C.   46
Laffont, J.-J., *see* Green, J.   626, 628, 736
LaMaster, Shawn, *see* Campbell, Joseph   27, 102, 228, 229
LaMaster, Shawn, *see* Van Boening, Mark V.   242
Langan, Loren, *see* Holt, Charles A.   63, 84, 138
Laskey, K., *see* Martignon, L.   1009, 1010
Laury, S.K.   798–800, 849n, 853, 854, 1050
Laury, S.K., *see* Goeree, Jacob K.   849n, 851
Laury, S.K., *see* Holt, Charles A.   1048, 1062, 1065
Lave, L., *see* Dolbear, F.T.   63
Leary, M.R., *see* Baumeister, R.F.   844
Ledyard, John O.   206, 625, 626, 636, 784, 802, 818, 836, 846n, 849, 850, 854, 898
Ledyard, John O., *see* Arifovic, J.   634
Ledyard, John O., *see* Carlson, Dale   656, 666
Ledyard, John O., *see* Easley, D.   20
Ledyard, John O., *see* Groves, Theodore   626, 630, 736, 803
Ledyard, John O., *see* Williams, Arlington W.   376
Lee, T.H., *see* Pearson, S.D.   981

Lei, Vivian   257, 260–262
Leininger, W.   560
Leonid, Hurwicz   626
Levin, Dan, *see* Jung, Yun Joo   180, 615
Levin, Dan, *see* Kagel, John H.   187, 188, 190, 191, 344
Levin, I.P.   1062
Levine, David K.   849
Levine, David K., *see* Fudenberg, Drew   585, 607, 612
Levine, Michael   858n
Levy, H.   1066, 1069
Levy, Haim, *see* Kroll, Yoram   914, 915
Lewis, David   520, 520n
Lian, P.   376
Lichtenstein, Sarah   929, 967, 968, 1026
Lichtenstein, Sarah, *see* Slovic, Paul   914, 930
Lieberman, A., *see* Dolbear, F.T.   63
Lieberman, B.   543
Liebrand, W.B.G.   818
Liljas, Bengt, *see* Johannesson, Magnus   760
Limberg, S., *see* Kachelmeier, Steven J.   55–58
Lind, H., *see* Bohm, Peter   725, 933
Lindén, J., *see* Bohm, Peter   956, 957
Lindman, H.   929
Lindsey, S.   1023, 1024
Lindsey, S., *see* Hoffrage, U.   1024
Linhart, Peter B.   560, 561
Linhart, Peter B., *see* Leininger, W.   560
Lipman, B., *see* Bagnoli, M.   626, 635, 637
Lipman, B.L., *see* Bergin, J.   479
List, J.   190n
Littlechild, Stephen   676
Livingston, J.W., *see* Griesinger, D.W.   818
Lo, A.   365
Loeb, Martin   156
Loeb, Martin, *see* Groves, Theodore   156, 626
Loewenstein, George, *see* Babcock, Lind   532n
Logan, J.A., *see* Kandel, D.B.   1061n
Lones, Smith, *see* Shimer, Robert   109n
Loomes, G.   929
Lopez, G.   552
López, Rafael   391n
Lopomo, G., *see* Brusco, S.   186, 193
Lorens, W., *see* Spigner, C.   1061
Lucas Jr., Robert E.   454, 993
Luce, R.D.   598, 1015, 1035
Lucking-Reiley, David H.   724n
Lucking-Reiley, David H., *see* List, J.   190n
Luke, Margaret, *see* Coursey, Don L.   71, 72, 74, 156, 200

Lundholm, Russell, *see* Forsythe, Robert   344
Lusardi, Annamaria, *see* Browning, Martin   923
Lutz, M., *see* Seguino, S.   510, 510n
Lutz, N.A., *see* Eckel, Catherine C.   1071
Lynch, M.   331, 331n, 333

MacGregor, D.   1061
MacKinlay, C., *see* Lo, A.   365
MacLeod, W. Bentley   123, 167
Madsen, M., *see* Kagan, S.   449
Magat, Wesley, *see* Loeb, Martin   156
Maier, Steven F., *see* Cohen, Kalman J.   25
Mailath, G.   626
Mailath, George, *see* Kandori, Michihiro   479
Malcomson, James   320
Malcomson, James, *see* MacLeod, W. Bentley   123
Malkiel, B.   364
Malouf, M.W.K., *see* Roth, Alvin E.   1087
Manelli, A.   190, 191, 192n
Mansfield, Carol, *see* Smith, V. Kerry   760
Maoz, Z., *see* Felsenthal, D.S.   889, 895
Maoz, Z., *see* Rapoport, Amnon   889, 895
Marcet, A.   303, 306
Mark, L.   625n
Marks, Melanie B.   637
Marks, Melanie B., *see* Croson, Rachel T.A.   637
Marmorstein, H., *see* Alba, J.W.   1015
Marrese, M., *see* Harstad, Ronald   627n, 630, 631, 634
Marshak, Jacob, *see* Becker, G.M.   950, 956, 969, 1093, 1094
Martignon, L.   1006, 1009–1013
Martignon, L., *see* Berretty, P.M.   981
Martignon, L., *see* Gigerenzer, G.   981, 984
Martin, Stephen, *see* Harstad, Ronald   164, 167
Marwell, Gerald   776, 793n
Maskin, Eric, *see* Fudenberg, Drew   488
Mason, R.G., *see* MacGregor, D.   1061
Massaro, D., *see* Kitzis, S.   303, 305
Mathur, S., *see* Van Huyck, John B.   521, 527–529
Matthews, S., *see* Mark, L.   625n
Maynes, E., *see* Cadsby, C.B.   510, 510n, 637
Mayo, D.   511n–528n
McAfee, R. Preston   103, 185, 670
McCabe, Kevin A.   46, 88, 102, 133, 143, 144, 186, 186n, 192n, 196n, 232, 266, 267, 425, 676, 703–705, 952, 953
McCabe, Kevin A., *see* Amden, Holly   779n, 789

McCabe, Kevin A., *see* Berg, Joyce E.   911, 1036
McCabe, Kevin A., *see* Hoffman, Elizabeth   411, 413–415, 417, 420, 423–426, 428, 430, 432–435, 488, 489n, 492, 492n, 915
McClelland, Gary H.   759, 915
McClintock, C.G.   449
McClintock, C.G., *see* Toda, M.   449
McClintock, C.G., *see* van Avermaet, E.   449
McClintock, E., *see* McClintock, C G.   449
McCue, Kenneth F., *see* Isaac, R. Mark   771, 795n, 832
McDaniel, Tanga M., *see* Harrison, Glenn W.   764
McGuckin, Thomas, *see* Neill, Helen R.   758, 760
McInnes, M.M., *see* Harrison, Glenn W.   1065
McKee, M., *see* Bagnoli, M.   636, 793n
McKee, Michael, *see* Harrison, Glenn W.   155, 157
McKee, Michael, *see* McClelland, Gary H.   915
McKelvey, Richard D.   403, 526n, 542, 543, 550, 551, 611, 781n, 850n, 872, 874, 878, 880, 881, 889
McKelvey, Richard D., *see* Guarnaschelli, Serena   341
McLeod, P.   978
McMillan, John, *see* McAfee, R. Preston   185, 670
McStay, J.R.   1061
Mehr, D.R., *see* Green, L.   981
Mellers, B.   1028, 1029
Menkhaus, D.   196n
Menkhaus, D., *see* Phillips, O.   196
Mertens, J.   132
Mertz, C.K., *see* Flynn, J.   1061
Messick, Samuel   914
Mestelman, Stuart   77, 78, 82, 656
Mestelman, Stuart, *see* Chan, Kenneth S.   796, 799, 831
Mestelman, Stuart, *see* Godby, Robert   656, 658, 666
Mestelman, Stuart, *see* Muller, R. Andrew   656, 665
Meszaros, J., *see* Johnson, E.J.   1028
Michelitsch, R., *see* Franciosi, Robert   57, 949, 951–953
Milgrom, Paul R.   185, 186, 319, 320, 585, 633
Milgrom, Paul R., *see* Glosten, Lawrence R.   25
Milgrom, Paul R., *see* Kreps, David M.   488, 598, 602, 776

Miller, G.F.   187n, 1043, 1044
Miller, G.F., *see* Todd, P.M.   1044
Miller, G.J., *see* Bottom, William   887
Miller, Gary J.   861, 862, 867–869
Miller, Gary J., *see* Eavey, Cheryl L.   859, 861, 863, 864
Miller, Gary J., *see* Hammond, Thomas H.   858, 865n, 867
Miller, Gary, *see* Bottom, William   864, 869n, 870
Miller, John H.   851, 854
Miller, John H., *see* Andreoni, James   483, 484n, 598, 781n, 782, 848n
Miller, John H., *see* Rust, John   39, 269
Miller, R.M., *see* Lynch, M.   331, 331n, 333
Misiolek, W.S.   144
Mitchell, Robert C.   755, 763n
Mitzkewitz, Michael   537n
Moir, Rob, *see* Chan, Kenneth S.   799, 831
Moir, Rob, *see* Mestelman, Stuart   656
Montalvo, Garcia J., *see* Bosch-Domenech, Antoni   395, 401, 408
Montgomery, M., *see* Kealy, Mary Jo   757
Montgomery, W. David   661
Moore, E.   1062, 1064–1067
Morgan, Peter, *see* Harrison, Glenn W.   318
Mori, T.   631, 634
Mori, T., *see* Kawagoe, T.   629, 630
Morris, Stephen   257
Morton, R.B., *see* Gerber, E.R.   890–892, 896
Moser, Donald, *see* Kagel, John H.   537n
Moskowitz, J.M., *see* McClintock, C.G.   449
Moulin, Herve, *see* Jackson, Matthew O.   626
Muench, T.   633
Muller, R. Andrew   656, 665
Muller, R. Andrew, *see* Chan, Kenneth S.   796, 799, 831
Muller, R. Andrew, *see* Godby, Robert   656, 658, 666
Muller, R. Andrew, *see* Mestelman, Stuart   656
Murnighan, J. Keith.   449, 598n
Murnighan, J. Keith., *see* Kahn, L.M.   444, 599, 599n
Murnighan, J. Keith., *see* Pillutla, M.M.   436–438, 440, 443, 444, 447
Murnighan, J. Keith., *see* Roth, Alvin E.   436, 598n
Murnighan, J. Keith., *see* Straub, Paul   436–440, 442, 444
Murphy, A.H.   818
Murphy, James, *see* Cummings, Ronald G.   762

Murphy, Kevin 120, 122
Murphy, Kevin M., *see* Becker, Gary S. 923
Muth, J.F. 993
Myagkov, M. 1051
Myerson, R.B. 891, 893, 895, 896
Myerson, R.B., *see* Forsythe, Robert 890, 891, 891n, 892, 895
Myerson, R.B., *see* Rietz, T.A. 890, 892, 895
Mysker, M. 636

Nagel, Rosemarie 393, 394, 401, 403, 404, 407
Nagel, Rosemarie, *see* Bosch-Domenech, Antoni 395, 401, 403, 408
Nagel, Rosemarie, *see* Duffy, J. 394, 406, 407
Nagel, Rosemarie, *see* Grosskopf, Brit 397
Nagel, Rosemarie, *see* Mitzkewitz, Michael 537n
Nagel, Rosemarie, *see* Selten, Reinhard 395, 403
Nakamura, H., *see* Saijo, T. 796n, 802, 803, 825, 846n, 849
Nash, J. 500–502
Neill, Helen R. 758, 760
Nelson, Brad, *see* Brewer, Paul J. 44
Nelson, F.D., *see* Berg, Joyce E. 742n, 748
Nelson, F.D., *see* Forsythe, Robert 743n, 749, 750
Nemeth, C. 605
Neumann, G.R., *see* Forsythe, Robert 743n, 749, 750
Newell, B. 1014
Nicoll, Jennifer, *see* Bottom, William 869n, 887
Niemi, R.G., *see* McKelvey, Richard D. 881
Nöldeke, G. 573, 574
Noll, Roger, *see* Hahn, Robert W. 662
Normann, Hans-Theo, *see* Harstad, Ronald 164, 167
Nöth, Markus 337n, 344, 720
Nöth, Markus, *see* Kraemer, Carlo 337n
Noussair, Charles N. 186, 358, 376
Noussair, Charles N., *see* Alsemgeest, P. 187
Noussair, Charles N., *see* Lei, Vivian 257, 260–262
Nowell, C. 510, 510n, 513

Oaxaca, Ronald L., *see* Cox, James C. 92, 96, 97, 311, 313–316, 318, 1078, 1080, 1084
O'Brien, J.R., *see* Berg, Joyce E. 1087, 1090, 1092–1094
O'Brien, John 256

Ochs, Jack 392, 436, 464, 549
Ockenfels, Axel 494
Ockenfels, Axel, *see* Bolton, Gary E. 489, 492n, 494n, 495, 496, 496n, 532, 533n, 535n, 537, 850
Ockenfels, Axel, *see* Selten, Reinhard 492, 494, 538, 539
Odean, T., *see* Barber, B. 1002
Odom, Sherry L., *see* Harrison, Glenn W. 764
Oechssler, Jörg, *see* Huck, Steffen 337n
Offerman, Theo 817, 818, 821n, 823, 824, 836, 841
Offerman, Theo, *see* Sonnemans, Joep 779, 819
Okuno-Fujiwara, Masahiro, *see* Roth, Alvin E. 494, 495, 537, 538
Oliven, K. 749, 750
Olmstead, Nancy, *see* Carlson, Dale 656, 666
Olson, Mark A. 677, 681, 690, 803, 817, 818
Olson, Mark A., *see* Alsemgeest, P. 187
Olson, Mark A., *see* Banks, J. 196n
Olson, P., *see* Mysker, M. 636
Olsson, H., *see* Juslin, P. 1026
O'Neill, B. 544
Önkal, D., *see* Ayton, P. 987, 990
Orbell, J.M., *see* Caporael, L.R. 821n
Ordeshook, P.C., *see* McKelvey, Richard D. 874, 889
Ortmann, A. 794n, 1001, 1042
Ortmann, A., *see* Borges, Bernhard F.J. 994–996, 997n, 998–1001
Ortmann, A., *see* Hertwig, R. 1053
Ortmann, A., *see* Van Huyck, John B. 521, 527–529
Ortner, G. 750
Osborne, Laura L., *see* Cummings, Ronald G. 762
Ostrom, E., *see* Walker, James M. 887
Ostroy, Joseph, *see* Friedman, Daniel 85, 112, 267
Otani, Y. 101
Otten, W., *see* van Lange, P.A.M. 836
Otto, P., *see* Rieskamp, J. 1013, 1014

Palfrey, Thomas R. 779–781, 785n, 823n, 825, 898
Palfrey, Thomas R., *see* Forsythe, Robert 376
Palfrey, Thomas R., *see* Goeree, Jacob K. 549
Palfrey, Thomas R., *see* Guarnaschelli, Serena 341
Palfrey, Thomas R., *see* Ledyard, John O. 626

Palfrey, Thomas R., *see* McKelvey, Richard D. 403, 526n, 542, 543, 550, 551, 611, 781n, 850n
Palmer, Richard, *see* Rust, John 39, 269
Panzar, John C., *see* Baumol, William J. 71, 155
Parnell, P., *see* Cooperstock, R. 1061n
Patterson, David A., *see* Duffield, John 757
Payne, J.W. 977, 984, 1014
Pearson, S.D. 981
Peleg, B. 626, 630, 635n
Peterson, G. 896
Phillips, L.D., *see* Lichtenstein, Sarah 1026
Phillips, O. 196
Phillips, O., *see* Menkhaus, D. 196n
Pillutla, M.M. 436–438, 440, 443, 444, 447
Pingry, David, *see* Franciosi, Robert 661, 662
Plott, Charles R. 19, 22n, 115, 116, 121, 200, 206, 208, 219, 223, 235, 264, 342, 344, 348n, 376, 661, 715, 720, 725, 750, 857, 860, 872, 874, 880, 889, 915, 1064, 1078
Plott, Charles R., *see* Aliprantis, C.D. 17
Plott, Charles R., *see* Anderson, C. 377–380
Plott, Charles R., *see* Asparouhova, Elena 24, 376
Plott, Charles R., *see* Banks, J. 639
Plott, Charles R., *see* Bossaerts, Peter L. 367, 376
Plott, Charles R., *see* Brewer, Paul J. 44
Plott, Charles R., *see* Carlson, Dale 656, 666
Plott, Charles R., *see* Casari, M. 849
Plott, Charles R., *see* Cason, Timothy N. 662, 725
Plott, Charles R., *see* Chen, Kay-Yut 349, 631, 634
Plott, Charles R., *see* Clauser, Laura 170, 185
Plott, Charles R., *see* Fiorina, Morris P. 860, 874, 878, 915
Plott, Charles R., *see* Forsythe, Robert 376
Plott, Charles R., *see* Goodfellow, J. 376
Plott, Charles R., *see* Grether, David M. 165, 175, 644–646, 914, 929, 968, 971
Plott, Charles R., *see* Guarnaschelli, Serena 344
Plott, Charles R., *see* Hong, James T. 619
Plott, Charles R., *see* Hung, Angela A. 337n, 340, 341, 344
Plott, Charles R., *see* Isaac, R. Mark 44, 46, 164, 170, 185, 223n, 235, 239, 771, 795n, 832
Plott, Charles R., *see* Jamison, Julian C. 20
Plott, Charles R., *see* Johnson, Michael D. 217

Plott, Charles R., *see* Kormendi, Roger C. 860, 862, 914n
Plott, Charles R., *see* Lei, Vivian 257, 260–262
Plott, Charles R., *see* Levine, Michael 858n
Plott, Charles R., *see* Lian, P. 376
Plott, Charles R., *see* Lynch, M. 331, 331n, 333
Plott, Charles R., *see* Miller, G.F. 187n
Plott, Charles R., *see* Myagkov, M. 1051
Plott, Charles R., *see* Noussair, Charles N. 358, 376
Poe, Gregory L., *see* Rondeau, Daniel 637
Pohlman, Larry, *see* Wolf, Charles 914
Polya, G. 977
Porter, David P. 188, 190, 247, 249, 252, 256
Porter, David P., *see* Banks, J. 196n, 545, 639
Porter, David P., *see* Carlson, Dale 656, 666
Porter, David P., *see* Ledyard, John O. 206
Porter, R., *see* Lynch, M. 331, 331n, 333
Porter, Robert H. 175
Porter, T., *see* Gigerenzer, G. 1019
Postlewaite, A., *see* Mailath, G. 626
Potter, Richard E., *see* Rapoport, Amnon 537n
Potters, J., *see* Jacobsen, B. 746n
Powell, M. 1066, 1068
Powell, P.L., *see* Johnson, J.E.V. 1070
Pozen, M.W. 981
Prasnikar, V. 438, 452, 1093n
Prasnikar, Vesna, *see* Roth, Alvin E. 494, 495, 537, 538
Prescott, E., *see* Dolbear, F.T. 63
Prisbrey, Jeffrey E., *see* Palfrey, Thomas R. 779–781, 785n, 823n, 825
Proulx, C., *see* Binmore, K. 60, 500, 505n

Rabin, Matthew 121, 415, 489, 492n, 495, 853n, 976, 1018, 1031
Radner, Roy 911
Radner, Roy, *see* Hurwicz, L. 31n, 37
Radner, Roy, *see* Leininger, W. 560
Radner, Roy, *see* Linhart, Peter B. 560, 561
Raiffa, H. 500n
Raiffa, H., *see* Luce, R.D. 598, 1035
Ramasubban, Radhika, *see* Griffin, Charles C. 758
Ramey, G., *see* Bagwell, Kyle 585
Ramey, Valerie, *see* Isaac, R. Mark 164, 170
Rangel, Antonio, *see* Ledyard, John O. 206
Rankin, F.W., *see* Van Huyck, John B. 458–460
Rankin, Frederick, *see* Van Huyck, John B. 521, 522

Rapoport, Amnon   273, 274, 281–287, 289–294, 509, 537n, 560, 561, 598, 889, 895, 1042
Rapoport, Amnon, *see* Daniel, T.E.   294, 560, 566, 570
Rapoport, Amnon, *see* Erev, Ido   273, 274
Rapoport, Amnon, *see* Felsenthal, D.S.   889, 895
Rapoport, Amnon, *see* Kroll, Yoram   914, 915
Rapoport, Amnon, *see* Seale, Darryl A.   1044
Rapoport, Amnon, *see* Sundali, James A.   273–283, 294
Rassenti, Stephen J.   644, 645, 1055
Rassenti, Stephen J., *see* Backerman, Steven R.   676, 700–702, 706
Rassenti, Stephen J., *see* Banks, J.   196n
Rassenti, Stephen J., *see* Denton, M.   677
Rassenti, Stephen J., *see* Durham, Yvonne   206, 209
Rassenti, Stephen J., *see* Kruse, Jamie Brown   63, 63n, 66–69, 139
Rassenti, Stephen J., *see* McCabe, Kevin A.   46, 88, 102, 133, 143, 144, 186, 186n, 192n, 196n, 232, 266, 267, 676, 703–705, 952, 953
Rassenti, Stephen J., *see* Olson, Mark A.   677, 681, 690
Rawls, J.   500, 500n
Raymond, E.L., *see* Boverie, P.E.   1061
Regan, D.T., *see* Frank, R.H.   450
Reilly, Robert J., *see* Davis, Douglas D.   68n, 555
Reiter, S., *see* Hurwicz, L.   31n, 37
Renninger, Suzann-Viola, *see* Fehr, Ernst   396
Reynolds, Stanley S.   144
Reynolds, Stanley S., *see* Franciosi, Robert   656, 661, 662, 664, 666
Reynolds, Stanley S., *see* Isaac, R. Mark   63
Reynolds, Stanley S., *see* Kruse, Jamie Brown   63, 63n, 66–69, 139
Rhodes, Carl M., *see* Wilson, Rick K.   466
Rich, Changhua Sun   109, 114, 665
Riedl, Arno, *see* Fehr, Ernst   123, 124, 325, 327, 329
Rieskamp, J.   1013–1015, 1036
Rietz, T.A.   744n, 889, 890, 892, 895, 1091
Rietz, T.A., *see* Berg, Joyce E.   742n, 743n, 746, 748–750, 1090
Rietz, T.A., *see* Forsythe, Robert   746, 749, 750, 890, 891, 891n, 892, 895, 896
Rietz, T.A., *see* Gerber, E.R.   890–892, 896
Rietz, T.A., *see* Oliven, K.   749, 750

Riezman, Raymond G., *see* Noussair, Charles N.   358, 376
Rigdon, Mary L., *see* Olson, Mark A.   677, 681, 690
Riker, W.R.   872, 880
Riley, John   585
Rob, Rafael, *see* Kandori, Michihiro   479
Roberson, Bruce, *see* Cox, James C.   92, 93, 95, 662, 1055, 1090
Roberts, John   626
Roberts, John, *see* Kreps, David M.   488, 598, 602, 776
Roberts, John, *see* Milgrom, Paul R.   319, 320, 585, 633
Roll, R.   19, 303
Romer, David   923
Romer, Thomas   858, 858n
Rondeau, Daniel   637
Rosenthal, H., *see* Palfrey, Thomas R.   898
Rosenthal, Howard, *see* Romer, Thomas   858, 858n
Rosenthal, R.W.   550, 551
Ross, Thomas W., *see* Cooper, Russell   164n, 500, 523
Ross, Thomas W., *see* Forsythe, Robert   746, 749, 750
Rotemberg, J.   144
Roth, Alvin E.   109n, 294, 407, 436, 437, 451, 488, 494, 495, 531, 533, 537, 538, 566, 598, 598n, 612, 1043, 1053, 1087
Roth, Alvin E., *see* Murnighan, J. Keith.   598n
Roth, Alvin E., *see* Ochs, Jack   436
Roth, Alvin E., *see* Prasnikar, V.   438, 452
Rousseau, D.   903
Rozef, M.S.   993
Rueter, F., *see* Dolbear, F.T.   63
Ruffle, Bradley J., *see* Kaplan, Todd   400
Rust, John   39, 269, 923
Rust, John, *see* Friedman, Daniel   206
Rustichini, Aldo   662
Rutström, E. Elisabet, *see* Blackburn, McKinley   763, 764
Rutström, E. Elisabet, *see* Cummings, Ronald G.   760, 761
Rutström, E. Elisabet, *see* Harrison, Glenn W.   1064, 1065

Safra, Zvi, *see* Karni, Edi   929, 969
Saijo, T.   796n, 802, 803, 825, 846n, 849
Saijo, T., *see* Brandts, Jordi   826, 829
Saijo, T., *see* Cason, Timothy N.   798n, 803, 810, 811, 813

Saltzman, Mark, see Goodman, Barbara 914
Samuelson, L., see Nöldeke, G. 573, 574
Samuelson, Larry, see Battalio, Raymond C. 521–523
Samuelson, Paul A. 481, 736
Samuelson, W., see Chatterjee, K. 560, 561
Sargent, T., see Marcet, A. 303, 306
Sargent, T.J. 976
Satorra, A., see Bosch-Domenech, Antoni 395, 401, 408
Satterthwaite, M. 84
Satterthwaite, M.A., see Linhart, Peter B. 560
Satterthwaite, Mark, see Rustichini, Aldo 662
Sauermann, H. 146, 147, 151, 152
Savin, N.E., see Forsythe, Robert 413–415, 417, 419–421, 423, 424, 426, 429–431, 433, 492, 915
Scarf, Herbert 376, 378
Schadewald, M., see Kachelmeier, Steven J. 55–58
Schelling, Thomas C. 464, 1035
Scherr, B. 628
Scheuffele, D.J., see Boverie, P.E. 1061
Schmalensee, Richard, see Joskow, Paul 664
Schmidt, Klaus, see Fehr, Ernst 532n, 850
Schmidtz, David, see Isaac, R. Mark 637
Schmittberger, Rolf, see Güth, Werner 412, 436
Schober, Michael F. 903
Schotter, A., see Linhart, Peter B. 561
Schoumaker, Francoise, see Roth, Alvin E. 436
Schram, Arthur 829, 898, 899
Schram, Arthur, see Brandts, Jordi 779, 825, 826, 829, 853, 854
Schram, Arthur, see Jacobsen, B. 746n
Schram, Arthur, see Offerman, Theo 818, 823, 836, 841
Schram, Arthur, see Sonnemans, Joep 779, 819
Schubert, R. 1062–1068
Schubert, R., see Gysler, M. 1066–1068
Schultz, Paul, see Christie, William 175
Schulze, William D. 637
Schulze, William D., see McClelland, Gary H. 759, 915
Schulze, William D., see Rondeau, Daniel 637
Schwartz, J.A., see Cramton, P. 185
Schwartz, Robert A. 232
Schwartz, Robert A., see Cohen, Kalman J. 25
Schwartze, Bernd, see Güth, Werner 412, 436
Schweppe, Fred, see Bohn, Roger E. 677, 678
Seagraves, J. 158

Seale, Darryl A. 1044
Seale, Darryl A., see Daniel, T.E. 294, 560, 566, 570
Seale, Darryl A., see Rapoport, Amnon 273, 274, 281–287, 289–294, 560
Seale, Darryl A., see Sundali, James A. 273–283, 294
Sedlmeier, P. 1025, 1031
Sefton, M. 794, 796
Sefton, M., see Manelli, A. 190, 191, 192n
Sefton, Martin, see Clark, Kenneth 523
Sefton, Martin, see Forsythe, Robert 413–415, 417, 419–421, 423, 424, 426, 429–431, 433, 492, 915
Segal, U. 929
Seguino, S. 510, 510n
Seip, K. 757, 758
Selker, H.P., see Pozen, M.W. 981
Sell, Jane 510, 510n, 513, 787
Selten, Reinhard 273, 395, 403, 407, 436, 488, 492, 494, 538, 539, 598, 611, 826, 981
Selten, Reinhard, see Gigerenzer, G. 976, 977, 981
Selten, Reinhard, see Harsanyi, John C. 521n
Selten, Reinhard, see Sauermann, H. 146, 147, 151, 152
Shachat, Keith, see Hoffman, Elizabeth 411, 413–415, 417, 420, 423, 425, 426, 428, 432, 433, 488, 489n, 492, 492n
Shafer, Wayne 959
Shaked, A., see Binmore, K. 437
Shanks, D., see Newell, B. 1014
Shapiro, Carl 123
Sharpe, W.F. 993
Shehata, Mohamed, see Kachelmeier, Steven J. 914, 915, 940, 1064
Shepsle, Kenneth 858n, 873, 880, 881
Sherman, R., see Dolbear, F.T. 63
Sherstyuk, K. 192–195
Sherstyuk, K., see Kwasnica, A. 193
Shiller, R.J. 1026
Shimer, Robert 109n
Shimomura, K., see Anderson, C. 377–380
Shin, S.Y., see Shogren, Jason F. 943, 949, 955
Shinotsuka, H., see Toda, M. 449
Shogren, Jason F. 943, 949, 955
Shogren, Jason F., see Fox, John A. 763, 764
Sholtz, Anne, see Carlson, Dale 656, 666
Shubik, M., see Fouraker, Lawrence 146
Sicilian, J., see Otani, Y. 101
Siegel, Alberta, see Siegel, Sidney 914, 916

Siegel, Sidney 914, 916, 1047
Siegel, Sidney, *see* Fouraker, Lawrence 66n, 146, 148–151, 413, 418, 914, 919, 920
Silverman, J.M. 1061
Simon, Carl P., *see* Bergstrom, Theodore 630n
Simon, Herbert A. 916, 976, 981, 1044
Sinden, J.A., *see* Knetsch, Jack L. 940
Singh, Bhanwar, *see* Griffin, Charles C. 758
Skaperdas, Stergios 127
Skogh, Goran 127
Slemrod, J. 750
Slonim, Robert 398, 401
Slovic, Paul 914, 930, 1062n, 1071
Slovic, Paul, *see* Flynn, J. 1061
Slovic, Paul, *see* Lichtenstein, Sarah 929, 967, 968
Slovic, Paul, *see* MacGregor, D. 1061
Slovic, Paul, *see* Tversky, Amos 929, 930, 936, 969, 972
Smith, Adam 164n, 170
Smith, Jared, *see* Plott, Charles R. 223
Smith, V. Kerry 760
Smith, Vernon L. 20, 25, 46, 52, 84, 85, 112, 136, 138, 153, 154, 170, 226n, 235, 239, 242, 247, 248, 251, 256, 260, 262, 266, 425, 619, 627n, 630, 634, 638, 639, 676, 792, 850, 914n, 916, 917, 919, 931, 949, 1047, 1054, 1058, 1059, 1078, 1087
Smith, Vernon L., *see* Backerman, Steven R. 676, 700–702, 706
Smith, Vernon L., *see* Banks, J. 196n
Smith, Vernon L., *see* Campbell, Joseph 27, 102, 228, 229
Smith, Vernon L., *see* Coursey, Don L. 71, 72, 74, 155, 156, 200, 235, 239
Smith, Vernon L., *see* Cox, James C. 92, 93, 95–97, 186n, 662, 1054–1056, 1090
Smith, Vernon L., *see* Denton, M. 677
Smith, Vernon L., *see* Durham, Yvonne 136, 206, 209
Smith, Vernon L., *see* Franciosi, Robert 57, 949, 951–953
Smith, Vernon L., *see* Hoffman, Elizabeth 411, 413–415, 417, 420, 423–426, 428, 430, 432–435, 488, 489n, 492, 492n, 915
Smith, Vernon L., *see* Isaac, R. Mark 178, 180, 183
Smith, Vernon L., *see* Ketcham, Jon 56, 63, 66n, 72, 139, 236n
Smith, Vernon L., *see* King, Ronald R. 242, 247, 254

Smith, Vernon L., *see* Kruse, Jamie Brown 63, 63n, 66–69, 139
Smith, Vernon L., *see* McCabe, Kevin A. 46, 88, 102, 133, 143, 144, 186, 186n, 192n, 196n, 232, 266, 267, 676, 703–705, 952, 953
Smith, Vernon L., *see* Olson, Mark A. 677, 681, 690
Smith, Vernon L., *see* Plott, Charles R. 915
Smith, Vernon L., *see* Porter, David P. 247, 249, 252, 256
Smith, Vernon L., *see* Rassenti, Stephen J. 644, 645, 1055
Smith, Vernon L., *see* Walker, James M. 1056, 1090–1092
Smith, Vernon L., *see* Williams, Arlington W. 376
Smorodinsky, M., *see* Kalai, E. 500
Snyder, M.A., *see* Levin, I.P. 1062
Sobel, J., *see* Blume, A. 573, 574
Solecki, W.D., *see* Cutter, S.L. 1061
Solis-Soberon, Fernando, *see* Holt, Charles A. 63, 139, 140
Solnick, S. 513, 514, 514n
Sonnegård, J., *see* Bohm, Peter 956, 957
Sonnemans, Joep 779, 819, 836
Sonnemans, Joep, *see* Offerman, Theo 818, 823, 836, 841
Sonnemans, Joep, *see* Schram, Arthur 898, 899
Sonnemans, Joep, *see* van Dijk, F. 794, 799, 836, 853
Sonnenschein, Hugo 959
Sonnenschein, Hugo, *see* Shafer, Wayne 959
Soros, G. 993
Sotomayor, Marilda, *see* Roth, Alvin E. 109n, 1043
Spence, A.M. 585
Spigner, C. 1061
Spitzer, Matthew, *see* Hoffman, Elizabeth 413, 417, 424
Sprinkle, G.B., *see* Blume, A. 575, 580, 903
Srivastava, Sanjay, *see* O'Brien, John 256
Stahl, Dale 393, 401, 403, 407, 612
Stallen, P.J.M. 1061
Starmer, C. 1061
Starmer, C., *see* Loomes, G. 929
Stech, F.J., *see* Toda, M. 449
Steinberg, R., *see* Sefton, M. 794, 796
Stengel, Daniel, *see* Miller, Gary J. 861
Stevens, T., *see* Seguino, S. 510, 510n
Stich, S.P. 1028
Stigler, G.J. 1042

Stiglitz, Joseph, *see* Shapiro, Carl 123
Stoecker, R., *see* Selten, Reinhard 407, 598
Strand, J., *see* Seip, K. 757, 758
Straub, Paul 436–440, 442, 444, 523, 524
Streater, A.L. 449
Stuart, Charles, *see* Skogh, Goran 127
Suchanek, Gerry L., *see* Smith, Vernon L. 20, 25, 242, 247, 248, 251, 256, 260, 425
Sugden, R., *see* Loomes, G. 929
Sugden, Robert 488, 520n, 525, 784, 785, 785n, 788, 790
Sugiyama, Alexandre Borges, *see* Plott, Charles R. 200
Sulloway, F.J., *see* Hertwig, R. 1042
Summers, Lawrence, *see* Katz, Lawrence 120
Summers, Lawrence, *see* Krueger, Alan 120, 122
Sundali, James A. 273–283, 294
Sundali, James A., *see* Rapoport, Amnon 273, 274, 281–286, 537n
Sundén, A.E. 1070
Sunder, Shyam 344, 406
Sunder, Shyam, *see* Bosch-Domenech, Antoni 370n
Sunder, Shyam, *see* Gode, Dhananjay K. 31, 37, 39, 44
Sunder, Shyam, *see* Plott, Charles R. 344, 376
Surette, B.J., *see* Sundén, A.E. 1070
Sutter, Matthias, *see* Gueth, Werner 399, 401
Sutter, Matthias, *see* Kocher, Martin G. 399
Sutton, J., *see* Binmore, K. 437
Swierzbinski, Joe, *see* Binmore, K. 60, 500, 505n
Swijtink, Z., *see* Gigerenzer, G. 1019
Sytkowski, P.A., *see* Pozen, M.W. 981
Szidarovszky, Ferenc, *see* Smith, Vernon L. 914n, 919

Tang, F.-F., *see* Chen, Kay-Yut 630–634
Tang, F.F., *see* Nagel, Rosemarie 403
Taylor, Laura O., *see* Cummings, Ronald G. 762
Telser, Lester G. 206, 211
Tetlock, P.E. 1035
Thaler, Richard H. 120, 395, 403, 939, 1018
Thaler, Richard H., *see* Debondt, W. 365
Thaler, Richard H., *see* Kahneman, Daniel 55–58, 61, 412, 413, 423, 424, 426, 429, 437, 940, 943, 945, 949–953, 955
Thaler, Richard H., *see* Tversky, Amos 930

the ABC Research Group, *see* Gigerenzer, G. 976, 1004
Thisse, J.F., *see* Chen, H.C. 552
Thompson, M.A., *see* Kruse, Jamie Brown 1066, 1069
Tian, G. 626, 630, 635n
Tideman, T.N. 628
Tiefenbacher, J., *see* Cutter, S.L. 1061
Tietz, R., *see* Güth, Werner 436
Tinkler, S., *see* Nowell, C. 510, 510n, 513
Tirole, Jean 247
Titus, Charles J., *see* Bergstrom, Theodore 630n
Toda, M. 449
Todd, P.M. 981, 1044
Todd, P.M., *see* Berretty, P.M. 981
Todd, P.M., *see* Davis, J.N. 1042
Todd, P.M., *see* Gigerenzer, G. 976, 1004
Todd, P.M., *see* Hertwig, R. 977
Todd, P.M., *see* Miller, G.F. 1043, 1044
Tomas, A., *see* Stallen, P.J.M. 1061
Tooby, John, *see* Cosmides, Leda 411, 415
Topel, Robert, *see* Murphy, Kevin 120, 122
Tougareva, E., *see* Fehr, Ernst 325, 329
Trivers, R.L. 1035
Tucker, W. 1007, 1008
Tullock, Gordon 858n
Turocy III, Theodore L., *see* Plott, Charles R. 19
Tversky, Amos 326n, 914–916, 926, 929, 930, 936, 969, 972, 981, 1015, 1028, 1029, 1031, 1047, 1050
Tversky, Amos, *see* Griffin, D. 1026
Tversky, Amos, *see* Kahneman, Daniel 281, 746n, 976, 977, 979, 1019, 1047, 1050
Tversky, Amos, *see* Rapoport, Amnon 1042

van Avermaet, E. 449
Van Boening, Mark V. 85, 206, 209, 211, 242
Van Boening, Mark V., *see* Archibald, Glen 211
Van Boening, Mark V., *see* Campbell, Joseph 27, 102, 228, 229
Van Boening, Mark V., *see* Cason, Timothy N. 664
Van Boening, Mark V., *see* Durham, Yvonne 206, 209
Van Boening, Mark V., *see* King, Ronald R. 242, 247, 254
Van Boening, Mark V., *see* Rassenti, Stephen J. 1055

van Damme, Eric, *see* Güth, Werner   436, 534, 534n, 539
van der Kragt, A.J.C., *see* Caporael, L.R.   821n
van Dijk, F.   794, 799, 836, 853
van Dijk, F., *see* Sonnemans, Joep   836
Van Huyck, John B.   293, 403, 455–461, 464, 500, 521, 522, 527–529, 556
Van Huyck, John B., *see* Battalio, Raymond C.   521–523
Van Huyck, P.P., *see* Van Huyck, John B.   521, 527–529
van Lange, P.A.M.   836
van Winden, F., *see* Jacobsen, B.   746n
van Winden, F., *see* Sonnemans, Joep   836
van Winden, F., *see* van Dijk, F.   794, 799, 836, 853
van Winden, Frans, *see* Keser, Claudia   779
VanDerhei, J.L., *see* Bajtelsmit, V.L.   1070
Vannoni, Michael, *see* Smith, Vernon L.   85, 112, 266
Varian, Hal R.   481n, 482, 626, 637, 959, 964
Varian, Hal R., *see* Andreoni, James   637
Varian, Hal R., *see* Bergstrom, Theodore   831
Vepsalainen, Ari, *see* Camerer, Colin F.   903
Vergnaud, Jean-Christophe, *see* Bounmy, Kene   341
Vesterlund, L., *see* Andreoni, James   516, 518
Vesterlund, L., *see* Harbaugh, W.T.   1051, 1062, 1064
Vesterlund, Lise   790
Vickrey, William S.   92, 186, 626, 644, 662, 1090
Villamil, Anne P., *see* Holt, Charles A.   63, 84, 138, 185
Vogelsang, Ingo, *see* Finsinger, Jörg   157
von Winterfeldt, D., *see* Edwards, W.   1026
Vragov, R., *see* Porter, David P.   188, 190

Walker, James M.   887, 1056, 1090–1092
Walker, James M., *see* Cox, James C.   92, 93, 95–97, 186n, 1054–1056, 1090
Walker, James M., *see* Isaac, R. Mark   175n, 185, 244, 637, 776, 789, 795n, 796, 804, 825, 832, 846n, 853, 914n
Walker, James M., *see* Laury, S.K.   798–800, 853
Walker, James M., *see* Smith, Vernon L.   136, 792, 850, 914n, 916, 917, 919, 1047, 1054, 1058, 1059
Walker, James M., *see* Williams, Arlington W.   242

Walker, M.   626, 630, 635
Walker, M., *see* Muench, T.   633
Wallsten, T.S., *see* Erev, Ido   1026
Walster, Elaine   831, 1036
Walster, G. William, *see* Walster, Elaine   831, 1036
Wärneryd, K.   573, 574
Warr, Peter   831
Wason, P.C.   1039
Watson, Joel   612
Weber, E.U.   1062n, 1066, 1071
Weber, E.U., *see* Blais, A.-R.   1062n
Weber, Martin, *see* Nöth, Markus   337n, 344, 720
Weber, R.   396
Weber, R.J., *see* Forsythe, Robert   890, 891, 891n, 892, 895, 896
Weber, R.J., *see* Myerson, R.B.   891, 893, 895, 896
Weber, R.J., *see* Rietz, T.A.   890, 892, 895
Weber, Roberto A.   903–906
Weibull, Jorgen W.   474, 525
Weichbold, A., *see* Fehr, Ernst   325, 328, 329
Weigelt, Keith, *see* Camerer, Colin F.   341, 344, 599n, 615, 781n
Weigelt, Keith, *see* Ho, Teck-Hua   392, 393, 400, 401, 407, 611
Weimann, Joachim   779
Weimann, Joachim, *see* Ockenfels, Axel   494
Weingast, B.R., *see* Shepsle, Kenneth   873, 881
Weitzman, Martin L.   235n
Welch, Ivo, *see* Bikhchandani, Sushil   335
Welland, J. Douglas, *see* Godby, Robert   656, 658, 666
Welland, J. Douglas, *see* Mestelman, Stuart   77, 78, 82
Wellford, Charissa P.   63
Werding, M., *see* Beckmann, K.   750
Wessen, Randii, *see* Ledyard, John O.   206
Whinston, Michael, *see* Bernheim, B. Douglas   165
Whitcomb, David K., *see* Cohen, Kalman J.   25
Wicksell, K.   736
Wilcox, Nathaniel T., *see* Archibald, Glen   195n, 211
Wilcox, Nathaniel T., *see* Durham, Yvonne   206, 209
Wilcox, Nathaniel T., *see* Van Boening, Mark V.   206, 209, 211
Wildenthal, J.M., *see* Van Huyck, John B.   403
Wilkes-Gibbs, D., *see* Clark, H.H.   903

Wilkie, Simon, *see* Corchon, Luis 626
Williams, Arlington W. 242, 303, 376
Williams, Arlington W., *see* Davis, Douglas D. 63, 74, 84, 138, 185
Williams, Arlington W., *see* Isaac, R. Mark 164, 170, 244, 825, 846n, 853, 914n
Williams, Arlington W., *see* Ketcham, Jon 56, 63, 66n, 72, 139, 236n
Williams, Arlington W., *see* King, Ronald R. 242, 247, 254
Williams, Arlington W., *see* Laury, S.K. 798–800, 853
Williams, Arlington W., *see* Mysker, M. 636
Williams, Arlington W., *see* Smith, Vernon L. 20, 25, 46, 52, 85, 112, 235, 239, 242, 247, 248, 251, 256, 260, 266, 425
Williams, Arlington W., *see* Van Boening, Mark V. 242
Williams, Melonie, *see* Harrison, Glenn W. 764
Williams, Steven, *see* Rustichini, Aldo 662
Williamson, Oliver 320
Willig, Robert D., *see* Baumol, William J. 71, 155
Willinger, Marc 337n
Willinger, Marc, *see* Bounmy, Kene 341
Wilner, B., *see* Manelli, A. 190, 191, 192n
Wilson, Bart J. 63, 66, 66n, 68, 144
Wilson, Bart J., *see* Davis, Douglas D. 63, 66, 68, 145, 175
Wilson, Bart J., *see* Reynolds, Stanley S. 144
Wilson, J.Q. 1061n
Wilson, K.N., *see* Desvousges, W.H 539n
Wilson, M., *see* Daly, M. 1061n
Wilson, P.W., *see* Stahl, Dale 403
Wilson, R., *see* Kreps, David M. 180, 598, 602
Wilson, R.K., *see* Haney, P. 874, 882
Wilson, R.K., *see* Sell, Jane 510, 510n, 513
Wilson, Rick K. 466
Wilson, Rick, *see* Sell, Jane 787
Wilson, Robert, *see* Kreps, David M. 488, 776

Winkler, R.L., *see* Murphy, A.H. 818
Winkler, Robin C., *see* Battalio, Raymond C. 960, 965
Winman, A., *see* Juslin, P. 1026
Winter, E., *see* Rapoport, Amnon 273, 274, 282, 287, 289–294
Winter-Ebmer, R., *see* Falkinger, J. 627n, 630, 633, 634
Wit, Jörgen, *see* Jacobsen, B. 746n
Wit, Jörgen, *see* Plott, Charles R. 342, 720
Wolf, Charles 914
Wright, J., *see* Forsythe, Robert 743n, 749, 750

Yamato, T., *see* Cason, Timothy N. 798n, 803, 810, 811, 813
Yamato, T., *see* Saijo, T. 803
Yang, C. Winston, *see* Plott, Charles R. 720
Yang, W.C., *see* Plott, Charles R. 342
Yellen, Janet L., *see* Akerlof, George 121, 325
Yeo, C., *see* Jedetski, J. 984
Yokotani, K., *see* Cason, Timothy N. 803, 810, 811
Young, H. Peyton 479, 520n

Zajac, E. 55
Zame, W., *see* Bossaerts, Peter L. 376
Zamir, Shmuel, *see* Roth, Alvin E. 494, 495, 537, 538
Zanella, Beatrice 323, 324n
Zarbatany, L. 449
Zeiler, K., *see* Plott, Charles R. 1064
Ziegelmeyer, Anthony, *see* Bounmy, Kene 341
Ziegelmeyer, Anthony, *see* Willinger, Marc 337n
Ziegler, Michael J., *see* Olson, Mark A. 677, 681, 690
Zona, J. Douglas, *see* Porter, Robert H. 175
Zwick, Rami, *see* Bolton, Gary E. 489, 491, 492, 495, 538, 539
Zych, Peter K., *see* Fehr, Ernst 923

SUBJECT INDEX OF VOLUME 1

2-person dilemma game   495
2SLS   1080–1085
37% rule   1043, 1044

absolute value of volume deviation   111
abundance   1011
abundant information   1013
adaptation   55, 60
adaptive behavior   457, 459, 461
adaptive dynamics   575
adaptive evolutionary responses   848
adaptive learning   282, 294, 565, 608
adjustment   1030
adjustment process   16
adverse selection   19, 669, 673
advertising   585
agenda control   858, 860–864
agenda setter   773, 858–860, 862–864, 867, 881, 882
agent's preferences   958, 959
aggregate   344
all-pay auction   553
allocation of private goods   625
allocative efficiency   669, 672–674
allowance market   661
allowance trading   661, 665–667
alternating offer bargaining   482
altruism   482, 555, 772, 780, 782, 784–786, 789, 790, 792, 804, 823, 848, 849, 851, 854, 1035
altruistic   779, 790, 849, 850
ambiguity   1065, 1067
ambiguity aversion   1062, 1065, 1067
anchoring   1030
anonymity   411
anonymity effect   492
anonymous open book trading   367
anti-competitive behavior   185
anticipation   611
antitrust   178
antitrust policy   138
appropriative   127, 128
AQRE   542, 543, 546
arbitrage   256–258

architectures   344
Areeda–Turner cost-based tests   178
Arrow–Debreu   344, 364
ascending price auctions   186, 193, 195
aspiration level   1043, 1044
asset market   260, 262, 335
asset pricing   364
asymmetric inequality aversion   850
asymmetric information   25
asymmetry   721, 722, 941, 944
Ausubel   186, 188, 190, 191
autarky   358
availability   977, 1018, 1030–1032, 1039
avoidable costs   206, 208, 209, 211

backward agenda   880, 885
backward voting agenda   882, 884–886
backward-bending   219, 226
bad intentions   496
balancing   215, 216
ball-and-urn   335
Banerjee model   340
banking   655, 656, 658
bargaining   436, 437, 448–450, 452, 453, 500
base rate fallacy   1018–1020, 1025
Bayes   1009, 1010
Bayes Law   345
Bayes' rule   336, 1025
Bayesian   136, 257, 258, 308, 608, 980, 1009, 1010, 1016, 1018–1021, 1024, 1028
Bayesian equilibrium   541
Bayesian inference tasks   1053
Bayesian methods   983
Bayesian Nash mechanisms   626
Bayesian posterior   337
Bayesian reasoning   1018
BDM choice experiments   952
BDM mechanism   956, 957, 971, 974
beacon   17
beauty contest   391, 392, 401, 403, 407
Becker, DeGroot, and Marschak (BDM)   950, 952, 956, 969, 974 1064, 1093
behavioral equilibrium   475

I-19

behavioral existence proof   181
belief   260, 817, 818, 821–824, 836
belief learning   609, 610, 612
believe   260, 262
Bellman's principle   923
Bernoulli process   916
Bernoullian framework   976
Bertrand competition   149
bias   746, 749, 750
bid/ask continuous market   46
bid/ask spread   25, 27, 30, 53, 228, 229, 232
bilateral bargaining   232, 560, 919
bilateral contracts   687
bilateral gift-exchange institutions   326
bilateral off-floor trading   229
bilateral trades   228
bimatrix   472
binary choice prediction experiment   916
binding   5, 7
blind two-sided auction   88
block transaction   644
boom   247
bounded   979
bounded rational reasoning model   407
bounded rationality   550, 850, 976
boundedly rational   585
breast cancer problem   1020
bubble   12, 13, 242, 244, 247–254, 256–258, 260–262, 348
bundled unit double auction (BUDA)   209, 211
buyer reserve   689
buyers' bid auction   8

cab problem   1020
calculation   850
calculation and recording   850
calculation errors   848
call markets   143, 144
capital asset pricing model (CAPM)   364, 993, 1003
cardinal ultimatum   490
cascade   344
CE   47–49, 52, 111, 113, 114, 269, 271, 662, 664
ceiling   46–49, 51, 53
centipede game   406
central exchange market   687
chains of markets   370
change-detection   610
cheap talk   116, 164, 167, 464, 465, 468, 470
cheap-riding   784

cheater detection   1037, 1040, 1041
cheating   413, 1037, 1038, 1040, 1041
children   449
Cho–Kreps intuitive criterion   585
choice reversals   973, 974
choice/reservation-price consistency   930
choice/reservation-price inconsistency   929, 936, 937
circle-test   837
classical model   214, 226
classical search theory   1042
coalition   857, 858, 862–869, 881, 883
coalitional relations   412
Cobb–Douglas economies   631
Cobb–Douglas utility function   802, 810
cobweb   217, 226
cognitive cost of effort   911
cognitive illusion   976, 978, 985, 1018, 1025, 1026, 1028, 1031, 1033
collective choice   872, 876, 878, 880, 887
collective ignorance   999
collusion   8, 10, 170–172, 174–176, 185, 186, 192, 193, 195–197, 202, 203, 211
collusive   170, 175, 176, 193–197
collusive agreements   170
combinatorial auction   644–647, 649, 650
combinatorial clock   10
combinatorial environment   645
combinatorial sealed-bid auction   644
common knowledge   260–263
comparative statics   772, 774, 784–786, 789, 790, 823
compensation mechanisms   637
compensatory   1011, 1014
competitive equilibrium   5–8, 11, 16, 17, 19, 25, 27, 46, 47, 49, 51, 56, 58, 60, 78, 84, 88, 89, 111, 113, 114, 116, 179, 193, 209, 211, 214, 217, 264, 267, 269, 271, 333, 345, 370, 662, 712, 1078–1084
competitive equilibrium allocation   690, 691
competitive pressure   320
competitors   818, 821, 836
complete information   150–152
complete information conditions   437
complete order flow information   104
complex multi-node networks   676
concave   312
Condorcet   874, 883
Condorcet Loser   889, 890, 892–895
conflict   127, 130, 131
conformity rewarding institution   340

confused   915
congestion   701, 708, 709
conjunction fallacy   1018, 1027, 1028, 1030
conjunction rule   1027–1030
conservation   375
consideration   608, 612
conspiracy   164, 167, 168, 170, 171, 173, 174
constant aggregate   662
constant relative risk averse model (CRRAM)   92, 95, 96, 1055
constant volume equilibrium environment   955
content effect   1039
contest success function   128
contestable market   155, 156
contestable market efficiency   156
continuous double auction (CDA)   30, 88, 170, 206, 260, 262, 264–267, 269, 271, 687, 690, 692–699, 710
continuous strategy space   500, 550
continuously updated nodal uniform price auction   703
contract   5, 6, 11, 77, 78
contract enforcement   319
contract enforcement problem   319
contribution function   826, 829
controlled error variables   1079
controls   7
convention   520–522, 525–529
convergence   214, 219
convergence behavior   472
convergence structure   370
convex policy space   872
cooperation   127, 128, 131–134, 136, 146, 149, 424–426, 772, 777, 780, 848, 852, 853, 1035–1037
cooperative   129–132, 134–136, 836, 848, 853, 854
cooperative behavior   412, 425, 479, 488
cooperative equilibrium   599, 601, 602, 604, 605
cooperative sequential equilibria   601
cooperatively   513
cooperators   818, 821, 823, 836, 849
coordinate   454, 455, 458, 459
coordination   273, 282, 288, 293, 294, 375, 463, 464, 466, 468, 470
coordination failure   454–459
coordination game   520
coordination problem   454, 463, 522, 525
Core   874–878
corporate culture   904

correct dominant strategy mechanism   644
corresponding equilibrium allocations   691
cost information asymmetry   669
cost plus contract   670
cost-sharing contract   670, 673, 674
country production possibility   359
Cournot   9, 146–152, 200, 201, 607, 609
Cournot adjustment   575
Cournot competition   553
Cournot duopoly   919
Cox and Isaac subsidy (C–I)   159, 160
crash   242, 244, 247, 249, 252–254, 260–262
curse of knowledge   611

data generating process (DGP)   1078, 1084, 1085
day-ahead sealed bid   690
DC   691
decision anomalies   976
decision behavior   560
decision cost   916, 917
decision cost model   1058
decision error   260, 262
decision-making   967
decision-making under uncertainty   967
decisions in sequence   335
decisiveness   127–131, 133, 135
decomposed game technique   836
defection   149
demand reduction   10, 185–188, 190–192, 197
demand revealing human buyers   74
detection   1041
dictator game   420–422, 429, 492, 431
directly revealed preferred   481
discrete choice behavior   541
discrete choice models   541
discriminative auctions   190
discriminative price rule   662
disequilibrium   454, 456, 458, 876, 880
distributive struggle   127
disturbance   541–543
disturbed   542
dominance solvable   391
dominant strategy   626, 772, 792–796, 798, 800, 802–804, 816
double auction (DA)   3–6, 8, 11, 12, 16, 22, 25, 30–32, 35, 37, 39, 44, 46–50, 52, 53, 77, 78, 82, 105, 138, 144, 153, 154, 170, 171, 185, 208, 209, 211, 217, 223, 226, 228, 229, 242, 326, 344, 661, 919, 1078–1085
double auction energy market   690
double oral auction   84, 235

double two stage minimum absolute deviation (D2SMAD) 1080–1085
drift 364
duopoly 151
Dutch auctions 92
Duverger 893, 895
Duverger-type 890
Duverger's Law 773, 889, 895

ecological 979, 983
ecological rationality 976, 978, 979, 983, 984, 1011
ecologically rational 984, 985
Edgeworth 6, 66, 69
Edgeworth box 946
Edgeworth cycles 139
education 585
Edward Chamberlain 200
effect 990
efficiency 9–11, 77, 78, 82, 100, 104, 105, 109, 111, 112, 153–156, 705–709
efficiency roller coasters 206
efficiency wage 120, 123, 125
efficiency wage theory 121–124
efficient market hypothesis 364, 993
effort enforcement problem 319
effort theory 1059
election markets 746, 749, 750
elections 742, 746, 747, 750
elimination of weakly dominated strategies 403
EMH 993
emission allowance trading 661, 665
emission allowances 662
emission quotas 725
emissions quota trade 726
emissions trading 655
emotional 836
empirical data fitting 607
employment policy 733
endogenous enforcement of contracts 319
endogenous inter-trader information 243
endogenous preferences 872
endowment 952
endowment effect 940, 943, 944, 946, 949, 950
English 92, 186
English clock (EC) 10, 186–188, 190, 192, 196
English clock auction 915, 971
enhanced cognition processes 243
entitlement 939–942, 946
entry limit-pricing game 585
equal increments solution 500

equality 413
equilibration 23, 214, 219, 348
equilibrium 190, 587, 611, 700, 702, 705–708, 873–878, 880–884, 917–920
equilibrium asset pricing theory 364
equilibrium consistency conditions 552
equilibrium convergence 5
equilibrium method 454
equity 413
equity theory 831, 832, 835
errors 850
estimators 1078–1084
event study 722
evolutionarily stable strategy (ESS) 811, 813
evolutionary adaptation 848
evolutionary assumption 472
evolutionary bargaining game 527
evolutionary coordination game 522
evolutionary equilibria 475
evolutionary game 520, 527
evolutionary game theory 475, 572
evolutionary models 851, 852
evolutionary psychology 411
evolutionary stag hunt game 521, 522
excess demand 100, 103
excludability 803
exogenously matched 328
expectations 411
expected utility theory 969, 971, 974
experience 1056, 1059
experience levels 1056
experience-weighted attraction (EWA) 607, 610–612
experimenter-subject anonymity condition 491
exploitation 608
exploited 510
exploration 608
extensive form game 542

factor price equalization 358
failure 6, 8, 9
fair 55, 57, 60, 61, 831, 849
fair behavior 531
fair distribution 493
fair reference wage 121
fair wage–effort hypothesis 122, 125, 325, 326
fairly 57
fairness 6, 55–58, 60, 61, 411, 412, 423, 429, 436–438, 440–442, 444, 445, 447, 448, 450–453, 488, 531, 792, 802, 831, 832, 835, 848–850, 878, 915, 1036
fairness norms 507

false consensus   611
false uniqueness   611
feedback   513
fictitious play   575, 607, 609
field applications   350
field environment   352
field testing   725
field tests   725
fighting   128–130, 132–136
financial asset markets   242
financial incentives   1053
finite search horizon   311
Finsinger–Vogelsang (F–V) subsidy   157–159
firm-specific   234, 235
first price auction   911, 1054
first price sealed bid auction   92, 1092
Fisher sign   316
fixed price contract   670, 673, 674
fixed total sacrifice effect   494
flat maximum   1056
floor   46–48, 50–53
focal point   500
forecast   303–306, 309
forecast rationality   303
forecasting   303, 748
foreign exchange markets   256
forward induction   585
forward moving agenda   880, 881, 884, 885
free ride   488, 736, 738, 776, 777, 780, 784, 785, 792, 798, 807, 846, 849, 852
free-rider incentives   736
free-rider problem   625, 803
full demand revelation   71
full rationality   4
full separation   574
fully separating equilibrium   574
fuzzed   501, 502

game method   518
games against nature   412
gender   513, 1066, 1071
general competitive equilibrium   370
general equilibrium models   376
general multi-market equilibrium   7
generalized axiom of revealed preference (GARP)   482, 959, 960, 964
generous   431, 434, 515
gift exchange game   325
giving behavior   492
Groves–Ledyard mechanism   630, 631, 633–635, 640

habit   923, 927
Hanneman hypothesis   949
Harsanyi   500
hawk–dove game   803, 811, 816
hawk–dove–bourgeois   472
herd-like behavior   341
herding   335
heuristic   976–985, 987, 1004–1009, 1011–1016, 1027, 1033, 1035–1037, 1041, 1044, 1045
human buyer   72, 74
hyperresponsive quantal response equilibrium (QRE)   611
hypothetical   914, 1049
hypothetical choice   914, 1048, 1053
hypothetical choice studies   1053
hypothetical incentives   1053
hypothetical payments   1047, 1049, 1050, 1053
hypothetical payoff   1048–1051
hysteresis   1092, 1095

ideal point   881–884
IEM   742, 743, 748–750
ignorance   994, 998–1000
imagination   608
imperfect incentive alignment   572
imperfect verification technology   323
impossibility theorems   91
impunity condition   491
incentive   705, 706, 1047, 1051, 1052
incentive compatible (IC)   190, 625, 627, 629, 630, 639, 640, 956
incentive compatible quadratic scoring rule   818
incentive-compatible mechanisms   627
incentive incompatibility   10
incentives for subjects units   47
income effects   950–952
incomplete information   149, 151, 152, 335
incomplete market   325
inconsistency   929–931, 933, 936, 938
increases in group size   243
increment/decrement   687
independence axiom   969–971
independent auction (IA)   646, 649, 650
Individual competitive equilibrium   47
individualists   818, 821, 823, 836
individually-oriented   509
inducing risk preferences   1087
industry demand function   147
inefficiency   77, 267, 269, 271
inefficient   7, 8, 11

inefficient representations   1018
inequality measure   849
information aggregation   342, 344
information aggregation mechanisms   348
information cascade   335
information economics   585
instability   214, 215, 217, 219, 223, 226, 857, 858
institutional differences   857
institutional effects   857
institutional features   857, 864
institutional rule   857, 858, 867
institutional structure   880, 887
institutional variation   857
institutions   857, 858, 867
instrument design   661
instrumental   898
interactive markets   370
international climate change   725
intertemporal   923
intertemporal behavior   923
intertemporal choice   923, 927
intertemporal dimension   923
intransitivity   972
intrinsic motivation   836, 837, 841
intuitive   546
intuitive equilibrium   545–547
inventory   77, 78, 82
inverse demand function   146, 147
investment choice   997, 1000
investment game   1036, 1037
investment heuristic   994
Iowa Electronic Markets   742
irrational   178, 251, 482
irrationality   976, 1016
iterated best reply model   401, 403, 407
iterated dominance   407
iterated elimination of weakly dominated strategies   391
iterated prisoner's dilemma   1035

jaws   22, 23
Joan Robinson   200
job search models   311
joint production   127, 128
Jonchkeere non-parametric order test statistic   435
judgmental bias   1016

Kalai–Smorodinsky   500
Kaplan   35

Kaplan's robots   35, 44
Kaplan's simple parasitic robots   39
Kendall's τ 1007
kindness   482, 802, 803
Kirchoff's law   710
knowledge validity   988, 989
Kolmogorov–Smirnov   93, 313
Kormendi and Plott experiments   861

laboratory environment   350
law of comparative advantage   358
law of one price   209
learning   148, 305, 306, 308, 309, 574, 823, 824
learning curves   309
learning model   566
legislative rules   858
lemons phenomenon   325
Leontief utility   484
less-is-more effect   988–990, 992
lexicographic heuristic (LEX)   1015
lexicographic strategy   1014
limited rationality   4
linear   818
linear altruism   829
linear contracts   670
linear demand function   149
linear equilibrium   561
linear equilibrium strategy (LES)   561–566
linear models   1008
linear payoff structure   792
linear payoffs   552
linear production function   359
linear program   712
linear programming problem   712
linear public good   817, 819, 823
linear utility   782
linear utility function   802
Loeb–Magat (L–M)   157, 158
Loeb–Magat mechanism   157, 158
Loehman–Whinston mechanism   628
log concave model (LCM)   92, 97, 98, 1055
log likelihood (LL)   612
logistic choice function   339
logistic error model   339
logistic QRE   543
logit   551
logit choice rule   552
logit differential equation   552
logit equilibrium   542, 852
logit equilibrium densities   552
logit quantal response equilibrium (QRE)   542, 543, 551

Subject Index of Volume 1 I-25

loop flow   710
loss aversion   326, 926
loss avoidance   927, 928
lottery   911, 929–936, 967, 968, 1063–1067
lottery choices   1048
lottery procedure   1094
lottery technique   1095
lottery-based induction procedure   1087, 1088
lump   370, 373

machine learning   608
majority coalition   878
majority rule   773, 857, 858, 860, 861, 864–868
majority rule institution   340
majority rule legislatures   857
manipulated   720, 723, 724
marginal per-capita return (MPCR)   846–854
marginal rate of substitution (MRS)   825, 826, 829
market allocations   1078
market efficiency   77, 82, 267
market entry games   585
market equilibrium   22
market imperfections   8
market institutions   1078
market jaws   23
market power   5, 6, 8–10, 62–64, 66, 68, 69, 138–145
market sequential choice task   971
market trading institution   170, 171
market trading institutions   153
marketing agreements   234
Marketscape   345
Marshall   200, 226
Marshallian   216, 219, 222, 223, 226
Marshallian path   35
matched-pair   721, 722
matching market   109, 111
matching market institution   665
mean absolute percent errors (MAPES)   1081–1084
mean matching (MM)   109–114, 473
measure of inequality   850
mechanism   956
message restriction   103, 104
message restriction rule   100
message space   572
microstructure   720
minimal information   104
minimalist   1004, 1007–1009, 1014

minimum absolute deviation (MAD)   1080–1083
minimum effort level   325
minimum information   103
minimum-effort coordination game   553
mixed equilibrium   142, 143
mixed motive games   403
mixed strategy   139, 140, 281, 466, 541, 549, 587
mixed-strategy equilibrium   139, 140, 274, 287
mixing   62–64, 67–69, 139
model   312, 358
model of rational addiction   923
monetary incentives   914, 915
monetary payments   914, 915
monetary payoffs   915
monetary rewards   914, 915
monetary stakes   423, 424
monopolistic agenda setters   860
monopolistic agenda setting   859
monopoly   6, 10, 11, 179, 181, 182, 184, 200–203, 205
monopoly agenda power   880
monopoly control   153
monotonicity   98
Monte Carlo study   1081
moral hazard   669, 671–673
motivational   836
multi-object auction markets   185
multi-unit auction   185, 186, 190–192
multinode   677
multinomial logit distribution   542
multiple buyer networks   677
multiple call market (MCM)   264–267, 269, 271
multiple equation structure   376
multiple equilibria   12, 273
multiple generator   677
multiple pure strategy equilibria   287
multiple regression   980, 983, 1008, 1009
multiple unit double auction (MUDA)   208, 209, 211, 264
multiple unit progressive auctions   10
must-serve inelastic loads   676
mutual consistency condition   520
mutual consistency problem   455
mutual consistency requirement   454
mutually consistent behavior   454
myopic voting   886

naive Bayesian model   823
naive decision rule   314
narrow norms   1018, 1033

Nash 6, 9, 13, 129–131, 134–136, 147, 150, 500, 611, 792, 795, 796, 798–800, 802–804, 811, 813, 848, 852, 854, 917, 1056
Nash equilibrium 62–64, 68, 69, 92, 93, 95–97, 101, 139–141, 273, 281, 288, 294, 463, 466, 475, 520, 521, 527, 529, 541–543, 549, 573, 598, 626, 627, 630, 631, 633–635, 639, 640, 671, 776, 792–796, 798, 800, 802, 817, 831, 832, 835, 838, 840, 846, 848, 850, 852, 853, 898, 899, 1090
Nash mixed strategy 63
Nash mixing predictions 63
Nash–Cournot reaction functions 128
Nash–Harsanyi incomplete information model 1054
Nash-predicted outcomes 68
Nathan Rothschild 720
natural monopoly 71, 155
natural monopoly cost structure 71, 73
neoclassical choice theory 482
network market 681
networks of markets 370
neutrality theorem 831
Newton 4, 115
Newton's method 23
node 700–706, 708, 709
noisy evolution model 552
noisy evolutionary adjustment 851
non-binding 5, 7, 46, 49, 53
non-binding ceiling 50
non-binding controls 5
non-binding price controls 46
non-collusive 193
non-compensatory 983, 1011–1014
non-convex cost structure 206
non-convexities 200, 203
non-cooperation 598, 600, 605
non-cooperative 273, 411, 598–601, 604, 605
non-cooperative equilibrium 132, 604
non-cooperative game theory 413
non-distorted buyer 956
non-dominant-strategy 796
non-Duverger 892
non-monetary reward structures 243
non-parametric test 172
non-rational behavior 802
non-satiated 958, 959
norm of equality 417, 421
normal form game 542
normative economics 967
normative model 916

NoSpec 261, 262
not binding 5

objective rationality 916
off-floor trading 228, 229, 232
offer auction 153, 154
oligopolies 146, 149, 151, 200, 203
oligopolistic market 146
oligopolists 146, 152, 164
oligopoly 63, 146, 148, 152
OLS 1080–1085
one-dimensional experiments 861
one-reason decision 985
one-reason decision making 978, 982, 983, 1004–1009, 1015
one-sided 326
one-sided auctions 185
one-sided multi-unit auctions 185
one-sided oral bid auction 327
open outcry 665
open-book call asset markets 242
optimal behavior 1047
optimal consumption 924–927
optimal individual trader choice 4
optimal search behavior 1042
optimization 976, 978–980
optimization algorithm 702
oral double auction 644, 661
order flow information 100, 103, 104
ordinary least squares 1078, 1080, 1082
organizational culture 903
oriented large-group markets 245
other-regarding 423, 488, 495
other-regarding behavior 411
other-regarding preferences 878
overconfidence 611, 612, 1018, 1026, 1027
overconfidence bias 1025–1027
overconsumption 925–928
overfits 1007
overfitting 1007, 1011
overresponse 306, 308, 309
overrevelation 106, 107
overweighting 1016

paired double auction 1078
pairwise Wilcoxon–Mann–Whitney rank sum tests 957
paradox of power (POP) 127, 130–132, 134–136
parallelism precept 931
Pareto 149–151, 232, 872
Pareto deficient 273, 281

Pareto efficient   777
Pareto optimal   147, 626, 630, 794–796, 832, 838, 866
Pareto-ranked   556
parimutuel betting   342
partial common interest   572
partial equilibrium   4, 9
partial information condition   437, 438, 441, 442, 447, 450
partial pooling   587
partial pooling equilibrium   575
partial pooling play   580
participation game   898, 899
payoff uncertainty   599, 605
perfect competition   8, 11
perfect rationality   551
performance-based incentives   1053
perversely shaped   223, 226
pivotal mechanism   628–630, 639
PLATO   72
play learning model   552
policy evaluation   733, 734
political markets   750
polls   742, 746–750
pooled information   347
pooling equilibrium   180
portfolio   993, 996–1003
post-auction cost uncertainty   671, 672, 674
posted bid   153, 154
posted bid market   320
posted bid pricing   56
posted offer   5–7, 56, 62–64, 68, 69, 71, 72, 74, 77, 78, 82, 138, 139, 141, 153, 154, 171, 209, 241, 1078–1085
posted offer market   164, 172, 174, 178
posted-offer auction   171
posted-offer exchange mechanism   236
posted-offer monopolies   170
posted-offer trading   170
power   6, 9, 63, 64, 66–68, 138–145
precommitment wage   314
predation   10, 178–181, 184
predatory   179–182, 184
predatory behavior   10
predatory intent   178, 181
predatory price range   179
predatory pricing   10, 178–184
predicted reversals   967, 968, 972
predictive hypothesis   911
preference   818, 873–878
preference axioms   942

preference induction   1089
preference relation   872
preference reversal   929–932, 935, 937, 938, 967–969, 971–975
preference-induced equilibrium   881
preferences   817, 818, 821–823, 929, 931, 933, 935
price adjustment   24
price bubble   11–13, 242
price ceiling   47–50, 53
price control   5, 7, 46–48, 235, 239–241
price control variable   48
price coordination   164
price cycle   64, 66, 67, 69
price discovery   3, 5, 11, 12, 22
price discovery process   115
price fixing   170, 174
price floor   47, 48, 51, 53
price formation   371
price movements   721
price signaling   164–168
price tunnel   101, 102, 105
primary sealed-bid auction   644
principal branch   543
principle of dual entitlements   55
prisoner's dilemma   406, 479, 482, 488, 599–601, 604, 605, 637, 803, 804, 811
privacy   243, 434
private goods   793
private information   273, 274, 288, 335
private signal   335
probabilistic choice model   850
procurement   669
procurement contracting   669
production possibilities frontier   360
profit maximization   31
property right   417, 418, 420–424, 428
proportional representation   929, 930, 933–937
prospect theory   1051
provision-point mechanism   636, 637
public   793, 798, 829
public good   482, 509, 771, 772, 776–780, 784, 785, 789, 790, 792, 793, 795, 796, 798–800, 802, 803, 810, 813, 817–821, 823, 825, 831, 832, 835–838, 840, 841, 844, 846, 848–853, 1084
public goods experiment   792, 793, 795, 800, 846
punish   132
punishing   58

punishment 55, 515
punishment parameter 631, 633–635, 640
pure strategies 62
pure strategy asymmetric equilibria 281
pure strategy equilibria 274
purification strategies 475
push–pull 637
pushing 19, 20, 22

Quadrant I 943
quadratic payoffs 553
quadratic utility 366
quantal response 612
quantal response equilibrium (QRE) 541–544, 610, 611
quantal response equilibrium model 551, 823
quantal response naive Bayesian model 823
quantity restriction 234, 236
quasi-experimental 733
quasi-symmetric mixed strategies equilibria 899
quota 234–241, 725, 727–730, 732
quota restrictions 234, 235
quota trade 726, 727, 730

radial network 700, 709
random bid or ask 31
random pairwise 473
random rematching 776
random selection problem 173
random shocks 850
random values environment 264, 266, 269, 271
random walk hypothesis 364
rank condition 780
rate of return 153
rational 9, 13, 223, 249, 252, 260, 319
rational choice model 898
rational choice theory 821, 829
rational expectations 252, 303, 345, 724
rational expectations equilibrium 720
rational expectations theory 251
rational forecasts 303
rational learning 575
rationality 31, 36, 37, 251, 260, 262, 263, 319, 328, 370, 500, 976, 978, 979, 983, 984, 1047
rationalizes 958–960
Rawls 500
real buyers 71, 72, 74, 75
real payments 1047, 1052
real payoff 1047–1052

recall 316
reciprocal altruism 825
reciprocal sharing 412
reciprocity 319, 328, 411, 413, 422, 429, 431, 772, 784–790, 848, 849
recognition heuristic 984, 987–994, 996–1003
recognition validity 988, 989
reconciliation market 655, 656
recording error 850
reduced form error 1084, 1085
reference transaction 55, 56, 60
regret 19
reinforcement model 609, 612
relevant revealed 962
remnants of regulation 239
repeated entry deterrence 615
repeated single-shot design 776
replicator dynamic 851, 854
representations 1018, 1019, 1023, 1025, 1033
representativeness 1030, 1031
reputation building 489
reputation effects 776, 781, 782
reputations 132, 411
required reserve (RR) 689
reservation price 929, 931–933, 935–938, 956, 957
resource endowments 831
restricted BUDA 209, 211
retaliation 193
revealed preference 481, 960, 961, 964, 965
revenue neutral 662
ring test 818, 821, 836, 837, 841
risk 7, 509, 911, 1061–1071, 1087, 1088, 1091, 1094, 1095
risk attitudes 1047
risk averse 93, 95–98, 248, 312, 363, 364, 502, 911, 914, 1048–1052, 1054–1056, 1058, 1059, 1061–1071, 1087, 1088, 1090, 1092–1095
risk dominance 479, 522
risk dominant equilibrium 521, 522
risk loving 1064, 1087
risk mitigation 1069
risk neutral 92–98, 274, 363, 1048, 1050, 1051, 1055, 1056, 1087, 1088, 1090–1092, 1094, 1095
risk neutral agent 311
risk neutral model (RNM) 92–96, 1059
risk perception 1062
risk preference 7, 1048, 1050, 1066
risk preference induction 1088, 1095

risk preferences   1066, 1087, 1088, 1093–1096
risk prone   1068, 1071
risk seeking   1087–1089, 1092–1095
riskier   1062
risky lottery   1048, 1049
robot   5, 6, 31–37, 39, 44, 983
rolling regressions   309
Rothschild   720
runs second-price sealed bid auctions   1090

safe lottery   1048
salient incentives   937
satisficing   1044
satisficing heuristic   981, 1044, 1045
sawtooth   16, 20
scarce information   1012, 1013
scarcity   958
sealed bid (SB)   185–188, 190, 192–194, 196, 344
sealed bid auction   92, 175, 1090, 1092
sealed bid day-ahead   687
sealed bid–offer (SBO)   8, 85, 86, 89, 685, 687, 692–695
sealed bid uniform-price   186
sealed-bid competitive auction   644
sealed-bid double auction mechanism   560
search duration tests   313
search horizon   311
secant   115, 116
second-price auction   936
second-price sealed bid auction   92, 1092, 1095
second-price sealed-bid auction market   975
secret discounts   171, 173, 174
secretary problem   1044
security   62, 63
selected sampling   1018
selection task   1039
self-centered fairness   489
self-interest   411, 790
selfish   319, 328, 484, 509
selfishness   319, 328
selfless   509
seller prices   956
sender–receiver games   572, 903
sentiments   836
separability   959
sequential   542, 545, 546
sequential auction submarkets   687
sequential equilibrium   543, 544, 546, 547, 585, 604
sequential move game   326

sequential search   1042
sequential voting   341
Seriatim process   631
sex difference   1061, 1063–1070
sexes   509
share trading   655, 656, 658
shared expectations   420–422
shirking   9, 120, 123–125
signal   132
signaling games   585
simple adaptive learning models   585
simple coordination   479
simple linear altruism   825
simple lotteries   929
simple majority   872
simple majority coalition   874
simple majority rule   857, 872, 873, 878
simple reinforcement   607
simulated buyers   71, 74
simultaneous equations estimators   1078, 1080–1085
simultaneous equations estimators, two stage least squares   1081
single call market (SCM)   109, 264–267, 271
single call market efficiency   271
single-cue parental investment   1045
single-peaked preferences   858
single-shot dominant strategy   776, 777
single-shot equilibrium   782
single-shot games   776
single-unit   185
single-unit auctions   185
Skew   877, 878
Skew Star   874
small-group   243
smart market   209, 211, 712
Smith auction   638, 639
social calibration   611
social choice   872, 873, 880, 881
social choice mechanism   857
social choice theory   880
social cognition   411
social contract   413, 1037–1042
social distance   429, 431, 433–435
social environments   1035
social goals   1035
social heuristic   1035–1037
social isolation   411
social maximizers   484
social norm   60, 411, 500
social rationality   1045

social tie   836, 837, 841, 844
social value orientation   836, 837, 841, 842, 844
socially rational   1045
socially-oriented   509
soft close   103
solidarity game   494
sophisticated   611, 612
sophisticated anticipation   611
sophisticated experience-weighted attraction (EWA)   607, 611, 612
spatial committee   873
spatial committee game   872, 878
spatial modeling   872
specialization   358
spite   437, 444, 445, 447, 448, 451, 453, 802–804, 807, 813, 815, 816, 831, 848, 849
spiteful behavior   771
split-majority voters   895
spot auction   676
spot market   676
stability   214, 216, 219, 222, 223, 226
stag hunt game   521
standard linear voluntary contributions game   848
standard open agenda procedure   881
Star   874–878
state contingent commodities   344
static equilibrium models   365
step-level   817, 818, 823, 836
stopping rule   1042
strategic   424–426
strategic advantage   417, 421
strategic behavior   71, 74, 472
strategic complementarity   454
strategic demand withholding   74
strategic misrepresentation   84
strategic reputation building   489
strategic teaching   612
strategic voting   773, 889, 892, 895
strategies   424, 426, 428
strategy coordination problem   459
strategy method   518
strategy-pooling equilibria   587
strategy-proof   84, 89
strategy-proof equilibrium   85, 88, 91
strategy-separating equilibria   587
strong ambiguity   1067
strong axiom of revealed preference   482
structure induced equilibrium (SIE)   880–882
stylized facts   550, 1078
stylized results   243

subgame perfect equilibrium   418, 436, 447, 449, 860, 1036
subject experience   1056
subjective rationality   916
sulfur dioxide allowances market   656
supermodular   633–635, 638, 640
supply and demand equations   1078
surplus split   111–113
symmetric   549
symmetric equilibrium   466
symmetric mixed equilibrium   529
symmetric mixed-strategy equilibrium   281, 282
system of equations   22, 23
systematic treatment effects   846

Take The Best   983, 984, 1004–1016
tatonnement   7, 8, 24, 102, 104, 115, 116
tatonnement auction   100
theory of rational addiction   925
thin market   271
three-stage treatment   320
tradable emission allowance   661
tradable quota   725, 726, 730, 732
trading emission allowances   665
trading in shares   658
trading institution   661
trading off-floor   228
trading spot power   676
trading volume   111, 114
traditional utility theory   784
transitivity   942
transmission   700–709
traveler's dilemma   549, 554
trembles   479
triopoly   149–152
trust games   615
turnout   898
twin study   734
two-node network   677
two-person sequential bargaining game   1036
two-prize gamble   1088
two-sided auction   88, 109
two-sided auction markets   185
two-sided bid–offer trading   7
two-sided incomplete information   560
two-sided sealed bid–offer auction   687
two-stage treatment   320
TwoMarket/NoSpec   262

ultimatum   411, 423, 436–438, 440, 444, 447, 448, 452, 453, 509

ultimatum bargaining   447, 449, 451–453, 849
ultimatum game   412, 417, 418, 420–423, 425, 429, 489, 849, 915
uncertainty   655, 656, 658, 1018, 1019
underconfidence   1026, 1027
underconsumption   925, 927
undercut   62, 66
underfitting   1007
underprovision of effort   323
underrespond   309
underresponse   306
underreveal   105, 107
underrevelation   105–107, 271
underweighting   1016
undominated Nash equilibrium   626
unfair   6, 55–58
unfairness   6, 445, 447, 448
unfairness aversion motive   491
ungenerous   515
uniform price (UP)   109, 111–114
uniform price auction   85, 662
uniform price double auction (UPDA)   85, 88, 89, 232, 264–267, 271, 703, 953, 955
uniform price sealed-bid auctions   646
uniform price sealed-bid/sealed-offer auction   662
uniform pricing   662
uniform-price sealed bid-offer auction   85, 89
UNIT   32, 34, 35
unit-weight linear model   1008, 1013
unit-weight linear rule   1011
unit-weight model   1008, 1015
unobserved preference shocks   550, 848
unpredicted reversals   967, 968, 972
utilitarian solution   500
utility hypothesis   958–960, 965
utility maximization   958, 963–965
utility maximizers   92
utility-maximizing agent   958
utility-maximizing choices   958, 963

valuation   911, 939–947
value orientation   818, 836, 837, 844
vertical markets   370
Vickrey–Clarke–Groves (VCG) mechanism   626, 628–630

Vickrey   7, 10, 92, 93, 186, 188, 190, 191
Vickrey auction   943
Vickrey risk neutral bid function   1055
violations of transitivity   972
volume deviation (VDVAB)   111
voluntary contribution mechanism (VCM)   802–804, 810, 825, 829, 835
voluntary contribution model   831
voluntary export restraints (VERs)   234
voluntary public goods provision   831
voter turnout   898
voting cycles   887
voting equilibria   891, 896

wage differentials   120–122, 124, 125
wage–effort relation   326
Walras   7, 115, 150, 151, 226
Walrasian   4, 8, 100, 102, 104, 105, 216, 219, 222, 223, 226
Walrasian adjustment   23
Walrasian auction   100–102, 105
warm glow   772, 779–782, 823, 825, 829
weak   1062
weak ambiguity   1064, 1067
weak axiom of revealed preference (WARP)   481
weighted additive model   1015
weighted additive rule   1013
weighted fictitious play   607, 608, 611, 612
weighted pros   1015
well-behaved   481
Wilcoxon   74
Wilcoxon rank-sum test   419
willing to pay   939–941
willingness to accept   949, 951, 954, 955
willingness to pay   84, 88, 208, 644, 694, 736–740, 949, 951, 954, 955
winner's curse   344
withholding   58
world production possibilities curve   360
wounded pride   445, 451

zero-intelligence (ZI) robots   31, 32, 34, 35, 37, 39, 44